RETIREMENT PLANNING
AND EMPLOYEE BENEFITS

Your unique textbook registration number is below. Please register your new textbook at www.money-education.com for access to our Student Practice Portal, updated errata, Money Tips, and other valuable resources.

VUEI176763

RETIREMENT PLANNING
AND EMPLOYEE BENEFITS

James F. Dalton

Michael A. Dalton

17th Edition

MONEY EDUCATION

3116 5th Street
Metairie, LA 70002
888-295-6023

This publication is designed to provide accurate and authoritative information in regard to the subject matter covered. It is sold with the understanding that the publisher, authors, and contributors are not engaged in rendering legal, accounting, tax, financial planning, or other professional services. If legal advice, tax advice, or other professional assistance is required, the services of a competent professional should be sought.

CFP®, CERTIFIED FINANCIAL PLANNER™, and CFP (with flame logo)® are certification marks owned by Certified Financial Planner Board of Standards Inc. These marks are awarded to individuals who successfully complete CFP Board's initial and ongoing certification requirements.

Printed in the U.S.A.

ISBN-13: 978-1-946711-49-6

ABOUT THE AUTHORS

James F. Dalton, MBA, MS, CPA/PFS, CFA®, CFP®
- CEO, Money Education
- Adjunct professor at George Mason University (2014 - 2017)
- Adjunct professor at Georgetown University (2002 - 2014)
- Former Executive Vice President, Assessment Technologies Institute LLC
- Former Senior Vice President, Kaplan Professional
- Former President, Dalton Publications LLC
- Former Senior Manager of KPMG, LLP, concentrating in personal financial planning, investment planning, and litigation consulting
- MBA from Loyola University New Orleans
- Master of Accounting in Taxation from the University of New Orleans
- BS in accounting from Florida State University in Tallahassee, Florida
- Member of the CFP Board of Standards July 1996, Comprehensive CFP® Exam Pass Score Committee
- Member of the AICPA and the Louisiana Society of CPAs
- Member of the Financial Planning Association
- Member of the *Journal of Financial Planning* Editorial Review Board
- Author of *Money Education's Quick Sheets*
- Author of *Investment Planning* (1st - 2nd Editions)
- Co-author of *Cases in Financial Planning: Analysis and Presentation* (1st - 4th Editions)
- Co-author of *Retirement Planning and Employee Benefits* (1st - 17th Editions)
- Co-Author of *Fundamentals of Financial Planning* (1st - 7th Editions)
- Contributing Author of *Insurance Planning* (1st - 7th Editions)
- Contributing Author of *Estate Planning* (1st - 12th Editions)
- Author of Kaplan Schweser's Personal Financial Planning Understanding Your Financial Calculator
- Author of Kaplan Schweser's Understanding Your Financial Calculator for the CFA® Exam
- Co-author of BISYS CFA® Study Notes Volumes I and II
- Co-author of Kaplan Schweser's Personal Financial Planning Cases and Applications
- Co-author of the Kaplan Schweser Review for the CFP® Certification Examination, Volumes I–VIII and Kaplan Schweser's Financial Planning Flashcards

Michael A. Dalton, Ph.D., JD, CPA, CLU, ChFC, CFP®

- Former Chair of the Board of Dalton Publications, L.L.C.
- Associate professor of Accounting and Taxation at Loyola University in New Orleans, Louisiana (retired)
- Adjunct professor at George Mason University (2014 - 2017)
- Adjunct professor at Georgetown University (2002 - 2014)
- Former Senior Vice President, Education at BISYS Group
- Ph.D. in Accounting from Georgia State University
- J.D. from Louisiana State University in Baton Rouge, Louisiana
- MBA and BBA in Management and Accounting from Georgia State University
- Former board member of the CFP Board's Board of Examiners, Board of Standards, and Board of Governors
- Former member (and chair) of the CFP Board's Board of Examiners
- Member of the Financial Planning Association
- Member of the *Journal of Financial Planning* Editorial Advisory Board
- Member of the *Journal of Financial Planning* Editorial Review Board
- Member of the LSU Law School Board of Trustees (2000 - 2006)
- Author of *Dalton Review for the CFP® Certification Examination: Volume I – Outlines and Study Guides, Volume II – Problems and Solutions, Volume III - Case Exam Book, Mock Exams A-1 and A-2* (1st - 8th Editions)
- Author of *Retirement Planning and Employee Benefits* (1st - 17th Editions)
- Author of *Estate Planning* (1st - 12th Editions)
- Author of *Fundamentals of Financial Planning* (1st - 7th Editions)
- Author of *Insurance Planning* (1st - 7th Editions)
- Co-author of *Income Tax Planning* (1st - 14th Editions)
- Co-author of *Cases in Financial Planning: Analysis and Presentation* (1st - 4th Editions)
- Co-author of *Dalton CFA® Study Notes Volumes I and II* (1st - 2nd Editions)
- Co-author of *Dalton's Personal Financial Planning Series – Personal Financial Planning Theory and Practice* (1st - 3rd Editions)
- Co-author of *Dalton's Personal Financial Planning Series – Personal Financial Planning Cases and Applications* (1st - 4th Editions)
- Co-author of *Cost Accounting: Traditions and Innovations* published by West Publishing Company
- Co-author of the *ABCs of Managing Your Money* published by National Endowment for Financial Education (NEFE)

ABOUT THE CONTRIBUTING AUTHOR

Sherri Donaldson, CFP®, ChFC®, MSFS, CASL®, CAP®, EA

- Editing Princess for Money Education
- Former Author/Editor/Lead instructor, Keir Educational Resources
- Former Assistant Vice President, Senior Training Specialist, M&T Securities
- Former Associate Financial Consultant, M&T Securities
- Former Financial Sales Specialist, Nationwide Financial
- Former Financial Services Representative, Nationwide Retirement Solutions
- MSFS from The American College Bryn Mawr, PA
- BS in business, concentration in financial services, Pennsylvania State University
- Member of the Financial Planning Association
- Contributing Author of *Cases in Financial Planning: Analysis and Presentation* (4th Edition)
- Contributing Author of *Estate Planning* (11th - 12th Editions)
- Contributing Author of *Fundamentals of Financial Planning* (6th - 7th Editions)
- Contributing Author of *Income Tax Planning* (13th - 14th Editions)
- Contributing Author of *Insurance Planning* (6th - 7th Editions)
- Contributing Author of *Investment Planning* (2nd Edition)
- Contributing Author of *Retirement Planning and Employee Benefits* (16th - 17th Editions)
- Co-Author/Editor of Keir *General Financial Planning Principles* textbook
- Co-Author/Editor of Keir *Risk Management and Insurance Planning* textbook
- Co-Author/Editor of Keir *Introduction to Financial Planning* textbook
- Co-Author/Editor of Keir *Retirement Savings and Income Planning* textbook
- Co-Author/Editor of Keir *Tax Planning* textbook
- Co-Author/Editor of Keir *Estate Planning* textbook
- Co-Author/Editor Keir *Investments Planning* textbook
- Editor Keir *Financial Plan Development* and *Practical Applications for Your Financial Calculator* textbook
- Co-Author/Editor Keir CFP® exam review books (*Core Knowledge Book 1* and *2*, *Essential Keys* book, *Case Studies* book), practice exams, flashcards, MP3 scripts, Key Concept Infograhics, and Quick Concept videos

Randal R. Cangelosi, JD, MBA
- Practicing litigator throughout Louisiana, in business/commercial law and litigation, products liability litigation, wills and trust litigation, environmental law and litigation, medical malpractice defense, and insurance law and litigation
- Has successfully defended numerous corporations, businesses, and doctors in jury and judge trials
- Juris Doctorate from Loyola University New Orleans
- Masters of Business Administration from Loyola University New Orleans
- BS in Finance from Louisiana State University
- Member of the American & Federal Bar Associations
- Member of the Bar of the State of Louisiana
- Member of the New Orleans and Baton Rouge Bar Associations
- Board Member of La Lupus Foundation
- Board Member of Baton Rouge Chamber of Commerce
- Former Board Member of the Baton Rouge Area Chapter of the American Red Cross
- Admitted to practice before US District Courts, Western, Eastern & Middle Districts of Louisiana
- Admitted to practice before the Federal 5th Circuit Court of Appeals
- Admitted to practice in USDC, Southern District of Iowa (Pro Hac Vice)
- Admitted to practice in Circuit Court of Wayne County, Mississippi (Pro Hac Vice)
- Admitted to practice in Circuit Court of Barbour County, Alabama (Pro Hac Vice)
- Admitted to practice in Court of Common Pleas, Darlington County, South Carolina (Pro Hac Vice)
- Admitted to practice in Los Angeles County Superior Court, California (Pro Hac Vice)
- Admitted to practice in Superior Court of New Jersey: Morris County (Pro Hac Vice)
- Admitted to practice in 17th Judicial Court, Broward County, Florida (Pro Hac Vice)
- Former Chairman of New Orleans Bar Association, Community Service Committee
- Former Chairman of New Orleans Bar Association, Food and Clothing Drives
- Co-author of *Personal Financial Planning: Theory and Practice* (1st - 3rd Editions)
- Co-author of *Professional Ethics for Financial Planners*

About the Reviewers and Contributors

We owe a special thanks to several key professionals for their significant contribution of time and effort with the current and previous editions of this text. These reviewers provided meticulous editing, detailed calculation reviews, helpful suggestions for additional content, and other valuable comments, all of which have improved this edition. To each of these individuals we extend our deepest gratitude and appreciation.

Brad Childs is an Associate Professor of Accounting at Belmont University, where he does research in the fields of taxation and financial planning. He has a Ph.D. from Purdue University and a J.D. from Suffolk University. Mr. Childs is currently a licensed attorney in Tennessee, a licensed CPA in Ohio, and a CFP Certificant.

Donna Dalton made a significant contribution to this textbook by her thoughtful and meticulous editing throughout the book. She provided many valuable improvements to both the textbook and instructor materials. We are extremely grateful for her contributions. This book would not have been possible without her extraordinary dedication, skill, and knowledge.

Randall Martinez is a Personal Financial Planner specializing in personal financial planning, estate, and individual income tax planning. He teaches retirement planning, estate planning, and income tax planning through various universities as well as comprehensive reviews for the Certified Financial Planner Examination.

Robin Meyer is a valuable member of our Money Education team. She worked diligently throughout this project by performing numerous reviews and revisions. Robin provided many valuable improvements to both the textbook and instructor materials and this book would not have been possible without her extraordinary dedication, skill, and knowledge. Robin is the joy in our office as she always works tirelessly with a great work ethic and an enormous sense of humor. We are always grateful for her contributions to our products as well as our office happiness.

Kristi Tafalla is an attorney and personal financial planner specializing in income tax and estate planning. She teaches estate planning, income tax planning and comprehensive case courses through various CFP® Board-Registered Programs as well as comprehensive reviews for the CFP® certification. She is a contributor to Money Education's *Estate Planning for Financial Planners*.

Bill Yurkovac has a private practice in Florida focusing on asset management and estate planning considerations for his clientele. Mr. Yurkovac holds a Master's Degree in Education, has more than twenty-five years experience in the financial services arena, and enjoys serving as an instructor for candidates preparing for the CFP® Certification Examination. Current community involvement includes assisting and counseling several nonprofit organizations and a chair on the local Estate Planning Council's Board of Directors.

Acknowledgments & Special Thanks

We are most appreciative for the tremendous support and encouragement we have received throughout this project. We are extremely grateful to the instructors and program directors of CFP Board-Registered programs who provided valuable comments during the development stages of this text. We are fortunate to have dedicated, careful readers at several institutions who were willing to share their needs, expectations, and time with us.

We would like to pay special thanks to Donna Dalton and Robin Meyer. It takes more than just the writer to produce a finished book and they are an essential element of our team.

We have received so much help from so many people, it is possible that we have inadvertently overlooked thanking someone. If so, it is our shortcoming, and we apologize in advance. Please let us know if you are that someone, and we will make it right in our next printing.

PREFACE

Retirement Planning and Employee Benefits is written for graduate and upperdivision undergraduate level students interested in acquiring an understanding of retirement planning from a professional financial planning viewpoint. The text is intended to be used in a Retirement Planning course as part of an overall curriculum in tax or financial planning. The text is also intended to serve as a reference for practicing professional advisors.

This textbook was also designed to meet the educational requirements for a Retirement/Employee Benefits Course in a CFP Board-Registered Program. Therefore, one of our goals is to assure CFP Board-Registered Program Directors, instructors, students, and financial planners that we have addressed every relevant topic covered by the CFP Board Exam Topic List and the most recent model curriculum syllabus for this course. The book will be updated, as needed, to keep current with any changes in the law, exam topic list, or model curriculum.

Special Features

A variety of tools and presentation methods are used throughout this text to assist the reader in the learning process. Some of the features in this text that are designed to enhance your understanding and learning process include:

- **Learning Objectives** – At the beginning of each chapter is a list of learning objectives to help you focus your studying of the material. These learning objectives will provide a preview of the important topics covered in the chapter.

- **Key Concepts** – At the beginning of each subsection are key concepts, or study objectives, each stated as a question. To be successful in this course, you should be able to answer these questions. So as you read, guide your learning by looking for the answers. When you find the answers, highlight or underline them. It is important that you actually highlight/underline and not just make a mental note, as the action of stopping and writing reinforces your learning. Watch for this symbol:

≔ *Key Concepts*

- **Quick Quizzes** – Following each subsection you will find a Quick Quiz, which checks and reinforces what you read. Circle the answer to each question and then check your answers against the correct answers supplied at the bottom of the quiz. If you missed any questions, flip back to the relevant section and review the material. Watch for this symbol:

☑ *Quick Quiz 1.1*

- **Examples** – Examples are used frequently to illustrate the concepts being discussed and to help the reader understand and apply the concepts presented.

- **Exhibits** – The written text is enhanced and simplified by using exhibits where appropriate to promote learning and application.

- **Cases** – Several chapters contain real world case summaries to help the reader appreciate the application of particular topics being discussed in the chapter.

- **End of Chapter Questions** – Each chapter contains a series of discussion questions and a sample of multiple-choice problems that highlight major topics covered in the chapter. The questions test retention and understanding of important chapter material and can be used for review and classroom discussion. Additional problems are available at money-education.com by accessing the Student Practice Portal.

- **Quick Quiz Explanations** – Each chapter concludes with the answers to the Quick Quizzes contained in that chapter, as well as explanation to the "false" statements in each Quick Quiz.

- **Glossary** – Key terms appear in **boldfaced type** throughout the text to assist in the identification of important concepts and terminology. A compilation of the key terms identified throughout the text is located at the end of the book

Student Practice Portal
available by registering your textbook at money-education.com

This book is dedicated to
the many members of the United States Armed Forces
including our family members

Lt. Col. James J. Dalton, U.S. Army (1912-1981)
Lt. Col. James J. Dalton II, USMC Retired
Lt. Col. Brian J. Dalton, USAF Retired
William "Billy" Delle, U.S. Navy (1941-2018)
Major Edwin C. Marotte, U.S. Army (1919-2009)
Laurence R. Means, U.S. Navy

for protecting our unalienable rights,
including Life, Liberty and the pursuit of Happiness.

Michael A. Dalton & James F. Dalton

TABLE OF CONTENTS

Chapter 3 | Qualified Plan Overview

Chapter 4 | Qualified Pension Plans

Chapter 6 | Stock Bonus Plans & Employee Stock Ownership Plans

Chapter 7 | Distributions from Qualified Plans

Chapter 8 | Installation, Administration, and Termination of Qualified Plans

Chapter 11 | Social Security, Medicare, and Medicaid

Chapter 15 | Item Sets and the Mike & Maria Roman Case

Appendix

1

INTRODUCTION TO RETIREMENT PLANNING

LEARNING OBJECTIVES

1. Explain alternative views on retirement.*
2. Define financial independence.
3. Understand various sources of money conflict.*
4. Explain why employers are interested in retirement planning.
5. Identify groups interested in the study of retirement planning.
6. Discuss factors related to Americans' confidence in their ability to retire comfortably.
7. Contrast the myths and realities regarding retirement age and working during retirement.
8. Explain why employers establish employee benefits and retirement plans.
9. Describe how government influences social policy.

Ties to CFP Certification Learning Objectives

INTRODUCTION

Retirement planning and employee benefits are challenging, but fascinating areas of study. Although complex, they provide tremendous career and intellectual opportunities for a wide variety of interested parties. Most individuals are interested in achieving financial security, which means achieving financial independence so that they are able to maintain their desired lifestyle without employment income. To become financially independent, one must generally forgo a certain level of immediate consumption to provide an opportunity for discretionary funds to grow and accumulate over time while avoiding catastrophic financial occurrences that could result in financial dependence. Retirement planning and employee benefits play an essential role in satisfying the need to save for future consumption and toward the goal of financial independence.

Employers are keenly interested in the areas of retirement planning and employee benefits because they consider and select employer-sponsored benefit plans, as a method of attracting and retaining high quality employees. As a result, they are impacted by both current and future benefits costs and the limitations of such plans. Employees are also interested because benefits are generally considered a part of an overall compensation package. The professional opportunities and vast amount of retirement assets attract a diverse group of professionals and members of the financial service industry to this area of study. Lastly, the U.S. government has a public, social, and tax policy interest in the area. When the government wants to promote social policy, such as health care benefits or promoting home ownership, it frequently utilizes tax policy to encourage plan selectors to adopt the programs desired by the government.

Be forewarned, the topics of study are neither simple nor entirely intuitive. Determining funding requirements for retirement requires an in-depth understanding of life expectancies, work life expectancies, retirement life expectancies, the projection of inflation and investment returns, and the determination of expenditure needs for particular persons far in advance of their occurrence. When a person reaches retirement age, the optimal distribution amount must be determined given a probability element that the distribution amount will provide sufficient income to maintain the retiree's lifestyle for the entire retirement period while having little or no risk of being depleted during the retiree's life.

A vast amount of study is needed to initially master the subject of qualified retirement plans because of the complexity of the federal legislation controlling the area. In addition, as one might expect, the rules governing qualified retirement plans are frequently amended by new legislation. Therefore, current rules and optimal choices today may change at any time. Thus, continuing study in the area is essential to maintain and improve your skill level. Tax-advantaged plans, other than qualified plans, are also government created or approved, have similar complexities, and also run the risk of legislative change.

While the first pension plans in the United States were established by the railroad industry in the 19th century, Congress has been legislating them since 1921. Because of the importance of retirement planning, Congress has provided oversight for these plans in an attempt to increase the protection of retirement benefits of workers. For example, the purpose of the Pension Protection Act of 2006 was to provide greater protection for workers with defined benefits and came after the bankruptcy and subsequent termination of United Airline's pension plan. It is important to stay abreast of legislation affecting pension and retirement plans.

This textbook also covers Social Security legislation and benefits, both of which are large and complex topics. Furthermore, after the implementation of employee benefit plans, the costs and benefits, as well as the employee censuses (age, income, length of services, etc.), do not remain static. Therefore, there will always be a need for monitoring, making changes, or terminating plans. As a result, one must learn the myriad of federal rules and stay current with changes in law and practice to become a master of the retirement planning field.

Before delving into the various retirement plans and employee benefits, this chapter provides an overview of how people view and define retirement, how emotion and psychological makeup can influence behavior related to money, various sources of conflict regarding money, and the interested parties in the retirement planning and employee benefits.

DEFINING RETIREMENT

The traditional concept of retirement (traditional retirement) in which an individual leaves the workforce at age 65 and pursues other initiatives during their remaining years until death, has developed over the last 50 to 100 years. For centuries before, farming and agriculture provided families with the foundation of their economic security. People remained on the farm and with the family until death. The farm provided food, shelter, and resources for families to survive. As family members aged, they were cared for on the farms. However, as the economy developed as part of the industrial revolution, more and more people began working outside of the family farm as an employee of another individual or company. This demographic shift continued such that a higher percentage of people began moving from multi-generational family farms to cities. As a result of this mobility and distance from family, senior family members were less capable of providing for their own welfare as they aged, especially in difficult economic times and when jobs were scarce.

These demographic shifts and the Great Depression set the stage for the Social Security system, which was signed into law by Franklin D. Roosevelt on August 14, 1935, and began the seeds of retirement planning. This process did not occur over night and was accompanied by limited company pensions and Social Security retirement benefits, both of which provide income during retirement - the remaining life expectancy after the working years. It should be noted, however, that Social Security retirement benefits do not, and were never intended to, provide sufficient income in retirement to replace the income earned prior to retirement.

Even today, the notion of retirement for most people in the United States is that it commences after they stop working and/or achieving financial independence. Retirement generally begins in the early to mid-sixties with an average retirement life expectancy of around 20 years. However, this period may be much shorter due to untimely death, or much longer due to better than average health, sometimes lasting into the 100s.

This duration of retirement is important as it is the time during which the retiree is, by definition, not working and income needs must generally be provided from savings, pension income, or Social Security. Although some retirees choose to work to supplement their savings and other income, many will find it difficult to do so due to their own health issues or the need to care for a family member. Another way to view retirement is as the time at which an individual achieves financial independence. **Financial independence** is the ability to live comfortably without having to work for an income. This ability to live without working may come from income generated from investments, Social Security, pension income, or other sources, such as a trust set up by a financially successful relative. For most people, financial independence typically occurs later in life, often in their late 50s to 60s.

While income and net worth tend to increase with age, health is inversely related to age and tends to decline as we age. The inverse relationship between wealth and health leads to the timeless quote, "youth is wasted on the young." People often sacrifice their youth and the prime of their life in an attempt to work hard and accumulate wealth and other assets (e.g., homes and cars). At the point of financial independence, people may be beyond their prime and their health may even be in noticeable decline.

Recognizing that time and youth cannot be preserved, some have attempted to achieve financial independence much earlier than the typical mid 60s by massively increasing savings. One such movement is called the FIRE movement, which stands for Financial Independence, Retire Early.

The FIRE movement is principled on early retirement, as well as flexibility and freedom from worrying about money. The primary driver of this early retirement is extreme savings, which is used to accumulate sufficient assets to generate investment income that covers living expenses. Under the FIRE movement, financial independence is reached when an individual has accumulated 25 times their estimated annual expenses. The multiple of 25 is derived from the well-known retirement withdrawal rate of four percent, which is a reasonably good withdrawal rate for many people in retirement.

Example 1.1

Scarlet has estimated expenses of $100,000. She accumulates $2.5 million or 25 times her annual expenses. Under the FIRE movement, she would be considered financially independent. Dividing $100,000 by $2.5 million equals 4%. As is discussed in Chapter 2, the 4% withdrawal strategy is a fairly common approach to preserving retirement funds.

Two important factors in this definition are annual expenses and accumulated assets. To increase savings, those following the FIRE lifestyle will choose less expensive living options, such as a scooter in lieu of a car. Scooters are less costly to buy, insure, and park, and have much greater fuel efficiency than a car. Another example would be to buy a smaller house, or even a mobile home. Naturally, lower costs allow for higher savings and a smaller required accumulated savings balance.

Following this lifestyle prioritizes saving over spending on luxury items or dinning out at fancy restaurants in order to have freedom from working for an income. At the core of this movement is the idea of discipline and sacrifice in terms of current spending in an attempt to reach a future state of financial independence. A couple might choose not to have children to avoid the associated costs and allow for more freedom. Ultimately, it is about priorities, spending, and control over one's life.

There are variations in the FIRE movement. Lean Fire is a very minimalistic lifestyle, while Fat Fire is the opposite and includes living anywhere in the world with few sacrifices. In between these two ends is what is referred to as Barista Fire, which is less minimalistic and less lavish. Each variation of the FIRE lifestyle is premised on saving significantly more than most people in a proactive attempt to accumulate enough income producing assets to retire early, avoid the stress of worry about money, and unlock the freedom of financial independence.

The FIRE movement is a more extreme version of working hard toward an early retirement in an attempt to get the most out of life. Another alternative to the traditional retirement model is to take mini-retirements, or sabbaticals, during working years.[1]

A mini-retirement is a trip that lasts an extended period of time, typically ranging from two to six months, often in a different part of the world, as opposed to taking a week-long vacation once a summer. Before dismissing the idea completely as impossible, consider 2020 and 2021. If nothing else, the COVID-19 pandemic has shown that work can be done remotely. If a job can be done at home, several miles from an office, it could be done from another part of the world. One could continue to work from Europe or South America while immersed in a different culture.

Funding for a mini-retirement could come from savings, just as one would save for a car or boat, or it could be managed by house swapping or other cost savings methods. Consider the following examples.

Example 1.2

Hayden and Hannah dated in college and planned to get married two years after graduation. Hayden studied biomedical engineering and Hannah studied accounting. After graduating, they both got jobs and saved most of their income. They shared a used car, leased a small apartment, and limited their spending. They spent two years saving for a year-long trip around the world. Their plan was to have a small, inexpensive wedding and travel for a full year. In effect, they would take a mini-retirement. They excelled at their jobs for the two years they worked and figured they could get new jobs after they returned from their worldwide expedition.

Example 1.3

Deke loved to travel. Every summer he would spend time in Italy or Prague. Deke also loved the Internal Revenue Code and helping individuals and small businesses prepare their tax returns. He decided he would arrange his tax practice such that he works in his office in Metairie, Louisiana during tax season, which extends from February through April. Then he would live in Italy May through mid-August. He would return to the United States and work through October 15th and then live in Prague through January. The key to Deke's success was that he managed his business and his clients so that he could accomplish his mini-retirements every year.

---

1. Tim Ferriss discusses the concept of mini-retirements in his book, The 4-Hour Workweek.

Example 1.4

Once Arax graduated college and law school, she became a litigator for the Department of the Treasury. She worked countless hours for years, but her passion was always rock climbing. Ultimately, she realized she hated working behind a desk all the time. As she had become more proficient at rock climbing, she changed her life. She quit the Treasury Department and got hired as a rock climbing guide. Because guide work does not pay much, she supplemented her income by teaching at the local law school and tutoring students preparing for the LSAT. Now, Arax has taken control over her life and her daily routine.

The FIRE movement and mini-retirement concepts are variations from the traditional idea about retirement. While most people in the United States will continue to retire in their early 60s, understanding these alternatives may help focus people on their priorities allowing them to find what is most important in their life. These variations can be somewhat aspirational. However, individuals and advisors attempting to plan for retirement should understand psychological considerations, especially as they relate to money and finance.

PSYCHOLOGICAL CONSIDERATIONS

Many people like to consider themselves devoid of emotion when it comes to making decisions, especially financial decisions. In reality, emotion drives many decisions in life whether we are conscious of it or not. Emotional issues greatly influence our relationship with money and by extension, work, family members, and more. Ultimately, nearly every decision one makes involving money makes sense to them at the time based on their own life experiences and their psychological makeup. One's childhood, upbringing, and the economic period in which one was raised all impact how a person deals with and manages money.[2]

While the emotional influence of money is almost obvious, it is not as well researched and documented as other areas of psychology. However, below are some common disorders impacting the relationship with money and, therefore, the likelihood of achieving financial and life goals.

Compulsive buying disorder (CBD) is found worldwide and is characterized by excessive preoccupation with shopping and spending that leads to distress. CBD behavior can be a response to negative feelings and events in one's life. Shopping and buying can provide initial relief with positive feelings that tend to be short lived. This sort of behavior can be detrimental to an attempt at financial discipline and financial independence. CBD can also lead to financial ruin and bankruptcy, often characterized by high credit card debt.

Example 1.5

Ivan and Irene are married and have serious financial difficulties, mostly from credit card and auto debt, which they financed over seven years. Irene's brother Beau is helping them manage the situation. However, on the way home from a meeting with the bankruptcy attorney, Ivan stops at Best Buy and purchases a new 75-inch TV because it is on sale and there is a deal for signing up for Best Buy's credit card. Ivan is clearly unable to manage his spending and does not understand the severity of his financial situation.

---

2. See Ulrike Malmendier & Stefan Nagel, 2011. "Depression Babies: Do Macroeconomic Experiences Affect Risk Taking?" The Quarterly Journal of Economics, Oxford University Press, vol. 126(1), pages 373-416 | link - https://www.nber.org/papers/w14813.

Hoarding is a disorder characterized by accumulating and being unable to discard possessions that most people would consider worthless. The accumulation of these types of worthless possessions often creates clutter that negatively impacts living and working spaces. Hoarding disorder can also be associated with money such that one is unwilling to spend money even after becoming successful. Additionally, this behavior may be associated with those who have been raised in poverty, such as those who grew up during the depression. While everyone has rational fears regarding money, the fear of running out of money can become irrational with hoarding behavior.

Gambling disorder is a recognized psychiatric condition. Continued problematic gambling often leads to impairment and distress. Everyone who has gambled knows the emotional highs and lows of winning and losing a bet. Gambling can be exciting. However, most people who go to a casino also know that in the long run, the house always wins; the odds are stacked in the house's favor.

Workaholism is a compulsive disorder that is often associated with anxiety or depression. Workaholics frequently fear not having enough money and as a result focus on their career at the expense of personal relationships. They often justify their focus on work and avoidance of family and friends.

Financial enabling often manifests itself as successful parents financially enabling adult children to the extent that it negatively affects their children's emotional wellbeing. This type of situation is relatively common with wealthy individuals who are successful and continue providing financial support to their adult children, thus depriving them of developing their own financial acumen and responsibility. Other examples of financial enabling include providing support to a sibling or parent who has self-inflicted chronic financial difficulties. Financial enabling can also be seen in many family businesses.

Example 1.6

Karen has two grown sons, Moe and Curley. She had Moe when she was 18 years old and has never been very responsible with money. Moe went to college and, through hard work over the decades, has become fairly successful. Although she has attended numerous financial education seminars and classes through the years, Karen has filed for bankruptcy three times and continues to mismanage her finances. She has no emergency fund and continues to call Moe when there is a financial crisis, such as a need for a new set of tires. Moe continues to enable her poor financial behavior.

Example 1.7

Olivia is a successful financial planner with her own practice and is recognized as a leader in the industry. She hires her two sons, Fitz and Huck, to help run and grow the business. Over a fairly short period of time, she ends up paying her boys several hundred thousand dollars each in salary. However, while Fitz is working fairly hard, he is clearly overpaid for what he is doing. Huck, on the other hand, rarely shows up for work. Olivia is enabling her sons and thus, depriving them of learning how to function in the real world. As she begins to think about retiring, she cannot trust Fitz and Huck to run the financial planning practice and ultimately purchase the business from her nor can she sell the firm to a third-party without the likelihood of the new owner firing at least Huck.

Financial infidelity is the act of engaging in significant financial transactions without the knowledge and support of a spouse or partner. While many people engage in financial transactions of some sort without the knowledge of a partner, it becomes problematic when the transactions are significant in amount, such as hiding money, accumulating debt, gambling, or investing in illiquid assets that require the use of debt and leverage.

The disorders mentioned above, as well as cognitive errors and emotional biases discussed in behavioral finance, can create friction when establishing financial plans, and especially long-term financial plans such as retirement.

When an advisor is working with a client, it is important for the advisor to identify a client's motivation for achieving their financial goals. It is helpful to understand and identify whether the client is subject to any of these money disorders. Often, financial and lifestyle decisions are motivated by fear of running out of money. This fear can be rational or irrational. Other clients may be motivated by developing a sense of control over their financial situation so that they are no longer dependent on someone else or need to have a job. By clarifying motivations and managing psychological deterrents to appropriate financial management, advisors can often assist clients in devising better financial plans and, ultimately, achieving their life goals. It is also important for advisors to understand potential sources of conflict with money when working with clients. Some of these are discussed below.

Potential Sources of Conflict with Money

Money is often one of the top sources of conflict both between spouses and among family members. Spouses who have differing philosophies from each other about money often have conflict. For example, if one spouse is a saver (hoarder) and one is a spender (CBD), there will most likely be conflict. The saver will likely resent the spender and vice-versa. Understanding these differences prior to marriage is ideal.

Marriages, as with other relationships, are predicated on honesty and transparency. Lack of transparency when it comes to financial decisions can be detrimental to marriages and other family relationships.

Example 1.8

Sue and Blue are a married couple saving for a down payment on a new home. Blue buys a new car that is relatively expensive, finances it over seven years, and intentionally deceives Sue about the size of the monthly car payment. This decision and lack of transparency may eventually cause friction between Sue and Blue. These types of financial infidelity over time can lead to resentment, as well as to the erosion of trust.

Some of the more common potential areas of conflict regarding finances between spouses and other family members are as follows:

Savings: Saving is an important process for achieving financial goals. Without savings, many goals would remain unachieved. It is important to understand the objective of the savings and how the savings is achieved, whether through payroll deductions in a 401(k) plan or in a bank savings account. Conflict often occurs when both spouses are not working together toward the same savings goal.

Spending: Spending is required in our society. However, conflict arises when the expenses that one spouse might categorize as frivolous (e.g., boat) or as a luxury item are categorized as necessities by the other spouse.

Priorities: The basic priority of work versus family time often creates conflict if not balanced properly. One spouse may be overly focused on work and providing for the financial needs of the family, while the other spouse may resent the lack of time spent with the family. Those with workaholism often spend the majority of their waking hours focused on their job and not on the family. This focus often creates tension with other family members.

Undue financial influence: Couples may agree that it is in the family's best interest for one spouse to stay home and raise children while the other spouse works for income. The spouse that stays home with the children can be at a financial disadvantage if the marriage ends and can be in a situation in which the working spouse withholds financial resources for various reasons. The stay-at-home spouse may feel trapped in a toxic relationship with limited prospects for a job after staying at home for 10 to 20 years.

Another example in which financial influence can appear is within a family business where parents employ children or other family members. It is difficult to separate the family relationship from the business relationship.

These sources of tension and conflict regarding financial matters should help to clarify the importance of identifying and agreeing on financial goals with spouses and other family members. Having a clear agreed upon plan for retirement, for example, may help spouses manage conflict when there is tension regarding work as a priority or savings as a means of funding an agreed upon retirement lifestyle. Without an underlying plan, there is little basis for these financial choices, other than "want." Only after the clients (who may be spouses or unmarried individuals in a long-term relationship planning for retirement together) agree on the retirement lifestyle or financial independence goal, and parameters and priorities for current lifestyle adjustments they are willing to make to accomplish the goal, can a financial planner proceed to the analysis required to assist the clients with retirement planning.

INTERESTED PARTIES

There are four primary parties that are interested in retirement plans and employee benefits. These are employees, employers, professionals and institutions, and government. These four parties are discussed below.

Employees

Retirement plans and employee benefits provide an essential role in the pursuit of financial security. Retirement plans, whether employer or employee funded, offer employees an opportunity to accumulate assets that can later be used to provide a stable standard of living and financial security during retirement.

Funding of retirement benefits has changed significantly over the last thirty years. Years ago, many large employers provided employees with a retirement benefit, typically in the form of a fixed pension that would continue for the life of the retiree. Over time these plans, which were generally noncontributory by employees and costly to employers, have been replaced by plans that place more of the burden of funding on employees and shift the investment risk and responsibility from the employer to the employees. Reasons for this trend include the costliness of defined benefit plans compared to defined contribution plans and the attractiveness of defined contribution plans with the addition of IRC 401(k) plans resulting from the Revenue Act of 1978. **Exhibit 1.1** and **Exhibit 1.2** illustrate these trends.

Exhibit 1.1 | Total Retirement Plans, Plan Participants, & Plan Assets (1975-2018)[3]

Year	Total Plans			Total Plans Participants (in thousands)			Total Plan Assets (in millions)		
	Total	Defined Benefit	Defined Contribution	Total	Defined Benefit	Defined Contribution	Total	Defined Benefit	Defined Contribution
1975	311,094	103,346	207,748	44,511	33,004	11,507	259,963	185,950	74,013
1980	488,901	148,096	340,805	57,903	37,979	19,924	563,551	401,455	162,096
1985	632,135	170,172	461,963	74,665	39,692	34,973	1,252,739	826,117	426,622
1990	712,308	113,062	599,245	76,924	38,832	38,091	1,674,139	961,904	712,236
1995	693,404	69,492	623,912	87,452	39,736	47,716	2,723,735	1,402,079	1,321,657
2000	735,651	48,773	686,878	103,329	41,613	61,716	4,202,672	1,986,177	2,216,495
2005	679,095	47,614	631,481	117,406	41,925	75,481	5,061,622	2,254,032	2,807,590
2006	694,550	48,579	645,971	121,995	42,146	79,849	5,684,302	2,468,142	3,216,160
2007	707,787	48,982	658,805	123,854	42,280	81,574	6,090,473	2,646,603	3,443,870
2008	717,530	48,374	669,156	124,851	42,342	82,509	4,703,461	2,040,925	2,662,537
2009	706,667	47,137	659,530	129,268	41,820	87,448	5,511,060	2,193,983	3,317,076
2010	701,012	46,543	654,469	129,724	41,423	88,301	6,281,749	2,448,361	3,833,388
2011	683,647	45,256	638,390	129,581	40,876	88,705	6,345,595	2,516,109	3,829,487
2012	676,622	43,601	633,021	130,584	39,809	90,775	6,966,261	2,701,856	4,264,405
2013	681,154	44,163	636,991	131,631	39,084	92,547	7,870,897	2,866,392	5,004,505
2014	685,203	44,869	640,334	132,434	37,749	94,685	8,307,434	2,985,476	5,321,958
2015	693,925	45,672	648,252	134,857	37,286	97,572	8,154,472	2,862,402	5,292,071
2016	705,540	46,300	656,241	136,179	36,028	100,152	8,614,940	2,923,233	5,691,707
2017	709,527	46,698	662,829	137,400	34,960	102,440	9,759,090	3,208,820	6,550,270
2018	721,876	46,869	675,007	139,814	33,967	105,846	9,233,060	2,968,452	6,264,608

Exhibit 1.2 | Defined Contribution vs. Defined Benefit Plans

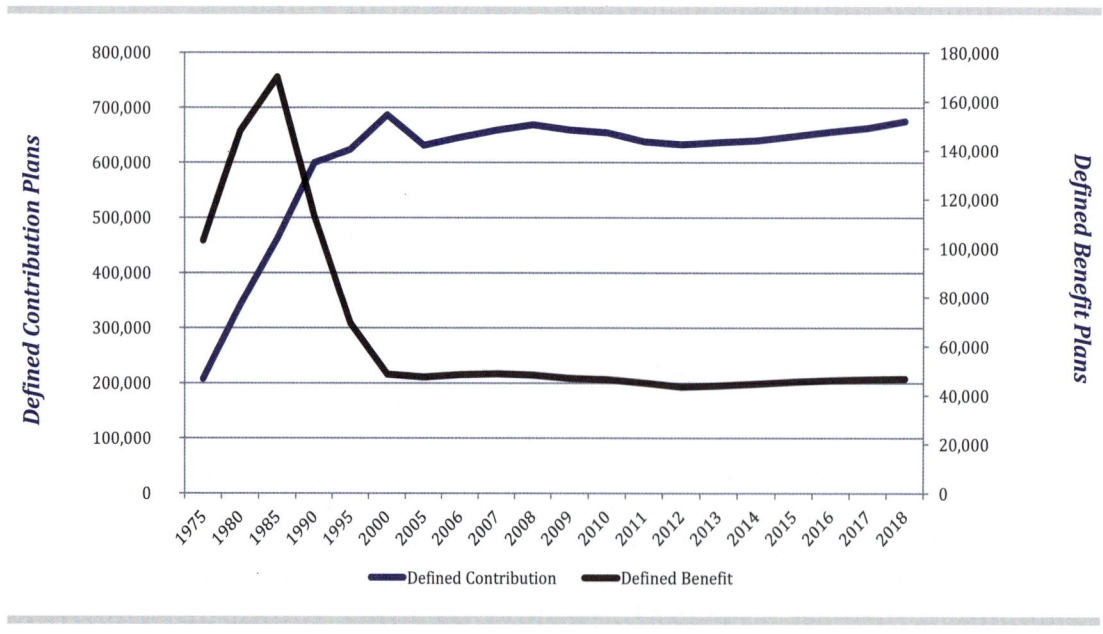

3. Form 5500 filings with the U.S. Department of Labor.

As employer funding has decreased and as life expectancy has increased, employees have begun to realize the importance of planning for retirement in hopes of achieving financial independence through their own savings and investments. Employees are also becoming more interested in risk management benefit plans (health insurance, disability insurance, life insurance, and long-term care insurance) because they are beginning to understand the risk and potential negative financial impact of a catastrophic event on their financial security. While it is the employer's responsibility to communicate employer-sponsored employee benefit and retirement plans provided to employees so that the employees have an opportunity to fully understand such benefits, the employee must take an active role in choosing and evaluating benefits available.

Many employees view retirement plan benefits and employee benefits (where employer contributions are present) as part of their overall compensation package. For example, employees realize that premiums paid for group health insurance are generally less costly than premiums paid for an individual plan with the same coverage and exclusions. Employees also realize that to the extent the employer contributes to the payment of such premiums, this value is not included in the employee's taxable income and, therefore, is less costly to the employee, who would have to purchase health insurance with after-tax dollars without such a plan.

Unfortunately, not all workers are covered by employee benefit plans, nor are they covered by retirement plans sufficient to produce adequate retirement income. While 91 percent of state and local government employees had access to retirement benefits, only 67 percent of all private industry employees had access to retirement benefits. In addition, the participation rates are lower than they should be at 83 percent for state and local government employees and only 51 percent for private industry employees.[4] These trends are illustrated in **Exhibit 1.3** along with the difference in retirement benefit access and participation for private industry employees of different size firms. While 83 percent of workers in private companies with 100 or more employees had access to retirement benefits, only 53 percent of workers in companies with less than 100 employees had access to retirement benefits. It is worth noting that the participation rate for employees in small companies is significantly lower at 37 percent compared to the participation rate for larger companies at 67 percent.

Exhibit 1.3 | Retirement Benefits: Access, Participation, and Take-Up Rates; National Compensation Survey, March 2020

	Private Industry			State and Local Government		
	Access	Participation	Take-Up Rate	Access	Participation	Take-Up Rate
1 to 99 Workers	53	37	69	88	83	95
1 to 49 Workers	49	34	69	85	80	94
50 to 99 Workers	69	46	68	91	87	95
100 Workers or More	83	67	81	92	83	89
100 to 499 Workers	80	60	76	91	84	92
500 Workers or More	88	77	88	93	82	88

Source: U.S. Department of Labor, BLS, National Compensation Survey, March 2020

4. U.S. Department of Labor, Bureau of Labor Statistics "National Compensation Survey: Employee Benefits in Private Industry in the United States, March 2020."

Americans' overall confidence in their ability to retire comfortably has increased somewhat from 2019 to 2020. The 2020 Retirement Confidence Survey by the Employee Benefit Research Institute indicates that approximately 69 percent of workers (up from 67 percent in 2019) are "somewhat" to "very confident" that they will have sufficient assets to live comfortably throughout retirement (a slight decline since 2007, when the percentage was 70 percent confident). **Exhibit 1.4** is a summary of the confidence of individuals over time. The question that was asked was, "Overall, how confident are you that you (and your spouse) will have enough money to live comfortably throughout your retirement years?"

Exhibit 1.4 | Confidence Survey[5]

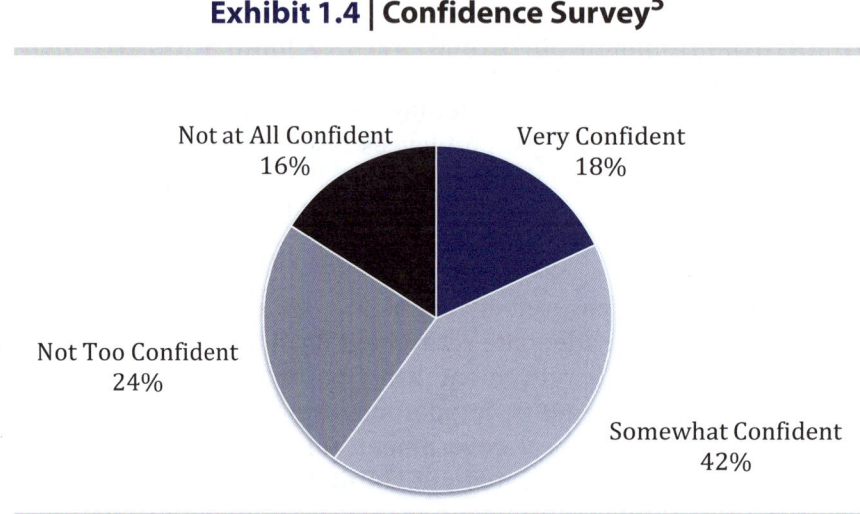

Mathew Greenwald's statement regarding a prior year's Retirement Confidence Survey (March 19, 2013) provides an insightful summary of the preparedness for retirement of the U.S. population, which has not significantly changed since then:

> "Savings rates of workers are disturbingly low and many are not saving at all. Only two-thirds of workers say they, or their spouse, have saved any money for retirement. At this point in time only 57% are actively saving money for retirement. As a result, the accumulated savings of many workers are quite low. Almost 3 in 5 (57%) of workers have financial assets that total to less than $25,000, not including their primary residence. Even when we just look at workers ages 45 and over, just under half (47%) have less than $25,000. Clearly, many are way behind in their financial preparation for retirement."

5. Employee Benefit Research Institute, 2020 Retirement Confidence Survey.

He also went on to discuss that the explanation most often given for not saving is the cost of living and the day-to-day expenses. However, many of the same participants agreed that there are expenses that could be cut out of their budgets, which would allow them to save more for retirement. The two expectations that contribute to not saving, even though there is an awareness of the need, are the expectation of working longer and the expectation of working during retirement. However, these two expectations are fraught with peril. There has historically been a significant difference between the expectation of working during retirement and actually working during retirement.

Possibly, the recognition of more realistic retirement needs has delayed the expected retirement age for many workers. The percentage of workers who expected to retire after age 65 increased from 11 percent in 1991 to 47 percent in 2020.

The 2020 study also points out the following myths and realities:

Myth: 74 percent of respondents say they plan to work during retirement.
Reality: Only 27 percent of retirees actually work during retirement.

Myth: 11 percent of respondents expect to retire before age 60 and 31 percent expect to retire at age 70 or later.
Reality: The average worker retires at age 62, which has remained constant for many years. 48 percent of retirees retired earlier than expected, and 70% of those who retired earlier than planned said that it was for some reason that was beyond their own control (e.g., due to health or changes in employment). 33 percent of workers retired before age 60 and only 6 percent actually waited until at least age 70 to retire.

It is also concerning that workers have very little saved for retirement, despite the dramatic trend away from traditional defined benefit pension plans that provide annuitized income for life. The survey provides the following facts:[6]

- Only 68 percent of workers have saved for retirement.
- 35 percent of workers have less than $25,000 in total savings and investments (excluding defined benefit plans and the value of their home).
- 18 percent of workers have less than $1,000 in total savings and investments.
- 47 percent of workers with a retirement plan (such as an IRA, defined contribution plan, or defined benefit plan) have $100,000 or more in retirement savings, versus only 8 percent of those without a retirement plan.
- 48 percent of workers have completed a retirement needs analysis or calculation.[7]

Unfortunately, even where employer-sponsored retirement plans exist, many of these plans are employee self-reliant plans requiring the participant to determine both the amount to save and the investments to choose from those offered. The ongoing need for assistance in the form of competent financial advice regarding retirement planning cannot be overemphasized.

---

6. EBRI 2020 Retirement Confidence Survey.
7. The topic of calculating needs is discussed in Chapter 2.

Exhibit 1.5 | Common Employee Perspectives of Retirement

- Employees view benefits as part of overall compensation.
- Employees would rather pay costs with pre-tax dollars.
- Employees generally understand retirement plans, and employee benefits are part of their overall financial plan.
- Employee confidence regarding their ability to retire comfortably is high, but inconsistent with reality.
- Employees generally do not really know the cost of retirement or how to achieve financial security.

Employers

Employers view employer-sponsored retirement plans and employee benefits as part of overall compensation costs. Employers are sensitive to the fact that once these plans are put into place, it is the employer that will have to manage these costs in the future, in spite of increasing rates of inflation associated with some of these benefits.

According to the 2020 Employer Health Benefit Survey, "The average annual premiums for employer-sponsored health insurance in 2020 are $7,470 (up from $7,188 in 2019) for single coverage and $21,342 (up from $20,576 in 2019) for family coverage. The average single premium increased four percent and the average family premium increased four percent over the past year. Workers' wages increased 3.4 percent and inflation increased 2.1 percent. The average premium for family coverage has increased 22 percent over the last five years and 55 percent over the last ten years" as indicated in the following chart:

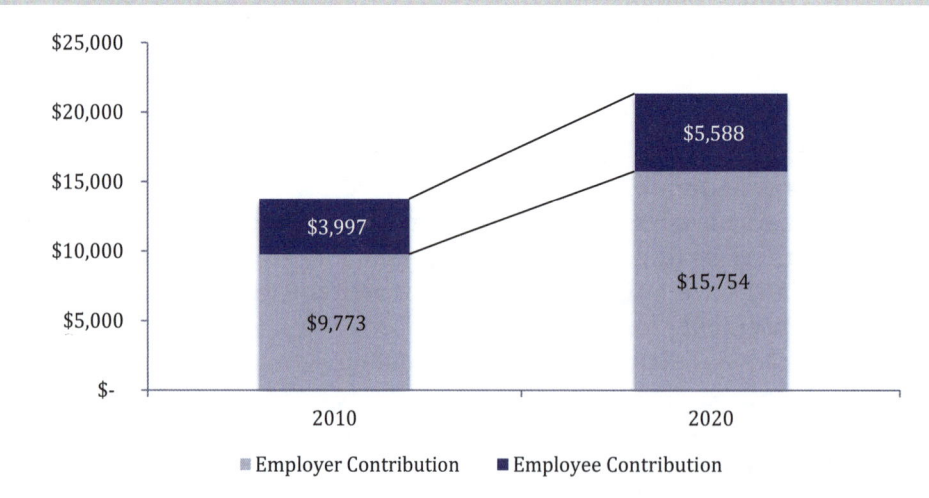

Example 1.9

The following is an example of how basic employee benefits (including health, life, and disability insurance; a 401(k) match; and reasonable vacation, personal, and holiday time) can increase employer payroll costs. In this case, the employer paid the employee a $40,000 salary and incurred $14,998 in additional benefits. These costs vary depending on the benefits offered, the age of the employee (insurance), and the salary received. There may also be other expenses, such as worker's compensation insurance and unemployment taxes (not intended to equal averages above).

	Amount	% of Compensation
Salary	**$40,000**	
Social Security	$3,060	7.65%
Health Insurance Premiums Paid	$6,500	16.25%
Life and Disability Insurance Premiums Paid	$700	1.75%
401(k) Employer Match	$1,200	3.00%
Vacation Time - 10 Days	$1,538	3.85%
Personal Time - 5 Days	$769	1.92%
Holiday Time - 8 Days	$1,231	3.08%
	$14,998	**37.50%**

The reasons that employers establish employee benefits and retirement plans are principally business related. Such plans have a positive impact on the ability to attract, reward, and retain qualified employees. The two leading reasons employers do not sponsor such plans are affordability and a lack of faith that such plans would have a positive effect on production and profitability.

Unfortunately, most small business owners are no more well informed about retirement plans and employee benefits than the workers they employ. There are a number of retirement plans that cost the employer little or nothing and would greatly benefit both the owner and the employees. Such plans are widely available but unknown or not understood by small business owners. Approximately one-third of small business owners have never heard of a SIMPLE plan, which has low costs and a positive impact on retirement planning.

Large employers are more likely than small employers to have a wide variety of employee benefits and a retirement plan. These employers have human resource departments that help select and administer employee benefit and retirement plans. The human resource departments make use of outside professional institutions and experts in plan selection, plan communication, and plan administration. The professionals include actuaries, pension experts, ERISA attorneys, employee benefit consultants, investment advisors, and plan administrators.

Exhibit 1.6 | Common Employer Perspectives of Retirement Plans

- Employers view retirement plans and employee benefits as part of overall compensation costs.
- Employee benefit expenses may add 30% - 40% to payroll costs.
- Employers use employee benefit plans to recruit, hire, and retain qualified workers.

Professionals and Institutions

There are a wide array of professionals and experts providing services in the areas of retirement planning, retirement plans, and employee benefits. There are also large financial institutions that manage plan assets (investments), administer plans, and communicate plan information to plan participants. Professionals within these financial institutions include personal financial planners or advisors who assist individuals and small business owners; actuaries whose primary role is in defined benefit or target benefit pension plans; pension experts and ERISA attorneys who assist in plan selection or creation, implementation, and communication; valuation experts who are used to value closely-held stock held in retirement plans; pension administrators who manage plan assets and communicate plan information to participants; Certified Public Accountants and other tax preparers who file required tax compliance reports; insurance planning professionals; and investment advisors who may advise either employers, plan participants, or both.

Major financial institutions play a role in the retirement plan area by providing prototype retirement plans for the convenience of customers, taking assets under management, and serving as custodians of assets. These institutions may also provide employee benefit plans and include insurance companies, banks, investment houses, and mutual fund companies.

Because of the complex nature of the entire field, any one of these experts may only be an expert in a small portion of the whole field. However, it is essential that advisors have a solid working knowledge of all of the areas and understand what each expert contributes so they can advise both employees and employers accordingly.

Exhibit 1.7 | Professionals and Institutions Interested in Retirement Planning

Interested Professionals
• Actuaries
• Pension Consultants
• Valuation Experts
• Financial Planners
• Employee Benefit Consultants
• ERISA Attorneys
• Certified Public Accountants
• Plan Administrators
• Insurance Professionals
Interested Institutions
• Banks
• Mutual Funds
• Insurance Companies
• Wirehouses and Brokerage Firms

According to the Investment Company Institute, there was approximately $33 trillion in retirement assets in the U.S. as of the end of the third quarter of 2020. This includes Individual Retirement Accounts (IRAs), SEP IRAs, Roth IRAs, employee-sponsored defined contribution plans, state and local government plans, private and federal defined benefit plans, and annuities, with the largest areas of growth being defined contribution plans and IRAs.

Exhibit 1.8 | Retirement Assets in the U.S., 2020 (Third quarter)[8]

IRAs (including rollovers)	$11.3 Trillion
Defined Contribution Plans	$9.3 Trillion
State and Local Government Retirement Plans	$4.8 Trillion
Private Defined Benefit Plans	$3.4 Trillion
Federal Pension Plans	$1.9 Trillion
Annuities	$2.4 Trillion
TOTAL	$33.1 Trillion (rounded)

8. https://www.ici.org/research/stats.

CASE STUDY 1.1

WWL is a talk radio station in New Orleans, Louisiana, broadcasting on 870 AM to the gulf coast and is now owned by Entercom Communications. The station has its beginnings at Loyola University, a Jesuit university that sought permission and was granted permission from the Vatican to own a radio station. It first began broadcasting in March 1922 and was finally sold in 1989 by Loyola to build the university's endowment fund.

From a tax perspective, WWL is an interesting example of how the government creates laws that may help or hinder certain industries or businesses. Internal revenue Code (IRC) §512 deals with unrelated business taxable income (UBTI). IRC §512(b)(15) is reproduced below:

Except as provided in paragraph (4), in the case of a trade or business -

512(b)(15)(A) **w**hich consists of providing services under license issued by a Federal regulatory agency,

512(b)(15)(B) **w**hich is carried on by a religious order or by an educational organization described in §170(b)(1)(A)(ii) maintained by such religious order, and which was so carried on before May 27, 1959, and

512(b)(15)(C) **l**ess than 10 percent of the net income of which for each taxable year is used for activities which are not related to the purpose constituting the basis for the religious order's exemption, there shall be excluded all gross income derived from such trade or business and all deductions directly connected with the carrying on of such trade or business, so long as it is established to the satisfaction of the Secretary that the rates or other charges for such services are competitive with rates or other charges charged for similar services by persons not exempt from taxation.

Notice that the first word for IRC §512(b)(15)(A),(B) and (C) begin with the letters WWL. The drafting of this code section was no accident. Nor is the code section an accident. The exclusion in this section was intended to benefit Loyola University specifically and its ownership of WWL and was attributed to Senator Russell Long of Louisiana. It also serves as an example of how the government can and does create laws that can help or hinder specific businesses or industries.

Exhibit 1.9 | Retirement Assets 1975 - 3Q 2020 (in trillions of dollars)

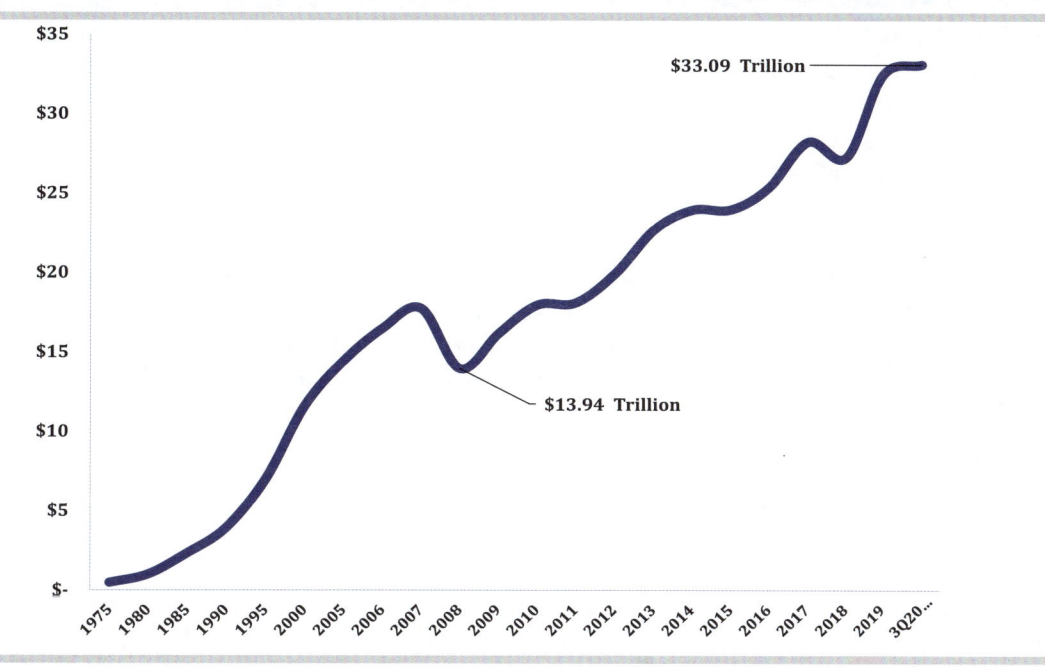

Government

The U.S. Government has a fundamental interest in employer-sponsored private retirement plans and privately-sponsored employee benefit plans. The government, as sponsor of the Social Security program and its benefits (retirement, disability, and survivorship) and health care benefits for retirees over age 65 through Medicare, is greatly concerned that Social Security contributions (funded through payroll taxes) may be insufficient to meet promised benefits. The government has a vested interest in promoting employee benefits such as employer-sponsored health care plans and retirement plans to mitigate the risk of more people ending up in the public welfare system. The government uses tax policy to make retirement plans and employee benefit plans sufficiently attractive so that a large number of employers will adopt them.

Keep in mind, however, that what the government gives out with one hand, it may take back with the other. Consider when studying these areas that while there are advantages to all these plans, usually in the form of current tax relief, there are also disadvantages, usually in the form of compliance, costs, and future taxes. The trillions in retirement assets combined with the annual contributions to retirement plans, is expected to grow significantly and will produce trillions in tax revenues. Both the Department of Labor and the Internal Revenue Service play an important role in these areas as does the Pension Benefit Guaranty Corporation (PBGC).

Exhibit 1.10 | Government Perspective of Retirement

- The government promotes social changes through tax legislation.
- The government sponsors the Social Security and Medicare systems, which act as a safety net for individual workers.
- The government has a vested interest in taxing deferred accounts.

PERSPECTIVE OF THE TEXT

The perspective of this text is that of a professional advisor who is providing professional services to workers and employers in the following areas:

- retirement funding
- retirement plan selection
- Social Security benefits
- employee benefits

In order to provide the highest level of service to the client, the advisor must have a thorough knowledge of retirement funding and forecasting. The advisor must also have a working knowledge of which qualified plans are appropriate for large employers given the goals and the employees census, which qualified plans are appropriate for small to medium size businesses, and which qualified plans are appropriate for single or few employee professionals.

The advisor needs to know the advantages and disadvantages of qualified plans and other tax-advantaged plans. The advisor needs to know when to use a nonqualified plan and how nonqualified plans fit into an employer's executive compensation plan.

Advisors need a deep understanding of retirement, disability, and survivorship benefits provided by Social Security and the benefits provided by Medicare to properly advise clients of the government sponsored safety net programs and to determine any gaps that need to be filled to meet client goals or needs.

Exhibit 1.11 | Overview of Text

The text covers retirement funding issues, a thorough understanding of qualified plans, other tax-advantaged plans, as well as Social Security, deferred compensation arrangements and employee benefits. It is organized as follows:

Chapter(s)	Topic
2	Retirement Accumulations and Distributions
3	Qualified Plan Overview
4	Qualified Pension Plans
5	Profit Sharing Plans
6	Stock Bonus Plans and Employee Stock Ownership Plans
7	Distributions from Qualified Plans
8	Installation, Administration, and Termination of Qualified Plans
9	IRAs and SEPs
10	SIMPLEs, 403(b) Plans, and 457 Plans
11	Social Security, Medicare and Medicaid
12	Deferred Compensation and Nonqualified Plans
13	Employee Benefits: Fringe Benefits
14	Employee Benefits: Group Benefits
15	Item Sets & the Mike and Maria Roman Case

Exhibit 1.12 | History of the Employment-Based Retirement System

Employers established retirement plans in the late 19th century in the absence of any tax advantages, although the government began granting tax-favored treatment to plans in the 1920s. After the Social Security system was established in 1935, employment-based retirement plans became widespread. In recent years, Congress has enacted legislation to regulate retirement plans more carefully and to allow employees to actively participate in certain types of employment-based plans.

Retirement Plans Prior to Tax Incentives

Formal retirement plans in the United States developed in tandem with shifts in family ties and in the nature of the business world. Urbanization weakened the extended family, which formerly had helped support those who were too old to work. In addition, the number of elderly people grew rapidly as earlier immigrants aged and life spans increased.

Large corporations needed systematic, publicly acceptable ways of moving elderly workers out of their jobs. Pensions were considered one solution that also provided an incentive to younger employees to stay with an employer throughout their working life. By 1929, about 15 percent of private-sector employees were covered by employment-based plans, which were concentrated in large corporations and in sectors in which government oversight tended to be the strongest.

The Government Gets Involved

The Revenue Acts of 1921, 1926, and 1928 initiated tax advantages for employment-based retirement plans. The 1921 law allowed employers to deduct contributions to profit-sharing and stock bonus plans from their taxable income. Employees, in turn, were allowed to delay recognizing contributions to those plans as taxable income until the contributions were withdrawn. The legislation also exempted the investment earnings of such plans until withdrawal. The 1926 law extended those advantages to pensions, while the 1928 law allowed sponsoring employers to deduct contributions for past as well as current service.

On the basis of the reported debate, it appears that Congress's exempting of the earnings of stock bonus and profit-sharing plans from taxation in 1921 was primarily intended to motivate workers to be more productive; increasing saving was a secondary consideration. Lawmakers' intentions in exempting pension plans in 1926 are less clear because there was no floor debate or discussion documented in committee reports. The provisions might have been intended to assist employers' nascent benefit plans or to resolve, in a purely technical way, the difficult problem of assigning trust income to a taxable entity.

Whatever the intent of those provisions, their enactment had little effect on the development of employment-based retirement plans in those years. Low tax rates held down the value of the benefits, so employers had little incentive to use them. Moreover, the provisions were barely in place when the Great Depression reversed the evolutionary trend of retirement plans: many employers terminated their plans, and a number of them failed to pay the benefits they had already promised to their workers.

Because employers' failure to pay promised benefits was exceptionally disruptive to the railroad industry, the federal government stepped in and established the Railroad Retirement system in 1935 to enable the depleted pension funds to meet their obligations. In that same year, lawmakers enacted the first Social Security legislation (although initially it covered only a portion of the labor force). Symptomatic of the general decline of employer-sponsored plans was the nearly total absence of any mention of them in the report of Congress's Committee on Economic Security in 1935.

History of the Employment-Based Retirement System Continued

By the late 1930s, however, retirement plans had revived enough to generate concerns about their being used primarily as tax-avoidance schemes for the wealthy. Accordingly, Congress passed the Revenue Act of 1938, which made pension and profit-sharing trusts irrevocable. The Revenue Act of 1942 established conditions that employer-sponsored plans had to meet before they qualified for tax-favored treatment. The 1942 law introduced the concepts of nondiscriminatory coverage and nondiscrimination in benefits and contributions, provisions that form the core of today's regulation of employment-based retirement plans. During World War II, pensions became a desirable form of compensation for two reasons: first, tax rates were very high and, second, contributions to pensions were exempted from wage controls. After the war, more and more employers began to offer pensions because tax rates remained high, Social Security benefits had been eroded by wartime inflation, and labor unions were successful in making pensions subject to collective bargaining.

Developments in the 1970s and 1980s

Changes in the tax code in recent years reflect evolving standards of adequacy and fairness in allocating the tax benefits associated with retirement plans. Lawmakers enacted plans in 1962 for self-employed workers and other noncorporate employers that were more tightly restricted than corporate plans. The Employee Retirement Income Security Act of 1974 (ERISA) considerably tightened the qualification rules for employers' plans. ERISA gave the federal government authority to prescribe a uniform meaning for plan rules and legislated minimum standards for participation, investing, the accrual of benefits, and funding.

Between 1974 and 1986, Congress pursued two different lines of policy. On one hand, it enhanced access to the tax-advantages of qualified plans in ways that emphasized individual decision making. The Revenue Act of 1978 sanctioned so-called salary-reduction arrangements in profit-sharing plans - now known as 401(k) plans - and in the state and local government sectors (§457 plans). Similarly flexible arrangements had already been possible in the nonprofit sector under §403(b) of the tax code. Then, in the Federal Employees Retirement System Act of 1986, Congress extended salary-reduction opportunities to all federal civilian employees. Although operated by employers, salary-reduction arrangements shift several key decisions from employers to workers, allowing participants to determine how much will be contributed and, in many cases, how that money will be invested.

On the other hand, lawmakers enacted changes that further constrained employer practices by emphasizing the collective or forced-saving aspects of pensions. Examples are the top-heavy plan rules in the Tax Equity and Fiscal Responsibility Act of 1982 (TEFRA) and the protections extended to widows in the Retirement Equity Act of 1984. TEFRA also eliminated differences between qualified plans maintained by corporate and noncorporate employers.

The Tax Reform Act of 1986 (TRA-86) reversed the trend toward individual control over retirement saving by lowering the maximum amount of compensation that could be deferred under 401(k) plans: whereas earlier law allowed annual deferrals of up to $30,000, TRA-86 limited them to only $7,000. But the law also extended a trend toward greater sharing of benefits among a firm's employees, primarily through stricter requirements for the inclusion of employees in retirement plans, faster vesting of benefits, and smaller offsets of plan benefits because of Social Security. Separately, the law's lowering of tax rates reduced the value of the tax advantages.

History of the Employment-Based Retirement System Continued

Recent Legislative Activity

During the 1990s, lawmakers sounded a theme of simplification. The various restrictions that the tax code placed on employers offering retirement plans were seen as placing an undue burden on small businesses that would probably discourage them from setting up plans. The Small Business Job Protection Act of 1996 established two new options (called SIMPLEs) for employers of 100 or fewer workers. Those plans allowed eligible employers to contribute to their employees' 401(k) plans or IRAs without being subject to nondiscrimination rules and the other tests that qualified plans must meet. In return for exempting employers from those requirements, the law specified formulas as the basis for employers' contributions.

In 2001, Congress passed the Economic Growth and Tax Relief Reconciliation Act (EGTRRA), which contained a variety of provisions that liberalized employment-based retirement plans. The law allows employers to contribute more to the retirement plans of high-income employees and to deduct more of what they contribute to all retirement plans. Employees are also allowed to contribute more to 401(k)-type plans on their own behalf. Additional provisions establish a credit for expenses incurred by small businesses in starting up a retirement plan and administering it for the first three years. They also enhance portability by permitting rollovers from one type of employment-based plan to another and from IRAs to employment-based plans.

In 2006, Congress passed The Pension Protection Act of 2006 (PPA), which was signed into law on August 17, 2006. The PPA 2006 was the most sweeping pension legislation in over 30 years and included a number of significant tax incentives to enhance and protect retirement savings for millions of Americans. One of its primary focal points was to force companies to fully fund obligations under defined benefit plans. The Small Business Jobs Act of 2010 provided for Roth Accounts in 457 Plans and created the in-plan Roth rollover, which allows plan balances in traditionally deferred accounts within qualified plans to be converted to Roth accounts. The American Taxpayer Relief Act of 2012 made permanent many of the provisions in EGTRRA 2001 and increased the funds that could be converted in an in-plan Roth rollover.

On December 20, 2019, the Setting Every Community Up for Retirement Enhancement (SECURE) Act was signed into law. While the SECURE Act provisions were broad in scope, many of the provisions were designed to encourage and make it easier for small businesses to establish and maintain retirement plans for the benefit of their employees. Along with other enhancements, the Act revised the rules regarding multiple-employer and pooled plans making it more attractive and accessible for small businesses to join together to establish a qualified retirement plan, increased the small employer startup cost credit, granted employers additional time to make the decision to initially establish a qualified plan by extending the due date for adopting the plan, and provided fiduciary protection to defined contribution plan sponsors offering lifetime income investment options within the qualified plan.

2

RETIREMENT PLANNING ACCUMULATIONS AND DISTRIBUTIONS

LEARNING OBJECTIVES

1. Identify the factors affecting retirement planning.*
2. Draw the exponential graph representing the required investment assets as a percent of gross pay from age 25 to age 65.
3. Explain why saving early is usually better than saving later.
4. Explain the impact of inflation on purchasing power.
5. Identify the costs that may decrease and those that may increase from pre-retirement to retirement.
6. Distinguish between the top-down and the bottom-up approaches in determining the wage replacement ratio.
7. Identify the various sources of retirement income.*
8. Calculate the capital needs analysis using the annuity approach, the capital preservation approach, the purchasing power preservation approach, and the capitalization of earnings approach.*
9. Discuss the various methods for sensitivity analysis as it is applied to capital needs analysis.*
10. Compare two of the common approaches to managing withdrawals for retirement income.*

Ties to CFP Certification Learning Objectives

INTRODUCTION

With nearly 35 percent of Americans having less than $25,000 in savings (excluding the value of their primary home and any defined benefit plans) and practically one in five with savings of less than $1,000, it is easy to make the case that most Americans are not financially prepared for retirement.[1] Financially prepared at retirement means that a person has:

1. Sufficient asset accumulation at retirement,
2. An appropriate investment plan, and
3. A plan for taking distributions from savings.

There are multiple factors to each of the three aspects of financial preparedness. This chapter examines the factors affecting retirement planning, the calculation of retirement needs, and methods of distributing assets during retirement.

FACTORS AFFECTING RETIREMENT PLANNING

Individuals face many decisions regarding retirement planning. In particular, they must decide what retirement means to them. Does retirement mean withdrawing from the workforce when financially able, or does it mean changes in lifestyle and family situations? For most, it is a momentous lifestyle change resulting from a significant shift in how they spend their time, money, and energy.

Individuals planning for retirement need to understand several basic factors that impact how much money is needed to fund retirement and how much money can be accumulated by the start of retirement. This chapter discusses the primary factors affecting retirement planning.

---

1. The 2020 Retirement Confidence Survey, EBRI, April 23, 2020.

The factors discussed in this chapter are:

- the remaining work life expectancy (RWLE)
- the savings amount and rate
- the wage replacement ratio (WRR)
- inflation expectations
- and other qualitative factors

- the annual income needed (needs) during retirement
- the retirement life expectancy (RLE)
- the sources of retirement income
- investment returns

A retirement plan must produce sufficient resources and income streams at retirement to ensure that a comfortable pre-retirement lifestyle is maintained throughout the retirement period. A discussion of each factor, its associated risks, and the calculations essential to retirement planning (capital needs analysis) is presented below.

Exhibit 2.1 | Factors Affecting Retirement Planning

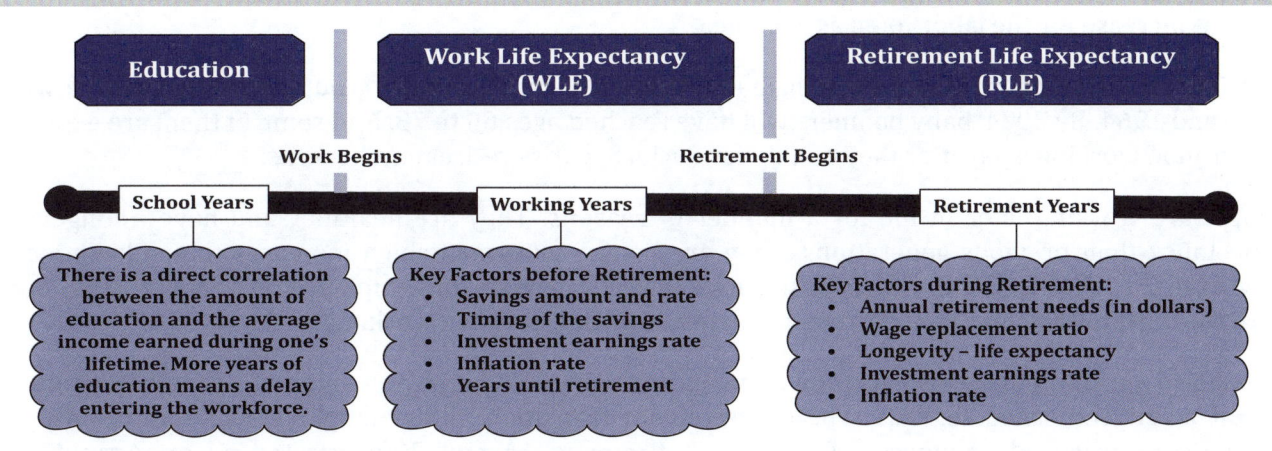

Remaining Work Life Expectancy (RWLE)

Work life expectancy (WLE) is the period of time a person is expected to be in the work force. This time period may last as long as 30 to 40 years and is essential in retirement planning because it is the period during which one saves and accumulates funds to use during retirement. Increasing or decreasing the work life expectancy impacts the time period over which individuals can save for retirement. The United States has seen a substantial decline in the overall WLE in the last several decades primarily due to individuals pursuing advanced education (undergraduate and graduate degrees), which delays their entry into the workforce, and those taking early retirement, which hastens their exit from the workforce.

Normal retirement has historically occurred near age 65 primarily because Social Security designated it as such and other employer provided retirement plans followed suit. The age at which recipients of Social Security can begin receiving benefits is age 62, but they must wait until Full Retirement Age to receive their full benefits under the system. Until recently, the average retirement age in the United States had steadily decreased since the 1970s due to a variety of factors including early retirement options from employer plans, early retirement under Social Security, and to some extent, positive investment performance during the 1980s and 1990s, which increased retirees' wealth.

However, Bureau of Labor (BLS) data show that the trend of earlier retirement is reversing and the age at which people are retiring has risen over the last several years. For example, in 2020, 22.3 percent of men aged 65 or older were employed, compared with 16.3 percent in 1990 and 17.5 percent in 2000. Among women 65 or older, 14.5 percent were working in 2020, compared with 8.6 percent in 1990 and 9.4 percent in 2000.[2]

Although they make up a smaller number of workers overall, the 65- to 74-year-old and 75-and-older age groups are projected to have faster rates of labor force growth annually than any other age groups. Over the entire 2014-24 decade, the labor force growth rate of the 65- to 74-year-old age group is expected to be about 55 percent, and the labor force growth rate of the 75-and-older age group is expected to be about 86 percent, compared with a 5-percent increase for the labor force as a whole.

This increase is being fueled by the aging baby-boom generation, a large group of people born between 1946 and 1964. By 2024, baby boomers will have reached ages 60 to 78. And some of them are expected to continue working even after they qualify for Social Security retirement benefits.

People are working later in life for a number of reasons. They are healthier and have a longer life expectancy than previous generations. They are better educated, which increases their likelihood of staying in the labor force. And changes to Social Security benefits and employee retirement plans, along with the need to save more for retirement, create incentives to keep working.

There also appears to be a recent trend of partial retirement, whereby an employee continues working but at a reduced schedule. This type of retirement transition allows employers to reduce cost but maintain experienced employees. The Pension Protection Act of 2006 created an opportunity for employees to begin receiving pension benefits while remaining employed after the attainment of age 62, and the Bipartisan American Miners Act of 2019 further expanded this opportunity by reducing the minimum age from 62 to 59½.

The trends discussed above are illustrated in **Exhibit 2.2**.

---

2. U.S. Department of Labor, Bureau of Labor Statistics.

Exhibit 2.2 | Labor Force Participation for Workers 65 and Older

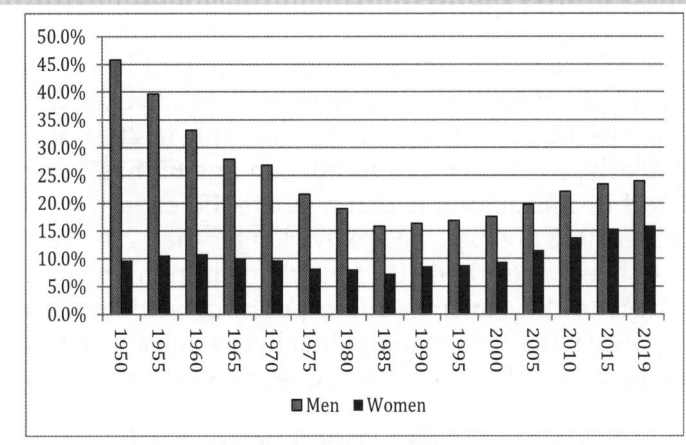

U.S. Bureau of Labor Statistics

Exhibit 2.2 illustrates that retirement age steadily declined over the last six decades, but is now increasing. According to research done by the Center for Retirement Research, based on US Census data, the average retirement age for men increased from age 62 to age 64 over the last 20 years. In addition, they found that the average age of retirement for women is age 62.[3] It is important for advisers to understand this information because it can provide them with a benchmark to use when calculating retirement needs. Thus, the adviser needs to talk with the client to determine the age the client is planning to retire.

The **remaining work life expectancy (RWLE)** is the work period that remains at a given point in time prior to retirement. For example, someone who is 30 years old and expects to retire at age 65 has a RWLE of 35 years. The RWLE is critical as it represents the remaining number of years over which savings can occur for the purpose of funding retirement.

Retirement Life Expectancy (RLE)

Retirement life expectancy (RLE) represents the total amount of time expected during retirement. This period begins at retirement and extends until death. Many retirees live as long as 20 to 40 years in retirement. However, this longevity has not always been the case. The average life expectancy for a newborn child in 1900 was 47 years, and many individuals worked as long as they were able.[4] During this time, the country was more agrarian and families lived together. As family members aged, they were cared for by the younger members of the family. There was not an official "retirement period." The concept of retirement, as we know it today, did not exist. **Exhibit**

> ### ✍ Quick Quiz 2.1
>
> 1. Approximately 80% of men work past age 65.
>   a. True
>   b. False
>
> 2. The RLE is the time period beginning at retirement and ending at death.
>   a. True
>   b. False
>
> 3. As the RLE increases because of early retirement, there is generally both an increased need of funds to finance the RLE and a shortened WLE in which to save and accumulate assets.
>   a. True
>   b. False
>
> False, True, True.

---

3. What is the Average Retirement Age?, Alicia H. Munnell, Center for Retirement Research at Boston College, August 2011.
4. It should be noted that the life expectancy in 1900 is biased due to a high infant death rate at the time.

2.3 presents data depicting the increase in life expectancy at birth from 1900 to 2018, and **Exhibit 2.4** depicts the increase in life expectancy at age 65.[5]

Population trends provide the adviser with a good understanding of how long a person might live in retirement. Women born in 2018 are expected to live on average 81.2 years, while men born in 2018 are expected to live on average 76.2 years. The average woman retiring in 2018 at age 65 has an average life expectancy of 20.7 years. Similarly, a man retiring in 2018 at age 65 has an average life expectancy of 18.1 years. The problem with this information is that average life expectancy is just that - an average. Fifty percent of women age 65 in 2018 are expected to live longer than 20.7 years and 50 percent of men age 65 in 2018 are expected to live longer than 18.1 years. In addition, the older an individual gets, the more likely they are to live beyond their average life expectancy as determined at birth or at age 65. Proper planning is needed because if the retired individual lives longer than he or she planned for, there is a risk of running out of money. This risk is known as **superannuation**.

Exhibit 2.3 | Life Expectancy at Birth

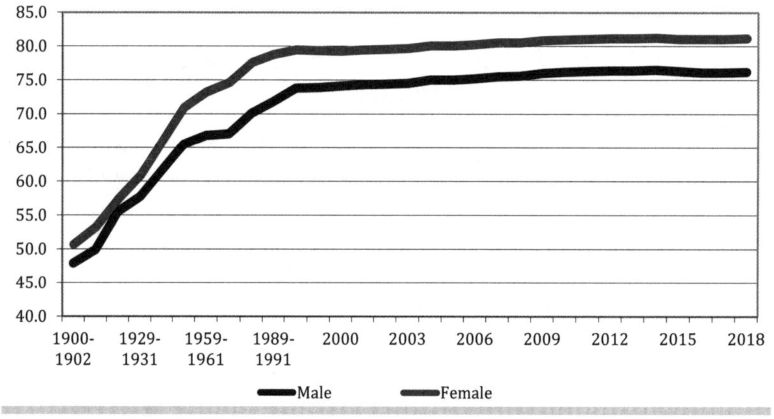

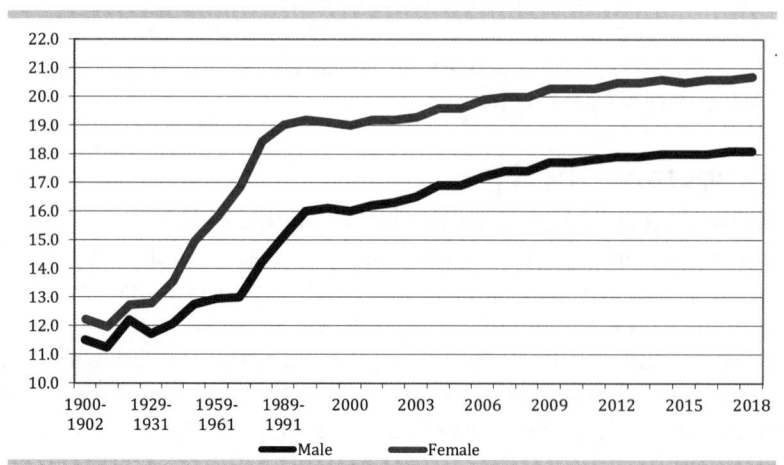

Source: Centers for Disease Control, NCHS, Mortality in the United States, 2018 (www.cdc.gov)

Exhibit 2.4 | Life Expectancy at Age 65

Source: Centers for Disease Control, NCHS, Mortality in the United States, 2018 (www.cdc.gov)

5. U.S. Department of Health & Human Services, CDC *NCHS, Mortality in the United States, 2018.*"

The Relationship Between The WLE and The RLE

The WLE and the RLE together make up a person's remaining life expectancy post education. Because this remaining period is effectively fixed, any change in one factor inversely impacts the other factor. If a person wants to increase their time during retirement, then that correspondingly shortens the WLE. A shortened WLE means less time to save and accumulate funds to satisfy a longer RLE. A person who is unable to save enough during their WLE to retire at a desired age, such as age 62, needs to consider delaying retirement, which is equivalent to increasing the WLE and decreasing the RLE. **Exhibit 2.5** visually depicts this relationship.

Exhibit 2.5 | The Relationship Between WLE and RLE

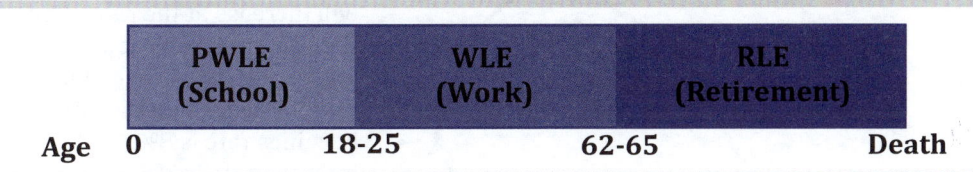

The prework life expectancy (PWLE) occurs prior to fully entering the work force and generally extends to some point between ages 18 and 25. The point at which the PWLE ends generally depends on the amount of education the person is undertaking. Some individuals may begin full time employment after high school graduation, while others may have four years of college education combined with years in post graduate study.

The WLE represents the time a person is working, saving, and accumulating wealth for retirement. This period begins once a person finishes their education, and it continues until retirement.

The RLE typically begins between age 62 and 65 and continues for the remainder of a person's life. As discussed earlier, the average life expectancy of someone who reaches the age of 65 is around 20 years. However, the RLE could last significantly longer, depending on the health of the person. Because life expectancy is unknown, retirement plans must be sufficiently flexible to allow for people who outlive the averages to not outlive their retirement income and savings.

Savings and Investment Issues

Retirees generally have multiple sources of income to pay for expenses during retirement. These sources generally include Social Security benefits, pension income, personal savings, and/or income from continued work during retirement. Most retirees cannot maintain their pre-retirement lifestyles on Social Security alone. Most need personal savings to sustain a relatively consistent standard of living during retirement. These sources of income are discussed in greater detail later in this chapter.

Personal savings is a critical element of most people's retirement funding plan and their ability to maintain their standard of living from their working years into their retirement years. The amount of personal savings a person has at retirement is dependent upon the following factors:
- The savings amount and the savings rate
- The timing of the savings and the period over which the savings grows
- The investment returns earned on the savings

In general, a person who begins saving between 10 percent and 13 percent of their income at or near age 25 will have sufficient funds accumulated at retirement, if the savings are invested in such a way as to earn a reasonable investment rate of return. Consider **Exhibit 2.6**, which illustrates a person saving 12 percent of their income from age 25 to age 65 earning eight percent, while inflation equals three percent. In this case, the savings accumulation takes care of their needs throughout retirement without the need for Social Security.

Exhibit 2.6 | Savings Balance from Age 25 to Age 100

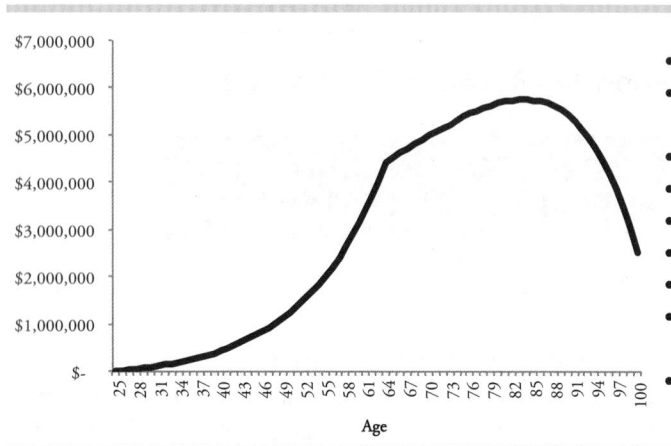

- Beginning age is 25
- Beginning salary is $100,000, which will increase at the rate of inflation
- Retirement begins at age 65
- Life expectancy is age 100
- Annual savings rate is 12%
- Earnings rate is 8%
- Inflation rate is 3%
- Distributions begin at age 65 based on a wage replacement ratio of 80%
- No Social Security benefits are included in the analysis

Regrettably, most individuals who are in their mid-twenties are unaware that funding for retirement is an important consideration, even though retirement may be forty years away. In addition, most people do not have a very good grasp of investment concepts and the total returns that are available through compounded annual returns.

The Savings Amount

The required amount of savings to fully or partially fund retirement is dependent on when a person begins to save for retirement. As mentioned, a person who begins to save 12 percent of their income at age 25 will accumulate an adequate amount of funds for retirement. Beginning to save early allows for compound investment returns that help savings grow significantly. However, when people delay saving for retirement, the amount of savings must be increased to overcome the lost contributions as well as the investment returns from lost years of annual compounding. **Exhibit 2.7** illustrates the percentage of income individuals must save if they begin saving at different ages.

≔ *Key Concepts*

1. What savings and investment concepts are important to retirement planning?

2. Why is it important to begin to save early for retirement?

3. Why is it important to understand investment decisions and their consequences in retirement planning?

4. How is inflation relevant to retirement planning?

Exhibit 2.7 | Required Savings Rate for Retirement
(Assume $0 of Accumulated Savings at the Beginning Age)

Age Regular Savings Begins*	Required Savings Rate*
25 - 35	10 - 13%
35 - 45	13 - 20%
45 - 55	20 - 40%**

*Assumes reasonable rate of return, normal raises, 80% wage replacement ratio, and Social Security benefits.

** At age 55, the person will realistically have to delay retirement until age 70.

Many people find it hard to begin any type of savings plan, let alone one that must continue for decades to be successful. Savings requires sacrificing current consumption for the purpose of higher future consumption. As **Exhibit 2.7** illustrates, the problem with delaying saving for retirement is that the rate that must be saved increases significantly over time. Saving 12 percent or even 15 percent at age 25 is generally easier than attempting to save 30 percent at age 50.

Exhibit 2.8 illustrates the required annual savings percentage necessary based on the time until retirement and the rate of return earned on invested assets.[6] Notice that if the RWLE is shortened from 40 years to 30 years and the portfolio continues to earn eight percent, the contribution increases from 12 percent to 22 percent. This example helps illustrate the importance of beginning a savings program early.

Exhibit 2.8 | Required Annual Savings Percentage[7]

Based on Exhibit 2.6 Assumptions		Number of Years Until Retirement						
		40	35	30	25	20	15	10
Rate of Return	4%	29%	34%	40%	50%	64%	87%	134%
	5%	23%	28%	35%	44%	58%	81%	128%
	6%	19%	24%	30%	39%	53%	76%	123%
	7%	15%	19%	25%	34%	48%	70%	117%
	8%	12%	16%	22%	30%	43%	66%	112%
	9%	9%	13%	18%	26%	39%	61%	107%
	10%	7%	11%	15%	23%	35%	57%	102%
	11%	6%	9%	13%	20%	31%	52%	98%
	12%	4%	7%	11%	17%	28%	49%	93%

---

6. **Exhibit 2.6** used future dollars whereas **Exhibit 2.8** uses today's dollars. The inflation rate remains at 3 percent, so the real rate of earnings at 8 percent is 4.8544 percent. The target future value is $1,399,103, which is the future value (in today's dollars) based on the same assumptions as **Exhibit 2.6**.
7. **Exhibit 2.8** uses the same assumptions as **Exhibit 2.6**. This result is the same as in **Exhibit 2.6**. Note also that as the time until retirement decreases, the required savings percentage increases significantly. Remember that this example includes zero savings at the beginning of the problem (PV = $0.00).

As an alternative to **Exhibit 2.7**, consider **Exhibit 2.9**, which assumes that each person is saving 10 to 13 percent of gross pay, including any employer retirement plan contribution. Assuming that the person saves 10 to 13 percent and also has an investment account balance equal to what they need at each age, they are making adequate progress toward the goal of financial security at retirement. If the person does not have the appropriate investment assets or has a lower savings rate than 10-13 percent, the shortfall will eventually emerge. Therefore, both investment assets on the balance sheet and the savings rate are relevant to achieving the desired capital balance for retirement.

Exhibit 2.9 | Benchmark for Investment Assets as a Percentage of Gross Pay

Age	Investment Assets as a Ratio to Gross Pay Needed at Varying Ages
25	0.20 : 1
30	0.6 - 0.8 : 1
35	1.6 - 1.8 : 1
45	3 - 4 : 1
55	8 - 10 : 1
65	16 - 20 : 1

The benchmarks as calculated consider incomes between $50,000 and $350,000, inflation at approximately two to three percent, a balanced investment portfolio of 60 / 40 equities to bonds returning five percent over inflation, a savings rate of 10 to 13 percent of gross pay, and a wage replacement ratio of 80 percent of gross pay. To the extent that any of these assumptions are incorrect for a particular person, the results may be misleading and require a specific personal calculation. These benchmarks are only a beginning.

Note that **Exhibit 2.9** illustrates that a person planning to retire at age 65 will need investment assets approximately 16 to 20 times the pre-retirement gross pay. A person at age 55 who plans to retire at 65 will need investment assets equal to eight times their current gross pay and will need to continue to save 10 to 13 percent of gross pay, including any employer contributions, and will need to earn an adequate investment rate of return on the retirement assets to achieve adequate retirement funding. More precise calculations are addressed throughout this chapter. While this schedule is only a benchmark, it works well for incomes between $50,000 and $350,000, inflation at two to three percent, and a balanced portfolio earning about five percent over inflation.

Exhibit 2.9 also illustrates that a tremendous amount of retirement asset accumulation occurs toward the end of the working years (ages 55 to 65). This increase is attributable to the compounding that occurs during the last ten years of work life expectancy based on the accumulation at age 55. Assuming that returns during this ten-year period are average, the accumulated assets should be what was expected. However, if the last ten years underperform from an investment return perspective, the investor may have to delay retirement or reduce spending during retirement.

Example 2.1

Assume Carrie, age 45, comes to you and is currently earning $100,000 per year. She has $350,000 (3.5 times her annual earnings) of investment assets (cash, mutual funds, retirement funds, etc.), not including personal use assets (equity in personal residence) and is saving $10,000 of her gross pay (10%). Carrie is concerned about making adequate progress towards her retirement goals. Assuming that Carrie is invested in an appropriate investment portfolio, she appears to be making adequate progress towards retirement if that is her only goal. Note that she will have to save more if she expects to live well beyond average life expectancy. Assume she can earn 8% with inflation of 3%. If she continues to spend as expected, she will run out of money at age 89. However, average expenditures for retirees tend to decline during retirement.

Step 1: Determine Future Income at Age 65

Current Earnings - PV	$100,000
Inflation - I	3%
WLE - N	20 years
Future Earnings - FV	$180,611

Step 2: Determine Needs at Retirement

WRR	80%
Retirement Payment	$144,489 ($180,611 x 80%)

Step 3: Project Savings at Retirement

Current Assets - PV	$350,000
Annual Savings - PMT	$10,000
Earnings Rate - I	8%
Work Life Expectancy - N	20 years
Assets at Retirement - FV	$2,088,955

Step 4: Determine Period of Time Funds will Last

Asset at Retirement - PV	($2,088,955)
Annual Inflation Adjusted Annuity Payment - PMT_{AD}	$144,489
Inflation Adjusted Earnings Rate - I	4.85437 ((1.08/1.03)-1) x 100
Funds at End - FV	$0
Years in Retirement that Funds will Last (Approximate)	24 Years

*Note that savings amount will increase each year with raises.

Savings Rate

The **U.S. personal savings rate** identifies the average savings amount in the U.S. The savings rate is interpreted as personal saving as a percentage of disposable personal income. The personal savings rate has declined significantly since the 1970s. In fact, the personal savings rate fell from a high of 13.5 percent in 1973 to 3.1 percent in 2005, increased to 8.8 percent in 2012 and was at 7.5 percent in 2019. **Exhibit 2.10** illustrates the historical trends.[8] The growth in personal expenditures may be the cause of the drop in savings over the past few decades and suggests that individuals are not saving enough for retirement. This low savings rate is extremely concerning. Recall that in order to meet just the retirement goal, a savings rate of 10 to 13 percent of gross pay over a long period is necessary. Unfortunately, most people are not well prepared for retirement, in terms of savings amount, savings rate, or accumulated savings.

Exhibit 2.10 | U.S. Personal Savings Rate

Timing of Savings

The timing of savings is also critical as it dictates the number of years over which savings can earn investment returns and grow. More compounding periods for savings to grow results in less total savings needed over the WLE. When individuals delay savings, the potential earnings that would have been achieved through compounding during those periods is lost. Consider **Example 2.2** which illustrates the power of compound returns.

Example 2.2

Peter saves $5,000 each year on his birthday, from age 35 through age 65, for a total of 30 payments. He invests the funds so that he earns an 8% rate of return over the 30 years. His friend, Lori, began saving the same amount on her birthday at age 25. She saved $5,000 each year from age 25 through age 34. She also earned an 8% rate of return on her investments. Surprisingly, Lori has a larger savings balance at age 65 than Peter. **Exhibit 2.11** summarizes their accumulated savings.

---

8. https://fred.stlouisfed.org/series/PSAVERT#.

Exhibit 2.11 | Time/Savings Example (Lori and Peter Example)

	Lori	Peter
Total Invested	$50,000 (10 years)	$150,000 (30 Years)
Balance at age 65	$728,867	$566,416
Earnings Rate	8%	8%
Investment Return Multiple	14.58x	3.78x

While Peter invested three times as much as Lori, Lori has 29 percent more than Peter at age 65. **Exhibit 2.12** graphically illustrates the power of saving early and compounding.

Exhibit 2.12 | Lori and Peter Investment and Accumulation

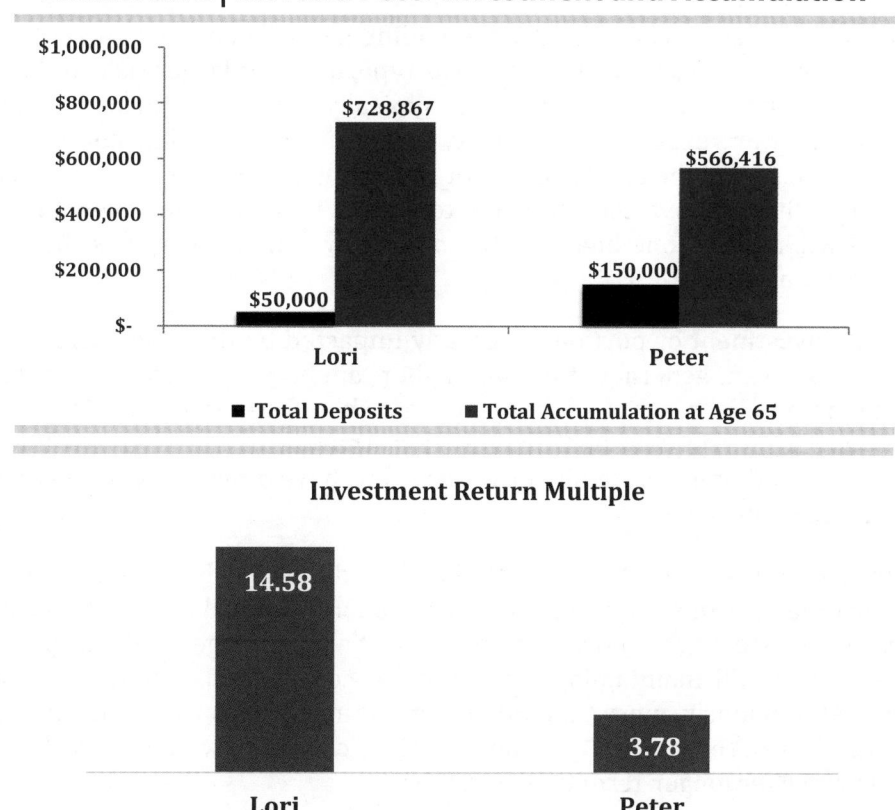

The second chart in **Exhibit 2.12** illustrates the final balance for Lori and Peter as a multiple of their respective savings totals. Lori accumulates 14.58 times what she saved, while Peter only accumulated 3.78 times what he saved. Essentially, by saving early, Lori is able to consume $100,000 more than Peter before retirement and accumulate more than Peter at retirement.

Investment Considerations

A successful retirement plan is dependent on a successful investment plan. A retirement plan is dependent on savings over time, but it is also dependent on the earnings and growth of those funds during the asset accumulation phase and throughout retirement. In **Exhibit 2.6**, with the 25-year old saving 12 percent of his income for 40 years earning eight percent, approximately 80 percent of the accumulated balance at retirement is derived from investment earnings, while 20 percent is from savings.

An investment plan must take into consideration the risk tolerance of the investor as well as the time horizon of the goal. Consideration must be given to historical and expected returns for the various asset classes, diversification, and the types of assets included in tax-deferred accounts versus taxable accounts. All of these factors go into constructing a portfolio to achieve specific goals, such as retirement planning.

The risk tolerance of an investor is essentially the willingness and ability to accept risk for potential returns. As indicated below, assets with larger returns typically have larger risks or larger variations in returns (standard deviation). Risk tolerance is typically assessed through questionnaires, an understanding of the investor's experience with risky assets and with the time horizon of the investment goal. If both the willingness and the ability to accept risk are high, the risk tolerance is high. If both the willingness and the ability are low, then the risk tolerance is low. If, however, there is a mismatch between ability and willingness (one high and the other low), then it suggests that the investor may need additional education.

The **suitability** of an investment or portfolio is greatly impacted by the time horizon of an investment goal. Longer-term goals can generally tolerate higher amounts of risk than shorter-term goals. Investments for the accomplishment of short-term goals should generally consist of relatively safe or stable assets, such as short-term debt instruments. Investments for the accomplishment of long-term goals can consist of assets that generate higher returns, but have a tendency to fluctuate more sharply when markets or the economy changes.

When investors are young, their investment portfolios should typically be dominated by common stocks because, due to long time horizons, young investors can generally afford the additional risk (fluctuation) of common stocks. As investors near retirement, their asset allocation generally begins to shift so that it becomes less risky while still maintaining some growth component to mitigate against the risk of inflation. As discussed previously, more than 50 percent of individuals who reach the age of 65 live for more than 20 years. Therefore, equities typically remain a critical part of a retiree's portfolio because they provide for growth over longer-term time horizons.

It is important to understand the return characteristics for asset classes that investors may include in a portfolio. **Exhibit 2.13** depicts selected investment returns over a long period of time.

Exhibit 2.13 | Historical Returns, Inflation-Adjusted Returns, and Standard Deviation of Asset Classes[9]

Asset Class	Historical Returns	Inflation-Adjusted Returns	Standard Deviation	Real Return After-Tax and Inflation
Small-Capitalization Stocks	12.0%	9.0%	32.0%	6.6%
Large-Capitalization Stocks	10.0%	7.0%	20.0%	5.0%
Long-Term Government Bonds	5.5%	2.5%	10.0%	0.9%
U.S. T-Bills	3.5%	0.5%	3.0%	(0.50%)
Consumer Price Index (CPI)	3.0%	N/A	N/A	N/A

Exhibit 2.13 illustrates that equities provide the best opportunity to have positive real returns, after taking into consideration taxes and inflation. Equities are generally an important element of a portfolio during asset accumulation as well as during retirement. Equities are important during retirement as it may last 20 to 40 years.

The risk tolerance and time horizon of the investor, as well as the expected risk and returns from various investment choices are considered in constructing an asset allocation and portfolio. The asset allocation is responsible for the majority of variation in returns within the portfolio and is a critical element in retirement planning.

Appropriate Assets for Tax Advantaged and Taxable Accounts

In addition to the asset allocation decision, investors should consider the appropriateness of assets for the different types of investment accounts. Income earned in a taxable account, such as a brokerage or bank account, is subject to current taxation, whereas income earned in a tax-deferred account, such as an IRA or 401(k) plan, is not subject to current taxation. Because there is a significant difference in the tax rates of capital gains and dividends compared to interest income from fixed income securities, such as bonds, it is logical to hold fixed income assets in tax-deferred accounts. This decision results in all fixed income securities residing in tax-deferred accounts. However, investors must also consider liquidity needs that are better met through fixed income investments and more easily accessed in taxable accounts. Therefore, there must be a balance between tax efficiency or tax optimization and the liquidity needs of the investor.

An investor must also consider limitations on the types of securities that can be held in various retirement accounts. Investors managing assets held in IRAs and qualified plans should also be aware of the rules relating to unrelated business taxable income, discussed below.

9. Approximations from 1926-2017. Assumes an equity tax rate of 20% and bond tax rate of 30%.

Unrelated Business Taxable Income

Unrelated business taxable income (UBTI) is a term used to describe income earned by a tax-exempt entity that is subject to taxation. The tax on unrelated business income applies to most organizations exempt from tax under §501(a). These organizations include charitable, religious, scientific, and other corporations described in §501(c), as well as employees' trusts forming part of pension, profit-sharing, and stock bonus plans described in §401(a). In addition, the following are subject to the tax on unrelated business taxable income:

1. Traditional IRAs
2. Roth IRAs
3. Simplified Employee Pensions (SEP-IRAs)
4. Savings Incentive Match Plans for Employees (SIMPLE IRAs)
5. State and municipal colleges and universities
6. Qualified state tuition programs
7. Medical savings accounts (MSAs)
8. Coverdell savings accounts

Because of the UBTI rules, IRAs and qualified plans, in addition to the other entities listed, are impacted if UBTI is earned within the entity. The impact is that the entity has to pay income tax on the UBTI and file Form 990-T if UBTI exceeds $1,000. The purpose of these rules is to prevent a tax-exempt entity from unfairly competing against tax paying businesses. This concept is reflected in the following excerpt from Treas. Reg. §1.513-1.

> "The primary objective of adoption of the unrelated business income tax was to eliminate a source of unfair competition by placing the unrelated business activities of certain exempt organizations upon the same tax basis as the nonexempt business endeavors with which they compete."

The term "unrelated business taxable income" generally means the gross income derived from any unrelated trade or business regularly carried on by an exempt organization, less the deductions directly connected with carrying on the trade or business. Previously, if an organization regularly carried on two or more unrelated business activities, its unrelated business taxable income was the total of gross income from all such activities less the total allowable deductions attributable to all the activities. However, for tax years beginning after December 31, 2017, the Tax Cuts and Jobs Act of 2017 requires that the UBTI from each unrelated trade or business be calculated separately, such that losses from one business can no longer offset income from another.

Generally, an unrelated trade or business includes one that meets the following three requirements:

1. It is a trade or business,
2. It is regularly carried on, and
3. It is not substantially related to furthering the exempt purpose of the organization.

Example 2.3

BU, an exempt scientific organization, enjoys an excellent reputation in the field of biological research. It exploits this reputation regularly by selling endorsements of various items of laboratory equipment to manufacturers. The endorsing of laboratory equipment does not contribute importantly to the accomplishment of any purpose for which the tax exemption is granted to BU. Accordingly, the income derived from the sale of endorsements is gross income from unrelated trade or business (UBTI).

Generally, income in the form of dividends, interest, payments with respect to securities loans, and annuities are excluded in computing unrelated business taxable income. In addition, royalties and rental income are generally not included in determining UBTI. However, investment income that is generally excluded from UBTI must be included to the extent it is derived from debt-financed property. The amount of income included is generally proportionate to the debt on the property.

Typically, a qualified plan, or an IRA, is subject to the UBTI rules if it:

- Operates a trade or business,
- Owns an interest in a pass through organization, such as a partnership or S corporation, that is operating a trade or business,
- Owns an interest in a master limited partnership, or
- Uses debt to generate portfolio income, as in the case of margin debt.

Quick Quiz 2.2

1. Our society tends to save at a rate that is adequate for retirement planning.
   a. True
   b. False

2. Fixed-income securities generally provide the best hedge against inflation and loss of purchasing power.
   a. True
   b. False

3. Individuals must consider the impact of inflation when projecting retirement needs.
   a. True
   b. False

False, False, True.

Example 2.4

Jamar's IRA owns an interest in Sushi & Saki LLC, a restaurant. The LLC is taxed as a partnership. Because the LLC interest is held in an IRA, the IRA's share of income from the LLC is subject to UBTI tax.

Inflation

Inflation represents a general increase in the price of goods and a corresponding decrease in the purchasing power of money. Inflation is an important factor for retirement planning because inflation erodes the purchasing power of money throughout a person's life, but especially during the retirement years. Because retirement can last 20 to 40 years, the erosion of purchasing power resulting from inflation can be substantial. **Exhibit 2.14** illustrates the decline in purchasing power of $100,000 over a 40-year period.

Exhibit 2.14 | Impact of Inflation: Purchasing Power Lost Over 40 Years

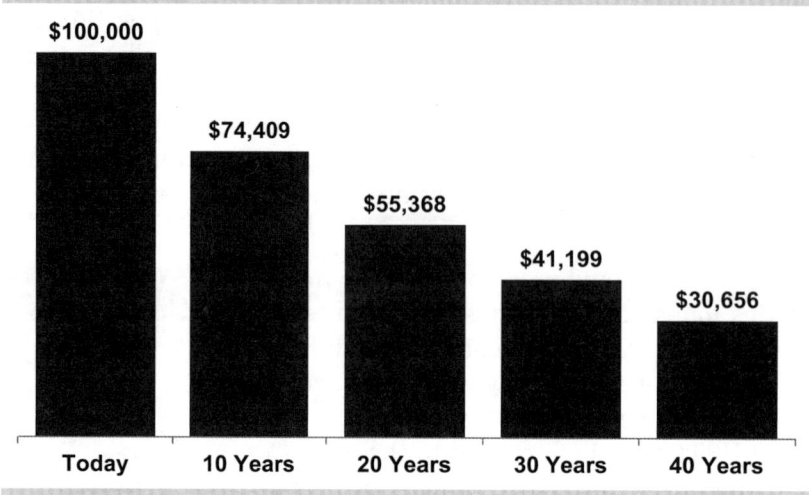

Example 2.5

Parker is 65 years old and spends $300 per month on groceries. If inflation is three percent, he can expect to spend over $540 when he is 85 years old for the same groceries. While an annual three percent increase is hardly noticeable in the short term, it amounts to an 80 percent increase over the 20 years.

As illustrated, in year 10 the $100,000 has lost 26 percent of its purchasing power. After 10 years, one can only buy $74,409 worth of items using $100,000 of today's dollars. More disturbing is the fact that in year 20, the same person would only be able to purchase $55,368 worth of assets for that same $100,000. Imagine a person with a fixed income who is expected to have a carefree retirement in 20 years with the same $100,000 income they have today.

The exhibit below provides an additional perspective of inflation over long periods of time. It depicts how many times greater the cost of an item was in 2013 compared to the price 100 years earlier.[10] 2013 marked the 100th anniversary for the Consumer Price Index. As depicted in the exhibit below, cheese was 26.27 times more expensive in 2013 compared to 1913.

Inflation over many years is a significant obstacle to overcome for retirees attempting to manage their finances and is an important factor to consider in retirement planning.

---

10. Stephen Reed,"One hundred years of price change: the Consumer Price Index and the American inflation experience," Monthly Labor Review, U.S. Bureau of Labor Statistics, April 2014.

Exhibit 2.15 | Impact of Inflation Over 100 Years

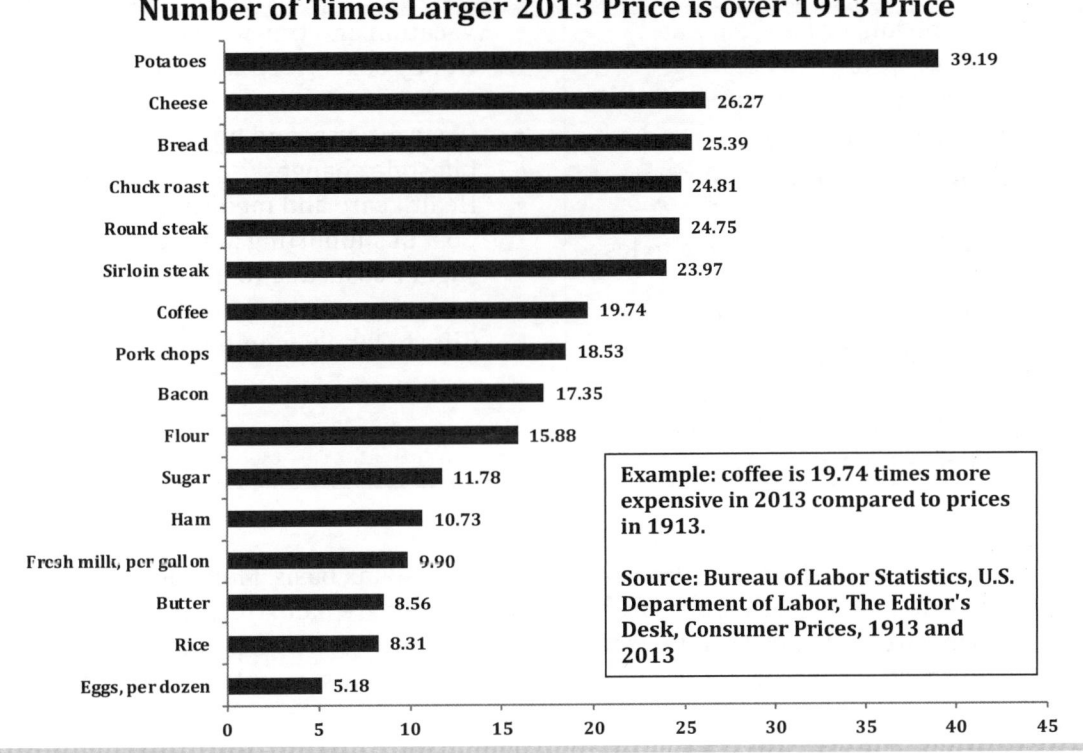

Number of Times Larger 2013 Price is over 1913 Price

Potatoes	39.19
Cheese	26.27
Bread	25.39
Chuck roast	24.81
Round steak	24.75
Sirloin steak	23.97
Coffee	19.74
Pork chops	18.53
Bacon	17.35
Flour	15.88
Sugar	11.78
Ham	10.73
Fresh milk, per gallon	9.90
Butter	8.56
Rice	8.31
Eggs, per dozen	5.18

Example: coffee is 19.74 times more expensive in 2013 compared to prices in 1913.

Source: Bureau of Labor Statistics, U.S. Department of Labor, The Editor's Desk, Consumer Prices, 1913 and 2013

Retirement Needs Analysis

Retirement needs analysis is the process of determining how much money a person needs to accumulate to be financially independent during retirement. One of the first steps is to determine the expenses a person will have when they retire. Most people prefer to maintain their pre-retirement standard of living during retirement. Therefore, the expenses they have when they are working will likely be similar to the expenses they have during retirement. However, there are some expenses that will increase during retirement, such as vacations and medical care, and expenses that will decrease during retirement, such as work related expenses, FICA expenses, and annual savings. **Exhibit 2.16** lists expenses that may increase or decrease during retirement.

Key Concepts

1. List the common factors that increase and decrease retirement income needs.

2. What is the wage replacement ratio?

3. Identify the two alternative methods for calculating the wage replacement ratio.

4. How is the WRR calculated utilizing the two applicable methods?

Exhibit 2.16 | Expenses that May Increase or Decrease During Retirement

Decreasing Expenses	Increasing Expenses
• Savings is no longer necessary at retirement • FICA payments are eliminated • Mortgage payments may end • Lower income means lower income taxes • Automobile costs are lower due to less driving • Work related expenses (clothes, coffees, lunches, etc.) are eliminated • Cost of insurance (life insurance may no longer be needed, limits might be reduced on property insurance)	• Vacation and travel costs • Hobby costs (race car driving, golf, etc.) • Costs for a second home • Lifestyle changes • Health care and medical costs • Cost of supporting adult children • Higher costs due to inflation (property tax, groceries, etc.) • Gifts to family members

Pre-Tax or After-Tax Planning for Retirement

Planning for retirement can be done on a pre-tax basis or an after-tax basis. Many people find it easier to plan on a pre-tax or gross income basis, out of which income taxes are paid. However, CPAs, accountants, and those who emphasize after-tax cash flows may plan on an after-tax basis. Either way works. In this text, the pre-tax approach is generally used because it is easier for most people to understand.

Wage Replacement Ratio (WRR)

Retirement needs analysis is the process of determining how much money a person needs to accumulate at the beginning of retirement to be financially independent during retirement. Part of this process is determining how much money will be spent in retirement on an annual basis. The amount of money needed in retirement as a percentage of income earned prior to retirement is called the **wage replacement ratio (WRR)**. It is calculated by dividing the retirement expenses by the pre-retirement income.

$$WRR = \frac{\text{Expenses in Retirement}}{\text{Pre-retirement Income}}$$

Generally, most individuals need less income during retirement compared to what they need while working. The reason for this decrease is that many expenses are eliminated. However, other expenses may increase during retirement. A WRR of 70 percent to 80 percent is often cited as an appropriate range for many people. While this range may work for many people, it is far from a uniform range that all people can rely on for a reasonable wage replacement ratio. Consider the following examples.

Example 2.6

Sheryl makes $100,000 per year and is about to retire. She has the following expenses that will be eliminated when she retires:

- House payment (annual) - $30,000 (the mortgage will be paid off when she retires)
- Savings into her 401(k) plan - $24,000
- Commuting costs to work - $5,000 (includes tolls, gas, parking, etc.)
- Work clothes per year - $2,000
- Lunches & coffees at work - $2,000
- FICA payments - $7,650

The total of these expenses that will be eliminated equals $70,650. Assume that she has other expenses that might increase, such as travel, which increases her expenses from $29,350 to $40,000. If that were the case, Sheryl's wage replacement ratio needed equals 40% ($40,000 divided by $100,000), which is dramatically different than the commonly cited 70% to 80% WRR.

Example 2.7

Rob makes $120,000 per year and is about to retire. He is the hotel manager for the Boston Zenith Hotel. Zenith Hotels is an international chain of luxury hotels based in the U.S. and Europe. As part of his compensation, he has the following benefits:

- He lives in the hotel with his family - he has never owned a home nor does he have homeowners insurance.
- He eats in the hotel with his family or eats at local hotels, both of which are paid for as part of his compensation.
- He has access to a vehicle when he needs it - he does not own a car nor does he have car insurance.
- He stays at Zenith properties when he vacations with his family.

Rob expects that when he retires, he will have to replace many of the benefits that he has received as part of his compensation. Here is a list of a few items on an annual basis:

- Housing costs - $35,000 (utilities, insurance, cable, etc.)
- Auto expenses - $15,000
- Vacation expenses - $10,000
- Food - $10,000

He has other expenses that will decrease, such as:

- Savings into his 401(k) plan - $20,000
- Work clothes per year - $2,000
- FICA payments - $9,180

If Rob adds the additional retirement costs to his compensation and subtracts the costs that will decrease, he ends up with retirement expenses needed of $158,820, which is 32.35% higher than his current salary and represents a WRR of 132%. Fortunately for Rob, he is able to save a great deal more during employment than most employees as a result of his employment perks.

Determining the WRR for a person is an individualized process in which specific expenses are considered for inclusion in the calculation. There are two frequently used methods to determine the WRR. The first, which was illustrated above, is called the top-down approach. The second approach is called the bottom-up approach or budgeting approach.

Top-Down Approach

The top-down approach begins with 100 percent of pre-retirement income and adjusts the percentage up or down depending on expenses that may be eliminated or added. This approach, which was illustrated in the two previous examples, is less precise than the bottom-up approach, but is generally quicker to calculate. The top-down approach is more appropriate for planning for people who are young and for those not close enough to retirement to worry about great precision.

Example 2.8

Marleen is 55 years old and makes $100,000 per year. She saves $12,350 per year and pays FICA expense of $7,650. She wants to assume that any other expense reductions will be offset by increased retirement expenditures, such as health care and vacations. Based on these assumptions, her WRR equals 80%.

$100,000	=	100.00%	of salary in % terms
(12,350)	=	(12.35%)	less: current savings in % terms
(7,650)	=	(7.65%)	less: payroll taxes in % terms (not paid in retirement)
$80,000	=	80.00%	wage replacement ratio in % terms

Marleen lives off about 80% of her pre-retirement income. Therefore, she will need about $80,000 in income during retirement. The remaining 20% or $20,000 is currently spent on retirement savings and FICA taxes.

Bottom-Up (Budgeting) Approach

The bottom-up approach to determining the WRR is also referred to as the budgeting approach because it determines total expenses in the same manner that is used to build a budget. This approach is more rigorous than the top-down approach, but is also more precise as it requires examining each category of expense to determine whether it will increase, decrease or remain the same during retirement. As a result, this approach is generally used by people who are very near retirement and can anticipate the expenses and changes that will occur once they retire. Keep in mind that some expenses will remain fixed, such as life insurance premiums and fixed mortgage payments, some will increase by inflation, and some will change differently.

Example 2.9

Assume Anna and Bart have the same amount of income and the same expenses and both are about to retire. They both want to determine their appropriate WRR. Anna's house and car will be paid off before retirement, while Bart will continue to have to make mortgage payments and car loan payments in retirement. They both have other expenses that will decrease by the same amount. Below is the bottom-up approach to calculating each WRR.

	Anna & Bart	Anna	Bart
	Current Budget	Retirement Budget	Retirement Budget
Income	$120,000	***	***
Expenses:			
Income Taxes (28%)	$33,600*	$33,600	$33,600
Social Security Taxes (FICA)	2,500	0	0
Health Insurance	2,000	2,000	2,000
Auto Insurance	1,200	1,200	1,200
Food (at home or away from home)	5,400	5,400	5,400
Utilities/Phone	6,000	6,000	6,000
Mortgage	18,000**	0	18,000
Auto Payment	6,000	0	6,000
Entertainment	6,000	6,000	6,000
Clothing	4,000	2,500	2,500
Auto Maintenance	1,000	750	750
Church Support	2,400	2,400	2,400
Retirement Savings	12,000	0	0
Other	19,900	17,850	17,850
Total Expenses (Needs)	**$120,000**	**$77,700**	**$101,700**
Wage Replacement Ratio (WRR)		**64.75%**	**84.75%**

*Assume for this example that Anna and Bart's income tax liability remains the same during retirement.
**Note that the mortgage of both is 15% of current income before retirement, but 0% for Anna and 18% of needs for Bart after retirement.
*** The current budget at retirement will be equal to the needs.

Spending By Age

Annual expenditures generally change as people age. Typically, people spend more as they move into middle age and then expenditures decrease. In retirement, expenses also decrease as individuals get older and approach life expectancy. Therefore, the WRR that is calculated for the beginning of retirement is likely to be higher than a WRR necessary in the later part of life.

While the amount of spending changes over a person's lifetime, as indicated in **Exhibit 2.17**, most of the categories of spending remain the same. In fact, many of the expenditures remain relatively constant on a percentage basis from younger to older ages. Consider the chart below from 2019.

Exhibit 2.17 | Average Annual Expenditures by Income and Age

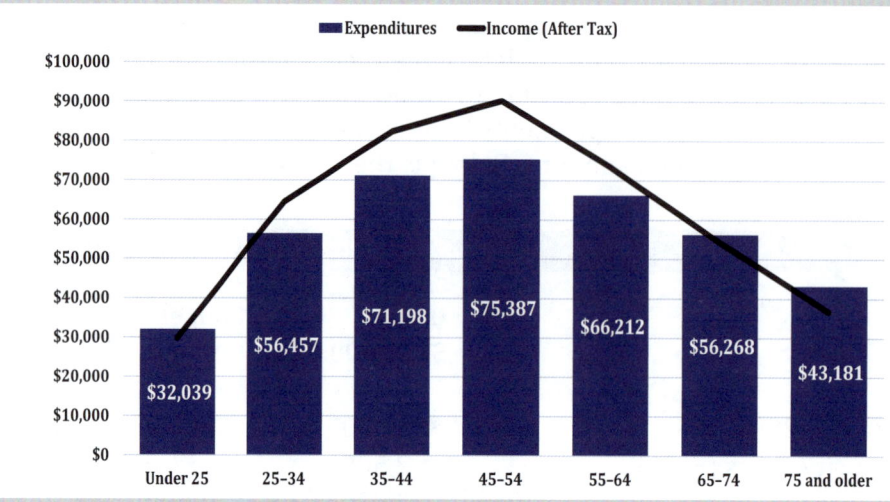

Bureau of Labor Statistics: Consumer Expenditure Survey 2019

Exhibit 2.18 | Consumer Spending by Age (In Percentages)

Spending category	Under 25 years	25-34 years	35-44 years	45-54 years	55-64 years	65 and older
Total	100%	100%	100%	100%	100%	100%
Housing	32.4	35.9	33.0	30.9	30.5	34.8
Transportation	21.1	18.0	18.3	17.3	16.4	14.9
Personal insurance and pensions	8.5	12.7	12.8	13.4	13.2	5.7
Food at home	7.0	6.7	7.3	7.3	7.3	8.1
Healthcare	3.8	5.5	6.4	6.9	8.6	13.6
Food away from home	7.9	6.2	5.7	5.7	5.0	5.0
Entertainment	3.5	4.2	4.9	5.0	5.7	4.7
Cash contributions	1.1	1.5	2.9	2.7	3.4	5.1
Apparel and services	3.6	3.3	3.3	3.1	2.6	2.6
Education	7.6	2.1	1.6	3.5	2.6	0.7
Miscellaneous	0.8	1.2	1.3	1.4	1.7	1.6
Personal care products and services	1.2	1.1	1.2	1.3	1.2	1.4
Alcoholic beverages	0.8	0.9	0.7	0.9	1.0	1.0
Tobacco products and smoking supplies	0.5	0.6	0.5	0.5	0.6	0.4
Reading	0.1	0.1	0.1	0.1	0.1	0.3

Note: The seven categories highlighted represent between 84% and 90% of total spending.
Source: BLS Consumer Expenditure Survey 2019

Naturally, some expenses vary on a percentage basis, such as healthcare and education. Healthcare increases as a percentage with age. Education tends to decrease as a percentage with age. However, housing tends to remain between 30 percent and 36 percent of total spending. Transportation tends to remain between 15 percent and 21 percent. Insurance and pension expenses start low, increase during mid-life, and taper off during retirement.

The determination of the appropriate WRR is a very useful process as it identifies the amount of money needed in retirement and forms the basis for determining the amount of money that must be accumulated by the time retirement occurs. While spending may decrease during retirement, most of the calculations presented in this text assume a level WRR. This assumption provides a certain built-in level of conservatism when it comes to the calculations.

Sources of Retirement Income

Most retirees rely on a combination of funds to finance retirement, including Social Security, employer-sponsored retirement plans, income from personal retirement plans (IRAs), income from personal savings, and in some cases, income from part-time employment (earnings). These sources of funds are intended to complement each other to provide adequate retirement income. **Exhibit 2.19** illustrates the percent of income for the average retiree from 1962 to 2015 from each of these sources.

Exhibit 2.19 | Retirement Income Sources for the Elderly

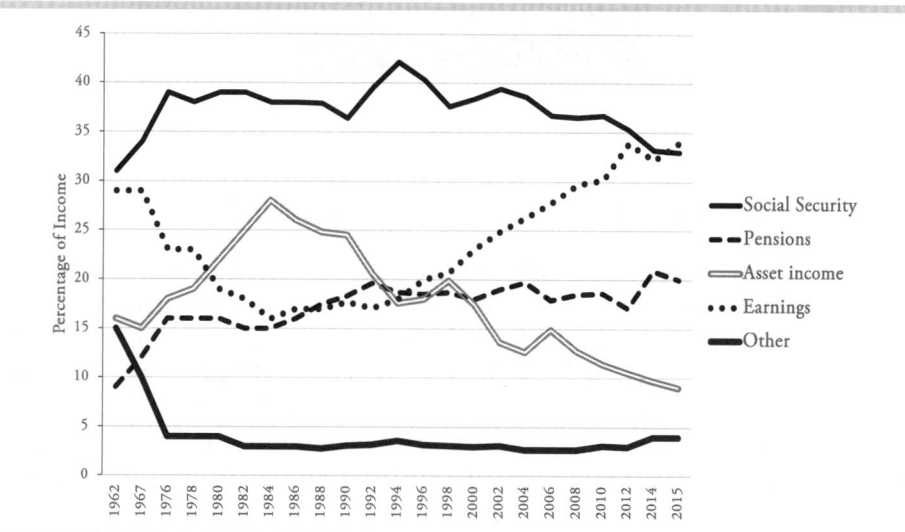

Source: Social Security Administration: Fast Facts & Figures About Social Security, 2017

Notice in the previous exhibit that the average retiree receives more than 30 percent of retirement income from Social Security. Social Security may provide a lower wage worker with a wage replacement ratio of 60 plus percent. However, Social Security only provides a wage replacement ratio of 18 to 27 percent for a worker with income of $200,000 (see **Exhibit 2.21**). Therefore, such a worker will need to look to other sources of funds to make up the amount of short-fall in wage replacement to maintain the worker's desired lifestyle.

Social Security

For most individuals, Social Security is the foundation of retirement income. Social Security provides benefits to nearly 90 percent of retirees. However, Social Security was never designed or intended to provide retirement benefits that would equate to a 100 percent WRR. It was signed into law in 1935 and was designed as a safety net for the "old-age" population. As **Exhibit 2.20** illustrates, Social Security is the major source of income for retired individuals and makes up more than 90 percent of income for a significant percentage of the retired population.

Exhibit 2.20 | Percentage of Retired Individuals Receiving Social Security Benefits by Relative Importance to Total Retirement Income

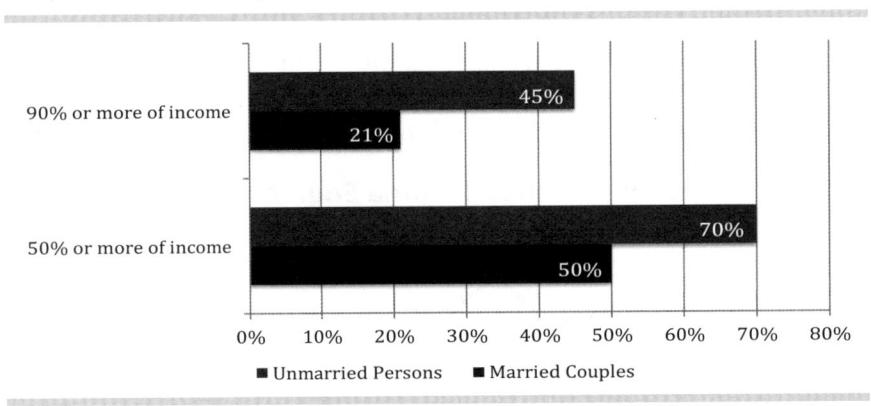

Source: Social Security Administration, Social Security Basic Facts (2020)

Most middle to higher income individuals planning for retirement should, therefore, consider Social Security as a foundation of income rather than depending on Social Security as their main source of retirement income. Social Security retirement benefits provide a wage replacement ratio ranging from less than 20 percent (for high-income earners) to approximately 80 percent (for low-income earners who have a same age, nonworking spouse). As illustrated in **Exhibit 2.21**, Social Security is an adequate wage replacement for lower wage earners, but is clearly inadequate to provide sufficient replacement income for middle-to-higher-wage earners. Keep in mind that Social Security was never meant to be the only source of income upon retirement. President Franklin D. Roosevelt implied this reality in his statement while signing the Social Security Act on August 14, 1935:

> "We can never insure one hundred percent of the population against one hundred percent of the hazards and vicissitudes of life, but we have tried to frame a law which will give some measure of protection to the average citizen and to his family against the loss of a job and against poverty-ridden old age."

Exhibit 2.21 | Wage Replacement Percentage for Social Security

Earnings	Worker WRR*	Worker with Same Age, Nonworking Spouse Total WRR	Comment
$15,000	78%	117%	Low Income
$20,000	67%	100%	(WRR Good)
$25,000	60%	90%	
$30,000	55%	83%	
$35,000	52%	78%	Middle Income (WRR Adequate)
$50,000	46%	69%	
$75,000	41%	61%	
$100,000	34%	51%	High Income
$200,000	19%	28%	(WRR Poor)

Estimated based on single person at normal retirement age (2021).
At same age, nonworking spouse can expect to receive 50 percent of the benefits of the covered worker.

Employer-Sponsored Retirement Plans

Most people in the United States have access to an employer sponsored retirement plan. These plans, which may be sponsored by private companies, public companies, or governmental entities, may be in the form of a defined contribution plan or a defined benefit plan. Today, there are significantly more defined contribution plans than defined benefit plans. Employees who participate in these plans can save part of their compensation on a pre-tax basis over many years. These savings can accumulate for decades and help provide a substantial amount of income during retirement.

Personal Assets and Savings

Personal assets and savings is another important source of retirement funds and the one that is almost completely influenced by the individual. This is a more difficult way to accumulate savings for retirement because savings may have to accumulate in a taxable account instead of a tax deferred account. While there are some tax deferred alternatives, such as traditional and Roth IRAs, there are limitations regarding how much can be contributed to these accounts. However, personal savings can be a significant source of retirement income.

Quick Quiz 2.4

1. Retirees generally rely on Social Security, private pension plans, and personal savings to fund their retirement incomes.
   a. True
   b. False

2. Social Security is an adequate wage replacement for most individuals.
   a. True
   b. False

3. Personal savings is the source of retirement income most influenced by the individual.
   a. True
   b. False

True, False, True.

There is a noticeable difference between retirees who have income from personal assets and those who do not. According to the Social Security Administration, 66 percent of those with income from personal assets have retirement income in the highest category ($30,000 or more), while only 25 percent of those without income from personal assets are in the highest category. It is in most people's best interest to accumulate wealth for retirement.

Exhibit 2.22 | Income of Retirees with and without Income from Personal Assets

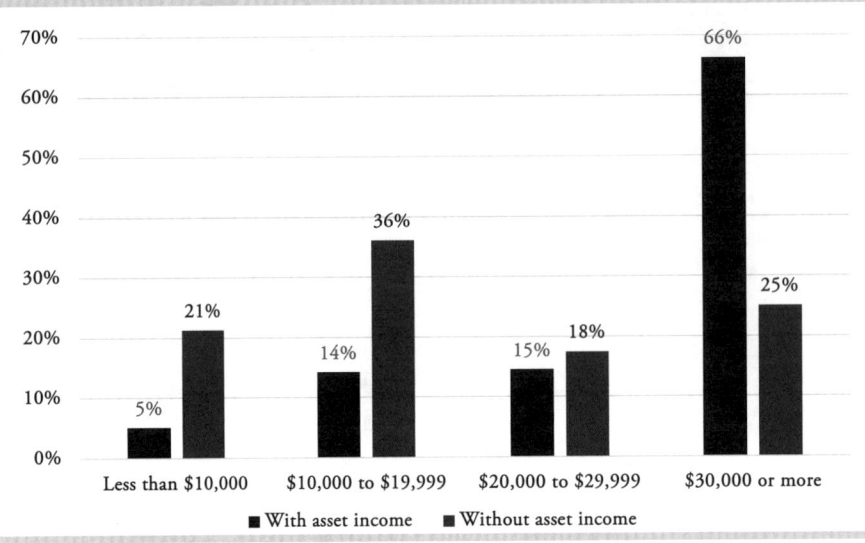

Source: Social Security Administration: Income of the Aged Chartbook 2014

The section below discusses the calculation of retirement needs, as well as the determination of required personal savings.

RETIREMENT FUNDING (CAPITAL NEEDS ANALYSIS)

Retirement funding (also known as retirement needs analysis or **capital needs analysis**) is the process of determining how much money a person needs to accumulate to be financially independent during retirement. Being financially independent means being able to maintain the pre-retirement lifestyle during retirement and manage the adverse effects of inflation.

The process of calculating the needed capital balance at retirement requires making assumptions about variables that cannot be known, such as future rates of return or life expectancy. These assumptions are discussed below, along with four methods of calculating retirement needs. These four methods are not the only methods for determining retirement needs and are relatively straight forward. Today's financial planning software certainly allows for more complicated assumptions. However, these four methods provide the foundation for estimating the needed capital at retirement.

Key Concepts

1. What is capital needs analysis and why is it important in retirement planning?

2. What are the four most common methods for analyzing capital needs?

3. How do each of these methods differ?

4. What assumptions must be made in capital needs analysis?

Accurate Assumptions

Retirement funding requires projecting savings amounts, spending patterns, investment returns, and inflation over extremely long periods of time. As a result, small changes in these assumptions can create large variations in retirement funding and annual savings requirements.

WRR - The wage replacement ratio should be calculated using the top-down approach for those who are more than a few years away from retirement. The bottom-up approach should be used when retirement is expected to take place within a few years and realistic retirement expenses can be estimated on a line item basis. It is important to consider the types of lifestyle changes that may take place in retirement and the cost considerations for those activities.

Life expectancy - While no one can predict with certainty how long any individual will live, life expectancy is an important variable to forecast. Life insurance companies, the Society of Actuaries, and the IRS have mortality tables that provide estimates of the average life expectancies for men and women. The life expectancy for men and women who attain the age of 65 are provided earlier in this chapter. However, it is generally far better to consider family longevity when estimating life expectancy.

Example 2.10

Roman is trying to prepare a retirement funding calculation. He is unsure about his life expectancy. Roman is healthy with no diseases or health concerns. He runs and swims regularly and maintains a healthy weight and good diet. Three of his grandparents lived into their 90s and his grandmother on his mother's side is still alive at age 99 and might live to age 110. Even though the average life expectancy for men is less than 80 years at birth, Roman should consider estimating a life expectancy of at least mid-90s, based on his family history. He might even consider a life expectancy of 100 for his retirement planning.

Earnings rate and inflation - Predicting rates of return and inflation is challenging over both short periods and long periods of time. Access to historical rates of return and inflation is widely available to professionals as well as non-professionals. While there is no indication that average historical returns or average inflation will necessarily continue, they do provide a basis for estimating these variables for the future.

The earnings rate used in retirement needs analysis should take into consideration the expected return of an individual's portfolio, based on the portfolio's asset allocation. More aggressive portfolios tend to have higher expected rates of return, while more conservative portfolios tend to have lower expected rates of return. Inflation should be estimated based on historical trends. It is wise to be somewhat conservative for both these variables, as the retirement calculation model is very sensitive to these inputs. The difference between the expected earnings rate and the expected inflation rate should also be considered and compared to historical real rates of return. If the difference between the two rates is significantly higher than historical real rates of return, then it is an indication that either the estimate for inflation is too low or the estimate for the expected return is too high.

Because these assumptions may not be precise, it is important to revisit a retirement needs analysis regularly to determine whether adequate progress is being made towards the retirement goal. In addition, it is important to periodically assess whether there are changes to the underlying assumptions that should be incorporated into the retirement analysis. A retirement needs calculation should not be performed only once and considered to be fixed in terms of required savings and/or needs analysis. Retirement planning is more of a dynamic process that extends over a person's work life expectancy and into retirement. In addition, retirement planning, or capital needs analysis, may incorporate a variety of assumptions about how much money is left or to be left at life expectancy. The section below discusses the most basic method of determining retirement needs, known as the annuity method, as well as three more conservative variations of capital needs analysis.

Annuity Method (4-Step Approach)

The **annuity method** is the simplest way to determine retirement needs, and is based on the **pure annuity concept**. The annuity method assumes the individual saves for a period of time, begins taking distributions at retirement, and then dies with a zero accumulation balance on the projected life expectancy date. Because the annuity method assumes that all funds will be consumed at the point of life expectancy, it does not provide any room for error if a person lives beyond life expectancy, nor does it generally provide for an estate for heirs. However, the annuity method is the basic method for capital needs analysis.

The annuity method can be calculated using one of two methods, the traditional 4-step approach or the uneven cash flow approach. Both methods work well for this type of calculation, as they are both methods of time value of money. However, the uneven cash flow method has a few limitations in comparison to the 4-step approach. The 4-step approach is designed to determine the amount of money that must be accumulated at retirement and the amount of money that needs to be saved each year up until retirement. The 4-step approach is outlined below:

Step 1: Determine the funding amount in today's dollars.

This step is designed to determine the amount of money in today's dollars that a person will need when they retire. At the most basic level, it adjusts the needs first by the wage replacement ratio and then reduces that resultant by the expected Social Security payments in today's dollars. The WRR reflects the change in needs during retirement in comparison to current earnings. Social Security payments are an income stream in retirement that does not need to be funded through personal savings. This approach assumes that the Social Security payments will increase because of the annual cost of living adjustment (COLA) at the same rate as inflation. While that assumption may not be exact, it is a reasonable assumption that simplifies the calculation.

Step 2: Inflate the needs from Step 1 to the beginning of retirement.

This step determines the needs in future dollars for the first year of retirement. It is determined by inflating the amount from Step 1 at the rate of inflation for the number of years until retirement. The amount that is needed in any subsequent year is increased by the rate of inflation from one year to the next.

Step 3: Determine the funding needs at retirement age.
This step calculates the amount of money that needs to be accumulated at retirement age, which is found by discounting the annuity from Step 2 for the number of years during retirement. The annual needs must be discounted at the earnings rate, while also being increased by the rate of inflation. To accommodate the simultaneous discounting and inflating of the annual needs, the inflation adjusted discount rate is used. The result of this step is the sum that should be accumulated at the time retirement begins. This calculation assumes the annuity stream during retirement is an annuity due because once retirement begins, funds are immediately needed.

Step 4: Determine the required annual savings amount.
This step calculates the amount of money needed to be saved each year to accumulate the funds determined in Step 3. The value from Step 3 is used as the future value (FV), while any funds set aside for retirement are the input for present value (PV) in the calculation. The earnings rate is used as the input for "i."

To determine the amount to save during the work life expectancy, discount the capital needed at retirement using the savings rate, being mindful as to whether the client is expected to save annually or more frequently and whether the client is expected to save under an annuity due or an ordinary annuity scheme.

Example 2.11 illustrates the use of the 4-step method. This example will also be used for the other retirement needs calculations in the chapter.

Example 2.11

Jordan, age 42, currently earns $70,000. Her wage replacement ratio is 80 percent. She expects that inflation will average 3 percent for her entire life expectancy. She expects to earn 9.5 percent on her investments and retire at age 62, possibly living to age 90. Her Social Security retirement benefit in today's dollars adjusted for early retirement is $15,000 per year.

1. Calculate Jordan's capital needed at retirement at age 62 and the amount Jordan must save at the end of each year, assuming she has no current savings accumulated for retirement.

Step 1: Determine the funding amount in today's dollars.		
	$70,000	Salary
	x 80%	WRR
=	$56,000	Total needs in today's dollars
	- 15,000	Less Social Security in today's dollars
=	$41,000	Annual amount needed in today's dollars
Step 2: Inflate the needs from Step 1 to the beginning of retirement.		
PV	=	41,000 (Step 1) Retirement needs in today's dollars
N	=	20 (62 - 42) Work Life Expectancy
i	=	3 (inflation)
PMT	=	0
FV	=	74,050.56 (to Step 3) First year needs for retirement

Step 3: Determine the funding needs at retirement age (use begin key).		
PMT_{AD}	=	74,050.56 (from Step 2) this is also an annuity due
N	=	28 (90 – 62) Retirement Life Expectancy (use begin key)
i	=	6.3107 [(1 + earnings rate) ÷ (1 + inflation rate)] – 1 x 100 [(1.095 ÷ 1.03) – 1] x 100
FV	=	0 (Annuity model is 0 at life expectancy)
$PV_{AD@62}$	=	1,022,625.85 (to Step 4 - amount needed at age 62)[1]
Step 4: Determine the required annual savings amount.		
$FV_{@62}$	=	$1,022,625.85 (from Step 3)
N	=	20
i	=	9.5
PV	=	0
PMT_{OA}	=	18,894.75 (annual savings)

1. $961,922 is the result of not using the begin key. This is not correct. To correct this error, change the setting on the calculator to "begin" or annuity due.

Note: The math in this example assumes unrounded numbers are used throughout the calculation. If the calculator is cleared at each step and a rounded number for i is used, the results will be slightly lower.

2. Calculate the amount she must save at the end of each year, assuming she presently has $50,000 in retirement savings.

$FV_{@62}$	=	$1,022,625.85
N	=	20
i	=	9.5
PV	=	($50,000)
PMT_{OA}	=	$13,220.91 (annual savings)

Exhibit 2.23 | Asset Accumulation and Distribution (Using Data from Example 2.11)

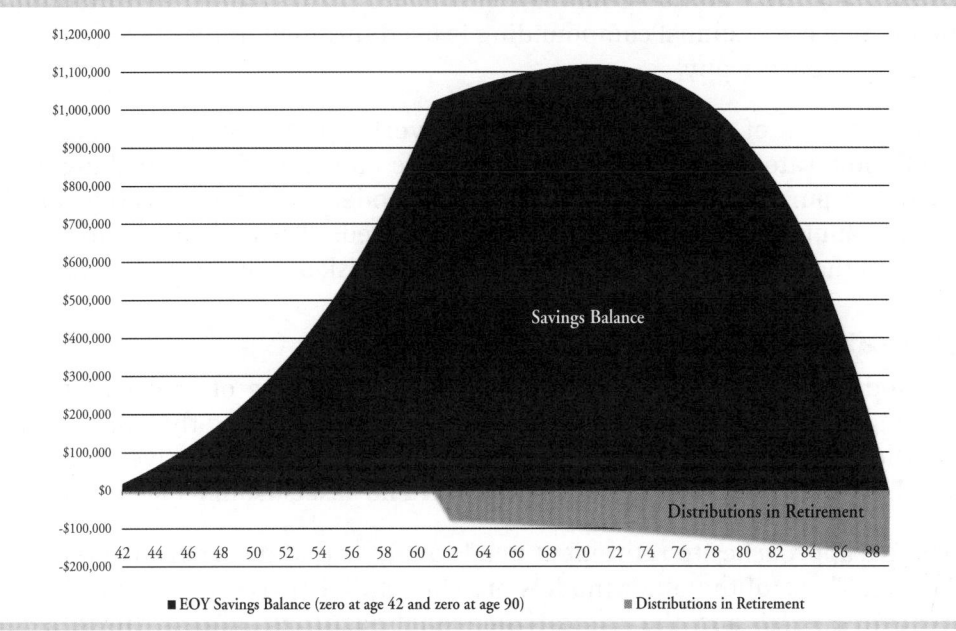

Uneven Cash Flow Method of Retirement Funding

This basic retirement needs calculation can also be performed using the uneven cash flow keys on a financial calculator. For this method, zeros are entered for each period up to the retirement age. Then, the needs in today's dollars (Step 1) are entered as the cash flow for the periods during retirement. The inflation adjusted discount rate is used to account for earnings and inflation over the entire period (WLE and RLE). Once these inputs are entered, net present value (NPV) is then calculated. The NPV equals the amount of funds necessary to pay for all of the retirement needs in today's dollars, based on the assumptions used. Consider the example of Jordan above. The time line below illustrates the cash flows and describes the calculations.[11]

Exhibit 2.24 | Uneven Cash Flow Method

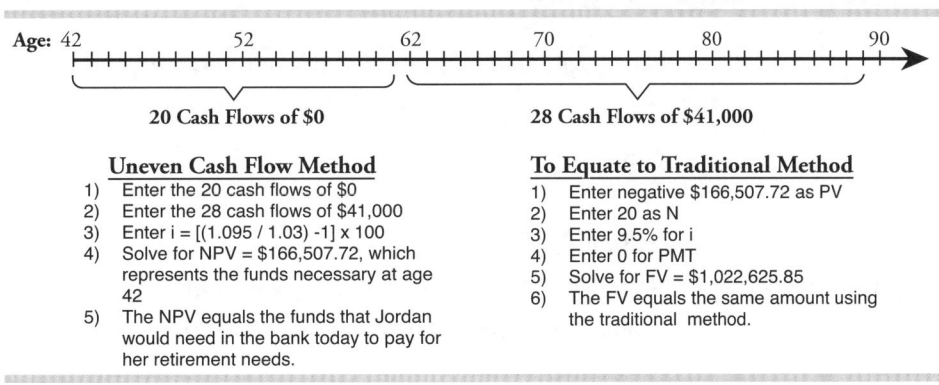

---

11. The uneven cash flow is effective for simple retirement needs calculations. It will not work when the earnings rate during retirement is different than the earnings rate during the accumulations phase.

Once the NPV is calculated, it can be used to determine the periodic funding amount. This amount is the same as calculated using the traditional method. However, mixing annual and monthly compounding causes the numbers to vary. If annual compounding is used throughout the two approaches, then there should be minimal difference, if any.

To mitigate against the risk of the assumptions being overly optimistic, changes can be made, such as adjusting the inflation rate upward, the earnings rate downwards, or making use of a capital preservation model, a purchasing power preservation model, or a capitalization of earnings model rather than a simple annuity model to determine capital needs. These three additional models help to overcome the risks of the pure annuity model (primarily the risk of running out of money).

Capital Preservation Model

The annuity method for retirement planning is the most basic type of retirement needs analysis. It results in exhausting all assets at the point of life expectancy, presuming that all assumptions occur as expected. Due to the nature of the assumptions of this model, a person who lives beyond their assumed life expectancy will be effectively destitute. They will have no assets from which to pay bills.

There are alternative approaches to retirement needs analysis that incorporate a level of conservatism into the calculations. Three of the other models are the **capital preservation model**, the **purchasing power preservation model**, and the **capitalization of earnings model**. These models provide a cushion in the event someone lives beyond their anticipated life expectancy. The capital preservation model assumes that the accumulated fund balance necessary under the annuity model is preserved until life expectancy. In other words, the balance that a retiree had at retirement under the annuity method is also expected at life expectancy. This approach necessarily requires that additional funds are accumulated by retirement so that the original needs are maintained until life expectancy. This additional calculation step is illustrated in **Example 2.12**.

Example 2.12

Recall that the amount needed for Jordan at age 62 calculated from **Example 2.11** was $1,022,625.85. If that amount is discounted at the expected earnings rate of 9.5 percent, then the result equals the additional amount of capital necessary to leave an estate of exactly $1,022,625.84 at life expectancy.

$FV_{@90}$	=	$1,022,625.85 (amount at life expectancy)
N	=	28
i	=	9.5
PMT	=	0
$PV_{@62}$	=	$80,560.37
$1,103,186.21	=	$80,560.37 + $1,022,625.85 (rounded)
		(amount needed for capital preservation model at retirement)

The capital preservation model requires Jordan to accumulate an additional $80,560 more at retirement than under the annuity model. However, it reduces her risk of superannuation, which is the risk that she outlives her available savings. This model requires a greater accumulation and therefore requires a larger annual savings amount.

The following chart compares the required annual savings under the capital preservation model with that of the annuity model for this example.

	Capital Preservation Model		Annuity Model		The Difference	
	Beginning Balance of Zero Savings	Beginning Balance of $50,000	Beginning Balance of Zero Savings	Beginning Balance of $50,000	Beginning Balance of Zero Savings	Beginning Balance of $50,000
$FV_{@62}$	1,103,186.21	1,103,186.21	1,022,625.85	1,022,625.85		
N	20	20	20	20		
i	9.5	9.5	9.5	9.5		
PV	0	- $50,000	0	- $50,000		
PMT_{OA}	20,383.24	14,709.40	18,894.75	13,220.91	1,488.49	1,488.49

The capital preservation model requires additional savings of approximately $1,500 per year, but mitigates against many of the risks in the traditional annuity approach.

Purchasing Power Preservation Model

The second model that mitigates superannuation is the **purchasing power preservation model**. The purchasing power model is even more conservative than the capital preservation model and assumes that the purchasing power of the accumulated fund balance necessary under the annuity model is preserved until life expectancy. This approach necessarily requires that additional funds are accumulated by retirement so that the purchasing power of the original needs are maintained until life expectancy. The required balance and the annual savings under this model are greater than what is required under the annuity model or the capital preservation model.

Example 2.13

Again recall **Example 2.11**. The capital balance of $1,022,625.85 is used as the future value, and then the entire calculation made in the original capital preservation model is repeated. By doing this, the $1,022,625.85 is simultaneously inflated at the rate of inflation and discounted at the earnings rate.

FV	=	$1,022,625.85
N	=	28
i	=	6.3107 [(1.095 ÷ 1.03) – 1] x 100
PMT_{AD}	=	$74,050.56 (amount needed the first year of retirement)
$PV_{@62}$	=	$1,206,942.14 (if i is not rounded, it will be $3 more)
		capital needed for purchasing power preservation model

The purchasing power preservation model requires Jordan to accumulate an additional $184,316 more at retirement than the annuity model. However, it reduces her risk of superannuation even more than the capital preservation model. This model requires a greater accumulation and therefore requires a larger annual savings amount. The chart below compares the required annual savings under the annuity model with the required savings under the purchasing power preservation model.

	Purchasing Power Model		Annuity Model	
	Beginning Balance of Zero Savings	Beginning Balance of $50,000	Beginning Balance of Zero Savings	Beginning Balance of $50,000
$FV_{@62}$	1,206,942.14	1,206,942.14	1,022,625.85	1,022,625.85
N	20	20	20	20
i	9.5	9.5	9.5	9.5
PV	0	- 50,000	0	- 50,000
PMT_{OA}	22,300.30	16,626.47	18,894.75	13,220.91

The purchasing power preservation model requires that Jordan save approximately $3,400 (18%) more each year compared with the annuity method. While this difference may or may not be significant to Jordan, the accumulation of assets and the risk mitigation are both significant.

Capitalization of Earnings Model

The third, and most conservative, model that mitigates superannuation is the capitalization of earnings model. The capitalization of earnings model is designed to produce a perpetual income stream. In the purchasing power preservation model illustrated in **Example 2.13** the desired income can continue to age 118, at which point the full account will have been liquidated. Since a capitalization of earnings calculation is based on the concept that the investments will produce sufficient income to support the desired withdrawal each year, the principal amount remains intact and withdrawals can continue through multiple generations. This, of course, requires an even higher level of savings.

The capitalization of earnings calculation is widely used to value investments that produce a perpetual income by simply dividing the annual income produced by the investment by the appropriate discount rate (expected rate of return). For example, if a preferred stock pays a dividend of $5 per year and the investor's required (or expected) return is 12 percent, the investor would be willing to pay $41.66. This investment of $41.66 earning 12 percent would produce income of $5 per year for an infinite number of years. This simple formula assumes that income earned throughout the year is distributed at the end of each year. For the purposes of the retirement needs analysis calculation, a few adjustments must be made. First, rather than dividing by the investment return, we must divide by the real return so that the annual income will increase with the rate of inflation. Second, the resulting need must be adjusted to account for beginning of year withdrawals, either by multiplying by the sum of 1 + the real return, or by adding an amount equal to the first year's payment.

Example 2.14

Recall in **Example 2.11** that Jordan's first year of retirement income needed at age 62 is $74,050.56.

If Jordan needed $74,050.56 as a flat dollar amount (not adjusted for inflation) at the end of each year, a simple capitalization of earnings calculation of $74,050.56 ÷ 0.095 = $779,479.58 would suffice. However, since Jordan needs her retirement income at the beginning of each year and needs the dollar amount to increase each year, adjustments must be made as follows:

$$\frac{\$74,050.56}{(1.095 \div 1.03) - 1} = \$1,173,416.56$$

Step 2: Adjust for beginning of year payments.

$$\$1,173,416.56 \ \times \ \frac{(1.095)}{(1.03)} = \$1,247,467.12$$

Note that the same result for Step 2 can be realized by adding the first-year income ($74,050.56) to the results of Step 1.[12]

If the assumptions for investment earnings and inflation remain constant, Jordan will have an income stream that can continue indefinitely, isolating her from the risk of superannuation.

The chart below compares the required annual savings under the annuity model with the required savings under the capitalization of earnings model.

Exhibit 2.25 | Capitalization of Earnings Model Comparison

	Capitalization of Earnings Model		Annuity Model	
	Beginning Balance of Zero Savings	Beginning Balance of $50,000	Beginning Balance of Zero Savings	Beginning Balance of $50,000
$FV_{@62}$	1,247,467.12	1,247,467.12	1,022,625.85	1,022,625.85
N	20	20	20	20
i	9.5	9.5	9.5	9.5
PV	0	-50,000	0	-50,000
PMT_{OA}	23,049.07	17,375.24	18,894.75	13,220.91

---

12. A common application of the capitalization of earnings concept is found in the constant growth dividend discount model used to value common stocks, V = D1/(r-g), where v is the current intrinsic value of the stock, D1 is the dividend (the income stream produced by the stock) one year from today, r is the required rate of return, and g is the growth rate of the dividend. Using this formula to calculate Jordan's capital needs at retirement, V = (74,050.56 x 1.03)/(0.095 - 0.03) = $1,173,416.56. This amount must then be multiplied by the sum of 1 + the real return to adjust for beginning of year payments. $1,173,416.56 x (1.095/1.03) = $1,247,467.12.

The capitalization of earnings model requires that Jordan save approximately $4,155 (22%) more each year compared with the annuity method. If Jordan has the wherewithal to accomplish this level of savings, and investment returns and inflation are as projected (or more favorable), her investments will produce an income stream that neither she nor her heirs will outlive

The exhibit below summarizes the required capital amount at retirement as well as the annual required savings amounts for each of the four models discussed.

Exhibit 2.26 | Capital Needs Analysis Comparison for Jordan Example[13]

	Annuity Model	Capital Preservation Model	Purchasing Power Preservation Model	Capitalization of Earnings Model
Capital needed at retirement	$1,022,625.85	$1,103,186.21	$1,206,942.14	$1,247,467.12
Annual savings with no initial balance	$18,894.75	$20,383.24	$22,300.30	$23,049.07
Annual savings with $50,000 initial balance	$13,220.91	$14,709.40	$16,626.47	$17,375.24

The Serial Payment Approach

The four models discussed so far are very similar except for the amount of money that remains at life expectancy. Each of these models assumes a level amount of annual savings over the remaining work life expectancy. Because each of the models assumes level funding, the savings amount over time should become a smaller percentage of annual income, as most people's income increases during their later working years. However, another method of funding the necessary retirement accumulation is to increase the savings amount each year, which often correlates to typical salary increases over a career. The increase from one year to another can be equal to inflation or can equal any other reasonable assumption. This type of approach is referred to as a serial payment.

Example 2.15

Consider the prior example with Jordan. The amount of money she needed to accumulate at retirement under the annuity method equals $1,022,625.85. That does not change with the serial payment approach. However, solving for the annual savings amount involves a few different calculations. The first adjustment is to convert the future retirement needs into today's dollars. The second adjustment is to determine the annual payment in today's dollars based on the annual increase in the savings amount. For this

13. Although we concentrate on the Annuity Model, Capital Preservation Model, and Purchasing Power Model in this textbook, the capital needed at retirement can also be calculated based on complex actuarial assumptions. In order to verify our results in the Jordan example, we sought the advice of an actuary who used a different approach (but one that we verified was competent), which assumed no particular start balance. He calculated the capital needed at retirement to be approximately $1,245,000. We do not present the details of this calculation due to the complexity of the assumptions and calculations. Suffice it to say that the capital needed is $1,200,000 to $1,250,000 regardless of the assumptions. If you are looking for a rule of thumb, it costs 10% more for the Capital Preservation Model and 20% more for the Purchasing Power Preservation Model as long as you have similar factors (e.g., 28 years and 3% inflation), but there is no substitution for exact calculations.

example, assume that Jordan would like to increase her annual savings amount by 8% each year.

Present value of retirement needs:	
FV	= $1,022,625.85
N	= 20
i	= 9.50%
PMT	= $0.00
PV	= ($166,507.72)

The $166,507.72 represents the amount of money needed today to fully fund the retirement needs for Jordan based on the annuity model.[14] The calculation below converts this amount into an annual savings amount.

PV	=	($166,507.72)
N	=	20
i	=	1.3889% [(1.095 ÷ 1.08) – 1] x 100
FV	=	$0.00
PMT_{OA}	=	$9,592.47 (in today's dollars)

The first payment at the end of year one equals $10,359.87, which represents an 8% increase over the PMT in today's dollars. The payment at the end of the second year, as well as each future years, will increase by 8% per year from the previous year.

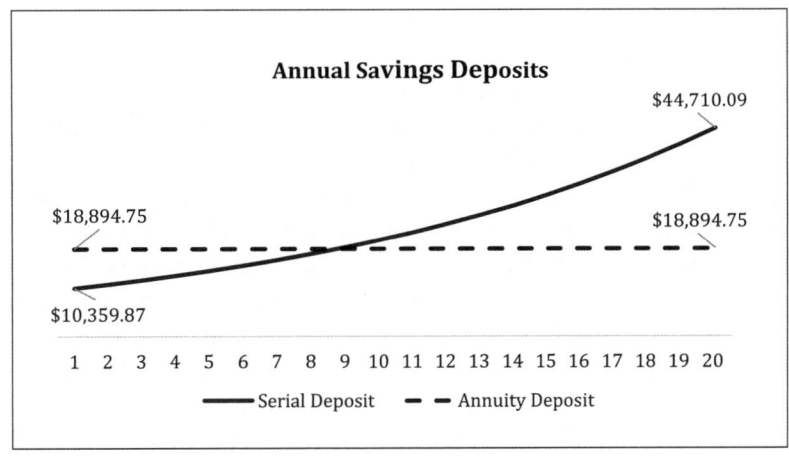

---

14. This number should look familiar. It is the same number calculated using the uneven cash flow keys.

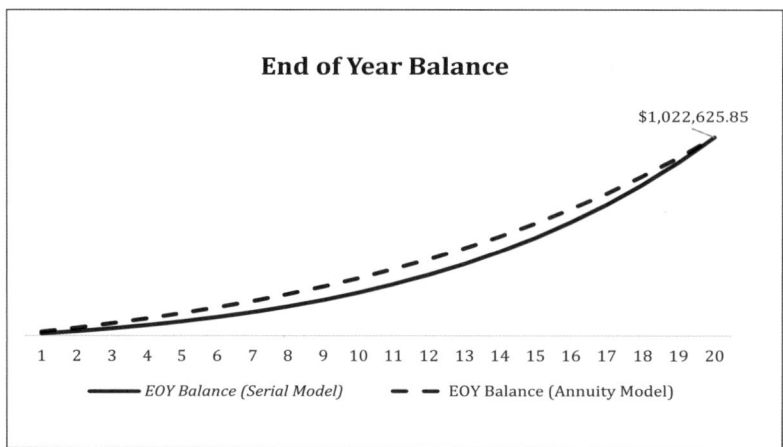

End of Year Balance

$1,022,625.85

1 2 3 4 5 6 7 8 9 10 11 12 13 14 15 16 17 18 19 20

———— EOY Balance (Serial Model)   — — EOY Balance (Annuity Model)

The charts graphically illustrate that the accumulation at retirement is the same for the annuity and serial payment approaches, but the annual funding for the serial payment starts lower than the annuity approach and then increases over the 20-year period. This funding method can be used with any of the three models discussed above.

Range Estimates, Sensitivity Analysis, Simulations, and Monte Carlo Analysis

As one might expect, small changes in assumptions regarding earnings, inflation, life expectancy, and retirement funding needs can have a dramatic impact on a retirement plan. One of the problems with traditional capital needs analysis is that advisers use deterministic estimates (i.e., the estimate is predetermined as opposed to a probability estimate) for each of the variables (needs, inflation, portfolio returns, life expectancies, etc.). While point estimates help the adviser create a plan for the client, it is unrealistic to

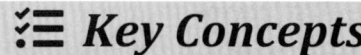 **Key Concepts**

1. Explain how sensitivity analysis is used.

2. What is a Monte Carlo Analysis?

think that these variables are really predictable to an exact deterministic point (given). Instead they may and will likely vary. Generally, point estimates used in deterministic models are the mean expectancy. For example, 10 percent on large capitalization common stocks is the mean expected return. While it is true that over the last 80 or so years large-cap stocks' average returns were 10 percent, there were only a few years out of 80 when the actual return was close to the mean expected return. It is unlikely that for any period going forward the investment return will replicate the historical return. A plan that only uses deterministic assumptions is likely to produce results that may range far from the original forecast. The adviser can employ various techniques to help begin to understand the effect of the range of probable outcomes for each variable in a plan. These techniques include range estimates, sensitivity analysis, and simulations such as Monte Carlo Analysis.

Range Estimates
Using range estimates allows the adviser to project the outcome using a range of assumptions (e.g., 2.5% to 3.5% inflation) for a variable as opposed to a single mean expectation (three percent inflation). A range estimate approach produces multiple outcomes that allow us to gain insight into the impact of a change in one variable or changes in a set of variables. Range estimate assumptions are usually conducted around the mean estimate, both lower and higher than the mean point estimates. If an adviser wanted to rotate the assumed coefficient of the variable toward the risk of an adverse outcome

(e.g., an investor who is more concerned with down side losses than upside potential returns may use semivariance analysis or alternatively, the number of months returns that were less than T-bill returns), then the technique to employ is sensitivity analysis rather than range estimating.

Sensitivity Analysis

Small deviations in one variable may significantly impact the entire plan. **Sensitivity analysis** consists of rotating each variable assumption toward the undesirable side of the risk to determine the impact of a small change in that variable on not achieving the overall plan.

For example:

1. One additional year of employment often makes a retirement plan work because there is one more year of savings, one more year of earnings accumulation, and one less year of consumption. The opposite is also true; one less year of work could make an otherwise achievable plan unworkable.
2. Small changes in the spread between the earnings rate and the inflation rate can have a significant impact on a plan, both positively and negatively.
3. A small increase in inflation can have a significant negative impact on an otherwise achievable retirement funding plan.

Understanding the importance of each individual variable and the risk involved if there is a change from the assumed number to a more conservative number allows the adviser to use sensitivity analysis to build a set of slightly worse case scenarios and then determine the impact of these more conservative assumptions on the overall plan.

Example 2.16

Recall the assumptions given in the Jordan annuity calculation (**Example 2.11**). The left columns below identify the given variables while the right columns below identify alternative variables that could be used.

Deterministic Example 2.11 Selected Assumptions		Sensitivity Analysis Conservative Assumptions
N	20 years to retirement	• Try 19 years
i	3% inflation	• Try 3.5% inflation
PV	$41,000 current needs	• Try $42,000 needs
PMT	$0	
FV	$74,050.56 future needs	

Deterministic Example 2.11 Selected Assumptions		Sensitivity Analysis Conservative Assumptions
N	28 years in retirement	• Use 30 years in retirement instead of 28
i	$[(1.095 \div 1.03) - 1] \times 100 = 6.3$	• Use a real rate of 5.75 instead of 6.3
PMT_{AD}	$74,050.56 future needs	• Use $80,745 as future needs rather than $74,050.56
$PV_{@62}$	$1,022,625.84 needed at retirement	
FV	$0	

Notice that slightly more conservative assumptions were used for the sensitivity analysis than were used in the original example in order to determine the robustness, or alternatively the sensitivity, of the previously calculated solution. If the retirement plan was recalculated using all of the sensitivity analysis assumptions previously identified, Jordan would need $200,000 more at retirement than originally expected, an increase of 20% just for the annuity model.

Annuity Model Solution with Conservative Assumptions Using Sensitivity Analysis	
N	19 years to retirement (instead of 20)
i	3.5 inflation (instead of 3.0)
PV	$42,000 current needs (instead of $41,000)
PMT	$0
FV	$80,745 future needs (instead of $74,050.56)
N	30 years in retirement (instead of 28)
i	5.75 real rate of return (instead of 6.3)
PMT_{AD}	$80,745 real payment (future dollars)
$PV_{@62}$	$1,207,472 (compared to $1,022,625) needed at age 62
FV	$0

Approximately $160,000 of the $184,847 change was caused by one variable, the inflation assumption being 3.5% instead of 3%.

Approximate Cause of Change		Explanation
1. Inflation 3.0 to 3.5	$158,916	• Inflations drives up future needs and drives down real return.
2. Change years 20 to 19	$15,857	• A shorter work life expectancy drives future needs higher, but over a shorter term.
3. Change years 28 to 30	$25,902	• A longer retirement period makes more annuity payments.
Total	$200,676	• The reconciliation is not exact because of the changes in terms and rates and the interaction of the variables.
Actual Change	$184,847	

Simulations and Monte Carlo Analysis

There is uncertainty associated with any retirement funding projection. The assumptions can be analyzed using the latest retirement planning software packages that incorporate simulations, such as Monte Carlo Analysis (MCA). As illustrated below, most retirement projections are based on fixed (deterministic) assumptions. While useful during retirement planning, deterministic projections do not account for variations. A **Monte Carlo Analysis** is a mathematical tool that illustrates the unpredictability of the "real" world and its effects on an individual's retirement plan. MCA uses a random number generator for inputs into a software package that will provide an output with specific probabilities of outcomes. MCA provides insight into the most likely outcome, but also provides other possible outcomes. It allows for a variety of alternative assumptions, such as changes in investment rates of return, the variability of inflation, adjustments to life expectancy, and many other market-condition scenarios. Such a method is invaluable to the adviser, as it allows the adviser to observe a large number of projections illustrating a potential range of future outcomes based on changing variables. Various software programs are available that allow the adviser to run simulations projecting various scenarios, thereby increasing the probability that the individual's retirement plan will be successful.

> **Quick Quiz 2.6**
>
> 1. Sensitivity analysis eliminates the risk of retirement planning.
>   a. True
>   b. False
>
> 2. Monte Carlo analysis predicts particular events.
>   a. True
>   b. False
>
> 3. Simulations allow for an unlimited number of simultaneous ranging variables.
>   a. True
>   b. False
>
> False, False, True.

A simulation calculates multiple scenarios of a model by repeatedly sampling values from probability distributions for uncertain variables. Traditional range estimates calculate outcomes on a best case, expected case, and worst case basis. Sensitivity analysis allows the model user to manipulate variables usually one at a time or one set of variables at a time. Simulations allow for an unlimited (or very large) number of simultaneous ranging of variables, possibly leading to more insight into the problem and into the impact of interacting variables.

Because retirement is frequently 20 to 30 years or longer and there are many historical patterns of investment returns for selected 20 to 30 year periods, the adviser simply does not know what the market conditions will be when the client retires, nor does the adviser know what pattern of market returns will follow a particular retirement date. Monte Carlo Analysis helps the adviser to understand the possibilities and probabilities. However, Monte Carlo Analysis cannot predict particular events. An excellent discussion of the problems with Monte Carlo Analysis was written in the Journal of Financial Planning by David Rawrocki (November 2001, Article 12) and is summarized in **Exhibit 2.27**.

Exhibit 2.27 | Selected Problems with Monte Carlo Analysis

- Assumes normal distributions, serial independence, and linear relationships for investment returns (none of which are true).
- Stock returns are not normally distributed - kurtosis is higher than expected. (Stock returns are actually **lepto-kurtic**, meaning that they do not have a normal distribution.)
- Means and standard deviations for stock returns vary over time rather than remaining static.
- Many Monte Carlo Analyses ignore income tax consequences.

Monte Carlo Analysis is a valuable tool and an interesting exercise. However, as with any analytical tool, it should not be used in a vacuum. It is useful to provide insight, but it should not take the place of professional judgment. As with most financial planning, retirement planning is a process that includes regular monitoring and adjustments to the plan as needed. Clients should visit their advisers regularly (at least annually) to modify and update their retirement plans to adjust for changes in the preselected variables so that their retirement objectives can be met.

Alternatives to Compensate for Projected Cash-Flow Shortfalls

Sometimes a retirement projection simply works. Occasionally, a person's assets are significantly greater than their needs, and they may actually need encouragement to spend some of their money, or they may need assistance transferring it to loved ones or donating it to charity. These situations are generally easier to deal with than those involving unrealistic expectations and shortfalls.

Situations can be challenging when the required annual savings amount is unrealistically high or the expressed needs of a client greatly exceed the assets available. In these situations, the plan simply does not work. There are several alternatives to consider, some of which have already been discussed briefly in this chapter. However, many of these alternatives are closely linked to the variables that are quite sensitive in the capital needs analysis model. These include the amount of retirement needs, the amount of the required savings, the length of the WLE, the length of the RLE, the earnings rate, and the rate of inflation. With that in mind, the plan may work if one or more of the following adjustments can occur:

1. The annual or monthly retirement needs are reduced
2. The annual or monthly savings amount is increased
3. Expected investment earnings are increased
4. Expected inflation is reduced
5. The WLE is increased
6. The RLE is decreased

Obviously, there are implications and limitations to each of the possibilities listed above. However, a combination of these adjustments may help to resolve the budget shortfall. For example, a solution might entail refining the needs a bit more precisely, resulting in a decrease in what is actually needed combined with working a few additional years and increasing the portfolio risk slightly, assuming of course that the portfolio is not already heavily weighted toward equities.

This solution reduces needs, increases the years of savings, decreases the years of needs, and increases the expected return from the portfolio.

Caution should be taken when adjusting the expected investment returns and inflation. The expected investment return should be based on reasonable expectations about the returns from risky assets and should generally be an output from an asset allocation model that incorporates the investor's risk tolerance and time horizon. Capital needs analysis models are extremely sensitive to changes in expected return and inflation and care should be taken when adjusting these input variables.

Example 2.17

BJ is 45 years old and plans on retiring at age 65 and living until age 95. Assume that he currently earns $100,000 and his wage replacement ratio is 70 percent and Social Security will provide $20,000 (in today's dollars) in retirement benefits. Also assume that he expects inflation to be 3 percent and expects that he can earn 6 percent on his investments.

Scenario 1: Step 1 of this problem is to determine the needs to be funded in today's dollars. His current income adjusted for the WRR and Social Security result in a funding need of $50,000 ($100,000 x 70% - $20,000) in today's dollars. Step 2 inflates this need until retirement. Based on inflation and when he is retiring, he will need $90,306 his first year of retirement. Step 3 determines the balance he needs in his investment accounts at retirement, which is $1,842,331. Finally, Step 4 calculates the required annual savings of $50,083. The annual funding is problematic because it is 50 percent of his income.

As would likely be the case, assume that Scenario 1 does not work for BJ. Scenarios 2, 3, 4, and 5 illustrate how changing the assumptions impact the annual funding requirements:

Scenario 2: Requires BJ to work an additional three years. This adjustment increases his accumulation period by three years and decreases his distribution period by three years.

Scenario 3: Requires a greater investment return from his portfolio increasing the return during his savings years from 6 percent to 9 percent. It does not change the return during retirement.

Scenario 4: Combines Scenarios 2 and 3.

Scenario 5: Combines Scenarios 2 and 3 and requires that he sell an asset, such as land or a boat, for $75,000 and uses the proceeds as the initial funding for his retirement plan.

		Scenario 1 (original projection)	Scenario 2 (work 3 more years)	Scenario 3 (increase investment return)	Scenario 4 (Scenarios 2 & 3 combined)	Scenario 5 (Scenario 4 & sale of asset)
Step 2: Inflate funds to retirement age	PV	($50,000)	($50,000)	($50,000)	($50,000)	($50,000)
	N	20	23	20	23	23
	i	3.00%	3.00%	3.00%	3.00%	3.00%
	PMT	0	0	0	0	0
	FV	$90,305.56	$98,679.33	$90,305.56	$98,679.33	$98,679.33
Step 3: PV of retirement annuity	PMT	$90,305.56	$98,679.33	$90,305.56	$98,679.33	$98,679.33
	N	30	27	30	27	27
	i	2.9126%	2.9126%	2.9126%	2.9126%	2.9126%
	FV	0	0	0	0	0
	PV	($1,842,330.85)	($1,880,625.32)	($1,842,330.85)	($1,880,625.32)	($1,880,625.32)
Step 4: Annual funding amount	FV	$1,842,330.85	$1,880,625.32	$1,842,330.85	$1,880,625.32	$1,880,625.32
	N	20	23	20	23	23
	i	6.00%	6.00%	9.00%	9.00%	9.00%
	PV	$0.00	$0.00	$0.00	$0.00	($75,000.00)
	PMT	($50,082.95)	($40,016.86)	($36,011.07)	($27,046.93)	($19,218.29)
Savings as a % of income		50%	40%	36%	27%	19.2%

The impact of these changes is that his annual savings requirement decreases from $50,083 in Scenario 1 to $19,218 in Scenario 5, which is certainly more reasonable based on his income. These changes may or may not be acceptable to BJ, nor are they necessarily all the choices or the best choices. However, they illustrate how a plan can be adjusted to more realistically achieve the level of funding desired. One obvious choice that was not included was to decrease the annual needs, which would result in a lower savings requirement. Another alternative is to maintain the same 9 percent investment assumption throughout his life. This adjustment combined with Scenario 5 results in an annual savings required amount of $12,363.45.

There are numerous other ways one might adjust a plan to help with its viability. Other considerations include potential inheritances that would offset future costs or reduced spending needs toward the later part of retirement, which is consistent with the spending patterns of many retirees (see **Exhibit 2.17** and **Exhibit 2.18**). Part time work may also be a possibility for those who are in good health. Finally, paying off mortgage debt (which often represents 30-35 percent of a budget) prior to retirement can significantly reduce required expenses during retirement. The examples above are not an exhaustive list. Instead, they should be considered as a starting point for situations in which a retirement plan initially does not work. Investors generally have to make a choice of sacrificing today, working longer, or sacrificing during retirement when there are projected shortfalls.

IMPLICATIONS OF CAPITAL NEEDS ANALYSIS

Once the question of how much money will be needed at retirement is determined, consideration must be given to how that goal will be achieved. Individuals have several sources of funding for retirement, including personal savings, retirement plans from work, Social Security, and working while in retirement. Personal savings can be accomplished through banks and brokerage accounts. However, these accounts are not "tax-advantaged," meaning that income earned on accumulated assets are subject to current taxation. It is generally accepted that in most cases, deferral of taxation is beneficial to the taxpayer. Taxpayers with earned income may be able to fund individual retirement accounts (IRAs) with pre-tax dollars up to $6,000 ($7,000 for those age 50 or over) for 2021. IRAs, which are covered in Chapter 9, are beneficial because they defer taxation until retirement. However, the IRA contribution limit is relatively small compared to what may need to be saved on an annual basis.

The other method to save on a pre-tax basis is through employer-sponsored retirement plans that permit employee salary deferrals, such as 401(k) plans, 403(b) plans, SARSEPs, 457 plans and SIMPLEs, which each permit employees to defer significantly more than can be contributed to an IRA. These plans, pension plans and other qualified plans are discussed in Chapters 3 through 8 with other tax-advantaged plans discussed in Chapter 9 and 10. Social Security benefits act as a base source of retirement funding and the amount received is influenced by the number of years that are worked as well as the amount of earnings. Social Security is discussed in Chapter 11.

OTHER CONSIDERATIONS

Most of this chapter has focused on factors that impact retirement needs and retirement funding. It is important to realize that retirees also face qualitative factors as they make the transition from the work force to retirement. In addition, risks can impede the best retirement plan. These two issues are briefly discussed below.

For many, work provides a sense of purpose and helps maintain mental wellness. When individuals retire, it is helpful to fill the void of work with activities that provide the person with a sense of purpose and help maintain cognitive functions. Ego and self-esteem are often tied to a person's occupation. However, work is not the only source of ego. Many people are successful at maintaining their self-esteem in retirement by becoming more involved with family, hobbies, charities, or through fulfilling long-term dreams or goals.

Example 2.18

Eric and Erica worked in private equity for the last twenty years and are retiring at age 60. They have amassed a sufficient amount of wealth to buy their retirement home in Punta Gorda, Florida. They plan on keeping their condominium in New York City and residing there part of the year to spend time with their grandchildren. During the winters, they plan on living in their retirement home on the water. Both Eric and Erica are volunteers with several charities. They are effectively managing their transition from a high pressure work environment to a meaningful retirement.

While **Example 2.18** illustrates a couple who is effectively transitioning to retirement, they do so while maintaining their primary home and support system. For many people, retiring to a new city or country is a lifelong dream. These types of decisions should be carefully planned. By moving away from the community they have lived in, retirees give up their support systems, which can often be undervalued until they are no longer available. In addition, relationships with physicians, professionals, and the like must be established. Relocating may necessitate travel to spend time with children, grandchildren, and other family members. Relocating can be a wonderful experience during retirement. However, it should be carefully considered.

In addition to factors that affect retirement planning, consideration must be given to the risks that can undermine a retirement plan. These risks include the factors discussed in the chapter, such as savings amounts and earnings rates. However, these risks also include untimely death, disability, and liability or creditor issues. These are examples of why a sufficient focus must be placed on risk management concerns.

MANAGING RETIREMENT DISTRIBUTIONS

One of the biggest challenges for retirees is determining how to manage their wealth once they retire. How much can they spend every year or week? How long will their money last? The risk of running out of money is referred to as superannuation, which is one of the primary concerns for most retirees. This issue is of paramount concern more today than in the past due to the decreased pensions and the increased number of defined contribution account type plans (e.g., 401(k) plan).

When defined benefit plans were prevalent, the risk of superannuation was pooled together among the plan participants. The defined benefit plan was responsible for paying a pension for as long as the retired participants lived. Naturally, some retirees would live longer than others and some would not live very long. Actuaries could mathematically estimate the average life expectancy of the pool of employees and determine the funding necessary to meet those needs. However, the pooling of risk ceased as defined benefit plans were replaced with defined contribution plans. No longer is the risk of outliving resources mitigated with shared risk. Now, retirees are responsible for the funds they have accumulated and must determine how to make those funds last throughout their retirement. While self-reliance is generally a great attribute, the reality is that many, if not most, retirees are ill-equipped to manage their portfolios themselves and will need the assistance of financial advisers. This responsibility can be daunting to retirees.

While managing one's assets in retirement has its challenges, there are ways to mitigate against superannuation. The simple answer is to shift the risk instead of retaining the risk. This risk shifting can be accomplished with annuities. Annuitized income is equivalent to the stream of income that was paid from defined benefit plans.

The simple fact is that annuities reduce the risk of superannuation. Whether from corporate or government pensions, insurance companies, or Social Security, annuities provide a base of cash flow that allows retirees to meet a certain percentage of necessities. There is published research that indicates a positive correlation between annuitized income and happiness. That correlation is not an endorsement for all annuities. Instead, it is a reflection of the risk averse nature of many investors and retirees and the simple fact that annuities reduce one aspect of risk. Those retirees who are extremely risk averse should have a larger portion of their assets annuitized compared to retirees who are less risk averse. While annuities have advantages, they also have disadvantages that investors must consider.

One of these disadvantages of purchasing an annuity or choosing an annuity is that the funds used for the annuity are no longer available for unexpected emergencies or unexpected desires. In addition, if the retiree does not live to at least his or her life expectancy, then the purchase of the annuity reduced the assets that would have been available to transfer to heirs. Annuities are by no means a panacea. However, they are a prodigious solution that can be partially implemented without much difficulty.

Assuming that a retiree is going to retain the risk or some of the risk, many different approaches can reduce the risks of outliving retirement accumulation. Two of the more common approaches are:
1. *4 Percent Per Year Approach:* Limit withdrawals from the capital accumulation to four percent per year.
2. *Multiple Portfolio Approach (Bucket Approach):* Divide capital into unequal tranches with each tranche representing five years of retirement. Invest the funds for each tranche in varying asset classes expected to produce inflation adjusted returns of about five to six percent per year.

4 Percent of Capital Balance Approach

Conceptually, this approach is relatively simple to understand and implement. It provides for distributions equal to four percent of the capital balance each year and generally has a very high success rate, especially when the assets are invested in a balanced portfolio, such as one with 60 percent equities and 40 percent fixed income. Such a portfolio should generally provide a good balance between income, growth, and downside protection.

However, one scenario that is a risk for retirees is when the retirement portfolio is subjected to several years of relatively large losses combined with distributions of four percent or more of the portfolio. In this scenario, the portfolio balance may decline so fast that it is irreparably impacted, without the retirees dramatically changing their lifestyles or going back to work.

It should be noted that some advisers and clients might choose to use a 3.5 percent model or a 4.5 percent model. Adjustments such as these provide more confidence or less confidence in the funds lasting through the retirement time period.

A four percent level of withdrawal initially indicates an account balance that is 25 times the income needed and implies a needed earnings rate of only 1.310 percent to pay out at a four percent rate for 30 years, assuming no inflation and annuity due payments. A four percent inflation adjusted withdrawal rate (assume inflation is three percent) would require an earnings rate of 4.349 percent annually for 30 years.

Required Earnings Rate			
Withdrawal Rate	*Fixed Payment Required Earnings Rate*	*Inflation Adjusted Required Earnings Rate*	*Portfolio Allocation*
3%	-0.711%	2.268%	Very Conservative
4%	1.310%	4.349%	Conservative
5%	3.079%	6.171%	Moderate Conservative
6%	4.696%	7.837%	Moderate
7%	6.218%	9.405%	Moderate Aggressive
8%	7.678%	10.908%	Aggressive

As mentioned above and implicit in the chart above, the investment of the retirement assets is critical to successfully managing the risk of superannuation. The four percent withdrawal rate is an appropriate approach that generally achieves the objectives of clients as long as the beginning retirement portfolio is large enough.

Multiple Portfolio Approach (Bucket Approach)

This approach divides assets into six five-year tranches and funds each tranche with sufficient money and the correct investment choices to provide retirement income for that period. The schedule below is an example that indicates the percent of capital necessary in each tranche, the expected investment return required for that tranche, and the type of asset class necessary to sustain this return.

Years	% of Capital	Rate of Return Required	Investments
1-5	28%	2%	Money Markets
6-10	26%	4%	Treasuries
11-15	20%	6%	Corporate Bonds
16-20	13%	8%	Balanced Fund
21-25	7%	10%	Large Cap & International Stock
26-30	6%	12%	Small Cap & International Stock

This approach is expected to produce a real overall return between five percent and six percent. The goal of this approach is to replenish the first five-year increment (the immediate income) every five years. It should be noted that this method is not a significant deviation from historical methods of managing assets. In fact, the overall portfolio allocation is similar to that of a moderately allocated portfolio. This model is a different way of accounting for the funds and retirement needs. It should also be noted that the investor and adviser might choose to change the percent of capital percentages as well as the number of tranches. For example, seven five-year tranches might be used in lieu of six. This approach helps the client focus on current needs, which are funded by the most stable types of investments, while longer term investments are invested to provide for growth and future needs.

These two approaches are effective for developing retirement income distribution strategies for clients. It is important to keep in mind that not all models work with all clients, and clients often have unique goals or needs that must be accounted for specifically.

DISCUSSION QUESTIONS

SOLUTIONS to the discussion questions can be found exclusively within the chapter. Once you have completed an initial reading of the chapter, go back and highlight the answers to these questions.

1. List the major factors affecting retirement planning.

2. Define work life expectancy.

3. Define retirement life expectancy.

4. What is the median retirement age for individuals in the U.S.?

5. Explain the work life expectancy/retirement life expectancy dilemma.

6. List the major savings and investment concepts that are important to retirement planning.

7. Explain the importance of beginning a retirement savings plan early.

8. Explain the importance of understanding investment decisions and their consequences in retirement planning.

9. How is inflation relevant to a retirement plan?

10. Why do an individual's needs increase or decrease during retirement?

11. List some of the common factors that increase an individual's retirement income needs.

12. List some of the common factors that decrease an individual's retirement income needs.

13. Define the wage replacement ratio.

14. What is the most common estimate range (in percentage terms) for the wage replacement ratio?

15. Describe why a person may or may not need the same wage replacement percentage dollar amount or purchasing power amount throughout their entire retirement period.

16. List the two alternative methods for calculating an individual's wage replacement ratio.

17. How is the WRR calculated utilizing the top-down approach?

18. How is the WRR calculated utilizing the budgeting approach?

19. List the three most common sources of an individual's retirement income.

20. Explain how Social Security affects an individual's retirement income.

21. Describe the importance of personal savings to an individual's retirement income needs.

22. List some of the qualitative considerations that are important in retirement planning.

23. List some of the common factors that negatively affect retirement planning.

24. Explain capital needs analysis and its importance to retirement planning.

25. List the four most common methods for analyzing an individual's capital needs.

26. Identify the main assumptions necessary for capital needs analysis.

27. Describe how Monte Carlo Analysis can be used in retirement planning.

28. Explain how the annuity model calculates retirement needs.

29. What assumption does the capital preservation model make to mitigate the risk of an individual outliving their retirement savings?

30. Why is sensitivity analysis important to retirement planning?

MULTIPLE CHOICE PROBLEMS

A sample of multiple choice problems is provided below. Additional multiple choice problems are available at money-education.com by accessing the Student Practice Portal.

1. Which of the following expenditures will most likely increase during retirement?
    a. Clothing costs.
    b. Travel.
    c. FICA.
    d. Savings.

2. Gemma, a 35-year-old client who earns $45,000 a year, pays 7.65% of her gross pay in Social Security payroll taxes, and saves 8% of her annual gross income. Assume that Gemma wants to maintain her exact pre-retirement lifestyle. Calculate Gemma's wage replacement ratio using the top-down approach (round to the nearest %) and using pre-tax dollars.
    a. 70%.
    b. 80%.
    c. 84%.
    d. 90%.

3. Omar would like to determine his financial needs during retirement. All of the following are expenditures he might eliminate in his retirement needs calculation except:
    a. The $200 per month he spends on drying cleaning for his work suits.
    b. The $1,500 mortgage payment he makes that is scheduled to end five years into retirement.
    c. The FICA taxes he pays each year.
    d. The $2,000 per month he puts into savings.

4. Scarlett has the following expenditures during the current year:

Expense	Amount
1. Health Care	$800
2. Savings	$4,000
3. Travel	$500
4. Gifts to Grandchildren	$1,000

    Which of these expenditures would you expect to decrease during Scarlett's retirement?
    a. 2 only.
    b. 1 and 3.
    c. 2 and 4.
    d. 1, 2, 3, and 4.

5. Niles and Daphne are near retirement. They have a joint life expectancy of 25 years in retirement. Daphne anticipates their annual income in retirement will need to increase each year at the rate of inflation, which they assume is 4%. Based on the assumption that their first year retirement need, beginning on the first day of retirement, for annual income will be $85,000, of which they have $37,500 available from other sources, and an annual after-tax rate of return of 6.5%, calculate the total amount that needs to be in place when Niles and Daphne begin their retirement.

    a. $743,590.43.
    b. $859,906.74.
    c. $892,478.21.
    d. $906,131.31.

QUICK QUIZ EXPLANATIONS

Quick Quiz 2.1
1. False. The average age men retire is age 64. Labor force participation for men over age 65 is under 30 percent.
2. True.
3. True.

Quick Quiz 2.2
1. False. Given that a savings rate of 10% to 13% of gross pay over a long period of time is necessary to meet the retirement goal, the savings rate in the U.S. is insufficient for retirement planning.
2. False. Common stocks provide the best hedge against inflation. The real economic returns for fixed-income securities are low and are not a good hedge against inflation.
3. True.

Quick Quiz 2.3
1. True.
2. True.

Quick Quiz 2.4
1. True.
2. False. Social Security is not a sufficient source of income replacement during retirement for most income levels. Social Security provides 100% of income to only 20% of individuals aged 65 or older receiving Social Security benefits.
3. True.

Quick Quiz 2.5
1. True.
2. True.
3. True.

Quick Quiz 2.6
1. False. While sensitivity analysis does not eliminate all risk associated with retirement planning, it does allow the adviser to build a slightly worse case scenario and to determine the impact of more conservative assumptions on the overall plan.
2. False. Monte Carlo Analysis does not predict particular events. Rather, it provides insight into the most likely outcome while also providing other possible outcomes, both good and bad.
3. True.

Chapter 2: Retirement Planning Accumulations and Distributions

3
QUALIFIED PLAN OVERVIEW

LEARNING OBJECTIVES

1. Understand the history of employer-sponsored retirement plans.
2. Understand the primary differences between pension plans and profit sharing plans.*
3. Understand the primary differences between defined benefit plans and defined contribution plans.*
4. Be able to explain the advantages of a qualified plan.*
5. Describe the requirements for a plan to be classified as a qualified plan under IRC §401(a).*
6. Determine whether a plan meets the coverage tests for a qualified plan.*
7. Determine whether an employee meets the definition to be classified as highly compensated or as a key employee.*
8. Identify employees who meet plan eligibility rules and those that can be excluded from the plan.*
9. Explain the impact of top-heavy status on defined benefit and defined contribution plans.*
10. Compare the vesting schedules for defined contribution, defined benefit and cash balance plans.*
11. Explain the funding limitations for defined contribution plans, defined benefit plans, and the limits on employers who sponsor both.*

Ties to CFP Certification Learning Objectives

HISTORY

Employer-sponsored pension and retirement plans have grown in terms of prevalence, protection and benefits over the last 100 years. In the United States, the first employer-sponsored pension plans were found in the railroad industry in the late 19th century. Pensions were not protected as they are today and were often paid out of current cash flow. Congress first provided preferential treatment to pension, profit sharing, and stock bonus plans in the Revenue Act of 1921. During the 1930s and 1940s, Congress provided that pension funds had to be used exclusively for the benefit of employees and their beneficiaries and that plans could not discriminate in favor of highly compensated employees.

Over time, with the increasing number of retirement plans, Congress realized that it was critical to further regulate pension and profit sharing plans. At the time, there was no legal recourse for employees of companies who did not pay pension benefits. ERISA (Employee Retirement Income Security Act) was signed into law by President Ford on September 2, 1974 and was designed to provide greatly enhanced protection for pension and retirement benefits. Congress wrote in §1001 of ERISA:[1]

- the Congress finds that the growth in size, scope, and numbers of employee benefit plans in recent years has been rapid and substantial;
- that the operational scope and economic impact of such plans is increasingly interstate; that the continued well-being and security of millions of employees and their dependents are directly affected by these plans; that they are affected with a national public interest; that they have become an important factor affecting the stability of employment and the successful development of industrial relations;

---

1. Chapter 18 of Title 29 of U.S. Code.

- that they have become an important factor in commerce because of the interstate character of their activities, and of the activities of their participants, and the employers, employee organizations, and other entities by which they are established or maintained;
- that a large volume of the activities of such plans are carried on by means of the mails and instrumentalities of interstate commerce; that owing to the lack of employee information and adequate safeguards concerning their operation, it is desirable in the interests of employees and their beneficiaries, and to provide for the general welfare and the free flow of commerce, that disclosure be made and safeguards be provided with respect to the establishment, operation, and administration of such plans;
- that they substantially affect the revenues of the United States because they are afforded preferential Federal tax treatment; that despite the enormous growth in such plans many employees with long years of employment are losing anticipated retirement benefits owing to the lack of vesting provisions in such plans;
- that owing to the inadequacy of current minimum standards, the soundness and stability of plans with respect to adequate funds to pay promised benefits may be endangered;
- that owing to the termination of plans before requisite funds have been accumulated, employees and their beneficiaries have been deprived of anticipated benefits; and
- that it is therefore desirable in the interests of employees and their beneficiaries, for the protection of the revenue of the United States, and to provide for the free flow of commerce, that minimum standards be provided assuring the equitable character of such plans and their financial soundness.

Congress believed that pension plans and the welfare of Americans was too important not to regulate employer-sponsored retirement plans. ERISA also set forth rules on disclosure, reporting, standards for fiduciaries, vesting, minimum benefits and provides for pension plan termination insurance, as afforded by the Pension Benefit Guarantee Corporation.

There is a large overlap of rules between ERISA and the Internal Revenue Code. Both ERISA and the IRC provide rules that employer-sponsored plans must comply with in the operation of retirement plans.

INTRODUCTION

Employers have many choices when selecting a retirement plan for the benefit of their company and its employees. Each retirement plan may have unique benefits and characteristics, but if the plan is to be a **qualified plan**, it must follow a standard set of rules and requirements to attain "qualified" status under Internal Revenue Code (IRC) §401(a). Once a plan has achieved qualified status, (provided it maintains the qualified status per §401(a)) the plan sponsor and the participants will benefit from tax deferral, asset protection, and several other advantages as discussed throughout this chapter and in Chapters 4, 5, and 6. Keep in mind that some employer-sponsored plans, such as 403(b) plans and SEPs, are tax-sheltered retirement arrangements, but are not "qualified" under IRC §401(a).

To help understand the unique advantages of each available qualified retirement plan and the specific requirements for the plans to attain qualified status, the universe of available qualified plans can be divided into four categories. Each of these four categories can be defined by its specific combination of certain qualities, benefits, and rules. First, qualified plans consist of **pension plans** and **profit sharing plans**. These plans are further divided into either **defined benefit** or **defined contribution** qualified plans, as depicted at **Exhibit 3.1**. (Note that "defined benefit" and "profit sharing" are category titles as well as plan names.)

As **Exhibit 3.1** illustrates, a qualified plan will always possess the characteristics of either a pension plan or a profit sharing plan with the characteristics of either a defined benefit plan or a defined contribution plan. For example, a money purchase pension plan has the qualities, advantages, disadvantages, and requirements of both a pension plan and a defined contribution plan, whereas a cash balance pension plan has the qualities of a pension plan and a defined benefit plan.

KNOW THE NUMBERS (2021)	
Covered Compensation	$290,000
Defined Benefit Maximum Limit	$230,000
Defined Contribution Maximum Limit	$58,000
401(k) Plan Deferral Limit	$19,500
Highly Compensated Employee	$130,000
Key Employee	$185,000
Social Security Wage Base	$142,800

Exhibit 3.1 | Qualified Plans

Pension Plans (4 Types)			Profit Sharing Plans (7 Types)	
Defined Benefit Pension Plans (2 Types)	Defined Benefit Pension Plans	Profit Sharing Plans		Defined Contribution Profit Sharing Plans (All 7)
	Cash Balance Pension Plans	Stock Bonus Plans		
		Employee Stock Ownership Plans		
Defined Contribution Pension Plans (2 Types)	Money Purchase Pension Plans	401(k) Plans		
		Thrift Plans		
	Target Benefit Pension Plans	New Comparability Plans		
		Age-Based Profit Sharing Plans		

Note: The DB(k) plan is not listed as it is a combination of a DB plan and a 401(k) plan.

PENSION PLANS VS. PROFIT SHARING PLANS

Historically, retirement plans paid benefits to retired employees until death. Some retirement plans continued the payment of retirement benefits even after the employee's death until the surviving spouse's death. Generally, the employee did not contribute to the plan, bear any responsibility for investment decisions, or participate in the management of the plan. The employee was simply promised a guaranteed benefit at retirement. Over the past 40 years, however, the number of these types of plans (noncontributory defined benefit plans) has decreased substantially as some employers have not fulfilled the promise of paying the retirement benefit and as employees have begun changing jobs frequently throughout their work life. In fact, between 1985 and 2000 the number of defined benefit pension plans declined from just over 170,000 to fewer than 50,000 and has remained fairly constant since then. Changing jobs even a few times in a lifetime could result in significantly limiting the growth of retirement benefits payable from these types of plans, which generally require many years of continuous service with the same employer to attain the expected or desired retirement benefit.

> ### ⋮≣ *Key Concepts*
>
> 1. Explain the reason for the change from pension plans to profit sharing plans.
>
> 2. From a global perspective, what are the differences between defined benefit and defined contribution plans?

With the decline of these "guaranteed" type plans, commonly known as defined benefit pension plans, came the addition of profit sharing plans. Under profit sharing plans, plan participants usually become responsible for the management of the plan's assets (investment decisions) and sometimes even responsible for personal contributions to the plan (contributory plans). The profit sharing plan also changed the employer's funding requirement and began to permit, subject to limitations, in-service withdrawals from qualified plans and investments in the employer's securities. **Exhibit 3.1** compares the basic characteristics between pension and profit sharing plans, which are discussed further in Chapters 3, 4, 5, and 6.

Exhibit 3.2 | The Differences Between Pension Plans and Profit-Sharing Plans

Characteristic	Pension Plan	Profit-Sharing Plan
Legal promise of the plan	Paying a pension at retirement	Deferral of compensation and taxation
Are in-service withdrawals permitted?	No*	Yes (after two years) if plan document permits
Is the plan subject to mandatory funding standards?	Yes**	No
Percent of plan assets available to be invested in employer securities	10%	Up to 100%
Must the plan provide qualified joint and survivor annuity and a qualified pre-survivor annuity?	Yes	No

Under the Pension Protection Act of 2006, pension plans could provide for in-service distributions to participants who are age 62 or older. The SECURE Act of 2019 amended the PPA rule to allow pension plans to provide for in-service distributions to participants who are age 59½ or older.
**For plan years beginning in 2008, the funding rules under IRC §412 have been amended by the Pension Protection Act of 2006.*

Exhibit 3.3 | Definitions of Qualified Plans (from the IRC and Treasury Regulations)

Pension Plan (Treas. Reg. 1.401-1(b))	• A pension plan within the meaning of §401(a) is a plan established and maintained by an employer primarily to provide systematically for the payment of definitely determinable benefits to his employees over a period of years, usually for life, after retirement. • Retirement benefits generally are measured by, and based on, such factors as years of service and compensation received by the employees. • A plan designed to provide benefits for employees or their beneficiaries to be paid upon retirement or over a period of years after retirement will, for the purposes of §401(a), be considered a pension plan if the employer contributions under the plan can be determined actuarially on the basis of definitely determinable benefits, or, as in the case of money purchase pension plans, such contributions are fixed without being geared to profits.
Profit Sharing Plan (Treas. Reg. 1.401-1(b))	• A profit-sharing plan is a plan established and maintained by an employer to provide for the participation in his profits by his employees or their beneficiaries. • The plan must provide a definite predetermined formula for allocating the contributions made to the plan among the participants and for distributing the funds accumulated under the plan after a fixed number of years, the attainment of a stated age, or upon the prior occurrence of some event such as layoff, illness, disability, retirement, death, or severance of employment. • A formula for allocating the contributions among the participants is definite if, for example, it provides for an allocation in proportion to the basic compensation of each participant. • A plan (whether or not it contains a definite predetermined formula for determining the profits to be shared with the employees) does not qualify under §401(a) if the contributions to the plan are made at such times or in such amounts that the plan in operation discriminates in favor of officers, shareholders, persons whose principal duties consist in supervising the work of other employees, or highly compensated employees.
Defined Contribution Plan (IRC 414(i))	• The term "defined contribution plan" means a plan which provides for an individual account for each participant and for benefits based solely on the amount contributed to the participant's account, and any income, expenses, gains and losses, and any forfeitures of accounts of other participants which may be allocated to such participant's account.
Defined Benefit Plan (IRC 414(i))	• The term "defined benefit plan" means any plan which is not a defined contribution plan.

DEFINED BENEFIT VS. DEFINED CONTRIBUTION

As illustrated in **Exhibit 3.1** qualified plans can be further divided into defined benefit plans and defined contribution plans. All defined benefit plans are pension plans, but defined contribution plans can be either pension or profit sharing plans. The primary differences between the classification of the plans as defined benefit or defined contribution are the assumption of the investment risk, the allocation of plan forfeitures, coverage under the Pension Benefit Guaranty Corporation (PBGC), the calculation of the accrued benefit or account balance, and the availability to grant credit to employees for prior service. Each of these differences is illustrated in **Exhibit 3.4** and discussed in detail below.

Under the Pension Protection Act of 2006, defined contribution plans that hold publicly traded securities of the employer must allow plan participants to diversify their pre-tax deferrals, after-tax contributions, and employer contributions that have been invested in those employer securities. The defined contribution plan must offer a choice of at least three investment options, other than employer securities, each of which must be diversified and have materially different risk and return characteristics (e.g., a money market fund, a bond fund, and a stock fund).

All plan participants must be allowed to diversify the investment of their elective deferrals and after-tax contributions. In addition, plan participants with three or more years of service must be allowed to diversify the investment of employer contributions made on their behalf. These requirements do not, however, apply to an ESOP if there are no contributions to the ESOP that are subject to the 401(k) nondiscrimination tests and the ESOP is a separate plan from any other qualified retirement plan.[2] As described in Chapter 6, ESOPs already require diversification under certain circumstances.

Quick Quiz 3.1

1. Pension plans are more common than profit sharing plans because individual workers remain longer with one employer and, therefore, can receive more benefits.
   a. True
   b. False

2. All pension plans are defined benefit plans.
   a. True
   b. False

False, False.

---

2. Pension Protection Act of 2006, §901.

Exhibit 3.4 | Characteristics of Defined Benefit vs. Defined Contribution Plans

Characteristics	Defined Benefit	Defined Contribution
What is the Annual Contribution Limit?	The greater of (1) the sum of the plan's funding target, target normal cost, and a cushion amount over the value of the plan asset, or (2) the minimum required contribution for the plan year.*	25% of covered compensation
Who assumes the investment risk?	Employer	Employee
How are forfeitures allocated?	Reduce plan costs	Reduce plan costs or allocate to other participants
Is the plan subject to Pension Benefit Guaranty Corporation (PBGC) coverage?	Yes (except professional firms with less than 25 employees)**	No
Does the plan have separate investment accounts?	No, they are commingled	Yes, they are usually separate
Can credit be given for prior service for the purpose of benefits?	Yes	No

*This is the annual contribution limit for defined benefit plans beginning in 2008 as a result of the PPA 2006.
See Chapter 4 for more detail.*
*** ERISA §4021, 29 U.S.C. §1321.*

Pension plans can be either defined benefit or defined contribution, while all profit sharing plans are defined contribution plans. The differences among various pension plans are discussed in more detail in Chapter 4.

ADVANTAGES OF QUALIFIED PLANS

The U.S. government offers several income tax advantages to both employers and employees who elect to maintain and participate in a qualified retirement plan. The purpose of these tax advantages is to encourage retirement savings by employers and employees. While retirees likely have benefits under the Social Security system, those benefits are generally not sufficient to maintain a lifestyle in retirement similar to that before retirement. Retirement savings helps to bridge that gap between retirement needs and benefits under the Social Security system.

A qualified plan must be designed and adopted in a fashion "approved" by the government, and the plan must meet certain requirements enumerated in IRC §401(a). Most of these requirements are established to ensure that a qualified plan is designed to protect and benefit rank-and-file employees. As distinguished from senior executives and owners, the rank-and-file are employees, such as the factory workers, counter clerks, mechanics, staff accountants, associate attorneys, etc. The government's primary motivation for the IRC requirements of §401(a) is to prevent employers from adopting qualified retirement plans that solely benefit executives and owners of the business. When a plan meets the qualification requirements and is considered a "qualified plan" under §401(a), the employer and the plan participants will benefit from income tax deferrals, payroll tax savings, and federally provided creditor asset protection. Each of these advantages is discussed below. The trade-offs for the tax advantages of qualified plans are the cost of the plan (both the operational expenses and contributions) and the compliance requirements, including vesting, funding, eligibility, non-discrimination testing, IRS reporting, and employee disclosure.

Taxation of Contributions to Plans

Income Tax

In almost all cases in the field of income taxation, when one individual or entity has a tax deductible expense, another entity or individual will have taxable income. This concept is referred to as the matching principle and is prevalent throughout the IRC.

Consider an office supply store that sells office supplies to a publishing company for $600. The office supply store has revenue, or taxable income, of $600 (subject to its costs), and the publishing company has a tax deductible expense of $600. This matching of income and expense especially holds true when an employer pays employees' wages, salaries, or bonuses for performance of services. The employees have taxable income and the employer has a tax deduction for the same amount. This concept is referred to as the matching principle because of the matching of income and deductions.

> **:≡ Key Concepts**
>
> 1. Explain the matching principle as between expenses and income and its application to qualified retirement plans.
> 2. How does the imposition of payroll taxes on contributions impact qualified retirement plans?
> 3. How are the investment earnings within a qualified plan taxed?

Example 3.1

Carla works 40 hours a week at Best Feed Supply for $8.00 per hour. In addition, if Carla sells more than 200 pounds of feed during the week, she receives a bonus of $200. In a week that Carla works 40 hours and sells 300 pounds of feed, Carla has taxable income of $520 (($8.00 x 40) + $200), and Best Feed Supply has a tax deductible wage expense of $520.

Contributions by employers to qualified plans, however, do not have to comply with this "matching" of taxable income with tax deductible expense. An employer may deduct an amount up to 25 percent (or as actuarially determined for defined benefit plans) of the total covered compensation paid to its employees as a contribution to a qualified plan. The employer will immediately have a deductible expense for income tax purposes, but the employee will not have taxable income related to the plan contribution until the funds are later distributed from the plan. This timing "mismatch" of income and expense is provided for in the IRC as a governmental incentive to entice employers to establish and fund qualified retirement plans for their employees. This mismatch is significant as it reduces the current tax revenue for the U.S. Treasury and defers the taxation of the funds until the plan participant receives a distribution from the qualified plan, generally many years later (during retirement).

This tax deferral is a benefit both to the participant and to society as it encourages the accumulation of assets specifically for retirement. As demographics have changed over the last several decades and life expectancies have increased, this tax deferral has become more important. However, because of this tax benefit and its potential abuse, the government has established, and continues to establish, certain limits for funding and deducting contributions to qualified retirement plans to minimize the reduction of tax revenue and to ensure that a substantial portion of the benefits are available to rank-and-file employees.

Example 3.2

Computer Connection, a C Corporation, employs fifteen service technicians, each earning $40,000 per year. The sole-shareholder of Computer Connection, Alexis, who is also a service technician and employee, pays herself $120,000 per year. For 2021, Computer Connection contributed 20 percent of each employee's salary to a qualified profit sharing plan. For 2021, Computer Connection will have a deductible business expense for contributions to the profit sharing plan of $144,000 ((15 x $40,000) x 20% + 20% x ($120,000)). Neither the employees nor Alexis will have current taxable income related to the contribution to the qualified profit sharing plan, but any distributions from the plan are taxable as ordinary income (and may be subject to penalties) to the recipients at the time of distribution. However, neither the employer contributions nor the distributions will ever be subject to payroll tax.

Payroll Taxes

In addition to income taxes, an employee who receives compensation for services rendered to an employer also incurs **payroll taxes** equal to 6.2 percent for Old Age Survivor and Disability Insurance (OASDI) on compensation up to $142,800 for 2021 and 1.45 percent for Medicare tax on 100 percent of the employee's compensation. The employer is also required to match any payroll taxes paid by the employee, creating a combined total payroll tax of 12.4 percent for OASDI up to $142,800 and 2.9 percent for Medicare on 100 percent of employee compensation.[3]

However, when the employer makes a contribution to a qualified retirement plan on behalf of its employees, the employer's contribution is not subject to payroll tax even though the contribution was on account of services rendered. This payroll tax savings acts to entice employers to fund qualified retirement plans and to view the combination of a qualified retirement plan and an employee's salary as part of an overall compensation package. Since the employee is not subject to payroll taxes on an employer's contribution to a qualified retirement plan either, a total savings of up to 15.3 percent (12.4 percent OASDI and 2.9 percent Medicare tax) on the employer

> ### ✓ *Quick Quiz 3.2*
>
> 1. Contributions to qualified retirement plans follow the IRC matching principle of the inclusion of income and the deduction of the expense at the same time.
>   a. True
>   b. False
>
> 2. The employer and employee are each responsible for their share of payroll taxes on the employee's compensation.
>   a. True
>   b. False
>
> 3. Distributions from a qualified retirement plan are generally taxable as ordinary income.
>   a. True
>   b. False
>
> False, True, True.

contribution may be realized. In **Example 3.2**, the alternative would have been to pay the $144,000 to the employees as additional salary instead of making the contribution to the qualified retirement plan. In that case, both the employer and the employee would have paid combined payroll taxes of up to 15.3 percent on most of the $144,000.

---

3. Chapter 11 discusses the Medicare taxes resulting from the Affordable Care Act for years 2013 and beyond. These taxes were not eliminated by TCJA 2017.

Example 3.3

If Butcher Block paid its two employees $50,000 each in wages and did not contribute to a qualified profit sharing plan for the year, Butcher Block would incur payroll taxes relating to the wages of $7,650 ($100,000 x 7.65%). Butcher Block's employees would have also incurred payroll taxes of $7,650 for total payroll taxes of $15,300.

Example 3.4

In comparison, if Butcher Block would have paid its two employees $45,000 each in wages and contributed $5,000 to a qualified profit sharing plan for each employee, Butcher Block would incur total payroll taxes relating to the wages and profit sharing plan contribution of $6,885 ($90,000 x 7.65%). In this case, Butcher Block's employees would also only incur $6,885 of payroll taxes for a total of $13,770 of payroll taxes. The combined payroll tax savings would be $1,530 ($15,300 - $13,770); however, Butcher Block's employees received total payments for services rendered equal to $50,000, $45,000 as cash compensation and $5,000 in contributions to a qualified profit sharing plan. Note that even at the time distributions are taken from the qualified profit sharing plan, the distributions will not be subject to any payroll taxes. The $1,530 of payroll tax that was saved is permanently avoided.

The payroll tax exclusion for contributions to qualified retirement plans does not pertain to employee elective deferrals to 401(k) plans, 403(b) plans, SIMPLEs, SARSEPs, and 457 plans. Therefore, if an employee defers income by making a pre-tax elective deferral contribution into one of these plans, then amounts deferred by the employee are subject to payroll taxes. However, if these employee contributions have employer-matching provisions, or the employer is making other contributions (such as profit sharing), the employer-matching contribution is not subject to payroll taxes. Note that 403(b) plans are not qualified plans and will be discussed in more depth in Chapter 10.

Example 3.5

Joseph earns $166,667 and is a participant in his employer-sponsored 401(k) plan that offers a 75 percent match for contributions up to three percent of salary. Joseph elects to defer three percent of his salary, or $5,000, into the qualified 401(k) plan, and his employer matches the contribution with a $3,750 (75% x $5,000) contribution into the plan. Joseph's contribution of $5,000 is subject to payroll taxes, but the employer's contribution of $3,750 is not subject to employee or employer payroll taxes. Note that because Joseph's earnings are in excess of the Social Security wage base and the OASDI of 6.2 percent is only paid on compensation up to the Social Security wage base, the employer and the employee are only saving the Medicare tax portion of 1.45 percent on the matching contribution to Joseph's 401(k) plan. However, in other cases where the employee's earnings are below the Social Security wage base, the employer and the employee are saving the full payroll taxes of 7.65 percent of the contribution by the employer.

Tax Deferral of Qualified Plan Earnings and Income

Assets contributed to a qualified retirement plan are held in a tax exempt trust by a fiduciary, the plan sponsor, or an appointee of the plan sponsor. The plan assets are invested per the direction of the fiduciary or the employee (as determined at the creation or by amendment of the qualified plan), and the earnings on the plan investments are not subject to current income tax.

Example 3.6

Juan's employer contributed $4,000 to a money purchase pension plan on his behalf. The funds were invested in a mutual fund that earned $300 in income during the year. The $300 is paid to Juan's money purchase pension plan account and reinvested in the mutual fund. Neither Juan nor his employer will currently recognize any taxable income resulting from the $300 of income from the mutual fund. Only upon distribution will the contribution ($4,000) and earnings ($300) be subject to income tax.

When funds are distributed from a qualified retirement plan, the recipient of the distribution will have taxable income. With a few exceptions (as discussed below), the entire distribution is taxed at the recipient's ordinary income tax rate at the time of the distribution regardless of whether the plan distributes cash, municipal bonds, Treasury bonds, or even stocks with "built-in" or unrealized capital gains.

It should be noted that because of the decrease in income tax rates over the last few decades as well as the reduction due to the Tax Cuts and Jobs Act of 2017 (TCJA), the advantages of tax deferral have been reduced. Specifically, the highest marginal income tax rate in 1986 was 50 percent while today's highest marginal income tax rate is 37 percent. Also, the tax rate on dividends and capital gains has been reduced to 20 percent (or less) for many equity investments and other capital assets. By deferring taxes today, an employee saves current income tax, but gives up favorable tax treatment on dividends and capital gains. For most employees, dividends and capital gains will be a large part of their earnings on funds used for retirement. These changes in tax rates should be considered as part of the analysis of whether a qualified plan is appropriate.

ERISA Protection

Because of various abuses by plan sponsors, Congress enacted the **Employee Retirement Income and Security Act (ERISA)** in 1974 to provide protection for an employee's retirement assets, both from creditors and from plan sponsors. Title I of ERISA ensures the employee's right to receive their dedicated benefits and is enforced by the Department of Labor.

> ### ⋮≡ *Key Concepts*
>
> 1. What protection does ERISA provide to participants in qualified plans?
>
> 2. Describe the special taxation options available for lump-sum distributions from a qualified plan.

Anti-Alienation Protection[4]

Because a qualified plan is designed to provide individuals with income during their retirement, ERISA provides **anti-alienation protection** over all assets within a qualified retirement plan. This anti-alienation protection prohibits any action that may cause the plan assets to be assigned, garnished, levied, or subject to bankruptcy proceedings while the assets remain in the qualified retirement plan. Assets in a retirement plan covered by ERISA can only be seized to pay federal tax liens. This protection is to ensure that the individual has income during retirement.

---

4. 29 U.S.C. §1056.

Example 3.7

Sofia has $4,000,000 in qualified retirement plan assets. Sofia's business failed and Sofia personally filed for federal bankruptcy (Chapter 7). At the time of the bankruptcy filing, Sofia had other assets totaling $250,000 and debts totaling $650,000. The court awarded Sofia's creditors $0.38 on the dollar and discharged Sofia of any remaining creditor claims. This judgment left Sofia with nothing except his qualified retirement plan assets. Because of ERISA afforded anti-alienation protection, the court could not award any of Sofia's $4,000,000 of qualified retirement plan assets to her creditors. Sofia will continue to have full rights over the assets of her qualified retirement plan.

Example 3.8

Nicole Brown Simpson's family and Ron Goldman's family won a civil judgment that exceeded $30 million dollars against O.J. Simpson in 1997. However, most of O.J.'s remaining assets (after the trial and his subsequent bankruptcy) were qualified retirement plan assets that are protected under ERISA. Because of the ERISA protection, the Brown and Goldman families have been unable to collect much, if any, of the $30 million dollar judgment even though the value of O.J.'s retirement assets is large enough to defray some of the debt. As of 2018, the judgment has grown, due to interest, to over $70 million.[5]

Once funds are distributed from a qualified retirement plan, the distributed assets are no longer protected by ERISA. Additionally, qualified retirement plan assets are not protected from alienation due to a **qualified domestic relations order** (QDRO - a court order related to divorce, property settlement, or child support), a federal tax levy, or from a judgment or settlement rendered upon an individual for a criminal act involving the same qualified plan. Individual Retirement Accounts (Traditional, Roth, SEP, or SIMPLE) are not afforded the same anti-alienation protection under ERISA, but as a result of the Bankruptcy Abuse Prevention and Consumer Protection Act of 2005 (BAPCPA 2005), IRAs are afforded similar creditor protection under Federal Bankruptcy law. Prior to the BAPCPA 2005, it was unclear whether IRAs were exempt from the debtor's estate. The Act clarifies that retirement accounts that are exempt from tax under the Internal Revenue Code are also exempt from the debtor's estate (up to $1 million).[6] See Chapter 9 for more details.

Protection from Employers

ERISA provides the laws, rules, and enforcement provisions to protect employees from abuse and misuse of qualified plan assets by employers as plan sponsors. Specifically, employers are prohibited by ERISA from discriminating against employees based on the benefits payable to the employee under the plan, from substantially altering the plan document without appropriate approval and notice, and from managing the qualified plan in a manner that is not in the best interest of the qualified plan participants and their beneficiaries.

---

5. Associated Press, January 30, 2018.
6. Bankruptcy Abuse Prevention and Consumer Protection Act of 2005, §224. This exemption is indexed to $1,362,800 as of April 2019. This limit is indexed every three years. Section 522(n). The limit applies to traditional and Roth IRAs. The bankruptcy exemption for SEP IRAs and SIMPLE IRAs is unlimited.

Special Taxation Option for Lump-Sum Distributions

As briefly discussed above (and thoroughly discussed in Chapter 7), the full value of a distribution from a qualified plan is usually subject to ordinary income tax at the date of the distribution (except for the return of a participant's adjusted basis from certain types of after-tax contributions). However, in certain circumstances, when an employee takes a lump-sum distribution from a qualified plan, that **lump-sum distribution** may be eligible to receive favorable income tax treatment on employer stock held within the plan.

A lump-sum distribution is a complete distribution of a participant's account balance within one taxable year of death, disability, attainment of age 59½, or separation from service. Specifically, a lump distribution of employer securities may be eligible for net unrealized appreciation treatment (NUA, discussed in detail in Chapter 7). The intent of this distribution option is to lower the overall income tax payable by the distribution recipient (but also functions to accelerate the tax revenue for the current administration by requiring the participant to pay tax in the year of distribution on the full cost of the employer securities purchased in the plan rather than just the yearly annuity amount needed during retirement). It is important to recognize, however, that NUA tax treatment does not always create the lowest overall income tax and may not be the best choice for eligible taxpayers.

Only lump-sum distributions from qualified plans qualify for the net unrealized appreciation taxation option. Distributions from an IRA, SEP IRA, or SIMPLE IRA do not qualify as lump-sum distributions for the purposes of NUA, and are taxed at ordinary income tax rates.

Exhibit 3.5 | Advantages of Qualified Plans

Advantages to the Employer
• Employer contributions are currently income tax deductible
• Employer contributions to the plan are not subject to payroll taxes
Advantages to the Employee
• Availability of pre-tax contributions
• Tax deferral of earnings
• ERISA protection
• Lump-sum distribution may qualify for NUA tax treatment

Exhibit 3.6 | Disadvantages of Qualified Plans

- Limited contribution amounts
- Contributions cannot be made after money is received
- Plans usually have limited investment options
- No or limited access to money while an active employee
- Distributions usually taxed as ordinary income (Basis = $0)
- Early withdrawal penalties may apply (prior to age 59½)
- Mandatory distributions at age 72 (unless still employed)*
- Only ownership permitted is by the account holder
- Cannot assign or pledge as collateral
- Limited enrollment periods (plan entrance dates)
- Considered to be an Income in Respect of a Decedent asset, subjecting distributions to both income and estate taxes with no step-up in basis
- Costs of operating the plan

Increased from age 70½ for those who attain age 70½ after December 31, 2019, by the SECURE Act 2019.

QUALIFICATION REQUIREMENTS

To benefit from the advantages of qualified plans, the IRC and ERISA impose requirements regarding eligibility, coverage, vesting, and plan funding limits for employers sponsoring qualified retirement plans. These requirements protect rank-and-file employees and ensure that qualified plans are not being used solely to provide additional benefits to owners and senior executives of the employer.

Plan Document

When a qualified plan is adopted, the terms of the plan are identified and described in the plan document. In order for the plan to maintain its qualified status, the plan document and the administration of the plan must be consistent with the IRC qualification requirements, which are discussed in this chapter. In some cases, plan adopters may choose between several options (such as vesting schedules and loans) and still maintain their qualified status. These selections must be identified and described in the initial plan document and the plan document must be amended if different options are later selected. The plan document is discussed in more detail in Chapter 8.

Eligibility

A qualified retirement plan must provide rules regarding when an employee becomes eligible for participation in the plan. The IRC provides **standard eligibility requirements** that state that an employee must be considered eligible to participate in the plan after:
- the employee has completed a period of service with the employer extending beyond the later of either the date on which the employee attains the age of 21, or
- the date on which the employee completes one year of service (defined as a 12 month period in which the employee works at least 1,000 hours).[7]

Any employer-provided qualified retirement plan may be more generous and provide that an employee is eligible to participate before one year of service or before the attainment of age 21, but this generally only occurs with 401(k) plans because a majority of contributions to 401(k) plans consist of employee elective deferrals and, thus, may only cost the employer a minimal matching amount. In fact, a plan that requires an employee to attain any age or term of service less than the standard eligibility requirements of the IRC will meet the eligibility requirements necessary to be a qualified retirement plan.

Note that an eligible employee is not automatically a participant in a qualified retirement plan. Other provisions of the plan may limit an employee's participation in the plan. Eligibility rules requiring age and service are established to ensure that employers are not requiring excessive years of service by employees or only allowing older employees to be eligible for the plan.

Plan Entrance Date

The eligibility rules could create an administrative burden for employers, requiring them to track eligible employees each day of the year. However, the IRC provides an elective grace period for the employer that states that even if an employee meets the requirements for eligibility listed above, an employer can make the employee wait until the next **plan entrance date** after the date on which the employee meets the eligibility requirements. The employer is allowed to follow this plan entrance date rule as long as the next available entrance date is not more than six months after the date of eligibility as determined above.[8] Because of this rule, most qualified retirement plans establish at least two plan entrance dates per year so that no eligibility date requires an employee to wait more than six months to enter the plan once the eligibility requirement has been met. Qualified retirement plans may have quarterly or monthly entrance dates that also meet the grace period requirement because they are more generous than twice per year and would always meet the six month requirement set forth by the IRC.

Example 3.9

Helium Limited operates a money purchase pension plan on behalf of its employees. The plan has entrance dates of January 1 and July 1 of each year. On April 12, 2021, Bob turned 21 years old and celebrated three years of service. On November 15, 2021, Cathy, age 25, celebrated her one-year anniversary of employment. Helium Limited considered Bob a participant in the plan at July 1, 2021 and Cathy a participant in the plan at January 1, 2022. Both employees were required to wait for entrance into the qualified retirement plan past their exact eligibility date, but neither was required to wait more than six months past their exact eligibility date. Thus, the plan meets IRC entrance requirements.

---

7. IRC §410(a)(1)(A).
8. IRC §410(a)(4).

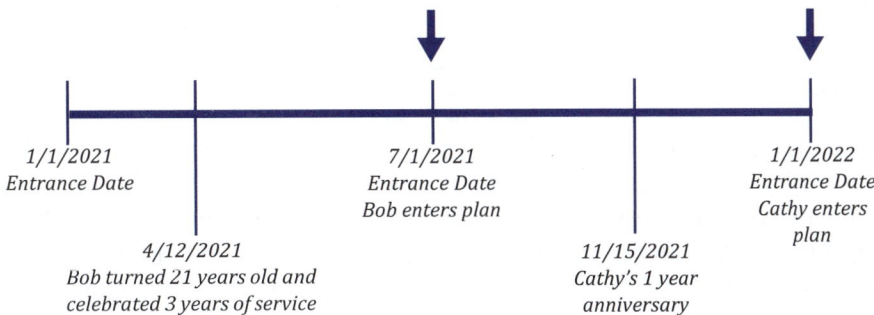

1/1/2021
Entrance Date

7/1/2021
Entrance Date
Bob enters plan

1/1/2022
Entrance Date
Cathy enters
plan

4/12/2021
Bob turned 21 years old and
celebrated 3 years of service

11/15/2021
Cathy's 1 year
anniversary

Special Eligibility Rules

Generally, qualified plans will follow the eligibility rule outlined above. However, there are several exceptions that are addressed below.

Long-Term Part-Time Employees

The SECURE (Setting Every Community Up for Retirement Enhancement) Act, passed in December 2019, amends the eligibility requirements to allow long-term part-time employees (age 21 and worked at least 500 hours per year for the employer for three consecutive years) to participate in the employer's 401(k) plan by making employee contributions to the plan, effective for plan years beginning after December 31, 2020. This new rule does not nullify the 1,000 hour requirement discussed above. Rather, it offers another eligibility requirement for employees to qualify to participate. See Chapter 5 for an additional discussion of these rules.

Two Year, 100 Percent Rule[9]

As an exception to the above eligibility rule, a qualified retirement plan could require that an employee complete two years of service to be eligible for participation into the qualified retirement plan. When an employer elects this special requirement for its qualified retirement plan, there are consequences. The plan must provide the plan participants with 100 percent immediate vesting of their accrued benefit or account balance upon completion of two years of service for the retirement plan to be considered qualified under §401(a). With this exception, the employer may still require that the employee attain the age of 21. Thus, such a plan would have an age 21 and two years of service requirement. The two-year eligibility election may be beneficial to employers that have high employee turnover during the first two years of employment. If the employer experiences higher turnover during the first two

---

Quick Quiz 3.4

1. Using the standard eligibility rules, an employee must be allowed to enter a qualified plan on the day after they attain the age of 21 and have completed one year of service.
   a. True
   b. False

2. If a company elects the two year eligibility rule, it can still require the employee to attain the age of 21 before being eligible for participation in the qualified retirement plan.
   a. True
   b. False

3. Tax-exempt educational institutions can require participants to attain the age of 26 before being eligible to participate in the qualified retirement plan.
   a. True
   b. False

4. XYZ sponsors a 401(k) plan for its employees. It can include a two-year service period for employees entering the plan.
   a. True
   b. False

False, True, True, False.

---

9. IRC §410(a)(1)(B)(i).

years, the two-year eligibility election can help the employer avoid covering employees who are not likely to remain with the employer for a significant amount of time.

Example 3.10

Doctor's Resource sponsors a stock bonus plan (a qualified plan) that requires that its employees be 21 years old and complete two years of service before being considered eligible to participate in the stock bonus plan. To retain qualified status for the stock bonus plan, Doctor's Resource's stock bonus plan must provide its plan participants with a 100 percent immediate vested account balance after completing two years of service. Therefore, any employer contributions to the plan will automatically be fully vested for the employee as of age 21 and 2 years of service.

The special **two-year eligibility election** is not available for 401(k) plans because most contributions to 401(k) plans are employee elective deferral contributions. As will be discussed in Chapter 5, a 401(k) plan may have employer-matching contributions, but these employer contributions usually account for a smaller portion of the total 401(k) account balance as compared to the employee elective deferral contributions. Because the government wants to provide employees with the maximum ability to save for their retirement and the 401(k) plan provides the employees with such a device, the government statutorily prohibits 401(k) plans from requiring two years of service for eligibility.[10]

Educational Institution

A tax-exempt educational institution with a qualified retirement plan maintained exclusively for its employees may delay eligibility in its qualified retirement plan until the later of the employee attaining age 26 or the completion of one year of service.[11] The IRC allows for this delayed age requirement to provide an incentive for tax-exempt institutions to establish and fund qualified retirement plans to benefit their employees. Otherwise, a tax-exempt institution is unlikely to establish a qualified plan for its employees because the tax-exempt institution does not, by nature, benefit from the tax deductions created by the contributions to a qualified retirement plan. From the organization's standpoint, a contribution to a qualified plan only creates additional costs to maintain the plan. It does not create additional tax deductions as a tax-exempt educational institution does not pay tax on its earnings but it may save payroll taxes. The organization's age requirement of 26 allows the tax-exempt educational institution, most of whose employees are teachers, the ability to deny eligibility to those new teachers that do not spend many years with the school. As discussed above, the employer could be more generous and consider employees eligible before attaining age 26 and one year of service, but unless the employer permits eligibility based on the general rule of completing one year of service and attaining the age of 21, the employees must be 100 percent vested in their account balance or accrued benefit after meeting the eligibility requirements of age 26 if that eligibility requirement is selected.

---

10. IRC §401(k)(2)(D).
11. IRC §410(a)(1)(B)(ii).

Example 3.11

A qualified profit sharing plan of a tax-exempt high school permits its employees to be eligible for the profit sharing plan after completing six months of service and attaining the age of 20. The qualified retirement plan follows a three-year cliff-vesting schedule. In this case, the profit sharing plan retains its qualified status under §401(a) even though participant account balances are not 100 percent vested after they complete one year of service because the plan did not increase the age requirement for eligibility to 26.

Example 3.12

A tax-exempt middle school sponsors a qualified money-purchase pension plan. To be considered eligible for the money purchase pension plan, the employees must complete one year of service and attain the age of 24. Because the money-purchase pension plan does not permit eligibility based on the general rule of completing one year of service and attaining the age of 21, the money purchase pension plan must provide 100 percent vesting to participant's accrued benefits.

Coverage

As described above, an employer is only required to consider those employees that meet the eligibility requirements (age and years of service) for participation in the plan. In addition, all employees covered under a collective bargaining agreement and nonresident alien employees who do not perform services in the U.S. are also excludable from the plan.[12] All other employees, those deemed **nonexcludable**, must be considered for participation in the qualified plan.

> **Key Concepts**
>
> 1. Which employees may be excluded from a qualified plan?
>
> 2. Which employees are highly compensated?

However, even after this determination, an employer is not required to adopt a plan that benefits each and every nonexcludable employee. In fact, many employer-provided plans are designed to benefit only select classes of nonexcludable employees. Provided the employer's selection of the beneficial class is not discriminatory (as defined below), the employer-provided plan may still be considered qualified if it meets the IRC coverage tests described below.

Participation in a qualified retirement plan counts as coverage in the plan. Specifically, an employee is **covered** under a qualified retirement plan when the employee receives a benefit from the plan.[13] For example:

- Profit sharing plan: In a profit sharing plan, the employee is considered benefiting if he receives a contribution to his profit sharing plan account for the year.
- Defined benefit plan: In a defined benefit plan, the employee is considered benefiting if the employee accrues a benefit for the plan year.
- 401(k) plan: In a 401(k) plan, an employee is treated as benefiting under the plan if the employee meets the eligibility requirements, without regard to whether the employee actually participates in the 401(k) plan.[14]

---

12. IRC §410(b)(3).
13. Treas. Reg. §1.410(b)-3.
14. Treas. Reg. §1.410(b)-3 and Treas. Reg. §1.401(k)-6

Nondiscriminatory Classification

The selection of the class of nonexcludable employees who will benefit under a qualified retirement plan must be reasonable and established based on the facts and circumstances of the business using objective business criteria. A few classifications considered reasonable are those based on whether the employee is hourly or salaried, the geographic location of the employee, or the employee's job description. For example, many law firms exclude their associate attorneys while some businesses exclude commissioned sales people from coverage under the qualified retirement plan. In these examples, the employers are excluding all employees who share a common job description from coverage. Provided the exclusion is uniform, the exclusion will be treated as nondiscriminatory. If, however, an employer bases coverage on age (other than according to the eligibility rules discussed above), sex, or any other non-business determination such as color of hair, eyes, or an employee's height, the classification will be considered discriminatory and the retirement plan will be disqualified, thus losing the tax benefits of qualified status.

When selecting the criteria to determine which employees benefit from the qualified retirement plan, an employer should always consider that a retirement plan is part of an employee's overall compensation package and should be viewed as a method of attracting, rewarding, and retaining employees. For example, if an employer chooses not to benefit those employees in its Atlanta office, the employees within that office may seek employment with competing employers in the local market who offer retirement plan benefits to their Atlanta employees. In this case, the employer may lose qualified employees to its competitor. The cost of the lost employees will likely far outweigh the cost of covering the employees under a qualified retirement plan.

Coverage Tests

The ability to determine which employees benefit under a qualified retirement plan is further governed by IRC requirements that a certain number of nonhighly compensated employees (defined below) must benefit from the plan for the plan to retain its qualified status. Specifically, to be qualified, the retirement plan must meet one of the three following coverage tests:[15]

1. the general safe harbor test,
2. the ratio percentage test, or
3. the average benefits test.[16]

---

15. A defined benefit plan must also satisfy another coverage test known as the 50/40 test.

Each of these tests only considers nonexcludable employees (as defined above), and each employer-provided retirement plan must only satisfy one of these tests (except defined benefit plans, which must also satisfy the 50/40 test) to meet the coverage requirements of the IRC.

Highly Compensated Employees

For purposes of several coverage test calculations, all nonexcludable employees are further divided into two classifications, **highly compensated** (HC) and nonhighly compensated (NHC).[17] The definition of a highly compensated employee provided by the IRC is an employee who is either:

- A more than five percent owner (defined below) at any time during the plan year or preceding plan year, or
- An employee with compensation in excess of $130,000 for the prior plan year (2021).

If the plan uses a fiscal year, calendar year compensation is used for the plan year that includes December 31. Notice that under this definition, an employee who meets either one of these requirements is considered a highly compensated employee. So, any owner with more than a five percent interest is a highly compensated employee, even if his compensation is the lowest of any employee.

5-Percent Owner Defined

Although the term "5-percent owner" seems relatively self-explanatory, it is actually a bit complicated. The IRC defines a "5-percent owner" as anyone who owns more than five percent of a company's stock or capital.[18] Therefore, if an employee owned exactly five percent of his employer's stock, that employee would not be considered a 5-percent owner, nor would he be considered highly compensated under this definition.

In addition to direct ownership, family attribution rules direct that an individual is considered as owning the shares of stock of certain relatives, including stock owned by the individual's:[19]

1. Spouse
2. Children
3. Grandchildren
4. Parents

Ownership of corporations, partnerships, estates, and trusts can also be attributed to individuals in the determination of whether one meets the definition of a 5-percent owner.

Example 3.13

Jeramy, his wife Hope, and his son Steve, each own one-third of the stock of the Great Corporation. For purposes of determining the amount of stock owned by Jeramy, Hope, or Steve, the amount of stock held by the other members of the family is added together. Thus, for coverage testing, each of them is deemed to own 100 percent of the stock of the Great Corporation.

---

16. IRC §410(b).
17. IRC §414(q).
18. IRC §416(i)(1)(B).
19. IRC §318(a).

Example 3.14

Jay, his wife Kristin, his son Camden, and his grandson (Camden's son) Jason, own the 100 outstanding shares of BWSG, Inc. stock, each owning 25 shares. Jay, Kristin, and Camden are each considered as owning 100 shares of BWSG, Inc. Jason is considered as owning only 50 shares (his own and his father's).

Example 3.15

Gisele and her husband Tom started Trophy Shop, Inc. many years ago. Together they owned 95% of the business and their only employee at that time, Bridget, owned the remaining 5%. Tom died last year and left his shares to Gisele. Gisele wanted to give up a majority of her responsibilities at the trophy shop and spend more time with her grandchildren. In the current year, Gisele sold all but a 5% interest to Bridget. Gisele now owns 5% of the business and Bridget owns 95%. Bridget recently had a baby and no longer wants to work full time. Bridget and Gisele each receive a salary of $50,000 for the limited amount of work they do. Bridget hired Brady, a successful salesman, to run the day-to-day operations and grow the business. Brady's salary is $150,000. Which of the three employees are considered highly compensated based on the qualified plan rules?

Employee	Salary	Ownership % Current year	Ownership % Last Year
Gisele	$50,000	5%	95%
Bridget	$50,000	95%	5%
Brady	$150,000	0	0

Even though Gisele does not own more than 5% in the current year, she is considered highly compensated because she owned greater than 5% last year. Bridget is highly compensated because she is a greater than 5% owner in the current year. Brady will be classified as highly compensated next year because his income exceeds the compensation limit. He will not be considered highly compensated for the current year as this is his first year and he does not have income for the prior year.

Highly Compensated Election

An employer election is available to reduce the number of employees considered highly compensated. This election, which is part of the definition of highly compensated employee within the plan document, allows an employer to only count those employees whose compensation is in excess of the dollar limit as highly compensated if that employee is also in the top 20 percent of all paid employees as ranked by compensation.[20] This exception does not exclude employees who are more than five percent owners because such employees are considered highly compensated based on ownership. An employer would consider this election when it would reduce the number of highly compensated employees as compared with the general highly compensated definition. An employer's overall goal is to reduce the number of employees classified as highly compensated and, thus, have more nonhighly compensated employees because the plan will be more likely to pass a coverage test and may help comply with the ADP test described in Chapter 5.

20. IRC §414(q)(1)(B)(ii) and IRC §414(q)(3).

Exhibit 3.7 | Determination of Highly Compensated

Owner Employees	Nonowner Employees
Either An owner of > 5%* for current or prior plan year *or* Compensation in excess of $130,000 for 2021** for prior plan year	Compensation in excess of $130,000 for 2021** for prior plan year

* 5% ownership may include ownership by spouse, children, grandchildren, or parents.
** If special employer election is made, add "and in top 20% of employees ranked by salary."

Example 3.16

Desk Emporium has the following 10 employees.

Employee	Salary	Ownership %
A	$200,000	65%
B	$150,000	35%
C	$145,000	-
D-J	$30,000	-

Utilizing the general definition of highly compensated (greater than five percent owner or compensation greater than $130,000 for 2021), employees A and B are highly compensated because both are greater than five percent owners of Desk Emporium. Employee C is also a highly compensated employee because his salary is in excess of $130,000 for 2021. So, in this example, three of the 10 employees are highly compensated.

If Desk Emporium elected to only count those employees as highly compensated if they were also in the top 20 percent of employees ranked by compensation, only employees A and B would be highly compensated. Employee C would not be highly compensated because he is not an owner of the company and if ranked by salary, C is not in the top 20 percent. In a company with 10 employees, only the top two ranked by salary would be in the top 20 percent. In this case, employee C is ranked third by salary and is therefore not highly compensated. By making the election, Desk Emporium reduced the number of highly compensated employees to two of the 10 employees. In a situation like this, the employer might make the 20 percent election and reduce the number of highly compensated employees to help pass the coverage tests.

	Desk Emporium Highly Compensated Test			
	General Rule		**20% Election**	
Employee	> 5% Owner	> $130,000 Compensation	> 5% Owner	Top 20% (ranked by compensation)
A	✓	✓	✓	✓
B	✓	✓	✓	✓
C		✓		
D - J				

General Safe Harbor Coverage Test

The general **safe harbor coverage test** is a straightforward test that considers the number of nonhighly compensated employees covered by the qualified retirement plan. A qualified retirement plan satisfies the general safe harbor coverage test if the plan benefits 70 percent or more of the nonexcludable, nonhighly compensated (NHC) employees.[21] Notice that this test only considers the nonhighly compensated employees, often called the rank-and-file, to determine the percent covered by the plan. The safe harbor test is not concerned with the percentage of highly compensated employees covered by the retirement plan.

☰ *Key Concepts*

1. What is the general safe harbor test for coverage in a qualified plan?

2. What is the ratio percentage test for coverage in a qualified plan?

3. What is the average benefits test and what are its component parts?

4. What is the defined benefit 50/40 test?

Example 3.17

Gerard's Automotive has 125 employees (26 highly compensated and 99 nonhighly compensated). 100 of these employees are nonexcludable and 25 of those are highly compensated (75 are nonhighly compensated). The company's qualified profit sharing plan benefits 21 of the highly compensated employees and 55 of the nonhighly compensated employees. The profit sharing plan meets the general safe harbor coverage test because it benefits 73.33 percent (55/75) of the nonhighly compensated eligible employees.

	Nonexcludable Employees		Excludable	Total
	Covered	**Not Covered**	**(Not 21&1, Union, etc)**	**All**
NHC	55	20	24	99
HC	21	4	1	26
Total	76	24	25	125

---

21. IRC §410(b)(1)(A).

General Safe Harbor Coverage Test			
	Nonexcludable Employees	Covered Employees	(%) Covered Employees
NHC	75	55	73.33%
HC	25	21	N/A
Total	100	76	General Safe Harbor Test % of NHC covered = 73.33% ≥ 70%

Only those employees considered nonexcludable were considered for the calculation of the safe harbor coverage test. Keep in mind that the plan does not cover each of those nonexcludable employees. In fact, 20 (75-55) of the nonexcludable NHC employees and four (25-21) of the nonexcludable HC employees are not covered by the plan. All of these employees meet the eligibility rules of the qualified retirement plan yet are not covered under the plan. Provided that the selection of the beneficial class was based on a nondiscriminatory classification (for example, the plan only benefits Gerard's Automotive mechanics), the plan will satisfy the safe harbor coverage test because it covers at least 70 percent of the NHC employees. If an employer only has HC employees, the plan will automatically meet the coverage test.[22]

Ratio Percentage Test

In the event a plan does not meet the safe harbor coverage test, the plan must meet one of two other coverage tests available or the plan risks disqualification. The first of these two tests is the ratio percentage test. The **ratio percentage test** compares the percentage of covered nonhighly compensated employees to the percentage of covered highly compensated employees. A plan satisfies the ratio percentage test if the plan covers a percentage of nonexcludable nonhighly compensated employees that is at least 70 percent of the covered nonexcludable highly compensated employees. The coverage percentage of each class is calculated simply by dividing the number of covered employees from that class by the total number of nonexcludable employees of that class. After these calculations are performed, the percentage of covered nonhighly compensated employees divided by the percentage of covered highly compensated employees equals the plan's ratio percentage test. If this percentage is at least 70 percent, the retirement plan satisfies the ratio percentage test.[23]

22. IRC §410(b)(6)(F).
23. IRC §410(b)(1)(B).

Example 3.18

A qualified profit sharing plan covers 60 of the 100 (60%) nonexcludable NHC employees and 40 of the 50 (80%) nonexcludable HC employees. This profit sharing plan's ratio percentage is 75 percent (60%/80%), and, thus, satisfies the ratio percentage test.

Ratio Percentage (%) Test			
	Nonexcludable Employees	Covered Employees	(%) Covered Employees
NHC	100	60	60%
HC	50	40	80%
Total	150	100	

$$\text{Ratio \% Test} = \frac{\text{\% of NHC Covered}}{\text{\% of HC Covered}} = \frac{60\%}{80\%} = 75\% \geq 70\% \text{ Pass}$$

In this example, the plan would not pass the general safe harbor coverage test because the plan only covered 60 percent (not 70%) of the nonhighly compensated employees. Remember, the plan only has to pass one coverage test and this one passed the ratio percentage test.

Example 3.19

A qualified profit sharing plan covers 40 percent of the nonexcludable (80 out of 200) NHC employees and 60 percent of the nonexcludable HC employees (30 out of 50). The plan's ratio percentage is 66.67 percent (40%/60%), failing the ratio percentage test. The plan also fails the safe harbor test because the plan does not cover ≥ 70 percent of the NHC.

Note: If the plan meets the general safe harbor test, then it will always meet the ratio percentage test.

Ratio Percentage (%) Test			
	Nonexcludable Employees	Covered Employees	(%) Covered Employees
NHC	200	80	40%
HC	50	30	60%
Total	250	110	

$$\text{Ratio \% Test} = \frac{\text{\% of NHC Covered}}{\text{\% of HC Covered}} = \frac{40\%}{60\%} = 67\% \leq 70\% \text{ Fails}$$

If a qualified plan fails to meet all of the coverage tests, it is subject to disqualification. The above plan has failed two tests, but gets a chance to pass the third test (the average benefits test).

Average Benefits Test

The third coverage test, the **average benefits test**, determines whether the plan adequately benefits the nonhighly compensated employees compared with the benefits received by the highly compensated employees and determines whether the employee classification is nondiscriminatory.[24] As such, the average benefits test actually consists of the following two tests:

1. The average benefits percentage test, and
2. The nondiscriminatory classification test.

A plan must pass both of these two tests, as described below, to be considered as passing the average benefits test and fulfilling the coverage requirement. If a plan does not pass both of these tests, it fails the average benefits test and must pass either the requirements of the general safe harbor coverage test or the ratio percentage test to satisfy the coverage requirements.

Average Benefits Percentage Test

A retirement plan satisfies the **average benefits percentage test** if the following ratio is at least 70 percent.[25]

$$\frac{\text{Average Benefit Percentage of Nonhighly Compensated Employees}}{\text{Average Benefit Percentage of Highly Compensated Employees}} \geq 70\%$$

The average benefit percentage of each class of employees is determined by first calculating the benefit percentage for each nonexcludable employee. To do this, the benefit provided to each nonexcludable employees is divided by that employee's annual compensation (i.e., an employee who has a $100,000 salary and receives a $10,000 benefit has a 10 percent average benefit). A benefit percentage is also determined for each nonexcludable employee who does not benefit from the plan (thus, a benefit percentage of zero). The calculated benefit percentages are then summed according to the employee's class (HC or NHC) and an average is calculated to determine the average benefit percentage. As expressed in the above formula, the average benefit percentage for the nonhighly compensated employees is then divided by the average benefit percentage of the highly compensated employees to arrive at a ratio that must be equal to or greater than 70 percent for the plan to pass the average benefits percentage test portion of the average benefits test.

Example 3.20

Employee	Status	Salary	Benefit $	Benefit %	Avg. Benefit %
A	HC	$150,000	$15,000	10%	10.00%
B	HC	$140,000	$14,000	10%	
C	NHC	$50,000	$3,000	6%	
D	NHC	$50,000	$5,000	10%	5.33%
E	NHC	$50,000	$0	0%	

HC = Highly Compensated
NHC = Non Highly Compensated

$$\frac{NHC\%}{HC\%} = \frac{5.33\%}{10.00\%} = 53\% \text{ (Fails Average Benefits Percentage Test)}$$

24. IRC §410(b)(2).
25. IRC §410(b)(2)(B).

Example 3.21

Waggaman's Meat Market employs 400 people and sponsors a money purchase pension plan for its employees. Of the 350 nonexcludable employees, 50 are HC employees and 300 are NHC employees. The HC have a calculated average benefit percentage of 10 percent, and the NHC have a calculated average benefit percentage of eight percent. This money purchase pension plan satisfies the average benefit percentage test of the average benefits test because the ratio of the average benefit of the nonhighly compensated (8%) to the average benefit of the highly compensated (10%) is 80 percent (8%/10%), which is greater than the requirement of 70 percent. This plan must also satisfy the nondiscriminatory classification test to satisfy the average benefits test.

Average Benefit Percentage (%) Test		
	Covered Employees	Average Benefit %
NHC	300	8%
HC	50	10%
Total	350	

$$AB\%\,Test = \frac{\%\text{ of NHC Covered}}{\%\text{ of HC Covered}} = \frac{8\%}{10\%} = 80\% \geq 70\% \text{ Pass}$$

Nondiscriminatory Classification Test

The second requirement of the average benefits test is the nondiscriminatory classification test. To satisfy this requirement, the method in which an employer chooses employees to cover under a qualified plan must meet both of the following requirements:

1. The classification must be reasonable and established, based on the facts and circumstances of the business, under objective business criteria that identify the category of employees who benefit under the plan (i.e., hourly or salaried, geographic location), and
2. The classification must be nondiscriminatory. In order for the classification to be nondiscriminatory, the plan must meet one of the following two tests:
   • Safe harbor test
   • Facts and circumstances test

The nondiscriminatory classification test is designed to guarantee that a plan truly provides benefits to a substantial group of the nonexcludable nonhighly compensated employees. If this nondiscriminatory test were not part of the average benefits test, it would be possible to satisfy the average benefits percentage test by benefiting only a very small group of nonhighly compensated employees with a substantial benefit. For example, if an employer chose to only provide a benefit to the janitors and the executives, the classification would satisfy the general nondiscrimination rule discussed above because it is a classification based on job description. The employer could then provide the janitors with a benefit sufficient enough to satisfy the average benefits percentage test and the plan would be considered qualified. This second nondiscriminatory classification test is included to protect against a classification selection such as this by requiring the employer to provide a benefit to at least a certain number of nonexcludable nonhighly compensated employees.

For a plan to satisfy the average benefits test, it must actually satisfy three requirements, the average benefits percentage test and the two nondiscriminatory classification requirements. If the plan satisfies the average benefit percentage test, the reasonable classification requirement, and the classification is nondiscriminatory, it will satisfy the coverage requirements and it will not be required to satisfy the general safe harbor coverage test or the ratio percentage test. Otherwise, if a plan does not pass the average benefits test, it must pass either the general safe harbor test or the ratio percentage test for it to satisfy the coverage requirement.[26]

A retirement plan is required to pass only one of these three coverage tests (general safe harbor, ratio percentage test, or average benefits test) to be a qualified retirement plan. Once it is determined that the plan passes one of these tests, the coverage requirement is met and no other test is performed. It is possible for a plan to fail one test and still meet the requirements of another and, thus, pass the coverage requirements.

Exhibit 3.8 | Coverage Tests Summary

A retirement plan must annually satisfy at least one of the following tests to be considered a qualified retirement plan.*

General Safe Harbor Test	% of NHC Covered $\geq 70\%$
Ratio Percentage Test	$\dfrac{\% \text{ of NHC Covered}}{\% \text{ of HC Covered}} \geq 70\%$
Average Benefits Test (Both Tests)	1. Average Benefit % Test $\dfrac{AB\% \text{ of NHC}}{AB\% \text{ of HC}} \geq 70\%$ 2. Nondiscriminatory Test

A defined benefit plan must also pass the 50/40 test described below.

Defined Benefit 50/40 Test

A defined benefit plan must satisfy the **50/40 coverage test** in addition to one of the other three coverage tests described in **Exhibit 3.8**.[27] The 50/40 coverage test requires the defined benefit plan to benefit the lesser of 50 nonexcludable employees or 40 percent of all nonexcludable employees on each day of the plan year. In the case of a defined benefit plan that has four or fewer nonexcludable employees, the plan must benefit at least two employees (or if there is only one nonexcludable employee, that employee must benefit from the defined benefit plan). This 50/40 coverage test does not segregate the calculation between highly compensated employees and nonhighly compensated employees.

---

26. More detailed information on the nondiscriminatory classification test can be found at money-education.com.
27. IRC §401(a)(26).

Exhibit 3.9 | 50/40 Coverage Test

Number of Nonexcludable Employees	How Many Must Be Covered
1 Employee	1 Employee
2 to 4 Employees	2 Employees
Less Than 125 Employees	40% of Employees
125 Employees or More	50 Employees

Example 3.22

A defined benefit plan sponsored by an employer with 125 nonexcludable employees must benefit at least 50 of the employees. This is calculated by determining the lesser of 50 employees or 40 percent of the employees. In this case, either calculation provides a requirement of exactly 50 employees. Note: A plan does not ever need to cover more than 50 employees to meet this test, but must still pass one of the other previously discussed coverage tests.

Example 3.23

A defined benefit plan being sponsored by an employer with 100 nonexcludable employees must benefit at least 40 employees. The determination is calculated by determining the lesser of 50 employees or 40 percent of the employees – in this case 40 employees (0.40 x 100 employees).

Example 3.24

A defined benefit plan being sponsored by an employer with three nonexcludable employees must benefit at least two employees. The determination is calculated based on the rule that states that a plan with less than four employees must benefit at least two of the employees.

Example 3.25

A defined benefit plan being sponsored by an employer with 5,000 nonexcludable employees must benefit at least 50 employees. The determination is calculated by determining the lesser of 50 employees or 40 percent of the employees – in this case 50 employees is less than 2,000 employees (40 percent of 5,000).

A defined benefit plan must satisfy either the general safe harbor test, the ratio percentage test, or the average benefit test and must also satisfy the 50/40 rule to satisfy the coverage requirements imposed by the IRC.

Example 3.26

Walker Brothers sponsors a defined benefit plan for its employees. Walker Brothers has 200 employees, 20 of which are excludable because they do not meet the age and service requirements set forth in the plan document. 15 of the nonexcludable employees are HC, and the remaining 165 are NHC employees. 10 of the HC employees are covered under the defined benefit plan, and 150 of the NHC employees are covered under the defined benefit plan. The average benefit percentage for the HC is 15 percent, and the average benefit percentage for the NHC is six percent. The selection of the covered class is determined to be nondiscriminatory. To be considered as passing the coverage test, Walker Brothers' defined benefit plan must pass either the general safe harbor test, the ratio percentage test, or the average benefits test and must also pass the 50/40 coverage test.

Employees	Nonexcludable	Covered	% Covered	AB%
NHC	165	150	90.91%	6%
HC	15	10	66.67%	15%
Total	180	160		

Coverage Test	Required to Pass	Plan Specific	Pass/Fail
Safe Harbor Test	$\geq 70\%$ of NHC covered	90.91% of NHC covered	Pass
Ratio Percentage Test	$\dfrac{\% \text{ of NHC Covered}}{\% \text{ of HC Covered}} \geq 70\%$	$\dfrac{90.91\%}{66.67\%} = 136.36\%$	Pass
Average Benefits Test	$\dfrac{\text{AB \% of NHC}}{\text{AB \% of HC}} \geq 70\%$	$\dfrac{6\%}{15\%} = 40\%$	Fail
50/40 Test	Plan must cover the lesser of: • 50 Employees • 40% of Employees	Plan covers 160 employees	Pass

Note: Since the plan passed the safe harbor test, it does not have to pass the ratio percentage test or the average benefits test. However, because it is a defined benefit plan, it is required to also pass the 50/40 test.

Vesting

Historically, some employers would require their employees to have many years of service for the employee to **vest** or receive ownership of employer benefits (employer contributions and the earnings on those contributions) provided by a retirement plan. The stringency of these requirements reduced the employer's final cost of providing the benefit to its employees because the employee did not receive the otherwise full benefit as determined without meeting the vesting requirement. In other words, the employer would segregate and deduct the employer contribution made on behalf of the employee to the plan each year as determined under the plan document, but unless the employee continued employment for a period of time equal to or greater than the vesting requirement, the employee would only receive a portion, if any, of the intended benefit. The loss of benefit upon termination would act as an incentive for employees to continue employment with the plan sponsor. Often, if the employee

> ### ☰ *Key Concepts*
>
> 1. What vesting schedules are available for qualified plans?
>
> 2. How is the vesting schedule of a qualified plan affected by the plan's top-heavy status?
>
> 3. At what point must the employee be 100% vested?
>
> 4. Define years of service.

terminated employment before retirement, the employee would not receive any benefit at retirement. If the benefit was not paid to the participant, it was forfeited. In such a case, the employer used these "forfeited" funds to contribute to the remaining employees' future benefits; thus, reducing the employer's overall future retirement plan costs (the expense of funding the employees' benefit). The IRC continues to allow qualified retirement plans to maintain a vesting requirement but limits the number of years of service that can be required by the employer for an employee to fully vest in employer contributions and associated earnings.

An employee's elective deferral contributions to a qualified plan and the earnings attributable (pro rata) to the employee's elective deferral contributions are not subject to any vesting requirements. Those contributions and earnings are always 100 percent vested in the employee's account. These funds are always the employee's funds because they are part of a salary reduction plan and were always owned by the employee.

Employer contributions will often vest using a cliff or graduated vesting schedule.

- A **cliff vesting schedule** provides an employee full rights to the plan's assets immediately upon the passage of a certain number of years of service, usually three years.
- A **graduated vesting schedule** provides an employee with full rights to a certain percentage benefit (less than 100%) after completing a certain number of years of service and provides the employee with an additional percentage for additional years of service.

In 1974, the year ERISA was enacted, employer contributions could vest under a 15-year graduated schedule, a 10-year cliff-vesting schedule, or under a method referred to as the "Rule of 45." However, since then, Congress has continued to reduce the years required for employees to fully vest in employer contributions.

Since the passage of the Pension Protection Act of 2006 (PPA 2006), all defined contribution plans (not defined benefit plans) must vest employer contributions under a 2-to-6-year graded or 3-year cliff schedule.[28] As a result, all employer contributions to defined contribution plans, including those made to top-heavy plans, are subject to a uniform set of vesting requirements (see **Exhibit 3.10**).

Minimum vesting in defined benefit plans remains at either 5-year cliff or 3-to-7-year graded vesting (see **Exhibit 3.11**), except when a defined benefit plan is classified as top-heavy, in which case the minimum vesting will be the same as for defined contribution plans.[29] Note that the vesting schedules defined here do not replace or modify the 100 percent vesting requirements for a plan that elects the two years of service for eligibility (as previously discussed).

Cash balance plans are a special type of defined benefit plan with hypothetical accounts. These plans are required to provide a 3-year cliff vesting schedule.[30] Thus, after three years of service, a participant has a nonforfeitable right to 100 percent of benefit derived from the employer contributions in a cash balance plan.

---

28. Prior to the Pension Protection Act of 2006, the IRC required that the employer's contributions and the earnings attributable (pro rata) to the employer's contributions follow a vesting schedule that provides a vested benefit to the employee at least as rapidly as a 5-year cliff vesting schedule or a 3-to-7-year graduated vesting schedule. When a plan was considered a top-heavy plan or when the employer's contributions were made as part of a matching contribution (such as in a 401(k) plan), the employee's accrued benefit or account balance under the plan had to vest at least as rapidly as a 3-year cliff or a 2-to-6-year graduated vesting schedule.
29. Pension Protection Act of 2006, §904; IRC §411.
30. IRC §411(a)(13)(B).

A plan must also vest an employee 100 percent in any accrued benefit or account balance when the employee attains normal retirement age (for vesting purposes, normal retirement age is the later of the age specified by the plan or the employee becoming age 65) or upon termination of the plan.[31]

Exhibit 3.10 | Defined Contribution Plan Vesting Schedules

| Years of Service | All Employer Contributions | | | Employee Contributions |
	2-to-6-Year Graduated	3-Year Cliff	2-Year Eligibility Election*	
1	0	0	0	100%
2	20%	0	100%	100%
3	40%	100%	100%	100%
4	60%	100%	100%	100%
5	80%	100%	100%	100%
6	100%	100%	100%	100%

Note: The two-year vesting schedule also applies to employer contributions under a 401(k) plan that makes use of an Automatic Enrollment Feature, as outlined in PPA 2006 (effective for years after 2007).

Exhibit 3.11 | Defined Benefit Plan Vesting Schedules

| Years of Service | All Employer Contributions | | | | | |
| | Non-Top-Heavy DB Plans | | 2-Year Eligibility Election | Top-Heavy DB Plan | | Cash Balance Plan* |
	3-to-7-Year Graduated	5-Year Cliff		2-to-6-Year Graduated	3-Year Cliff	
1	0	0	0	0	0	0
2	0	0	100%	20%	0	0
3	20%	0	100%	40%	100%	100%
4	40%	0	100%	60%	100%	100%
5	60%	100%	100%	80%	100%	100%
6	80%	100%	100%	100%	100%	100%
7	100%	100%	100%	100%	100%	100%

Note that under IRC §411(a)(13)(B), a cash balance pension plan provides for 100% vesting of employer contributions after three years of employee service.

Example 3.27

Miesha has been employed by Blue Cliff Supply Stores for two years. After meeting the plans eligibility rules, she is a benefiting participant of Blue Cliff's qualified profit sharing plan, which consists of employer contributions only and follows a 3-year cliff vesting schedule. The current balance of Miesha's profit sharing plan is $14,000. The $14,000 will be forfeited if Miesha terminates employment before reaching three years of service. Any forfeited funds will then be used by the plan to either reduce current plan costs or to increase the benefit provided to remaining participants.

31. Treas. Reg. §1.411(d)-2(a)(1).

Example 3.28

Anderson has attained three years of service with Stone Corporation. Over those three years, Anderson has received employer contributions to a qualified profit sharing plan in the amount of $60,000. If the plan follows a 2-to-6-year graduated vesting schedule, Anderson has a vested account balance of $24,000 (40% of $60,000).

Example 3.29

Ronda has attained four years of service with Pharmex Corporation. Pharmex sponsors a defined benefit plan that is not top-heavy and does not permit employee contributions. Ronda has an accrued benefit to date under the plan of $30 per month at retirement. If the plan follows a 3-to-7-year graduated vesting schedule and Ronda terminates her employment today, she would be entitled to a benefit of $12 (40% x $30) per month at her normal age retirement.

Vesting Schedule Options

Vesting schedules ensure that nonhighly compensated employees will benefit under the plan and that it does not require an unreasonable amount of time to become vested. The employer may always elect to provide the employee with a vested benefit faster than the standard schedules. For example, a defined contribution plan may vest an employee's benefit 100 percent after 18 months of service, or the vesting schedule may be based on a 3-year vesting schedule that provides for equal vesting in each of the three years. When an employer elects a faster vesting schedule, however, the vested benefit must always be at least as great as the corresponding statutory schedule (3-year cliff if full vesting occurs by year 3, or 2-to-6-year graduated for vesting schedules in which full vesting occurs after 3 years) in each and every year. The charts that follow list several examples of permitted vesting schedules and non-permitted vesting schedules for qualified plans. **Example 3.30** illustrates permitted vesting schedules for a defined contribution plan and **Example 3.31** illustrates permitted vesting schedules for a defined benefit plan.

Example 3.30

The following chart illustrates four various sample vesting schedules for a *defined contribution plan* and whether they meet the qualified plan vesting requirements.

Years of Service	Permitted 2-to-6-Year Graduated	Permitted 3-Year Cliff	Permitted Schedule (A)	Not Permitted Schedule (B)	Permitted Schedule (C)	Not Permitted Schedule (D)
1	0	0	5%	5%	33%	0
2	20%	0	25%	25%	66%	**0**
3	40%	100%	45%	**35%**	100%	50%
4	60%	100%	75%	60%	100%	75%
5	80%	100%	100%	80%	100%	100%
6	100%	100%	100%	100%	100%	100%
7	100%	100%	100%	100%	100%	100%

The permitted vesting schedules (A and C) for a defined contribution plans are at least as rapid as either the 2-to-6-year graduated vesting schedule or the 3-year cliff vesting schedule. The "not permitted" vesting schedules (B and D) provide a vesting schedule that is at least as rapid in some years but not in all years. Specifically, Vesting Schedule A provides a greater vested percentage in every year compared to the 2-to-6-year graduated vesting schedule. Vesting Schedule B provides a greater vested percentage than the 2-to-6-year graduated vesting schedule in years 1 and 2, but it is not as rapid as the 2-to-6-year vesting schedule in Year 3.

Vesting Schedule C provides full vesting by year 3 so it is compared to the 3-year cliff statutory schedule. Vesting is at least as rapid as compared to the 3-year cliff; therefore it meets the requirements and is considered a permitted vesting schedule. Vesting Schedule D provides full vesting after 3 years, so it is compared to the 2-to-6-year graduated schedule. It provides a better benefit than the 2-to-6-year graduated schedule except for year 2 which is a lower benefit than the statutory schedule. Therefore, it is not permissible.

Example 3.31

The following chart illustrates four various sample vesting schedules for a *defined benefit plan* and whether they meet the qualified, non-top-heavy plan vesting requirements.

Years of Service	Permitted 3-to-7-Year Graduated	Permitted 5-Year Cliff	Permitted Schedule (A)	Not Permitted Schedule (B)	Permitted Schedule (C)	Not Permitted Schedule (D)
1	0	0	5%	5%	0	0
2	0	0	10%	10%	5%	5%
3	20%	0	20%	**15%**	10%	20%
4	40%	0%	60%	60%	15%	**30%**
5	60%	100%	80%	80%	100%	60%
6	80%	100%	100%	100%	100%	80%
7	100%	100%	100%	100%	100%	100%

Note that under IRC §411(a)(13)(B), a cash balance pension plan provides for 100% vesting of employer contributions after three years of employee service.

The permitted vesting schedules (A and C) for a defined benefit plan that is not top-heavy are at least as rapid as either the 3-to-7-year graduated vesting schedule (when full vesting occurs after 5 years) or the 5-year cliff vesting schedule (if full vesting occurs at or before 5 years). Whereas, the "not permitted" vesting schedules (B and D) provide a vesting schedule that is at least as rapid as the corresponding statutory schedule in some years but not in all years. Specifically, Vesting Schedule A provides a greater vested percentage in every year compared to the 3-to-7-year graduated vesting schedule. Vesting Schedule B also provides full vesting after 5 years, so it is compared to the 3-to-7-year statutory schedule. The vesting is not at least as great as the statutory schedule in year 3; thus, it is not a permitted vesting schedule. Vesting Schedule C provides full vesting by year 5, so it is compared to the 5-year cliff statutory schedule. It provides a greater vested percentage in each year as compared to the 5-year cliff; therefore it meets the requirements and is considered a permitted vesting schedule. Vesting Schedule D provides full vesting after 5 years, so it is compared to the 3-to-7-year graduated statutory schedule. Since it is not at least as great in year 4, it is not a permitted vesting schedule.

Example 3.32

Lisa works for Pacific United and was hired three and a half years ago. She is a participant in her company's cash balance plan and has a hypothetical account balance of $12,000. If she were to leave today for another job, she would be able to take 100 percent of her account balance because cash balance plans must vest at least as rapidly as three-year cliff vesting.

Years of Service

As illustrated in **Exhibit 3.10** and **Exhibit 3.11**, employees earn a certain percentage benefit based on the applicable vesting schedule and after the employee attains a certain number of years of service. The **years of service** determination is based on the number of years, defined as a 12-month consecutive period with at least 1,000 hours worked for the employer. The determination is based on the employee's beginning date of employment and not on the date the employee becomes eligible to participate in the plan. For example, an employee who has worked 1,200 hours within a 12 month period has attained one year of service for purposes of vesting even though they may have just become eligible to participate in a qualified retirement plan that follows the general eligibility rule. This means that an employee will generally accrue years of service from the beginning of employment even though the employee is not yet eligible for the plan.

An employer does not have to count for purposes of vesting: (1) years of service the employee acquired with the employer before reaching the age of 18 if the employee was not participating in the plan at that time, (2) years of service the employee attained before the employer sponsored a qualified plan, or (3) years of service the employee attained during years when he did not contribute to an employee-contributory qualified plan.[32] If the employer desires, the employer can count any of these otherwise excludable years towards the employee's vesting requirement as long as all employees are treated the same.

Example 3.33

Taters Restaurant sponsors a defined benefit plan that does not permit employee contributions. Brian has been employed by Taters Restaurant for the past five years and has an accrued benefit to date under the plan of $20 per month at retirement. The Tater Restaurant's defined benefit plan is considered top-heavy and follows the least generous graduated vesting schedule. If Brian terminated his employment with Taters Restaurant today, he would be entitled to a benefit of $16 ($20 x 80%) per month at his retirement, an 80 percent vested accrued benefit. Taters Restaurant follows the 2-to-6-year graduated vesting schedule and not the 3-to-7-year graduated vesting schedule because Taters Restaurant's plan is considered top-heavy (see below for more information on top-heavy plans) and is a defined benefit plan.

---

32. IRC §411(a)(4).

Example 3.34

The employees of Tax Heaven are given the opportunity to contribute to a 401(k) plan after six months of continuous service. As part of the benefit, Tax Heaven matches employee elective deferral contributions with an amount equal to 25 percent. The plan maintains the least generous graduated vesting schedule for the employer matching contributions. Mike has four years of service with Tax Heaven and has contributed $18,000 to his 401(k) account over those four years. Mike has received $4,500 (25% of $18,000) of employer matching contributions to the 401(k) plan, has earnings of $9,500, and has a current balance of $32,000. As of today, Mike has a vested balance of $29,440 as illustrated in the chart below.

Calculation of Mike's vested account balance:

Contributions		Vested Percentage	Vested Balance
Employee	$18,000	100%	$18,000
Employer	$4,500	60%*	$2,700
Total Contributions	$22,500		
Earnings ($32,000 - $22,500 = $9,500)			
Employee	$9,500 \times \dfrac{18,000}{22,500} = \$7,600$	100%	$7,600
Employer	$9,500 \times \dfrac{4,500}{22,500} = \$1,900$	60%*	$1,140
Earnings Total	$9,500		
Total Account Balance	**$32,000**	**Total Vested Balance**	**$29,440**

* *Employer matching contributions for a 401(k) plan must vest at least as rapidly as 2-to-6-year graduated or 3-year cliff vesting schedules.*

Top-Heavy Plans

The **top-heavy** rules were designed to ensure that qualified plans that significantly benefit owners and executives of the company must provide some minimum level of benefits for the rank-and-file employees. The top-heavy requirements are most commonly applicable to small employer plans, age-based profit sharing plans, and any other plans that provide owners and executives with a disproportionate level of benefit from the plan. Most often the top-heavy rules are not applicable because the benefits provided to the non-key employees are generally greater than the required minimums of the top-heavy rules. The impact of the top-heavy rules has been lessened as a result of the PPA 2006's shortened vesting schedules. A plan is considered top-heavy under either of the following two definitions:

≡ Key Concepts

1. What is a top-heavy plan?

2. Which employees are considered key employees?

3. If a qualified plan is deemed top-heavy, how does it affect the vesting and funding of a plan?

- Top Heavy Defined Benefit Plan: A defined benefit plan is considered top-heavy when the present value of the total accrued benefits of key employees (defined below) in the defined benefit plan exceeds 60 percent of the present value of the total accrued benefits of the defined benefit plan for all employees.[33]
- Top Heavy Defined Contribution Plan: A defined contribution plan is top-heavy when the aggregate of the account balances of key employees in the plan exceeds 60 percent of the aggregate of the accounts of all employees.[34]

When a qualified retirement plan is determined to be top-heavy, the plan must: (1) use top-heavy vesting schedules[35] and (2) provide a minimum level of funding to non-key employees.[36] These top-heavy provisions attempt to ensure that non-key employees are actually benefiting from the qualified retirement plan and that the key employees are not benefiting in a disproportionate way.

Key Employee
A **key employee** is any employee who is any one or more of the following:
- A greater than five percent owner,[37] or
- A greater than one percent owner with compensation in excess of $150,000 (not indexed), or
- An officer (defined below) with compensation in excess of $185,000 for 2021 as determined last year.[38]

Example 3.35

John owns five percent of the stock of Market Resources, Inc. and receives an annual salary of $110,000. Even though John is an owner, he is not considered a key employee because his ownership percentage is not greater than five percent, and even though he is a greater than one percent owner, his income is not greater than $150,000.

Example 3.36

Claudia is an officer of Whinny National Bank. She earns $500,000 per year in annual compensation. Claudia is a key employee because she is an officer with compensation in excess of the annual limit of $185,000 for 2021.

Officer
Whether an individual is an officer is determined upon the basis of all the facts, including the source of his authority, the term for which elected or appointed, or the nature and extent of his duties. Generally, the term "**officer**" means an administrative executive who is in regular and continued service.[39]

---

33. IRC §416(g)(1)(A)(i).
34. IRC §416(g)(1)(A)(ii).
35. IRC §416(b)(1). Note that under the PPA 2006, all defined contribution plans must vest on a 3-year cliff or 2-to-6-year graded vesting schedule, without regard to the plan's top-heavy status.
36. IRC §416(c).
37. The definition of a five-percent owner under top-heavy rules is the same as it is for determining whether an employee is highly compensated and includes family attributions.
38. IRC §416(i)(1).
39. Treasury Regulation §1.416-1, Q&A T-13.

An employee who merely has the title of an officer but not the authority of an officer is not considered an officer for purposes of the key employee test. Similarly, an employee who does not have the title of an officer but has the authority of an officer is an officer for purposes of the key employee test.

No more than 50 employees must be treated as officers. If the number of officers, as defined above, exceeds 50, then only the first 50 ranked by compensation will be considered officers under the key employee definition.

Top-Heavy Vesting

If the qualified defined benefit retirement plan is top-heavy, the plan must accelerate the vesting from the standard vesting schedules to either a 2-to-6-year graduated or a 3-year cliff vesting schedule. All qualified defined contribution retirement plans now vest on a 3-year cliff or 2-to-6-year graduated vesting schedule, without regard to the plan's top-heavy status.[40] Therefore, the impact of the top-heavy rules regarding vesting is now limited to defined benefit plans. The employer may provide a vesting schedule that provides a vested benefit to its employees faster than that required by the top-heavy rules, but if so, the employer must utilize a vesting schedule that is always comparatively more rapid than one of the permitted vesting schedules.

Top-Heavy Funding

The sponsor of a top-heavy plan must also provide its non-key employees with a minimum level of funding. The amount of the minimum level of funding depends on whether the plan is a defined contribution plan or a defined benefit plan. These differences are discussed below.

Minimum Funding for Defined Contribution Plans

A defined contribution plan that is considered top-heavy must provide each of its nonexcludable, non-key employees a contribution equal to at least three percent of the employee's compensation. The benefit is payable to all eligible employees of the plan sponsor. An exception to the three percent minimum funding requirement occurs when the largest funding made on behalf of all key employees is less than three percent.[41] In such a case, all of the non-key employees must receive a minimum benefit percentage equal to the funding for the key employee with the highest percentage benefit for the year.

40. Pension Protection Act of 2006.
41. IRC §416(c)(2)(B)(i).

Example 3.37

The qualified profit sharing plan of MakeUps, LLP is considered top-heavy for the year. James, a plan participant, has annual compensation equal to $65,000 and James is not a key employee. The minimum amount that MakeUps, LLP must contribute to the qualified profit sharing plan on James' behalf is $1,950 ($65,000 x 3%) assuming that it contributes at least 3% to key employees.

Example 3.38

Erasers, Inc. sponsors a qualified age-based profit sharing plan. For the plan year, Eraser made contributions to its two key employees of one percent of compensation to Key Employee A and two percent of compensation to Key Employee B based on the formula provided under the plan document. The qualified profit sharing plan is top-heavy; therefore, all eligible nonexcludable, non-key employees must receive at least a two percent contribution to the qualified age-based profit sharing plan on their behalf because the two percent is the largest funding percent made to a key employee (Employee B).

Defined Benefit Plan

A top-heavy defined benefit plan must provide a benefit to its non-key employees equal to two percent per the employee's years of service multiplied by the employee's average annual compensation over the testing period.[42] A participant's testing period shall be the period of consecutive years (not exceeding five) during which the participant had the greatest aggregate compensation from the employer.[43] The maximum top-heavy requirement is a minimum benefit of 20 percent (or 10 years of service at two percent each year) of the employee's average annual compensation for the period of consecutive years not exceeding five. If the employer's benefit funding equation provides a greater percentage than the minimum funding level calculated for the year, the employer's funding equation will be used to determine the employee's benefits. **Example 3.39** provides an illustration of possible funding schedules compared with the minimum funding requirements of top-heavy plans.

42.IRC §416(c)(1).
43.IRC §416(c)(1)(D).

Example 3.39

Jocko, Echo, and Grecko Corporations sponsor defined benefit plans providing benefits based on years of service and an employee's average annual salary. Jocko, Echo, and Grecko provide benefits of 1%, 1.5%, and 3% respectively for each year of service.

		Defined Benefit Plans Accrued Benefit Percentage After Years of Service - Minimum Funding for Top-Heavy Plans		
		Funding Schedules		
Years of Service	Jocko Corp. (A)	Echo Corp. (B)	Grecko Corp. (C)	Minimum Funding Requirement for Non-Key Employees if the Plan is Top-Heavy (D)
1	1.0%	1.5%	3.0%	2.0%
2	2.0%	3.0%	6.0%	4.0%
3	3.0%	4.5%	9.0%	6.0%
4	4.0%	6.0%	12.0%	8.0%
...				
10	10.0%	15.0%	30.0%	20.0%
11	11.0%	16.5%	33.0%	20.0%
12	12.0%	18.0%	36.0%	20.0%
13	13.0%	19.5%	39.0%	20.0%
14	14.0%	21.0%	42.0%	20.0%
15	15.0%	22.5%	45.0%	20.0%

* Beyond 20%, the top-heavy rules no longer apply.

If the plans are top-heavy, Jocko Corp. and Echo Corp. must provide a benefit of 2.0% per year of service up to 20% (D) for non-key employees, rather than the 1.0% (A) and 1.5% (B) per year of service, as defined in their plan documents. Notice that in Year 14, the funding schedule for non-key employees of Echo Corp. reverts back to the original schedule (B). Key employees with Jocko Corp. and Echo Corp. will not be impacted and will simply receive the benefits provided for in their plans (A) and (B). Grecko Corp. benefits are more generous than those provided by the top-heavy rules; therefore, the top-heavy rules would not apply and both key and non-key employees would receive benefits as provided under their plan.

Example 3.40

Entertainment Hourly, Inc. sponsors a defined benefit plan for its employees. The plan benefit formula is 1.5 percent multiplied by the employee's years of service multiplied by the average of the employee's three highest consecutive years of compensation. The plan is determined to be top-heavy for the year. Charlotte, a participant of the plan, has been employed by Entertainment Hourly, Inc. for eight years. Under the current benefit formula, Charlotte should have an accrued benefit in the defined benefit plan of 16 percent (2% x 8 years) times her three highest consecutive years of compensation. The defined benefit plan funding formula is based on two percent times years of service in this case because the defined benefit plan is considered top-heavy and the benefit provided under the plan is less than that provided by the top-heavy rules.

Example 3.41

A defined benefit plan's benefit formula is 25 percent of an employee's average three highest consecutive years compensation at retirement. The plan has been determined to be top-heavy for the year. An employee with 30 years of service and an average three highest consecutive years of compensation of $40,000 has an accrued benefit equal to $10,000 (25% x $40,000). In this case, the top-heavy formula is not applicable because it would have only provided the employee with a 20 percent benefit (the minimum funding formula always tops out at a 20 percent benefit). When the plan benefit formula provides a greater benefit than the top-heavy benefit formula, the plan benefit formula is used.

Exhibit 3.12 | Top-Heavy Plan Summary

	Defined Benefit Plan	**Defined Contribution Plan**
Definition	More than 60% of the total accrued benefits of the defined benefit plan are for the benefit of key employees.	More than 60% of the total account balances of the defined contribution plan are for the benefit of key employees.
Funding	Must be at least 2% x years of service x compensation factor (up to 20%)	3% minimum to all eligible non-key employees or less if less provided to the key employees
Vesting	The plan participant's benefits must vest at least as rapidly as a 2-to-6-year graduated vesting schedule or a 3-year cliff vesting schedule. For years after 2006, this only impacts defined benefit plans.	

CASE STUDY 3.1

In the case of Snyder v. Elliot W. Dann Co., Inc., top-heavy minimum benefits were at issue. In the case, Snyder, a vested participant in an employee pension plan, filed a lawsuit against the Plan, its administrators, and its fiduciaries seeking, among other things, minimum top-heavy benefits.

The court first addressed whether the Plan was top-heavy. Section 416(c) of the Internal Revenue Code of 1986 and Section 7.3 of the Plan provided that a member of the Plan who was not a "key employee" was entitled to a "top-heavy minimum benefit," also referred to as a "minimum annual pension," equal to the product of two percent of compensation multiplied by his or her "years of service." The Plan was deemed to be "top-heavy" because the present value of the cumulative accrued benefits under the plan for key employees exceeded 60 percent of the present value of the cumulative accrued benefits under the plan for all employees. Snyder was not a "key employee" as defined by IRC §416(i)(1) and §2.18 of the Plan.

The court next addressed whether Snyder was entitled to top-heavy minimum benefits for his last incomplete year of service. Dann Co. conceded that Snyder was entitled to top-heavy minimum benefits under the Plan for prior years, but contested his claim for his final year of employment on the basis that Snyder did not complete a "year of service." Snyder had been actively employed by defendant Dann Co. during all of 1984 and 1985. Snyder resigned from his employment on September 15, 1986, but he continued to render service to Dann Co. on a regular basis through December 15, 1986.

Snyder submitted evidence indicating that he conducted extensive efforts, including series of telephone conferences, correspondence, and meetings that culminated in a property sale on December 10, 1986, which generated a fee of $475,000 to Dann Co., one-half of which was paid to Snyder on December 15, 1986. The court reasoned that because Snyder was compensated on a commission basis, he may be considered employed for Plan purposes through the final date of his remuneration. Because Snyder put forth sufficient evidence to establish his claim that he worked past September 1986 and into December 1986, the court granted top-heavy minimum benefits for all three years at issue, including 1986.

Actual Deferral Percentage/Actual Contribution Percentage

Any qualified plan that includes a cash or deferred arrangement (CODA), such as a 401(k) plan, must also satisfy each of the two following tests:
- the Actual Contribution Percentage (ACP) Test for employer matching contributions (and employee after-tax contributions), and
- the Actual Deferral Percentage (ADP) Test for employee elective deferrals.

Both of these tests compare the benefits derived from the CODA plan by the nonhighly compensated employees to the benefits attributable to the highly compensated employees to ensure that the plan is not benefiting the highly compensated employees by an impermissible disproportionate amount.

As these tests are specific to CODA-type plans, the requirements of the ADP and ACP tests are explained and discussed in detail in Chapter 5.

Plan Limitations on Benefits and Contributions

To retain its qualified status and to benefit from the qualified plan advantages discussed earlier, an employer-sponsored qualified plan is limited in the benefits and/or contributions that it is permitted to provide to its employees. The various types of plans (defined benefit or defined contribution) have different methods by which the plan's benefits are provided to its participants. A defined benefit plan promises a definable payment at retirement whereas a defined contribution plan provides a contribution to a plan for each year of employment or at least on a regular basis. For this reason, the contribution limits differ for each type of plan. Defined benefit plans limit the distributions provided at retirement, and defined contribution plans limit the annual contributions to each employee's account for the year.

<aside>

⚙ Key Concepts

1. What is the covered compensation limit for qualified plans?

2. What are the plan limits for defined benefit plans?

3. What are the plan limits for defined contribution plans?

4. What are the plan limits for combined qualified plans?

</aside>

Covered Compensation[44]

The benefits payable under a qualified plan are based on the employee's compensation from the employer. However, the maximum amount of compensation that can be considered for the plan year is $290,000 for 2021, and is referred to as the **covered compensation limit**. Before applying any of the rules or limitations discussed below, the covered compensation limit must be taken into account. For example, an employee whose compensation is $350,000 for the year may only consider compensation up to the limit of $290,000 for 2021. As such, any plan funding formula that requires the use of the employee's compensation cannot consider any compensation above the covered compensation limit.[45]

Exhibit 3.13 | Covered Compensation Limit

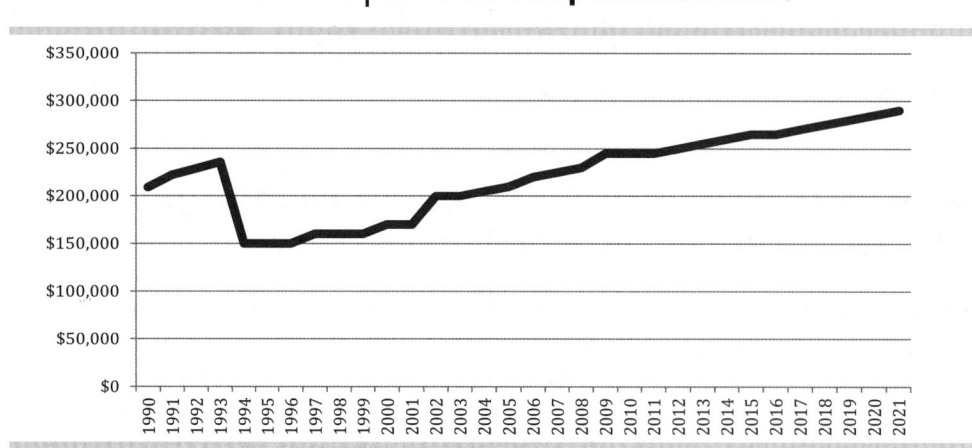

44.In 1993, Congress enacted the Omnibus Budget Reconciliation Act of 1993, which reduced the annual compensation limit from $235,840 in 1993 to $150,000 in 1994. This change was an attempt by Congress to limit contributions to higher income employees and/or increase contributions to rank-and-file employees. It has taken almost twenty years to return to the compensation limits from 1993.

45.IRC § 401(a)(17).

Defined Benefit Plans

As will be fully discussed in Chapter 4, a defined benefit plan is designed to provide a benefit to an employee at normal retirement age, approximately age 65, and will not provide the employee with any benefit during the term of employment or prior to his separation from service with the employer. As such, the employer determines when designing the plan the amount of benefit desired to provide to employees for this future date. The statutory requirements generally limit the employer to providing an employee with the following maximum annual expected benefit at retirement:

The lesser of:
- $230,000 for 2021, or
- 100 percent of the average of the employee's three highest consecutive years compensation during the time of plan participation (considering the covered compensation limit).

Exhibit 3.14 | Defined Benefit Limit

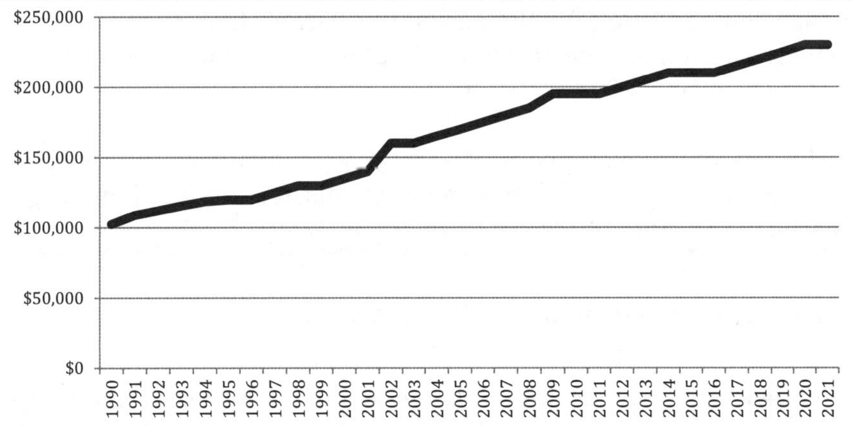

Accordingly, the greatest annual amount an employee can expect to receive as a benefit from a defined benefit plan at normal retirement will not exceed the lesser of $230,000 (adjusted periodically for inflation) or the average of the employee's three highest consecutive years compensation. A defined benefit plan may always provide a lesser benefit based on its formula but can never provide a greater benefit than $230,000 per year for 2021 (at normal age retirement).

Example 3.42

Trinity Audio has employed Ronald for 12 years. Trinity Audio operates a defined benefit plan that provides a benefit to its employees equal to one percent per year of service of the average of employee's three highest consecutive years compensation. Ronald's highest consecutive years of compensation are $275,000 (2019), $325,000 (2020), and $350,000 (2021). An employee's maximum annual compensation for any year is limited to the lesser of the employee's compensation for that year or the maximum covered compensation limit for that year.[46] In this case, Ronald's annual compensation exceeds the covered compensation limit each of the three years. Therefore, his maximum compensation for these purposes is equal to the covered compensation limit for 2019, 2020, and 2021, which is $280,000, $285,000, and $290,000, respectively. The average of these amounts equals $285,000. Therefore, the maximum benefit Trinity Audio can

---

46. Treas. Reg. §1.401(a)(17)-1

provide Ronald with at retirement, considering the plan formula and the compensation limits, is $34,200 (1% x 12 years x $285,000) annually.

To ensure that qualified retirement plans do not benefit only certain employees with very few years of plan participation, an individual who participates in a defined benefit plan for less than 10 years must reduce the calculated maximum benefit by 10 percent for every year of participation less than 10.[47]

Example 3.43

Charlie begins employment with Employer Avant on January 1, 2014, at the age of 58. Avant maintains a noncontributory defined benefit plan, which provides for a straight life annuity beginning at age 65 and uses the calendar year for the plan year. Charlie becomes a participant in Avant's plan on January 1, 2014, and works through December 31, 2020, when he is age 65. Charlie begins to receive benefits under the plan in 2021. Charlie's average compensation for the period of Charlie's high three years of service is $40,000. Furthermore, under the terms of Employer A's plan, Charlie has only seven years of service with Avant (2014 through 2020).

Because Charlie has only seven years of service with Avant at the time he begins to receive benefits under the plan, the maximum permissible annual benefit payable with respect to Charlie is $28,000 ($40,000 multiplied by 7/10).[48]

Distribution Before or After Normal Age Retirement

Defined Benefits Plan

Distributions from defined benefit plans should begin at the normal retirement age of the employee. However, employers may provide in the plan document that the benefit be payable to the employee before the normal retirement age, perhaps as a method to encourage early retirement. In these situations where the benefit payments begin prior to normal retirement age, the calculated maximum benefit is actuarially reduced to an equivalent maximum benefit for the payment year. Other circumstances may create the need for an employer to establish an incentive to continue employment past the normal retirement age and allow the employee to accrue additional benefits in the defined benefit plan. Accordingly, where an individual's benefit payments begin after the normal retirement age, the maximum payment can be actuarially increased to an equivalent maximum benefit for the payment year. The depth and detail of these actuarial calculations are reserved for an advanced course in retirement planning.

Example 3.44

Jose, age 68, has been employed by Whole Drinks Store for 39 years. He began employment as a grocery clerk and is now the President of the company. Jose has calculated that under the company's defined benefit plan, he will receive $230,000 per year after his retirement. However, because Jose has continued to work past his normal retirement age, his benefit will increase to an amount actuarially equivalent to what it would have been if he had taken it at his normal retirement age.

---

47. IRC §415(b)(5).
48. Treas. Reg. §1.415(b)-1.

Defined Contribution Plans

Similar to the defined benefit plan, the defined contribution plan also has a maximum benefit it may provide to its participants. However, the maximum benefit of a defined contribution plan is the maximum amount that may be contributed to an employee's defined contribution account for the year, not the amount payable to the employee at retirement, as in the case for defined benefit plans. This "annual additions limit" is a statutory ceiling that consists of employee deferrals, employer matching contributions, employer discretionary contributions, employee after-tax contributions, and forfeitures.[49]

In general, the maximum contribution per participant to a defined contribution plan is the lesser of:

- 100 percent of an employee's compensation for the plan year, or
- $58,000 for 2021.[50] Catch-up contributions increase this limit to $64,500 for 2021.

> **Quick Quiz 3.9**
>
> 1. The covered compensation limit for 2021 is $290,000.
>   - a. True
>   - b. False
>
> 2. The defined benefit plan limit is $230,000 for 2021.
>   - a. True
>   - b. False
>
> 3. The defined contribution plan limit is the lesser of 25% of compensation or $58,000 for 2021.
>   - a. True
>   - b. False
>
> True, True, False.

Only those employees whose compensation is less than $58,000 (2021) are affected by the percentage limitation of 100 percent of compensation. For example, an employee whose compensation for the plan year is $30,000 could potentially receive a $30,000 contribution to a defined contribution plan. However, an employee whose compensation for the plan year is $150,000 could only receive a maximum $58,000 contribution to a defined contribution plan in 2021.

Exhibit 3.15 | Defined Contributions Annual Additions Limit

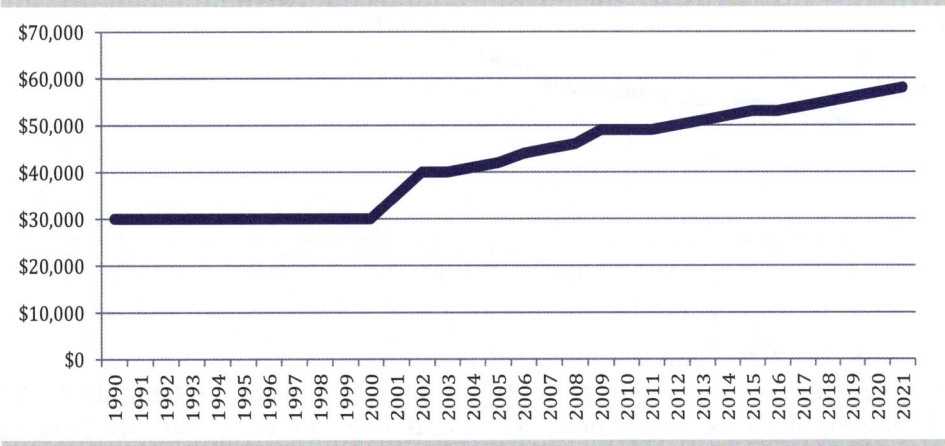

The maximum contribution is an aggregate amount consisting of:
1. The employer contributions to the plan, plus
2. The employee contributions to the plan, plus
3. Any forfeitures allocated from non-vested employees who terminated employment during the year.

49. IRC §415(c).
50. Does not include the catch-up contribution for those age 50 and older, which is $6,500 in 2021. Therefore, the limit for these individuals is $64,500 for 2021.

The maximum contribution discussed here should not be confused with the employer's maximum tax-deductible amount of 25 percent of the employer's total covered compensation paid (discussed below). The limit under IRC §415(c) is an individual limit, while the 25 percent limit is a plan limit. Both limits must be complied with while operating the qualified plan.

Employer Contributions to the Plan

The total employer contributions to a defined contribution plan include any mandatory contributions, discretionary contributions, and matching contributions. If the employer maintains multiple defined contribution plans, the limit is based on the aggregate of all contributions to all of the qualified retirement plans.

Employee Contributions to the Plan

The total employee contributions to a defined contribution plan include any mandatory contributions, elective deferral contributions, and any after-tax contributions. The maximum employee elective deferral, as discussed in Chapter 5, is included within the defined contribution account maximum annual contribution. The limit for employee salary deferrals is $19,500 for 2021. This limit is an individual annual limit and includes 401(k) plans, 403(b) plans, SARSEPs and SIMPLEs.[51] Therefore, if an individual has access to more than one of these plans during a year, the maximum that could be contributed to all the combined plans is $19,500 for 2021, even if the plans are offered by different employers.[52] Catch-up contributions made by the participant are not limited by the $58,000 for 2021 limit and allow an individual age 50 or over to contribute up to $64,500 for 2021.[53]

Exhibit 3.16 | 401(k) Deferral Limit

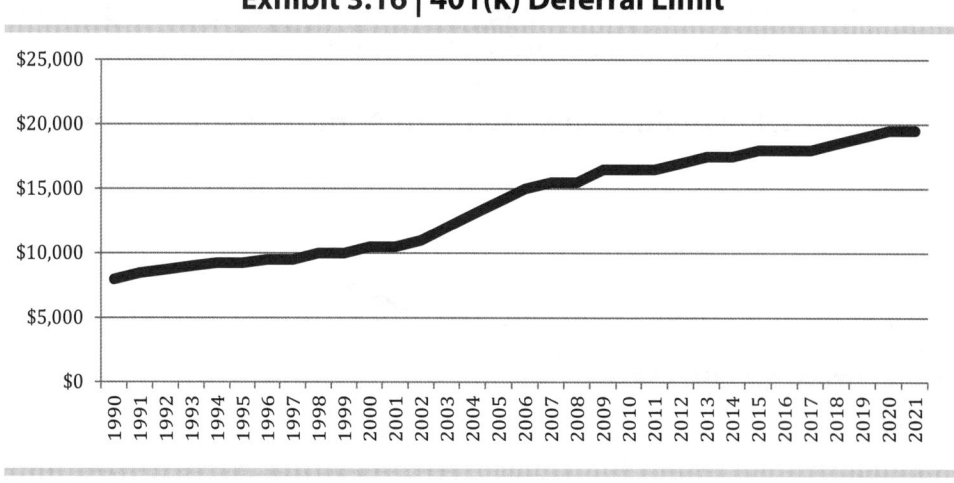

Forfeitures from Non-Vested Employees

If an employee terminates employment prior to being fully vested, the employee's benefits or a percentage of the employee's benefits will be forfeited and may then either be used to reduce future plan costs or increase the other plan participants' account balances. Any **forfeiture** allocated to an employee's defined contribution plan account during the year is included as a contribution to the plan when determining the maximum annual additions limit.

---

51. SIMPLEs have a lower limit than the 401(k) plans, 403(b), plans and SARSEPs, but deferrals to a SIMPLE will count against the annual deferral limit.

52. Note that 457(b) plans have the same deferral limit as the plans mentioned. However, the deferrals to the 457(b) plans are not counted against the salary deferral limit. Therefore, someone with a 401(k) plan and a 457(b) plan could defer twice the annual limit. See Chapter 10 for more on 457 plans.

53. Catch up contributions (IRC §402(g)(1)(C)) are discussed in Chapter 5 relating to contributions to a 401(k) plan.

Example 3.45

Pretzels, Inc. sponsors a defined contribution plan for its employees. Ashley, age 46, a long-term employee with compensation of $150,000 for 2021, has received a $40,000 profit sharing plan contribution and $2,000 of forfeiture allocations. Ashley could still defer $16,000 ($58,000 - $40,000 - $2,000) in the 401(k) plan to maximize her annual contribution limit of $58,000 for the plan year.

Exhibit 3.17 | Maximum Plan Limitations

	Defined Benefit	Defined Contribution
Covered Compensation	$290,000 for 2021	$290,000 for 2021
Maximum Benefit	Lesser of: • $230,000 for 2021 or • Average of 3 highest consecutive years of compensation	Lesser of: • 100% of compensation or • $58,000 for 2021

Exhibit 3.18 | Coordination of Maximum Defined Contribution Limit (2021)

	Employer Contributions
+	Employee Contributions
+	Plan Forfeitures
=	Lesser of $58,000 or 100% of compensation

Employer Contribution Limit

In addition to the limits per employee as detailed above, another limit applies to the maximum tax deductible amount allowed by an employer. Generally, an employer cannot deduct contributions to defined contribution plans in excess of 25 percent of the employer's total covered compensation. Covered compensation includes compensation up to $290,000 (2021) for all those employees included in the plan. The 25 percent rule does not apply to defined benefit pension plans because the employer is required to fund the defined benefit plan to the minimum funding standard determined by the actuary.

Multiple Plan Limitations

When an employer maintains both a defined benefit plan and a defined contribution plan, the general rule is that the total amount deductible in a taxable year under such plans shall not exceed the greater of:[54]

- 25 percent of the compensation otherwise paid or accrued during the taxable year to the beneficiaries under such plans, or
- the amount of contributions made to or under the defined benefit plans to the extent such contributions do not exceed the amount of employer contributions necessary to satisfy the minimum funding standards.

Effectively, the defined benefit plan must be funded, even if the contributions exceed 25 percent of covered compensation. If the funding does not exceed 25 percent of covered compensation, then additional contributions can be made to the defined contribution plan. However, PPA 2006 made the rules less stringent with several exceptions introduced. This combined limit does not apply in the following cases:[55]

---

54. IRC §404(a)(7).

1. If there are no employees who benefit under both the defined benefit and defined contribution plans, then the combined limit does not apply.
2. If the plan is subject to PBGC insurance, the combined limit does not apply. The defined benefit plan would be subject to the minimum funding standards and the defined contribution plan would be limited to 25 percent.
3. If one or more of the plans is a multiemployer plan, then that plan is not considered for purposes of these rules.
4. Salary deferrals are not considered for purposes of determining the combined limits.[56]
5. If contributions do not exceed six percent of the compensation otherwise paid or accrued during the taxable year to the beneficiaries under the plans, then these limitations do not apply.

Regarding exception number five above, if the defined benefit plan is not covered by PBGC and if contributions do exceed six percent, then only the excess beyond the six percent limit will be subject to the limitation.[57] In essence, when employer contributions to a defined contribution plan exceed six percent of compensation, then the combined limit would apply. Another way to view these limits is that if the contribution to the defined benefit plan exceeds 19 percent of covered compensation, then the defined contribution plan is limited to six percent.

Example 3.46

Mary's Carpentry Supplies (MCS) operates a defined benefit plan not covered by PBGC insurance and a defined contribution plan. The annual covered compensation for MCS is $1,000,000. The actuary has determined that a contribution of $120,000 must be made to the defined benefit plan. In this case, MCS can make a tax deductible profit sharing plan contribution on behalf of its employees up to $130,000 (($1,000,000 x 25%)-$120,000) for the current year. Notice that the contributions to the defined contribution plan are in excess of 6%.

Example 3.47

Consider the same facts as above except that the actuary determined that a contribution of $400,000 had to be made to the defined benefit plan. In this case, MCS can make a tax deductible contribution to the profit sharing plan of up to 6% or $60,000 for a total deduction of $460,000 or 46%.

Example 3.48

Cheryl owns Notlad, which sponsors both a defined benefit plan (not covered by the PBGC) and a profit-sharing plan. The covered compensation for Notlad is $500,000. If the required funding for the defined benefit plan is $50,000, then how much can be contributed to the profit-sharing plan? The answer is $75,000, or the difference between 25% of $500,000 and the $50,000 for the defined benefit plan.

---

55. IRC §404(a)(7)(C).
56. IRC §404(n).
57. IRC §404(a)(7)(C)(iii)(II).

Example 3.49

Saben LLC sponsors both a defined benefit plan and a profit sharing plan with a cash or deferred arrangement. The defined benefit plan is covered by the PBGC. The covered compensation for Saben LLC is $900,000. Salary deferrals total $50,000. If the required funding for the defined benefit plan is $200,000, then how much can be contributed to the profit-sharing plan? The answer is $225,000 (25% of $900,000) since the plan is covered by the PBGC and the multiple plan limits do not apply. If the plan was not insured with the PBGC, then $54,000 (6% of $900,000) could be contributed to the profit sharing plan.

On March 13, 2007, the Internal Revenue Service issued Notice 2007-28, which provides guidance with regard to the 2006 changes. Notice 2007-28 states that the 2006 changes exclude multiemployer plans from consideration and provide that the combined limit only applies in the case of employer contributions to one or more defined contribution plans to the extent that such contributions exceed six percent of the compensation otherwise paid to or accrued during the taxable year to the beneficiaries under the plan. The Notice further states that matching contributions and nonelective employer contributions are taken into account for the purpose of applying the limits of §404(a)(7), but elective deferrals are not.

CONTROLLED GROUP

A controlled group consists of two or more commonly owned corporations. These commonly owned entities generally take one of two forms. A controlled group will be classified as a parent-subsidiary group or as a brother-sister group. However, a group of related entities may be classified as a combined controlled group of corporations.

There are a variety of tax benefits that are available to corporations and other taxable entities, such as lower tax brackets, expensing of depreciable business assets (IRC §179), and tax deductions for contributions to qualified plans. Except for the controlled group rules under IRC §1561, savvy business owners could double or even triple these and other tax benefits by splitting current companies into two or three companies and still maintaining complete ownership. The controlled group rules cause multiple entities that are commonly owned to be treated as one entity for purposes of certain tax limits and tax benefits. The controlled group rules are intended to prevent business owners from simply splitting a company into separate companies with identical ownership so as to double or even triple certain benefits that are provided under the Internal Revenue Code.

Fully understanding the controlled group rules may allow a family to structure entity ownership in such a way as to avoid falling within the controlled group rules, thus being able to benefit by having multiple entities.

The Internal Revenue Code (specifically IRC §414(b)) also provides that companies belonging to a controlled group be treated as a single employer for purposes of qualified plans, specifically for purposes of:

- IRC §401 – qualification
- IRC §404 – deductions
- IRC §410 – participation
- IRC §415 – contribution and benefit limitations
- IRC §416 – top-heavy rules

It should also be noted that while the controlled group rules under IRC 1563 relate specifically to corporations, IRC §414(c) provides for similar treatment for purposes of qualified plans, SEPs, and SIMPLEs as it relates to non-incorporated businesses (such as partnerships and LLCs).

Therefore, companies belonging to a controlled group must comply with the qualification rules, participation rules, and the other rules relating to qualified plans as if the companies were a single employer. In the event that such businesses fail to meet these requirements, the qualified plan(s) will be subject to disqualification. More information on the controlled group rules can be found in the Appendix to this chapter.

If two or more corporations, trades or businesses are part of a controlled group of businesses, the controlled group members are treated as a single employer when applying certain employee plan benefits requirements. These requirements are:

1. Nondiscrimination, IRC §401(a)(4),
2. Compensation dollar limit under IRC §401(a)(17),
3. Minimum participation test under IRC §401(a)(26),
4. Eligibility, IRC §401(a)(3) and §410(a),
5. Coverage, IRC §410(b),
6. Vesting, IRC §401(a)(7) and IRC §411,
7. Section 415 limits,
8. Top heavy rules IRC §416, and
9. SEP's under 408(k) and SIMPLE-IRA plans under IRC §408(p).

IRC Sections 414(b) & (c) were added to the Code because, in the words of the Senate Committee Report on ERISA: "The Committee, by this provision, intends to make it clear that the coverage and nondiscrimination provisions cannot be avoided by operating through separate corporations instead of separate branches of one corporation." A plan that is maintained by an employer, within a group of employers that are under common control, must meet the requirements of IRC Section 401(a) as if a single employer employed all employees of the group.

Employee Plans Compliance Resolution System (EPCRS)

If a qualified plan does not meet any one of the necessary requirements discussed throughout this chapter, the plan could lose its qualified status and its tax-favored status. In this case, the employer will lose its tax deductions for contributions to the plan, and the employees (usually only highly-compensated and key employees) would be taxed on the value of the plan's assets, including any earnings in their accounts.

To avoid the total loss of its tax advantages, a plan sponsor may voluntarily correct any problems with its qualified plan following the **Employee Plans Compliance Resolution System** (EPCRS) before two years from the end of the plan year in which the problem occurred. By voluntarily correcting the problem, the IRS will be more lenient and, provided the plan sponsor retroactively benefits all employees as if the problem had not occurred, will more likely than not allow the continuance of the plan's qualified status.[58]

---

58. More information on the EPCRS can be found on the IRS website, IRS.gov.

CHAPTER
3
APPENDIX

LEASED EMPLOYEES

Qualified and other tax-advantaged retirement plans, such as SEPs and SIMPLEs, have specific guidelines as to which persons must benefit under the plan. Generally, only an employee of the sponsor organization will benefit under the plan. Independent contractors and temporary or leased employees are usually not covered by a company's retirement plan. However, there are specific rules that determine when a leased employee must be treated as an employee for purposes of the plan. If these rules were not in place, a company could simply hire temporary employees (leased employees) to fill the majority of positions within the company and avoid having to provide them with retirement benefits. This would create the illusion of a nondiscriminatory plan even though such a plan would be discriminatory. To avoid this possibility, the IRC provides guidance on who is to be considered leased employees and the employer's (sponsor) requirements as it relates to these employees.

Any person who provides services to the employer and is not an employee will be considered a leased employee if the following criteria are met:

- The services provided are pursuant to an agreement between the employer and a leasing organization;
- Such person has performed services for the employer on a substantially full-time basis for a period of at least one year; and
- Such services are performed under the primary control of employer.[59]

The significance of these rules is that leased employees must be considered a common law employee for purposes of meeting coverage rules, top-heavy rules, contribution and benefit rules, as well as a variety of other rules.[60]

---

59. IRC §414(n)(2).
60. IRC §414(n)(3) states that a leased employee is considered an employee for purposes of the following code sections: §§401(a)(3), (4), (7), (16), (17), and (26); §408(k); §408(p); §410; §411; §415; §416; §79; §106; §117(d); §120; §125; §127; §129; §132; §137; §274(j); §505; and §4980(B).

Example 3.50

ABC company, sponsor of a qualified plan, hires a receptionist, Diana, through a temporary service and employs Diana for a period in excess of one year. In such a case, Diana is treated the same as any employee of the organization for certain requirements related to qualification of the retirement plan. For example, Diana must be considered for purposes of meeting the coverage rules if she was otherwise eligible (e.g., 21/1). Although the general rule is that only 70 percent of the non-highly compensated employees must be covered, the addition of Diana may cause the plan to violate the coverage rules.

The IRC provides that if certain requirements are met (safe harbor rules) by the leasing organization, someone meeting the definition of a leased employee will not have to be treated as an employee. The leased employee(s) must be covered by a plan that is maintained by the leasing organization and the leased employee(s) must not represent more than 20 percent of the employer's nonhighly compensated work force. However, the plan that is sponsored by the leasing organization must also meet certain requirements, including:

- The plan must be a money purchase pension plan with a nonintegrated employer contribution rate for each participant of at least 10 percent of compensation;
- Such plan provides for full and immediate vesting; and
- Each employee of the leasing organization (other than employees who perform substantially all of their services for the leasing organization) immediately participates in such plan.[61]

Although the above rules provide a safe harbor for an employer who uses leased employees, the requirements are so stringent that they are unlikely to be met.

CONTROLLED GROUP (ADDITIONAL INFORMATION)

There are a variety of tax benefits that are available to corporations and other taxable entities, such as lower tax brackets, expensing of depreciable business assets (IRC §179), and tax deductions for contributions to qualified plans. Except for the controlled group rules under IRC §1561, savvy business owners could double or even triple these and other tax benefits by splitting current companies into two or three companies and still maintaining complete ownership. The controlled group rules cause multiple entities that are commonly owned to be treated as one entity for purposes of certain tax limits and tax benefits. The controlled group rules are intended to prevent business owners from simply splitting a company into separate companies with identical ownership so as to double or even triple certain benefits that are provided under the Internal Revenue Code.

However, fully understanding the controlled group rules may allow a family to structure entity ownership in such a way as to avoid falling within the controlled group rules, thus being able to benefit by having multiple entities.

The Internal Revenue Code (specifically IRC §414(b)) also provides that companies belonging to a controlled group be treated as a single employer for purposes of qualified plans, specifically for purposes of:

- IRC §401 – qualification
- IRC §404 – deductions

---

61. IRC §414(n)(5).

- IRC §410 – participation
- IRC §415 – contribution and benefit limitations
- IRC §416 – top-heavy rules

Therefore, companies belonging to a controlled group must comply with the qualification rules, participation rules, and the other rules relating to qualified plans as if the companies were a single employer. In the event that such businesses fail to meet these requirements, the qualified plan(s) will be subject to disqualification. In addition to the rules for qualified plans, the rules under IRC §408(k) relating to Simplified Employee Pensions (SEPs) are also subject to the same limitations.

Definition of a Controlled Group

A controlled group consists of two or more commonly owned corporations. These commonly owned entities generally take one of two forms. A controlled group will be classified as a parent-subsidiary group or as a brother-sister group. However, a group of related entities may be classified as a combined controlled group of corporations.

Parent-Subsidiary Controlled Group[62]

A parent-subsidiary controlled group of businesses consists of a group of entities with common controlling ownership and a common parent. A controlling interest generally implies an 80 percent ownership interest. However, for purposes of IRC §415 (limitation on contributions and benefits), the 80 percent limit is reduced to 50 percent. **Example 3.51** through **Example 3.53** help illustrate this point.

Example 3.51

P corporation owns stock representing 80 percent of the total combined voting power of all classes of stock entitled to vote of S corporation. P is the common parent of a parent-subsidiary controlled group consisting of member corporations P and S.

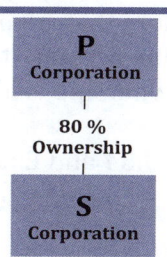

Example 3.52

Assume the same facts as above. Assume further that S owns stock representing 80 percent of the total value of shares of all classes of stock of T Corporation. P is the common parent of a parent-subsidiary controlled group consisting of member corporations P, S, and T. The result would be the same if P, rather than S, owned the T stock.

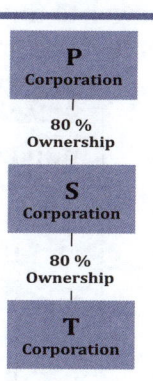

---

62. Treas. Reg. §1.1563-1(a)(2).

Example 3.53

L Corporation owns 80 percent of the only class of stock of M Corporation, and M, in turn, owns 40 percent of the only class of stock of O Corporation. L also owns 80 percent of the only class of stock of N Corporation, and N, in turn, owns 40 percent of the only class of stock of O. L is the common parent of a parent-subsidiary controlled group consisting of member corporations L, M, N, and O.

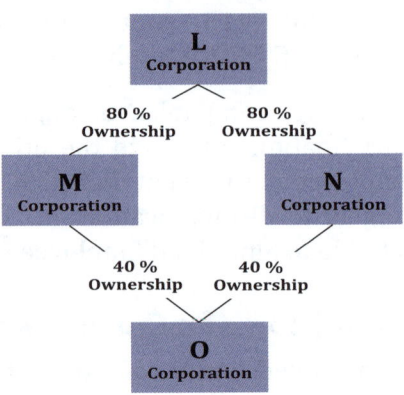

Brother-Sister Controlled Group

A brother-sister controlled group consists of two or more companies that share common owners. There are two tests that must be met for a group of entities to be considered a controlled group: the 50 percent test and the 80 percent test. Two or more entities are a brother-sister controlled group if the same five or fewer persons who are individuals, estates, or trusts own stock possessing:

- At least 80 percent of the total combined voting power of all classes of stock entitled to vote or at least 80 percent of the total value of shares of all classes of the stock of each corporation; and
- More than 50 percent of the total combined voting power of all classes of stock entitled to vote or more than 50 percent of the total value of shares of all classes of stock of each corporation, taking into account the stock ownership of each such person only to the extent that such stock ownership is identical with respect to each such corporation.

Example 3.54 and **Example 3.55** illustrate the concept of a brother-sister controlled group.

Example 3.54

Assume that individuals A, B, C, D, and E own corporations P, Q, R, S, and T as follows. Are these corporations or some of these corporations considered a controlled group? The answer to this question depends on whether or not both the 80 percent test and the 50 percent test are met.

Individuals	Corporations					Identical Ownership
	P	Q	R	S	T	
A	55%	51%	55%	55%	55%	**51%**
B	45%	49%	-	-	-	**45%***
C	-	-	45%	-	-	
D	-	-	-	45%	-	
E	-	-	-	-	45%	
Total	100%	100%	100%	100%	100%	

(P & Q only)

The 50 percent test is met for all five corporations (P through T). However, corporations R, S, and T are not members of a controlled group because at least 80 percent of the stock of each of the corporations is not owned by the same five or fewer individuals whose ownership is considered for purposes of the 50 percent test. Only corporations P and Q are classified as a controlled group in the above example.

Example 3.55

Individuals	Scenario 1		Scenario 2		Scenario 3	
	P	Q	P	Q	P	Q
A	100%	-	80%	20%	70%	30%
B	-	100%	20%	80%	30%	70%
C	-	-	-	-	-	-
D	-	-	-	-	-	-
E	-	-	-	-	-	-
Total	100%	100%	100%	100%	100%	100%

Clearly, Companies P and Q in Scenario 1 are not a controlled group. A owns 100 percent of the stock of Company P, while B owns 100 percent of the stock of Company Q. In Scenario 2, the 80 percent test is met; however, the 50 percent test is not met. A has 20 percent common ownership of Companies P and Q and B has 20 percent common ownership of Companies P and Q. Thus, the identical ownership is 40 percent, not the required greater than 50 percent. In Scenario 3, both tests are met, which means that Companies P and Q are members of a brother-sister controlled group.

AFFILIATED SERVICE GROUPS

Affiliated service groups are groups of entities that perform services together on a regular basis. The importance of affiliated service groups to retirement planning is that the entities that constitute an affiliated service group are treated as one organization or entity for purposes of the qualified plan rules. Prior to these rules, elaborate structures of entities could be established to provide higher qualified plan benefits to certain groups of owners at the expense of the rank-and-file employees. The affiliated service group rules were enacted to prevent such abuses.

A classic example of an affiliated service group is a two person law firm that is structured as a partnership with two corporations as the partners. Each corporation is solely owned by an individual attorney, who is also the only employee of such corporation. The three organizations, the partnership and the two corporations, constitute the affiliated service group.

An "affiliated service group" is a particular type of group of related employers. The affiliated service group designation refers to two or more organizations that have a service relationship and, in some cases, an ownership relationship.[63] There are three types or categories of affiliated service groups, including A-Organization groups, B-Organization groups, and management groups.

---

63. IRC §414(m).

Example 3.56

A doctor is the 100% shareholder of Corporation X, a medical corporation that specializes in sports injuries. She also owns a 40% interest in Corporation Y, which performs such medical diagnostic services as X-rays and MRIs. The doctor regularly refers patients to Y for such services. Under the attribution rules of §318(a)(3), the doctor's 40% ownership interest in Corporation Y is attributed to Corporation X. The corporations are regularly associated in providing medical services to patients; thus, constitute an affiliated service group. Under the A-Org test, Corporation Y is the FSO and X is the A-Organization. Y has ownership interest in X and the organizations regularly perform services for patients.

Example 3.57

Jones, an attorney, is a 25% shareholder in a law firm. Jones also has a 25% interest in corporation X, which provides word processing and other clerical and secretarial services. The law firm engages the services of corporation X on a regular basis. X derives at least 10% of its gross receipts from this relationship. The law firm and corporation X constitute an affiliated service group.

Example 3.58

Cameron is the former owner of Company P. She sells her interest in the company but continues to provide management consulting services to Company P through a new wholly owned entity, Company Q. Company Q provides management functions to P on a regular basis with all of the income for Company Q derived from Company P. Companies P and Q constitute an affiliated service group.

Example 3.59

Assume the same facts as above except that Company Q also provides management functions to 2 other businesses (total of 3) and that the revenue received from each of the companies is approximately equal. In this case, there is not an affiliated service group. Since no one company is the principal business of Company Q, there is no affiliated service group.

Impact of Affiliated Service Groups

As with the controlled group rules, when a group of companies are classified as an affiliated service group, the group of companies is treated as a single employer for purposes of qualified plans rules. The qualified plan rules that are impacted include eligibility, coverage, vesting, non-discrimination (including ADP and ACP), contribution/benefit limits under IRC §415, top-heavy rules, and other rules.

SEPARATE LINE OF BUSINESS

Eligible employees within the same company are generally required to be treated uniformly with regard to qualified retirement plans. However, companies that maintain separate lines of business may be permitted to treat the employees of one line of business different than employees of another line of business.[64]

Usually, a separate line of business will have a separate organizational unit, separate accounting, separate employee group, and separate management. A firm can provide different benefits, including qualified retirement plan benefits, to employees of a separate line of business than to other parts of a business. This provision may allow a firm to reduce company expenses.

For an employer to treat various parts of a business as separate lines of business, there must be a valid business purpose and certain rules must be met. The employer must have at least 50 employees within a line of business and notify the Secretary (IRS) that such line of business is going to be treated as a separate line of business for purposes of IRC §129(d)(8) and 410(b). Form 5310-A (Notice of Merger or Consolidation, Spinoff, or Transfer of Plan Assets or Liabilities; Notice of Qualified Separate Line of Business) is used to notify the IRS that a company intends to maintain separate lines of business. In addition, such lines of business must meet certain guidelines prescribed by the Secretary or the employer must receive a determination letter permitting the line of business to be treated as a separate line of business.

Certain safe harbor provisions will satisfy the previous requirement of meeting prescribed guidelines established by the Secretary.[65] A line of business will meet the safe harbor requirements if the percentage of highly compensated employees is not less than one-half and not more than twice the percentage that highly compensated employees are of all employees of the employer. There are also a variety of administrative safe harbor rules that will permit a separate line of business.

BREAK IN SERVICE RULES

In some cases an employee may leave their job and return at a later time. This may occur because an individual quits and then is later rehired, or the individual may take a leave of absence due to the birth of a child or for military service. These types of leaves from the employer may create what is referred to as a "break in service." The consequences of a break in service depend on the length of time the employee is away, whether their retirement benefit was fully vested, and, in some cases, the reason that the employee took the leave.

A one year break in service is defined as a "calendar year, plan year, or other 12-consecutive-month period designated by the plan during which the participant has not completed more than 500 hours of service."[66] In the case of a plan utilizing the elapsed time method, the term "1-year break in service" generally means a 12-consecutive month period beginning on the severance from service date or any anniversary thereof and ending on the next succeeding anniversary of such date.

64. IRC §414(r).
65. IRC §414(r)(3).
66. IRC §411(a)(6)(A).

Example 3.60

Fischer and Company maintains a qualified plan. The plan requires 2 years of service to become eligible for the plan. Paul was hired on January 1, 2021 and works 40 hours per week for the rest of the year. Paul takes a leave of absence from February 1, 2023 to December 31, 2023 to care for his aging father. Paul returns to work January 1, 2024. Since Paul only worked 160 hours in 2023, a one year break in service occurred for 2023.

In general, a qualified plan must count all of the employee's years of service for eligibility purposes since the employee's date of hire. However, for an employee who has incurred a 1-year break in service, years of service completed before such break are not required to be taken into account until the employee has completed one year of service after his return to service.[67] In addition, if a plan requires two years of service before an employee can enter the plan, then the plan can, if properly elected in the plan document, disregard years of service before a "one year break" in service.

Example 3.61

In the previous example, Paul had one year of service before he had a one year break in service. Since the plan requires two years of service for eligibility the plan is not required to take into account Paul's service for 2021. Thus, when Paul returns to work in 2024 his years of service for eligibility will start over.

If an employee is already eligible for the qualified plan then a break in service can affect the employee's vesting in the plan. In the case of a nonvested participant who has incurred a 1-year break in service, years of service completed before such break are not required to be taken into account with regard to vesting if the employee has the greater of five consecutive one year breaks in service or the participant's years of service before the break.

Example 3.62

Fischer Company maintains a qualified plan. The plan utilizes a calendar year 3-year cliff vesting schedule. Paul was hired on January 1, 2021. After two years of service Paul separated from service. One year later Paul returns to Fischer Company and reenters the plan. If Paul completes one year of service after reentering the plan then the plan must credit Paul for his previous years of service. Thus, when Paul has completed one year of service after reentering the plan, he will have 3 years accumulated toward meeting the vesting requirement.

Example 3.63

Assume instead Paul returns five years later instead of one year later. Since Paul has five one year breaks in service, the plan is not required to credit Paul for his previous years of service. Therefore, when Paul has completed one year of service after reentering the plan, he will only have 1 year towards the 3 year requirement.

---

67. IRC §1.411(a)-6.

In the case of a participant in a defined contribution plan who has incurred a 1-year break in service, years of service completed after such break are not required to be taken into account for purposes of determining the nonforfeitable percentage of the participant's right to employer-derived benefits that accrued before the break if the employee has five consecutive one year breaks in service or receives a distribution of the account balance.

Example 3.64

Fischer Company maintains a defined contribution plan. The plan utilizes a calendar year 2-to-6-year graduated vesting schedule. Paul was hired on January 1, 2021. After three years of service Paul separated from service with a vested balance of 40% that was not distributed from the plan. One year later Paul returns to Fischer Company and reenters the plan. If Paul completes one year of service after reentering the plan, then the plan must credit Paul's pre-break in service account for years of service after the break. Thus, Paul's account balance will be 60% vested in all funds in the account at his initial separation. In addition, the contributions made for Paul after he reenters the plan will benefit from the prior years of service. Thus, when Paul has completed one year of service after reentering the plan, he will also be 60% vested in that year's contributions.

Example 3.65

Assume instead Paul returns five years later instead of one year later. Since Paul has five one year breaks in service, the plan is not required to credit Paul's pre-break in service account for years of service after the break. Thus, the 60% unvested portion in his pre-break account is forever lost. In addition, contributions made after Paul's return do not benefit from Paul's prior service. Therefore, when Paul has completed two years of service after reentering the plan, he will only be 20% vested in his post break account balance.

For purposes of determining the employee's accrued benefit under a plan, the plan may not disregard service due to distribution unless the plan provides an opportunity for the participant to repay the full amount of the distribution after returning to service. A defined benefit plan can also require the repayment to include interest no greater than 120 percent of the federal midterm rate on the first day of the plan year that the repayment occurs. The plan provision required may provide that such repayment must be made in the case of a withdrawal because of separation from service, before the earlier of five years after the first date on which the participant is subsequently re-employed by the employer, or the close of the first period of five consecutive 1-year breaks in service commencing after the withdrawal; or in the case of any other withdrawal, five years after the date of the withdrawal.

Example 3.66

Fischer Company maintains a defined contribution plan. The plan utilizes a calendar year 2-to-6-year graduated vesting schedule. Paul was hired on January 1 of this year. After three years of service Paul separated from service with a vested balance of 40%, which was distributed from the plan. One year later Paul returns to Fischer Company and reenters the plan. Since Paul took the distribution from the plan, the plan does not have to credit Paul for pre-break service unless he repays the distribution.

Employees wanting to take a leave of absence should carefully examine their plan document so that they do not inadvertently and unnecessarily lose retirement benefits.

Military Service

If an employee leaves employment for qualified military service and is then reemployed after such service, then the employee is treated as not having incurred a break in service. The term "qualified military service" means any service in the uniformed services (as defined in Chapter 43 of Title 38, United States Code) by any individual if such individual is entitled to reemployment rights under such chapter with respect to such service. Each period of qualified military service served by an individual is, upon reemployment, deemed to constitute service with the employer maintaining the plan for the purpose of determining the nonforfeitability of the individual's accrued benefits under such plan and for the purpose of determining the accrual of benefits under such plan.[68]

There is no requirement for the employer to make contributions to the military employee's defined contribution plan while they are on active duty. However, once the military employee returns from military duty and is reemployed, the employer must make the employer contributions that would have been made if the military employee had been employed during the period of military duty. If employee contributions are required or permitted under the plan, the employee has a period equal to the lesser of three times the period of military duty or five years, whichever ends first, to make up the contributions. If the employee makes up the contributions, the employer must make up any matching contributions. There is no requirement that the employer contributions include earnings or forfeitures that would have been allocated to the employee had the contributions been made during their military service.[69]

Maternity/Paternity Leave

For vesting and eligibility purposes, an employee who is absent from work due to pregnancy or the birth or adoption of a child is treated as having completed the number of hours that would have been credited but for the absence up to 501 hours of service. The credit for hours of service during the absence is only for determining if a break in service has occurred.[70]

Example 3.67

Donna works 10 hours a week for Mad Scientist Inc. Mad Scientist Inc. has a qualified plan and Donna participates in the plan. For the current year Donna worked 36 weeks and was on maternity leave for 16 weeks. While Donna only worked 360 hours for the year, for purposes of the break in service rules she is credited with the 160 hours she would have worked had she not been on maternity leave. Therefore, Donna will not have a break in service since she is deemed to have worked 520 hours for the year.

---

68. IRC §414(u)(8).
69. IRC §414(a)(2)(A).
70. IRC §410(a)(5)(E)(i).

DISCUSSION QUESTIONS

SOLUTIONS to the discussion questions can be found exclusively within the chapter. Once you have completed an initial reading of the chapter, go back and highlight the answers to these questions.

1. Describe the historical change from pension plans to profit sharing plans.

2. Describe the overall differences between defined benefit and defined contribution plans.

3. Explain the matching principle of expenses and income and its impact on qualified plans.

4. What are payroll taxes and how do they impact qualified retirement plans?

5. How are contributions to, earnings within, and distributions from qualified plans taxed?

6. Describe the anti-alienation protection afforded to qualified plans.

7. How are assets of a qualified plan protected for employees from the employer?

8. Describe the special taxation option available for lump-sum distributions which include employer stock.

9. Explain the standard eligibility rules for qualified plans.

10. What is the "Two-Year" eligibility rule?

11. Explain how eligibility rules are used to encourage tax-exempt educational institutions to sponsor qualified plans.

12. Which employees may be excluded from a qualified plan?

13. Define "highly compensated."

14. Describe the general safe harbor coverage test.

15. Describe the ratio percentage coverage test.

16. Describe the average benefits test and its component parts.

17. Describe the defined benefit 50/40 coverage test.

18. Explain the available vesting schedules for qualified plans.

19. Define "years of service" for qualified plans.

20. Define a "top-heavy qualified plan."

21. Define "key employee."

22. How are the vesting and funding requirements of a qualified plan affected by it being a top-heavy status plan?

23. What is the current covered compensation limit?

24. What is the maximum annual benefit that may be provided to an employee from a defined benefit plan?

25. What is the maximum allowable contribution to an individual's account under a defined contribution plan for 2021?

26. What are the funding limits when a company sponsors a defined benefit plan and a defined contribution plan?

MULTIPLE CHOICE PROBLEMS

A sample of multiple choice problems is provided below. Additional multiple choice problems are available at money-education.com by accessing the Student Practice Portal.

1. Which of the following is not an example of a qualified retirement plan?
   a. ESOP.
   b. Age-based profit sharing plan.
   c. ESPP.
   d. 401(k) plan.

2. Stevie has a qualified plan with an account balance of $2,000,000. In which of the following circumstances would a third party be able to alienate the assets within Stevie's qualified plan?
   1. A QDRO in favor of a former spouse.
   2. A federal tax levy.
   3. Creditors in a personal bankruptcy.
      a. 3 only.
      b. 1 and 2.
      c. 1 and 3.
      d. 1, 2, and 3.

3. Barry's Graphic Arts Studio sponsors a qualified profit sharing plan. The plan requires employees to complete one year of service and be 21 years old before entering the plan. The plan has two entrance dates per year, January 1st and July 1st. Assuming that today is December 15, 2022 and the Studio has the following employee information, which of the following statements is correct?

Employee	Age	Start Date
Barry	35	1/1/2021
Del	34	8/1/2021
Karen	24	6/1/2022
Jenn	18	5/1/2021

   a. Two people have entered the plan.
   b. The qualified plan must provide participants with 100% vesting upon entering the plan because of the eligibility requirements of the plan.
   c. Del has not yet entered the plan.
   d. Jenn entered the plan on July 1, 2022.

4. Which of the following people would be considered a highly compensated employee for 2021?
    1. Tiana, a 1% owner whose salary last year was $150,000.
    2. Ariel, a 6% owner whose salary was $42,000 last year.
    3. Belle, an officer, who earned $105,000 last year and is the 29th highest paid employee of 96 employees.
    4. Jasmine, who earned $142,000 last year and is in the top 20% of paid employees.
        a. 1 and 4.
        b. 1, 2, and 4.
        c. 1, 3, and 4.
        d. 1, 2, 3, and 4.

5. Cheque Company has 100 eligible employees and sponsors a defined benefit pension plan. The company is unsure if they are meeting all of their testing requirements. How many employees (the minimum) must be covered by Cheque Company's defined benefit pension plan for the plan to conform with ERISA?
        a. 40.
        b. 50.
        c. 70.
        d. 100.

> **Additional multiple choice problems**
> **are available at**
> **money-education.com**
> **by accessing the**
> **Student Practice Portal.**
> **Access requires registration of the title using**
> **the unique code at the front of the book.**

QUICK QUIZ EXPLANATIONS

Quick Quiz 3.1
1. False. Pension plans are now less common than profit sharing plans. Pension plans are less common because workers tend to not stay as long with one employer.
2. False. Pension plans can be either defined contribution or defined benefit plans.

Quick Quiz 3.2
1. False. Contributions by employers to qualified plans do not have to comply with the matching principle. When a contribution is made, the employer has a current deduction, but the employee does not have taxable income related to the contribution until the funds are distributed from the plan.
2. True.
3. True.

Quick Quiz 3.3
1. False. ERISA does not protect qualified plan assets from alienation due to a QDRO, a federal tax levy, or from a judgment or settlement rendered upon an individual for a criminal act involving the same qualified plan.
2. False. An advantage of a qualified plan is that ERISA provides the laws, rules, and enforcement provisions to protect employees from the employer's wrong doings.
3. True.

Quick Quiz 3.4
1. False. Using the standard eligibility rules, an employee must be allowed to enter a qualified plan within six months of becoming eligible.
2. True.
3. True.
4. False. This exception is not available to 401(k) plans.

Quick Quiz 3.5
1. True.
2. False. The selection of a class of excludable employees must be reasonable and established based on the facts and circumstances of the business under objective business criteria.
3. False. In 2021, a highly compensated employee is one who earned at least $130,000 in the previous plan year.
4. False. Bobby will be classified as a highly compensated employee since he is a "5% owner."
5. False. She might not be classified as a highly compensated employee if she is not in the top 20% of paid employees or if it were her first year of employment.
6. True.

Quick Quiz 3.6
1. False. To be a qualified retirement plan, a plan only needs to pass one of the coverage tests. A qualified retirement plan is not required to pass all three coverage tests.
2. False. The average benefits test is comprised of two tests and both tests must be passed.
3. True.

QUICK QUIZ EXPLANATIONS

Quick Quiz 3.7

1. True.
2. True.
3. False. The employee does not attain one year of service until he has worked for a 12-month period with at least 1,000 hours.
4. True.
5. True. [($15,000 / $45,000) x $60,000 x 60%] = $12,000

Quick Quiz 3.8

1. False. In 2021, an officer must have compensation in excess of $185,000 to be considered a key employee.
2. False. Qualified defined benefit plans that are top-heavy must use a 2-to-6-year graduated or 3-year cliff vesting schedule.

Quick Quiz 3.9

1. True.
2. True.
3. False. The defined contribution plan employer contribution limit is 25% of covered compensation. The maximum annual additions limit for an employee under a defined contribution plan is the lesser of 100% of compensation or $58,000 for 2021.

4

QUALIFIED PENSION PLANS

LEARNING OBJECTIVES

1. Explain the characteristics of pension plans.*
2. Differentiate between pension plans and profit sharing plans.*
3. Explain the difference between defined benefit pension plans and defined contribution pension plans.*
4. Evaluate the appropriateness of each of the pension plans discussed in the chapter relative to the needs and goals of a specific company.*
5. Describe the limitations of using life insurance within qualified plans and the tax impact when life insurance is included in these plans.
6. Understand how the Pension Benefit Guarantee Corporation helps to protect the pensions of workers who are participants or beneficiaries of defined benefit plans.

Ties to CFP Certification Learning Objectives

INTRODUCTION

The traditional **pension plan** pays a formula-determined benefit beginning at retirement, usually in the form of an annuity, to a plan participant for the participant's remaining life. In some cases, a lump-sum option may be available. Historically, pension plans were offered by many employers; however, over the last 30 years, many employers have replaced their pension plans with profit sharing plans in an attempt to reduce employers' costs, eliminate mandatory funding requirements, and shift the investment responsibility from the employer to the employees.

The legal promise of a pension plan is to pay a pension. There are defined benefit pension plans, including both defined benefit and cash balance pension plans, characterized by annual funding requirements, actuarial needs, Pension Benefit Guaranty Corporation (PBGC) insured benefits, and investment risk retained by the employer. There are also two defined contribution pension plans characterized by separate individual accounts, investment risks borne by the participants, and no government-insured benefits. All of these issues will be discussed in this chapter.

Pension Plans (4 Types)	
DEFINED BENEFIT PENSION PLANS (2 TYPES)	Defined Benefit Pension Plans
	Cash Balance Pension Plans
DEFINED CONTRIBUTION PENSION PLANS (2 TYPES)	Money Purchase Pension Plans
	Target Benefit Pension Plans

Recall from Chapter 3 that there are numerous dollar limits that qualified plans must comply with including contribution limits, limits on distributions, limits on covered compensation and others. Many of these limits are illustrated below in the "Know The Numbers" table.

KNOW THE NUMBERS (2021)	
Covered Compensation Limit for Qualified Plans	$290,000
Defined Benefit Maximum Limit	$230,000
Defined Contribution Maximum Limit	$58,000
401(k), SARSEP, 457, 403(b)	$19,500
PBGC Monthly Benefit at Age 65	$6,034.09
PBGC Yearly Benefit at Age 65	$72,409

Traditional defined benefit pension plans continue to exist today but are primarily used in mature, well-established companies (often publicly traded) that have not changed to profit sharing plans.[1] In 2020, the PBGC paid monthly retirement benefits to more than 984,000 retirees in more than 5,000 pension plans that no longer exist.[2] Fewer new pension plans are being established today because employers have shifted the retirement planning burden from the employer to the employee. As illustrated in **Exhibit 4.1**, the number of defined benefit plans has decreased dramatically since 1985, while there has been a substantial increase in defined contribution plans.

Despite the expense associated with pension plans, many governmental agencies continue to provide pensions plans (although these are not qualified plans) as the predominant form of retirement benefit, but the benefits payable from these pension plans have been reduced over the years. Many governmental agencies have begun shifting some of the responsibility for retirement funding and planning to the individual employee through self-reliant contributory plans. For example, the Federal government Thrift Savings Plan, which is discussed in more detail in Chapter 5, is nearly identical to a 401(k) plan.

Traditional pension plans promise a certain defined benefit amount available at the time of a participant's retirement. This benefit, the present value of which can be calculated at any given point during an employee's service, is commonly based on a combination of the participant's years of service with the company and the participant's salary.[3] A participant's salary for these purposes is usually defined as the participant's final salary, the average of the participant's highest salaries, or the average of the participant's salaries over their career. If, however, a career average salary is used in the formula, there will be a significant loss of purchasing power when the benefit is received as compared to the final salary method.

The following is an example of a common pension plan benefit formula.

1.5%	x	# of Years of Service	x	The Average of the 3 Highest Consecutive Years Salary	=	Annual Pension Benefit Amount ($)
1.5%	x	40 years	x	$100,000	=	$60,000

1. It should be noted that there are many planning opportunities with defined benefit plans for small businesses. Some of these are discussed in this chapter.
2. www.pbgc.gov/about/who-we-are.html.
3. It may also be based on years of participation in the pension plan and the participant's salary.

Exhibit 4.1 | Total Plans by Type 1975 - 2018

Year	Total Plans		
	Total	Defined Benefit	Defined Contribution
1975	311,094	103,346	207,748
1980	488,901	148,096	340,805
1985	632,135	170,172	461,963
1990	712,308	113,062	599,245
1995	693,404	69,492	623,912
2000	735,651	48,773	686,878
2005	679,095	47,614	631,481
2006	694,550	48,579	645,971
2007	707,787	48,982	658,805
2008	717,530	48,374	669,156
2009	706,667	47,137	659,530
2010	701,012	46,543	654,469
2011	683,647	45,256	638,390
2012	676,622	43,601	633,021
2013	681,154	44,163	636,991
2014	685,203	44,869	640,334
2015	693,925	45,672	648,252
2016	705,540	46,300	656,241
2017	709,527	46,698	662,829
2018	721,876	46,869	675,007

Source: Form 5500 filings with the U.S. Department of Labor

Example 4.1

Assume that Eric works for ABC Company, which sponsors a defined benefit plan with a benefit formula of 1.5% times the years of service times the final salary. Assuming that Eric worked for ABC for 40 years and that his final salary is $100,000, he would be entitled to an annual benefit of $60,000 per year (1.5% x 40 x $100,000) during retirement. If Eric were to live for 30 years in retirement, ABC would have to pay a total of $1.8 million ($60,000 x 30 years) in retirement benefits to Eric. (Note that corporate pension benefit payments are not usually adjusted for inflation.)

Assume Dane also works for ABC Company. If Dane works for the company for ten years and has a final salary of $60,000, then his annual retirement benefit would be $9,000 (1.5% x 10 x $60,000).

There are many possible variations for the benefit formula of a pension plan resulting in a promise to pay the employee a defined benefit during retirement. Generally, pension plans do not include employee contributions (**noncontributory plans**). However, it is possible, especially in a not-for-profit or governmental institution, to have a defined benefit plan with mandatory employee contributions. In the more general case of a noncontributory plan, the full funding burden is on the employer. The plan document defines the formula that will be used to determine the pension benefit.

PENSION PLAN CHARACTERISTICS

An employer who establishes a pension plan promises to pay a defined benefit to an employee. In some cases, the funds necessary to pay benefits are not available upon the employee's retirement. If this occurs, it is usually the result of the employer's bankruptcy, cash flow problems, poor investment decisions, or some combination of the above. In any case, the employee will not receive the promised retirement benefit. As a result of the employer's promise to pay a retirement benefit and the employee's reliance on this expected retirement benefit, the government established several requirements to increase the likelihood that a pension plan has the funds required to pay the promised defined benefit throughout the employee's retirement.

For qualified pension plans, the government requires mandatory annual funding, disallows most in-service withdrawals, limits the investment of the plan assets in employer's securities, and limits the investment of plan assets in life insurance.[4] Each of these requirements is designed to provide protection for the employee's promised benefit. In addition, the Pension Benefit Guaranty Corporation (PBGC) was established in 1974 as part of ERISA to provide additional protection for lower-wage participants of defined benefit plans. The PBGC is discussed in more detail later in this chapter.

Exhibit 4.2 | Pension Plan Requirements

1. Mandatory annual funding
2. Disallow most in-service withdrawals
3. Limited investment in employer securities
4. Limited investment in life insurance

Anti-Cutback Rule

ERISA provides a rule prohibiting a plan sponsor from amending a plan such that the accrued benefit of an employee is decreased or reduced by such amendment or change.[5] This rule is intended to protect employees and participants from changes made by the employer with the intent of simply reducing the cost of the plan. However, this rule does not prevent the plan from freezing benefits, reducing future benefits, or eliminating future benefits. It simply provides that benefits already accrued cannot be retroactively reduced through amendment. This rule is referred to as the anti-cutback rule.

4. Under the Pension Protection Act of 2006, pension plans may allow in-service withdrawals for workers age 62 or older.
5. 29 U.S.C. §1054(g).

Mandatory Funding

ERISA and the IRC provide rules to ensure that there are or will be sufficient assets available to pay the promised benefits from pension plans to participants and their beneficiaries. The PPA 2006 significantly enhanced these rules in an attempt to provide better protection to participants and their beneficiaries. These changes followed and were likely a result of several high profile corporate bankruptcies, especially in the airline industry in the early 2000s. There continues to be a balance between insuring that the promised pension benefits are properly funded and limiting the employer's ability to over-fund retirement plans as a means of sheltering current taxable income. However, it appears that the pendulum has swung toward protecting benefits with these changes, as one of the primary themes of PPA 2006 was to ensure that pension plans were working toward fully funding their pension liabilities by 2015. Despite that objective, along with the positive investment returns on the S&P 500 from 2009 through 2020, defined benefit plans remain largely underfunded.[6]

There are many issues regarding defined benefit funding that must be considered by plan sponsors and actuaries that are also contemplated by ERISA. The liabilities of a defined benefit plan or pension plan are long-term in nature and should therefore be funded over a longer period of time. As with any long period of time, there is uncertainty regarding future costs of pension plans due to unknown information, including information about earnings, inflation, mortality, disability, and salary increases. Each of these factors impacts the actual cost of funding pension plan obligations.

A good example of this uncertainty is the investment market and economic declines beginning in 2008, known as the Great Recession. These declines resulted in many pension plans, including government pension plans, becoming significantly underfunded. However, there are also periods in which investment returns significantly exceed assumptions built into pension liability projections.

The calculation of the **mandatory funding requirement** differs for defined benefit pension plans and defined contribution pension plans, but in both cases, the employer is required to fund the plan with the determined amount (or within a range of amounts for defined benefit pension plans) regardless of the current investment market situation. The application of the mandatory funding standard requirement for both defined benefit pension plans and defined contribution pension plans is described below.

Defined Benefit Pension Plans

A **defined benefit plan** is a plan that focuses on the benefit payable to participants during retirement. Based on those expected payments, an actuary determines the amount of current funding necessary when compounded to the retirement period to fund that future benefit. The mandatory funding requirements of a defined benefit pension plan, either a defined benefit plan or a cash balance pension plan, require that the plan sponsor fund the plan on an annual basis with an amount within the range provided by an actuary (whose services are required annually). The range provided by the actuary is statutorily defined in the IRC as an amount that is between the accumulated funding deficiency and the full funding limitation.

---

6. http://us.milliman.com/PFI/

ERISA requires companies sponsoring defined benefit pension plans to fully fund the plans every year. The minimum required contribution to a single-employer defined benefit pension plan for a plan year generally depends on a comparison of the value of the plan's assets with the plan's funding target and target normal cost.

Funding Target

A plan's funding target for a plan year is the present value of all benefits accrued or earned under the plan as of the beginning of the plan year. For this purpose, all benefits (including early retirement or similar benefits) are taken into account. Benefits accruing during the plan year are not taken into account in determining the plan's funding target.

Target Normal Cost

The minimum required contribution for a plan year generally includes the plan's target normal cost for the plan year. A plan's target normal cost is the present value of all benefits expected to accrue or be earned under the plan during the plan year (the "current" year). For this purpose, an increase in any benefit attributable to services performed in a preceding year by reason of a compensation increase during the current year is treated as having accrued during the current year.

The minimum required contribution for a plan year, based on the value of plan assets compared to the funding target, is shown in the following table.

Exhibit 4.3 | Minimum Contribution for a Plan Year

If the value of plan assets	The minimum required contribution is:
is <u>less than</u> the funding target,[1]	the sum of: (1) target normal cost; (2) any shortfall amortization charge; and (3) any waiver amortization charge.
<u>equals or exceeds</u> the funding target,	the target normal cost, reduced (but not below zero) by the excess of: (1) the value of plan assets, over (2) the funding target.

1. The value of the plan assets is generally reduced by any prefunding balance and funding standard carryover balance. These balances may be used to offset the minimum contribution for the current year.

If the plan assets are greater than the funding target or PV of accrued benefits at the beginning of the year, then the minimum contribution equals the target normal cost reduced by the excess of the plan assets over the funding target. However, if the assets are less than the funding target, then the shortfall will generally have to be amortized. Therefore, the minimum contribution equals the target normal cost plus any shortfall amortization charge. The amortization period was seven years under PPA 2006. However, the ARPA of 2021, modified the rules and extended the amortization period to 15 years beginning after 2018.[7]

In addition, contributions in excess of the required minimum contributions generally are credited to a prefunding balance that may be used in certain circumstances to reduce otherwise required minimum contributions in the future. The value of the prefunding balance is usually deducted from the plan assets when determining if a plan has met the funding target.

7. ARPA (American Rescue Plan Act of 2021); IRC §430(c)(8)

While comparing assets to liabilities should be rather straight forward, that is not always the case when the valuation of those assets or liabilities involves discounted cash flows. ERISA and the IRC provide rules for determining the funding target, which is the process of determining the present value of the accrued benefits at the beginning of the year. Pension plans are required to discount future benefits using specific discount rates based on when the benefits are expected to be paid.

Small changes in interest rates can result in large swings in the present value of future pension benefits. These changes can result in large underfunded pension obligations. Congress has attempted to address this issue by providing for "pension smoothing" by tying discount rates to 25-year interest rate averages. This smoothing results in higher interest rates and lower present values. The ARPA extends these rules through 2029.

At-Risk Plans

Plans that are not current with their funding obligations and are thus deemed to be at risk of defaulting on their liabilities must use specific actuarial assumptions and may have increased current liabilities. In other words, plans that do not maintain funding are penalized. These rules are intended to be an incentive to maintain funding of pension obligations.

A plan is in at-risk status for a plan year if it does not meet either of two tests.[8] Under the first test, a plan is at-risk unless the funding target attainment percentage for the preceding plan year is at least 80 percent. Under the second rule, a plan is at-risk unless the funding target attainment percentage for the preceding plan year (determined by using additional "worst case" actuarial assumptions in computing the funding target) is at least 70 percent.

There is an exception to the at-risk rules for smaller plans. Plans with 500 or fewer participants on each day of the preceding year are not treated as in at-risk status for the plan year.

Plans that have been in at-risk status for at least two of the preceding four years are subject to an additional cost referred to as a loading factor. This loading factor increases the current cost of the plan and equals four percent of the plan's liabilities plus $700 per participant. This penalty for not maintaining the funding status is consistent with the theme from the PPA 2006 of providing more protection for participants and beneficiaries.

For plan years beginning in 2010 and later, a combined plan is permitted with elements of a defined benefit pension plan together with a 401(k) plan arrangement. The combined single plan is known as a DB(k) plan and is discussed further in Chapter 5.

Defined Contribution Pension Plans

There are two types of defined contribution pension plans, money purchase pension plans and target benefit pension plans. The mandatory funding requirements for a defined contribution pension plan, either a money purchase pension plan or a target benefit pension plan, require that the plan sponsor fund the plan annually with an amount as defined in the plan document.

---

8. IRC §430(i).

Example 4.2

An employer who establishes a money purchase pension plan requiring a 17% annual contribution must make an annual contribution of 17% of each employee's covered compensation to the money purchase pension plan to meet the mandatory funding requirement.

Underfunding

The plan sponsor of a pension plan that does not meet the mandatory funding requirements may apply to the IRS for a funding waiver. The IRS grants the waiver in most cases when the employer is temporarily experiencing hardships that limit the availability of funding and when not waiving the requirement would negatively impact the interests of the plan participants. For example, if the requirement was not waived, the company may become bankrupt. Any funding waiver merely postpones the employer's required contribution (as determined under the mandatory funding requirements) but does not eliminate the funding requirement of the plan. In fact, the employer will be required to fund the plan with the "waived" amount and any additional amounts that accrue during the waiver period.

Example 4.3

If an employer receives a waiver to fund the plan when the funding requirement contribution is $40,000 and the employer has not funded the $40,000 by the following year, the employer will be required to fund the plan with the $40,000 and also fund the current year's determined mandatory funding amount.

Long periods of poor investment performance in the equity market may cause pension plans to become underfunded, but the underfunded status may change because of reversing market conditions.

Disallowance of In-Service Withdrawals

An **in-service withdrawal** is any withdrawal from the plan while the employee is a participant in the plan other than a loan (which requires a defined term, interest accrual, and repayment provisions as discussed in Chapter 7). Because the fundamental promise of a pension plan is to pay the employee a benefit at retirement, the plan cannot permit in-service withdrawals or it would risk not having enough money to pay the retirement benefit. Any such provision would be inconsistent with the promise to pay the pension benefit at retirement. Plan loans are not in-service withdrawals because they are required to be paid back. Although loans are allowed by the IRC, most pension plans do not permit plan loans because the contributions are generally funded exclusively by the employer.

Under the Pension Protection Act of 2006, pension plans were permitted to provide for in-service distributions to participants age 62 or older. The SECURE Act of 2019 further expanded the ability for participants to receive in-service distributions by reducing the minimum age from 62 to 59½.[9] This type of distribution, also known as phased retirement, is intended to enable older workers to become part-time employees and receive partial benefits to maintain their current earnings level. This provision is a beneficial option for employees and plan sponsors.

---

9. IRC §401(a)(36).

Limited Investment in Employer Securities

The assets of a pension plan may be invested in the securities of the employer/plan sponsor provided the aggregate value of the employer securities does not exceed 10 percent of the fair market value of the pension plan assets at the time the employer securities are purchased.[10] Employer securities are any securities issued by the plan sponsor or an affiliate of the plan sponsor, including stocks, bonds, and publicly traded partnership interests.

The purpose of this limitation is to protect the ability of the plan to pay the promised retirement benefit. The value of the plan sponsor's securities are tied to the value of the company. If the company performs poorly, its securities will likely decrease in value. In the case where there was no limit on investment in the employer's securities, the defined benefit plan assets would also decrease substantially. Any such decrease could subsequently create a large funding requirement from the same employer that is in the financial difficulty (the cause of the plan's decrease in value).

If the company is struggling financially and the pension plan assets were heavily invested in the employer's securities, several problems may occur. The company would already have cash flow problems due to the financial situation and the reduction in the plan assets attributable to the decrease in the company's stock price would further exacerbate the cash flow problem by increasing the minimum amount necessary to fund the plan. Therefore, it is not reasonable to have a significantly large percentage of plan assets in a pension plan invested in employer securities. The 10 percent limitation of investment of a pension plan's assets in the employer's securities is designed to protect the employer's promise to pay a pension to the employee.

A significant exposure to any one security is inconsistent with the concept of asset allocation and portfolio diversification. A basic understanding of asset management and portfolio management supports the notion of limiting the exposure to the employer's securities to promote risk reduction through diversification in the investment portfolio.

Diversification

In addition to the 10 percent limitation, defined contribution plans holding publicly traded employer securities must allow plan participants to diversify their pre-tax deferrals, after-tax contributions, and employer contributions that have been invested in employer securities. The defined contribution plan must offer a choice of at least three investment options, other than employer securities, each of which must be diversified and have materially different risk and return characteristics. This requirement is consistent with that found in ERISA and generally implies that a plan must provide at least one type of stock, bond, and cash fund as investment options. All plan participants must be allowed to diversify the investment of their elective deferrals and after-tax contributions. In addition, plan participants with

---

10. ERISA §407(a)(2); 29 U.S. Code §1107(a)(2).

three or more years of service must be allowed to diversify the investment of employer contributions made on their behalf. [11]

Limited Investment in Life Insurance

One exception to the retirement benefit promise is the ability to use the assets of a pension plan to provide incidental death benefits to a participant's beneficiary through the purchase of life insurance.[12] In fact, any qualified plan may purchase life insurance (subject to these limitations). As long as life insurance is not the primary focus of the pension plan, the government allows this exception from the ultimate retirement benefit promise because the death benefit of the life insurance policy is payable to the employee's spouse and other survivors at the employee's death. The beneficiaries of the policy are usually the same beneficiaries who would receive the remainder of the employee's retirement benefits at the employee's death; therefore, purchasing life insurance allows employees to leverage the amount they will leave to their survivors in the event of an untimely death.

Whether the life insurance is the primary focus of the qualified plan or is an incidental death benefit is determined by a series of tests that limit the amount of life insurance coverage provided by a qualified plan or the cost of the life insurance provided by the plan. To maintain its qualified plan status, a qualified plan that includes life insurance must pass either the (1) 25 percent test or (2) the 100 to 1 ratio test.

25 Percent Test[13]

The 25 percent test consists of two tests, a 25 percent test and a 50 percent test. The test used depends upon the type of life insurance provided by the plan. If a **term insurance** or **universal life insurance** policy is purchased within the qualified plan, the aggregate premiums paid for the life insurance policy cannot exceed 25 percent of the employer's aggregate contributions to the participant's account. If a **whole life insurance policy** is purchased within a qualified plan, the aggregate premiums paid for the whole life insurance policy cannot exceed 50 percent of the employer's aggregate contributions to the participant's account. In addition, for any permanent life insurance policy, the entire life insurance policy must be converted to cash or an annuity at or before retirement to avoid taxation. Alternatively, the policy can be distributed to the participant; however, the participant will be taxed on the fair market value of the policy as a distribution from the retirement plan.[14] In the case of term insurance, the policy cannot be maintained in a qualified plan after retirement, but can be distributed to the participant as a taxable distribution from the plan if the participant wishes to retain the policy. The IRS treats whole life policies different from term and universal life policies. Term and universal policies must meet the 25 percent rule while whole life policies must meet the 50 percent rule, and the mortality cost alone cannot exceed 25 percent of the contributions. In general, the 25%/50% rule will be applied to defined contribution plans, including defined contribution pension plans. A qualified plan that meets the 25 percent test (either the 25 percent test or the 50 percent test) does not have to meet the 100 to 1 ratio test to retain its qualified status.

11. IRC §401(a)(35).
12. Treas. Reg. §1.401-1(b)(1)(i).
13. Revenue Ruling 74-307.
14. See Rev. Proc. 2005-25 for safe harbor methods to determine the fair market value of a life insurance policy distributed by a qualified retirement plan.

Example 4.4

Jolene is a participant in a qualified plan sponsored by her employer. The employer has made aggregate contributions for Jolene of $100,000. Her plan holds a $90,000 term life insurance policy on her life. The total premiums that have been paid for the policy are $4,000. Because this policy is a term life insurance policy, the premiums paid cannot exceed $25,000 ($100,000 x 25%) per the 25% test. Since the premiums for this policy have been $4,000, the plan meets the 25% test.

100 to 1 Ratio Test

A defined benefit plan may have life insurance in the plan and retain its qualified status by meeting the 100 to 1 ratio test, which provides limits based on the benefits provided by the life insurance protection rather than the cost of the life insurance protection. Specifically, the 100 to 1 ratio test limits the amount of the death benefit of life insurance coverage purchased to 100 times the monthly-accrued retirement benefit provided under the same qualified plan's defined benefit formula. It is quite common to use the 100 to 1 ratio test for a defined benefit pension plan because of the ease of calculating the monthly accrued retirement benefit. Most qualified defined contribution plans, including pension and profit sharing plans, will use the 25%/50% tests. Although, if the defined contribution plan benefit is an annuity, it would be possible to use the 100 to 1 ratio test (unusual). In any case, the objective of these rules is to insure that life insurance death benefits are incidental to the retirement benefit and not the primary focus of the plan.

Example 4.5

As a participant in her employer's defined benefit plan, Dory has accrued a retirement benefit of $4,000 per month. Based on the 100 to 1 ratio test, the plan is limited to utilizing plan assets to purchase life insurance up to a face amount of $400,000 ($4,000 x 100).

Tax Issues with Life Insurance in Qualified Plans

The proceeds from life insurance policies are typically not subject to income tax to the beneficiary and funds in a qualified plan are typically contributed on a pre-tax basis. Therefore, premiums paid by the employer for the life insurance policy are taxable to the employee at the time the premium is paid.[15] The amount that is taxable to the employee is determined from Table 2001, which reflects one-year term premiums per $1,000 of life insurance coverage. [16]

---

15. Treas. Reg. §1.72-16(b)(2).

16. The premium cost of life insurance protection provided by a qualified plan is considered to be the one-year term premium for the amount of insurance provided for the participant. According to IRS Notice 2002-8, the one-year term premiums may be determined from Table 2001, which shows the premium per $1,000 of life insurance. Table 2001 premiums effectively replace the older P.S. 58 rates set forth in Rev. Rul. 55-747.

Example 4.6

Marlin works for Appletosh, which sponsors a qualified plan. The plan purchased a life insurance policy on Marlin's life. The cost of the insurance (from Table 2001) purchased in the plan is taxable to Marlin. Because the insurance is taxable, it creates basis in his qualified plan assets.

Example 4.7

An annual premium policy purchased by a qualified trust for an employee (age 50) provides an annuity of $100 per month upon retirement at age 65, with a minimum death benefit of $10,000. The insurance payable if death occurred in the first year would be $10,000. The cash value at the end of the first year is $0. The net insurance is therefore $10,000 minus $0, or $10,000. Assuming the premium cost for the employee's age is $2.30 per $1,000, the premium for $10,000 of life insurance is therefore $23.00, and this is the amount to be reported as income by the employee for the taxable year in which the premium is paid. Assuming that the cash value at the end of the second year is $500, the net insurance would then be $9,500 for the second year. With a net 1-year term rate of $2.52 for the employee's age in the second year, the amount to be reported as income to the employee would be $23.94.

As mentioned, generally the proceeds from life insurance are not taxable to a beneficiary. Qualified plans are permitted to purchase cash value life insurance in qualified plans. The limit for whole life insurance is 50 percent because part of the premium is used to fund the cash value of the policy, similar to deferred compensation. Because of this, the beneficiary of a life insurance policy purchased within a qualified plan must include into taxable income the proceeds of life insurance to the extent of cash value of the policy.[17]

---

17. Treas. Reg. §1.72-16(c)(2).

Exhibit 4.4 | Table 2001: Table of One-Year Term Premiums for $1,000 of Life Insurance Protection

Attained Age	Section 79 Extended and Interpolated Annual Rates	Attained Age	Section 79 Extended and Interpolated Annual Rates	Attained Age	Section 79 Extended and Interpolated Annual Rates
0	$0.70	35	$0.99	70	$20.62
1	$0.41	36	$1.01	71	$22.72
2	$0.27	37	$1.04	72	$25.07
3	$0.19	38	$1.06	73	$27.57
4	$0.13	39	$1.07	74	$30.18
5	$0.13	40	$1.10	75	$33.05
6	$0.14	41	$1.13	76	$36.33
7	$0.15	42	$1.20	77	$40.17
8	$0.16	43	$1.29	78	$44.33
9	$0.16	44	$1.40	79	$49.23
10	$0.16	45	$1.53	80	$54.56
11	$0.19	46	$1.67	81	$60.51
12	$0.24	47	$1.83	82	$66.74
13	$0.28	48	$1.98	83	$73.07
14	$0.33	49	$2.13	84	$80.35
15	$0.38	50	$2.30	85	$88.76
16	$0.52	51	$2.52	86	$99.16
17	$0.57	52	$2.81	87	$110.40
18	$0.59	53	$3.20	88	$121.85
19	$0.61	54	$3.65	89	$133.40
20	$0.62	55	$4.15	90	$144.30
21	$0.62	56	$4.68	91	$155.80
22	$0.64	57	$5.20	92	$168.75
23	$0.66	58	$5.66	93	$186.44
24	$0.68	59	$6.06	94	$206.70
25	$0.71	60	$6.51	95	$228.35
26	$0.73	61	$7.11	96	$250.01
27	$0.76	62	$7.96	97	$265.09
28	$0.80	63	$9.08	98	$270.11
29	$0.83	64	$10.41	99	$281.05
30	$0.87	65	$11.90		
31	$0.90	66	$13.51		
32	$0.93	67	$15.20		
33	$0.96	68	$16.92		
34	$0.98	69	$18.70		

In effect, the use of funds from a qualified plan to purchase life insurance is deemed a distribution.[18] This taxation does create taxable basis in the plan, which is further discussed in Chapter 7.

---

18. IRC §402(a). However, this distribution is not subject to any penalties.

Example 4.8

Donald died suddenly in a freak accident. Fortunately for his girlfriend, Daisy, there was a life insurance policy payable to her that was purchased in Donald's qualified plan. The face amount of the policy is $25,000 and the cash value of the contract just before his death was $11,000. Therefore, $14,000 is treated as life insurance paid by reason of the death of the insured and is income tax free, and $11,000 is a death benefit, which is taxable to Daisy. However, the taxable portion may be reduced by Donald's basis, that is, the aggregate of the amounts that were currently taxable to him because they represented the portion of premiums paid by employer for the life insurance protection. This aggregate amount represents the employee's contribution to the plan. Assuming that the basis is $1,000, it reduces the taxable portion from $11,000 to $10,000.

As mentioned and will be discussed further in Chapter 7, distributions from qualified plans are generally taxable as ordinary income.[19] The distribution of life insurance is subject to taxation except to the extent that, within 60 days after the distribution of the contract, all or any portion of such value is irrevocably converted into a contract under which no part of any proceeds payable on death at any time would be excludable as life insurance proceeds under IRC §101(a).[20] In other words, the contract must be converted to an annuity contract to avoid taxation as a distribution.

412(e) Plan (Formerly 412(i) Plan)

A "section 412(e) plan," set forth in IRC §412(e), is a specific type of defined benefit pension plan that is funded entirely by a life insurance contract or an annuity. The employer claims tax deductions for contributions that are used by the plan to pay premiums on an insurance contract covering an employee. The plan may hold the contract until the employee dies or it may distribute or sell the contract to the employee at a specific point, such as when the employee retires.

The typical candidate for this type of plan is a sole proprietor with only a few employees. The 412(e) plan allows greater contributions to the plan than a traditional defined benefit plan because of the need to fund the life insurance or annuity. In addition, the plan is easier to explain to employees because the insurance/annuity is fixed and provides less risk due to the certainty of the insurance/annuity. The plan is also less costly than a traditional defined benefit plan. Because of the exclusive use of life insurance or annuities as a funding vehicle, no actuarial calculations are necessary, reducing administrative requirements and associated expenses. Unfortunately, the plan does not provide alternative investment choices, thus sacrificing the opportunity for significant long-term appreciation. In addition, the employer does not have much flexibility with regard to plan design and the plan cannot permit loans.

Although originally thought to be beneficial, some advisors have determined that 412(e) plans generally are not growth or cash flow beneficial. The lack of growth potential for 412(e) plans often overshadows the ability for greater funding. In addition, 412(e) plans have been the focus of IRS controversy over the last few years, prompting narrowing regulations and rulings.

In 2004, the IRS and the Treasury Department issued guidance intended to shut down abusive transactions involving 412(e) plans. The guidance covers three specific issues. First, a new proposed regulation states that any life insurance contract transferred from an employer or a qualified plan to an employee must be taxed at its full fair market value. This provision was designed to counteract

---

19. IRC §402(a).
20. Treas. Reg. §1.402(a)-1(a)(2).

arrangements in which an employer establishes a 412(e) plan, makes contributions to the plan (which are then deducted by the employer), purchases life insurance, and then sells the policy to the covered employee for less than the full fair market value of the policy.

Second, Revenue Ruling 2004-20 states that an employer cannot buy excessive life insurance in order to claim large tax deductions. These arrangements are considered listed transactions for tax-shelter reporting purposes.

Third, Revenue Ruling 2004-21 states that a 412(e) plan cannot use differences in life insurance contracts to discriminate in favor of highly paid employees. While 412(e) plans may initially appear beneficial to defer taxes, costs and cash flow requirements have slowed their growth. While caution should be taken when considering this type of plan, it remains a viable tool in certain circumstances.

DEFINED BENEFIT PENSION PLANS vs. DEFINED CONTRIBUTION PENSION PLANS

The defined benefit pension plan and the cash balance pension plan are both defined benefit pension plans whereas the money purchase pension plan and the target benefit pension plan are both defined contribution pension plans. Each of these plans share the characteristics attributable to pension plans but differ between the categorization of defined benefit and defined contribution. The primary differences between the two categorizations of the plans include the following:
- the use of an actuary (annually, at inception, or not needed)
- assumption of the investment risk (to the employer or to the employee)
- the disposition of plan forfeitures (reduce plan costs or allocate to remaining employees)
- coverage under the Pension Benefit Guaranty Corporation (PBGC)
- the use of Social Security integration (offset or excess)
- the calculation of the accrued benefit or account balance
- the ability to grant credit for prior service for funding
- the use of commingled funds versus separate, individual investment accounts

The Actuary

Defined benefit and cash balance pension plans require the use of annual actuarial services to determine the proper annual funding of the plan. The target benefit pension plan uses actuarial assumptions only at the inception of the plan and does not require annual actuarial work. The money purchase pension plan has no need for actuarial services because the annual contribution is predefined (usually as a percentage of covered compensation) in the plan documents.

Exhibit 4.5 | Actuary

Plan Type	Actuary Required
Defined Benefit & Cash Balance	Annually
Target Benefit	At Inception Only
Money Purchase	Not Used At All

The **actuary** makes assumptions about future inflation, expected wage increases, life expectancy of the assumed retirees, expected investment returns on plan assets, expected mortality rates for retirees, and expected forfeitures resulting from termination. Each of these assumptions has an impact and relationship to plan costs and plan funding.

Exhibit 4.6 | Actuary Assumptions and Relationship to Plan Costs

Actuarial Assumption About	Direct Relationships			Indirect Relationships		
	Expected Inflation	Expected Wage Increases	Life Expectancy	Expected Investment Returns	Expected Mortality	Expected Forfeiture / Employee Turnover
Change	↑	↑	↑	↑	↑	↑
Impact on Plan Costs	↑	↑	↑	↓	↓	↓

Inflation affects plan costs directly and includes such costs as actuarial services, plan supplies, and the cost of providing service and summary plan documents for the plan. As wages increase, plan costs increase because benefits are almost always paid as an annuity derived from a formula that includes some measure of the last or highest salaries. Because the pension is a life or joint life annuity, any increase in life expectancy will increase plan costs. On the indirect side, plan costs are reduced when actual investment returns are higher than what was assumed. If the retiree's mortality rate increases faster than expected, payouts are lessened and plan costs are reduced. In addition, if there are more forfeitures than originally expected, plan costs are reduced because forfeitures in defined benefit plans must be used to reduce future plan costs.

Investment Risk

A defined benefit pension plan is designed to pay a promised benefit to a plan participant at the participant's retirement, whereas a defined contribution pension plan only guarantees that contributions based on a defined formula will be made to the plan per the plan document. In other words, the participant in a defined contribution plan is entitled to the value of the defined contribution plan account balance at retirement, including any investment gains or losses. The participant in a defined benefit plan is entitled to the promised defined benefit at retirement, regardless of the actual investment performance. Consider employees A and B who earn equal salaries, are the same age, and have the same length of service. Each will receive exactly the same pension benefit as calculated under any one of the defined benefit funding formulas at their retirement. If, however, A and B were participants in a defined contribution plan, they would have each received the same contribution each year to their defined contribution accounts, but their individual investment performance may vary widely based on their investment selections, resulting in different account balances at their retirement. Because of the nature of the benefit to be provided (a promised benefit or a promised contribution), the investment risk while the plan assets are within the qualified plan is borne by the plan sponsor for a defined benefit pension plan and generally borne by the individual plan participant for a defined contribution pension plan.

Exhibit 4.7 | Investment Risk

Plan Type	Burden of Investment Risk
Defined Benefit & Cash Balance	Employer
Target Benefit & Money Purchase	Employee

Defined Benefit Plan

The plan sponsor of a defined benefit plan must ensure that the guaranteed benefit as provided in the plan document is available to pay the employee at the time of the employee's retirement. After meeting the mandatory funding standards as required for all pension plans (as discussed above), plan assets are invested and will experience investment returns dependent upon the investment selections made by the plan sponsor or investment manager. If the plan's investments experience positive returns and the assets grow to a level exceeding the plan's mandatory funding requirement, the plan is said to be overfunded, and the employer benefits from the excess growth by being able to offset the required funding amount for future years by the excess growth. Conversely, if the value of the plan's assets decrease due to less than expected investment returns, the employer is responsible for contributing additional amounts to maintain the mandatory funding requirement. Any deficiency in funding is the employer's responsibility regardless of how low the value of the plan's assets have decreased in comparison to the minimum required funding amount as determined by the actuary.

Key Concepts

1. How does the investment risk differ for defined contribution plans as compared with defined benefit plans?

2. How are forfeitures treated in defined benefit and defined contribution plans?

3. Which types of qualified plans are covered by the PBGC?

4. How is the accrued benefit of a defined benefit plan calculated?

5. Which qualified plans allow credit for prior service?

Example 4.9

If an employer funds a defined benefit pension plan with the required mandatory funding for 2021 of $100,000, and subsequently the fair market value of the pension plan assets declines in value to $80,000, the employer is required to contribute additional funds to restore the pension assets to the required level. However, any deficit will generally be amortized over a period not to exceed seven years.

Example 4.10

If an employer funded a defined benefit pension plan with the mandatory funding standard amount of $100,000 for 2021 and the fair market value of the pension plan assets grows to $180,000, the plan sponsor can utilize the growth of the assets to offset future plan funding requirements. If, in the subsequent year, the mandatory funding amount was $190,000, the employer would only be required to contribute $10,000 to meet the requirement. Any excess investment growth reduces the employer's future plan costs.

One advantage for participants of a defined benefit pension plan is that they do not bear any of the investment risk. Their benefit is guaranteed to be the amount determined by the benefit formula in the plan document.[21] The fact that the employer bears this investment responsibility is viewed as a disadvantage for the employer because it is required to fund whatever amount as determined by the actuary to meet the mandatory funding requirements. This funding requirement increases the cost of providing retirement benefits to employees in years when the market performs poorly and, thus, could disrupt the projected cash flows of the employer.

Despite the positive investment returns on the S&P 500 from 2009 through 2019, many defined benefit plans remain underfunded today. Fortune 500 companies that once sponsored overfunded plans now find that they have unfunded liabilities. Today, the PBGC has increased the cost of maintaining defined benefit plans, as well as increased the cost of sponsoring an underfunded plan. As the cost of maintaining defined benefit plans increases, along with the longevity risk associated with increasing life expectancy, defined benefit plan sponsors must consider whether or not to maintain these plans or simply offer a defined contribution plan.

Defined Contribution Pension Plans

The investment risk of plan assets within a defined contribution pension plan is generally borne by each participant in the plan. To a large extent, the plan sponsor's responsibility ends after the contribution required in the plan document is made to the defined contribution plan account on behalf of the participant. As such, if the value of the investments in the account increases, the plan participant benefits from all of the increase in the account value. Conversely, if the value of the account decreases, the plan participant bears the sole responsibility and risk for this decrease. The employer is not required to subsequently contribute any additional amounts to make up for any decline in value of the account.

Defined contribution pension plans require the employer to fund the plan annually per the plan document, but the employer is not required to continuously maintain any minimum value in an individual participant's account. After the employer contribution is made, a defined contribution pension plan generally permits the individual employee participant to select investments. A poor performing investment market will not affect the employer's cash flows in the same way they might be affected under a defined benefit pension plan.

Example 4.11

If an employer sponsors a defined benefit pension plan with a target normal cost of $100,000 for 2021 and the plan's assets are less than the plan's funding target, the plan sponsor would have a minimum required contribution of $100,000 plus any shortfall amortization charge. If the value of the plan assets exceeds the plan's funding target, then the $100,000 minimum contribution is reduced by the amount that the value of the plan assets exceed the plan's funding target. Therefore, any excess investment growth will still offset future plan funding requirements.

The shift from defined benefit pension plans to defined contribution pension plans has gradually resulted in a shifting of investment risk to employees, who may not be in the best position to manage their own investments. Defined benefit plans generally have a professional investment advisor or an investment

---

21. Assuming the company has the requisite funds to pay the benefit. Even though defined benefit plans are generally covered by the PBGC, participants may not receive full benefits, especially if they have higher incomes.

committee that helps manage the plan's assets. Individuals are generally given a choice of funds from which to invest, without understanding risk and return of various asset classes over time.

Guaranteed sources of income, whether from a pension or from Social Security, provide a fairly reliable foundation for retirement needs. The final benefit for employees who have defined contribution plans is no longer defined, as under a defined benefit plan, but rather dependent upon contributions and investment performance. As a result, similarly situated employees may have drastically different outcomes from similar contributions.

Example 4.12

Kayo and Zhong both worked for Suni Enterprises for 30 years. They have the same compensation and have received a company contribution to their money purchase pension plan of $10,000 annually. Kayo invested in a guaranteed income fund averaging 3% per year, while Zhong invested in a more aggressive portfolio averaging 8% per year. Their balances at the end of 30 years are $475,754 and $1,132,832, respectively. Despite the same compensation level and savings amount, their retirement balances are drastically different.

Example 4.13

Amelia's Flight School sponsors a 15% money purchase pension plan. In the current year, Amelia's contributed $15,000 to the plan on behalf of Joann. If the value of the $15,000 contribution decreases to $10,000 in the subsequent year, Amelia's is not responsible for the loss. If Joann is still employed by Amelia's at the end of the subsequent year, Amelia's must make another contribution of 15% of covered compensation on Joann's behalf for that subsequent year.

Allocation of Forfeitures

When an employee terminates employment before being fully vested (discussed in Chapter 3), those benefits allocated to the employee that are not yet vested are known as **forfeitures**. For a defined benefit pension plan, the forfeited funds can only be used to reduce future plan funding costs of the employer. The forfeitures within a defined benefit plan cannot increase the benefit of any other plan participant, nor may the forfeited funds be allocated for any other purpose. The plan sponsor of a defined contribution pension plan, however, can choose to utilize plan forfeitures in one of two ways, either by reducing future plan funding costs or by allocating the forfeitures to other remaining participants in a nondiscriminatory manner; thus increasing the participants' account balances. The total contributions to a participant's defined contribution plan, including any forfeitures, are limited to the maximum annual contribution as discussed in Chapter 3.

Example 4.14

Adele has an accrued benefit from her employer's defined benefit plan equal to $6,000 per month at retirement. However, based on the plan's vesting schedule, Adele has a vested accrued benefit equal to $4,800 per month at retirement. If Adele terminates employment today, the non-vested assets in the defined benefit plan must be used to offset future plan funding costs.

Example 4.15

Carmela has a defined contribution pension plan with an account balance equal to $100,000, but she is only 20% vested in the account balance. If Carmela terminates employment today, the nonvested amount (forfeiture amount) of $80,000 could be allocated to the other plan participants or it could be used to reduce future plan costs. The treatment of forfeitures is reflected in the plan document.

Exhibit 4.8 | Forfeitures

Plan Type	Forfeitures
Defined Benefit & Cash Balance	Must Reduce Plan Costs
Target Benefit & Money Purchase (and all other Defined Contribution Plans)	Can Reduce Plan Costs or Allocate to Remaining Participants

Pension Benefit Guaranty Corporation Insurance

The **Pension Benefit Guaranty Corporation (PBGC)** was established in 1974 when President Gerald R. Ford signed the Employee Retirement Income Security Act (ERISA) into law. The PBGC acts, just as its name implies, to guarantee pension benefits. It is a federal corporation that acts as an insurance provider to maintain the benefits promised to employees by their defined benefit pension plans. The plan sponsors of defined benefit and cash balance pensions plans pay premiums for the insurance coverage, but the PBGC only provides plan participants with a limited retirement benefit if the plan completely or partially terminates with an unfunded or underfunded liability.

The PBGC does not insure defined contribution pension or profit sharing plans, nor does it insure defined benefit pension plans of professional service corporations with 25 or fewer participants. The PBGC does insure all other defined benefit plans and covered plans are required to pay a flat-rate, per participant premium. In addition, previously underfunded plans must pay a variable-rate premium (VRP) equal to 4.6 percent (or $46 per $1,000 for 2021) of unfunded vested benefits. For 2021, the VRP is capped at $582 times the number of participants.

The Pension Protection Act of 2006 limits the variable-rate premiums owed by employers with 25 or fewer employees to $5 per participant for plan years after 2006. Note that this limitation only applies to employers that are not professional service corporations because the PBGC does not insure the plans of professional service corporations with 25 or fewer participants. Additionally, there is a flat-rate premium for all defined benefit plans of $86 per participant for single-employer pension plans (for 2021) with indexing based on increases in average wages.

Example 4.16

Daniel is one of three partners in SueMe Law Corporation, which employs five other attorneys and six staff members. A defined benefit plan sponsored by SueMe would not be covered by the PBGC because it is a professional services corporation with less than 25 employees.

Example 4.17

ABC has a defined benefit pension plan with 1,000 participants, and it has unfunded liabilities payable to the plan of $2 million dollars. The PBGC insurance premium is $86,000 ($86 x 1,000) + $92,000 ($46 per $1,000 of underfunding) for a total of $178,000 for 2021. In 2020, the same plan would have paid $173,000. This difference represents an increase of 2.9%

Exhibit 4.9 | Maximum PBGC Pension Guarantee for 2021

	Guarantee Limit at Age 65	Guarantee Limit at Age 62	Guarantee Limit at Age 60	Guarantee Limit at Age 55
Monthly	$6,034.09	4,766.93	3,922.16	2,715.34

In the event that a defined benefit plan terminates or partially terminates with an unfunded amount, the calculation of the benefit payment is not equal to the calculation under the terminated plan document. Instead, the PBGC benefits have a maximum limit that is indexed to inflation. As discussed in Chapter 3, a defined benefit pension plan may provide a benefit to a plan participant with a maximum of $230,000 for 2021 at retirement. However, the maximum annual benefit paid to plan participants at retirement by the PBGC is $72,409 per year for 2021. This lower amount can create a significant deficiency in expected retirement benefits for employees with higher compensation levels. Earning the maximum benefit based on the terminated pension plan document does not equate to the plan participant earning the maximum under a plan managed by the PBGC. The payment from the PBGC is based upon:

1. the form of the benefit as payable under the terminated plan,
2. the participant's age, and
3. any amounts that PBGC recovered from the employer in the case that the plan was underfunded.

Example 4.18

In April of 2003, the PBGC became the trustee of the defined benefit pension plan for the U.S. Airways pilots. Many of these pilots had salaries in excess of the covered compensation limit and had accrued benefits at their retirement equal to the maximum defined benefit pension plan amount of the plan. However, the PBGC will only pay out the maximum amount based on the termination date. For plans terminated in 2003 (as U.S. Airways was), the max benefit at age 65 was $43,977, and $28,585 for age 60. Age 60 was the mandatory retirement age for pilots in 2003. These amounts are significantly less than what the pilots would have expected from their defined benefit plan.

Example 4.19

In July 2009, the Pension Benefit Guaranty Corporation announced it would assume responsibility for the pension plans of 70,000 workers and retirees of Delphi Corp., the nation's largest producer of automotive parts. The PBGC took on unfunded liabilities in excess of $6 billion. Delphi was spun off from General Motors in 1999.

Example 4.20

In 2020, PBGC announced it assumed responsibility for The McClatchy Company Retirement Plan, which covers 24,000 current and future retirees and is underfunded by $1 billion. This California-based newspaper publisher operates 30 media companies in 14 states. PBGC also took responsibility for J.C. Penny Corporation's Pension Plan, which covers about 36,000 current and future retirees and is underfunded by $270 million.

Example 4.21

In December 2017, the PBGC announced it would pay retirement benefits for nearly 8,000 current and future retirees who participated in the Avaya, Inc. Pension Plan for Salaried Employees. Avaya filed for Chapter 11 protection. The termination of its pension plan went into effect on November 30, 2017. The Avaya salaried plan was 63% funded, with plan assets of $1.6 billion and liabilities for future benefits of $2.5 billion, and thus was underfunded by $938 million. Benefit accruals under the plan have been frozen since 2003. Avaya is a spinoff of Lucent Technologies.

Example 4.22

In January 2019, the PBGC announced it was taking steps to assume responsibility for Sears Holdings Corporation's two defined benefit pension plans, which cover about 90,000 people. The national retail chain headquartered in Hoffman Estates, Illinois, operates through its subsidiaries, which include Sears, Roebuck and Co. and Kmart Corporation. PBGC has worked with Sears for several years to improve funding for the company's plans. PBGC estimated that the Sears' plans were underfunded by $1.4 billion leaving them 64 percent funded.

Exhibit 4.10 | PBGC Insurance

Plan Type	PBGC Insurance
Defined Benefit & Cash Balance	Yes
Target Benefit & Money Purchase	No

As discussed, the objective of the PBGC is to insure pension benefits for participants and beneficiaries of defined benefit plans. However, it only insures benefits up to the annual limit. In addition, it has taken over many defined benefit plan over the last ten years such that the liabilities of the PBGC exceed its assets by billions of dollars. In response to this situation, the PBGC has increased annual premiums and has increased the risk within its asset portfolio.

Exhibit 4.11 | PBGC Net Position (assets minus liabilities) Over Time

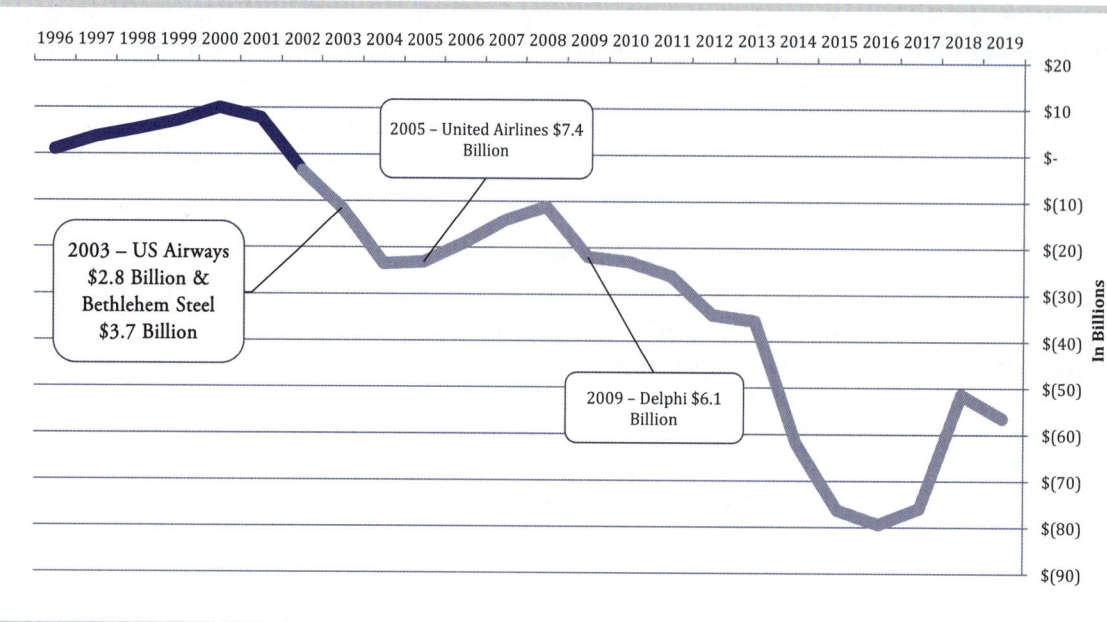

Effective in 2018, the Pension Benefit Guaranty Corporation began expanding its Missing Participants Program to terminated 401(k) and other plans in an effort to connect more people to their retirement savings. Beginning in January 2018, terminating defined contribution plans will have the option of transferring missing participants' benefits to PBGC instead of establishing an IRA at a financial institution. Participant accounts will not be diminished by ongoing maintenance fees or distribution charges, and PBGC will pay out benefits with interest when participants are found. The enhanced program will make it easier for people to locate their retirement benefits after their plan terminates.

Exhibit 4.12 | Top 10 Firms Presenting Claims

Table S-5
Top 10 Firms Presenting Claims (1975-2017)
Single-Employer Program

Top 10 Firms	Number of Plans	Fiscal Year(s) of Plan Termination(s)	Claims (by firm)	Vested Participants	Average Claim Per Vested Participant	Percent of Total Claims
1. United Airlines	4	2005	$7,304,186,216	122,483	$59,634	14.7%
2. Delphi	6	2009	4,820,168,215	66,614	72,360	9.7%
3. Bethlehem Steel	1	2003	3,702,771,655	92,174	40,172	7.5%
4. US Airways	4	2003, 2005	2,708,976,605	60,585	44,714	5.5%
5. LTV Steel*	6	2002, 2003, 2004	2,134,985,884	83,782	25,483	4.3%
6. Delta Air Lines	1	2006	1,710,043,418	13,237	129,187	3.5%
7. National Steel	7	2003	1,319,009,116	35,152	37,523	2.7%
8. Pan American Air	3	1991, 1992	841,082,434	53,624	15,685	1.7%
9. Trans World Airlines	2	2001	668,377,105	32,197	20,759	1.3%
10. Weirton Steel	1	2004	640,480,970	9,825	65,189	1.3%
Top 10 Total	35		$25,850,081,619	569,673	$45,377	52.2%
All Other Total	4,810		23,679,088,131	1,719,418	13,772	47.8%
Total	4,845		$49,529,169,749	2,289,091	$21,637	100.0%

Benefits - Accrued Benefit/Account Balance

At any given time, based on the provisions of each specific plan, a plan participant has accrued a benefit within his qualified pension plan. How the accrued benefit is calculated depends upon the type of plan sponsored by the participant's employer. A participant in a defined benefit plan has an accrued benefit roughly equal to the present value of the expected future payments at retirement (discussed further below). In contrast, a participant in a defined contribution plan has an accrued benefit equal to the account balance of the qualified plan consisting of any combination of employer and employee contributions plus the earnings on the respective contributions reduced by any non-vested amounts.

Accrued Benefit

A defined benefit plan is subject to the mandatory funding requirement as calculated by an actuary. An employee who terminates participation in the plan, usually through termination of employment before full retirement age, will be entitled to a benefit payable from the plan equal to the retirement benefit earned to date. This benefit is the actuarial equivalent of the benefit that would have been provided to the participant had the participant waited until retirement to receive the payments. As each plan document will detail the plan benefit formula (as discussed below), the calculation of the participant's accrued benefit utilizes all information at the date of termination. Communicating the value of the accrued benefit to the participants of a defined benefit plan is difficult because participants generally do not understand the funding process and the plan benefit formula. Also, an employee who is far from retirement and whose accrued benefit is quite small, will likely not grasp the true value of the ultimate benefit.

Account Balance

Calculating the accrued benefit for the participant in a defined contribution plan is usually much easier than calculating the accrued benefit for the participant of a defined benefit plan because the benefit in a defined contribution plan is simply the participant's account balance reduced by any non-vested amounts. The participant's account balance is the sum of the employer contributions to the plan and the employee contributions to the plan plus or minus any investment earnings or losses. This balance is communicated to the plan participants with periodic investment statements. These statements explain to the participants the exact amount of any plan benefit, which is the total amount of assets in the participant's account.

The SECURE Act, passed in December 2019, created a new requirement that defined contribution account statements provided more often than every 12 months include a lifetime income disclosure at least once every 12 months. The lifetime income projection will be based upon prescribed assumptions and is designed to assist participants with retirement planning by illustrating the hypothetical monthly income benefits the participant would receive if the entire account balance were used to provide a lifetime income stream. Plan sponsors will have no liability if the illustrated lifetime income is not actually available for the participant and are not responsible for ensuring any particular monthly benefit amount. Ultimately, the benefit will continue to be based upon the account balance and investment or annuitization options available at the time of the employee's retirement.

Exhibit 4.13 | Benefits

Plan Type	Benefits
Defined Benefit and Cash Balance	Accrued Benefit
Target Benefit & Money Purchase	Account Balance

Credit for Prior Service

At the creation of a retirement plan, every employee's accrued benefit or account balance is zero. However, an employer who establishes a defined benefit plan may elect to give employees credit for their service prior to the establishment of the plan. A defined benefit plan can easily incorporate the prior years of service into the defined benefit formula. If the plan is established in the current year, an owner who is also an employee can be credited for all of his years of service since the inception of the company. Granting **credit for prior service** must be nondiscriminatory, but in any case may benefit an older owner employer who does not have many long-term employees. The benefit of giving oneself credit for prior years of service may outweigh the additional cost of giving the other short-term employees' credit.

Example 4.23

Darcy started Dirty Day Car Wash 12 years ago. Her company is finally profitable, and she would like to establish a defined benefit plan to benefit herself and her employees. The plan will provide the employees with a benefit equal to 1.5% x years of service x final salary. If Darcy elects when she establishes the plan to give credit for prior service, immediately Darcy's benefit would be based on 12 years of service; however, the plan must then count prior years of service for all employees. Alternatively, Darcy could choose not to count prior years of service in the calculation of the benefit, but then her benefit would only be calculated on years of service after the establishment of the defined benefit plan.

A defined contribution plan cannot grant credit for prior service.

Example 4.24

Washboard Industries, Inc. established a defined contribution plan today that provides for a 20% of compensation annual contribution to all of its employees. As a defined contribution plan, contributions can only be made to participants' accounts based on compensation for plan years after the establishment of the plan.[22]

Exhibit 4.14 | Credit for Prior Services

Plan Type	Credit for Prior Service
Defined Benefit & Cash Balance	Yes
Target Benefit & Money Purchase Pension Plan	No

Integration with Social Security - Permitted Disparity for Defined Benefit Plans

The Social Security system is intentionally designed to be discriminatory towards lower income workers. The system, which is discussed in detail in Chapter 11, replaces a higher percentage of income for lower income workers than for higher income workers.[23] Qualified plans have been able to provide higher benefits to higher paid workers to offset the structure of the Social Security system since the Revenue Act of 1942 through what is know as Social Security integration or permitted disparity.

Permitted disparity (often referred to as Social Security Integration) is a technique or method of allocating plan contributions or benefits to employees that provides higher contributions to those employees whose compensation is in excess of the Social Security wage base for the plan year. All qualified pension plans may utilize permitted disparity as a method of allocating benefits to plan participants.[24] Permitted disparity allows the qualified plan to consider the Social Security benefits that will be provided to plan participants in the calculation of the participant's accrual of benefit or contribution amount.

The two primary parts of the Social Security system are OASDI (Old Age Survivor Disability Insurance) and Medicare taxes. Both employers and employees each contribute to the system through FICA[25] payments that consist of 6.2 percent for OASDI and 1.45 percent for Medicare.[26] The OASDI portion of 6.2 percent applies to income up to the Social Security wage base ($142,800 for 2021), while the Medicare portion applies to all income with no limit. In effect, the Social Security system does not consider income that exceeds the wage base for purposes of retirement benefits. Therefore, an individual who earns $142,800 will be treated exactly the same as someone who earns $1,000,000 for

---

22. However, credit could be provided to employees for purposes of vesting.
23. This disparity is due to two factors: income over the wage base is not considered for purposes of benefits and income at the lower level is counted at a higher percentage through the PIA (primary insurance amount) calculation.
24. All qualified plans can make use of permitted disparity except ESOPs and CODAs.
25. FICA stands for Federal Insurance Contributions Act.
26. Beginning in 2013, there is an additional Medicare tax of 0.9 percent on all earned income above $200,000 for single taxpayers and $250,000 for taxpayers filing jointly.

purposes of retirement benefits and for purposes of the amount of income that is subject to the 6.2 percent OASDI tax.

Consider Employee A who earns $142,800 for 2021 and Employee B who earns $285,600 (twice the Social Security wage base). In this case, their employer will make a 6.2 percent contribution to the governmental retirement plan (OASDI) on 100 percent of Employee A's income and only a 3.1 percent contribution on Employee B's total income. Stated another way, the 6.2 percent contribution or payment applies to 100 percent of Employee A's income and only 50 percent of Employee B's income. Social Security taxes are only paid on earned income up to the wage base and Social Security benefits are only based on Social Security covered earnings. However, because of this disparity in treatment between lower and higher paid workers in the Social Security system, the IRC permits qualified plans to provide higher contributions or benefits to employees with income that exceeds the Social Security wage base.

The two methods of permitted disparity are the offset method and the excess method. Defined benefit plans can utilize the excess method or the offset method (both discussed below), while defined contribution plans are only permitted to utilize the excess method (see Chapter 5).

Excess Method – Defined Benefit Pension Plans

The excess method provides an increased percentage benefit, referred to as the excess benefit, to those plan participants whose earnings are in excess of an average of the Social Security wage bases over the 35 year period prior to the individual's Social Security Retirement Age. This average is called the covered compensation limit, which is $86,052 for 2020 and $91,764 for 2022.[27] The covered compensation limit can be found in an annual Revenue Ruling from the IRS.

The increased percentage benefit only applies to income that exceeds the covered compensation limit and is limited to the lesser of (1) 0.75 percent per year of service or (2) the benefit percentage for earnings below the covered compensation limit per year of service. This additional benefit only applies up to 35 years. Therefore, the maximum increase in benefits for compensation over the covered compensation limit is 26.25 percent, which is found by multiplying 0.75 percent by 35 years.

---

27. Revenue Ruling 2021-3. This year's revenue ruling does not include an amount for 2021 due to how the IRS calculates retirement age under the Social Security system. Any partial years for Social Security full retirement age are rounded up. For example, FRA for someone born in 1955 is 66 years and 2 months, which rounds to 67. The year 1955 plus 67 years equals the year 2022.

Example 4.25

Katy is a participant of Button World's defined benefit pension plan, earns $100,000 per year, and has been employed with Button World for 30 years. The base funding formula for Button World's defined benefit plan is 1% per year of service multiplied by final salary. Under this formula, Katy would have a benefit equal to $30,000 (1% x 30 x $100,000).

In addition, Button World also provides an additional benefit of 0.75% per year of service for income that exceeds the covered compensation limit. Assume for this problem (and simplicity) that the covered compensation limit is $90,000, Katy would be entitled to an additional benefit of $2,250 (0.75% x 30 x $10,000).[28] Therefore, by integrating the plan with Social Security, Katy receives $4,500 more during retirement than she would have received if the plan had not been integrated.

Offset Method – Defined Benefit Pension Plans

To provide an increased benefit to those individuals whose earnings are in excess of the covered compensation limit, the offset method applies a benefit formula to all earnings and then reduces the benefit on earnings below the covered compensation limit. It simply takes a different approach compared to the excess method, which provides additional benefits for earnings above the covered compensation limit. The reduction of the benefit is limited to the lesser of (1) 0.75 percent per year of service up to 35 years or (2) 50 percent of the overall benefit funding percentage per year of service.[29] As with the excess method, the total reduction is limited to 26.25 percent of the earnings below the covered compensation limit.

Example 4.26

Consider the same facts as above, except that Button World's defined benefit funding formula is 1.75 percent per year of service multiplied by final salary and includes an offset reduction that reduces the benefit for earnings below the covered compensation limit by 0.75 percent. In this case, Katy would receive a benefit equal to $32,250 [(1.75% x 30 x $100,000)-(0.75% x 30 x $90,000)].

Example 4.25 and **Example 4.26** were designed to illustrate that the same outcome could be reached whether the excess benefit method or the offset method was used. However, the important concept is that defined benefit plans can be structured in such a way as to provide higher benefits to those employees who have compensation above the Social Security wage base.

28. The actual number changes each year. This assumption simply makes the math a little easier to follow.
29. Treas. Reg. 1.401(l)-3: These regulations provide additional modifications to the reduction in benefits discussed above. For example, the 0.75% is adjusted to the extent that benefits are paid prior to Social Security age. In addition the 50% limitation is reduced by multiplying it by the fraction (not to exceed 1.0), the numerator of which is the employee's average annual compensation, and the denominator of which is the employee's final average compensation up to the offset level.

Example 4.27

Otis has worked for Ex-On for the last 30 years.[30] Ex-On's basic formula is 1.6% times years of service times final salary minus the Social Security offset. The Social Security offset amount equals 1.5% times years of service (up to a maximum of 33½ years) times the Social Security benefit. Otis's salary is $70,000 and he expects to receive $2,000 per month from Social Security. His benefit is as follows:

Benefit Formula: 1.6% x 30 years x $70,000 = $33,600

Less Social Security offset (1.5% x 30 years x $2,000 x 12 months) = $10,800

Annual pension benefit = $22,800

There are several reasons to justify permitted disparity or Social Security integration. The first is that employers pays half of FICA and being able to offset the benefits provided under Social Security allows employers to reduce part of the cost of offering a pension plan. This accommodation provides an incentive to establish and offer pension plans. In addition, permitted disparity allows for higher benefits for those higher paid workers, which is a method of attracting, retaining and rewarding key employees.

While integration can help employees and employers, it can add to the confusion of the value of the benefit to be received during retirement, specifically with defined benefit plans. Participants may believe that they are receiving a higher benefit and not realize that their pension is being offset by benefits provided under the Social Security system.

Exhibit 4.15 | Integration

Plan Type	Method of Integration
Defined Benefit & Cash Balance	Excess or Offset
Target Benefit & Money Purchase (and all other Defined Contribution Plans)	Excess Only

Commingled vs. Separate Individual Investment Accounts

Defined benefit pension plans use a commingled investment account, but send individual summaries to participants showing their accrued benefit to a certain date. Most defined contribution plans, including target benefit and money purchase pension plans, utilize separate, individual investment accounts and require that the individual participant invest his own retirement assets. In some cases in a defined contribution plan, the employer will direct the investments or hire an outside investment advisor to manage the investments, in which case the funds may be commingled.

---

30. Example is adapted from the ExxonMobile Pension Plan Formula detailed in the 2012 summary plan description.

Exhibit 4.16 | Commingled vs. Separate Accounts

Plan Type	Accounts
Defined Benefit & Cash Balance	Commingled
Target Benefit & Money Purchase (and all other Defined Contribution Plans)	Usually Separate

Exhibit 4.17 | Summary of Characteristics of Defined Benefit Pension Plans vs. Defined Contribution Pension Plans

Characteristic	Defined Benefit Plans	Defined Contribution Plans
Actuary (Annually)	Yes	No (Except Target Benefit at Inception)
Investment Risk Borne by	Employer	Employee
Treatment of Forfeitures	Must Reduce Plan Costs	Reduce Plan Costs or Allocate to Other Plan Participants
PBGC Insurance	Yes	No
Credit for Prior Service	Yes	No
Social Security Integration	Offset or Excess	Excess Only
Separate Investment Accounts	No - Commingled	Yes - Separate (Usually)

DEFINED BENEFIT PENSION PLANS

The various qualified retirement plans have been initially divided into pension and profit sharing type plans and further subdivided into defined benefit and defined contribution plans. Beyond the requirements and characteristics detailed above, the defined benefit pension plan is unique as compared to the other pension plans.

Establishing the Formulas for Benefits

To determine the retirement benefit provided by a defined benefit pension plan, first the plan funding and allocation formula must be established. The IRC offers several methods of calculating the participant's ultimate retirement benefit, but the most common benefit formulas are:

1. the flat amount formula
2. the flat percentage formula
3. the unit credit formula

Regardless of which formula is used, it is important to keep in mind that in order to receive the maximum benefit under a defined benefit pension plan, the employee must have at least 10 years of participation in the plan. If an employee has less than 10 years of participation in the plan, then the maximum benefit is determined by multiplying $230,000 (the 2021 maximum benefit permissible for defined benefit plans) by the employee's number of years of participation divided by 10.[31]

Example 4.28

Jonas has worked for Nicholas Toy Corporation for eight years. Nicholas Toy Corporation sponsors a defined benefit pension plan. The maximum benefit that Jonas is eligible to receive under the defined benefit pension plan is $230,000 x (8 years/10 years) or $184,000.

Example 4.29

Malik begins employment with Employer Alpha on January 1, Year 1, at the age of 58. Alpha maintains only a noncontributory defined benefit plan that provides for a straight life annuity beginning at age 65 and uses the calendar year for the plan year. Malik becomes a participant in Alpha's plan on January 1, Year 2, and works through December 31, Year 7, when Malik is age 65. Malik begins to receive benefits under the plan in Year 8. Malik's average compensation for the period of Malik's high-3 years of service is $40,000. Furthermore, Malik has only 7 years of service with Employer Alpha (Year 1-Year 7).

Because Malik has only 7 years of service with Alpha at the time he begins to receive benefits under the plan, the maximum permissible annual benefit payable with respect to Malik is $28,000 ($40,000 multiplied by 7/10).[32]

Flat Amount Formula

A defined benefit pension plan that provides its participants with a benefit calculated under the **flat amount formula** provides each participant with an equal dollar benefit at retirement. The formula provides an amount that each plan participant will receive at retirement, such as $250 per month. The formula is not based on years of service with the employer or the participant's salary. From the highest paid plan participant to the lowest paid plan participant, each participant will receive the same amount at retirement.

A plan that utilizes the flat amount formula protects the employer from having to provide increased benefits as salaries increase. Such a plan does not provide the participant with any incentive to attain additional years of service with the employer

☷ *Key Concepts*

1. What are the common funding allocation methods for a defined benefit plan?

2. How are participant accounts treated within a defined benefit plan?

3. Which age group benefits more from the establishment of a defined benefit plan?

because the benefit will not increase with any additional years of service beyond the minimum number required to receive the benefit. This formula is used more commonly in union plans and collective bargaining agreements.

An employer wishing to utilize a defined benefit plan to improve employee retention would generally not choose a flat amount formula. Also, highly paid employees, usually the persons selecting the qualified plan for the employer, are unlikely to choose a flat amount formula because, as a proportion of income,

---

31. IRC Section 415(b)(5). However, IRC Section 415(b)(4) states that such reduction is not required for total annual benefits that do not exceed $10,000.
32. Treas. Reg. §1.415(b)-1.

they would benefit less than the lesser paid employees. However, a flat amount formula may be used in combination with a unit credit formula or some other benefit formula.

Flat Percentage Formula

The **flat percentage formula** provides all plan participants with a benefit equal to a specific percentage of the participant's salary, usually the final salary or an average of the participant's highest salaries. The percentage remains the same throughout participation in the plan and does not increase based on additional years of service or age. The flat percentage formula will provide a plan participant with an increasing benefit as salary increases simply based on the fact that the benefit will be calculated based on the increased salary. Usually the participant must attain a required minimum number of years of service to be eligible to receive the benefit. This type of benefit formula is not widely used because it does not give credit for long service. However, the flat percentage formula can be used to provide benefits to older owners who are attempting to fund defined benefit plans with larger amounts of additional cash flow.

Unit Credit Formula

When a defined benefit plan utilizes both a participant's years of service and salary to determine the participant's accrued benefit, the plan is using a **unit credit formula**. Unit credit formulas provide a fixed percentage of a participant's salary multiplied by the number of years (the unit) the participant has been employed by the employer. Examples include two percent per year of service multiplied by the participant's annual compensation or 1.5 percent per year of service multiplied by the average of the participant's three highest annual consecutive salaries. A unit credit formula gives credit for both a participant's term of employment and salary in the awarding of the benefit. A participant without substantial years of employment will not accrue a benefit comparable to the participant's annual salary. Generally, a unit credit formula is more likely to retain employees than the flat amount formula or the flat percentage formula. The unit credit formula approach is widely used in defined benefit pension plans.

Example 4.30

CE Corporation uses a unit credit formula for calculation of benefits as follows:

2% x # of Years of Service x	The Average of the 3 Highest Consecutive Annual Salaries

Ray, Debra, Frank, and Marie are retiring this year. Each person's benefit is calculated below based on their years of service and compensation.

	Years of Service	Average of 3 Highest Years of Compensation	Annual Benefit	Wage Replacement Ratio
Ray	28	$100,000	$56,000	56%
Debra	30	$120,000	$72,000	60%
Frank	40	$150,000	$120,000	80%
Marie	33	$60,000	$39,600	66%

Exhibit 4.18 | Summary of Defined Benefit Plan Funding Formulas

Funding Formula	Benefit Calculation	Example	Comments
Flat Amount Formula	Flat amount per month	$250 per month	No incentive for participants to continue employment after attaining maximum flat amount
Flat Percentage Formula	Flat percentage based on compensation	10% of compensation per year at retirement	Incentive to increase compensation through raises but not to continue employment after attaining a desired benefit
Unit Credit Formula	Benefit determined on a combination of service and compensation	2% x years of service x average 3 highest consecutive years of pay	Incentive to attain additional years of service and additional compensation to increase ultimate benefit

Benefit Accrual

Defined benefit plans may use a flat amount, flat percentage, unit credit formula or a combination of these methods in structuring the benefit to participants. However, ERISA and the IRC provide for three primary methods of benefit accrual for defined benefit plans to ensure against what is referred to as **back loading**.

Back loading is a practice of delaying the accrual of benefits until late in someone's career so that, if they were to leave the company, they would forfeit all or a large portion of their benefits. Consider **Example 4.31**.

Example 4.31

BackLoad Inc. sponsors a defined benefit plan. Assume that the earliest someone could enter the plan is age 21, normal retirement is age 65 and the benefit accrual rate is as follows:

Years of Service (YOS)	Benefit Accrual
Age 21 through 60	0.1% x YOS
Age 61 through 65	15% x YOS

In this example, an employee who worked for 40 years and terminated would accrue a benefit of just four percent (0.1% times 40 years), whereas if that employee worked five more years, the benefit would be 79 percent. This is an example of extreme back loading.

The three permitted benefit accrual methods provided for in the IRC are:
1. 3 Percent Method
2. $133\frac{1}{3}$ Percent Rule
3. Fractional Rule

All defined benefit plans, other than excluded 412(e) plans, must satisfy one of the above accrual methods.

3-Percent Method

A plan will satisfy the 3-percent method if the accrued benefit to which each participant is entitled upon the participant's separation from the service is at least three percent of the normal retirement benefit to which the participant would be entitled if he or she commenced participation at the earliest possible entry age under the plan and served continuously until the earlier of age 65 or the normal retirement age specified under the plan, multiplied by the number of years (not in excess of $33\frac{1}{3}$) of participation in the plan.

This rule means that at any point a participant separates from service, the participant should receive a benefit that is at least three percent per year of participation times the full benefit assuming that the participant entered the plan at the earliest point and left at normal retirement.

Example 4.32

X corporation's defined benefit plan provides an annual retirement benefit, commencing at age 65, of 2% of the average of the three highest consecutive years of compensation (AC) for each year of service (YOS) in the Plan (not to exceed 30). As a condition of participation, the plan requires that an employee should have attained age 21 and has one year of service. Does the plan formula satisfy the "3% rule?"

Answer:
For a plan to satisfy the 3% method, as of the end of each year, the employee's accrued benefit should equal to 3% x YOS x normal retirement benefit (NRB), which is calculated as if the participant entered the plan at the earliest possible entry age and terminated from service as of the earlier of the plan's normal retirement age (which in this case is 65) or age 65.

In this case, at the end of the first year of participation, the participant would have accrued a benefit of two percent of AC. Under the three percent method, if the employee had entered the Plan at age 21 and terminated from service at age 65, the employee would have had 44 years of service. Based on that, the NRB provided by the Plan is two percent of AC x 30 YOS = 60% of AC.[33]

---

33. Note that years in excess of the maximum 30 years are ignored because the plan benefit limits benefit accrual to 30 years.

At the end of year 1, the participant's accrued benefit should be at least as great as 3% x 1 x 60% of AAC = 1.8% of AC. At the end of year 1, the participant's accrued benefit (2% of AAC) is greater than what is required under the three percent method (1.8% of AC). The participant's accrued benefit would exceed the accrued benefit required under the three percent method for all other years. For example, in Year 5, the participant's accrued benefit would be 10 percent of AC. Under the three percent rule, the participant would be required to have an accrued benefit that is at least as great as 3% x 5 x (60% of AC)= 9% of AC. Therefore, the Plan accruals comply with the "3% method."

$133^1/_3$ Percent Rule

A defined benefit plan satisfies the requirements of the $133\,^1\!/_3$ rule if the accrued benefit payable at the normal retirement age is equal to the normal retirement benefit and the annual rate at which any participant can accrue the retirement benefits payable at normal retirement age under the plan for any later plan year is not more than $133\,^1\!/_3$ percent of the annual rate at which the participant can accrue benefits for any prior plan year.

Example 4.33

Y corporation's defined benefit plan provides an annual retirement benefit based on years of participation and AC. The plan provides that a participant will accrue his benefits as follows:

- 2% of AC for the first 15 years of participation
- 3% of AC for the next 15 years of participation

The Normal Retirement Benefit payable at age 65 will be equal to the accrued benefit calculated for the participant based on the accrual rates provided above. Does the plan formula satisfy the "$133\,^1\!/_3$ percent" rule?

Answer:

For the plan to comply with the $133\,^1\!/_3$ percent rule, a subsequent year's accrual cannot exceed $133\,^1\!/_3$ percent of a prior year's accrual. Because 3% is 1.5 times 2%, the plan does not pass the $133\,^1\!/_3$ percent rule. If however the first accrual rate was 1.5% and the second accrual rate was 2%, then the plan would meet the $133\,^1\!/_3$ percent rule.

Fractional Rule

A defined benefit plan satisfies the Fractional Rule if the accrued benefit to which any participant is entitled upon separation from the service is not less than a fraction of the annual benefit commencing at normal retirement age to which he or she would be entitled under the plan as in effect on the date of separation if the participant continued to earn annually until normal retirement age the same rate of compensation upon which the participant's normal retirement benefit would be computed under the plan, determined as if the participant had attained normal retirement age on the date on which any such determination is made. The fraction cannot exceed 1.

This rule is satisfied if the benefit is proportional to the years of participation relative to the full benefit that would have been received if the participant had remained in service until normal retirement.

Example 4.34

ABC defined benefit plan provides for a Normal Retirement Benefit of 60% of high-3 consecutive years' average compensation (AC) payable in the form of a life annuity at the Plan's NRA of 65. The Plan provides that the participant's Accrued Benefit will be based on the fractional rule. Employee A commences participation in the Plan at age 35 and separates from service at age 50. Assume his AC is $40,000. What is the amount of A's accrued benefit?

Answer:
Benefit at NRA = 60%
Years of participation 15 (50 – 35)
Years of participation until NRA 30 (65 – 35)
Accrued benefit = 60% benefit x 15/30 x $40,000 = $12,000

Commingled Accounts

Even though a participant in a defined benefit pension plan may have a calculated accrued benefit, a defined benefit pension plan does not have separate accounts for each participant. All of the assets of a defined benefit plan are managed as a group, and it is impossible to segregate any individual participant's funds. Benefits are simply paid from the pool of assets.

Younger/Older

A defined benefit pension plan is generally considered to benefit older participants because at the creation of the plan, the largest percentage of the overall contribution to the plan will often be attributable to the older participant(s). Older employees entering the plan require higher accrued benefits because of fewer compounding periods to retirement.

Eligibility/Coverage/Vesting

Defined benefit plans follow the eligibility, coverage, and vesting rules described in Chapter 3.

Distributions

Distributions from defined benefit pension plans are subject to the rules for distributions from qualified plans described in Chapter 7.

CASH BALANCE PENSION PLANS

A **cash balance pension plan** is a defined benefit pension plan that shares many of the characteristics of defined contribution plans, but provides specific defined retirement benefits. From the participant's perspective, a cash balance pension plan is a qualified plan that consists of an individual account with guaranteed earnings attributable to the account balance. However, the account that the employee sees is merely a **hypothetical account** displaying hypothetical allocations and hypothetical earnings. The accounts are hypothetical because the cash balance pension plan assets are managed by the plan sponsor in the same manner as a defined benefit pension plan. This commingled account consists of the assets that will be used to fund the benefits promised to the plan participants on their account statements.

Because the cash balance pension plan is a defined benefit pension plan, it is subject to all of the requirements of defined benefit plans and pension plans. Most notably, the plan sponsor of a cash balance pension plan is subject to mandatory funding (the guarantee that the participant will have a benefit at retirement), insurance from PBGC, the investment risk of the plan's assets, and must obtain an annual actuarial valuation of the plan.

Contributions and Earnings

When a cash balance plan is established, the plan sponsor must develop a benefit formula. A cash balance formula typically includes two elements – a pay credit and an interest (or earnings) credit:

Pay credit – the plan specified amount that is contributed in the hypothetical account, which is generally stated as a percent of compensation. The pay credit will often be a fixed percent of compensation, such as four percent or five percent. However, the pay credit may also be different for different age groups, employee classifications, or by other methods. Pay credits may be designed to benefit older employees or higher paid employees or owners. However, benefits must be non-discriminatory. In addition, benefits can be integrated with Social Security.

Interest credit – the amount of earnings applied to the balance in the hypothetical account. The interest credit may be a fixed rate, such as three percent, or a variable rate tied to an index, such as the one-year Treasury bill rate. The formula for the interest credit can certainly be more complicated including a minimum interest rate combined with a variable component that is higher or lower than a specified rate by a specified number of basis points.[34]

The PPA 2006 provided new rules for cash balance plan interest credits. These rules, described in Treasury Regulation §1.411(b)(5)-1(d) (market rate of return) provide that a cash balance plan cannot provide an interest credit rate in excess of a "market rate of return." This term permits a cash balance plan to base the crediting rate on actual rates of return assuming diversification, the returns of a mutual fund assuming the returns are not more volatile than the market, certain fixed percentage rates, other fixed income rates, and combinations of permitted rates.[35]

Participants receive annual statements detailing the additions to the account during the year. The statement looks very much like that of a defined contribution plan in that it will have an opening balance and include the contributions during the year. The opening balance simply equals the ending value from the prior year. The contributions include the pay credit and the interest credit. The sum of the three will equal the ending value for the year. **Exhibit 4.19** provides an example of a cash balance plan statement.

---

34. One basis point is equal to 0.01%.
35. Applies to plan years that begin on or after January 1, 2017.

Exhibit 4.19 | Cash Balance Statement

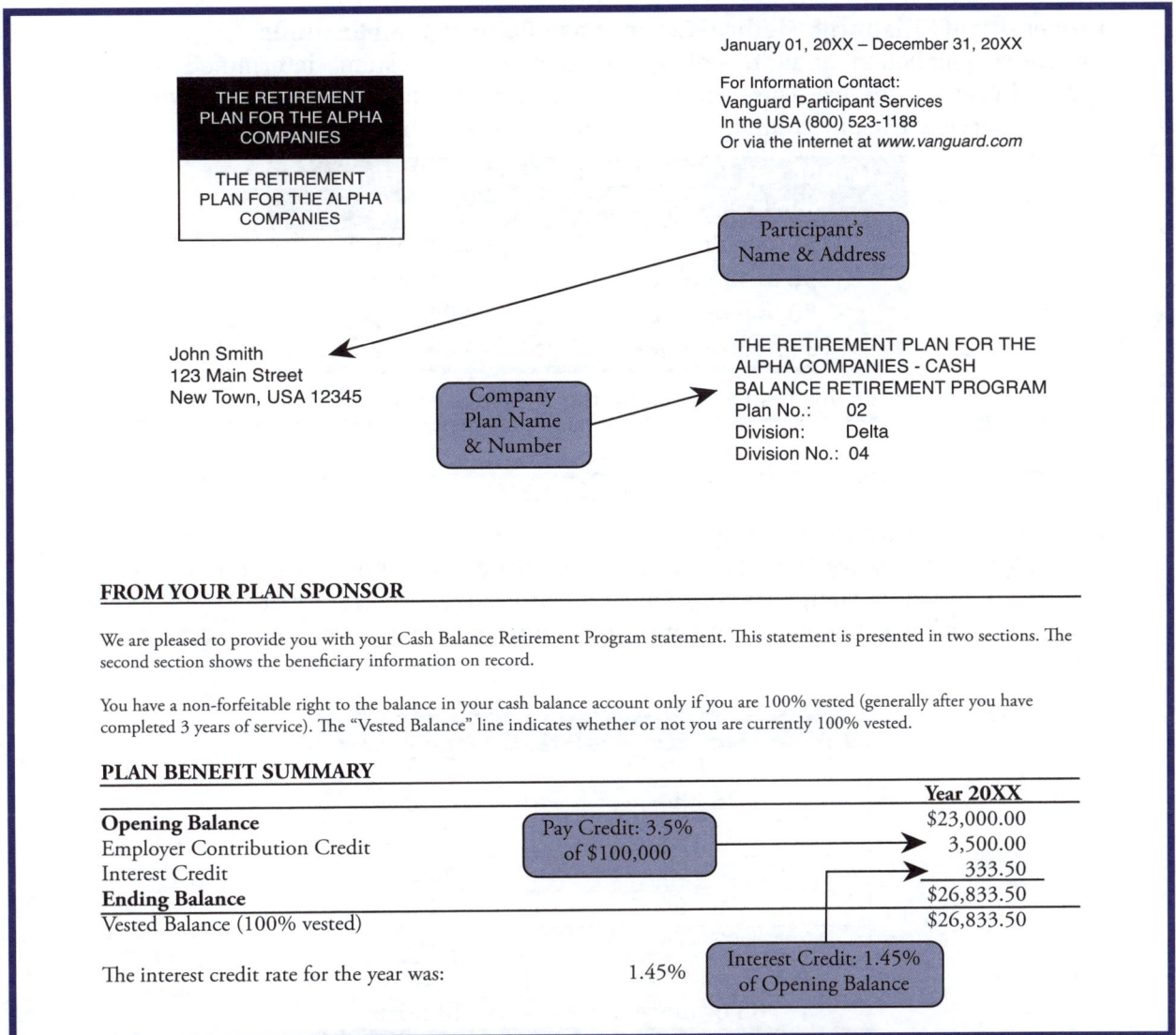

January 01, 20XX – December 31, 20XX

For Information Contact:
Vanguard Participant Services
In the USA (800) 523-1188
Or via the internet at *www.vanguard.com*

THE RETIREMENT
PLAN FOR THE ALPHA
COMPANIES

THE RETIREMENT
PLAN FOR THE ALPHA
COMPANIES

Participant's
Name & Address

John Smith
123 Main Street
New Town, USA 12345

Company
Plan Name
& Number

THE RETIREMENT PLAN FOR THE
ALPHA COMPANIES - CASH
BALANCE RETIREMENT PROGRAM
Plan No.:   02
Division: Delta
Division No.: 04

FROM YOUR PLAN SPONSOR

We are pleased to provide you with your Cash Balance Retirement Program statement. This statement is presented in two sections. The second section shows the beneficiary information on record.

You have a non-forfeitable right to the balance in your cash balance account only if you are 100% vested (generally after you have completed 3 years of service). The "Vested Balance" line indicates whether or not you are currently 100% vested.

PLAN BENEFIT SUMMARY

		Year 20XX
Opening Balance		$23,000.00
Employer Contribution Credit	Pay Credit: 3.5% of $100,000	3,500.00
Interest Credit		333.50
Ending Balance		$26,833.50
Vested Balance (100% vested)		$26,833.50

The interest credit rate for the year was: 1.45%

Interest Credit: 1.45% of Opening Balance

Example 4.35 through **Example 4.37** illustrate three different cash balance formulas from actual plans. These examples should help demonstrate how companies might implement a cash balance plan.

Example 4.35

Glatfelter Cash Balance Plan SPD Example[36]
The Glatfelter pay credit (contribution credit) equals 5.5 percent of pay contributed on a monthly basis. The interest credit is based on the Moody's Aa nominal bond yield, also credited monthly.

---

36. Glatfelter SPD Glatfelter Retirement Plan for Salaried Employees Cash Balance Benefit Effective January 1, 2014.

Example 4.36

University of Pittsburgh Medical Center Cash Balance Plan Example[37]

The retirement benefit under this plan is based on a "point system" determined by adding age and years of service. The formula benefits older participants and those with more years of service. The pay credit is based on the following table:

If Your Age Plus Benefit Service Equals:	Annual Retirement Credit
Less than 36 points	2.5% of pay
36 to 49 points	3.0% of pay
50 to 69 points	4.0% of pay
70 or more points	5.0% of pay

The interest credit for this plan is based on the 30-year Treasury bond rate.

Example 4.37

KPMG Cash Balance Plan Example[38]

The KPMG cash balance formula consists of service credits and interest credits. Service credits are based on compensation, age, and service. Interest credits are based on each individual's balance in their account at the beginning of each plan year. The service credits are as follows:

Age Plus Years of Service	Service Credit
Less than 25	2.25%
25 - 34	2.50%
35 - 44	3.25%
45 - 54	4.25%
55 - 64	5.50%
65 - 74	7.00%
75 - 84	9.25%
85 or more	11.50%

Assume Reese is a five-year accountant at KPMG and is 27 years old. She would receive a service credit of 2.50% of her compensation because the sum of her age and years of service is 32. Seth, who has been with the firm for 27 years and turned 50 this year, would receive a service credit of 9.25% of his compensation into the plan.

Interest credits for the plan are based on the average yield on the 30-year Treasury bond.

---

37. UPMC Cash Balance Plan (Urban) Summary Plan Description 2019.
38. KPMG SPD May 1, 2016.

Practical Considerations

Cash balance plans are often found in large companies and may have been established to provide a pension benefit that is easier to communicate to employees and easier to manage costs of the plan versus a traditional defined benefit plan. These plans are often found in large publicly traded companies and may be a result of a company converting its traditional defined benefit plan to a plan with a cash balance formula.

Small businesses may establish a cash balance plan, often in conjunction with a profit sharing plan such that the combination of plans benefits the owners of the business at a significantly higher rate than for the rank-and-file employees. While the plans require relatively advanced actuarial testing, it is important to know that these types of plans can provide significantly higher benefits than what is permitted under the IRC 415(c) limits.[39]

When a cash balance pension plan is established, the plan sponsor develops a formula to fund the cash balance hypothetical allocation. Usually, the promised funding is based on a percentage of a participant's salary, such as four percent of salary, and earnings on the contributions are guaranteed to be at least a fixed amount, such as two percent earnings per year, or may be tied to a variable rate, such as the U.S Treasury Bond rate. The contributions may be integrated with Social Security to produce a higher benefit percentage to those participants who earn a salary above the Social Security wage base or may be based on a combination of age and years of service – thus rewarding participants for longer service.

In any case, participants receive a statement each year detailing the additions to their account, which are equal to the promised contribution and the promised earnings for the plan year. This statement communicates the participant's benefit to the employee in an understandable format, but this account statement only portrays a hypothetical account. The value detailed to the participant is the benefit that will be payable to the participant based on the funding formula set forth in the plan document by the plan sponsor but not until the participant's retirement.

The plan sponsor does not fund a cash balance pension plan with the full benefit as detailed by the participant's hypothetical account; instead, the plan sponsor will fund the cash balance pension plan with the actuarial equivalent of the benefit (allocations plus earnings) that will be payable from the cash balance pension plan to the participant at the participant's normal retirement age. This actuarial equivalent is calculated by an actuary (whose services are required annually) considering mortality, disability, turnover, and salary growth.

Like all defined benefit plans, the plan sponsor is responsible for the investment performance of the plan's assets and earnings. The benefit, as determined under the plan document, will be payable to the participant at retirement regardless of the plan's true earnings, whether greater than or less than the benefit provided by the plan formula.

---

39. Treas. Reg. §1.401(a)(4)-9(b)(2)(v)(D)(3) discusses non-discrimination rules for plan aggregation (two or more plans tested together) and provides that a plan is deemed to satisfy the minimum aggregate allocation gateway of this paragraph (b)(2)(v)(D) if the aggregate normal allocation rate for each NHCE is at least 7½ % of the NHCE's compensation within the meaning of §415(c)(3), measured over a period of time permitted under the definition of plan year compensation.

Quasi-Separate Accounts

A cash balance pension plan does not have a separate account for each participant even though the plan participant receives a statement detailing a separate account in his name. A cash balance pension plan consists of a commingled account that has a value equal to the actuarial equivalent of the present value of the expected future benefits that will be paid from the cash balance pension plan to the participants (the promised contribution and earnings).

Younger/Older

A cash balance pension plan is generally more beneficial for younger participants because the formula is generally based on the number of years the participant is employed by the plan sponsor with a guaranteed rate of return. Younger participants have more years of contributions and earnings than older participants. However, benefits under a cash balance plan can be structured such that older employees receive higher pay credits than younger employees.

Eligibility/Coverage/Vesting

The cash balance pension plan follows the rules and requirements for eligibility, coverage, and vesting required under the Pension Protection Act of 2006 and described in Chapter 3. Cash balance plans must use a 3-year cliff vesting formula or a vesting schedule that is at least as generous as a 3-year cliff formula.

Distributions

The available and required distribution options of qualified plans are discussed in Chapter 7, but of particular concern for lump-sum distributions from cash balance pension plans is the guaranteed interest rate used to determine the value of the participant's accrued lump-sum value. Under prior law, where the hypothetical earnings credit rate was greater than the interest rate required by ERISA (to calculate the lump-sum payment), the required payment to the participant was greater than provided under the plan benefit formula. As a result of the Pension Protection Act of 2006, however, this calculation discrepancy has been eliminated.

To determine the value of the lump-sum payment under prior law, first calculate the annuity that the participant would have received for continued employment through retirement using the interest rate provided under the plan document. This is the hypothetical account balance. Second, the present value of this annuity is then calculated utilizing the interest rates provided under ERISA, usually a rate tied to the 30-year Treasury rate. A number of courts concluded that the participant entitled to a lump-sum distribution must be paid the greater of the present value calculated under the ERISA rate or the hypothetical account balance. A cash balance pension plan with interest credits tied to the same rate provided by ERISA or with a rate lower than the ERISA rate would not experience a difference in the calculation value of the lump-sum distributions. But those cash balance pension plans that utilize a higher (more generous) guaranteed earnings rate credit under the above formula may be required to provide a lump-sum payment greater than the payment calculated under the plan document. This effect on the distribution is sometimes referred to as "interest rate whipsaw." The whipsaw results in terminating employees being paid amounts far in excess of their hypothetical account balance. This, of course, is detrimental to the plan and plan sponsor.

Under the PPA 2006, for distributions after August 17, 2006 (the date of enactment), no distribution in excess of a participant's hypothetical account balance is required.

CASE STUDY 4.1

In *Cooper v. IBM Personal Pension Plan*, a class action suit was filed against the IBM Personal Pension Plan ("IBM Plan").[1] Various plaintiffs claimed that IBM's defined benefit plan violated the age discrimination prohibitions of ERISA.[2] Plan amendments were made that converted the IBM defined benefit plan to a cash balance plan. The court calculated that a 49-year-old employee with 20 years of service would accrue $8,093 in age-65 annuity benefits in 2000 under that employer's cash balance plan, an additional $622 in benefits in 2001, and $282 per year in benefits by 2010.[3] Thus, the employee's benefit accrual is reduced for each year he ages.

The court acknowledged that a defined benefit plan violates ERISA's age discrimination prohibition if "an employee's benefit accrual is ceased, or the rate of an employee's benefit accrual is reduced, because of the attainment of any age."[4] The court explained that the theory that cash balance plans violate this provision is based on a series of premises. The court said that when evaluating defined benefit plans, ERISA directs that accrued benefits are calculated in terms of "an annual benefit commencing at normal retirement age," or in other words, in terms of a traditional annuity beginning at age 65.[5] In order to apply this definition to a cash balance plan, the current hypothetical balance in an employee's account must be translated into the equivalent age-65 annuity that those sums could purchase. The court reasoned that age discrimination arises because money contributed to a younger employee will be worth more (when expressed as an annuity starting at age 65) than the same amount of money contributed to an older employee because the contribution to the younger employee will have more years to accrue interest before normal retirement age.[6] Stated another way, if any employer contributes the same amount to an employee's cash balance account every year, the value of those annual benefits when expressed as an annuity starting at age 65 decreases with every passing year.[7] This inevitably results in a declining benefit accrual rate as an employee ages, an apparent violation of ERISA.

The court ultimately ruled that IBM's cash balance plan conversion was a violation of ERISA because it impermissibly discriminated against participants based on age. Under the ruling of the case, all cash balance plans per se violate the ERISA age discrimination provision by virtue of their design. Interestingly, there are other cases in the federal case law that lead to a different result. See for example *Eaton v. Onan Corp.*, 117 F.Supp.2d 812, 817 (S.D.Ind.2000)(finding cash balance plan did not violate ERISA); see also *Campbell v. BankBoston*, N.A., 327 F.3d 1, 9-10 (1st Cir. 2003) (noting problems with the age discrimination theory to attack cash balance plans).

1. *Cooper v. IBM Personal Pension Plan*, 274 F.Supp.2d 1010 (S.D.Ill. July 31, 2003).
2. Employee Retirement Income Security Act, 29 U.S.C. Sections 1001-1461.
3. *Cooper*, 274 F.Supp.2d at 1021-22.
4. 29 U.S.C. §1054(b)(1)(H)(i). See also *Cooper*, 274 F.Supp.2d 1010, 1021-22.
5. 29 U.S.C. §1002(23)(A).
6. *Cooper*, 274 F.Supp.2d at 1021.
7. *Cooper*, 274 F.Supp.2d at 1021-22.

Conversions to a Cash Balance Plan

A cash balance "conversion" occurs when an employer changes from a traditional defined benefit pension plan into a cash balance plan. Current law does not prevent companies from converting to cash balance plans. The law does prevent an employer from taking away or reducing the value of a pension benefit that has already been earned by a worker, whether or not there is a cash balance conversion.[40] This law is referred to as the anti-cutback rule and prohibits an employer from amending a plan such that employees loose benefits accrued to date or benefits are reduced. A cash balance plan conversion has no effect on current retirees.

During the 1990s, a number of companies converted their defined benefit plans into cash balance plans, prompting charges from older workers that the change violated age-discrimination laws. The Treasury proposed regulations in December 2002 to address this issue. The proposed regulations provided guidance under the statutory age-discrimination rules for all qualified plans, including cash balance pension plans. The proposed regulations set forth specific conditions under which cash balance plans and cash balance conversions would not be considered to violate these age-discrimination rules. Thousands of comment letters were submitted on the proposed regulations, including comments from older and longer-service employees who stated that they had been adversely affected by cash balance conversions. Other comments set forth employer concerns that the regulations would create issues for certain traditional defined benefit plans that had not previously been considered age-discriminatory.

Section 205 of the Consolidated Appropriations Act, 2004, Pub. L. 108-199, eliminated funding to implement the proposed age-discrimination regulations or any regulations reaching similar results. Additionally, the Act required the Secretary of the Treasury propose legislation providing transition relief for older and longer-service participants affected by cash balance conversions. In response, the Treasury set forth a proposal addressing cash balance plans and conversions to cash balance plans. The legislative proposal would require companies converting to cash balance plans to protect current employees through a five-year "hold harmless" period and would prohibit any benefit wear-away. The proposal also would provide rules under which cash balance formulas would not be considered age-discriminatory. The proposal would eliminate the "whipsaw" effect, which acts as a cap on the interest credits that cash balance plans can provide to workers. This would permit companies to give higher interest credits, allowing larger retirement accumulations for workers.[41] The proposal would provide similar rules for other types of hybrid plans and hybrid plan conversions.[42]

In July of 2004, the Treasury withdrew the proposed age-discrimination regulations issued in December 2002 to provide Congress an opportunity to review and consider the Administration's legislative proposal and to address cash balance and other hybrid plan issues through legislation. The PPA 2006 sets forth the circumstances under which hybrid plans can avoid discrimination claims. In addition, the PPA 2006 also sets forth the standards for conversions from defined benefit plans to hybrid plans. The new provisions apply to hybrid plan conversions or hybrid plans adopted after June 29, 2005. Under the PPA 2006, a hybrid plan must meet three main requirements.

40.https://www.irs.gov/retirement-plans/plan-participant-employee/retirement-topics-employer-converts-an-existing-retirement-plan-to-another-type-of-plan.

41.http://www.ustreas.gov/press/releases/js1132.htm.

42.http://www.irs.gov/irb/2004-27_IRB/index.html.

The first requirement is that a participant's accrued benefit, as determined as of any date under the terms of the plan, would be equal to or greater than that of any similarly situated, younger participant. For this purpose, an individual is similarly situated to a participant if the individual and the participant are (and always have been) identical in every respect (including period of service, compensation, position, date of hire, work history, and any other respect) except for age.

The second requirement is that the interest rate used to determine the interest credit on the account balance in the hybrid plan must not be greater than a market rate of return, to be determined under regulations to be issued.

The third requirement is that for plan years beginning after 2007, the hybrid plan must provide 100 percent vesting after three years of service.

The PPA 2006 also addresses the "whipsaw" effect by providing that the distribution of a participant's hypothetical cash balance account is sufficient to satisfy the participant's benefit entitlement from distributions after the date of enactment. Thus, employers are no longer penalized for using a higher interest credit.

> ### ✏ *Quick Quiz 4.4*
>
> 1. Participants in a cash balance pension plan have separate accounts.
>   a. True
>   b. False
>
> 2. The establishment of a cash balance pension plan generally benefits the younger employees more than the older employees.
>   a. True
>   b. False
>
> 3. A cash balance plan can be structured to benefit owners and higher compensated employees under certain circumstances.
>   a. True
>   b. False
>
> False, True, True.

Pension Equity Plans

Pension equity plans (PEP) are a type of hybrid plan similar to a cash balance plan. These plans have not received the attention of cash balance plans and are certainly less popular. However, they become more popular when RJR Nabisco implemented one in 1993 recognizing that its work force had become more mobile and it wanted to attract more experienced employees that would not benefit as much under a traditional defined benefit plan.

Two important distinctions of pension equity plans compared to cash balance plans are the salary used as part of the benefit and interest credits. The final lump-sum benefit for a PEP is based on a final average salary, whereas cash balance plan pay credits are effectively career average since they are credited each year. The second issue is that PEPs do not typically provide for interest credits prior to termination. Rather, the benefit is structured in such a way that it references years of service and final pay. Both types of plans define the benefits in terms of lump-sum benefits.

Example 4.38

Colin is a participant in the Davidson plan and retires after 30 years of service. The plan provides for a benefit equal to 5 percent per year of service multiplied by the final pay average. If Colin's final pay was $100,000, then the lump-sum benefit would be equal to 150 percent or $150,000.

Similar to cash balance plans, PEPs can provide more complicated benefit formulas that provide higher benefits to those workers with a greater number of years of participation.

Example 4.39

Jackie works for Pearson and is a participant in the Pearson Pension Equity Plan. It provides for the following benefits:

Age	PEP Percentage
Under 30	3%
30 - 39	4%
40 - 49	5%
50 - 59	6%
60 and over	8%

Jackie started working at age 40 and continued until last year when she retired at age 65. Her benefit is determined as follows:

Age	Benefit				
Under 30	3%	x	0 years	=	0%
30 - 39	4%	x	0 years	=	0%
40 - 49	5%	x	10 years	=	50%
50 - 59	6%	x	10 years	=	60%
60 and over	8%	x	5 years	=	40%
	Total				**150%**

Benefit = PEP Percentage x Years of Service

Assuming Jackie's final average salary is $60,000, her lump-sum benefit is $90,000 or 150 percent of her final average salary.

Example 4.40

Colie works for Caterpillar, Inc., which offers a Pension Equity Plan. The PEP formula produces a single lump sum benefit based on salary, years and months of Credited Service. The lump sum benefit is equal to the Final Average Monthly Earnings (FAME), multiplied by 12 to obtain an annual amount, multiplied by the sum of the percentages determined below based on Credited Service.

Credited Service	Benefit Accrual
Up to 5 years	4% per year of corresponding Credited Service x FAME x 12, plus
More than 5, but less than 10 years	5% per year of corresponding Credited Service x FAME x 12, plus
More than 10, but less than 15 years	7% per year of corresponding Credited Service x FAME x 12, plus
More than 15, but less than 20 years	8% per year of corresponding Credited Service x FAME x 12, plus
More than 20	9% per year of corresponding Credited Service x FAME x 12, plus

> Assuming Colie's FAME when she retires is $5,000 and she has 22 years of service, her lump sum PEP benefit is $5,000 x 12 x 138% = $82,800. The 138% is calculated by adding the benefit accrual for each period of vesting (138% = 20% + 25% + 35% + 40% + 18%). For example, the benefit accrual for more than 10 years equals 35% (7% x 5 years).

These examples should help to clarify how PEPs are presented to employees and how they differ from cash balance plans and traditional defined benefit plans.

MONEY PURCHASE PENSION PLANS

A **money purchase pension plan** is a defined contribution pension plan that provides for a contribution to the plan each year of a fixed percentage of the employees' compensation. Specifically, the employer promises to make a contribution to the plan for the plan year, but the employer is not required to guarantee a specific retirement benefit. The limitations and characteristics of money purchase pension plans are discussed below.

Contribution Limit

As a defined contribution plan, money purchase pension plans are limited in the amount of contributions that an employer can make on behalf of the participants. An employer cannot deduct contributions to the plan in excess of 25 percent of the employer's total covered compensation paid. As discussed in Chapter 3, a defined contribution plan is limited in the contribution to the plan each year on behalf of each participant to the lesser of 100 percent of the participant's compensation or $58,000 for 2021. This limit is an aggregate per person limit for all contributions to defined contribution plans for the year for that employer and includes employer contributions, employee contributions, and any forfeitures allocated to a participant's account for the year.

The funding formula of the money purchase pension plan is stated in the plan document. A common funding formula is a percentage of a participant's salary, similar to the cash balance pension plan but without the promise of a guaranteed earnings rate. For example, a money purchase pension plan might promise a contribution of 10 percent of each participant's salary per year. The plan may be integrated with Social Security (as detailed in Chapter 5) or otherwise designed in such a way to provide disproportionate contributions to a certain class of participants, perhaps based on a combination of age and years of service.

> :≡ *Key Concepts*
>
> 1. What is the contribution percentage limitation for money purchase pension plans?
>
> 2. How are participant accounts treated in money purchase pension plans?
>
> 3. At the establishment of a money purchase pension plan, which age group generally benefits the most?
>
> 4. Describe the impact of EGTRRA 2001 on money purchase pension plans.

Separate Accounts

When the employer makes a contribution on behalf of each participant to a money purchase pension plan, the contribution is made to a separate account on behalf of each participant. As such, participants know exactly the value of their benefit from the stated value on the account statement – allowing the plan benefits to be communicated to the plan participants more easily than with a defined benefit pension plan.

The plan sponsor can choose to manage the funds of each participant but usually does not do so. The plan usually requires that participants manage their own investments. In either case, employees retain their own separate account.

Younger/Older

A money purchase pension plan, like all defined contribution plans, benefits younger participants more than older participants because of the increased number of contributions and compounding periods. The younger participants will have the benefit of receiving more contributions to the account over time and the benefit of the tax-deferred growth. An older participant simply has fewer years to accumulate assets within the retirement plan.

Impact of the Economic Growth and Tax Relief Reconciliation Act of 2001 (EGTRRA 2001)

After the enactment of EGTRRA 2001, most employers interested in establishing a defined contribution plan would establish a profit sharing plan instead of a money purchase pension plan. Before EGTRRA 2001, employers could deduct contributions to money purchase pension plans up to 25 percent of the total employer's compensation paid but could only deduct contributions to profit sharing plans up to 15 percent of the total employer's compensation paid. Under these old limits, some employers (especially single practitioner professionals) would establish two plans, a money purchase pension plan and a profit sharing plan. Commonly, the employer would set the funding limit of the money purchase pension plan at 10 percent (the mandatory component) and would have discretionary contributions to the profit sharing plan up to 15 percent for a total 25 percent limit. This combination of the pension plan and the profit sharing plan is known as a **Tandem Plan** and would provide the employer with the maximum deductibility for contributions to employee retirement plans with the greatest flexibility in the funding for the plans. With the Tandem plan, the employer was only required to make a 10 percent contribution to the money purchase pension plan each year, but because the profit sharing plan contributions are discretionary, the employers' contributions to the profit sharing plan only have to be "substantial and recurring" allowing the employer to forgo contributions in certain years (discussed fully in Chapter 5).

> ### ☑ *Quick Quiz 4.5*
>
> 1. A plan sponsor cannot deduct more than 25 percent of their covered compensation as a contribution to a money purchase pension plan.
>   a. True
>   b. False
>
> 2. Each participant has a separate account in a money purchase pension plan.
>   a. True
>   b. False
>
> 3. The establishment of a money purchase pension plan generally benefits older employees more than younger employees.
>   a. True
>   b. False
>
> 4. EGTRRA 2001 increased the popularity of money purchase pension plans.
>   a. True
>   b. False
>
> True, True, False, False.

EGTRRA 2001 increased the contribution limit for profit sharing plans to 25 percent and created an equal deduction limit for both defined contribution pension and profit sharing plans of 25 percent. Employers now wishing to establish a defined contribution plan will likely establish a profit sharing plan because they will be able to deduct the maximum amount in any given year (25 percent of employer compensation), but the contribution will not be mandatory as is the case of money purchase pension plans. Consequently, some employers with money purchase pension plans converted their plans to profit sharing plans (or terminated their money purchase pension plans) to avoid the future mandatory funding requirements.

Many of EGTRRA 2001's provisions were scheduled to sunset for tax years beginning after 2010. However, the Pension Protection Act of 2006 has made the provisions of EGTRRA 2001 permanent.

Eligibility/Coverage/Vesting

The money purchase pension plan is subject to all of the eligibility, coverage, and vesting rules applicable to defined contribution pension plans, which are described in Chapter 3. Note that because money purchase pension plans are a type of defined contribution plan, they are subject to the shorter vesting requirements for defined contribution plans under the PPA 2006. In other words, employer contributions to a money purchase pension plan must vest at least as rapidly as a 2-to-6-year graduated or 3-year cliff vesting schedule.

Distributions

Chapter 7 describes the distribution options, availability, and requirements for all qualified plans.

TARGET BENEFIT PENSION PLANS

A special type of money purchase pension plan, known as a **target benefit pension plan**, determines the contribution to the participant's account based on the benefit that will be paid from the plan at the participant's retirement. The plan formula may be written to provide a contribution to each participant during the plan year that is actuarially equivalent to the present value of the benefit at the participant's retirement. An actuary is required at the establishment of the target benefit pension plan, but unlike a defined benefit plan or a cash balance pension plan, an actuary is not required on an annual basis. The actuary will create a funding formula for participants entering the plan at various ages. Once established, the funding formula is generally not recalculated for changes in assumptions. The target benefit pension plan considers the formula as the "target," the benefit the employer hopes the employee will have at retirement.

Instead of funding the plan with the amount necessary to attain the target and ensuring that the target is met, the employer promises a contribution to the participant's individual account based on the original actuarial assumptions. Once the contribution has been made, the participant is responsible for choosing investments. Like any defined contribution plan, the participant, at retirement, is entitled to the plan balance regardless of its value, be it greater than or less than the intended target benefit.

The actuarial equivalent contribution will vary from participant to participant because of age and salary differences. In fact, the contribution will be greatest for the oldest participants because the discounting period (contribution date to retirement date) is less than the discounting period for younger participants. Accordingly, target benefit pension plans are utilized to disproportionately benefit older participants because the target benefit funding formula will allocate a greater contribution to the older participants.

The target benefit pension plan is a form of money purchase pension plan; consequently, the target benefit pension plan is subject to all of the same contribution, eligibility, coverage, vesting, and distribution limitations as the money purchase pension plan.

Mainly due to the increase of the profit sharing deductibility limits to 25 percent under EGTRRA 2001, target benefit pension plans have lost some of their attractiveness. Instead, employers are establishing age-weighted profit sharing plans (see Chapter 5) so that the contributions to the plan each year are discretionary rather than mandatory but still favor older employees.

Example 4.41

Ken, a business owner, is age 50 and earns $290,000 per year. The company's target benefit plan has a benefit formula equal to 132.18391% of compensation reduced by 1/25th for each year of participation less than 25 years. Therefore, since Ken plans to retire at age 65, his contribution is reduced by 40% because he only has 15 years until retirement (15/25 = 60%). The plan also benefits Melissa, an employee age 25 earning $25,000 per year. Melissa has more than 25 years until retirement, so her contribution is not reduced. The first year contribution is determined as follows, assuming a normal retirement age of 65 and 8% interest:

	Ken	Melissa
Age	50	25
Compensation	$290,000	$25,000
Target Benefit	$230,000	$33,045.98
Actuarial Factor for Age	2.338	0.304
PV of Benefit	$537,740	$10,046
Factor	0.1075	0.0812
Theoretical Contribution	$57,807	$816
Annual Additions Limit (the lesser of 100% of payroll or $58,000)	$58,000	$25,000
Top-Heavy Minimum (3% of compensation)	$0	$0
Actual Contribution	57,807	$816
Contribution Rate	19.93%	3.26%
Percent of Contribution	98.61%	1.39%

The benefit for the business owner is 132.18391% x $290000 x (15 ÷ 25) = $230,000.
**The benefit for the employee is 132.18391% of $25,000 = $33,045.98.*

The plan permits the benefits to be principally contributed to Ken, the owner. The target benefit plan can still be used to reduce overall plan costs. However, as you will see in Chapter 5, profit sharing plans allow contributions up to 25% of covered compensation and discretionary funding. In some cases, age-based profit sharing plans and new comparability plans can produce similar results to the target benefit plan without the mandatory funding and compliance issues.

DISCUSSION QUESTIONS

SOLUTIONS to the discussion questions can be found exclusively within the chapter. Once you have completed an initial reading of the chapter, go back and highlight the answers to these questions.

1. Explain the mandatory funding requirement and its impact on defined contribution plans and defined benefit plans.

2. Define "in-service withdrawal."

3. Explain the investment limitations for pension plans.

4. Compare the investment risk of defined contribution plans to the investment risk of defined benefit plans.

5. Compare the treatment of forfeitures within defined benefit plans and defined contribution plans.

6. What is the PBGC and what plans are covered by the PBGC?

7. How is a participant's accrued benefits calculated for defined benefit and defined contribution plans?

8. List and describe the common funding formulas of a defined benefit plan.

9. How are a participant's accrued benefits managed in defined benefit plans?

10. Which age group generally benefits the most from the establishment of a defined benefit pension plan?

11. List the advantages of cash balance pension plans.

12. Which age group generally benefits the most from the establishment of a cash balance pension plan?

13. What is the contribution limit for money purchase pension plans?

14. How are participant account balances managed in money purchase pension plans?

15. Which age group generally benefits the most from the establishment of a money purchase pension plan?

16. What impact did EGTRRA 2001 have on money purchase pension plans?

17. List the characteristics of a target benefit pension plan.

MULTIPLE CHOICE PROBLEMS

A sample of multiple choice problems is provided below. Additional multiple choice problems are available at money-education.com by accessing the Student Practice Portal.

1. Which of the following is not a characteristic of pension plans?
    a. Mandatory funding.
    b. In-service withdrawals for employees under the age of 62.
    c. Limited investment in life insurance.
    d. A limit of 10 percent investment in the employer's securities.

2. Which one of the following statements is true for a defined benefit plan?
    a. A defined benefit plan generally favors older age entrants.
    b. The maximum retirement benefit payable from a defined benefit plan is the lesser of 100 percent of the participant's compensation or $230,000 for 2021.
    c. A defined benefit plan with 100 employees is required to pay PBGC insurance premiums.
    d. All of the above are true.

3. If a participant's accrued benefit from a qualified defined benefit pension plan is $2,000 per month, what is the maximum life insurance death benefit coverage that the plan can provide based on the 100 to 1 ratio test?
    a. $0.
    b. $2,400.
    c. $200,000.
    d. $240,000.

4. Which of the following statements regarding defined benefit plans is true?
    a. A defined benefit plan can allocate forfeitures to other plan participants.
    b. A defined benefit plan can use forfeitures to reduce future plan costs.
    c. A defined benefit plan cannot give credit for prior service.
    d. Each participant of a defined benefit plan has an individual account.

5. Which of the following is not a common defined benefit plan funding formula?
    a. Flat amount formula.
    b. Flat percentage formula.
    c. Unit credit formula.
    d. Excludable amount formula.

> **Additional multiple choice problems are available at money-education.com by accessing the Student Practice Portal. Access requires registration of the title using the unique code at the front of the book.**

QUICK QUIZ EXPLANATIONS

Quick Quiz 4.1

1. False. While a pension plan may request a funding waiver, such a waiver only postpones the employer's funding obligation. The funding waiver does not eliminate the funding needed for that particular year.
2. False. Prior to the SECURE Act, the statement was true. However, under the SECURE Act, in-service distributions can be made to an employee who has attained the age of 59½.
3. False. Only ten percent of a pension plan's assets may be invested in employer securities.

Quick Quiz 4.2

1. False. In a defined benefit pension plan, the employer bears the investment risk.
2. False. Defined benefit pension plans must use forfeitures to reduce plan costs. Defined contribution pension plans can use forfeitures to either reduce plan costs or the forfeitures can be allocated to the other remaining plan participants.
3. False. In the event that a defined benefit pension plan cannot pay the promised amount, the PBGC will pay the employee an amount based on (1) the form of the benefit as payable under the terminated plan, (2) the participant's age, and (3) any amounts the PBGC recovered from the employer in the case that the plan was underfunded. The PBGC benefit is not guaranteed to be equal to the amount of the benefit that would have been paid under the defined benefit pension plan.
4. True.

Quick Quiz 4.3

1. True.
2. False. Defined benefit plans do not maintain separate accounts for each participant. All of the assets of a defined benefit plan are managed as a group and it is impossible to segregate any individual participant's funds.
3. True.

Quick Quiz 4.4

1. False. Participants in a cash balance pension plan do not have separate accounts even though the plan participant receives a statement detailing a separate account in his name. Rather, the account balance on the statement is a hypothetical amount that has a value equal to the actuarial equivalent of the present value of the expected future benefit that will be paid to the participant.
2. True.
3. True.

QUICK QUIZ EXPLANATIONS

Quick Quiz 4.5

1. True.
2. True.
3. False. The establishment of a money purchase pension plan generally benefits younger employees because younger employees have the benefit of a greater number of contributions and compounding periods.
4. False. EGTRRA 2001 increased the popularity of profit sharing plans by increasing the contribution limit for profit sharing plans to 25 percent of the employer's total compensation paid.

Quick Quiz 4.6

1. False. A target benefit pension plan is a defined contribution pension plan, not a defined benefit pension plan. A target benefit pension plan is a special type of money purchase pension plan.
2. True.

5
PROFIT SHARING PLANS

LEARNING OBJECTIVES

1. Explain the basic purpose of profit sharing plans.*
2. Understand the primary differences between pension plans and profit sharing plans.*
3. Discuss the various methods of allocating profit sharing contributions to employee accounts including advantages and disadvantages of each method.*
4. Explain why Social Security integration is permitted and how to apply it to a profit sharing plan.*
5. Illustrate the impact of an age based formula on the allocation of contributions to a profit sharing plan.*
6. Describe the basic elements of a new comparability plan.*
7. Recommend an appropriate allocation method for a profit sharing plan based on a desired outcome.*
8. Describe a 401(k) plan and determine when it would be an appropriate retirement plan for a business.*
9. Explain the 401(k) deferral limits and how they impact the limits under IRC §415(c).*
10. Describe the differences between Roth accounts and Roth IRAs.
11. Describe the rules for and tax treatment of hardship distributions from 401(k) plans.

Ties to CFP Certification Learning Objectives

PROFIT SHARING PLANS

Profit Sharing Plans (7 Types)
Profit Sharing Plans
Stock Bonus Plans
Employee Stock Ownership Plans
401(k) Plans
Thrift Plans
Age-Based Profit Sharing Plans
New Comparability Plans

The term profit-sharing plan is defined in Treasury Regulation §1.401-1(b) as follows:

A **profit-sharing plan** is a plan established and maintained by an employer to provide for the participation in profits by employees or their beneficiaries. The plan must provide a definite predetermined formula for allocating the contributions made to the plan among the participants and for distributing the funds accumulated under the plan after a fixed number of years, the attainment of a stated age, or upon the prior occurrence of some event such as layoff, illness, disability, retirement, death, or severance of employment. A formula for allocating the contributions among the participants is definite if, for example, it provides for an allocation in proportion to the basic compensation of each participant. A plan (whether or not it contains a definite predetermined formula for determining the profits to be shared with the employees) does not qualify under Section 401(a) if the contributions to the plan are made at such times or in such amounts that the plan in operation discriminates in favor of officers, shareholders, persons whose principal duties consist in supervising the work of other employees, or highly compensated employees. For the rules with respect to discrimination, see §§1.401-3 and 1.401-4. A profit-sharing plan within the meaning of IRC §401 is primarily a plan of deferred compensation, but the amounts allocated to the account of a participant may also be used to provide for him or his family incidental life, accident, or health insurance.

The key points from this regulation are as follows:
- The purpose of the plan is to provide for participation in profits by employees and beneficiaries,
- The plan must have a predefined formula for contributions and distributions, and the plan cannot be discriminatory.

KNOW THE NUMBERS (2021)

Covered Compensation Limit	$290,000
Defined Contribution Maximum Limit	$58,000
401(k), SARSEP, 457, 403(b) Catch-Up	$6,500
401(k), SARSEP, 457, 403(b) Employee Deferral Limit	$19,500
Highly Compensated Employee	$130,000
Social Security Wage Base	$142,800

Exhibit 5.1 | Basic Differences Between Pension Plans and Profit-Sharing Plans

Characteristic	Pension Plan	Profit-Sharing Plan
Legal Promise of the Plan	To pay a pension at retirement	To defer compensation and thus tax deferral
Are in-service withdrawals permitted?	No*	Yes (after two years)
Is the plan subject to mandatory funding standards?	Yes	No
Percent of plan assets allowed to be invested in employer securities	10 percent	100 percent
Employer annual contribution limit of covered compensation	25 percent**	25 percent***

* Pension plans may allow in-service withdrawals for participants age 59½ or older as a result of the SECURE Act of 2019.
** The plan must meet minimum funding standards. Defined benefit pension plans may exceed 25%.
*** Increased from 15 percent by the EGTRRA 2001 for years after 2001.

Profit-sharing plans allow employers to make contributions to a qualified plan on behalf of employees of the company. A pure profit sharing plan is a noncontributory plan (employees do not contribute). As with all qualified plans, earnings within a profit sharing plan are not subject to income tax until the funds are distributed from the plan. Because profit sharing plans are not subject to mandatory funding requirements, contributions can be, and generally are, made on a discretionary basis from year to year. However, any contributions made to the plan must be made to participants' accounts on a nondiscriminatory basis. In other words, contributions cannot discriminate against the rank-and-file employees for the benefit of shareholders, officers, and highly compensated employees. That, however, does not mean that the contributions to rank-and-file employees have to be equal to the contributions to shareholders, officers, and highly compensated employees.

Although contributions must be made on a **nondiscriminatory** basis, there are types of profit sharing plans available that provide for larger allocations of contributions to shareholders, officers, and highly compensated employees. Among these types of plans are age-based profit sharing plans, integrated plans, and new comparability plans. The use of such plans is permitted by the IRS because they are within the anti-discrimination permissible limits.

Contributions and Deductions

Under prior law, qualified plans were required to be established by the end of the tax year (December 31 for calendar year entities). For tax years beginning after December 31, 2019 the SECURE (Setting Every Community Up for Retirement Enhancement) Act created additional flexibility for plan sponsors wishing to adopt a new qualified plan by allowing a plan established by the due date of the company's tax return (including extensions) for the year for which the employer will be contributing to the plan to be treated as having been established as of the last day of the taxable year. Contributions can be made to the plan as late as the due date of the company income tax return (including extensions). Tax returns for partnerships and S-corporations are due by the 15th day of the third month following the end of the tax year and can be extended by six months by properly filing for the extension by the due date of the tax return. C-corporation tax returns are due by the 15th day of the 4th month following the end of the tax year, and can be extended for up to six months (5 months for calendar year C-corporations until tax years after December 31, 2025, when it changes to 6 months) by properly filing for the extension by the due date of the tax return.

Example 5.1

Tasso partnership, a calendar year taxpayer, wants to establish a profit sharing plan for the current year. It must do so by September 15 of next year (partnership returns are due by the 15th day of the third month following the end of the tax year, and can be extended by six months). Contributions must be made no later than September 15 of next year assuming that it has properly filed all extensions for its tax return.[1]

---

1. IRC §401(b) as amended by the SECURE Act of 2019 and Revenue Ruling 66-144.

Contributions to profit sharing plans are generally discretionary but funding must be "substantial and recurring."[2] Contributions can be in the form of employer stock, but proxy voting rights remain with the plan trustee.[3] A plan that does not make any contributions for an extended period of time risks disqualification.

Although most contributions to profit sharing plans are made in cash and are related to profits of the company, there is no requirement that a company must contribute to the plan in a year in which it has profits nor is there a prohibition against contributions to the plan in years in which the company does not have profits.[4]

Profit sharing plans have an employer contribution limit of 25 percent of covered compensation.[5] Covered compensation is considered to be the compensation of all eligible employees.[6] Therefore, if an employer's total covered compensation paid to its employees is $1,000,000, then the largest income tax deduction that can be taken by the employer for contributions to the plan is $250,000 ($1,000,000 x 25%).[7]

In some cases, an employer may contribute more than the permitted 25 percent. In such a case, the employer will currently deduct the 25 percent (on the tax return) and may carry forward the contribution amount in excess of the 25 percent limit and deduct this amount in a future year. However, the amount carried forward when added to the contribution made for the future year cannot exceed 25 percent. Additionally, the employer is required to pay a 10 percent excise tax on the portion of the contribution that exceeds 25 percent of covered compensation for the current year.[8]

> **Quick Quiz 5.1**
>
> 1. A profit sharing plan is a plan established and maintained by an employer to provide participation in the profits of the company solely for officers and shareholders.
>   a. True
>   b. False
>
> 2. A pension plan can be funded using 100% employer securities.
>   a. True
>   b. False
>
> 3. Profit sharing plans must be established by, and contributions made by, the due date of the tax return including extensions for the tax year for which the employer wants to make contributions
>   a. True
>   b. False
>
> False, False, True.

Conceptually, the deduction limit simply creates a big bucket of money, which must then be distributed among the participating employees in a nondiscriminatory manner. There is not a requirement that all employees who receive the same salary receive the same contribution to their individual account so long as the allocation is nondiscriminatory and the contribution to each employee's account is not more than the maximum permitted for the year ($58,000 for 2021). The various methods to skew contributions toward certain employees in a nondiscriminatory manner are discussed below.

---

2. Treasury Regulation §1.401-1(b)(2). As a rule of thumb, contributions during 3 out of 5 years or 5 out of 10 years will usually gain IRS approval. See Revenue Ruling 80-144.

3. IRC §401(a)(22) provides that, to qualify under IRC §401, a defined contribution plan other than a profit-sharing plan (i.e., a stock bonus plan or a money purchase pension plan) must satisfy the pass-through voting requirements of IRC §409(e).

4. The determination of whether the plan under which any contributions are made is a profit sharing plan shall be made without regard to current or accumulated profits of the employer and without regard to whether the employer is a tax-exempt organization. IRC §401(a)(27).

5. IRC §404(a)(3).

6. The compensation considered cannot exceed the compensation limit for each covered employee - $290,000 for 2021.

7. The overall plan compensation limitation does not include employee 401(k) deferrals after EGTRRA 2001. However, prior to EGTRRA 2001, employee deferrals, such as in a 401(k) plan, counted against the plan limit.

8. IRC §4972(a).

Allocations

A profit sharing plan must provide a definite predetermined formula for allocating plan contributions to employees' accounts. This predetermined formula, which must be non-discriminatory, will be part of the qualified plan document and is used as the basis for determining the contributions allocated to each participants' account. There are several permitted methods that are deemed non-discriminatory. Allocations based on the same percentage of compensation or allocations that are equal in terms of dollars are permitted. In addition, allocation methods that skew contributions based on income or age may also be permitted. Ultimately, employers are limited to a contribution of 25 percent of the overall covered compensation for covered employees, but there are many methods for allocating this contribution to employees' accounts. Several of these methods are discussed in this chapter. Consider **Exhibit 5.2** below, which illustrates possible allocations for a company with four employees and total compensation of $400,000.

Exhibit 5.2 | Profit Sharing Allocation Example

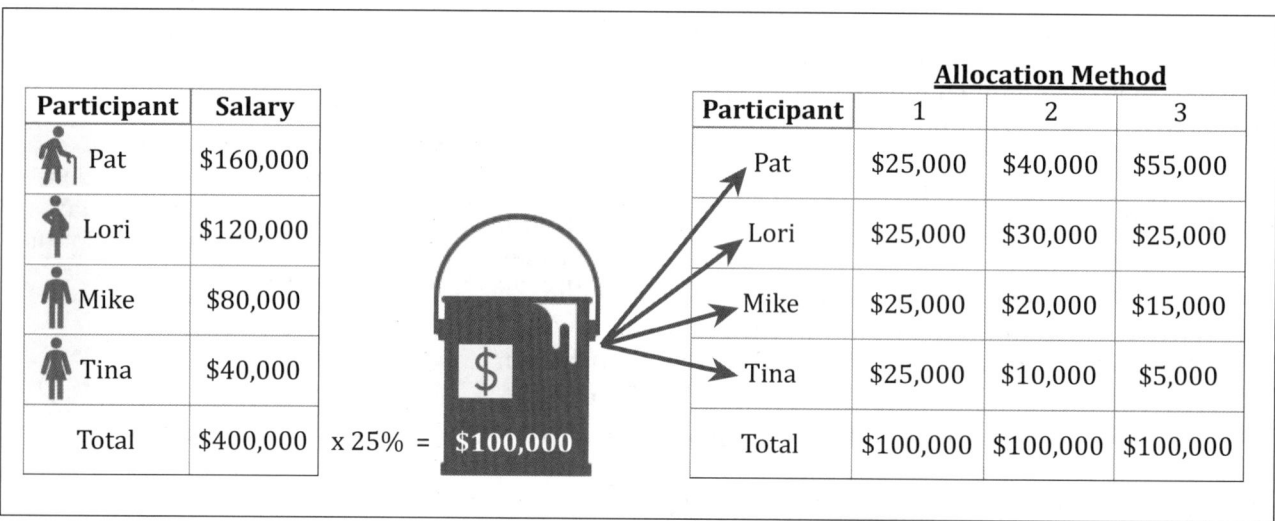

Participant	Salary
Pat	$160,000
Lori	$120,000
Mike	$80,000
Tina	$40,000
Total	$400,000

x 25% = $100,000

Participant	Allocation Method 1	2	3
Pat	$25,000	$40,000	$55,000
Lori	$25,000	$30,000	$25,000
Mike	$25,000	$20,000	$15,000
Tina	$25,000	$10,000	$5,000
Total	$100,000	$100,000	$100,000

In the exhibit above, the maximum employer contribution is 25 percent of $400,000 or $100,000. This $100,000 could be allocated in a variety of ways. In allocation 1, all employees receive the same dollar amount. In allocation 2, all employees receive the same percentage of their respective salaries. In allocation 3, the contributions might be skewed based on the participant's income and / or age. Several allocation methods are discussed throughout the remainder of this chapter.

Standard Allocations

The standard method of allocating contributions to a profit sharing plan is to simply allocate the contribution based on a percentage of each employee's covered compensation. **Example 5.2** illustrates this method.

Example 5.2

Acme Co. has 7 employees (A-G), ages 25-55 with compensation ranging from $30,000 to $250,000.

Employee	Age	Covered Compensation*	Contribution Percent	Overall Contribution	Percent of Total Contribution
A (owner)	55	$250,000	14.0%	$35,000	47.6%
B	45	$60,000	14.0%	$8,400	11.4%
C	40	$60,000	14.0%	$8,400	11.4%
D	35	$50,000	14.0%	$7,000	9.5%
E	30	$40,000	14.0%	$5,600	7.6%
F	25	$35,000	14.0%	$4,900	6.7%
G	25	$30,000	14.0%	$4,200	5.7%
		$525,000		$73,500	100.0%

ACME Standard Profit Sharing Allocation

Recall that there is a covered compensation limit.

In this example, each employee receives a contribution of 14% of their covered compensation. The 14% was selected by the employer based on the amount of money the employer wanted to contribute to the plan, which was approximately $73,500. Note that the contribution percentage could have ranged from 0% to 25% of the total covered compensation, or an overall maximum contribution of $131,250 (25%). Assuming that employee A is the owner of the business as well as an employee, A receives a contribution of $35,000 or almost 48% of the total plan contribution.

This methodology benefits the highly compensated more than the non-highly compensated in terms of absolute dollars but is nondiscriminatory with regard to percentages of the total contribution because the contributions are based on a straight percentage of total covered compensation.

Permitted Disparity (Social Security Integration)

Social Security retirement benefits are designed to replace a greater percentage of wages for lower-income workers than for higher-income workers. For a low income worker, Social Security replaces a large percent (50% to 75%) of pre-retirement earnings, while for a higher wage earner, it will replace a smaller percent (10% - 25%) of pre-retirement earnings. With the Revenue Act of 1942, private pension plans are permitted to provide larger benefits to higher paid workers than to lower paid workers in an attempt to reduce the gap in total wage replacement. Plans may consider the benefits provided by Social Security in the design of their benefit formula. Plans can integrate their retirement benefit formulas with Social Security under an "offset method" or an "excess method." However, a defined contribution plan may only use the "excess method."

Permitted disparity (often referred to as **Social Security Integration**) is a technique or method of allocating plan contributions to employees' accounts that provides higher contributions to employees whose compensation is in excess of the Social Security wage base for the plan year. In the standard allocation example (**Example 5.2**), all plan participants received a contribution of 14 percent of their covered compensation. However, an integrated (permitted disparity) formula provides an even higher percentage contribution for the higher compensated employees (those above the Social Security wage base) when compared to lower compensated employees (those below the Social Security wage base).

For defined contributions plans, such as profit sharing plans, an integration level is chosen by the plan sponsor (employer). This integration level is usually the Social Security wage base, which is $142,800 for the year 2021.[9] With an integrated formula, there are two profit sharing plan contribution rates established, the base contribution percentage rate and the excess contribution percentage rate. The base rate is applied on income earned up to the integration level, while the excess rate is applied to income earned above the integration level but only up to the maximum **covered compensation limit** for the year, $290,000 for 2021. The excess rate is generally 5.7 percentage points higher than the base rate.[10] The excess rate is limited to the lesser of twice the base rate or a maximum difference of 5.7 percent. In other words, the maximum disparity equals the lesser of the base rate or 5.7 percent. Consider the following table:

Base Rate	Excess Rate	Maximum Disparity
1.0%	2.0%	1.0%
2.0%	4.0%	2.0%
3.0%	6.0%	3.0%
5.0%	10.0%	5.0%
5.7%	11.4%	5.7%
8.0%	13.7%	5.7%
10.0%	15.7%	5.7%
12.0%	17.7%	5.7%

9. The integration level may be less than the Social Security wage base; however, if so, the excess percentage will be reduced.
10. If the base rate is less than 5.7 percent, then the excess rate cannot be more than twice the base rate. If the base rate is equal to or greater than 5.7 percent, then the excess rate can be no more than 5.7 percentage points greater than the base percentage rate. In addition, if the integration level is not at the Social Security wage base, then the 5.7 percent rate will generally be lower.

Example 5.3

Assume that Tantalus Inc. sponsors an integrated profit sharing plan that provides for a 10 percent base contribution percentage and an excess contribution percentage of 15.7 percent. If Dave earns $50,000, he would receive a contribution of $5,000 (10% x $50,000). If Mike earned $200,000 and the Social Security wage base was $142,800, then Mike would receive a contribution of $23,260 [10% x $142,800 plus 15.7% x ($200,000 - $142,800), rounded to the nearest dollar]. It is important to understand that integration has increased Mike's contribution by $3,260 ($23,260 - $20,000) over a straight 10 percent plan. This higher contribution is a result of the higher excess contribution rate for compensation above the integration level.

Tantalus Integrated Profit Sharing Plan								
Employee	**Covered Comp.**	**Base Comp.**	**Excess Comp.**	**Base Cont. 10%**	**Excess Cont. 15.7%**	**Total Cont.**	**Percent of Comp.**	**Percent of Total Cont.**
Mike	$200,000	$142,800	$57,200	$14,280	$8,980	$23,260	11.63%	82.31%
Dave	$50,000	$50,000	$0	$5,000	$0	$5,000	10.00%	17.69%
Totals	**$250,000**	**$192,800**	**$57,200**	**$19,280**	**$8,980**	**$28,260**		**100.00%**

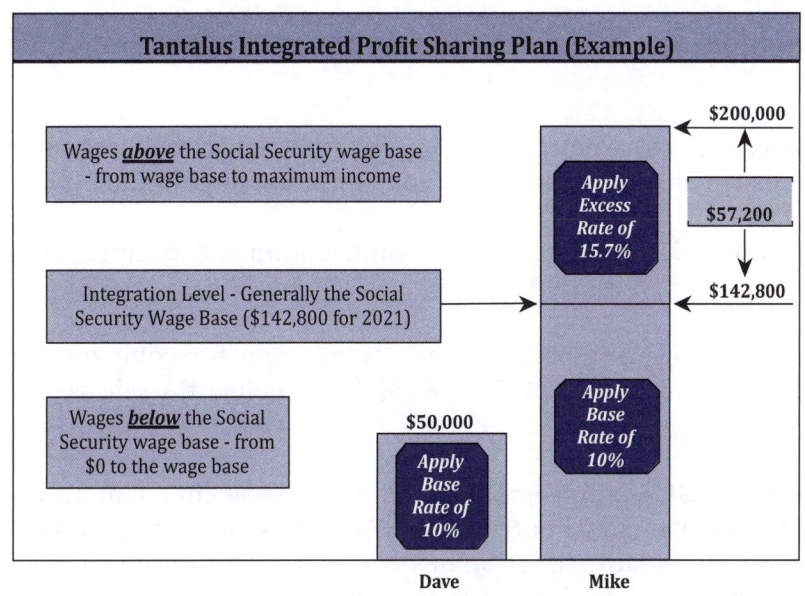

Example 5.4

Consider the same facts as in **Example 5.2** (they want to contribute approximately the same amount in total), except with an integrated profit sharing plan and a base contribution rate chosen by the employer of 13% (the excess rate is 18.7% (13% + 5.7% = 18.7%)).

Employee	Covered Comp.	Base Comp.	Excess Comp.	Base Cont. 13.0%	Excess Cont. 18.7%	Total Cont.	Percent of Comp.	Percent of Total Cont.
A (Owner)	$250,000	$142,800	$107,200	$18,564	$20,046	$38,610	15.44%	51.92%
B	$60,000	$60,000	$0	$7,800	$0	$7,800	13.00%	10.49%
C	$60,000	$60,000	$0	$7,800	$0	$7,800	13.00%	10.49%
D	$50,000	$50,000	$0	$6,500	$0	$6,500	13.00%	8.74%
E	$40,000	$40,000	$0	$5,200	$0	$5,200	13.00%	6.99%
F	$35,000	$35,000	$0	$4,550	$0	$4,550	13.00%	6.12%
G	$30,000	$30,000	$0	$3,900	$0	$3,900	13.00%	5.24%
Totals	$525,000	$417,800	$107,200	$54,314	$20,046	$74,360	14.16%	100.00%

Figures are rounded to the nearest dollar.

Base compensation ($) – represents compensation up to the integration level, $142,800 for 2021.

Excess compensation ($) – represents compensation above the integration level, (over $142,800 for 2021) but below the covered compensation limit ($290,000 for 2021).

Base contribution ($) – represents the contribution for compensation up to the integration level (12% in this example).

Excess contribution ($) – represents the contribution for compensation above the integration level [rate of 18.7% (13% + 5.7%)] and below the covered compensation limit.

Total contribution ($) – represents the sum of the base contribution and the excess contribution. The total amount contributed ($74,360) is close to what would have been contributed using a standard allocation of 14% ($73,500). This amount was chosen by management as what they could afford to contribute to the plan.

In this example, the base rate equals 13%. Therefore, all employees will receive a contribution of 13% of their own compensation earned up to $142,800, the integration level for 2021. Notice that the column "Percent of Comp" is the same for employees B through G; all have a contribution of 13% of their compensation. None of them have compensation above the integration level, so none will have a contribution at the higher excess contribution rate of 18.7%.

Because employee A has compensation in excess of the integration level, he will have a contribution for both the base compensation and an additional contribution for the excess compensation. His base contribution equals $18,564 ($142,800 x 13%), while his excess contribution equals $20,046 [($250,000 - $142,800) x 18.7%]. His excess contribution is based on the $107,200 ($250,000 - $142,800) of compensation over the integration level.

Notice that in this example, the company has contributed $74,360 to the plan and the owner A receives an allocation of $38,610; whereas in **Example 5.2**, the total contribution was $73,500 and the owner A received $35,000. Integration has allowed the owner to increase his contribution by $3,610. The $3,610 has come from reducing the contributions of B-G from 14% to 13% each to reflect that employer contributions to Social Security are part of the overall retirement plan and by increasing the total contributions slightly.

Although the integration level is generally equal to the Social Security wage base, it can be reduced to allow for larger amounts of income to be subject to the higher excess rate. However, as the integration level is reduced, so is the maximum difference between the base rate and the excess rate. Higher income employees will generally have higher contributions as the integration level is reduced, but this may also result in additional contributions for other employees.

If the integration level is less than the Social Security wage base, but more than 80 percent of the wage base, then the 5.7 percent is reduced to 5.4 percent. If the integration level is less than or equal to 80 percent of the wage base and greater than 20 percent of the wage base, then the 5.7 percent is reduced to 4.3 percent. At 20 percent or less, the rate remains at 5.7 percent.[11]

Exhibit 5.3 | Integration Level and Maximum Excess Percentage

Social Security Integration Level	Excess Percentage
100% of wage base	2 times the base limited to 5.7%
More than 80% of wage base but less than 100% of wage base	2 times the base limited to 5.4%
More than 20% of wage base but not more than 80% of wage base	2 times the base limited to 4.3%
Below 20% of wage base	2 times the base limited to 5.7%

Integration is generally used when the owner wants to increase or skew the contributions toward higher paid employees (those whose earnings are above the wage base) or himself. Social Security integration is not considered discriminatory because the employees who are receiving the excess contributions are not receiving Social Security retirement contributions on their wages in excess of the Social Security wage base.

---

11. Treas. Reg. §1.401(l)-2.

Age-Based Profit Sharing Plans

Age-based profit sharing plans use both age and compensation as the basis for allocating contributions to an employee's account. An age-based plan is chosen when the employee census is such that the owner or key employee is older than most or all other employees and the company wants to tilt the contribution toward those older employees. The concept of using an age-weighting formula in the allocation of benefits is based on a theory of comparable benefits for employees at normal age retirement (usually 65). Because older employees are closer to normal retirement age, current contributions must be higher than those for younger employees. While this initially appears to be discriminatory when comparing the current contributions to the plan, it seems relatively fair after comparing the ultimate benefits derived from the plan at the time of each of the employee's retirement.

It is possible that employees may perceive an inequity in the contributions to the plan under an age-based profit sharing formula. For example, if two employees are performing the same duties and are paid the same salary but are of different ages, the older employee will receive a higher current contribution to the plan than the younger employee. An illustration of an age-based profit sharing plan is provided in **Example 5.5**.

Example 5.5

This example uses the same facts as earlier Acme example, in which there are seven employees (A-G), ages 25-55 and with compensation ranging from $30,000 to $250,000. The employer contributed $73,000 because it is enough to maximize Employee A's contribution to the plan.

Acme Age-Based Profit Sharing Plan						
Employee	Age	Covered Comp	PV of $1**	Allocation Factor (age-weighted compensation)	Percent of Total Contribution**	Dollar Contribution**
A (Owner)	55	$250,000	0.4423	$110,571	79.417072%	$57,974.46
B	45	$60,000	0.1956	$11,737	8.430003%	$6,153.90
C	40	$60,000	0.1301	$7,806	5.606335%	$4,092.62
D	35	$50,000	0.0865	$4,326	3.107056%	$2,268.15
E	30	$40,000	0.0575	$2,302	1.653067%	$1,206.74
F	25	$35,000	0.0383	$1,339	0.961944%	$702.22 *
G	25	$30,000	0.0383	$1,148	0.824523%	$601.90 *
		$525,000		$139,229	100.00%	$73,000.00

Note that this plan is most likely a top-heavy plan. Therefore, employees F and G would have to be allocated 3% of their salary ($347.78 and $298.10, respectively). This top-heavy contribution would reduce the amount available to the owner or increase the overall cost of the plan.
*** Rounded using a discount rate of 8.5%.*

The initial step in calculating the contribution under an age-based profit sharing plan is to determine the present value of one dollar of benefit at the normal retirement age, usually age 65. For example, to determine this present value factor for employee A, the following calculation is performed:

FV = 1.0

N = 10 (65–55)(difference in current age from normal age retirement 65)

i = 8.5

PMT = 0

PV = 0.44229 (the contribution factor for this employee)

The term (N) is determined by subtracting the current age from the normal retirement age. In this case, the employee (A) has 10 years until he attains the age of 65. The interest factor is generally permitted by the IRS to be between 7.5% and 8.5%. This calculation, using 8.5%, results in a present value of 0.4423, which means that for employee A to receive a benefit of $1.00 at age 65, the plan sponsor would have to contribute $0.4423 today.

Notice that the present value factor decreases for younger age participants reflecting the longer period until retirement. For example, employee C's present value factor is 0.1301, whereas employee E's factor is 0.0575. The result is that contributions are higher for those employees who are older because the present value factor increases each year for each employee as they approach retirement.

The next step in the calculation is to weight the present value factor by the employee's compensation to arrive at an age-weighted compensation. For employee A, the allocation factor equals $110,571 ($250,000 x 0.4423). Once this process is completed for each employee, the resulting allocation factors are used to prorate the total contribution to the plan to the individual employees. Employee A's allocation factor over the total age-weighted compensation equals 79.42 percent ($110,571 ÷ $139,229), a significantly higher percentage relative to the other employees. The percentage of total age-weighted compensation is then multiplied by the total dollar contribution to the plan ($73,000).

The age-weighted profit sharing formula provides an amazing result. The owner, employee A, increases his allocation of the employer's contribution from $35,000 in **Example 5.2** to $57,974 and at a slightly lower total contribution. Because the 2021 limit for any particular employee is $58,000, his allocation will not be limited for 2021. This method of allocating contributions works extremely well when the owner is older than the other employees and when his compensation is relatively high. **Exhibit 5.4** summarizes the benefits of an integrated plan over a standard allocation, as well as the amazing results that an age weighted plan can produce under the right circumstances.

Exhibit 5.4 | Comparison of Acme Allocation Methods

Technique for Plan Contributions	Allocation of Contribution to Owner*	Total Employer Contribution to Plan*	Owner's Percentage of Contribution	Impact of the Change Over Standard Allocation (%)
Standard Allocation (Equal %)	$35,000	$73,500	47.62%	N/A
Permitted Disparity (Integration)	$38,610	$74,360	51.92%	10.32%
Age-Weighted Plan	$57,974	$73,000**	79.42%	65.64%

Figures are rounded to the nearest dollar.
** Employer will need to increase the contribution to comply with the top-heavy 3% rule.

Unfortunately, most business owners are unaware of the availability of these favorable contribution methods for a retirement plan. Advisors who understand the outcome for these types of allocations can add significant value to their client relationships.

New Comparability Plans

A **new comparability plan** is a profit sharing plan in which contributions are made to an employee's account based on their respective classification in the company as defined by the plan sponsor (employer). The contributions for the "owner" category classification will always be higher than the contributions for other employee classifications.

The higher contributions are based on the concept of cross-testing, in which contributions to a defined contribution plan are determined to be non-discriminatory in terms of benefits, rather than contributions. IRC §401(a)(4) states that, for a plan to be qualified, the contributions or benefits provided under the plan must not discriminate in favor of highly compensated employees.[12] The key word in that sentence is the word "or." Either the contributions or the benefits must be non-discriminatory, not both.

The regulations provide several methods for a new comparability plan to meet the non-discrimination rules.[13] The regulations provide that a plan will meet the non-discrimination rules if the plan conforms to one of the two "minimum allocation gateways." The general rule is that a plan satisfies the minimum allocation gateway if each NHCE has an allocation rate that is at least one third of the allocation rate of the HCE with the highest allocation rate. The second gateway provides that a plan is deemed to satisfy the minimum allocation gateway if each NHCE receives an allocation of at least five percent of the NHCE's compensation (within the meaning of IRC §415(c)(3)).

12. IRC §401(a)(4).
13. Treas. Reg. §1.401(a)(4)-8.

Exhibit 5.5 | Minimum Allocation Gateway

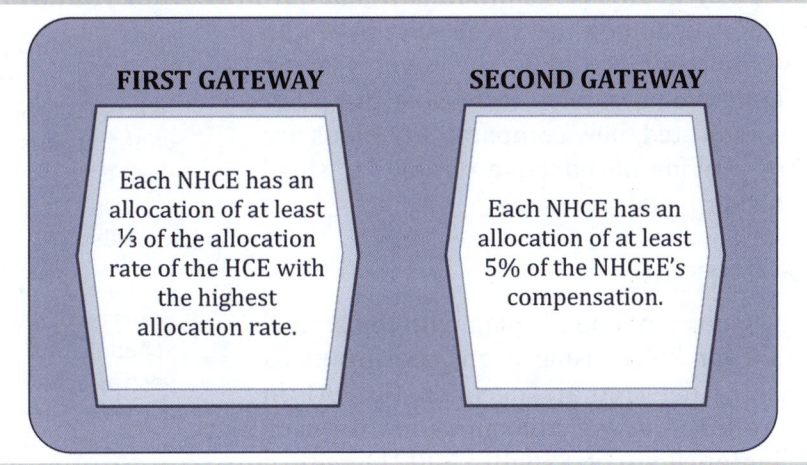

In addition, the regulations provide that if a plan does not meet either of the minimum allocation gateways, then it can still meet the non-discriminatory requirements if the plan has "broadly available" allocation rates or if the plan has age-based allocation rates that are based on either a gradual age or service schedule. These alternatives are discussed in detail within the Treasury regulations.

While new comparability plans are generally more expensive to administer, they allow for higher contributions for owners. **Example 5.6** illustrates a business with seven employees in which an owner would benefit from a new comparability allocation compared to a traditional profit sharing plan or an integrated profit sharing plan.

Example 5.6

Employee	Age	Salary	Profit Sharing Plan 13.64% Allocation	Integrated Profit Sharing Plan with Base Percentage of 12.15%	New Comparability Allocation
Owner	50	$290,000	$39,568	$43,632	$58,000
Manager	45	$150,000	$20,466	$18,639	$15,000
Staff 1	30	$40,000	$5,458	$4,861	$2,000
Staff 2	25	$35,000	$4,775	$4,253	$1,750
Staff 3	20	$30,000	$4,093	$3,646	$1,500
Staff 4	20	$25,000	$3,411	$3,038	$1,250
Staff 5	20	$20,000	$2,729	$2,430	$1,000
Totals		$590,000	$80,500	$80,500	$80,500

Notice that the total employer contribution in **Example 5.6** is same for all three allocation methods. The difference is in how that contribution is allocated among the seven employees. In the case of the new comparability plan, the owner would receive $58,000, while he would receive less using the other allocation methods. As indicated, new comparability plans are more complicated, but provide an effective option for small businesses to benefit higher paid owners.

Other Allocation Methods

A highly compensated owner can fund his plan with the annual additions limit, $58,000 for 2021, using profit sharing plans with or without a cash or deferred arrangement (CODA). In many cases, the use of a CODA may enable an owner to reach the maximum contribution limit of $58,000 (2021) with a lower total employer contribution. 401(k) profit sharing plans are used in most cases to fulfill this need.

Forfeitures

When employment is terminated and the employee has funds in a profit sharing plan that are less than 100 percent vested, the employee forfeits the amount not vested. **Forfeitures** in a profit sharing plan may either be used to reduce future plan contributions or be reallocated to the remaining participants' accounts.[14] However, any such reallocation of the forfeiture amounts must not be discriminatory in favor of highly compensated employees, owners, or officers.

Forfeitures can be allocated to remaining employees' accounts based on account balances as long as the allocation method does not discriminate. Alternatively, the forfeitures could be allocated on current year compensation – the same as normal contributions to the plan. Forfeitures cannot be reallocated to participants' accounts that have already reached their annual additions limit for the year. Therefore, an owner who has managed to have current contributions of $58,000 for 2021 made to his account will likely consider having forfeitures reduce future contributions to the plan since he cannot personally benefit from forfeitures. Alternatively, a forfeiture policy of reallocation can be combined with integration or an age-based approach to assist the owner in receiving the maximum contribution allowed.

Quick Quiz 5.3

1. A profit sharing plan can require the participants to wait three years before entering the plan, but all contributions must then be 100% vested.
   a. True
   b. False

2. Under PPA 2006, profit sharing plans must use a 5-year cliff vesting schedule or a 3-to-7-year graduated vesting schedule.
   a. True
   b. False

3. Profit sharing plans may permit in-service withdrawals after a participant has attained two years of service in the plan.
   a. True
   b. False

False, False, True.

Example 5.7

Georgia has a $30,000 account balance and is 80% vested in her profit sharing plan when she terminates employment. Georgia's vested balance in the profit sharing plan is $24,000, and she will forfeit the remaining $6,000. This forfeiture could be used to reduce future plan contributions. For example, the $68,000 contribution to the age-based profit sharing plan in **Example 5.5** could be reduced to $62,000 ($68,000 - $6,000). Alternatively, in the previous example demonstrating the profit sharing plan that utilized

---

14. IRC §401(a)(8).

the standard allocation formula, the $6,000 could be distributed to the remaining participants with the largest allocation to employee A.

Eligibility

Profit sharing plans are subject to **standard eligibility** rules of other qualified plans. Therefore, the standard eligibility of age 21 and one year of service will generally apply to profit sharing plans. As discussed before, plan sponsors may always relax the eligibility requirements.

In addition, profit sharing plans may also require a two year waiting period before an employee is eligible; however, all employer contributions must then be 100 percent vested. The two year eligibility rule is not a common choice for most businesses due to the 100 percent vesting requirement.

Vesting

The vesting rules for profit sharing plans are the same as for defined contribution plans. The standard 3-year cliff or 2-to-6-year graduated vesting apply unless the plan requires a two-year waiting period, in which case all contributions must then be 100 percent vested.[15] As discussed before, the plan sponsor is always permitted to be more generous but may not exceed these vesting requirements.

Distributions

Generally, profit sharing plans do not permit employees to receive distributions from the plan except upon termination, hardship, disability, or retirement. However, profit sharing plans may permit in-service withdrawals after the participant has fulfilled two years of service in the plan. Chapter 7 fully explains the taxation of distributions from qualified plans and the application of any penalties for early withdrawal.

CASH OR DEFERRED ARRANGEMENTS [401(k) PLANS]

A **cash or deferred arrangement (CODA)**, generally referred to as a 401(k) plan, is a feature that attaches to certain types of qualified plans to create a contributory component to the plan. Specifically, a CODA is permitted with profit sharing plans and stock bonus plans.[16] The CODA permits employees to defer a portion of their salary on a pre-tax basis to the qualified plan, thereby reducing their current income tax liability. These employee elective deferral contributions are tax-deferred - meaning that the earnings are not subject to income taxation until such time as the employee receives a distribution from the plan. Note that in the case of a Roth account, the deferral contribution occurs on an after-tax basis. It is referred to as a cash or deferred arrangement because employees are given the option to receive their current salary in cash (in their payroll) or make an elective deferral contribution into the 401(k) plan.

> **Key Concepts**
>
> 1. What are the general characteristics of a cash or deferred arrangement?
>
> 2. List the advantages for employees to have a 401(k) plan.
>
> 3. Which type of entities may establish a 401(k) plan?

---

15. PPA 2006 increased the vesting for all defined contribution plans beginning in 2007.
16. CODAs can also be used with pre-1974 money purchase pension plans.

Cash or deferred arrangements were introduced to the Internal Revenue Code in The Revenue Act of 1978 with an effective date of January 1, 1980. Since then, the number of 401(k) plans has increased dramatically. 401(k) plans are attractive to employers because these plans are employee self-reliant plans and provide a means of establishing a qualified retirement plan for employees without requiring the employer to make contributions to the plan (although employer contribution matches are a common option).

Exhibit 5.6 | Growth of 401(k) Plans from 1984 to 2018[17]

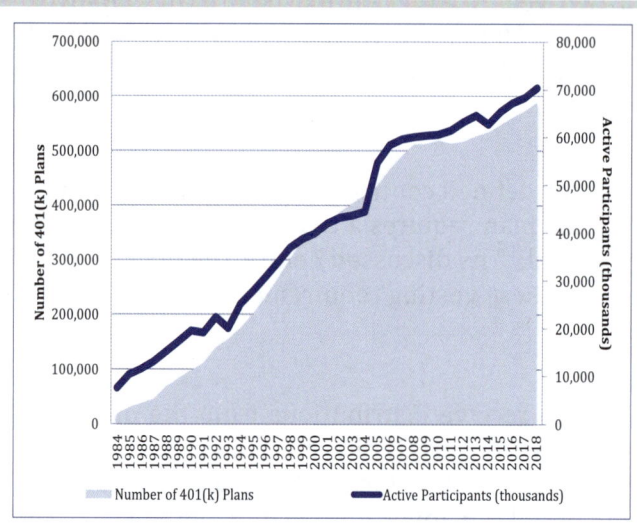
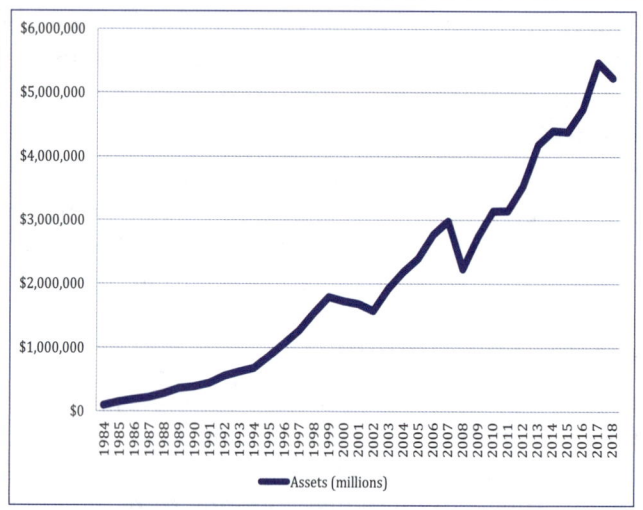

Exhibit 5.7 | Advantages of 401(k) Plans

To Employees	To Employers
• Shelter current income from taxation in a qualified plan • Self-directed investments • Earnings grow tax-deferred until distributed	• Minimal expense • No annual contribution commitment required • Owner employees may participate

401(k) plans are the most popular type of newly installed qualified retirement plans today. Cash or deferred arrangements are so prevalent because employers have begun to shift from plans in which the employees are dependent on the employer for the funding of retirement benefits to plans in which the employees are responsible for the funding of retirement benefits. Employers can, but are not obligated to, provide contributions to such plans (usually in the form of a match based on the employee's deferral); nonetheless, as with any profit sharing, such employer contributions are discretionary.

17. Form 5500 filings with the U.S. Department of Labor.

Establishing a 401(k) Plan

As with any qualified plan, plan sponsors may use prototype plans (see Chapter 8) or custom designed plans to establish a cash or deferred arrangement. Because these cash or deferred arrangements are qualified plans, the procedures to establish one are similar to other qualified plans. However, there are certain differences in terms of which types of entities can establish CODAs.

Which Entities May Establish a 401(k) Plan?

Only certain types of entities are permitted to establish and sponsor a 401(k) plan. Employers, such as corporations, partnerships, LLCs, and proprietorships may establish such a plan. In addition, for years after 1996, tax-exempt entities are permitted to establish 401(k) plans. Traditionally, tax-exempt entities (such as 501(c)(3) organizations) have established tax sheltered annuities (403(b) plans), but today, these types of entities may establish either the traditional tax sheltered annuity (403(b) plan) or a 401(k) plan. Over the past few years, these two types of plans have become very similar in nature. A governmental entity may no longer establish a 401(k) plan; however, certain grandfathered government plans that were in existence prior to May 6, 1986 may continue to be maintained. In addition, self-employed individuals and owner-only businesses with no employees may establish individual 401(k) plans, which will be discussed below.[18]

A 401(k) plan is typically a profit sharing plan (although it may be arranged as a stock bonus plan) that permits employees to make contributions from their salary to the plan on a pre-tax basis.

Entities Which May Establish a 401(k) Plan
Corporations
Partnerships
LLCs
Proprietorships
Tax-exempt entities

Because of their qualified status, 401(k) plans must comply with the rules discussed in Chapter 3 regarding eligibility, coverage, nondiscrimination, vesting, etc. However, some of the rules that relate to 401(k) plans are different than the standard rules relating to qualified plans. These differences are discussed below.

Eligibility

401(k) plans, like other qualified plans, have rules regarding who is eligible to participate in the plan. As you recall, the standard eligibility rules for qualified plans are that the employee must have attained the age of 21 and worked **one year of service** (defined as 1,000 hours within a 12 month period).[19] The

---

18. IRC §401(k)(4)(B).

exception to the one year of service rule is that an employer may make an employee wait two years to enter the plan if upon entrance into the plan, all benefits are fully vested. This two year exception is not available for 401(k) plans because an employee cannot be required to complete more than one year of service as a condition of participation in a section 401(k) arrangement.[20] The reason for this exception is that the employee elective deferral contributions are already 100 percent vested.

As with any qualified plan, the eligibility rules may always be more liberal to benefit the employees but cannot be more restrictive.

Once the eligibility requirements are met, the employee will enter the plan upon the next plan entrance date. As discussed in Chapter 3, most qualified plans have two entrance dates or more to meet the qualification requirement, which limits the waiting period to six months or less after eligibility.

Example 5.8

Dirk, age 35, has just taken a job at Advanced Technologies, which sponsors a 401(k) plan that requires one year of service and has entrance dates on January 1 and July 1. If Dirk started work on February 15, 2021, he will be entering the plan on July 1, 2022.

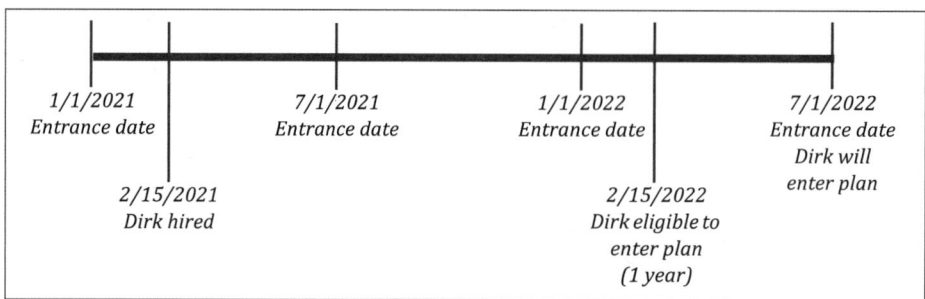

Long-Term, Part-Time Employee Eligibility

The SECURE (Setting Every Community Up for Retirement Enhancement) Act, passed in December 2019, amends the eligibility requirements for 401(k) plans to allow long-term part-time employees (age 21 and worked at least 500 hours per year for the employer for three consecutive twelve month periods) to participate in the employer's 401(k) plan by making employee contributions to the plan, effective for plan years beginning after December 31, 2020. Twelve month periods beginning before January 1, 2021 are not taken into account for eligibility purposes, but are taken into account for vesting purposes if the employer elects to make employer contributions on behalf of eligible part-time employees (the employee is credited with one year of service for vesting purposes for each year with at least 500 hours of service).[21] Once a long-term part-time employee has met the age 21 and three consecutive years with 500 hours of service requirement, the employee may enter the plan at the earlier of (1) the first day of the plan year beginning after the age and service requirements are met, or (2) six months after the date the requirements are met, as described previously.

---

19. Rule is generally referred to as "21 and 1."

20. IRC §401(k)(2)(D).

21. IRC §401(k)(15) and IRS Notice 2020-68.

This new eligibility requirement provides another method for employees to participate in a 401(k) plan. It does not replace the 1,000 hour requirement; therefore, employees with less than 1,000 hours of service may continue to be treated as ineligible for employer nonelective or matching contributions. In addition, these long-term, part-time employees do not have to be considered in discrimination testing, ADP testing, or in top-heavy testing.

Example 5.9

Dominick celebrates his 19th birthday the week before starting at Southeastern University in Hammond, LA. He is studying finance and realizes he needs a job. He is hired by Fat Boys Pizza and works approximately 600 hours in 2021, 2022, and 2023. Fat Boys sponsors a 401(k) plan with standard eligibility, which Dominick would not meet as he did not work at least 1,000 hours. However, under the long-term, part-time eligibility rules, he would be able to participate after 2023. He would have attained age 21 and worked at least three years with 500 or more hours per year.

Vesting

The vesting requirements for 401(k) plans are the same as those for other defined contribution plans. Contributions to 401(k) plans consist of employee elective deferrals and if applicable, employer matching contributions. If the 401(k) plan is sponsored in conjunction with a profit sharing plan or stock bonus plan, contributions to those plans are considered separate from the 401(k) plan contributions. For vesting purposes, all employee deferral contributions and the earnings on those contributions are always 100 percent vested. The employer matching contributions, employer discretionary profit sharing contributions, and the earnings on employer contributions must vest under a schedule at least as generous as the 2-to-6-year graduated or 3-year cliff schedules.

Example 5.10

The total balance of Trish's 401(k) profit sharing plan is $200,000. Of this balance, $60,000 is attributable to employer profit sharing plan contributions and $40,000 is attributable to earnings on the employer profit sharing plan contributions. $39,000 consists of Trish's elective deferral contributions to the 401(k) plan and $21,000 is the earnings on Trish's elective deferral contributions. The remainder of the balance consists of employer matching contributions and the earnings on the employer match. If the 401(k) plan uses a graded vesting schedule and Trish has completed two years of service with her employer, what is her vested balance in this 401(k) profit sharing plan?

To calculate this, first separate all of the contributions to determine the proper type of vesting schedule to use with each type of contribution, and then apply the appropriate vesting percentage.

Profit Sharing Plan		Vested %		Vested Amount
Employer contribution	$60,000	20%	2 to 6 graduated vesting	$12,000
Earnings or employer contributions	$40,000	20%	2 to 6 graduated vesting	$8,000
Total	$100,000	20%	Vested profit sharing plan	$20,000
401(k) Plan				
Trish's deferral contributions	$39,000	100%	100% vested	$39,000
Earnings on Trish's contributions	$21,000	100%	100% vested	$21,000
Employer matching contributions and earnings	$40,000	20%	2-to-6-year graduated vesting	$8,000
Total 401(k)	$100,000			$68,000
TOTAL	**$200,000**	**Vested 401(k) Account Balance**		**$88,000**

Participation

Employee enrollment meetings are typically held after the establishment of a 401(k) plan to inform the employees of the plan details and to encourage participation in the plan.[22] These educational meetings also help the plan sponsor comply with their ERISA 404(c) fiduciary requirements.[23] The most popular form of election under a CODA is a salary reduction agreement in which the employee agrees to reduce compensation in exchange for the elective deferral contribution into the plan. The salary reduction agreement may apply to current salary; to a salary increase; or to a bonus, commission, or other form of compensation for services. The employee's election to defer is generally made as a percentage of income or a dollar amount that will be contributed to the plan for the current year and usually directs the funds to be invested in a specific manner.

Example 5.11

Sam agrees (elects) to reduce her $50,000 salary by 20% ($10,000) if the funds are deposited in the 401(k) plan. She receives a W-2 showing taxable compensation of $40,000 with the remainder ($10,000) of her salary contributed to the 401(k) plan. Typically, she will choose how the funds are invested – whether stocks, bonds, cash, or other investments.[24] Plans that provide for employee self-direction of plan assets generally permit the employees to change their investments on a regular basis, in many cases on a daily basis.

22. Participation is encouraged for the benefit of the employee and for ADP/ACP testing.
23. ERISA 404(c).
24. While most 401(k) plans provide for self-direction, some plans may provide for outside management of the plan assets.

Employee Contributions

Contributions to 401(k) plans can be made as employee elective deferral contributions (either as a traditional elective deferral or as a contribution to a Roth account), employee after-tax contributions, employer matching contributions, employer profit sharing contributions, or employer contributions used to solve an ADP/ACP problem (discussed below).

Employee Deferrals

Employee elective deferral contributions are limited per year to the amounts in **Exhibit 5.8**.

Exhibit 5.8 | 401(k) Annual Elective Deferrals Limits for 2021

Year	Annual Elective Deferral Limit	Catch-Up Contributions **	Total Elective Deferral Limit
2021	$19,500	$6,500	$26,000

The same limits apply to SARSEPs, 403(b) Plans, and governmental 457(b) Plans.
** Age 50 or older.

Tax Impact

Besides the mere accumulation of benefits towards retirement, pre-tax funds deferred in a 401(k) plan are not currently subject to federal income tax and are not currently subject to state income tax. This tax deferral reduces current tax payments and allows for greater compounding of the funds contributed and the earnings over time.

Although employee elective deferrals (other than to a Roth account) are not subject to income tax, these deferral amounts are subject to payroll taxes. This means that the employee and the employer must pay payroll taxes on the employee elective deferral amounts contributed to a 401(k) plan. This will result in a Form W-2 that has different amounts in the various boxes on the form.

Exhibit 5.9 | W-2 Example

22222	**a** Employee's social security number 123-45-6789	OMB No. 1545-0008	
b Employer identification number (EIN) 35-1234567		**1** Wages, tips, other compensation 130,500.00	**2** Federal income tax withheld 30,000.00
c Employer's name, address, and ZIP code Best Employer 99 Company Drive City, GA 12345		**3** Social security wages 142,800.00	**4** Social security tax withheld 10,924.20
		5 Medicare wages and tips 150,000.00	**6** Medicare tax withheld 2,175.00
		7 Social security tips	**8** Allocated tips
d Control number 35-1234567		**9**	**10** Dependent care benefits
e Employee's first name and initial Last name Greatest Employee 100 Greatest Drive City, GA 12345	Suff.	**11** Nonqualified plans	**12a** C | 81.28
		13 Statutory employee ☐ Retirement plan ☒ Third-party sick pay ☐	**12b** D | 19,500.00
		14 Other	**12c**
			12d
f Employee's address and ZIP code			

15 State	Employer's state ID number	**16** State wages, tips, etc.	**17** State income tax	**18** Local wages, tips, etc.	**19** Local income tax	**20** Locality name
GA	9876543210	130,500.00	6,200.00			

Form W-2 Wage and Tax Statement

Department of the Treasury—Internal Revenue Service

Copy 1—For State, City, or Local Tax Department

Notice, in the Form W-2 above, Medicare wages (box 5) represents the total income for the employee. Subtracting the 401(k) deferral of $19,500 (box 12b) from Medicare wages results in the taxable wages found in box 1. Box 4 (Social Security tax withheld) equals 6.2 percent of box 3 (Social Security Wages) and box 6 equals 1.45 percent of box 5 (Medicare wages). Recall that the Medicare tax applies to all wages, while the Social Security tax (OASDI) is limited to the Social Security wage base ($142,800 for 2021). (Box 12a indicates the taxable component of the insurance premiums for the employee's group term life coverage.)

Employer Deposits of Employee Deferrals

Employee elective deferrals must be deposited and segregated from the employer's assets by the earliest date that is reasonably possible. However, the segregation of the funds must be completed by the 15th day of the month following the deferral from the employee's compensation. It is important to note that the 15th day is not a safe harbor. The employer has a responsibility to deposit the funds as soon as it is reasonably possible.

Catch-Up Contributions

One of the helpful provisions from EGTRRA 2001 was the allowance for higher contributions for older workers, which provides the opportunity to better prepare and save for retirement. Employees who are at least 50 years old during the plan year may increase their elective deferral limit by up to $6,500 for 2021. The additional deferral is called a **"catch-up" contribution** and allows those nearing retirement to increase their deferral contributions to improve their financial situation in anticipation of retirement.

In 2021, the employee elective deferral catch-up contribution may increase an employee's deferral limit from $19,500 to $26,000. In addition, these employee deferral catch-up contributions are not limited by plan limits, limits on annual accumulations, or by the ADP/ACP testing (discussed below). In other words, as long as the plan provides for equal treatment among participants (both HC and NHC), there are virtually no restrictions on using these catch-up contributions for employees age 50 and older.

Employee deferrals are included as part of the employee's annual funding limit of the lesser of 100 percent of income or $58,000 for 2021. However, the catch-up contributions do not count against this limit and, therefore, allow a participant who is age 50 or older to increase the maximum contributions to qualified plans to $64,500 for 2021.

> ### ✍≡ Key Concepts
>
> 1. Identify the methods employees can contribute to 401(k) plans and the applicable deferral contribution limits.
>
> 2. What is the income tax impact of 401(k) employee deferral contributions?
>
> 3. When must the employer deposit employee deferral contributions into the 401(k) plan?
>
> 4. Discuss the application of the catch-up contribution rules and the limits on catch-up contributions.
>
> 5. Identify the participation rules and negative elections.

Example 5.12

Dia, age 50, is employed by Ace, Inc. and has a salary of $200,000. Ace sponsors a 401(k)/ profit-sharing plan and contributes 20% for each employee. For Dia, the employer contribution equals $40,000. Since the annual contribution limit is $58,000 for 2021, Dia can only defer $18,000 to the 401(k) plan and not the maximum of $19,500. However, DIA is at least 50 years old and can therefore contribute $6,500 as a catch up contribution for a total deferral of $24,500. It is important to note that the catch up provision is only employee funded. An employer cannot make the contribution for the employee and an employee that did not have access to a cash or deferred arrangement could not exceed the IRC §415(c) limit.[25]

Employee After-Tax Contributions - Thrift Plans[26]

Although much less popular today, some 401(k) plans still permit employees to make after-tax contributions to the plan. These types of contributions have historically been called **thrift plan** contributions and were utilized by those who wanted to save more than the elective deferral limit or more than the amount allowed under the ADP/ACP test (discussed below). Any earnings on the after-tax contribution grow tax-free until distribution just as the earnings on pre-tax contributions. As will be discussed in Chapter 7, these after-tax contributions (Thrift Plan) give the plan participant an adjusted basis in their 401(k) plan.

Roth Contributions (Roth Accounts)[27]

Roth accounts were first introduced by EGTRRA 2001 for years beginning after 2005. IRS regulations for designated Roth contributions under qualified cash or deferred arrangements described in Section 401(k) were adopted effective January 3, 2006 and apply to plan years beginning on or after January 1, 2006. However, even today, Roth accounts are not as widely adopted as expected, based on their benefits.

Under IRC §402A, a plan may permit an employee who makes elective contributions under a qualified cash or deferred arrangement to designate some or all of those contributions as Roth contributions. Designated Roth contributions are elective contributions under a qualified cash or deferred arrangement that are:

1. designated irrevocably by the employee at the time of the cash or deferral election as designated Roth contributions that are being made in lieu of all or a portion of the pre-tax elective deferral contributions the employee is otherwise eligible to make under the plan;
2. treated by the employer as includible in the employee's gross income at the time the employee would have received the contribution amount in cash if the employee had not made the cash or deferral election; and
3. maintained by the plan in a separate account.

---

25. $58,000 VAR for 2021 VAR
26. These thrift plans are different than the governmental Thrift Savings Plan (TSP), which is a retirement savings and investment plan for Federal employees and members of the uniformed services, including the Ready Reserve. It was established by Congress in the Federal Employees' Retirement System Act of 1986 and offers the same types of savings and tax benefits that many private corporations offer their employees under 401(k) plans.
27. IRC §402A.

The same dollar limits that apply to employee pre-tax deferrals also apply to Roth contributions in total. Therefore, for 2021, an employee could contribute up to $19,500 to a 401(k) plan Roth account or to a pre-tax account, but not to both. Similarly, a catch-up contribution can be contributed to a Roth account or to the pre-tax account of a 401(k) plan. This treatment is the same for catch-up contributions for 403(b) plans and governmental 457(b) plans.

Designated Roth contributions to a 401(k) account bear some similarity to contributions to a Roth IRA (discussed in Chapter 9). Contributions to either type of account are after-tax contributions and qualified distributions from either type of account are excludable from gross income. In addition, both Roth IRAs and Roth 401(k) plans are subject to the qualified distribution rules under IRC §408A(d)(2)(A).

However, there are several significant differences between these types of arrangements. For example, contributions to a Roth account (unlike contributions to a Roth IRA) are not subject to modified adjusted gross income limitations. In addition, the contribution limit for designated Roth account contributions is $19,500 in 2021, which is significantly higher than the limits for contributions to traditional and Roth IRAs. Furthermore, distributions from a Roth account are not subject to the same favorable ordering rules that apply to Roth IRA distributions. Instead, distributions from a Roth account are subject to the rules under IRC §72, which provide for a pro-rata distribution of income and basis in the event the distribution fails to be a qualified distribution.Finally, unlike Roth IRAs, Roth 401(k) account balances are subject to minimum distributions requirements and are available for loans.

Exhibit 5.10 | Comparison of Roth IRA and Roth Accounts (2021)

Characteristic	Roth IRA	Roth Account
Participation	Anyone with earned income under limit	Anyone who is a participant in a 401(k), 403(b) or 457 plan that permits Roth contributions
Contribution Limits	IRA Annual limit - for 2021, $6,000 plus $1,000 catch up if age 50 or older. Subject to AGI limit: Single ($125,000-$140,000); MFJ ($198,000-$208,000)	Deferral limit - for 2021, $19,500 plus $6,500 if age 50 or older. No AGI limits.
Rollover/Conversion Recharacterization Permitted	No longer permitted after 2017.[1]	No - not permitted. Once the rollover takes place, it cannot be undone.
Minimum distributions	Only after death of participant	Yes - required[2]
Requirements for qualified distribution	Five years & on account of death, disability, age 59½ or first time home purchase (up to $10,000)	Five years & on account of death, disability or age 59½
Tax for nonqualified distributions (early distribution penalties may apply to part of the distribution)	Nonqualified distributions are distributed in order: contributions (basis), conversions (basis), then earnings (taxable)	Nonqualified distributions are prorated between Roth contributions (basis) and earnings (taxable)

1. Recharacterization of conversions are no longer permitted as a result of the TCJA 2017. However, other recharacterizations are still possible.
2. Minimum distribution requirements can be delayed until the death of the participant if rolled to a Roth IRA.

Under the final regulations, there are a number of requirements that must be met by an employer sponsoring a qualified cash or deferred arrangement in which employees may make designated Roth contributions. First, if the employer/plan sponsor offers designated Roth elections, it must also offer pre-tax elective contributions (i.e., traditional contributions). Second, separate accounting must be maintained for any contributions designated as Roth contributions. Consequently, no contributions other than designated Roth contributions and certain rollover contributions may be allocated to a designated Roth account. In other words, matching contributions and forfeiture allocations may not be allocated to a designated Roth account.[28] Third, a designated Roth contribution must satisfy the requirements applicable to any other elective contributions made under a qualified cash or deferred arrangement (e.g., nonforfeitability and distribution restrictions) and is taken into account under the actual deferral percentage test (ADP test) in the same manner as pre-tax contributions.[29]

The Small Business Jobs Act of 2010

The Small Business Jobs Act (SBJA) of 2010 signed by the President on September 27, 2010 made several changes to the IRC §402A, which sets forth the rules for elective deferrals to Roth accounts. SBJA 2010 added IRC §402A(c)(4) to the Code, effective for distributions made after September 27, 2010, to permit plans that include a qualified Roth contribution program to allow individuals to roll over amounts from their accounts other than designated Roth accounts to their designated Roth accounts in the plan. This option, which can be accomplished as a direct rollover or as an indirect rollover, is akin to converting funds in a traditional IRA to a Roth IRA. In addition, SBJA 2010 permits governmental 457(b) plans to include designated Roth accounts for years after 2010. These rules are discussed in greater detail in Chapter 7.

Individual 401(k) Plan (Also Known As Solo 401(k))

An **individual 401(k) plan** is an easy-to-administer, low-cost retirement plan designed for self-employed individuals and owner-only businesses. An individual 401(k) may also be known as a self-employed 401(k), solo 401(k), or a 401(k)I. An individual 401(k) plan offers many of the same advantages of a traditional 401(k), but has fewer administrative costs and requirements due to its small size. An individual 401(k) may be used by a sole proprietorship or business owner (including S and C corporations and partnerships) with no employees other than a spouse. Note that business owners must have at least a five percent ownership share to be eligible for an individual 401(k). Individual 401(k) plans are subject to the same elective deferral limits as traditional 401(k) plans, but annual funding is

> ### ☑ *Quick Quiz 5.6*
>
> 1. The employee 401(k) plan deferral limit is indexed for inflation after 2006.
>   a. True
>   b. False
>
> 2. Employee deferral contributions to 401(k) plans are subject to payroll taxes at the time of contribution.
>   a. True
>   b. False
>
> 3. An employer is not required to deposit the employee's 401(k) plan deferral contributions until the 15th day of the month following the deferral.
>   a. True
>   b. False
>
> 4. As a maximum, an individual over 50 years old can defer $26,000 in 2021 to a 401(k) plan.
>   a. True
>   b. False
>
> 5. A negative election is an election the employee can make that states that they want to participate in the plan.
>   a. True
>   b. False
>
> True, True, False, True, False.

---

28. Treasury Regulation §1.401(k)-1(f)(2).
29. IRC §402A, Treasury Regulation §1.401(k)-1(f).

not required. Individual 401(k) plans are also eligible for the Roth account feature. Individual 401(k) plans that allow both (1) voluntary after-tax contributions and (2) in-plan Roth rollovers or in-service distributions enable the participant an opportunity known as a "mega backdoor Roth" strategy. Since after-tax contributions (not Roth contributions) are permitted up to the maximum Sec. 415(c) limit of $58,000 (in 2021), utilizing the after-tax contributions in combination with an in-plan Roth rollover allows for the accumulation of a larger amount of Roth funds within the plan. This strategy is best suited for Individual 401(k) plans due to the lack of ADP/ACP testing (discussed below).

Employer Contributions

Matching Contributions

Employers and plan sponsors often provide a matching contribution based on the **employee elective deferral contributions** to the 401(k) plan. These **employer matching contributions** act as an incentive for plan participants to defer larger portions of their compensation than they may have otherwise contributed. Examples of methodologies for matching contributions are:

- 50 percent match up to six percent of compensation. If an employee contributes six percent or more of his compensation, the employer would match with a three percent contribution.
- Dollar-for-dollar match up to four percent. For every dollar of employee elective deferral, the employer will contribute (match) equally up to four percent of the employee's compensation.

Example 5.13

In 2021, Rita elects to defer 8% of her $40,000 salary to a 401(k) plan. Her employer matches 50% of her deferral up to a maximum of 6% of compensation. For the year, Rita contributes 8% of her salary ($3,200) and her employer contributes 3% (50% of 6% or $1,200), for a total contribution of $4,400. Employer matching contributions are typically capped. In this case, the match is capped at 3%, which is 50% of the 6%.

Example 5.14

Assume Jonah is 50 and attempting to maximize his employee deferral contributions. He has a $50,000 salary and his employer matches dollar for dollar up to 4% of salary. Jonah can elect to defer $19,500 (2021) and he can elect to defer the catch-up of $6,500 (2021). Jonah's total elected deferral contribution to the 401(k) plan would be $26,000. In addition, the employer match would be $2,000 ($50,000 x 4%) for a total contribution of $28,000. Jonah's W-2 would show $24,000 ($50,000 - $26,000) subject to federal income tax, although he and his employer would pay payroll taxes on the full $50,000. The employer match would not be subjected to payroll tax or current income tax.

While employee elective deferral contributions are always 100 percent vested, employer matching contributions must vest at least as rapidly as either a three-year cliff vesting schedule or a 2-to-6-year graduated vesting schedule. These are the same maximum vesting schedules that are required for all defined contribution plans. Remember, plan sponsors can always be more generous by reducing years of service requirements for employees to achieve full vesting but may not extend the vesting period. Some matching contributions are applied simultaneously with employee deferral contributions. Other plans may require active employment as of December 31 to qualify for the employer match, so matching contributions occur after year end.

⋮☰ *Key Concepts*

1. What are matching contributions and their allowed vesting schedules?

2. How can profit sharing plan contributions be used with the 401(k) plan?

3. What are the requirements for a 401(k) plan to offer a Roth Account?

Profit Sharing (Stock Bonus) Contributions

Because 401(k) plans consist of a CODA attached to a profit sharing plan or stock bonus plan, employers may also make a contribution to the profit sharing (or stock bonus) plan. These contributions are often referred to as the nonelective employer contribution. The employee elective deferral contributions do not count against the plan contribution limit of 25 percent, so large contributions can be made as a nonelective profit sharing contribution. The total contributions to qualified plans for the year is still limited to $58,000 per person for 2021 ($64,500 if the participant is age 50 and over).

Exhibit 5.11 | 401(k) Plan for 2021

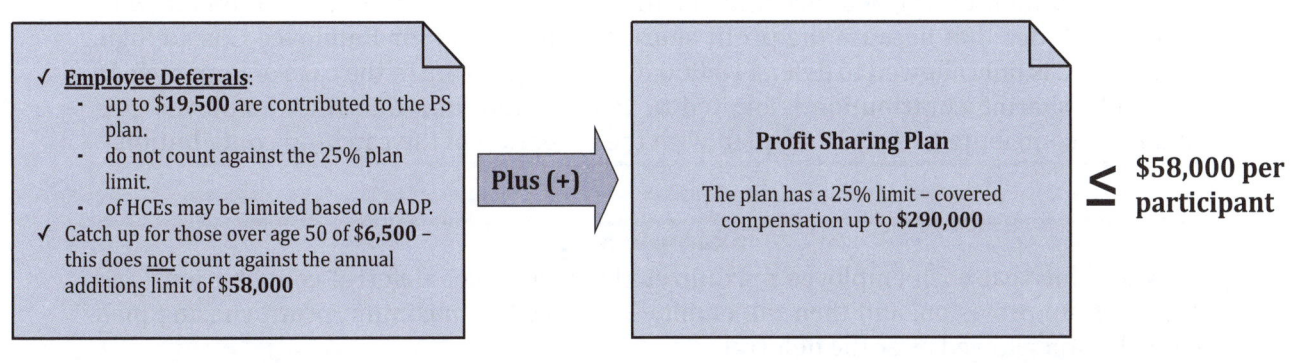

Example 5.15 illustrates how profit sharing contributions, employee deferral contributions, and catch-up contributions work in unison. This example also illustrates how the annual additions limit works in harmony with the 401(k) limit and plan contribution limit.

Example 5.15

Assume that each employee wants to maximize his employee deferral contributions and the employer is already making a 25% of employee compensation contribution to a profit sharing plan on behalf of each employee.

Consider Employees A through D with compensation ranging from $40,000 to $290,000. Also assume that each employee is over the age of 50.

Profit Sharing, Elective Deferrals, and Catch-Up Contributions				
	Employee A	**Employee B**	**Employee C**	**Employee D**
Salary	$40,000	$100,000	$160,000	$290,000
Catch-up contribution	$6,500	$6,500	$6,500	$6,500
401(k) plan deferral	$19,500	$19,500	$18,000	$0
P/S contribution (25%)	$10,000	$25,000	$40,000	$58,000
Total Contributions	**$36,000**	**$51,000**	**$64,500**	**$64,500**

Notice, if the employer makes a 25% contribution, that limits the elective deferral for C and D but will not affect the catch-up contribution.

The profit sharing contribution is assumed to be 25% of the employee's salary limited to the annual additions limit of $58,000, as in the case of Employee D. The 401(k) deferral is assumed to be limited to the lesser of the difference between the annual additions limit or the maximum deferral for the year. In the case of Employee A, he cannot reach either the $58,000 limit or 100% of his annual compensation because of how the limits work together. Notice that because the profit sharing contribution for Employee C is so high, Employee C is only allowed to defer $18,000 in the 401(k) plan. In the case of Employee D, the profit sharing contribution is limited to the $58,000 limit and thus Employee D is unable to contribute to the 401(k) plan with the exception of the catch-up contribution.

Example 5.16

Now assume that each employee maximizes their employee deferral contributions and the catch-up provision, and then the employer makes the maximum profit sharing plan contribution allowed after the deferral.

	Employee A	**Employee B**	**Employee C**	**Employee D**
Salary	$40,000	$100,000	$160,000	$290,000
Catch-up contribution	$6,500	$6,500	$6,500	$6,500
401(k) deferral	$19,500	$19,500	$19,500	$19,500
P/S contribution	$10,000	$25,000	$38,500	$38,500
Total Contributions	**$36,000**	**$51,000**	**$64,500**	**$64,500**

In this case, the profit sharing contributions are limited for C and D rather than the employee deferral contributions, but each employee (C and D) still reaches the maximum contribution to qualified plans for the year.

Nondiscrimination Testing

All qualified plans are required to meet certain nondiscrimination tests, but qualified plans that maintain a CODA must also meet two special nondiscrimination tests known as the actual deferral percentage test (ADP) and the actual contribution percentage test (ACP). However, because of the burdensome nature of annually complying with these rules, the IRC provides a safe harbor provision that eliminates the requirement of annual testing. In addition, the Pension Protection Act of 2006 has provided an optional nondiscrimination safe harbor for automatic enrollment plans. Thus, after December 31, 2007, employers will have three options with respect to 401(k) nondiscrimination testing. They can:

1. perform the ADP and ACP tests and take corrective action if the plan fails the test;
2. institute a qualified automatic enrollment feature and comply with the new safe harbor;[30] or
3. comply with the old safe harbor.

Actual Deferral Percentage Test (ADP)

The **Actual Deferral Percentage (ADP) test** limits employee elective deferrals for the highly compensated employees (HC) based on the elective deferrals of non-highly compensated employees (NHC). A qualified plan with a CODA does not fail the ADP test simply because all eligible employees are highly compensated.[31]

IRC §401(k)(3) states that the actual deferral percentage for eligible highly compensated employees for the plan year is limited by the actual deferral percentage for all other eligible employees for the preceding plan year and must meet either of the following tests:

- **Test 1:** The actual deferral percentage for the group of eligible highly compensated employees is not more than the actual deferral percentage of all other eligible employees multiplied by 1.25 (the 1.25 requirement).
- **Test 2:** The excess of the actual deferral percentage for the group of eligible highly compensated employees over that of all other eligible employees is not more than two percentage points, and the actual deferral percentage for the group of eligible highly compensated employees is not more than the actual deferral percentage of all other eligible employees multiplied by 2 (the 200% / 2% test).

> ### Quick Quiz 5.7
>
> 1. Matching contributions vest at either a 2-to-6-year graduated vesting schedule or a 5-year cliff vesting schedule.
>   a. True
>   b. False
>
> 2. A catch-up contribution can allow an eligible employee to defer more than the annual additions limit of $58,000 for 2021.
>   a. True
>   b. False
>
> 3. An employee can contribute the maximum deferral limit of $19,500 to the 401(k) pre-tax account and another $19,500 to the Roth account, if both accounts are available in the plan?
>   a. True
>   b. False
>
> False, True, False.

Although the ADP test above may appear rather convoluted and difficult to follow, the test can be interpreted rather easily with the following exhibits.

---

30. IRC §401(k)(13).
31. IRC §401(k)(3).

Exhibit 5.12 | ADP Schedule

ADP Schedule	
If the ADP for NHC Employees is:	**The Permissible ADP for HC Employees is:**
0% to 2%	2 times ADP for NHCs
2% to 8%	2% plus ADP for NHCs
8% and over	1.25 times ADP for NHCs

Exhibit 5.13 | Explanation of ADP Schedule

The Rule	ADP of NHC	ADP Limit for HC
2 times ADP of NHC	1%	2.00%
	2%	4.00%
Plus 2 percentage points of ADP of NHC	3%	5.00%
	4%	6.00%
	5%	7.00%
	6%	8.00%
	7%	9.00%
	8%	10.00%
1.25 times ADP of NHC	9%	11.25%
	10%	12.50%
	11%	13.75%
	12%	15.00%
	13%	16.25%
	14%	17.50%
	15%	18.75%

As indicated in the above exhibits, the elective deferral contributions of the highly compensated employees are limited based on the elective deferrals of the nonhighly compensated employees. Generally, the current plan year ADP for the highly compensated employees is tested against the ADP of the nonhighly compensated employees for the prior plan year. Using this approach will generally minimize excess contributions by highly compensated employees. In other words, knowing the ADP for the nonhighly compensated employees for the prior plan year will allow the highly compensated employees to comply with the ADP test for the current plan year.

Plans can choose either the Current Year Method or Prior Year Method for ADP testing. The Prior Year Method calculates the maximum permissible deferral for highly compensated employees by using the nonhighly compensated employee's ADP from the previous year. Although the highly compensated employees have less certainty in knowing their deferral limits by using the Current Year Method, this approach may give the highly compensated employees a slightly higher deferral ceiling. The Current Year Method also provides more flexibility to the plan sponsor in the event of ADP failures.

n the first year of a 401(k) plan or the year that such plan is established, there is obviously no prior year on which to base the ADP for the highly compensated employees. In the first plan year, the ADP for the nonhighly compensated employees will be either three percent (as provided for in the regulations) or the actual ADP for the current year.[32]

How is the ADP Calculated?

To determine whether the requirements of the ADP test have been met, the first step is to separate the eligible employees into highly compensated and nonhighly compensated groups. The only employees included in the calculation are those who meet the eligibility requirements of the 401(k) plan. It is important to note that this also includes those employees that have met eligibility but have chosen not to defer any of their compensation.

Next, calculate the actual elective deferral ratio (ADR) for each of the eligible employees by dividing the elective deferral contribution by the employee's compensation. Once the ADR is determined for each eligible employee, the amount of the ADP is calculated by averaging the ADRs for the employees within each group (HC or NHC). Once the ADP for each group is determined, they are compared to determine that the qualified plan complies with either the 1.25 test or the 200%/2% test.

Example 5.17

Boo Company sponsors a 401(k) plan with ten eligible employees. Each employee can defer up to 70 percent of their compensation limited to the annual deferral limit. The employees made the following deferral elections:

Basic Data				
Employee	Ownership	Compensation	Elective Deferral	ADR
A	60%	$200,000	$11,000	5.5%
B	30%	$160,000	$11,200	7.0%
C	5%	$150,000	$15,000	10.0%
D	3%	$80,000	$8,000	10.0%
E	2%	$50,000	$2,500	5.0%
F	-	$30,000	$3,000	10.0%
G	-	$25,000	-	0.0%
H	-	$25,000	$1,000	4.0%
I	-	$25,000	-	0.0%
J	-	$20,000	$500	2.5%

32. Treas. Reg. §1.401(k)-1(g)(11).

Employee	Alternative A HC definition without 20% election*		Alternative B HC definition with 20% election*	
	HC	NHC	HC	NHC
A	5.5%		5.5%	
B	7.0%		7.0%	
C	10.0%			10.0%
D		10.0%		10.0%
E		5.0%		5.0%
F		10.0%		10.0%
G		0.0%		0.0%
H		4.0%		4.0%
I		0.0%		0.0%
J		2.5%		2.5%
Average	7.5%	4.5%	6.25%	5.19%

Election to include only top 20% of employees as determined by compensation as HC.

Who is highly compensated in the example?
- Employee A and B are clearly highly compensated because of their ownership percentage.
- Employee C is highly compensated based on his income of $150,000. However, if the definition for highly compensated includes the election of being in the top 20 percent of paid employees, then Employee C would be classified as a NHC. Although Employee C owns 5% of the company, he is not a "5% owner" because he is not a <u>more</u> than 5% owner of the company.[33]
- Employees D through J are all NHC employees.

Alternative A and Alternative B demonstrate the difference of treatment depending upon whether the top 20% election is made or not. The election is made as part of the definition of highly compensated employee in the plan document.

Following Alternative A (without the top 20% election), the ADP of the HCs is 7.5%, while the ADP for the NHCs is 4.5%. Referring to the table above, with the NHCs ADP equal to 4.5%, the ADP for the HCs should be no greater than 6.5% - two percentage points more than the ADP for the NHCs. Therefore, the plan fails the ADP test.

See the discussion below for remedies.

---

33. IRC §416(i)(1)(B).

HC	NHC
ADP of HC - 7.5	ADP of HC must be no more than 6.5 = NHC ADP of 4.5% + 2%

Following Alternative B (with the top 20% election), the ADP of the HCEs is 6.25%, while the ADP for the NHC employees is 5.19%. Based on these figures, the plan complies with the ADP test. Notice that in this example, the difference between passing the ADP and not passing is how the plan defined the definition of highly compensated. By electing the top 20% of paid employees, Employee C shifted from the HC category to the NHC category. This example illustrates one reason an employer might choose the 20% election as the definition of highly compensated.

Failing the ADP Test

If the ADP test is not met, then there has been an excess elective deferral contribution by the highly compensated employees. An excess contribution occurs when the HCs defer more than is permitted under the ADP test. When this happens, there are four alternative remedies that the plan may use to bring the plan into compliance:

- corrective distributions,
- recharacterization,[34]
- qualified nonelective contributions (QNEC), or
- qualified matching contributions (QMC).

If a plan does not meet the ADP test, there are two explanations on why the plan did not meet the nondiscrimination test:

- the highly compensated employees deferred too much, or
- the non-highly compensated employees deferred too little (or some combination of the two).

This is a question of whether the "glass is half full or half empty." As discussed below, the negative election is often used to entice participation and increase the deferral for the NHC. In either case, the plan must be corrected to meet the ADP test by either reducing the HC employees elective deferral contributions or by increasing the NHC employees elective deferral contributions. Corrective distributions and recharacterizations are methods to reduce the HC employees' elective deferrals, while QNECs and QMCs are methods to increase the ADP of the NHC employees.

When there are excess contributions, the 401(k) plan must correct the situation within 2½ months (75 days) after the plan year for which the contributions were made. If the correction is not made, then the employer is subject to a 10 percent penalty on the excess deferral contribution amount. In addition, if the correction is not made within twelve months, the plan may be deemed disqualified.

If the employer chooses to use a QNEC or QMC, then these contributions can be made beyond the 2½ month period.

---

34. IRC §401(k)(8)(A).

Corrective Distribution

When a plan fails the ADP test, the most common method of correcting the situation is to reduce the elective deferrals of the HCs by distributing or returning funds to the HCs. This distribution is referred to as a **corrective distribution** because it corrects the elective deferrals with regard to the ADP test. Corrective distributions must be completed within 2½ months after the end of the plan year; otherwise, a 10 percent excise tax is imposed on the amount that should have been distributed.

Example 5.18

Recall Alternative A of the Boo Company example above in which the ADP for the HC was 7.5% while the ADP for the NHCs was 4.5%. With the NHC's ADP equal to 4.5%, the ADP for the HCs must equal no more than 6.5%. Therefore, the plan would have to distribute enough from the HCs to reduce the ADP to 6.5% from 7.5%. The leveling method is used to determine the total excess contributions based on the dollar amount of the deferrals.

	Employee A	Employee B	Employee C	Total
Compensation	**$200,000**	**$160,000**	**$150,000**	**$510,000**
Deferral	$11,000	$11,200	$15,000	$37,200
Initial ADR	5.50%	7.00%	10.00%	7.50%
Initial Deferral	$11,000	$11,200	$15,000	$37,200
First Reduction <1>	-	-	($3,800)	($3,800)
Net	$11,000	$11,200	$11,200	$33,400
Next Reduction <2>	-	($200)	($200)	($400)
Net	$11,000	$11,000	$11,000	$33,000
Final Reduction <3>	($100)	($100)	($100)	($300)
Corrected deferral	**$10,900**	**$10,900**	**$10,900**	**$32,700**
Total Corrective Distribution	($100)	($300)	($4,100)	($4,500)
Compensation	$200,000	$160,000	$150,000	$510,000
Deferral	$10,900	$10,900	$10,900	$32,700
Corrected ADR	**5.45%**	**6.81%**	**7.27%**	**6.51%**

* Rounded

Under the leveling method, the elective deferral of the HC employee with the highest deferral, Employee C is reduced by the amount, <1>, necessary to reduce the deferral to the highest deferral to the next highest dollar deferral, $11,200. The process continues to reduce to the next highest deferral, <2>. If the total excess contribution is not fully allocated, the process continues, <3>, until the full amount is distributed.

This process results in Employee A reducing his deferral by $100, Employee B reducing his deferral by $300, and Employee C reducing his deferral by $4,100. Averaging the ADR for each HC employee results in an ADP of 6.51% rounded to 6.5% – a deemed acceptable level.

In addition to the excess contributions being returned to the HC employees, any earnings on those contributions must also be returned or distributed to the HC employees.

Tax Treatment of Corrective Distributions

Corrective distributions are intended to properly adjust the HCE's deferral amount. Therefore, if the HCE deferred too much, the corrective distribution returns the excess deferral back resulting in a lower deferral, which corresponds with the ADP test. However, the distribution may be taxable in the year in which the deferral was taken or the following year, depending on when the distribution is received by the HCE.

If the distribution is received within 2½ months after the plan year end, then the distribution will be taxable to the HCE in the year in which the deferral was taken. In effect, it is as if the HCE deferred the proper amount. However, if the distribution is received after the 2½ month period, then it is taxable in the following year. Thus, the HCE would have received a larger deduction than should have been allowed in one plan year and more income the next.

Example 5.19

Randy defers $10,000 in the current year. However, after the ADP test is calculated, Randy is determined to have deferred $2,000 more than permitted under the test. Therefore, Randy needs to receive a corrective distribution of the $2,000 by March 15 of the next year. If this happens, then the $2,000 will be included in Randy's taxable income for the previous year. If the distribution is received after March 15 of the next year, then it is taxable to Randy in the next year and the employer must pay a 10 percent penalty on the amount not distributed within 2½ months after the plan year end, in this case $2,000.

Recharacterization

If a plan fails the ADP test, the plan sponsor may choose to recharacterize the excess deferrals (pre-tax) as after-tax employee contributions. This **recharacterization of deferrals** must be completed within 2½ months after the end of the plan year, at which time these recharacterized contributions are taxable to the employee.[35] If the excess contributions are not recharacterized within 2½ months of the plan year end, then the employer is subject to a 10 percent excise tax (penalty) on the amount of excess contributions (the amount that should have been recharacterized).

Quick Quiz 5.8

1. The elective deferrals of the highly compensated employees may be limited based on the elective deferrals of the non-highly compensated employees.
   a. True
   b. False

2. All eligible employees are included in the calculations for the ADP test including those employees who elect not to defer.
   a. True
   b. False

3. If a CODA plan fails the ADP test, the plan will be terminated.
   a. True
   b. False

4. The pre-PPA 2006 safe harbor provisions require that a 401(k) plan use top-heavy vesting schedules to avoid calculating the ADP test.
   a. True
   b. False

5. Orange Co. has a non-safe harbor 401(k) plan with five NHCEs who defer 4%, 0%, 10%, 0%, and 6%. As a result, the HCEs are limited to a deferral of 8%.
   a. True
   b. False

True, True, False, False, False.

35. These after-tax employee contributions would then be subject to the ACP test.

One potential problem with recharacterization is that the pre-tax contributions that are recharacterized to after-tax contributions may cause the plan to fail the actual contribution percentage (ACP) test. The ACP test is the exact same mathematical test as the ADP test except that instead of testing employee elective deferrals (actual deferral percentage, ADP), it tests employer matching contributions and employee after-tax contributions (actual contribution percentage). In addition, these after-tax contributions will be counted against the employee's annual additions limit of the lesser of $58,000 for year 2021 or 100 percent of compensation.

Qualified Nonelective Contributions

An employer may choose to make a **qualified nonelective contribution (QNEC)** to NHC employees' CODA plan accounts to increase the ADP of the NHC employees for purposes of passing the ADP test. The QNEC is made by the employer without regard to any elective deferral election made by the employee, so the contribution is made on behalf of all eligible employees. The contribution is treated as if deferred by the employee and therefore is included in the calculation of the ADP test to increase the ADP of the NHC. Since the contribution is treated as an employee elective deferral, it is also 100 percent vested in the employee.

Example 5.20

The ADP of the HC employees is six percent and the ADP of the NHC employees is 3.75%. To pass the ADP test, the NHC employees must have an ADP at least equal to 4%. To increase the ADP of the NHC employees, the plan sponsor may elect to make a QNEC to all eligible employees that will increase the ADP of the NHC employees to 4%. Whatever amount of QNEC contributions is made will be considered 100% vested in the NHC employees.

Qualified Matching Contributions

A **qualified matching contribution (QMC)**, like a QNEC, increases the ADP of the NHC employees. However, unlike the QNEC, the QMC is only made to those eligible employees who had elected to defer during the plan year. Essentially, the QMC is an additional match from the employer to increase the deferral percentage of the NHC employees. Because the contributions are treated as being made by the employee, the QMC is 100 percent vested.

Example 5.21

The ADP of the NHC employees was 6% for the plan year, and the ADP of the HC employees was 8.20% for the year. To pass the ADP nondiscrimination test, the plan sponsor would make QMCs to all NHC employees who had elected to defer during the plan year to increase the ADP of the NHC employees to 6.20%. Those employees who had not deferred during the year would not receive any QMC. The QMC is 100% vested in the employee.

Actual Contribution Percentage (ACP)

The **actual contribution percentage test (ACP)** is calculated the same way as the ADP test except that instead of testing the employee elective deferral contributions, the ACP test calculates a contribution percentage based on the sum of the following:[36]

1. employee after-tax contributions, and
2. employer matching contributions.

After calculating the ACP for both NHC employees and HC employees, the two are compared using the same scale as the ADP test. If the plan does not pass the ACP test, the same corrective measures as used for the ADP test are used to either reduce the ACP of the HC or increase the ACP of the NHC.

Safe Harbor 401(k) Plans

Plans that provide for a CODA are subject to the nondiscrimination rules discussed above as well as the top-heavy rules discussed in Chapter 3. For many employers and plan sponsors, the annual testing required to comply with these rules is administratively burdensome and costly. Fortunately, the IRC provides a **safe harbor** provision whereby the employer is not required to comply with the ADP test, the ACP test, or the top-heavy testing if the plan meets the safe harbor test.

To comply with safe harbor status, the plan must provide a minimum contribution that must be immediately 100 percent vested. The permissible contributions can either be a three percent minimum nonelective contribution or a matching contribution (discussed below). Under the nonelective contribution, all eligible employees would receive a 100 percent vested contribution equal to three percent of their compensation from the employer.

Under prior law, a plan sponsor wishing to amend a plan to provide a three percent nonelective safe harbor provision was required to provide a contingent notice prior to the beginning of the plan year and to make the election no later than 30 days before the end of the plan year. Under the SECURE Act of 2019 the rules regarding the election of a nonelective safe harbor provision were somewhat allayed. For plan years beginning after December 31, 2019, the contingent notice is no longer required, however, the amendment to the nonelective safe harbor must still be completed no later than the 30th day before the close of the plan year. The SECURE Act permits a nonelective safe harbor amendment after the 30th day before the close of the plan year, but before the last day for distributing excess contributions for the plan year, if the nonelective contribution is at least four percent.

If the employer elects to use a match rather than the nonelective contribution, the standard safe harbor match formula requires the employer to match 100 percent of the first three percent of employee elective deferrals and 50 percent of employee elective deferrals greater than three percent and less than five percent. For a safe harbor plan providing a matching contribution, an election must be made 60 days prior to the beginning of the plan year to convert a 401(k) plan to the safe harbor match.

---

36. IRC §401(m).

Exhibit 5.14 | Safe Harbor Employer Contributions

Employee Elective Deferral	Employer Safe Harbor Match	Employer Nonelective Contribution
0%	0.0%	3%
1%	1.0%	3%
2%	2.0%	3%
3%	3.0%	3%
4%	3.5%	3%
5% or more	4.0%	3%

Alternatively, the employer can provide for any formula that is at least as generous as this formula and satisfy the safe harbor provisions. A common formula found in many CODA safe harbor adoption agreements is a match of 100 percent up to four percent of compensation. This formula is slightly more generous than the one discussed above and is easier to communicate to employees.

Although matching contributions or nonelective contributions are required to be 100 percent vested, safe harbor plans allow the employer to avoid the ADP test, the ACP test, and the top-heavy rules and thus have become quite popular.

Automatic Enrollment Safe Harbor 401(k) Plans

Some 401(k) plans have an "automatic enrollment" or "negative election" feature. Such plans provide that elective contributions by the employee are made at a specified rate unless the employee elects otherwise (i.e., elects not to make contributions or to make contributions at a different rate). However, the employee must have an effective opportunity to elect to receive cash in lieu of contributions. This feature has been approved by the IRS and is used to increase the elective deferrals of the NHC employees in an attempt to meet the nondiscrimination tests applicable to 401(k) plans.

The negative election can apply to both current employees as well as recently hired employees or employees who meet eligibility requirements.

Example 5.22

After one year of service, Adrian meets the eligibility requirements for the ABC company 401(k) plan. The plan provides for a negative election in which the employer will deposit five percent of participants' compensation to the 401(k) plan. If Adrian earns $40,000, the plan sponsor will contribute $2,000 of her compensation to the plan unless she affirmatively elects to increase or decrease the contribution.

Under the Pension Protection Act of 2006, plans that contain a "qualified automatic enrollment feature" are eligible for a new nondiscrimination safe harbor and are treated as meeting the ADP test and the ACP test, and are not subject to the top-heavy rules. This type of plan is known as a **Qualified Automatic Contribution Arrangement (QACA)**. The PPA automatic enrollment provisions are effective for plan years after 2007. A QACA must meet certain requirements with respect to:
1. automatic deferral
2. matching or nonelective contributions
3. notice to employees

Key Concepts

1. Why would an employer want to elect to convert a 401(k) plan to a safe harbor status?

2. What are the permissible employer contributions necessary to comply with safe harbor status?

3. What are the features of a Qualified Automatic Contribution Arrangement (QACA)?

Automatic Deferral

To satisfy the automatic deferral requirement, a QACA must provide that, unless an employee elects otherwise, the employee is treated as making an election to make elective deferrals equal to a stated percentage of compensation not in excess of 10 percent for plan years beginning prior to January 1, 2020 (15% for plan years beginning after December 31, 2019; SECURE Act) and at least equal to: three percent of compensation for the first year the deemed election applies to the participant; four percent during the second year; five percent during the third year; and six percent during the fourth year and thereafter. The stated percentage must be applied uniformly to all eligible employees.

Exhibit 5.15 | Qualified Automatic Enrollment Arrangement

Elective Deferrals	
Period	**Required Deferral Percentage**
Year 1	At least 3%
Year 2	At least 4%
Year 3	At least 5%
Year 4 and thereafter	At least 6%

The QACA satisfies the contribution requirement if the employer either:
- meets the matching contribution requirement detailed below; or
- makes a nonelective contribution to a defined contribution plan of at least three percent of an employee's compensation on behalf of each nonhighly compensated employee who is eligible to participate in the automatic enrollment feature.

Matching Contribution Requirement

A plan generally satisfies the matching contribution requirement if, under the arrangement:
1. the employer makes a matching contribution on behalf of each nonhighly compensated employee that is equal to 100 percent of the employee's elective deferrals up to one percent of compensation and 50 percent of the employee's elective deferrals between one and six percent of compensation; and
2. the rate of match with respect to any elective deferrals for highly compensated employees is not greater than the rate of match for nonhighly compensated employees.

Any matching or other employer contributions taken into account in determining whether the requirements for a qualified automatic enrollment feature are satisfied must vest at least as rapidly as under two-year cliff vesting. In other words, employees with at least two years of service must be 100 percent vested with respect to such contributions.

Exhibit 5.16 | QACA Employer Contribution

Employee Elective Deferral	Employer Safe Harbor Match	Employer Nonelective Contribution
0%	0.0%	3%
1%	1.0%	3%
2%	1.5%	3%
3%	2.0%	3%
4%	2.5%	3%
5%	3.0%	3%
6% or more	3.5%	3%

Notice Requirement

To satisfy the notice requirement for matching contributions (the SECURE Act eliminated the notice requirement for employer nonelective contributions, as described above), each employee eligible to participate in the QACA must receive notice of the feature informing the employee of such rights and obligations and is written in a manner calculated to be understood by the average employee. The notice must explain:

1. the employee's right under the arrangement to elect not to have elective contributions made on the employee's behalf or to elect to have contributions made in a different amount; and
2. how contributions made under the automatic enrollment arrangement will be invested in the absence of any investment election by the employee.

The employee must be given a reasonable period of time after receipt of the notice and before the first election contribution is to be made to make an election with respect to contributions and investments.

With this new additional safe harbor created by the PPA 2006, plan sponsors have three methods of dealing with the ADP / ACP nondiscrimination testing: either perform the tests and take corrective measures (if necessary), adopt a Safe Harbor Plan, or use the automatic enrollment provisions provided for in PPA 2006 (see **Exhibit 5.17**).

Reduction of Safe Harbor Contributions

In November 2013, the IRS issued regulations for 401(k) plans that provide guidance on permitted mid-year reductions or suspensions of safe harbor nonelective contributions in certain circumstances.[37] Companies are permitted to reduce contributions if the business is operating at an economic loss for the plan year or the company provides a statement in the required notification to employees that the plan may be amended during the year to reduce or suspend safe harbor matching contributions and notice is actually provided prior to any reduction or suspension.[38]

Eligible Automatic Contribution Arrangement[39]

Under an eligible automatic contribution arrangement (EACA), a participant is treated as having elected to have the employer make contributions in an amount equal to a uniform percentage of compensation. This automatic election will remain in place until the participant specifically elects not to have such deferral percentage made (or elects a different percentage). There is no required deferral percentage and there is no required matching or non-elective contribution as is required with a qualified automatic contribution arrangement.

> ### ≔ *Key Concepts*
>
> 1. Under what circumstances may individuals take distributions from their 401(k) plan?
>
> 2. Define "hardship distributions."

Under an EACA, participants are permitted to withdraw their automatic contributions to the plan if there is an election to do so no later than 90 days after the date of the first elective contributions under the EACA. In addition, the participant must withdraw the entire amount of EACA default contributions, including any earnings thereon.

If the plan allows withdrawals under the EACA, the amount of the withdrawal other than the amount of any designated Roth contributions must be included in the employee's gross income for the tax year in which the distribution is made. The additional 10 percent tax on early distributions will not apply to the distribution.

---

37. Under Treas. Reg. §1.401(k)-3.
38. As described in IRC §412(c)(2)(A).
39. IRC 414(w).

Exhibit 5.17 | 401(k) Non-Discrimination Testing

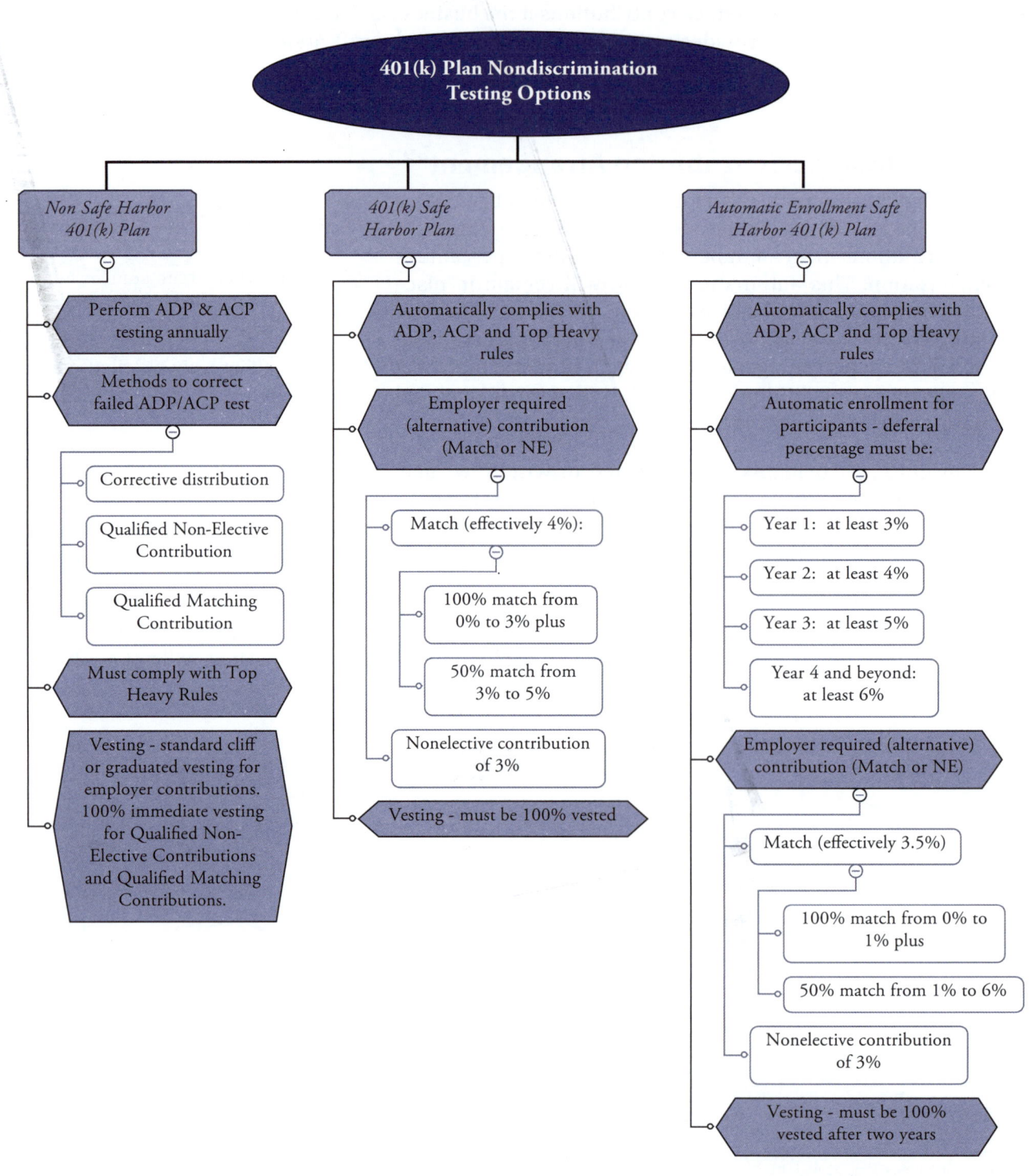

Plan Loans

Although distributions to employees are generally not permitted until retirement or termination, qualified plans are permitted to make loans to plan participants. However, plan loans must be made available to all participants and beneficiaries on an effectively equal basis, must be limited in amount, must be paid back within a certain time period, must bear a reasonable rate of interest, must be adequately secured, may not be made through the use of a credit card or similar arrangement (for plan loans made after December 20, 2019; SECURE Act), and the administrator must maintain proper accounting for the loans. Although any qualified plan could establish a loan provision, they are generally only found in CODA type plans, such as 401(k) plans and 403(b) plans. Chapter 7 includes a full discussion of the rules related to qualified plan loans.

Distributions

Participants of 401(k) plans can generally take distributions from the plan following the same rules as provided to other qualified plans (discussed in Chapter 7). However, all CODA type plans, including 401(k) plans, provide that in addition to the normal distribution options, plan participants may take distributions for hardships. Specifically, distributions may occur after:

- the retirement, death, or separation of service of the participant,
- the termination of the plan without the establishment of another plan, ·
- certain acquisitions of the company or company assets,
- the attainment of age 59½ by the participant, or
- certain hardships.

Distributions on account of any of these items are taxable as ordinary income to the extent the participant does not have an adjusted basis in the 401(k) plan and may also be subject to a 10 percent penalty. The full distribution rules and the application of the 10 percent early withdrawal penalty are discussed in Chapter 7.

It is important to note that distributions of elective deferrals from a 401(k) plan cannot take place merely by reason of the completion of a stated period of participation or the lapse of a fixed number of years. Profit sharing plans may permit distributions after a stated period of time; however, this is not the case for 401(k) plans.[40]

---

40. IRC §401(k)(2)(B)(ii).

CASE STUDY 5.1

In **Sternberg v. IRS**, the plaintiff, Irwin Sternberg ("Sternberg") brought an action against the Internal Revenue Service ("IRS") seeking a refund of taxes he paid for the 1997 tax year and a release from taxes still owed for that year.[1]

In 1990, Sternberg retired from the Harris Company. In July 1990, Sternberg received a lump-sum distribution of $147,512 from his employer's 401(k) plan and timely rolled over this distribution into an IRA.

In 1997, Sternberg withdrew $211,007 from his IRA, representing the original rollover of $147,512 plus deferred earnings from 1990 to 1997. On his 1997 tax return, Sternberg showed a tax liability of $40,956, primarily the result of a withdrawal of $211,007 from his IRA. Thereafter, Sternberg re-read the printed instructions accompanying IRS Form 1040 and "became aware of IRS Publication 590 and Form 8606 which were to be used in the determination of taxable distributions" from IRAs. On Form 8606 for "Nondeductible IRAs," Sternberg treated the original rollover of $147,512 as a nondeductible contribution to his IRA. After following the remaining instructions on Form 8606, Sternberg calculated his taxable IRA distribution for 1997 as being $83,347, not $211,007.

Based on this new number, Sternberg then filed an amended Form 1040 tax return in June 2000 that reported a total tax assessment of only $1,819 for the 1997 tax year. Accordingly, Sternberg claimed that the IRS owed him $36,741 in overpaid taxes. By letter, the IRS disallowed Sternberg's amended tax return on the grounds that, under IRC §408(d), the IRA distribution taken in 1997 was fully taxable.

Both parties agreed that Sternerg rolled over $147,512 from his employer's 401(k) into an IRA in 1990 without having to pay tax on the 401(k) distribution. Both parties also agreed that Sternberg received a distribution of $211,007 in 1997 (the original rollover plus earnings from 1990 to 1997) from the IRA, and reported the distribution as taxable on his 1997 tax return. The court found that Sternberg erroneously characterized his $147,512 rollover in 1990 as a nondeductible contribution to his IRA, when the relevant statutes, regulations, and publications establish that the rollover only deferred the taxes that he would have owed had he elected to keep the 401(k) distribution.

Under the Internal Revenue Code, if "any amount ... distributed from an individual retirement or individual retirement annuity" is paid to the owner of the annuity, and the entire amount is then rolled over into an individual retirement account within 60 days, the amount distributed is not subject to income tax at that time.[2]

1. **Sternberg v. Internal Revenue Service,** 2004 WL 790219 (E.D.N.Y.), 93 A.F.T.R.2d 2004-1388 (Feb. 9, 2004).
2. IRC §402(c); 26 C.F.R. §1.408 4(b).

rdship Distributions

ributions on account of hardship must be limited to the maximum distributable amount. Under prior the maximum distributable amount was equal to the employee's total elective deferral contributions the date of distribution, reduced by the amount of previous distributions of elective contributions. the maximum distributable amount did not include earnings, Qualified Nonelective Contributions

(QNECs) or Qualified Matching Contributions (QMCs), unless certain grandfather rules applied. These grandfather rules related to amounts that were credited to an employee's account prior to December 31, 1988.[41] The Bipartisan Budget Act of 2018 amended the rules such that, for distributions made on or after January 1, 2020, the amount available as a hardship distribution now includes employee elective deferrals, Qualified Nonelective Contributions (QNECs), Qualified Matching Contributions (QMCs), and earnings attributed to these contributions regardless of when contributed or earned, reduced by the amount of previous distributions.[42]

Exhibit 5.18 | Maximum Hardship Distributions

Employee Deferral Contribution at Date of Distribution
Plus: QNECs + QMCs + Earnings on These Amounts
Less: (Previous Distributions)
Equals: Maximum Distributable Amount

Example 5.23

Hardy defers $5,000 of his annual compensation into the company 401(k) plan every year. He has been doing so for the last ten years. The earnings attributable to his contributions are $8,000. Therefore, his maximum distributable amount is equal to his total elective deferrals plus the earnings attributable to his contributions, or $58,000. If he had previously received a hardship distribution, then the amount of that distribution would reduce the $58,000 maximum distributable amount.

Hardship distributions can only be provided if there is an immediate and heavy financial need and the withdrawal is necessary to satisfy such need. Whether an employee has an immediate and heavy financial need is to be determined based on all the relevant facts and circumstances. Generally, for example, the need to pay funeral expenses of a family member would constitute an immediate and heavy financial need. A distribution made to an employee for the purchase of a boat or television would generally not constitute a distribution made on account of an immediate and heavy financial need. A financial need may be immediate and heavy even if it was reasonably foreseeable or voluntarily incurred by the employee.[43]

A distribution is deemed to be on account of an immediate and heavy financial need of the employee if the distribution is for any of the following:[44]
- **Medical** - expenses for medical care described in IRC §213(d) previously incurred by the employee, the employee's spouse, any dependents of the employee (as defined in IRC §152), or a primary beneficiary under the plan or necessary for these persons to obtain medical care described in IRC §213(d);
- **Residence** - costs directly related to the purchase of a principal residence for the employee (excluding mortgage payments);

---

41. Treas. Reg. §1.401(k)-1(d)(3).
42. IRC §401(k)(14)(A)
43. Treas. Reg. §1.401(k)-1(d)(3).
44. Treas. Reg. §1.401(k)-1(d)(3)(ii)(B), as amended by PPA 2006.

- **Education** - payment of tuition, related educational fees, and room and board expenses for up to the next 12 months of post-secondary education for the employee or the employee's spouse, children, dependents (as defined in IRC §152), or a primary beneficiary under the plan;
- **Eviction** - payments necessary to prevent the eviction of the employee from the employee's principal residence or foreclosure on the mortgage on that residence;
- **Funeral** - payments for burial or funeral expenses of the employee's deceased parent, spouse, child, dependent (as defined in IRC §152), or for a deceased primary beneficiary under the plan;
- **Casualty Loss** - expenses for the repair of damage to the employee's principal residence that would be deductible under IRC §165 (without regard to the 10% of AGI floor, and without regard to the limitations in IRC §165(h)(5) added by the TCJA); or
- **Disaster** - expenses and losses (including loss of income) incurred by the employee on account of a FEMA-declared disaster, provided that the employee's principal residence or principal place of employment at the time of the disaster was located in the FEMA-designated disaster area.

A distribution is treated as necessary to satisfy an immediate and heavy financial need of an employee only to the extent the amount of the distribution is not in excess of the amount required to satisfy the financial need. For this purpose, the amount required to satisfy the financial need may include any amounts necessary to pay any federal, state, or local income taxes or penalties reasonably anticipated to result from the distribution.

A distribution is not treated as necessary to satisfy an immediate and heavy financial need of an employee to the extent the need may be relieved from other resources that are reasonably available to the employee. This determination generally is to be made on the basis of all the relevant facts and circumstances. For these purposes, the employee's resources are deemed to include those assets of the employee's spouse and minor children that are reasonably available to the employee. Thus, for example, a vacation home owned by the employee and the employee's spouse, whether as community property, joint tenants, tenants by the entirety, or tenants in common, generally will be deemed a resource of the employee. However, property held for the employee's child under an irrevocable trust or under the Uniform Gifts to Minors Act (or comparable State law) is not treated as a resource of the employee.

An immediate and heavy financial need generally may be treated as one not capable of being relieved from other resources that are reasonably available to the employee. An employer can rely upon the employee's written representation (including use of electronic medium or oral representation on a recorded phone line) that the employee has insufficient cash or other liquid assets reasonably available to satisfy the need unless the employer has actual knowledge to the contrary. Plans are permitted to provide that additional conditions, such as a requirement that the employee must obtain all nontaxable loans available under the plan and all other plans maintained by the employer, be met prior to becoming eligible for a hardship distribution. A plan may not, however, require the suspension of the employee's elective contributions as a condition for obtaining the hardship distribution.[45]

Hardship distributions are taxed as ordinary income and may be subject to the 10 percent early withdrawal penalty (discussed in Chapter 7). Distributions are not subject to the 20 percent statutory withholding requirements (discussed in Chapter 7) since hardship distributions are not eligible for rollover treatment. Under prior law, those taking a hardship distribution were suspended from making future contributions to the plan for six months. The rule on suspension of contributions was eliminated by the Bipartisan Budget Act of 2018, thus allowing the employee to continue to contribute to the plan in

---

45. Treas. Reg. §1.401(k)-1(d)(3), as amended by the Bipartisan Budget Act of 2018.

spite of the hardship distribution, allowing for a greater opportunity to rebuild the retirement funds necessary for a secure retirement.

Example 5.24

Dalmart Co. maintains Plan Y, a profit sharing plan that includes a CODA that does not permit participant loans. However, Plan Y provides that elective contributions under the arrangement may be distributed to an eligible employee on account of hardship using the deemed immediate and heavy financial need provisions. Amanda is an eligible employee in Plan Y with an account balance of $50,000. The total amount of elective deferral contributions made by Amanda, who has not previously received a distribution from Plan Y, is $20,000. Amanda requests a $15,000 hardship distribution of her elective deferral contributions to pay six months of college tuition and room and board expenses for her dependent child. At the time of the distribution request, Amanda's sole asset (that is reasonably available to Amanda within the meaning of the code) is a savings account with an available balance of $10,000.

A distribution is made on account of hardship only if the distribution is made both on account of Amanda's immediate and heavy financial need. A distribution for payment of up to the next 12 months of post-secondary education and room and board expenses for Amanda's dependent child is deemed to be on account of an immediate and heavy financial need of Amanda.

However, the distribution is only treated as necessary to satisfy Amanda's immediate and heavy financial need to the extent the need may not be relieved from other resources reasonably available to Amanda. Since Amanda has a $10,000 savings account as a reasonably available resource, it must be taken into account in determining the amount necessary to satisfy Amanda's immediate and heavy financial need. Thus, Amanda may only receive a distribution of $5,000 ($15,000 - $10,000) of her elective deferral contributions on account of this hardship plus an amount necessary to pay any federal, state, or local income taxes or penalties reasonably anticipated to result from the hardship distribution.

Example 5.25

The facts are the same as in **Example 5.24**, Doug, another employee of Dalmart Co. has a vested account balance of $25,000. The total amount of elective deferral contributions made by Doug, who has not previously received a distribution from Plan Y, is $15,000. Doug requests a $10,000 distribution of his elective deferral contributions to pay six months of college tuition and room and board expenses for his dependent child. Doug makes a written representation (with respect to which Dalmart Co. has no actual knowledge to the contrary) that he does not have sufficient cash or other liquid assets reasonably available to satisfy the need.

A distribution for payment of up to the next 12 months of post-secondary education and room and board expenses for Doug's dependent child is deemed to be on account of Doug's immediate and heavy financial need. In addition, because Dalmart Co. can rely on

> Doug's written representation, the distribution is considered necessary to satisfy Doug's immediate and heavy financial need. Therefore, Doug may receive a $10,000 distribution of his elective contributions on account of hardship plus an amount necessary to pay any federal, state, or local income taxes or penalties reasonably anticipated to result from the distribution.

It is important to note that while the above rules are guidelines in the IRC, individual plans may choose to restrict the types of contributions that are available for hardship distributions and can allow distributions for some or all of the seven safe harbor needs. It is important for participants and advisors to read the plan document to determine specific elements of a particular plan.

DB(k) RETIREMENT PLANS

Combined Defined Benefit and Qualified Cash or Deferred Arrangements Plan

A **DB(k) retirement plan** incorporates, under one single plan with a single trust, a defined benefit plan combined with a 401(k) arrangement. For plan years beginning in 2010 and later, a DB(k) plan can be established by a sponsoring employer who employs an average of 2 to 500 workers in the preceding calendar year and employs at least two workers at the beginning of the plan year (for a new employer the determination is based on the average number of employees anticipated to employ during the current calendar year). The defined benefit and defined contribution components must meet the benefit, contribution, vesting, and nondiscrimination requirements under IRC §414(x). Note: Under IRC §414(x), after three years of service the employee has a nonforfeitable right to 100 percent of employee's accrued benefits derived from employer contributions under the defined benefit portion of the plan, and to employer nonelective contributions made under the defined contribution portion of the plan.

The annual reporting requirements of the DB(k) plan are somewhat simplified. While plan sponsors offering different types of plans are generally required to annually a Form 5500 for each plan type, the DB(k) files only one Form 5500 annually. Details regarding annual filing requirements are discussed in Chapter 8.

Defined Benefit Component of DB(k)

The minimum benefit provided by the defined benefit portion of the plan, must provide each participant with an annual retirement amount that is not less than the worker's final average pay times the lesser of: (1) one percent multiplied times the participant's years of service, or (2) 20 percent. The participant's final average pay is computed by averaging up to five consecutive years of the worker's highest compensation. A plan participant must be fully vested in the defined benefit plan after completion of three years of service.

DB(k) plans are permitted to offer a cash balance formula as the defined benefit part of the plan. In such a case, the pay credits must not be less than the following table, which is based on the age of the employee:

30 or less	.....	2%
Over 30 but less than 40	.....	4%
40 or over but less than 50	.....	6%
50 or over	.....	8%

The DB(k) plan design will either provide a normal defined benefit or one with a hypothetical account (i.e., cash balance).

Defined Contribution Component of DB(k)

The 401(k) portion of the combined plan is considered an automatic contribution arrangement if it meets notice and election requirements and if the plan provides that each worker eligible to participate is treated as having elected to participate in a contribution amount equal to four percent of the worker's compensation (unless the employee elects out or selects a lower rate of contribution). Employer matching contributions must be made in an amount equal to 50 percent of the employee elective contributions up to four percent of compensation. Participants must be immediately fully vested in any required employer matching contributions. After completion of three years of service, a participant is fully vested in any employer nonelective contributions. A DB(k) plan is deemed to satisfy the top-heavy rules, as well as the rules for ADP and ACP.

Small companies that are currently managing both a benefit pension plan and a 401(k) plan may consider the DB(k) plan to reduce plan costs and paperwork. In addition, small companies that employ skilled workers, such as engineering, law, and accounting firms, may consider the plan to competitively attract talented employees. In order to offer the plan, a small company needs adequate cash to pay the costs of adopting the DB(k). Because the DB(k) retirement plan may have limited application, the individual 401(k) (covered earlier in this chapter) may be an attractive alternative to the DB(k) plan.

> ### ✎ Quick Quiz 5.9
>
> 1. A distribution from a 401(k) plan is not available until the plan participant either retires or dies.
>   a. True
>   b. False
>
> 2. A hardship distribution can be taken from a 401(k) plan for an amount equal to the employee's total elective contribution, QNECs, QMCs, and earnings on these amounts, less the value of any previous hardship distributions.
>   a. True
>   b. False
>
> 3. Hardship withdrawals are available if there is an immediate and heavy financial burden even if the participant has other assets available to satisfy the need.
>   a. True
>   b. False
>
> False, True, False.

Exhibit 5.19 | DB(k) Plans

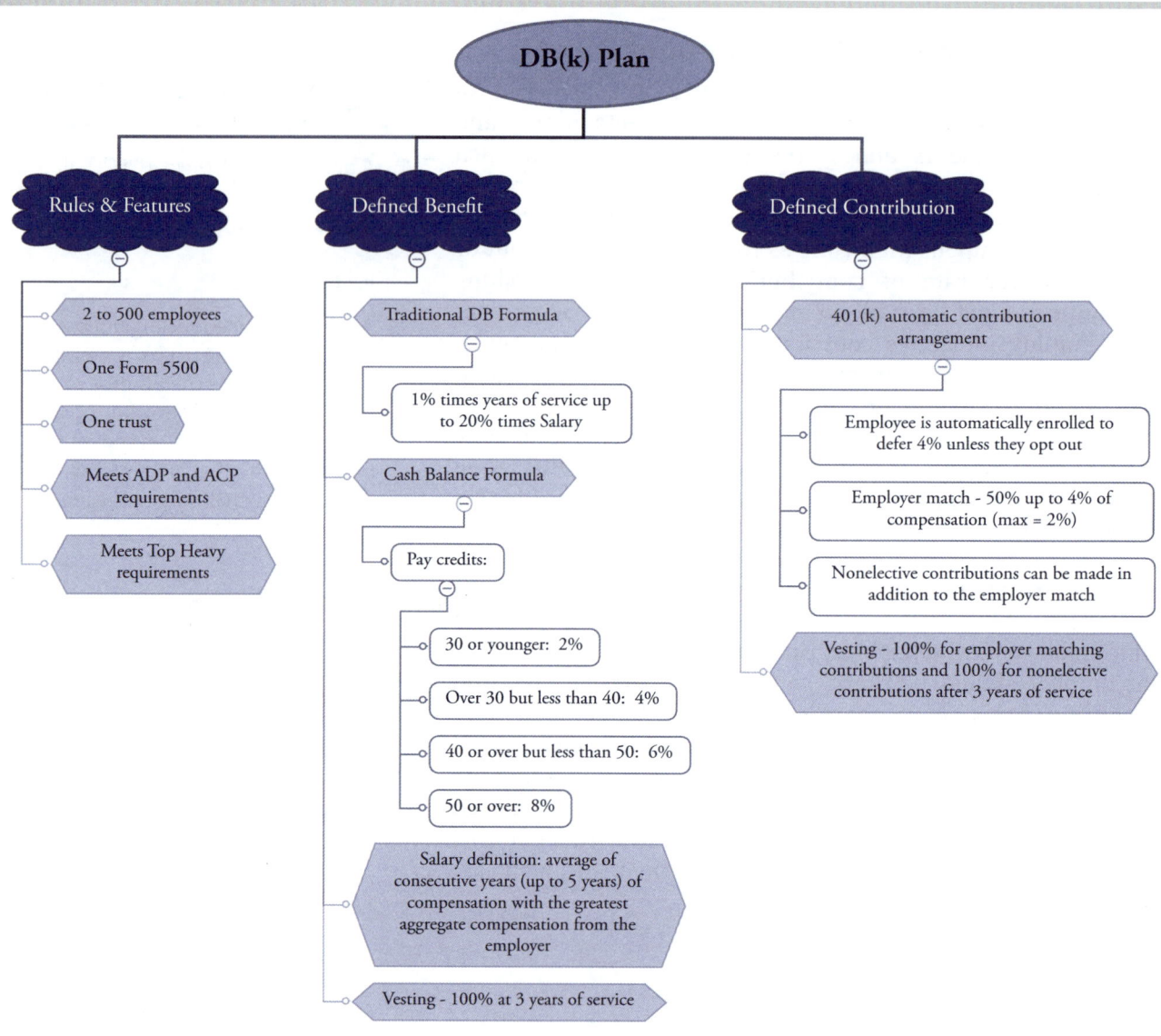

DB(k) Plan

Rules & Features
- 2 to 500 employees
- One Form 5500
- One trust
- Meets ADP and ACP requirements
- Meets Top Heavy requirements

Defined Benefit
- Traditional DB Formula
  - 1% times years of service up to 20% times Salary
- Cash Balance Formula
  - Pay credits:
    - 30 or younger: 2%
    - Over 30 but less than 40: 4%
    - 40 or over but less than 50: 6%
    - 50 or over: 8%
- Salary definition: average of consecutive years (up to 5 years) of compensation with the greatest aggregate compensation from the employer
- Vesting - 100% at 3 years of service

Defined Contribution
- 401(k) automatic contribution arrangement
  - Employee is automatically enrolled to defer 4% unless they opt out
  - Employer match - 50% up to 4% of compensation (max = 2%)
  - Nonelective contributions can be made in addition to the employer match
- Vesting - 100% for employer matching contributions and 100% for nonelective contributions after 3 years of service

US GOVERNMENT THRIFT SAVINGS PLANS

The **Thrift Savings Plan** (TSP) is a retirement savings and investment plan for Federal employees and members of the uniformed services, including the Ready Reserve. It was established by Congress in the Federal Employees' Retirement System Act of 1986 and offers the same types of savings and tax benefits that are provided in 401(k) plans, including traditional and Roth deferrals.

Contributions

There are three sources of contributions to the TSP:
1. employee contributions
2. agency automatic contributions
3. matching contributions

The employee contributions are the same as 401(k) salary deferrals and have the same limit, including catch up contributions for those who have attained the age of 50 within the year. The TSP includes an automatic enrollment into the plan, which can be changed by the participant. Employees hired on or after October 1, 2020 are automatically enrolled in the TSP at five percent of their salary, entitling them to a full match.

Certain employees, including those covered by the Federal Employees' Retirement System (FERS), automatically receive contributions of one percent of basic pay to the TSP. These contributions are called Agency Automatic (1%) Contributions and generally vest after three years, but may vest as fast as two years in some cases.

The third type of contribution is a matching contribution. Employee deferrals are matched dollar-for-dollar up to three percent of pay and 50 percent from three percent to five percent.[46] With an employee deferral of five percent or more, the match is four percent of compensation. Matching contributions are always fully vested.

The contribution limit is the same as with 401(k) plans at $19,500 (2021) with a maximum deferral of $26,000 (2021) for those who have attained age 50.[47] Total contributions are also limited to the IRC §415(c) limit of $58,000 (2021).

Other similarities of the TSP and 401(k) plans are rollover rules, both in and out of the plan, loan provisions, and hardship withdrawals. In addition, participants in the TSP have an array of investment options to choose from ranging from government securities to international equities. Ultimately, the TSP is very much a government version of the standard safe harbor 401(k) plan.

---

46. This is the same formula as for a safe harbor 401(k) plan.
47. Contributions to the TSP by uniformed service members in a combat zone are contributed to the TSP as "tax-exempt" are not subject to the IRC elective deferral limit, but are considered for purposes of the IRC §415(c) limit. The term "uniformed services" means the Armed Forces, the Army National Guard and the Air National Guard when engaged in active duty for training, inactive duty training, or full-time National Guard duty, the commissioned corps of the Public Health Service, and any other category of persons designated by the President in time of war or national emergency.

DISCUSSION QUESTIONS

SOLUTIONS to the discussion questions can be found exclusively within the chapter. Once you have completed an initial reading of the chapter, go back and highlight the answers to these questions.

1. Describe the key elements of a profit sharing plan as discussed in Treasury Regulation 1.401-1(b).

2. List the differences between pension plans and profit sharing plans.

3. For years after 2019, what is the last date during the year that a profit sharing plan may be established and by when must contributions be made to a profit sharing plan?

4. Explain the differences between the standard allocation formula, permitted disparity, age-based profit sharing plans, and new comparability plans.

5. How can forfeitures be used within a profit sharing plan?

6. What are the eligibility requirements for profit sharing plans?

7. What are the applicable vesting rules for profit sharing plans?

8. When may distributions be taken from a profit sharing plan and how will they be taxed?

9. Describe the characteristics of a cash or deferred arrangement.

10. List the advantages of 401(k) plans to both employees and employers.

11. Which entities may establish a 401(k) plan?

12. Describe the eligibility rules for 401(k) plans.

13. What are the entrance dates rules for 401(k) plans?

14. Define "participation" and "negative elections" with regard to 401(k) plans.

15. How can employees make contributions to a 401(k) plan and what are the applicable limits?

16. What is the income tax impact of employee elective deferrals?

17. When must the employer deposit employee elective deferrals?

18. Describe the catch-up contribution available for some employees.

19. How are employee after-tax contributions taxed?

20. Describe matching contributions and their associated vesting schedules.

21. How can a profit sharing contribution be used with a 401(k) plan?

22. What is the purpose of the ADP test and how does it work?

23. How is the ADP test calculated?

24. What are the remedies available if a company fails the ADP test?

25. What are corrective distributions and how are they used to correct the ADP test?

26. What is recharacterization and how is it used to correct the ADP test?

27. What are qualified nonelective and matching contributions and how are they used to correct the ADP test?

28. Explain the safe harbor rules and how they affect 401(k) contributions.

29. When may distributions be taken from a 401(k) plan?

30. Describe the hardship distribution rules.

A sample of multiple choice problems is provided below. Additional multiple choice problems are available at money-education.com by accessing the Student Practice Portal.

1. Which of the following is not true regarding profit sharing plans?
    a. The plan is established and maintained by the individual employee.
    b. Allows employees to derive benefit from profits of the company.
    c. Profit sharing plans cannot discriminate in favor of officers and shareholders.
    d. Profit sharing plans provide a definite predetermined formula for allocating the contributions made to the plan among the participants and for distributing the funds accumulated under the plan.

2. Which of the following statements is true?
    a. Profit sharing plans may not offer in-service withdrawals.
    b. Pension and profit sharing plans are both subject to mandatory funding requirements.
    c. Profit sharing plans allow annual employer contributions up to 25 percent of the employer's covered compensation.
    d. The legal promise of a profit sharing plan is to pay a pension at retirement.

3. Andi, the 100 percent owner of Andi's Day Care, a C-corporation, would like to establish a profit sharing plan. Andi's Day Care's tax year ends July 31 to coincide with the school year. What is the latest day Andi can establish and contribute to the plan?
    a. Andi must establish and contribute to the plan by December 31 of the year in which she would like to establish the plan.
    b. Andi must establish the plan and make the contribution by April 15 of the following year assuming she filed the appropriate extensions.
    c. Andi must establish the plan by July 31 of the year in which she would like to establish the plan and contribute by December 31.
    d. Andi must establish the plan by December 31 of the year in which she would like to establish the plan and contribute to the plan by April 15 of the following year.

4. Which of the following statements is true regarding CODAs?
    a. A 401(k) plan must be established in such a way that employers are required to contribute to the plan permitting only employee contributions to the plan.
    b. A CODA is allowed with a profit-sharing plan, stock bonus plan, and a cash balance pension plan.
    c. Contributions can only be made after-tax.
    d. CODAs are employee self-reliant plans.

5. All of the following are advantages of a 401(k) plan except:

    a. Employees are permitted to shelter current income from taxation in a 401(k) plan.

    b. Employers can sponsor 401(k) safe harbor plans without committing to annual contributions and without creating a deferred liability.

    c. Earnings grow tax-deferred until distributed.

    d. Employers can establish 401(k) plans with minimal expense.

> **Additional multiple choice problems
> are available at
> money-education.com
> by accessing the
> Student Practice Portal.
> Access requires registration of the title using
> the unique code at the front of the book.**

QUICK QUIZ EXPLANATION

Quick Quiz 5.1
1. False. A profit sharing plan allows all eligible employees to participate in the profits of the company. An eligible employee does not have to be an officer or shareholder to participate in a profit sharing plan.
2. False. A pension plan may not invest more than 10 percent of its assets in employer securities.
3. True.

Quick Quiz 5.2
1. False. Permitted disparity is a technique of allocating plan contributions to employees' accounts that will provide higher contributions to those employees whose compensation is in excess of the Social Security wage base (or integration level) for the plan year.
2. True.
3. False. The regulations associated with new comparability plans restrict their flexibility and require minimum allocations to NHCEs.

Quick Quiz 5.3
1. False. A profit sharing plan, like other qualified plans, may not require participants to wait more than two years to become eligible.
2. False. Under the PPA 2006, profit sharing plans must use a 3-year cliff vesting schedule or a 2-to-6-year graduated vesting schedule.
3. True.

Quick Quiz 5.4
1. False. For tax years after 1996, tax-exempt entities are permitted to establish 401(k) plans.
2. True.
3. True.

Quick Quiz 5.5
1. True.
2. False. A 401(k) must generally have two entrance dates per year to meet the requirements of a qualified plan.

Quick Quiz 5.6
1. True.
2. True.
3. False. Employee elective deferrals must be deposited and segregated from the employer's assets by the earliest date that is reasonably possible. However, the segregation of the funds must be completed by the 15th day of the month following the deferral from the employee's compensation.
4. True.
5. False. A negative election requires an employee to proactively opt-out of the plan.

QUICK QUIZ EXPLANATION

Quick Quiz 5.7
1. False. Matching contributions vest on a 3-year cliff or 2-to-6-year graded vesting schedule.
2. True.
3. False. The annual deferral limit of $19,500 for 2021 is the maximum that could be contributed to either account or in combination. A taxpayer cannot defer $19,500 to the pre-tax account and another $19,500 to the Roth account.

Quick Quiz 5.8
1. True.
2. True.
3. False. If a CODA fails the ADP test, there are four alternative remedies to bring the plan into compliance: corrective distributions, recharacterization, qualified nonelective contributions (QNEC), or qualified matching contributions (QMC).
4. False. The pre-PPA 2006 safe harbor provisions require that matching contributions or nonelective contributions must be 100% vested to avoid calculating the ADP test.
5. False. The ADP for the NHCEs is 4% (20% / 5). The HCEs are limited to 6%, which is 2% above the 4% average.

Quick Quiz 5.9
1. False. In addition to the normal distribution options, 401(k) participants may also take distributions for hardships.
2. True.
3. False. Hardship distributions can only be provided if there is an immediate and heavy financial need and the withdrawal is necessary to satisfy the need (i.e., the participant does not have other resources that could be used to satisfy the need).

6

STOCK BONUS PLANS &
EMPLOYEE STOCK
OWNERSHIP PLANS

1. Explain the similarities and differences between stock bonus plans and profit sharing plans.*
2. Explain the similarities and differences between a stock bonus plan and an ESOP.*
3. Determine whether the advantages of an ESOP are appropriate for a given situation.*
4. Explain how the ESOP trustee may have a potential conflict of interest while attempting to execute the trustee's duties.
5. Describe how ESOPs work when adopted by an S corporation.

Ties to CFP Certification Learning Objectives

INTRODUCTION

As discussed in the previous chapter, profit sharing plans allow employers to contribute to a qualified plan on behalf of employees of the organizations. However, a profit sharing plan may not be the best option for an organization or company that has limited cash resources. For example, a company might be unable to contribute large amounts of cash to a profit sharing plan due to internal cash needs. In such an situation, a stock bonus plan or employee stock ownership plan (ESOP) may be a viable short to intermediate term alternative to a profit sharing plan, while still providing the advantages of a qualified plan.

A **stock bonus plan** is a plan established and maintained by an employer to provide benefits similar to those of a profit sharing plan.[1] While contributions by the employer are similar in deductibility to a profit sharing plan, a stock bonus plan is not dependent upon profits. Both contributions to and distributions from a stock bonus plan are generally in the form of employer stock. Thus, a stock bonus plan does not require the corporation to fund the plan with cash that is better utilized for other obligations or opportunities. For purposes of allocating and distributing the stock of the employer, which is to be shared among the employees or their beneficiaries, such a plan is subject to the same basic qualified plan requirements as profit sharing plans.

An Employee Stock Ownership Plan (ESOP) is a qualified plan that invests primarily in "qualifying employer securities," typically shares of stock in the corporation creating the plan.[2] ESOPs were first enacted into federal legislation in 1974 under ERISA. At the time, Congress wanted to give employers an incentive to provide rank-and-file employees an ownership stake in the corporation for which they worked. Consequently, Congress established laws creating stock bonus plans and ESOPs, which provide an incentive to invest primarily in employer securities. This chapter discusses both the stock bonus plan and the ESOP in detail.

KNOW THE NUMBERS (2021)

ESOP Account Balance	$1,165,000
Covered Compensation	$290,000

---

1. The term "stock bonus plan" is defined in the Treas. Reg. at §1.401-1(b)(1)(iii) as follows: A stock bonus plan is a plan established and maintained by an employer to provide benefits similar to those of a profit-sharing plan, except that the contributions by the employer are not necessarily dependent upon profits and the benefits are distributable in stock of the employer company. For the purpose of allocating and distributing the stock of the employer which is to be shared among his employees or their beneficiaries, such a plan is subject to the same requirements as a profit-sharing plan.
2. IRC §1107 (d)(6)(A).

STOCK BONUS PLANS

Stock bonus plans are defined contribution profit sharing plans that allow employers to contribute stock to a qualified plan on behalf of their employees. As with all qualified plans, earnings within a stock bonus plan are tax deferred until the stock, its value in cash, or other securities are distributed from the plan. Because stock bonus plans are not subject to mandatory funding, contributions can and generally are made on a discretionary basis. However, when contributions are made, they must be made to participant's accounts on a nondiscriminatory basis. The contributions cannot discriminate against the **rank-and-file employees** for the benefit of shareholders, officers, and highly compensated employees. Thus, a stock bonus plan is a variation of a profit sharing plan, yet it has some distinct differences from other profit sharing plans.

Generally, stock bonus plans must satisfy the following requirements:[3]
- Unlike profit sharing plans, stock bonus plan participants must have pass through voting rights on employer stock held by the plan.[4]
- Participants must have the right to demand employer securities on plan distributions.
- Participants must have the right to demand that the employer repurchase the employer's securities if they are not publicly traded (the put option).[5]
- Participants must be able to elect to have distributions begin within one year of normal retirement age, death, or disability, or within five years for other modes of employment termination.[6]
- Distributions must be fully paid within five years of commencement of distributions.[7]

Advantages and Disadvantages of Stock Bonus Plans

Stock bonus plans are profit sharing plans for which an employer makes contributions of employer stock on behalf of a participant to a qualified plan as part of the employee's overall compensation package. Similar to profit sharing plans, stock bonus plans are designed to provide benefits to both employers and employees. The fair market value of contributions of employer stock are tax deductible to the employer, which can result in decreased income tax costs for the corporation. The contributions are not required to be fixed in amount, as there is no annual mandatory contribution requirement for stock bonus plans, which allows the corporation flexibility in funding. Stock bonus plans also promote productivity within the corporation because participants, as shareholders, have a vested financial interest in the growth and success of the corporation (although this does not always lead to an increase in stock prices).

Disadvantages to the Employees

While the advantages of stock bonus plans are attractive, stock bonus plans do have drawbacks. To the employee, there is the risk associated with the non-diversified investment portfolio. The employee earns income from the employer and also has an investment in the stock of the employer. In other words, if the corporation were to fail, the entire value in the employee retirement accounts may be lost as well as the employee's job and source of income (wages).

---

3. IRC §§401(a)(22) and 401(a)(23).
4. IRC §409(e).
5. IRC §409(h).
6. There are certain expectations. See IRC §409(o).
7. IRC §409(o).

Disadvantages to the Employer

One disadvantage to the employer is that the ownership and control of the corporation is diminished or "**diluted**" as shares are granted to the employees. This has a greater impact on smaller, closely held corporations.

With stock bonus plans, the required "**repurchase option**" **(put option)** could deplete the cash of the corporation. A repurchase option allows a terminating employee the choice to receive the cash equivalent of the employer's stock if the stock is not readily tradeable on an established market. If the repurchase occurs at an unexpected time (e.g., upon the death of participant), the forced sale of stock back to the corporation may drain the corporation's cash flow as well as result in a costly appraisal of the stock to determine the value to pay the employee-participant's heirs. In such a situation, the strain on the cash flow of the employer may have a negative impact on the corporation as a whole.

Features of Stock Bonus Plans as Compared to Profit Sharing Plans

As discussed above, stock bonus plans are a particular type of profit sharing plan and have many profit sharing characteristics. The features of stock bonus plans will be discussed in relation to profit sharing plans in order to identify the similarities and differences between the two types of plans.

Contributions and Deductions

As with all qualified plans, stock bonus plans and profit sharing plans must be established by, and contributions to the plan made by, the due date of the income tax return including permitted extensions.

Contributions to stock bonus plans and profit sharing plans are **discretionary**, but must meet the general profit sharing plan requirement of "**substantial and recurring**." While most contributions to stock bonus plans are tied to the corporation's profitability, there is no requirement that a corporation must contribute to the plan in a year in which it has earnings nor is there a prohibition against contributions to the plan in years in which the corporation has losses.

Like profit sharing plans, stock bonus plans have a deductible contribution limit of 25 percent of covered compensation (limited to $290,000 for 2021) per employee.[8] When stock is contributed, the fair market value of the stock, as determined by a qualified appraiser, is deductible. In some instances, an employer may contribute more than the permitted 25 percent, in which case the employer would deduct the 25 percent and could carry forward the amount which exceeds the 25 percent limit and deduct the excess in a future year. However, the amount carried forward when added to the contribution made for the future year cannot exceed 25 percent, and the employer must pay a 10 percent excise tax on the portion of the contribution that exceeds 25 percent of covered compensation for the current year.[9]

---

8. IRC §404(a)(3).
9. IRC §4972(a).

Valuation of Employer Stock in Stock Bonus Plans

An important area of plan administration for a stock bonus plan is the valuation or appraisal of the employer's securities. Valuations are performed to determine the value of the contribution for the corporation's income tax deduction purposes and the corporation's financial statements. Valuations are also completed to periodically inform the participants of the stock's value. The employer will track the value of the contributions and therefore the amount of ordinary income that the employee will have to recognize upon distribution. A valuation also allows the employee to determine the sales price of the stock if the employee is exercising the repurchase option (put option).

For private or closely held corporations, determining the value of securities is often difficult. The law requires valuations of employers' securities and if those securities are not readily tradeable on an established securities market, then these valuations must be undertaken by independent appraisers.[10] The appraiser must be an uninterested, independent party. The valuation must be done in good faith and must be based on all factors relevant to determining the securities' fair market value.[11] The valuation therefore involves an assessment of what a willing buyer would pay to a willing seller for the securities or business.[12] These valuations, which can be costly, are used on an annual basis to determine the value of the securities, that, for example, were contributed by the employer for tax deduction purposes or that were subjected to a repurchase option of a departing employee.

Eligibility

Stock bonus plans are subject to standard eligibility rules discussed in Chapter 3, the same as other qualified plans, including profit sharing plans. The standard eligibility of age 21 and one-year of service generally applies to stock bonus plans. As discussed before, plan sponsors can choose to make the eligibility requirements less restrictive.

Like other qualified plans, stock bonus plans may require a two year waiting period before the employee is eligible. However, if the employer requires a two year waiting period, then all contributions must be 100 percent vested after the two year waiting period.

Allocation Methods

The allocation methods for contributions to participants' accounts in stock bonus plans are the same as those for profit sharing plans. The difference is that, normally, employer stock is contributed to the stock bonus plan rather than cash.

10. IRC §401 (a)(28)(C).
11. Regulations §54.4975-11(d)(5). See also *Donovan v. Cunningham* 541 ESOPs 246 (S.D. Texas 1982).
12. Revenue Ruling 59-60.

The standard allocation method for a stock bonus plan is to allocate contributions based on a percentage of each employee's compensation. Whenever stock is contributed, the stock must be valued by a qualified appraiser as discussed previously. Cash is generally only contributed when the plan expects cash distribution elections or the plan needs cash to meet its obligation to provide a market for the stock.

The percentage of compensation method is not the only acceptable allocation method for stock bonus plans. The formulas discussed for profit sharing plans based on age and past service also apply to stock bonus plans, as does the new comparability plan based on the employees' respective classifications in the corporation. These methods apply as long as they do not discriminate in favor of highly compensated employees. As discussed in Chapter 5, stock bonus plans are also permitted to use the technique or method of permitted disparity, also known as Social Security Integration, which allocates plan contributions to employees' accounts and provides greater contributions to those employees whose earnings exceed the Social Security wage base.

> **Key Concepts**
>
> 1. Define net unrealized appreciation.
>
> 2. What is the advantage to an employee of receiving a stock distribution from a stock bonus plan rather than receive the distribution in cash?

Vesting

Similar to profit sharing plans, the vesting rules for stock bonus plans are the same as for other qualified plans as discussed in Chapter 3. The standard three-year cliff vesting schedules and the graduated 2-to-6-year vesting schedules for defined contribution plans as required by the Pension Protection Act of 2006 apply unless the employer selects a two year eligibility rule. The plan sponsor may not exceed these vesting requirements, yet is always permitted to be more generous if desired.

Portfolio Diversification

Profit sharing plans are generally designed to invest in **diversified investment portfolios**. Consequently, the assets in these plans are not usually invested exclusively in employer stock. Unlike profit sharing plans, stock bonus plans are usually funded with one hundred percent employer stock. Profit sharing plans assist the employee in preparing for retirement through the growth of the individual participant's account with deferred compensation and tax deferral on earnings. As such, these plans are generally well-diversified investment portfolios. In contrast, stock bonus plans are initially "cash free" to the employer as they are predominately funded with the employer's stock in order to provide benefits to employees without the need to use the corporation's cash. The exclusive use of employer stock as contributions results in an undiversified portfolio for the participant.

To the extent that a stock bonus plan is sponsored by a publicly traded company, the Pension Protection Act of 2006 requires the plan to allow plan participants to diversify their pre-tax deferrals, after-tax contributions, and employer contributions that have been invested in employer securities. Like other defined contribution plans, the plan must offer a choice of at least three investment options, other than employer securities, each of which must be diversified and have materially different risk and return characteristics. This requirement is consistent with that found in ERISA and generally implies that a plan must provide at least one type of stock, bond, and cash fund as investment options. All plan participants must be allowed to diversify the investment of their elective deferrals and after-tax contributions. In addition, plan participants with three or more years of service must be allowed to diversify the investment of other contributions made on their behalf.

Exhibit 6.1 | PPA 2006 Diversification Requirements for Public Companies

	Employee Contributions*		Employer Contributions
	Pre-tax Elective Deferrals	**After-tax Contributions**	
Participant with less than 3 years of service	Immediate right to diversify	Immediate right to diversify	No requirement to diversify
Participant with 3 years or more of service			Immediate right to diversify

Employee contributions typically occur in 401(k) plans and thrift plans. Cash or deferral arrangements (CODAs) can be added to stock bonus plans and ESOPs.

Voting Rights

If a profit sharing plan consists of employer stock, the plan participant generally does not have voting rights in the stock held by the plan. However, participants in a stock bonus plan must have pass through voting rights on employer stock that is held by the plan on their behalf.[13] **"Pass through" voting rights** mean that the voting rights of the stock pass through from the plan all the way down to the participant. In this case, the participant could vote the shares of stock allocated to his stock bonus plan account. There are exceptions for closely held corporations to limit voting to only those matters that are material. Also, unallocated shares are usually voted by the plan trustee. Unallocated shares are those shares in the trust that have not yet been allocated to individual participants.

Distributions

Stock bonus plan distributions are generally made in the form of employer stock. The distribution of stock provides additional income tax benefits because there is a deferral of income tax on the stock's appreciated value until the stock is later sold. Although the stock in the stock bonus plan is usually distributed to the employee, the plan may provide the employee with the choice of receiving the cash equivalent of the shares of stock at the time of distribution. However, if a cash equivalent is received, the deferral of income tax on the stock's appreciated value until the stock is sold is lost.

Generally, stock bonus plans do not permit employees to receive in-service withdrawal distributions from the plan except upon termination, hardship, disability, or retirement. However, stock bonus plans may permit, but are not required to allow, in-service withdrawals after a participant attains two years of participation in the plan. Similar to profit sharing plans, employee/participant loans are available from a stock bonus plan if the plan permits and the loans are available in a nondiscriminatory manner. Generally, employers choose not to permit loans from stock bonus plans.

The taxation of a distribution of employer stock or securities from a stock bonus plan depends on whether the distribution is a lump-sum distribution or a partial distribution. If there is a lump-sum distribution, the employee is subject to ordinary income tax in the year of the distribution based on the fair market value of the employer stock at the time of the original contribution. The net unrealized appreciation (NUA) of the stock (i.e., the appreciation of the stock while held in the plan) is not taxed at the time of the lump-sum distribution but rather is taxed as a long-term capital gain when the stock is ultimately sold (discussed below).

13. IRC §§401(a)(22) and 409(e).

On the other hand, if the distribution of the employer stock or securities is made in installments (a partial distribution), the fair market value of all employer securities distributed in the installment distribution attributable to employer contributions will be taxable as ordinary income. This treatment clearly contrasts with the taxation of a lump-sum distribution.[14] The exception to this rule provided in IRC §401(e)(4)(A) is that NUA excluded from gross income does include any amount attributable to employee nondeductible contributions. NUA attributable to employee deferrals are subject to ordinary taxation.

Distributions may be subject to the 10 percent early withdrawal penalty if the participant is under the age of 59½. Distributions of stock may also be rolled into an IRA account or to another qualified plan that accepts stock and is willing to accept the rollover. Note that if the employer securities are rolled over to another tax-advantaged account, the ability to benefit from the NUA treatment is lost.

Net Unrealized Appreciation (NUA)

One of the principal benefits of stock bonus plans is net unrealized appreciation (NUA) treatment. **Net unrealized appreciation** is the appreciation in the value of employer stock from the time of contribution to the plan until the time that the stock is distributed to the plan participant. The NUA of the stock (i.e., the gain while being held in the plan) is not taxed as ordinary income at the time of the distribution, but rather is taxed as a long-term capital gain when the stock is sold. There are no holding period requirements to qualify this gain for the preferential long-term capital gains tax treatment. The cost basis of the stock (as provided by the plan administrator on Form 1099-R, Box 6) at the date of contribution is taxable as ordinary income at the date of distribution.

Example 6.1

Lana is 65 years old. Over her career while working at ABC Corporation (a privately held corporation), she received stock contributions of ABC Corporation to her account in the stock bonus plan. ABC's tax deduction was $20,000, or the combined value of contributions of stock valued at the time of contribution. Lana decides that she will retire, and she no longer wants to assume the risk that ABC Corporation will remain as an ongoing solvent entity; thus, she decides to take a full distribution from the plan and then sells all of her stock for cash. At distribution, Lana's ABC stock is valued by an independent appraiser at $100,000. Upon distribution of the stock, Lana has $20,000 of ordinary income representing the total value of the employer's contribution. The remaining $80,000 ($100,000 - $20,000) of NUA will be taxed at the time of the sale as a long-term capital gain.

---

14. IRC §402(e)(4)(A).

If Lana instead sells the stock two years after distribution for $165,000, she will have a basis of $20,000 (the ordinary income recognized at distribution), $80,000 of NUA (long-term capital gain), and $65,000 of long-term capital gain representing the appreciation of the stock since the date of distribution. If the sale occurs before one year and a day from the distribution, any post-distribution appreciation would be taxed as short-term capital gain, but the long-term capital gain on the NUA would not be affected unless the sale was for less than $100,000.

This example not only stresses the tax implications involved, but it also points out that with an investment in ABC Corporation, Lana assumes the risk that ABC Corporation will continue as a viable entity. If ABC Corporation goes bankrupt or becomes insolvent, Lana's stock investment could be completely lost or seriously devalued. Thus, investment risk is an important consideration for a participant in a stock bonus plan.

	Value	Comment
FMV of stock when distributed	$100,000	Stock will generally be transferred to a brokerage account.
Value of stock when contributed over career	$20,000	Must be included as ordinary income in the year of distribution.
Net unrealized appreciation (NUA)	$80,000	Treated as LTCG when the stock is sold. The basis of the stock equals the amount taxed as ordinary income in the year of distribution.

If Lana sells the stock immediately, then she has an $80,000 LTCG.	If Lana holds the stock and sells two years later for $165,000, then she has a gain of $145,000 consisting of NUA of $80,000 and additional appreciation after distribution of $65,000.

As illustrated, the benefit of NUA treatment is that the deferral of taxation on the stock is treated as a capital gain instead of ordinary income. The employee is taxed at ordinary income rates in the year of distribution only on the value of the securities deducted by the employer at the time of contribution to the plan. The net unrealized appreciation (i.e., the gain of the value of the stock while being held in the plan) is not taxed at the time of distribution but is taxed as a long-term capital gain when the stock is later sold by the participant.[15] In order to receive NUA treatment, the distribution must qualify as a lump-sum distribution. Lump-sum distributions and NUA are discussed in more detail in Chapter 7.

---

15. IRC §402(e)(4)(B); see also *Villarroel v. Commissioner*, 1998-247 T.C. Memo (1988), aff'd, 202 F.3d 271 (6th Cir. 2000).

Put Options

Stock bonus plans and ESOPs are required, under the same rules, to provide employees with a "put option" or repurchase option whereby the employer buys back the employer stock distributed at a fair market value. These rules are discussed in greater depth later in this chapter under ESOPs.

Exhibit 6.2 | Comparison of Stock Bonus Plans to Profit Sharing Plans*

	Stock Bonus Plans	Profit Sharing Plans
Plan Establishment	Due date of tax return plus extensions	Due date of tax return plus extensions
Date of Contribution	Due date of tax return plus extensions	Due date of tax return plus extensions
Type of Contributions	*Generally stock*	*Generally cash*
DeductibleContribution Limit	25% of covered compensation	25% of covered compensation
Valuation	*Generally needed annually*	*Generally unnecessary*
Eligibility	Same as other Qualified Plans (age 21 and one year of service or two years with 100% vesting)	Same as other Qualified Plans (age 21 and 1 year of service or two years with 100% vesting)
Allocation Method	% of compensation or formula based on age, service of classification	% of compensation or formula based on age, service of classification
Vesting	Same as other Defined Contribution Qualified Plans (3-year cliff or 2-to-6-year graduated vesting)**	Same as other Defined Contribution Qualified Plans (3-year cliff or 2-to-6-year graduated vesting)**
Portfolio Diversification	*No***	*Generally yes*
Voting Rights	*Generally yes*	*Generally no*
Type of Distributions	*Generally in stock*	*Generally in cash*
In-Service Withdrawals	May be allowed after two years	May be allowed after two years
Loans	May be allowed (but not usually)	May be allowed (but not usually)
Taxation of Distributions	*Lump-sum distributions will qualify for NUA treatment. Other distributions are treated as ordinary income.*	*Generally full distribution is ordinary income*

* Differences are highlighted in blue.
**Effective for plan years after 2006 under the Pension Protection Act of 2006.
*** Diversification may be required as a result of the PPA 2006.

Exhibit 6.3 | Form 1099-R

9898	☐ VOID	☐ CORRECTED		

PAYER'S name, street address, city or town, state or province, country, ZIP or foreign postal code, and telephone no.	**1** Gross distribution $	OMB No. 1545-0119 **2021** Form **1099-R**	**Distributions From Pensions, Annuities, Retirement or Profit-Sharing Plans, IRAs, Insurance Contracts, etc.**
	2a Taxable amount $		
	2b Taxable amount not determined ☐	Total distribution ☐	**Copy A**
PAYER'S TIN	RECIPIENT'S TIN	**3** Capital gain (included in box 2a) $	**4** Federal income tax withheld $	**For Internal Revenue Service Center**
				File with Form 1096.
RECIPIENT'S name	**5** Employee contributions/ Designated Roth contributions or insurance premiums $	**6** Net unrealized appreciation in employer's securities $	For Privacy Act and Paperwork Reduction Act Notice, see the **2021 General Instructions for Certain Information Returns.**
Street address (including apt. no.)	**7** Distribution code(s)	IRA/ SEP/ SIMPLE ☐	**8** Other $ %	
City or town, state or province, country, and ZIP or foreign postal code	**9a** Your percentage of total distribution %	**9b** Total employee contributions $	
10 Amount allocable to IRR within 5 years $	**11** 1st year of desig. Roth contrib.	**12** FATCA filing requirement ☐	**14** State tax withheld $ $	**15** State/Payer's state no. 	**16** State distribution $ $
Account number (see instructions)		**13** Date of payment	**17** Local tax withheld $ $	**18** Name of locality	**19** Local distribution $ $

Form **1099-R** Cat. No. 14436Q www.irs.gov/Form1099R Department of the Treasury - Internal Revenue Service

Do Not Cut or Separate Forms on This Page — Do Not Cut or Separate Forms on This Page

Employee Stock Ownership Plans, referred to as ESOPs, are a special form of stock bonus plans that reward employees with both ownership in the corporation and provide owners with substantial tax advantages. An ESOP is controlled through a trust. The sponsor company receives tax deductions for contributions of stock from the corporation. The ESOP then allocates the stock to separate accounts for the benefit of individual employee-participants.

Employee ownership in the context of ESOPs refers to ownership in the stock of the corporation through an employee benefit plan by most or all of the corporation's employees. ESOPs provide corporate owners with a way to transfer significant ownership interests to their employees while benefiting from favorable tax advantages. One underlying rationale for promoting employee ownership is that the long-term health of the free economy is best served through providing employees with ownership of corporate securities beyond normal salaries and wages. Congress envisioned that ESOPs would function both as "an employee retirement benefit plan and a 'technique of corporate finance' that would encourage employee ownership."[16] Because of these dual purposes, ESOPs are not necessarily designed to guarantee retirement benefits because they place employee retirement assets at greater risk than the usual diversified ERISA qualified plans.[17]

> ## ☷ *Key Concepts*
>
> 1. What are ESOPs and why are they used?
>
> 2. List the parties of a typical leveraged ESOP.
>
> 3. List the requirements necessary for the owners of a closely held corporation to qualify for nonrecognition of capital gain at the creation of an ESOP.
>
> 4. Discuss three advantages and disadvantages of an ESOP.

A key characteristic of the ESOP is that the trust may borrow money from a bank or other lender to purchase the employer stock. The corporation generally repays the loan through tax deductible contributions to the ESOP. Both the interest and the principal repayments for the loan are income tax deductible. The ESOP can thus be "leveraged." ESOPs with borrowings are referenced as LESOPs, which stands for "Leveraged" Employee Stock Ownership Plans (discussed below). When used in conjunction with financial and estate planning techniques and tax savings strategies, there can be substantial tax and investment benefits gained from utilization of an ESOP. ESOPs are, as one court wrote, "employee benefit plan(s) designed to invest primarily or when certain safeguards are present, solely in securities issued by the sponsoring corporation."

To become eligible for these tax advantages, the ESOP must satisfy various rules of the IRC and of ERISA. Like other qualified plans, the ESOP must satisfy applicable rules of employee vesting, participation, eligibility, and coverage. The ESOP must also have a trustee who is charged with a fiduciary duty to handle and maintain the plan in the best interest of plan participants and their beneficiaries.

---

16. *Martin v. Feilen,* 965 F.2d 660, 664 (8th Cir. 1992), *cert. denied*, 506 U.S. 1054, 113 S.Ct. 979, 122 L.Ed.2d 133 (1993).
17. *Moench v. Robinson,* 62 F.3d 553, 568 (3rd Cir. 1995) (quoting *Martin v. Feilen*, 965 F.2d 660, 664).

Exhibit 6.4 | Facts about ESOPs

According to the ESOP Association:[1]
- There were roughly 10,000 ESOPs in the United States covering more than 10 million participants.
- ESOPs controlled about $940 billion in assets at the end of 2011.
- Of these ESOPs, roughly 97 percent were for closely held corporations while about three percent were for publicly traded corporations.
- About 5,000 corporations are now majority employee-owned by the ESOP.
- At least 75 percent of the ESOPs are or were leveraged.

The ESOP Association, which represents approximately 1,400 ESOP corporations, touts the following information concerning ESOPs:[2]
- Approximately 99 percent of the members of the ESOP Association are private, closely held corporations.
- Approximately two-thirds of the members of the ESOP Association have less than 250 employees, although there are ESOPs in large businesses as well.
- While ESOPs exist in a broad range of industries, roughly 23 percent of the members of the ESOP Association are in manufacturing, followed by 15 percent in construction.
- The ESOP Association's members had, on average, annual sales revenue ranging from 20 million to 50 million.
- Approximately 65 percent of the members of the ESOP Association report that their ESOPs have been in place for at least 10 years.
- Roughly 83 percent of the members of the ESOP Association have corporations that are more than 50 percent owned by the ESOPs.
- Roughly 94 percent of the members of the ESOP Association provide a supplemental benefit plan as well as the ESOP, including 401(k) plans, pension plans, and profit sharing plans.
- Research shows that the implementation of an ESOP results in more information sharing, communications, and involvement in decision making for the employee-owners.
- Roughly 83 percent of the members of the ESOP Association report that motivation and productivity increased as a result of the ESOPs.
- ESOP Association members have, on average, an account balance of $113,318.

1. See www.esopassociation.org and its resource library for more information. The ESOP Association, founded in 1978, is a national association of corporations with employee stock ownership plans and service providers with a professional commitment to employee ownership through ESOPs. The ESOP Association has a library that is informative and provides much information concerning ESOPs. According to its website, the ESOP Association is the leading voice in America for employee ownership through ESOPs, and devotes considerable time to creating and maintaining favorable ESOPs legislation. Further, the ESOP Association is a prime source for educational materials necessary for successful implementation and administration of an ESOP.
2. Source: The ESOP Association, "2015 Company Survey" (most current, conducted every five years).

The ESOP Transaction

The corporation, the principal shareholder of the corporation, the ESOP trust, the trustee or trustees, a lender, and employees are all part of the process of establishing an ESOP. Most ESOPs are leveraged because money must be borrowed to purchase the stock from the principal shareholder. In a **leveraged ESOP**, the corporation makes tax deductible contributions to the trust in the form of both principal and interest for the loan. The trust receives these funds and the trust, through a trustee, then repays the acquisition loan from a bank or other lender. The trust purchases shares of the corporate stock from the principal shareholder, and these shares are normally pledged as security for the bank loan. The corporation and generally the principal shareholder (seller) guarantee the loan, and the corporation's assets are pledged as collateral for the loan. Prior to the allocation of the actual shares to the participant's account within the trust, the pledged shares are held in a separate holding account (suspense) and referred to as unallocated.

As the trust repays the bank loan, an appropriate allocation of shares are withdrawn from the holding account and allocated to the account of the individual participant. Once a share of stock has been withdrawn from the holding account, that share may no longer act as pledged collateral for the debt. However, a proportionate amount of the loan was repaid; therefore, there is no need for additional cash or funds from the corporation to maintain the loan. There may, however, be a need for cash if the trust needs or wants to redeem distributed shares.

The following diagram illustrates the various relationships and transactions regarding a leveraged ESOP.

Exhibit 6.5 | Various Relationships and Transactions in a Leveraged ESOP

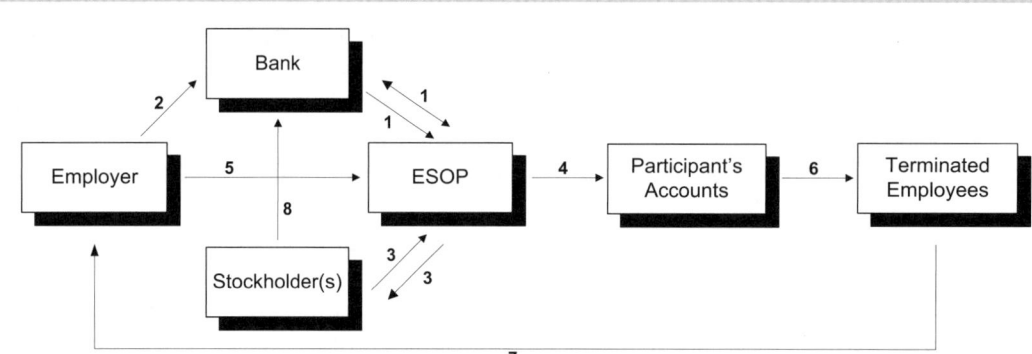

1. An ESOP obtains a loan from a bank or other outside lender. The ESOP signs a promissory note for the money.
2. The employer guarantees the loan on behalf of the ESOP.
3. The ESOP uses the money from the loan to buy stock from existing shareholder (or employer).
4. The stock purchased by the ESOP is held in an ESOP suspense account, and is released for allocation to participant accounts over time as the loan is repaid with funds contributed to the ESOP by the employer. These allocations are in lieu of a cash contribution that could have been made to a retirement plan.
5. The employer contributes funds to the ESOP so that the ESOP can make its annual debt repayment to the bank (or other lender).
6. Employees are entitled to receive distributions of employer stock in kind upon termination or retirement.
7. Employees are entitled to sell back or "put" the stock back to the employer.
8. Shareholders may also be required to guarantee the ESOP loan.

Practical Uses of ESOPs and Nonrecognition of Gain Treatment

Most commonly, an ESOP is used to buy the stock of the retiring or departing owner or owners of a closely held corporation in order to achieve deferral of federal income taxes. The establishment of ESOPs allow owners of closely held businesses to sell all or part of their interest in the corporation and defer recognition of the capital gain. This tax benefit is known as **nonrecognition of gain treatment** and is provided for by §1042 of the Internal Revenue Code.[18] In order to qualify for nonrecognition of gain treatment, the following requirements apply:[19]

1. The ESOP must own at least 30 percent of the corporation's stock immediately after the sale (notice that the controlling interest may remain owned elsewhere, but if this occurs the ESOP share should have been valued using a minority share discount).
2. The seller or sellers must reinvest the proceeds from the sale into qualified replacement securities (defined below) within 12 months after the sale.
3. The corporation that establishes the ESOP must have no class of stock outstanding that is tradable on an established securities market.
4. The seller or sellers, relatives of the seller or sellers, and 25 percent shareholders in the corporation are precluded from receiving allocations of stock acquired by the ESOP through the rollover (sale to the ESOP).
5. The ESOP may not sell the stock acquired through the rollover transaction for three years. The requirement, however, will not apply if the corporation is sold. The three-year period is called a "holding" period, which prevents unnecessary, duplicative rollovers by the corporation.
6. The stock sold to the ESOP must be common or convertible preferred stock and must have been owned by the seller for at least three years prior to the sale.

If all of these requirements are satisfied, the sellers (usually former principals of the corporation) may reinvest the proceeds from the sale within 12 months of the sale into qualified replacement securities (securities of domestic corporations as defined below), and carry over their former adjusted basis from the corporation into the qualified replacement securities. As long as the seller retains these replacement securities, there will be no taxable event. If the seller later sells some or all of these replacement securities, the seller will have capital gains or losses determined by the carry over basis. If the seller dies, then the seller's heirs (or estate) are entitled to a new adjusted basis equal to the date of death fair market value, thus avoiding capital gains taxation altogether. The nonrecognition of gain treatment is not available to the seller of an S Corporation that establishes an ESOP because IRC §1042 only allows owners of closely held C Corporations to do so.[20]

For the deferral of capital gain recognition to occur, the reinvestment must be made into qualified replacement securities. **Qualified replacement securities** are securities in a domestic corporation, including stocks, bonds, debentures, or warrants, which receive no more than 25 percent of their income from passive investments. The qualified replacement securities can be in the form of stock in an S Corporation. However, stock of the corporation that issued the employer securities (or a corporation that is part of a control group with that corporation) cannot serve as a qualified replacement security.

---

18. IRC §1042.
19. IRC §1042(c)(3); see also Temp. Regulations §1.1042-IT, Q and A-3(c).
20. IRC §1042(c)(1)(A).

Advantages and Disadvantages of ESOPs

There are many reasons why the ESOP is the most common type of stock bonus plan. ESOPs benefit the employer-corporation and its participants in various ways. From the corporation's perspective, the ESOP creates a market for the stock of privately held corporations. It is crucial for shareholders to have a market for their stock for financial planning and estate planning issues.

Advantages to the Employer

The shareholders, often owners who will soon retire, may sell shares to the plan, which is a ready and available buyer. Hence, ESOPs are frequently used as estate planning vehicles for closely held corporations and their owners. Without the ESOP, there may not be a market for the privately held corporate stock. Also, the corporation or trust is allowed to borrow money in order to provide contributions resulting in funds being provided immediately to the ESOP, while the employer repays the loan to the ESOP with tax deductible contributions. Not only do these tax deductions save the corporation cash, the cash flow of the corporation is further strengthened because in the ESOP exchange, the trust allocates shares to the employees' accounts while the corporation is paying cash to the bank (in a leveraged ESOP) and deducting such payments for both principal and interest. By providing employees with a stake in the corporation, employers give economic incentives to employees, which increases motivation and improves employee retention.

Advantages to the Employees

From the employees' perspective, the ESOP provides them with a type of retirement vehicle. The ESOP provides them with ownership in the corporation where they work, which tends to improve a worker's attitude, motivation, sense of loyalty, and belonging to the corporation. The employee-participant may also benefit from net unrealized appreciation (NUA) at the time of stock distributions because of favorable capital gains rates and deferred recognition.

Disadvantages to the Employees

There are disadvantages to ESOPs as well. There is an inherent lack of diversification of the individual "investment" portfolio because ESOPs must invest primarily in the stock of the corporation. As a result, an employee-participant's account is susceptible to fluctuations or drastic drops in value because of the corporation's stock. This means that a long-time employee who has received large allocations of the stock has significant nondiversified portfolio risk. This risk can be mitigated somewhat for ESOP participants who are at least 55 years of age and who have completed at least 10 years of participation in the plan. This special diversification treatment is discussed later in this chapter.

Disadvantages to the Employer

From the shareholder's perspective, ESOPs "dilute" ownership in the corporation by reducing the concentration of shares from the sellers to broaden the employees' holdings. Moreover, the repurchase option for stock that is not readily tradable can create cash flow problems and administrative concerns.[21] With the repurchase option, an employee can force the corporation to repurchase the stock originally issued and distributed to the employee-participant. In addition, the corporation creating the ESOP has substantial costs in setting up the plan, drafting plan documents, and administering the plan.

Plan administration can also be costly, and the annual appraisals create significant and recurring expenses for closely held corporations. These appraisals are necessary to determine the value of the tax

---

21. See previous section on Repurchase Option.

deduction for the employer and to determine the price that an employer or trust would pay for the repurchase of ESOP distributed shares.

Employer-corporations must also be ready to purchase the shares of departing employees, which can further diminish or stretch the cash flow of a corporation. The lender involved with a leveraged ESOP may also place more scrutiny or requirements upon the employer, especially for annual valuations, which add to administrative costs of the plan.

ESOPs can generally use any allocation method permitted by profit sharing plans or stock bonus plans. However, ESOPs cannot be integrated with Social Security. This limitation is somewhat unique as most other qualified plans can be integrated with Social Security.[22]

Exhibit 6.6 | Advantages and Disadvantages of ESOPs

	Advantages	Disadvantages
Employer	• Creates a market for stock in a private/ closely held corporation • Helps retain employees • Improves employee loyalty • Employer-owners may create a diversified portfolio without recognition of capital gain • Corporation can borrow against stock • Corporation can improve the current cash flow of the corporation by taking a tax deduction on stock contributions	• Dilutes ownership • Administrative costs • May strain employer cash flow to meet payout requirements to departing employees at uncertain times • Periodic appraisal costs are expensive • Personal liability concerns for officers or management who also serve as trustees of ESOPs • Creates cash flow uncertainty in the future • Social Security integration is not permitted
Employee	• Acquires ownership in employer corporation • Employees have better perception of or attitude towards employer corporation • Favorable tax treatment on stock distributions (NUA) • Can force employer to repurchase stock at end of employment (put option) • Receives stock as form of compensation	• Employee bears risk of employer's insolvency (nondiversification) • Value of stock subject to appraiser • Stock value subject to fluctuation • Stock not liquid

Voting

Generally, ESOP participants have the same voting rights with their allocated shares as other shareholders, including the right to vote the shares and the right to earn dividends. For public ESOP corporations registered with the Securities and Exchange Commission, participants have full voting rights. However, ESOPs of privately held corporations are not required to provide full voting rights for these shares. The law merely requires that participants possess voting rights on major corporate decisions. Such major corporate decisions are considered to be mergers, acquisitions, consolidation, reclassification, liquidation, dissolution, recapitalization, or sale.

---

22. Social Security integration is also not available with respect to elective deferrals or matching contributions, such as in a 401(k) plan. Treas. Reg. §1.401(l)-1(a)(4).

The trustee of the ESOP votes the shares on behalf of these participants on regular corporate matters beyond those listed above. For stock in a privately held corporation under these circumstances, the IRC allows the plan to authorize the ESOP trustee to vote the stock as one vote for each participant.[23]

ESOP trustees must discharge their duties by evaluating the best interests of the beneficiaries in the abstract as beneficiaries, not as directors who may lose control of the corporation nor should they discharge their duties as employees, some of whom may lose their jobs if control of the corporation changes hands.[24] Courts have commented that it is appropriate for trustees to put aside personal judgment in favor of carrying out the wishes of the trust participants.[25] The trust documents concerning an ESOP must be construed in light of ERISA's policies, and trust documents cannot excuse trustees from their fiduciary duties under ERISA.[26]

Contributions to ESOPs

ESOPs can provide generous tax benefits. These tax benefits were created to provide an incentive for employers and corporations to implement ESOPs and build work forces comprised of many employee-owners. Contributions to ESOPs are undertaken by the corporation and are made to the trust though the trustee. The corporation contributes cash or stock to the trust so that the trust can buy new or existing shares. The trust also has the option to borrow funds to buy shares while the corporation makes cash contributions to the plan so that the loan can be repaid. While there are significant tax benefits with ESOPs, there are limitations to contributions to an ESOP. Contributions to ESOPs may be in cash or in the form of employer securities. The employer may deduct the value of the stock contributed and in the process, increase the corporation's cash profits by the taxes avoided.

Employer contributions to ESOPs are deductible by the employer just like any contribution to a qualified profit sharing plan or stock bonus plan, but contributions are subject to the 25 percent limit of covered compensation.[27] However, if the employer's stock is obtained by virtue of a loan (leveraged ESOP), then the permissible deductions for the employer are increased for the interest on the loan. In other words, the employer is allowed to deduct all interest paid on the loan over and above the 25 percent deduction of total eligible payroll of the plan participants.[28] The interest deduction is unlimited.

> ### ☑ Quick Quiz 6.3
>
> 1. In a leveraged ESOP, the corporation makes after-tax contributions to a trust on behalf of its employees.
>   a. True
>   b. False
>
> 2. Foreign securities may qualify as qualified replacement securities.
>   a. True
>   b. False
>
> 3. The creation of an ESOP may dilute ownership in the corporation.
>   a. True
>   b. False
>
> False, False, True.

Example 6.2

If XYZ Corporation contributes 33% of covered compensation to the ESOP for principal and interest on the loan to the ESOP, this entire amount is deductible if 25% was applied to pay principal and 8% was applied to pay for interest payments.

---

23. IRC §409(e)(3). See also *Schoenholtz v. Doniger*, 657 F.Supp. 899 (S.D.N.Y. 1987).
24. *Danaher Corp. v. Chicago Pneumatic Tool Co.*, 635 F. Supp. 246, 249-250 (S.D.N.Y. 1986).
25. Id.
26. *Central States, Southeast and Southwest Areas Pension Fund v. Central Transport*, 472 U.S. 559, 568 (1985).
27. IRC §404(a)(3).
28. IRC §404(a)(9)(B).

Employers are further allowed tax deductions for dividends paid on stock held by an ESOP under various circumstances. This deduction was made permanent under the Pension Protection Act of 2006. Dividends that are paid in cash for stock purchases with an ESOP securities purchase loan are tax deductible by the employer/plan sponsor. Dividends, regardless of whether received outright or reinvested, are taxable as current ordinary income to the employee. Cash dividends on stock purchased with an ESOP securities acquisition loan are included in the 25 percent contribution limit for leveraged ESOPs. Also, employers may take a deduction on dividends applied to loan payments to a leveraged ESOP. Finally, if employees voluntarily reinvest dividends in the corporation's stock held by an ESOP, then these dividends are deductible by the employer.

> ## ⋮≡ *Key Concepts*
>
> 1. Explain the voting rights of ESOP participants of public corporations.
>
> 2. Discuss the scenario in which the employer's deduction related to an ESOP may exceed 25% of the total covered compensation.
>
> 3. If securities are not readily tradable, how is the value of the security determined for purposes of the ESOP contribution?

Distributions

Distributions from ESOPs, much like those from stock bonus plans, are largely subject to the same restrictions applicable to distributions from any qualified plan. Therefore, the distribution rules for stock bonus plans discussed earlier in this chapter generally apply to ESOPs as well. The exceptions to the general treatment are discussed below. Aside from the general exceptions, distributions before age 59½, death, disability, or retirement are subject to the 10 percent penalty. There is no requirement for an ESOP or stock bonus plan to provide a joint and survivor annuity or a spousal death benefit.

An ESOP may pay distributions in a lump sum or in installments. By using lump sum distributions, a company accelerates its repurchase obligation, allows current employees who participate to share in potential growth of the company, and protects former employees from absorbing future losses in company value. Installment distributions allow former participants to continue ownership in the company while the stock remains in the account of the participant.

An ESOP is subject to the minimum distribution requirements of IRC §401(a)(9) (as discussed in Chapter 7). However, plan participants can elect to receive substantially equal periodic payments (installment payments) of their account balance not less than once per year after the participant separates from service. The substantially equal periodic payments must be for a period no longer than five years,[29] unless the participant's account balance is valued at more than $1,165,000 for 2021, in which case the distribution period may be extended one year for each additional $230,000 for 2021 of account value up to a total of ten years.[30] If the participant's separation from service is due to the participant's attainment of the plan's normal retirement age, death, or disability, these substantially equal periodic payments must begin within one year after the participant's separation from service. If the participant's separation is for any other reason, these substantially equal periodic payments must begin within one year after the fifth year after the participant's separation.[31]

These rules simply provide the plan participant with a level of protection from the plan sponsor spreading out distributions over an extended period of time.

---

29. IRC §409(o)(1)(C).
30. IRC §409(o)(1)(C)(ii).
31. IRC §409(o)(1).

Any distribution from an ESOP that is not a lump distribution of the employer securities will not be eligible to receive NUA treatment and will be taxed as ordinary income. These distributions may also be subjected to the 10 percent early withdrawal penalty unless the distribution complies with one of the exceptions detailed in Chapter 7.

Example 6.3

Joel retires, at normal retirement age, from his career with Risky Business in 2021. At his retirement, the value of Joel's ESOP is $400,000. Joel may have several options:

1. The plan may allow Joel to take distributions from the plan at his discretion.
2. The plan may allow Joel to roll over the account balance into an IRA rollover account.
3. Joel may leave the assets in his ESOP until he attains the age of 70½ (age 72 if age 70½ is attained after December 31, 2019), at which time he will be required to begin taking his required minimum distributions.
4. The plan must allow Joel, if he elects, to begin taking annual substantially equal periodic payments in 2022.

In any case, if Joel's distribution is not a lump-sum distribution of his employer's securities, the distribution will be taxed as ordinary income.

Valuation of Employer Stock in ESOPs

Valuation of the employer's securities is an important area of ESOP administration. Valuations are necessary for various reasons, which include:

- When contributions are made to an employee's account, the employer must know the value of the contribution for the corporation's tax deduction purposes.
- When contributions are made to an employee's account, the employee must know the value of the contribution for future NUA calculation.
- If a lender lends money to leverage the ESOP, the lender must know the value of the stock to determine if and how much money to lend to the corporation.
- If an employee exercises the put or repurchase option, the value of the stock must be determined.
- Valuations are needed for financial statements and reports.

Valuations for ESOP transactions should be guided by current appraisals by outside, independent valuation experts. Publicly traded stock is readily valued by looking to the stock's market price, whereas determining the value of a closely held corporation's securities is much more involved and costly. If securities are not readily tradable on an established securities market, then valuations must be undertaken by independent appraisers, who must be uninterested, independent parties.[32] The corporation's lender may also place further requirements on the corporation regarding the valuation of the stock. The valuation must be done in good faith and must be based on all factors relevant to determining the securities' fair market value, resulting in an assessment of what a willing buyer would pay to a willing seller for the securities.[33]

If a valuation is overstated, the corporation may be penalized. Any tax deduction based on these valuations can be lost if the value used is later determined to be overstated. Also, if the securities are purchased by the ESOP for an amount higher than their fair market value, then the corporation may be subject to excise tax.[34] In some extreme cases, the ESOP may be disqualified altogether, losing its status as an ESOP and as a qualified plan. If the trustee is found to have caused the ESOP to buy stock at a price greater than its fair market value, the trustee may be deemed to have violated his fiduciary obligations and can be personally liable to the ESOP participants for the amount of the overpayment.

ERISA requires the ESOP to purchase the stock using an **adequate consideration standard**. Adequate consideration has been defined as fair market value determined in good faith.[35] **Fair market value** in the context of fiduciary breaches in ERISA cases has been defined as "the price that a willing buyer would pay a willing seller, both having reasonable knowledge of the pertinent facts."

Example 6.4

Percy has owned a toy train business for 30 years. He wants to retire early. The business is worth approximately $10 million. Percy cannot find a third-party buyer for his business; thus, he has been advised to consider the establishment of an ESOP. Percy hires an appraiser, who values the stock at $10 million. A banker agrees that the corporation is worth approximately $10 million, and the bank lends money to Percy's train business to establish an ESOP. Percy can, in effect, sell his stock to the ESOP and receive non-recognition of gain treatment if the ESOP holds the stock for more than three years, the ESOP owns more than thirty percent (30%) of the stock, and Percy purchases qualified replacement property within twelve months of the sale.

In the scenario above, Percy was able to eliminate his concentrated portfolio and was also able to reduce his business risk in the train corporation by diversifying his portfolio without incurring taxation and related costs. Percy was also able to align the economic incentives of the employees to that of the business by making employees part owners in the train business. Unfortunately, both Percy and the corporation will probably be required by the bank to be guarantors of the loan to the trust; thus, Percy will retain some risk until the loan is repaid.

32. IRC §401(a)(28)(C).
33. Regulations §54.4975-11(d)(5). See also *Donovan v. Cunningham* 541 ESOPs 246 (S.D. Texas 1982).
34. Revenue Ruling, 69-494, 1969-2 C.B. 88.
35. 29 U.S.C. §1002 (18)(B).

Example 6.5

Assume the same facts as above except that Percy has an adjusted basis of $300,000 in the corporation, and he sells seventy percent (70%) of his stock in the corporation to the ESOP and uses those funds to obtain a diversified portfolio of common stock by purchasing $1 million of stock in corporations A, B, C, D, E, F, and G ($1 million for each), for a total of $7 million. The basis of the $7 million is $210,000 (70% of $300,000). The qualified replacement property is all stock in domestic corporations. Assume that after the transactions and within applicable time periods, Percy sells stock A for $1.5 million and sells stock B for $850,000. What is the tax treatment for the sale of A and B?

Percy will be taxed once he sells the stock. His adjusted basis is his "carry over basis" in the original shares of stock. The basis in stock A is $30,000, 1/7th of 70% of $300,000. With an adjusted basis of $30,000, the first $30,000 is a return of basis. The remaining $1,470,000 is taxed as a long-term capital gain. As for stock B, his adjusted basis again is $30,000, 1/7th of 70% of $300,000. The first $30,000 is a return of basis, while the remaining $820,000 ($850,000 - $30,000) is taxed as a long-term capital gain.

Example 6.6

Assume that Percy bequeaths stock in corporations C, D, and E to Gordon, his brother. At the time of Percy's death, the stock in C, D, and E were worth $2 million each. If Gordon inherits and then sells these stocks, what would his basis be?

With capital assets, there is a "step to fair market value" or an adjustment to fair market value of the adjusted basis at the time of death. The "step up" in this case occurs at death, and Percy's original adjusted basis $300,000 is not taken into account. Therefore, Gordon's (the heir of the stock) basis is $2 million dollars for each stock C, D, and E.

Diversification Issues

ESOPs are permitted to hold 100 percent of the corporate stock in the trust. Most, if not all, of the stock in the ESOP trust is stock in the corporation where the employee-participant works. If the corporation files for bankruptcy or becomes insolvent, then the employee-participant will likely lose his entire investment. Employees with corporate stock in ESOPs are prohibited from selling their shares to diversify their holdings while employed unless they meet certain requirements. Under the IRC, qualified participants may force diversification of their holdings if they are a **qualified participant** during the **qualified election period**.

- *Qualified participant* - the term "qualified participant" means any employee who has completed at least 10 years of participation under the plan and has attained age 55.
- *Qualified election period* - the term "qualified election period" means the 6-plan-year period beginning with the first plan year in which the individual first became a qualified participant.

Exhibit 6.7 | ESOP Diversification

Qualified Participant
1) 10 years of service and
2) Attainment of age 55

Qualified Election Period

Year 1	Year 2	Year 3	Year 4	Year 5	Year 6
25% diversification limit in years 1 through 5					50%

If the participant meets these qualification requirements, the ESOP must provide the participant with either the opportunity to receive a distribution from the ESOP or alternative investment options for a percentage of his account. The qualified participant must be offered a diversification election within 90 days after the close of each plan year beginning with the year after the employee becomes qualified.[36] The participant may elect to diversify up to 25 percent of the total shares of employer stock contributed to the plan into non-employer stock at this time. The election to diversify is cumulative; therefore, if an election is made to diversify 10 percent of the shares in the first eligible year, an election could be made in the following year to diversify an additional 15 percent of the total number of shares of employer stock contributed to the plan (assuming no additional shares were contributed). The final election year is the last year of the 6-plan-year period. In the final election year, the cumulative diversifiable percentage is increased to 50 percent.[37]

The plan documents may satisfy the requirements of diversification of investments if the plan documents offer at least three investment options (consistent with regulations prescribed under the Internal Revenue Code, e.g., a cash fund, a bond fund, and a stock fund) to each participant making a diversification election. Within 90 days after the period during which the election was chosen, the plan must invest the portion of the participant's account covered by the election.[38]

Example 6.7

Kerstin is a participant in Smith Corporation's ESOP. She has been with the company for 20 years. Kerstin turns 55 this year. The ESOP must allow Kerstin to diversify up to 25% of her shares of employer stock for the current year. Assume she has the plan diversify 15% for the current year, next year she could diversify the remaining 10% allowed for a total of 25%.

---

36. IRC §401(a)(28)(B)(i).
37. IRC §401(a)(28) and Notice 88-56, Q&A 9.
38. IRC §401(a)(28)(B)(ii).

Example 6.8

Ben has 10 years of participation in the Blackrock Corporation ESOP and turns age 55 in November of the 2021 plan year. The ESOP uses a calendar year plan. During the 90-day period beginning on January 1, 2022, and ending on March 31, 2022, Ben may direct the trustee to diversify up to 25% of his shares of employer stock. If he elects to diversify the 25% maximum amount, then he could only elect to diversify amounts attributable to increases (from additional contributions) during the 2023, 2024, 2025 and 2026 election periods. From January 1, 2027, to March 31, 2027, Ben must be given the opportunity to diversify up to a cumulative 50% of the total number of shares of employer stock contributed to his account, as of the end of the 2026 plan year.

If Ben did not elect to diversify any portion of the ESOP account balance during the 2022 election period, a similar election would be available during the 2023, 2024, 2025 and 2026 election periods. In each year, he could elect to diversify the portion of his account that, when aggregated with prior amounts for which diversification was elected, did not exceed 25% of the cumulative number of shares contributed as of the end of that year. If Ben did not elect any diversification during the 2022 - 2026 election periods, a final election would be available in 2027 (the election period following the plan year in which he reaches age 60) to diversify as much as 50% of his shares of employer stock.

Example 6.9

Assume Ben, in **Example 6.8** , has 120 shares of Blackrock Corporation stock in his ESOP on December 31, 2021 (the first year in which he is a qualified participant). During the 90-day period beginning on January 1, 2022, and ending on March 31, 2022, the maximum number of shares Ben may diversify is 25% x 120 shares = 30 shares. Ben directs the trustee to diversify 22 shares. During 2022 another 20 shares are allocated to Ben's account, making the total number of Blackrock shares contributed during Ben's participation in the plan 140 shares as of December 31, 2022. During the 90-day period beginning on January 1, 2023, and ending on March 31, 2023, the maximum number of shares Ben may diversify is: 25% x 140 shares = 35 shares, less the 22 shares previously diversified. Therefore, Ben may diversify up to 13 shares during this election period. A similar calculation continues through the 2026 election period. In the 2027 election period (the election period following the plan year in which he reaches age 60), the calculation to determine the number of shares which may be diversified is performed in the same manner, but substitutes 50% for 25%. Assume another 20 shares is added to his account each year, that he does not diversify any additional shares until the final year, and he fully diversifies all eligible shares in the final year.

Election Period (Jan 1 - Mar 31 of following year)*	2021	2022	2023	2024	2025	2026
Cumulative shares contributed to Ben's Accounts	120	140	160	180	200	220
Total shares that may be diversified (25% / 50% in 6th year)	30	35	40	45	50	110
Total shares actually diversified by Ben	22	22	22	22	22	110
Difference (shares that could have been diversified)	8	13	18	23	28	0

The election period is the year following the qualification year.

Although the Pension Protection Act of 2006 mandates certain investment diversification requirements for defined contribution plans (for plan years beginning after 2006), the diversification requirements do not apply to an ESOP if:

1. there are no contributions to the ESOP (or earnings thereunder) that are subject to the special nondiscrimination tests that apply to elective deferrals, employee after-tax contributions, and matching contributions; and

2. the ESOP is a separate plan from any other qualified plan of the employer.

Therefore, while many ESOPs will qualify for the above exception and will thus only be subject to the general ESOP diversification requirements discussed above, ESOPs that provide for elective deferrals will need to comply with the diversification requirements for defined contribution plans, which are discussed in greater depth in Chapter 4.

Put Options

Once a plan meets the distribution requirements and a participant is entitled to a distribution from the plan, the participant has the right to demand that the benefits be distributed in the form of employer securities. If the employer securities are not readily tradeable on an established market, the participant has the right to require that the employer repurchase the employer securities under a fair market valuation formula. This is referred to as a "put option" or "repurchase option" under ESOPs. This also applies equally with stock bonus plans.

The put or repurchase option is a substantial benefit to an employee-participant of an ESOP. A closely held or private corporation that sponsors an ESOP must provide for a "put option" on corporate stock that is distributed to employee-participants.[39] The rank-and-file employees are protected with the put option because the employee may force the corporation to "buy back" the stock at the fair market value when there otherwise would be no market for the stock. If no put option is provided, then the corporation could choose not to purchase the departing employee's stock, leaving the employee with stock that cannot be sold or liquidated. Indeed, this rule applies to closely held or private corporations because the inherent nature of closely held or private corporations is that there is no readily established securities market for the stock. ESOPs may offer the right of first refusal to the corporation to buy back the stock from participants to prevent the stock from being owned and controlled by outside entities. At a minimum, the put option must be available during two time periods, first, for no less than sixty days immediately following the distribution and the second, if the put option is not exercised within such 60-day period, for an additional period of at least 60 days in the following plan year.[40]

If a corporation is forced to repurchase the stock that was distributed to the employee as part of a total distribution,[41] then the corporation's repurchasing of that stock under a fair valuation formula[42] is satisfied if the corporation pays the participant in substantially equal periodic payments over a period beginning no later than 30 days after the exercise of the put option. However, this periodic payment must not be paid less frequently than annually and must be completed within five years.[43] For periodic repayments, reasonable interests and adequate security must be given.[44] If a put option is exercised

---

39. IRC §409(h).
40. IRC §409(h)(4).
41. Total distribution is defined as the distribution within one tax year of the balance of the recipient's account. IRC §409(h)(5).
42. IRC §409(h)(1)(B).
43. IRC §409(h)(5), 409(h)(5)(A) and 409(h)(5)(B).
44. IRC §409(h)(5)(B).

after an installment distribution of the employer stock, then the employer must repurchase the stock within 30 days to fulfill the put option.[45]

Example 6.10

Molly, an employee of KAC corporation, receives a stock distribution of ten shares of stock in KAC corporation on October 10, 2021 as a participant of an ESOP. KAC is a closely held corporation. If Molly exercises her put option ninety days after distribution, is KAC corporation required to honor her put option?

The answer is initially no, but ultimately yes. Molly must exercise her put option within 60 days following the distribution according to IRC §409(h)(4); however, IRC §409(h)(4) also provides an additional 60 day period in the following plan year, which would start on January 1, 2022 and continue through February 28, 2022, and thus Molly's exercise of her put option would be timely under IRC §409(h)(4) with respect to the additional 60 days within the following taxable year of the plan.

CASE STUDY 6.1

The case of **Roth v. Sawyer-Cleaton Lumber Co.**,[1] dealt with the ESOP trustees' decisions concerning put options. Roth was a former employee of Sawyer-Cleaton, a closely held corporation engaged in lumber sales. Under the corporation's ESOP plan documents, each participant had one account consisting of corporation stock and another consisting of other investments, and participants could exercise a put option on stock issued. At the time of Roth's retirement in 1988, Roth chose to exercise his put option. The stock sale was accomplished through a promissory note and stock pledge agreement. The Plan obligated itself to make payments to Roth over ten years with Roth retaining a security interest in his stock under the stock pledge agreement. Roth received partial payment of the sums due under the promissory note, but the corporation began to experience financial troubles. In 1990, the corporation terminated its business operations, and the Plan defaulted on payments due under the promissory note.

By 1991, the corporation was forced into Chapter 7 bankruptcy and Roth's stock and security became worthless.[2] Roth sued the ESOP and its trustees, claiming breach of fiduciary duty because of the failure to adequately secure notes given from the Plan and the assumption of the notes by the Plan. The court ultimately concluded that Roth's loss was caused by the trustees' decision to secure the plaintiff's promissory note with corporation stock and to make the ESOP the obligated party on the plaintiff's notes. Therefore, the trustees in that case could be liable for breach of fiduciary duty.[3]

---

1. *Roth v. Sawyer-Cleaton Lumber Co.*, 61 F.3d 599 (8th Cir. 1995).
2. *Roth*, 61 F.3d 599, 601.
3. *Id.* at 605.

45.IRC §409(h)(6).

The ESOP Trustee and "Inherent" Conflicts

The ESOP is created by written plan documents, which are responsible for the establishment of the trust. The plan sponsor establishes the plan and the trust, and in some cases the trust borrows from a bank or other type of lender. The tax deductible contributions are paid to the trust, and in some cases the trust repays funds to the bank or lender. Under this complicated set of transactions, the trust must use the loan proceeds to acquire the employer stock. The trust is administered by the trustee, who, depending on the specific plan and the documents creating it, is an individual, a group of individuals, committee, or entity.[46] The trustee holds funds "in trust" for the benefit of employees, participants, and their beneficiaries. The trustee purchases employer securities, deals with the corporation, interacts with the bank or lender, and keeps the employee-participants apprised of the status and value of their accounts. In addition to all of these duties, the ESOP trustee must strive to preserve the ESOP's fundamental goal of investing plan assets into employer securities. The trustee is held to the standard of a fiduciary.

Key Concepts

1. Under what circumstances can an ESOP participant require the employer to diversify the participant's holdings?

2. When must a closely held corporation provide a put option to the participants of an ESOP?

3. Explain the inherent conflict of interest within an ESOP.

4. Discuss the impact of an S Corporation ESOP participant demanding a stock distribution.

There are times where the interests of the employees, the interests of the corporation, and the interests of the management of the corporation are different or even in conflict. Often, the trustee is forced to navigate these complicated and perplexing issues and bear the brunt of criticism or claims. There has been much litigation over these issues in the case law.[47] Occasionally, individuals serve in a dual capacity concerning the ESOP, both as trustees of the ESOP and as officers, directors, or employees of the corporation. The corporation is the plan sponsor and a potential conflict of interest can arise. Here, as detailed in **Shoen v. Americo, 885 F.Supp. 1332**, the ideal course of action for the trustee could be that "trustees of an [ESOP] must discharge their duties by evaluating the best interest of the beneficiaries in the abstract as beneficiaries, not as directors who may lose control of the corporation nor as employees, some of whom may lose their jobs if control of the corporation changes hands."[48] The courts have generally concluded that if the conflict of interest is so great that it is virtually impossible for the fiduciary to discharge the duties with "an eye to the beneficiaries' interests," then the preferred course of action for a fiduciary of a plan holding or acquiring the stock of a target, who is also an officer, director, or employee of a party in interest seeking to acquire or retain control of the target, is to resign and clear the way for the appointment of a genuinely neutral trustee to manage the assets involved in the control contest.[49]

There are cases in which the conflict of interest, although substantial, is not so great as to require the trustee's resignation. The question in these cases becomes whether the fiduciary engaged in an intensive and independent investigation of alternatives to insure that the action taken was in the shareholders' best interests. One element of this inquiry is the extent to which the use of the trust's assets track the best interest of another party. The bottom line is, considering the duty imposed on the fiduciary under

46. Interestingly, the corporation may have its own ESOP committee that is part of the corporation and not the ESOP, and the ESOP committee could have been charged with establishing and drafting the documents that formed the ESOP and its trustee.
47. See, for example, *Shoen v. Americo,* 885 F.Supp. 1332, 1348 (D. Nev. 1994); *Chas v. Archer,* 827 F.Supp. 159, 169 (W.D.N.Y. 1993).
48. *Central Trust Corporation, N.A. v. American Avents Corp.,* 771 F.Supp. 871, 874-875 (S.D. Ohio 1989).
49. Danaher Corp. v. Chicago Pneumatic Tool Co., 635 F. Supp. 246, 250 (S.D.N.Y. 1986) (quoting *Leigh v. Engle*, 727 F.2d 113, 122 (7th Cir. 1984)).

these circumstances, trustees must avoid placing themselves in a position where their acts as officers or directors of the corporation will prevent their functioning with the complete loyalty to participants demanded of them as trustees of the pension plan.[50] For instance, ESOP trustees will probably be found to have breached their fiduciary duties if they form a separate corporation designed to compete with the corporation where they are an ESOP trustee.[51]

The court in the *Shoen* decision also noted a second problem that is common in litigation concerning control of the corporation as it relates to the trustee's duty to monitor communications to participants. ESOPs, the court acknowledged in *Shoen*, typically contain provisions for "pass through" voting by the participants to qualify for favorable tax treatment under IRC §409. Basically each participant can direct the ESOP trustees on how to vote the shares allocated to the participant's individual account in the ESOP if it is a closely held corporation not concerning major corporate decisions. The court in *Shoen* explained that the contesting parties desired to communicate quickly and frequently with the participants, and in such a situation, according to the Department of Labor, the trustee's fiduciary duty mandates that the trustee insure that necessary information is given to participants, that misleading or false information is not provided to participants, and that participants render an independent decision free from duress or pressure from their employer as to how to vote.[52] The court also indicated that ESOPs have been known to be established to serve as anti-takeover devices, with the theory being that the ESOP will own a significant amount of the corporation's stock and will, because the voting of that stock is directed by the corporation's employees through the "pass through" framework, be friendlier in a contest of control to the incumbent management than to an outside, hostile force or entity.[53]

For an investment advisor to be deemed a "fiduciary" under ERISA's "renders investment advice" definition, the investment advisor must render advice pursuant to an agreement, be paid for such advice, and have influence approaching control over benefit plan's investment decisions.[54] The trustee must also be prudent. ERISA's "prudence" requirement commands a fiduciary to act "with the care, skill, prudence, and diligence under circumstances then prevailing that a prudent man acting in a like capacity and familiar with such matters would use in the conduct of an enterprise of a like character and with like aims."[55]

---

50. *Shoen, 885 F.Supp. at 1348; Donovan v. Bierwirth,* 680 F.2d 263, 271 (2nd Cir. 1982).
51. See *Neyer, Tisco & Hindo, Ltd. v. Russell,* 1993 WL 52552 (E.D. Pa. 1993).
52. *Shoen,* 885 F.Supp. at 1349.
53. *Id.* at 1355 n.35.
54. ERISA, 29 U.S.C.A. §1002(21)(A)(ii).
55. 29 U.S.C. §1104(a)(1)(B).

CASE STUDY 6.2

In **Kuper v. Iovenko**,[1] the plaintiffs filed claims under ERISA for breach of fiduciary duty against the ESOP trustees and administrators. The plaintiffs were employees of the Emery Division of Quantum Chemical Corp. These employees were participants in the corporation's ESOP. Quantum entered into an agreement to sell its Emery Division to Henkel Corporation. Henkel Corporation, in the meantime, agreed to employ existing employees of Emery Division under comparable terms and to accept the trust-to-trust transfer of the ESOP assets of those employees who continued employment with Henkel Corporation following the sale. Although the sale was effective on April 17, 1989, the trust-to-trust transfer of ESOP assets was not completed until roughly a year and a half later. During this 18-month period, Quantum's stock declined in value from more than $50 per share to approximately $10 per share. Plaintiffs contended that Quantum's acknowledged failure to consider diversifying or liquidating the ESOP constituted a breach of fiduciary duty owed to the plan and its participants.

Finally, the United States Sixth Circuit conducted a balancing act of the competing concerns. After this delicate balancing of varying interests, the Court held that an ESOP fiduciary's decision to continue investing in employer securities is reviewed for abuse of discretion. This balancing act is done with the purpose of ERISA on the one hand and the nature of ESOPs on the other. In this scenario, the courts may presume that a fiduciary's decision to remain invested in employer securities was reasonable. A plaintiff may rebut this presumption of reasonableness by showing that a prudent ESOP fiduciary acting under similar circumstances would have made a different investment decision.[2]

In defending the case, the defendants in **Kuper** asserted that the terms of the ESOP did not give them discretion to diversify or to liquidate the ESOP funds. The United States Sixth Circuit Court of Appeals discussed the duties of ERISA fiduciaries in general and the exemptions from those duties for ESOP fiduciaries.[3]

Fiduciary duties under ERISA, the court explained, have three components:
- the duty of loyalty, which requires the fiduciary to make all decisions regarding an ERISA plan "with an eye single to the interests of the participants and beneficiaries;"[4]
- the "prudent man" obligation, which requires the fiduciary to act as a prudent person would act in a similar situation or under similar circumstances; and
- the exclusive purpose obligation, which requires the fiduciary to act for the exclusive purpose of providing benefits to plan beneficiaries.[5]

The United States Sixth Circuit reasoned that an ESOP fiduciary is exempt from the duty to diversify investments and cannot be held liable for failing to diversify investments even if diversification would be prudent under the terms of a non-ESOP plan. These statutory exemptions, however, do not relieve a fiduciary from the general fiduciary responsibilities enumerated above.[6] "Thus, ESOP fiduciaries must, then, wear two hats and are expected to administer ESOP investments consistent with the provisions of both a specific employee benefits plan and ERISA... These competing concerns make it more difficult to delineate the responsibilities of ESOP trustees."[7]

1. *Kuper v. Iovenko*, 66 F.3d 1447 (6th Cir.1995).
2. See also *Keach v. United States Trust Co., N.A.*, 222 F.Supp.2d 1224 (C.D.Ill. Dec. 30, 2002), 2002 WL 31887909.
3. *Kuper v. Iovenko*, 66 F.3d 1447, 1458 (6th Cir.1995).
4. *Kuper*, 66 F.3d at 1458.
5. *Id.*
6. *Id.* (citing *Martin v. Feilen*, 965 F.2d 660, 665 (8th Cir.1992)).
7. *Id.*

CASE STUDY 6.3

In some situations, an ESOP trustee may be deemed to have been required to obtain advice from a separate independent party. In **Leigh v. Eagle**,[1] plan administrators played a role in having the plan they directed to invest, along with corporations they controlled, into the stock of corporations that the plan administrators, i.e., fiduciaries, were attempting to acquire. The plan administrators did not perform an independent, diligent investigation into the investment options available to the trust. Nor did these fiduciaries seek out independent advice from separate third parties concerning investment options. Even though the trust did not lose money and the trust did not decrease in value based on the actions of these fiduciaries, the court found that the fiduciaries nonetheless breached their duty by failing to seek out independent advice or embark on an independent, diligent investigation into investment options available to the trust.

1. *Leigh v. Eagle*, 727 F.2d 113, 129 (7th Cir. 1984).

CASE STUDY 6.4

In **Wright v. Oregon Metallurgical Corp.**,[1] an Oregon District Court was asked to evaluate an ESOP trustee's fiduciary obligations. The fiduciary duties in that case arose with the creation of an ESOP designed to finance the leveraged buyout of the owner's shares. The Court explained that under ERISA, a fiduciary is required to discharge his duties:

- "Solely in the interest of the participants and beneficiaries;" and
- with the exclusive purpose of providing benefits to participants and their beneficiaries and defraying reasonable expenses of administering the plan [the exclusive purpose requirement];
- with the care, skill, prudence, and diligence under circumstances then prevailing that a prudent man acting in a like capacity and familiar with such matters would use in the conduct of an enterprise of a like character and with like aims [the prudence requirement];
- by diversifying the investments of the plan in order to minimize the risk of large losses, unless under the circumstances it is clearly prudent not to do so [the diversification requirement]; and
- in accordance with the documents and instruments governing the plan insofar as such documents and instruments are consistent with the provisions of ERISA.

1. *Wright v. Oregon Metallurgical Corp.*, 222 F. Supp. 2d 1224, 28 Employee Benefits Cas. 2006 (D. Oregon, Aug. 6, 2002).

The law and jurisprudence relating to trustees shows that the ESOP trustee must strive to preserve the ESOP's fundamental goal of investing plan assets into employer securities, all the while being held to the standard of a fiduciary while purchasing employer securities, dealing with the corporation, interacting with the bank or lender, and keeping employee-participants updated as to the value of their accounts and status of the ESOP as a whole.

S Corporations' Role as an Owner of ESOPs

IRC §1361 was amended in 1996 by the Small Business Job Protection Act, which allowed qualified plan trusts and §501(c)(3) organizations to be shareholders of S Corporations. Therefore, S Corporations may establish ESOPs, and ESOPs are permitted to own the stock of an S Corporation.[56] **S Corporations** are generally small corporations that:

- have no more than 100 shareholders,
- have shareholders that are individuals, and[57]
- have only one class of stock.

A significant change in the law occurred when an ESOP maintained by an S Corporation was treated as not violating the Code's qualification requirements nor as engaging in a prohibited transaction. In accordance with plan documentation, distributions of S Corporation stock that constitute qualifying employer securities held by the ESOP may be used to make interest and principal payments on loans utilized to acquire securities.

At first, it would appear that the 100 shareholder limitation would create an issue with respect to the number of participants in the ESOP. Nonetheless, the participants in the ESOP are not counted towards the 100 shareholder limit for an S Corporation. Instead, the ESOP is deemed to be only one shareholder.

Example 6.11

Matthew, Patrick, Michael, and American ESOP all hold shares in the same S Corporation. American ESOP has seven employee-participants in its ESOP. Matthew, Patrick and Michael are not employee-participants of American ESOP. Based on this factual scenario, how many shareholders are there of the S Corporation?

The answer is four. Matthew, Patrick, and Michael count as three shareholders and American ESOP is considered to be one shareholder. American ESOP is not deemed to be seven shareholders because the employee-participants are not counted towards the aggregate number of shareholders in the S Corporation.

The Taxpayer Relief Act of 1997 also added several beneficial changes to the way ESOPs and S Corporations are treated, including an amendment to §409(h)(2) of the IRC. This amendment allowed ESOPs the power to prevent participants from demanding stock distributions. Otherwise, a participant could terminate a corporation's S Corporation status by demanding a stock distribution and then placing that stock in an IRA, which is not permitted to hold stock in an S Corporation.[58] This law was somewhat modified concerning banks that are S Corporations. Section 1361 of the Internal Revenue Code now provides that an IRA or Roth IRA may be a shareholder of a bank that is an S Corporation, but only to the extent of bank stock held by the IRA as of the date of enactment of the provision, which is October 22, 2004.[59] With respect to dividends, the IRC prohibits S Corporations from deducting dividends paid from employer securities that are held by ESOPs.[60]

---

56. IRC §1361.
57. The shareholders can be individuals, an estate, some trusts, a qualified retirement plan, or other qualified entities, but generally must be an individual. Also, a nonresident alien cannot serve as a shareholder of an S Corporation.
58. IRC §409(h)(2).
59. IRC §1361(c)(2)(A)(vi).
60. IRC §404(k)(1).

The income of an S Corporation passes through to the ESOP, and because an ESOP is tax exempt, no tax is paid on the income until it is distributed to the ESOP participant. ESOPs are advantageous in S Corporations to the extent that, among the S Corporation owners, the ESOP is not required to pay federal income taxes on its profits. In sum, it is important to note in the financial planning and estate planning process that ESOPs used in conjunction with S corporations can provide significant financial benefits to owners and employees. The same is likewise true for stock bonus plans.

Ultimately, the attractiveness of flow-through income from an S corporation avoiding taxation in an ESOP until distributed was too much for some taxpayers and resulted in significant abuse during the late 1990s. As a result, Congress added IRC §409(p) in 2001, entitled Prohibited Allocations of Securities in an S corporation, which is designed to limit a concentration of the benefits of an ESOP to a small number of persons.

The general rule under this section is that no allocations of stock within the ESOP can accrue to a disqualified person in a nonallocation year. Below are the definitions of disqualified persons and a nonallocation year.

Disqualified persons - any person who:
1. owns with other family members 20 percent or more of the stock of the company, or
2. in the case of someone without other family ownership, owns 10 percent or more of the stock of the company.

Nonallocation year - any plan year of an employee stock ownership plan that holds employer securities consisting of stock in an S corporation, and disqualified persons own at least 50 percent of the number of shares of stock in the S corporation.[61]

In effect, the owners of a closely held S corporation are prohibited from benefiting under an ESOP arrangement when there is a significant concentration of ownership. However, these rules should not be considered as a reason to avoid consideration of an ESOP for an S corporation. On the contrary, Congress purposely changed the Internal Revenue Code to allow S corporations to benefit from ESOP arrangements. These rules that were put in place in 2001 were intended to minimize the abusive transactions involving ESOPs and S corporations.

61.IRC §409(p)(3)(A).

CASE STUDY 6.5

Ries Enterprises, Inc. v. Commissioner, U.S. Tax Court, Dkt. No. 9941-11, TC Memo. 2014-14 (January 27, 2014).

John Ries ("Ries") incorporated the subject company ("Petitioner") in 2002 to engage in the rental and leasing business. In the same year, Petitioner elected to be treated as an S corporation. With this election, in 2002 Petitioner filed a Form 1120S, U.S. Income Tax Return for an S Corporation, and did not pay federal income tax. Petitioner had two classes of stock outstanding at the time it elected to be treated as an S corporation.

In its ruling, the Tax Court found that, for purposes of Section 409(p), 2002 was a "nonallocation" year. A nonallocation year, the Tax Court reasoned, includes any plan year of an ESOP holding shares of an S corporation where a disqualified person owns at least 50 percent of the S corporation's outstanding stock. See Ries Enterprises, TC Memo Ruling, at p. 13 (citing Section 409(p)(3)(A)) et seq. A taxpayer is treated as owning the shares that his or her spouse owns. Id. (citing Section 409(p)(3)(B). A taxpayer is also treated as owning deemed-owned shares. A Trust held 80 percent of Petitioner's stock during 2002, and Mr. Ries and his wife owned the remaining 20 percent. Mr. Ries, a disqualified person, was therefore treated as owning all of Petitioner's stock for 2002. Id. at 13-14 (citing Section 409(p)(3)).

Based on the foregoing, the court ruled that the plan made an impermissible allocation of Petitioner's stock in 2002, thereby violating Section 409(p). In short, the S corporation's sole owner was a disqualified person in an nonallocation year, and hence the prohibited transaction tax applied.

Summary

Stock bonus plans provide benefits similar to those of profit sharing plans, except that benefits are normally distributed in the form of employer securities. ESOPs are the most common type of stock bonus plans. An ESOP can be a very powerful tool for closely held businesses. ESOPs provide tax benefits and satisfy the employer's goals of having motivated, loyal, and long-term employees. Meanwhile, the employees are provided with value for services rendered and are able to accumulate assets that are provided over time towards retirement. Employees also become part owners of a corporation in which they work, which should increase their productivity, efficiency, and motivation. A key ingredient of the ESOP is that the corporation has the ability to borrow (leverage) to purchase the employer stock.

The leveraging aspect of ESOPs, along with the tax deductibility of the payments, make ESOPs a very attractive tool in the financial planning and estate planning areas. On the other hand, because the investments of ESOPs are primarily in employer securities, it is a highly non-diversified and risky investment depending on the strength, standing, and goodwill of the corporation as an on going entity. If the corporation were to fail, the ESOP and the accounts of the individual employee-participants may be rendered worthless. Nonetheless, depending on each individual situation, financial planning advice and estate planning advice must be given with these advantages and disadvantages in mind. The ESOP trustees may be the ones named in subsequent lawsuits if ESOPs fail, or the businesses with which they are affiliated fail.

Stock bonus plans and ESOPs are primarily used to avoid putting cash into a qualified plan while a corporation is growing and needs the cash for growth. The problem with these plans is that eventually cash must be contributed to diversify the 55-year olds, those terminating participants, and in the case of a closely held corporation, to provide a market for those retirees or plan participants who wish to sell their shares. It is also important to remember that stock bonus plans and ESOPs are "pay me now or pay me later" qualified plans and as the employer stock becomes more valuable, the plan will need more and more cash to redeem any outstanding shares. Sponsors considering adopting a stock bonus or ESOP plan should carefully consider not only the initial tax deduction and cash flow impact but the ultimate necessity to fund the plan with sufficient cash to redeem shares under the put option and diversify the investment portfolios for those participants age 55 or older.

Exhibit 6.8 | Comparison of Stock Bonus Plans to ESOPs

	Stock Bonus Plans	ESOPs
Plan Establishment	Due date of tax return plus extensions	Due date of tax return plus extensions
Date of Contribution	Due date of tax return plus extensions	Due date of tax return plus extensions
Type of Contributions	Generally stock	Generally stock
Deductible Contribution Limit	*25% of covered compensation*	*25% of covered compensation plus interest paid on loan*
Valuation	Generally needed	Generally needed plus dividends (in certain circumstances)
Eligibility	Same as other Qualified Plans (21 and one year of service or two years with 100% vesting)	Same as other Qualified Plans (21 and one year of service or two years with 100% vesting)
Allocation Method	% of compensation or formula based on age, service of classification	% of compensation or formula based on age, service of classification
Integration with Social Security	*Yes*	*No*
Vesting	Same as other Defined Contribution Qualified Plans (3-year cliff or 2-to-6-year graduated vesting)	Same as other Defined Contribution Qualified Plans (3-year cliff or 2-to-6-year graduated vesting)
Portfolio Diversification	No*	Yes, up to 25% (or 50% in final year) if at least 55 years old and 10 years of participation
Voting Rights	Generally yes	Generally yes
Distributions	Generally stock	Generally stock
In-Service Withdrawals	May be allowed after two years of participation	May be allowed after two years of participation
Loans	May be allowed (but not usually)	May be allowed (but not usually)
Taxation of Distributions	Ordinary income with NUA treatment available	Ordinary income with NUA treatment available

Note: The differences between Stock Bonus Plans and ESOPs are highlighted in blue.
* Diversification may be required under PPA 2006 for stock bonus plans of publicly traded companies.

DISCUSSION QUESTIONS

SOLUTIONS to the discussion questions can be found exclusively within the chapter. Once you have completed an initial reading of the chapter, go back and highlight the answers to these questions.

1. List the required characteristics of a stock bonus plan.

2. List advantages and disadvantages of stock bonus plans.

3. List at least three distinctions between profit sharing plans and stock bonus plans.

4. Why are valuations of the employer's securities completed each year for the plan sponsor of a stock bonus plan?

5. What are the eligibility requirements for stock bonus plans?

6. Describe the standard method of allocating contributions to a stock bonus plan.

7. Explain the stock voting rights of stock bonus plan participants.

8. Define net unrealized appreciation and discuss the tax advantages related to it.

9. Define ESOPs and discuss when they are used.

10. Discuss how the leveraged ESOP works.

11. For the owner of a closely held business to qualify for the nonrecognition of capital gain treatment certain requirements must be met. List these requirements.

12. Define qualified replacement securities.

13. List several advantages of an ESOP.

14. List several disadvantages of an ESOP.

15. Describe the voting rights of ESOP participants.

16. Discuss the limitations on contributions to ESOPs.

17. What are the requirements necessary for an employee to force diversification of his holdings in the ESOP?

18. Describe the requirements of the "put option" for an ESOP.

19. Discuss how the changes created by the Taxpayer Relief Act of 1997 with regard to ESOPs impact S Corporations.

MULTIPLE CHOICE PROBLEMS

A sample of multiple choice problems is provided below. Additional multiple choice problems are available at money-education.com by accessing the Student Practice Portal.

1. Which of the following are requirements for a qualified stock bonus plan?
    1. Participants must have pass through voting rights for stock held by the plan.
    2. Participants must have the right to demand employer securities at a distribution, even if the plan sponsor is a closely held corporation.
    a. 1 only.
    b. 2 only.
    c. Both 1 and 2.
    d. Neither 1 nor 2.

2. Byron, age 60, is a participant in the stock bonus plan of Tally, Inc., a closely held corporation. Byron received contributions in shares to the stock bonus plan and Tally, Inc. took income tax deductions as follows:

Year	# of Shares	Value per Share (At Time of Contribution)
Year 1	100	$10
Year 2	125	$12
Year 3	150	$13
Year 4	200	$15
Year 5	400	$18

Byron terminates employment and takes a distribution from the plan of 975 shares of Tally, Inc., having a fair value of $19,500. What are Byron's tax consequences?
    a. There are no immediate tax consequences because he has not sold the stock.
    b. Byron has ordinary income of $14,650 at distribution.
    c. Byron has net unrealized appreciation of $19,500 at distribution.
    d. Byron has ordinary income of $19,500 at distribution.

3. Brianna sells stock several years after she received it as a distribution from a qualified stock bonus plan. When the stock was distributed, she had a net unrealized appreciation of $7,500. Brianna also had ordinary income from the distribution of $29,000. The fair market value of the stock and the sale price at the time of sale was $81,000. How much of the sale price will be subject to long-term capital gain treatment?
    a. $7,500.
    b. $44,500.
    c. $52,000.
    d. $73,500.

4. Which of the following are costs of a stock bonus plan?
    1. Periodic appraisal costs.
    2. Periodic actuarial costs.
        a. 1 only.
        b. 2 only.
        c. Both 1 and 2.
        d. Neither 1 nor 2.

5. Patrick and Kevin own Irisha Corporation and plan to retire. They would like to leave their assets to their children; therefore, they transfer 70 percent of the stock to a trust for the benefit of their 10 children pro rata. Patrick and Kevin then plan to sell the remaining Irisha shares to a qualified ESOP plan. Which of the following is correct?
    1. The stock transfer to the ESOP is not a 50 percent transfer and therefore will not qualify for nonrecognition of capital gains.
    2. Any transfer to an ESOP of less than 50 percent ownership may be subject to a minority discount on valuation.
        a. 1 only.
        b. 2 only.
        c. Both 1 and 2.
        d. Neither 1 nor 2.

> **Additional multiple choice problems**
> **are available at**
> **money-education.com**
> **by accessing the**
> **Student Practice Portal.**
> **Access requires registration of the title using**
> **the unique code at the front of the book.**

QUICK QUIZ EXPLANATIONS

Quick Quiz 6.1
1. True.
2. False. A valuation of an employer's securities must generally be performed annually in order to determine the employer's tax deduction and for the purposes of the employer's financial statements.
3. False. Stock bonus plans are subject to the same eligibility rules as other qualified plans. Therefore, the standard eligibility criteria of age 21 and one year of service applies to stock bonus plans.

Quick Quiz 6.2
1. True.
2. True.
3. False. Net unrealized appreciation treatment is one of the principal benefits of stock bonus plans. The NUA of the stock is not taxed as ordinary income at the time of distribution, but rather is taxed as a long-term capital gain when the stock is sold.
4. True.

Quick Quiz 6.3
1. False. In a leveraged ESOP, the corporation makes tax deductible contributions to the trust in the form of both principal and interest for the loan that has been used to finance the purchase of stock for the benefit of participants/employees.
2. False. Qualified replacement securities are securities in a domestic corporation, including stocks, bonds, debentures, or warrants.
3. True.

Quick Quiz 6.4
1. False. The majority of ESOPs are established by closely held corporations in order to help create a market for the corporation's stock.
2. True.
3. True.
4. False. An ESOP is subject to the minimum distribution requirements of IRC §401(a)(9).

Quick Quiz 6.5
1. True.
2. True.
3. False. Under IRC §1361, S Corporations are allowed to establish ESOPs.

7

DISTRIBUTIONS FROM QUALIFIED PLANS

LEARNING OBJECTIVES

1. Explain the distribution options available to participants from qualified plans.*
2. Understand the differences among QJSAs, QPSA and QOSAs.*
3. Understand how distributions from qualified plans are taxed and the exceptions to the general rule.*
4. Describe the rules regarding rollovers, including rollovers attributable to Roth IRAs and Roth accounts.*
5. Calculate the taxable portion of a distribution that partially consists of after-tax contributions or other basis.*
6. Discuss the rules surrounding loans from qualified plans.*
7. Understand the additional 10 percent penalty on premature distributions from qualified plans and the exceptions to the penalty.*
8. Understand and calculate minimum distributions for participants and beneficiaries.*
9. Understand the creditor issues surrounding inherited IRAs and how to plan for the issue.

Ties to CFP Certification Learning Objectives

INTRODUCTION

This chapter focuses on distributions from qualified plans and, as discussed in previous chapters, the relationship between the government, the participant, and the plan sponsor (employer). The government allows the participant and/or the plan sponsor to deposit pre-tax funds into an account that will grow tax-free until distribution to the participant (or the participant's beneficiaries), at which time the funds will be subject to income tax.[1]

To receive the tax-free growth of the assets within the plan, the plan participant must follow precise rules and requirements regarding distributions from the plan. This chapter covers the requirements, benefits, stipulations, and consequences of taking distributions for retirement, as well as the impact of taking distributions prior to retirement or not using the funds during retirement.

While this chapter focuses on distributions from qualified plans, distributions from other tax-advantaged accounts, such as IRAs, SIMPLEs, 403(b) plans, and 457 plans will be discussed in Chapters 9 and 10.

DISTRIBUTION OPTIONS

Distributions are disbursements of assets from a qualified plan with no intention by the participant of returning the assets to the plan. Distributions include in-service withdrawals, payments made upon termination or retirement, and may also include certain distributions related to qualified domestic relations orders. Loans taken from a qualified plan are not distributions unless the loan is not repaid and the transaction is deemed a distribution (discussed below).

A qualified plan may, by law, offer a wide range of distribution options, but each plan document establishes the options actually available to the participants of a particular plan. Generally, qualified plans offer a variety of distribution options including a lump-sum distribution, a rollover distribution, a single

---

1. Elective deferrals to Roth accounts and contributions to thrift savings plans may be made on an after-tax basis. Roth contributions and earnings generally grow tax-free and qualified distributions are tax free.

life annuity, or a joint life annuity option. The plan may also offer in-service distributions and hardship withdrawals before retirement (discussed below).

Exhibit 7.1 | Distribution Options

- Annuities
- Lump-sum distributions
- Rollovers
- In-service withdrawals
- Non-repaid loans

Pension Plans

Pension plans are generally not permitted to offer in-service withdrawals to participants unless the participant is participating in a phased-in retirement beginning at age 59½ or older. A phased retirement is intended to enable older workers to become part-time employees and receive benefits to maintain their current earnings level; however, because of the continued accrual of benefits, plans often do not permit such withdrawals. Thus, distributions from pension plans are normally made because of the participant's termination of employment, early retirement, normal retirement, disability, or death.

Early Termination

A participant who terminates employment before normal retirement age may have up to three options:
1. receive a lump-sum distribution of the qualified plan assets,
2. roll the assets over to an IRA or other qualified plan, or
3. leave the funds in the pension plan.

However, these options depend on the plan document. Many pension plans do not have lump-sum options.

If the participant's vested account balance is less than $5,000, then the law permits, but does not require, the plan to distribute the balance to the participant if the participant does not make a timely election. This situation is called a forced payout. Before March 28, 2005, a plan could simply distribute the account balance and still meet its fiduciary duty. However, the Department of Labor issued final regulations that changed the responsibilities of plan administrators with regards to forced payouts. Section 2550.404a-2 of the Department of Labor

> ### Key Concepts
> 1. What are the distribution options for pension plans?
> 2. What are the distribution options for profit sharing plans?

regulations now require that forced payouts between $1,000 and $5,000 be directly rolled to an IRA if the participant has not made a timely election and the plan requires a forced payout. A forced payout for amounts less than $1,000 are not affected by this change.

Normal Retirement

At the participant's normal retirement age, a pension plan will typically distribute retirement benefits through an annuity payable for the remainder of the participant's life. The plan may also provide for a lump-sum distribution option that pays the participant an amount equal to the present value of the annuity. Under PPA 2006, the interest rate to be used in determining the value of lump-sum distributions from defined benefit plans after 2006 is based on the corporate bond yield curve of investment-grade corporate bonds of varying maturities.[2] While the plan document dictates the distribution options available to the participant, a single life annuity is generally the automatic form of benefit for a single participant. However, married individuals must be offered a qualified joint and survivor annuity (QJSA). Other annuity options may include term certain features, which ensure that payments will continue even after death, for the number of years specified as the term certain. Regardless of the form, distributions from qualified pension plans are generally characterized as ordinary income for income tax purposes.

Qualified Joint and Survivor Annuity (QJSA)

A **Qualified Joint and Survivor Annuity (QJSA)** must be provided, but can be waived, to married participants of a pension plan and must also be provided to married participants of profit sharing plans unless the plan meets the following criteria:

1. The plan provides that the participant's nonforfeitable accrued benefit is payable in full, upon the participant's death, to the participant's surviving spouse (unless the participant elects, with spousal consent, that such benefit be provided instead to a designated beneficiary).
2. The participant does not elect the payment of benefits in the form of a life annuity.

In order to meet the first requirement, two additional requirements must be met. First, the benefit must be available to the surviving spouse within a reasonable time after the participant's death. A "reasonable time" is defined by the IRC to mean within the 90-day period following the date of death. Longer periods may be deemed a reasonable time based on the particular facts and circumstances. Second, the benefit payable to the surviving spouse must be adjusted for gains or losses occurring after the participant's death in accordance with plan rules governing the adjustment of account balances for other plan distributions.[3]

> ### ✏ Quick Quiz 7.1
>
> 1. Pension plans generally provide a lump-sum distribution.
>   a. True
>   b. False
>
> 2. A qualified joint and survivor annuity and qualified pre-retirement survivor annuity are required for pension plans.
>   a. True
>   b. False
>
> 3. Profit sharing plans may allow for in-service withdrawals.
>   a. True
>   b. False
>
> False, True, True.

The QJSA pays a benefit to the participant and spouse as long as either lives. At the death of the first spouse, the surviving spouse's annuity payments can range from 50 percent to 100 percent of the joint life benefit, depending on the plan provisions and the participant election. Because the annuity is paid as long as either spouse is living, the QJSA is actuarially reduced compared to an annuity payment that would have been derived using the participants' single life expectancy. The reduction is to actuarially compensate for the continuing payments to the surviving spouse after the first spouse's death. The nonparticipant spouse beneficiary may choose to waive his right to a QJSA by executing a notarized or otherwise official waiver of benefits. The waiver may be made during the 90-day period beginning 90 days before the annuity start date.

---

2. Prior to the Pension Protection Act of 2006, the interest rate used to determine the present value of the annuity was generally the 30-year Treasury security rate for the month before the date of distribution.
3. Treas. Reg. §1.401(a)-20 Q-A #3.

Exhibit 7.2 | Sample Waiver of Qualified Joint and Survivor Annuity

Participant Information	Employer Plan Name: _____ Full Name of Participant: _____ Social Security Number: ___ - __ - ____ Daytime Phone Number: (___)___ - ____
Participant's Authorized Signature	I have made an election for distribution of benefits in a form other than a Qualified Joint and Survivor Annuity. The plan administrator has provided me with a written explanation of the effect of this election, my right to waive the joint and survivor payment form and the financial effect of selecting an alternate payment form. I understand that this election is revocable up until the beginning distribution date, and anytime thereafter for assets that are not yet distributed. I hereby waive the distribution of plan benefits in the form of a Qualified Joint and Survivor Annuity ("QJSA"). I hereby waive the QJSA 30-day notice period under Internal Revenue Code sections 401(a)(11) and 417(a)(7). _____ **Signature of Participant** **Date**
Consent of Spouse	I, _____[insert your name], am the spouse of _____ [insert name of Participant]. I understand that I have the right to have my spouse's Employer's Plan pay my spouse's retirement benefits in the form of a Qualified Joint Survivor Annuity ("QJSA"), and I agree to waive that right. I understand that by signing this agreement, I may receive less money than I would have received under the QJSA payment form and I may receive nothing after my spouse dies depending on the payment form that my spouse chooses. I understand that by signing this waiver, my spouse can choose any retirement benefit form that is allowed by the Plan without telling me and without getting my agreement. I also understand that my spouse can change the retirement benefit form selected at any time without telling me and without getting my agreement. I understand that I can limit my spouse's choice to a particular retirement benefit form and that I am waiving that right. I understand that I do not have to sign this agreement. I am signing voluntarily. I understand that if I do not sign this agreement, then my spouse and I will receive payments from the plan in the form of a QJSA. I hereby consent to my spouse's waiver of the QJSA 30-day notice period under Internal Revenue Code sections 401(a)(11) and 417(a)(7). I have executed this consent this _____ day of _____, 20_____, which is no more than 90 days from the beginning payment date requested by my spouse. _____ **Signature of Spouse of Participant**
Witnessed By: Employer's Plan Representative OR Notary Public	Signature of Spouse witnessed this _____day of _____ , 20 _____. _____ **Employer's Plan Representative** Subscribed and sworn to before me this _____day of _____, 20 _____. _____ **My commission expires** _____ **Notary Public** **(SEAL)**

Qualified Pre-Retirement Survivor Annuity (QPSA)

A **qualified pre-retirement survivor annuity (QPSA)** must also be provided to married participants of a pension plan or a profit sharing plan utilizing the same criteria as discussed above.[4] A QPSA provides a benefit to the surviving spouse if the participant dies before attaining normal retirement age. A QPSA is essentially a term insurance policy paid for by a reduction in the ultimate pension plan retirement benefit that the participant would have received from the plan at normal retirement age.

The nonparticipant spouse is offered the QPSA and may choose whether to accept or waive the option. The QPSA may be waived by the nonparticipant spouse via a written notarized waiver. (In some cases, the signature can be witnessed by a plan official instead of being notarized.) The waiver may be made beginning the first day of the plan year in which the participant attains age 35 until the day the participant dies.[5] In addition, the waiver can be revoked at any time during this period. Since any waiver is generally executed when the participant is age 35, this waiver or acceptance decision is critical, as it may impact the family's overall future financial plan. Advisors should carefully review the couple's life insurance situation before making a determination as to whether they should waive the QPSA. Assuming the QPSA is elected and the surviving spouse receives the benefit, there is no adjusted basis in the benefit. Thus, the full value of distribution under the QPSA is subject to ordinary income tax in addition to estate tax.

Exhibit 7.3 | QPSA Benefit Comparison

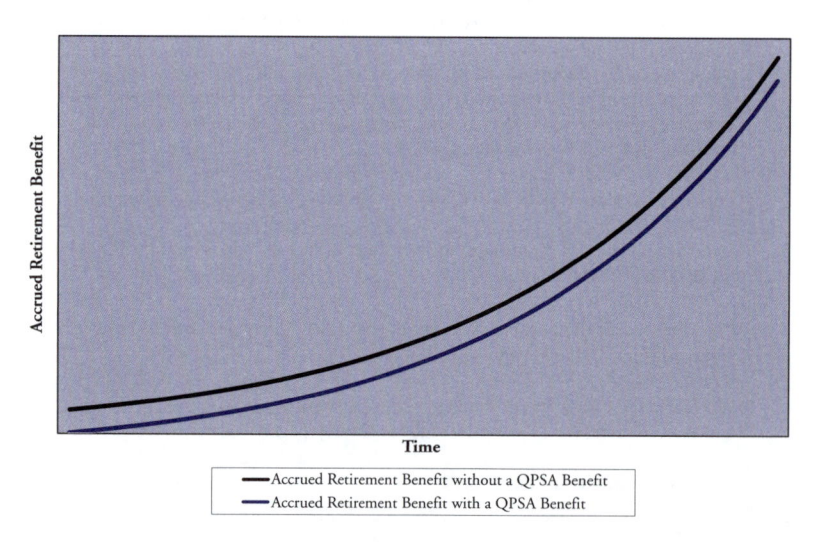

The difference between the two lines is the premium cost of life insurance associated with the QPSA.

Exhibit 7.4 | Pension Plan Normal Retirement Age Distribution Options

- Qualified Joint and Survivor Annuity (QJSA)
- Single Life Annuity if QJSA is waived or no spouse
- Lump-Sum

---

4. IRC §401(a)(11).
5. IRC §417(a)(6)(B).

Exhibit 7.5 | Characteristics of an Effective Waiver QPSA or QJSA Benefits

- In writing
- Clearly indicates that the QPSA or QJSA will be waived and the consequences of the waiver
- Signed by the nonparticipant spouse
- Notarized or witnessed by a plan official

PPA 2006 amends IRC Section 417 that requires a plan subject to the annuity requirement under IRC Section 401(a)(11) to offer a **qualified optional survivor annuity (QOSA)** to a plan participant who has waived the QJSA. A QOSA is an annuity for the life of a participant with a survivor annuity for the life of the participant's spouse that is equal to a specified applicable percentage of the amount of the annuity that is payable during the joint lives of the participant and the spouse (and that is actuarially equivalent to a single life annuity for the life of the participant). Written explanation of the terms and conditions of the QOSA must be provided to participants.

The level of the spouse survivor annuity under the QOSA depends on a plan's level of spouse survivor annuity under the QJSA. For the married participant under a plan, if the QJSA provides a survivor annuity for the life of the participant's spouse that is less than 75 percent of the amount of the annuity that is payable during the joint lives of the participant and the participant's spouse, then the QOSA must provide a spouse survivor annuity of 75 percent. In the same situation, if the QJSA provides a survivor annuity for the life of the participant's spouse that is greater than or equal to 75 percent of the amount of the annuity that is payable during the joint lives of the participant and the participant's spouse, the QOSA must provide a spouse survivor annuity of 50 percent.[6]

Exhibit 7.6 | QJSA vs. QOSA

QJSA	QOSA
Participant / Survivor Nonparticipant Spouse	Participant / Survivor Nonparticipant Spouse
If 100% / < 75%	then, 100% / 75%
If 100% / ≥ 75%	then, 100% / 50%

The QOSA must be actuarially equivalent to a single annuity for the life of a participant, and applies to distributions for annuity start dates in plan years beginning after December 31, 2007. Further information on this topic is available in IRS Notice 2008-30.

Rollover

A distribution from a pension plan may be rolled over into another qualified plan or an IRA provided the participant is not required to begin taking the required minimum distributions. If the assets are rolled over, the participant defers recognition of ordinary income until the assets are distributed from the rollover account. However, in certain situations when a distribution is taken as a lump-sum distribution, the recipient may receive favorable tax treatment on the distribution (Net Unrealized Appreciation (NUA), 10-year forward averaging, and/or pre-74 capital gain treatment) as discussed below. These

6. IRC §417(g).

favorable tax treatments will be lost if the distribution is rolled over to an IRA or to a plan that is not a qualified plan.

Profit Sharing Plans

Profit sharing plans generally provide participants with a distribution of the plan's assets at the participant's termination. At termination, the participant may be able to take a lump-sum distribution taxed as ordinary taxable income, annuitize the value of the account (if the plan document permits), or roll the assets over into a rollover qualified plan or IRA to continue the deferral of the income tax depending on the options available. In contrast to pension plans, profit sharing plans are not required to offer survivor benefits if the plan does not pay the participant in the form of a life annuity benefit and the participant's nonforfeitable accrued benefit is payable to the surviving spouse upon the participant's death. (See discussion in QJSA above.) Profit sharing plans also differ from pension plans because profit sharing plans may allow for in-service withdrawals for participants of any age (plan dependent) and most 401(k) plans generally allow plan loans to participants in the plan document.

TAXATION OF DISTRIBUTIONS

Distributions from qualified retirement plans are generally subject to ordinary income tax because the plans usually contain both contributions and earnings that have never been subjected to income tax. The contributions to the plan were effectively wages that would have been taxed at ordinary income tax rates had they been paid directly to the participant. These contributions have not yet been subjected to income tax because the benefits were held in a qualified plan. Therefore, when the plan assets are distributed, they are included in the participant's income and are taxed as ordinary income at the value upon distribution.

Key Concepts

1. What are rollovers and when and how are they used?

2. Under what circumstances will a participant have an adjusted basis in their qualified plan?

3. What special options are available for lump-sum distributions?

Just as the government requires an employer to withhold a specific amount of tax from an employee's wages to ensure that the government receives the income tax, a distribution from a qualified retirement plan is also subject to income tax withholding requirements. Generally, the plan custodian is required to withhold a mandatory 20 percent from most non-periodic distributions (any payment that is not part of an annuity) made to the participant (the 20 percent withholding requirement does not apply to hardship distributions or loans).[7] If income tax is not withheld or insufficient income tax is withheld, the recipient may be required to make estimated tax payments or otherwise be subject to penalties for insufficient withholdings or estimated tax payments. This withholding requirement only pertains to qualified plans and not to distributions from IRAs.

Rollovers

Even when the participant has the option of taking a lump-sum distribution, the participant is not required to withdraw the account balance. Instead, the participant may elect to **rollover** or transfer the balance of the account into another tax-advantaged qualified plan or an IRA account to continue to defer the recognition of income taxes until the ultimate distribution of the assets from the new plan. Generally, a participant will elect to rollover an account balance when the participant has terminated employment

7. IRC §§3405(c) and 402(c)(4).

but would like to continue to benefit from the tax-deferred growth of the assets and plan for retirement. A participant may also elect a rollover to increase his investment choices or to have more control over the plan assets. It is important to note that the rules regarding rollovers have been significantly broadened over the years, including the expanded rules for SIMPLE IRAs, 403(b) and 457 plans as discussed in Chapter 10.[8]

The decision to rollover qualified plan assets into an IRA should be considered carefully. Once the assets are deposited into the IRA, the assets will continue to benefit from the tax-deferred growth until a distribution is taken from the IRA account. However, any assets deposited into the IRA lose the ERISA alienation protection, the benefit of **10-year forward averaging**, the benefit of **pre-1974 capital gain treatment**, and the benefit of **net unrealized appreciation** (NUA).[9] The opportunity to benefit from 10-year forward averaging, pre-1974 capital gain treatment, and net unrealized appreciation does not exist for distributions from IRAs. All of these topics are discussed in detail below.

There are two primary reasons that funds rolled over to an IRA from a qualified plan should be segregated from other IRA assets. The first reason is that funds that are rolled from a qualified plan can later be rolled over into another qualified plan, assuming the receiving plan permits such contributions. While funds from a traditional IRA can also be rolled over, not all plans permit such rollovers. Secondly, rollovers, unlike traditional IRAs, are fully protected under bankruptcy law and therefore rollover funds should be segregated to maintain this protection.[10] Accounts that hold rollover funds are often referred to as IRA rollover accounts or **Conduit IRAs**, as they provide a conduit to another qualified plan.

Exhibit 7.7 | The Cost of a Rollover from a Qualified Plan to an IRA

- Lose ERISA anti-alienation protection (but not protection under federal bankruptcy laws)
- Lose potential 10-year forward averaging
- Lose potential Net Unrealized Appreciation (NUA)
- Lose potential pre-1974 capital gain treatment

These considerations, along with potentially higher account or investment fees and other material differences must be reconciled when recommending a rollover from a qualified plan to an IRA.[11]

Rollovers may be accomplished in one of the two following ways:
1. Direct rollover
2. Indirect rollover

---

8. EGTRRA 2001, PPA 2006, and the PATH Act of 2015 provided more flexibility to move qualified and tax deferred funds from one plan to another.
9. Although assets rolled over into an IRA lose ERISA protection, as a result of the Bankruptcy Abuse Prevention and Consumer Protection Act (BAPCPA 2005), rollover IRAs are fully protected so long as they are not commingled with traditional IRA assets or contributions. In addition, assets in IRAs are protected up to $1 million ($1,362,800 as indexed for 2019-2021) under federal bankruptcy laws (11USC §522). Therefore, the loss of ERISA protection is not as significant as it was before the BAPCPA 2005. Note, however, that IRA protection from other judgments outside of bankruptcy is determined by state law.
10. 11 USC 522(n).
11. Note that, under the DOL's PTE 2020-02 *Improving Investment Advice for Workers and Retirees,* investment advisers and representatives of banks, insurance companies, and broker-dealers are generally held to a fiduciary standard when recommending a rollover from a qualified plan to an IRA and must meet the disclosure and best interest requirements set forth in relation to PTE 2020-02. Answers to frequently asked questions may be found at https://www.dol.gov/agencies/ebsa/about-ebsa/our-activities/resource-center/faqs/new-fiduciary-advice-exemption.

Direct Rollover

A **direct rollover** occurs when the plan trustee distributes the account balance directly to the trustee of the recipient account. A direct rollover is usually completed with a wire transfer from the old custodian to the new custodian or a check is issued from the old custodian negotiable only by the custodian of the new account. All qualified plans must provide for the availability of direct rollovers of certain distributions. If the participant elects a direct rollover, then the original plan custodian is not required to withhold 20 percent of the distribution for federal income tax.

Under the Pension Protection Act of 2006, direct rollovers from qualified plans to Roth IRAs are allowed after 2007. Under previous law, a rollover from a qualified plan to a Roth IRA generally required the use of a conduit traditional IRA. The following exhibit contrasts direct rollovers and indirect rollovers.

Exhibit 7.8 | Direct vs Indirect Rollovers

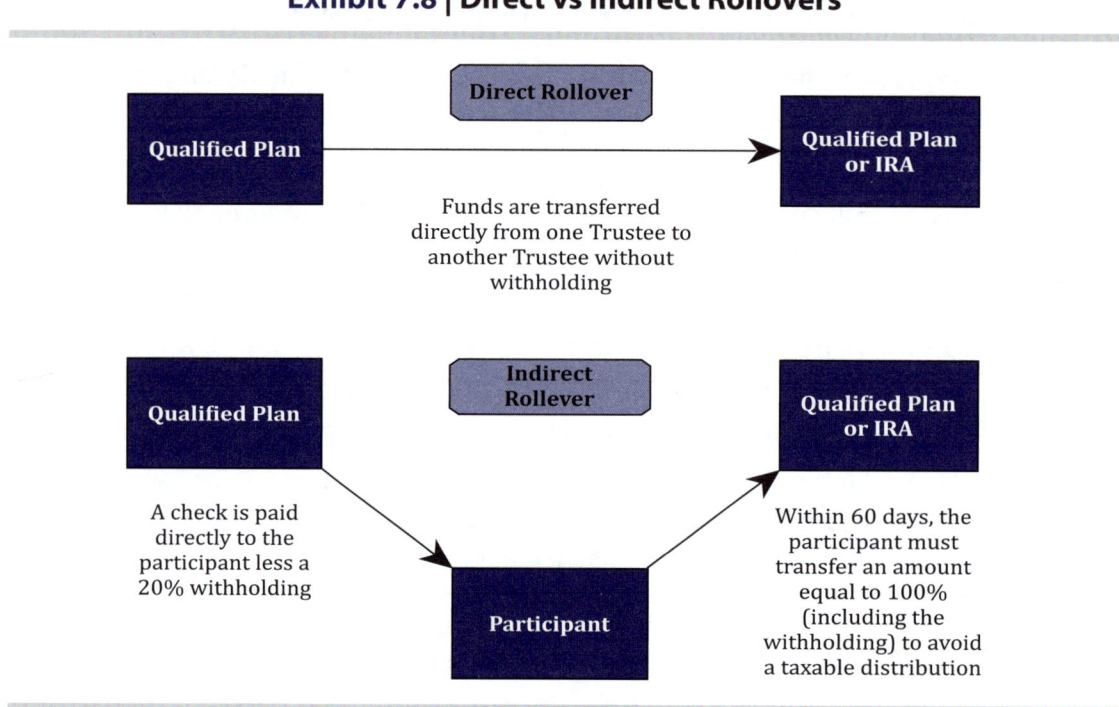

Indirect Rollover

The second method of completing a rollover is indirectly through a distribution to the participant with a subsequent transfer by the participant to another account. In this instance the original custodian issues a check to the participant in the amount of the full account balance reduced by the 20 percent mandatory withholding allowance. In order to complete the rollover, the participant must then reinvest the full original account balance of the qualified plan (including the 20 percent mandatory withholding) within 60 days of the original distribution into the new qualified plan or IRA. The 60-day clock starts with the participant's constructive receipt of the distribution (usually upon receipt of the check). The PPA 2006 makes permanent EGTRRA rules giving the IRS authority to extend the 60-day rollover period when a person's failure to comply is due to events beyond the reasonable control of that person.

In determining whether to grant such a waiver, the IRS will consider all relevant facts and circumstances, including:

- errors committed by a financial institution,
- inability to complete a rollover due to death, disability, hospitalization, incarceration, restrictions imposed by a foreign country or postal error,
- the use of the amount distributed (for example, in the case of payment by check, whether the check was cashed), and
- the time elapsed since the distribution occurred.[12]

If the 60-day deadline is missed, there are three ways to avoid the distribution being taxable (plus a penalty if applicable):

1. Automatic waiver
2. Private letter ruling
3. Self-certification

An automatic waiver of the 60-day deadline will apply if: (1) the correct procedures set forth by the financial institution for depositing the rollover were followed, but the funds were not actually deposited within the 60-day period solely due to an error on the part of the financial institution, and (2) the funds are deposited into the plan or IRA within one year from the beginning of the 60-day rollover period.

If the 60-day deadline is missed due to a hardship, the taxpayer can request a hardship waiver under a private letter ruling. The fee for a private letter ruling waiver of the 60-day rollover requirement is $10,000. Fortunately, the self-certification procedure described below will eliminate the need for a private letter ruling for many taxpayers.

Revenue Procedure 2016-47 (as modified by Revenue Procedure 2020-46) provides a self-certification procedure for taxpayers who miss the 60-day rollover deadline to a qualified plan, 403(b), 457 plan, or IRA for specific reasons.

Self-certification to the plan administrator or IRA trustee may be used if:

- The IRS has not previously denied a waiver for that rollover; **and**
- The rollover contribution satisfies all of the requirements to be valid (except the 60-day deadline); **and**
- The contribution is made to the plan or IRA as soon as possible after the circumstances causing the delay no longer prevent the taxpayer from making the contribution (the safe-harbor time frame is within 30 days); **and**

The reason for the delay is one of the following:

1. The distributing or receiving financial institution made an error related to the rollover; or
2. The distribution was made in the form of a check, which was misplaced and never cashed; or
3. The taxpayer deposited the distribution into an account which he or she mistakenly thought was an eligible retirement plan (and the funds remained in that account); or
4. The taxpayer's principal residence was severely damaged; or
5. The taxpayer's family member died; or
6. The taxpayer (or a member of the taxpayer's family) was seriously ill; or
7. The taxpayer was incarcerated; or
8. A foreign country imposed restrictions; or

12. Revenue Procedure 2003-16.

9. The was a postal error; or
10. The distribution was made due to a levy under §6331 (for unpaid taxes), and the proceeds of the levy were returned to the taxpayer; or
11. There was a delay in receiving the information regarding the rollover from the distributing entity, which the receiving plan or IRA required in order to complete the rollover (and the taxpayer made reasonable efforts to obtain the information).
12. The distribution was made to a state unclaimed property fund.[13]

Exhibit 7.9 | Waiver of 60-Day Rollover Requirement

In *PLR 201143027*, the IRS waived the 60-day rollover requirement due to an error by the taxpayer's financial advisor. The financial advisor acknowledged that he misunderstood the taxpayer and deposited the rollover amount into a taxable account instead of a self-directed IRA.

In *PLR 201143029*, the IRS waived the 60-day rollover requirement when funds were transferred to a financial institution that was involved in a plan to defraud investors in a Ponzi scheme. The criminal charges were upheld and the president of the financial institution pled guilty and was convicted in a U.S. District Court on charges of securities and mail fraud.

In *PLR 201143031*, the IRS waived the 60-day rollover requirement due to a failure to comply with the requirement as a result of the taxpayer's diminished mental capacity. The taxpayer represented that he has limited memory retention and moderate dementia, which caused problems with his judgment, and that he did not understand the implications of the withdrawal from his IRA.

In *Blake Sime Atkin and Susan M. Atkin v. Commissioner, T.C. Memo. 2008-93, 95 T.C.M. 1364, (Apr. 10, 2008)*, the Tax Court held that the taxpayer was liable for income tax, the 10 percent early withdrawal penalty and accuracy related penalties for failing to rollover funds from a SEP IRA within the permitted 60-day period.

Facts:
- Mr. Atkin (age 45) received a distribution in 2002 of $25,000 from his SEP IRA and deposited it into his law firm operating account.
- Within 60 days, he instructed his bookkeeper to send a check in the amount of $25,000 to his broker (Mr. Barben), who never received the funds.
- The Atkins did not report the original distribution on their tax return.
- In 2006, Mr. Atkin segregated the $25,000 into a separate taxable account.

Findings:
- The Atkins argued against the accuracy related penalty. The court wrote, "We disagree and find that petitioners failed to exercise due care or to act as a reasonable person would under the circumstances. Petitioners were allegedly unaware that the $25,000 check was not cashed until respondent brought it to their attention after years had passed. Petitioners never received monthly statements from the IRA and never followed up with Mr. Barben to make sure that he had opened the IRA. Further, Mr. Atkin should have been aware that his law firm's operating account had $25,000 more than he thought it should have. After Mr. Atkin told his bookkeeper to write a check to open an IRA, he took no steps to follow up in over two years."
- The court found the Atkins responsible for the income tax, early withdrawal penalty and the accuracy related penalty.
- The court also noted that the Atkins failed to apply to the Secretary for a waiver.

13. Distribution to state unclaimed property fund added by Revenue Procedure 2020-46.

Rev. Proc. 2020-46 includes a model letter that may be used for self-certification. There is no fee for using the self-certification procedure. The model letter should be retained to be presented upon audit, since the self-certification itself is not a waiver (the IRS may grant a waiver upon examination of the income tax return). Taxpayers may report the rollover as valid, unless the IRS later informs them otherwise. IRA trustees report on Form 5498 rollover contributions that are received after the 60-day deadline and certified by the participant.

The time for making a rollover may also be postponed under Section 7508 for service in a combat zone, in the case of a terroristic or military action, or in the case of a Presidentially declared disaster.

One of the problems with the **indirect rollover** method is that the distribution is subject to the mandatory withholding of 20 percent, but 100 percent of the account balance must be deposited in the new qualified plan or IRA within 60 days of the date of distribution. Thus, the participant must utilize funds from other sources in the amount of the 20 percent withheld and deposit 100 percent of the distribution amount into the rollover account.

Example 7.1

Terrance, age 28, took a distribution from his 401(k) plan of his entire account balance of $85,000. He intended to rollover the $85,000 to an IRA at a brokerage company, but decided to receive the check himself rather than have the custodian do a direct trustee-to-trustee rollover. The custodian of the 401(k) plan withheld 20% of the account balance ($17,000) (as required by law) and sent Terrance a check in the amount of $68,000. In order to avoid having to recognize any taxable income, Terrance must open the IRA and deposit $85,000 (not $68,000) within 60 days of receiving the $68,000 check. Terrance will then receive a tax refund of the $17,000 withheld when he files his federal income tax return. To avoid the 20% withholding requirement, Terrance could have initiated a direct rollover (trustee-to-trustee transfer) from the 401(k) to his new IRA.

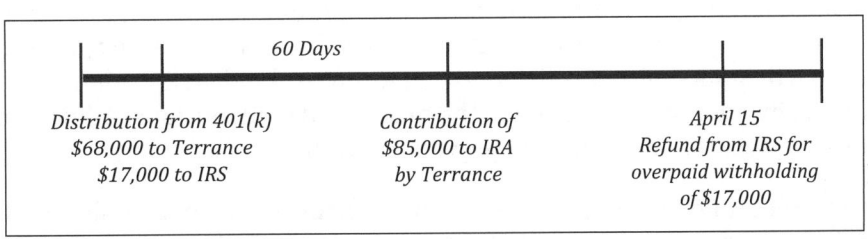

60 Days		
Distribution from 401(k) $68,000 to Terrance $17,000 to IRS	Contribution of $85,000 to IRA by Terrance	April 15 Refund from IRS for overpaid withholding of $17,000

Indirect rollovers usually occur due to poor planning or because the account owner wants to use the funds during the 60-day period. To prevent potential abuse, the IRS only permits an individual to have one indirect rollover from an IRA per year.[14] This limit previously applied on an individual account basis. However, that is no longer the case. As of January 1, 2015, individuals are only permitted one annual (rolling 12-month) 60-day rollover from any of the individual's IRAs, including SEP and SIMPLE IRAs.[15] This change is a significant departure from the previous interpretation of this rule. The one year waiting

---

14. A Tax Court opinion, Bobrow v. Commissioner, T.C. Memo. 2014-21, held that the limitation applies on an aggregate basis, meaning that an individual can not make an IRA-to-IRA rollover if he or she had made such a rollover involving any of the individual's IRAs in the preceding 1-year period.
15. IRC §408(d)(3)(B).

period does not apply to indirect rollovers to or from qualified plans, nor does it apply to conversions from traditional IRA to Roth IRA.[16] There can also be an unlimited number of direct rollovers during the year.

Example 7.2

Odette, who is 42 years old, has five IRAs. On January 25th of Year 1, she takes a distribution of $45,000 from IRA 1. On March 20th, she deposits the $45,000 into IRA 4. Based on her actions, she has made use of the 60-day rollover rule. There is no tax impact to this scenario. On December 15th of the same year, Odette takes a distribution of $25,000 from IRA 3. She rolls over the funds on February 2nd of Year 2. In this case, Odette has violated the one indirect IRA rollover per year rule. As a result, Odette has made a taxable distribution from IRA 3 in the amount of $25,000. The $25,000 is taxable in Year 1 and will likely be subject to the 10% early withdrawal penalty. In addition, she has made an impermissible IRA contribution, which will need to be removed from the IRA.

Example 7.3

Cindy, who is 42 years old, has five IRAs. On January 12th, she converts IRA 2, which is a traditional IRA, into a Roth IRA. On March 25th, she takes a distribution of $20,000 from IRA 1. On May 20th, she rolls over the $20,000 into IRA 4. She has made use of the 60-day rollover rule. The conversion is subject to income tax. However, there is no tax impact to the rollover.

Planning for a Rollover

As mentioned above, plan sponsors are required to offer the participant the choice of a direct rollover at the time of the distribution, but qualified plans are not required to accept rollovers from other qualified plans or IRAs. Thus, without proper planning, an individual who takes a distribution from a qualified plan with the intention of completing an indirect rollover into another qualified plan may fail to meet the 60 day requirement if their new qualified plan does not accept rollovers from other plans. Qualified plans are required to provide participants with a written explanation of the distribution options, the mandatory withholding rules, and any other rules relating to the taxation of distributions. Additionally, any necessary spousal waivers must be secured in advance of any distribution.

Neither direct nor indirect rollovers may consist of any distribution from a qualified plan that is one of a series of substantially equal periodic payments (not less frequently than annually) made for the life of the participant, the joint lives of the participant and the participant's designated beneficiary, or for a period of 10 years or more. In addition, any distribution on account of a required minimum distribution (discussed below), a substantially equal periodic payments election under IRC Section 72(t), and hardship withdrawals may not be rolled over into another qualified plan or IRA.

---

16. IRS Announcement 2014-32.

Exhibit 7.10 | Summary of Allowable Rollovers

					Roll To			
		Roth IRA	**Traditional IRA**	**SIMPLE IRA**	**SEP-IRA**	**Government 457(b)**	**Qualified Plan**	**403(b)**	**Designated Roth Account 401(k), 403(b), 457(b)**
Roll From	**Roth IRA**	Yes	No	No	No	No	No	No	No
	Traditional IRA	Yes. Must include in income.	Yes*	Yes, after 2 years.*	Yes*	Yes, must have separate accounts.	Yes	Yes	No
	SIMPLE IRA	Yes, after 2 years. Must include in income.	Yes, after 2 years.*	Yes*	Yes, after 2 years.*	Yes, after 2 years. Must have separate accounts.	Yes, after 2 years.	Yes, after 2 years.	No
	SEP-IRA	Yes. Must include in income.	Yes*	Yes, after 2 years.*	Yes*	Yes, must have separate accounts.	Yes	Yes	No
	Government 457(b)	Yes. Must include in income.	Yes**	Yes, after 2 years.**	Yes**	Yes	Yes**	Yes**	Yes as in plan rollover. Must include in income.
	Qualified Plan	Yes. Must include in income.	Yes	Yes, after 2 years.	Yes	Yes, must have separate accounts.	Yes	Yes	Yes as in plan rollover. Must include in income.
	403(b)	Yes. Must include in income.	Yes	Yes, after 2 years.	Yes	Yes, must have separate accounts.	Yes	Yes	Yes as in plan rollover. Must include in income.
	Designated Roth Account, 401(k), 403(b), 457(b)	Yes	No	No	No	No	No	No	Yes, if a direct trustee to trustee transfer.

*One within 12 months. **While rollovers from 457(b) plans to other types of plans are permitted, they result in loss of the ability to take penalty-free distributions upon separation from service prior to age 59½.

After-Tax Contributions

If a qualified plan consists of employee after-tax contributions, these contributions may be rolled over into another qualified plan that accepts after-tax dollars or into a traditional IRA. In the case of a rollover of after-tax contributions from one qualified plan to another qualified plan, the rollover can only be accomplished through a direct rollover. A qualified plan is not permitted to accept rollovers of after-tax contributions unless the plan provides separate accounting for such contributions and the applicable earnings on those contributions. Conversely, after-tax contributions are not permitted to be rolled over from an IRA into a qualified plan.[17]

IRS Notice 2014-54 provides rules for allocating pre-tax and after-tax amounts among disbursements that are made to multiple destinations from a qualified plan. For example, a retiree who has pre-tax and after-tax funds in a 401(k) plan may want to rollover the pre-tax portion to a traditional IRA and the after-tax funds to a Roth IRA. The IRS, in Notice 2014-35, finally acquiesced to this type of arrangement. Following are two general rules to keep in mind:
- Each distribution from a retirement plan will include a pro-rata share of both after-tax and pre-tax amounts.
- Under IRC Section 402(c)(2), a direct rollover first consists of the pre-tax amount.

Example 7.4

Bob participates in a qualified plan that does not contain a designated Roth account. Bob's $250,000 account balance consists of $200,000 of pre-tax amounts and $50,000 of after-tax amounts. Bob separates from service and is entitled to, and requests, a distribution of $100,000. The pre-tax amount with respect to the distribution is $80,000 ($100,000 x ($200,000/$250,000)).

	Pre-Tax	After-Tax
QP Balance $250,000	$200,000	$50,000
Distribution $100,000 (pro-rata)	($80,000)	($20,000)
Remaining in QP	$120,000	$30,000

Bob specifies that $70,000 is to be directly rolled over to the qualified plan maintained by his new employer and that $30,000 is to be paid to Bob. Because the pre-tax amount exceeds the amount directly rolled over, the amount directly rolled over to the new plan consists entirely of pre-tax amounts. The amount paid to Bob (prior to application of withholding) consists of $10,000 in pre-tax amounts and $20,000 in after-tax amounts.

	Pre-Tax	After-Tax
Distribution (from above)	$80,000	$20,000
Direct Rollover to IRA*	($70,000)	
Paid to Bob	$10,000	$20,000

Rollovers are pre-tax first, then after-tax.

---

17. IRC §408(d)(3)(A)(ii).

Prior to the 60th day after the distribution, Bob chooses to roll over $12,000 to an IRA. Because the amount rolled over in the 60-day rollover exceeds the remaining pre-tax amounts, the amount rolled over to the IRA consists of $10,000 of pre-tax amounts and $2,000 of after-tax amounts.

	Pre-Tax	After- Tax
Paid to Bob (from above)	$10,000	$20,000
60-day Rollover to IRA $12,000*	($10,000)	($2,000)

* Rollovers are pre-tax first, then after-tax.

Example 7.5

Assume the same facts as in **Example 7.4**, except that Bob chooses to make a direct rollover of $80,000 to a traditional IRA and $20,000 to a Roth IRA.

Bob is permitted to allocate the $80,000 that consists entirely of pre-tax amounts to the traditional IRA so that the $20,000 rolled over to the Roth IRA consists entirely of after-tax amounts.

Rollovers to Roth IRAs and Roth Accounts

Roth IRAs continue to be a hot topic, although they have been available for over 20 years, since their creation by the Taxpayer Relief Act of 1997. The enthusiasm is largely driven by the fact that qualified distributions from Roth IRAs and Roth accounts are not subject to income taxation or penalties. **Exhibit 7.11** highlights the legislative history of Roth IRAs and Roth accounts.

Today, taxpayers have several options to fund Roth-type vehicles: They can contribute to Roth IRAs assuming they meet the AGI limits and can defer compensation into a Roth account assuming that it is an option provided by their employer's 401(k), 403(b) or governmental 457(b) plan (the only plans that permit Roth accounts). In addition, taxpayers have several options available to convert pre-tax money, such as in a qualified plan or traditional IRA, to Roth money. This section discusses benefits and implications of converting pre-tax retirement funds as well as the available conversion options.

Exhibit 7.11 | History of Roth IRAs and Accounts

1997	Roth IRA created by Taxpayer Relief Act of 1997.
2001	Economic Growth and Tax Relief Reconciliation Act of 2001 (EGTRRA) created Roth Accounts for 401(k) plans and 403(b) plans effective in 2006.
2005	The Tax Increase Prevention and Reconciliation Act of 2005 eliminated the AGI limit of $100,000 for conversions effective after 2009.
2006	Pension Protection Act 2006 provided for direct rollovers from qualified plans to Roth IRAs.
2010	The Small Business Jobs and Credit Act of 2010 provided for Roth accounts in governmental 457(b) plans and provided for in-plan Roth Rollovers.
2012	The American Taxpayer Relief Act of 2012 added IRC Section 402A(c)(4)(E), which permits transfers of any amounts not otherwise distributable under the qualified plan to a designated Roth account for the benefit of the individual.
2013	The IRS issued Notice 2013-74, which provides guidance on the funds that can be rolled over to a designated Roth account within the same qualified plan. For the most part, any funds that are vested can be rolled over to a designated Roth account.
2014	The IRS issued Notice 2014-54, which provides rules for allocating pre-tax and after-tax amounts among disbursements that are made to multiple destinations from a qualified plan. These rules provide authority for allocating the pre-tax portion of a rollover from a qualified plan to a traditional IRA and allocating the after-tax portion to a Roth IRA.
2017	The Tax Cuts and Jobs Act of 2017 eliminated the ability to recharacterize conversions to a Roth IRA after 2017.

As discussed in Chapter 5 and Chapter 9, a qualified distribution is tax free and penalty free. Two tests must be met for a distribution to be considered a qualified distribution: (1) the five-year rule and (2) the distribution rule.

Five-Year Rule

The distribution must be made after a five-taxable-year period which begins January 1st of the taxable year for which the first regular contribution is made to a Roth IRA or Roth account of the individual or, if earlier, January 1st of the taxable year in which the first rollover or conversion contribution is made to any Roth IRA of the individual. The five-year clock for Roth IRAs is based on the earliest Roth IRA if the taxpayer has multiple Roth IRAs. For each Roth account (within a qualified plan), the five-year rule is based on the specific Roth account. Roth accounts are not grouped like Roth IRAs. The five-year period ends on the last day of the fifth consecutive taxable year.[18]

Example 7.6

On March 5, 2021, Isabella made a Roth IRA contribution for the 2020 tax year. Isabella had made no Roth IRA contributions in any prior year. The five-year period begins on January 1, 2020 (the year for which the contribution was made). The five year period ends on December 31, 2024. Distributions made on or after January 1, 2025 will meet the five-year rule.

---

18. Treas. Reg. §1.408A-6, Question 2.

Example 7.7

Assume the same facts as in **Example 7.6**. In August 2026, Isabella withdraws the entire balance from her Roth IRA. Isabella makes a contribution to a new Roth IRA at a different financial institution in May 2027, and withdraws the full amount in 2028. Because Isabella has previously satisfied the five-year requirement in a Roth IRA, the 2028 distribution also meets the five-year requirement.

Example 7.8

Assume the same facts as in **Example 7.6** and **Example 7.7**, but that rather than making contributions to a Roth IRA Isabella made the 2020 contribution to a designated Roth account in her 401(k) at Employer A during 2020 and that she made the 2027 contribution to a designated Roth account in her 401(k) at Employer B. Each designated Roth account has its own five-year clock; therefore, the distribution from the designated Roth account at employer B in 2028 does not meet the five-year requirement.

In order to be a qualified distribution in which earnings are both tax free and penalty free, the distribution must satisfy both the five-year rule and the distribution rule.

Distribution Rule

The distribution must satisfy one of the following requirements for Roth IRAs or one of the first three requirements for Roth accounts:

- made on or after the date on which the owner attains the age 59½,
- made to a beneficiary or estate of the owner on or after the date of the owner's death,
- is attributable to the owner being disabled, or
- for first time home purchase (lifetime cap of $10,000 for first time homebuyers (includes taxpayer, spouse, child, or grandchild) who has not owned a house for at least two years).

Funds from a Roth account can be rolled over tax-free to a Roth IRA, but the time (holding period) the funds were held in the Roth account will not carry over to the Roth IRA. The five-year rule for the Roth IRA begins at the earliest of a contribution, conversion, or rollover to the Roth IRA. If a taxpayer already had a Roth IRA established, then the rollover funds from a Roth account will have the same holding period as the other Roth IRA funds. If a taxpayer did not already have a Roth IRA established, then the five-year period for the newly established Roth IRA begins on January 1st of the year in which the Roth account was rolled over to the Roth IRA.

Example 7.9

When Shane graduates from college in the year 20X1, he begins to contribute to a Roth 401(k) offered by his employer. Shane does not intend to stay at that employer for more than seven years, and plans to roll the funds from the Roth 401(k) to a Roth IRA upon separating from service from the employer. He may then want to use some of the funds to purchase a condo, his first home.

If Shane opens a Roth IRA with a nominal contribution during the year 20X1, then rolls from the Roth 401(k) to the Roth IRA in year 20X7, he will have fulfilled the 5-year requirement for qualified distributions from the combined funds. The original Roth IRA contribution sets the clock for both the Roth IRA and the rollover from the Roth 401(k). If, however, Shane does not make any Roth IRA contributions and then rolls from the Roth 401(k) to a Roth IRA in year 20X7, he will not have fulfilled the 5-year requirement because his first contribution to a Roth IRA was from the rollover in 20X7, making the clock start January 1, 20X7.

Benefits and Implications of a Roth Conversion

There are two basic types of "conversions" that permit a taxpayer to change pre-tax retirement funds into Roth funds:

1. A qualified rollover contribution (we will use the word conversion for short), which generally means transferring assets from a traditional IRA or qualified plan to a Roth IRA.[19, 20]
2. An in-plan Roth rollover, whereby pre-tax funds in a qualified plan are converted or rolled over into a Roth account in a 401(k) plan, 403(b) plan, or governmental 457 plan.

While there are differences between the two, effectively they accomplish the same objective and both types have several advantages and implications. It is important to understand that when funds are converted, it requires that the pre-tax conversion amount be included into taxable income in the year of conversion. The converted amount will generally be reported on Form 1099-R. To the extent there are after-tax funds in the account that is being converted, these funds are not subject to taxation.

Benefits of Conversion

The benefits of conversion include the possibility of:

- tax reduction/tax diversification,
- tax-deferred funds transfer,
- minimum distribution avoidance, and
- possible estate tax reduction.

Tax Reduction / Tax Diversification: It may be possible for a taxpayer to reduce the total tax on retirement plan assets in certain situations through a Roth type conversion. The easiest case to make is for those taxpayers who are in a relatively low tax bracket today but expect to be in a higher bracket in the future. A conversion under this scenario results in the taxpayer paying income tax today at a lower rate than if the funds were deferred until the future. However, it is not always possible to know the income tax rates in the future, which could be higher or lower. In addition, the funds within the Roth could be deferred until the next generation, who might be paying income tax at a higher rate (prime earning years) or at a lower rate. Converting provides possible total tax reduction, but certainly provides for tax diversification.

Funds distributed from a Roth IRA or Roth account during retirement will generally not be subject to income tax or penalties.[21] The conversion effectively reduces the income during retirement that would have been subject to income tax if the funds were distributed from a traditional IRA or qualified plan. This reduction may also reduce the overall tax rate on other retirement income sources, such as deferred compensation or Social Security.

---

19. The PPA 2006 expanded the definition of a qualified rollover contribution, which is defined in IRC §408A(e), to include qualified plans, annuities and 457 plan amounts.
20. Technically, conversions are transfers from a traditional IRA to a Roth IRA, however, the term is being used for simplicity.
21. Generally after age 59½.

Earnings on investments held in a taxable account are taxable in the year earned, while earnings on investments held in an IRA are only taxable when distributed. Earnings within a Roth IRA or Roth account will never be taxed assuming a qualified distribution.[22] This benefit actually offsets the potential risk of paying tax today at a higher rate than during retirement.

For taxpayers who have net operating loss (NOL) carryforward amounts, Roth conversions can be accomplished with no direct tax cost. This strategy is helpful since it accomplishes the objective of conversion with little or no income tax cost. In addition, it may be helpful to the individual to use up the remaining NOL, which can only be carried forward (and not back), after changes in the law from TCJA 2017.[23]

Tax-Deferred Funds Transfer: Assets in a traditional IRA or qualified plan are tax deferred, meaning that the funds will be subject to tax when distributed. Therefore, the deferred assets have a corresponding liability attached, which is the future tax that will be paid. By converting and paying tax with assets outside of an IRA or qualified plan, a taxpayer ends up with a Roth account that has no future tax liability. Effectively, the taxpayer has shifted funds to a tax exempt account.

Example 7.10

Assume Liza has $100 in a traditional IRA and her effective tax rate is 30 percent. Prior to the conversion, the IRA is worth $70 after tax. After the conversion, the Roth IRA is worth $100 after-tax, since all distributions will be tax-free. In effect, there has been a transfer or shift to the Roth account of $30.

Minimum Distribution Avoidance: Traditional IRAs and qualified plans are subject to minimum distributions, which are discussed in depth later in this chapter and require that distributions occur after attainment of age 72. However, Roth IRAs are not subject to minimum distributions while the account owner is alive. Minimum distributions force taxpayers to take distributions so that the government can generate tax revenue. Roth IRAs do not have this same requirement until after the owner dies. Minimum distributions are not required for Roth IRAs, but are required for Roth accounts.

Estate Tax Reduction: As discussed above, tax deferred assets have an inherent liability representing the tax that must ultimately be paid on the tax deferred funds. Converting these tax-deferred funds into Roth funds requires that tax be paid in the year of conversion. This payment of tax reduces the assets that will be included in the taxpayer's gross estate at death resulting in potentially lower estate tax.[24] Clearly with the increased lifetime exemption that is currently in place, this benefit is only applicable to high net worth individuals.

Consequences and Implications

As mentioned above, Roth conversions and in-plan Roth rollovers both require that the taxpayer include the conversion amount into taxable income in the year of conversion. The converted amount is reported on Form 1040 and will result in higher income taxes. In addition, it may cause the taxpayer's income to

---

22. A qualified distribution will generally occur after five years and after attainment of age 59½ - see **Exhibit 7.13** for the differences between Roth IRAs and Roth Accounts.
23. The CARES Act of 2020 allows net operating losses arising in tax years beginning after December 31, 2017 and before January 1, 2021 to be carried back up to five years.
24. There is an itemized deduction under IRC §691(c) that allows heirs to deduct estate tax attributable to income in respect of a decedent (IRD) included in the gross estate. This deduction is intended to reconcile the inherent liability attributable to tax deferred funds, but does not do so perfectly.

increase such that deductions and exemptions are phased out or credits are lost. Because the tax liability is accelerated, the taxpayer is out of pocket these funds. In addition, there is the risk that tax rates will be lower in the future, which could greatly reduce the benefits of the conversion.

There is a clear monetary advantage to converting if it can be accomplished at a current tax rate that is lower than future tax rates. Therefore, taxpayers should consider converting over time when the value of the pre-tax assets is low, such as on market drops or corrections, and in years that taxable income is low. This strategy is helpful in minimizing the tax attributable to conversions.

Recharacterizing Roth Conversions

One of the great features of Roth IRAs was that taxpayers could recharacterize (undo) conversions if it was advantageous. This rule allowed a taxpayer a certain amount of flexibility and a bit of relief in the event that the value of the converted funds (and the value that was reported for income tax purposes) declined subsequent to the conversion. The taxpayer effectively had the ability to undo the conversion if it had adverse effects. However, the TCJA 2017 eliminated the ability of taxpayers to recharacterize conversions for years after 2017.

Exhibit 7.12 | Benefits of a Roth Conversion

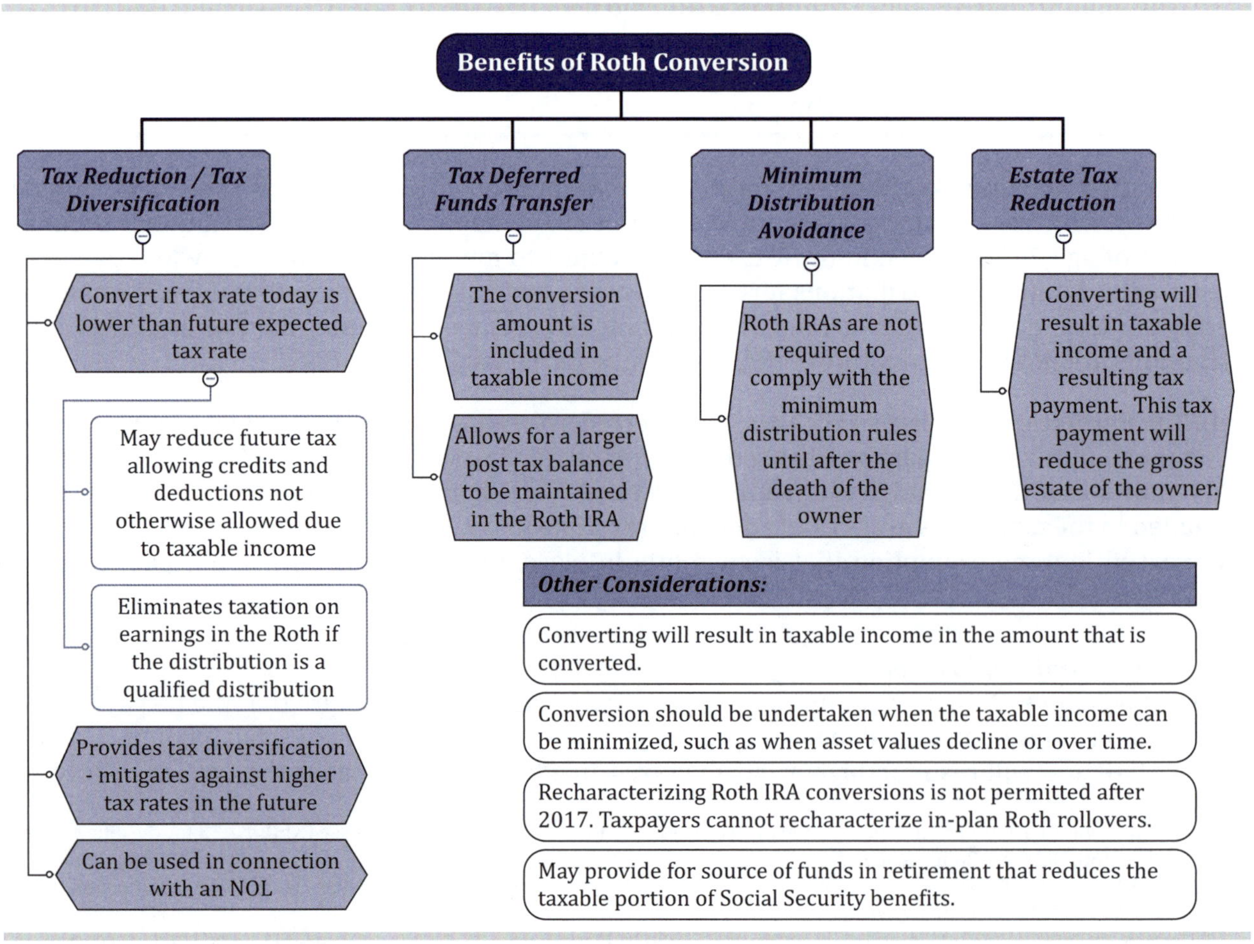

Recharacterization is still permitted with respect to Roth IRA contributions. For example, an individual may make a contribution for a year to a Roth IRA and, before the due date for the individual's income tax return (including extensions) for that year, recharacterize it, along with the earnings on that contribution (determined as a pro rata amount if the contribution was to an existing Roth IRA), as a contribution to a traditional IRA.[25] In addition, an individual may still make a contribution to a traditional IRA and convert the traditional IRA to a Roth IRA, but the individual is precluded from later unwinding the conversion through a recharacterization.

Example 7.11
Recharacterization example for years prior to 2018.

In May 2017, Colin converts $100,000 in his traditional IRA to a Roth IRA. The value of the assets in the Roth IRA drops by 40 percent due to a significant decline in the stock market that occurs in October 2017. The Roth conversion results in Colin incurring $100,000 of taxable income, when he could have waited and converted only $60,000 (after the 40 percent drop). Accordingly, prior to the due date (plus extensions) for filing his Federal income tax return for 2017, Colin decides to recharacterize the conversion contribution. He instructs the trustee of the Roth IRA to transfer in a trustee-to-trustee transfer the amount of the contribution, plus net income, to the trustee of a new traditional IRA. Colin notifies the trustee of the Roth IRA and the trustee of the traditional IRA that he is recharacterizing his IRA contribution. On his Federal income tax return for 2017, he treats the original amount of the conversion as having been contributed to the traditional IRA and not the Roth IRA. As a result, for Federal tax purposes, the contribution is treated as having been made to the traditional IRA and not to the Roth IRA.

For tax years after 2017, Colin would not be able to recharacterize the conversion due to the changes from TCJA 2017.

In-Plan Roth Rollover

The Small Business Jobs Act (SBJA) of 2010 made several important changes to the Internal Revenue Code dealing with elective deferrals in Roth accounts. SBJA 2010 added IRC Section 402A(c)(4) to the Code to permit plans that include a qualified Roth contribution program to allow individuals to roll over amounts from their accounts to their designated Roth accounts in the plan.[26] This option, which can be accomplished as a direct rollover or as an indirect rollover, is akin to converting funds in a traditional IRA to a Roth IRA. In addition, SBJA 2010 permits governmental 457(b) plans to include designated Roth accounts for years after 2010.

An "in-plan Roth rollover" is a distribution from an individual's plan account, other than a designated Roth account, that is rolled over to the individual's designated Roth account in the same plan, pursuant to new IRC Section 402A(c)(4).[27] The rollover may be accomplished by a direct rollover or by a distribution of funds to the individual who then rolls over the funds into the individual's designated Roth account in the plan within 60 days. An in-plan Roth rollover is generally not considered a distribution from the plan, but will result in the individual being taxed on the amount of the rollover.

---

25. Treas. Reg. §1.408(a)-5 Q-A #1&2.
26. Effective for distributions made after September 27, 2010.
27. After September 27, 2010.

In-plan Roth rollovers are a great option for individuals who are interested in converting pre-tax funds to Roth status. Before this law, taxpayers could only convert pre-tax funds in a qualified plan to a Roth IRA by distributing the funds from the qualified plan. Distributions from qualified plans lose the benefits available to ERISA funds and resulted in what the industry calls "leakage" or the transfer of assets from the employer plans to IRAs. The SBJA 2010 protects against leakage by allowing employees the ability to have in-plan Roth rollovers and employers to restrict in-service withdrawals solely to Roth rollovers. In addition, this law is a revenue accelerator for the federal government.

Rollover contributions, after-tax contributions, employer profit sharing contributions and employee deferrals continue to be eligible rollover amounts.

Example 7.12

DeeDee worked for Big Co for many years and accumulated a sizable balance in her retirement plan that was subsequently rolled into the qualified plan of Small Co, her current employer. Small Co sponsors a 401(k) plan with a Roth account. If permitted by the plan, DeeDee can convert the pre-tax rollover to the Roth account via an in-plan Roth rollover election. Assuming that the amount rolled over to the Roth account was $100,000, she would have taxable income of $100,000 in the year of the in-plan Roth rollover. The $100,000 is not subject to any penalties, regardless of her age. In addition, she would not have the ability to change her mind or recharacterize the $100,000. However, all qualified distributions from this account will be tax-free.

The taxable amount of a distribution that an individual rolls over in an in-plan Roth rollover is includible in gross income in the taxable year in which the distribution occurs. However, the rollover amount is not subject to the 10 percent early withdrawal penalty.

IRC Section 402A(c)(4)(E) - More Liberal In-Plan Roth Rollover Options (New Rules)

The American Taxpayer Relief Act of 2012 added IRC Section 402A(c)(4)(E), which permits transfers of any amounts not otherwise distributable under the qualified plan to a designated Roth account for the benefit of the individual. It appears that Congress felt that the rules that were in place were too restrictive and it wanted to permit more individuals to take advantage of the ability to convert pre-tax funds into Roth funds within a designated Roth account.[28]

Notice 2013-74 clarifies the rules for in-plan Roth rollovers after ATRA 2012:
- To be eligible for an in-plan Roth rollover, an amount must be vested.
- Amounts no longer have to be distributable to be rolled over. The following can now be rolled over without regard to whether they satisfy the conditions for distribution:
  - Elective deferrals in 401(k) plans and 403(b) plans;
  - Matching contributions and nonelective contributions, including qualified matching contributions and qualified nonelective contributions described in Prop. Reg. Section 1.401(k)-6; and
  - Annual deferrals made to governmental 457(b) plans.
  - Note: The federal government's Thrift Savings Plan is treated as a 401(k) plan for this purpose.

28.Note that the result of more in-plan Roth rollovers is an acceleration of tax revenue.

Based on this IRS Notice and the law, most vested amounts within an eligible plan can be rolled over as an in-plan Roth rollover to a Roth Account. However, there is no ability to recharacterize an in-plan Roth rollover.

Taxation Rules Applicable to a Distribution from a Designated Roth Account that is Rolled Over[29]

A distribution from a Roth account is permitted to be rolled over into another designated Roth account or a Roth IRA without inclusion into gross income. Rollovers from a Roth account to another Roth account must generally be accomplished through a direct rollover (i.e., not using the 60-day rollover).[30]

If a distribution from a designated Roth account is made to an employee, the employee would still be able to rollover the entire amount (or any portion thereof) into a Roth IRA within 60-days.

If less than 100 percent of a distribution is rolled over from a Roth Account and it is not a qualified distribution, then the part that is rolled over is deemed to consist first of the portion of the distribution that is attributable to income under section IRC Section 72(e)(8). This treatment is a benefit to the taxpayer as the taxable portion is rolled over first.

If an employee receives a distribution from a designated Roth account, the portion of the distribution that would be includible in gross income is permitted to be rolled over into a designated Roth account under another plan. The employee's period of participation under the distributing plan is not carried over to the recipient plan for purposes of satisfying the five-taxable-year period of participation requirement under the recipient plan. Generally, the taxable year in which the recipient plan accepts such rollover contribution is the taxable year that begins the participant's new five-taxable-year period of participation. However, if the participant is rolling over to a plan in which the participant already has a pre-existing designated Roth account with a longer period of participation, the starting date of the recipient account is used to measure the participant's five-taxable-year period of participation.

Example 7.13

Employee B receives a $14,000 eligible rollover distribution that is not a qualified distribution from B's designated Roth account, consisting of $11,000 of investment in the contract and $3,000 of income. Within 60 days of receipt, Employee B rolls over $7,000 of the distribution into a Roth IRA. The $7,000 is deemed to consist of $3,000 of income and $4,000 of investment in the contract. Because the only portion of the distribution that could be includible in gross income (the income) is rolled over, none of the distribution is includible in Employee B's gross income.

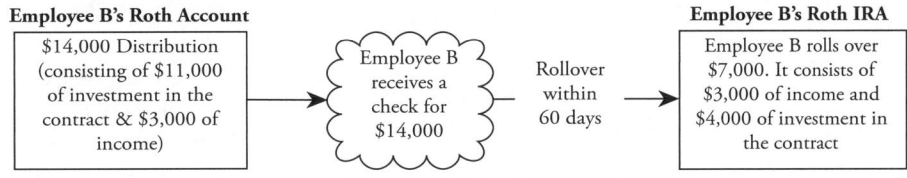

---

29. Treas. Reg. §1.402A-1.
30. If a distribution from a designated Roth account is rolled over to another designated Roth account in a direct rollover, the amount of the rollover contribution allocated to investment in the contract in the recipient designated Roth account is the amount that would not have been includible in gross if the distribution had not been rolled over. Thus, if an amount that is a qualified distribution is rolled over, the entire amount of the rollover contribution is allocated to investment in the contract. If the entire account balance of a designated Roth account is rolled over to another designated Roth account in a direct rollover, and, at the time of the distribution, the investment in the contract exceeds the balance in the designated Roth account, the investment in the contract in the distributing plan is included in the investment in the contract of the recipient plan.

Rolling Over Funds from Inherited IRAs and Qualified Plans to a Roth IRA or Roth Account

There are several recent changes to the law that permit inherited IRAs or qualified plans to be rolled over to a Roth IRA or account. With the PPA 2006 expansion of the term, qualified rollover contribution, inherited assets in a qualified plan can now be rolled directly to a Roth IRA by the beneficiary.[31] While the beneficiary will be required to include the conversion amount into taxable income and will be responsible for taking minimum distributions from the account, it may be a strategy that should be considered. However, the considerations regarding minimizing tax during the conversion still apply.

An in-plan Roth rollover can be elected by a beneficiary if he or she is a surviving spouse, but cannot be elected by a non-spouse beneficiary. In addition, an inherited IRA from a spouse can be converted to a Roth IRA.[32]

Exhibit 7.13 | Characteristics of Roth IRAs and Roth Accounts

Characteristic	Roth IRA	Roth Account
Participation	Anyone with earned income under limit.	Anyone who is a participant in a 401(k), 403(b) or 457 plan that permits Roth contributions.
Contribution limits	IRA Annual limit - for 2021, $6,000 plus $1,000 catch up if age 50 or older. Subject to AGI limit: Single ($125,000-$140,000); MFJ ($198,000-$208,000)	Deferral limit - for 2021, $19,500 plus $6,500 if age 50 or older. No AGI limits.
Recharacterization permitted	Not permitted after 2017 (TCJA 2017), except for contributions.	No - not permitted. Once the rollover takes place, it cannot be undone.
Minimum distributions	Only after death of participant	Yes - required
Requirements for qualified distribution	Five years & on account of death, disability, age 59 ½ or first time home purchase (up to $10,000).	Five years & on account of death, disability or age 59½.
Tax for nonqualified distributions (early distributions penalties may apply to part of the distribution)	Nonqualified distributions are distributed in order: (1) contributions (basis), (2) conversions (basis), then (3) earnings (taxable).	Nonqualified distributions are prorated between Roth contributions (basis) and earnings (taxable).
Five year holding period for qualified distributions	Begins Jan 1 of the year for which a contribution is made to any Roth IRA.	Each Roth account has a separate beginning date, which starts Jan. 1 of the year for which a contribution if first made.
Loans	Not permitted	Allowed if provided for in the plan document.
Withdrawals	Withdrawals can occur anytime - nonqualified distribution may be subject to tax and penalty.	Withdrawals are only allowed if permitted by the plan. Nonqualified distribution may be subject to tax and penalty.
Beneficiary	Anyone	Anyone, but for a nonspouse beneficiary, spouse must consent.
Conversion from a qualified plan to:	Permitted - no income limitations	Permitted as an in-plan Roth rollover
Conversion from a traditional IRA to:	Permitted - no income limitations	Not permitted

---

31. See IRS Notices 2008-30 and 2009-75.
32. See IRS Notice 2010-84.

Adjusted Basis

A participant will have an **adjusted basis** in distributions received from a qualified plan if either of the following have occurred:

- the participant made after-tax contributions to a contributory qualified plan, or
- the participant was taxed on the premiums for life insurance held in the qualified plan.

When a plan participant contributes after-tax funds to a qualified plan, the participant will have an adjusted basis in the qualified plan equal to the amount of after-tax funds contributed to the plan during participation. Distributions from qualified plans that have an adjusted basis will be partially treated as a nontaxable return of basis while the remaining portion of the distribution will be taxed as ordinary income. The calculation will vary depending upon whether a distribution is taken as an annuity or lump-sum. Lump-sum distributions are discussed in a later section.

Annuity Payments

Amounts distributed as an annuity are taxable to the participant of a qualified plan in the year in which the annuity payments are received. Each annuity payment is considered a partially tax-free return of adjusted basis and partially ordinary income using an inclusion/exclusion ratio. Annuity distributions made after November 18, 1996 from qualified plans use a simplified method for the calculation of the excludable amount. The investment in the contract is divided by the number of anticipated payments for a life annuity or joint life annuity as set forth in IRC Section 72(d):[33]

Single Life Annuity	
If the age of the annuitant on the annuity starting date is:	The number of anticipated payments is:
Not more than 55	360
More than 55 but not more than 60	310
More than 60 but not more than 65	260
More than 65 but not more than 70	210
More than 70	160

Joint Life Annuity	
If the combined ages of the annuitants are:	The number of anticipated payments is:
Not more than 110	410
More than 110 but not more than 120	360
More than 120 but not more than 130	310
More than 130 but not more than 140	260
More than 140	210

$$\frac{\text{Cost Basis in the Annuity}}{\text{Anticpated \# of Payments}} = \text{Excludable amount}$$

33. The simplified calculation method outlined in IRC §72(d) does not apply if the primary annuitant has attained age 75 on the annuity starting date unless there are fewer than 5 years of guaranteed payments under the annuity. Where a fixed number of installment payments are to be made in lieu of a life annuity, the number of installment payments determines the number of anticipated payments.

Example 7.14

Kim, who is single and age 62, is a participant in a qualified plan from which she is to receive annuity payments of $3,000 per month. Kim has an adjusted basis in the qualified plan in the amount of $180,000. How much of each annuity distribution to Kim is subject to ordinary income?

$$\frac{\text{Cost Basis in the Annuity}}{\text{Anticpated \# of Payments}} = \text{Excludable amount}$$

$$\frac{\$180,000}{260} = \text{Excludable Amount of Each Payment}$$

$$\frac{\$180,000}{260} = \$692.31$$

$692.31 of each monthly payment is return of adjusted basis.

$3,000 - $692.31 = $2,307.69 of each monthly payment is subject to ordinary income tax.

Once the participant has recovered the entire cost basis of the annuity, all future monthly payments will be fully taxed.[34] In the event that the participant dies before recovering all of the cost basis, a deduction (miscellaneous itemized deduction not subject to two percent) will be available on the participant's final income tax return for the unrecovered investment.[35] Distributions that are not lump-sum and are not part of an annuity are taxed pro rata to the account balance in comparison to the pre-taxed portion.

Lump-Sum Distributions

Participants may take a full distribution, often called a lump-sum distribution, from a plan upon termination of employment. Any after-tax contributions will simply offset the taxable distribution. Lump-sum distributions are discussed in detail below.

Lump-Sum Distributions

Distributions from qualified plans are generally taxed as ordinary income, however, **lump-sum distributions** from a qualified pension or profit sharing plan may receive special income tax treatment. When a distribution is considered a lump-sum distribution, the distribution may qualify for one of the following special tax treatments:

- 10-year forward averaging
- Pre-1974 capital gain treatment
- Net Unrealized Appreciation (NUA)

However, simply because a distribution may qualify for one of the special tax treatments does not mean that it is the best choice for the individual receiving the distribution. In many cases, the best choice may be to rollover the distribution into an IRA (or another qualified plan) and defer taxation. However, it is always important to evaluate the options that are available.

---

34. IRC §72(b)(2).
35. IRC §72(b)(3).

Under 10-year forward averaging, the income tax due on a lump-sum distribution is calculated by dividing the taxable portion of the lump-sum distribution by 10 and then applying the 1986 individual income tax rates to the result (one-tenth of the total taxable distribution). This result is then multiplied by 10 to determine the total income tax due on the distribution. Participants born prior to January 2, 1936 are also eligible to treat the portion of a lump-sum distribution attributable to pre-1974 participation in a qualified plan as a long-term capital gain (taxable at 20 percent, not eligible for special 15 percent capital gains rate).

Ten-year forward averaging and Pre-1974 capital treatment are applicable only to qualified plan participants born before January 2, 1936 and are, therefore, of limited application or nearly obsolete today. Our discussion in this chapter will primarily focus on the special tax treatment available regarding net unrealized appreciation (NUA) in employer securities held within a qualified plan.[36]

NUA tax treatment requires a "lump sum distribution." A lump sum distribution does not require that all assets be distributed at the same time and to the same account. A lump-sum distribution must meet the following three requirements:

1. the distribution must represent the employee's entire accrued benefit in the case of a pension plan or the full account balance in the case of a defined contribution plan.
2. a distribution of the balance of a participant's entire accrued benefit or account balance must be made within one taxable year.
3. the distribution must be on account of either the participant's death, attainment of age 59½, separation from service (does not apply to self-employed individuals in the plan), or disability.[37]

All three requirements must be met in order for the distribution to qualify as a lump-sum distribution and therefore qualify for NUA tax treatment.

Net Unrealized Appreciation (NUA)[38]

Taxpayers who receive a lump-sum distribution of employer securities (such as stock) may receive special tax treatment on the distribution. This tax treatment consists of favorable capital gain treatment instead of ordinary income tax treatment on the NUA portion of the distribution as well as deferral of recognition of the gain on the NUA portion until the distributed employer securities are sold. Although this treatment certainly applies to lump-sum distributions of employer securities from any qualified plan, it is most likely to occur from a stock bonus plan or ESOP. While the lump sum distribution rules require a full distribution, they do not preclude the ability to roll the remaining assets in the plan, other than the employer securities for which NUA treatment is desired, to an IRA to retain tax deferral on those amounts, nor do they preclude the ability to distribute only a portion of the employer securities under NUA and roll the remaining portion to an IRA to retain tax deferral. The portion of the distribution to which NUA tax treatment applies will be reported in Box 6 of Form 1099-R.

---

36. More detailed information on 10-year forward averaging and pre-1974 capital gain treatment, as well as other resources for the Retirement Planning textbook, can be found at money-education.com.
37. IRC §402(e)(4)(D)(i).
38. IRC §402(e)(4).

Exhibit 7.14 | Form 1099-R

9898 ☐ VOID ☐ CORRECTED		
PAYER'S name, street address, city or town, state or province, country, ZIP or foreign postal code, and telephone no.	**1** Gross distribution $ **2a** Taxable amount $	OMB No. 1545-0119 20**21** Form **1099-R** **Distributions From Pensions, Annuities, Retirement or Profit-Sharing Plans, IRAs, Insurance Contracts, etc.**
	2b Taxable amount not determined ☐ Total distribution ☐	**Copy A** **For Internal Revenue Service Center**
PAYER'S TIN **RECIPIENT'S TIN**	**3** Capital gain (included in box 2a) $ **4** Federal income tax withheld $	File with Form 1096.
RECIPIENT'S name	**5** Employee contributions/ Designated Roth contributions or insurance premiums $ **6** Net unrealized appreciation in employer's securities $	For Privacy Act and Paperwork Reduction Act Notice, see the **2021 General Instructions for Certain Information Returns.**
Street address (including apt. no.)	**7** Distribution code(s) IRA/SEP/SIMPLE ☐ **8** Other $ %	
City or town, state or province, country, and ZIP or foreign postal code	**9a** Your percentage of total distribution % **9b** Total employee contributions $	
10 Amount allocable to IRR within 5 years $ **11** 1st year of desig. Roth contrib. **12** FATCA filing requirement ☐	**14** State tax withheld $ **15** State/Payer's state no. **16** State distribution $	
Account number (see instructions) **13** Date of payment	**17** Local tax withheld $ **18** Name of locality **19** Local distribution $	

Form **1099-R**   Cat. No. 14436Q   www.irs.gov/Form1099R   Department of the Treasury - Internal Revenue Service

Do Not Cut or Separate Forms on This Page — Do Not Cut or Separate Forms on This Page

Employer securities generally include stocks, bonds, and debentures of the employer corporation as well as securities of a parent company or subsidiary. However, distributions generally consist of employer stock.

Net unrealized appreciation (NUA) is defined as the excess of the fair market value of the employer securities at the date of the lump-sum distribution over the cost of the employer securities at the date the securities were contributed to the qualified plan.

$$\begin{array}{rl} & \text{Fair Market Value at Date of Distribution} \\ - & \underline{\text{Value of Securities at the Date of the Employer Contribution}} \\ = & \text{Net Unrealized Appreciation} \end{array}$$

The portion of the lump-sum distribution attributable to the cost of the employer securities (the value of the employer's tax deduction) will be taxable as ordinary income (eligible for 10-year forward averaging if the participant was born before January 2, 1936) to the participant in the year of the distribution and this value is considered the participant's adjusted basis in the employer securities. At the date of the subsequent sale of the employer securities, the participant will be required to recognize the long-term capital gain deferred since the date of the distribution.[39] Any subsequent gain after the distribution date will be treated as either short-term capital gain or long-term capital gain based on the holding period beginning at the date of the distribution. If at the date of the subsequent sale the value of the employer securities has decreased since the date of the initial distribution, the participant will decrease the recognition of the deferred long-term capital gain to an amount equal to the differences between the fair market value of the stock at the date of the subsequent sale and the adjusted basis of the securities.

---

39. The 3.8% Medicare Tax on net investment income does not apply to distributions from retirement plans. IRC §1411(c)(5) and Treas. Reg. §1.1411-8(b)(4)(ii).

Exhibit 7.15 | Illustration of Net Unrealized Appreciation

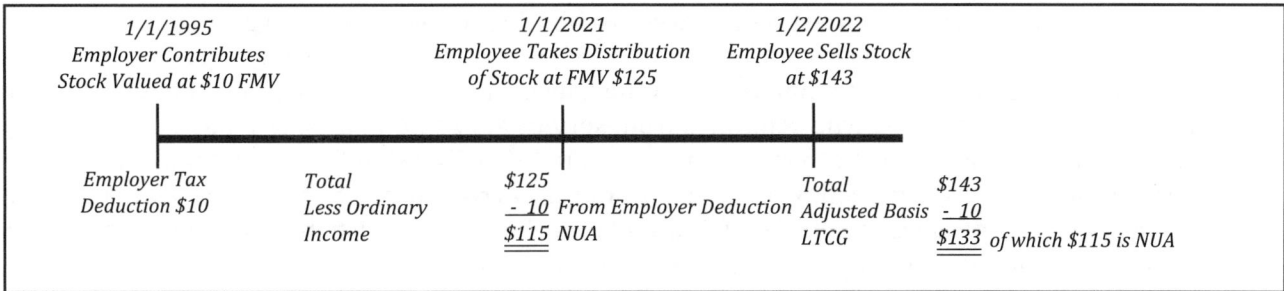

Example 7.15

Cody received a lump-sum distribution of his employer's stock from his qualified plan. The lump-sum distribution consisted of 1,000 shares of the employer's stock valued at $2,000,000 as of the date of the distribution. The value of the stock at the date the employer contributed the stock to the plan was $500,000. When Cody receives the $2,000,000 lump-sum distribution of the employer stock, $500,000 of the distribution will be taxed as ordinary income in the year of the lump-sum distribution. The remaining gain of $1,500,000 will not be recognized until the employer stock is sold. At the date the employer stock is sold, Cody's adjusted basis in the stock will be $500,000, the amount taxed as ordinary income in the year of distribution. If he subsequently sells the stock for any amount greater than $500 per share, then Cody will have a capital gain. The first $1,500,000 of gain will be taxable as long-term capital gain and any gain in excess will be short or long-term capital gain depending on the holding period after the distribution date. Thus, if he sold it at the date of distribution for $2,000,000 then he would have a long-term capital gain of $1,500,000, the NUA.

Assume, utilizing the facts above, that Cody sells the stock two years after the distribution date for $2,120 per share. What would be the tax consequences?

$2,120,000	Sales price ($2,120 x 1,000 shares)
$500,000	Adjusted basis (taxed as ordinary income in the year of distribution)
$1,620,000	Long-term capital gain (NUA ($1,500,000) and subsequent long-term capital gain ($120,000))

If Cody had held the stock for less than one year and one day (the long-term holding period requirement), the tax consequences would be different and as follows:

$2,120,000	Sales price ($2,120 x 1,000 shares)
$500,000	Adjusted basis (taxed as ordinary income in the year of distribution)
$1,620,000	Total capital gain
$1,500,000	Long-term capital gain (NUA)
$120,000	Short-term capital gain on sale held less than 1 year and 1 day

There are several issues involved in this type of transaction:

1. The participant must qualify for lump-sum distribution treatment.
2. The lump sum distribution must be the first distribution following the triggering event (it must be paid on account of death, disability, age 59½, or separation from service). No other distribution may occur in the time between the triggering event and the lump sum distribution. For example, an employee who separates from service at age 56 and takes a partial distribution at that time cannot later choose to take a "lump sum" distribution of the remaining balance that qualifies for NUA tax treatment since distributions occurring in two different tax years following a triggering event does meet the definition of a lump sum distribution. The employee is disqualified until or unless another triggering event occurs, such as attaining age 59½. On the other hand, an employee who retired at age 56 and took no distributions at that time or any time until several years later could then take a lump sum distribution (full distribution in one tax year) and receive the favorable tax treatment under NUA.
3. Employer securities must be transferred in-kind (not sold and the cash used to repurchase the securities).
4. The NUA portion must be relatively high in comparison to the cost basis portion; otherwise, the recipient may be paying too much immediate ordinary income tax for the benefit of future long-term capital gain treatment.
5. The next issue concerns whether the stock is to be held by the recipient. If so, then the investment risks of holding a large concentration of a single security must be considered.
6. Cash flow considerations must be evaluated to determine the impact of holding the securities versus selling the securities. Note: The amount of the distribution subject to ordinary income tax is also subject to a penalty if there is no exception in the Code. A penalty would apply if a taxpayer received a lump-sum distribution, was under the age of 59½ and did not qualify for an exception.
7. Funds distributed from a qualified plan will no longer be protected from creditors under ERISA.

In the event that this type of transaction does not make economic sense for a participant, the assets in the qualified plan can be rolled over into an IRA. However, if these assets are rolled into an IRA, the benefits of NUA are lost because distributions from IRAs are always characterized as ordinary income.[40] The loss of the special tax treatment may not be that important if the NUA portion is relatively small compared to the ordinary income element, and the rollover allows for the continued deferral of income tax.

Inherited Securities with NUA Resulting from a Qualified Plan Distribution

Stock that was part of a distribution from a qualified plan may be transferred upon the death of the participant to a beneficiary or heir. The question arises, "How should this stock be treated by the beneficiary for tax purposes?" There are two competing concepts in the IRC that must be considered. First is the concept of adjustment to FMV at the date of death. If this rule is applied, the stock, which is a capital asset, would simply have the same adjusted basis to the heir as the fair market value reported for estate tax purposes. The second concept is that of income in respect to a decedent, which is income earned at death yet not recognized for tax purposes prior to death. Such income will not receive an adjustment to FMV at date of death. For example, the adjusted basis of assets in a qualified plan or IRA are not adjusted to fair market value as a result of the death of the owner.

---

40. The only exception to ordinary income in an IRA is basis.

The appropriate tax treatment is a fair application of the competing concepts. The inherited stock will receive an adjustment of basis to FMV at date of death less any unrecognized NUA. The tax will be paid when the assets are disposed of by the heirs.

Example 7.16

Assume the same facts from **Example 7.15**, except that Cody dies shortly after the lump-sum distribution. At his death, the total value of the stock is $2,750,000. There is still $1,500,000 of NUA that has not been taxed. Cody's heirs would generally receive stock with a new adjusted basis equal to the fair market value at the date of death (a step to the fair market value). However, when received as part of a lump-sum distribution of employer securities, the heirs' adjusted basis in the stock is equal to the fair market value of the stock at the date of death less the NUA (the heirs will pay the deferred LTCG on the NUA upon sale of the stock). Therefore, in this example, Cody's heirs will have an adjusted basis in the stock of $1,250,000 ($2,750,000 - $1,500,000).

Qualified Domestic Relations Order

ERISA generally prevents a participant's qualified plan assets from being assigned or alienated in favor of a third party. However, a spouse or former spouse may be entitled to a portion of a participant's qualified plan benefits. An exception to the ERISA anti-alienation rules has been made if the assignment or alienation is at the direction of a **Qualified Domestic Relations Order (QDRO)**.

A QDRO is an order, judgment, or decree pursuant to a state domestic relations law that creates or recognizes the right of a third party alternate payee (nonparticipant) to receive benefits from a qualified plan. QDROs can be used for the provision of child support, alimony, or marital property rights to a spouse, former spouse, child, or other dependent of a participant. A QDRO can be issued by a judge or state agency that has the authority to issue orders, judgments, or decrees.

Although there is not a particular form that must be followed, a QDRO must specify the name and last known mailing address of the participant and the name and mailing address of each third party alternate payee covered by the order. It must also specify the amount or percentage of the participant's benefits to be paid by the plan to each third party alternate payee or the manner in which the amount or percentage is to be determined, the number of payments or period to which such order applies, and each plan to which the QDRO applies. A QDRO can give the third party payee all or part of the retirement benefits. The QDRO cannot, however, provide for any distribution mechanism or benefit not allowed by the retirement plan itself.

Quick Quiz 7.2

1. Rollovers can consist of distributions of any kind including those from a qualified plan that are part of a series of substantially equal periodic payments.
   a. True
   b. False

2. Distributions from qualified plans are always treated as ordinary income.
   a. True
   b. False

3. QDROs allow retirement benefits to be distributed to a payee spouse without triggering a tax consequence.
   a. True
   b. False

False, False, False.

The administrator of the qualified plan is responsible for determining whether a domestic relations order is qualified. Therefore, the plan document must establish reasonable procedures to determine the qualified status. Administrators are required to notify participants and alternate payees when they receive a domestic relations order and to furnish a copy of the plan's procedures for determining the qualified status of such orders. Once the administrator determines the plan is qualified, the administrator must follow the plan's procedures for making QDRO distributions.

QDROs are often used either to provide support payments to the alternate payee or to divide marital property pursuant to divorce. There are two basic approaches that may be used to divide the benefit depending on the reason the QDRO is being used. One approach, often called the "**shared payment approach**," splits the actual benefit payments made between the participant and the alternate payee. Thus, each payment that would be made to the participant under the plan is split such that the alternate payee receives part of the payment and the participant receives the remaining portion of the payment. Under this approach, the alternate payee will not receive any payments unless the participant receives a payment or is already in pay status. This approach is often used when a participant has already begun to receive a stream of payments from the plan, usually at retirement, such as a life annuity.

Example 7.17

After many years of marriage, Ryan and Scarlett filed for divorce. Ryan has a qualified retirement plan from his previous employer. He currently receives $800 per month in retirement benefits. Assume the qualified plan allows for a shared payment approach for QDRO distributions. If Ryan and Scarlett's QDRO allocated 50% of the benefit to be paid to each, then each month Ryan will receive $400 and Scarlett will receive $400.

The second approach, often called the "**separate interest approach**," divides the participant's retirement benefit into two separate portions. Depending on the plan document, this may give the alternate payee the right to receive a lump-sum distribution equal to the present value of the account balance or a separate right to receive their portion of the retirement benefit payable at a later time similar to that of the participant. This approach is often used when the retirement plan is being divided pursuant to divorce but before the participant retires.

Example 7.18

After several years of marriage, Nick and Mariah have filed for divorce. Nick has a qualified retirement plan through his current employer with an account balance of $100,000. Assume the qualified plan allows for a separate interest approach for QDRO distributions. The plan states that if a QDRO is issued, then the QDRO must provide for a lump-sum distribution of a percentage of the account balance to the nonparticipant as ordered by the court. If Nick and Mariah's QDRO states that Mariah is to receive 40% of the account balance, then a lump distribution will be made by the plan to Mariah in the amount of $40,000.

Note: The plan document, and not the court, determines how the retirement plan will satisfy QDROs (i.e., split account, payout the present value). As long as the QDRO complies with the plan document, the participant and the alternate payee can agree to the approach utilized.

Example 7.19

After several years of marriage, Gavin and Gwen filed for divorce. Gwen has a qualified retirement plan through her current employer. Assume the qualified plan allows for a separate interest approach for QDRO distributions. The qualified plan documents provide that if a QDRO is issued, then the QDRO can provide for any one of the following:

- A lump-sum distribution to the alternate payee of the present value of the estimated future benefit.
- A lump-sum distribution of a percentage of the account balance.
- A separation of the account balance where a percentage of the account is allocated to each party and is maintained by the plan provider for each party payable when the participant reaches retirement age regardless of whether the participant actually retires.

Gavin and Gwen's QDRO can utilize any one of these three methods to separate the plan interest.

A distribution pursuant to a QDRO will not be considered a taxable distribution to the third party alternate payee as long as the assets are deposited into the recipient's IRA or qualified plan. If a distribution pursuant to a QDRO is not deposited in an IRA or other qualified plan, the third party alternate payee will be subjected to tax at ordinary income tax rates on the value of the distribution. However, the distribution is not subject to the 10 percent early withdrawal penalty if it is not deposited into the recipient's IRA or qualified plan, as this is one of the exceptions to the 10 percent penalty.[41]

Exhibit 7.16 | Sample QDRO

QUALIFIED DOMESTIC RELATIONS ORDER
RYAN AND SCARLETT SMITH

Parties

The Participant is Ryan Smith. The Participant's address is 123 Blueberry Lane, Any City, All States, 12345. The Participant's Social Security number is 123-45-6789.

The Alternate Payee is Scarlett Smith. The Alternate Payee's address is 987 Strawberry Lane, Any City, All States, 12345. The Alternate Payee's Social Security number is 987-65-4321. The Alternate Payee is the former spouse of the Participant.

Plan

This order applies to benefits under the ABC Retirement Plan, herein called the Plan.

Amount of Benefits to be Paid to Alternate Payee

The Alternate Payee shall receive 50% of each benefit payment made from the Plan.

Form and Commencement of Payment to Alternate Payee

The Alternate Payee shall receive payments from the Plan of the benefits assigned to the Alternate Payee under this Order (including payments attributable to the period in which the issue of whether this Order is a qualified domestic relations order is being determined) commencing as soon as practicable after this Order has been determined to be a qualified domestic relations order or, if later, on the date the Participant commences receiving benefit payments from the Plan. Payment to the Alternate Payee shall cease on the earlier of: Alternate Payee's remarriage, or the date that payments from the Plan with respect to the Participant cease.

---

41. IRC §72(t)(2)(C).

Exhibit 7.17 | Qualified Domestic Relation Order

A "qualified domestic relations order" (QDRO) is:
- A domestic relations order
- That creates or recognizes the existence of an "alternate payee's" right to receive, or assigns to an alternate payee the right to receive, all or a portion of the benefits payable with respect to a participant under a retirement plan, and contains specific information and does not require the plan to do specific things as follows.

QDROs must contain the following information:[1]
- The name and last known mailing address of the participant and each alternate payee;
- The name of each plan to which the order applies;
- The dollar amount or percentage (or the method of determining the amount or percentage) of the benefit to be paid to the alternate payee, and
- The number of payments or time period to which the order applies.

QDRO must <u>not</u> contain: [2]
- The order must not require a plan to provide an alternate payee or participant with any type or form of benefit, or any option, not otherwise provided under the plan,
- The order must not require a plan to provide for increased benefits (determined on the basis of actuarial value),
- The order must not require a plan to pay benefits to an alternate payee that are required to be paid to another alternate payee under another order previously determined to be a QDRO, and
- The order must not require a plan to pay benefits to an alternate payee in the form of a qualified joint and survivor annuity for the lives of the alternate payee and his or her subsequent spouse.

1. ERISA §206(d)(3)(C)(i)-(iv); IRC §414(p)(2)(A)-(D).
2. ERISA §§206(d)(3)(D)(i)-(iii), 206(d)(3)(E)(i)(III); IRC §§414(p)(3)(A)-(C), 414(p)(4)(A)(iii).

Qualified Coronavirus-Related Distributions

Section 2202 of the CARES Act of 2020 provides for an exception to the 10 percent early distribution penalty for up to $100,000 in aggregate distributions from a qualified plan, IRA, 403(b) or 457 plan between January 1, 2020 and December 31, 2020 to a qualified individual. A qualified individual is an individual:[42]

1. who has been diagnosed with SARS-CoV-2 or COVID-19 (by a test approved by the Centers for Disease Control and Prevention), or
2. whose spouse or dependent has been diagnosed with SARS-CoV-2 or COVID-19 (by a test approved by the Centers for Disease Control and Prevention), or
3. who experiences adverse financial consequences as a result of being quarantined, being furloughed or laid off or having work hours reduced due to such virus or disease, being unable to work due to lack of child care due to such virus or disease, or closing or reducing hours of a business owned or operated by the individual due to such virus or disease, or
4. who experiences adverse financial consequences as a result of a reduction in pay (or self-employment income) due to COVID-19 or having a job offer rescinded or job start date delayed due to COVID-19, or

42. CARES Act Section 2202(a)(4)(A)(ii) and IRS Notice 2020-50.

5. who experiences adverse financial consequences as a result of the individual's spouse or a member of the individual's household being quarantined, being furloughed or laid off, or having work hours reduced due to COVID-19, being unable to work due to lack of childcare due to COVID-19, having a reduction in pay (or self-employment income) due to COVID-19, or having a job offer rescinded or start date for a job delayed due to COVID-19, or

6. who experiences adverse financial consequences as a result of closing or reducing hours of a business owned or operated by the individual's spouse or a member of the individual's household due to COVID-19.

Qualified Coronavirus-related distributions are not subject to the 20 percent mandatory withholding, and are taxed ratably over a period of three years beginning with the year of distribution (unless the taxpayer elects otherwise). If the distributee dies within the 3-year period, the remaining untaxed amount will be included in income in the year of death; however, a surviving spouse electing to treat the retirement account as her own will continue to be taxed over the 3-year period.

In addition, the Coronavirus-related distribution may be paid back to the retirement plan within the 3-year period beginning on the day after the distribution is received. Repayments are treated as eligible rollover contributions and do not count against annual contribution limits. As with other distributions, the distribution is reported by the plan administrator on Form 1099-R. Distributions and repayments are reported by the taxpayer on Form 8915-E.[43]

Plan Loans

Although distributions of qualified plan assets to participants are generally not permitted until retirement or termination, qualified plans are allowed but not required to provide loans from the plan to participants. A loan must be evidenced by a legally enforceable agreement that complies with the requirements in the IRC.

> **≔ Key Concepts**
>
> 1. What is the maximum amount a participant can borrow from a 401(k) plan?
>
> 2. When must loans from a 401(k) plan be repaid?
>
> 3. Discuss the impact of plan termination on plan loans.

Loans are utilized typically to increase plan participation and help the plan pass its nondiscrimination testing (ADP and ACP testing). **Plan loans** must be made available to all participants and beneficiaries on an effectively equal basis, must be limited in amount, must be repaid within a certain time period, must bear a reasonable rate of interest, must be adequately secured, may not be made through the use of a credit card or similar arrangement (for plan loans made after December 20, 2019; SECURE Act), and the administrator must maintain proper accounting for the loans. Although any qualified plan could establish a loan provision, loan provisions are common only in cash or deferred arrangement (**CODA**) type plans such as 401(k) and 403(b) plans. Loans are prohibited on other tax-sheltered retirement savings vehicles, such as IRAs, SEPs, and SIMPLE IRAs (discussed later).

43.See IRS Notice 2020-50 for details regarding reporting requirements.

Amount of Loan

A loan from a qualified plan is considered a distribution, which is subject to taxation and possibly the early withdrawal penalty, unless the loan amount is less than or equal to a certain limit set forth by IRC Section 72(p). The limit for a new loan is the lesser of:[44]

1. $50,000 less the highest outstanding loan balance within the previous twelve months, or
2. The difference between the greater of:
   - One-half of the vested accrued benefit under the plan, or
   - $10,000

   and the value of any outstanding loan balance from the plan at the time of a new loan.

Consider examples (A through F) in the following table. These examples illustrate the basic limits on loan amounts without the additional complication of an outstanding loan.

	Vested Accrued Benefit	Maximum Permissible Loan
A	$1,000,000	$50,000
B	$120,000	$50,000
C	$80,000	$40,000
D	$24,000	$12,000
E	$18,000	$10,000
F	$9,000	$9,000

Reduction of $50,000 limit: If the participant had an outstanding loan balance within the previous twelve months, the otherwise maximum permissible loan of $50,000 is reduced by the highest outstanding loan balance during the twelve month period ending the day prior to when the current loan is made.

Example 7.20

Deana has $125,000 in vested plan benefits. She borrowed $40,000 on January 1, 2021 from her 401(k) plan and repaid $25,000 on August 14, 2021. On December 31, 2021, Deana's maximum permissible loan from the plan would be $10,000. Deana is subjected to this limitation because her highest outstanding balance within twelve months of December 30, 2021 (the day before the date of the calculation) is $40,000. The otherwise maximum permissible loan amount of $50,000 must be reduced by $40,000 to determine the ultimate maximum loan amount available of $10,000.

If instead, Deana calculated her maximum permissible loan on August 16, 2022, she could borrow $35,000 because of the previous repayment. This amount is calculated by

---

44. The federal government occasionally increases the maximum loan amount from $50,000 to $100,000 and eliminates the 50% of vested account limitation for loans and/or extends repayment terms for those affected by certain federally declared disasters (including the COVID-19 pandemic in 2020 - see CARES Act Sec. 2202(b) and IRS Notice 2020-50), so research on current tax and retirement plan rules applicable to disaster situations is warranted when plan advisors are working with clients affected by such disasters.

reducing the maximum loan of $50,000 by the highest outstanding loan balance within the prior twelve months of $15,000 ($40,000 loan - $25,000 repayment).

Reduction of one-half of the vested accrued benefit under the plan: If the participant has an outstanding loan balance from the plan and is attempting to take an additional loan, then the limit of one-half of the vested balance must be reduced by the outstanding loan balance at the time of the new loan. If not, then the new loan, when added to the outstanding balance, would exceed the permitted limits. Consider **Example 7.21**.

Example 7.21

Melanie has a vested account balance in her employer-sponsored qualified profit sharing plan of $90,000. Melanie had an outstanding loan balance within the prior 12 months of $30,000 that has been reduced to $15,000. What is the maximum loan Melanie could take from this qualified plan, assuming the plan permitted loans?

The maximum loan an individual can take is the lesser of $50,000 or 50% of his or her vested account balance. The $50,000 maximum is reduced by the highest outstanding balance within 12 months of $30,000. This reduction nets to $20,000. Melanie's vested amount is $90,000. Half of this amount is $45,000. However, since Melanie has an outstanding loan balance of $15,000, the maximum loan available is the lesser of $20,000 or $30,000 ($45,000 minus $15,000).

For purposes of the loan calculation, all plans under the same employer are treated as one for the employer.

Exhibit 7.18 | Maximum Plan Loan

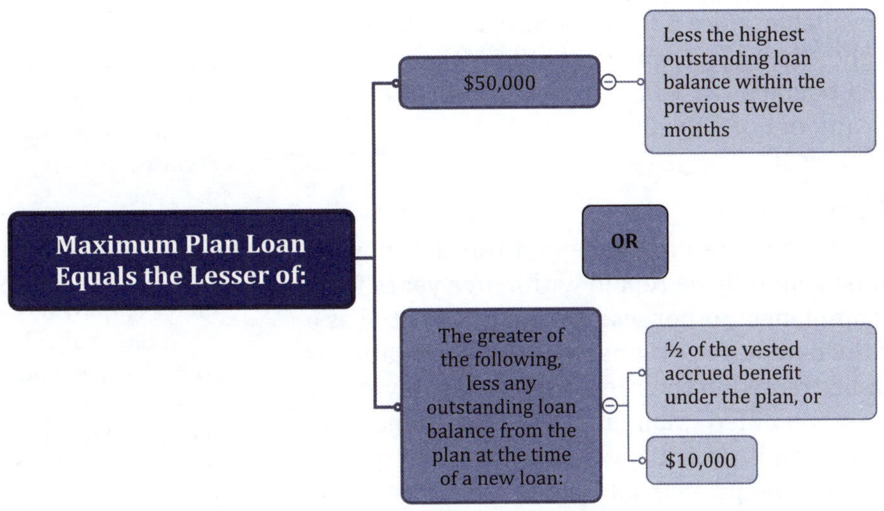

Example 7.22

Duke has a vested account balance in his employer-sponsored qualified profit sharing plan of $66,000. Duke had an outstanding loan balance within the prior 12 months of $25,000 that has been reduced to $7,000. What is the maximum loan Duke could take from this qualified plan, assuming the plan permitted loans?

The maximum loan an individual can take is the lesser of $50,000 or 50% of his or her vested account balance. The $50,000 maximum is reduced by the highest outstanding balance within 12 months of $25,000. This reduction nets to $25,000. Duke's vested amount is $66,000. Half of this amount is $33,000. However, since Duke has an outstanding loan balance of $7,000, the maximum loan available is the lesser of $25,000 or $26,000 ($33,000 minus $7,000).

As long as the maximum loan amount has not been reached, participants may be able to borrow additional funds in the form of multiple loans. However, there are two ways the IRS permits the interpretation of the maximum loan amount. The IRS will look to see consistent application of the loan administration. Consider **Example 7.23**.

Example 7.23

Tasha borrowed $30,000 in February which was fully repaid in April, and $20,000 in May which was fully repaid in July before applying for a third loan in December. The plan may determine that no further loan would be available, since $30,000 + $20,000 = $50,000. Alternatively, the plan may identify "the highest outstanding balance" as $30,000 and permit the third loan in the amount of $20,000.[45]

Repayment of Loans

Loans from qualified plans are usually repaid through payroll deductions and must generally be repaid within five years from the date the loan commences; otherwise, the loan is treated as a distribution as of the date of the original loan. Loans treated as a distribution will be treated in the same manner as any other distribution from a qualified plan and will be subject to ordinary income tax and potentially the early withdrawal penalty of 10 percent if the participant fails to meet one of the exceptions (discussed below).

The five-year repayment rule does not apply to loans that are used for the purchase of a principal residence. In such a case, the IRC provides that the loan must be repaid over "a

> ### Quick Quiz 7.3
>
> 1. Loans from qualified plans can never exceed 50% of the participant's vested account balance.
>   a. True
>   b. False
>
> 2. Loans from qualified plans must always be repaid within five years.
>   a. True
>   b. False
>
> 3. The law requires loans from qualified plans to be repaid upon the participant's termination of employment from the plan sponsor.
>   a. True
>   b. False
>
> 4. Sam has a vested account balance in her employer-sponsored qualified profit sharing plan of $18,000. Sam had an outstanding loan balance within the prior 12 months of $9,000 that has been reduced to $6,000. The maximum loan Sam could take from this qualified plan is $4,000.
>   a. True
>   b. False
>
> False, False, False, True.

45. IRS Memorandum, Computation of Maximum Loan Amount under IRC§ 72(p)(2)(A).

reasonable time" determined at the time of the loan. Presumably, the repayment of loans for purposes of a purchase of a personal residence could be over 30 years (the life of the mortgage), but 10 years is a typical maximum repayment period. As each plan may have different loan provisions, it is important to determine the provisions that are provided in the plan document and determine the policies from the loan administrator.

Loans are not only required to be repaid within a specific period of time, but are also required to be repaid in a specific manner over the repayment period. Substantially level amortization of the loan is required over the term of the loan.[46] Loan repayments must be level over the repayment period and must be made at least quarterly. In other words, the loan cannot be repaid in full with a payment (or payments) at the end of the five-year period. Generally, employers require that loans be repaid only through payroll deduction, which alleviates the likelihood of late payments. Late loan payments may cause a deemed distribution to occur. Plan documents commonly include cure periods (grace periods) of 30 or 60 days for payments to be made, and the maximum cure period permitted is no later than the last day of the calendar quarter after the calendar quarter in which the loan payment was due.[47] If this deadline is missed, a deemed distribution subject to income tax and possibly an early withdrawal penalty will occur.

Example 7.24

Adam has a vested accrued benefit of $200,000 and receives $70,000 to be repaid in level quarterly installments over five years. Adam has a deemed distribution of $20,000 (the excess of $70,000 over $50,000) at the time of the loan because the loan exceeds the $50,000 maximum permissible loan limit. The remaining $50,000 loan is not a deemed distribution.

Example 7.25

Ginger has a vested accrued benefit of $30,000 and borrows $20,000 from her plan as a loan repayable in level monthly installments over five years. Ginger's maximum permissible loan is $15,000 (50% of $30,000), so her loan is $5,000 more than permissible. In this case, Ginger has a deemed distribution of $5,000 at the date of the loan. The remaining $15,000 is a permissible loan and would not be a deemed distribution. The $5,000 will be taxed as ordinary income and potentially subject to a 10% early withdrawal penalty unless Ginger meets one of the exceptions.

Example 7.26

Byron has a vested accrued benefit of $100,000, and he takes a $50,000 loan. The loan is repayable in level quarterly installments over seven years, and Byron is using the proceeds to buy a new car. Because the repayment period of the loan exceeds the maximum term of five years, Byron has a deemed distribution of $50,000 at the date the loan is made. The $50,000 will be taxed as ordinary income and potentially subject to a 10% early withdrawal penalty unless Byron meets one of the exceptions.

---

46. IRC §72(p)(2)(C).
47. Treas. Reg. §1.72(p)-1

Interest on Loans

When a loan is made, securities are sold and funds are removed from the participant's account. This loan amount must be paid back to the participant's account using a level amortization that includes interest. The interest charged on the loan must be at a commercially reasonable rate of interest. It should be noted that the interest is paid to the participant's account, and it is paid with after-tax dollars from the participant.

Because the loan interest is paid back with after-tax dollars, those dollars will be taxed twice. The first taxation is when the participant earns the funds. Then the after-tax dollars are paid to the plan. However, these contributions do not create basis inside the qualified plan and will be taxable upon distribution.

Exhibit 7.19 | Loan Summary

- Qualified plans may permit loans up to the lesser of one-half of the vested plan accrued benefit up to $50,000.
- If the vested accrued benefit is less than or equal to $20,000, then a loan is permitted up to the lesser of $10,000 or the vested accrued benefit.
- Reduce maximum loan of $50,000 by maximum outstanding loan within the past year.
- Loans are usually associated with 401(k) and 403(b) plans.
- Loans must generally be repaid within five years with an exception for loans associated with the purchase of personal residences, which must be reasonable and could be as long as 30 years.
- Loan interest must be at a commercially reasonable rate and is paid back to the participant's account.

Impact of Loans When an Employee is Terminated

Most plan documents require that loans be repaid upon termination of employment; however, this is not a requirement under the law. Loan repayments are generally accommodated through payroll deduction, which, of course, is unavailable after termination occurs. If a participant fails to repay a loan from a qualified plan before termination or before the end of a grace period (cure period) following termination if the plan allows for one, the employer will generally declare the unpaid portion a deemed distribution, which will be subject to ordinary income tax and possibly the ten percent early withdrawal penalty.

However, plans may provide that the outstanding loan balance reduce the amount of a direct rollover distribution. This reduction is called a **loan offset**. A loan offset is treated as an actual distribution from the plan equal to the unpaid loan balance (rather than a deemed distribution), and (unlike a deemed distribution) the amount of the distribution is eligible for tax-free rollover to another eligible retirement plan. Historically, the rollover had to occur within 60 days. However, TCJA 2017 extended the rollover period for qualified plan loan offset amounts after 2017 from 60 days to the due date (including extensions) for filing the Federal income tax return for the taxable year in which the plan loan offset occurs, that is, the taxable year in which the amount is treated as distributed from the plan.

The TCJA 2017 defines a **qualified plan loan offset amount** as a plan loan offset amount that is treated as distributed from a qualified retirement plan, a section 403(b) plan or a governmental section 457(b) plan solely by reason of the termination of the plan or the failure to meet the repayment terms of the loan because of the employee's severance from employment. This extension of time to roll over a loan offset allows taxpayers with a loan from a retirement plan more time to avoid the harsh treatment of ordinary income and possible penalty for a loan that is not paid back, often at the time when the taxpayer's job has been eliminated.

Example 7.27 through **Example 7.30** illustrate this available option.

Example 7.27

In 2021, Alina has a vested account balance of $10,000 in Plan Y, of which $3,000 is invested in a plan loan to Alina that is secured by the remainder of her vested account balance. Upon termination of employment in 2021, Alina, who is under the age of 72 (and was not yet age 70½ as of December 31, 2019), elects a direct rollover distribution of her entire account balance of Plan Y, and the outstanding plan loan is offset against the distributable account balance.

Plan Y must pay $7,000 ($10,000 - $3,000) directly to the eligible retirement plan chosen by Alina in the direct rollover. When Alina's account balance was offset by the amount of the $3,000 unpaid loan balance, Alina received a plan loan offset amount (equivalent to $3,000), an eligible rollover distribution. Alina must roll over $3,000 to an eligible retirement plan by the due date of the return including extensions, or else the $3,000 distribution will be treated as any other distribution from a qualified plan, subject to ordinary income tax and possibly early withdrawal penalty.[48]

Example 7.28

Assume the same facts as **Example 7.27** except that the terms governing the plan loan to Alina provide that upon termination of employment, Alina's account balance is automatically offset by the amount of any unpaid loan balance to repay the loan. Alina terminates employment but does not request a distribution from Plan Y. Nevertheless, pursuant to the terms governing the plan loan, Alina's account balance is automatically offset by the amount of the $3,000 unpaid loan balance.

The $3,000 plan loan offset amount attributable to the plan loan in this example is treated in the same manner as the $3,000 plan loan offset amount in the prior example. Alina will have ordinary income and possible early withdrawal penalty.

Example 7.29

Again assume the same facts as the previous example except that Alina elects to receive the distribution of the account balance that remains after the $3,000 offset to repay the plan loan instead of electing a direct rollover of the remaining account balance.

In this case, the taxable amount of the distribution to Alina is $10,000, not $3,000. Because the amount of the $3,000 offset attributable to the loan is included in determining the amount that equals 20 percent of the eligible rollover distribution received by Alina, withholding in the amount of $2,000 (20 percent of $10,000) is required. The $2,000 is required to be withheld from the $7,000 to be distributed to Alina in cash so that Alina actually receives a check for $5,000.

Alina would still be entitled to roll over $7,000 within 60-days and $3,000 by the due date of the return including extensions and avoid applicable income tax and penalties.

---

48. IRC §402(c)(3).

Alina's Vested Account Balance = $10,000		
Loan = $3,000		
Terminates and Rolls Over	**Terminates and Does Not Rollover**	**Terminates Takes Distribution of Vested Account Balance**
Alina must roll over $3,000 to an eligible retirement plan by the due date of the return including extensions, or the $3,000 will be subjected to ordinary income tax and possibly the 10 percent early withdrawal penalty.		Alina receives a distribution in the amount of $5,000, $10,000 less withholding and less the outstanding loan. To avoid taxation on the full $10,000, Alina must contribute $7,000 within 60 days and $3,000 by the due date of the tax return to a new retirement plan or IRA.

Example 7.30

Freddie, age 40, has an account balance in Plan Z, a qualified profit sharing plan that includes a CODA. Plan Z does not permit after-tax employee contributions. In 2021, Freddie receives a loan from Plan Z. In 2023, Freddie stops repayment, and is therefore taxed on a deemed distribution equal to the amount of the unpaid loan balance. The deemed distribution is not an eligible rollover distribution because Freddie has not separated from service or experienced any other event that permits the distribution of the elective contributions that secure the loan. Plan Z is prohibited from executing on the loan. Accordingly, Freddie's account balance is not offset by the amount of the unpaid loan balance at the time he stops repayment on the loan. Thus, there is no distribution of an offset amount that is an eligible rollover distribution in 2023. The deemed distribution is also subject to the 10% early withdrawal penalty.

Exhibit 7.20 | Loan Summary for Failure to Repay Loan or Termination of Employment

- Many qualified plans treat an outstanding loan as a distribution from the plan and issue the participant a Form 1099-R (distributions from a retirement plan). The participant will then report this distribution as ordinary income, and it may be subject to the 10% early withdrawal penalty if the participant does not meet one of the exceptions.

- A qualified plan may provide that the employee has a certain period of time to repay the loan after termination, or it will otherwise treat the loan as a distribution.

- Qualified plans may provide that the loan is simply an offset of the distribution, and this offset can either be treated as a taxable distribution or may be rolled over by the participant to another qualified plan.

- Plan loan offsets occurring between January 1, 2020 and December 31, 2020 may be treated as qualified Coronavirus-related distributions (as discussed previously in this chapter) if the individual is a qualifying individual.

DISTRIBUTIONS PRIOR TO 59½

In some cases, individuals may want or need to take distributions from a qualified plan before their retirement. To discourage taxpayers from using the funds before retirement, taxable distributions before the age of 59½ will generally be subject to a 10 percent early withdrawal penalty. Most plans also limit the ability of participants to take early distributions from a qualified plan except in the case of the participant's termination, death, or retirement. However, some plans may permit rollovers and substantially equal periodic payments as distributions before the age of 59½. Although not common, profit sharing plans may permit in-service distributions from the plan after the participant has participated in the plan for at least two years. This provision may be included in a plan to encourage plan participation within a company by alleviating the employees' fear of not being able to access the funds.

> ### ≔ *Key Concepts*
>
> 1. What is the penalty for taking distributions from a qualified plan before the participant attains the age of 59½?
>
> 2. List the exceptions to the early withdrawal penalty.

Early Withdrawal Penalty

In any case, a distribution prior to the participant attaining the age of 59½ may be subjected to a 10 percent **early withdrawal penalty** unless the distribution is on account of one of several exceptions.[49] All of the exceptions coincide with the government's intention that participants use the plan assets for their retirement, but in circumstances like death and disability, it makes sense to allow the participant (or the participant's beneficiaries) to withdraw the assets prior to their scheduled retirement.

The general rule under IRC Section 72(t) is that any distribution from a qualified plan (or IRA) that is taxable will result in an additional tax of 10 percent applied to the amount that is includible in gross income.

Example 7.31

Kris, who is 40 years old, takes a distribution from his IRA to purchase a new ski boat. The distribution is in the amount of $10,000. However, 20 percent of the distribution is not taxable because it is deemed a return of basis, which is from Kris making non-deductible IRA contributions in prior years. In this case, Kris will have ordinary income of $8,000 and the 10 percent early withdrawal penalty will be applied to the $8,000 taxable amount. Therefore, the penalty is $800.

Exceptions to the 10 Percent Early Withdrawal Penalty

As mentioned above, the general rule of a 10 percent early withdrawal penalty will apply unless there is a valid exception. These exceptions are discussed below.

---

49. With SIMPLE plans, the early withdrawal penalty is increased to 25% if the withdrawal occurs within the first two years of plan participation.

Exhibit 7.21 | Summary of 10 Percent Penalty Exceptions

Exceptions to 10% Early Withdrawal Penalty
• Attainment of age 59½
• Death
• Disability
• Substantially equal periodic payments (Section 72(t))
• Separated from service after attainment of age 55
• Dividends paid from an ESOP
• IRS tax levy on a plan
• Medical expenses that exceed 7.5% percent of AGI
• Qualified Domestic Relations Order (QDRO)
• Individuals called to active duty
• Qualified public safety employee who separates from service after age 50
• Qualified birth or adoption distributions*

Added by the SECURE Act of 2019

Age 59½

Any distribution from a qualified plan that is made on or after the date on which the employee attains age 59½ is not subject to the 10 percent penalty. This exception is intended to encourage individuals to save for their retirement and not use the funds before such time.

Death

Any distribution made to a beneficiary (or to the estate of the employee) on or after the death of the employee is not subject to the 10 percent penalty. Therefore, any inherited qualified plan interest can be distributed without regard to the age of the beneficiary and avoid the 10 percent penalty.

Disability

The 10 percent penalty will not apply in case of a participant's disability. An individual is considered to be disabled if he is unable to engage in any substantial gainful activity by reason of any medically determinable physical or mental impairment which can be expected to result in death or to be of long-continued and indefinite duration. An individual must be able to furnish proof of the disability in such form and manner as the Secretary may require.[50] Whether or not impairment in a particular case constitutes a disability is to be determined with reference to all the facts in the case.

The Treasury regulations provide the following list of impairments that are generally considered to prevent substantial gainful activity:[51]

1. Loss of use of two limbs;
2. Certain progressive diseases which have resulted in the physical loss or atrophy of a limb, such as diabetes, multiple sclerosis, or Buergers disease;
3. Diseases of the heart, lungs, or blood vessels which have resulted in major loss of heart or lung reserve as evidenced by X-ray, electrocardiogram, or other objective findings, so that despite medical treatment breathlessness, pain, or fatigue is produced on slight exertion, such as walking several blocks, using public transportation, or doing small chores;

50. IRC §72(m)(7).
51. Treas. Reg. §1.72-17A.

4. Cancer which is inoperable and progressive;
5. Damage to the brain or brain abnormality which has resulted in severe loss of judgment, intellect, orientation, or memory;
6. Mental diseases (e.g., psychosis or severe psychoneurosis) requiring continued institutionalization or constant supervision of the individual;
7. Loss or diminution of vision to the extent that the affected individual has a central visual acuity of no better than 20/200 in the better eye after best correction, or has a limitation in the fields of vision such that the widest diameter of the visual fields subtends an angle no greater than 20 degrees;
8. Permanent and total loss of speech; and
9. Total deafness uncorrectible by a hearing aid.

The regulations go on to state that one or more of the impairments listed above will not automatically permit a finding that the individual is disabled. The impairment must be evaluated in terms of whether it does in fact prevent the individual from engaging in customary or any comparable substantial gainful activity.

CASE STUDY 7.1

In *Gillette, Kathryn, (2018) TC Memo 2018-195*, the tax court found that Ms. Gillette, who was a former police officer and military veteran, was liable for the 10% additional tax on a premature distribution under section 72(t) despite the fact that she suffered from a gambling addiction, possibly caused by prescription medication.

IRC Section 72(t) provides that a taxpayer is disabled if he or she is unable to engage in any substantial gainful activity by reason of any medically determinable physical or mental impairment which can be expected to result in death or to be of long-continued and indefinite duration. An individual's substantial gainful activity is the activity, or a comparable activity, in which the individual customarily engaged prior to the arising of the disability.

Ms. Gillette argued that her gambling addiction falls under two examples enumerated in section 1.72-17A(f)(2). The first is damage to the brain or brain abnormality which has resulted in severe loss of judgment, intellect, orientation, or memory. The second is mental diseases (e.g. psychosis or severe psychoneurosis) requiring continued institutionalization or constant supervision of the individual. Notwithstanding these two examples, an impairment which is remediable does not constitute a disability within the meaning of section 72(m)(7). An impairment is remediable if the taxpayer can treat the impairment "with reasonable effort and safety to himself," and where the taxpayer will not be prevented by the impairment from engaging in his customary or any comparable substantial gainful activity.

Even accepting that Ms. Gillette suffered an impairment in 2012, the court nonetheless found that any impairment was remediable and not a disability under section 72(m)(7). Ms. Gillette was treated in a reasonable and safe manner with the help of her family and medical professionals. She was able to return to managing her rental properties and financial affairs and has not gambled since 2015. Any impairment that affected Ms. Gillette during the year at issue was remediable; she was not disabled under section 72(m)(7) and does not qualify for an exception under section 72(t)(2).

Exhibit 7.22 | Form 5329

Form **5329**	**Additional Taxes on Qualified Plans (Including IRAs) and Other Tax-Favored Accounts**	OMB No. 1545-0074
Department of the Treasury Internal Revenue Service (99)	▶ Attach to Form 1040, 1040-SR, or 1040-NR. ▶ Go to *www.irs.gov/Form5329* for instructions and the latest information.	20**20** Attachment Sequence No. **29**

Name of individual subject to additional tax. If married filing jointly, see instructions. | Your social security number

Fill in Your Address Only if You Are Filing This Form by Itself and Not With Your Tax Return ▶

Home address (number and street), or P.O. box if mail is not delivered to your home | Apt. no.

City, town or post office, state, and ZIP code. If you have a foreign address, also complete the spaces below. See instructions.

If this is an amended return, check here ▶ ☐

Foreign country name | Foreign province/state/county | Foreign postal code

If you **only** owe the additional 10% tax on early distributions, you may be able to report this tax directly on Schedule 2 (Form 1040), line 6, without filing Form 5329. See the instructions for Schedule 2 (Form 1040), line 6.

Part I   **Additional Tax on Early Distributions.** Complete this part if you took a taxable distribution (other than a distribution related to a qualified disaster or a coronavirus-related distribution) before you reached age 59½ from a qualified retirement plan (including an IRA) or modified endowment contract (unless you are reporting this tax directly on Schedule 2 (Form 1040)—see above). You may also have to complete this part to indicate that you qualify for an exception to the additional tax on early distributions or for certain Roth IRA distributions. See instructions.

1	Early distributions included in income. For Roth IRA distributions, see instructions	**1**	
2	Early distributions included on line 1 that are not subject to the additional tax (see instructions).		
	Enter the appropriate exception number from the instructions: _____	**2**	
3	Amount subject to additional tax. Subtract line 2 from line 1	**3**	
4	**Additional tax.** Enter 10% (0.10) of line 3. Include this amount on Schedule 2 (Form 1040), line 6 . .	**4**	
	Caution: If any part of the amount on line 3 was a distribution from a SIMPLE IRA, you may have to include 25% of that amount on line 4 instead of 10%. See instructions.		

Part II   **Additional Tax on Certain Distributions From Education Accounts and ABLE Accounts.** Complete this part if you included an amount in income, on Schedule 1 (Form 1040), line 8, from a Coverdell education savings account (ESA), a qualified tuition program (QTP), or an ABLE account.

5	Distributions included in income from a Coverdell ESA, a QTP, or an ABLE account	**5**	
6	Distributions included on line 5 that are not subject to the additional tax (see instructions)	**6**	
7	Amount subject to additional tax. Subtract line 6 from line 5	**7**	
8	**Additional tax.** Enter 10% (0.10) of line 7. Include this amount on Schedule 2 (Form 1040), line 6 . .	**8**	

Part III   **Additional Tax on Excess Contributions to Traditional IRAs.** Complete this part if you contributed more to your traditional IRAs for 2020 than is allowable or you had an amount on line 17 of your 2019 Form 5329.

9	Enter your excess contributions from line 16 of your 2019 Form 5329. See instructions. If zero, go to line 15		**9**	
10	If your traditional IRA contributions for 2020 are less than your maximum allowable contribution, see instructions. Otherwise, enter -0-	**10**		
11	2020 traditional IRA distributions included in income (see instructions) . . .	**11**		
12	2020 distributions of prior year excess contributions (see instructions) . . .	**12**		
13	Add lines 10, 11, and 12		**13**	
14	Prior year excess contributions. Subtract line 13 from line 9. If zero or less, enter -0-		**14**	
15	Excess contributions for 2020 (see instructions)		**15**	
16	Total excess contributions. Add lines 14 and 15		**16**	
17	**Additional tax.** Enter 6% (0.06) of the **smaller** of line 16 **or** the value of your traditional IRAs on December 31, 2020 (including 2020 contributions made in 2021). Include this amount on Schedule 2 (Form 1040), line 6		**17**	

Part IV   **Additional Tax on Excess Contributions to Roth IRAs.** Complete this part if you contributed more to your Roth IRAs for 2020 than is allowable or you had an amount on line 25 of your 2019 Form 5329.

18	Enter your excess contributions from line 24 of your 2019 Form 5329. See instructions. If zero, go to line 23		**18**	
19	If your Roth IRA contributions for 2020 are less than your maximum allowable contribution, see instructions. Otherwise, enter -0-	**19**		
20	2020 distributions from your Roth IRAs (see instructions)	**20**		
21	Add lines 19 and 20		**21**	
22	Prior year excess contributions. Subtract line 21 from line 18. If zero or less, enter -0-		**22**	
23	Excess contributions for 2020 (see instructions)		**23**	
24	Total excess contributions. Add lines 22 and 23		**24**	
25	**Additional tax.** Enter 6% (0.06) of the **smaller** of line 24 **or** the value of your Roth IRAs on December 31, 2020 (including 2020 contributions made in 2021). Include this amount on Schedule 2 (Form 1040), line 6		**25**	

For Privacy Act and Paperwork Reduction Act Notice, see your tax return instructions.   Cat. No. 13329Q   Form **5329** (2020)

Form 5329 Continued

Form 5329 (2020)   Page **2**

Part V   **Additional Tax on Excess Contributions to Coverdell ESAs.** Complete this part if the contributions to your Coverdell ESAs for 2020 were more than is allowable or you had an amount on line 33 of your 2019 Form 5329.

26	Enter the excess contributions from line 32 of your 2019 Form 5329. See instructions. If zero, go to line 31	**26**	
27	If the contributions to your Coverdell ESAs for 2020 were less than the maximum allowable contribution, see instructions. Otherwise, enter -0-	**27**	
28	2020 distributions from your Coverdell ESAs (see instructions)	**28**	
29	Add lines 27 and 28	**29**	
30	Prior year excess contributions. Subtract line 29 from line 26. If zero or less, enter -0-	**30**	
31	Excess contributions for 2020 (see instructions)	**31**	
32	Total excess contributions. Add lines 30 and 31	**32**	
33	**Additional tax.** Enter 6% (0.06) of the **smaller** of line 32 **or** the value of your Coverdell ESAs on December 31, 2020 (including 2020 contributions made in 2021). Include this amount on Schedule 2 (Form 1040), line 6	**33**	

Part VI   **Additional Tax on Excess Contributions to Archer MSAs.** Complete this part if you or your employer contributed more to your Archer MSAs for 2020 than is allowable or you had an amount on line 41 of your 2019 Form 5329.

34	Enter the excess contributions from line 40 of your 2019 Form 5329. See instructions. If zero, go to line 39	**34**	
35	If the contributions to your Archer MSAs for 2020 are less than the maximum allowable contribution, see instructions. Otherwise, enter -0-	**35**	
36	2020 distributions from your Archer MSAs from Form 8853, line 8	**36**	
37	Add lines 35 and 36	**37**	
38	Prior year excess contributions. Subtract line 37 from line 34. If zero or less, enter -0-	**38**	
39	Excess contributions for 2020 (see instructions)	**09**	
40	Total excess contributions. Add lines 38 and 39	**40**	
41	**Additional tax.** Enter 6% (0.06) of the **smaller** of line 40 **or** the value of your Archer MSAs on December 31, 2020 (including 2020 contributions made in 2021). Include this amount on Schedule 2 (Form 1040), line 6	**41**	

Part VII   **Additional Tax on Excess Contributions to Health Savings Accounts (HSAs).** Complete this part if you, someone on your behalf, or your employer contributed more to your HSAs for 2020 than is allowable or you had an amount on line 49 of your 2019 Form 5329.

42	Enter the excess contributions from line 48 of your 2019 Form 5329. If zero, go to line 47	**42**	
43	If the contributions to your HSAs for 2020 are less than the maximum allowable contribution, see instructions. Otherwise, enter -0-	**43**	
44	2020 distributions from your HSAs from Form 8889, line 16	**44**	
45	Add lines 43 and 44	**45**	
46	Prior year excess contributions. Subtract line 45 from line 42. If zero or less, enter -0-	**46**	
47	Excess contributions for 2020 (see instructions)	**47**	
48	Total excess contributions. Add lines 46 and 47	**48**	
49	**Additional tax.** Enter 6% (0.06) of the **smaller** of line 48 **or** the value of your HSAs on December 31, 2020 (including 2020 contributions made in 2021). Include this amount on Schedule 2 (Form 1040), line 6	**49**	

Part VIII   **Additional Tax on Excess Contributions to an ABLE Account.** Complete this part if contributions to your ABLE account for 2020 were more than is allowable.

50	Excess contributions for 2020 (see instructions)	**50**	
51	**Additional tax.** Enter 6% (0.06) of the **smaller** of line 50 **or** the value of your ABLE account on December 31, 2020. Include this amount on Schedule 2 (Form 1040), line 6	**51**	

Part IX   **Additional Tax on Excess Accumulation in Qualified Retirement Plans (Including IRAs).** Complete this part if you did not receive the minimum required distribution from your qualified retirement plan.

52	Minimum required distribution for 2020 (see instructions)	**52**	
53	Amount actually distributed to you in 2020	**53**	
54	Subtract line 53 from line 52. If zero or less, enter -0-	**54**	
55	**Additional tax.** Enter 50% (0.50) of line 54. Include this amount on Schedule 2 (Form 1040), line 6	**55**	

Sign Here Only if You Are Filing This Form by Itself and Not With Your Tax Return

Under penalties of perjury, I declare that I have examined this form, including accompanying attachments, and to the best of my knowledge and belief, it is true, correct, and complete. Declaration of preparer (other than taxpayer) is based on all information of which preparer has any knowledge.

▶ Your signature   ▶ Date

Paid Preparer Use Only

Print/Type preparer's name	Preparer's signature	Date	Check ☐ if self-employed	PTIN
Firm's name ▶			Firm's EIN ▶	
Firm's address ▶			Phone no.	

Form **5329** (2020)

Substantially Equal Periodic Payments

If the distribution is part of a series of substantially equal periodic payments, also called Section 72(t) distributions, made at least annually for the life or life expectancy of the participant or the joint lives or joint life expectancies of the participant and his designated beneficiary, the payments will not be subjected to the 10 percent early withdrawal penalty. The payments must begin after the participant has separated from service (for qualified plans; IRAs do not have this requirement), and to be considered substantially equal periodic payments, the payments must be made in any one of the following three ways: [52]

1. **Required Minimum Distribution Method.**

    The payments are calculated in the same manner as required under minimum distribution rules (discussed below).[53] Note that payments are recalculated annually.

2. **Fixed Amortization Method.**

    The payment is calculated over the participant's life expectancy if single, or the joint life expectancy if married, and the interest rate is reasonable (not to exceed 120% of the federal midterm rate). This method creates a series of installment payments that remain the same in subsequent years.

3. **Fixed Annuitization Method.**

    The participant takes distributions of the account over a number of years determined by dividing the account balance by an annuity factor using a reasonable interest rate and mortality table. Under this method, the payment does not change in future years.

Example 7.32

Mr. B, age 50, would like to explore his distribution options under IRC Section 72(t) rules. His account balance is $400,000.[54]

Option 1 - Required Minimum Distribution Method

Assume the required minimum distribution factor was 34.2 years.[55]

$$\frac{\$400,000}{34.2} = \$11,695.91 \text{ per year (1st year)}$$

Option 2 -Fixed Amortization Method

Assume the interest rate is 2.0%, and the single life expectancy is 34.2 years.[56] The annual distribution amount is calculated by amortizing the account balance of $400,000 over Mr. B's single life expectancy (34.2 years) at an interest rate of 2.0%. If an end-of-the year payment is calculated, then the annual distribution amount is $16,260.57.[57]

---

52. These three methods are set forth in Notice 89-25 as modified by Rev. Ruling 2002-62. An alternate method may be used, but must be approved through the use of a private letter ruling.

53. As discussed in the Required Minimum Distribution section later in this chapter, in 2020 the IRS issued final regulations updating the life expectancy tables used to calculate lifetime minimum distribution amounts and provided guidance regarding a reset of life expectancy for those who had previously begun distributions. These final regulations indicate that the IRS intends to issue separate guidance regarding the application of the new life expectancy tables (which become effective beginning in 2022) to substantially equal periodic payments. As of the time of printing this guidance was not yet available.

54. This example is derived from "Retirement Plan FAQs Regarding Rev. Ruling 2002-62," available at https://www.irs.gov/retirement-plans/retirement-plans-faqs-regarding-substantially-equal-periodic-payments#7.

55. The factor is determined by the "Single Life Table" in Reg. §1.401(a)(9) - 9, as applicable for distribution years prior to January 1, 2022. See footnote 53 regarding the change to updated tables applicable to distribution years after 2021.

56. The interest rate is 120% of the applicable midterm rate. The interest rate in this example is provided for illustration purposes.

Option 3 - Fixed Annuitization Method

Under this method, the annual distribution amount is equal to the account balance of $400,000 divided by the cost of an annuity factor that would provide one dollar per year over Mr. B's life, beginning at age 50. The age 50 annuity factor (24.683) is calculated based on the mortality table in Appendix B of Revenue Ruling 2002-62 and an interest rate of 2.0%. Such calculations would normally be made by an actuary.

$$\frac{\$400,000}{24.683} = \$16,205.49$$

Notice that Options 2 and 3 provide a larger payment than Option 1. For example, a person may want the larger payment to help finance a new business venture. The participant can choose any of the methods.

In the case above, Mr. B may choose Option 1 if he needs some current income but does not want to significantly deplete his account balance. He must continue to withdraw until he is 59½ (as discussed below). Mr. B could choose Option 2 or 3, which provide larger payments, if, for example, he were starting a new business and needed the extra cash flow, or expected that business losses from a flow-through entity would shelter part of the distributions.

Summary of 72(t) Distributions*			
	RMD Method	**Fixed Amortization Method**	**Fixed Annuitization Method**
Annual Payment	$11,695.91	$16,260.57	$16,205.49

* Based on an individual at age 50 with an account balance of $400,000, an expected interest rate of 2.0%, and a life expectancy of 34.2 years.

The payment calculated under one of the methods determined above must continue exactly as calculated for the later of five years from the date of the first payment or the participant attaining the age of 59½.[58] If the payments change in any way, the participant will be considered to have made a distribution equal to the full account balance of the qualified plan in the first year of the substantially equal periodic payments. The addition of this amount to the participant's taxable income will also subject the participant to an early withdrawal penalty as well as penalties and interest for the years passed since the first year of the distribution.

Revenue Ruling 2002-62 allows a taxpayer to make a one-time irrevocable switch from the fixed amortization or fixed annuitization methods to the required minimum distribution method. If the switch is made then the required minimum distribution method must be used for all subsequent years. The change would be useful in cases where the value of the account had declined substantially and the taxpayer wanted to reduce the required annual payments for future years.

57. When comparing these three methods, it is easiest to use one of the many 72(t) calculators available online, such as the calculator provided Bankrate.com (available at https://www.bankrate.com/calculators/retirement/72-t-distribution-calculator.aspx).
58. Rev. Ruling 2002-62: Permits a participant a one-time election to change from the 2nd or 3rd method to the 1st (RMD) method.

Once the distribution under Section 72(t) has been elected, the rules must be followed precisely to avoid being subject to the 10 percent penalty. If a mistake is made, the results are often irreversible and costly including unnecessary tax and penalties. Errors typically will disqualify all prior year distributions under Section 72(t), subjecting them to the 10 percent penalty and interest. Revenue Ruling 2002-62 states that additional contributions cannot be made to the account (other than investment gains) nor can amounts from the plan be rolled over tax-free into another account without subjecting the account to the 10 percent penalty.

From a planning perspective, taxpayers can, prior to initiating the substantially equal payments, separate retirement accounts to control the amount of the substantially equal payments. Taxpayers do not have to take these payments on the entire combined balance of all IRAs. This flexibility allows taxpayers to increase the distributions over time and Revenue Ruling 2002-62 allows them to decrease it one time by changing to the RMD method.

Example 7.33

Assume the same facts as in **Example 7.32**, and that Mr. B wants to use the fixed annuitization method, but only needs $8,102.75, not $16,205.49 per year. Mr. B can separate his $400,000 IRA into two $200,000 IRAs and take substantially equal periodic payments from only one them. This would result in a payment of $8,102.75,

$$\frac{\$200,000}{24.683} = \$8,102.75 \text{ per year}$$

providing him with the income he needs without depleting the total amount in his IRAs faster than necessary.

Separated From Service After Attainment of Age 55

A distribution to an employee from a qualified plan will avoid the 10 percent early withdrawal penalty if it is made after the employee has separated from service for the employer maintaining the plan and such separation from service occurred during or after the calendar year in which the employee attained age 55.[59]

This exception may be extremely helpful to those employees who take an early retirement package and need funds from their retirement plan prior to receiving Social Security benefits. It is important to note that this exception is only applicable to distributions from qualified plans and is not available to distributions from IRAs.

It should be noted that this exception will not apply if an individual separates from service before age 55 and defers distributions until after the attainment of age 55. In other words, the employee must turn age 55 (or older) within the year of separation of service.

59. IRC §72(t)(2)(A)(v) and IRS Notice 87-13.

Dividends Paid from an ESOP

The government provides an exception to the 10 percent early withdrawal penalty if the distributions are dividends paid within 90 days of the plan year end from an ESOP.

IRS Tax Levy on the Plan

If the distribution is made to pay certain unpaid income taxes because of a tax levy on the plan, the distribution will not be subject to the 10 percent penalty.

CASE STUDY 7.2

In *Gregory T. and Kim D. Benz v. Commissioner., U.S. Tax Court, 132 T.C. No. 15, (May 11, 2009)*, the Tax Court held that a distribution from an IRA for qualified higher education expenses is not an impermissible modification of a series of substantially equal periodic payments.

Facts:
- In 2002, Petitioner's wife elected to receive a series of substantially equal periodic payments from her IRA that qualified for a statutory exception to the 10 percent early withdrawal penalty.
- IRC §72(t)(4) provides that a modification of a series of periodic payments within the first five years (other than by reason of the employee's death or disability) or before age 59½ will be subject to the 10 percent penalty. It also results in all payments under the substantially equal periodic payment exception to be subject to the 10 percent penalty.
- In 2004, Petitioners wife received additional distributions to pay for qualified higher education costs for her son.
- Petitioners reported all distributions on their Form 1040 as taxable, but not subject to the 10 percent penalty.

Issues:
- The sole issue for decision is whether a distribution for qualified higher education expenses is an impermissible modification of a series of substantially equal periodic payments.

Arguments:
- The IRS argues that an employee who elects a series of substantially equal periodic payments is not allowed any further distributions within the first five years of the election irrespective of whether the distribution would qualify for another statutory exception to the §72(t) tax unless the employee dies or becomes disabled.
- Petitioners argue that a distribution used for a purpose that qualifies for a statutory exception is not a modification of a series of substantially equal periodic payments that triggers the recapture tax under §72(t)(4).
- In *Arnold v. Commissioner*, 111 T.C. 250, 255-256 (1998), the Court held that an additional distribution that did not qualify for a statutory exception was an impermissible modification to a series of substantially equal periodic payments.

Findings:
- The court held that a distribution for qualified higher education expenses is not a modification of a series of substantially equal periodic payments.
- It considered the *Arnold v. Commissioner* case, but also considered the language in the IRC that allows for multiple exceptions to the 10 percent penalty.
- The court noted that the legislative purpose of the 10-percent additional tax is that premature distributions from IRAs frustrate the intention of saving for retirement, and §72(t) discourages this from happening." This legislative purpose is not frustrated where an employee receives distributions for more than one of the purposes that Congress has recognized as deserving special treatment.

CASE STUDY 7.3

In *Francisco A. Murillo v. Commissioner, (1998-13 Tax Court Memo Ruling, 75 TCM 1564)*, the tax court found that a forfeited IRA account for the purpose of a tax levy is not subject to the 10 percent penalty.

Mr. Murillo was indicted with: (1) Conspiracy to structure cash deposits into bank accounts in the New York area for the purpose of avoiding Federal currency transaction reporting requirements; (2) 22 substantive structuring counts relating to approximately $1,026,855 in U.S. currency deposited into various bank accounts during the period January 19, 1988, through August 23, 1989; and (3) 10 counts alleging violations of customs reporting requirements.

In contrast to the Murillo case above, the Tax Court found in *James A. and Linda A. Willhite v. Commissioner*, T.C. Memo. 2009-263, 98 T.C.M. 470 that the petitioner was liable for the 10 percent penalty because he received the distribution before receiving the notice to levy from the IRS.

The conclusion can be drawn that this exception should only apply in the event that a taxpayer receives a distribution directly as a result of an IRS levy.

Medical Expenses in Excess of 7.5 Percent of AGI

There is no 10 percent penalty if the distribution is made to the participant for certain medical expenses paid during the year greater than 7.5 percent of the participant's adjusted gross income (whether the person itemizes or not). Naturally, these expenses cannot be reimbursed by a health care provider or employer.

Qualified Domestic Relations Orders (QDRO)

Distributions to an alternate payee pursuant to a QDRO are not subject to the 10 percent early withdrawal penalty. The QDRO must relate to child support, alimony payments, or marital property rights to a spouse, former spouse, child, or other dependent. In addition the QDRO must specify:[60]

- The name and the last known mailing address (if any) of the participant and the name and mailing address of each alternate payee covered by the order,
- The amount or percentage of the participant's benefits to be paid by the plan to each such alternate payee, or the manner in which such amount or percentage is to be determined,
- The number of payments or period to which such order applies, and
- Each plan to which the order applies.

In addition the order cannot require the plan to pay in a manner not provided for in the plan document nor can it provide that the plan provide higher benefits than are due to the participant.

Note that the exception to the 10 percent penalty applies only to distributions from the qualified plan related to the QDRO, and does not extend to all subsequent distributions. If the alternate payee rolls the funds under the QDRO to an IRA, the penalty exception will not apply to distributions from the IRA.

Individuals Called to Active Duty

IRC Section 72(t)(2)(G) provides that distributions from an IRA or attributable to deferrals by anyone called to active duty for a period in excess of 179 days or for an indefinite period are not subject to the 10 percent penalty. This exception applies for individuals ordered to active duty after September 11, 2001.

---

60. IRC §414(p).

This exception also provides these active duty personnel an opportunity to repay the distribution back to the IRA or plan within two years after the end of the active duty period. However, this contribution cannot be deducted.

Distributions to Qualified Public Safety Employees in Governmental Plans

Under the Pension Protection Act of 2006, the 10 percent early withdrawal tax does not apply to distributions from a governmental defined benefit pension plan paid to a qualified public safety employee who separates from service after age 50. A qualified public safety employee is an employee of a State or political subdivision of a State if the employee provides police protection, fire fighting services, or emergency medical services for any area within the jurisdiction of such State or political subdivision. This provision is effective as of August 17, 2006.

The Trade Priorities and Accountability Act of 2015 (the TPA Act) expanded the category of government workers who qualify for the Section 72(t)(10) penalty exception, effective for distributions made after December 31, 2015. Under the TPA Act, certain federal employees, such as federal law enforcement officers, customs and border protection officers, federal firefighters, and air traffic controllers, are also eligible for the penalty exception if they have separated from federal service at age 50 or after. In addition, the TPA Act expanded the types of plans to which the penalty exception applies to include defined contribution plans and other types of government plans.

The ability to take advantage of this penalty exception is lost if the funds are rolled out of the government plan to a new custodian.

Qualified Birth or Adoption Distribution

The SECURE Act of 2019 created a new penalty exception for qualified birth or adoption distributions made after December 31, 2019. A qualified distribution is one made from an eligible retirement plan (including IRAs, 401(k), 403(b) and 457(b) plans, and qualified defined contribution plans) to an individual during the 1-year period beginning on the date on which a child of the individual is born or on which the legal adoption by the individual of an eligible adoptee is finalized.[61] There is an aggregate limit on qualified distributions of $5,000 per individual (allowing each parent up to $5,000 as a qualified distribution from their own eligible retirement plan) per child.[62] The 20 percent mandatory withholding on distributions from qualified plans does not apply.

Example 7.34

Karl and Salina became the proud parents of twin girls on March 3, 2021. On January 4, 2022, Karl and Salina each take a distribution of $10,000 ($5,000 per child) from their respective qualified plan. The entire $20,000 qualifies for the penalty exception.

---

61. Eligible plans are those listed under IRC §402(c)(8)(B). Defined benefit plans are not eligible.
62. IRS Notice 2020-68.

An eligible adoptee is any individual, other than a child of the taxpayer's spouse, who had not attained age 18 or who is physically or mentally incapable of self-support. The taxpayer is required to include the name, age, and Taxpayer Identification Number (TIN) of the child or adoptee on the tax return for the year of the distribution.

An individual who receives an eligible birth or adoption distribution is permitted to later repay up to the amount of the distribution to an eligible retirement plan to which a rollover contribution could be made.[63] The contribution is treated as if it were an eligible rollover contribution made within 60 days of distribution. Qualified birth or adoption distributions from IRAs that are repaid are treated as having been transferred to the eligible retirement plan in a direct trustee-to-trustee transfer within 60 days of distribution.

Exhibit 7.23 | Summary of 10 Percent Penalty Exceptions for Qualified Plans

- Distribution is made after the participant is age 59½.
- Distribution is made on account of death of the participant.
- Distribution is made on account of disability of the participant.
- Distribution is part of a series of substantially equal periodic payments made at least annually for the life or life expectancy of the participant or the joint lives or joint life expectancies of the participant and his designated beneficiary (§72(t)).
- Distribution is made after separation from service after the participant attains age 55.
- Distributions are dividends paid within 90 days of the plan year from an ESOP.
- Distribution is made to pay certain unpaid income taxes because of a tax levy on the plan.
- Distributions made to the participant for certain medical expenses paid during the year greater than 7.5 percent of adjusted gross income.
- Distributions pursuant to a Qualified Domestic Relations Order (QDRO).
- Individuals called to active duty.
- Distributions to qualified public safety employees in governmental plans.
- Qualified birth or adoption distributions.

Other exceptions to the 10 percent early withdrawal penalty are plan rollovers and plan loans. As discussed previously, these withdrawals receive preferential treatment. In addition, other exceptions discussed in Chapter 9 apply specifically to IRAs.

---

63. For plans other than IRAs, the individual must be otherwise eligible to make rollover contributions to the plan.

Exhibit 7.24 | Summary of Exceptions for Qualified Plans and IRAs

Exception to 10% Penalty	Qualified Plan	IRA	IRC §(s)
After participant/IRA owner reaches age 59	Yes	Yes	72(t)(2)(A)(i)
After death of the participant/IRA owner	Yes	Yes	72(t)(2)(A)(ii)
Total and permanent disability of the participant/IRA owner	Yes	Yes	72(t)(2)(A)(iii)
Series of substantially equal payments	Yes	Yes	72(t)(2)(A)(iv)
Separation from service during or after year employee reaches age 55 (age 50 for public safety employees)	Yes	No	72(t)(2)(A)(v) and 72(t)(10)
Dividend pass through from an ESOP	Yes	N/A	72(t)(2)(A)(vi)
Because of an IRS levy of the plan	Yes	Yes	72(t)(2)(A)(vii)
Amount of your unreimbursed medical expenses (>7.5% AGI)	Yes	Yes	72(t)(2)(B)
To an alternate payee under a Qualified Domestic Relations Order	Yes	No	72(t)(2)(C)
Payment of health insurance premiums paid while unemployed	No	Yes	72(t)(2)(D)
Qualified higher education expenses	No	Yes	72(t)(2)(E)
Qualified first-time homebuyers up to $10,000	No	Yes	72(t)(2)(F)
Certain distributions to qualified military reservists called to active duty	Yes	Yes	72(t)(2)(G)
Qualified Birth or Adoption Distributions	Yes	Yes	72(t)(2)(H)
Corrective distributions	Yes	No	401(k)(8)(D), 401(m)(7), and 402(g)(2)(C)
Rollovers	Yes	Yes	402(c), 403(a)(4),403(b)(8), 408(d)(3)and 408A(d)(3)(A)
Governmental 457(b) distributions are not subject to the 10% additional tax except for distributions attributable to rollovers from another type of plan or IRA.			

MINIMUM DISTRIBUTIONS

Assets in qualified plans and other tax-advantaged plans enjoy tax-deferred growth. However, this favorable tax treatment is for the purpose of encouraging individuals to save for retirement. In the past, the IRC has established age 70½ as the maximum deferral age before distributions must begin. The SECURE Act of 2019 increased the mandatory distribution age to 72 for in individuals who attain age 70½ after December 31, 2019. Once a taxpayer attains the age of 70½ (or 72 if age 70½ is reached after December 31, 2019), the minimum distribution rules must be complied with by the taxpayer. The minimum distribution rules require individuals to begin taking minimum distributions when the participant attains the age of 70½ (or 72 if age 70½ is reached after December 31, 2019). If the funds are not distributed by the required date, a 50 percent excise tax will be levied on the participant for failure to take the **required minimum distribution (RMD)**. The penalty is calculated on the amount equal to the RMD less any distribution that was taken, but the result cannot be less than zero. It is important to note that the minimum distribution is in fact a minimum amount. Distributions in excess of the minimum distribution can certainly be taken by the participant or owner.

> ### ☰ *Key Concepts*
>
> 1. When must minimum distributions begin?
> 2. How is the minimum distribution calculated?
> 3. What effect does death of the participant have on minimum distributions?

Minimum distributions apply to assets in a qualified plan, IRA, 403(b), SEP, SIMPLE, or 457 plan. While minimum distribution rules do not apply to Roth IRAs, they do apply to Roth accounts in a 401(k) or 403(b) plan.[64]

The first distribution is for the year in which the participant attains the age of 72 (for those who did not reach age 70½ before December 31, 2019) but may be delayed until the **required beginning date (RBD)** which is April 1 of the following year. However, for each year thereafter, the RMD must be taken by December 31 of the tax year. The special first year option allows a participant to delay the first payment until April 1 following the year in which the participant turns 72. However, such a delay only applies to the first distribution and could cause a bunching of income in the year after the participant attains the age of 72 since the second RMD must still be taken by December 31 of that same year.

Exhibit 7.25 | RBD Summary Post SECURE Act

Required Beginning Date (RBD)	
Attained age 70½ prior to January 1, 2020	April 1st of the year following the year the participant attains age 70½
Attained age 70½ after December 31, 2019	April 1st of the year following the year the participant attains age 72

---

64. Minimum distribution rules also apply to inherited Roth IRAs.

Example 7.35

Paul turned 70½ in March of 2021. He was a participant in a qualified plan with his previous employer but has not received any distributions since retirement. Since Paul turned 70½ after December 31, 2019, his first distribution year will be 2022, the year he turns age 72 (he will turn age 72 in September 2022). The last date he can take his distribution for 2022 without incurring a minimum distribution penalty is April 1 of 2023. The last date he can withdraw his distribution for 2023 is December 31 of 2023.[65]

For the sake of ease, refer to the mandatory distribution age as age 72 (as applicable for those who attain age 70½ after December 31, 2019) in the following paragraphs and examples. Note that, using age 72 (rather than age 70½) as the focal point corresponds to turning age 72 on or after July 1, 2021. Those who turn age 72 before July 1, 2021 would have attained age 70½ by December 31, 2019 and begun taking required distributions under the old rules at that time. The new rules delaying the first distribution year to the year in which age 72 is attained apply to those who turn age 72 on or after July 1, 2021, since these participants would have attained age 70½ after December 31, 2019.

An exception to the general RMD for qualified plans exists if a participant is still employed by the plan sponsor of a qualified plan upon attainment of age 72. A participant that is still employed by the plan sponsor of the qualified plan does not have to begin taking RMDs until April 1 of the year after the participant terminates employment with the plan sponsor. The exception is not available for any participant that owns more than five percent of the ownership of the plan sponsor in the year the participant reaches the age of 72. In addition, if the participant is a more than five percent owner and begins taking the RMD, he cannot discontinue taking the distributions should he no longer own greater than five percent of the company at some future date. However, while the law permits the delay, a qualified plan may require all individuals, even those participants that have continued employment past the age of 72, to take RMDs at 72; the discretion is given to the plan's sponsor.

---

65. Since Paul is already 72, he will have to take a minimum distribution before he rolls over the balance to an IRA because he is in what is called "a distribution year." The minimum distribution must be satisfied before a rollover may occur.

CASE STUDY 7.4

In the case of ***Lee v. California Butchers' Pension Trust Fund,***[1] Lee (the pensioner) who retired at age 73 brought an action against pension trust fund ("Fund"), claiming that the Fund violated, among other things, ERISA by underpaying his pension. The United States Ninth Circuit Court of Appeals concluded that the Fund improperly denied increased benefits to the pensioner.

Lee worked at Safeway as a butcher for 30 years. He retired in 1992 at age 73. The dispute in this case dealt with the amount of money that Mr. Lee was entitled to be paid every month in his pension. He wanted to be paid as though he had worked 30 years and retired in 1992. The Fund insisted on paying him as though he had retired in 1990 instead of 1992, and then started working again. The effect of the Fund decision was to pay Mr. Lee $815.50 per month instead of $1,498.20. The Internal Revenue Code requires pension plans to begin paying people their pensions after they attain age 70½ whether they keep working or not. Thus, the plan started paying Lee his pension in 1990 because he had reached age 70½.

A collective bargaining agreement increased pensions for people who retired beginning in 1992. When the 1992 increases came into effect, Lee obviously wanted them calculated on all his years of service. However, the Fund did not pay him on the basis that he had worked almost 30 years. Instead, it just applied the higher amounts to his two years of service following the 1990 beginning date of his distributions, as though he had only worked as a butcher covered by the plan for two years, resulting in his obtaining the pre-1992 calculation applied to almost all his years of work, and the post-1992 calculation only on his post-age-70½ work. Lee's lawyer initiated correspondence with the Fund about the calculation in December of 1991. After repeated inquiry, Lee's lawyer was told that the plan deemed him to have retired April 1, 1990.

Lee filed suit, claiming that the Fund discriminated against him based on his age (i.e., that he had turned 70½ before the 1992 increase) and violated the plan provisions because the tax provision just meant that Lee had to start drawing his pension so he would start paying income tax on the money, not that he had to retire at age 70½. Because Lee was not required to retire at age 70½ and had not in fact retired, he could not be "deemed" to have retired. The Fund argued that it correctly denied Lee's claim because the Internal Revenue Code required them to distribute his entire interest at age 70½. Congress amended the Internal Revenue Code in 1986 to require pension plans to begin distributing benefits when the pensioner reaches age 70½.[2]

The Fund read this to mean that a person must be treated as having retired at age 70½ and referred to such an employee's status as "legally retired" and distinguished it from "physically retired." The Court disagreed with the Fund and ruled in Lee's favor, explaining that there were no words in the statute or plan to support what the trustees did. Lee was not "legally" or "physically" retired in 1990; rather, he was indeed working at Safeway as a butcher. IRC §401(a)(9) limited use of pension funds as tax shelters beyond age 70½, but did not say a word about requiring people to quit working or authorizing plans to deprive them of increases and accruals following age 70½ when they are still working. The Court concluded that the law did not require the employee to be retired, just that his money be "distributed," beginning by the specified date. As no possible reading of the plan language could "deem" Lee to have retired in 1990, under the plan, Lee was to be "deemed retired" after he quit working in 1992, at which time he was entitled to the increased benefits available to all employees who stopped working after January 1, 1992. The Fund's denial of the increase to Lee was therefore considered to be an abuse of discretion.

1. *Lee v. California Butchers' Pension Trust Fund*, 154 F.3d 1075 (9th Cir. 1998).
2. See IRC §401(a)(9)(A)(ii) (1990).

Exhibit 7.26 | Required Minimum Distributions

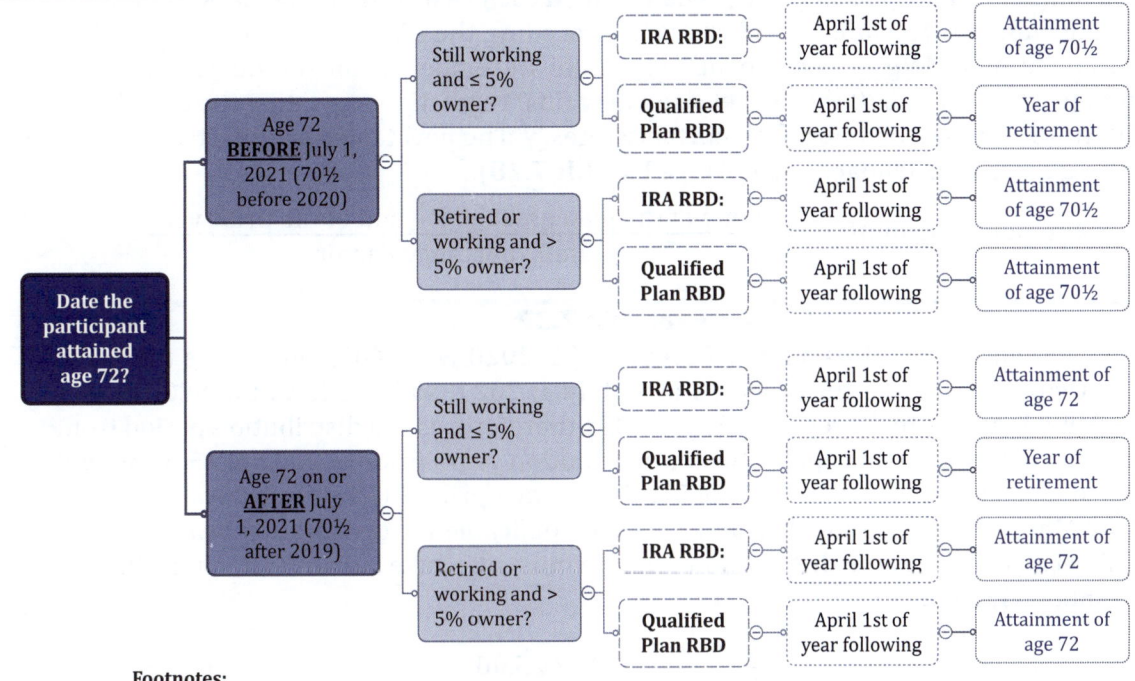

Footnotes:

1. Qualified plans include 403(b) plans and 457 plans.
2. Exception for being employed at age 70½ (or 72) only applies to the retirement plan of the current employer. All prior retirement plans follow the RBD for IRAs.

Example 7.36

Mary, age 74, works at the local grocery store. She is a participant in the grocer's profit sharing plan but has not begun taking RMDs. If Mary terminates employment on August 1 of this year, she must take her first RMD by April 1 of next year.

Exhibit 7.27 | Minimum Distribution Summary

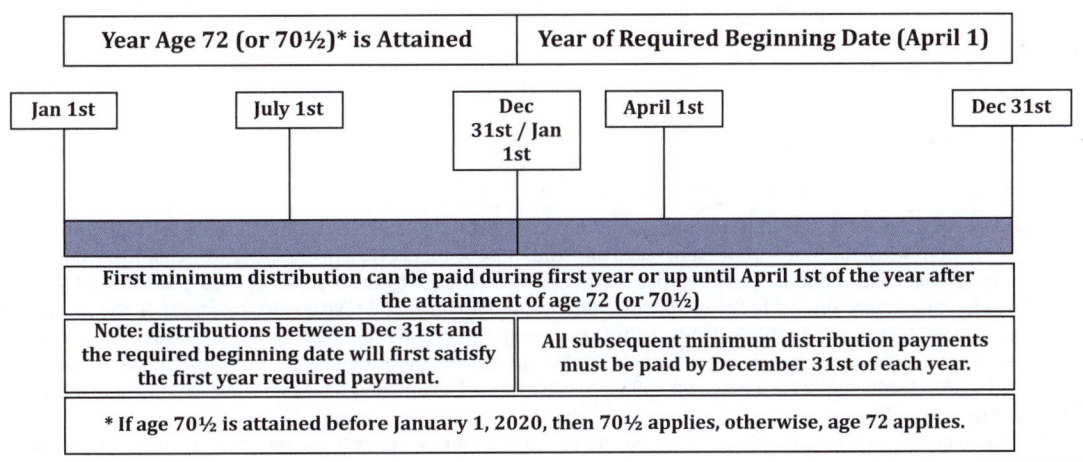

Calculating the Required Minimum Distribution

The required minimum distribution (RMD) is determined each year by dividing the account balance as of the close of business on December 31 of the year preceding the distribution year by the distribution period determined according to participant's age as of December 31 of the distribution year in the uniform lifetime table.[66] In 2020 the IRS released new final regulations updating the distribution tables under §1.401(a)(9)-9 based on improved mortality rates.[67] The new tables are effective for distribution years beginning on or after January 1, 2022 (See **Exhibit 7.28**).

$$\text{Minimum Distribution} = \frac{\text{Value of the plan asset at the end of the prior year}}{\text{Life Expectancy Factor}}$$

Example 7.37

Assume Eddie's account balance at December 31, 2020 was $400,000, and he turns age 72 in October 2021 (he turns age 72 after July 1, 2021, so he follows the SECURE Act rules) and is age 72 on December 31, 2021. He, therefore, uses a distribution period from the uniform lifetime table applicable for distribution years prior to 2022 of 25.6 and will need to take a distribution for 2021 of $15,625.00 by April 1, 2022. If he delays until April 1, 2022, he will still use the distribution table applicable for distribution years prior to 2022 because 2021 is the distribution year. He must also take a distribution for 2022 by December 31, 2022.

$$\frac{\$400,000}{25.6} = \$15,625.00$$

Assume Eddie's account balance at December 31, 2021 was $480,000, and he took his 2021 distribution in April of 2022. He will need to take $18,113.21 by December 31, 2022 for 2022, in addition to his April 1, 2022 distribution ($15,625.00). For the 2022 distribution, Eddie will use a factor of 26.5 based on age 73 in the updated tables in effect beginning in 2022. Note that when two distributions are combined in one year, it can cause the recipient to move up in the progressive tax brackets due to the stacking of two payments.

$$\frac{\$480,000}{26.5} = \$18,113.21$$

---

66. Treas. Reg. §1.401(a)(9)-9. In the past, the above calculation permitted an exception. An alternate calculation was used for the second year of RMD when the first RMD was not taken until the subsequent tax year. In this case, to calculate the RMD for the second year, the plan account balance at the end of the preceding year was reduced by the first year's RMD that had not been taken at that time. This adjustment only applied to the second distribution, and it was to the taxpayer's benefit. When the revised regulations were promulgated (Treas. Reg §1.401(a)(9)-5, A-3(c)) this exception was not part of the revised regulations, thus requiring all distributions to be calculated the same regardless of whether the first distribution was delayed until the second year.

67. The tables in effect through 2021 are based on 2003 mortality rates. The updated tables effective beginning in 2022 are based on mortality rates for 2022.

68. The life expectancy factor is determined based on the age at the end of the year for which minimum distributions are being determined.

Example 7.38

Kendal attained the age of 70½ in October 2019. Since she turned age 70½ before January 1, 2020 (age 72 before July 1, 2021) she falls under the old rules in effect prior to the SECURE Act. She retired several years ago but has not taken any distributions as of December 31, 2019. Her account balance on December 31, 2018 was $100,000, and her balance on December 31, 2019 was $110,000. The first year for which Kendal must take a minimum distribution is 2019 (although she may wait until April 1, 2020 to actually take the first distribution). To calculate the 2019 distribution, determine the factor from the uniform lifetime table based on her age at December 31, 2019 (70). The distribution period is 27.4. Utilizing the end of the prior year's account balance of $100,000, Kendal's required minimum distribution for 2019 is $3,649.64.

$$\frac{\$100,000}{27.4} = \$3,649.64$$

For 2020, the distribution will be $4,150.94. Each year after that, the end of the prior year account balance and the age related distribution period at current year end will be used to determine the RMD.

$$\frac{\$110,000}{26.5} = \$4,150.94$$

Beginning in 2022, Kendal's distributions will be calculated using the updated Uniform Lifetime Table. On December 31, 2022 Kendal will be age 72. To calculate her required distribution amount for 2022, divide the account balance on December 31, 2021 by 27.4 (the factor for age 72 under the revised life expectancy tables). As illustrated in **Exhibit 7.28**, the percentage of the account that must be distributed at age 72 is reduced from 3.91% to 3.65% for distribution years after 2021.

Example 7.39

John is 72 on October 15, 2022. Since he turns age 72 on or after July 1, 2021 he will follow the SECURE Act required distribution rules. John's year-end account balance for 2021, 2022, 2023, and 2024 are $300,000, $360,000, $420,000, and $502,000 respectively. Calculate John's minimum distribution for years 2021, 2022, 2023, 2024, and 2025. (See **Exhibit 7.28**.)

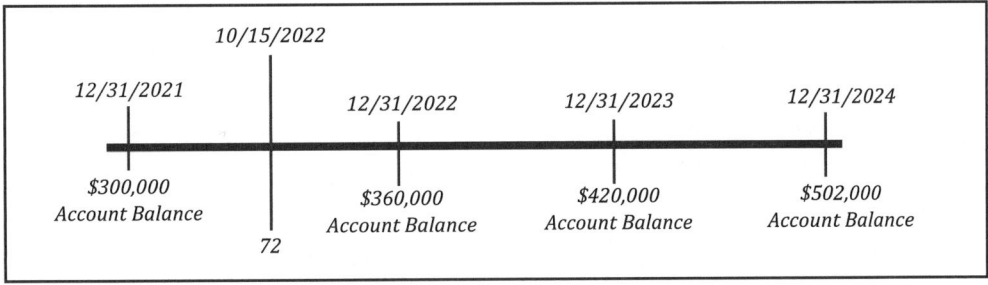

Minimum distribution calculation for 2021:
There is no minimum distribution required for 2021 because John is not yet 72.

Minimum distribution calculation for 2022:

$$\frac{\$300,000}{27.4} = \$10,948.91$$

Minimum distribution calculation for 2023:

$$\frac{\$360,000}{26.5} = \$13,584.91$$

Minimum distribution calculation for 2024:

$$\frac{\$420,000}{25.5} = \$16,470.59$$

Minimum distribution calculation for 2025:

$$\frac{\$502,000}{24.6} = \$20,406.50$$

Exhibit 7.28 | Uniform Lifetime Table - Before 2022 vs. After 2021

Age	RMD Factor For Distribution Years After 2021	RMD Factor For Distribution Years Before 2022	RMD as % of Account Balance After 2021	RMD as % of Account Balance Before 2022
70	N/A	27.4		3.65%
71	N/A	26.5		3.77%
72	27.4	25.6	3.65%	3.91%
73	26.5	24.7	3.77%	4.05%
74	25.5	23.8	3.92%	4.20%
75	24.6	22.9	4.07%	4.37%
76	23.7	22.0	4.22%	4.55%
77	22.9	21.2	4.37%	4.72%
78	22.0	20.3	4.55%	4.93%
79	21.1	19.5	4.74%	5.13%
80	20.2	18.7	4.95%	5.35%
81	19.4	17.9	5.15%	5.59%
82	18.5	17.1	5.41%	5.85%
83	17.7	16.3	5.65%	6.13%
84	16.8	15.5	5.95%	6.45%
85	16.0	14.8	6.25%	6.76%
86	15.2	14.1	6.58%	7.09%
87	14.4	13.4	6.94%	7.46%
88	13.7	12.7	7.30%	7.87%
89	12.9	12.0	7.75%	8.33%
90	12.2	11.4	8.20%	8.77%
91	11.5	10.8	8.70%	9.26%
92	10.8	10.2	9.26%	9.80%
93	10.1	9.6	9.90%	10.42%
94	9.5	9.1	10.53%	10.99%
95	8.9	8.6	11.24%	11.63%
96	8.4	8.1	11.90%	12.35%
97	7.8	7.6	12.82%	13.16%
98	7.3	7.1	13.70%	14.08%
99	6.8	6.7	14.71%	14.93%
100	6.4	6.3	15.63%	15.87%
101	6.0	5.9	16.67%	16.95%
102	5.6	5.5	17.86%	18.18%
103	5.2	5.2	19.23%	19.23%
104	4.9	4.9	20.41%	20.41%
105	4.6	4.5	21.74%	22.22%
106	4.3	4.2	23.26%	23.81%
107	4.1	3.9	24.39%	25.64%
108	3.9	3.7	25.64%	27.03%
109	3.7	3.4	27.03%	29.41%
110	3.5	3.1	28.57%	32.26%
111	3.4	2.9	29.41%	34.48%
112	3.3	2.6	30.30%	38.46%
113	3.1	2.4	32.26%	41.67%
114	3.0	2.1	33.33%	47.62%
115	2.9	1.9	34.48%	52.63%
116	2.8	1.9	35.71%	52.63%
117	2.7	1.9	37.04%	52.63%
118	2.5	1.9	40.00%	52.63%
119	2.3	1.9	43.48%	52.63%
120+	2.0	1.9	50.00%	52.63%

When calculating the RMD for the plan participant, always use the **uniform lifetime table**, which accounts for the age of the account holder and one other person who is 10 years younger. One exception to this rule occurs when the participant's sole designated beneficiary is the participant's spouse and that spouse is more than 10 years younger than the participant. In that case, use the **joint life expectancy table** to calculate the RMD. Utilizing the joint life expectancy tables will result in a longer life expectancy and decrease the RMD. An excerpt of the joint life expectancy chart in effect for distribution years prior to 2022 is provided below. For distribution years beginning in 2022 and after, the joint life table has been updated to reflect improved mortality rates, increasing the life expectancy and decreasing the required minimum distribution amounts at each age. The complete chart can be found at Treas. Reg. Section 1.401(a)(9)-9, and in IRS Publication 590.

Example 7.40

Assume the same facts as **Example 7.38** except that Kendal is married, and her husband Brody, age 69 at December 31, 2019, is the sole beneficiary. The minimum distribution will be calculated exactly as it was previously because Brody is not more than 10 years younger than Kendal.

Example 7.41

Now, assume the same facts as the above example except that Kendal is married, and her husband Brody, age 39 at December 31, 2019, is the sole beneficiary. Now the joint and survivor tables are used to determine the life expectancy because Brody is more than 10 years younger than Kendal. Their joint life expectancy is 44.9 (age 70 and 39). Under this scenario, Kendal's RMD will be $2,227.17 ($100,000/44.9).

Example 7.42

Assume the same facts as the above example except that Kendal's daughter Kylie, age 22 on December 31, 2019, is the sole beneficiary. In this case, the uniform table is used to determine the distribution period. Therefore, the RMD is the same as **Example 7.38** ($100,000/27.4 = $3,649.64).

Exhibit 7.29 | Excerpt from the Joint and Last Survivor Table (Used by Participants with Spouses More than 10 Years Younger than the Participant, For Distribution Years Prior to 2022)

Ages	30	31	32	33	34	35	36	37	38	39
30	60.2	59.7	59.2	58.8	58.4	58.0	57.6	57.3	57.0	56.7
31	59.7	59.2	58.7	58.2	57.8	57.4	57.0	56.6	56.3	56.0
32	59.2	58.7	58.2	57.7	57.2	56.8	56.4	56.0	55.6	55.3
33	58.8	58.2	57.7	57.2	56.7	56.2	55.8	55.4	55.0	54.7
34	58.4	57.8	57.2	56.7	56.2	55.7	55.3	54.8	54.4	54.0
35	58.0	57.4	56.8	56.2	55.7	55.2	54.7	54.3	53.8	53.4
36	57.6	57.0	56.4	55.8	55.3	54.7	54.2	53.7	53.3	52.8
37	57.3	56.6	56.0	55.4	54.8	54.3	53.7	53.2	52.7	52.3
38	57.0	56.3	55.6	55.0	54.4	53.8	53.3	52.7	52.2	51.7
39	56.7	56.0	55.3	54.7	54.0	53.4	52.8	52.3	51.7	51.2
40	56.4	55.7	55.0	54.3	53.7	53.0	52.4	51.8	51.3	50.8
41	56.1	55.4	54.7	54.0	53.3	52.7	52.0	51.4	50.9	50.3
42	55.9	55.2	54.4	53.7	53.0	52.3	51.7	51.1	50.4	49.9
43	55.7	54.9	54.2	53.4	52.7	52.0	51.3	50.7	50.1	49.5
44	55.5	54.7	53.9	53.2	52.4	51.7	51.0	50.4	49.7	49.1
45	55.3	54.5	53.7	52.9	52.2	51.5	50.7	50.0	49.4	48.7
46	55.1	54.3	53.5	52.7	52.0	51.2	50.5	49.8	49.1	48.4
47	55.0	54.1	53.3	52.5	51.7	51.0	50.2	49.5	48.8	48.1
48	54.8	54.0	53.2	52.3	51.5	50.8	50.0	49.2	48.5	47.8
49	54.7	53.8	53.0	52.2	51.4	50.6	49.8	49.0	48.2	47.5
50	54.6	53.7	52.9	52.0	51.2	50.4	49.6	48.8	48.0	47.3
51	54.5	53.6	52.7	51.9	51.0	50.2	49.4	48.6	47.8	47.0
52	54.4	53.5	52.6	51.7	50.9	50.0	49.2	48.4	47.6	46.8
53	54.3	53.4	52.5	51.6	50.8	49.9	49.1	48.2	47.4	46.6
54	54.2	53.3	52.4	51.5	50.6	49.8	48.9	48.1	47.2	46.4
55	54.1	53.2	52.3	51.4	50.5	49.7	48.8	47.9	47.1	46.3
56	54.0	53.1	52.2	51.3	50.4	49.5	48.7	47.8	47.0	46.1
57	54.0	53.0	52.1	51.2	50.3	49.4	48.6	47.7	46.8	46.0
58	53.9	53.0	52.1	51.2	50.3	49.4	48.5	47.6	46.7	45.8
59	53.8	52.9	52.0	51.1	50.2	49.3	48.4	47.5	46.6	45.7
60	53.8	52.9	51.9	51.0	50.1	49.2	48.3	47.4	46.5	45.6
61	53.8	52.8	51.9	51.0	50.0	49.1	48.2	47.3	46.4	45.5
62	53.7	52.8	51.8	50.9	50.0	49.1	48.1	47.2	46.3	45.4
63	53.7	52.7	51.8	50.9	49.9	49.0	48.1	47.2	46.3	45.3
64	53.6	52.7	51.8	50.8	49.9	48.9	48.0	47.1	46.2	45.3
65	53.6	52.7	51.7	50.8	49.9	48.9	48.0	47.0	46.1	45.2
66	53.6	52.6	51.7	50.7	49.8	48.9	47.9	47.0	46.1	45.1
67	53.6	52.6	51.7	50.7	49.8	48.8	47.9	46.9	46.0	45.1
68	53.5	52.6	51.6	50.7	49.7	48.8	47.8	46.9	46.0	45.0
69	53.5	52.6	51.6	50.6	49.7	48.7	47.8	46.9	45.9	45.0
70	53.5	52.5	51.6	50.6	49.7	48.7	47.8	46.8	45.9	44.9
71	53.5	52.5	51.6	50.6	49.6	48.7	47.7	46.8	45.9	44.9
72	53.5	52.5	51.5	50.6	49.6	48.7	47.7	46.8	45.8	44.9
73	53.4	52.5	51.5	50.6	49.6	48.6	47.7	46.7	45.8	44.8
74	53.4	52.5	51.5	50.5	49.6	48.6	47.7	46.7	45.8	44.8
75	53.4	52.5	51.5	50.5	49.6	48.6	47.7	46.7	45.7	44.8
76	53.4	52.4	51.5	50.5	49.6	48.6	47.6	46.7	45.7	44.8
77	53.4	52.4	51.5	50.5	49.5	48.6	47.6	46.7	45.7	44.8
78	53.4	52.4	51.5	50.5	49.5	48.6	47.6	46.6	45.7	44.7
79	53.4	52.4	51.5	50.5	49.5	48.6	47.6	46.6	45.7	44.7

Excerpt from the Joint and Last Survivor Table (Continued)

Ages	40	41	42	43	44	45	46	47	48	49
40	50.2	49.8	49.3	48.9	48.5	48.1	47.7	47.4	47.1	46.8
41	49.8	49.3	48.8	48.3	47.9	47.5	47.1	46.7	46.4	46.1
42	49.3	48.8	48.3	47.8	47.3	46.9	46.5	46.1	45.8	45.4
43	48.9	48.3	47.8	47.3	46.8	46.3	45.9	45.5	45.1	44.8
44	48.5	47.9	47.3	46.8	46.3	45.8	45.4	44.9	44.5	44.2
45	48.1	47.5	46.9	46.3	45.8	45.3	44.8	44.4	44.0	43.6
46	47.7	47.1	46.5	45.9	45.4	44.8	44.3	43.9	43.4	43.0
47	47.4	46.7	46.1	45.5	44.9	44.4	43.9	43.4	42.9	42.4
48	47.1	46.4	45.8	45.1	44.5	44.0	43.4	42.9	42.4	41.9
49	46.8	46.1	45.4	44.8	44.2	43.6	43.0	42.4	41.9	41.4
50	46.5	45.8	45.1	44.4	43.8	43.2	42.6	42.0	41.5	40.9
51	46.3	45.5	44.8	44.1	43.5	42.8	42.2	41.6	41.0	40.5
52	46.0	45.3	44.6	43.8	43.2	42.5	41.8	41.2	40.6	40.1
53	45.8	45.1	44.3	43.6	42.9	42.2	41.5	40.9	40.3	39.7
54	45.6	44.8	44.1	43.3	42.6	41.9	41.2	40.5	39.9	39.3
55	45.5	44.7	43.9	43.1	42.4	41.6	40.9	40.2	39.6	38.9
56	45.3	44.5	43.7	42.9	42.1	41.4	40.7	40.0	39.3	38.6
57	45.1	44.3	43.5	42.7	41.9	41.2	40.4	39.7	39.0	38.3
58	45.0	44.2	43.3	42.5	41.7	40.9	40.2	39.4	38.7	38.0
59	44.9	44.0	43.2	42.4	41.5	40.7	40.0	39.2	38.5	37.8
60	44.7	43.9	43.0	42.2	41.4	40.6	39.8	39.0	38.2	37.5
61	44.6	43.8	42.9	42.1	41.2	40.4	39.6	38.8	38.0	37.3
62	44.5	43.7	42.8	41.9	41.1	40.3	39.4	38.6	37.8	37.1
63	44.5	43.6	42.7	41.8	41.0	40.1	39.3	38.5	37.7	36.9
64	44.4	43.5	42.6	41.7	40.8	40.0	39.2	38.3	37.5	36.7
65	44.3	43.4	42.5	41.6	40.7	39.9	39.0	38.2	37.4	36.6
66	44.2	43.3	42.4	41.5	40.6	39.8	38.9	38.1	37.2	36.4
67	44.2	43.3	42.3	41.4	40.6	39.7	38.8	38.0	37.1	36.3
68	44.1	43.2	42.3	41.4	40.5	39.6	38.7	37.9	37.0	36.2
69	44.1	43.1	42.2	41.3	40.4	39.5	38.6	37.8	36.9	36.0
70	44.0	43.1	42.2	41.3	40.3	39.4	38.6	37.7	36.8	35.9
71	44.0	43.0	42.1	41.2	40.3	39.4	38.5	37.6	36.7	35.9
72	43.9	43.0	42.1	41.1	40.2	39.3	38.4	37.5	36.6	35.8
73	43.9	43.0	42.0	41.1	40.2	39.3	38.4	37.5	36.6	35.7
74	43.9	42.9	42.0	41.1	40.1	39.2	38.3	37.4	36.5	35.6
75	43.8	42.9	42.0	41.0	40.1	39.2	38.3	37.4	36.5	35.6
76	43.8	42.9	41.9	41.0	40.1	39.1	38.2	37.3	36.4	35.5
77	43.8	42.9	41.9	41.0	40.0	39.1	38.2	37.3	36.4	35.5
78	43.8	42.8	41.9	40.9	40.0	39.1	38.2	37.2	36.3	35.4
79	43.8	42.8	41.9	40.9	40.0	39.1	38.1	37.2	36.3	35.4
80	43.7	42.8	41.8	40.9	40.0	39.0	38.1	37.2	36.3	35.4
81	43.7	42.8	41.8	40.9	39.9	39.0	38.1	37.2	36.2	35.3
82	43.7	42.8	41.8	40.9	39.9	39.0	38.1	37.1	36.2	35.3
83	43.7	42.8	41.8	40.9	39.9	39.0	38.0	37.1	36.2	35.3
84	43.7	42.7	41.8	40.8	39.9	39.0	38.0	37.1	36.2	35.3
85	43.7	42.7	41.8	40.8	39.9	38.9	38.0	37.1	36.2	35.2
86	43.7	42.7	41.8	40.8	39.9	38.9	38.0	37.1	36.1	35.2
87	43.7	42.7	41.8	40.8	39.9	38.9	38.0	37.0	36.1	35.2
88	43.7	42.7	41.8	40.8	39.9	38.9	38.0	37.0	36.1	35.2
89	43.7	42.7	41.7	40.8	39.8	38.9	38.0	37.0	36.1	35.2

Effect of Multiple Qualified Plans or IRAs

As discussed, upon reaching age 72, taxpayers are required to begin taking minimum distributions. However, it is important to understand that a minimum distribution must be taken from each qualified plan in which the taxpayer has an account balance. Therefore, if the taxpayer had three qualified plans resulting from previous jobs, then three minimum distributions would have to be taken.

Many taxpayers have multiple IRAs; however, taxpayers are permitted to combine the value of all of their IRAs in determining the required minimum distribution. In addition, the amount distributed for purposes of complying with the minimum distribution rules can be taken from one IRA or multiple IRAs depending on the wishes of the taxpayer.[69] Inherited IRAs, however, require a separate distribution from each inherited IRA.

Qualified Longevity Annuity Contract

With the increased popularity of defined contribution plans, one problem many retirees will face is the possibility of outliving their money, known as superannuation. This risk can potentially be managed by using a lump-sum of money to purchase a deferred annuity earmarked to be annuitized when the retiree reaches a certain age, such as 80 or 85. This strategy for ensuring that the retiree does not outlive his or her income becomes problematic, however, when the majority of retirement savings is inside a qualified defined contribution plan because qualified retirement plans have required minimum distributions (RMDs) beginning at age 72. The requirement to start withdrawals at age 72 eliminates the ability to wait until a later age to annuitize the deferred annuity.

Fortunately, the Treasury issued Regulation 1.401(a)(9)-6 allowing the purchase of longevity annuities inside qualified defined contribution plans (including 401(k), 403(b), and 457(b) plans) and IRAs. The regulations define a qualified longevity annuity contract (QLAC), which is excluded from consideration when calculating the minimum distributions. A QLAC is an annuity contract (that is not a variable annuity, equity-indexed contract, or similar contract) that is purchased from an insurance company for an employee which states that it is intended to be a QLAC and that satisfies each of the several requirements.

Distributions from the annuity must begin no later than the specified annuity starting date nor after the owner turns age 85. Premiums for the QLAC cannot exceed the lesser of $$135,000 (2021) (as adjusted for inflation) or 25 percent of the employee's account balance under the plan. The 25 percent limit is separately determined for each plan in which the employee participates. For IRAs (as opposed to qualified defined contribution plans), the amount of premiums paid for the QLAC may not exceed the lesser of $135,000 or 25 percent of the aggregate account balances as of December 31st of the year before the calendar year in which the QLAC premium is paid.

Contracts are permitted to offer a return of premium (ROP) feature both before and after the annuity start date such that a lump-sum death benefit may be paid to a beneficiary to the extent that the premium payments made with respect to the QLAC exceed the payments made to the employee. When a QLAC is providing a life annuity to a surviving spouse, it may also provide a similar ROP benefit after the death of both the employee and the spouse. When a beneficiary receives payment from the QLAC it will follow the same tax and distribution rules as other qualified plan inheritances.

---

69. Treas. Reg. §1.408-8, Q-9.

Variable and indexed annuities are not permitted to be QLACs. In addition, QLACs are not permitted to offer a cash surrender value. If the QLAC satisfies these rules (and others), the value of the contracts is not considered for purposes of minimum distributions.

Example 7.43

Assume the same facts as **Example 7.37**, but that Eddie's account balance at December 31, 2020 was $400,000, of which $100,000 was invested in a QLAC. Eddie's minimum distribution for 2021 is calculated as:

$$\frac{\$300,000}{25.6} = \$11,718.75$$

This is significantly less than the $15,625 minimum distribution without the QLAC, and the QLAC will provide Eddie with at least a guaranteed minimum amount of income for the rest of his life, no matter how long he lives.

Minimum Distributions for Beneficiaries

Minimum distributions are still required to be taken even after a participant dies. In some cases, an important distinction is made depending on whether the participant died before or after beginning minimum distributions. In either case, in the year of the participant's death, the RMD is calculated as if the participant has not died.

Note that the beneficiary of a qualified plan may withdraw all of the assets of the qualified plan after the death of the participant with no penalty. Recall that the 10 percent early withdrawal penalty does not apply to distributions taken after death. The RMD rules only apply when the beneficiary wants to delay withdrawing the assets of the qualified plan.

The SECURE Act of 2019 changed the rules for beneficiary required minimum distributions, effective for deaths occurring after December 31, 2019. We will begin with a review of the post-death RMD rules for participants who died before January 1, 2020, then will discuss the rules applicable to beneficiaries where the participant died after December 31, 2019.

Death Before January 1, 2020: Death after Beginning of Minimum Distributions
If the participant dies before January 1, 2020 and after beginning to take minimum distributions, then the calculation of subsequent minimum distributions uses the designated beneficiary's single life expectancy factor as determined on the last day of the year following the year of the participant's death. This life expectancy factor is reduced by one in each succeeding year to determine the required distribution amount.

Qualified plans may disregard any beneficiary eliminated by an effective disclaimer or distribution of the benefit during the period between the participant's death and September 30 of the following year.[70] If there is more than one designated beneficiary, the beneficiary with the shortest life expectancy (usually the oldest beneficiary) is used as the measuring life, but the plan may also be divided into a separate account for each beneficiary to utilize the life expectancy of each beneficiary for the calculation of the required minimum distribution.[71]

If a trust is named as the beneficiary, the beneficiaries of the trust will be treated as the designated beneficiaries provided:
- the trust is valid under state law;
- the trust is irrevocable or will become so upon the participant's death (e.g., inter vivos trust);
- the trust beneficiaries are identifiable from the trust instrument; and
- appropriate documentation has been provided to the plan administrator.

Spouse Beneficiary (Death Before January 1, 2020/After RBD)
If the surviving spouse is a beneficiary of the plan, then the surviving spouse can receive distributions over his remaining single-life expectancy (see **Exhibit 7.30**), recalculated each year based on the single life expectancy table. Distributions must begin, however, in the year following the year of the participant's death.

Alternatively, if the surviving spouse is the sole beneficiary, the surviving spouse may rollover the plan balance to her own account and wait until she attains age 70½ (or age 72 if age is 70½ attained after December 31, 2019) to begin taking minimum distributions utilizing the uniform life table for her own life expectancy at that point.

There are a number of reasons why a surviving spouse would choose to either leave the deceased spouse owner's account intact or, alternatively, roll the account over to the surviving spouse's name. If the account remains in the decedent's name, it will be retitled after death "Mr. John Doe Plan for the Benefit of Mrs. Jane Doe." If rolled over and put into spouse's name, the title of the account will be Mrs. Jane Doe, IRA. If placed in the surviving spouse's own name, then the surviving spouse can name the beneficiary. If left intact as a qualified plan, the ERISA protection remains. If rolled over to an IRA, ERISA protection is lost, but bankruptcy creditor protection is provided up to certain limits under the BAPCPA 2005.

In the case of a spouse who is much younger than the decedent owner, leaving the account intact if distributions have begun will assure continuing cash flows. If a surviving spouse needs the money, this approach would provide penalty-free funds because the surviving spouse would otherwise have to wait until retirement to collect the funds (penalty-free) if the assets are rolled over into the surviving spouse's name. Keep in mind that the spouse is not limited to taking just the minimum distributions. Alternatively, if the surviving spouse is older than the owner, leaving the account intact will allow the surviving spouse to stretch out the distributions. In the case of a surviving spouse who is younger than the decedent and does not need the cash flow, rolling the account over to the surviving spouse's name allows for continual deferral and the designation of a new beneficiary; thus, creating the opportunity to stretch out the minimum distributions far into the future.

---

70. Treas. Reg. §1.401(a)(9)-84, A-4.
71. See Treas. Reg. §1.401(a)(9)-8 for more information on establishing separate accounts.

Example 7.44

Louise, age 72, had been taking minimum distributions from her qualified plan for the past two years. Louise died in 2018, and the sole beneficiary of her qualified plan was her husband, Harry, age 68. The RMD for the year of Louise's death is calculated based on the uniform life table and Louise's age at the end of the year. After that RMD is taken, Harry could choose to either roll Louise's qualified plan balance into an IRA for himself and wait until he is 72 to begin taking the required minimum distributions, or Harry could begin taking minimum distributions based on his life expectancy as calculated by the single life expectancy table in the year after Louise's death.

Assuming the following account balances and information:

Date	Account Balance	Louise's Age	Harry's Age
12/31 of Year 1 (Before Death)	$400,000	72	68
12/31 of Year 2 (Death)	$425,000	Year of Death	69
12/31 of Year 3 (After Death)	$490,000	-	70

The RMD for Year 2, the year in which Louise died, is based on Louise's life expectancy utilizing the uniform life table for that year and the account balance at the end of the previous year as follows:

$$\frac{\$400,000}{24.7 \text{ (at age 73)}} = \$16,194.33$$

For Year 3, Harry could roll the remaining plan balance to an IRA for himself, take a full taxable distribution of the account balance, or, alternatively, he may begin taking RMDs over his life expectancy as determined by the single life expectancy table as follows:

$$\frac{\$425,000}{17.0 \text{ (at age 70)}} = \$25,000.00$$

For Year 4, Harry's RMD would be calculated using the recalculated single life expectancy as follows:

$$\frac{\$490,000}{16.3 \text{ (at age 71)}} = \$30,061.35$$

Nonspouse Beneficiary (Death Before January 1, 2020/After RBD)

If the beneficiary is someone other than the participant's surviving spouse, then the distribution period is the remaining single, non-recalculated life expectancy of the designated beneficiary. If the beneficiary is significantly younger than the decedent, the minimum distribution rules permit the beneficiary to "stretch out" the distributions taken. If more than one nonspouse beneficiary exists, the shortest life expectancy of the beneficiaries is used. As always in the year of the participant's death, the RMD is calculated based on the participant's life expectancy (Uniform Lifetime table). Subsequently, however, the life expectancy for the nonspouse beneficiary is calculated using the age of the designated beneficiary in the year following the year of the participant's death (Single Life Expectancy for Beneficiaries table **Exhibit 7.30**). In subsequent years, the beneficiary's life expectancy is not recalculated. Instead, the life expectancy factor for the first year is reduced by one for each subsequent year.

As with the Uniform Lifetime Table, the Single Life Expectancy table has been updated for distribution years after 2021 (**Exhibit 7.30**). A special transition rule applies for beneficiaries who began distributions under the old table prior to 2022. In this case, the beneficiary's life expectancy will be reset in 2022 by referencing the life expectancy in the updated tables for the age of the beneficiary in the year distributions first began and subtracting one for each subsequent year.

Exhibit 7.30 | Single Life Table - Before 2022 vs. After 2021

Age	RMD Factor After 2021	RMD Factor Before 2022	RMD as % of Account Balance After 2021	RMD % of Account Balance Before 2022	Age	RMD Factor After 2021	RMD Factor Before 2022	RMD as % of Account Balance After 2021	RMD % of Account Balance Before 2022
0	84.6	82.4	1.18%	1.21%	61	26.2	24.4	3.82%	4.10%
1	83.7	81.6	1.19%	1.23%	62	25.4	23.5	3.94%	4.26%
2	82.8	80.6	1.21%	1.24%	63	24.5	22.7	4.08%	4.41%
3	81.8	79.7	1.22%	1.25%	64	23.7	21.8	4.22%	4.59%
4	80.8	78.7	1.24%	1.27%	65	22.9	21.0	4.37%	4.76%
5	79.8	77.7	1.25%	1.29%	66	22.0	20.2	4.55%	4.95%
6	78.8	76.7	1.27%	1.30%	67	21.2	19.4	4.72%	5.15%
7	77.9	75.8	1.28%	1.32%	68	20.4	18.6	4.90%	5.38%
8	76.9	74.8	1.30%	1.34%	69	19.6	17.8	5.10%	5.62%
9	75.9	73.8	1.32%	1.36%	70	18.8	17.0	5.32%	5.88%
10	74.9	72.8	1.34%	1.37%	71	18.0	16.3	5.56%	6.13%
11	73.9	71.8	1.35%	1.39%	72	17.2	15.5	5.81%	6.45%
12	72.9	70.8	1.37%	1.41%	73	16.4	14.8	6.10%	6.76%
13	71.9	69.9	1.39%	1.43%	74	15.6	14.1	6.41%	7.09%
14	70.9	68.9	1.41%	1.45%	75	14.8	13.4	6.76%	7.46%
15	69.9	67.9	1.43%	1.47%	76	14.1	12.7	7.09%	7.87%
16	69.0	66.9	1.45%	1.49%	77	13.3	12.1	7.52%	8.26%
17	68.0	66.0	1.47%	1.52%	78	12.6	11.4	7.94%	8.77%
18	67.0	65.0	1.49%	1.54%	79	11.9	10.8	8.40%	9.26%
19	66.0	64.0	1.52%	1.56%	80	11.2	10.2	8.93%	9.80%
20	65.0	63.0	1.54%	1.59%	81	10.5	9.7	9.52%	10.31%
21	64.1	62.1	1.56%	1.61%	82	9.9	9.1	10.10%	10.99%
22	63.1	61.1	1.58%	1.64%	83	9.3	8.6	10.75%	11.63%
23	62.1	60.1	1.61%	1.66%	84	8.7	8.1	11.49%	12.35%
24	61.1	59.1	1.64%	1.69%	85	8.1	7.6	12.35%	13.16%
25	60.2	58.2	1.66%	1.72%	86	7.6	7.1	13.16%	14.08%
26	59.2	57.2	1.69%	1.75%	87	7.1	6.7	14.08%	14.93%
27	58.2	56.2	1.72%	1.78%	88	6.6	6.3	15.15%	15.87%
28	57.3	55.3	1.75%	1.81%	89	6.1	5.9	16.39%	16.95%
29	56.3	54.3	1.78%	1.84%	90	5.7	5.5	17.54%	18.18%
30	55.3	53.3	1.81%	1.88%	91	5.3	5.2	18.87%	19.23%
31	54.4	52.4	1.84%	1.91%	92	4.9	4.9	20.41%	20.41%
32	53.4	51.4	1.87%	1.95%	93	4.6	4.6	21.74%	21.74%
33	52.5	50.4	1.90%	1.98%	94	4.3	4.3	23.26%	23.26%
34	51.5	49.4	1.94%	2.02%	95	4.0	4.1	25.00%	24.39%
35	50.5	48.5	1.98%	2.06%	96	3.7	3.8	27.03%	26.32%
36	49.6	47.5	2.02%	2.11%	97	3.4	3.6	29.41%	27.78%
37	48.6	46.5	2.06%	2.15%	98	3.2	3.4	31.25%	29.41%
38	47.7	45.6	2.10%	2.19%	99	3.0	3.1	33.33%	32.26%
39	46.7	44.6	2.14%	2.24%	100	2.8	2.9	35.71%	34.48%
40	45.7	43.6	2.19%	2.29%	101	2.6	2.7	38.46%	37.04%
41	44.8	42.7	2.23%	2.34%	102	2.5	2.5	40.00%	40.00%
42	43.8	41.7	2.28%	2.40%	103	2.3	2.3	43.48%	43.48%
43	42.9	40.7	2.33%	2.46%	104	2.2	2.1	45.45%	47.62%
44	41.9	39.8	2.39%	2.51%	105	2.1	1.9	47.62%	52.63%
45	41.0	38.8	2.44%	2.58%	106	2.1	1.7	47.62%	58.82%
46	40.0	37.9	2.50%	2.64%	107	2.1	1.5	47.62%	66.67%
47	39.0	37.0	2.56%	2.70%	108	2.0	1.4	50.00%	71.43%
48	38.1	36.0	2.62%	2.78%	109	2.0	1.2	50.00%	83.33%
49	37.1	35.1	2.70%	2.85%	110	2.0	1.1	50.00%	90.91%
50	36.2	34.2	2.76%	2.92%	111	2.0	1.0	50.00%	100.00%
51	35.3	33.3	2.83%	3.00%	112	2.0	1.0	50.00%	100.00%
52	34.3	32.3	2.92%	3.10%	113	1.9	1.0	52.63%	100.00%
53	33.4	31.4	2.99%	3.18%	114	1.9	1.0	52.63%	100.00%
54	32.5	30.5	3.08%	3.28%	115	1.8	1.0	55.56%	100.00%
55	31.6	29.6	3.16%	3.38%	116	1.8	1.0	55.56%	100.00%
56	30.6	28.7	3.27%	3.48%	117	1.6	1.0	62.50%	100.00%
57	29.8	27.9	3.36%	3.58%	118	1.4	1.0	71.43%	100.00%
58	28.9	27.0	3.46%	3.70%	119	1.1	1.0	90.91%	100.00%
59	28.0	26.1	3.57%	3.83%	120+	1.0	1.0	100.00%	100.00%
60	27.1	25.2	3.69%	3.97%					

Example 7.45

Chery dies in August 2019 at the age of 73 (her 74th birthday would have been December 1, 2019). The beneficiary of her qualified plan is her daughter, Elizabeth, who was 42 when Cheryl died (Elizabeth's birthday is September 3). Assuming the facts below, calculate the RMD for 2019, 2020, and 2021.

Date	Account Balance	Cheryl's Age	Elizabeth's Age
12/31/2018	$100,000	73	42
12/31/2019	$95,000	-	43
12/31/2020	$87,000	-	44

For 2019, the RMD is calculated utilizing the uniform life table life expectancy based on the age Cheryl would have been at 12/31/2019 and the account balance at 12/31/2018.

$$\frac{\$100,000}{23.8 \text{ (at age 74)}} = \$4,201.68$$

For 2020, the RMD is calculated based on Elizabeth's life expectancy utilizing the single life expectancy table for Elizabeth's age at 12/31/2020 and the plan account balance at 12/31/2019.

$$\frac{\$95,000}{39.8 \text{ (at age 44)}} = \$2,386.93$$

For 2021, the RMD is calculated utilizing the account balance at 12/31/2020 and Elizabeth's life expectancy as calculated in the prior year reduced by one.

$$\frac{\$87,000}{39.8 - 1 \text{ (at age 45)}} = \$2,242.27$$

The RMD calculations for all subsequent years would continue to reduce Elizabeth's life expectancy calculated in 2020 by one for each year after 2020. The life expectancy would normally not be recalculated; however, due to the update of the life expectancy table beginning in 2022, the life expectancy must be reset in 2022. Elizabeth's age as of 12/31/2020 (her first distribution year, the year following the year of Cheryl's death) was 44. The corresponding life expectancy under the new tables, as seen in **Exhibit 7.30**, is 41.9. The updated life expectancy is then reduced by one for each year following the first distribution year. Since 2022 is two years later, the factor used for the 2022 calculation will be 39.9 (41.9 - 1 -1 = 39.9). Assuming the account balance as of December 31, 2021 is $90,000, the 2022 minimum distribution is:

$$\frac{\$90,000}{41.9 - 2 \text{ (at age 46)}} = \$2,255.64$$

In this example, Elizabeth can withdraw all of the account balance after Cheryl's death as a lump-sum or in payments larger than the RMD, but in no case would Elizabeth be able to withdraw less than the RMD in any year.

Under the Pension Protection Act of 2006, the benefits of a nonspouse beneficiary may be transferred directly into an IRA. The IRA is treated as an inherited IRA of the nonspouse beneficiary. Thus, distributions from the inherited IRA are subject to the normal distribution rules applicable to beneficiaries. This provision applies to amounts payable to a beneficiary under a qualified retirement plan, 457 plan, or tax-sheltered annuity and is effective for tax years after 2006.

No Beneficiary (Death Before January 1, 2020/After RBD)

If no beneficiary has been named by September 30 of the year following the owner's death (or the beneficiary is the decedent's estate or a charity), then distributions must continue over the remaining life expectancy of the deceased owner. The remaining life expectancy is reduced by one each year and is reset in 2022 based on the updated single life expectancy tables, as illustrated in **Example 7.45**.

Example 7.46

Robin began taking the RMD from her profit sharing plan in 2017. In 2019, Robin died after suffering a heart attack. She had not named a beneficiary of her profit sharing plan at the time of her death. Robin's estate may choose to take a full distribution of Robin's profit sharing plan account balance or, alternatively, may choose to defer distributions from the plan to the RMD. In the year of Robin's death, the RMD would be calculated as if Robin had not died. In the year after Robin's death, the RMD would be calculated based on the account balance at the end of the prior year, and Robin's life expectancy is calculated in the year of her death from the single life table reduced by one. In 2022 the life expectancy factor will reset based on the updated life expectancy table, as illustrated in **Example 7.45**.

Death Before January 1, 2020: Death Before Required Beginning Date

If death occurred before January 1, 2020 and the participant died before the required beginning date (before minimum distributions have begun), then the minimum distribution rules will depend on the designated beneficiary.

Spouse Beneficiary (Death Before January 1, 2020/Before RBD)

If the surviving spouse is the beneficiary of the plan, the surviving spouse can receive distributions over his remaining single-life expectancy, recalculated each year under the **single life expectancy table**.[72] Distributions must begin in the year in which the owner would have attained age 70½ (72 if age 70½ is attained after December 31, 2019). Alternatively, if the surviving spouse is the sole beneficiary, the surviving spouse can roll the plan balance over and wait until he attains age 70½ (72 if age 70½ is attained after December 31, 2019) to begin taking minimum distributions. The surviving spouse can also elect to distribute the entire account balance within five years after the year of the owner's death.

---

72. IRC §401(a)(9)(B)(iv)(II) and Treas. Reg. §1.401(a)(9)-5 Q&A-5(c)(1) and (2).

Example 7.47

Ross died at the age of 37 in 2019. His wife, Rachel, was the sole beneficiary of his profit sharing plan. Since Ross had not begun taking RMDs before his death, Rachel has four options in relation to Ross's profit sharing plan.

1. Rachel may withdraw Ross's entire account balance immediately.
2. Rachel may choose to leave the assets in the plan, but she must take a distribution of the account balance before the end of the fifth year after Ross's death.
3. Rachel may choose to roll the account balance to an IRA for her benefit. In this case, the RMD would begin when Rachel attained the age of 70½ (or 72 if Rachel turned age 70½ after December 31, 2019) and would be based on Rachel's life expectancy as determined by the uniform life expectancy table. In addition, she could not take a distribution until age 59½ without having the 10 percent early withdrawal penalty apply.
4. Rachel may elect to take distributions from the plan based on her recalculated life expectancy (single life expectancy table) each year. Rachel may choose to begin the distribution immediately or wait until Ross would have been 70½ (72 if age 70½ is attained after December 31, 2019).

Nonspouse Beneficiary (Death Before January 1, 2020/Before RBD)

If the beneficiary is someone other than the surviving spouse, then the beneficiary has two options. The first distribution period option is the remaining single, non-recalculated life expectancy of the designated beneficiary. Life expectancy is calculated using the age of the designated beneficiary in the year following the year of the employee's death, reduced by one for each subsequent year. For this option to apply, distributions must begin by December 31 of the year following the year of death. If the beneficiary has chosen the lifetime distribution option, the special transition rule between the pre-2022 single life expectancy and the post-2021 single life expectancy applies in the same manner as applies for deaths after the RBD. In 2022 the beneficiary's life expectancy will be reset by referencing the life expectancy in the updated tables for the age of the beneficiary in the year distributions first began (the year following the year of death) and subtracting one for each year after.

Alternatively, the beneficiary can elect to distribute the entire account balance within five years after the year of the owner's death. In this case, the beneficiary may choose to leave assets in the account and not take distributions from the plan until the fifth year after the participant's death. In the fifth year, however, the beneficiary must take a distribution of the entire account balance. The beneficiary cannot start taking distributions over their life expectancies at that time. The 5-year rule allows the beneficiary to forgo taking distributions for the four years after the death of the participants; whereas, in all other cases, the beneficiary must take at least the annual minimum distributions calculated based on his non-recalculated single life expectancy.

No Beneficiary (Death Before January 1, 2020/Before RBD)

If no beneficiary has been named by September 30 of the year following the owner's death (or the beneficiary is the decedent's estate or charity), the account must be fully distributed before the end of the fifth year following the year of death. The account balance may be distributed anytime before the end of the fifth year but may never extend beyond.

Multiple Beneficiaries (Death Before January 1, 2020)

Determining who is to receive assets upon one's death is a very personal decision. Often, individuals will select multiple beneficiaries as the primary beneficiaries for retirement accounts. However, selecting multiple beneficiaries can adversely impact minimum distributions for one or more of the beneficiaries once the owner dies.

If there are multiple beneficiaries on an IRA, they must each take minimum distributions from the account based on the life expectancy of the oldest beneficiary. While this rule does not adversely impact the oldest beneficiary's minimum distribution, it does impact the younger beneficiary or beneficiaries. They will have to take out larger distributions than if they used their respective life expectancies.

The solution to this issue is to have separate IRAs for each beneficiary. This separation can be accomplished prior to death or after death, at which point the inherited IRA could be separated so that each beneficiary has his or her own account. Once the accounts are separate, each beneficiary will take minimum distributions based on their respective single life expectancies. If the account is not separated prior to death, then the separate accounts must be established on a date no later than the last day of the year following the calendar year of the employee's death.[73]

Example 7.48

Billie, who died prior to January 1, 2020, named her brother Cisco (age 70), her son Wally (age 39), and her daughter Iris (age 30) as equal beneficiaries of her Roth IRA. Upon her death, each of the three beneficiaries would have to take minimum distributions based on Cisco's single life expectancy. However, if, before the end of the year following Billie's death, the Roth IRA account was separated into three accounts, then the beneficiaries would take minimum distributions based their respective single life expectancies.

---

73. Treas. Reg. §1.409(a)(9)-8.

Exhibit 7.31 | Death of Participant Occurs Prior to January 1, 2020 Summary

	Options After Minimum Distributions Begin*
Spouse Beneficiary	1. Spouse can receive distributions over the surviving spouse's remaining single life expectancy as <u>recalculated</u> using the single life table. 2. Rollover plan balance to an IRA in surviving spouse's name and delay distributions until spouse is 70½ (72 if age 70½ is attained after December 31, 2019).
Nonspouse Beneficiary	1. Distribution period is the longer of the remaining single life expectancy (not recalculated) of the designated beneficiary (reduced by one year) or the remaining life expectancy of the participant. 2. Rollover plan balance to an IRA in the name of the deceased IRA owner for the benefit of the beneficiary and distribute over the longer of the remaining single life expectancy of the beneficiary or the remaining life expectancy of the participant (not recalculated).
No Beneficiary	1. Distributions must continue over the remaining life expectancy of the deceased owner (single life table). The decedent's remaining distribution period is reduced by one each year.
	Options Before Minimum Distributions Begin*
Spouse Beneficiary	1. Distribution over surviving spouse's remaining single life expectancy as <u>recalculated</u> using single life expectancy table beginning when the participant would have turned 70½ (72 if age 70½ is attained after December 31, 2019). 2. Distribute participant's account within 5 years. 3. Roll plan assets to an IRA in surviving spouse's name and wait until surviving spouse is 70½ (or 72 if surviving spouse attains age 70½ after December 31, 2019) to begin RMD.
Nonspouse Beneficiary	1. Distribute participant's account within five years. 2. Remaining single life expectancy (not recalculated) of designated beneficiary (reduced by one each year). 3. Roll plan assets to an IRA in the name of the deceased IRA owner for the benefit of the beneficiary and then distribute within five years or over the remaining single life expectancy of the beneficiary (not recalculated). (PPA 2006)
No Beneficiary	1. Distribute participant's account within five years.

* In all cases, the beneficiary can take more than the minimum distribution.

Death After December 31, 2019[74]

If the participant dies after December 31, 2019, the SECURE Act limits the ability to stretch distributions over the beneficiary's lifetime to only certain eligible beneficiaries. When death occurs after December 31, 2019, designated beneficiary distribution options are no longer dependent upon whether the participant died before or after the required beginning date (RBD). If required minimum distributions had already begun prior to death, as applicable for deaths prior to January 1, 2020, the RMD for the year of death is calculated based on the uniform lifetime table and the deceased participant's age as of December 31 of the year of death and must be distributed if not yet distributed prior to death. Beneficiary distribution options depend on whether the beneficiary is an eligible designated beneficiary, an ineligible designated beneficiary, or there is a no designated beneficiary (the beneficiary is an estate, a charity, or a non-eligible trust).

74.These new rules apply to government plans (as defined in §414(d)) for deaths occurring after December 31, 2021 (rather than December 31, 2019).

Ineligible Designated Beneficiary (Death After December 31, 2019)

The SECURE Act generally requires that a designated beneficiary receive a full distribution of the inherited account no later than December 31 of the year containing the 10th anniversary of the death of the participant.

Example 7.49

Jeremiah died on February 1, 2021, at the age of 57. He left his entire qualified plan balance to his 28-year-old daughter, Latisha. Since Latisha is not an eligible beneficiary (as described below), she must distribute the entire account balance by December 31 of the year containing the 10th anniversary of Jeremiah's death. Latisha may choose to take distributions of any amount, or $0, each year during the first nine years, so long as the full account value is distributed by the end of the 10th year.

Had Jeremiah instead died prior to January 1, 2020, Latisha could have begun distributions in the year following the year of Jeremiah's death and spread them over her life expectancy of 54.3 years. She would have been required to receive a minimum distribution each year, but could also elect to receive higher distributions in some years. (Note that if Jeremiah's death was prior to January 1, 2020, Latisha's life expectancy would have initially been calculated using the single life table for distribution years prior to 2022, and then reset based on the updated tables beginning in 2022, as described previously in **Example 7.45**.

As illustrated by the example above, the new post-death RMD rules imposed by the SECURE Act drastically limit the ability of ineligible beneficiaries to stretch distributions over a long period of time to maintain tax deferred growth and allow the beneficiary flexibility in controlling the taxation of distributions. For deaths prior to January 1, 2020 the RMD over lifetime created a minimum distribution each year, potentially spread over a large number of years, but the beneficiary could choose to take higher distributions in years where she was in a lower tax bracket. For deaths after December 31, 2019 an ineligible beneficiary has limited flexibility in the timing of distributions.

Eligible Designated Beneficiary (Death After December 31, 2019)

If the designated beneficiary is one of the four types of eligible designated beneficiaries, then distributions to the beneficiary may be made over the lifetime of the beneficiary. The four categories of eligible beneficiaries are outlined in **Exhibit 7.32**.

Exhibit 7.32 | Eligible Designated Beneficiaries

Eligible Designated Beneficiaries
1. The surviving spouse of the deceased participant
2. A minor child of the deceased participant
3. An individual who is disabled[1,3] or chronically ill[2,3]
4. An individual who is not more than 10 years younger than the deceased participant

1. As defined in §72(m)(7).
2. As defined in §7702B(c)(2).
3. Must obtain certification that the period of inability is indefinite and reasonably expected to be lengthy in nature.

While an eligible designated beneficiary is permitted to receive minimum distributions based on her life expectancy (using the single life table and the beneficiary's age in the year following the year of death), upon the death of that beneficiary any remaining balance must be distributed within 10 years of the death of that beneficiary. If the original account owner died before January 1, 2020 and the beneficiary began taking distributions over her lifetime and that beneficiary dies after December 31, 2020, the subsequent beneficiary must distribute within 10 years of the death of the original beneficiary. The pre-SECURE Act distribution rules that would have allowed the subsequent beneficiary to continue distributions on the same schedule as the original beneficiary will no longer apply.

Example 7.50

Elvis died on January 15, 2021, leaving his 401(k) to his sister Petunia, who is six years younger than Elvis. Since Petunia was an eligible designated beneficiary, she chose to receive minimum distributions over her lifetime of 30.6 years (based on the single life expectancy table and her age on December 31, 2022, and reducing by one each year). If Petunia dies 3 years later, leaving the remaining balance to her daughter Lily, Lily is not required to continue receiving distributions each year, but the entire value must be distributed to her no later than December 31 of the year containing the 10th anniversary of Petunia's death.

Had Elvis instead died in December 2015, under the old rules Petunia, as a designated beneficiary, would have been able to stretch the distributions over her lifetime (reducing by one each year). If Petunia then died in 2019, Lily would have been able to continue the distribution schedule based on the remainder of Petunia's life (reducing by one each year). However, if Petunia dies after December 31, 2019, Lily must take a full distribution of the remainder of the account by December 31 of the year containing the 10th anniversary of Petunia's death.

If the eligible beneficiary is the surviving spouse and the participant dies before the required beginning date, the surviving spouse may delay distributions until the deceased participant would have attained age 72, and then receive distributions based on the surviving spouse's recalculated life expectancy. If the surviving spouse dies before distributions begin, the surviving spouse will be treated as if she were the employee (owner), allowing an eligible designated beneficiary of the surviving spouse to stretch distributions over his lifetime. A surviving spouse may also, as was the case for deaths prior to January 1, 2020, roll the qualified plan or IRA to her own IRA. Eligible designated beneficiaries other than the surviving spouse must begin distributions by December 31 of the year following the year of death.

Example 7.51

When George died in 2021 at the age of 55 he left his IRA to his wife, Elaine, age 58. Elaine is an eligible designated beneficiary, so she will be permitted to stretch RMDs over her lifetime, and as a surviving spouse can delay distributions until the year George would have turned age 72. Elaine subsequently names her best friend, Jerry, age 49, as her beneficiary. If Elaine dies prior to beginning distributions (in the year George would have turned age 72), Jerry can receive RMDs over his lifetime. Jerry is an eligible designated beneficiary because Elaine is treated as the employee (owner) and Jerry is less than ten years younger than Elaine.

If the eligible designated beneficiary is the minor child of the deceased participant, the child may initially receive distributions over her life expectancy, however, upon reaching the age of majority the child will cease to be an eligible beneficiary and any remaining portion of that child's interest must be distributed within 10 years of reaching the age of majority. Note also that a minor child is an eligible designated beneficiary, but a minor grandchild is not.

Example 7.52

Rakesh died on September 3, 2021 and left his entire 401(k) balance to his daughter Aiesha, age 5. Since Aiesha is an eligible designated beneficiary her required minimum distribution will be calculated based on a life expectancy of 78.8 years (based on her age of 6 in the year following the year of death and the single life table for distribution years after 2021). When Aiesha reaches the age of majority, however, the lifetime-based minimum distributions cease and the full account balance must be distributed within 10 years of reaching the age of majority.

To qualify as a disabled eligible beneficiary, the beneficiary must be unable to engage in any substantial gainful activity by reason of a medically determinable physical or mental impairment which can be expected to result in death or to be of long-continued and indefinite duration. Certification of the existence of the disability may be required by the Secretary.[75]

To qualify as a chronically ill eligible beneficiary, a licensed healthcare practitioner must certify that the beneficiary is unable to perform (without substantial assistance from another individual) at least two activities of daily living for an indefinite period of time which is expected to be lengthy in nature.[76]

The SECURE Act also created a special rule for trusts established for disabled or chronically ill individuals under which the disabled or chronically ill beneficiaries may be treated as eligible beneficiaries, allowing distributions to be spread over the beneficiary's lifetime. For this rule to apply, the terms of an applicable multi-beneficiary trust1 must include one of the following:[77]

1. the trust must be divided immediately upon the death of the employee into separate individual trusts, or
2. no individual other than an eligible disabled or chronically ill beneficiary has any right to an interest in the trust until the death of all disabled or chronically ill beneficiaries.

Example 7.53

Gigi dies in March 2021, leaving her profit sharing plan to a trust. Her two children, Alex and Rebecca (who is permanently disabled) are the beneficiaries of the trust. The trust is a special needs trust, solely for the benefit of Rebecca while she is alive, with Alex as the remainder beneficiary upon Rebecca's death. Since the trust is an applicable multi-beneficiary trust meeting the requirements of §409(a)(9)(H)(iv), the required minimum distributions for Rebecca are calculated based on her life expectancy and any remaining balance attributable to the qualified plan must be distributed to Alex within 10 years of Rebecca's death.

---

75. IRC §72(m)(7)
76. IRC §7202B(c)(2) and §409(a)(9)(E)(ii)(IV), as amended by the SECURE Act.
77. An applicable multi-beneficiary trust is one in which all beneficiaries are designated beneficiaries and at least one beneficiary is an eligible disabled or chronically ill beneficiary.

No Designated Beneficiary (Death After December 31, 2019)

If there is no designated beneficiary, the RMD rules are the same as they were prior to the SECURE Act.

If the participant dies before the required beginning date and no beneficiary has been named by September 30 of the year following the owner's death (or the beneficiary is the decedent's estate or charity), the account must be fully distributed before the end of the fifth year following the year of death. The account balance may be distributed anytime before the end of the fifth year but may never extend beyond.

If the participant dies after the required beginning date and no beneficiary has been named by September 30 of the year following the owner's death (or the beneficiary is the decedent's estate or a charity), then distributions must continue over the remaining life expectancy of the deceased owner. The remaining distribution period is reduced by one each year.

Exhibit 7.33 | Post-Death RMD Chart

Participant/IRA Owner Death After December 31, 2019 (Regardless of Age)		
Beneficiary	**Required Distribution**	**Additional Rules**
Ineligible Designated Beneficiary	Distribute within 10 years of death of the participant.	
Eligible Designated Beneficiaries (4):	General Rule: Distribute over life expectancy (LE) of eligible beneficiary (beginning in the year following the year of death).	Account balance must be distributed within 10 years of the death of the eligible beneficiary.
1. Surviving Spouse	General rule above/Recalculate each year.[1,2]	If death is before RBD, spouse can delay distribution until deceased participant would have been age 72.
2. Minor Child	General rule above/Use LE in year following year of death and reduce by one each year.[2]	Account balance must be distributed within 10 years of reaching age of majority.
3. Disabled or Chronically Ill	General rule above/Use LE in year following year of death and reduce by one each year.[2]	
4. Individual Not More Than 10 Years Younger Than Deceased Participant/IRA Owner	General rule above/Use LE in year following year of death and reduce by one each year.[2]	
Participant/IRA Owner Death Before or After December 31, 2019 (No Change Made by SECURE Act of 2019)		
Beneficiary	**Required Distribution - Participant Dies BEFORE RBD**	**Required Distribution - Participant Dies AFTER RBD**
No Designated Beneficiary	Distribute within five years of date of death	Distribute based on deceased owner's life expectancy in year of death (reduce by one)[2]

1. A surviving spouse may also choose to roll to her own IRA, as was the case for deaths prior to January 1, 2020.
2. In 2022, life expectancy is reset by determining the life expectancy under the tables for distribution years after 2021, based on the age of beneficiary in their first distribution year and then subtracting one for each succeeding year.

STRETCH IRAS

Stretch IRAs have been a topic in estate and financial planning for years, if not decades. The concept of a stretch IRA is to minimize distributions from the IRA so that tax deferred assets can grow as much as possible unimpaired from income tax. This minimization strategy occurs not only during the life of the owner (or participant), but also during the life of the beneficiary. For the taxpayer attempting to "stretch out" an IRA for the longest period of time, it is important to select the most appropriate beneficiary.

As discussed in this chapter, taxpayers are required to take distributions from their retirement accounts after age 70½ (or 72 if age 70½ is reached after December 31, 2019) and beneficiaries are required to take distributions from inherited IRAs. Each time a distribution is taken from a traditional IRA, it is subject to ordinary income tax. Distributions from a Roth IRA or Roth Account are not subject to income tax, but the earnings on the funds distributed from the Roth IRA or Account may be taxable. These required distributions reduce the value of the IRA over time. Thus, the objective of "stretching" is to reduce these distributions as much as possible.

For deaths prior to January 1, 2020, accomplishing the objective of reducing required distributions after the death of the participant was best achieved by choosing a very young beneficiary. Beneficiaries taking minimum distributions use the single life expectancy table. Consider the required distribution from an inherited IRA for a 45 year-old compared to a 10 year-old, based on the life expectancy tables for distribution years prior to 2022. The life expectancy factor for a 45 year-old is 38.8, which results in a required distribution of 2.57 percent of the account value. The life expectancy factor for a 10 year-old is 72.8, which results in a required distribution of 1.37 percent of the account value. While the difference between the two distributions does not seem significant, it makes a significant difference, especially over time. For example, after ten years, the life expectancy factor (without consideration of the reset in 2022) for the now 55 year-old is 28.8, which results in a required distribution of 3.47 percent of the account value. The life expectancy factor for the now 20 year-old is 62.8, which results in a required distribution of 1.59 percent of the account value.

Example 7.54

This example compares the balances of an inherited IRA valued at $100,000 left to a 45 year old and one that is left to a 10 year old assuming death occurred prior to 2020 and, for simplicity, assuming no reset based on the updated life expectancy tables in 2022. Minimum distributions will be taken at the end of each year based on the required distribution. These distributions will be reduced by a tax rate of 30 percent and will accumulate in a taxable account. Both the IRA and the taxable account will earn a rate of return of nine percent on account balances, but the earnings within the taxable account are subject to a 30 percent income tax rate. The following table depicts the account value after 15, 25, and 35 years:

Year	45 Year-Old			10 Year-Old		
	Traditional IRA Balance	Value of Distributions in a Taxable Account	Total Value of IRA & Taxable Account	Traditional IRA Balance	Value of Distributions in a Taxable Account	Total Value of IRA & Taxable Account
0	$100,000	$0	$100,000	$100,000	$0	$100,000
15	$232,776	$77,762	$310,538	$294,799	$41,050	$335,850
30	$341,289	$494,440	$835,728	$815,294	$255,467	$1,070,760
45	-	$1,916,849	$1,916,849	$1,999,839	$1,212,313	$3,212,152
60	-	$4,792,774	$4,792,774	$3,581,575	$5,222,862	$8,804,437

The value of the two accounts for the 10 year-old beneficiary is significantly greater than the value of the accounts for the 45 year-old.[78] This increased value illustrates the value of "stretching" the IRA. The two graphs illustrate the account balances in the IRAs. Notice that, since the 45 year-old had a life expectancy of 38.8 years upon inheriting the IRA, the IRA balance is reduced to zero after 38 years while the IRA balance for the 10 year-old is still growing exponentially on a tax deferred basis.

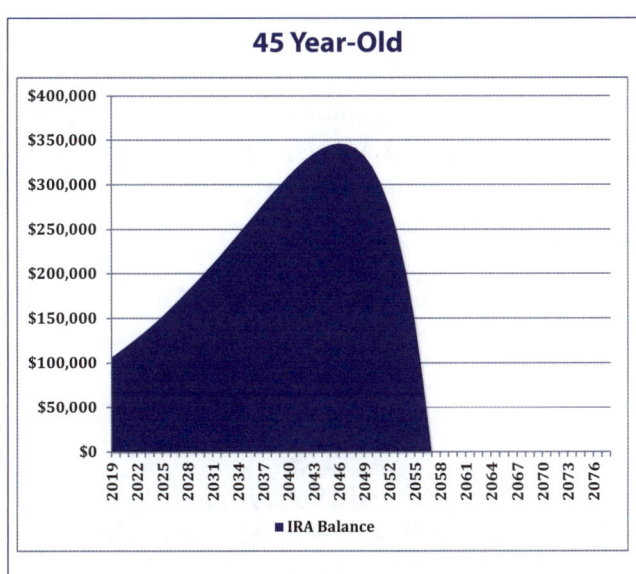

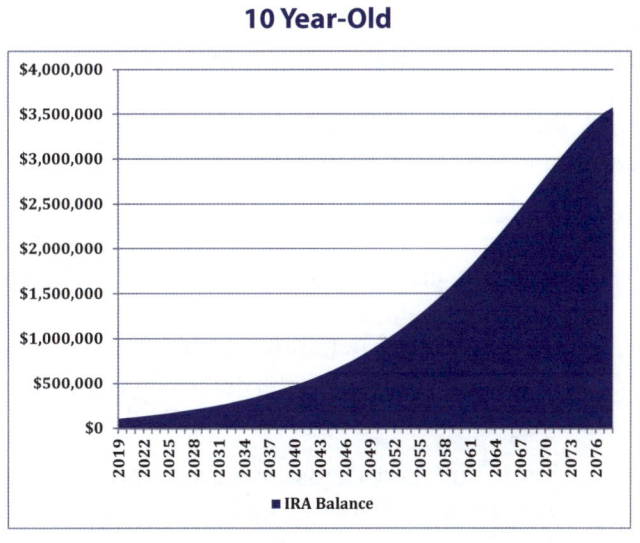

---

78. The IRA account assets are pre-tax. However, even adjusting for the tax owed on these funds, the value of the accounts for the 10 year-old are significantly higher.

The table below uses the same assumptions as above, except that it assumes that the accounts are Roth IRAs, which reduces income taxes paid by the beneficiaries and results in larger account balances.

Year	45 Year-Old			10 Year-Old		
	Roth IRA Balance	Value of Distributions in a Taxable Account	Total Value of IRA & Taxable Account	Roth IRA Balance	Value of Distributions in a Taxable Account	Total Value of IRA & Taxable Account
0	$100,000	$0	$100,000	$100,000	$0	$100,000
15	$232,776	$111,089	$343,865	$294,799	$58,643	$353,442
30	$341,289	$706,342	$1,047,631	$815,294	$364,952	$1,180,246
45	-	$2,738,356	$2,738,356	$1,999,839	$1,731,876	$3,731,715
60	-	$6,846,820	$6,846,820	$3,581,575	$7,461,232	$11,042,806

The table depicting the account values with the Roth IRA helps to explain the value of converting today a traditional IRA to a Roth IRA. This benefit holds even when the income tax that would have been used to pay the tax on the conversion is incorporated into the comparison.

Example 7.54 illustrates the power of stretching an IRA and why it has been a topic with planners for years. The SECURE Act change to a distribution period of 10 years for ineligible beneficiaries severely limits the ability to stretch and will require more careful planning and analysis than was previously required when selecting beneficiaries if the goal is to stretch over the longest period of time possible.

Example 7.55

Phylicia, age 60 has three loved ones she would like to consider as beneficiaries for her qualified plan:
1. Cliff, her spouse, age 62
2. Theo, her son, age 28, and
3. Denise, her sister, age 58.

Both Cliff and Denise would name Phylicia's son, Theo, as the beneficiary upon their subsequent death. Assuming that Phylicia has other assets which will be used to provide for the loved ones who are not selected as the beneficiary of the qualified plan, which beneficiary would allow for the longest period over which minimum distributions must be paid?

Assume Phylicia's death will occur after 2021; therefore, the life expectancy tables for distribution years after 2021 will be used. If she names Cliff, he can delay distributions for 12 years, until Phylicia would have reached age 72. At that time Cliff will be age 74 and can spread distributions over his life expectancy of 15.6 years (if he lives beyond 15.6 years, the account will not have been depleted due to the recalculation of life expectancy each year). If we assume Cliff will live to age 89, the total distribution period is 27 years. However, if Cliff were to die just five years after Phylicia, he is treated as the employee.

His beneficiary is Theo, who is not an eligible beneficiary, so the full balance must be distributed within 10 years of Cliff's death, for a total stretch of only 15 years. Alternatively, Cliff can roll the balance to his own IRA and begin distributions after 10 years when he is age 72. At age 72 his distribution period based on the Uniform Lifetime Table is 27.4 years, but is recalculated each year. If he lives beyond 27.4 years, the account will not be fully depleted due to the recalculation each year. However, as with the first option, if Cliff were to die just five years after Phylicia, Theo must receive a full distribution within 10 years, creating only a 15 year distribution period.

If Phylicia names Theo as her beneficiary, the distribution period will be just 10 years since Theo is not an eligible beneficiary.

Since Denise is not more than 10 years younger than Phylicia, if Phylicia names Denise as her beneficiary, Denise can stretch distributions over her life expectancy of 28 years. If Denise dies prior to receiving a full distribution, the remaining balance must be paid to Theo within 10 years of Denise's death.

If Cliff and Denise both live to their full life expectancy and Cliff elects to delay until Phylicia would have been age 72, the distribution period is nearly the same (27 years versus 28 years). If Cliff elects to roll to his own IRA, the distribution period could potentially be longer. Their current health and family history of longevity may become a deciding factor in this case since death prior to life expectancy could result in a much shorter distribution period in both cases.

However, in reality, beneficiaries often distribute and spend money far faster than owners intended. In addition, stretching is not always the highest priority for account owners.

In reality, only about 20.5 percent of beneficiaries are expected to take only the required minimum distribution in the year 2021, presumably due to the need for the additional funds to provide support during their lifetime.[79] However, for the 20.5 percent who wish to take the least amount possible, careful planning can yield much greater family wealth over time.

Participants with high value qualified plans or IRAs who have both charitable intent and a goal of stretching distributions over the life of an ineligible beneficiary may find the use of a charitable remainder trust to be an attractive strategy to accomplish these goals in light of the new RMD rules. This strategy would allow distributions, and the taxation of them, to be distributed over the life expectancy of the noncharitable beneficiary's lifetime with the remainder going to a charity of the participant-grantor's choice.[80]

In light of the shortened distribution period, but flexibility in timing distributions during the 10 years following death, if ineligible beneficiaries are likely to be in their peak earning years in the 10 years after inheriting an IRA or qualified plan, it may make sense for the participant to gradually convert from pre-tax to Roth during their lifetime if they are in lower tax bracket than the beneficiary is likely to be in the 10 years following the death of the participant. While beneficiaries of Roth IRAs and Roth accounts must

79. Preamble to Proposed Regulations 132210-18
80. A detailed discussion of charitable remainder trusts is beyond the scope of this textbook, but is covered in detail in Money Education's Estate Planning textbook.

follow the RMD rules upon the death of the participant, if the 5-year holding period has been met the distributions will be tax-free to the beneficiary. Since distributions will not be required until the 10th year, even if the participant has not met the 5-year period, the beneficiary could simply delay distributions until the full 5 years has been met, thus ensuring tax-free distributions.

PLANNING FOR QUALIFIED PLANS AND IRA BENEFICIARIES

Creditor Protection

One of the benefits of qualified plans and IRAs is that the funds are protected from creditors. It is important to keep in mind that no one anticipates having creditor problems, so pro-actively accumulating wealth in these vehicles is wise. Remember that the U.S. Bankruptcy code, as a result of the Bankruptcy Abuse Prevention and Consumer Protection Act, provides for the following exemptions related to retirement plans:

1. All ERISA type retirement plans and rollovers from them to IRAs are exempt for an unlimited amount (so long as regular IRA contributions are not commingled with the rollover).
2. SEP and SIMPLE IRAs are exempt up to an unlimited amount.
3. Traditional and Roth IRAs are exempt up to $1,000,000, which is adjusted for inflation every three years ($1,362,800 as of 2019).

Note that while rollovers from qualified plans to IRAs retain unlimited bankruptcy protection, they do not retain the ERISA protection from other types of judgments. IRA protection from other types of judgments is determined by state law and varies widely from state-to-state.

IRAs and qualified plans are beneficial in terms of deferring taxation and planning is often done to "stretch" these accounts far into the future to the next generation. The question arises as to how an inherited IRA is treated in terms of creditor protection.

The issue of inherited IRAs being part of bankrupt estates is becoming more prevalent since there are more assets in IRAs today and bankruptcy filings have become commonplace. Several court cases over a period of years had ruled on this issue inconsistently.

While the trend in the court cases appeared to be heading toward affording creditor protection for inherited IRAs under the federal bankruptcy laws, the question has been answered by the U.S. Supreme Court in the Clark v. Rameker case in 2014.

In Clark *v.* Rameker, the Supreme Court ruled that the funds in an inherited IRA are not protected from creditors and that the funds are part of the bankruptcy estate assets. The court stated that the Bankruptcy Code makes clear that funds held in inherited IRAs are not "retirement funds" within the meaning of Section 522(b)(3)(C)'s bankruptcy exemption. The court went on to say in the opinion that there are three legal characteristics of inherited IRAs that lead to the conclusion that funds held in such accounts are not objectively set aside for the purpose of retirement.

- First, the holder of an inherited IRA may never invest additional money in the account. 26 U. S. C. Section 219(d)(4). Inherited IRAs are thus unlike traditional and Roth IRAs, both of which are quintessential "retirement funds." For where inherited IRAs categorically prohibit contributions, the entire purpose of traditional and Roth IRAs is to provide tax incentives for account holders to contribute regularly and over time to their retirement savings.

- Second, holders of inherited IRAs are required to withdraw money from such accounts, no matter how many years they may be from retirement. Under the Tax Code, the beneficiary of an inherited IRA must either withdrawal of the funds in the IRA within five years after the year of the owner's death or take minimum annual distributions every year. That the tax rules governing inherited IRAs routinely lead to their diminution over time, regardless of their holders' proximity to retirement, is hardly a feature one would expect of an account set aside for retirement.

- Finally, the holder of an inherited IRA may withdraw the entire balance of the account at any time—and for any purpose—without penalty. Whereas a withdrawal from a traditional or Roth IRA prior to the age of 59½ triggers a 10 percent tax penalty subject to narrow exceptions—a rule that encourages individuals to leave such funds untouched until retirement age—there is no similar limit on the holder of an inherited IRA. Funds held in inherited IRAs accordingly constitute "a pot of money that can be freely used for current consumption," not funds objectively set aside for one's retirement.

The court went on to say the following:

- As a general matter, those provisions [in the bankruptcy code] effectuate a careful balance between the interests of creditors and debtors. On the one hand, we have noted that "every asset the Code permits a debtor to withdraw from the estate is an asset that is not available to creditors." On the other hand, exemptions serve the important purpose of "protect[ing] the debtor's essential needs."

- Allowing debtors to protect funds held in traditional and Roth IRAs comports with this purpose by helping to ensure that debtors will be able to meet their basic needs during their retirement years. At the same time, the legal limitations on traditional and Roth IRAs ensure that debtors who hold such accounts (but who have not yet reached retirement age) do not enjoy a cash windfall by virtue of the exemption - such debtors are instead required to wait until age 59½ before they may withdraw the funds penalty-free.

- The same cannot be said of an inherited IRA. For if an individual is allowed to exempt an inherited IRA from her bankruptcy estate, nothing about the inherited IRA's legal characteristics would prevent (or even discourage) the individual from using the entire balance of the account on a vacation home or sports car immediately after her bankruptcy proceedings are complete. Allowing that kind of exemption would convert the Bankruptcy Code's purposes of preserving debtors' ability to meet their basic needs and ensuring that they have a "fresh start," *Rousey*, 544 U. S., at 325, into a "free pass." We decline to read the retirement funds provision in that manner.

> ## ✏️ Quick Quiz 7.6
>
> 1. Stretch IRAs are available for all designated beneficiaries.
>   a. True
>   b. False
>
> 2. For deaths prior to January 1, 2020, stretch IRAs were best accomplished by choosing young beneficiaries.
>   a. True
>   b. False
>
> 3. Leaving an IRA to a spouse could be a better way to stretch an IRA than leaving it to a child.
>   a. True
>   b. False
>
> 4. The eligible beneficiaries of an inherited IRA will use the life expectancy of the youngest beneficiary on the account.
>   a. True
>   b. False
>
> False, True, True, False.

With this ruling, the Court has resolved the conflict between the Seventh Circuit's ruling and the Fifth Circuit's decision in Chilton. Inherited IRAs are NOT protected under 11 U. S. C. Section 522(b)(3)(C). However, debtors may find protection under state bankruptcy statutes. For example, Texas enacted SB 181061 in 2011, which affords the same level of creditor protection to inherited IRAs as to traditional IRAs.

Controlling and Protecting Inherited IRAs

In 2020, assets in individual retirement accounts (IRAs) exceeded $12.2 trillion and was the largest component of the more than 34 trillion in retirement assets in the United States.[81] For many Americans, IRAs are a significantly large portion of their net worth. In some cases, IRAs may contain substantial balances and should be part of an overall financial and estate plan.

> ### ⁝☰ *Key Concepts*
>
> 1. Describe the risks of an inherited custodial IRA.
>
> 2. Explain the advantages of a trusteed IRA and a See-Through trust.

There are two significant risks that are associated with inherited IRAs. These risks include the depletion of the IRA assets by the beneficiary and the creditor risk associated with inherited IRAs.

As discussed above, one of the benefits of an IRA is the ability to stretch out the distributions over the life of two individuals (the owner and the beneficiary, if the beneficiary is an eligible designated beneficiary). This stretching of the IRA allows for larger tax-deferred growth. However, beneficiaries of IRAs have full control over the IRA assets and can take out more than the required minimum distributions or even liquidate the IRA. Taking larger than required distributions is very common and is often in conflict with the wishes of the IRA owner, who is now deceased. There is no mechanism to prevent a beneficiary from simply taking the money out of a traditional custodial inherited IRA.

The second risk applies to non-spousal IRAs who have immediate or potential creditor problems and was discussed above. For deaths prior to January 1, 2020 there are two possible solutions to the above risks: the trusteed IRA and the "See Through" Trust as a beneficiary to the IRA.

To understand how to resolve the above issues, it is important to realize how IRAs are set up. IRAs may be structured as a custodial IRA (under IRC Section 408(h)) or as a trusteed IRA (under IRC Section 408(a)). Custodial IRAs, which are most common today, can be set up with a see-through trust as a beneficiary. This type of arrangement creates a trust between the IRA and the beneficiary and resolves both of the above issues. The other alternative is to create a Trusteed IRA, which is effectively an IRA within a trust. Both of these alternatives may resolve the two risks discussed above.

Trusteed IRAs

Trusteed IRAs, which can be either traditional or Roth IRAs, are trusts established within the United States. They are IRAs and trusts, and therefore, have the same advantages of IRAs, including creditor protection and tax deferral while the owner is alive, and the same advantages of trusts. The structure of the trust allows for the unique advantage of being able to control the distributions from the IRA after the owner dies, which provides creditor protection and reduces the likelihood of the assets being prematurely consumed (when death of the participant occurred prior to January 1, 2020 and the designated trust beneficiary's lifetime could be used to determine the amount of the RMD).

---

81. ICI.org (as of 12/31/2020).

When established, trusteed IRAs are structured to make pre-defined payments to beneficiaries. These amounts might be limited to:

1. The required minimum distribution,
2. The required minimum distribution plus additional amounts under an ascertainable standard for the benefit of the beneficiaries (generally for health, education, maintenance, or support), or
3. The greater of income or the required minimum distribution.

In addition to controlling the distributions to beneficiaries, a trusteed IRA can be set up to control who receives the funds after the death of the primary beneficiary. Typically, the beneficiary of an inherited custodial IRA will choose the person to receive the assets after he or she dies.

Trusteed IRAs are established with an institutional trustee who will generally manage the trust and often the assets of the IRA. Trusteed IRAs are more expensive than custodial assets, but less expensive than a See-Through trust. There is often a 100 to 150 basis point fee as well as an asset minimum (generally $500,000 to $1 million).

For participant deaths occurring after December 31, 2019, the trusteed IRA could be problematic for ineligible beneficiaries in that limiting distributions with reference to the RMD as described above could result in no distributions for the first nine years, and a very large distribution in the 10th year, since for ineligible beneficiaries there is no distribution required until the 10th year following the death of the participant. The problem could potentially be solved by creating trust terms that allow for distributions during the first nine years, however, the end result is still a shortened distribution period versus under prior law and once the distribution is made in the 10th year there is no mechanism to protect the assets from the beneficiary's creditors or from a beneficiary's spendthrift tendencies. While the trusteed IRA may still be beneficial for eligible designated beneficiaries, it could backfire if the beneficiary later becomes ineligible, such as when a minor child reaches age of majority or a disabled beneficiary no longer meets the definition of disabled, triggering full distribution within 10 years.

"See-Through" Trust

Owners of IRAs can name a see-through trust as a beneficiary. A see-through trust is a stand-alone trust used as a beneficiary of a retirement (IRA) account. The IRS has four minimum distribution trust rules that must be followed in naming a trust as the beneficiary of an IRA.

- The trust must be valid under state law.
- The trust is irrevocable or will by its terms, become irrevocable upon the death of the IRA owner.
- The beneficiaries of the trust are identifiable.
- A copy of the trust documents must be provided to the IRA custodian by October 31 of the year immediately following the year in which the IRA owner died.

A see-through trust allows the custodian to determine the required minimum distribution (RMDs) by looking through the trust to the life expectancies of the trust beneficiaries. The trust can have the strongest spendthrift provisions permitted by law. The trustee can be empowered to direct the custodian's investments and direct the custodian to distribute more but not less than the RMDs at the trustee's discretion.

> **📝 Quick Quiz 7.7**
>
> 1. Inherited IRAs are protected in bankruptcy because they are IRAs.
>   a. True
>   b. False
>
> 2. Trusteed IRAs allow IRA owners to control how distributions from the IRA will be paid out and to whom the assets will pass to after the death of the primary beneficiary.
>   a. True
>   b. False
>
> 3. See-through trusts are the same as trusteed IRAs.
>   a. True
>   b. False
>
> False, True, False.

Exhibit 7.34 | See-Through Trust

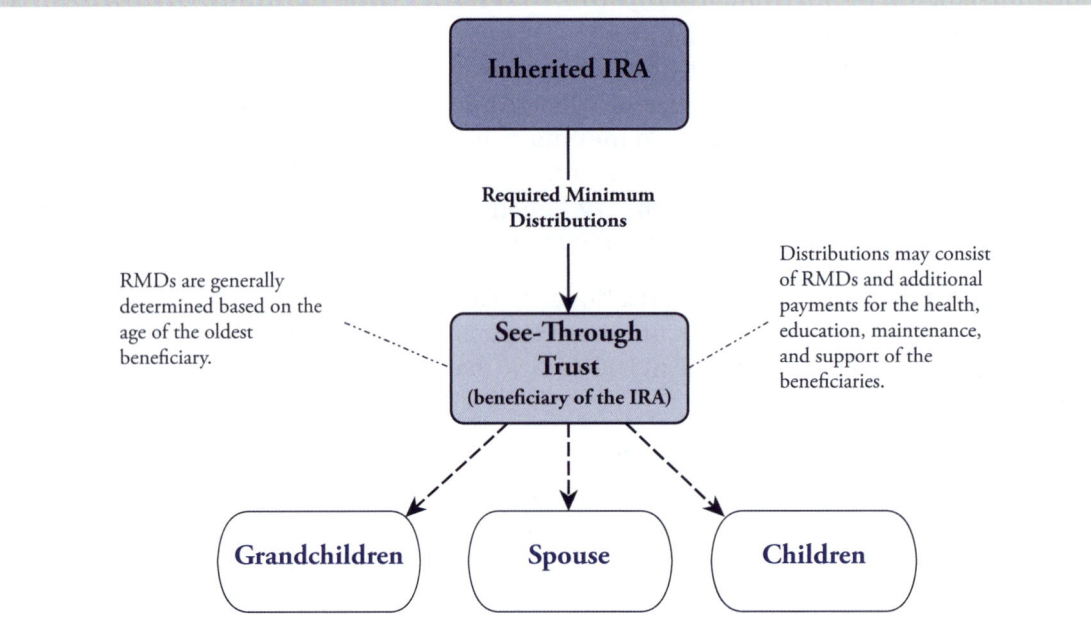

The see-through trust can be either a conduit trust (distribution by custodian is exactly distributed by trustee to beneficiary) or an accumulation trust. The accumulation trust is much more complex and requires specialized tax knowledge to properly draft. The accumulation trust is especially useful if the IRA is a Roth IRA and deferral and growth are objectives as well as creditor protection. An accumulation trust can also be used as a special needs trust. However, it is important to keep in mind that the tax brackets for trusts are massively compressed with income above $13,050 taxed at 37 percent.

As with the trusteed IRA, potential problems arise under the new RMD rules for deaths after December 31, 2019 when the beneficiary is an ineligible beneficiary or when a previously eligible beneficiary loses that status and must then receive a full distribution within 10 years. Roth conversions by the participant during lifetime can mitigate the unfavorable tax consequences, but a conduit see-through trust would still have the problem of distributing assets after ten years, making them susceptible to the beneficiary's creditors or spendthrift tendencies. A properly drafted accumulation trust as beneficiary of a Roth IRA may still be a viable solution for overcoming these problems.

Life Insurance Trusts

For deaths occurring after December 31, 2019, the use of life insurance trusts may become more favorable for passing wealth to ineligible beneficiaries while retaining control over distributions and providing creditor protection. As discussed in Chapter 4, qualified plans are permitted to invest in an incidental amount of life insurance and these policies may be distributed (subject to taxation) to the participant upon retirement and placed into a life insurance trust. In addition, the required minimum distributions, or higher amounts if the participant is in a low tax bracket and wishes to leverage the distributions from the IRA or qualified plan, can be used to pay premiums on a life insurance policy owned by or payable to a trust upon the death of the participant. The life insurance death benefit will be paid to the trust free of income tax, free of estate tax if properly drafted, and the trust terms will determine how and when distributions are to be made as well as provide for protection from the creditors of the beneficiary.[82]

DISCUSSION QUESTIONS

SOLUTIONS to the discussion questions can be found exclusively within the chapter. Once you have completed an initial reading of the chapter, go back and highlight the answers to these questions.

1. Describe the distribution options for pension plans.

2. Describe the distribution options for profit sharing plans.

3. Describe rollovers and when and how they are used.

4. Discuss the circumstances that will result in a qualified retirement plan participant having adjusted basis in plan assets.

5. List the three special options available for lump-sum distributions from a qualified plan.

6. Describe qualified plan loans and their limitations.

7. How are Qualified Domestic Relations Orders (QDRO) treated with regard to qualified retirement plans?

8. Discuss the penalty for distributions from a qualified plan before age 59½.

9. Explain when minimum distributions must begin.

---

82. A full discussion of life insurance trusts is beyond the scope of this textbook, but are discussed in detail in Money Education's Estate Planning textbook.

MULTIPLE CHOICE PROBLEMS

A sample of multiple choice problems is provided below. Additional multiple choice problems are available at money-education.com by accessing the Student Practice Portal.

1. Which of the following distributions from a qualified plan would not be subject to the 10 percent early withdrawal penalty, assuming the participant has not attained age 59½?
    1. A distribution made to a spouse under a Qualified Domestic Relations Order (QDRO).
    2. A distribution from a qualified plan used to pay the private health insurance premiums of a current employee of Clinical Trials Company.
    3. A distribution to pay for costs of higher education.
    4. A distribution made immediately after separation from service at age 57.
        a. 1 and 2.
        b. 1 and 3.
        c. 1 and 4.
        d. 2 and 3.

2. Viola, who is 75 years old, requested from the IRS a waiver of the 60-day rollover requirement. She indicated that she provided written instructions to her financial advisor that she wanted to take a distribution from her IRA and roll it over into a new IRA. Her financial advisor inadvertently moved the funds into a taxable account. Viola did not make the request of the IRS until five years after the mistake was made. Will the IRS permit the waiver?
    a. No. The IRS never waives this requirement, except under the most extreme of circumstances.
    b. Yes. The mistake was the fault of the financial advisor and the IRS regularly grants waivers in these circumstances.
    c. No. Viola waited beyond the one-year period for filing such a request.
    d. No. Viola waited an unreasonable amount of time before filing the request.

3. Owen turned 72 on November 1 of 2021 and must receive a minimum distribution from his qualified plan. The account balance had a value of $409,216 at the end of 2020. The distribution period for a 72 year old is 25.6, and for a 73 year old it is 24.7 under the Uniform Lifetime Table effective for distribution years prior to 2022. The distribution period for a 72 year old is 27.4, and for a 73 year old it is 26.5 under the Uniform Lifetime Table effective for distribution years after 2021. If Owen takes a $15,000 distribution on April 1, 2022, what is the amount of the minimum distribution tax penalty associated with his first year's distribution?
    a. $0.
    b. $230.
    c. $492.
    d. $985.

4. Laura, age 43, has several retirement accounts and wants to know what accounts can be rolled over to other accounts. Which of the following statements regarding rollovers is not correct?
   a. She could take a distribution from her SEP IRA and roll it over to a qualified plan without incurring a 20% withholding.
   b. She could rollover her government 457(b) plan to her new employer's qualified plan.
   c. She could rollover the funds from her old employer's qualified plan to her new employer, who sponsors a 401(k) plan with a Roth account, and be able convert the funds in an in-plan Roth rollover.
   d. She could rollover her traditional IRA to her designated Roth account in her 403(b) plan.

5. In May 2021, Seth converts $100,000 in his traditional IRA to a Roth IRA. The value of the assets in the Roth IRA drops by 40 percent due to a significant decline in the stock market that occurs in October 2021. The Roth conversion results in Seth incurring $100,000 of taxable income, when he could have waited and converted only $60,000 (after the 40 percent drop). Which of the following statements is correct?
   a. Seth cannot recharacterize the conversion.
   b. Seth can recharacterize as long as it is done within six months from the date of the conversion.
   c. Seth can recharacterize after December 31, 2021.
   d. Seth can recharacterize at any time before the due date of his tax return, including extensions.

> **Additional multiple choice problems
> are available at
> money-education.com
> by accessing the
> Student Practice Portal.
> Access requires registration of the title using
> the unique code at the front of the book.**

Quick Quiz 7.1

1. False. Pension plans typically distribute retirement benefits through an annuity payable for the remainder of the participant's life. The plan may provide for a lump-sum distribution option.
2. True.
3. True.

Quick Quiz 7.2

1. False. Neither direct nor indirect rollovers may consist of any distribution from a qualified plan that is one of a series of substantially equal periodic payments. In addition, distributions on account of a required minimum distribution and hardship withdrawals may not be rolled over into another qualified plan or IRA.
2. False. Distributions from qualified plans are generally taxed as ordinary income, but when a distribution is considered a lump-sum distribution, the distribution may qualify for 10-year forward averaging, pre-1974 capital gain treatment, or Net Unrealized Appreciation (NUA).
3. False. A distribution pursuant to a QDRO that is not deposited into an IRA or other qualified plan will be subjected to tax at ordinary income rates on the distribution.

Quick Quiz 7.3

1. False. If the vested accrued benefit is less than or equal to $20,000, then a loan is permitted up to the lesser of $10,000 or the vested accrued benefit. Therefore, if an individual had an account balance of $17,000 with a vested accrued benefit of $15,000, he would be eligible for a loan of $10,000, which is greater than 50 percent of the account balance.
2. False. Although loans from qualified plans must generally be repaid within five years, the five-year repayment rule does not apply to loans that are used for the purchase of a principal residence.
3. False. Most plan documents require that loans be repaid upon termination of employment; however, this is not a requirement under the law. Any portion of a loan that is not repaid will be treated as a taxable distribution.
4. True.

Quick Quiz 7.4

1. True.
2. False. The 10 percent penalty exception applies if the participant separates from service after age 55. There is no exception for situations where the participant separates from service before age 55, but waits until age 55 to receive distributions.

Quick Quiz 7.5

1. False. The first minimum distribution must be made by April 1 of the year after the year in which the participant attains the age of 72 unless the participant is still employed by the plan sponsor and is not a greater than five percent owner, in which case the first minimum distribution must be taken by April 1 of the year after the participant terminates service with the plan sponsor.
2. True.
3. True.

QUICK QUIZ EXPLANATIONS

Quick Quiz 7.6

1. False. For deaths prior to January 1, 2020, all designated beneficiaries had the option to stretch distributions over their lifetime. However, under the new rules established by the SECURE Act, when death occurs after December 31, 2019, only certain eligible designated beneficiaries are permitted to stretch distributions over their lifetime.
2. True.
3. True.
4. False. The beneficiaries must use the life expectancy of the oldest not youngest beneficiary.

Quick Quiz 7.7

1. False. The Supreme Court ruled in Clark v. Ramaker that inherited IRAs are not retirement plans and therefore, are subject to claims of creditors in bankruptcy.
2. True.
3. False. A see-through trust is a beneficiary of a custodial IRA, whereas a trusteed IRA is the IRA itself, as well as being a trust.

8

INSTALLATION, ADMINISTRATION, AND TERMINATION OF QUALIFIED PLANS

LEARNING OBJECTIVES

1. Use the plan selection process to identify the best plans for a business to adopt.*
2. Understand the requirements for establishing a qualified plan.*
3. Describe the documents that must be provided to employees and other interested parties related to qualified plans.*
4. Compare the investment options available to a plan sponsor.*
5. Determine the requirements for a self-employed plan participant.*
6. Discuss prohibited transactions and the penalties for engaging in such a transaction.*
7. Understand the various Form 5500 filing requirements for qualified plans.*
8. Calculate the maximum contribution for a self-employed plan participant.*
9. Identify the types of qualified plan terminations.*
10. Determine the implications for assets reverting back to the plan sponsor upon plan termination.*

Ties to CFP Certification Learning Objectives

INTRODUCTION

In today's economic environment, retirement plans are an essential component of the overall compensation package of an employer and are designed to attract, retain, and reward talented employees. The selection of an appropriate qualified plan can be both time-consuming and expensive. Depending on the plan selected, numerous initial and continuing requirements must be met to ensure that the plan retains its qualified, and thus tax-advantaged, status. Once a plan is established, annual testing, yearly contributions, and yearly filings may also be required. Special rules also apply to plan amendments and terminations of qualified plans when needed. This chapter will discuss plan selection, installation, administration, and amending and terminating a qualified plan.

QUALIFIED PLAN SELECTION

Selecting a qualified plan begins with the consideration of a number of relevant issues including business, financial, and sometimes personal goals. Other issues that impact plan selection are the employee census, employee turnover, funding requirements, philosophy about employee savings, and the cost to adopt, implement, and maintain the plan. The retirement plan decision-makers in a small company are usually the owners, while executive management and human resources management usually make the decisions for a large company. Decision-makers are often assisted in plan selection by qualified plan experts who help the decision-makers consider the many factors at issue when selecting a plan. For large companies, the decisions are usually based on the business objectives of the company, but for small or closely held businesses, plan choice is often based on both the owner's business and personal objectives.

⦂≣ *Key Concepts*

1. What business and personal issues should be considered when making a qualified plan selection?

2. What is an employee census and why is it important?

3. What are the general characteristics of qualified plans?

Business Objectives

The first step in plan selection is to determine the business objectives for establishing a qualified plan. Although they can vary, the typical objectives of a large company include being competitive in the labor market by offering a qualified plan that fits within an overall compensation package. For a smaller company, the ability to assist the small business owner with tax-deferred savings is frequently a primary personal objective. Other common reasons companies establish qualified plans are to attract, reward, and retain employees, assist employees in saving for retirement, or simply to benefit the employees through the adoption of a tax-advantaged plan.

Exhibit 8.1 | Steps in Qualified Retirement Plan Selection

Concept Summary
1. Establish the objectives for the plan (Sample Objectives).
• To benefit owners of a small businesses
• To benefit all employees
• To benefit select employees
• To attract, retain, or reward employees
• To encourage early retirement
• To provide a tax-advantaged benefit
2. Prepare an employee census to identify the beneficiaries of various plans and the financial impact of alternative plans on the employer sponsor.
3. Identify the types of plans that can meet both the qualitative and quantitative objectives.
4. Assess each plan's financial characteristics:
• Contribution costs
• Costs of administration
• Flexibility of contributions
• Burden of investment risks
• Necessity of mandatory funding
5. Select plan.

Employee Census

An important first step to consider when selecting a qualified plan is to prepare an employee census. If the primary goal of having a plan is to simply provide a savings vehicle such as a 401(k) plan, the **employee census** may not be important. However, if the purpose of the plan is to benefit the small business owner, the employee census is essential. The census will identify each employee, their age, compensation, number of years of employment, and any ownership interest. Each element of the census is important to consider because plans can be structured to benefit highly compensated employees, nonhighly compensated employees, older or younger employees, employees who have a certain length of service, a group of employees, or some mix of these employees. The census helps to identify which employees will benefit (and to what extent) from using various possible types of plans. In addition to a current census, a review of employee turnover is essential to plan selection because such a review can help determine the appropriate vesting schedules and how to deal with forfeitures resulting from employee termination.

Example 8.1

Sample Employee Census				
Employee	Age	Compensation	Ownership Interest	Length of Service
Sylvester	30	$200,000	100%	10 Years
Adrian	35	$35,000	0	5 Years
Paulie	30	$30,000	0	1 Year
Mickey	30	$30,000	0	1 Year
Total		$295,000	100%	

Expected Turnover 0 for Sylvester and Adrian and by year 3 for Paulie and Mickey.

Consider the Sample Employee Census above. Suppose Sylvester (the owner) wanted to establish a plan to benefit all employees who would save for their own retirement. He should consider a 401(k) plan with an employer match of up to 3% of covered compensation. Sylvester could simply reduce future compensation raises by 3% and thus have a net zero cost of funding the plan. The 401(k) employer match is also discretionary, leaving the sponsor with cash flow flexibility.

Suppose an additional objective was to benefit only those who are employed by the company for at least three years. Because the plan utilizes an employer match, the longest cliff vesting schedules Sylvester could use is a 3-year cliff vesting schedule. This would still only require Sylvester to provide a vested match to those employees who remained employed for three years.

If Sylvester was much older than Adrian, Paulie, and Mickey, he might consider using an age-weighted profit sharing plan, so that most of the contributions and benefits would be contributed to the plan on his behalf.

An employee census is an essential tool in determining which employees will benefit and how much they will benefit using various plans. The employee census is then used to help select the best plan to accomplish the goals of the company and its owners.

Cash Flow Considerations

The decision maker should always consider the company's financial stability and the predictability of its cash flows prior to plan selection. The company's cash flows dictate how committed the company can be with regard to mandatory contributions, such as those required for pension plans. For example, if cash flows fluctuate widely from year to year, it is probably not prudent to adopt a pension plan because of the **mandatory funding requirement**. In the case of fluctuating cash flows, it is more prudent to select some type of qualified profit sharing plan because profit sharing plans have **discretionary contributions** each year. However, if cash flows are stable and predictable, then the company may want to consider either pension or profit sharing plans.

Administration Costs

When a company implements a qualified plan, there are numerous costs associated with adopting and administering the plan. Establishing a plan generally requires an advisor or retirement plan expert to assist the company in selecting and adopting the plan. In addition, once the plan has been adopted, the company must pay for the actual funding of the plan if the plan includes employer contributions. If the plan is large and has many participants, the sponsor may need to hire employees to administer the plan during the year and file the necessary compliance forms or outsource this function to an outside vendor such as a **third party administrator** (TPA).

A company's ability to afford such costs impacts the type of plan chosen. For example, profit sharing plans are often very easy to set up with many prototype plans available, have discretionary contributions and minimal annual testing; therefore, they are relatively inexpensive to establish and maintain. Adding a 401(k) feature (**CODA**) to a profit sharing plan increases the cost slightly because of the annual **ADP** and **ACP** testing (as discussed in Chapter 5) and the matching contributions. The testing and its associated cost could be avoided by adopting a safe harbor 401(k) plan, which does not require certain nondiscrimination tests (such as ADP and ACP testing) but does require either an employer match or employer nonelective contribution (discussed in Chapter 5).

> ### 📝 *Quick Quiz 8.1*
>
> 1. Plan selection should only focus on the needs of the company and should never focus on the needs of the small business owner as this would be a conflict of interest.
>   a. True
>   b. False
>
> 2. While an employee census is generally essential, it may not be critical if the only objective is to provide a savings vehicle.
>   a. True
>   b. False
>
> 3. An employer with fluctuating cash flows will generally choose a pension plan.
>   a. True
>   b. False
>
> False, True, False.

Stock bonus plans and ESOPs often require annual valuations of the stock of the business by a valuation expert, making the administration of this type of plan more expensive than a simple profit sharing plan. Defined benefit plans require PBGC insurance premiums, and actuaries are needed annually to determine plan contributions, making the defined benefit plan potentially the most expensive plan to adopt. Large companies may be able to absorb the substantial costs associated with a defined benefit plan, while small companies may be more sensitive to controlling plan costs. However, today there is a trend for large companies to convert defined benefit plans to cash balance pension plans in an attempt to reduce certain costs and for newer companies to avoid defined benefit plans altogether. This illustrates the need for consideration to be given to plan costs for adoption and administration during plan selection.

Exhibit 8.2 | Common Plan Administration Costs

- Consultation and plan set-up/implementation expenses
- Funding
- Recordkeeping
- Administration
- Nondiscrimination Testing
- Reporting/Disclosure to Participants (including statements and summary annual reports)
- IRS/Department of Labor Reporting (Form 5500)
- Fiduciary Duties (such as fulfilling ERISA §404(c) requirements with education programs and enrollment meetings)

Exhibit 8.3 | TPA or Bundled Providers' Functions

- Trustee Duties
- Recordkeeping
- Administration
- Investment Management
- Reporting and Disclosure

Owner's Business and Personal Objectives

If the company is a small or closely held company, then the owner's personal and business objectives are critical in plan selection. Small business owners typically want to reduce their current taxes and save for their own financial future. For example, key owners of small companies generally want a majority of plan benefits for themselves and less for the rank-and-file employees, especially those who do not stay with the employer for a long period. The owners may select a plan that will meet this need or use various techniques to modify the plan to primarily benefit owners and/or key employees. Since these are the decision-makers that advisors will be working with, it is important to understand and try to achieve their goals.

Exhibit 8.4 | Qualified Plan Summary of Characteristics

Qualified Plan	Who Generally Contributes	Mandatory Funding	Investment Risk	Company Stock %[1]	Permits Soc. Sec. Integration	Required Expert	Who is Generally Favored?[2]	QJSA / QOSA/ QPSA[3]
Pension Plans								
Defined Benefit Pension Plan	ER	Yes	ER	≤ 10%	Yes	Actuary and Pension Expert	Older Age Entrants	Yes
Cash Balance Pension Plan	ER	Yes	ER	≤ 10%	Yes	Actuary and Pension Expert	Younger Persons	Yes
Target Benefit Pension Plan	ER	Yes	EE	≤ 10%	Yes	Actuary once and Pension Expert	Older Age Entrants	Yes
Money Purchase Pension Plan	ER	Yes	EE	≤ 10%	Yes	None[4]	Younger Persons	Yes
Profit Sharing Plans								
Profit Sharing Plan	ER	No	EE	≤ 100%	Yes	None[4]	Highly Compensated and Younger Persons	No
Stock Bonus Plan	ER	No	EE	≤ 100%	Yes	Valuation Specialist and Pension Expert	Highly Compensated and Long Length of Service	No
ESOP	ER	No	EE	≤ 100%	No	Valuation Specialist and Pension Expert	Highly Compensated and Long Length of Service	No
401(k) Plan/ 401(k) Roth Account	EE and ER	No[5]	EE	≤ 100%	No[6]	Pension Expert	Savers and Younger Persons	No
Thrift Plan	EE	No	EE	≤ 100%	Yes	Pension Expert	Savers and Younger Persons	No
Age-Based Profit Sharing Plan	ER	No	EE	≤ 100%	Yes	Pension Expert	Older Highly Compensated	No
New Comparability Plan	ER	No	EE	≤ 100%	Yes	Pension Expert	Owners	No

EE = Employee, ER = Employer

1. Note that as a result of PPA 2006, certain defined contribution plans holding publicly traded employer securities are subject to new diversification requirements, which requires that employees be permitted to diversify 100% of their contributions and 100% of employer contributions after 3 years. See Chapter 3 for more detail.
2. Where younger persons are favored, it is because they benefit from a greater number of compounding periods. However, through cross-testing and other methods, most plans can be structured to benefit the owners and highly compensated employees.
3. Qualified Joint and Survivor Annuity/Qualified Optional Survivor Annuity/Qualified Pre-Survivor Annuity.
4. Many prototype plans are available.
5. 401(k) plans may have mandatory funding if there is a matching contribution for a safe harbor plan.
6. If a CODA feature is a part of the profit sharing plan then, the profit sharing plan can be integrated, but not the CODA portion.

Plan Selection Application

After evaluating each of the above issues, a financial advisor/pension expert can assist the owner or key decision maker in determining which plan suits the owner and the company's needs. **Exhibit 8.4** summarizes some of the important issues to consider in plan selection.

Example 8.2 through **Example 8.4** demonstrate the plan selection process.

Example 8.2

Assume Sylvester owns a small company with the following employee census information:

Employee Census				
Employee	**Age**	**Compensation**	**Ownership**	**Length of Service**
Sylvester	30	$200,000	100%	10 Years
Adrian	35	$35,000	0	5 Years
Paulie	30	$30,000	0	1 Year
Mickey	30	$30,000	0	1 Year
Total		**$295,000**	**100%**	

Assuming the company has sufficient cash flow to fund a plan, the most obvious plan recommendation would be a profit sharing plan. The plan could be integrated with Social Security, thus providing Sylvester an even greater share of the contributions than a non-integrated plan. A profit sharing plan would allow a contribution of up to 25% of covered compensation and would help maximize contributions to Sylvester.

The profit sharing plan could also include a CODA (401(k)) feature if Sylvester wanted the employees to contribute to the plan. The CODA feature would allow employees to make elective deferrals into the plan. The company could then match employee contributions to encourage employee participation.

Assume instead that Sylvester is 51 years old and wants to maximize contributions for his own benefit. Since, in this case, Sylvester is significantly older than the other employees, a defined benefit plan or age-weighted profit sharing plan may be more appropriate than a straight profit sharing plan or an integrated profit sharing plan. Either of these plans would allow for higher contributions on behalf of Sylvester because of his age. In choosing between a defined benefit and an age-weighted profit sharing plan, Sylvester is choosing between mandatory funding for the defined benefit plan and discretionary funding for the age-based plan. Also, the costs of maintaining the plans will be quite different because a defined benefit plan requires annual actuarial determinations and a profit sharing plan does not utilize actuaries. Sylvester will have to compare the advantages and disadvantages of each of the plans in making his decision.

Example 8.3

Tyson and Laila each own 50% of a small company with the following employee census.

Employee Census				
Employee	**Age**	**Compensation**	**Ownership**	**Length of Service**
Tyson	55	$300,000	50%	10 Years
Laila	30	$300,000	50%	10 Years
Manny	35	$30,000	0	1 Year
Miesha	30	$30,000	0	1 Year
Total		**$660,000**	**100%**	

The age difference between Tyson and Laila (owners) makes the plan selection slightly more challenging. An age-weighted plan would be beneficial for Tyson. However, because Laila is much younger than Tyson, such a plan would not equally benefit Laila. Assuming they both wanted to benefit equally and did not want to consider a defined benefit plan, a 401(k) plan would be most appropriate because it would allow them to each receive the maximum contribution up to the annual additions limit ($58,000 for 2021). In addition, the plan could be integrated with Social Security to provide higher benefits for the highly compensated employees, Tyson and Laila.

Assumptions: Wage Base $142,800, Base Rate 6.30%, 401(k) Limit $19,500					
	Tyson	**Laila**	**Manny**	**Miesha**	**Total**
Compensation	$290,000	$290,000	$30,000	$30,000	$640,000
401(k) Deferral	$19,500	$19,500	$10,000	-	$49,000
401(k) Match at 4%	$11,600	$11,600	$1,200	-	$24,400
Integrated Profit Sharing Contribution					
Base	$8,996	$8,996	$1,890	$1,890	$21,773
Excess	$17,664	$17,664	-	-	$35,328
Total	$26,660	$26,660	$1,890	$1,890	$57,101
Total	**$57,760**	**$57,760**	**$13,090**	**$1,890**	**$130,501**
% of Total	**44.3%**	**44.3%**	**10.0%**	**1.4%**	**100%**
Analysis					
Integration Benefit	$8,390	$8,390	-	-	$16,781
Percentage - Total	19.9%	19.9%	43.6%	6.3%	
Percentage - Employee	6.7%	6.7%	33.3%	0.0%	
Percentage - Employer	13.2%	13.2%	10.3%	6.3%	
Total ER Contribution	**$38,260**	**$38,260**	**$3,090**	**$1,890**	**$81,501**
% of Total	**46.9%**	**46.9%**	**3.8%**	**2.3%**	**100%**

The chart above illustrates a safe harbor integrated 401(k) plan. Tyson and Laila are almost able to reach their IRC Section 415(c) limit of $58,000 (2021). In addition, Tyson could defer even more for his catch up contribution because he is over the age of 50.

The plan requires a four percent match, which is available to all employees deferring into the plan. Notice that Manny receives a matching contribution, while Miesha does not. In addition, the plan provides for an integrated profit-sharing plan contribution. The base percentage of 6.3 percent has been selected to allow the owners to almost reach their annual additions limit. Notice that the owners are the only two that enjoy the excess benefit and that 93 to 94 percent of the benefit of the employer contribution is going to the owners.

As an alternative, a new comparability plan would permit them to create classes of employees such that higher contributions were allocated to the owner group and lower contributions were allocated to the rank-and-file group. New comparability plans are discussed in more detail in Chapter 5.

If they were open to considering a defined benefit plan or cash balance plan, Tyson and Laila could likely increase the amounts contributed on their behalf significantly without much additional contribution for the other employees.

Example 8.4

Irene has been the owner of Irene's Pet Shop for 10 years. She decided to establish a retirement plan for her corporation. She has come to you and indicated that she wants to make all initial contributions to the plan using company stock. She may also want to integrate the plan with Social Security.

Either a qualified profit sharing or stock bonus plan would be an appropriate plan for Irene since she wants to use 100% company stock for the initial and subsequent contributions. Both plans also allow integration with Social Security.

Exhibit 8.5 | Taxonomy of Plan Selection

1. Assume that the sponsor company wants a qualified plan. The sponsor must be willing to comply with the qualified plan requirements, including:
   - Nondiscrimination and broad coverage
   - Eligibility rules
   - Coverage rules
   - Reporting rules
   - Testing rules
   - Disclosure rules
   - Vesting rules
2. Prepare an employee census
3. Determine if (A) mandatory or (B) discretionary funding is appropriate
   A. Mandatory funding:
      - Determine whether investment risk will be borne by the employer or the employee:
        - Employer: Either defined benefit pension plan or cash balance pension plan
          - If the plan favors older age entrants - defined benefit pension plan
          - If the plan favors younger age entrants - cash balance pension plan
        - Employee: Either target benefit pension plan or money purchase pension plan
          - If the employer is willing to endure larger establishment costs and wants to benefit older employees - target benefit pension plan
          - If the employer wants low establishment costs - money purchase pension plan
   B. Discretionary funding:
      - If employee contributions to the qualified plan are desired (self reliance - contributory):
        - Pre-tax: 401(k) Plan
        - After-tax: Thrift Plan/401(k) Roth
      - If only the employer contributes to the qualified plan (noncontributory):
        - Contributions of company stock: profit sharing plan, stock bonus plan, ESOP
        - Test benefits for discrimination rather than contributions (cross-test): Age-based profit sharing plan, new comparability plan
      - If the employer wants low initial costs - profit sharing plan
      - If the employer is willing to pay additional costs - stock bonus plan, ESOP, age-based profit sharing plan, or new comparability plan
      - If the employer wants integration - profit sharing plan or stock bonus plan

Exhibit 8.6 | Plan Selection Flow Chart

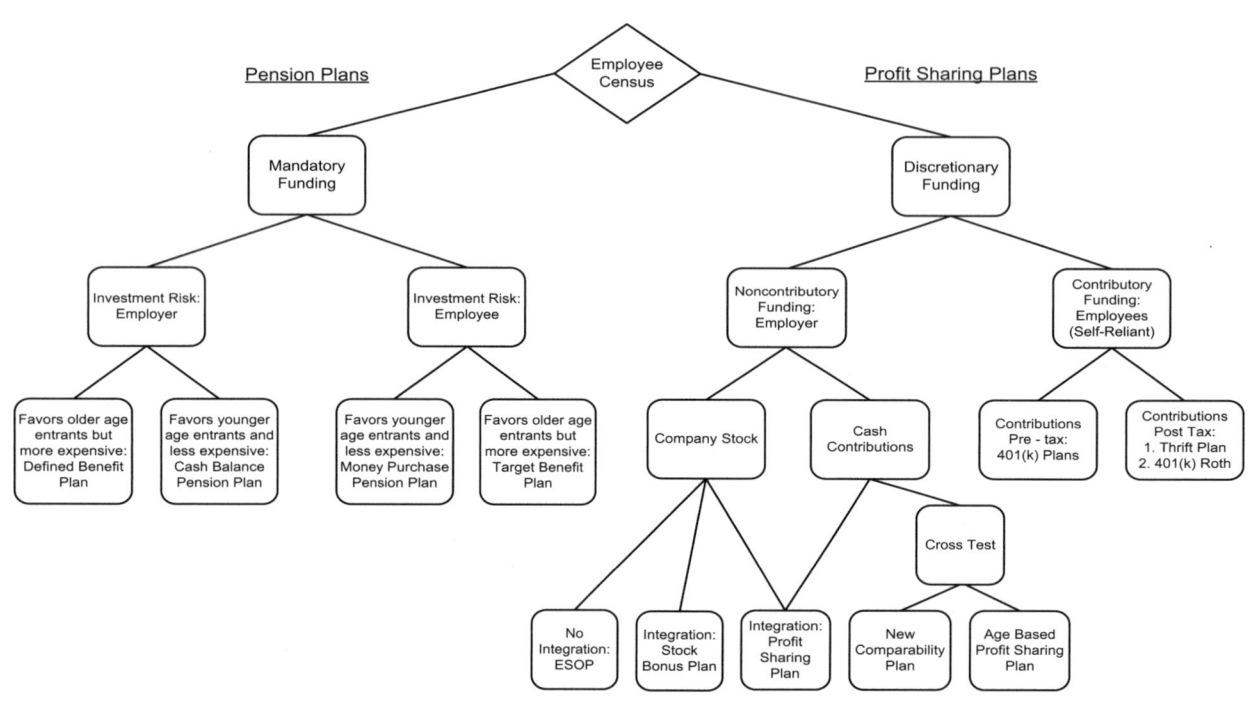

ESTABLISHING A QUALIFIED PLAN

The employer-sponsor is responsible for setting up and maintaining the qualified plan. There are several steps involved in establishing a qualified plan. First, the employer must select and adopt the appropriate plan. Next, the employer must communicate the plan to employees and establish a procedure for funding and administering the plan. Remember that the employer (owner) does not necessarily need to have employees other than himself to establish a qualified plan. A self-employed person who has no other employees can establish a qualified plan.

> ### ✒ *Key Concepts*
>
> 1. What are the requirements for establishing a qualified plan?
>
> 2. How and when should employees be notified when a qualified plan is established?
>
> 3. Who may manage the qualified plan assets?

Adopting a Written Plan

A qualified plan must be detailed in a written plan that is adopted by the company. To take an income tax deduction for contributions for a particular tax year, the plan must be adopted by the due date of the tax return, including extensions (changed from the last day of the tax year by the SECURE Act). Tax returns for partnerships and S-corporations are due by the 15th day of the third month following the end of the tax year and can be extended by six months by properly filing for the extension by the due date of the tax return. C-corporation tax returns are due by the 15th day of the 4th month following the end of the tax year, and can be extended for up to 6 months by properly filing for the extension by the due date of the tax return.

In some cases, the company may elect for the plan to have a different tax year than the company.

Example 8.5

If a partnership is on a calendar year basis, then the plan must be adopted by September 15 of the year following the year in which the deduction is desired. If, instead, the partnership is on a fiscal year ending August 31, then the plan should be adopted by May 15 of the following year.

The company can individually design the plan using an **ERISA attorney** (expensive), or the company can use an IRS-approved master or prototype plan (very inexpensive). Once adopted, information about the plan must be communicated in writing to the employees as detailed below.

Master or Prototype Plans

The majority of qualified plans follow standard forms called master or prototype plans. These plans have been pre-approved by the IRS and are available for employers to simply adopt. **Master plans** provide a single trust or custodial account that is jointly used by all adopting employers. **Prototype plans** allow each employer to establish their own separate trust or custodial account. IRS approved master or prototype plans can often be obtained from banks, trade or professional organizations, insurance companies, investment houses, or mutual funds. These organizations will assist the employer by offering them a basic plan and trust document. They will also use an adoption agreement, so that the employer can elect, by checking the box, various options such as participation requirements, vesting schedules, contribution limits, investment options, and conditions for withdrawals.

Individually Designed Plans

If the company has specific needs that are not addressed in a master or prototype plan, or if they so choose, the company can have their own individually drafted plan. However, in order to be considered a qualified plan, the plan must be permanent and for the exclusive benefit of the employees and their beneficiaries. The adopted plan should detail the procedure for amending and identify who can amend the plan should it be necessary.

Individually designed plans are less common because of the cost to design and draft and because of the wide availability of prototype plans. While advance IRS approval is not required to adopt an individually drafted plan, approval can and usually is sought from the IRS. This approval is accomplished by requesting a determination letter and paying the required fee. Creating an individually designed plan usually requires the services of an ERISA attorney, making the plan much more expensive than prototype plans.

Exhibit 8.7 | Types of Plans

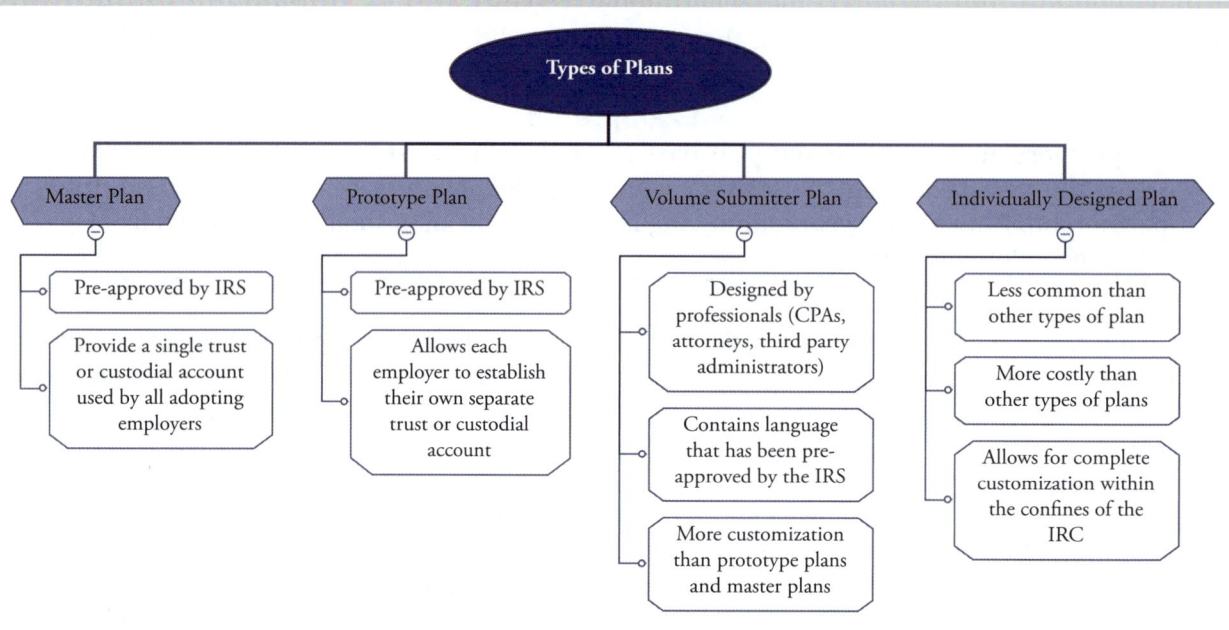

Volume Submitter Plan

A volume submitter plan falls in between a prototype plan and an individually designed plan. It is a plan that is designed by a professional, such as an attorney, CPA or third party administrator, which contains language that has been pre-approved by the IRS. This type of plan allows for more customization than a standard prototype plan, but is generally much less costly than an individualized plan.

Determination Letters

Determination letters may be used when a retirement plan is adopted, amended, or terminated. They may be filed in advance of the plan being adopted or immediately thereafter, usually by filing Form 5300. While they are not required in any of these circumstances, they are useful to the plan sponsor because they allow the plan sponsor to rely on the response from the IRS. If the IRS has any issues with the plan design, the plan can be amended immediately to ensure compliance.

Determination letters are usually accompanied by the appropriate fee. The fee is based on the type of transaction involved. Some small employers may be exempt from paying the fee if they meet certain criteria. The fee is determined on IRS Form 8717.[1]

Determination letters are generally narrow in scope and address particular issues. For example, a favorable determination letter may be received that indicates that the plan meets the qualified plan rules, but the determination letter may or may not verify that certain types of contributions to the plan are income tax deductible. Just because a plan receives a favorable determination letter does not mean that it cannot lose its qualified status if it does not continue to comply with provisions of the plan document as well as with the IRC and ERISA. It is critical to understand that the sponsor must follow the provisions established in the plan document. It is also equally important that a plan be amended to reflect current law so that it continues to comply and does not risk losing its qualified status.

1. Form 8717 no longer lists the user fees but is used to file and pay the fee. User fees for 2021 are listed in Rev. Proc. 2021-4.

Exhibit 8.8 | Form 8717

| Form **8717**
(Rev. September 2017)
Department of the Treasury
Internal Revenue Service | **User Fee for Employee Plan Determination Letter Request**
▶ Attach to determination letter application.
▶ Go to *www.irs.gov/Form8717* for the latest information. | For IRS Use Only | OMB No. 1545-1772

Amount paid _____ |

1 Name of plan sponsor (employer if single-employer plan)

| **2** Sponsor's employer identification number | **3** Plan number | **4** Plan name |

Caution: If you qualify for the exemption from user fees for small business employers, complete only the certification below. See the instructions on page 2 for details. For all other applications, leave the certification blank and check the appropriate box and enter the user fee in column B of line 5.

Certification

I certify that the application for a determination letter on the qualified status of the plan listed above meets the conditions for exemption from user fees described in section 7528(b)(2)(B) of the Internal Revenue Code.

Sign Here ▶ _____ Date ▶ _____

Type or print name and title ▶ _____

	Form Submitted		User Fee A	User Fee B
5a	**Form 5300:**			☐ $
b	**Form 5307:**			☐ $
c	**Form 5310:**			☐ $
d				
e	Multiple employer plans **(Form 5300)**			☐ $
f	Multiple employer plans **(Form 5310)**			☐ $
g	Reserved			
	(1a)			
	(1b)			
	(2a)			
	(2b)			
	(3)			
	(4)			
h	Reserved			
	(1a)			
	(1b)			
	(2)			
	(3)			
	(4a)			
	(4b)			
	(5)			
	(6)			
	(7)			
i	**Form 5316:**			☐ $

Attach Check or Money Order Here

Cat. No. 64727O

Form **8717** (Rev. 9-2017)

Exhibit 8.9 | Sample Plan Adoption Agreement

Sample Plan Adoption Agreement
401(k) Plan

Employer Information

Name: _____   Telephone: _____

Address: _____   EIN: _____

_____   Plan Administrator: _____

Plan Information

Name of Plan: _____

Plan Number: _____   Plan Year: ❏ Calendar year   ❏ Fiscal year ending

Effective Date: ❏ January 1, _____; or ❏ _____ (For initial plan year enter a date between January 1 and October 1.)
 ❏ This is a restatement of a prior plan known as:
    The restated effective date of the plan is:

Coverage Information

The eligibility requirements for participation in the Plan will be:

1. Eligibility Service Requirement (check one)
  ❏ No eligibility service requirement.
  ❏ Six months of employment. (If this option is selected, an Employee will not be required to complete any specified number of Hours of Service in the six-month period.)
  ❏ One year of service.

2. Age Requirement
  ❏ No minimum age requirement
  ❏ ____ Years (cannot be more than 21).

The requirements listed above are (check one):
  ❏ Applicable to all Employees.
  ❏ Applicable to all Employees except those Employees employed on the Effective Date. Such Employees will participate immediately. All other Employees will need to satisfy the requirements listed above.

Employer Contribution Information

The Employer shall contribute on behalf of each Participant for each Plan Year in accordance with one of the following as indicated in the Summary Plan Description:
  ❏ Matching Contributions in the amount of the Participant's Elective Deferral up to 4%.
  ❏ Nonelective Contribution of 2% of each Participant's Compensation.

Vesting Information

A participant's vested interest in his or her Employer Contribution Account will be:
  ❏ 100% immediately vested at all times.
  ❏ 100% vested after ____ Years of Service (not to exceed 3 years). A Participant will be 0% vested prior to completing this period.
  ❏

Years of Service	Vested Percentage
1	0%
2	20%
3	40%
4	60%
5	80%
6	100%

Signatures

Employer: _____   Trustee (optional): _____

By (Authorized Signature): _____   By (Authorized Signature): _____

Date: _____   Date: _____

Notifying Eligible Employees

Information regarding the qualified plan must be distributed to employees who might be eligible for the plan. In addition, the information must be furnished to the ineligible employees working at the same facility. This information helps to inform the employee of his rights under ERISA and the qualified retirement plan.

Before the IRS can issue a determination letter on the qualified status of a retirement plan, the employer must provide the IRS with satisfactory evidence that it has notified the persons who qualify as interested parties. **Interested parties** with regard to notification are present employees who are eligible to participate in the plan and present employees who are not eligible for the plan but whose principal place of employment is the same as the principal place of employment of any employee who is eligible to participate.

Example 8.6

Loupili company wants to establish a qualified retirement plan that requires one year of service to participate. Loupili has two offices, one on the north side of town called the North office and one on the south side of town called the South office. The North office has 32 employees, and the South office has 10 employees. The North office has been operational for several years, and half of its employees are eligible to participate in the qualified retirement plan. The South office was recently opened, and none of the employees have met the service requirement to be eligible. Loupili must notify all of the employees in the North office because some of them are eligible and the others work in the same office as eligible individuals. The employees in the South office do not need to be notified at this time because none of them are eligible for the plan.

Proper advance notice can be made in person, via e-mail or mail, or by posting a notice in a location generally used for posting notices to employees. The notice must be provided at least ten days before, but not more than 24 days before, the determination application is mailed to the IRS.[2] Below is a sample form taken from Revenue Procedure 2021-4 that can be used to notify employees.

---

2. Rev. Proc. 2021-4.

Exhibit 8.10 | Sample Notice to Interested Parties

APPENDIX B

SAMPLE NOTICE TO INTERESTED PARTIES

The sample notice set forth below may be used to satisfy the requirements of section 20 of this revenue procedure.

SAMPLE NOTICE TO INTERESTED PARTIES

1. Notice To:_____[describe class or classes of interested parties]

An application is to be made to the Internal Revenue Service for an advance determination on the qualification of the following employee pension benefit plan:

2. _____

    (name of plan)

3. _____

    (plan number)

4. _____

    (name and address of applicant)

5. _____

    (applicant EIN)

6. _____

    (name and address of plan administrator)

7. The application will be filed on _____ for an advance determination as to whether the plan meets the qualification requirements of § 401 or § 403(a) of the Internal Revenue Code (Code), with respect to the plan's _____ [initial qualification, termination, or partial termination]. The application will be filed with:

> • Internal Revenue Service
>
> • Attention: EP Determination Letters
>
> • P.O. Box 12192
>
> • TE/GE Stop 31A Team 105
>
> • Covington, KY 41012-0192

8. The employees eligible to participate under the plan are:

9. The Internal Revenue Service [has/has not] previously issued a determination letter with respect to the qualification of this plan.

RIGHTS OF INTERESTED PARTIES

10. You have the right to submit to EP Determinations, either individually or jointly with other interested parties, your comments as to whether this plan meets the qualification requirements of the Code. Label your comments "Interested Party Statement". Include the EIN, plan name, and plan number in your correspondence. Also include your contact information (mailing address and phone number) in case we need to contact you. Your comments to EP Determinations should be submitted to:

> • Internal Revenue Service
>
> • EP Determinations

Bulletin No. 2021–1   241   **January 4, 2021**

• Attn: Customer Service Manager

• P.O. Box 2508

• Cincinnati, OH 45202

You may instead, individually or jointly with other interested parties, request the DOL to submit, on your behalf, comments to EP Determinations regarding qualification of the plan. If the DOL declines to comment on all or some of the matters you raise, you may, individually, or jointly if your request was made to the DOL, submit your comments on these matters directly to EP Determinations at the Cincinnati address above.

REQUESTS FOR COMMENTS BY THE DOL

11. The DOL may not comment on behalf of interested parties unless requested to do so by the lesser of 10 employees or 10 percent of the employees who qualify as interested parties. The number of persons needed for the DOL to comment with respect to this plan is _____. If you request the DOL to comment, your request must be in writing and must specify the matters upon which comments are requested, and must also include:

(1) the information contained in items 2 through 5 of this Notice; and

(2) the number of persons needed for the DOL to comment.

A request to the DOL to comment should be addressed as follows:

• Deputy Assistant Secretary

• Employee Benefits Security Administration

• U.S. Department of Labor,

• 200 Constitution Avenue, N.W.

• Washington, D.C. 20210

• Attention: 3001 Comment Request

COMMENTS TO THE INTERNAL REVENUE SERVICE

12. Comments submitted by you to EP Determinations must be in writing and received by it by _____. However, if there are matters that you request the DOL to comment upon on your behalf, and the DOL declines, you may submit comments on these matters to EP Determinations to be received by it within 15 days from the time the DOL notifies you that it will not comment on a particular matter, or by _____, whichever is later, but not after _____. A request to the DOL to comment on your behalf must be received by it by _____ if you wish to preserve your right to comment on a matter upon which the DOL declines to comment, or by _____ if you wish to waive that right.

ADDITIONAL INFORMATION

13. Detailed instructions regarding the requirements for notification of interested parties may be found in sections 19 and 20 of Rev. Proc. 2021–4. Additional information concerning this application (including, where applicable, an updated copy of the plan and related trust; the application for determination; any additional documents dealing with the application that have submitted to the Service; and copies of section 19 of Rev. Proc. 2021–4) are available at _____ during the hours of _____ for inspection and copying. (There is a nominal charge for copying and/or mailing.)

The employer is required to provide, free of charge, a summary of the details of the qualified retirement plan, called a **Summary Plan Description**, to employees, participants, and beneficiaries under pay status (receiving benefits).[3] The summary must be furnished within 90 days after the person becomes a participant, or first receives benefits as a beneficiary, or within 120 days after the plan is established under ERISA. The Summary Plan Description explains in plain language what the plan provides and how it operates. It provides information on when an employee can begin to participate in the plan, how service and benefits are calculated, when benefits become vested, when and in what form benefits are paid, and how to file a claim for benefits. The Summary Plan Description is needed because the plan document is lengthy and has substantial legal jargon that many employees may not understand. The Summary Plan Description must be re-issued every 10 years (the interval decreases to five years if the plan was amended).

The employer should ensure that the Summary Plan Description accurately reflects what is included in the actual plan to avoid potential liability. Many employers use disclaimers in the Summary Plan Description that state that in the event that the Summary Plan Description is different than the plan document, the plan document controls the provisions of the qualified plan. This strategy has been effective for some companies in the past; however, it has and will continue to be a source of litigation until it is legislatively decided.

The employer is also required to provide the plan participants notices of any plan amendments or changes. This notice can be provided either through a revised Summary Plan Description or in a separate document, called a **Summary of Material Modifications**. This document must be given to participants free of charge within 210 days after the end of the plan year in which a change is adopted and applies when there are substantive changes in the plan.

In addition to the Summary Plan Description, the employer must automatically provide the participants, free of charge, a copy of the plan's **Summary Annual Report** each year. The Summary Annual Report is a summary of the annual financial report that the plan files with the Department of Labor each year (Form 5500 discussed later in this chapter). Participants may also ask the plan administrator for a copy of the plan's annual report in its entirety if they wish to learn more about the plan. See **Exhibit 8.11**.

---

3. ERISA §1022.

Exhibit 8.11 | Sample Summary Annual Report

Summary Annual Report
ABC Company Defined Contribution Retirement Plan

This is a summary of the annual report for the **ABC Company Defined Contribution Retirement Plan** EIN XX-XXXXXXX, for the period January 1, 2020 through December 31, 2020. The annual report has been filed with the Employee Benefits Security Administration, as required under the Employee Retirement Income Security Act of 1974 (ERISA).

Basic Financial Statement

Benefits under the plan are provided by trust and insurance. Plan expenses were $XX,XXX,XXX. These expenses included $XX,XXX,XXX in administrative expenses and $XX,XXX,XXX in benefits paid to participants and beneficiaries. A total of XX,XXX persons were participants in or beneficiaries of the plan at the end of the plan year, although not all of these persons had yet earned the right to receive benefits.

The value of the plan assets, after subtracting liabilities of the plan was $XXX,XXX,XXX as of December 31, 2020, compared to $XXX,XXX,XXX as of January 1, 2020. During the plan year, the plan experienced a decrease in its net assets of $XX,XXX,XXX.

This decrease included unrealized depreciation in the value of plan assets; that is, the difference between the value of the plan's assets at the end of the year and the value of those assets at the beginning of the year. The plan had a total negative income of $X,XXX,XXX, including employer contributions of $X,XXX,XXX, realized losses of $X,XXX,XXX from the sale of assets, and negative net earnings from investments of $X,XXX,XXX (which includes unrealized losses on assets).

Minimum Funding Standards

Enough money was contributed to the plan to keep it funded in accordance with the minimum funding standards of ERISA.

Your Rights To Additional Information

You have the right to receive a copy of the full annual report, or any part thereof, on request. The following items are included in the report:
1. an accountant's report;
2. assets held for investment;
3. financial information; and
4. insurance information.

To obtain a copy of the full annual report, or any part thereof, write or call ABC Company, 123 Lovers Lane, Anytown, USA, telephone number (555) 555-2004. The charge to cover copying will be 25 cents per page or any part thereof.

You also have the right to receive from the plan administrator, on request and at no charge, a statement of the assets and liabilities of the plan and accompanying notes, or a statement of income and expenses of the plan and accompanying notes, or both. If you request a copy of the full annual report from the plan administrator, these two statements and accompanying notes will be included as part of that report. The charge to cover copying costs given above does not include a charge for the copying of these portions of the report because these portions are furnished without charge.

You also have the legally protected right to examine the annual report at ABC Company, 123 Lovers Lane, Anytown, USA, telephone number (555) 555-2004 and at the U.S. Department of Labor in Washington, D.C., or to obtain a copy from the U.S. Department of Labor upon payment of copying costs. Requests to the Department should be addressed to: Public Disclosure Room, Pension and Welfare Benefit Administration, Department of Labor, 200 Constitution Avenue, N.W., Washington, D.C. 20210.

Exhibit 8.12 | Sources of Plan Information[4]

Document	Type of Information	To Whom	When
Summary Plan Description (SPD):	Primary vehicle for informing participants and beneficiaries about their plan and how it operates. Must be written for average participant and be sufficiently comprehensive to apprise covered persons of their benefits, rights, and obligations under the plan. Must accurately reflect the plan's contents as of the date not earlier than 120 days prior to the date the SPD is disclosed. See 29 CFR §§2520.102-2 and 2520.102-3 for style, format, and content requirements.	Participants and those pension plan beneficiaries receiving benefits. (Also see "Plan Documents" below for persons with the right to obtain SPD upon request). See 29 CFR §2520.102-2(c) for provisions on foreign language assistance when a certain portion of plan participants are literate only in the same non-English language.	Automatically to participants within 90 days of becoming covered by the plan and to pension plan beneficiaries within 90 days after first receiving benefits. However, a plan has 120 days after becoming subject to ERISA to distribute the SPD. Updated SPD must be furnished every 5 years if changes made to SPD information or plan is amended. Otherwise must be furnished every 10 years. See 29 CFR §2520.104b-2.
Summary of Material Modification (SMM)	Describes material modifications to a plan and changes in the information required to be in the SPD. Distribution of updated SPD satisfies this requirement. See 29 CFR §2520.104b-3.	Participants and those pension plan beneficiaries receiving benefits. (Also see "Plan Documents" below for persons with the right to obtain SMM upon request).	Automatically to participants and pension plan beneficiaries receiving benefits; not later than 210 days after the end of the plan year in which the change is adopted.
Summary Annual Report (SAR)	Narrative summary of the Form 5500. See 29 CFR §2520.104b-10(d) for prescribed format.	Participants and those pension plan beneficiaries receiving benefits. For plan years beginning after December 31, 2007, the SAR is no longer required for defined benefit pension plans, which now instead provide the annual funding notice (see below).	Automatically to participants and pension plan beneficiaries receiving benefits within 9 months after end of plan year, or 2 months after due date for filing Form 5500 (with approved extension).
Plan Documents	The plan administrator must furnish copies of certain documents upon written request and must have copies available for examination. The documents include the latest updated SPD, latest Form 5500, trust agreement, and other instruments under which the plan is established or operated.	Participants and beneficiaries. Also see 29 CFR §2520.104a-8 regarding the Department's authority to request documents.	Copies must be furnished no later than 30 days after a written request. Plan administrator must make copies available at its principal office and certain other locations as specified in 29 CFR §2520.104b-1(b).

---

4. Reporting and Disclosure Guide for Employee Benefit Plans, U.S. Department of Labor, September 2017.

Sources of Plan Information Continued

Document	Type of Information	To Whom	When
Periodic Pension Benefit Statement	Content of statements varies depending on the type of plan. In general, all statements must indicate total benefits and total nonforfeitable pension benefits, if any, which have accrued, or earliest date on which benefits become nonforfeitable. Benefit statements for an individual account plan must also provide the value of each investment to which assets in the individual account have been allocated. Benefit statements for individual account plans that permit participant investment direction must also include an explanation of any limitation or restriction on any right of the participant or beneficiary under the plan to direct an investment; an explanation of the importance of a well-balanced and diversified portfolio, including a statement of the risk that holding more than 20 percent of a portfolio in the security of an entity (such as employer securities) may not be adequately diversified; and a notice directing the participant or beneficiary to the Internet Website of the Department of Labor for sources of information on individual investing and diversification. See ERISA § 105.	Participants and beneficiaries.	In general, at least once each quarter for individual account plans that permit participants to direct their investments; at least once each year, in the case of individual account plans that do not permit participants to direct their investments; and at least once every three years in the case of defined benefit plans or, in the alternative, defined benefit plans can satisfy this requirement if at least once each year the administrator provides notice of the availability of the pension benefit statement and the ways to obtain such statement. In addition, the plan administrator must furnish a benefit statement to a participant or beneficiary upon written request, limited to one request during any 12-month period.
§404(c) Plan Disclosures	Investment-related and certain other disclosures for participant-directed individual account plans described in 29 CFR §2550.404c-1, including blackout notice for participant-directed individual account plans described in ERISA §404(c)(1)(A)(ii), as described below. Special rules apply for qualified investment options under ERISA section 404(c)(4)(C).	Participants or beneficiaries, as applicable.	Certain information should be furnished to participants or beneficiaries before the time when investment instructions are to be made; certain information must be furnished upon request.
Notice of Blackout Period for Individual Account Plans	Notification of any period of more than 3 consecutive business days when there is a temporary suspension, limitation or restriction under an individual account plan on directing or diversifying plan assets, obtaining loans, or obtaining distributions.	Participants and beneficiaries of individual account plans affected by such blackout periods and issuers of affected employer securities held by the plan.	Generally at least 30 days but not more than 60 days advance notice. See ERISA §101(i) and 29 CFR §2520.101-3 for further information on the notice requirement.

https://www.dol.gov/sites/dolgov/files/EBSA/about-ebsa/our-activities/resource-center/publications/reporting-and-disclosure-guide-for-employee-benefit-plans.pdf

Qualified Trust

The assets of the qualified plan must be placed in a qualified trust or a custodial account.[5] IRC §401(a) describes the specific requirements for a qualified trust. Generally, a **qualified trust** is a trust established or organized in the United States that is maintained by an employer for the exclusive benefit of the employer's employees. The trust must distribute assets to employees and not discriminate against certain employees. **Custodial Accounts** are generally maintained by a bank or other financial institution.

Exhibit 8.13 | 401(a) Summary of Qualified Trust[6]

- The trust must be established or organized in the United States and maintained at all times as a domestic trust in the United States.

- The trust must be part of a pension, profit-sharing, or stock bonus plan established by an employer for the exclusive benefit of his employees or their beneficiaries.

- The trust must be formed for the purpose of distributing to the employees or their beneficiaries the corpus and income of the fund accumulated by the trust in accordance with the plan.

- It must be impossible under the trust instrument at any time before the satisfaction of all liabilities with respect to employees and their beneficiaries under the trust, for any part of the corpus or income to be used for, or diverted to, purposes other than for the exclusive benefit of the employees or their beneficiaries.

- The trust must be part of a plan that benefits prescribed percentages of the employees or which benefits such employees as qualify under a classification set up by the employer and found by the Commissioner of the IRS not to be discriminatory in favor of certain specified classes of employees.

- The trust must be part of a plan under which contributions or benefits do not discriminate in favor of certain specified classes of employees.

- The trust must be part of a plan that provides certain nonforfeitable rights.

- If the trust forms part of a pension plan, the plan must provide that forfeitures must not be applied to increase the benefits any employee would receive under such plan.

- The trust must, if the plan benefits any self-employed individual who is an owner-employee, satisfy the additional requirements for qualification.

---

5. IRC §401(a).
6. IRC §401(a) summarized.

Investing Plan Assets

Investing plan assets is a critical element of overall plan management. Plan assets will either be managed by the plan sponsor (or an asset management firm hired by the plan sponsor) or individually by the plan participants. In many cases, the type of plan and who retains the investment risk will dictate whether the plan assets are managed by the plan sponsor or self-directed by the plan participants. Defined benefit plan sponsors are responsible for funding a determined retirement benefit for plan participants based upon a specific formula and therefore retain the investment risk. As a result, the sponsor will generally hire an outside asset management firm to invest the plan assets in such a way as to fund the pension liabilities over time. Cash balance pension plans function in a similar manner to defined benefit plans, and the assets are generally managed in a similar function.

Defined contribution plan participants bear the investment risk for the assets in their accounts. Despite this, plan sponsors may choose to manage the plan assets or hire an outside asset management firm to manage the assets for the plan participants.

Plan sponsors are generally considered fiduciaries of qualified plans. Being classified as a fiduciary requires a certain level of responsibility and prudence. Employers and plan sponsors have attempted to shift some or all of the fiduciary responsibility regarding investment of plan assets from the sponsor to the employees following the guidelines under ERISA §404(c).[7]

> ## ☑ Quick Quiz 8.2
>
> 1. To take a deduction for contributions for a particular year, the qualified plan must be adopted by the due date of the tax return for the plan year including extensions.
>   a. True
>   b. False
>
> 2. Notification of the adoption of a qualified plan may be made in person, via e-mail, or by posting notice at the place of business.
>   a. True
>   b. False
>
> 3. If the plan sponsor shifts the investment responsibility to the plan participants, then the sponsor no longer has any fiduciary responsibility.
>   a. True
>   b. False
>
> True, True, False.

Even when plan sponsors choose to shift the management responsibility of the investment assets to the plan participants, the plan sponsor still retains certain responsibilities over the choices and alternative investments available to the participants.

Retirement plan sponsors must provide a broad range of investment choices for participants to manage their retirement assets. A plan must offer a broad range of investment alternatives (at least three) that are sufficient to provide participants or beneficiaries with a reasonable opportunity to materially affect the potential return on amounts in his individual account. If employer stock is offered, it cannot be one of the three core investment options. Generally, a plan will provide at least one diversified stock investment option, one diversified bond investment option, and one cash or money market type investment option. This combination of security options allows an investor to create relatively efficient portfolios by allocating different amounts to the three funds.

---

7. 29 USC §1104(c)(1)(A)(ii) provides that: no person who is otherwise a fiduciary shall be liable under this part for any loss, or by reason of any breach, which results from such participant's or beneficiary's exercise of control, except that this clause shall not apply in connection with such participant or beneficiary for any blackout period during which the ability of such participant or beneficiary to direct the investment of the assets in his account is suspended by a plan sponsor or fiduciary.

The plan must therefore provide the participants with at least three alternatives to invest in within the retirement plan. These alternatives must meet the following criteria:
- be diversified,
- have materially different risk and return characteristics, which in the aggregate enable the participant or beneficiary to achieve a portfolio with aggregate risk and return characteristics at any point within the range normally appropriate (efficient frontier) for the participant or beneficiary, and
- each alternative, when combined with investments in the other alternatives tends to minimize through diversification the overall risk of a participant's or beneficiary's portfolio.

IRS regulations, directing the types of investments that should be included in a retirement plan, are consistent with concepts and notions that competent advisors use in advising clients regarding investing, diversification, and the balance between increasing returns and reducing risk within a portfolio

In the past, one issue facing plan fiduciaries of defined contribution plans has been the liability associated with meeting the prudent investor standard described above in respect to the selection of an insurance company to offer a guaranteed retirement income contract as an investment option in the plan. Since annuity contracts are backed by the issuing insurance company, plan fiduciaries have feared being held accountable if the insurer could not fulfill the payments promised under the annuity. As a result, most defined contribution plans simply have not offered annuities as investment options. Since more employers are offering defined contribution plans in lieu of the traditional defined benefit plans that promise a particular retirement benefit to participants, the lack of an annuity option within defined contribution plans limits a participant's ability to receive a guaranteed life income. To address this issue, the SECURE Act of 2019 created a safe harbor under which the prudent man standards of ERISA Section 404(a)(1)(B) will be deemed satisfied in respect to selection of an insurer to offer a guaranteed retirement income contract if the fiduciary:
- engages in an objective, thorough, and analytical search to identify potential insurers from which to purchase the contacts; and
- considers the financial capability of each insurer to satisfy its obligations under the guaranteed retirement income contract; and
- considers the cost (including fees and commissions) of the contract in relation to the benefits, product features, and administrative services provided under the contract; and
- on the basis of the above considerations, concludes that at the time of selection, the insurer is financially capable of satisfying its obligations under the contract and that the relative cost is reasonable.

The SECURE Act amendment to ERISA does not require that the insurer with the lowest cost be selected. Rather, it specifies that the above considerations be reviewed in conjunction with the cost. If the plan fiduciary follows the prescribed requirements they will not be liable for any losses that may result to the participant or beneficiary due to the insurer's inability to satisfy its financial obligations under the annuity contract.

The SECURE Act also provides that, for plan years beginning after December 31, 2019, if the defined contribution plan fiduciary changes the investment options available in the plan such that a lifetime income investment (annuity) is no longer available the plan may allow (1) a direct trustee-to-trustee transfer to another employer-sponsored retirement plan or IRA, or (2) distribution of a lifetime income investment in the form of a qualified plan distribution annuity contract (an annuity contract purchased for a participant and distributed to the participant), to be made on or after the date which is 90 days prior to the removal the annuity from the plan's investment options.

ADMINISTRATION

Qualified retirement plans require ongoing administration and maintenance. Informational compliance tax returns, such as IRS Form 5500, must be filed annually. The allocation of contributions to employees' accounts or determination of accrued benefits must also be completed at least annually. Other administrative duties include annual testing to comply with IRS regulations and amending the plan document for tax law changes. Besides performing the administrative duties, the plan sponsor frequently retains and is responsible for an investment adviser to assure that plan assets are managed for the sole benefit of participants and their beneficiaries. The plan sponsor may outsource each of these tasks to a third party administrator or other provider.

Operating the Plan

Covering Eligible Employees
Recall from Chapter 3 that a qualified retirement plan must benefit a broad range of rank-and-file employees, not just the highly compensated or key employees. The company can establish age and service requirements (within the guidelines prescribed by the IRC) in order to control the number of individuals eligible to be in the plan. In addition, qualified plans require annual coverage testing to ensure that the rank-and-file employees (nonhighly compensated and nonkey) are sufficiently covered. Recall from Chapter 5 that some 401(k) plans have an "automatic enrollment" or "negative election" feature. These features help to increase coverage of nonhighly compensated employees. Refer to Chapter 3 for more specific information on the coverage rules and Chapters 3 through 6 for detailed information on each plan's specific annual testing requirements.

Making Appropriate Contributions

Minimum Funding Requirement
In general, sponsors of money purchase pension plans, cash balance pension plans, defined benefit pension plans, and target benefit pension plans must contribute enough money into the plan to satisfy the minimum funding requirements as determined by an actuary for each year.

Example 8.7
Loopili Corporation has a money purchase pension plan for which they contribute two percent of covered compensation each year. Loopili has four employees that each make $20,000. By the required contribution date (tax return due date plus extensions) Loopili must contribute $1,600 to the plan ($20,000 x 4 employees x 2%).

Determining the amount needed to satisfy the minimum funding standard for a defined benefit plan is complicated. The amount is based on what should be contributed under the plan formula using actuarial assumptions and formulas. Actuaries work with the plan sponsor to determine the minimum funding for a defined benefit plan. The actuarial assumptions will take into account factors such as life expectancy, likelihood of early retirement, mortality rates, inflation rates, investment return rates, and the expected rate of forfeitures.

Defined benefit plans must make quarterly installment payments of the required contributions. If installment payments are not made on time, then the company must pay interest on any underpayment for the period of the underpayment. The installment payment due dates are 15 days after the end of each quarter. For a calendar-year plan, the installment payments are due April 15, July 15, October 15, and January 15 (of the following year). Each quarterly installment payment must be 25 percent of the required annual payment.

Key Concepts

1. What are the minimum funding requirements for qualified plans, and when may contributions be deducted by the employer?

2. How are forfeitures treated in qualified plans?

3. What transactions are prohibited for a qualified plan?

4. What regulatory bodies and filing requirements are involved with the operation of a qualified plan?

Contributions in General

A qualified plan is generally funded by employer contributions (often called a noncontributory plan because employees do not contribute to the plan), but employees participating in the plan may also be permitted to make contributions (a contributory plan). As explained earlier, one of the benefits of qualified plans is that the employer is allowed to take a deduction in the year of contribution, but the employee does not have to include the income as taxable income in that year. The deductibility of these contributions in effect reduces the overall cost to the employer of the qualified plan.

A company can make deductible contributions for a tax year up to the due date of their tax return (plus extensions) for the year of contribution. A promissory note made out to the plan for contributions is a prohibited transaction and is not a payment that qualifies for an income tax deduction.

While the employer generally applies contributions in the year in which they are paid, the employer may apply the payment to the previous year if all the following requirements are met:
1. The contributions are made by the due date of the tax return for the previous year (plus extensions).
2. The plan was established by the end of the previous year (the plan year) if the plan was adopted before January 1, 2020. For plans adopted for tax years after December 31, 2019, the SECURE Act allows a plan adopted by the due date of the tax return (including extensions) to treat the plan as adopted as of the last day of the tax year.
3. The plan treats the contributions as though it had received them on the last day of the previous year.
4. The company specifies in writing to the plan administrator or trustee that the contributions apply to the previous year, or the company takes a deduction for the amount of the contributions on the tax return for the previous year.

Self-employed individuals can make contributions on behalf of themselves only if they have positive net earnings (compensation) from self-employment in the trade or business for which the plan was established. The net earnings must be from the self-employed individual's personal services and not from investments. A self-employed individual cannot make a contribution for himself in a year in which he has a loss, but he can still make contributions for other employees based on the employees' compensation.

There are certain limits on the contributions and other annual additions a company can make each year on behalf of plan participants (discussed in Chapter 3). There are also limits on the deductible amount of plan contributions. The limits differ depending on whether the plan is a defined contribution plan or a defined benefit plan.

For 2021, the annual benefit for a defined benefit plan participant cannot exceed the lesser of 100 percent of the participant's average compensation for his highest three consecutive calendar years or $230,000. For 2021, a defined contribution plan's annual contributions and other additions (excluding the earnings of the plan assets) to a participant account cannot exceed the lesser of 100 percent of the participant's compensation or $58,000. Catch-up contributions for those participants age 50 and over are not subject to the annual defined contribution limit and thus can be in addition to these limits.

In the event that more money is contributed to a defined contribution plan than is allowed under the limits above, the excess amount is called the excess annual addition. A plan can correct excess annual additions if the excess was caused by a reasonable error in estimating a participant's compensation, determining the elective deferrals permitted, or because of forfeitures allocated to participants' accounts. To do so, the plan can allocate the excess to other participants in the plan to the extent of their unused limits for the year. If these limits are exceeded, they can hold the excess in a separate account and allocate it to participants' accounts in later years before making any contributions for that year, or they can return employee after-tax contributions or elective deferrals. Returning employee after-tax contributions or distributing of elective deferrals to correct excess annual additions is considered a corrective distribution rather than a distribution of accrued benefits. The penalties for early distributions and excess distributions do not apply.

Exhibit 8.14 | Correcting Excess Annual Additions

- Allocate the excess annual additions to other plan participants.
- Hold excess annual additions in a separate account and allocate in future years.
- Make corrective distributions.

Participants may be permitted to make nondeductible contributions to a plan in addition to the employer's contributions. Even though these employee contributions are not deductible, the earnings will accrue tax-free until distributed in later years. These contributions must satisfy certain nondiscrimination tests.

Taking Deductions

Employer Deduction

The employer can usually deduct, subject to certain limitations, contributions made to a qualified plan, including those made for their own retirement. The contributions (and the attributable earnings and gains) are generally not taxed to the employee until distributed by the plan. The deduction limit for contributions to a qualified plan depends on the type of plan.

The deduction for contributions to a defined contribution plan cannot exceed 25 percent of the covered compensation paid or accrued during the year to eligible employees participating in the plan. If the individual is self-employed, he must reduce this limit in figuring the deduction for contributions made to his own account. Recall that the maximum compensation that can be taken into account when calculating plan funding for each employee is the covered compensation limit, $290,000 for 2021.

The deduction for contributions to a defined benefit plan is based on actuarial assumptions and computations. Consequently, an actuary must calculate the appropriate amount of mandatory funding.

Deduction Limit for Self-Employed Individuals (Keogh Plans)

Sole proprietors who file a Schedule C, partners of a partnership, and members of an LLC taxed as a partnership are generally treated as self-employed individuals for tax purposes. In contrast, owners of C-corporations and S-corporations may also be employees of those entities. While self-employed individuals may adopt basically any qualified plan (generally not a stock bonus plan or an ESOP since there is no stock involved with sole proprietorships, partnerships, or LLCs), the plan they choose to adopt will be referred to as a **Keogh plan**. A Keogh plan is simply a qualified plan for a self-employed person. An important distinction of Keogh plans is the reduced contribution that can be made on behalf of the self-employed individual. The employees of a firm that maintains a Keogh plan will generally be treated in the same manner as if the plan was not a Keogh plan. Employees will generally receive a benefit based on their W-2 income. The reason for the distinction is that self-employed individuals do not receive a form W-2 and will instead file a Schedule C or receive a schedule K-1, which details the owner's earnings.

There is a special computation needed to calculate the maximum contribution and tax deduction for a Keogh plan on behalf of self-employed individuals. Since self-employed individuals do not have W-2s, the IRC uses the term "earned income" to denote the amount of compensation that is earned and can be considered by the self-employed individual.

Earned income is defined as net earnings from self-employment less one-half of self-employment tax less the deduction for contributions to the qualified plan on behalf of the self-employed person. Through this process, the IRC attempts to treat self-employed individuals as if they were corporations instead of self-employed. Both employers and employees each pay one-half of self-employment taxes; however, in the case of self-employed individuals, they are required to pay both halves. If the company was a corporation, then it would deduct one half of the self-employment taxes paid on behalf of the individual in arriving at net income. Therefore, earned income for self-employed individuals is the self-employment income reduced by one-half of self-employment tax. Similarly, a corporation would deduct the contribution made to a qualified retirement plan in arriving at net income. Therefore, calculating earned income for a self-employed individual also requires a reduction for the amount of the contribution to the Keogh plan.

Recall from Chapter 4 that the two primary parts of the Social Security system are OASDI (Old Age Survivor Disability Insurance) and Medicare. Both employers and employees contribute to the system through FICA payments that consist of 6.2 percent for OASDI and 1.45 percent for Medicare. The OASDI portion of 6.2 percent applies to income up to the Social Security wage base ($142,800 for 2021) while the Medicare portion applies to all income with no limit.

The deduction for the self-employed person's contributions and net earnings is interrelated and depends on each other. For this reason, the self-employed person must determine the deduction for their own contributions by using simultaneous equations or a circular calculation or by using the simpler method described below that adjusts the plan contribution rate for the self-employed person.

To calculate the self-employed individual's 2021 contribution to the Keogh plan, utilize the following formulas:

1. Calculate the self-employed individual's contribution rate:

$$\text{Self-Employed Contribution Rate} = \left(\frac{\text{Contribution Rate to Other Participants}}{1 + \text{Contribution Rate to Other Participants}} \right)$$

2. Calculate Self-Employment Tax:

> Net Self-Employment Income
> Times: 92.35%
> **Net Earnings subject to Self Employment Tax**
> Times: 15.3% up to $142,800 + 2.9% over $142,800
> **Equals: Self-Employment Tax**

3. Calculate the self employed individual's contribution:

> Net Self-Employment Income
> Less: ½ of Self-Employment Taxes
> **Equals: Adjusted Net Self-Employment Income (Earned Income)**
> Times: Self-Employed Contribution Rate
> **Equals: Self-Employed Individual's Qualified Plan Contribution**

Example 8.8

Jack has Schedule C net income of $200,000 and wants to know the maximum amount he can contribute to a Keogh profit sharing plan. In this instance Jack can contribute $37,694 to the plan for 2021. The contribution is calculated as follows:

1. Calculate the self employed individual's contribution rate:

    $$\text{Self-Employed Contribution Rate} = \left(\frac{25\%}{1 + 25\%}\right)$$

    Self-Employed Contribution Rate = 20%

2. Calculate Self-Employment Tax:

$200,000	Net Self-Employment Income
x 0.9235	Times: 92.35%
$184,700	**Net Earnings subject to Self-Employment Tax**
x 15.3%/2.9%	Times: 15.3% up to $142,800 + 2.9% over $142,800 ($41,900)
$23,064	**Equals: Self-Employment Tax**

3. Calculate the self-employed individual's contribution:

$200,000	Net Self-Employment Income
$11,532	Less: ½ of Self-Employment Taxes (50% x $23,064)
$188,468	**Equals: Adjusted Net Self-Employment Income**
x 0.20	Times: Self-Employed Contribution Rate
$37,694	**Equals: Self-Employed Individual's Qualified Plan Contribution**

    Check figure:

    $$\frac{\$37,694}{\$188,468 - \$37,694} = 25\%$$

When solving the Keogh contribution calculation, it is important to understand that while 25 percent is the limit for employee compensation, the self-employed individual maximum is 25 percent of the self-employed individual's earned income. The 25 percent of earned income effectively translates to 20 percent of net self-employed income less one-half of self employment tax. The reason is because the self-employed individual is responsible for the employer's share of self-employment taxes, and the self-employed individual's ultimate compensation is relative to the retirement contribution made on his behalf.

Example 8.9

Thus, in **Example 8.8**, Jack's earned income is calculated as follows:

$200,000	Schedule C net income
- $11,532	Less: ½ self-employment taxes
- $37,694	Less: Keogh contribution
$150,774	Earned income
x 0.25	Times: 25% to determine Keogh contribution
$37,694	**Total Keogh contribution**

Notice that the maximum Keogh contribution is exactly 25 percent of the earned income.

If the contribution rate for other employees is less than 25 percent, then the rate used is calculated in the same manner as discussed above.

Contribution Rate	Self-Employed Contribution Rate
5.0%	4.7619%
10.0%	9.0909%
15.0%	13.0435%
20.0%	16.6667%
25.0%	20.0000%

Exhibit 8.15 | Form 1040 Schedule SE

SCHEDULE SE
(Form 1040)

Department of the Treasury
Internal Revenue Service (99)

Self-Employment Tax

▶ Go to *www.irs.gov/ScheduleSE* for instructions and the latest information.
▶ Attach to Form 1040, 1040-SR, or 1040-NR.

OMB No. 1545-0074

2020

Attachment
Sequence No. **17**

Name of person with self-employment income (as shown on Form 1040, 1040-SR, or 1040-NR)

Social security number of person
with **self-employment** income ▶

Part I — Self-Employment Tax

Note: If your only income subject to self-employment tax is **church employee income,** see instructions for how to report your income and the definition of church employee income.

A If you are a minister, member of a religious order, or Christian Science practitioner **and** you filed Form 4361, but you had $400 or more of **other** net earnings from self-employment, check here and continue with Part I . . . . ▶ ☐

Skip lines 1a and 1b if you use the farm optional method in Part II. See instructions.

1a	Net farm profit or (loss) from Schedule F, line 34, and farm partnerships, Schedule K-1 (Form 1065), box 14, code A . . .	**1a**	
b	If you received social security retirement or disability benefits, enter the amount of Conservation Reserve Program payments included on Schedule F, line 4b, or listed on Schedule K-1 (Form 1065), box 20, code AH	**1b**	( )

Skip line 2 if you use the nonfarm optional method in Part II. See instructions.

2	Net profit or (loss) from Schedule C, line 31; and Schedule K-1 (Form 1065), box 14, code A (other than farming). See instructions for other income to report or if you are a minister or member of a religious order	**2**	
3	Combine lines 1a, 1b, and 2	**3**	
4a	If line 3 is more than zero, multiply line 3 by 92.35% (0.9235). Otherwise, enter amount from line 3 .	**4a**	
	Note: If line 4a is less than $400 due to Conservation Reserve Program payments on line 1b, see instructions.		
b	If you elect one or both of the optional methods, enter the total of lines 15 and 17 here	**4b**	
c	Combine lines 4a and 4b. If less than $400, **stop;** you don't owe self-employment tax. **Exception:** If less than $400 and you had **church employee income,** enter -0- and continue . . . . ▶	**4c**	
5a	Enter your **church employee income** from Form W-2. See instructions for definition of church employee income	**5a**	
b	Multiply line 5a by 92.35% (0.9235). If less than $100, enter -0-	**5b**	
6	Add lines 4c and 5b	**6**	
7	Maximum amount of combined wages and self-employment earnings subject to social security tax or the 6.2% portion of the 7.65% railroad retirement (tier 1) tax for 2020	**7**	137,700
8a	Total social security wages and tips (total of boxes 3 and 7 on Form(s) W-2) and railroad retirement (tier 1) compensation. If $137,700 or more, skip lines 8b through 10, and go to line 11	**8a**	
b	Unreported tips subject to social security tax from Form 4137, line 10 . . .	**8b**	
c	Wages subject to social security tax from Form 8919, line 10	**8c**	
d	Add lines 8a, 8b, and 8c	**8d**	
9	Subtract line 8d from line 7. If zero or less, enter -0- here and on line 10 and go to line 11 . . . ▶	**9**	
10	Multiply the **smaller** of line 6 or line 9 by 12.4% (0.124)	**10**	
11	Multiply line 6 by 2.9% (0.029)	**11**	
12	**Self-employment tax.** Add lines 10 and 11. Enter here and on **Schedule 2 (Form 1040), line 4** . .	**12**	
13	**Deduction for one-half of self-employment tax.** Multiply line 12 by 50% (0.50). Enter here and on **Schedule 1 (Form 1040), line 14**	**13**	

Part II — Optional Methods To Figure Net Earnings (see instructions)

Farm Optional Method. You may use this method **only** if **(a)** your gross farm income[1] wasn't more than $8,460, **or (b)** your net farm profits[2] were less than $6,107.

14	Maximum income for optional methods	**14**	5,640
15	Enter the **smaller** of: two-thirds (⅔) of gross farm income[1] (not less than zero) **or** $5,640. Also, include this amount on line 4b above	**15**	

Nonfarm Optional Method. You may use this method **only** if **(a)** your net nonfarm profits[3] were less than $6,107 and also less than 72.189% of your gross nonfarm income,[4] **and (b)** you had net earnings from self-employment of at least $400 in 2 of the prior 3 years. **Caution:** You may use this method no more than five times.

16	Subtract line 15 from line 14	**16**	
17	Enter the **smaller** of: two-thirds (⅔) of gross nonfarm income[4] (not less than zero) **or** the amount on line 16. Also, include this amount on line 4b above	**17**	

[1] From Sch. F, line 9; and Sch. K-1 (Form 1065), box 14, code B.
[2] From Sch. F, line 34; and Sch. K-1 (Form 1065), box 14, code A—minus the amount you would have entered on line 1b had you not used the optional method.
[3] From Sch. C, line 31; and Sch. K-1 (Form 1065), box 14, code A.
[4] From Sch. C, line 7; and Sch. K-1 (Form 1065), box 14, code C.

For Paperwork Reduction Act Notice, see your tax return instructions.   Cat. No. 11358Z   **Schedule SE (Form 1040) 2020**

Form 1040 Schedule SE Continued

Schedule SE (Form 1040) 2020   Attachment Sequence No. **17**   Page **2**

Part III	**Maximum Deferral of Self-Employment Tax Payments**		
If line 4c is zero, skip lines 18 through 20, and enter -0- on line 21.			
18	Enter the portion of line 3 that can be attributed to March 27, 2020, through December 31, 2020 . .	18	
19	If line 18 is more than zero, multiply line 18 by 92.35% (0.9235); otherwise, enter the amount from line 18	19	
20	Enter the portion of lines 15 and 17 that can be attributed to March 27, 2020, through December 31, 2020	20	
21	Combine lines 19 and 20	21	
If line 5b is zero, skip line 22 and enter -0- on line 23.			
22	Enter the portion of line 5a that can be attributed to March 27, 2020, through December 31, 2020 . .	22	
23	Multiply line 22 by 92.35% (0.9235)	23	
24	Add lines 21 and 23	24	
25	Enter the smaller of line 9 or line 24	25	
26	Multiply line 25 by 6.2% (0.062). Enter here and see the instructions for line 12e of Schedule 3 (Form 1040)	26	

Schedule SE (Form 1040) 2020

Example 8.10

Robbins Co., a sole proprietorship, employs B, C, D, and E as well as the sole proprietor, A, who files a Schedule C for his business.

	Compensation	Contributions
A*	$150,000	See note below
B	$100,000	$15,000
C	$80,000	$12,000
D	$50,000	$7,500
E	$20,000	$3,000

*A's compensation is Schedule C net income

Robbins maintains a Keogh profit sharing plan with a 15% contribution to each employee (not the owner). In spite of the fact that each employee receives exactly 15%, A is limited to receiving 13.0435% (0.15/1.15) of $150,000 less one-half of the self-employment taxes due on his earnings.

$150,000	Schedule C net income
- $6,000	Less: ½ self-employment taxes ($12,000 assumed for ease of calculation)
$144,000	Self-employment income
x 0.130435	Contribution rate (0.15/1.15)
$18,782.64	**Contribution on behalf of A ***

* Rounding was not utilized when applying the contribution rate (0.130434783).

The special calculation is required because Schedule C net income is presumed to include the qualified plan contribution and because one-half of the self-employment taxes are deductible for self-employed persons after the calculation of the Schedule C net income. For all of the other employees, their contribution is calculated based upon 15% of their compensation.

Where To Deduct Contributions

Deductions for contributions to qualified plans made for employee-participants are taken on the employer's tax return. For example, sole proprietors deduct contributions on Form 1040, either Schedule C (Profit or Loss From Business) or Schedule F (Profit or Loss From Farming). Partnerships and most LLCs deduct contributions on Form 1065 (U.S. Return of Partnership Income Tax Return), Form 1120-A (U.S. Corporation Short-Form Income Tax Return), or Form 1120S (U.S. Income Tax Return for an S Corporation). Sole proprietors and partners deduct contributions for themselves on Form 1040, Schedule 1. If the self-employed person is a partner, then contributions for that partner from the partnership are shown on Form 1065, Schedule K-1 (Partner's Share of Income, Credits, Deductions, etc.).

Exhibit 8.16 | Adjusted Gross Income Section of Form 1040 Schedule 1

10	Educator expenses	10	
11	Certain business expenses of reservists, performing artists, and fee-basis government officials. Attach Form 2106	11	
12	Health savings account deduction. Attach Form 8889	12	
13	Moving expenses for members of the Armed Forces. Attach Form 3903	13	
14	Deductible part of self-employment tax. Attach Schedule SE	14	
15	Self-employed SEP, SIMPLE, and qualified plans	15	
16	Self-employed health insurance deduction	16	
17	Penalty on early withdrawal of savings	17	
18a	Alimony paid	18a	
b	Recipient's SSN . . . . ▶		
c	Date of original divorce or separation agreement (see instructions) ▶		
19	IRA deduction	19	
20	Student loan interest deduction	20	
21	Tuition and fees deduction. Attach Form 8917	21	
22	Add lines 10 through 21. These are your **adjustments to income.** Enter here and on Form 1040, 1040-SR, or 1040-NR, line 10a	22	

Carryover of Excess Contributions

If the employer contributes more to the qualified plan than the permitted deduction for the year, the excess contribution can be carried over and deducted in future years, combined with, or in lieu of, contributions for those years. The combined deduction in a later year is limited to 25 percent of the participating employees' compensation for that year. This percentage limit must be reduced to figure the maximum deduction for contributions made for the self-employed individual.

The amount that can be carried over and deducted may be subject to an excise tax. If the employer contributes more than the deductible amount to a retirement plan, the employer has made a nondeductible contribution and may be liable for an excise tax. In general, a 10 percent excise tax applies to nondeductible excess contributions made to qualified pension and profit sharing plans.

The 10 percent excise tax does not apply to any contribution made for a self-employed individual to meet the minimum funding requirements in a defined benefit plan. Even if that contribution is more than the earned income from the trade or business for which the plan is set up, the difference is not subject to this excise tax.

If the employer maintains a defined benefit plan, the following exceptions may enable them to avoid the 10 percent penalty on certain nondeductible contributions. If contributions to one or more defined contribution plans are not deductible only because they are more than the combined plan deduction limit, the 10 percent excise tax does not apply to the extent the difference is not more than the greater of six percent of the participants' compensation (including elective deferrals) for the year or the sum of employer matching contributions and the elective deferrals to a 401(k) plan. [8]

In figuring the 10 percent excise tax, the employer can choose not to take into account as nondeductible contributions for any year contributions to a defined benefit plan that are not more than the full funding limit figured without considering the current liability limit. The employer applies the overall limits on deductible contributions first to contributions to defined contribution plans and then to contributions to defined benefit plans. If the employer uses this exception, the employer cannot also use the exception discussed above regarding contributions to one or more defined contribution plans.

8. See Chapter 3 for more information on combined limits for defined contribution plans and defined benefit plans.

Forfeitures

Generally, **forfeitures** occur when employees terminate employment. In the event that there are forfeitures from a defined contribution plan, the forfeited amounts can be used to either reduce the employer's contributions under the plan or can be reallocated to the remaining plan participants. Employers often anticipate the effect of forfeitures on remaining plan participants in determining the costs of a qualified plan.

Example 8.11

Loopili Corporation recently established a profit sharing plan that requires three years of service before obtaining a vested right to benefits under the plan. Lucy, one of the company's employees, resigned from her position after two years of service and has an unvested account balance of $8,000. Loopili Corporation may reduce its next contribution to the plan by $8,000 or reallocate the $8,000 to the remaining participants.

Defined benefit plans are required to use forfeitures to reduce plan costs. Forfeitures cannot be allocated to the participant's accounts because participants of defined benefit plans do not have individual accounts. Contributions to defined benefit plans are made yearly to keep the plan actuarially on target to pay the expected required benefits. If the plan is over-funded one year, then the company pays less in the subsequent year. The over-funded amount is not returned to the employer until all claims from the plan have been paid, and the plan document allows the plan to distribute the assets to the employer.

Example 8.12

Assume for this example Loopili Corporation established a defined benefit plan in favor of its employees based on years of service. Last year the plan assets were $1,000,000, and the actuary estimated that the plan assets needs to be $1,200,000 to fund the required benefits. The company contributes the necessary $200,000 bringing the account balance to $1,200,000 for the current year. During the year, Andy, a long time employee, died prematurely. At the end of the year the actuary estimates that the plan only needs $1,180,000 to fund the needed benefits. The company is not able to take back the excess $20,000. That amount will stay in the plan and reduce contributions in future years.

Exhibit 8.17 | Treatment of Forfeitures from Terminations

Defined Benefit Plans	Defined Contribution Plans
• Forfeitures may reduce plan costs	• Forfeitures may reduce plan costs or • Allocate forfeitures to remaining participants

Prohibited Transactions

Prohibited transactions are transactions between the plan and a disqualified person that are prohibited by law. The prohibited transaction rules usually pertain to related party activities and are imposed to address potential conflicts with parties-in-interest. If a disqualified person takes part in a prohibited transaction, that disqualified person will be subject to a tax as discussed below.

Exhibit 8.18 | Definition of Disqualified Person

A disqualified person is any of the following:
1. A fiduciary of the plan.
2. A person providing services to the plan.
3. An employer, any of whose employees are covered by the plan.
4. An employee organization, any of whose members are covered by the plan.
5. Any direct or indirect owner of 50% or more of any of the following:
   - The combined voting power of all classes of stock entitled to vote, or the total value of shares of all classes of stock of a corporation that is an employer or employee organization described in (3) or (4).
   - The capital interest or profits interest of a partnership that is an employer or employee organization described in (3) or (4).
   - The beneficial interest of a trust or unincorporated enterprise that is an employer or an employee organization described in (3) or (4).
6. A member of the family of any individual described in (1), (2), (3), or (5). (A member of a family is the spouse, ancestor, lineal descendant, or any spouse of a lineal descendant.)
7. A corporation, partnership, trust, or estate of which (or in which) any direct or indirect owner described in (1) through (5) holds 50% or more of any of the following:
   - The combined voting power of all classes of stock entitled to vote or the total value of shares of all classes of stock of a corporation.
   - The capital interest or profits interest of a partnership.
   - The beneficial interest of a trust or estate.
8. An officer, director (or an individual having powers or responsibilities similar to those of officers or directors), a 10% or more shareholder, or highly compensated employee (earning 10% or more of the yearly wages of an employer) of a person described in (3), (4), (5), or (7).
9. A 10% or more (in capital or profits) partner or joint venture of a person described in (3), (4), (5), or (7).
10. Any disqualified person, as described in (1) through (9) above, who is a disqualified person with respect to any plan to which a §501(c)(22) trust is permitted to make payments under §4223 of ERISA.

Prohibited transactions generally include actions by a disqualified person that potentially could have adverse consequences to the plan or participants. A transfer of plan income or assets to, use of them by, or for the benefit of a disqualified person is a prohibited transaction. A prohibited transaction is also any act of a fiduciary that uses plan income or assets in his own interest. The receipt of consideration by a fiduciary for his own account from any party dealing with the plan in a transaction that involves plan income or assets is prohibited. Selling, exchanging with, or leasing property, as well as lending money or extending credit to a disqualified person by the plan is prohibited.

Exhibit 8.19 | Prohibited Transactions

> A fiduciary with respect to a plan shall not cause the plan to engage in a transaction, if the fiduciary knows or should know that such transaction constitutes a direct or indirect-
> - sale or exchange, or leasing, of any property between the plan and a party in interest;
> - lending of money or other extension of credit between the plan and a party in interest;
> - furnishing of goods, services, or facilities between the plan and a party in interest;
> - transfer to, or use by or for the benefit of a party in interest, of any assets of the plan; or
> - acquisition, on behalf of the plan, of any employer security or employer real property in violation of ERISA §1107 (a).

Certain transactions are exempt from being treated as prohibited transactions. For example, a prohibited transaction does not take place if a disqualified person receives any benefit that they are entitled as a plan participant or beneficiary. However, the benefit must be figured and paid under the same terms as for all other participants and beneficiaries.

In the past, ERISA fiduciary standards and prohibited transaction rules often discouraged employers from furnishing investment advice and information to plan participants. The Pension Protection Act of 2006 created a new exception to the prohibited transactions rule permitting plan fiduciaries to be compensated for giving participants investment advice through an eligible investment advice arrangement, subject to rules intended to limit the possibility of abuse.[9] For employer-sponsored plans subject to ERISA, a fiduciary that is a registered investment company, bank, insurance company or registered broker-dealer is engaged in an eligible investment advice arrangement if either: (1) its fee does not vary depending on the investment choices that participants make, or (2) its recommendations are based on a computer model certified by an independent third party. Under either approach, the PPA 2006 requires several safeguards, including an annual audit of the arrangement. If these requirements are met, the following are exempt from prohibited transaction treatment: (1) the provision of investment advice; (2) an investment transaction (e.g., sale of a security); and (3) the direct or indirect receipt of fees or other compensation in connection with the provision of the advice or an investment transaction pursuant to the advice. This exemption is available for advice provided after December 31, 2006.

The initial penalty on a prohibited transaction is a 15 percent excise tax on the amount involved for each year (or part of year) in the taxable period. Under the PPA 2006, no excise tax will be assessed if the transaction is corrected within 14 days of the date the disqualified person (or other person knowingly participating in the transaction) discovers, or reasonably should have discovered, the transaction was a prohibited transaction. If the transaction is not corrected within the taxable period, an additional tax of 100 percent of the amount involved is imposed.[10]

---

9. IRC §4975(f)(8).
10. See Form 5330 and instruction for Form 5330.

The term "correct" means, with respect to a transaction:
- to undo the transaction to the extent possible and in any case to make good to the plan or affected account any losses resulting from the transaction; and
- to restore to the plan or affected account any profits made through the use of assets of the plan.

Both taxes (the 15 percent tax and the 100 percent tax) are payable by any disqualified person who participated in the transaction (other than a fiduciary acting only as such). If more than one person takes part in the transaction, each person can be jointly and severally liable for the entire tax. The amount involved in a prohibited transaction is the fair market value of any property received or given. If services are performed, the amount involved is any excess compensation given or received.

The taxable period starts on the transaction date and ends on the earliest of the following days:
- The day the IRS mails a notice of deficiency for the tax.
- The day the IRS assesses the tax.
- The day the correction of the transaction is completed.
- Payment of the 15 percent tax with Form 5330.

If a disqualified person participates in a prohibited transaction, that person can avoid the 100 percent tax by correcting the transaction as soon as possible. Correcting the transaction means rectifying it to the fullest extent without putting the plan in a worse financial position than if the fiduciary had originally acted under the highest fiduciary standards.

Example 8.13

Ortez Inc. sponsors a 401(k) plan that allows participant contributions. The company pays its employees and withholds the contributions on a bi-weekly basis. The plan does not allow participants to direct their investments. The plan fiduciary invests the plan assets in a diversified portfolio of investments. Assume employee contributions were not deposited into the plan for the first pay period of the year. Therefore, the participant contributions that normally would have been deposited remained in Ortez Inc.'s general assets. Since the employer was able to use the money that belonged to the participants, they engaged in a prohibited transaction (the use of assets for the benefit of a disqualified person - the employer). Ortez Inc. realized the error a month later. To avoid the 100% penalty, Ortez Inc. must not only deposit the employee contributions into the participant's account, but they must also deposit additional funds to compensate for the earnings on the contribution the participants did not receive (the amount required is determined using the IRC §6621 rate compared to the plan's earning rate).[11]

If the prohibited transaction is not corrected during the taxable period, the disqualified person usually has an additional 90 days after the day the IRS mails a notice of deficiency for the 100 percent tax to correct the transaction. This correction period (the taxable period plus the 90 days) can be extended if the IRS grants reasonable time needed to correct the transaction or the disqualified person petitions the Tax Court. If the disqualified person corrects the transaction within this period, the IRS will abate, credit, or refund the 100 percent tax.

11.https://www.dol.gov/agencies/ebsa/employers-and-advisers/plan-administration-and-compliance/correction-programs/vfcp

ERISA and Filing Requirements

ERISA

The **Employee Retirement Income Security Act of 1974** (ERISA) places several burdens on retirement plan administration. One of the key obligations ERISA imposes is that of fiduciary responsibility. While several people may be imposed with the fiduciary duty, the duty is generally imposed on those individuals that have authority over the plan's management, administration, or disposition of the plan's assets. The duty is also imposed on individuals that render investment advice on the plan's assets for a fee. Plan fiduciaries may include plan administrators, plan trustees, and members of the plan's investment committee.

Things a Fiduciary Must Do

First, the **fiduciary** must exercise the care, skill, and diligence of a prudent person acting solely in the interest of plan participants and their beneficiaries.[12] Second, the fiduciary also has an obligation to diversify the plan's assets to reduce the risk of loss. Third, the fiduciary must also act in accordance with the plan's provisions and must refrain from acts forbidden under the law. Effectively, the fiduciary must "do the right thing" and not violate the provisions of the plan or the laws.

Things a Fiduciary Must Not Do

Fiduciaries are prohibited from engaging in certain activities. First, they may not be paid for their services if they are already receiving full-time pay from an employer or union whose employees or members are participants. Second, they cannot act in any transaction involving the plan on behalf of a party whose interests are adverse to those of the plan, its participants, or beneficiaries. Third, they may not receive any consideration for their own personal account from any party dealing with the plan in connection with a transaction involving the assets of the plan. Fourth, they may not cause a plan to engage in certain transactions with parties in interest. Fifth, they may not permit more than 10 percent of a pension plan's assets to be invested in employer securities.

If a plan fiduciary does not exercise the necessary care, skill, and diligence of a prudent person or engages in prohibited transactions, the fiduciary may be held personally liable for any losses the plan suffers. The plan fiduciary may also be required to remit to the plan any profits earned through improper use of the assets. In some instances, a court may relieve a fiduciary of his services to the plan due to fiduciary misconduct.

Periodic Pension Benefit Statements

As a result of the Pension Protection Act of 2006, the administrator of a defined contribution plan is required (beginning in 2007) to provide a benefit statement:
1. to a participant or beneficiary who has the right to direct the investment of assets in his account, at least quarterly,
2. to any other participant or other beneficiary who has his own account under the plan, at least annually, and
3. to other beneficiaries, upon written request, but limited to one request during any 12-month period.

12.29 USC§1104.

A benefit statement provided with respect to a defined contribution plan must include the value of each investment to which assets in the individual's account are allocated, including the value of any assets held in the form of employer securities.

The SECURE Act of 2019 created a new requirement that defined contribution individual account statements provided more often than every 12 months include a lifetime income disclosure at least once every 12 months. The lifetime income projection must be based upon assumptions prescribed by the Department of Labor and is designed to assist participants with retirement planning by illustrating the hypothetical monthly income benefits the participant would receive if the entire account balance were used to provide a lifetime income stream. Projections must include a qualified joint and survivor annuity with a spouse of equal age and a single life annuity. Plan sponsors will have no liability if the illustrated lifetime income equivalent is not actually available for the participant and are not responsible for ensuring any particular monthly benefit amount. Ultimately, the benefit will continue to be based upon the account balance and investment or annuitization options available at the time of the employee's retirement. The disclosure is simply to create awareness of the amount of retirement benefit that may be possible based on current savings. Since many participants underestimate the amount needed to fund retirement, these disclosures may encourage participants to save more diligently in situations where the projected income stream is lower than what the participant may have expected. Inclusion of the lifetime income illustrations will begin with benefit statements furnished after September 18, 2021.

Example 8.14[13]

Cris, who is 40 years old and single, has an account balance on December 31, 2021 of $125,000. The 10-year constant maturity Treasury rate (10-year CMT rate) is 1.83% as of the first day of December. Cris's lifetime benefit illustration is as follows:

Current Account Balance		$125,000
Single Life Annuity	Assumes participant is age 67 on December 31, 2021 when the annuity commences	$645 per month for life
Qualified Joint and 100% Survivor Annuity	Assumes participant and hypothetical spouse are both age 67 on December 31, 2021 when the annuity commences	$533 per month for the participant's life and $533 per month for the life of the spouse following the participant's death

13. Example derived from the Department of Labor's Factsheet *Pension Benefit Statements - Lifetime Income Illustrations.* https://www.dol.gov/agencies/ebsa/about-ebsa/our-activities/resource-center/fact-sheets/pension-benefit-statements-lifetime-income-illustrations. See DOL Interim Final Rule on Lifetime Income Disclosures (at the same web address) for details regarding assumptions used. Note: This example and corresponding assumptions are based on an interim final rule and assumptions may change when the final rule is published.

As a result of the Pension Protection Act of 2006, the administrator of a defined benefit plan is required either:

1. to furnish a benefit statement at least once every three years to each participant who has a vested accrued benefit under the plan and who is employed by the employer at the time the benefit statements are furnished to participants; or

2. to furnish at least annually to each participant notice of the availability of a benefit statement and the manner in which a participant can obtain it.

The administrator of a defined benefit pension plan is also required to furnish a benefit statement to a participant or beneficiary upon written request, limited to one request during any 12-month period.

For both a defined contribution plan and a defined benefit plan, a benefit statement must be written in a manner calculated to be understood by the average plan participant.

Department of Labor

The **Department of Labor** administers and enforces more than 180 federal laws covering many workplace activities for about 10 million employers and 125 million workers. The Employee Benefits Security Administration (EBSA), an agency of the Department of Labor, oversees plan administration, primarily focusing on being an advocate for the employee. Applicable to this text, the Department of Labor is charged with enforcing the rules governing the conduct of plan managers, investment of plan assets, reporting and disclosure of plan information, enforcement of the fiduciary provisions of the law, and workers' benefit rights as regulated by ERISA.

Pension Benefit Guaranty Corporation

Recall from Chapter 4 that the **Pension Benefit Guaranty Corporation** was established in 1974 when President Gerald R. Ford signed ERISA into law. The PBGC, just as its name implies, acts to guarantee pension benefits. It is a federal corporation that acts as an insurance provider to maintain the benefits promised to employees by their defined benefit pension plans. The plan sponsors of defined benefit and cash balance pensions plans pay premiums for the insurance coverage, but the PBGC only provides plan participants with a limited benefit in the case of the plan completely or partially terminating with an unfunded or underfunded liability.

The PBGC does not cover defined contribution plans, nor does it cover defined benefit pension plans of professional services corporations with 25 or fewer participants. The PBGC does cover all other defined benefit plans at a cost to the plan sponsor of $86 (2021) per plan participant per year and $46 (2021) per $1,000 of plan underfunding for the year.

Reporting Requirements

The employer generally must file an annual report with the Department of Labor. Generally, this is accomplished by filing Form 5500, which is primarily an informational return. Some employers are allowed to file an abbreviated form called Form 5500-EZ, and other organizations are exempt from filing altogether. If a report is due, then it must be filed with the Department of Labor by the last day of the 7th month after the plan year end. The Department of Labor will then provide the necessary information to the IRS and PBGC. In addition, the Pension Protection Act of 2006 requires any PBGC-insured plans to provide participants, the PBGC, and any union that represents employees covered by the plan with an annual funding notice. The notice must include information about the plan's funded status and the allocation of its assets. The PPA 2006 further requires that certain Form 5500 information be made available on the Internet and on the employer's intranet (if applicable). Below is a discussion of Form 5500.

Form 5500–EZ

Form 5500–EZ is used if the plan only provides benefits for the employer, the employer and their spouse, or one or more partners and their spouses. A plan that benefits employees other than an owner, spouse, partner or partner's spouse cannot use Form 5500-EZ. Form 5500-EZ can be used for defined benefit plans and defined contribution plans, but not for ESOPs. A plan that covers a business that is a member of an affiliated service group, a controlled group of corporations, or a group of businesses under common control, or a plan that covers a business that leases employees cannot file a Form 5500-EZ.

Form 5500-SF

The Form 5500-SF, Short Form Annual Return/Report of Small Employee Benefit Plan, is a simplified annual reporting form for use by certain small pension and welfare benefit plans. To be eligible to use Form 5500-SF, the plan must:

- be a small plan (i.e., generally have fewer than 100 participants at the beginning of the plan year),
- meet the conditions for being exempt from the requirement that the plan's books and records be audited by an independent qualified public accountant (IQPA),
- have 100 percent of its assets invested in certain secure investments with a readily determinable fair value, such as mutual fund shares, investment contracts with insurance companies and banks valued at least annually, publicly traded securities held by a registered broker dealer, cash and cash equivalents,
- hold no employer securities (ESOPs not permitted), and
- not be a multi-employer plan.

Form 5500

All other employers, unless exempt from filing, must file a Form 5500. Form 5500 contains the basic identifying information of the plan. For small plans with fewer than 100 participants at the beginning of the year that do not qualify to file Form 5500-SF, they must file 5500, but do not have to file as many schedules as larger plans with 100 or more participants. As detailed in **Exhibit 8.21** there are several schedules that may also have to be completed depending on the type and nature of the plan.

Exemption from Filing Form 5500

Form 5500–EZ and Form 5500 are not required if the employer has only a one-participant plan that had total plan assets of $250,000 or less for a plan year.

Annual Reporting Requirements for Code Section 403(b) Plans

The Department of Labor (DOL) repealed, starting with the 2009 annual return/report, the special limited financial reporting rules that applied to Code §403(b) plans. Thus, beginning with the 2009 plan year, administrators of 403(b) plans subject to Title I of ERISA, like administrators of 401(k) plans, must file financial and other compliance information about the plans annually with the government on a Form 5500 or Form 5500-SF. Large 403(b) plans (generally those with 100 or more participants) also must include a report of an independent qualified public accountant (IQPA) with their Form 5500. The IRS has a website for administrators of 403(b) plans: https://www.irs.gov/retirement-plans/irc-403b-tax-sheltered-annuity-plans.

Exhibit 8.20 | Summary of Form 5500

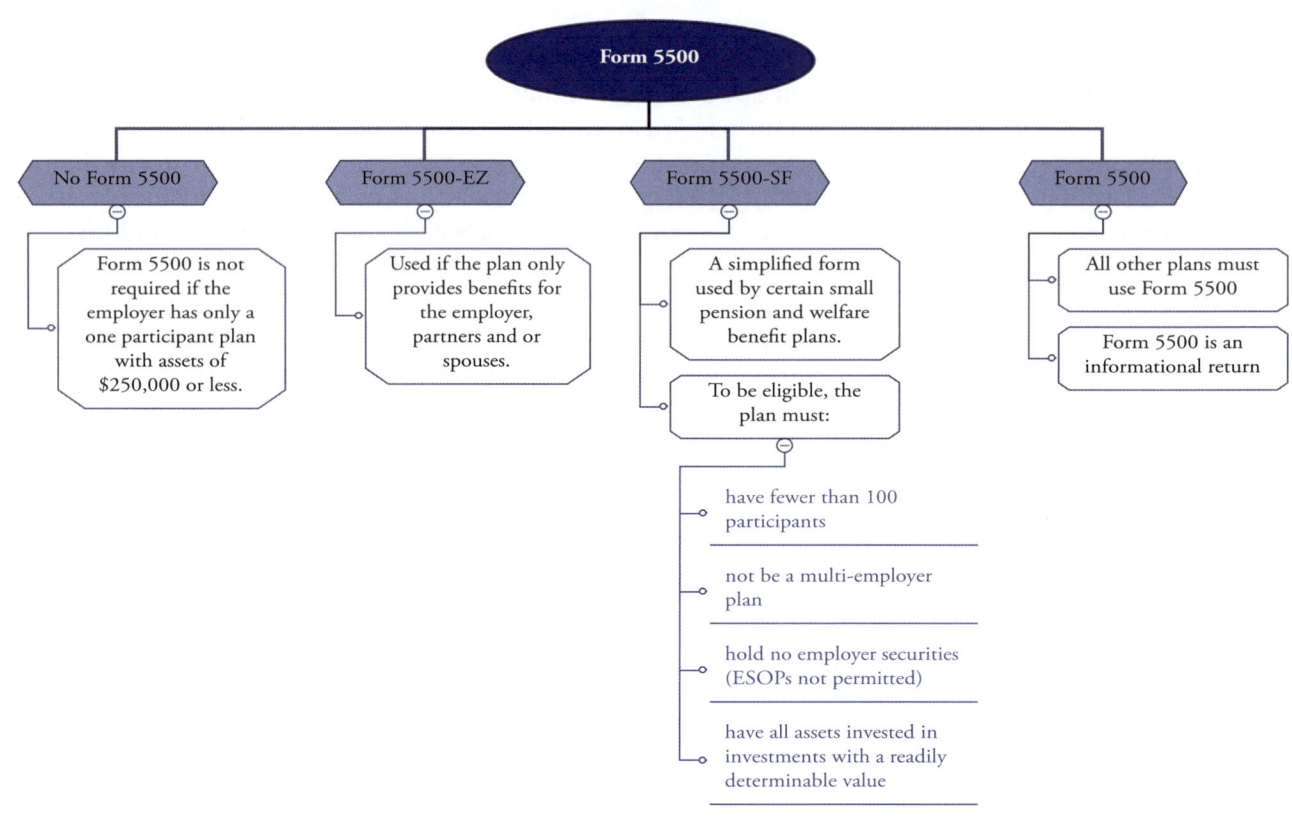

EFAST2 Processing System

Effective January 1, 2010, all pension and welfare plans that are required to submit an annual return/report under Title I of ERISA (Form 5500 or Form 5500-SF) must do so electronically for all plan years using the new EFAST2 Processing System.[14] The Form 5500-EZ cannot be submitted electronically and must be filed using paper based forms.

---

14. See https://www.efast.dol.gov/welcome.html.

Exhibit 8.21 | Quick Reference Chart for Form 5500

	Large Pension Plan[1]	Small Pension Plan[1]
Form 5500	Must complete.	Must complete.
Schedule A (Insurance Information)	Must complete if plan has insurance contracts for benefits or investments.	Must complete if plan has insurance contracts for benefits or investments.
Schedule C (Service Provider Information)	Must complete if service provider was paid $5,000 or more and/or an accountant or actuary was terminated.	Not required.
Schedule D (DFE/Participating Plan Info.)	Must complete Part I if plan participated in a CCT, PSA, MTIA, or 103-12 IE.	Must complete Part I if plan participated in a CCT, PSA, MTIA, or 103-12 IE.
Schedule G (Financial Transaction Schedules)	Must complete if Schedule H, line 4b, 4c, or 4d is "Yes."[2]	Not required.
Schedule H (Financial Information)	Must complete.[2]	Not required.
Schedule I (Financial Information - Small Plan)	Not required.	Must complete.
Schedule MB (Actuarial Information)	Must complete if multi-employer defined benefit plan or money purchase plan subject to minimum funding standards.[3]	Must complete if multi-employer defined benefit plan or money purchase plan subject to minimum funding standards.
Schedule R (Retirement Plan Information)	Must complete.[4]	Must complete.[4]
Schedule SB (Actuarial Information)	Must complete if single-employer or multi-employer defined benefit plan, including an eligible combined plan and subject to minimum funding standards.	Must complete if single-employer or multi-employer defined benefit plan, including an eligible combined plan and subject to minimum funding standards.
Accountant's Report	Must attach.	Not required unless Schedule I, line 4k, is checked "No."

1. This chart provides only general guidance. Not all rules and requirements are reflected. A large plan is defined as a plan that covered 100 or more participants as of the beginning of the plan year. A small plan is a plan that covered fewer than 100 participants as of the beginning of the plan year.
2. Schedules of assets and reportable (5%) transactions also must be filed with the Form 5500 if Schedule H, line 4i or 4j is "Yes," but use of printed form not required.
3. Money purchase defined contribution plans that are amortizing a funding waiver are required to complete lines 3, 9, and 10 of the Schedule MB in accordance with the instructions. Also see instructions for line 5 of Schedule R and line 12a of Form 5500-SF.
4. A pension plan is exempt from filing Schedule R if all of the following four conditions are met:
    - The plan is not a defined benefit plan or otherwise subject to the minimum funding standards of Code §412 or ERISA §302.
    - No in-kind distributions reportable on line 1 of Schedule R were distributed during the plan year.
    - No benefits were distributed during the plan year that are reportable on Form 1099-R using an EIN other than that of the plan sponsor or plan administrator.
    - In the case of a plan that is not a profit sharing, ESOP, or stock bonus plan, no plan benefits were distributed during the plan year in the form of a single sum distribution.

Exhibit 8.22 | Form 5500

Form **5500-EZ**	**Annual Return of A One-Participant (Owners/Partners and Their Spouses) Retirement Plan or A Foreign Plan**	OMB No. 1545-1610

Form **5500-EZ**

Department of the Treasury
Internal Revenue Service

Annual Return of A One-Participant (Owners/Partners and Their Spouses) Retirement Plan or A Foreign Plan

This form is required to be filed under section 6058(a) of the Internal Revenue Code.
Certain foreign retirement plans are also required to file this form (see instructions).

▶ **Complete all entries in accordance with the instructions to the Form 5500-EZ.**
▶ **Go to** *www.irs.gov/Form5500EZ* **for instructions and the latest information.**

OMB No. 1545-1610

2020

This Form is Open
to Public Inspection.

Part I Annual Return Identification Information

For the calendar plan year 2020 or fiscal plan year beginning (MM/DD/YYYY)   **and ending**

A   This return is: (1) ☐ the first return filed for the plan   (3) ☐ the final return filed for the plan
                         (2) ☐ an amended return   (4) ☐ a short plan year return (less than 12 months)

B   If filing under an extension of time, check this box (see instructions). . . . . ▶ ☐

C   If this return is for a foreign plan, check this box (see instructions) . . . . ▶ ☐

D   If this return is for the IRS Late Filer Penalty Relief Program, check this box (see instructions) . . . . ▶ ☐

Part II Basic Plan Information — enter all requested information.

1a   Name of plan

1b   Three-digit plan number (PN) ▶

1c   Date plan first became effective (MM/DD/YYYY)

2a   Employer's name

Trade name of business (if different from name of employer)

In care of name

Mailing address (room, apt., suite no. and street, or P.O. box)

City or town, state or province, country, and ZIP or foreign postal code (if foreign, see instructions)

2b   Employer Identification Number (EIN)
(Do not enter your Social Security Number)

2c   Employer's telephone number

2d   Business code (see instructions)

3a   Plan administrator's name (if same as employer, enter "Same")

In care of name

Mailing address (room, apt., suite no. and street, or P.O. box)

City or town, state or province, country, and ZIP or foreign postal code (if foreign, see instructions)

3b   Administrator's EIN

3c   Administrator's telephone number

4   If the employer's name, the employer's EIN, and/or the plan name has changed since the last return filed for this plan, enter the employer's name and EIN, the plan name, and the plan number for the last return in the appropriate space provided

a   Employer's name

4b   EIN

4c   Plan name

4d   PN

5a(1) Total number of participants at the beginning of the plan year	**5a(1)**	
a(2) Total number of active participants at the beginning of the plan year	**5a(2)**	
b(1) Total number of participants at the end of the plan year	**5b(1)**	
b(2) Total number of active participants at the end of the plan year	**5b(2)**	
c Number of participants who terminated employment during the plan year with accrued benefits that were less than 100% vested	**5c**	

Part III Financial Information

		(1) Beginning of year	**(2)** End of year
6a	Total plan assets		
b	Total plan liabilities		
c	Net plan assets (subtract line **6b** from **6a**)		

For Privacy Act and Paperwork Reduction Act Notice, see the Instructions for Form 5500-EZ.   Cat. No. 63263R   Form **5500-EZ** (2020)

Form 5500 Continued

Form 5500-EZ (2020) Page 2

Part III — Financial Information (continued)

7 Contributions received or receivable from: | Amount

a Employers. — 7a

b Participants — 7b

c Others (including rollovers) — 7c

Part IV — Plan Characteristics

8 Enter the applicable two-character feature codes from the List of Plan Characteristics Codes in the instructions.

[ ][ ] [ ][ ] [ ][ ] [ ][ ] [ ][ ] [ ][ ] [ ][ ] [ ][ ] [ ][ ] [ ][ ]

Part V — Compliance and Funding Questions

		Yes	No	Amount
9 During the plan year, did the plan have any participant loans? If "Yes," enter amount as of year end	9			
10 Is this a defined benefit plan that is subject to minimum funding requirements? If "Yes," complete Schedule SB (Form 5500) and line 10a below (see instructions)	10			
a Enter the unpaid minimum required contributions for all years from Schedule SB (Form 5500), line 40	10a			
11 Is this a defined contribution plan subject to the minimum funding requirements of section 412 of the Code?	11			
If "Yes," complete lines 11a or 11b, 11c, 11d, and 11e below, as applicable.				
a If a waiver of the minimum funding standard for a prior year is being amortized in this plan year, enter the month, day, and year (MM/DD/YYYY) of the letter ruling granting the waiver (see instructions)	11a			
b Enter the minimum required contribution for this plan year	11b			
c Enter the amount contributed by the employer to the plan for this plan year	11c			
d Subtract the amount in line 11c from the amount in line 11b. Enter the result (enter a minus sign to the left of a negative amount)	11d			

		Yes	No	N/A	
e Will the minimum funding amount reported on line 11d be met by the funding deadline?	11e				

Caution: A penalty for the late or incomplete filing of this return will be assessed unless reasonable cause is established.

Under penalties of perjury, I declare that I have examined this return including, if applicable, any related Schedule MB (Form 5500) or Schedule SB (Form 5500) signed by an enrolled actuary, and, to the best of my knowledge and belief, it is true, correct, and complete.

Sign Here ▶

_____ Signature of employer or plan administrator

_____ Date

_____ Type or print name of individual signing as employer or plan administrator

Form **5500-EZ** (2020)

AMENDING AND TERMINATING A QUALIFIED PLAN

Just as adopting a qualified plan often makes good business sense, terminating or changing a qualified plan may also make good business sense. Employers may (and should) reserve the right to change or terminate the plan and to discontinue contributions within the plan document. There are many reasons for changing provisions of a qualified plan. Changes (amendments) are often used to solve original defects in the plan document, maximize benefits to key employees, or comply with a new tax law requirement. In addition, there are other reasons for terminating a qualified plan. Terminations often occur when a law change occurs that makes one type of plan less

📋 *Key Concepts*

1. Why would a qualified plan be amended or terminated?

2. How is a qualified plan amended?

3. How is a qualified plan terminated?

advantageous than it was previously, the company can no longer financially maintain the plan, or the company realizes the plan no longer meets the needs of the employees or the company.

Reasons to Amend or Terminate a Plan

Qualified plans, especially for small employers, are often changed to maximize the provision of benefits to key employees. Some plans allow forfeitures to be reallocated to other plan participant's or may be used to reduce plan costs. Small business owners frequently change this election based on the benefits they are able to receive from the plan. For example, consider an owner who has compensation of $100,000 when the plan is first established. Due to the amount of his compensation, the owner is unable to receive the maximum contribution allowed for the year ($58,000 for 2021); therefore, the logical choice would be to allow forfeitures to be reallocated to remaining participants, so that his contributions can be increased by the other's forfeitures. In later years, when his compensation is $400,000 and he is able to receive the maximum contribution, it no longer makes sense from his perspective to allow reallocation of forfeitures. Since he has already reached his annual additions limit, the reallocated forfeitures could not be used to increase his account. In such an instance, he may amend the plan to require that forfeitures only reduce future plan costs.

Another reason a plan may be changed or terminated is that a law change may make an entire plan or plan provision obsolete. For example, before the Economic Growth and Tax Relief and Reconciliation Act of 2001 (EGTRRA 2001) was enacted, the contribution limit for a profit sharing plan was 15 percent of employer compensation. An extra 10 percent was available for employers to increase their total contribution through the adoption of pension plans (namely money purchase pension plans). To do this, many employers selected what is referred to as a **Tandem Plan** (typically combined a 10 percent money purchase pension plan with a 15 percent profit sharing plan so that owners would be able to receive the maximum contribution each year into their qualified plan), while only exposing themselves to a 10 percent mandatory contribution. When EGTRRA 2001 passed, it increased the contribution limit for profit sharing plans to 25 percent, which virtually made Tandem Plans obsolete. The reason is simple. Recall the money purchase pension plan requires a mandatory fixed contribution each year, while the profit sharing plan allows the employer the discretion to determine the contribution percentage each year. With the profit sharing plan able to reach the maximum limit of 25 percent, it becomes unnecessary for the employer to take the risk involved with the fixed contribution of the money purchase pension plan. Therefore, many plans were amended so that the money purchase pension plan was terminated and the plan remaining consisted solely of a profit sharing plan.

A qualified plan may also be terminated when the employer finds that they can no longer financially support the plan they have in place. Sometimes the decision is made by the employer, while other times the decision is made by the PBGC. The employer will frequently reach out for debt relief when it has filed for bankruptcy (Chapter 7) or reorganization (Chapter 11). The PBGC also has the right to step in to terminate a plan if the plan is under-funded and the PBGC feels that it needs to protect its risk that the plan will go under.

A plan may also be terminated simply because the employer finds that the plan is not meeting the needs of the employees or the company. Sometimes the plan benefits are so small that the cost of administering the plan is prohibitive. The employer may realize that a simple increase in compensation for the employees will satisfy the same goodwill as a qualified plan and at a lower cost.

Exhibit 8.23 | Amending or Terminating a Qualified Plan

- To maximize benefits for key employees
- Law changes
- Employer is unable to support
- Benefits were not sufficient

Amending a Qualified Plan

Plan changes are very common due to tax law changes, business changes, or to solve a defect in the plan. Changes are often easily implemented by amending the plan document. When the plan document is amended, the administrator must also revise the Summary Plan Description. The employer is also required to provide the plan participants notices of any plan amendments or changes. Notice can be made either through a revised Summary Plan Description or in a separate document called a Summary of Material Modifications. This document must also be provided to participants free of charge within 210 days after the end of the plan year in which a change is adopted.

Terminating a Qualified Plan

When a qualified plan is terminated, and presuming that sufficient funds are available, all of the participants in the plan become fully vested in their benefits as of the date of termination.[15] Sponsors that terminate a qualified plan must discontinue all contributions and benefit accruals and must distribute all plan assets within a reasonable period of time after the termination of the plan. The method of obtaining a termination and the requirements that need to be met are different for defined-benefit plans and defined-contribution plans.

Permanency Requirement

Although qualified plans are required to be permanent, permanency does not necessarily require that the plan never terminate or continue in existence forever. Permanency in this context just means that the plan must not be established as a temporary program. The goal behind the "permanency" requirement is to dissuade owners from creating plans that will only benefit the owners and key employees and then having the plan vanish before benefits can be accrued by rank-and-file employees. Unfortunately, the abandonment of the plan for any reason other than business necessity within the first few years after it is established will be evidence that the plan was not a bona fide program for the

---

15. Treas. Reg. 1.411(d)-2(a)(1).

exclusive benefit of employees. This is especially true when a pension plan is abandoned soon after pensions have been fully funded for officers or shareholders. The permanency of the plan is indicated by all of the surrounding facts and circumstances, including the likelihood of the employer's ability to continue contributions as provided under the plan.

Defined Benefit Plan Terminations

Because the PBGC is responsible for under-funded defined benefit plans, there are more requirements for terminating a defined benefit plan than for a defined contribution plan. Title IV of ERISA requires that a defined benefit plan terminate under a standard, distress, or involuntary termination. See **Example 8.15**.

Standard Termination

A **standard termination** is voluntary and may occur when the employer has sufficient assets to pay all benefits (liabilities) at the time of final distribution. To terminate a defined benefit plan this way, the administrator must first notify all affected parties between 60 and 90 days before the proposed termination date.

An affected party is:
1. a plan participant,
2. a beneficiary of a deceased participant or an alternate payee under a qualified domestic relations order, and
3. any employee organization representing plan participants.

The termination date can be any date selected by the administrator, including a weekend or holiday. The administrator must then notify the PBGC. The PBGC must approve the termination because it will be liable should the organization not be able to pay the intended debts. Assuming the plan has met the PBGC requirements, then the date of termination will generally be the date proposed by the administrator in the notice of intent to terminate.

Distress Termination

A **distress termination** is voluntary and occurs when the employer is in financial difficulty and is unable to continue with the plan financially. Generally a distress termination occurs when the company is in liquidation, in bankruptcy (Chapter 7), or has filed for reorganization (Chapter 11). It can also occur when the company can no longer pay debts or the pension costs are simply unreasonable. The administrator must also notify the affected parties and the PBGC, as discussed above.

Example 8.15

US Airways is an example of a company that decided it could no longer fund the plan it had in place. In 2003, US Airways filed for Chapter 11 bankruptcy and requested that the bankruptcy court allow them to terminate the pension plan they had in place for the pilots. At the time, the plan was underfunded by approximately $2.5 billion dollars, and the company claimed that fulfilling this obligation would prevent them from successfully reorganizing and emerging from bankruptcy. The court allowed the termination and left the company free to establish a more conservative defined contribution plan. The impact was that the PBGC took over the plan and only protected benefits up to the 2003 PBGC limit, approximately $43,000 (2004 benefits were approximately $44,000). Many pilots saw their benefits reduced from as much as $144,000 annually to approximately $19,000 annually for those age 55, due to the PBGC limit and the actuarial reduction from normal

---

retirement age of 65 to 55. Note that the 2021 maximum annual benefit for retirement for PBGC purposes at age 65 is $72,409.

Involuntary Termination

An **involuntary termination** may be initiated by the PBGC for a plan that is unable to pay benefits from the plan in order to limit the amount of exposure to the PBGC. The PBGC may terminate a pension plan, even if a company has not filed to terminate a plan on its own initiative, if:
- the plan has not met the minimum funding requirements;
- the plan cannot pay current benefits when due;
- a lump-sum payment has been made to a participant who is a substantial owner of the sponsoring company; or
- the loss to PBGC is expected to increase unreasonably if the plan is not terminated.[16]

The PBGC must terminate a plan if assets are unavailable to pay benefits currently due. Under the Pension Protection Act of 2006, the plan sponsor or plan administrator of a plan that has received notice from the PBGC of a determination that the plan should be involuntarily terminated is required to provide an affected party with any information provided to the PBGC in connection with the plan termination.

Defined Contribution Plan Terminations

Compared to defined benefit plans, terminating a defined contribution plan is relatively easy. Defined contribution plans are already funded and not subject to PBGC. Essentially, all the employer must do to terminate the plan is pass a corporate resolution to do so. At that point, any final promised contributions must be completed and the assets must be distributed from the plan.

Partial Terminations

In some instances, a plan, by operation of law, will experience a partial termination. This can occur when the employer changes the plan so that it is very adverse to the employees, or there is a significant severance of employees covered by the plan (i.e., a layoff). A partial termination is decided on a facts and circumstances test; therefore, companies who plan to make decisions that will affect a large number of employees should consider how their actions will affect their qualified plans. Similar to a full termination, the benefits of the plan participants will be 100 percent vested in the event there is a partial termination.

> ### ✎ Quick Quiz 8.4
>
> 1. Qualified plans are often amended to maximize benefits to key employees.
>   a. True
>   b. False
>
> 2. Qualified plan amendments are difficult and require approval by ERISA.
>   a. True
>   b. False
>
> 3. Qualified plans may never terminate without losing their qualified status retroactively to inception.
>   a. True
>   b. False
>
> True, False, False.

Plan Freeze

In some cases, an employer may find that they no longer want to contribute to a plan but do not want to fully terminate the plan. This can be accomplished by freezing the plan (**plan freeze**). For defined contribution plans, a freeze simply means that the employer will no longer make any contributions. For a

16. www.pbgc.gov.

defined benefit plan, participants will no longer accrue additional benefits but the plan sponsor must maintain the previously accrued benefits. The plan will continue to benefit from the tax deferral on the plan's earnings until the plan distributes its assets according to the plan document.

Tax on Reversion of Qualified Plan Assets to Employer[17]

While plan sponsors are prohibited under ERISA from withdrawing assets from a qualified plan, they can recoup assets in the plan that exceed the liabilities and obligations provided for under the plan upon plan termination. There is a 20 percent excise tax on any amount of assets that revert back to the employer from a qualified plan. If certain requirements are not met, then the excise tax is increased to 50 percent of the reversionary amount. These requirements include:
- the employer establishes a qualified replacement plan, or
- provides for specific benefit increases.

This 50 percent excise tax does not apply in the event that the plan sponsor is in bankruptcy. It should be evident that it is unlikely that assets will revert back to the employer in or out of bankruptcy and it is costly when it occurs.

17. IRC §4980.

CASE STUDY 8.1

A request for a distress termination was made in the Chapter 11 bankruptcy reorganization in *In re* **Diversified Industries, Inc.**[1] The Chapter 11 debtor-employer filed a motion with the Bankruptcy Court for authorization to file a notice of intent with Pension Benefit Guaranty Corporation ("PBGC") to terminate five defined benefit plans. The facts showed that the plans were underfunded. The total unpaid minimum contributions for all of these plans as of December 31, 1992 was $2,841,000. The Debtor gave notice of its intent to seek termination of all pension plans. Since there were no objections to the termination of four of these plans, the Court granted authorization and the Debtor initiated the process with PBGC to terminate those four. The benefits for all the participants in those four plans were fully guaranteed by PBGC. The Debtor elected to seek authorization from the PBGC to terminate the remaining plan ("the Plan") pursuant to ERISA's distress termination procedure.

The Plan provided substantial pension benefits for Mr. Ben Fixman and certain other present and former members of the Debtor's senior management team, but a large portion of these benefits were not guaranteed by the PBGC. It was uncontested that if the senior management pension plans were terminated, Mr. Fixman would lose a greater sum than any other employee. Mr. Fixman's pension plan provided him with an annual payment of approximately $136,000. If the Plan were to be terminated, his annual pension would drop to approximately $27,000, the maximum payment that PBGC insured. Mr. Fixman filed an objection to the Debtor's motion, claiming in part that the Debtor was required under ERISA to have the Bankruptcy Court determine whether the Plan could be terminated.

The Bankruptcy Court concluded that due to the Plan's insolvency, the only method of termination was by means of distress termination, which required the plan administrator to provide 60 days' advance notice of intent to terminate to the affected parties, to submit to the PBGC various information as required by ERISA, and to submit information for the PBGC to determine whether the distress criteria had been met.[2] Before submitting the request to terminate the Plan to the PBGC, the Bankruptcy Court explained that the Debtor must satisfy a "business judgment" test and show that the decision is a reasonable exercise of its business judgment. At a hearing, the Debtor proved that it was in its best interest to seek termination of the Plan because, unless the Plan was terminated, the Debtor and its subsidiaries would be unable to pay their debts when due, resulting in the Debtor being unable to continue in business outside the Chapter 11 reorganization process. Accordingly, the court ordered that the Debtor submit the appropriate notices under ERISA to the PBGC to institute the proceedings at that agency to terminate the Plan.

1. In *re Diversified Industries, Inc.*, 166 B.R. 141 (Bkrtcy. E.D. Mo. 1993).
2. Employee Retirement Income Security Act of 1974, §4041(c); 29 U.S.C.A. §1341(c).

SOLUTIONS to the discussion questions can be found exclusively within the chapter. Once you have completed an initial reading of the chapter, go back and highlight the answers to these questions.

1. Describe the business and personal issues that should be considered when making a qualified plan selection.

2. What is an employee census and why is it important?

3. Explain the steps involved in adopting a qualified plan.

4. How and when should employees be notified when a qualified plan is established?

5. What are the minimum funding requirements for qualified plans?

6. When may contributions to a qualified plan be deducted by the employer?

7. Explain how forfeitures are treated in qualified plans.

8. List the transactions that are prohibited in a qualified plan and the exceptions.

9. Describe the regulatory bodies, other than the IRS, and filing requirements involved with the operation of a qualified plan.

10. Under what circumstances would a qualified plan be amended or terminated?

11. Describe how a qualified plan is amended.

12. Describe how a qualified plan is terminated.

13. List and describe the three types of terminations.

14. Describe under what conditions assets from a qualified plan can revert to the employer.

MULTIPLE CHOICE PROBLEMS

A sample of multiple choice problems is provided below. Additional multiple choice problems are available at money-education.com by accessing the Student Practice Portal.

1. Generally, which of the following are contributory plans?
    a. 401(k) and money purchase pension plans.
    b. 401(k) and thrift plans.
    c. Thrift plans and ESOPs.
    d. Money purchase pension plans and profit sharing plans.

2. Which of the following generally contribute to defined benefit plans, profit sharing plans, and money purchase pension plans?
    a. Employees only.
    b. Employer only.
    c. Both employer and employees.
    d. Employer, employees, and government.

3. Who generally makes elective deferrals to a 401(k) plan?
    a. Employees only.
    b. Employer only.
    c. Employees and employer.
    d. Employees, employers, and forfeitures.

4. Plans that require mandatory funding are generally funded by?
    a. The employee.
    b. The employer.
    c. The employee and the employer.
    d. For PBGC insured plans, the employee and the employer.

5. The target benefit pension plan and the money purchase pension plan provide some employee/participant investment diversification protections by limiting the investment amount in employer stock to less than or equal to:
    a. 5%.
    b. 10%.
    c. 20%.
    d. 100%.

> **Additional multiple choice problems
> are available at
> money-education.com
> by accessing the Student Practice Portal.
> Access requires registration of the title using
> the unique code at the front of the book.**

QUICK QUIZ EXPLANATIONS

Quick Quiz 8.1

1. False. With a small business, the plan selection process must focus on both the needs of the company and the needs of the small business owner. Meeting the owner's needs as well as the company's needs is critical to establishing a successful retirement plan.
2. True.
3. False. An employer with fluctuating cash flows would be more likely to choose some type of qualified profit sharing plan that has discretionary contributions each year rather than a pension plan that has mandatory funding requirements.

Quick Quiz 8.2

1. True.
2. True.
3. False. Even when plan sponsors choose to shift the management responsibility of the investment assets to the plan participants, the plan sponsor still retains certain responsibilities over the choices and alternative investments available to the participants.

Quick Quiz 8.3

1. True.
2. False. Defined benefit plans may only use forfeitures to reduce plan costs.
3. True.

Quick Quiz 8.4

1. True.
2. False. Plan changes are very common due to tax law changes, business changes, or to solve a defect in the plan. Changes are often easily implemented by amending the plan document. When the plan document is amended, the administrator must also revise the Summary Plan Description.
3. False. Termination of a qualified plan does not necessarily mean that the plan retroactively loses its qualified status.

9

IRAS AND SEPS

LEARNING OBJECTIVES

1. Contrast the characteristics of IRAs with qualified plans.*
2. Explain the impact of compounding on the ending value of an IRA account after years of continuous funding.
3. Describe the funding limits for traditional and Roth IRAs.*
4. Describe the impact of converting funds in a traditional IRA or qualified plan to a Roth IRA.*
5. Determine the deductibility of contributions to a traditional IRA including taking into consideration the characterization of active participant status.*
6. Calculate the penalties associated with overfunding traditional and Roth IRAs.*
7. Understand the importance of Form 8606.
8. Describe the nature of the taxation of distributions from traditional and Roth IRAs.*
9. Understand the exceptions to the 10 percent early withdrawal penalty that apply to IRAs.*
10. Explain the types of investments that are permitted to be held within an IRA.*
11. Describe the advantages and rules associated with Simplified Employee Pensions (SEPs).*

Ties to CFP Certification Learning Objectives

INTRODUCTION

IRAs, SEPs, SARSEPs, SIMPLEs, and tax sheltered annuities (403(b) plans) are not qualified plans, do not meet the requirements under IRC §401(a), and are not entitled to all of the same benefits as qualified plans. They are referred to as "other tax-advantaged plans" to indicate that, while not qualified plans, they have many of the same benefits and features as qualified plans. While all of these plans have many of the benefits of qualified plans, they also have certain advantages over qualified plans. Similar to qualified plans, tax-advantaged plans are all tax deferred, meaning that earnings within the trust or plan are not taxed until a distribution occurs. In addition, all of these tax-advantaged plans provide for sheltering of current income from taxation.

However, IRAs, SEPs, and SIMPLEs have many key differences from qualified plans. First, IRAs, SEPs, and SIMPLEs are not subject to the same federal reporting requirements as qualified plans. Second, lump-sum distribution options such as NUA, pre-74 capital gain treatment, and 10-year forward averaging are not permitted for distributions from IRAs, SEPs, SIMPLEs, or 403(b) plans. Third, these plans also do not have the same non-alienation of benefits protection found under ERISA. Fourth, these plans, with the exception of the 403(b) plan, are not permitted to offer loans to participants. Fifth, whereas qualified plans typically have specific vesting schedules for contributions made by the employer on behalf of the employee, other tax-advantaged plans always provide for 100 percent vesting, with the exception of some employer contributions to 403(b) plans.

This chapter discusses the rules surrounding Traditional IRAs, IRA annuities, Roth IRAs, SEPs, and SARSEPs. SIMPLE plans, 403(b) plans, and 457 plans are discussed in the following chapter.

Exhibit 9.1 | Characteristics of Qualified Plans and Other Tax-Exempt Plans

Characteristic	Qualified Plans	IRAs	SEP IRAs	SIMPLE IRAs**	403(b) Plans
Provides for tax deferral for deposits and savings	✓	✓	✓	✓	✓
Provides shelter for current income	✓	✓	✓	✓	✓
Annual reporting – Form 5500	✓	✗	✗	✗	Maybe***
Vesting required	✓	✗	✗	✗	Maybe
Loans are permitted	✓	✗	✗	✗	✓
Protection under ERISA	✓	✗****	✗****	✗****	Maybe*
10-year averaging permitted	✓	✗	✗	✗	✗
Pre-74 capital gain treatment	✓	✗	✗	✗	✗
Distributions eligible for NUA	✓	✗	✗	✗	✗

✓ *YES* ✗ *NO*

Many 403(b) plans provide for ERISA protection; however, some do not.
*** There are very few, if any, SIMPLE 401(k)s.*
****Employer maintained 403(b) plans must file Form 5500.*
**** *Although federal bankruptcy protection is available under the Bankruptcy Abuse Prevention and Consumer Protection Act of 2005.*

KNOW THE NUMBERS (2021)

	Traditional IRA	Roth IRA	SEP	SARSEP
Contribution Limit	$6,000	$6,000	25% or $58,000	$19,500
Catch-Up (Over age 50)	$1,000	$1,000	N/A	$6,500
Contribution Phaseout 2021	N/A	Single: $125,000 – $140,000 MFJ: $198,000 – $208,000 MFS: $0,000 – $10,000	N/A	N/A
Deduction Phaseouts 2021	Not an Active Participant: No Limit Active Participant: Single: $66,000 – $76,000 MFJ: $105,000 – $125,000 One Spouse is an Active Participant: $198,000 – $208,000	N/A	N/A	N/A
Provide to Employee With	N/A	N/A	Compensation > $650	N/A

INDIVIDUAL RETIREMENT ACCOUNT

The Individual Retirement Account (IRA) has been available since 1974.[1] The amount that could be contributed on a tax-deferred basis per person per year was once limited to $1,500, but that has now been increased to $6,000 for 2021 with an additional deferral of $1,000 for 2021 for persons age 50 or older. The rules regarding deductibility have also changed as will be explained in this chapter. The IRA has great potential as an accumulation device for retirement when started early and funded annually. Consider an individual who makes annual year-end deposits of $6,000 in a mutual fund earning a 10

percent return each year for 40 years (age 25-65). The future accumulated balance of the account at age 65 is $2,655,555 even though the individual only deposited a total of $240,000. The compound growth potential of such accounts often makes the tax deductibility of the contribution a less significant issue than the accumulation, as illustrated in the graph below.

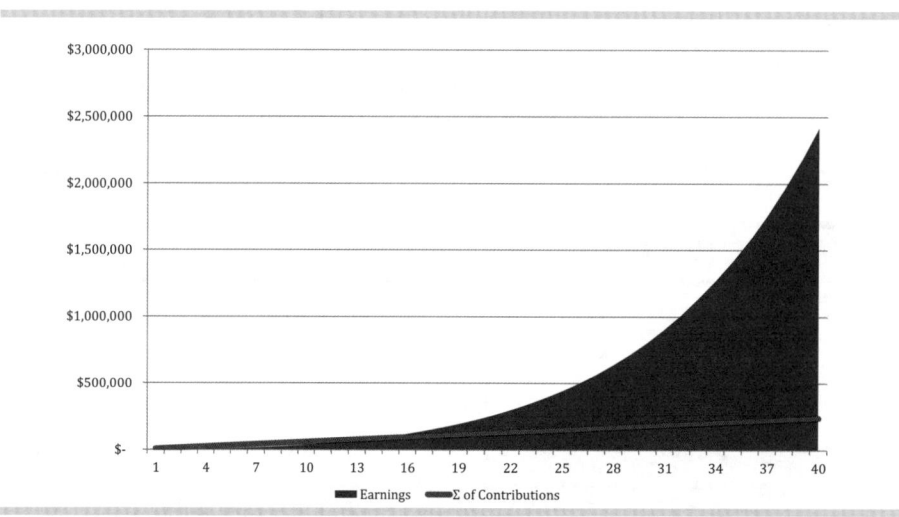

There are two general types of **individual retirement accounts** (IRAs) under present law: traditional IRAs, to which both deductible and nondeductible contributions may be made, and Roth IRAs, to which only nondeductible contributions may be made.[2] Many of the rules relating to traditional IRAs and Roth IRAs are the same and will be discussed together under traditional IRAs. The differences between the types of IRAs are discussed later in this chapter.

Traditional IRAs

Traditional IRAs have been available for many years and as the limits on both contributions and deductions have increased, these retirement vehicles remain an important part of retirement planning for individuals. IRAs take one of two forms, an individual retirement account or an **individual retirement annuity**. An IRA account can hold a wide variety of investments and can be held by a wide variety of **custodians** (e.g., brokerage, bank, mutual fund, etc.). An IRA annuity is usually held by an insurance

---

1. IRC §408.
2. This chapter does not consider Coverdell Education Savings Accounts (formerly known as Education IRAs).

company as custodian. As a result of the increased contribution limits established under EGTRRA 2001, and made permanent by PPA 2006, IRAs have become a more significant part of planning for retirement.

Exhibit 9.2 | History of IRAs[3]

Individual retirement accounts were introduced in 1974 with the enactment of the Employee Retirement Income Security Act (ERISA). As the Congress originally conceived the accounts, participants could contribute up to $1,500 a year and reduce their taxable income by the amount of their contributions. Initially, ERISA restricted IRAs to workers who were not covered by a qualified employment-based retirement plan. But the 1981 Economic Recovery Tax Act allowed all taxpayers under the age of 70½ to contribute to an IRA, regardless of their coverage under a qualified plan. It also raised the maximum annual contribution to $2,000 and allowed participants to contribute $250 on behalf of a nonworking spouse. The Tax Reform Act of 1986 reversed the trend toward expanded participation by phasing out the deduction for IRA contributions among higher-earning workers who are covered by an employment-based retirement plan themselves or who have a covered spouse.

In the 1990s, the Congress raised some of the limits it had previously placed on IRA contributions and also created the Roth IRA - a new type of account that features nondeductible contributions and tax-exempt withdrawals. The Small Business Job Protection Act of 1996 raised the limit on contributions on behalf of nonworking spouses from $250 to $2,000. Further changes came in the Taxpayer Relief Act of 1997. In addition to creating Roth IRAs, it increased the income threshold above which deductible contributions are phased out and distinguished between taxpayers who are covered by an employment-based plan and those who are not but whose spouses are covered. The income thresholds for the latter category of taxpayers are now higher than those for the former, which allows more people who are not covered by an employer's retirement plan to make tax-deductible contributions.

Additional changes to IRAs resulted from the Economic Growth and Tax Relief Reconciliation Act of 2001 (EGTRRA). The law raised the limit on contributions beginning in 2002 and allowed "catch-up" contributions by people ages 50 and above. It also provided a nonrefundable credit for certain contributions to an IRA or a 401(k)-type plan.

The Setting Every Community Up for Retirement Enhancement Act of 2019 (SECURE) further expanded the ability to contribute to IRAs by removing the age cap (formerly 70½) for contributions to traditional IRAs and increasing the mandatory distribution starting age from 70½ to 72.

Contribution Limits

Prior to EGTRRA 2001, contributions to a traditional IRA were limited each year to the lesser of $2,000 or earned income. EGTRRA 2001, however, increased the maximum contribution over several years. As a result, individuals could contribute a maximum of $3,000 or earned income in 2004, $4,000 or earned income in 2005-2007, and $5,000 or earned income in 2008. Beginning in 2009, the $5,000 contribution limit is subject to adjustment for inflation (the contribution limit is $6,000 for 2021).[4] In addition, individuals who have attained the age of 50 before the end of the current taxable year are also eligible to

---

3. http://www.cbo.gov/OnlineTaxGuide/Page_2A.htm. Note: Link is no longer active. SECURE Act information added by Money Education.
4. IRC §219(b)(5)(D).

make catch-up contributions, thereby further increasing the annual IRA contribution limit. These contribution limits, which are combined for both traditional and Roth IRAs, are summarized in the following chart. Note that the catch-up contribution is not adjusted for inflation.

Exhibit 9.3 | Contribution Limit for IRAs (Traditional & Roth)

Year	Annual Limit	Catch-Up Limit (for those over age 50)	Maximum Contribution
2021	$6,000	$1,000	$7,000

Example 9.1

The following chart and graph depict the accumulation over time in an IRA assuming a $6,000 contribution was made to the account at the beginning of each year and without considering the availability of the catch-up contribution and the increase in the limits. Notice that after ten years, $60,000 of deposits have accumulated to $105,187 assuming a 10 percent rate of return. After thirty years, $1,085,661 has accumulated assuming a 10 percent rate of return.

Years	Amount Deposited	8% Return	10% Return	12% Return
1-5	$30,000	$38,016	$40,294	$42,691
1-10	$60,000	$93,873	$105,187	$117,927
1-15	$90,000	$175,946	$209,698	$250,520
1-20	$120,000	$296,538	$378,015	$484,192
1-25	$150,000	$473,726	$649,091	$896,004
1-30	$180,000	$734,075	$1,085,661	$1,621,756

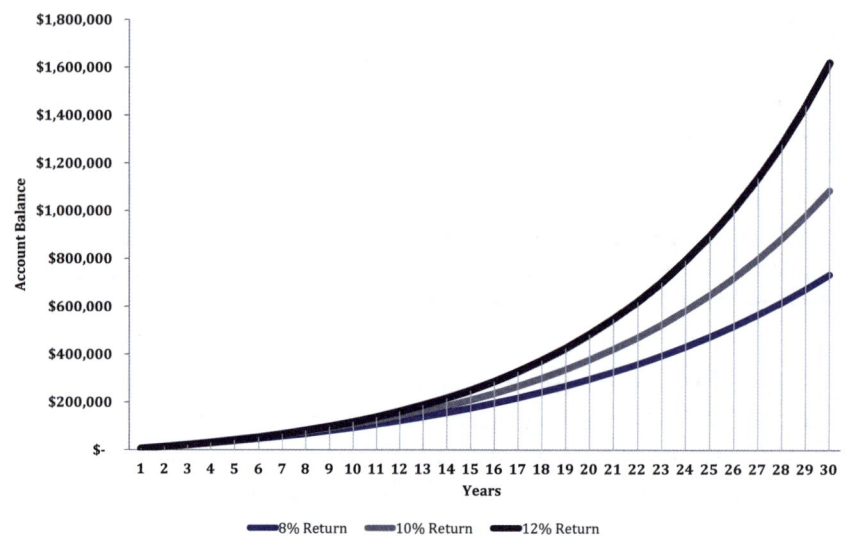

Example 9.2

A straight deposit equal to $6,000 per year assuming contributions are made at the end of each year at various earning rates for 30 and 40 years are:

Years (N)	Rate (i)	Annual PMT	Amount Deposited	FV
30	8%	$6,000	$180,000	$679,699.27
30	10%	$6,000	$180,000	$986,964.14
30	12%	$6,000	$180,000	$1,447,996.11
40	8%	$6,000	$240,000	$1,554,339.11
40	10%	$6,000	$240,000	$2,655,555.33
40	12%	$6,000	$240,000	$4,602,548.52

Earned Income - Individual IRA

The annual contributions to an IRA are limited to the lesser of an individual's earned income or the annual limit in effect. **Earned income** includes any type of compensation where the individual has performed some level of services for an employer or is considered self-employed. Compensation includes earnings for W-2 employees or those individuals who are self-employed, whether they operate a sole proprietorship, partnership, or an LLC taxed as a sole proprietorship or partnership.

Earned income may also include alimony received by the taxpayer. For federal income tax purposes, **alimony** is deductible by the payor and is includible as earned income by the recipient if it pertains to a divorce agreement signed before 2019. Alimony attributable to divorce agreements signed after 2018 is not included in income and thus not earned income.[5] For tax years beginning after December 31, 2019, the SECURE Act of 2019 expands the definition of earned income for IRA contributions to include any amount included in gross income when paid to an individual in the pursuit of graduate or postdoctoral study (e.g., taxable fellowship or stipend payments). **Exhibit 9.4** provides a list of earned income and a separate list of what is not earned income.

Example 9.3

In Letter Ruling 9202003, the IRS ruled that hogs transferred from a husband to his wife (a bona fide employee) did in fact constitute compensation (earned income) and could be used as the basis for contributions to an IRA.

Earned Income - Spousal IRA

Individuals who do not have any earned income may still be eligible to establish an IRA if their spouse has sufficient earned income. An IRA for a spouse who has no earned income is generally referred to as a spousal IRA and can be established provided the other spouse has sufficient earned income. The necessary level of earned income is equal to the total amount that is to be contributed to both spouses' IRAs. **Spousal IRAs** can be established up to the contribution limit for the year in question ($6,000 for 2021). The catch-up contribution is also available for those individuals age 50 and over.

---

5. These rules were modified by the TCJA 2017.

Example 9.4

Jody, age 48, and Sydney, age 43, have been married for 20 years and are currently retired. Although Jody is unemployed, Sydney earns $15,000 from part-time work at the local market during 2021. Because Sydney has income of $12,000, both Jody and Sydney can contribute up to $6,000 to each of their IRAs in 2021.

Example 9.5

Rico, age 54, and Lola, age 52, have been married for 20 years and are planning to retire in six years. Although Rico is currently unemployed, Lola earns $38,000 from her work at the local school. Lola's income of $38,000 would allow each of them to contribute up to $6,000 to each of their IRAs during 2021. In addition, each of them can contribute an extra $1,000 for 2021 as a catch-up contribution because they are both age 50 or over.

Exhibit 9.4 | Examples of Earned Income and What Is Not Earned Income

Earned Income:
• W-2 income
• Schedule C net income
• K-1 income from a partnership (or an LLC taxed as a partnership) where the partner is a material participant
• Alimony (attributable to divorce agreements signed before 2019)
• Taxable fellowship and stipend payments for graduate or postdoctoral study (for tax years after December 31, 2019)

Not Earned Income:
• Earnings and profits from property, such as rental income, interest income, and dividend income
• Capital gains
• Pension and annuity income
• Deferred compensation received (compensation payments postponed from a past year)
• Income from a partnership for which you do not provide services that are a material income producing factor
• Any amounts excluded from income, such as foreign income and housing costs
• Unemployment benefits
• Investment returns as a limited partner in a partnership
• Income flowing from an S-corporation via Schedule K-1
• Social Security benefits
• Workers' compensation

CASE STUDY 9.1

In *Gary H. and L. Marianne Bell v. Commissioner, T.C. Summary Opinion 2006-146*, the court ruled against the Bells when they attempted to take a deduction for an IRA contribution based on income from a defined contribution plan.

Earned Income - Attainment of 70½

For tax years prior to January 1, 2020, contributions to a traditional IRA were not permitted in the year or any years after the year in which an individual attained age 70½.[6] This limitation for traditional IRAs did not apply to Roth IRAs. Individuals who have sufficient earned income may continue to contribute to a Roth IRA after the attainment of age 70½. The SECURE Act of 2019 repealed the maximum age for traditional IRA contributions, allowing those over age 70½ who are still working to continue to contribute to either a traditional or Roth IRA for tax years beginning after December 31, 2019.

Example 9.6

Billy and Jean have been married for many years. Although Billy is currently retired, he has a part-time position at the local superstore earning $13,000 each year. Billy turned 70 on March 8th of 2019. Jean is 40 and is a stay-home mom. Because Billy attained the age of 70½ during 2019, he is not permitted to contribute to a traditional IRA for 2019. However, if he is still working in 2020 he will be permitted to make a traditional IRA contribution for 2020. Alternatively, Billy can contribute $6,000 to a Roth IRA (plus a $1,000 catch-up contribution) in 2019 or 2020. Jean may contribute $6,000 for both 2019 and 2020 to a spousal IRA (either traditional or Roth).

Excess Contributions

Contributions that exceed the limits discussed above ($6,000 for 2021) are subject to an excise tax penalty of six percent. This penalty is charged each year that the excess contribution remains in the IRA.[7] The taxpayer can avoid the excise penalty on excess contributions by withdrawing the excess contribution and the earnings attributable to the excess contributions by the due date (including extensions) of the federal income tax return (April 15th for calendar year taxpayers; October 15 with a properly filed extension).[8] These excess contributions rules and the penalty apply to both traditional and Roth IRAs.

Example 9.7

In 2021, Priscilla, age 32, contributed $6,500 to her IRA. She made an excess contribution of $500 that will be subject to a six percent penalty if she does not withdraw the excess contribution and any related earnings by April 15, 2022 or by October 15th, 2022 if extended.

---

6. IRC §219(d)(1); prior to repeal by the SECURE Act.
7. IRC §4973.
8. IRC Section 408(d)(4).

Example 9.8

In 2021, Aidan, age 32, contributed $5,000 to his traditional IRA and $1,500 to his Roth IRA. He has made an excess contribution of $500. He can avoid the six percent penalty by withdrawing the excess contribution and any related earnings from either the IRA or the Roth IRA account (or both) by April 15, 2022 or by October 15th, 2022 if extended.

The calculation of earnings attributable to the excess IRA contribution is based on a prorated portion of the earnings accrued by the IRA while the excess contribution remained in the IRA.

Timing of Contributions to IRAs

As discussed in Chapter 8, contributions to qualified plans can be made as late as the due date of the tax return including extensions. For most entities with a calendar year end, the final date a contribution can be made to a qualified plan is September 15th. For self-employed individuals, the final date a contribution can be made to a qualified plan is October 15th. However, for IRAs, contributions must be made to both traditional and Roth IRA accounts by the due date of the individual federal income tax return without considering extensions. For most taxpayers, this due date is April 15th of the year following the tax year end.

Finally, with the exception of rollover contributions from other IRAs, a contribution to a traditional IRA or Roth IRA must be made in cash.[9] No other type of asset may be contributed to an IRA.

Deductibility of IRA Contributions

Provided an individual has sufficient earned income, the individual may contribute the maximum amount to a traditional IRA on an annual basis. However, the deductibility of the traditional IRA contribution on an individual's federal income tax return is dependent on several factors, including coverage or participation in a qualified plan or other retirement plan, which is referred to as whether the individual is an **active participant**, and the amount of the individual's **adjusted gross income** (AGI). If the individual and spouse (if any) are not active participants in a qualified plan or retirement plan (defined later), they may contribute to a deductible IRA to the lesser of the IRA contribution limit or earned income. Even if the individual or their spouse is an active participant, they still may be able to contribute to a deductible IRA if the AGI of the taxpayer (and spouse, if any) is below certain threshold limits as discussed below.

Not Active Participants of Qualified or Other Retirement Plan

An individual who is not an active participant does not have an income limitation for purposes of deducting his IRA contributions. Therefore, if an individual earns a substantial amount of income (e.g., $1,000,000) and is not an active participant, then the individual may fully deduct a contribution (within the contribution limit) to his or her traditional IRA account.

> ### ☑ Quick Quiz 9.1
>
> 1. A 55-year old individual can contribute a maximum of $6,000 to an IRA in 2021.
>   a. True
>   b. False
>
> 2. Annual contributions to an IRA are limited to the lesser of a single individual's earned income or the annual limit in effect.
>   a. True
>   b. False
>
> 3. Persons who do not have any earned income are never permitted to contribute to an IRA.
>   a. True
>   b. False
>
> False, True, False.

---

9. IRC §408(a)(1).

Exhibit 9.5 | Who Can Deduct Contributions to a Traditional IRA

Taxpayer is not an active participant	Taxpayer(s) is an active participant		One spouse is an active participant, the other is not
No AGI Limit	**Single**	**AGI Phaseout** $66,000 – $76,000 (2021)	The spouse who is not an active participant may have a deductible traditional IRA contribution as long as their joint AGI does not exceed $208,000. The deductible IRA contribution is phased out between $198,000 and $208,000 for 2021.
	MFJ	**AGI Phaseout** $105,000 – $125,000 (2021)	

Active Participants of Qualified or Other Retirement Plans

For individuals or married couples filing jointly who are considered active participants (defined below) of a qualified plan or other retirement plan, there is an income test to determine the deductibility of IRA contributions. If the taxpayer's AGI is greater than the upper limit of the phaseout, no deduction is permitted. If the taxpayer's AGI is less than the lower limit of the phaseout, then a full deduction is permitted. If the taxpayer's AGI is between the limits, then the deduction is ratably phased out.

Married couples filing separately are effectively phased out between an AGI of $0 and $10,000. Individuals falling within these phaseout ranges must calculate the deductible amount of the contribution utilizing the calculation discussed below.

As illustrated in **Exhibit 9.6**, simply because one spouse is covered by a qualified plan does not prohibit the other spouse from deducting a contribution to a traditional IRA. However, this ability to deduct the contribution is phased out for married individuals with AGI beginning at $198,000 and is completely phased out for AGI at or above $208,000.

Exhibit 9.6 | Can I Deduct my Traditional IRA Contribution (2021)?

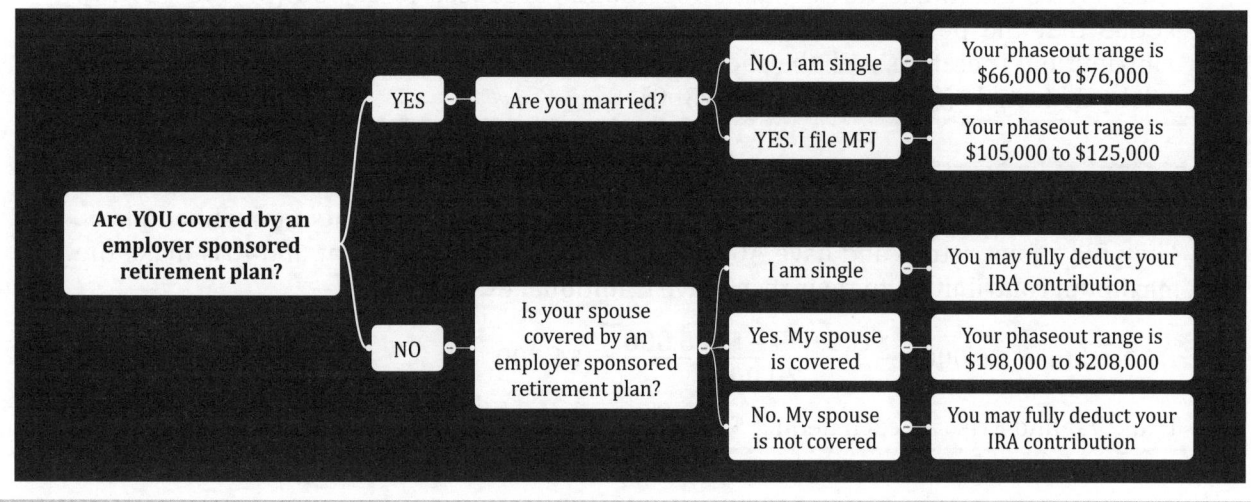

Calculation of IRA Deduction – Subject to Phaseout

An individual who is an active participant in a retirement plan and has an AGI within the **phaseout** range will have a reduced maximum deductible IRA contribution. The deduction limit ($6,000 for 2021) will be reduced based on a proportion equal to the amount by which the individual's AGI exceeds the lower limit of the phaseout range divided by $10,000 (or $20,000 in the case of a joint return). The calculation of this reduction in the IRA deductibility limit is as follows:[10]

$$\text{Reduction} = \text{Contribution Limit**} \times \frac{\text{AGI} - \text{Lower Limit}}{\$10,000*}$$

* $20,000 for joint returns
** Including catch-up contribution

Consider the following examples:

Example 9.9

Fred is single, age 38, and an active participant in his employer's qualified retirement plan. His AGI for 2021 is $67,000, and he makes the maximum contribution to his traditional IRA.

$$\text{Reduction} = \$6,000 \times \frac{\$67,000 - \$66,000}{\$10,000} = \$600$$

Thus, Fred's traditional IRA deduction for 2021 is reduced by $600 to $5,400 ($6,000 - $600).

Example 9.10

Assume the same facts as above except that Fred is over the age of 50 and is eligible for the catch-up contribution of $1,000. In this case, the traditional IRA deduction is reduced by $700.

$$\text{Reduction} = \$7,000 \times \frac{\$67,000 - \$66,000}{\$10,000} = \$700$$

Thus, Fred's traditional IRA deduction for 2021 is reduced to $6,300 ($7,000 - $700). Notice that the portion that is phased out represents 10 percent of the allowable contribution. Therefore, with the additional $1,000 contribution, only 90 percent or $900 will be deductible ($5,400 + $900 = $6,300).

Example 9.11

Pat, age 32, and Kris, age 31, are married and are active participants in qualified plans. They file a joint return and have AGI of $108,000 for 2021. Both Pat and Kris make the maximum contribution to their respective traditional IRAs in 2021.

$$\text{Reduction} = \$6,000 \times \frac{\$109,000 - \$105,000}{20,000} = \$1,200$$

Thus, Pat and Kris can each deduct $4,800 ($6,000 - $1,200).

---

10. IRC §219(g)(2)(A).

Example 9.12

Doyle and Vanessa are married and file jointly. Vanessa is an attorney who earns $100,000 per year and is an active participant in the firm's qualified plan. Doyle earns $15,000 for the year gambling at the local country club. If Doyle and Vanessa are both 42 years old, how much can they contribute and deduct to a traditional IRA? The phaseout range for 2021 is $105,000 – $125,000. Since Vanessa is an active participant, their joint income of $114,000 is compared to the joint phaseout range. As a result, half of Vanessa's contribution can be deducted (since the joint income is in the middle of the phaseout range). Doyle, on the other hand, is not an active participant and can therefore fully deduct an IRA contribution since their joint income is below the $198,000 threshold. Notice that married individuals filing jointly can have two different phaseout ranges for the deductibility of their IRA contributions even though they file their taxes on the same return.

Where is the Traditional IRA Deduction Taken

The deduction for contributions to traditional IRAs is a deduction for AGI. The deduction is listed on line 19 of Schedule 1 for Form 1040.

Exhibit 9.7 | Schedule 1 (Form 1040) Adjustments to Income

10	Educator expenses	10
11	Certain business expenses of reservists, performing artists, and fee-basis government officials. Attach Form 2106	11
12	Health savings account deduction. Attach Form 8889	12
13	Moving expenses for members of the Armed Forces. Attach Form 3903	13
14	Deductible part of self-employment tax. Attach Schedule SE	14
15	Self-employed SEP, SIMPLE, and qualified plans	15
16	Self-employed health insurance deduction	16
17	Penalty on early withdrawal of savings	17
18a	Alimony paid	18a
b	Recipient's SSN	
c	Date of original divorce or separation agreement (see instructions) ▶	
19	IRA deduction	19
20	Student loan interest deduction	20
21	Tuition and fees deduction. Attach Form 8917	21
22	Add lines 10 through 21. These are your **adjustments to income.** Enter here and on Form 1040, 1040-SR, or 1040-NR, line 10a	22

Active Participant Status

As discussed above, the deductibility of traditional IRA contributions may be reduced if the taxpayer is an active participant in a retirement plan for the year of contribution to the traditional IRA. An active participant is an employee who has benefited under one of the following plans through a contribution or an accrued benefit:[11]

- qualified plan
- annuity plan
- tax sheltered annuity (403(b) plan)
- certain government plans[12]
- simplified employee pension plans (SEPs)
- simple retirement accounts (SIMPLEs)

11. IRC §219(g)(5).
12. Does not include 457 plans – IRC §219(g)(5). In addition, certain Armed Forces reserve members and volunteer firefighters may not be considered active participants.

Active participant status for an employee depends on the type of retirement plan. For a defined benefit plan, an individual who is not excluded under the eligibility provisions of the plan is considered to be an active participant in the plan, regardless of whether such individual has elected to decline participation in the plan, has failed to make a mandatory contribution specified under the plan, or has failed to perform the minimum service required to accrue a benefit under the plan.[13] For example, when a participant completes an additional year of service in a defined benefit plan that calculates the benefit based on years of service, then, the participant has accrued additional benefits in that year.

An individual is an active participant in a money purchase pension plan or target benefit pension plan if the employer is required to make a contribution on behalf of that employee. Since these plans must comply with mandatory funding requirements, most employees who are eligible for such plans and are covered will be active participants.

Because contributions to profit sharing plans (and stock bonus plans) are discretionary from the employer, the determination of active participant status is dependent on whether the participant receives a contribution for the year. Remember the contribution may come from the employer, employee, or from a plan forfeiture allocation. Also, qualified nonelective contributions, as well as qualified matching contributions, will qualify as a contribution to the plan for the year. Any of these contributions will cause an individual to be classified as an active participant for the year for which the contribution was made. An employee is considered an active participant even if the contributions to the account are completely forfeitable. In other words, even if the employee is not vested in any benefit, he will still be considered an active participant if he receives a contribution to his account for the current year. An employee who is an active participant will receive a Form W-2 from the employer with box 13 checked to indicate active participant status. See **Exhibit 9.8**.

> ### ☰ *Key Concepts*
>
> 1. What is the penalty for excess contributions to an IRA?
>
> 2. List the factors that affect the deductibility of IRA contributions on an individual's federal tax return.
>
> 3. What are the required minimum distribution rules for IRAs?

As previously discussed, contributions to traditional IRAs are required to be made by April 15th for the previous year, while contributions to qualified plans can be made as late as the due date of the company's income tax return including extensions. With a profit sharing plan, an individual may not know whether or not he will be an active participant for a particular year until after he is required to make the contribution to the IRA account. Because of the timing difference, certain provisions permit such qualified plan contributions to be considered for the following year for purposes of traditional IRA deductibility.[14]

---

13. Internal Revenue Bulletin 1987-5, Notice 87-16.
14. Treas. Reg. §1.219-2.

Exhibit 9.8 | Form W-2

22222	VOID ☐	a Employee's social security number	For Official Use Only ▶ OMB No. 1545-0008	

b Employer identification number (EIN)	1 Wages, tips, other compensation	2 Federal income tax withheld

c Employer's name, address, and ZIP code	3 Social security wages	4 Social security tax withheld
	5 Medicare wages and tips	6 Medicare tax withheld
	7 Social security tips	8 Allocated tips

d Control number	9	10 Dependent care benefits

e Employee's first name and initial	Last name	Suff.	11 Nonqualified plans	12a See instructions for box 12

13 Statutory employee ☐ Retirement plan ☒ Third-party sick pay ☐

12b

14 Other

Active Participant Status ↑

12c

12d

f Employee's address and ZIP code

15 State	Employer's state ID number	16 State wages, tips, etc.	17 State income tax	18 Local wages, tips, etc.	19 Local income tax	20 Locality name

Form W-2 Wage and Tax Statement **2021**

Department of the Treasury—Internal Revenue Service
For Privacy Act and Paperwork Reduction Act Notice, see the separate instructions.
Cat. No. 10134D

Copy A—For Social Security Administration. Send this entire page with Form W-3 to the Social Security Administration; photocopies are **not** acceptable.

Do Not Cut, Fold, or Staple Forms on This Page

Example 9.13

George is employed by Hone Company, which sponsors a profit-sharing plan. The plan was established in 2001. Hone decides in August of 2022 to make a contribution to the plan for the year 2021. Since Hone made the contribution in 2022, George would be considered an active participant for the year 2022, not 2021. However, if a contribution was made for George in 2021, then George would be an active participant for 2021.

As discussed, an employee who makes an employee elective deferral contribution to a plan, such as a 401(k) plan, is considered an active participant for the current year. However, just because an employee is eligible to defer a portion of his salary into a 401(k) plan does not automatically make the employee an active participant for the current year (e.g., the employee does not defer).[15]

For spouses filing jointly, the active participation status of one spouse does not constitute active participant status of the other spouse.[16] If only one spouse is an active participant, then the spouse that is not an active participant may make a deductible IRA contribution as long as the couple's joint income (adjusted gross income) does not exceed $208,000 (the ability to take a deduction phases out from $198,000 to $208,000).

---

15. Treas. Reg. §1.219-2(e).
16. IRC §219(g)(7).

Example 9.14

Kin's employer sponsors a money purchase pension plan with a contribution level of seven percent of compensation. Kin meets the eligibility requirements. Therefore, Kin is an active participant for purposes of IRA deductibility.

Example 9.15

Brooklyn is a participant of his company's profit sharing plan. However, the company had a bad year and did not make a contribution to the profit sharing plan, and no employees terminated employment with non-vested benefits during the current year. Brooklyn did not receive an employer contribution or a forfeiture allocation and is therefore not an active participant in the plan.

Example 9.16

Sawyer is employed with Kensington Company where he is eligible to defer up to 80 percent of his salary into the 401(k) plan. Sawyer does not defer any of his salary into the 401(k) plan, nor does he receive a contribution by the employer or a forfeiture allocation. Sawyer is not an active participant for purposes of IRA deductibility for that year.[17]

Example 9.17

Lamar, who is a non-highly compensated employee, is employed with Kensington Company where he is eligible to defer up to 80 percent of his salary into the 401(k) plan. Lamar does not defer any of his salary into the 401(k) plan, nor does he receive a forfeiture allocation. However, Lamar does receive a small contribution from the employer in the form of a qualified nonelective contribution.[18] Lamar is considered an active participant for purposes of IRA deductibility.

Example 9.18

Kennedy and Stacey are married and file a joint income tax return. Their joint AGI in 2021 is $165,000. Stacey is a dentist who earns a salary of $120,000 per year, and defers the maximum into the company 401(k) plan. Kennedy is a personal trainer earning $45,000 in fees per year. Kennedy files a Schedule C on their federal income tax return. Stacey is an active participant in a qualified plan, but Kennedy is not. Although Kennedy should probably establish a Keogh plan for the personal training self-employment income, Kennedy is not currently an active participant. Because their joint AGI is less than $198,000 and Kennedy is not an active participant in a qualified plan, Kennedy can make a fully deductible traditional IRA contribution. Stacey could make a non-deductible IRA contribution or a contribution to a Roth IRA.

---

17. However, Deanna is considered covered for purposes of the coverage rules.
18. Qualified nonelective contributions (QNECs) are contributions made to non-highly compensated employees so that the plan sponsor meets the ADP requirements.

Non-Deductible IRA Contributions

Although one of the advantages of an IRA contribution is that it is often income tax deductible for AGI, contributions to an IRA can be non-deductible.[19] Generally, taxpayers make non-deductible contributions to traditional IRAs if they are active participants in a qualified plan and their income exceeds the phaseout limits for both a deductible traditional IRA and for contributions to a Roth IRA. However, any taxpayer can make a non-deductible contribution as long as they have earned income. These non-deductible contributions receive the benefit of the deferral of income tax on the current earnings within the IRA.

When an individual makes a non-deductible contribution to an IRA, the individual has an adjusted basis in the IRA. Withdrawals from the IRA will consist partially of account earnings that have not been subject to income tax and partially of return of adjusted basis for which the individual has already paid income tax.

Individuals who have non-deductible IRA contributions should file Form 8606 with their federal income tax return. This form should be filed each year to track the adjusted basis of an individual's IRA account (see lines 1 and 2 on Form 8606). The most recent copy of the Form 8606 should be retained on an ongoing basis, as this is where the cost basis information is located for determining the tax-free portion of future withdrawals.

According to the form instructions, taxpayers who are required to file Form 8606 to report a nondeductible contribution to a traditional IRA, but do not do so, must pay a $50 penalty. Overstating nondeductible contributions will result in a $100 penalty.[20]

---

19. IRC §408(o)(2)(B)(ii).
20. Instructions to Form 8606.

Exhibit 9.9 | Form 8606

Form 8606

Department of the Treasury
Internal Revenue Service (99)

Nondeductible IRAs

▶ Go to *www.irs.gov/Form8606* for instructions and the latest information.
▶ For coronavirus-related distributions, see the instructions.
▶ Attach to 2020 Form 1040, 1040-SR, or 1040-NR.

OMB No. 1545-0074

2020

Attachment
Sequence No. **48**

Name. If married, file a separate form for each spouse required to file 2020 Form 8606. See instructions. | Your social security number

Fill in Your Address Only if You Are Filing This Form by Itself and Not With Your Tax Return

Home address (number and street, or P.O. box if mail is not delivered to your home) | Apt. no.

City, town or post office, state, and ZIP code. If you have a foreign address, also complete the spaces below (see instructions).

Foreign country name | Foreign province/state/county | Foreign postal code

---

Part I   **Nondeductible Contributions to Traditional IRAs and Distributions From Traditional, SEP, and SIMPLE IRAs**

Complete this part only if one or more of the following apply.

- You made nondeductible contributions to a traditional IRA for 2020.
- You took distributions from a traditional, SEP, or SIMPLE IRA in 2020 **and** you made nondeductible contributions to a traditional IRA in 2020 or an earlier year. For this purpose, a distribution does not include a rollover (other than a repayment of a qualified disaster distribution (see 2020 Forms 8915-C, 8915-D, and 8915-E)), qualified charitable distribution, one-time distribution to fund an HSA, conversion, recharacterization, or return of certain contributions.
- You converted part, but not all, of your traditional, SEP, and SIMPLE IRAs to Roth IRAs in 2020 **and** you made nondeductible contributions to a traditional IRA in 2020 or an earlier year.

1	Enter your nondeductible contributions to traditional IRAs for 2020, including those made for 2020 from January 1, 2021, through April 15, 2021. See instructions	**1**
2	Enter your total basis in traditional IRAs. See instructions	**2**
3	Add lines 1 and 2	**3**

> In 2020, did you take a distribution from traditional, SEP, or SIMPLE IRAs, or make a Roth IRA conversion?
>
> **No** ──▶ Enter the amount from line 3 on line 14. Do not complete the rest of Part I.
>
> **Yes** ──▶ Go to line 4.

4	Enter those contributions included on line 1 that were made from January 1, 2021, through April 15, 2021	**4**
5	Subtract line 4 from line 3	**5**
6	Enter the value of **all** your traditional, SEP, and SIMPLE IRAs as of December 31, 2020, plus any outstanding rollovers. Subtract any repayments of qualified disaster distributions (see 2020 Forms 8915-C, 8915-D, and 8915-E) . . .	**6**
7	Enter your distributions from traditional, SEP, and SIMPLE IRAs in 2020. **Do not** include rollovers (other than repayments of qualified disaster distributions (see 2020 Forms 8915-C, 8915-D, and 8915-E)), qualified charitable distributions, a one-time distribution to fund an HSA, conversions to a Roth IRA, certain returned contributions, or recharacterizations of traditional IRA contributions (see instructions)	**7**
8	Enter the net amount you converted from traditional, SEP, and SIMPLE IRAs to Roth IRAs in 2020. Also enter this amount on line 16	**8**
9	Add lines 6, 7, and 8	**9**
10	Divide line 5 by line 9. Enter the result as a decimal rounded to at least 3 places. If the result is 1.000 or more, enter "1.000"	**10** × .
11	Multiply line 8 by line 10. This is the nontaxable portion of the amount you converted to Roth IRAs. Also enter this amount on line 17	**11**
12	Multiply line 7 by line 10. This is the nontaxable portion of your distributions that you did not convert to a Roth IRA	**12**
13	Add lines 11 and 12. This is the nontaxable portion of all your distributions	**13**
14	Subtract line 13 from line 3. This is **your total basis in traditional IRAs for 2020 and earlier years** .	**14**
15a	Subtract line 12 from line 7	**15a**
b	Enter the amount on line 15a attributable to qualified disaster distributions from 2020 Forms 8915-C, 8915-D, and 8915-E (see instructions). Also, enter this amount on 2020 Form 8915-C, line 23; 2020 Form 8915-D, line 22; **or** 2020 Form 8915-E, line 13, as applicable	**15b**
c	**Taxable amount.** Subtract line 15b from line 15a. If more than zero, also include this amount on 2020 Form 1040, 1040-SR, **or** 1040-NR, line 4b	**15c**

Note: You may be subject to an additional 10% tax on the amount on line 15c if you were under age 59½ at the time of the distribution. See instructions.

For Privacy Act and Paperwork Reduction Act Notice, see separate instructions.   Cat. No. 63966F   Form **8606** (2020)

Form 8606 Continued

Part II   2020 Conversions From Traditional, SEP, or SIMPLE IRAs to Roth IRAs

Complete this part if you converted part or all of your traditional, SEP, and SIMPLE IRAs to a Roth IRA in 2020.

16	If you completed Part I, enter the amount from line 8. Otherwise, enter the net amount you converted from traditional, SEP, and SIMPLE IRAs to Roth IRAs in 2020	**16**
17	If you completed Part I, enter the amount from line 11. Otherwise, enter your basis in the amount on line 16 (see instructions)	**17**
18	**Taxable amount.** Subtract line 17 from line 16. If more than zero, also include this amount on 2020 Form 1040, 1040-SR, or 1040-NR, line 4b	**18**

Part III   Distributions From Roth IRAs

Complete this part only if you took a distribution from a Roth IRA in 2020. For this purpose, a distribution does not include a rollover (other than a repayment of a qualified disaster distribution (see 2020 Forms 8915-C, 8915-D, and 8915-E)), qualified charitable distribution, one-time distribution to fund an HSA, recharacterization, or return of certain contributions (see instructions).

19	Enter your total nonqualified distributions from Roth IRAs in 2020, including any qualified first-time homebuyer distributions, and any qualified disaster distributions (see instructions). Also see 2020 Forms 8915-C, 8915-D, and 8915-E	**19**
20	Qualified first-time homebuyer expenses (see instructions). **Do not** enter more than $10,000 reduced by the total of all your prior qualified first-time homebuyer distributions	**20**
21	Subtract line 20 from line 19. If zero or less, enter -0-	**21**
22	Enter your basis in Roth IRA contributions (see instructions). If line 21 is zero, **stop here**	**22**
23	Subtract line 22 from line 21. If zero or less, enter -0- and skip lines 24 and 25. If more than zero, you may be subject to an additional tax (see instructions)	**23**
24	Enter your basis in conversions from traditional, SEP, and SIMPLE IRAs and rollovers from qualified retirement plans to a Roth IRA. See instructions	**24**
25a	Subtract line 24 from line 23. If zero or less, enter -0- and skip lines 25b and 25c	**25a**
b	Enter the amount on line 25a attributable to qualified disaster distributions from 2020 Forms 8915-C, 8915-D, and 8915-E (see instructions). Also, enter this amount on 2020 Form 8915-C, line 24; 2020 Form 8915-D, line 23; **or** 2020 Form 8915-E, line 14, as applicable	**25b**
c	**Taxable amount.** Subtract line 25b from line 25a. If more than zero, also include this amount on 2020 Form 1040, 1040-SR, **or** 1040-NR, line 4b	**25c**

Sign Here Only if You Are Filing This Form by Itself and Not With Your Tax Return

Under penalties of perjury, I declare that I have examined this form, including accompanying attachments, and to the best of my knowledge and belief, it is true, correct, and complete. Declaration of preparer (other than taxpayer) is based on all information of which preparer has any knowledge.

▶ Your signature   ▶ Date

Paid Preparer Use Only

Print/Type preparer's name	Preparer's signature	Date	Check ☐ if self-employed	PTIN
Firm's name ▶			Firm's EIN ▶	
Firm's address ▶			Phone no.	

Form **8606** (2020)

Saver's Credit (Retirement Savings Contribution Credit)

The **retirement savings contributions credit** is intended to encourage lower-income taxpayers to save for retirement. The rate used in calculating the credit is reduced as modified adjusted gross income (MAGI) increases, until the rate reaches zero percent at MAGI of $66,000 on a joint return for 2021, $49,500 for a head of household for 2021, and $33,000 in all other cases for 2021. For purposes of this credit, MAGI is defined in IRS Publication 590 as adjusted gross income less any exclusion or deduction claimed for the year for foreign earned income, foreign housing costs, income for bona fide residents of American Samoa, or income from Puerto Rico.

The retirement savings contributions credit is available to an eligible individual who makes qualified retirement savings contributions of up to $2,000 for a tax year. An eligible individual is a person who is 18 or older at the end of the tax year if that person is not allowed to be claimed as a dependent of another person for the year and is not considered to be a full-time student.

The amount of the credit is determined by multiplying a taxpayer's qualified retirement savings contributions (after the reduction for certain distributions) by the applicable percentage from **Exhibit 9.10**.

Exhibit 9.10 | Applicable Percentage for Savers Credit (2021)

Joint Return Modified AGI		Head of a Household Modified AGI		All Other Cases Modified AGI		Applicable Percentage
Over	Not over	Over	Not over	Over	Not over	
$0	$39,500	$0	$29,625	$0	$19,750	50%
$39,501	$43,000	$29,626	$32,250	$19,751	$21,500	20%
$43,001	$66,000	$32,251	$49,500	$21,501	$33,000	10%
$66,000	--	$49,500	--	$33,000	--	0%

The maximum credit is $1,000 per person each year, or $2,000 on a joint return. Any credit that cannot be used in the current year is lost.

Example 9.19

Kiley contributed $4,000 to her Roth IRA for 2021. She had MAGI of $15,000 for 2021 and used the single filing status. She has never taken a distribution from a retirement plan. Her maximum credit for 2021 is $1,000 ($2,000 x 50%).

Assume the same facts, except that Kiley contributes $5,000 to her Roth IRA for 2021. Also assume that her MAGI was $21,000 for 2021, then her maximum credit is $400 ($2,000 x 20%).

Example 9.20

Reese, who works at a retail store, is married and earned $30,000 in 2021. Reese's husband was unemployed in 2021 and did not have any earnings. Reese contributed $1,000 to her IRA in 2021. After deducting her IRA contribution, the adjusted gross income shown on her joint return is $29,000. Reese may claim a 50% credit, $500, for her $1,000 IRA contribution.

Example 9.21

Seth, who is an architect, is married and earned $42,000 in 2021. Seth's wife, Morgan, is an actress, but did not have any earnings in 2021. Seth, who is concerned about their retirement, contributed $2,000 to each of their Roth IRAs in 2021. The adjusted gross income shown on their joint return is $42,000. Seth and Morgan may claim a 20% credit, $800 (20% up to $4,000), for their contributions to the Roth IRAs.

If Seth would have established traditional IRAs for Morgan and himself, then he would have reduced his AGI to $38,000 ($42,000 - $4,000) and therefore would have had a credit of 50% of $4,000 or $2,000.

Achieving a Better Life Experience (ABLE) accounts

ABLE accounts are designed to help people with disabilities and their families save and pay for disability-related expenses. Though contributions are not deductible, distributions, including earnings, are tax-free to the designated beneficiary if used to pay qualified disability expenses. These expenses can include housing, education, transportation, health, prevention and wellness, employment training and support, assistive technology and personal support services and other disability-related expenses.

Normally, contributions totaling up to the annual gift-tax exclusion amount, currently $15,000 for 2021, may be made to an ABLE account each year for the benefit of an eligible person with a disability, known as a designated beneficiary. Starting in 2018, if the beneficiary works, the beneficiary can also contribute part, or all, of their income to their ABLE account.

This additional contribution is limited to the poverty-line amount for a one-person household. The designated beneficiary is not, however, eligible to make this additional contribution if their employer contributes to a workplace retirement plan on their behalf.

Also starting in 2018, ABLE account beneficiaries can qualify for the Saver's Credit based on contributions they make to their ABLE accounts. Up to $2,000 of these contributions may qualify for this special credit designed to help low- and moderate-income workers.

In addition, some funds may now be rolled into an ABLE account from the designated beneficiary's own 529 plan or from the 529 plan of certain family members.

Rollover contributions (money that is moved from another ABLE account or from a Qualified Tuition Plan (QTP) account) do not qualify for the credit. Also, eligible contributions may be reduced by any recent distributions received from an ABLE account.

Distributions from Traditional IRAs

Generally, distributions from traditional IRAs are taxed as ordinary income. The one exception is for distributions consisting of a combination of tax-deferred earnings and the return of adjusted basis that results from either non-deductible IRA contributions or rollovers of contributions from qualified plan balances that included after-tax contributions (such as thrift plans). In such cases, each distribution will consist of a combination of return of **adjusted basis** (AB) and ordinary income. The ratio of return of AB is equal to the ratio of the total AB of the account before the withdrawal to the fair market value of the total account balance. The calculation will be made each year on Form 8606 (see Part 1).

Example 9.22

Nat has a traditional IRA with an account balance of $100,000. Over the years, Nat made after-tax contributions of $25,000, and the remaining $75,000 is attributable to pre-tax contributions and earnings. Therefore, Nat has an adjusted basis of $25,000, the total amount contributed after tax. When Nat begins receiving distributions, the distribution will be partially a return of basis and partially ordinary income. The ratio is calculated by dividing the AB over the fair market value ($25,000/$100,000 = ¼). Thus, if Nat took a $10,000 distribution then ¼ ($2,500) would be a return of basis and ¾ ($7,500) would be ordinary income. For purposes of this calculation, all traditional IRA account balances, including rollover IRAs, are aggregated and treated as a single account.

Example 9.23

Assume the same facts as **Example 9.22**, except that Nat also has a rollover IRA with a balance of $50,000. The total IRA balance is now $150,000, and the ratio is calculated as ($25,000/$150,000 = 16.67%). Thus, if Nat took a $10,000 distribution then 16.67% ($1,667) would be a return of basis and $8,333 ($10,000 - $1,667) would be ordinary income.

The same pro rata distribution calculation is used when converting a traditional IRA to a Roth IRA. This tax treatment makes the so-called "backdoor" Roth IRA strategy (discussed later in this chapter) less attractive for clients who already have funds in a traditional IRA. Rather than simply converting the nondeductible contribution and incurring no tax, the client will pay tax based on the pro rata calculation. Additional details regarding Roth IRAs and conversions are discussed later in this chapter.

$$\text{Ratio of AB} = \frac{\text{AB before withdrawal}}{\text{FMV of account at withdrawal}}$$

Required Minimum Distributions

Traditional IRA distributions can be taken at anytime, but the **required minimum distribution** (RMD) rules require that the distributions must (except Roth IRAs) begin by April 1st of the year following the year in which the owner attains the age of 70½ (or age 72 if age 70½ is attained after December 31, 2019; SECURE Act).[21] The minimum distribution rules require that traditional IRA owners begin receiving distributions from their accounts based on the same factors as discussed in Chapter 7 for qualified plans. These rules prohibit a taxpayer from continuing to indefinitely accrue tax-deferred earnings within their traditional IRA. Required distributions that are not taken are subject to a 50 percent excise tax.

The 10 Percent Penalty and its Exceptions for Early Withdrawals

By allowing deductions for traditional IRA contributions and by allowing balances in IRAs (both traditional and Roth) to grow on a tax-deferred basis, the government forfeits current income (tax revenue) to encourage taxpayers to save for retirement in their IRAs. The government also encourages taxpayers to leave funds in their traditional and Roth IRAs until retirement by imposing a 10 percent premature withdrawal penalty on taxable distributions prior to age 59½. Therefore, traditional and Roth IRA distributions before the age of 59½ will generally be subject to the 10 percent penalty unless a specific exception applies. **Exhibit 9.11** summarizes the exceptions to the 10 percent withdrawal penalty for distributions from IRAs and qualified plans.

Quick Quiz 9.2

1. IRA contributions that exceed the contribution limits are subject to an excise tax of six percent.
   a. True
   b. False

2. Individuals who are active participants in a qualified retirement plan or SEP may be subject to a reduced maximum deductible IRA contribution.
   a. True
   b. False

3. Lump-sum IRA distributions may be taken at any time without being subject to penalty.
   a. True
   b. False

4. The saver's credit is generally available to all taxpayers who save in a 401(k) plan or an IRA, regardless of income.
   a. True
   b. False

True, True, False, False.

---

21. The minimum distribution rules do not apply to Roth IRAs.

Exhibit 9.11 | Summary of 10 Percent Penalty Exceptions

Applies to Distributions from:	Exception to 10% Early Withdrawal Penalty
Both Qualified Plans & IRAs	• Death • Attainment of age 59½ • Disability • Substantially equal periodic payments (§72(t)) • Medical expenses that exceed 7.5% of AGI for 2021 • Rollover • Because of an IRS tax levy • Certain distributions to qualified military reservists called to active duty • Qualified birth or adoption distributions*
Only Qualified Plans	• Qualified Domestic Relations Order (QDRO) • Attainment of age 55 and separation from service • Public safety employee who separates from service after age 50 • Dividend pass through from an ESOP
Only IRAs	• Higher education expenses • First time home purchase (up to $10,000) • Payment of health insurance premiums by unemployed

Added by the SECURE Act of 2019

The 10 percent penalty does not apply if a distribution is received after the owner attains the age of 59½, by a beneficiary after the account owner's death, because of the account owner's disability, for medical expenses in excess of 7.5 percent (in 2021) of the participant's AGI, if the distribution is part of a series of substantially equal periodic payments, if the distribution is within one year following a qualified birth or adoption, because of an IRS tax levy, or received by a qualified military reservist. The final exceptions from the 10 percent penalty apply only for withdrawals from IRAs (not qualified plans) for higher education expenses, for acquisition costs of a first home (up to $10,000), and for health insurance premiums paid by the unemployed.

Higher Education Expenses

The education expense exception is for higher education expenses (post-secondary educational institutions) for the benefit of the taxpayer, taxpayer's spouse, child, or grandchild at an eligible educational institution. Qualified expenses include tuition, fees, books, supplies. Room and board will also be included if the student is at least half time.[22]

First Time Home Purchase

The first time home purchase exception applies up to a lifetime maximum of $10,000 for the acquisition of a home for the taxpayer, taxpayer's spouse, child, grandchild, or ancestor of such taxpayer or taxpayer's spouse. A first time home buyer is defined as an individual (and if married, such individual's spouse) that had no present ownership interest in a principal residence during the 2-year period ending on the date of acquisition of the principal residence to which the exception applies.[23]

22. IRC §529(e)(3).
23. IRC §72(t)(8)(D)(i)(I).

Health Insurance Premiums

The payment of health insurance premiums by an unemployed individual is not subject to the 10 percent penalty. The individual must have received unemployment compensation for 12 consecutive weeks under any federal or state unemployment compensation law.[24] The exception no longer applies when the individual has regained employment and has been employed for 60 days.

IRA Annuity vs. IRA Accounts

An individual retirement annuity is different than a traditional IRA because it is an annuity contract or endowment contract issued by an insurance company. However, an IRA annuity must meet certain similar requirements regarding transferability, nonforfeitability, premiums, and distributions.

Transferability and Nonforfeitability

An IRA annuity is not transferable by the owner and the benefits must not be forfeitable. The proceeds from an IRA annuity must be received by the owner or by a beneficiary of the contract. Similar to traditional IRAs, these IRA annuities cannot be pledged as collateral nor can loans be taken from the contract.

Premiums

The annual premiums for an IRA annuity may not exceed $6,000 for 2021. The premiums for the IRA annuity cannot be fixed. In the event that premium payments cease, the owner must be given the right to receive a paid up annuity and the owner of the annuity must also be allowed to forego payment of the annuity premium.

> ### ≔ *Key Concepts*
>
> 1. What is the difference between a traditional IRA and an individual retirement annuity?
>
> 2. How does a Roth IRA differ from a traditional IRA?
>
> 3. What are the income limits for Roth IRA contributions?
>
> 4. How can qualified plan assets be converted to a Roth IRA?
>
> 5. What issues should taxpayers consider when considering a "backdoor Roth?"
>
> 6. What are the requirements for a distribution from a Roth IRA to be classified as a qualified distribution?

Distributions

The distribution rules for IRA annuities are the same as for traditional IRAs. This includes the required minimum distribution beginning April 1st of the year following the year the owner attains the age of 70½ (or age 72 if age 70½ is attained after December 31, 2019) and the 10 percent penalty for distributions before age 59½.

Roth IRAs

Roth IRAs were created by the Taxpayer Relief Act of 1997. Roth IRAs are very attractive because, although the contributions to a Roth IRA are not deductible, qualified distributions (defined below) from Roth IRA accounts consist solely of tax-free income. In other words, the tax-deferred earnings may be distributed without ever being subjected to income tax. Additionally, Roth IRAs may be funded after the owner attains the age of 70½ (as can traditional IRAs for tax years after December 31, 2019) and are not subject to the required minimum distribution rules during the owner's life.

24.IRC §72(t)(2)(D)(i).

Roth IRAs and traditional IRAs share many of the same features and characteristics. The same contribution limitations that apply to traditional IRAs also apply to Roth IRAs, and this limit is an aggregate limit that includes contributions to both types of IRAs. Roth IRAs and traditional IRAs also share the prohibited transaction rules (as discussed below), the permitted investment rules, and the definition of earned income.

Exhibit 9.12 | Similarities and Differences of Traditional vs. Roth IRAs

	Traditional IRA	**Roth IRA**
Earned Income	✓	✓
Contributions	Contributions **can** be made beyond 70½ (for tax years after December 31, 2019)	Contributions **can** be made beyond 70½
Deductions	✓	N/A
Investment Choices	✓	✓
Minimum Distribution Rules	During life and after death	Only after death
Prohibited Transactions	✓	✓
Distributions	Usually taxable	Usually tax free

✓ = same

Taxpayers can fund Roth IRAs by either making cash contributions or by converting traditional IRAs or qualified plan balances into Roth IRAs.[25] When funding a Roth IRA, dollar limitations prevent contributions beyond certain income levels. As a result, high income and high net worth taxpayers generally cannot establish or fund Roth IRAs. However, they may be able to fund Roth accounts in 401(k) plans, 403(b) plans or governmental 457(b) plans.

Contributions

Both Roth IRAs and traditional IRAs share an annual single contribution limit and use the same definition for earned income. However, taxpayers may only contribute to a Roth IRA if they fall within the prescribed income limits. For single individuals, the 2021 limit, based on AGI, ranges from $125,000 to $140,000. If a single taxpayer's adjusted gross income is below $125,000, then a full contribution can be made to a Roth IRA. If the taxpayer's AGI exceeds $140,000, then the taxpayer may not contribute to a Roth IRA. If the taxpayer's AGI falls between the limits, then the contribution is limited based on a phaseout calculation. For married taxpayers filing jointly, the AGI limit ranges from $198,000 to $208,000 (for 2021), so a couple (both below the age of 50) filing jointly could contribute $12,000 to their Roth IRAs for the year 2021 if their income is below $198,000.

Exhibit 9.13 | Funding Roth IRAs (2021 AGI Limits)

Contribution AGI Phaseout Limit ($)	
Single	$125,000 – $140,000
Married Filing Jointly	$198,000 – $208,000
Married Filing Separate	$0,000 – $10,000

25. With the changes of the PPA 2006, qualified plans can be converted directly to Roth IRAs after December 31, 2007.

Roth Accounts

The TRA 2001 created what is referred to as Roth accounts. These accounts permit employees to defer current income (on an after-tax basis) into the account with qualifying distributions being free from income tax. Today, Roth accounts are permitted in 401(k) plans, 403(b) plans, and governmental 457(b) plans. This topic is discussed in more detail in Chapter 5.

Conversions[26]

Both qualified plan balances and traditional IRAs can be converted to a Roth IRA. By converting a traditional IRA to a Roth IRA, a taxpayer hopes to receive distributions that are completely income tax-free. However, at the time of the conversion, the taxpayer must include the value of the **conversion** amount in their taxable income. Therefore, the taxpayer is making the choice to forego funds (those used to pay the tax) by paying tax today to save tax in the future. Generally, this is an effective strategy when the person converting to the Roth has lower current income tax rates than their future expected income-tax rates, or when the account owner is unlikely to need to IRA funds during their own retirement years and the beneficiary is likely to be in a higher tax bracket upon inheriting the IRA than the current owner is today.

Qualified plan balances can also be directly converted into a Roth IRA without regard to the level of income of the taxpayer. Therefore, even high-income taxpayers can choose to convert IRAs or qualified plan balances to Roth IRAs. Whether or not taxpayers with higher income levels will choose to convert their IRAs will depend on many factors, including current marginal tax rates and future expected tax rates.

Conversions to a Roth IRA will likely result in reduced taxable income during retirement, which may result in less Social Security benefits being subject to income tax.

Recharacterized Contributions

IRA owners may **recharacterize** certain **contributions** made to one type of IRA as made to a different type of IRA for a taxable year.[27] For example, this may occur if a contribution is made to a traditional IRA, and the owner subsequently decides that it is better to contribute the funds to a Roth IRA. The individual can transfer the contribution (or a portion of the contribution) and its attributable earnings in a trustee-to-trustee transfer from the trustee of the traditional IRA to the trustee of the Roth IRA, and the individual can elect to treat the contribution as having been made to the Roth IRA, instead of to the traditional IRA, for federal income tax purposes.

These types of recharacterizations must be made by the due date of the individual's tax return (including extensions). However, the IRS has made exceptions in certain cases. The IRA custodian reports contributions to, and recharacterizations of, IRAs to both the account owner and the IRS on Form 5498. Custodians report distributions from an IRA to both the account owner and the IRS on Form 1099-R.

---

26. For tax years before 2010, taxpayers were permitted to convert traditional IRAs to Roth IRAs only if their AGI was less than or equal to $100,000. This same dollar limitation applied to single taxpayers and married taxpayers filing jointly.
27. Treas. Reg. §1.408A.

Exhibit 9.14 | Form 5498

2828	☐ VOID	☐ CORRECTED		
TRUSTEE'S or ISSUER'S name, street address, city or town, state or province, country, and ZIP or foreign postal code		**1** IRA contributions (other than amounts in boxes 2–4, 8–10, 13a, and 14a) $	OMB No. 1545-0747 **2021** Form **5498**	**IRA Contribution Information**
		2 Rollover contributions $		
		3 Roth IRA conversion amount $	**4** Recharacterized contributions $	**Copy A**
TRUSTEE'S or ISSUER'S TIN	PARTICIPANT'S TIN	**5** FMV of account $	**6** Life insurance cost included in box 1 $	**For Internal Revenue Service Center** File with Form 1096.
PARTICIPANT'S name		**7** IRA ☐ SEP ☐	SIMPLE ☐ Roth IRA ☐	
		8 SEP contributions $	**9** SIMPLE contributions $	For Privacy Act and Paperwork Reduction Act Notice, see the **2021 General Instructions for Certain Information Returns.**
Street address (including apt. no.)		**10** Roth IRA contributions $	**11** Check if RMD for 2022 ☐	
		12a RMD date	**12b** RMD amount $	
City or town, state or province, country, and ZIP or foreign postal code		**13a** Postponed/late contrib. $	**13b** Year **13c** Code	
		14a Repayments $	**14b** Code	
Account number (see instructions)		**15a** FMV of certain specified assets $	**15b** Code(s)	

Form **5498**   Cat. No. 50010C   www.irs.gov/Form5498   Department of the Treasury - Internal Revenue Service

Do Not Cut or Separate Forms on This Page — Do Not Cut or Separate Forms on This Page

Exhibit 9.15 | Form 1099-R

9898	☐ VOID	☐ CORRECTED		
PAYER'S name, street address, city or town, state or province, country, ZIP or foreign postal code, and telephone no.		**1** Gross distribution $	OMB No. 1545-0119 **2021** Form **1099-R**	**Distributions From Pensions, Annuities, Retirement or Profit-Sharing Plans, IRAs, Insurance Contracts, etc.**
		2a Taxable amount $		
		2b Taxable amount not determined ☐	Total distribution ☐	**Copy A**
PAYER'S TIN	RECIPIENT'S TIN	**3** Capital gain (included in box 2a) $	**4** Federal income tax withheld $	**For Internal Revenue Service Center** File with Form 1096.
RECIPIENT'S name		**5** Employee contributions/ Designated Roth contributions or insurance premiums $	**6** Net unrealized appreciation in employer's securities $	For Privacy Act and Paperwork Reduction Act Notice, see the **2021 General Instructions for Certain Information Returns.**
Street address (including apt. no.)		**7** Distribution code(s) IRA/SEP/SIMPLE ☐	**8** Other $ %	
City or town, state or province, country, and ZIP or foreign postal code		**9a** Your percentage of total distribution %	**9b** Total employee contributions $	

| **10** Amount allocable to IRR within 5 years $ | **11** 1st year of desig. Roth contrib. | **12** FATCA filing requirement ☐ | **14** State tax withheld $ $ | **15** State/Payer's state no. | **16** State distribution $ $ |
| Account number (see instructions) | | **13** Date of payment | **17** Local tax withheld $ $ | **18** Name of locality | **19** Local distribution $ $ |

Form **1099-R**   Cat. No. 14436Q   www.irs.gov/Form1099R   Department of the Treasury - Internal Revenue Service

Do Not Cut or Separate Forms on This Page — Do Not Cut or Separate Forms on This Page

---

Example 9.24

Andrea contributes $6,000 to her traditional IRA for 2021. Prior to the due date (plus extensions) for filing her federal income tax return, she decides that she would prefer to contribute to a Roth IRA instead. Andrea instructs the trustee of the traditional IRA to transfer in a trustee-to-trustee transfer the amount of the contribution, plus attributable earnings, to the trustee of a Roth IRA. She notifies the trustee of the traditional IRA and the trustee of the Roth IRA that she is recharacterizing the $6,000 contribution. Andrea will receive both a Form 5498 (contribution to the IRA) and 1099-R (distribution from the IRA) from the trustee of the traditional IRA, and will receive a Form 5498 (contribution to the Roth) from the trustee of the Roth IRA. On her federal income tax return, Andrea treats the $6,000 as having been contributed to the Roth IRA and not the traditional IRA.

Contributions to Roth IRAs can also be recharacterized as traditional IRA contributions. This type of recharacterization might apply in the event that a taxpayer made a contribution to a Roth IRA because she anticipated meeting the income limitations and later realized that her income exceeded the income limits.

Example 9.25

Cassidy, who is single, contributes $6,000 to her Roth IRA for 2021. However, she receives a significantly larger bonus because of her hard work and dedication to the firm. This unusually large bonus causes her income to exceed $140,000 (the 2021 income limit for contributions to Roth IRAs). As a result, she recharacterizes the contribution to the Roth IRA as a contribution to her traditional IRA. If Cassidy is not an active participant, she can deduct this contribution on her federal tax return. However, if she is an active participant, then she would effectively be making an after-tax contribution to her traditional IRA and would be required to file Form 8606.

As discussed in Chapter 7, Conversions from a traditional IRA or qualified plan to a Roth IRA were able to be recharacterized prior to 2018.[28] If a taxpayer converted a traditional IRA and the value of the account subsequently dropped, the taxpayer could recharacterize the conversion. This option would likely reduce the taxpayer's tax attributable to the conversion. However, this type of recharacterization was eliminated in TCJA 2017 for years after 2017.

"Backdoor Roth" Contributions

As discussed above, taxpayers with higher levels of income are prohibited from making contributions to Roth IRAs. The backdoor Roth technique may be employed by taxpayers to fund Roth IRAs while circumventing the income limits for contributions to Roth IRAs. The technique is typically accomplished in two steps:

- **Step 1: contribute to a non-deductible Traditional IRA** – since no deduction is taken, the IRA has basis equal to the contribution.
- **Step 2: convert the Traditional IRA to a Roth IRA** – any conversion from a Traditional IRA to a Roth IRA must include the conversion amount into income. However, because the conversion amount consists of after-tax contributions, the income that would be picked up equals the after-

---

28. Recall that in-plan Roth rollovers cannot be recharacterized.

tax basis. Thus, if the taxpayer has no other traditional IRAs and there have not yet been any earnings on the amount contributed, the conversion results in the Roth IRA being funded and no income being recognized by the taxpayer on her tax return.

Taxpayers can convert any IRA funds to a Roth IRA. However, the concept of the backdoor Roth is to contribute to a traditional IRA and then convert to a Roth IRA without increasing taxable income.

Example 9.26

Brisco has AGI of $300,000 and therefore cannot directly contribute to a Roth IRA. He has no existing traditional IRA accounts when he contributes the $6,000 to a Traditional IRA. Because he is an active participant in his company's 401(k) plan, he cannot take a deduction for the IRA contribution. As a result, he has $6,000 of basis in the Traditional IRA. Brisco then converts the Traditional IRA into a Roth IRA prior to the accumulation of any earnings. He will not have to report any income because the funds consist entirely of after-tax funds. Through the backdoor Roth, Brisco is able to fund a Roth IRA even though he has income above the contribution limits.

As **Example 9.26** illustrates, the basic backdoor Roth is easy to implement. However, an important issue that taxpayers must consider before attempting one of these is what is known as the IRA aggregation rule. Under this rule, taxpayers must combine the value of all IRA accounts when determining the pro-rata portion of a distribution that consists of return of basis. In other words, if the taxpayer does not have any other IRA accounts, then the backdoor Roth works well. However, if the taxpayer has other IRA accounts or other assets in IRA accounts, then the taxpayer may not receive the full benefit of the backdoor Roth.

Example 9.27

Assume the same facts as **Example 9.26** except that Brisco has $94,000 in his traditional IRA with no basis. When he contributes $6,000 to the IRA account, it has a balance of $100,000 and basis of $6,000. If Brisco converts $6,000 to a Roth IRA, the basis of $6,000 must be pro-rated over the entire value of his IRA balances. Therefore, the portion of the $6,000 distribution that consists of return of basis equals 6.0% ($6,000 divided by $100,000). The conversion consists of $360 of return of basis and $5,640 of taxable income. Therefore, the aggregation rules have undermined the benefit of the backdoor Roth for Brisco. He could have first initiated a reverse rollover (rolled his traditional IRA balances to his employer retirement plan (if permitted)) and then attempted the backdoor Roth.

As **Example 9.27** illustrates, the aggregation rule may prevent a taxpayer from receiving the full benefit of a backdoor Roth if the taxpayer already has funds in a traditional IRA. However, taxpayers may be able to eliminate this issue by rolling traditional IRA funds into an employer retirement plan. In such a case, those funds would no longer be included in the IRA balance.

For many years, there was a concern about the IRS's step transaction doctrine, which subjects a set of transactions to IRS scrutiny. Under this doctrine, individual steps in a transaction may be permitted, but the net result of all of the steps taken in total can be considered as violating certain provisions of the IRC. In the case of a backdoor Roth, the steps involved, while permitted, clearly are designed to circumvent the contribution limits. However, the step transaction doctrine appears to not be an issue for the backdoor

Roth transaction, as the 2017 TCJA Joint Explanatory Statement explains that taxpayers are free to engage in the steps involved in a backdoor Roth.[29]

While the step transaction doctrine no longer appears to be a risk, taxpayers should take care to consider the aggregation rules. In addition, as a result of the TCJA 2017, taxpayers can no longer recharacterize Roth conversions after 2017. Previously, the backdoor Roth could only be used with taxpayers who had not attained the age of 70½, however, with the repeal of the maximum age for contributions to traditional IRAs beginning in 2020, a taxpayer of any age who has earned income can use the backdoor Roth strategy.

Distributions

Distributions from IRAs and other retirement plans are generally treated as ordinary income. However, distributions from Roth IRAs are designed to be tax-free in retirement. A distribution from a Roth IRA is not included in the owner's gross income and is not subject to the 10 percent early withdrawal penalty if it is a "**qualified distribution.**" Distributions that do not meet the definition of a qualified distribution may be subject to income tax and the 10 percent early withdrawal penalty.

Qualified Distributions

A qualified distribution is a distribution from a Roth IRA that satisfies both of the following tests:

1. **Five-Year Test:** The distribution must be made after a five-taxable-year period (which begins January 1st of the taxable year for which the first regular contribution is made to any Roth IRA of the individual or, if earlier, January 1st of the taxable year in which the first conversion contribution is made to any Roth IRA of the individual), **AND**

2. **Distribution Test:** The distribution satisfies one of the following four requirements:
   - made on or after the date on which the owner attains age 59½,
   - made to a beneficiary or estate of the owner on or after the date of the owner's death,
   - is attributable to the owner being disabled, or
   - for first time home purchase (lifetime cap of $10,000 for first time homebuyers includes taxpayer, spouse, child, or grandchild who has not owned a house for at least two years).

29. See Joint Explanatory Statement of the Committee of Conference for the 2017 TCJA, footnotes 268, 269, 276, and 277, beginning on page 114 of the PDF.

Exhibit 9.16 | Roth 5-Year Rule

Year 1	Year 2	Year 3	Year 4	Year 5	Year 6+
5 Taxable-Year-Period					After 5 Years
Not a Qualified Distribution					Qualified Distribution

Example 9.28

On July 5, 2021, Yvonne established a Roth IRA for year 2021 with a $1,200 contribution. Since this was her first contribution to a Roth IRA, her five-year period begins on January 1, 2021. The five year period ends on December 31, 2025. Therefore, Yvonne cannot have a qualified distribution prior to 2026. If Yvonne took a $1,000 distribution in 2026 and was 60 years old, then the distribution would be characterized as a qualified distribution.

Example 9.29

On February 16, 2022, Melissa made an initial contribution of $900 to a Roth IRA. She made the contribution for the 2021 tax year (recall that a taxpayer can make contributions until April 15 of the following year to a traditional or Roth IRA for the prior tax year). Melissa's five-year period begins on January 1, 2021 even though she made her initial contribution in 2022 because the contribution was for the 2021 tax year.

Example 9.30

Colin decides that he wants a sailboat as a present for his 60th birthday. He decides to liquidate his Roth IRA to make the purchase. His first contribution to a Roth IRA was in 2001. Since he established the Roth IRA more than five years before the distribution and he is over the age of 59½, the distribution is a qualified distribution and is not subject to income tax or penalty.

The five-taxable-year period is not re-determined when the owner of a Roth IRA dies. Thus, the beneficiary of the Roth IRA would need to wait until after the end of the original five-taxable-year period for the distribution to be a qualified distribution. Prior to the end of the five-year period, minimum distributions could be taken from the contribution and conversion layers (discussed below) without tax or penalty. However, these distributions would not be qualified distributions.

Example 9.31

Jay first contributes to a Roth IRA three years ago. He also converted a traditional IRA to his Roth IRA last year. Unfortunately, a meat truck accidentally tips over and crushes him to death. His son inherits the IRA and needs to begin taking minimum distributions. Although the distribution is on account of the death of the owner, it is not a qualified distribution because the five-year period has not elapsed. Therefore, he will need to take distributions from the inherited Roth IRA from the contribution and conversion layers to avoid income tax until the five-year period is met. Note that, due to the change in RMD rules made by the SECURE Act, his son is not required to take any distributions until the 10th year following Jay's death, at which time the entire account balance must be distributed. Therefore, Jay's son could elect to wait until the 5-year requirement has been met before receiving distributions that are subject to the 5-year requirement.

Nonqualified Distributions

Any amount distributed from an individual's Roth IRA that is not a qualified distribution is treated as made in the following order (determined as of the end of a taxable year and exhausting each category before moving to the following category):

1. from regular contributions (i.e., the $6,000 for 2021 annual contributions),
2. from conversion contributions on a first-in-first-out basis, and then
3. from earnings.

In the event a distribution is not a qualified distribution, the first layer will be return of adjusted basis from after-tax contributions. These distributions are tax and penalty free regardless of age. After all contributions have been distributed, the next layer of distributions is from post-tax conversion contributions. Since these contributions have already been taxed there will be no income tax consequences (although there may be a penalty). The final layer consists of the tax-deferred earnings on contributions and conversions within the Roth IRA, which will be subject to tax (and possibly a penalty) if the distribution is not a qualified distribution.

Distributions will generally not be taxable to the extent that total distributions do not exceed total contributions and conversions. However, if an individual takes a distribution that is not a qualified distribution and the amount of the distribution is neither contributed to another Roth IRA in a qualified rollover contribution nor constitutes a corrective distribution, part of the distribution may be includible in the individual's gross income. The amount included in the owner's gross income is the amount by which the total of all distributions (qualified or not) taken through the years exceeds the amount of all contributions and conversions to all of the individual's Roth IRAs.

Exhibit 9.17 | Roth IRA Distributions

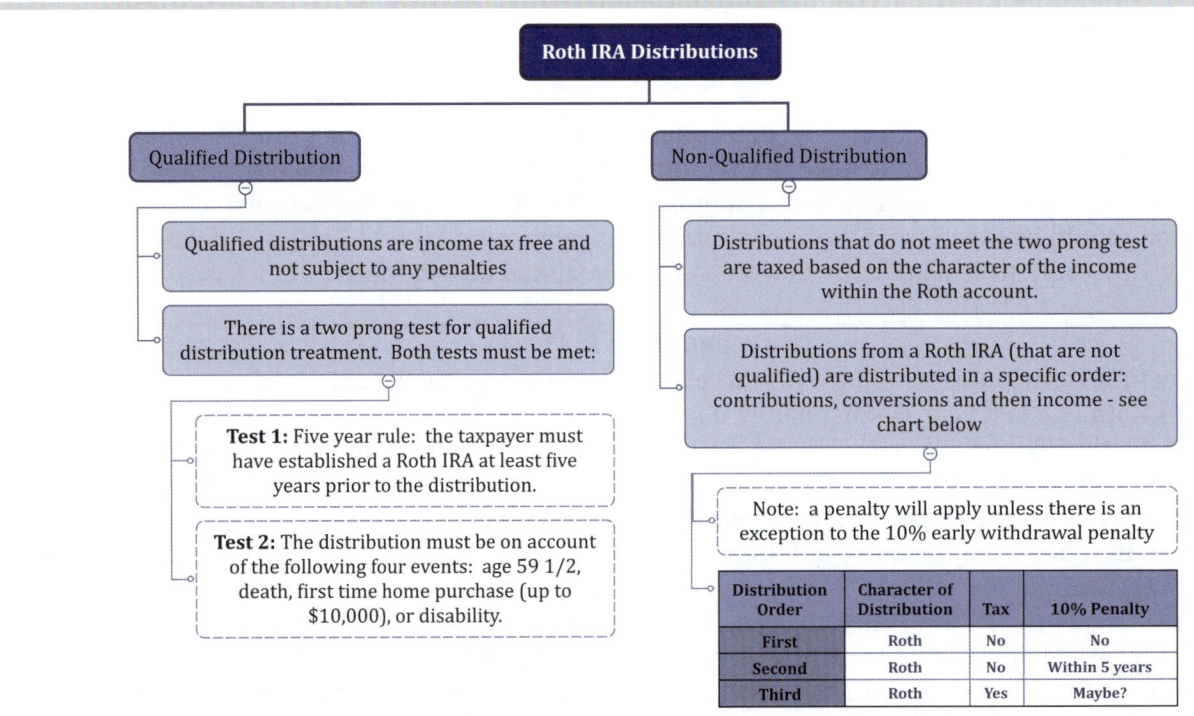

10 Percent Early Withdrawal Penalty

The 10 percent early withdrawal penalty will generally apply to any portion of a distribution from a Roth IRA that is includible in gross income (such as distributions that consist of earnings within the Roth IRA). The penalty also applies to a nonqualified distribution, even if it is not includible in gross income, to the extent it is allocable to a conversion contribution if the distribution is made within the five-taxable-year period beginning with the first day of the individual's taxable year in which the conversion contribution was made. For purposes of this rule, each conversion has its own five-year period; it does not follow the five-year clock set by making the first Roth contribution or conversion. The separate five-year period requirement for conversions is necessary to prevent abuse of the privilege to convert. Without this requirement, a young person (significantly under age 59½ with a traditional IRA who wanted to take a distribution to buy a new car (not a penalty exception) could simply convert to Roth and then take a penalty-free distribution. To prevent this abuse, each conversion will have a separate five-year requirement in order to avoid a penalty associated with a distribution from the converted amounts.

It is important to note that although a nonqualified distribution may be subject to the 10 percent penalty based on the Roth IRA rules, the penalty may be avoided if the distribution falls within one of the exceptions for IRAs discussed earlier in this chapter.

For example, a distribution could avoid the 10 percent penalty if the proceeds were used for qualified higher education expenses or to pay for certain medical costs. The following table summarizes the treatment from the standpoint of taxation and penalties of distributions from a Roth IRA to the extent the distribution is not a qualified distribution.

Exhibit 9.18 | Summary of Nonqualified Roth IRA Distributions

	Subject to Taxation?	Subject to 10% Penalty?
Contributions	No	No
Conversions	No	Yes Within five years of conversion*
Earnings	Yes	Yes*

* Penalty will not apply if the distribution falls within the exceptions listed above.

Example 9.32

Fenix, age 45, contributed a total of $10,000 to her Roth IRA beginning six years ago. She also converted a traditional IRA with a balance of $25,000 to a Roth IRA two years ago. Her current account balance in both Roth IRAs is $43,000. If she receives a complete distribution from both of these Roth IRAs and uses the proceeds to pay for her son's college tuition, then the distribution will have the following tax treatment:

The distribution does not meet both of the requirements of a qualified distribution. Therefore, the earnings portion of the distribution ($8,000) is subject to ordinary income tax, but none of the distribution will be subject to the 10 percent early withdrawal penalty. The penalty does not apply because the proceeds are being used for qualified higher education expenses, one of the exceptions to the 10 percent early withdrawal penalty for IRAs.

Distribution Layer	Pre-Distribution Amount/Time	Distribution from This Category (Total Distribution Amount $43,000)	Tax/Penalty Treatment	Explanation
1st: Contributions	$10,000 Six years ago	$10,000	No tax, no penalty	Contributions can be withdrawn at any time without tax or penalty.
2nd: Conversions	$25,000 Two years ago	$25,000	No tax, no penalty	Withdrawals of converted amounts are always tax-free. While the 5-year clock on conversions has not been met (which would make the penalty apply), there is a penalty exception for higher education expenses.
3rd: Earnings	$8,000	$8,000	Taxed, no penalty	Disqualified distribution since higher education expenses is not one of the triggering events that creates a qualified distribution. However, higher education is a penalty exception.

Example 9.33

Assume the same facts as above, except that Fenix took the distribution from her Roth IRAs to be used as a down payment on her son's new Porsche sports car. The distribution will have the following tax treatment:

The distribution does not meet both of the requirements of a qualified distribution. Therefore, the earnings portion of the distribution ($8,000) is subject to ordinary income tax. In addition, the 10 percent early withdrawal penalty applies to the conversion portion of the distribution because she has converted from a traditional IRA to a Roth IRA within the last five years. The $8,000 of earnings that is considered taxable income is also subject to the 10 percent early withdrawal penalty and the $25,000 conversion is subject to the 10 percent penalty but is not taxable.

Distribution Layer	Pre-Distribution Amount/Time	Distribution from This Category (Total Distribution Amount $43,000)	Tax/Penalty Treatment	Explanation
1st: Contributions	$10,000 Six years ago	$10,000	No tax, no penalty	Contributions can be withdrawn at any time without tax or penalty.
2nd: Conversions	$25,000 Two years ago	$25,000	No tax, 10% penalty	Withdrawals of converted amounts are always tax-free. The 5-year clock on conversions has not been met (which makes the penalty apply), and there is no penalty exception available.
3rd: Earnings	$8,000	$8,000	Taxed, 10% penalty	Disqualified distribution since purchase of car is not one of the triggering events that creates a qualified distribution. No penalty exception applies.

If Fenix was over the age of 59½, then the distribution would have been a qualified distribution and none of the distribution would be subject to ordinary income tax or penalty. The year of the conversion is only a factor when the distribution is not a qualified distribution. In this case, the Roth IRA was established six years ago, and Fenix was over 59½, thus the distribution was a qualified distribution.

Example 9.34

Brad is 61 years old and first contributed to a Roth IRA three years ago. His contributions to the Roth IRA total $6,000. In addition, Brad converted his traditional IRA to a Roth IRA last year. The conversion was in the amount of $20,000. If Brad takes a $35,000 distribution from the Roth IRA, it will have the following tax treatment:

The distribution has not met the five-year requirement to be a qualified distribution. Therefore, the portion of the distribution that consists of earnings ($9,000) is subject to ordinary income tax, but none of the distribution will be subject to the 10 percent early withdrawal penalty. The penalty does not apply because Brad is over the age of 59½, one of the exceptions to the 10 percent early withdrawal penalty.

Distribution Layer	Pre-Distribution Amount/Time	Distribution from This Category (Total Distribution Amount $35,000)	Tax/Penalty Treatment	Explanation
1st: Contributions	$6,000 Three years ago	$6,000	No tax, no penalty	Contributions can be withdrawn at any time without tax or penalty.
2nd: Conversions	$20,000 One year ago	$20,000	No tax, no penalty	Withdrawals of converted amounts are always tax-free. While the 5-year clock on conversions has not been met (which would make the penalty apply), there is a penalty exception for over age 59½.
3rd: Earnings	$9,000	$9,000	Taxed, no penalty	Disqualified distribution since the 5-year requirement has not been met. However, there is a penalty exception for over age 59½.

Comparing Roth IRAs to Traditional IRAs

Two important distinctions when comparing Roth IRAs to traditional IRAs are:

1. Qualified Roth distributions are tax-free, allowing greater control of taxation and flexibility of withdrawals in the retirement years since large lump sum distributions for large purchases (such as a car, gift to a loved one, or dream trip around the world) do not increase AGI when distributed from a Roth IRA. This type of distribution translates to lower tax brackets and less potential of reaching an AGI level that causes the 3.8 percent Medicare tax to apply to investment income, and may avoid increasing the amount of Social Security benefits subject to taxation or increased IRMAA premiums for Medicare Part B.[30]
2. The required minimum distribution rules do not apply to Roth IRAs during the life of the original account owner, but, like traditional IRAs, do apply to the beneficiaries after the death of the owner.

Other IRA Issues

Investments

Individuals have a plethora of options regarding the investment choices for assets purchased or held in an IRA. Investments in cash, stocks, bonds, and even options are permitted. However, custodians often limit IRA owners from investing in certain option contracts, especially naked options, within an IRA.

Although there is great freedom of investment choices, certain types of investments are prohibited. Life insurance and collectibles are not allowed to be held within an IRA.[31] If either life insurance or collectibles are purchased within an IRA, the value of the purchase is treated as a distribution from the IRA account and is subject to tax and/or penalty.

Collectibles include all of the following:[32]
*   any work of art
*   any rug or antique
*   any metal or gem
*   any stamp or coin
*   any alcoholic beverage

> ### ☷ *Key Concepts*
>
> 1. What are the limitations on the types of investments that can be held in an IRA?
>
> 2. What are the rollover rules for transferring balances from a qualified plan to an IRA?
>
> 3. What are the distribution rules for an IRA?
>
> 4. What transactions are considered prohibited for an IRA?

An exception to the collectibles rule exists for certain coins and bullion. U.S. gold, silver, and platinum minted coins, such as American Gold, Silver, and Platinum Eagle coins, are permitted to be held in an IRA account. However, coins of most foreign countries, such as South African Krugerrands, are considered collectibles and are therefore not permissible investments for an IRA. In addition, investments in gold, silver, platinum, or palladium bullion are permitted.

---

30. Details regarding these items are covered in Chapter 11.
31. IRC §408(a)(3).
32. IRC §408(m).

Tax-Free Distributions for Charitable Purposes

First introduced under the Pension Protection Act of 2006 for years 2007 through 2014 and made permanent by the Protecting Americans from Tax Hikes Act of 2015 (PATH 2015), qualified charitable distributions from a traditional or Roth IRA may be excluded from gross income.[33] The exclusion may not exceed $100,000 per taxpayer per tax year. A qualified charitable distribution is any distribution from an IRA (qualified plans are not eligible) directly by the IRA trustee to a charitable organization. Qualified charitable distributions (QCDs) are taken into account for purposes of the minimum distribution rules applicable to traditional IRAs to the same extent the distribution would have been taken into account under such rules had the distribution not been directly distributed under this provision. Distributions are eligible for this exclusion only if made on or after the date the IRA owner attains age 70½. The distribution is reported on Form 1099-R, and is entered as a distribution from an IRA on the Form 1040; however, the "taxable" amount on the Form 1040 is reported as $0 (if the full distribution was a qualified charitable distribution), with "QCD" written on that line to denote the reason.

This provision is extremely helpful for those taxpayers with charitable intent. Without this law change, a taxpayer would take a distribution from his IRA, which would be subject to tax as ordinary income, and then contribute that amount to charity. Although the taxpayer might be able to take a charitable deduction, that deduction is "below-the-line" and subject to phase-out limits, and does not completely offset the inclusion into income. The old rules actually result in a cost to the taxpayer who gives away funds from his or her IRA to a charity. This exclusion makes it easier and tax-free, thus benefiting both charities and taxpayers.

As a result of the SECURE Act of 2019 repeal of the maximum age for contributions to traditional IRAs, the QCD rules have been amended to prevent a "double dipping" of tax advantages, as would result if a taxpayer could, in the same tax year, deduct a contribution to and take advantage of a tax-free qualified charitable distribution from an IRA. For QCDs made after December 31, 2019, the amount of charitable distributions excluded from gross income is reduced by the excess of:
1. the aggregate amount of IRA deductions taken for all taxable years after the date the taxpayer attains age 70½, over
2. the amount of reductions under this rule for all taxable years preceding the current taxable year.

Example 9.35

Wanda, who is age 71 in 2021 and still working, contributed $5,000 to a deductible IRA. She also made a charitable distribution directly from her IRA to her church in the amount of $4,000. Wanda will not qualify for QCD treatment on the $4,000 distribution because it is reduced (but not below zero) by the deductible contribution. She will report the $4,000 distribution as taxable income on her tax return. If Wanda itemizes her deductions on Schedule A, she can claim the $4,000 charitable contribution below-the-line. The result would be the same if she took the $4,000 distribution in 2022 or 2023 because the rule considers all years after attainment of age 70½.

---

33. IRC §408(d)(8).

Example 9.36

Assume the same facts as the previous example. In 2022, Wanda is still working and contributes $6,000 to a deductible IRA. She also makes a charitable contribution to the animal shelter (a qualified charity) of $15,000 directly from her IRA. Wanda's QCD reduction is equal to the total of all of her IRA deductions since turning age 70½ ($5,000 in 2021 + $6,000 in 2022 = $11,000), less the amount of QCDs denied in prior years ($4,000). Therefore her QCD reduction for this year is $7,000 ($11,000 - $4,000). Of her $15,000 donation, $8,000 is a qualified charitable contribution which is not taxable income on her tax return. The remaining $7,000 is taxed as a distribution but can be deducted below-the-line if Wanda itemizes deductions.

Reconciliation from age 70½:

Total charitable contributions from IRA: $19,000 ($4,000 + $15,000)

Total deductible IRA contributions: $11,000 ($4,000 + $7,000) - denied QCD treatment

Allowed QCD treatment (nontaxable): $8,000

IRA Rollovers

There are a variety of rollover rules that facilitate taxpayers transferring their retirement balances from one type of plan or account to another. These rules address transfers from qualified plans and from IRAs. EGTRRA 2001 greatly enhanced the portability and flexibility of transferring retirement funds.

Exhibit 9.19 | Summary of Allowable Rollovers

		Roll To							
		Roth IRA	Traditional IRA	SIMPLE IRA	SEP-IRA	Government 457(b)	Qualified Plan	403(b)	Designated Roth Account 401(k), 403(b), 457(b)
Roll From	**Roth IRA**	Yes	No	No	No	No	No	No	No
	Traditional IRA	Yes. Must include in income.	Yes*	Yes, after 2 years.*	Yes*	Yes, must have separate accounts.	Yes	Yes	No
	SIMPLE IRA	Yes, after 2 years. Must include in income.	Yes, after 2 years.*	Yes*	Yes, after 2 years.*	Yes, after 2 years. Must have separate accounts.	Yes, after 2 years.	Yes, after 2 years.	No
	SEP-IRA	Yes. Must include in income.	Yes*	Yes, after 2 years.*	Yes*	Yes, must have separate accounts.	Yes	Yes	No
	Government 457(b)	Yes. Must include in income.	Yes	Yes, after 2 years.	Yes	Yes	Yes	Yes	Yes as in plan rollover. Must include in income.
	Qualified Plan	Yes. Must include in income.	Yes	Yes, after 2 years.	Yes	Yes, must have separate accounts.	Yes	Yes	Yes as in plan rollover. Must include in income.
	403(b)	Yes. Must include in income.	Yes	Yes, after 2 years.	Yes	Yes, must have separate accounts.	Yes	Yes	Yes as in plan rollover. Must include in income.
	Designated Roth Account, 401(k), 403(b), 457(b)	Yes	No	No	No	No	No	No	Yes, if a direct trustee to trustee transfer.

One within 12 months.

Distributions from Qualified Plans

When an individual terminates employment with the plan sponsor of a qualified plan, the individual may roll the qualified plan balance over into an IRA. Typically, an IRA that holds funds that have been transferred from a qualified plan is referred to as a "conduit" IRA or an IRA rollover account. The funds in such a conduit IRA are allowed to be rolled back into another qualified plan, assuming the new plan permits such rollovers.

Example 9.37

Craig leaves his employer, Planet Source, where he was a participant in a qualified plan. Craig can rollover his balance in his qualified plan into an IRA, which is generally referred to as a conduit IRA. Once Craig finds a new employer, he can rollover the funds in the conduit IRA into the new qualified plan (assuming that the plan permits such a rollover contribution). Alternatively, Craig could maintain the conduit IRA until he turns age 70½ (or age 72 if age 70½ is attained after December 31, 2019), at which point he would be required to begin taking minimum distributions.

It is important to consider the assets that are being transferred from the qualified plan to the IRA. If assets that are not permitted to be held in an IRA, although allowed in a qualified plan, are rolled into an IRA, then there may be a deemed distribution that will be subject to taxable income and possibly the 10 percent premature withdrawal penalty. For example, life insurance can be held in a qualified plan but not in an IRA.

If a participant in a qualified plan wishes to convert to a Roth IRA through a rollover, it is no longer necessary that the participant first roll the qualified plan proceeds into a traditional IRA and then to the Roth IRA. As of 2008, a participant can roll directly from a qualified plan to a Roth IRA.[34] However, the rolled over amount will be includible in taxable income.

Many taxpayers and advisors often leave funds in a conduit IRA and never roll the funds over to another qualified plan because there are few real benefits (other than creditor protection and potentially lower expense ratios on mutual fund investments) to having funds in a qualified plan versus having funds in an IRA. **Exhibit 9.20** identifies some of the benefits of a qualified plan versus an IRA.

---

34. Under the PPA 2006, direct rollovers from qualified plans to Roth IRAs are allowed after 2007. Under previous law, a rollover from a qualified plan to a Roth IRA generally required the use of a conduit traditional IRA.

Exhibit 9.20 | Comparison of Benefits for Qualified Plans vs. IRAs

Benefits	Qualified Plan	IRA
NUA tax treatment available*	Yes	No
Loans may be permitted?	Yes, if plan permits loans	No
Assets are protected from creditors (ERISA or state law)?	Yes, ERISA	Yes, under the federal bankruptcy laws.**
Assets can be invested in life insurance?	Yes	No
Participants/owners have complete discretion of investment decisions?	Generally No	Yes
60 day rollover?	No	Yes, once per year

*Applies only to the stock of the employer sponsoring the qualified plan.
**Except inherited IRAs may not be protected from creditors in bankruptcy. (See Chapter 7)

As discussed in Chapter 7, although 10-year forward averaging and capital gain treatment for pre-1974 participation is available for lump-sum distributions from a qualified plan, it is only available for those taxpayers born prior to January 2, 1936. Thus, the number of taxpayers who would qualify for **10-year forward averaging** or **pre-1974 capital gain treatment** is minimal. One advantage of a qualified plan is that participants may be able to withdraw a portion of the plan balance as a loan. However, the plan must provide for this feature and many plans do not permit loans. Although IRAs do not allow for loans, they do permit a rollover of 60 days that can, in effect, be a short-term loan (see discussion below). One of the most advantageous features of a qualified plan is the creditor protection that is provided by ERISA. This type of protection is not available to IRAs, however federal bankruptcy law now protects certain IRA accounts.[35]

Employee after-tax contributions from a qualified plan may be rolled over into another qualified plan or a traditional IRA for years after December 31, 2001. In the case of a rollover from a qualified plan to another qualified plan, the rollover is permitted only through a direct transfer. In addition, a qualified plan is not permitted to accept rollovers of after-tax contributions unless the plan provides separate accounting for such contributions and earnings. After-tax contributions, including nondeductible contributions to an IRA, are not permitted to be rolled over from an IRA into a qualified plan or 403(b) plan.

60-day Period

Taxpayers have the ability to take a distribution from an IRA at any time. However, distributions from IRAs will generally be taxed as ordinary income and may be subject to the 10 percent early withdrawal penalty if the distribution is not rolled back into another IRA within 60 days from the original distribution. (Although, the IRS may waive the 60-day requirement in the event the delay is caused by casualty, disaster, or other events beyond the taxpayers control.) This rule permits taxpayers to receive a distribution, make use of the funds for a period of 60 days, and then redeposit the funds into an IRA without any tax consequences. The PPA 2006 makes permanent EGTRRA rules giving the IRS authority to extend the 60-day rollover period when a person's failure to comply is due to events beyond the reasonable control of that person. There are many examples of the IRS waiving or extending the 60-day period. The following example from a private letter ruling illustrates this point.

35. Bankruptcy Abuse Prevention and Consumer Protection Act of 2005.

Example 9.38

IRS Letter Ruling 200925047 (Mar. 26, 2009)

Taxpayer A, asserts that on Date 3, Taxpayer A received a distribution of Amount L from Plan X. Taxpayer A asserts that her failure to accomplish a rollover of Amount L within the 60 day period prescribed by section 402(c)(3)(A) of the Code was due to the failure of her tax service provider, Attorney V, to provide correct advice regarding the distribution of Amount L from Plan X.

On Date 1, Taxpayer A's husband, Decedent D, died having designated Taxpayer A as the beneficiary of his account balance in Plan X, a plan intended to be qualified under Section 401(a) of the Internal Revenue Code. In addition to her husband's sudden and unexpected death at age 55, Taxpayer A had lost her father and uncle earlier in the year. After her husband's death, Taxpayer A began exhibiting signs of depression such as sleeplessness, extreme weight loss, and potentially dangerous lapses of concentration due to her grief.

During this period on Date 2, three months after Decedent D's death, Plan X distributed a check in Amount M, (Amount L minus tax withholding) which Taxpayer A deposited in a money market account for safe keeping. Taxpayer A sought professional treatment for anxiety and depression during the 60 day period after the distribution of Amount L from Plan X. Taxpayer A was prescribed drugs to alleviate depression and anxiety. Taxpayer A has submitted documentation from health care providers Dr. L, Health Care Provider O, Instructor C, and Individual K attesting to Taxpayer A's depression and out of character behavior during the 60-day rollover period.

Decedent D and Taxpayer A retained Attorney V to prepare their wills. Attorney V took control of Decedent D's estate tax planning from Taxpayer A after Decedent D's death and was in charge of Decedent D's estate inventory both before and after the Date 2 distribution from Plan X and throughout the following 60-day rollover period. In Fact, the distribution of Amount M was included as an asset on the Estate Inventory filed with the Probate Court of the county of Decedent D's last residence. Before the end of the 60-day rollover period Taxpayer A was assured by Attorney V that she would have no income tax liabilities as a result of Taxpayer A's inheritance of assets from Decedent D.

Taxpayer A submits that during the depression treatment period which included all of the 60-day rollover period, she relied on Attorney V to handle the financial affairs of Decedent D and Attorney V failed to timely inform Taxpayer A of the availability of a rollover option for Amount L from Plan X and failed to properly advise her and to properly manage the distribution of Amount L until after the 60-day period for a rollover to an IRA had expired. Taxpayer A was notified of her lost opportunity for a rollover of the Amount L Plan X distribution by Certified Financial Planner M after the expiration of the 60-day rollover period who advised Taxpayer A to write the Internal Revenue Service for a 60-day rollover waiver request.

Based on the above information, the Service waived the 60-day rollover period found in section 402(c)(3)(A). As a result Taxpayer A is granted a period of 60 days from the issuance of this ruling letter to contribute Amount L, or any portion thereof, to an IRA.

Generally, if the taxpayer makes a tax-free rollover of any part of a distribution from a traditional IRA they cannot make another tax-free rollover from that same IRA or any other of their IRAs within a one-year period. The one-year period begins on the date the taxpayer received the IRA distribution, not on the date they rolled it back into an IRA.[36]

Example 9.39

Kendra has two traditional IRAs: IRA-1 and IRA-2. She makes a tax-free rollover of a distribution from IRA-1 into a new traditional IRA (IRA-3). Kendra cannot within one year of the distribution from IRA-1, make a tax-free rollover of any distribution from any of her IRAs into another traditional IRA.

Rollover to Qualified Plans

In the past, only funds held in a conduit IRA could be rolled back into a qualified plan. However, distributions after December 31, 2001 from an IRA are now permitted to be rolled over into a qualified plan, §403(b) annuity, or governmental §457 plan. Although it is now permissible to roll an IRA balance into a qualified plan, 403(b), or 457 plan, these plans are not required to accept such rollovers.

Lump-sum distributions from qualified plans may receive special tax treatment, including pre-74 capital gains treatment and 10-year forward averaging. However, a distribution from a qualified plan is not eligible for capital gains or averaging treatment if there was a rollover to the plan that would not have been permitted under present law. Thus, in order to preserve capital gains and averaging treatment for a qualified plan distribution that is rolled over, the rollover would have to be made to a conduit IRA and then rolled back into a qualified plan. In effect, the IRS does not permit taxpayers to receive special tax treatment on funds held in an IRA that would never have qualified for special tax treatment.

ERISA Protection vs. State Law Protection

As discussed in Chapter 3, qualified plans are protected by ERISA, which provides that a participant's accounts and benefits under the plan may not be alienated or assigned.[37] However, IRAs are not afforded this same protection because IRAs are not exempt from creditor's claims under ERISA. The Supreme Court ruled on April 4, 2005 that IRAs can be exempt property in a bankruptcy proceeding. Although providing some protection where there was none previously, the ruling does not provide blanket protection for IRAs.

---

36. IRC Section 408(d)(3)(A)(i) provides generally that any amount distributed from an IRA will not be included in the gross income of the distributee to the extent the amount is paid into an IRA for the benefit of the distributee no later than 60 days after the distributee receives the distribution. This type of rollover is generally referred to as an indirect rollover. Section 408(d)(3)(B) provides that an individual is permitted to make only one rollover described in the preceding sentence in any 1-year period. Previously, Proposed Regulation § 1.408-4(b)(4)(ii) and IRS Publication 590, Individual Retirement Arrangements (IRAs), provided that this limitation is applied on an IRA-by-IRA basis. However, a Tax Court opinion, Bobrow v. Commissioner, T.C. Memo. 2014-2, held that the limitation applies on an aggregate basis, meaning that an individual could not make an IRA-to-IRA rollover if he or she had made such a rollover involving any of the individual's IRAs in the preceding 1-year period. In Announcement 2014-32, the IRS made clear that it would follow the Tax Court's opinion and the new interpretation would apply beginning Jan. 1, 2015. Although an eligible IRA distribution received on or after Jan. 1, 2015 and properly rolled over to another IRA will still get tax-free treatment, subsequent distributions from any of the individual's IRAs (including traditional and Roth IRAs) received within one year after that distribution will not get tax-free rollover treatment.

37. ERISA § 206(d).

CASE STUDY 9.2

Rousey Et Ux v. Jacoway: Several years after petitioners deposited distributions from their pension plans into Individual Retirement Accounts (IRAs), the Rouseys filed a joint petition under Chapter 7 of the Bankruptcy Code. They sought to shield portions of their IRAs from their creditors by claiming them as exempt from the bankruptcy estate under 11 U. S. C. §522(d)(10)(E), which provides, inter alia, that a debtor may withdraw from the estate his "right to receive . . . a payment under a stock bonus, pension, profit sharing, annuity, or similar plan or contract on account of . . . age." Respondent Jacoway, the Bankruptcy Trustee, objected to the Rouseys' exemption and moved for turnover of the IRAs to her. The Bankruptcy Court sustained her objection and granted her motion, and the Bankruptcy Appellate Panel (BAP) agreed. The Eighth Circuit affirmed, concluding that, even if the Rouseys' IRAs were "similar plans or contracts" to the plans specified in §522(d)(10)(E), their IRAs gave them no right to receive payment "on account of age," but were instead savings accounts readily accessible at any time for any purpose.

However, the Supreme Court held that the Rouseys can exempt IRA assets from the bankruptcy estate because the IRAs fulfill both of the §522(d)(10)(E) requirements at issue here—they confer a right to receive payment on account of age and they are similar plans or contracts to those enumerated in §522(d)(10)(E).

However, as a result of the Bankruptcy Abuse Prevention and Consumer Protection Act of 2005 (BAPCPA 2005), IRAs are now afforded similar protection to qualified plans under Federal Bankruptcy law. The Act clarifies that retirement accounts that are exempt from tax under the Internal Revenue Code are also exempt from the debtor's estate. The aggregate value of the assets in a traditional IRA or a Roth IRA that may qualify for this exemption cannot exceed $1 million (indexed to $1,362,800 for 2019-2021 for an individual debtor.[38] However, the assets subject to the $1 million cap do not include amounts attributable to rollover contributions or earnings on these amounts. This exemption is generally available to all debtors, regardless of whether they choose the federal bankruptcy exemptions or the exemptions available under the laws of their state. Despite this expanded protection for IRAs, consideration should still be given to all of the facts and circumstances surrounding a rollover from a qualified plan to an IRA since IRAs are still not provided the same anti-alienation protection provided under ERISA.[39] Note that inherited IRAs with a nonspouse beneficiary may not be protected in bankruptcy. Additional information on inherited IRAs with a nonspouse beneficiary is available in Chapter 7.

38. This amount is periodically indexed.
39. Bankruptcy Abuse Prevention and Consumer Protection Act of 2005 (BAPCPA 2005), §224.

CASE STUDY 9.3

The ***In re Dubroff***[1] case involved Dubroff, a Chapter 7 debtor, who claimed an exemption under New York law for the entire value of his IRA.[2] The creditors and bankruptcy trustee objected. Ultimately, the United States Second Circuit Court of Appeals held that the debtor could claim exemption for his IRA pursuant to a New York bankruptcy exemption statute. The Court reasoned that the Chapter 7 debtor could claim the exemption for his IRA under the New York bankruptcy exemption statute that exempted pension plans that qualify as an IRA under Internal Revenue Code and make payment on account of age. A subsequent statutory amendment to the New York law also explicitly exempted IRAs from satisfaction of money judgments. This case illustrates the importance of an IRA plan complying with all requirements of the Internal Revenue Code because, if such requirements are not met, the state protection afforded IRA assets of being free from seizure to satisfy money judgments or creditors in bankruptcy may otherwise be lost.

1. *In re Dubroff*, 119 F.3d 75 (2nd Cir. 1997).
2. Under Chapter 7 of the United States Bankruptcy Code, 11 U.S.C. §§101-1330, the debtor claimed an exemption under N.Y. Debt. & Cred. Law §282(2)(e) for the entire value of his IRA, which amounted to $43,974.

Prohibited Transactions

There are certain transactions that an owner or beneficiary is not permitted to engage in with an IRA. An IRA loses its tax exemption when the account ceases to be an IRA by reason of a **prohibited transaction**. If an individual or beneficiary of an IRA engages in any of the following transactions, then the account will cease to be an IRA as of the first day of the current taxable year:[40]

- selling, exchanging, or leasing of any property to an IRA,
- lending money to an IRA,
- receiving unreasonable compensation for managing an IRA,
- pledging an IRA as security for a loan,
- borrowing money from an IRA, or
- buying property for personal use (present or future) with IRA funds.

In the event that a prohibited transaction has occurred, the account ceases to be an IRA as of the beginning of the year and the entire balance in the IRA is treated as having been distributed.[41] In this case, the taxpayer will be subject to ordinary income tax on the entire balance and will also be subject to the 10 percent early withdrawal penalty if not otherwise exempted, as discussed above.

> ### 📝 Quick Quiz 9.4
>
> 1. Cash, stock, bonds, life insurance, and collectibles are all permitted investments for IRAs.
>   - a. True
>   - b. False
>
> 2. Funds in an IRA may be transferred to a qualified plan.
>   - a. True
>   - b. False
>
> 3. IRAs are exempt from creditor's claims by ERISA.
>   - a. True
>   - b. False
>
> 4. Loans from an IRA are considered prohibited transactions.
>   - a. True
>   - b. False
>
> False, True, False, True.

---

40. IRC §408(e)(2).
41. IRC §408(e)(2)(B).

A similar rule applies to an IRA annuity. If an individual borrows money against an IRA annuity contract, the individual must include the fair market value of the annuity contract as of the first day of the tax year in his gross income. The distribution may also be subject to the 10 percent early withdrawal penalty.

CASE STUDY 9.4

Lawrence F. Peek And Sara L. Peek, and Darrell G. Fleck And Kimberly J. Fleck (Taxpayers) vs. Commissioner of the Internal Revenue Service (IRS)

In 2001 Taxpayers established new traditional IRAs. Taxpayers formed FP Corp. and directed their new IRAs to use rolled-over cash to purchase 100% of FP Corp.'s newly issued stock. Taxpayers used FP Corp. to acquire the assets of AFS Corp. Taxpayers personally guaranteed loans of FP Corp. that arose out of the asset purchase. In 2003 and 2004 Taxpayers undertook to roll over the FP Corp. stock from their traditional IRAs to Roth IRAs, including in Taxpayers' income the value of the stock rolled over in those years. In 2006 after the FP Corp. stock had significantly appreciated in value, Taxpayers directed their Roth IRAs to sell all of the FP stock. Taxpayers' personal guaranties on the loans of FP Corp. persisted up to the stock sale in 2006. IRS contends that Taxpayers' personal guaranties of the FP Corp. loan were prohibited transactions, and, as a result, the gains realized in 2006 and 2007 from the 2006 sales of FP stock should be included in Taxpayers' income.

The Tax Court Held:
- Each of Taxpayers personal guaranties of the FP Corp. loan was an indirect extension of credit to the IRAs, which is a prohibited transaction; and under IRC Section 408(e), the accounts that held the FP Corp. stock ceased to be IRAs.
- The gains realized on the sale of the FP Corp. stock are included in Taxpayers' income.
- Taxpayers are liable for the accuracy-related penalty under IRC Section 6662.

Since the Court held that the loan guaranties were prohibited transactions, it did not need to address nor did it address two other issues that appear problematic for the Taxpayers:
- FP Company made payments of wages to Mr. Fleck and Mr. Peek, which the IRS contends were prohibited transactions under section 4975(c)(1)(D).
- FP Company made payments of rent to an entity owned by Mrs. Fleck and Mrs. Peek, which the IRS contends were prohibited transactions under section 4975(c)(1)(E).

Transfers Incident to Divorce

If an interest in an IRA is transferred from a spouse or former spouse (transferor) to an individual (transferee) by reason of divorce, **qualified domestic relations order (QDRO)**, separate maintenance decree, or a written document related to such a decree, starting from the date of the transfer, the interest in the IRA is treated as the individual's (transferee's) IRA.[42]

However, if an owner receives a distribution from an IRA and subsequently transfers the distributed funds to the other spouse pursuant to a divorce decree, the distribution is subject to ordinary income tax and, potentially, a 10 percent early withdrawal penalty.

42.IRC §408(d)(6).

If an individual is required to transfer some or all of the assets of his traditional IRA to a spouse or former spouse, there are two commonly used methods to make the transfer. The individual can instruct the custodian to simply change the name on the account to the name of the spouse or former spouse, or one spouse can direct the trustee of his IRA to transfer the funds directly to the trustee of the other spouse's IRA.

SIMPLIFIED EMPLOYEE PENSION (SEPS)

A **simplified employee pension (SEP)** is a practical retirement plan alternative to a qualified plan that can be used by small businesses and sole proprietors. SEPs are easier to establish than qualified plans and have practically no filing requirements. Because SEPs use IRAs as the receptacle for contributions, there is no trust accounting for the plan sponsor. In addition, SEPs have similar characteristics to profit sharing plans in terms of funding limits.

Because a SEP is not a qualified plan, it has some unique rules compared to the rules for qualified plans. For example, SEPs have more liberal participation requirements than qualified plans and have different contribution, distribution, and vesting rules.

Participation

Employers that sponsor SEPs must provide benefits to almost all employees. The requirements for coverage include the following:
- Attainment of age 21 or older
- Performance of services for three of the last five years
- Received compensation of at least $650 during the year

> ### ⁝☰ *Key Concepts*
>
> 1. List the coverage requirements for an employee to participate in a SEP.
> 2. How does an employer establish a SEP?
> 3. When is the latest date that an employer can establish a SEP?
> 4. Identify the contribution rules for SEPs.
> 5. When may an employee withdraw funds from his SEP?

The participation rules for SEPs mean that an employer must cover all employees who are 21 years of age, have worked for the company for a period of three years or more, and have earned more than $650 during the current year. Based on this definition, even part-time employees must be covered. However, the three-year requirement allows the employer to exclude anyone who has not worked for at least three years. Therefore, if a company has high employee turnover, a SEP may be used to exclude employees who do not remain employed for a period of at least three years.

It is important to note that contributions must be made on behalf of all employees who meet the participation rules during the calendar year whether or not they are still employed as of the end of the year and whether or not they are still alive. For example, an employee who resigned in March and earned more than $650 would be entitled to a contribution based on the employee's earnings through his termination date.

In addition, those employees over the age of 70½ (age 72 if age 70½ is attained after December 31, 2019) who meet the eligibility rules must also receive an employer contribution to their SEP.

As with qualified plans, the employer may impose less restrictive participation requirements for its employees than those discussed above but not more restrictive requirements.

Employees can also be excluded from participation in a SEP if they are members of either of the following groups:
- Employees covered by a union agreement if their retirement benefits were bargained for in good faith by their union and their employer.
- Nonresident alien employees who have no U.S. source earned income from their employer.

Establishment of a SEP

SEPs can be established, as well as funded, for a plan year as late as the due date of the federal income tax return including extensions. Therefore, SEPs can be established for the following entities as late as the date indicated below:

Entity	Due date of return	Final extension
Sole proprietorship (Schedule C)	April 15th	October 15th
Partnership (Form 1065)	March 15th	September 15th
Corporation (Form 1120)	April 15th	September 15th
S-Corporation (Form 1120S)	March 15th	September 15th

This establishment feature allows an advisor to recommend establishing a retirement plan and implementing it for the previous year.

To establish a SEP, the employer must complete three basic steps:
1. A formal written agreement to provide benefits to all eligible employees must be executed.
2. All eligible employees must be given notice about the SEP.
3. A SEP-IRA (the receptacle account) must be set up for each eligible employee.

The standard method of complying with the first requirement is to adopt the IRS model SEP using Form 5305-SEP (See **Exhibit 9.21**). Using Form 5305-SEP allows the plan to be established without IRS approval or a determination letter, and the form does not have to be filed with the IRS or the Department of Labor. The plan sponsor should keep the original form. Most financial service companies, including banks, mutual funds, brokerage houses, and insurance companies, have prototype SEP documents that can be used by employers.

Exhibit 9.21 | Form 5305-SEP[43]

| Form **5305-SEP** (Rev. December 2004) Department of the Treasury Internal Revenue Service | **Simplified Employee Pension—Individual Retirement Accounts Contribution Agreement** (Under section 408(k) of the Internal Revenue Code) | OMB No. 1545-0499 **Do not** file with the Internal Revenue Service |

_____ makes the following agreement under section 408(k) of the
(Name of employer)   Internal Revenue Code and the instructions to this form.

Article I—Eligibility Requirements (check applicable boxes—see instructions)

The employer agrees to provide discretionary contributions in each calendar year to the individual retirement account or individual retirement annuity (IRA) of all employees who are at least _____ years old (not to exceed 21 years old) and have performed services for the employer in at least _____ years (not to exceed 3 years) of the immediately preceding 5 years. This simplified employee pension (SEP) ☐ includes ☐ **does not** include employees covered under a collective bargaining agreement, ☐ includes ☐ **does not** include certain nonresident aliens, and ☐ includes ☐ **does not** include employees whose total compensation during the year is less than $450*.

Article II—SEP Requirements (see instructions)

The employer agrees that contributions made on behalf of each eligible employee will be:

A. Based only on the first $205,000* of compensation.
B. The same percentage of compensation for every employee.
C. Limited annually to the smaller of $41,000* or 25% of compensation.
D. Paid to the employee's IRA trustee, custodian, or insurance company (for an annuity contract).

_____   _____
Employer's signature and date   Name and title

Most recent version available at time of printing.

According to the IRS, Form 5305-SEP cannot be used in the following situations:

- The employer currently maintains another qualified retirement plan. However, this does not prevent the employer from sponsoring a SEP.
- If IRAs have not been established for any eligible employees.
- If the employer is a member of any of the following groups (unless all eligible employees of all the members of these groups, trades, or businesses participate in the SEP):
  - An affiliated group described in §414(m),
  - A controlled group of corporations described in §414(b),
  - Trades or businesses under common control described in §414(c), or
  - The employer does not pay the cost of the SEP contributions.

The employer must provide eligible employees with a copy of Form 5305-SEP, its instructions, and other information. This notification is a key element in establishing a SEP and is consistent with the establishment of qualified plans. Employees must be given notice of their rights relating to the employer's retirement plan.

---

43. The Form 5305-SEP is current. The numbers in the form with an asterisk are indexed.

Contributions

Similar to profit sharing plans, employer contributions to SEPs are discretionary from year to year, however, unlike profit sharing plans, there is no requirement that SEP contributions be substantial and recurring. Because of the discretionary nature of the contributions, SEPs are often used by small businesses that cannot or do not wish to commit to a mandatory contribution every year. However, in years that a contribution is made to a SEP, a contribution must be made for all employees eligible during the year, whether or not they are employed or alive as of the end of the year.

Contributions to SEPs are made by the employer and must be made to employees' IRA accounts based on a written formula that does not discriminate in favor of highly compensated employees. However, contributions to SEPs may be integrated with Social Security (permitted disparity). The contribution, subject to the limits discussed below, made for the employee is excluded from the employee's gross income and not subject to FICA or FUTA.

The limit for contributions to a SEP is the lesser of 25 percent of an employee's compensation or $58,000 for 2021.[44] As with qualified plans, no more than $290,000 of compensation for 2021 can be considered for purposes of contributions to a SEP. Therefore, the maximum contribution for any employee in year 2021 is $58,000. It is important to understand that an employee might receive more than 25 percent of his compensation in a qualified plan through integration or cross-testing, but an employee cannot receive more than 25 percent of his compensation in a SEP.

For self-employed individuals, the 25 percent limit converts to 20 percent (0.25 ÷ 1.25) of net self-employment income. Recall that the 25 percent limit for self-employed individuals is based on earned income, not total income.[45]

Contributions to a SEP are included under IRC §415(c) for purposes of determining the annual contributions limit under IRC §415(c). Therefore, if the employer maintains a defined contribution qualified plan in addition to a SEP, both the SEP contribution and the qualified plan contribution are added together to determine whether or not the annual contributions limit ($58,000 for 2021) has been violated.

If the employer maintains a profit sharing plan in addition to a SEP, then contributions to the SEP reduce the 25 percent limit of the profit-sharing plan. In other words, the maximum that could be contributed to a SEP and a profit-sharing plan in total cannot exceed 25 percent of total covered compensation.

> ### Quick Quiz 9.5
>
> 1. Requirements for coverage in a SEP include an employee's performance of service for three of the last five years.
>   a. True
>   b. False
>
> 2. Part-time employees are exempt from being included in a SEP.
>   a. True
>   b. False
>
> 3. Employer contributions to SEPs are discretionary and do not have to be made each year.
>   a. True
>   b. False
>
> 4. Employer contributions to a SEP are always 100% vested.
>   a. True
>   b. False
>
> True, False, True, True.

---

44. IRC §§402(h)(2) and 408(j).
45. See Chapter 8 for more information on contribution for self-employed taxpayers.

Excess contributions are contributions in excess of the 25 percent or $58,000 limit for 2021. These excess contributions cannot be deducted in the current year but may be carried forward and deducted in a future year. However, excess contributions are generally subject to a 10 percent excise tax. This treatment is the same as with qualified plans.

Deductions

Contributions to a SEP are deductible for the employer and excludable for the employees up to the limits discussed above. The employer's deduction for contributions to a SEP is generally claimed on the following forms:

Entity	Where to Deduct Contribution
Unincorporated business	Schedule C or Schedule F of Form 1040
Partnership	Form 1065
Corporation	Form 1120
S-Corporation	Form 1120S

The employer's deduction for contributions to a SEP is claimed on line 15 of Form 1040 Schedule 1 if self-employed. This includes both sole proprietors and partners. Partnerships must distribute Schedule K-1 to all of its partners and passes its deduction for contributions to a SEP to the partner by way of Schedule K-1.

Exhibit 9.22 | Schedule 1 (Form 1040) Adjustments to Income

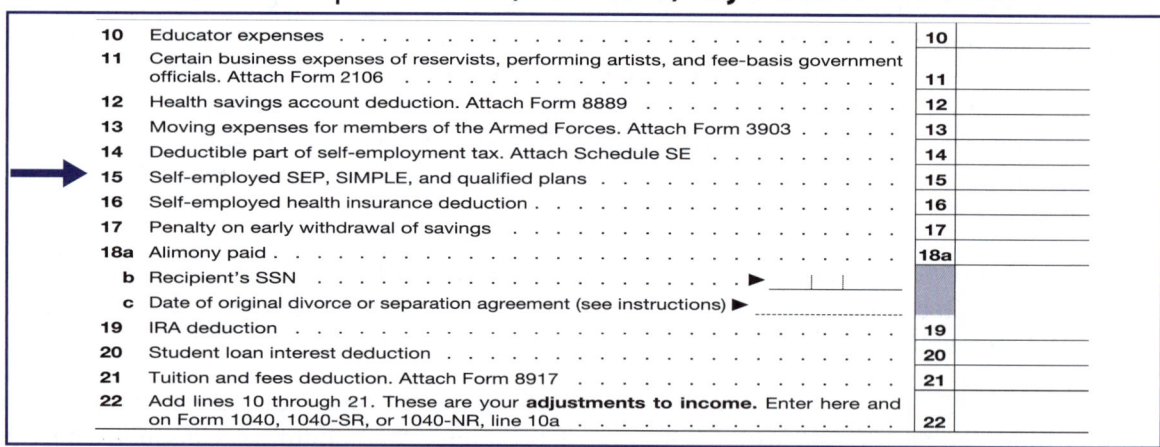

The deduction for contributions made to a SEP on behalf of the employer will be deducted on the tax return for corporations and S-corporations as with the deduction for contributions made on behalf of the employees.

Vesting and Withdrawals

Contributions for a SEP are made to IRA accounts on behalf of employees. As a result, there is no vesting for employer contributions. Once the contribution is made to an employee's SEP-IRA, the funds within that account immediately belong to the employee.

Further, employees are able to withdraw funds in any amount from their SEP-IRA because of the nature of the account – that is, because it is an IRA. This ability to withdraw funds is available at all times, including while the employee is still employed. However, if the employee does receive a distribution from the SEP-IRA, the distribution will be subject to ordinary income tax and may be subject to the early withdrawal penalty unless the distribution qualifies for any of the exceptions to the 10 percent early withdrawal penalty as discussed earlier for IRAs and Roth IRAs.

Note that contributions to SEPs are made to traditional IRA accounts and cannot be made to Roth IRA accounts.

SALARY REDUCTION SIMPLIFIED EMPLOYEE PENSION (SARSEPS)

Although SIMPLE plans were introduced by Congress to replace **SARSEPs**, which are not permitted to be established for years after 1996, many of the SARSEPs in existence prior to 1997 are still in operation. SARSEPs allow employees to elect to defer a portion of their current salary into a SEP-IRA in a similar fashion to 401(k) plans. In fact, the SARSEP deferral limit is the same as 401(k) plans. However, the SARSEP was very easy to establish and had minimal reporting and testing requirements.

Key Concepts

1. What provisions were required in order for an employer to establish a SARSEP?

2. How do elective deferrals into a SARSEP work with other salary deferral type plans?

To establish a SARSEP, an employer had to meet the following provisions:

- At least 50 percent of the employees eligible to participate must choose to defer a portion of their salary.
- The employer had to have no more than 25 eligible employees.
- The elective deferrals of the highly compensated employees had to meet the SARSEP ADP test (discussion follows).

SARSEP ADP Test

Under this test, the amount deferred each year by each eligible highly compensated employee as a percentage of pay (the deferral percentage) cannot be more than 125 percent of the average deferral percentage (ADP) of all nonhighly compensated employees eligible to participate.[46]

The deferral percentage equals:

$$ADP = \text{Elective employee deferral} \div \text{Employee's compensation}$$

---

46. The ADP test for 401(k) plans consists of three separate tests, one of which is the 125 percent test.

Example 9.40

Consider the following example for Affordable Company:

Employee	Ownership	Compensation	Elective Deferral	ADP
A	60%	$200,000	$11,000	5.50%
B	30%	$140,000	$9,800	7.00%
C	5%	$85,000	$3,400	4.00%
D	3%	$80,000	$5,000	6.25%
E	2%	$50,000	$2,500	5.00%
F	-	$40,000	$2,000	5.00%

Employees A and B are the only highly compensated employees. Their actual deferral percentage equals 6.25 percent [(5.50 + 7.00) ÷ 2]. The other four employees are nonhighly compensated and have an actual deferral percentage of 5.06 percent [(4.00 + 6.25 + 5.00 + 5.00) ÷ 4]. The plan meets the ADP test because the ADP of the HCs is less than 1.25 times the ADP of the NHCs. The ADP of the NHCs times 1.25 equals 6.33, whereas the ADP for the HCs equals 6.25 percent.

Elective Deferral Limit

An employee cannot defer more than $19,500 for 2021 of their compensation into a SARSEP. However, those taxpayers who have attained the age of 50 by the end of the tax year may make additional catch-up contributions as detailed in the chart that follows.

Exhibit 9.23 | Summary of Elective Deferral Limits (2021)

SARSEPs, 401(k) Plans, 403(b) Plans, 457 Plans		Roth 401(k) Plans		SIMPLE Plans	
Annual Deferral Limit	Catch-Up Contributions	Annual Deferral Limit	Catch-Up Contributions	Annual Deferral Limit	Catch-Up Contributions
$19,500	$6,500	$19,500	$6,500	$13,500	$3,000

It is important to note that the $19,500 deferral limit for 2021 applies to the aggregate elective deferrals the employee makes for the year to a SARSEP and any of the following plans:
- Cash or deferred arrangement (401(k) plan)
- Salary reduction arrangement under a tax-sheltered annuity plan (403(b) plan)
- SIMPLE IRA plan

This rule prevents an employee of a company who defers the maximum into his employer's 401(k) plan from also deferring salary from another source into one of the above plans. However, other income sources may be eligible to be considered for some other type of qualified plan arrangement or simplified employee pension.

If the employer makes nonelective contributions to the SARSEP, the combined employee and employer contributions cannot exceed the lesser of 25 percent of the employee's compensation or $58,000 for 2021.

Excess Deferrals

Excess deferrals in a SARSEP are elective contributions made by highly compensated employees that violate the SARSEP ADP test. The highly compensated employees must be given notice within 2½ months after the end of the plan year of their excess contributions. These deferral contributions must then be removed from the SARSEP. If the employer does not inform the highly compensated employees, then the employer must pay a 10 percent excise tax on the excess portion.

Comparison of IRA, SEP, and SIMPLE

SEP IRAs and SIMPLE IRAs (discussed in Chapter 10) sometimes follow the rules for traditional IRAs, sometimes follow rules similar to qualified plans, and sometimes have rules that are distinctive to the SEP or SIMPLE. The following chart provides a side-by-side summary of these three types of IRAs.

Exhibit 9.24 | Comparison of Traditional IRA vs SEP and SIMPLE

Comparison of Traditional IRA, SEP IRA, and SIMPLE IRA Plans for 2021			
	Traditional IRA	**SEP IRA**	**SIMPLE IRA**
Deadline to Establish the Plan	Due date of return, with no extensions	Due date of return, including extensions	October 1st of the year the plan starts
Contribution Limits	$6,000 plus $1,000 catch-up for individuals aged 50 and older	Lesser of 25% of earned income or up to $58,000 in 2021; no catch-up; maximum income to be considered is $290,000 in 2021	Employee maximum $13,500, plus $3,000 catch-up for individuals aged 50 and older; Employer choice: 2% nonelective contribution on compensation up to $290,000 in 2021 or 3% match (no compensation maximum)
Deadline for Contributions to be made	Due date of return, with no extensions	Due date of return, including extensions	Employee contributions: as soon as reasonably possible (but no later than 30 days after the end of the month for which they are withheld); Employer contributions: by due date of tax return, including extensions
Are Contributions Allowed After Age 70½ (72 if age 70½ is attained after December 31, 2019)?	Yes, if still working	Yes, if still working	Yes, if still working

Comparison of Traditional IRA, SEP IRA, and SIMPLE IRA Plans for 2021, continued			
	Traditional IRA	**SEP IRA**	**SIMPLE IRA**
Investments	No life insurance and no collectibles except gold, silver, and platinum coins issued in the U.S., and gold, silver, platinum, and palladium bullion; no margin accounts	Same as traditional IRA	Same as traditional IRA
Loans	No	No	No
Premature Distribution Penalty (Prior to Age 59½)	10%	10%	10%; increased to 25% in the first two years of participation in the plan
Penalty Exceptions	See list previously discussed in this chapter	Same as traditional IRA	Same as traditional IRA
Required Minimum Distributions	RMDS Required Beginning Date (RBD) is April 1st of the year following the year age 70½ (72 if age 70½ is attained after December 31, 2019) is attained. No delay permitted, even if still working * If still working, RMDs and contributions may occur in same year	Same as traditional IRA * If still working, RMDs and contributions may occur in same year	Same as traditional IRA * If still working, RMDs and contributions may occur in same year
Qualified Charitable Distributions After age 70½	Yes	No	No
Federal Bankruptcy Protection	Limited to $1,362,800 (as of 2019; indexed for inflation every 3 years)	Unlimited	Unlimited
Creditor Protection for other Judgment	Varies based on state law; may not be as comprehensive as qualified plan protection under ERISA	Same as traditional IRA	Same as traditional IRA

DISCUSSION QUESTIONS

SOLUTIONS to the discussion questions can be found exclusively within the chapter. Once you have completed an initial reading of the chapter, go back and highlight the answers to these questions.

1. What is the limit on contributions to an IRA for 2021?

2. List items of income that are considered earned income for purposes of IRA contributions.

3. What is a spousal IRA?

4. How are excess contributions to an IRA penalized?

5. Discuss the ability to deduct a contribution made to a traditional IRA given a person who is not covered by a qualified retirement plan.

6. Discuss the ability to deduct a contribution made to a traditional IRA when an employee is covered by a qualified retirement plan.

7. Discuss the ability to deduct a contribution made to a traditional IRA given an employee covered by a qualified retirement plan who has a spouse who is not covered by a qualified retirement plan.

8. Define active participant status for purposes of deducting IRA contributions.

9. What are the minimum distribution rules for traditional IRAs?

10. When is the early withdrawal penalty applicable to traditional IRAs?

11. How do individual retirement annuities differ from a traditional IRA account?

12. Compare and contrast a traditional IRA to a Roth IRA.

13. How does the definition of earned income for a Roth IRA compare with the definition of earned income for a traditional IRA?

14. Identify the 2021 AGI income limits for contributions to a Roth IRA.

15. What are the income limits for converting a traditional IRA to a Roth IRA?

16. How can the assets of a qualified plan be converted into a Roth IRA?

17. What is a "qualified distribution" from a Roth IRA?

18. How is a nonqualified distribution from a Roth IRA taxed?

19. What are the minimum distribution rules relating to Roth IRAs?

20. What types of investments may be held in an IRA and what investments are specifically prohibited from being held in an IRA?

21. What types of coins are permitted IRA investments?

22. Discuss the impact of violating the prohibited transaction rules of an IRA.

23. What are the SEP coverage requirements?

24. What employees may be excluded from participation in a SEP?

25. What is the 2021 contribution limit for a SEP?

26. How and when is a SEP established?

27. What vesting options are available for a SEP?

28. Compare and contrast a SEP and a profit sharing plan.

29. How are the elective deferrals into a SARSEP considered in relation to other salary deferral type plans?

MULTIPLE CHOICE PROBLEMS

A sample of multiple choice problems is provided below. Additional multiple choice problems are available at money-education.com by accessing the Student Practice Portal.

1. Which statements are generally correct regarding penalties associated with IRA accounts?
    1. Distributions made prior to 59½ are subject to the 10% premature distribution penalty.
    2. There is a 50% excise tax on a required minimum distribution not made by <u>April 1</u> of the year following the year in which age 70½ is attained (or age 72 if age 70½ is attained after December 31, 2019).
        a. 1 only.
        b. 2 only.
        c. Both 1 and 2.
        d. Neither 1 nor 2.

2. David took a lump-sum distribution from his employer's qualified plan at age 56 when he terminated his service. He rolled over his distribution using a direct rollover to an IRA. Assuming David has met 10-year forward averaging requirements, which of the following is/are correct regarding tax treatment of the transaction?
    1. If at age 59 he distributes the IRA, he benefits from 10-year forward averaging.
    2. If he rolls the entire IRA to a new employer's qualified plan, he may be eligible for forward averaging treatment in the future.
    3. If he rolls over a portion of the IRA to a new employer's qualified plan, he may preserve any eligibility for forward averaging on that portion that was rolled over.
    4. If David immediately withdraws the entire amount from his IRA, he may benefit from 10-year forward averaging.
        a. 2 only.
        b. 2 and 3.
        c. 2, 3, and 4.
        d. 1, 2, 3, and 4.

3. Robbie and Robin, both age 45, are married and filed a joint return for 2021. Robin earned a salary of $100,000 in 2021 and is covered by her employer's 401(k) plan. Robbie and Robin earned interest of $40,000 in 2021 from a joint savings account. Robbie is not employed, and the couple had no other income. On April 15, 2022, Robin contributed $6,000 to an IRA for herself and $6,000 to an IRA for Robbie. The maximum allowable IRA deduction on the 2021 joint return is:
    a. $0.
    b. $4,500.
    c. $6,000.
    d. $12,000.

4. Gloria, divorced and age 55, received taxable alimony of $50,000 in 2021. In addition, she received $1,800 in earnings from a part-time job. Gloria is not covered by a qualified plan. What was the maximum deductible IRA contribution that Gloria could have made for 2021?
    a. $1,800.
    b. $2,800.
    c. $6,000.
    d. $7,000.

5. Axel, who is currently age 52, made his only contribution to his Roth IRA in 2021 in the amount of $6,000. If he were to receive a total distribution of $11,000 from his Roth IRA in the year 2026 to purchase a new car, how would he be taxed?
    a. Since Axel waited five years, the distribution will be classified as a "qualified distribution" and will therefore not be taxable or subject to the 10% early distribution penalty.
    b. Since Axel waited five years, the distribution will be classified as a "qualified distribution" and will therefore not be taxable but will be subject to the 10% early distribution penalty.
    c. Although Axel waited five years, the distribution will not be classified as a "qualified distribution" and will therefore be taxable and will be subject to the 10% early distribution penalty.
    d. Although Axel waited five years, the distribution will not be classified as a "qualified distribution" and will therefore be taxable to the extent of earnings and will be subject to the 10% early distribution penalty on the amount that is taxable.

> **Additional multiple choice problems**
> **are available at**
> **money-education.com**
> **by accessing the**
> **Student Practice Portal.**
> **Access requires registration of the title using**
> **the unique code at the front of the book.**

QUICK QUIZ EXPLANATIONS

Quick Quiz 9.1

1. False. A 55-year old individual can contribute the maximum amount of $6,000 for 2021 plus an additional deferral of $1,000 for 2021 for persons age 50 or older.
2. True.
3. False. Individuals who do not have any earned income may still be eligible to establish an IRA if their spouse has sufficient earned income.

Quick Quiz 9.2

1. True.
2. True.
3. False. Generally, distributions from traditional IRAs are taxed as ordinary income. In addition, the government encourages taxpayers to leave funds in their IRAs until retirement by imposing a 10 percent premature withdrawal penalty for distributions prior to age 59½.
4. False. The saver credit is intended for those taxpayers with relatively low income.

Quick Quiz 9.3

1. True.
2. False. As a result of the SECURE Act of 2019, for tax years beginning after December 31, 2019, both traditional and Roth IRAs may be funded after the account owner attains age 70½.
3. True.
4. True.
5. True.

Quick Quiz 9.4

1. False. Collectibles and life insurance are not permitted investments for IRAs.
2. True.
3. False. IRAs are not exempt from creditor's claims as a result of ERISA. However, IRA account balances up to $1 million (indexed) are protected from creditors under federal bankruptcy law as a result of the Bankruptcy Abuse Prevention and Consumer Protection Act of 2005.
4. True.

Quick Quiz 9.5

1. True.
2. False. Part-time employees must be covered by a SEP as long as they have attained the age of 21, performed services for three of the last five years, and have received compensation of at least $650 during the year.
3. True.
4. True.

Quick Quiz 9.6

1. False. An employer was not permitted to establish a SARSEP if he had more than 25 employees.
2. True.

10

SIMPLE, 403(b), AND 457 PLANS

1. Identify other tax-advantaged plans.*
2. Compare and contrast qualified plans with other tax-advantaged plans.*
3. Explain how SIMPLEs work and when they should be considered.*
4. Understand the similarities and differences between 403(b) plans and 401(k) plans.*
5. Describe how the deferral limits for SIMPLEs, SARSEPs, 401(k) plans and 403(b) plans work together.*
6. Differentiate between private and public eligible 457 plans as well as ineligible 457 plans.*

Ties to CFP Certification Learning Objectives

INTRODUCTION

A company may wish to establish a retirement plan but may be unable or unwilling to incur the costs associated with a qualified plan. The IRC provides for "other tax-advantaged plans" that provide favorable tax treatment but are not qualified plans. These plans are often easier and less costly to administer. This chapter discusses in detail three of these "other tax-advantaged plans," SIMPLEs, 403(b)s, and 457 plans.

SIMPLEs (Savings Incentive Match Plans for Employees) provide incentives to "small employers" (100 or fewer employees)[1] to adopt retirement plans for employees with less administrative costs and fewer set-up procedures than qualified plans and no annual filing requirements. SIMPLEs were created by the American Jobs Creation Act of 1996.[2]

Section 403(b) plans, also called "Tax Sheltered Annuities" (TSAs) or "Tax-Deferred Annuities" (TDAs), are plans available to certain non-profit organizations and to employees of public educational systems. The limits for employee elective deferral contributions to 403(b) plans were increased and catch-up provisions for those persons over 50 years old were added, allowing for employee elective deferrals equal to that of 401(k) plans.

Section 457 plans resemble deferred compensation plans that allow certain employees of state and local governments and of nongovernmental tax-exempt entities the ability to defer compensation free from current income taxation. These employee deferral contributions to 457 plans are separate and not combined with other deferral contributions to retirement plans such as SARSEPs, 401(k)s, SIMPLEs, or 403(b)s for purposes of overall contribution limits.

KNOW THE NUMBERS (2021)

SIMPLEs	**Total Elective Contribution** $13,500	**Catch-Up > 50** $3,000	
403(b) Plans	**Annual Deferral Limit** $19,500	**Catch-Up > 50** $6,500	
457 Plans	**Annual Deferral Limit** $19,500	**Catch-Up > 50** $6,500	**Final 3-Year Catch-Up** $19,500

---

1. IRC §408(p).
2. Pub.L.No.104-188, 110 Stat.1755 (1996) (Codified at IRC §408(p)(2001)).

SIMPLES

Savings Incentive Match Plans for Employees, referred to as "SIMPLEs," are retirement plans for small employers. Many smaller employers are reluctant to set up qualified retirement plans because of the complicated rules and administrative costs that accompany qualified plans. SIMPLEs, however, are both easy to establish and maintain and provide an incentive to small employers to adopt retirement plans because they possess tax advantages similar to qualified plans. In addition, SIMPLE plans are attractive to employers because they are not required to meet all of the nondiscrimination rules applicable to qualified retirement plans and they do not have burdensome annual filing requirements.

> **≔ Key Concepts**
>
> 1. What are SIMPLE plans?
> 2. What types of SIMPLE plans are available?
> 3. List the requirements to establish a SIMPLE plan.

A SIMPLE allows employees to make elective deferral contributions similar to a 401(k) plan. The employer/sponsor is required to match employee elective deferral contributions made by employees or, alternatively, to make nonelective contributions for all employees who are eligible. The employer and employee enter into a written agreement that directs the employer to make employee elective deferral contributions to the accounts of eligible employees in exchange for a salary reduction.

Example 10.1

Karli makes an election to reduce her salary from $50,000 to $45,000 and have her employer deposit the $5,000 into a SIMPLE IRA. The employer will also match the employee's contribution up to three percent of salary ($50,000 x 0.03 = $1,500) into the SIMPLE IRA.

Exhibit 10.1 | A Summary of the Characteristics of SIMPLEs

- Employer establishes SIMPLE plan.
- Employer contracts with employee to have salary reduction.
- Employer withholds employee deferral over the course of a year.
- Employee elective deferrals are not subject to income tax but are subject to payroll tax.
- Employer deposits match on a regular basis tax deferred without payroll tax.
- Earnings grow tax deferred on all contributions.

Types of SIMPLEs

When establishing a SIMPLE, the sponsor company has two choices in determining the vehicle used to hold the assets of the plan. A company may choose either an IRA or 401(k) for the plan. Therefore, a sponsor company may establish the SIMPLE as either a SIMPLE IRA plan or a SIMPLE 401(k) plan. In most instances, the company will establish a SIMPLE IRA because there are fewer administrative burdens than for SIMPLE 401(k) plans. SIMPLE 401(k) plans are very rare in practice.

The SIMPLE IRA

A **SIMPLE IRA** is a SIMPLE plan that utilizes an IRA account as the funding vehicle of the plan. The SIMPLE IRA is established utilizing an individual retirement account (or an individual retirement annuity). The plan is established by the employer via a written plan that allows each employee to choose between directing the employer to make contributions to the SIMPLE IRA plan or allowing the employee to receive such payments directly in cash (a CODA feature) as compensation. SIMPLE IRAs require the employer to either match the employee contributions of those that participate or provide nonelective contributions to all employees who are eligible. All contributions made under a SIMPLE IRA must be paid to a SIMPLE IRA, not to any other type of IRA. SIMPLE IRA plans can be established by for-profit entities, tax-exempt employers, and governmental entities.

The SIMPLE 401(k)

A **SIMPLE 401(k)** is a SIMPLE plan that utilizes a 401(k) plan as the funding vehicle of the plan. Unlike the SIMPLE IRA, plan loans are permitted with a SIMPLE 401(k). SIMPLE 401(k) plans must be maintained by an eligible employer and satisfy contribution requirements, eligibility requirements, and vesting requirements. A SIMPLE 401(k) plan must be maintained on a calendar year basis and not a fiscal year basis. An employer may adopt a SIMPLE 401(k) plan if it has 100 or fewer employees. A SIMPLE 401(k) is not subject to nondiscrimination requirements or top-heavy restrictions if it meets certain contribution and other requirements that are discussed in this chapter, but the administrative requirements are greater as compared to a SIMPLE IRA.

Establishing a SIMPLE

A SIMPLE IRA plan can be maintained only on a calendar year basis. As such, plan contributions to the SIMPLE IRA, as well as the eligibility of employers who establish the SIMPLE IRA, are determined on a calendar year basis.[3]

SIMPLEs are designed for the small employer. A SIMPLE is very easy to establish and maintain, as it has minor administrative costs and does not have any annual filing requirements. There are definite advantages for SIMPLEs compared to qualified plans. As discussed throughout this book, qualified plans have significant administrative costs and burdensome rules and requirements.

Who Can Establish a SIMPLE?

SIMPLE plans can only be established for companies who employ 100 or fewer employees who earned at least $5,000 of compensation from the employer for the preceding calendar year. The employer can be a C corporation, partnership, S corporation, limited liability company, sole proprietorship, tax-exempt entity, or governmental entity. Whether the employees are eligible to participate in the SIMPLE or not, all employees who earned $5,000 or more in the previous year that are employed at any time during the calendar year are taken into consideration for purposes of counting the 100 employee limitation. Accordingly, even employees that can be excluded, such as nonresident aliens or those employees who do not meet the plan's minimum eligibility requirements, must all be considered in the 100 employee limitation to avoid a company that truly has more than 100 employees being eligible to establish a

---

3. IRC §408(p)(6)(C).

SIMPLE. Leased employees or self-employed individuals who received earned income from the employer in the preceding calendar year are also included in the calculation for the 100 employee limitation rule.[4]

Example 10.2

Z-Mart Corporation employed 150 employees in 2021, 115 of whom were nonresident aliens. For calendar year 2022, the company would only have 35 employees eligible to participate in the year 2022, but Z-Mart Corporation may not establish a SIMPLE IRA plan in calendar year 2021 because the company employed 150 employees (though 115 of them were nonresident aliens). The company had fewer than 100 eligible participants, but for purposes of the 100 employee limitation, nonresident aliens must be considered for the preceding calendar year in the calculation of the eligibility of the company as a whole.

Exhibit 10.2 | Entities That Can Establish SIMPLE Plans

C Corporations
S Corporations
Limited Liability Companies (LLC)
Partnerships
Proprietorships
Government Entities

Two-Year Grace Period for Employers Who Cease to Comply with 100 Employee Limit

If an employer meets the 100 employee limitation in a given year, then the employer will have a two year "**grace period**" where the employer can exceed the limitation without losing eligibility to maintain the SIMPLE. In other words, if an employer in a calendar year satisfies the 100 employee limitation, that employer is treated as if it satisfied the 100 employee limitation for two calendar years immediately after the calendar year for which it last satisfied the 100 employee limitation.[5]

However, if the employer undergoes an acquisition, disposition, or other similar transaction, the employer will retain eligibility (i.e., not deemed as exceeding the 100 employee limitation) for the year of the transaction plus the two subsequent years, only if both of the following two rules are met:
1. the plan coverage has not significantly changed during the grace period, and
2. the SIMPLE plan would have continued to qualify after the transaction if the employer had remained as a separate employer.[6]

If, at any time within the two years, the employer does not meet the requirements listed above, neither the employer nor the employee will be permitted to make contributions to the plan.

---

4. IRC §408(p)(2)(C)(i)(I).
5. IRC §408(p)(2)(C)(i)(II).
6. IRC §408(p)(4), §408(p)(10).

Other Plans Not Allowed

An employer may not establish a SIMPLE if the employer contributes to a defined contribution plan for its employees during the year, if its employees accrue a benefit from a defined benefit plan during the year, or if the employer contributes to a SEP or 403(b) plan during the year.[7]

If an employer maintains another qualified plan solely to benefit union employees whose retirement benefits were the subject of good faith bargaining, the employer can make contributions to a SIMPLE plan. All the eligibility and contribution rules will apply and the SIMPLE must exclude those union employees.

How is a SIMPLE Established?

SIMPLEs are easy to establish and maintain in comparison to other types of qualified retirement plans. There are few administrative costs associated with the SIMPLE plan because there are no annual filing requirements. At the inception, an employer files **Form 5304-SIMPLE** or **Form 5305-SIMPLE** to establish a SIMPLE IRA plan. These are model SIMPLE plan documents. Form 5304 applies to employers who allow plan participants to select the financial institution that will receive their contributions while Form 5305 applies to those SIMPLEs that require initial contributions to be deposited at a designated financial institution. As a further illustration of the relaxed administrative rules and required paperwork, Forms 5304-SIMPLE and 5305-SIMPLE by themselves: (1) satisfy employer notification requirements for SIMPLEs, (2) maintain the SIMPLE plan records, and (3) establish proof that the employer set up a SIMPLE plan for its employees.

> ### ✎ Quick Quiz 10.1
>
> 1. SIMPLE plans may operate on a calendar or fiscal year basis.
>   a. True
>   b. False
>
> 2. SIMPLE IRA plans are permitted for tax-exempt employers and governmental entities.
>   a. True
>   b. False
>
> 3. SIMPLE plans can only be established for companies who employ 100 or fewer employees.
>   a. True
>   b. False
>
> False, True, True.

An employer can establish a SIMPLE IRA plan any time between January 1 and October 1 of the year in which it wants the plan to begin unless the employer or one of its predecessors previously maintained a SIMPLE IRA plan. If the employer previously maintained a SIMPLE IRA plan, then the employer must establish the SIMPLE IRA by January 1 of the year in which it wants the plan to begin. New employers who begin business after October 1 of the year may establish a SIMPLE IRA after October 1 if the SIMPLE is established as soon as administratively feasible. In any case, the employer must provide the participants with a 60-day period of time during which they can make their deferral elections. This 60-day period must occur every plan year between November 2 and December 31. If a plan is established during the year, or an employee becomes eligible during the year, the participant's 60-day election period must include the date of eligibility.

---

7. IRC §408(p)(2)(D).

Exhibit 10.3 | Form 5304-SIMPLE

Form **5304-SIMPLE** (Rev. March 2012) Department of the Treasury Internal Revenue Service	**Savings Incentive Match Plan for Employees of Small Employers (SIMPLE)—Not for Use With a Designated Financial Institution**	OMB No. 1545-1502 **Do not** file with the Internal Revenue Service

_____ establishes the following SIMPLE
Name of Employer

IRA plan under section 408(p) of the Internal Revenue Code and pursuant to the instructions contained in this form.

Article I—Employee Eligibility Requirements _(complete applicable box(es) and blanks—see instructions)_

1 **General Eligibility Requirements.** The Employer agrees to permit salary reduction contributions to be made in each calendar year to the SIMPLE IRA established by each employee who meets the following requirements (select either 1a or 1b):

a ☐ **Full Eligibility.** All employees are eligible.

b ☐ **Limited Eligibility.** Eligibility is limited to employees who are described in both (i) and (ii) below:

    (i) **Current compensation.** Employees who are reasonably expected to receive at least $ _____ in compensation (not to exceed $5,000) for the calendar year.

    (ii) **Prior compensation.** Employees who have received at least $ _____ in compensation (not to exceed $5,000) during any _____ calendar year(s) (insert 0, 1, or 2) preceding the calendar year.

2 **Excludable Employees.**

    ☐ The Employer elects to exclude employees covered under a collective bargaining agreement for which retirement benefits were the subject of good faith bargaining. **Note:** _This box is deemed checked if the Employer maintains a qualified plan covering only such employees._

Article II—Salary Reduction Agreements _(complete the box and blank, if applicable—see instructions)_

1 **Salary Reduction Election.** An eligible employee may make an election to have his or her compensation for each pay period reduced. The total amount of the reduction in the employee's compensation for a calendar year cannot exceed the applicable amount for that year.

2 **Timing of Salary Reduction Elections**

a For a calendar year, an eligible employee may make or modify a salary reduction election during the 60-day period immediately preceding January 1 of that year. However, for the year in which the employee becomes eligible to make salary reduction contributions, the period during which the employee may make or modify the election is a 60-day period that includes either the date the employee becomes eligible or the day before.

b In addition to the election periods in 2a, eligible employees may make salary reduction elections or modify prior elections _____ , _____ . If the Employer chooses this option, insert a period or periods (for example, semi-annually, quarterly, monthly, or daily) that will apply uniformly to all eligible employees.

c No salary reduction election may apply to compensation that an employee received, or had a right to immediately receive, before execution of the salary reduction election.

d An employee may terminate a salary reduction election at any time during the calendar year. ☐ If this box is checked, an employee who terminates a salary reduction election not in accordance with 2b may not resume salary reduction contributions during the calendar year.

Article III—Contributions _(complete the blank, if applicable—see instructions)_

1 **Salary Reduction Contributions.** The amount by which the employee agrees to reduce his or her compensation will be contributed by the Employer to the employee's SIMPLE IRA.

2 a **Matching Contributions**

    (i) For each calendar year, the Employer will contribute a matching contribution to each eligible employee's SIMPLE IRA equal to the employee's salary reduction contributions up to a limit of 3% of the employee's compensation for the calendar year.

    (ii) The Employer may reduce the 3% limit for the calendar year in (i) only if:

        (1) The limit is not reduced below 1%; **(2)** The limit is not reduced for more than 2 calendar years during the 5-year period ending with the calendar year the reduction is effective; and **(3)** Each employee is notified of the reduced limit within a reasonable period of time before the employees' 60-day election period for the calendar year (described in Article II, item 2a).

b **Nonelective Contributions**

    (i) For any calendar year, instead of making matching contributions, the Employer may make nonelective contributions equal to 2% of compensation for the calendar year to the SIMPLE IRA of each eligible employee who has at least $ _____ , (not more than $5,000) in compensation for the calendar year. No more than $250,000* in compensation can be taken into account in determining the nonelective contribution for each eligible employee.

    (ii) For any calendar year, the Employer may make 2% nonelective contributions instead of matching contributions only if:
        (1) Each eligible employee is notified that a 2% nonelective contribution will be made instead of a matching contribution; and
        (2) This notification is provided within a reasonable period of time before the employees' 60-day election period for the calendar year (described in Article II, item 2a).

3 **Time and Manner of Contributions**

a The Employer will make the salary reduction contributions (described in 1 above) for each eligible employee to the SIMPLE IRA established at the financial institution selected by that employee no later than 30 days after the end of the month in which the money is withheld from the employee's pay. See instructions.

b The Employer will make the matching or nonelective contributions (described in 2a and 2b above) for each eligible employee to the SIMPLE IRA established at the financial institution selected by that employee no later than the due date for filing the Employer's tax return, including extensions, for the taxable year that includes the last day of the calendar year for which the contributions are made.

* _This is the amount for 2012. For later years, the limit may be increased for cost-of-living adjustments. The IRS announces the increase, if any, in a news release, in the Internal Revenue Bulletin, and on the IRS's internet website at_ **IRS.gov.**

For Paperwork Reduction Act Notice, see the instructions. Cat. No. 23377W Form **5304-SIMPLE** (Rev. 3-2012)

Form 5304-SIMPLE Continued

Article IV—Other Requirements and Provisions

1   **Contributions in General.** The Employer will make no contributions to the SIMPLE IRAs other than salary reduction contributions (described in Article III, item 1) and matching or nonelective contributions (described in Article III, items 2a and 2b).

2   **Vesting Requirements.** All contributions made under this SIMPLE IRA plan are fully vested and nonforfeitable.

3   **No Withdrawal Restrictions.** The Employer may not require the employee to retain any portion of the contributions in his or her SIMPLE IRA or otherwise impose any withdrawal restrictions.

4   **Selection of IRA Trustee.** The Employer must permit each eligible employee to select the financial institution that will serve as the trustee, custodian, or issuer of the SIMPLE IRA to which the Employer will make all contributions on behalf of that employee.

5   **Amendments To This SIMPLE IRA Plan.** This SIMPLE IRA plan may not be amended except to modify the entries inserted in the blanks or boxes provided in Articles I, II, III, VI, and VII.

6   **Effects Of Withdrawals and Rollovers**

a   An amount withdrawn from the SIMPLE IRA is generally includible in gross income. However, a SIMPLE IRA balance may be rolled over or transferred on a tax-free basis to another IRA designed solely to hold funds under a SIMPLE IRA plan. In addition, an individual may roll over or transfer his or her SIMPLE IRA balance to any IRA or eligible retirement plan after a 2-year period has expired since the individual first participated in any SIMPLE IRA plan of the Employer. Any rollover or transfer must comply with the requirements under section 408.

b   If an individual withdraws an amount from a SIMPLE IRA during the 2-year period beginning when the individual first participated in any SIMPLE IRA plan of the Employer and the amount is subject to the additional tax on early distributions under section 72(t), this additional tax is increased from 10% to 25%.

Article V—Definitions

1   **Compensation**

a   **General Definition of Compensation.** Compensation means the sum of the wages, tips, and other compensation from the Employer subject to federal income tax withholding (as described in section 6051(a)(3)), the amounts paid for domestic service in a private home, local college club, or local chapter of a college fraternity or sorority, and the employee's salary reduction contributions made under this plan, and, if applicable, elective deferrals under a section 401(k) plan, a SARSEP, or a section 403(b) annuity contract and compensation deferred under a section 457 plan required to be reported by the Employer on Form W-2 (as described in section 6051(a)(8)).

b   **Compensation for Self-Employed Individuals.** For self-employed individuals, compensation means the net earnings from self-employment determined under section 1402(a), without regard to section 1402(c)(6), prior to subtracting any contributions made pursuant to this plan on behalf of the individual.

2   **Employee.** Employee means a common-law employee of the Employer. The term employee also includes a self-employed individual and a leased employee described in section 414(n) but does not include a nonresident alien who received no earned income from the Employer that constitutes income from sources within the United States.

3   **Eligible Employee.** An eligible employee means an employee who satisfies the conditions in Article I, item 1 and is not excluded under Article I, item 2.

4   **SIMPLE IRA.** A SIMPLE IRA is an individual retirement account described in section 408(a), or an individual retirement annuity described in section 408(b), to which the only contributions that can be made are contributions under a SIMPLE IRA plan and rollovers or transfers from another SIMPLE IRA.

Article VI—Procedures for Withdrawals *(The Employer will provide each employee with the procedures for withdrawals of contributions received by the financial institution selected by that employee, and that financial institution's name and address (by attaching that information or inserting it in the space below) unless: (1) that financial institution's procedures are unavailable, or (2) that financial institution provides the procedures directly to the employee. See **Employee Notification** in the instructions.)*

Article VII—Effective Date

This SIMPLE IRA plan is effective _____ . See instructions.

*   *   *   *   *

_____
Name of Employer

By: Signature   Date

_____
Address of Employer

Name and title

Form **5304-SIMPLE** (Rev. 3-2012)

Form 5304-SIMPLE Continued

Model Notification to Eligible Employees

I.   Opportunity to Participate in the SIMPLE IRA Plan

You are eligible to make salary reduction contributions to the _____ SIMPLE IRA plan. This notice and the attached summary description provide you with information that you should consider before you decide whether to start, continue, or change your salary reduction agreement.

II. Employer Contribution Election

For the _____ calendar year, the Employer elects to contribute to your SIMPLE IRA *(employer must select either (1), (2), or (3)):*

☐ **(1)** A matching contribution equal to your salary reduction contributions up to a limit of 3% of your compensation for the year;

☐ **(2)** A matching contribution equal to your salary reduction contributions up to a limit of _____ % *(employer must insert a number from 1 to 3 and is subject to certain restrictions)* of your compensation for the year; or

☐ **(3)** A nonelective contribution equal to 2% of your compensation for the year (limited to compensation of $250,000*) if you are an employee who *makes at least $* _____ *(employer must insert an amount that is $5,000 or less)* in compensation for the year.

III. Administrative Procedures

To start or change your salary reduction contributions, you must complete the salary reduction agreement and return it to

_____ (employer should designate a place or

individual by _____ *(employer should insert a date that is not less than 60 days after notice is given).*

IV. Employee Selection of Financial Institution

You must select the financial institution that will serve as the trustee, custodian, or issuer of your SIMPLE IRA and notify your Employer of your selection.

Model Salary Reduction Agreement

I.   Salary Reduction Election

Subject to the requirements of the SIMPLE IRA plan of _____ *(name of employer)* I authorize _____ % or $ _____ (which equals _____ % of my current rate of pay) to be withheld from my pay for each pay period and contributed to my SIMPLE IRA as a salary reduction contribution.

II. Maximum Salary Reduction

I understand that the total amount of my salary reduction contributions in any calendar year cannot exceed the applicable amount for that year. See instructions.

III. Date Salary Reduction Begins

I understand that my salary reduction contributions will start as soon as permitted under the SIMPLE IRA plan and as soon as administratively feasible or, if later, _____ . *(Fill in the date you want the salary reduction contributions to begin. The date must be after you sign this agreement.)*

IV. Employee Selection of Financial Institution

I select the following financial institution to serve as the trustee, custodian, or issuer of my SIMPLE IRA.

_____

Name of financial institution

_____

Address of financial institution

_____

SIMPLE IRA account name and number

I understand that I must establish a SIMPLE IRA to receive any contributions made on my behalf under this SIMPLE IRA plan. If the information regarding my SIMPLE IRA is incomplete when I first submit my salary reduction agreement, I realize that it must be completed by the date contributions must be made under the SIMPLE IRA plan. If I fail to update my agreement to provide this information by that date, I understand that my Employer may select a financial institution for my SIMPLE IRA.

V.   Duration of Election

This salary reduction agreement replaces any earlier agreement and will remain in effect as long as I remain an eligible employee under the SIMPLE IRA plan or until I provide my Employer with a request to end my salary reduction contributions or provide a new salary reduction agreement as permitted under this SIMPLE IRA plan.

Signature of employee _____   Date _____

* This is the amount for 2012. For later years, the limit may be increased for cost-of-living adjustments. The IRS announces the increase, if any, in a news release, in the Internal Revenue Bulletin, and on the IRS website at **IRS.gov.**

Form **5304-SIMPLE** (Rev. 3-2012)

Eligibility

To be eligible for a SIMPLE, an employer cannot have more than 100 employees and all employees considered eligible must benefit from the SIMPLE. Eligible employees are those employees who earned at least $5,000 in compensation from the employer during any two preceding calendar years and who are reasonably expected to earn at least $5,000 in compensation during the current calendar year.[8] Employers have the option to choose less restrictive eligibility requirements. Air pilots, nonresident aliens, and union employees whose retirement benefits were the subject of good faith bargaining may be excluded from the eligibility requirements of a SIMPLE IRA plan by the employer.

The employer and employee eligibility for a SIMPLE is determined based on the calendar year, January 1 to December 31. A SIMPLE plan cannot use any other fiscal years (other than those that mimic calendar years) to determine eligibility requirements.

Exhibit 10.4 | Eligibility Characteristics

- Employees who earned $5,000 during any two preceding calendar years.
- Employees who are expected to earn $5,000 or more during the current calendar year.

Vesting

All employer contributions to SIMPLE IRA accounts on behalf of employees and the related earnings are fully (100%) and immediately vested and cannot be forfeited by the employee.[9] All contributions under the SIMPLE 401(k) plan are likewise fully and immediately vested.

SIMPLE IRAs

Employee Elective Deferral Contributions

With the exception of certain rollover contributions, the only contributions that may be made under a SIMPLE IRA plan are the employee's elective deferral contributions and the required employer matching contributions or nonelective contributions.[10] Similar to other cash or deferred arrangement (CODA) type plans, rather than have funds paid directly in cash to the employee through payroll, an employee's elective deferral contribution or salary reduction contribution is made to the employee's SIMPLE IRA account.

The SIMPLE IRA permits employees to defer a percentage or a dollar amount of their compensation for the year. Within 60 days prior to the beginning of the plan year, the employee elects the amount to defer under the plan. The employer is not allowed to place any restriction on the employee's elective deferral unless the annual limit on the salary reduction amount is reached, $13,500 for 2021.[11]

---

8. IRC §408(p)(4).
9. IRC §408(p)(3).
10. IRC §408(p)(2)(A), §408(p)(2)(A)(iii).
11. IRC §408(p)(2)(A)(ii).

Exhibit 10.5 | SIMPLE Characteristics

- Employee elective deferral (optional)
- Employer match (or nonelective contribution)
- 100% vesting in all contributions and earnings
- Employer must have ≤ 100 employees

Annual Limit on Employee Elective Contributions for SIMPLE IRAs

Employees may make annual elective deferrals to a SIMPLE IRA plan for 2021 and thereafter, in the amount of $13,500 adjusted for inflation.

Year	Total Elective Contribution	Catch-Up
2021	$13,500	$3,000

The $13,500 limitation is adjusted for inflation in increments of $500 (the inflation adjustment is rounded downward to the nearest $500). The base period for calculating the inflation adjustment is the calendar quarter beginning July 1, 2004.[12]

Salary Reduction Catch-up Contributions for SIMPLE IRAs

For employees who have attained the age of 50 by the end of the calendar year and if there are no other elective contributions that can be made for them during the calendar year, such employees are permitted to make additional elective contributions, also known as "catch-up contributions," to the plan for that calendar year. The maximum catch-up contribution for such an eligible employee for the calendar year is the lesser of:

- the catch-up contribution limit of $3,000 for 2021,[13] or
- the employee's compensation for the year reduced by all of the employee's other elective deferrals for the year to other SIMPLEs, or 401(k) plans, SEPs, and 403(b) plans.

Example 10.3

In July of 2021, Huey, age 54, began working for Knowledger Contributions, which sponsors a SIMPLE. Between July and December of 2021, Huey earns $14,000. He defers $13,500 to the SIMPLE. Therefore, he can only defer an additional $500 ($14,000 - $13,500) to the SIMPLE under the catch-up provision because of his compensation reduced by the elective deferral.

Employer Contributions

An employer who sponsors a SIMPLE IRA is required to make either matching contributions to those employees who make elective deferrals or, alternatively, to make nonelective contributions to all eligible employees.

---

12. IRC §408(p)(2)(A)(ii), as amended by EGTRRA 2001, §611(f)(1); §408(p)(2)(E), as amended by EGTRRA 2001, §611(f)(2); EGTRRA 2001, §611(i)(1).
13. After the 2006 calendar year, the $2,500 limitation was adjusted for inflation in increments of $500, and the base period for calculating the inflation adjustment was the calendar quarter starting July 1, 2005. IRC §414(v), as amended by EGTRRA, 2001, §631(a).

Employer Matching Contributions

If the employer elects to make matching contributions, the employer is generally required to match the employee's elective deferral contributions on a dollar-for-dollar matching basis up to three percent of the compensation of the employee (without regard to the covered compensation limit) for the entire calendar year.[14] The employer's matching contribution is limited to the maximum dollar limit for employee deferrals ($13,500 in 2021).

The employer may reduce the three percent matching contribution requirement for a calendar year, but only under all of the following circumstances:[15]
- the limit is reduced to no less than one percent,
- the limit is not reduced for more than two years out of the five year period that ends with (and includes) the year for which the election is effective, and
- employees are notified of the reduced limit within a reasonable period of time before the sixty day election period for a salary reduction agreement.

This only applies to SIMPLE IRAs, and hence is not available for SIMPLE 401(k)s.[16]

Example 10.4

An employer normally must match each employee's elective deferral contribution dollar-for-dollar up to 3% of the employee's compensation. Irma is employed by Thomas Company in 2021. Irma earned $30,000 and elected to defer 10% of her salary. Thomas was self-employed and his net earnings were $300,000. Thomas elects to defer 3% of his earnings to his SIMPLE IRA. Thomas Company makes a 3% matching contribution. The total contribution to Irma's SIMPLE IRA for 2021 is $3,900 as calculated below. Notice that the match for Thomas is not limited to 3% of $290,000 (the covered compensation limit for qualified plans). The limit is $9,000 (3% of $300,000).

Irma's elective deferral contribution ($30,000 x 10%)	$3,000
Matching contribution by Thomas Co. ($30,000 x 3%)	$900
2021 Total SIMPLE IRA Contribution	**$3,900**

Using the same facts as above, the total contribution for 2021 to Thomas's SIMPLE IRA is $18,000 as calculated below:

Thomas's elective deferral contribution ($300,000 x 3%)	$9,000
Matching contribution by Thomas Co. ($300,000 x 3%)	$9,000
2021 Total SIMPLE IRA Contribution	**$18,000**

Nonelective Contributions by Employer

The alternative for the employer who chooses not to match employee elective deferrals is to make nonelective contributions for all eligible employees. If the employer chooses to make **nonelective contributions**, then the employer must contribute two percent of each eligible employee's compensation (up to the covered compensation limit of $290,000 for 2021) to the SIMPLE IRA. The contribution must be made for all eligible employees who earn at least $5,000 from the employer for the year, or less if

---

14. IRC §408(p)(2)(A)(iii).
15. IRC §408(p)(2)(C)(ii).
16. IRC §401(k)(11)(B)(i).

elected by the employer. If the employer decides to make nonelective contributions, the employer is required to make those nonelective contributions whether or not the employee chooses to make any elective deferral contributions. The employees must be notified within a reasonable time period before the 60 day election period of the employer's choice of the two percent nonelective contribution method or the matching contribution.

Example 10.5

Matthew, an employee of Perry's Company, earned $40,000 in 2021 and agreed to make elective deferral contributions of 9% of his salary to his SIMPLE IRA. Perry earned $60,000 net self-employment income and chose to make elective deferral contributions of 10% of her earnings. Perry's Company, as the employer, made a nonelective contribution of 2% to each eligible employee. The total contribution to Matthew's SIMPLE IRA for 2021 is $4,400 as calculated below.

Matthew's elective deferral contribution ($40,000 x 0.09)	$3,600
Nonelective contribution by Perry Co. ($40,000 x 0.02)	$800
2021 Total Contribution for Matthew	**$4,400**

Using the same facts as above, the total contribution to Perry's SIMPLE IRA for 2021 is $7,200 as calculated below.

Perry's elective deferral contribution ($60,000 x 0.10)	$6,000
Nonelective contribution by Perry Co. ($60,000 x 0.02)	$1,200
2021 Total Contribution for Perry	**$7,200**

Taxation of Contributions

SIMPLE IRA contributions are contemporaneously tax deductible for the small employer. The deductible amount includes the employee elective deferral contributions (as compensation) and any employer match or nonelective contribution. The contributions to a SIMPLE IRA are not subject to a limitation based on a percentage of compensation, but the employee's elective deferral is limited to $13,500 for 2021.

Employer Contributions	Employee Elective Deferrals
• 3% match, or • 2% nonelective contribution for all eligible employees	• % or $ contribution up to $13,500 plus $3,000 for age 50 and over for 2021

Employers are allowed to deduct contributions for the taxable year only if the contributions are made on or before the date that the employer's tax return is due. The elective contributions of the employee that are being made into the SIMPLE IRA account must be contributed by the employer no later than 30 days following the last day of the month of the contributions. [17] The employer must also make any matching contributions or nonelective contributions by the date that its tax return is due for that tax year, including extensions.

Employee elective deferral contributions and employer contributions made to SIMPLE IRAs are excluded from an employee's taxable income and are not subject to federal income tax withholding. An employee's elective deferral contributions are, however, subject to payroll taxes (OASDI and Medicare), but the employer matching or nonelective contributions made to SIMPLE IRA accounts are not subject to payroll tax (OASDI and Medicare).

Withdrawals and Distributions

Distributions from a SIMPLE IRA plan are includible as ordinary income in the individual employee's taxable income in the year in which they are withdrawn. SIMPLE IRA plan distributions are taxed in the same manner as distributions from a traditional IRA. As a general rule, trustee-to-trustee transfers (direct), and rollovers of SIMPLE IRAs are not taxable distributions. SIMPLE distributions may be subjected to an early withdrawal penalty of 10 percent if received prior to age 59½. The exclusions from the 10 percent penalty for SIMPLE IRAs are the same as described in Chapter 9 for IRAs.

A distribution or transfer made from a SIMPLE IRA during the first two years of an employee's participation in the SIMPLE must be contributed to another SIMPLE IRA to avoid taxation and penalty. After the two year participation period, a SIMPLE IRA can be transferred or rolled over tax-free to:
- an IRA other than a SIMPLE IRA,
- a qualified plan,
- a 403(b) account or tax sheltered annuity, or
- a deferred compensation plan of a State or local government (457 plan).

If a distribution is taken from a SIMPLE IRA plan during the first two years of an employee's participation in the plan and if the distribution is subject to the early withdrawal penalty, the penalty tax increases from 10 percent to 25 percent. If the distribution is made on account of a penalty exception (as described in Chapter 9), then the 25 percent penalty tax will not apply.[18] After the employee's first two years of plan participation, the 10 percent penalty for early withdrawal will apply if the distribution is not because of a penalty excluded reason.

The Consolidated Appropriations Act (CAA) of 2016, which became law on December 18, 2015, expanded the list of account types from which SIMPLE IRA plans can accept rollovers. Historically, a SIMPLE IRA plan could only accept rollover contributions from another SIMPLE IRA plan. The CAA of 2016 expands portability of retirement assets by permitting taxpayers to roll over assets from traditional and SEP IRAs, as well as from employer- sponsored retirement plans, such as a 401(k), 403(b), or 457(b) plan, into a SIMPLE IRA plan for years after 2015. As with distributions from SIMPLE IRA plans, this change applies only to rollovers made after the two-year period beginning on the date the participant first participated in their employer's SIMPLE IRA plan.

---

17. IRC §408(p)(5)(B).
18. IRC §72(t)(6).

SIMPLE 401(k) Plans

A SIMPLE 401(k) plan is a qualified plan and must generally satisfy the same requirements as 401(k) plans and SIMPLE IRA plans. The differences between SIMPLE 401(k)s and SIMPLE IRAs or between SIMPLE 401(k)s and 401(k)s are discussed below, along with other attributes of SIMPLE 401(k)s.

Under a SIMPLE 401(k) plan, an employee may choose to reduce his salary in return for "salary reduction contributions" or deferrals to a SIMPLE 401(k) account. This salary reduction contribution is expressly stated as a percentage of the employee's compensation but may not exceed $13,500 for 2021. The employer may, but is not required to, permit certain employees to use the catch-up feature, under which employees age 50 and over may defer a contribution of up to $3,000 for 2021.

The rules concerning contributions for employers to regular 401(k) plans, discussed in Chapter 5, also apply to SIMPLE 401(k)s. The limitation of $13,500 for 2021 or employee elective deferral contributions to the SIMPLE IRA plans (discussed above) also apply to the SIMPLE 401(k)s.

A participant of a SIMPLE 401(k) may take a loan (plan permitting) from a SIMPLE 401(k), unlike a participant of a SIMPLE IRA. The amount of the loan is subject to the same restrictions, discussed in Chapter 7, as loans from qualified plans.

Employers who sponsor SIMPLE 401(k) plans must make either: (1) a matching contribution, or (2) a nonelective contribution to the plan. An employer is required to match the elective deferral contribution of the employee on a dollar-for-dollar basis up to three percent of the employee's compensation for the calendar year.[19] In contrast to a SIMPLE IRA plan, the employer does not have the available option of reducing matching contributions to less than three percent of the compensation of each employee.

As an alternative to matching elective deferral contributions, an employer that has established a SIMPLE 401(k) plan may elect to provide nonelective contributions of two percent of each eligible employee's compensation. The nonelective contributions of the employer are required to be made for each eligible employee, regardless of whether that employee elects to make any salary reduction deferral contributions. Under these circumstances, the employer is permitted, but is not required, to limit nonelective contributions to only those eligible employees (those employees who meet the eligibility rules).[20] Unlike the SIMPLE IRA, for which the annual covered compensation limit of $290,000 (for 2021) applies only to employer non-elective contributions, the annual covered compensation limit of $290,000 for 2021 applies to all contributions made to the SIMPLE 401(k).

19. IRC §401(k)(11)(B)(i)(II).
20. IRC §401(k)(11)(B)(ii).

No other contribution may be made to the trust comprising the SIMPLE 401(k) account. No contributions can be made nor may benefits accrue for services during the year pursuant to any other qualified retirement plan of the employer for any employee participating in the SIMPLE 401(k) plan. The ADP test, ACP test, and top-heavy rules, explained in prior chapters, do not apply to SIMPLE 401(k)s because they are essentially safe harbor plans. Furthermore, annual filings of the Form 5500 are not required for SIMPLE 401(k) plans. Once again, though, there are few SIMPLE 401(k) plans that have been established.

Conclusion

SIMPLEs are retirement plans for small employers, and like their name implies, are very easy to establish and maintain, have less administrative costs than other retirement plans, and do not have any annual filing requirements. As discussed, SIMPLEs can take the form of a SIMPLE IRA or SIMPLE 401(k), both of which essentially share the same rules. In practice, most employers chose the SIMPLE IRA instead of the SIMPLE 401(k). Although the 401(k) version has loans as an available option, it also has greater administrative requirements.

Exhibit 10.6 | Concept Summary - SIMPLE Plans

SIMPLE	Savings Incentive Match Plan for Employees
Application	Small employers (limit of 100 employees with compensation ≥ $5,000)
Style	Self-reliant employee elective deferral contributions and employer match
Type	Could be SIMPLE 401(k), but almost all are SIMPLE IRAs
Established By What Date	Generally, October 1 of year the plan starts
Characteristics	No annual filing requirement, minor costs No other retirement plans are permitted
Employee Elective Deferral Contribution Limit	Lesser of $13,500 for 2021 salary reduction or 100% salary
Catch-Up Contribution for Age 50	Yes, $3,000 for 2021
Available Employer Contributions	Dollar-for-dollar match up to the lesser of 3% of compensation (without regard to covered compensation limit for SIMPLE IRA) or $13,500 or 2% of compensation (up to covered compensation limit of $290,000 for 2021) nonelective contribution for each eligible employee regardless of deferral
Penalties for In-Service Withdrawals	For SIMPLE IRA, 25% if within first two years, unless penalty exception applies; 10% after two years unless penalty exception applies. For SIMPLE 401(k), the penalty is 10% unless penalty exception applies.
Loans Permitted	No - SIMPLE IRA; Yes - SIMPLE 401(k)
In-Service Withdrawals	Yes, subject to income and penalties

Exhibit 10.7 | SIMPLE IRA, SIMPLE 401(k), and 401(k) Plan Comparison

	SIMPLE IRA	SIMPLE 401(k)	401(k) Plans
Application	Small employers (limit of 100 employee's with compensation ≥ $5,000)	Same as SIMPLE IRA	Most employers
Style	Self-reliant employee elective deferral contributions and employer match		
Established By What Date	Generally, October 1 of the year the plan starts	Same as SIMPLE IRA	By due date of tax return (including extensions)
Ability to have Other Plans	Must not have another retirement plan	Same as SIMPLE IRA	There may be other plans
Filings and Costs	No annual filing requirement, minor costs	Same as 401(k) Plan	Annual filing required and administrative costs
Annual Testing	None required if meet contribution requirements	None required if meet contribution requirements	Required
Vesting	All contributions are fully vested	All contributions are fully vested	Vesting schedules allowed
Employee Elective Deferral Contribution Limit	$13,500 for 2021	Same as SIMPLE IRA	$19,500 for 2021
Catch-Up Contribution for Age 50 and over	$3,000 for 2021	Same as SIMPLE IRA	$6,500 for 2021
Employer Contribution	The employer must generally make: • A dollar-for-dollar match up to 3% of pay or • A 2% nonelective contribution for each eligible employee.	Same as SIMPLE IRA except for the employer-match cannot be reduced to as low as 1% for no more than 2 out of 5 years, including the year of election.	Employer may contribute
Loans Permitted	No	Same as 401(k) Plan	Yes
In-Service Withdrawals	Permitted, but 10% penalty if under age 59½ (unless penalty exception applies). If withdrawals are made within the first two years of participation, the 10% additional tax is increased to 25% (unless penalty exception applies).	Same as 401(k) Plan	Permitted, but possible 10% penalty if under age 59½ (unless penalty exception applies)

403(b) PLANS OR TAX SHELTERED ANNUITIES (TSAs)

Under §403(b) of the IRC, plans called **tax sheltered or deferred annuities**, or "**403(b) plans**," are available to the employees of certain qualified nonprofit organizations, public educational systems, cooperative hospital service organizations, and to certain ministers. The employee elective deferral contributions limits of 403(b) plans, along with the catch-up provisions, allow for the deferral of significant amounts for those employees who are age 50 or older.

> ### Key Concepts
>
> 1. What are 403(b) plans?
> 2. When does ERISA apply to 403(b) plans?
> 3. Who is eligible for a 403(b) plan?
> 4. What rules are applicable to employee contributions to 403(b) plans?

Definition of a 403(b) Plan

A 403(b) plan is a retirement plan for certain employees of public schools, certain ministers, and employees of various tax-exempt organizations. It is a tax-sheltered retirement plan, but not a qualified plan. The 403(b) plan is established by the employer and the employee has an individual account earmarked as his or her 403(b) plan account. Many consider 403(b) plans of nonprofit entities to be the counterpart to the 401(k) plans of for-profit entities. Sometimes, 403(b) plans are termed "401(k) plans for nonprofits." Though not considered qualified plans, many 403(b) plans offer similar attributes as qualified defined contribution plans. There are two basic types of 403(b) plans. The first type is a salary reduction plan, which only accepts employee deferrals. This is the most common type of plan. The second type of plan is an employer-funded plan, which accepts employee and employer contributions. This type of 403(b) plan is less common.

Entities that can Establish 403(b) Plans

Only employers may set up 403(b) accounts. Individuals cannot establish 403(b) accounts on their own. Interestingly, however, self-employed ministers (discussed briefly below) are considered both employees and employers, and thus are able to contribute to a retirement 403(b) income account for their own benefit. Generally, employers that are eligible to establish 403(b) plans are nonprofit religious, charitable, scientific, educational, and other public interest organizations such as private schools, colleges, universities, and teaching hospitals.

Technically, the two types of entities that can establish 403(b) plans are:
1. Tax-exempt organizations under IRC §501(c)(3), or
2. Public schools or public educational organizations.

Section 501(c)(3) Organizations

Section 501(c)(3) organizations are nonprofit tax-exempt organizations that are established under IRC §501(c)(3) of the Internal Revenue Code. Section 501(c)(3) organizations are nonprofit entities such as corporations, community chests, funds, or foundations. They are organized exclusively (1) for religious, charitable, scientific, literary, or educational purposes, (2) to foster amateur sports competition nationally or internationally, unless any of their activities involve providing athletic equipment or facilities, or (3) to prevent cruelty to children or animals. Net earnings of the organization may not inure to the benefit of private shareholders. Further, no lobbying activities (other than by public charities) can comprise a substantial part of the organization's activities, nor can the organization participate in any political campaign for any candidate for public office.[21]

Public Schools or Public Educational Organizations

In general, public schools can establish 403(b) plans, and most often the public educational system of a state or community will establish a 403(b) plan. A public educational system is an organization run by a state, political subdivision, or agency that maintains a faculty and curriculum and has regularly enrolled students in attendance where educational activities are conducted.[22]

ERISA Applicability

The issue of whether ERISA applies to a 403(b) plan is important. If ERISA applies, then the plan requirements change. ERISA applies if the 403(b) plan is considered to be an "employee benefit pension plan." An employee benefit pension plan is defined as any plan, fund, or program established or maintained by an employer that provides retirement income to employees or defers income of employees for periods until termination of employment or beyond. Governmental TSAs and church-related TSAs are not subject to ERISA, but plans of §501(c)(3) organizations may be subject to ERISA unless employer involvement is so minimal that it falls short of the requirement that a plan be sponsored by an employer (as discussed below).

It is very common for a 403(b) plan to be a part of an overall pension or retirement plan. The 403(b) portion may be referred to as the supplemental retirement plan. If this is the case, then the plan is subject to ERISA requirements.

Generally 403(b) plans are not subject to ERISA rules if the following are true:
- employee participation is voluntary,
- there are no employer contributions,
- employee has solely enforceable rights under the plan,
- employer's involvement is limited in scope, and
- sponsored by a government or religious institution.

Example 10.6

Suppose Loyola University had a retirement plan that required employees to contribute 3.5 percent of their salary to the plan and the university contributed eight percent to the plan. Loyola also maintained a 403(b) plan that allowed employees to choose elective deferrals up to the maximum provided by the law. In this case, Loyola's 403(b) plan would be subject to ERISA requirements because it is maintained as an "employer benefit pension plan."

If a 403(b) plan only provides for salary reduction agreements, then the plan is not considered to be established or maintained by the employer and ERISA is inapplicable. If ERISA applies, nonelective deferral contributions must satisfy nondiscrimination requirements, matching contributions must satisfy the ACP test, and the plan is subject to pre-retirement joint and survivor annuity elections and joint and survivor elections at retirement as distribution requirements.

To illustrate this point, consider the scenario of a 403(b) plan that only provides for elective deferrals (i.e., salary reduction contributions). In such a case, only one nondiscrimination requirement will apply: If one employee has the right to elect to have the employer make salary reduction contributions under a

---

21. IRC §501(c)(3).
22. IRC §403(b)(1)(A)(ii).

salary reduction agreement, then all employees must be permitted to elect salary deferral contributions. If, however, the plan contains employer contributions beyond salary reduction contributions, then contributions to the 403(b) plan are subject to the general nondiscrimination rules applicable to qualified retirement plans and may not discriminate in favor of the HCE.

Employee deferrals to a 403(b) plan are not subject to the actual deferral percentage (ADP) test discussed in Chapter 5. However, a 403(b) plan must generally allow all eligible employees to make elective deferrals to the plan under what is referred to as the universal availability rule. Under this rule, if an employer permits one employee to defer salary by contributing it to a 403(b) plan, the employer must extend this offer to all employees with the following exceptions:
- employees who will contribute $200 or less annually,
- employees who participate in a 401(k) or 457(b) plan or in another 403(b) plan of the employer,
- nonresident aliens,
- employees who normally work less than 20 hours per week, and
- students who are enrolled and regularly attending classes at such school, college, or university.

Eligibility

Eligible employees can participate in a 403(b) plan sponsored through an employer. 403(b) plans with immediate vesting may require a maximum waiting period of two years and the attainment of age 21, or one year and the attainment of age 26 (educational institutions only). Plans that do not offer immediate vesting may not have a waiting period longer than one year and the attainment of age 21. The following are considered eligible employees (who must meet the age and service requirements) to participate in a 403(b) plan:
1. Employees of tax-exempt organizations as defined under IRC §501(c)(3).
2. Employees who are involved in the day-to-day operations of a public school or public school system.
3. Employees of cooperative hospital service organizations.[23]
4. Ministers who meet one of the following criteria:
   - Ministers that are employed by §501(c)(3) organizations (discussed above).
   - Ministers that are self-employed. A self-employed minister is deemed as employed by a tax-exempt organization that is a qualified employer.
   - Ministers who are employed by organizations that are not §501(c)(3) organizations and function as ministers in their day-to-day responsibilities with their employer.

Self-employed ministers must report total contributions to 403(b) accounts as a tax deduction on their tax returns.

Notes on Employees
When the term "employee" is used in discussing these rules, an employer-employee relationship must exist to allow the employee to be eligible to participate. The individual must be an employee, not an independent contractor. There are many IRS guidelines for characterizing someone as an employee or independent contractor based on the relationship between the individual and the company. Some emphasis is placed on the amount of control, direction, and supervision that the employer has over the individual.

23.Cooperative hospital service organizations are codified in IRC §501(e). They are deemed to be §501(c)(3) organizations, and thus are allowed to form a 403(b) plan for employees.

CASE STUDY 10.1

In **Azad v U.S.,**[1] a radiologist was on salary at a hospital. The radiologist's work at the hospital was not supervised nor was it directed by the hospital. The Court concluded that the radiologist was not an employee as defined by the IRC, and was not permitted to exclude from his gross income those amounts contributed to an annuity contract by the employer.

1. *Azad v. U.S.*, 277 F. Supp. 258 (D.C. Minn. 1966), *aff'd*, 388 F.2d 74 (8th Cir. 1968).

Employee Contributions

Employees' elective deferral contributions to 403(b) accounts are very similar to employee elective deferral contributions to 401(k) plans, SARSEPs, and 457 plans. While a 403(b) plan is established by the employer, the employee has an individual 403(b) account for his own benefit. Only the employer is allowed to make contributions to the 403(b) account on behalf of the employee (usually through employee salary reduction), but some plans may also allow employees to make after-tax contributions similar to a thrift plan.

The following contributions are permissible contributions (but are not required) for 403(b) accounts:
- employee elective deferrals
- nonelective contributions
- after-tax contributions
- any combination of the above

With employee "elective deferrals," contributions can be made under a salary reduction agreement where the employee agrees that the employer will withhold money from the employee's paycheck so that these funds can be contributed directly into the 403(b) account for the benefit of the employee. The employee is not subject to income tax on the contribution until the funds are withdrawn from the 403(b) account by the employee. However, the elective deferral amounts are subject to payroll taxes exactly as are 401(k) elective deferrals. For 2021, an employee can electively defer no more than $19,500, subject to catch-up provisions discussed later in this chapter. Deferrals can also be made to a Roth account if it is part of the 403(b) plan, but these deferrals consist of after-tax contributions.

Unlike employee elective deferrals, "nonelective contributions" are not made under a salary reduction agreement. Instead, nonelective contributions are matching contributions, mandatory contributions from the employer, or even discretionary contributions by the employer. Again, the employee does not pay taxes on these contributions until withdrawn by the employee from the account.

Finally, an employee may contribute after-tax or non-deductible funds to a 403(b) account. Although after-tax contributions to 403(b) accounts are allowed, they are unusual in practice, other than to Roth accounts, discussed below. Unlike the elective deferral and nonelective contributions, however, the amounts contributed in after-tax contributions are not excluded from the income of the employee and will therefore create an adjusted basis in the 403(b) account. When the participant takes a withdrawal from such an account, some of the funds will be return of capital and, therefore, nontaxable.

Limits on Elective Deferrals

An elective deferral is basically an employee's contribution to an employee's account through a voluntary salary reduction agreement. While technically only employers can actually make contributions into the 403(b) accounts on behalf of the employees, employees voluntarily elect or decide to reduce their salary by a certain amount, and that forgone amount is contributed by the employer for the benefit of the employees into the 403(b) account. Commonly, this is referred to as a cash or deferred arrangement (CODA) because the employee has the choice of receiving the funds in cash or deferring the income. Therefore, the employee is directing the employer to place these deferral amounts into this account on his behalf.

During a given year, an employee may enter into more than one salary reduction agreement. If elective deferrals are made to more than one 403(b) account for a given employee (irrespective of whether the contributions were made by the same employer) in the same year, then there must be a summary of all such elective deferrals to determine if the aggregate amount exceeds the employee's limit for that year, $19,500 for 2021. If elective deferrals are made to other retirement plans on behalf of the employee, then the limit on elective deferrals applies to the total, aggregate amount. Other accounts that are included in the aggregate total are 401(k) plans, SIMPLEs, SARSEPs, and all 403(b) plans.[24] If an amount contributed exceeds the limit, the employee must include the excess in gross income on his tax return for the year contributed.

Exhibit 10.8 | 403(b) Annual Elective Deferrals Limits*

Year	Annual Deferral Limit	Catch-Up Contributions **	Total Deferral
2021	$19,500	$6,500	$26,000

The same limits apply to SARSEPs, 401(k) plans, and 457 plans.
** Age 50 or older

The limit on elective deferrals for 2021 that can be contributed to a 403(b) account through a salary reduction agreement is $19,500. There are certain exceptions to the general limit of $19,500 for 2021 for contributions to 403(b) plans. Those age 50 and over, and those with at least 15 years of service to the employer can make additional, or catch-up, contributions.

Catch-Up Contributions

Age 50 Catch-Up Provisions

There are "catch-up" provisions for certain employees participating in a 403(b) plan. In addition to the contribution limits to a 403(b) plan, employees age 50 and over at the end of the year may make additional contributions under the catch-up provisions of IRC §403(b). An employee is eligible to make catch-up contributions if the employee has reached age 50 by the end of the year, and the maximum amount of elective deferrals that can be made to the employee's account have been satisfied for the year. If these two elements exist, then the total amount of "catch-up contributions" for the employee age 50 and over would be the lesser of $6,500 for 2021, or includible compensation (explained below) subtracted by other elective deferrals for the year. When determining what catch-up contributions are allowable under 403(b), all catch-up contributions made by the employer on behalf of the employee must be combined, and these amounts include contributions made to qualified retirement plans, 401(k) plans, 403(b) plans, SEPs, and SIMPLEs.

---

24. Also included are §501(c)(18) plans and trusts established prior to June 25, 1959.

"15-Year Rule" Exception

There is a special catch-up rule, in addition to the $6,500 catch-up for participants age 50 and over, that applies only for 403(b) plans for employees who have at least 15 years of service with a public school system, hospital, home health service agency, health and welfare service agency, church, or convention or association of churches (or associated organization).[25] Note that the 15 years of service are not required to be consecutive. If an employee has worked for 15 years with an organization that qualifies for eligibility under a 403(b) plan, then the limit of elective deferrals to the 403(b) account is increased by the lesser of the following:

- $3,000,
- $15,000, reduced by increases to the general limit that were allowed in previous years due to the **15-year rule**, or
- $5,000 times the number of years of service for the organization by the employee, reduced by the total elective deferrals made by the employer on behalf of the employee for earlier years [($5,000 x years of service) - total prior elective deferrals].

If an employee qualifies for the 15-year rule, the maximum elective deferrals for the 403(b) plan for the plan year may be as high as $29,000 for 2021 ($19,500 maximum deferral plus $3,000 from the 15-year rule plus $6,500 for the 50 and over catch-up rule).

Employee	Age	Years of Service	Maximum Deferral
A	25	2	$19,500
B	52	3	$26,000
C	52	16	$29,000

Roth Contributions (Roth Accounts)

403(b) plans, along with and 401(k) plans and 457(b) plans, may allow employees to make contributions to Roth accounts. These contributions are not excludable from the employee's gross income. Instead, these contributions will consist of after-tax dollars, just like contributions to Roth IRAs. Distributions attributable to these Roth contributions will be non-taxable and will not be subject to penalties if the distribution is a qualifying distribution. The qualifying distribution rules are discussed in Chapter 7 and are virtually the same as those for distributions from Roth IRAs as discussed in Chapter 9. Plans that establish Roth accounts are required to maintain separate accounts and maintain separate records for these Roth contributions and earnings allocable to the contributions.

These Roth contributions provide a great opportunity for employees to save for retirement. Although the contributions are not pre-tax, all qualifying distributions will be tax-free and penalty free. The contribution limit for Roth accounts in 2021 is $19,500, significantly higher than the limits for contributions to Roth IRAs. In addition, catch-up contributions can be directed to the Roth account, as well as the traditional account. Contributions to Roth IRAs are also limited based on annual income, but Roth accounts within 403(b) plans do not have such income limitations. Therefore, a highly compensated employee would be able to fund a Roth only through a Roth account, not a Roth IRA.

25. IRS Publication 571.

As discussed in Chapter 7, The Small Business Jobs Act (SBJA) of 2010 made several important changes to the Internal Revenue Code dealing with elective deferrals in Roth accounts. SBJA 2010 added IRC §402A(c)(4) to the Code to permit plans that include a qualified Roth contribution program to allow individuals to roll over amounts from their accounts to their designated Roth accounts in the plan.[26] This option, which can be accomplished as a direct rollover or as an indirect rollover, is akin to converting funds in a traditional IRA to a Roth IRA. In addition, SBJA 2010 permits governmental 457(b) plans to include designated Roth accounts for years after 2010.

An "in-plan Roth rollover" is a distribution from an individual's plan account, other than a designated Roth account, that is rolled over to the individual's designated Roth account in the same plan, pursuant to new IRC §402A(c)(4).[27] An in-plan Roth rollover is generally not considered a distribution from the plan, but will result in the individual being taxed on the amount of the rollover. The American Taxpayer Relief Act of 2012 expanded the amounts that are permitted to be rolled over in an in-plan Roth rollover.

> ### ✎ Quick Quiz 10.3
>
> 1. Employers or individuals can establish a 403(b) plan.
>   a. True
>   b. False
>
> 2. 403(b) plans may be covered under ERISA.
>   a. True
>   b. False
>
> 3. Additional catch-up contributions to a 403(b) plan may be after-tax contributions from the employee.
>   a. True
>   b. False
>
> False, True, False.

Employer Contributions

Nonelective contributions are matching contributions, mandatory contributions, or even discretionary contributions from the employer. Employer matching contributions are based on the employee's deferral, and the employer may make other contributions without regard to the employee's elective deferral. Unlike employee elective deferrals, nonelective contributions are not made under a salary reduction agreement. As discussed earlier, the nonelective employer contributions (other than salary reduction contributions) to the 403(b) account subject the plan to ERISA.

The Limit on Annual Additions

There is a limit on "annual additions" or amounts added to an account over the course of a year for an employee in a 403(b) plan to comply with IRC §415(c). The limitation applies to an aggregate of all contributions. The total contributions are comprised of elective deferrals, nonelective contributions, and after-tax contributions. The maximum for 2021 is the lesser of $58,000, or 100 percent of the employee's covered compensation for the employee's most recent year of service. If an employee contributed to more than one 403(b) account, all employer contributions to the accounts must be combined when determining if they exceed acceptable limits.

Includable Compensation for the Most Recent Year of Service

The definition of **includable compensation** for the most recent year of service is that amount of taxable wages and benefits that are received by the employee from the employer. When figuring includable compensation for the most recent year of service, it could be that the most recent year of service is not the same as the employer's most recent annual work period. In such a case, the most recent year of service is determined by calculating the previous full year of service for the employee's position.

---

26. Effective for distributions made after September 27, 2010.
27. After September 27, 2010.

A full year of service is equal to full time employment for the annual work period of the employer. For instance, if an employee worked the last four months of 2021 and the next nine months of 2022, then the most recent year of service would have been the first nine months of 2022 and the last three months of 2021, totaling the most previous 12-month period of work.

Once the most recent year of service has been identified, the next step is to quantify the includable compensation earned during that full year of service. Includable compensation is the total of income and benefits received from an employer maintaining a 403(b) account and the amount included in the income of the employee. The following amounts are considered as includible compensation:
- elective deferrals
- amounts contributed by an employer under a Cafeteria Plan
- amounts contributed under an eligible Section 457 nonqualified deferred compensation plan
- wages, salaries, and fees for personal services earned with the employer maintaining the 403(b) account
- income excluded under the Foreign Earned Income exclusion
- qualified transportation or fringe benefits

Meanwhile, the following items are not considered includible compensation:
- the employer's contributions to the employee's 403(b) account
- compensation earned while the employee was not eligible
- the employer's contributions to a qualified plan on behalf of the employee that are excluded from income
- the cost of incidental life insurance

Vesting

403(b) plans will often provide for full and immediate vesting on all amounts contributed to the plan. Employee contributions are always fully vested. However, employers that make contributions to a 403(b) plan must make a choice about whether to impose a vesting schedule or not. If the employer chooses to include vesting, it must be consistent with the requirements for 401(k) plans and other defined contribution plans. These vesting requirements permit an employer to choose between the 3-year cliff and the 2-6 graduated methods.

Final regulations under IRC §403(b) generally became effective January 1, 2009. One of the requirements of these regulations is that sponsors of 403(b) plans are required to maintain a written plan.

> ### Key Concepts
>
> 1. What are the available investment choices for 403(b) plans?
>
> 2. How are loans and distributions from a 403(b) plan taxed?
>
> 3. What rollover, distribution, and minimum distribution rules apply to 403(b) plans?

Investment Choices and Limitations

Funds within a 403(b) account can only be invested in either insurance annuity contracts or mutual funds. Specifically, individual accounts in 403(b) plans must be one of the following forms:
- A contract provided through an insurance company called an annuity contract;
- An account invested in mutual funds only, which is referred to as a custodial account; or
- An account for church employees that is a retirement income account, which invests in either annuities or mutual funds.

Annuity Contracts

"**Annuity contracts**" are not specifically defined in the Internal Revenue Code. An annuity contract must be purchased for the employee from an insurance company and may give a fixed benefit or a variable benefit depending on the performance of the investment.[28] Any contract or certificate that is transferable to a person other than a trustee is not an annuity contract.

CASE STUDY 10.2

In ***Corbin v. U.S.***,[1] the Court was faced with whether an annuity must be purchased from an insurance company in order to qualify for this special treatment. The United States Eighth Circuit Court of Appeals noted that the IRS had issued Revenue Ruling 82-102, 1982-1, C.B., revoking prior rulings that seemed to extend to non-insurance company-purchased annuities the special benefits of IRC §403(b)(1). The Court concluded that the wording of the statute using the word "premiums" indicated that the privilege is limited to annuities purchased from insurance companies.

---

1. *Corbin v. U.S.*, 760 F.2d 234, 6 Employee Benefits Cas. 1417 (8th Cir. 1985).

Loans

While in-service withdrawal distributions to employees are generally not permitted until retirement or termination, ERISA plans are permitted to make loans to plan participants. Non-ERISA 403(b) plans are also permitted to offer optional features, such as loans and hardship withdrawals, provided that the 403(b) annuity provider (rather than the employer) takes all responsibility for making discretionary determinations involving the transactions. Loans to 403(b) employee-participants are allowed and are subject to the same limitations and requirements applicable to loans from qualified retirement plans (e.g., 401(k) plan). Although any qualified plan may establish a loan provision, they are generally found only in 401(k) plans and 403(b) plans. As discussed fully in Chapter 7, plan loans must be made available to all participants and beneficiaries on an effectively equal basis, must be limited in amount, must be repaid within a certain time period, must bear a reasonable rate of interest, must be adequately secured, and the administrator must maintain proper accounting for the loans.

When an employee is terminated or if the TSA is terminated, then any outstanding loan will be affected. Loan repayments are generally accomplished through payroll deduction, which of course is unavailable after employee termination occurs. If an employee fails to repay a loan from a qualified plan upon termination, the employer will generally declare the unpaid portion a deemed distribution, which will be subject to ordinary income tax and possibly an early withdrawal penalty of 10 percent if under the age of 59½. However, plans may provide alternatives such as reducing the amount of a direct rollover distribution and providing the employee a certain period of time to repay the loan before it will be treated as a distribution.

---

28. Treasury Regulation §1.403(b)-1(c)(3).

Distributions

Because 403(b) plans fall within the ERISA plan area, they follow many of the same rules regarding distributions applicable to other qualified plans. Generally, distributions can be paid from a 403(b) account only after the following events:

- the employee turns age 59½,
- the employee is separated from service,
- the employee dies,
- the employee becomes disabled, or
- for salary reduction contributions, the employee endures a severe hardship.[29]

These restrictions apply only to contributions from salary reduction agreements. Nonelective deferral contributions have no such restrictions upon distribution. However, if distributions attributable to salary reduction contributions or nonelective deferrals occur before the employee turns 59½, then a 10 percent penalty for early withdrawal may apply. Under the CARES Act and TCDTRA of 2020, certain qualifying individuals are eligible to receive disaster-related distributions in 2020 and 2021 without penalty, with taxes paid over three years, and with the ability to repay the distribution within three years, as discussed in Chapter 7.

Hardship distributions are permitted in 403(b) plans. Therefore, the hardship rules discussed in Chapter 5 for CODAs can be used for guidance, with the exception that earnings attributed to elective deferrals in a 403(b) account are not available for hardship distributions, and QNEC and QMC contributions to custodial 403(b) accounts are not available for hardship distributions.[30] However, distributions of QNEC and QMC amounts are available for noncustodial 403(b) annuities. Hardship distributions from TSAs cannot be rolled over to an IRA and are not subject to the 20 percent income tax withholding rules as discussed in Chapter 7.

Rollovers to and from 403(b) Plans

Employee-participants can generally roll over tax-free all or any part of a distribution from a 403(b) plan to a qualified plan, a traditional IRA, or to another 403(b) retirement plan. Since January 1, 2008, 403(b) distributions may also be rolled into a Roth IRA.[31] Any rollover that is not a direct trustee-to-trustee rollover will be subject to mandatory 20 percent withholding and 100 percent of the distribution must be deposited into the new account by the 60th day following the day on which the employee receives the distribution.

---

29. IRC §403(b)(11).
30. The Bipartisan Budget Act of 2018, which expanded hardship distributions to include earnings, QNEC, and QMC contributions in 401(k) accounts, did not make the same amendments to 403(b) hardship distributions.
31. Pension Protection Act of 2006. See Chapter 9 for more detail.

Hardship Exception to Rollover Rules

The IRS may waive the 60-day rollover period if the participant's failure to waive such requirement would be against equity or good conscience, including cases of casualty, disaster, or other events beyond the reasonable control of the individual. To obtain a hardship exception, the participant must apply to the IRS for a waiver of the 60-day rollover requirement. In its determination as to the grant of a waiver, the IRS will consider all relevant facts and circumstances, including:

- whether errors were made by the financial institution facilitating the rollover,
- whether the participant was unable to complete the rollover due to death, disability, hospitalization, incarceration, restrictions imposed by a foreign country or postal error,
- whether the participant used the amount distributed, and
- the time passed since the date of distribution.

There are many exceptions granted by the IRS as a result of "errors" or poor advice or execution made at least in part by a financial institution. In these instances where there is an error, the IRS will waive or extend the 60-day rule.

Minimum Distribution Requirements

403(b) plans are subject to the same minimum distribution requirements applicable to IRAs and qualified plans, which require that an individual begin taking withdrawals from the plan by April 1st of the year after the participant attains the age of 70½ (age 72 if age 70½ is attained after December 31, 2019). These rules include the latest time that distributions from 403(b) plans may begin and the minimum amount that may be distributed from the 403(b) plan, which are similar to the rules for IRAs and for qualified retirement plans. For a more complete explanation of the minimum distribution requirements, see Chapter 7.

Excess Employer Contributions

If a distribution from a 403(b) plan consists of income that was previously included in income as an excess employer contribution, then that portion of the transfer is not eligible as a rollover distribution to an IRA. This transfer does not affect the rollover treatment of the eligible portion of the transferred amounts; however, the ineligible portion is subject to the traditional IRA contribution limits and may create an excess IRA contribution subject to a six percent excise tax. Chapter 9 discusses the traditional IRA contribution limits and the six percent excise tax.

Taxation of 403(b) Distributions

The tax rules that apply to 403(b) distributions are basically the same tax rules that apply to distributions from other qualified retirement plans and IRAs. In most instances, the distributions from 403(b) accounts received by participants are taxable as ordinary income in the year received; however, the employee-participant's return of adjusted basis is not subject to tax. This basis includes the employee's voluntary after-tax contributions, life insurance protection costs, employer contributions previously includible in the employee's income, and loans to the employee secured by the TSA that were deemed as taxable distributions.

Qualified Joint and Survivor Annuity

As discussed in Chapter 7, a **qualified joint and survivor annuity (QJSA)** is an immediate annuity for the life of the participant coupled with an annuity for the surviving spouse of the participant for the remainder of the spouse's life. The survivor annuity may not be less than 50 percent, nor more than 100 percent, of the payable amount of the annuity during the lifetime of the participant and spouse. While the IRC does not specifically provide that QJSA apply to 403(b) plans, ERISA will control whether the QJSA requirement is applicable to the 403(b) plan. Recall that ERISA will apply if the 403(b) plan is an employee benefit pension plan or provides employer contributions beyond salary deferrals. If ERISA does apply to the 403(b) plan, then the QJSA requirements will generally apply.

The Benefits of 403(b) Plans and Contributing to 403(b) Plans

There are some significant benefits to making employee elective deferral contributions to 403(b) plans. First, the employee does not pay income taxes on the contributions to the plan. This, of course, does not apply to any after-tax contribution but does apply to the elective deferral and the nonelective contributions from the employer. The employee only pays taxes on allowable contributions once withdrawals from the plan are taken. Second, earnings and gains on the amounts placed in a 403(b) account are not subjected to income tax until withdrawn by the employee. Third, the benefits are similar to those in 401(k) plans (as discussed in Chapter 5) and other retirement vehicles because the employees have tax-deferred benefits of growth over time, along with a vehicle where an employer may match benefits and may provide for other incidental contributions for an employee's benefit.

Similarities and Differences Between 401(k) Plans and 403(b) Plans

403(b) plans for nonprofit organizations are similar to the 401(k) plans used by for-profit businesses. Like 401(k) plans, 403(b) plans allow employees to defer a portion of their salary. The funds accumulate and grow over time and are not subjected to income taxation by federal or state governments until distributed to the employee.

The tax advantages associated with 401(k) qualified defined-contribution plans are the same as those for 403(b) plans, namely that allowable contributions and the earnings of these contributions are not subject to federal income taxation until withdrawn. The amount of contributions to 401(k) plans and to 403(b) plans may consist of employee elective deferrals, employer contributions, and after-tax employee contributions. 403(b) plans may provide for employer matching contributions, much like 401(k) plans. Participants in 403(b) plans have the same contribution limits each year as 401(k) plan participants, and the early withdrawal rules are basically the same for both types of plans.

> ### ☑ *Quick Quiz 10.4*
>
> 1. For 403(b) plans the "most recent year of service" is always based on a calendar year of service.
>   a. True
>   b. False
>
> 2. Funds within a 403(b) plan may only be invested in either annuity contracts or mutual funds.
>   a. True
>   b. False
>
> 3. 403(b) plans generally provide for 100% immediate vesting of contributions.
>   a. True
>   b. False
>
> False, True, True

Obviously, there are differences between the two types of plans. However, with the changes to the Code over the last twenty years, the differences between 401(k) plans and 403(b) plans are rather limited. Some of the differences are investment choices and the additional catch-up rules for 403(b) plans.

Exhibit 10.9 | Concept Summary - 403(b) Plans

Application	Not-For-Profit institution (large universities)
Style	Self reliance plans; employee only contributions
Subject to ERISA	Maybe (if organized as a qualified plan)
Established By What Date	End of year
Characteristics	Self-reliant savings plan
Elective Deferral Contribution Limit	$19,500 + $6,500 catch-up contribution (2021)
Available Contribution	$58,000 for 2021 or 100% of compensation including elective deferrals
Additional After-Tax Contributions Permitted	Permissible by plan document
Investment Risk	Employee has investment choices and risks
Investment Alternatives	Limited to Insurance Annuities and Mutual Funds
Penalties	10% early withdrawal (if applicable)
Loans Permitted	Yes (regular qualified plan rules on loans if plan permits)
Rollovers	Yes, to IRA, qualified plan, or other 403(b)*
ERISA Protected	Yes, if ERISA plan. ERISA not applicable if governmental or church TSA.
In-Service Withdrawals	Generally no, except hardships, which are plan specific
Vesting	100% for all employee contributions. Employer contributions may be subject to standard vesting (post PPA 2006).

* Rollovers to Roth IRAs are permitted after December 31, 2007.

457 PLANS

Under §457 of the Internal Revenue Code, employees of state and local governments and of nongovernmental tax-exempt entities may participate in tax-free deferred compensation plans to aid employees in saving for retirement. Employee elective deferrals into a **457 plan** do not count against deferrals into 401(k) or 403(b) plans.

☰ *Key Concepts*

1. What are 457 plans and which entities may establish them?

2. To what extent is ERISA applicable to 457 plans?

3. Who is eligible to establish a 457 plan?

4. What are the applicable rules for employee contributions to 457 plans?

Definition of a 457 Plan

Section 457 of the Internal Revenue Code allows employees of state and local governments and employees of tax-exempt nongovernmental entities to save tax-deferred compensation for retirement. 457 plans work in many ways like 401(k) and 403(b) plans. Employees contribute a portion of their salary through a payroll reduction. The annual amount that an employee may contribute is limited (except for ineligible 457(f) plans explained below), and employee elective deferral contributions are not includible in an employee's gross income in the year earned but are deferred until paid out or made available to the employee. 457 plans are not "qualified plans" and, thus, are not subject to many of the eligibility standards of IRC 401(a), including such requirements as nondiscrimination, minimum participation, and funding and vesting standards. A 457 plan is a "nonqualified" deferred compensation plan.[32]

---

32. *Rheal v. Commissioner*, T.C. Memo 1989 - 525.

There are three types of 457 plans: (1) eligible governmental plans under IRC §457(b), (2) eligible tax-exempt plans under IRC §457(b), and (3) "ineligible plans" under IRC §457(f). **Exhibit 10.10** illustrates how these three types of 457 plans are related.

Exhibit 10.10 | Relationship Between 457 Plans

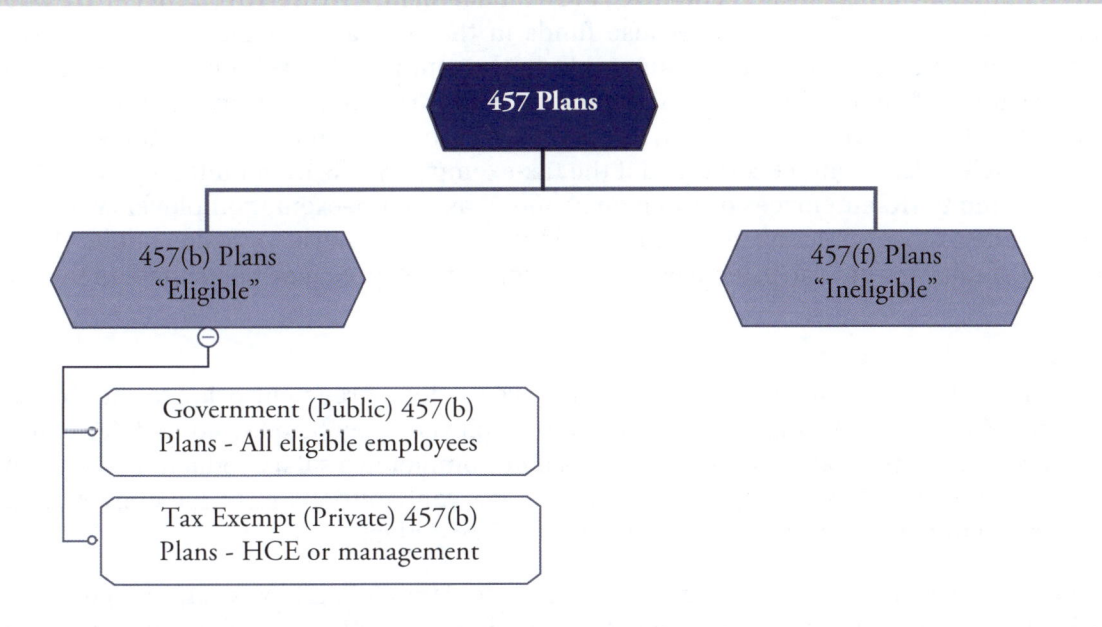

Plans that are "eligible" under **457(b)** allow employees of sponsoring organizations to defer income taxation on savings for retirement into future years. Plans that are "ineligible," found under §**457(f)**, may trigger different tax treatment under §457(f). The main distinction between eligible plans (457(b) plans) and ineligible plans (457(f) plans) is that ineligible plans provide for greater deferral of funds. Most of this section on 457 plans will address rules applicable to 457(b) plans. Ineligible plans and their differences compared to 457(b) plans will be addressed later in the chapter.

Entities That Can Establish 457(b) Plans

457(b) plans may only be formed and maintained by employers that are "eligible" as defined under §457.[33] The term eligible employer is defined as a State, a political subdivision of a State, or any agency or instrumentality of a State or political subdivision of a State, and any other organization other than a governmental unit that is exempt from tax.[34] These tax-exempt organizations include trade associations, religious organizations, private hospitals, rural electric cooperatives, farmers' cooperatives, private schools and foundations, labor unions, and charitable organizations. Churches[35] and qualified church-controlled organizations[36] are not considered eligible employers under §457.[37]

---

33. IRC §457(e)(1).
34. IRC §457(e)(1)(A)(B).
35. IRC §3121(w)(3)(A).
36. IRC §3121(w)(3)(B).
37. Note that while churches and qualified church-controlled organizations may not establish 457 plans, tax-exempt church-related entities such as schools and hospitals may still be eligible employers for 457 plans.

ERISA Applicability

457(b) plans sponsored by governmental employers are also called "public 457(b) plans." 457(b) plans for tax-exempt employers are called "private 457(b) plans." Public 457(b) plans are required to be funded through a trust holding all assets and income for the exclusive benefit of plan participants and their beneficiaries.[38] Under private 457(b) plans for tax-exempt employers, ERISA limits participation to a select group of highly compensated employees or management. Private 457(b) plans are offered only to HC employees or top management because funds in the plan are not placed in trust. The private 457(b) plan is "unfunded" and remains vulnerable to the employer's creditors. This poses a potential conflict between ERISA and §457. As a general matter, ERISA requires that private retirement plans be funded through a trust or annuity contract, yet private 457(b) plans must not be funded to receive tax benefits. Nonetheless, this conflict is avoided if the tax-exempt organization under a private 457(b) plan limits participation to HC employees or top management, as the tax-exempt employer would be exempt from ERISA under those circumstances. An employer does not have to make public 457(b) plans available to all employees but can selectively choose which employees may participate in the plan.

Eligibility

Participants in 457(b) plans must enter into a salary reduction agreement prior to the first day of the month in which compensation will be deferred. New employees may be allowed to defer compensation during the calendar month that the employee starts if he completed a salary reduction agreement before his first day of work. A 457 plan may not accept after-tax contributions from the employee, except for contributions to a Roth account under a governmental 457(b) plan.

Contributions made by the employer are generally not vested immediately. Vesting with eligible plans can create problems with the annual limits. However, for ineligible 457(f) plans, the employer agrees to pay the participant a certain amount of money after a specified period of employment, at which time the employee is no longer at "substantial risk of forfeiture" of the funds (discussed below).

Employee Contributions

Limits

457(b) plans generally operate with employees deferring compensation on a pre-tax basis through salary reduction agreements with their employer. However, as a result of The Small Business Jobs Act (SBJA) of 2010, governmental 457(b) plans can establish Roth accounts. The deferral amount, instead of being paid as income to the employee, is paid directly to the 457 plan. The annual amount deferred by an employee for an eligible 457(b) plan must not exceed the lesser of 100 percent of the employee's compensation or of the applicable dollar limit for the given calendar year. Stated differently, employees are able to contribute up to the lesser of the following amounts:
- the employee elective deferral of $19,500 for 2021, or
- up to 100 percent of includible compensation, but this amount must be less than the employee elective deferral limit.

---

38. IRC §457(g).

Age 50 Catch-Up Contributions for Governmental 457(b) Plans

Section 457(b) permits governmental entities to allow for catch-up contributions for employees age 50 and over. Employees age 50 or over may contribute an additional $6,500 above the elective deferral limit of $19,500 for 2021. Thereafter, the catch-up amount will be increased for cost-of-living adjustments in increments of $500. This catch-up benefit is available only for eligible governmental (public) 457(b) plans.[39] The age 50 catch-up is not available to employees of eligible tax-exempt (private) 457(b) plans.

Exhibit 10.11 | Applicable Elective Deferral Limits and Catch-Up Amounts

Year	Employee Elective Deferral Limit	Catch-Up Amounts (Age 50 or Over)
2021	$19,500	$6,500

Special "Final 3-Year" Additional Catch-Up Provision

457(b) plans may also have a special catch-up option that is termed the **"final 3-year" catch-up provision**. It applies to both public and private 457(b) plans. It is designed for employees approaching retirement that have not contributed the maximum amount to a 457 plan in previous years. It effectively doubles the employee deferral limit of IRC §402(g), but is limited to prior year employee deferrals not taken. It allows these employees to make up for previously missed contributions as follows: Three years prior to normal retirement age (as defined by the plan) an employee may contribute an additional amount equal to the elective deferral limit, which for 2021 is $19,500 ($18,000 for 2015 - 2107, $18,500 for 2018, $19,000 for 2019, and $19,500 for 2020). Thus, an employee with adequate compensation could defer $19,500 under the regular deferral limitation and $19,500 as catch-up for a total of $39,000 in 2021. The limits are listed as follows:

Exhibit 10.12 | Maximum Employee Elective Deferral Limits with the "Final 3-Year" Catch-Up

Year	Normal Deferral	Catch-up Deferral	Total Annual Deferral in the Final 3-Years
2021	$19,500	$19,500	$39,000

This "final 3-year" catch-up option is further limited to prior unused maximum deferral amounts.

Example 10.7

Robby has worked for New York City for the last 20 years. His normal retirement age, as defined under New York City's 457(b) plan, will be at the end of 2021. Robby has a prior unused maximum deferral amount of $39,000 as of December 31, 2018. How much can Robby contribute as his final three-year catch-up contributions and when?

Robby can contribute "final 3-year" catch-up contributions of up to $19,000 in 2019, up to $19,500 in 2020, and up to $500 in 2021. He is limited to $500 in 2021 because his prior unused maximum deferral amount of $39,000 has been exhausted ($39,000 - $19,000 - $19,500 - $500 = 0). Notice, during the three years prior to his normal retirement age, Robby could also defer up to the regular elective deferral contribution limits.

---

39. IRC §414(v).

Employers that sponsor 457 plans are not required to offer the "final 3-year" catch-up option. Furthermore, participants who utilize the "final 3-year" catch-up cannot simultaneously use the age 50 or older catch-up provisions. When the participant is eligible for both the final 3-year catch-up and the age 50 catch-up, the maximum deferral is the based on the greater of the two amounts.

Example 10.8

Assume that Robby, in **Example 10.7**, is age 50 or older. His catch-up contributions for 2019 and 2020 are $19,000 and $19,500, respectively. For 2021 he can take the greater of (1) the final 3-year catch-up, which is limited to $500, or (2) the age 50 catch-up, which is $$6,500. In 2021 he will use the age 50 catch-up of $$6,500.

The final 3-year catch-up provision is limited to the prior unused deferrals and cannot be combined with the age 50 or older catch-up provision. In the case in which a participant cannot make use of the 3-year catch up provision, the age 50 option is still available. A participant age 50 or older who has always contributed the annual maximum will not be eligible for the final 3-year catch-up, but is permitted the age 50 catch-up (the age 50 catch-up is, fundamentally, an additional contribution limit, rather than a true "catch-up").

Normal Retirement Age

A governmental Sec. 457(b) plan's normal retirement age may, in some cases, be earlier than the normal retirement age permitted for qualified plans. In general, a Sec. 457 plan may define normal retirement age as the earlier of 1) age 65, or 2) the age at which participants have the right to receive benefits under the employer's basic defined benefit plan (or money purchase plan if the employer does not offer a defined benefit plan) without an actuarial reduction because of retirement before a specified age; but no later than age 70½.[40] Alternatively, the 457 plan may provide that a participant is permitted to designate a normal retirement age within these ages.[41]

A special rule is available for eligible plans of qualified police or firefighters (defined under § 415(b)(2)(H)(ii)(I) of the Code). These plans may designate a normal retirement age that is earlier than the general rule, but no earlier than age 40.

Employer Contributions

As with other retirement plans, an employer may make matching contributions or nonelective deferrals into the 457 plan. Interestingly, the 457(b) contribution limit of $19,500 for 2021 includes both employee contributions and employer

Quick Quiz 10.5

1. Churches may establish 457 plans.
   a. True
   b. False

2. A 457 plan may accept after-tax contributions from employees.
   a. True
   b. False

3. The 457 deferral limit for 2021 is $19,500.
   a. True
   b. False

4. 457 plans have a special final three year catch-up provision that allows employees to contribute up to 100% of their compensation in the last three years.
   a. True
   b. False

False, False, True, False.

---

40. At the time of printing, the IRS had not yet provided guidance on whether the maximum age will be amended to age 72 to conform with the SECURE Act increase in age for required minimum distributions.
41. Rev. Proc. 04-56

matching contributions. This is a significant difference between 457(b) plans and 401(k) or 403(b) plans. As a result, matching contributions by employers in 457 plans are very infrequent compared to those for 401(k) or 403(b) plans. Many 457 plans do not offer a matching contribution at all.

No Integration with Other Salary Deferral Plans

A vital and substantial benefit of contributing to a 457 plan is that the contributions to the 457 plan are not aggregated or combined with contributions to other tax-deferred retirement plans. An employee may contribute the maximum amount to a 401(k) plan, 403(b) plan, SARSEP, or SIMPLE IRA, in addition to the deferral limits for 457(b)s. This means that an employee could contribute up to $19,500 for 2021 to a 457(b) plan and up to $19,500 for 2021 to another 403(b) or 401(k) plan if available. Beginning in 2002, the law separated the 457(b) deferral limit from the limit on other retirement plans, resulting in a boost in popularity of the 457 plan. Deferrals to the 457 plan of one employer are, however, aggregated with deferrals to the 457 plan of a different employer to determine the maximum annual contribution ($19,500 in 2021) to a 457 plan for any individual.

Exhibit 10.13 | Summary of Contribution Limits

Year	457 Contribution	403(b)/401(k)/ SARSEP Contribution	Aggregate Total for the Year
2021	$19,500	$19,500	$39,000

Example 10.9

Mike, age 35, works for the State of California and earns a salary of $50,000. The State of California offers a 403(b) and a 457(b) plan to its employees. What is the maximum amount that Mike can defer into both plans in 2021? The answer is $39,000, $19,500 into the 457(b) plan and another $19,500 into the 403(b) plan.

Example 10.10

Kathryn, age 64, works for Florida Atlantic University, which offers a 403(b) plan and a 457 plan. Kathryn could defer the following amounts:
- $19,500 as salary deferral into the 403(b) plan
- $19,500 as salary deferral into the 457(b) plan
- $6,500 as a catch-up contribution into the 403(b) plan
- $6,500 as a catch-up contribution into the 457(b) plan

In addition, she could potentially defer up to $3,000 more into the 403(b) plan if she met the requirements and could double her deferral into the 457(b) plan in lieu of the age 50 catch-up contribution if she had prior unused deferral amounts.

Distributions

Generally, amounts deferred under an eligible 457 plan may not be paid to a participant or beneficiary before the participant terminates employment with the eligible employer or when the participant attains the age of 70½ (age 72 if age 70½ is attained after December 31, 2019), if earlier. However, there are certain exceptions for loans and distributions resulting from unforeseeable emergencies. These exceptions are discussed below.

Distributions from 457 plans are generally treated in the same manner as distributions from qualified plans or IRAs. These distributions are taxed as ordinary income in the year they are received, or in the case of a private 457 plan, at the earlier of when the funds are received or when the funds are made available to the participant. The exceptions to ordinary income treatment that are available to distributions from qualified plans are not available to distributions from 457 plans.

Under the CARES Act and TCDTRA of 2020, certain qualifying individuals are eligible to receive disaster-related distributions in 2020 and 2021 without penalty, with taxes paid over three years, and with the ability to repay the distribution within three years, as discussed in Chapter 7.

Loans

Loans may be permitted from public 457(b) plans, but not private 457(b) plans. Loans from public eligible plans must follow the rules under IRC Section 72, which were discussed in Chapter 7. If a participant or beneficiary receives (directly or indirectly) any amount deferred as a loan from an eligible plan of a tax-exempt entity, that amount will be treated as having been paid or made available to the individual as a distribution under the plan.

Example 10.11

The State of Georgia sponsors an eligible 457 plan, Plan X, which permits an employee's account balance to be paid in a single sum at severance from employment with the State of Georgia. Plan X includes a loan program under which any active employee with a vested account balance may receive a loan. Loans are made pursuant to plan provisions regarding loans that are set forth in the plan under which loans bear a reasonable rate of interest and are secured by the employee's account balance. The Plan X loan rules limit the amount of loans and require loans to be repaid in level installments as required under IRC section 72(p)(2).

Jacques' vested account balance under Plan X is $50,000. Jacques receives a loan from the plan in the amount of $5,000 on December 1, Year 1, to be repaid in level installments made quarterly over the 5-year period ending on November 30, Year 5. Jacques makes the required repayments until he terminates employment in Year 3 and subsequently fails to repay the outstanding loan balance of $2,250. The $2,250 loan balance is offset against Jacques' $80,000 account balance benefit under Plan X, and Jacques elects to be paid the remaining $77,750 in Year 3.

The making of the loan to Jacques is not treated as a violation of the requirements of section 457(b) or the regulations. The cancellation of the loan at severance from employment does not cause Plan X to fail to satisfy the requirements for plan eligibility under section 457. In addition, because the loan satisfies the maximum amount and repayment requirements of section 72(p)(2), Jacques is not required to include any amount in income as a result of the loan until Year 3, when he has income of $2,250 as a result of the offset (which is a permissible distribution under this section) and income of $77,750 as a result of the distribution made in Year 3.[42]

Unforeseeable Emergency[43]

An eligible plan may permit a distribution to a participant or beneficiary for an unforeseeable emergency. An unforeseeable emergency must be defined in the plan as a severe financial hardship of the participant or beneficiary resulting from one of the following:

- An illness or accident of the participant or beneficiary, the participant's or beneficiary's spouse, or the participant's or beneficiary's dependent;
- A loss of the participant's or beneficiary's property due to casualty (including the need to rebuild a home following damage to a home not otherwise covered by homeowner's insurance, such as damage that is the result of a natural disaster);
- Other similar extraordinary and unforeseeable circumstances arising from events beyond the control of the participant or the beneficiary. For example, the imminent foreclosure of or eviction from the participant's or beneficiary's primary residence may constitute an unforeseeable emergency.
- The need to pay for medical expenses, including non-refundable deductibles, as well as for the cost of prescription drug medication, may constitute an unforeseeable emergency.
- The need to pay for the funeral expenses of a spouse or a dependent of a participant or beneficiary may also constitute an unforeseeable emergency.

Whether a participant or beneficiary is faced with an unforeseeable emergency permitting a distribution under this exception is determined based on the relevant facts and circumstances of each case, but, in any case, a distribution on account of an unforeseeable emergency may not be made to the extent that such emergency is or may be relieved through reimbursement or compensation from insurance or otherwise, by liquidation of the participant's assets, to the extent the liquidation of such assets would not itself cause severe financial hardship, or by cessation of deferrals under the plan.

Distributions because of an unforeseeable emergency must be limited to the amount reasonably necessary to satisfy the emergency need (which may include any amounts necessary to pay for any federal, state, or local income taxes or penalties reasonably anticipated to result from the distribution). The purchase of a home and the payment of college tuition are not unforeseeable emergencies under this paragraph.

10% Early Withdrawal Penalty

The early withdrawal penalty applies when a taxpayer receives any amount from a qualified retirement plan, which includes qualified plans, annuity plans, and IRA accounts (which include SIMPLEs and SEPs). Distributions from either eligible or ineligible 457 plans are generally not subject to the early

---

42. Treas. Reg. §1.457-6.
43. Treas. Reg. §1.457-6.

withdrawal penalty. An exception to this rule applies when a distribution or part of a distribution is attributable to a rollover contribution to a governmental 457(b) plan from another retirement plan that is subject to the early withdrawal penalty, and the distribution does not qualify for one of the exceptions to the penalty.

Minimum Distribution Rules

Eligible 457 plans must meet the same minimum distribution rules as qualified plans, which are found under IRC Section 401(a)(9). These rules require that the participant generally begin taking distributions from the plan by age 70½ (age 72 if age 70½ is attained after December 31, 2019).

Rollovers

The rules for rollovers from 457(b) plans are the same as those that apply to rollovers from qualified plans. The important distinction is whether the 457 plan is a public (governmental) 457(b) plan. Public 457(b) plans allow funds to be rolled over into a new employer's 403(b), 401(k), or 457(b) plan if that plan accepts such transfers. Otherwise, the assets can be rolled into an IRA. However, 457(b) plans for nongovernmental tax-exempt entities may allow funds only to be rolled over from the 457(b) plan into another tax-exempt organization's 457(b) plan if the plan accepts such transfers. However, these funds cannot be rolled into an IRA or any another type of employer-sponsored retirement plan.

The absence of an early withdrawal penalty for a governmental Sec. 457 plan distribution is an important consideration when the taxpayer is contemplating a rollover of a 457 plan to an IRA or qualified plan. If the participant is under age 59½, a rollover is generally not advisable since doing so will subject the assets to an early withdrawal penalty which would have been avoided had the assets remained in the 457 plan.

Certain types of employees should also use caution when considering a rollover from a 457 plan to an IRA. Retired (by reason of attainment of normal retirement age or disability) public safety employees who are employees of states and political subdivisions such as counties and cities (e.g., law enforcement officers, firefighters, chaplain, rescue squad, ambulance crew) can apply distributions from eligible governmental plans to the purchase of qualified health or long-term care insurance and exclude such distributions from gross income (up to $3,000 per year in aggregate for all eligible plans).[44] Payment must be directly from the governmental plan to the insurer, so rolling to an IRA will eliminate the ability to take advantage of this tax-saving opportunity.

Benefits and Disadvantages of a Section 457 Plans

Pre-tax deferrals into a 457 plan reduce current taxable income. They allow the participant to save on a tax-deferred basis for retirement. The contributions and earnings are able to grow tax deferred. The participant has the ability to contribute to a 457(b) plan, in addition to a 403(b) or a 401(k) plan, depending on whether or not it is offered by the employer. The 457(b) plan also provides "portability" for the participant. Offering portability allows the employee-participant to rollover savings to another public sector employer's 457 plan, if applicable. In other words, a public 457(b) plan may rollover funds into a new employer's 457(b) plan, or even a 401(k) or 403(b) plan, if the plan accepts such transfers. Such funds can also be rolled into an IRA.

---

44. IRC §402(l).

In addition, as a result of The Small Business Jobs Act (SBJA) of 2010, governmental 457(b) plans can establish Roth accounts that permit employees to save on an after-tax basis with qualifying distributions being free of tax and penalties. The SBJA also provides for in-plan Roth rollovers, which are discussed in detail in Chapter 7.

One significant drawback to a non-governmental tax-exempt organization offering a 457 plan is that there is a lack of creditor protection concerning the plan assets. A public 457(b) plan for governmental entities requires funds to be placed in a trust for the exclusive benefit of the participant and beneficiaries. However, there is no such requirement for private 457(b) plans for non-governmental, tax-exempt organizations, and therefore private 457(b) plan assets are available to the employer's creditors and the employee may lose access to the funds. This is one very important distinction that should be considered in the financial planning process.

Section 457(f) "Ineligible" Plans

Ineligible plans, under IRC §457(f), are nonqualified deferred compensation plans for state and local governmental employers and for tax-exempt employers. These ineligible plans are also called "top-hat" plans. Only highly compensated employees or top management may participate in a 457(f) plan. Ineligible plans are those plans under §457 that fail to meet one or more requirements of the "eligible plan." 457(f) plans are frequently intentionally ineligible while some are unintentionally ineligible. With ineligible plans under 457(f), there is no limit on the amount of deferral because 457(f) plans are effectively deferred compensation plans.

However, the amounts contributed to 457(f) plans are subject to a "substantial risk of forfeiture." This means that the participant is considered to be a general unsecured creditor of the plan sponsor or employer. The substantial risk of forfeiture is conditioned upon (1) the unsecured status of the employee, and (2) the employee's future performance of substantial services for the employer. The employer agrees to pay the participant a certain amount of money after a specified period of employment, at which time the employee is no longer at "substantial risk of forfeiture" of the funds.

Taxation of funds in an ineligible plan occurs when there is no risk of forfeiture. Amounts may therefore be taxable prior to the actual payment or distribution to the participant. The amounts that are taxable prior to actual payment are included in the gross income of the participant in the first year that the deferral amount is not subject to a substantial risk of forfeiture. The typical deferred compensation arrangement for ineligible 457(f) plans is for presidents, CEOs, and coaches.

Example 10.12

In 2021, X, a tax-exempt entity, agrees to pay deferred compensation to employee D. The amount payable is $100,000 to be paid 10 years later in 2031. The commitment to make the $100,000 payment is not subject to a substantial risk of forfeiture. In 2021, the present value of the $100,000 is $50,000. In 2031, X pays D the $100,000 that is due.

In this example, D has income of $50,000 in 2021.[45] In 2031, D has income of $50,000, the remaining income from the 2021 commitment. If there was a substantial risk of forfeiture, then there is no tax consequence until the payment is made in 2031.

45.Treas. Reg. §1.457-11.

Disadvantages to 457(f) Plans

If the participant terminates employment before the stated payment period, the participant may forfeit all of the 457(f) plan funds. Also, because the funds in the plan remain the employer's property until vested, the employee-participant may lose all the 457(f) account and the funds if the employer goes bankrupt. Also, even though a distribution may not occur, the participant may be taxed on the value of the plan once the funds vest in the participant or are no longer subject to substantial risk of forfeiture.

457(f) plans essentially provide special benefits to executives or individuals that companies or universities want to retain. For instance, in the highly competitive world of college sports, many schools with winning coaches desire to provide such coaches with an incentive to stay through use of 457(f) plans. The college is able to contribute any amount, as there are no limits. As the assets are retained by the employer until paid to the employee, the 457(f) plan creates a tax shelter for the executive or coach. It is protected from claims against the executive or coach, but not from the creditors of the organization.

In conclusion, 457 plans allow employees of tax-exempt organizations and of governments to defer compensation into retirement savings plans. Public 457(b) plans hold funds in trust and are available to all employees while private 457(b) plans are not funded and are available only to high compensated employees or upper management. Salary deferrals into 457(b) plans are not aggregated or combined with salary deferrals to other retirement plans such as 401(k) and 403(b) plans. 457(f) plans are ineligible but allow for an unlimited amount of contributions to the plan. Nonetheless, the participant's funds in a 457(f) plan are subject to a substantial risk of forfeiture.

Exhibit 10.14 | 457 Plan Comparison

	Public 457(b) Plans	Private 457(b) Plans	457(f) Plans
Eligible/Ineligible	Eligible	Eligible	Ineligible
Employer/Sponsors	Governmental Entities	Tax-Exempt Organizations under 501(c)	Governmental Entities (Rare) & Tax-Exempt Entities under 501(c)
Assets in Plan	Protected by Trust	Not Protected by Trust; Available to Employer's Creditors	Not Protected by Trust; Available to Employer's Creditors
Elective Deferral Contribution Limits	2021 - $19,500	2021 - $19,500	No Limit
Loans	May be permitted	Not Available	Not Available
Employees that Participate	Rank and File Employees and Key Management	Key Management and HCs for Tax Exempt Organizations; All Employees if Church-Related Organization	Key Management and HCs
Pre-tax Contribution	Yes	Yes	Yes
Roth Account Contributions	Yes	No	No
Funds Grow Tax Deferred	Yes	Yes	Yes
Age 50 and Over Catch-Up Provisions	Yes	No	No
3-Year Catch-Up Provisions	Yes 2021 - $19,500	Yes 2021 - $19,500	No
Rollovers	Permitted to 401(k), 403(b), 457(b), or IRA plans*	Not Permitted Unless Rolled Into Another 457(b)	Not Permitted
In-Plan Roth Rollover	Yes	N/A - No Roth Accounts	N/A - No Roth Accounts
10% Penalty for Early Withdrawal	No, except for distributions attributable to rollovers from another type of plan or IRA	Not Applicable	Not Applicable

Rollovers to Roth IRAs are permitted after December 31, 2007.

DISCUSSION QUESTIONS

SOLUTIONS to the discussion questions can be found exclusively within the chapter. Once you have completed an initial reading of the chapter, go back and highlight the answers to these questions.

1. Describe SIMPLE plans.

2. List and define the different types of SIMPLE plans.

3. What are the rules for establishing a SIMPLE plan?

4. Identify the characteristics of SIMPLE IRAs.

5. Identify the characteristics of SIMPLE 401(k) plans.

6. Describe 403(b) plans.

7. When does ERISA apply to a 403(b) plan?

8. Who is eligible to establish a 403(b) plan?

9. What are the applicable rules regarding employee contributions to 403(b) plans?

10. What are the applicable rules regarding employer contributions to 403(b) plans?

11. What investment options are available for 403(b) plans?

12. How are distributions from 403(b) plans taxed?

13. What are the rollover, distribution, and minimum distribution rules applicable to 403(b) plans?

14. What are 457 plans and what entities may establish them?

15. Who is eligible to establish a 457 plan?

16. What are the applicable rules regarding employee contributions to 457 plans?

17. What are the applicable rules regarding employer contributions to 457 plans?

18. How does a participant's salary deferral to a 457 plan affect his contributions to a qualified plan?

19. How are distributions from a 457 plan taxed?

20. What are the benefits and disadvantages of a 457 plan?

21. What are §457(f) plans and how are the distributions taxed?

MULTIPLE CHOICE PROBLEMS

A sample of multiple choice problems is provided below. Additional multiple choice problems are available at money-education.com by accessing the Student Practice Portal.

1. Monique, age 42, earns $300,000 annually as an employee for CTM, Inc. Her employer sponsors a SIMPLE retirement plan and matches all employee contributions made to the plan dollar-for-dollar up to 3% of compensation. What is the maximum contribution (employer and employee) that can be made to Monique's SIMPLE account in 2021?
    a. $22,050.
    b. $22,500.
    c. $25,500.
    d. $27,000.

2. Which of the following is/are correct regarding SIMPLE plans?
    1. A SIMPLE plan does not require annual testing.
    2. A SIMPLE IRA must follow a 3-year cliff vesting schedule if the plan is top-heavy.
    3. A 25% early withdrawal penalty may apply to distributions taken within the first two years of participation in a SIMPLE plan.
    4. The maximum elective deferral contribution to a SIMPLE 401(k) plan is $19,500 for 2021 and $26,000 for 2021 for an employee who has attained the age of 50.
    a. 3 only.
    b. 1 and 3.
    c. 1, 2, and 3.
    d. 2, 3, and 4.

3. All of the following statements is/are correct regarding tax-sheltered annuities (403(b) plans) except?
    1. The non-age-based catch-up provision is available to employees of all 501(c)(3) organization employers that sponsor a TSA.
    2. Active employees who take withdrawals from TSAs prior to 59½ are subject to a 10% penalty tax.
    3. TSAs are available to all employees of 501(c)(3) organizations who adopt such a plan.
    4. If an employee has had at least 15 years of service with an eligible employer, an additional catch-up contribution may be allowed.
    a. 1 only.
    b. 1 and 2.
    c. 1, 2, and 3.
    d. 2, 3, and 4.

4. Which of the following statements is/are correct regarding TSAs and 457(b) deferred compensation plans?

   1. Both plans require contracts between an employer and an employee.
   2. Participation in either a TSA or a 457 plan will cause an individual to be considered an "active participant" for purposes of phasing out the deductibility of Traditional IRA contributions.
   3. Both plans allow a special "final 3-year" catch-up contribution.
   4. Both plans must meet minimum distribution requirements that apply to qualified plans.

      a. 1 only.
      b. 1 and 4.
      c. 2, 3, and 4.
      d. 1, 2, and 4.

5. Rex works for New Orleans Museum of Art, which sponsors a 403(b) plan. If Rex is 45 years old and has worked at the museum for the last 20 years, what is his maximum elective deferral for 2021?

      a. $19,500.
      b. $22,500.
      c. $26,000.
      d. $29,000.

> **Additional multiple choice problems**
> **are available at**
> **money-education.com**
> **by accessing the**
> **Student Practice Portal.**
> **Access requires registration of the title using**
> **the unique code at the front of the book.**

QUICK QUIZ EXPLANATIONS

Quick Quiz 10.1
1. False. SIMPLE plans may only operate on a calendar year basis.
2. True.
3. True.

Quick Quiz 10.2
1. True.
2. True.
3. False. An employer may, but is not required to, allow for catch-up contributions for participants age 50 and older.

Quick Quiz 10.3
1. False. Only employers may establish 403(b) plans. Individuals may not establish 403(b) plans.
2. True.
3. False. Catch-up contributions may not be made with employee after-tax contributions.

Quick Quiz 10.4
1. False. The most recent year of service is not necessarily equal to a calendar year.
2. True.
3. True.

Quick Quiz 10.5
1. False. Churches may not establish 457 plans.
2. False. After-tax contributions to 457 plans are not permitted.
3. True.
4. False. The final three year catch-up provision essentially allows participants to double their contributions in the last three years, but is limited by the deferrals not taken in prior years.

Quick Quiz 10.6
1. False. The 457 contribution limit includes both employee contributions and employer matching contributions.
2. True.

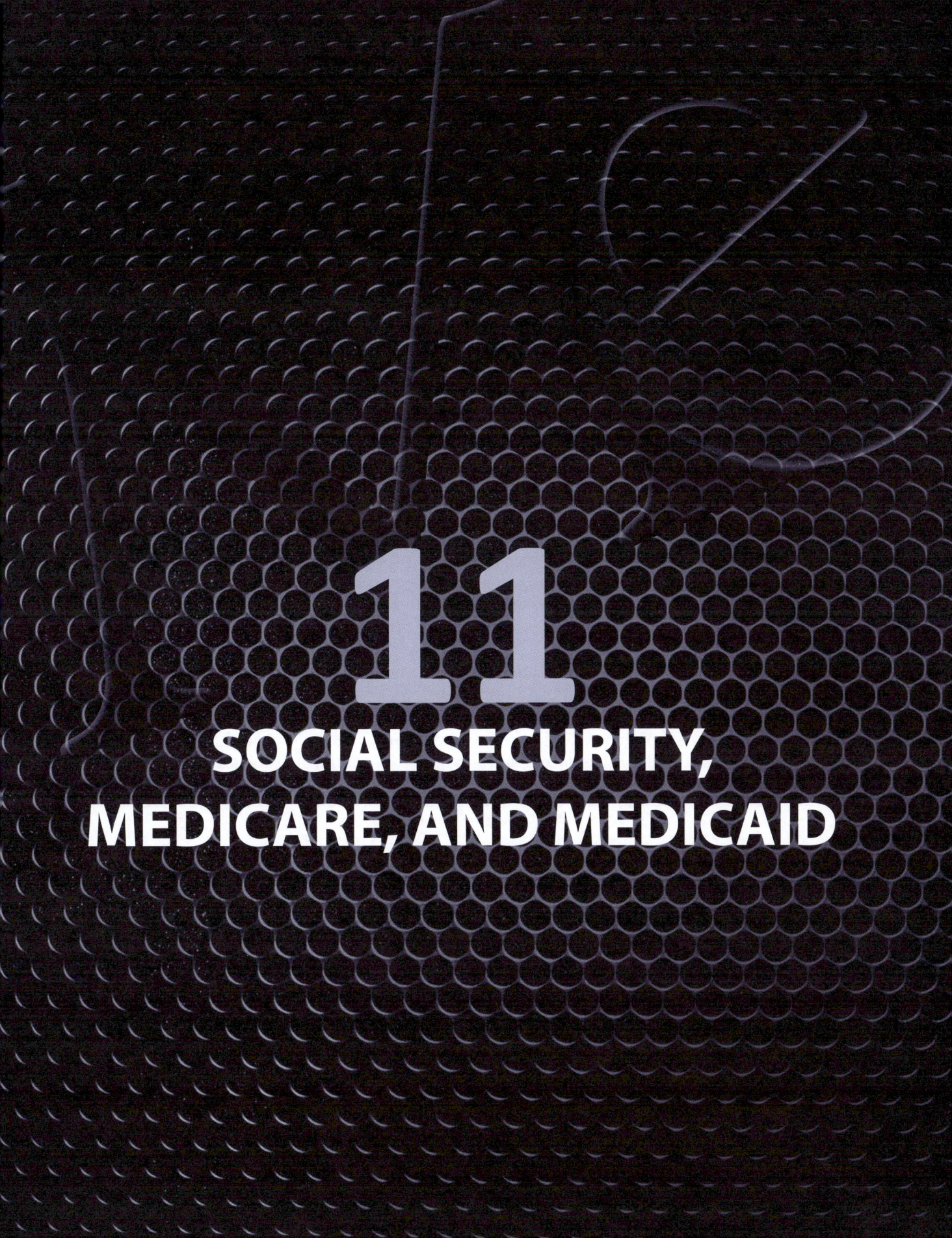

11
SOCIAL SECURITY, MEDICARE, AND MEDICAID

LEARNING OBJECTIVES

1. Understand the history and purpose of the Social Security program and the conditions under which it was enacted.
2. Provide an overview of the Social Security system, including payroll taxes, benefits, and qualifications.*
3. Explain if and how a client may qualify for Social Security benefits.*
4. Identify possible beneficiaries under the Social Security system and the types of benefits they may be entitled to receive.*
5. Explain the computation of the Average Indexed Monthly Earnings (AIME) and the Primary Insurance Amount (PIA) and the impact on benefits relative to historical earnings.*
6. Explain disability benefits, survivor benefits, and maximum family benefits under the Social Security system.*
7. Advise clients in choosing the optimal date to begin receiving Social Security benefits, considering the impact of taxation, benefit reductions and credits, reductions under the earnings test, as well as life expectancy.*
8. Understand proposed or possible changes to the Social Security system and the possible impact on retirement and other financial planning.*
9. Describe the taxation of Social Security benefits.*
10. Explain the windfall elimination and government pension offset on retirement benefits.*
11. Provide an overview of the Medicare program, including the payroll taxes and eligibility structure.*
12. Identify the four Parts of Medicare coverage, the benefits provided by each, common out-of-pocket costs required for insured individuals, and alternative insurance options to cover the gaps associated with Medicare.*
13. Assist a client in selecting proper Medicare coverage and any supplemental coverage with careful attention to appropriate deadlines.*
14. Understand the enrollment requirements and timing deadlines for Medicare enrollment.*
15. Provide an overview of the Medicaid program structure, benefits and funding sources.*
16. Identify Medicaid eligibility requirements and Medicaid planning strategies to maximize client benefits and available resources.*

* Ties to CFP Certification Learning Objectives

Social Security and other forms of social insurance were born out of changes in economies and in families. For centuries, farming and agriculture provided families with the foundation of their economic security. Farms provided food, shelter, and resources for families to survive. As family members aged, they were cared for on the farms. However, as economies changed as part of the industrial revolution, more and more people became employees working for someone else. This demographic shift continued such that a higher percentage of people began moving from the farms to the cities. As a result, people were less capable of providing for their own welfare as they aged, especially in difficult economic times.

These demographic shifts and the Great Depression set the stage for the Social Security system, which was signed into law by Franklin D. Roosevelt on August 14, 1935. At the signing of the law, President Roosevelt made the following statement:

"Today a hope of many years' standing is in large part fulfilled. The civilization of the past hundred years, with its startling industrial changes, has tended more and more to make life insecure. Young people have come to wonder what would be their lot when they came to old age. The man with a job has wondered how long the job would last.

This Social Security measure gives at least some protection to thirty millions of our citizens who will reap direct benefits through unemployment compensation, through old-age pensions and through increased services for the protection of children and the prevention of ill health.

We can never insure one hundred percent of the population against one hundred percent of the hazards and vicissitudes of life, but we have tried to frame a law which will give some measure of protection to the average citizen and to his family against the loss of a job and against poverty-ridden old age."

Today, the Social Security system is significantly different than what it was envisioned more than 80 years ago in terms of the programs offered and the size of the program. The system provides tremendous benefits to millions of Americans, as indicated in **Exhibit 11.1**. However, the system also has significant fiscal problems that must be addressed and resolved if there is any chance that it continues for generations to come. Two of the primary issues with the program are the number of workers paying into the system relative to the number of retirees and other beneficiaries and the significant increase in the life expectancy of our current and future population.

Exhibit 11.1 | Social Security Basic Facts[1]

1.	In 2020, over 65 million Americans will receive over one trillion dollars ($1,000,000,000,000.00) in Social Security benefits.
2.	An estimated 178 million workers are covered under Social Security. • 49% of the workforce has no private pension coverage. • 33% of workers report that they and/or their spouse have no savings set aside specifically for retirement.
3.	Social Security is the major source of income for most of the elderly. • Nine out of ten individuals age 65 and older receive Social Security benefits. • Social Security benefits represent about 33% of the income of the elderly. • Among elderly Social Security beneficiaries, 50% of married couples and 70% of unmarried persons receive 50% or more of their income from Social Security. • Among elderly Social Security beneficiaries, 21% of married couples and about 45% of unmarried persons rely on Social Security for 90% or more of their income.
4.	In 1940, the life expectancy of a 65-year-old was almost 14 years; today it is just over 20 years.
5.	By 2035, there will be almost twice as many older Americans as today - from 56 million today to 78 million.
6.	There are currently 2.8 workers for each Social Security beneficiary. By 2035, there will be 2.3 workers for each beneficiary.

---

1. Social Security Basic Facts, June 2020.

KNOW THE NUMBERS (2021)

Social Security Wage Base	$142,800
Social Security Quarter of Coverage	$1,470
Social Security Bottom Bend Point	$996
Social Security Top Bend Point	$6,002
Social Security Maximum Monthly Benefit	$3,148
Social Security Medicare Part A Deductible Days 1-60	$1,484 per benefit period
Social Security Medicare Part A Deductible Days 61-90	$371 per day
Social Security Medicare Part A Deductible Days 91 and Over	$742 per day
Social Security Medicare Part B Deductible	$203
Social Security Skilled Nursing Care Deductible Days 21-100	$185.50 per day
Social Security Disability Monthly Earnings Limit	$1,310
Social Security Disability Monthly Earnings Limit if Blind	$2,190
Social Security Death Benefit	$255
Social Security Earnings Limitation (under full retirement age)	$18,960
Social Security Earnings Limitation (full retirement age)	$50,520

INTRODUCTION

Social Security benefits were never intended to provide total pre-retirement wage replacement upon retirement. Social Security was created to supplement a covered worker's pension, savings, investments, and other earnings from assets to make up an appropriate wage replacement ratio (e.g., 70 percent). Individuals who retire may need 70 to 80 percent of their pre-retirement income during their retirement to maintain their pre-retirement standard of living.

Low wage earners receive Social Security retirement benefits averaging 60 percent of pre-retirement income. Average wage earners receive an average of 42 percent of pre-retirement income from Social Security benefits, whereas high wage earners receive an average of 26 percent of pre-retirement income (see **Exhibit 11.2**).

From a financial planning standpoint, it is important to understand Social Security law and the various benefits that are available from Social Security. This chapter provides an overview of the Social Security system and its benefits. The six major categories of benefits administered by the Social Security Administration are:

1. Retirement benefits
2. Disability benefits
3. Family benefits
4. Survivors' benefits
5. Medicare
6. Supplemental Security Income (SSI) benefits. SSI benefits are not funded by Social Security taxes but are funded by general funds from the Treasury.

The **retirement benefit** is the most well-known benefit from Social Security. Full retirement benefits are payable at "full retirement age" (reduced benefits are available as early as age 62) to anyone who has obtained a minimum amount (40 quarters) of Social Security credits. Based on the Social Security law in 1983, the age when full retirement benefits are paid began to rise from age 65 in the year 2000, and increases to age 67 by the year 2027. Workers who delay retirement beyond the full retirement age receive a special scheduled increase (**Exhibit 11.14**) in benefits for each delayed year extending until age 70.[2]

Exhibit 11.2 | Social Security Benefits as a Percentage of Pre-Retirement Income

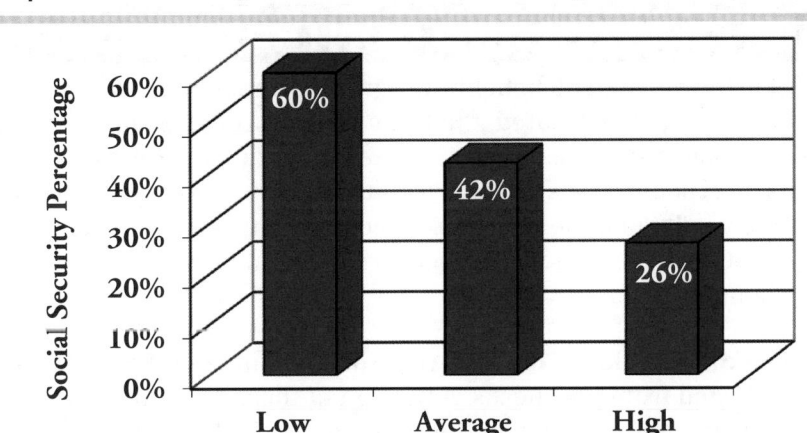

The **disability benefit** is payable at any age to workers who have sufficient credits under the Social Security system to qualify for disability benefits. Recipients must have a severe physical or mental impairment that is expected to prevent them from performing "substantial" work for at least a year or to result in their death. Monthly earnings of $1,310 for 2021 (if the individual is blind, then the amount is increased to $2,190 per month for 2021) or more is considered substantial. The disability insurance program has built-in incentives to smooth the transition back to the workforce including continuation of benefits and health care coverage.

> **Key Concepts**
>
> 1. What are the six major categories of benefits administered by the Social Security Administration?
>
> 2. How are funds collected for Social Security?

The **family benefit** is provided to certain family members of workers eligible for retirement or disability benefits. Such family members include spouses age 62 or older, spouses under age 62 but caring for a child under age 16, unmarried children under 18, unmarried children under age 19 and full-time students, and unmarried children of any age who were disabled before age 22.

Survivors' benefits apply to certain members of the deceased worker's family if the worker earned sufficient Social Security credits. Family members entitled to survivors' benefits include those listed for family benefits and may also include the worker's dependent parents if the worker was their primary means of support. A special one-time payment of $255 may be made to the spouse or minor children upon the death of a Social Security covered worker.

---

2. The increases are not compounded, and there are no increases for delay beyond age 70.

Medicare provides hospital and medical insurance. Those who have attained age 65 or those who receive disability benefits for at least two years automatically qualify for Medicare. Others must file an application to become qualified.

Finally, **Supplemental Security Income (SSI)** (funded by general tax revenues and not by Social Security taxes) is another benefit that provides monthly payments to those disabled or at full retirement age who have a low income and few assets. Generally, those who receive SSI also qualify for **Medicaid**, food stamps, and other governmental assistance.

SOCIAL SECURITY TAXES AND CONTRIBUTIONS

Although the Social Security retirement benefits program is thought by many to be one of the most complicated and confusing programs created, the basic concept is quite simple. Employees, employers, and self-employed individuals pay Social Security taxes, known as FICA taxes, during their working years. These payments are pooled in special trust funds. Contributing workers become "covered" workers, meaning that they will fall under the Social Security umbrella of benefits after contributing for approximately 10 years (40 quarters) and will receive retirement benefits based on those contributions and the Social Security benefits formula.

The **Federal Insurance Contributions Act (FICA)** is the law allowing Social Security taxes, including Medicare taxes, to be deducted from paychecks. A portion of these FICA taxes pays part of the Medicare coverage. Both employers and employees pay the taxes for Social Security and Medicare. For the year 2021, an employer and employee each pay 6.2 percent of the employee's gross salary up to a limit of $142,800 for **OASDI (Old Age, Survivor, and Disability Insurance)**. The salary limit rises annually based on annual increases in average wages. Self-employed workers pay 12.4 percent (6.2 percent x 2) of their taxable income up to the same salary limit. The Medicare portion of the Social Security tax is 1.45 percent for both employers and employees and is 2.9 percent for self-employed workers with no limit on the amount of compensation taxed.

Example 11.1

If an employee earns a salary of $150,000 in 2021, the first $142,800 of the employee's salary will be subject to a tax of 7.65 (6.2 + 1.45) percent while the remaining $7,200 will be subject to a tax of only 1.45 percent. The employer pays the same amount as the employee.

	Taxable Amount	x	Tax Rate	Total Tax
Employee - Social Security	$142,800		6.20%	$8,853.60
Employee - Medicare	$150,000		1.45%	$2,175.00
Total Tax				$11,028.60

Additional Medicare Taxes Beginning in 2013

The Affordable Care Act created two additional Medicare taxes that impact wealthier taxpayers. The first is an additional Medicare tax of 0.9 percent on wages or self-employment income. The second is a 3.8 percent tax on certain amounts of net investment income.

The additional Medicare tax equal to 0.9 percent applies to wages or self-employment income that is above the following threshold amounts:

Married Filing Jointly	$250,000
Married Filing Separately	$125,000
Single	$200,000
Head of Household	$200,000

Only employees pay this Medicare tax. Employers do not pay this tax, but must withhold the tax from wages if the taxpayer has income in excess of $200,000.

Example 11.2

Carlos, a single filer, has $130,000 in wages and $145,000 in self-employment income. IIis wages are not in excess of the $200,000 threshold for single filers, so Carlos is not responsible for Additional Medicare Tax on these wages.

Before calculating the Additional Medicare Tax on self-employment income, the $200,000 threshold for single filers is reduced by his $130,000 in wages, resulting in a reduced self-employment income threshold of $70,000. Carlos is required to pay Additional Medicare Tax on $75,000 of self-employment income ($145,000 in self-employment income minus the reduced threshold of $70,000). Carlos has total earnings of $275,000, which is $75,000 over the $200,000 threshold.

Example 11.3

Franklin and Aretha are married and file jointly. Franklin has $150,000 in wages and Aretha has $175,000 in self-employment income. Franklin's wages are not in excess of the $250,000 threshold for joint filers, so Franklin and Aretha are not responsible for Additional Medicare Tax on Dave's wages.

Before calculating the Additional Medicare Tax on Aretha's self-employment income, the $250,000 threshold for joint filers is reduced by Franklin's $150,000 in wages resulting in a reduced self-employment income threshold of $100,000. Franklin and Aretha are required to pay Additional Medicare Tax on $75,000 of self-employment income ($175,000 in self-employment income minus the reduced threshold of $100,000). Franklin and Aretha have total earnings of $325,000, which is $75,000 over the $250,000 threshold.

The 3.8 percent Medicare tax is imposed on the lesser of net investment income or modified AGI over the following threshold amounts:

Married Filing Jointly	$250,000
Married Filing Separately	$125,000
Single	$200,000
Head of Household	$200,000

Net investment income is a broadly defined term that includes gross income from interest, dividends, annuities, royalties, and rents other than such income derived from the ordinary course of a trade or business, **plus** other trade or business income, for which the entity is a passive activity (or if the entity is trading financial instruments or commodities), **plus** net gain attributable to the disposition of property other than property held in a trade or business. It should be noted that net investment income does not include any distribution from a 401(k), 403(b), 457(b) plan or an IRA or Roth IRA. However, such distributions may cause a taxpayer to exceed the threshold amounts.

Example 11.4
In 2021, Dan and Mary (MFJ) have $250,000 of dividend income. In this case, they are not subject to the 3.8% surtax.

Example 11.5
Same as **Example 11.4** but Dan and Mary convert a traditional IRA to a Roth IRA. The taxable amount of the conversion is $100,000. Thus, they will have AGI of $350,000, and $100,000 will hence be subject to the 3.8% surtax.

Example 11.6
Same as **Example 11.4** but Dan and Mary also take minimum distributions of $50,000. They will be subject to the 3.8% tax on $50,000, which is the lesser of Net Investment Income and the AGI above $250,000.

Exhibit 11.3 | 3.8% Medicare Tax

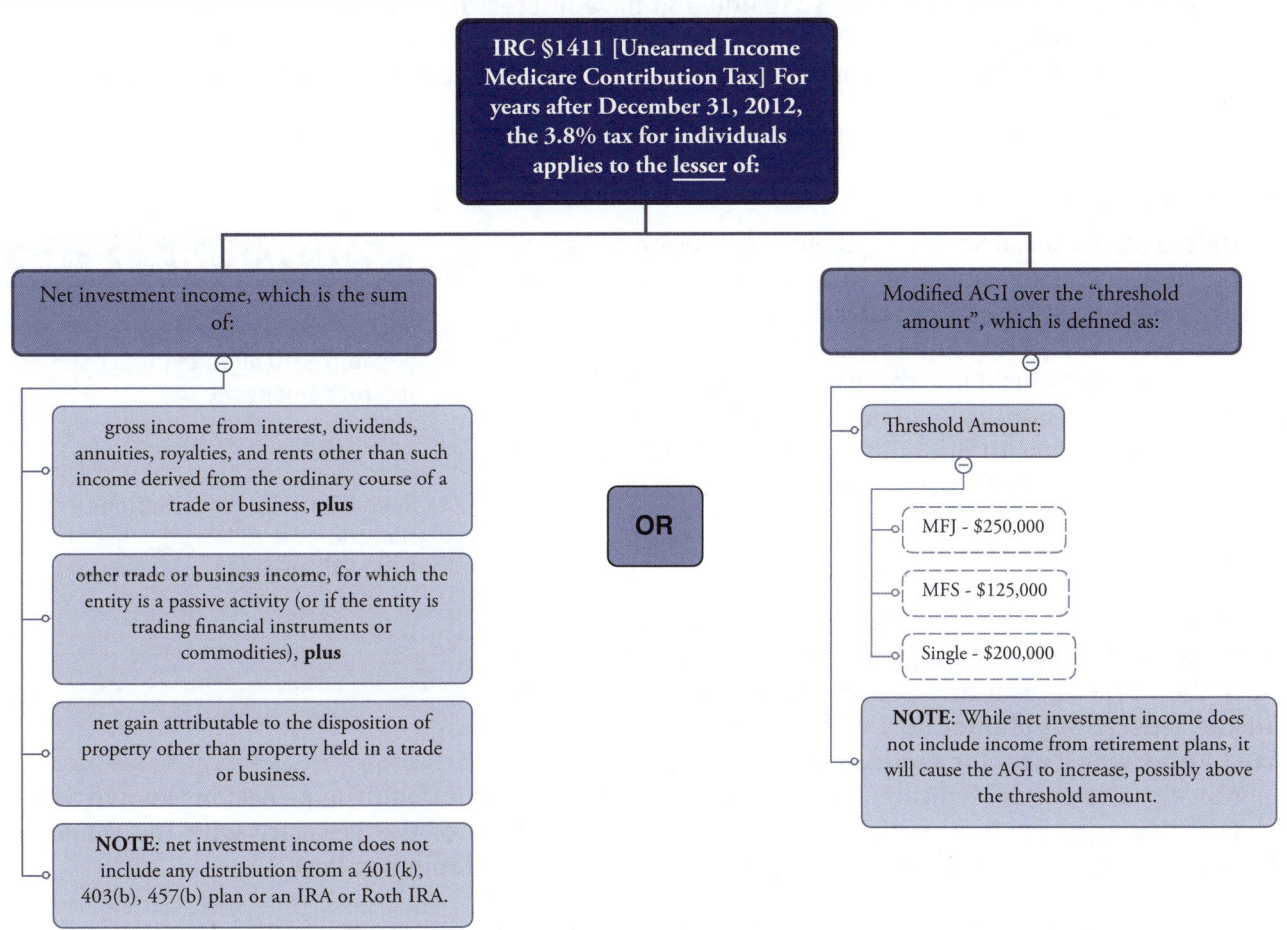

Example 11.7

In 2021, Steve and Ashley (MFJ) have $100,000 of dividend income and $100,000 of wages. In this case, they are not subject to the 3.8% surtax because they are not over the $250,000 limit.

Example 11.8

Same as **Example 11.7** but Steve and Ashley convert a traditional IRA to a Roth IRA. The taxable amount of the conversion is $100,000. Thus, they will have AGI of $300,000. The lesser of $50,000 (the AGI in excess of the $250,000 threshold) or $100,000 (the dividend income) will be subject to the 3.8% surtax.

Example 11.9

Jack and Jill (MFJ) each earn $250,000 and have interest income of $1,000. The $1,000 would be subject to the 3.8% tax. The answer would not change if they each made $125,000, $500,000, or $1 million. In each case, there would be $1,000 subject to the 3.8% tax.

Trust Funds

The United States Social Security system operates on a "pay-as-you-go" basis. Social Security taxes are collected and divided among several trust funds. The federal **Old Age and Survivors Insurance ("OASI") Trust Fund** pays retirement and survivors' benefits. The OASI Trust Fund receives 5.30 percent of the FICA tax. The federal **Disability Insurance ("DI") Trust Fund** pays benefits to workers with disabilities and their families. The DI Trust Fund receives 0.90 percent of the FICA tax. OASI and DI are the two trust funds used for payment of Social Security benefits (total 6.2 percent).

The two Medicare trust funds are the federal **Hospital Insurance ("HI") Trust Fund**, which pays for services covered under the hospital insurance provisions of Medicare (Part A), and the federal **Supplementary Medical Insurance ("SMI") Trust Fund**, which pays for services covered under the medical insurance provisions of Medicare, known as Part B and the prescription drug provisions known as Part D.[3] The SMI Trust Fund is partially funded by the general fund of the Treasury with the remaining funding coming from monthly premiums paid by the individuals enrolled in Part B.

> ### 🖉 *Quick Quiz 11.1*
>
> 1. Social Security benefits are not payable until an individual reaches full retirement age.
>   - a. True
>   - b. False
>
> 2. Social Security contributions are placed in the following trust funds: OASI, DI, and SMI.
>   - a. True
>   - b. False
>
> False, False.

Exhibit 11.4 | Sources Of Funding To Social Security Trust Funds

OASI Trust Fund	5.30 percent (limited to the maximum taxable earnings)
DI Trust Fund	0.90 percent (limited to the maximum taxable earnings)
HI Trust Fund	1.45 percent (all earnings are taxed) (In 1993, the Omnibus Budget Reconciliation Act of 1993 abolished the ceiling on taxable earnings for Medicare.)
SMI Trust Fund	-0- (no FICA taxes used; funded by general federal tax revenues and monthly premiums paid by enrollees)

---

3. Medicare Prescription Drug. Improvement and Modernization Act of 2003 (PL 108-173).

CASE STUDY 11.1

The case of ***Veterinary Surgical Consultants, P.C. v. C.I.R.***, involved an owner of an S corporation who attempted to avoid FICA and FUTA taxes by declaring his remuneration as a K-1 distribution of corporate net income and not W-2 wages.[1] Dr. Sadanaga performed substantial services for the S corporation, Veterinary Surgical Consultants, P.C. ("VSC"). Dr. Sadanaga worked approximately 33 hours per week for VSC. He was the only individual working for VSC. Tellingly, all of VSC's income was generated from the consulting and surgical services provided by Dr. Sadanaga. As officer and sole shareholder, Dr. Sadanaga declared all remuneration he received on a K-1 form, not on a W-2 form, thus avoiding FICA and FUTA taxes.

VSC claimed that the amounts paid to Dr. Sadanaga were distributions of its corporate net income, rather than wages, and that as an S corporation it passed its net income to Dr. Sadanaga as its sole shareholder. Not surprisingly, the Court disagreed with VSC, i.e., Dr. Sadanaga, and concluded that an S corporation cannot avoid federal FICA and FUTA employment taxes by characterizing compensation paid to its sole director and shareholder as distributions of the S corporation's net income rather than wages. The Court's analysis focused on whether payments represented remuneration for services rendered. To characterize the payments to Dr. Sadanaga as distributions of VSC's net income was "but a subterfuge for reality." The payments constituted remuneration for services performed by Dr. Sadanaga on behalf of VSC. Regardless of how an employer may choose to characterize payments made to its employees, the true analysis is whether the payments represent remuneration for services rendered.[2] Dr. Sadanaga's reporting of the distributions as nonpassive income from an S corporation had no bearing on the Federal employment tax treatment of those wages. He was VSC's sole source of income, thereby requiring treatment as an employee. In short, while an S corporation is permitted to pass through items of income in calculating its income tax liability, it may not pass through its tax liability for federal employment taxes.

1. *Veterinary Surgical Consultants, P.C. v. C.I.R.*, 117 T.C. No. 14, 117 T.C. 141, 2001 WL 1242120 (U.S. Tax Ct.), Tax Ct. Rep. (CCH) 54,527, Tax Ct. Rep. Dec. (RIA) 117.14 (U.S. Tax Ct. 2001).
2. See also *Spicer Accounting, Inc. v. United States*, 918 F.2d 90 (9th Cir. 1990); *Joseph Radtke, S.C. v. United States*, 895 F.2d 1196 (7th Cir. 1990).

SOCIAL SECURITY BENEFITS – ELIGIBILITY AND CALCULATIONS

Covered Workers and Insured Status

To qualify for retirement benefits, a worker must be **"fully insured,"** which means that a worker has earned a certain number of quarters (credits) of coverage under the Social Security system. Since 1978, quarters of coverage have been determined based on annual earnings. In other words, earning a designated amount of money, regardless of when it was earned during the year, will credit the worker with a quarter of coverage for that year. In 2021, the designated amount for a quarter of coverage is $1,470. Thus, workers who earn at least $5,880 are credited with four quarters of coverage for 2021. No worker may earn more than four quarters in one year, regardless of earnings. The following is a list of the designated amounts for a quarter of coverage dating back to 1990.

≔ *Key Concepts*

1. Who are covered workers with regard to Social Security?

2. Who are beneficiaries of Social Security benefits?

Exhibit 11.5 | Designated Amounts for a Quarter of Social Security Coverage

Year	Amount Needed to Receive a Credit for One Quarter	Year	Amount Needed to Receive a Credit for One Quarter
1990	$520	2006	$970
1991	$540	2007	$1,000
1992	$570	2008	$1,050
1993	$590	2009	$1,090
1994	$620	2010	$1,120
1995	$630	2011	$1,120
1996	$640	2012	$1,130
1997	$670	2013	$1,160
1998	$700	2014	$1,200
1999	$740	2015	$1,220
2000	$780	2016	$1,260
2001	$830	2017	$1,300
2002	$870	2018	$1,320
2003	$890	2019	$1,360
2004	$900	2020	$1,410
2005	$920	2021	$1,470

For most persons, 40 quarters of coverage (10 years of work in employment covered by Social Security) or one quarter per year from age 21 to age 62 will fully insure a worker for life. Fully insured workers are entitled to the benefits under the Social Security system. Some benefits, like survivors' benefits, are available to "currently" (although not necessarily fully) insured individuals. **"Currently" insured workers** are those individuals who have at least six quarters of coverage out of the previous 13 quarters.

Example 11.10

In 2021, Winnie earned $10,000 from employment subject to Social Security between January 1 and March 31. She was then unemployed for the remainder of the year. How many quarters of coverage did she earn for Social Security 2021?

For 2021, a worker receives one quarter credit for each $1,470 in annual earnings on which Social Security taxes are withheld up to a maximum of four quarters. It is irrelevant that Winnie earned the $10,000 all in the first quarter. Winnie has earned four quarters for the year.

Example 11.11

How is a worker's insured status determined under Social Security?

It is determined by the number of quarters of coverage received. To achieve currently insured status under Social Security, a worker must have at least six quarters of coverage out of 13 calendar quarters prior to retirement, disability, or death. Any worker with 40 covered quarters is fully insured.

Social Security Beneficiaries

Social Security benefits are paid upon retirement, disability, or death if the eligibility requirements are satisfied. The worker's spouse and children may also be eligible to receive benefits when the worker satisfies eligibility requirements. Generally, monthly Social Security benefits can be paid to:

- A disabled insured worker under age 65.
- A retired insured worker at age 62 or older.
- The spouse of a retired or disabled worker who:
  - is at least 62 years old, or
  - is caring for a child who is under age 16 or disabled.
- The divorced spouse of a retired or disabled worker entitled to benefits if the divorced spouse is age 62 or older and was married to the worker for at least 10 years.
- The divorced spouse of a fully insured worker who has not yet filed a claim for benefits if both are at least age 62, were married for at least 10 years, and have been finally divorced for at least two continuous years.
- The dependent, unmarried child of a retired or disabled worker or of a deceased insured worker if the child is:
  - under age 18;
  - under age 19 and a full-time elementary or secondary school student; or
  - age 18 or over but disabled (if the disability began before age 22).
- The surviving spouse (including a surviving divorced spouse) of a deceased insured worker if the widow(er) is age 60 or older.
- The disabled surviving spouse (including a surviving divorced spouse in some cases) of a deceased insured worker if the widow(er) is age 50 or older.
- The surviving spouse (including a surviving divorced spouse) of a deceased insured worker, regardless of age, if caring for an entitled child of the deceased who is either under age 16 or disabled before age 22.
- The dependent parents of a deceased insured worker at age 62 or older.

> ### ✑ Quick Quiz 11.2
>
> 1. "Fully insured" means that a worker has earned a certain number of quarters (generally 40) of coverage under the Social Security system.
>   a. True
>   b. False
>
> 2. Social Security benefits can be paid to the dependent parents of a deceased insured worker at age 62.
>   a. True
>   b. False
>
> True, True.

In addition to monthly survivors' benefits, a lump-sum death payment of $255 is payable upon the death of an insured worker.

Exhibit 11.6 | Survivors Benefits: Currently vs. Fully Insured

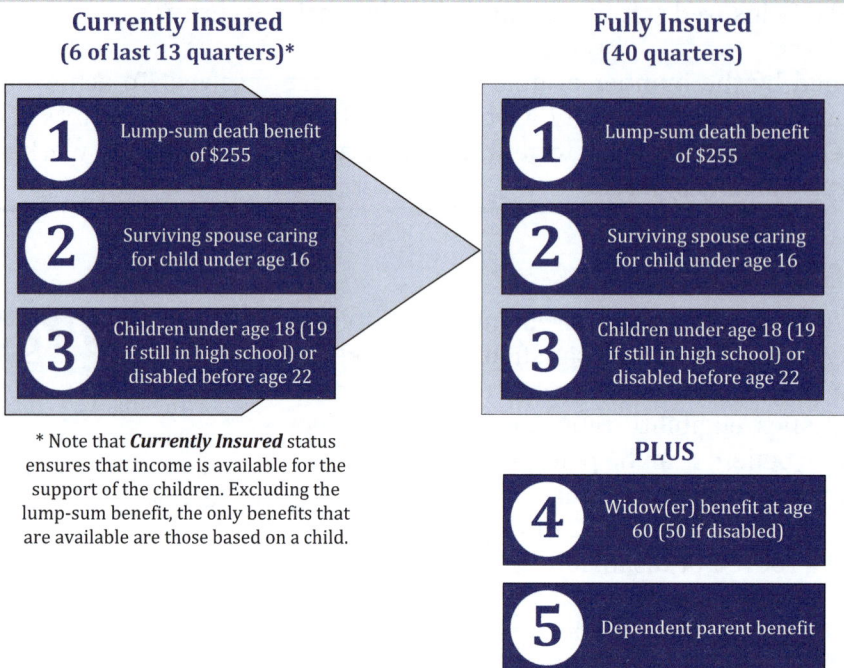

Currently Insured
(6 of last 13 quarters)*

1. Lump-sum death benefit of $255
2. Surviving spouse caring for child under age 16
3. Children under age 18 (19 if still in high school) or disabled before age 22

* Note that ***Currently Insured*** status ensures that income is available for the support of the children. Excluding the lump-sum benefit, the only benefits that are available are those based on a child.

Fully Insured
(40 quarters)

1. Lump-sum death benefit of $255
2. Surviving spouse caring for child under age 16
3. Children under age 18 (19 if still in high school) or disabled before age 22

PLUS

4. Widow(er) benefit at age 60 (50 if disabled)
5. Dependent parent benefit

Exhibit 11.7 provides a summary of those eligible for OASDI benefits and the percentages of the worker's primary insurance amount ("PIA") that each beneficiary will receive. The PIA is the retirement benefit that the worker would receive if the worker retires at full retirement age.

Example 11.12

Guy, age 38, has just died. He has been credited with the last 35 consecutive quarters of Social Security coverage since he left college. He did not work before leaving college. Which of the following persons are eligible to receive Social Security survivor benefits as a result of Guy's death?

1. Richie, Guy's 16-year-old son
2. Grace, Guy's 18-year-old daughter
3. Olivia, Guy's 38-year-old widow
4. Arline, Guy's 60-year-old dependent mother

Answer: Grace is too old; Olivia does not have a child under 16 and she is too young; and Arline is not eligible because she is too young. Thus, only Richie is eligible.

Example 11.13

Under Social Security (OASDI), what benefits are available to the survivors of a deceased but only currently insured worker?

A $255 lump-sum death benefit, which is generally payable to the insured's spouse, and 75 percent of the worker's PIA is available to a child under 18 or to a surviving spouse with a dependent child under the age of 16.

Exhibit 11.7 | Summary of Social Security OASDI Benefits (As a Percentage of PIA)

	Assuming Full Retirement Age of the Worker			
	Retirement	Survivorship		Disability
	Fully Insured[2]	Fully Insured[2]	Currently Insured[3]	Disability Insured[4]
Participant	100%	Deceased	Deceased	100%
Child Under 18[6]	50%	75%	75%	50%
Spouse with child under 16[7]	50%	75%	75%	50%
Spouse - Full Age Retirement[1]	50%	100%	0%	50%
Spouse - Age 62[1,8]	32.5% to 35%	80% to 81%[9]	0%	32.5% to 35%
Spouse - Age 60[1]	N/A	71.5%	0%	N/A
Dependent Parent (age 62)	0%	75/82.5%[5]	0%	0%

1. Includes divorced spouse if married at least 10 years (unless they have remarried). Survivorship benefits are also available to divorced spouse if remarried after age 60.
2. Fully insured is 40 quarters of coverage or one quarter for each year after age 21 but before age 62 (with at least six quarters of coverage).*
3. Currently insured is at least six quarters of coverage in the last 13 quarters.
4. Disability insured is based on age as follows:
   - Before age 24 - Must have 6 quarters of coverage in the last 12 quarters.
   - Age 24 through 30 - Must be covered for half of the available quarters after age 21.
   - Age 31 or older - Must be fully insured and have 20 quarters of coverage in the last 40 quarters.
5. Parent benefit is 82.5 percent for one parent and 75 percent for each parent if two parents.
6. Child under age 19 and a full-time student or of any age and disabled before age 22 also qualifies.
7. Spouse with child disabled before age 22 also qualifies.
8. A spouse can choose to retire as early as age 62, but doing so may result in a benefit as little as 32.5 percent of the worker's primary insurance amount. A spousal benefit is reduced 25/36 of one percent for each month before normal retirement age, up to 36 months. If the number of months exceeds 36, then the benefit is further reduced 5/12 of one percent per month.
9. The reduction for a widow(er) is 28.5 percent at age 60. It is prorated for months between full retirement age and age 60.

Note: Notice that when the participant worker is alive (retirement and disability), beneficiaries who qualify for a benefit, qualify for 50% of PIA. When the participant dies, all qualified beneficiaries generally receive 75% of PIA with the exceptions being the spouse who replaces the participant at 100% (benefit reduced below PIA if deceased worker retired before FRA, and benefit above PIA due to delayed retirement credits (DRCs) if worker delayed retirement beyond FRA) and any qualified dependent parents. See note 5.

* 42 U.S.C. 414.

Social Security Retirement Benefits – A Closer Look

The most well known Social Security benefit is the Retirement Benefit. Until 2000, normal age retirement, the age where full retirement benefits are available to the retiree, was 65 years. The age at which full benefits are paid began to rise in the year 2000. **Exhibit 11.8** illustrates the gradual increase of the normal age retirement with full benefits to age 67.

Exhibit 11.8 | Age Full Retirement Benefits Begin (Normal Age Retirement)

Full Retirement Age With Full Benefits	Year Born
65 years	Before 1938
65 years, 2 months	1938
65 years, 4 months	1939
65 years, 6 months	1940
65 years, 8 months	1941
65 years, 10 months	1942
66 years	1943-1954
66 years, 2 months	1955
66 years, 4 months	1956
66 years, 6 months	1957
66 years, 8 months	1958
66 years, 10 months	1959
67 years	1960-present

People who delay receiving Social Security retirement benefits beyond full retirement age receive an increase in their benefit when they do retire. People who take early retirement, currently as early as age 62, receive an actuarially reduced monthly benefit. (Early and late retirement options are discussed later in this chapter.)

When planning for an individual, it may be appropriate to calculate the individual's expected Social Security retirement benefit or to ask the client to request a Social Security statement and consider the benefit in that individual's retirement plan. Some advisors, however, choose not to consider the estimated retirement benefit in order to be conservative in developing a retirement plan. Others justify the exclusion of Social Security retirement benefits from retirement planning based on the belief that there will be drastic changes to the Social Security system through legislative action or through economically-driven forces.

≔ *Key Concepts*

1. How is a person's Social Security retirement benefit calculated?

2. How does retiring early or retiring late affect Social Security retirement benefits?

The Retirement Benefit Calculation

Determining a worker's Social Security retirement benefit requires specific, detailed information pertaining to the person's age, actual earnings history that was subject to Social Security taxes, and the worker's retirement date. Social Security benefits are based on earnings averaged over most of a worker's lifetime. Actual earnings, in historical dollars, are first adjusted or "indexed" to current dollars to account for changes in average wages and inflation since the year the earnings were received. Then, the Social Security Administration calculates **average indexed monthly earnings ("AIME")** during the 35 years in which the applicant earned the most. The Social Security Administration applies a formula to these earnings and arrives at a basic benefit, which is referred to as the **primary insurance amount (PIA)**. The Social Security retirement benefit is based on the worker's PIA. The PIA determines the amount the applicant will receive at his full retirement age, but the dollar amount of the benefit depends on the year in which the worker retires. The PIA is indexed to the consumer price index (CPI) annually.

Figuring the Worker's Average Indexed Monthly Earnings (AIME)

To determine a worker's AIME, the worker's actual annual earnings from age 22 to 62 must be converted into current dollars by multiplying the worker's total annual earnings for each year by an indexing factor. The indexing factor is the result of dividing the national average wage for the year in which the worker attains age 60 by the national average wage for the actual year being indexed. The following exhibit provides national average wages from 1951 to 2019.

Exhibit 11.9 | National Average Wage Indexing Series, 1951- 2019

Year	Amount	Year	Amount	Year	Amount
1951	$2,799.16	1974	$8,030.76	1997	$27,426.00
1952	$2,973.32	1975	$8,630.92	1998	$28,861.44
1953	$3,139.44	1976	$9,226.48	1999	$30,469.84
1954	$3,155.64	1977	$9,779.44	2000	$32,154.82
1955	$3,301.44	1978	$10,556.03	2001	$32,921.92
1956	$3,532.36	1979	$11,479.46	2002	$33,252.09
1957	$3,641.72	1980	$12,513.46	2003	$34,064.95
1958	$3,673.80	1981	$13,773.10	2004	$35,648.55
1959	$3,855.80	1982	$14,531.34	2005	$36,952.94
1960	$4,007.12	1983	$15,239.24	2006	$38,651.41
1961	$4,086.76	1984	$16,135.07	2007	$40,405.48
1962	$4,291.40	1985	$16,822.51	2008	$41,334.97
1963	$4,396.64	1986	$17,321.82	2009	$40,711.61
1964	$4,576.32	1987	$18,426.51	2010	$41,673.83
1965	$4,658.72	1988	$19,334.04	2011	$42,979.61
1966	$4,938.36	1989	$20,099.55	2012	$44,321.67
1967	$5,213.44	1990	$21,027.98	2013	$44,888.16
1968	$5,571.76	1991	$21,811.60	2014	$46,481.52
1969	$5,893.76	1992	$22,935.42	2015	$48,098.63
1970	$6,186.24	1993	$23,132.67	2016	$48,642.15
1971	$6,497.08	1994	$23,753.53	2017	$50,321.89
1972	$7,133.80	1995	$24,705.66	2018	$52,145.80
1973	$7,580.16	1996	$25,913.90	2019	$54,099.99

Source: Social Security Administration (www.ssa.gov)

Example 11.14

For a worker age 62 in 2020, the indexing factor for the year 1980 is determined by dividing the national average wage for 2018 (when the worker attained age 60), which was $52,145.80, by the national average wage for 1980 (the year being indexed), which was $12,513.46, yielding a factor of 4.1672.

Year	AWI	Age 62 in 2020		Age 66 in 2020	
		Age	Factor	Age	Factor
1954	3,155.64		16.5246	0	14.7297
1955	3,301.44		15.7949	1	14.0792
1956	3,532.36		14.7623	2	13.1588
1957	3,641.72		14.3190	3	12.7636
1958	3,673.80	0	14.1940	4	12.6522
1959	3,855.80	1	13.5240	5	12.0550
1960	4,007.12	2	13.0133	6	11.5997
1961	4,086.76	3	12.7597	7	11.3737
1962	4,291.40	4	12.1512	8	10.8313
1963	4,396.64	5	11.8604	9	10.5721
1964	4,576.32	6	11.3947	10	10.1570
1965	4,658.72	7	11.1932	11	9.9773
1966	4,938.36	8	10.5593	12	9.4123
1967	5,213.44	9	10.0022	13	8.9157
1968	5,571.76	10	9.3589	14	8.3423
1969	5,893.76	11	8.8476	15	7.8866
1970	6,186.24	12	8.4293	16	7.5137
1971	6,497.08	13	8.0260	17	7.1542
1972	7,133.80	14	7.3097	18	6.5157
1973	7,580.16	15	6.8792	19	6.1320
1974	8,030.76	16	6.4933	20	5.7879
1975	8,630.92	17	6.0417	21	5.3855
1976	9,226.48	18	5.6518	22	5.0378
1977	9,779.44	19	5.3322	23	4.7530
1978	10,556.03	20	4.9399	24	4.4033
1979	11,479.46	21	4.5425	25	4.0491
1980	12,513.46	22	4.1672	26	3.7145
1981	13,773.10	23	3.7861	27	3.3748
1982	14,531.34	24	3.5885	28	3.1987
1983	15,239.24	25	3.4218	29	3.0501
1984	16,135.07	26	3.2318	30	2.8808
1985	16,822.51	27	3.0998	31	2.7631
1986	17,321.82	28	3.0104	32	2.6834
1987	18,426.51	29	2.8299	33	2.5225
1988	19,334.04	30	2.6971	34	2.4041
1989	20,099.55	31	2.5944	35	2.3126
1990	21,027.98	32	2.4798	36	2.2105
1991	21,811.60	33	2.3907	37	2.1310
1992	22,935.42	34	2.2736	38	2.0266
1993	23,132.67	35	2.2542	39	2.0093
1994	23,753.53	36	2.1953	40	1.9568
1995	24,705.66	37	2.1107	41	1.8814
1996	25,913.90	38	2.0123	42	1.7937
1997	27,426.00	39	1.9013	43	1.6948
1998	28,861.44	40	1.8068	44	1.6105
1999	30,469.84	41	1.7114	45	1.5255
2000	32,154.82	42	1.6217	46	1.4456
2001	32,921.92	43	1.5839	47	1.4119
2002	33,252.09	44	1.5682	48	1.3979
2003	34,064.95	45	1.5308	49	1.3645
2004	35,648.55	46	1.4628	50	1.3039
2005	36,952.94	47	1.4111	51	1.2579
2006	38,651.41	48	1.3491	52	1.2026
2007	40,405.48	49	1.2906	53	1.1504
2008	41,334.97	50	1.2615	54	1.1245
2009	40,711.61	51	1.2809	55	1.1417
2010	41,673.83	52	1.2513	56	1.1154
2011	42,979.61	53	1.2133	57	1.0815
2012	44,321.67	54	1.1765	58	1.0487
2013	44,888.16	55	1.1617	59	1.0355
2014	46,481.52	56	1.1219	60	1.0000
2015	48,098.63	57	1.0841	61	1.0000
2016	48,642.15	58	1.0720	62	1.0000
2017	50,321.89	59	1.0362	63	1.0000
2018	52,145.80	60	1.0000	64	1.0000
2019		61	1.0000	65	1.0000
2020		62	1.0000	66	1.0000

Next, each year's annual earnings must be multiplied by its indexing factor to arrive at the indexed earnings for the years from age 22 to 60. Note that the indexing factor will always equal one for the years in which the worker is 60 or older. After all annual earnings are indexed, or converted to current dollar amounts, the highest 35 years of indexed earnings are added together for a total. The sum of the highest 35 years is then divided by 420 (which represents 35 years multiplied by 12 months per year). This calculation yields the average amount of monthly earnings for all indexed years, hence the name Average Indexed Monthly Earnings (AIME). Once the worker's AIME is determined, the next step in determining the worker's retirement benefit is to calculate the primary insurance amount (PIA) for the worker.

Example 11.15

Assume Ronnie and Karen both retired in 2020. Ronnie retired at age 62. Karen retired at her normal (or full) retirement age. Assume Karen had covered earnings from 1978 through 2020, as shown in columns labeled "nominal earnings" and Ronnie had covered earnings from 1978 through 2020.

Indexing adjusts nominal earnings to near-current wage levels. For each case, the table shows columns of earnings before and after indexing. Between these columns is a column showing the indexing factors. A factor will always equal one for the year in which the person attains age 60 and all later years. The indexing factor for a prior year Y is the result of dividing the average wage index for the year in which the person attains age 60 by the average wage index for year Y. For example, Ronnie's indexing factor for 1978 (4.9399) is the average wage for 2018 ($52,145.80; as provided in the National Average Wage Indexing Table in Exhibit 11.8) divided by the average wage for 1978 ($10,556.03; as provided in the National Average Wage Indexing Table in **Exhibit 11.9**).

The highest 35 years of indexed earnings are used in the benefit computation. The selected indexed amounts are bold. Below the indexed earnings are the sums for the highest 35 years of indexed earnings and the corresponding average monthly amounts of such earnings. (The average is the result of dividing the sum of the 35 highest amounts by the number of months in 35 years.) Such an average is called the "Average Indexed Monthly Earnings" (AIME).

As reflected in the following chart, Ronnie's AIME was $2,872 and Karen's AIME was $3,753.

Year	Ronnie					Karen			
	Age	Nominal earnings	Indexing factor	Indexed earnings	Top 35	Age	Nominal earnings	Indexing factor	Indexed earnings	Top 35
1978	20	$5,167	4.9399	$25,524		24	$5,194	4.4033	$22,871	
1979	21	$5,525	4.5425	$25,097		25	$5,747	4.0491	$23,270	
1980	22	$5,847	4.1672	$24,365		26	$6,262	3.7145	$23,260	
1981	23	$6,140	3.7861	$23,246		27	$6,746	3.3748	$22,766	
1982	24	$6,452	3.5885	$23,153		28	$7,253	3.1987	$23,200	
1983	25	$7,088	3.4218	$24,254		29	$8,135	3.0501	$24,813	
1984	26	$7,535	3.2318	$24,352		30	$8,815	2.8808	$25,394	
1985	27	$7,988	3.0998	$24,761		31	$9,511	2.7631	$26,279	
1986	28	$8,589	3.0104	**$25,856**	✓	32	$10,396	2.6834	**$27,897**	✓
1987	29	$9,186	2.8299	**$25,996**	✓	33	$11,293	2.5225	**$28,487**	✓
1988	30	$9,742	2.6971	**$26,275**	✓	34	$12,151	2.4041	**$29,213**	✓
1989	31	$10,521	2.5944	**$27,295**	✓	35	$13,305	2.3126	**$30,769**	✓
1990	32	$11,447	2.4798	**$28,387**	✓	36	$14,667	2.2105	**$32,421**	✓
1991	33	$12,485	2.3907	**$29,848**	✓	37	$16,197	2.1310	**$34,517**	✓
1992	34	$13,748	2.2736	**$31,257**	✓	38	$18,051	2.0266	**$36,583**	✓
1993	35	$14,513	2.2542	**$32,715**	✓	39	$19,273	2.0093	**$38,726**	✓
1994	36	$15,228	2.1953	**$33,430**	✓	40	$20,445	1.9568	**$40,007**	✓
1995	37	$16,131	2.1107	**$34,047**	✓	41	$21,887	1.8814	**$41,178**	✓
1996	38	$16,827	2.0123	**$33,860**	✓	42	$23,063	1.7937	**$41,368**	✓
1997	39	$17,335	1.9013	**$32,960**	✓	43	$23,994	1.6948	**$40,665**	✓
1998	40	$18,450	1.8068	**$33,335**	✓	44	$25,779	1.6105	**$41,517**	✓
1999	41	$19,369	1.7114	**$33,148**	✓	45	$27,311	1.5255	**$41,663**	✓
2000	42	$20,146	1.6217	**$32,671**	✓	46	$28,659	1.4456	**$41,428**	✓
2001	43	$21,087	1.5839	**$33,400**	✓	47	$30,257	1.4119	**$42,719**	✓
2002	44	$21,884	1.5682	**$34,318**	✓	48	$31,663	1.3979	**$44,260**	✓
2003	45	$23,024	1.5308	**$35,245**	✓	49	$33,582	1.3645	**$45,823**	✓
2004	46	$23,234	1.4628	**$33,986**	✓	50	$34,155	1.3039	**$44,534**	✓
2005	47	$23,869	1.4111	**$33,683**	✓	51	$35,360	1.2579	**$44,478**	✓
2006	48	$24,839	1.3491	**$33,511**	✓	52	$37,071	1.2026	**$44,581**	✓
2007	49	$26,067	1.2906	**$33,641**	✓	53	$39,188	1.1504	**$45,081**	✓
2008	50	$27,602	1.2615	**$34,821**	✓	54	$41,790	1.1245	**$46,993**	✓
2009	51	$29,061	1.2809	**$37,223**	✓	55	$44,305	1.1417	**$50,584**	✓
2010	52	$30,696	1.2513	**$38,409**	✓	56	$47,115	1.1154	**$52,550**	✓
2011	53	$32,410	1.2133	**$39,322**	✓	57	$50,076	1.0815	**$54,156**	✓
2012	54	$33,200	1.1765	**$39,061**	✓	58	$51,629	1.0487	**$54,145**	✓
2013	55	$33,551	1.1617	**$38,976**	✓	59	$52,503	1.0355	**$54,367**	✓
2014	56	$34,388	1.1219	**$38,579**	✓	60	$54,148	1.0000	**$54,148**	✓
2015	57	$36,400	1.0841	**$39,463**	✓	61	$56,092	1.0000	**$56,092**	✓
2016	58	$37,900	1.0720	**$40,630**	✓	62	$56,408	1.0000	**$56,408**	✓
2017	59	$38,113	1.0362	**$39,494**	✓	63	$57,103	1.0000	**$57,103**	✓
2018	60	$39,551	1.0000	**$39,551**	✓	64	$59,955	1.0000	**$59,955**	✓
2019	61	$40,000	1.0000	**$40,000**	✓	65	$60,000	1.0000	**$60,000**	✓
2020	62	$42,000	1.0000	**$42,000**	✓	66	$62,000	1.0000	**$62,000**	✓
		Highest-35 total		$1,206,394				Highest-35 total	$1,576,415	
	Total ، 420 Months		AIME	$2,872				AIME	$3,753	

Calculating the Worker's Primary Insurance Amount (PIA)

Generally, the PIA is the actual Social Security retirement benefit for the single retiree who retires at full retirement age. For those who retire early or late and for family or surviving beneficiaries, the PIA is not the actual amount of the benefit but the PIA is used to determine their actual benefit.

The PIA is a result of applying the AIME to the PIA formula. This benefit formula changes the dollar amounts (by CPI), but not the percentages, from year to year and depends on the worker's first year of eligibility, that is, when the worker turns 62, becomes disabled, or dies.

The PIA is the sum of three separate percentages of portions of the AIME. These portions are also known as "bend points." For the year 2021, these portions are the first $996 of AIME, the amount of AIME between $996 and $6,002, and the AIME over $6,002. The bend points for 2021 are thus $996 and $6,002. For individuals who first become eligible for retirement benefits or disability insurance benefits in 2021 or who die in 2021 before becoming eligible for benefits, their PIA will be the sum of:

> 90 percent of the first $996 of their AIME, *plus*
> 32 percent of their AIME over $996 up to $6,002, *plus*
> 15 percent of their AIME that exceeds $6,002.
> (Maximum PIA for 2021 is $3,148.)

The sum of these three calculations is rounded down to the next lower multiple of $0.10 (if it is not already a multiple of $0.10). For calculations in subsequent years, it is useful to know how to determine a given year's bend points. **Exhibit 11.10** shows the established bend points from 1983 through 2021.

Exhibit 11.10 | Bend Point Table

Dollar Amounts (bend points) in PIA Formula		
Year	First	Second
1983	$254	$1,528
1984	$267	$1,612
1985	$280	$1,691
1986	$297	$1,790
1987	$310	$1,866
1988	$319	$1,922
1989	$339	$2,044
1990	$356	$2,145
1991	$370	$2,230
1992	$387	$2,333
1993	$401	$2,420
1994	$422	$2,545
1995	$426	$2,567
1996	$437	$2,635
1997	$455	$2,741
1998	$477	$2,875
1999	$505	$3,043
2000	$531	$3,202
2001	$561	$3,381
2002	$592	$3,567
2003	$606	$3,653
2004	$612	$3,689
2005	$627	$3,779
2006	$656	$3,955
2007	$680	$4,100
2008	$711	$4,288
2009	$744	$4,483
2010	$761	$4,586
2011	$749	$4,517
2012	$767	$4,624
2013	$791	$4,768
2015	$826	$4,980
2016	$856	$5,157
2017	$885	$5,336
2018	$895	$5,397
2019	$926	$5,583
2020	960	5,785
2021	$996	$6,002

Source: Social Security Administration (www.ssa.gov)

These figures for the PIA rise each year based on a cost-of-living adjustment (**COLA**) that is applied to reflect changes in the cost of living. Recent COLAs, which are based on inflation, are shown in **Exhibit 11.11**.

Exhibit 11.11 | Cost-of-Living Adjustment (COLA) Per Year

Year	COLA	Year	COLA	Year	COLA
1994	2.8%	2003	2.1%	2012	1.7%
1995	2.6%	2004	2.7%	2013	1.5%
1996	2.9%	2005	4.1%	2014	1.7%
1997	2.1%	2006	3.3%	2015	0.0%
1998	1.3%	2007	2.3%	2016	0.3%
1999	2.5%	2008	5.8%	2017	2.0%
2000	3.5%	2009	0.0%	2018	2.8%
2001	2.6%	2010	0.0%	2019	1.6%
2002	1.4%	2011	3.6%	2020	1.3%

* Source: www.ssa.gov/oact/cola/colaseries.html

As mentioned, the calculation of the Social Security retirement benefit skews benefits toward the low-income worker. This design is evident in the PIA calculation with a 90 percent wage replacement for extremely low income and only a 15 percent wage replacement for higher income. The following exhibit illustrates the wage replacement ratio provided by Social Security at full retirement age based on the annualized income, which is AIME multiplied by 12 months.

Exhibit 11.12 | Wage Replacement Ratio from Social Security

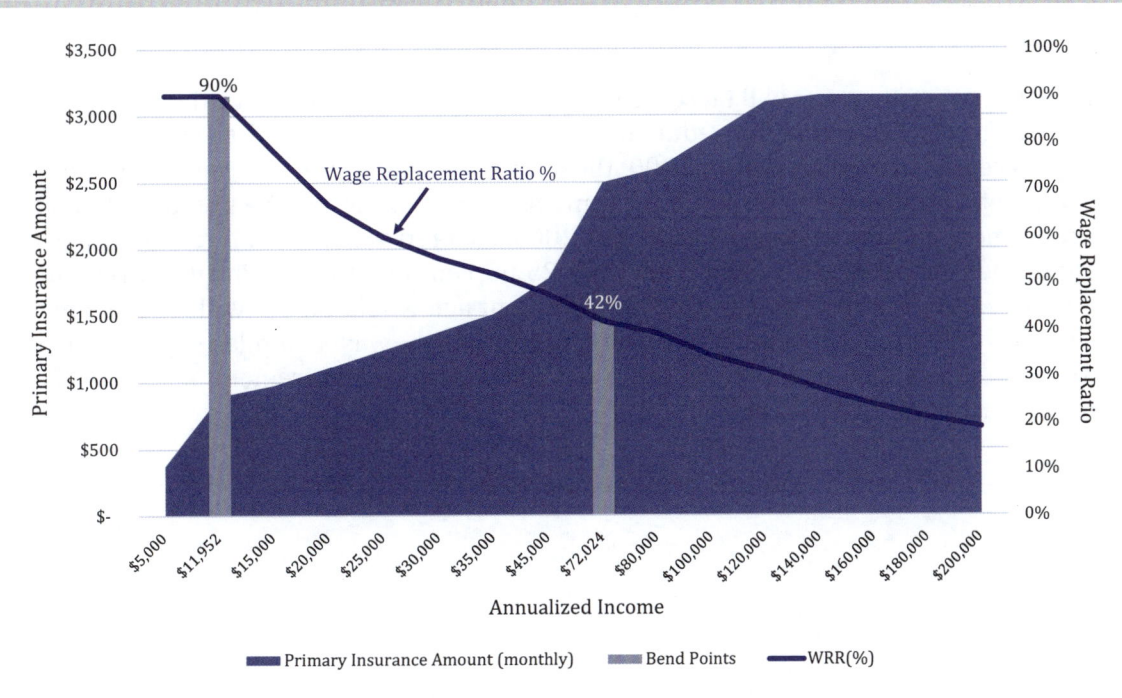

Annual COLA increases are determined by October of each year and go into effect in time so that they first appear on monthly benefit checks received in the following January. In 2021, the maximum monthly retirement benefit for retirees at full retirement age is $3,148, compared to $3,011 in 2020.

Early and Late Retirement Options

Workers entitled to retirement benefits can currently take early retirement benefits as early as age 62. The worker will receive a reduced benefit because he will receive more monthly benefit payments than if the worker had waited and retired at full retirement age. The reduction to one's monthly benefit for early retirement is permanent. Conversely, a delayed or postponed retirement will permanently increase the monthly retirement benefit for a worker.[4]

For each month of early retirement, workers will receive a reduction in their monthly retirement benefit of 5/9 of one percent for up to the first 36 months. For subsequent months of early retirement, the permanent reduction percentage is 5/12 of one percent per month.

Example 11.16

Assume Henry begins receiving benefits at the earliest possible age, which is age 62. Then, the benefit amount for Henry is reduced for 48 months of retirement before his normal retirement age, which is 66 years. Assume his PIA before reduction is $1,421.90. The PIA is thus reduced to a monthly benefit of $1,066.43 (rounded to $1066.40).

PIA	$1,421.90
5/9 x 1% x 36 months	Less 20% reduction
5/12 x 1% x 12 months	Less 5% reduction
Monthly Benefit	$1,066.43

Although the full retirement age will increase to age 67, workers will still have the option of taking early retirement at age 62. However, the reduction percentage that is applied to the monthly retirement benefit will increase until 2027. Before 2000, those who retired at age 62 received 80 percent of their retirement benefit, but the increase in full retirement age has increased the number of months from 62 until full retirement age. For instance, in the year 2009, covered workers who retired at age 62 received 75 percent of their monthly retirement benefit, or 25 percent less than their full retirement benefit. By 2027, covered workers retiring at age 62 (full retirement age would be 67) will receive only 70 percent of their monthly retirement benefit. **Exhibit 11.13**, which was compiled by the Social Security Administration, shows the phase-in of the Social Security full retirement age and accompanying reductions for early retirement at age 62.

---

4. A spouse can choose to retire as early as age 62, but doing so may result in a benefit as little as 32.5 percent of the worker's primary insurance amount. A spousal benefit is reduced 25/36 of one percent for each month before normal retirement age, up to 36 months. If the number of months exceeds 36, then the benefit is further reduced 5/12 of one percent per month. Source: SSA.gov.

Exhibit 11.13 | Social Security Full Retirement and Reductions by Age*

Year of Birth	Full Retirement Age	Age 62 Reduction Months	Monthly Percent Reduction	Total Percent Reduction
1937 or earlier	65	36	0.555	20.00
1938	65 & 2 months	38	0.548	20.83
1939	65 & 4 months	40	0.541	21.67
1940	65 & 6 months	42	0.535	22.50
1941	65 & 8 months	44	0.530	23.33
1942	65 & 10 months	46	0.525	24.17
1943-1954	66	48	0.520	25.00
1955	66 & 2 months	50	0.516	25.84
1956	66 & 4 months	52	0.512	26.66
1957	66 & 6 months	54	0.509	27.50
1958	66 & 8 months	56	0.505	28.33
1959	66 & 10 months	58	0.502	29.17
1960 and later	67	60	0.500	30.00

*Percentage monthly and total reductions are approximate due to rounding. The actual reductions are 0.555 or 5/9 of one percent per month for the first 36 months and 0.416 or 5/12 of one percent for subsequent months.
Source: Social Security Administration (www.ssa.gov)

No matter what the full retirement age is, a worker may start receiving benefits as early as age 62 and can also retire at any time between age 62 and full retirement age. However, if a worker starts benefits at one of these early ages, the benefits are reduced a fraction of a percent for each month before the full retirement age.

Example 11.17

Assume that Josephine, a worker born in 1956, decided to retire on her 63rd birthday. Assume that her full retirement benefit would have been $1,429.20 at age 66 and four months, her full retirement age. If she retires at age 63, what is her monthly retirement benefit?

The answer is $1,119. Josephine retired 40 months early. The monthly retirement benefit reduction percentage is 1/180 (5/9 x 1% = 1/180 = 0.0056) for the first 36 months (1/180 x 36 = 20 percent) and 1/240 (5/12 x 1% = 1/240 = 0.0042) for the four subsequent months of early retirement (1/240 x 4 = 1.6668 percent), yielding a total permanent reduction to Josephine's monthly retirement benefit of 21.6667 percent. 21.6667 percent x $1,429.20 = $309.66. $1,429.20 - $309.66 = $1,119.50 (rounded).

Example 11.18

What if Josephine retired at age 65 and six months? What is her permanent monthly retirement benefit (subject to COLA increases)? Note she retired 10 months early from normal retirement age.

The answer is $1,349. 1/180 x 10 = 5.5556 percent. 5.5556 percent x $1,429.20 = $79.40. $1,429.20 - $79.40 = $1,349.80 (rounded).

For those covered individuals who take late retirement, or when benefits are lost due to the earnings limitation, the monthly retirement benefit and the benefit paid to the surviving spouse will increase each year (until age 70) as follows:

Exhibit 11.14 | Percentage Increases for Delayed Retirement

Increase For Year Born	Annual Percentage Increase Each Year Of Late Retirement	After Age
1917-1924	3.0%	65
1925-1926	3.5%	65
1927-1928	4.0%	65
1929-1930	4.5%	65
1931-1932	5.0%	65
1933-1934	5.5%	65
1935-1936	6.0%	65
1937	6.5%	65
1938	6.5%	65 and 2 months
1939	7.0%	65 and 4 months
1940	7.0%	65 and 6 months
1941	7.5%	65 and 8 months
1942	7.5%	65 and 10 months
1943 or later	8.0%	66

Example 11.19

Jeanette's full retirement age is 66. She is considering taking Social Security retirement benefits at age 62, 66, or 70. Assume her monthly expected benefit is $1,000 at full retirement age, expected inflation is 4%, and her life expectancy is 90. Calculate the present value of her benefits at ages 62, 66, and 70 (A, B, or C).

Choice A – Begin Benefits at age 62.

PMT	$750	($1,000 less 25% reduction)
N	336	(90-62) x 12
i	0.3333	4/12
FV	0	
PV$_{@62}$	$151,450.19	

Choice B – Begin Benefits at age 66.

PMT	$1,000	Full benefit at full retirement age
N	288	(90-66) x 12
i	0.3333	4/12
FV	0	
PV$_{@66}$	$184,948.61	

Discount to age 62 for comparison.

PMT	$0	
N	4	(66-62)
i	4	
FV	$184,948.61	
PV$_{@62}$	$158,094.84	

Choice C – Begin Benefits at age 70.

PMT	$1,320	($1,000 plus 8% x 4 years increase)
N	240	(90-70) x 12
i	0.3333	4/12
FV	0	
PV$_{@70}$	$217,828.85	

Discount to age 62 for comparison.

PMT	$0	
N	8	(70-62)
i	4	
FV	$217,828.85	
PV$_{@62}$	$159,165.41	

As you can see, even though the benefit is reduced if Jeanette begins her benefit early, the PV of the total benefit at age 62 is not much less than if she took the benefit at age 66. Similarly, if she begins her payments later, her yearly payments will be higher but the PV of the benefit at age 62 is not much more than if she had taken benefits at age 66. The significance here is that all things being equal, the acceleration or delay of benefit generally has little impact on the PV of the benefit at age 62. However, the choice of retirement age is significant when considering the annual income needed to maintain one's standard of living.

Another critical factor in this analysis is the life expectancy of the worker. If the life expectancy is significantly less than what was assumed it might not make sense to delay benefits. Another factor that was not considered is the tax impact of benefits, which is discussed later in this chapter.

Although the calculations explained above can provide estimates of the Social Security benefits a retiring worker may receive, an advisor should have the client obtain his entire Social Security earnings history up to the moment of retirement from the Social Security Administration to get the most accurate benefit estimate.

Exhibit 11.15 depicts the percent of PIA that a participant will receive based on the age benefits begin. The increase in the monthly benefit over time compensates for the decrease in life expectancy, such that an individual living to average life expectancy will be expected to receive the same dollar amount of benefits over their lifetime. To the extent an individual expects to live beyond the average life expectancy, delaying benefits is beneficial. To the extent an individual does not expect to reach average life expectancy, beginning benefits at an early age is beneficial.

Exhibit 11.15 | Social Security Benefits at Different Ages

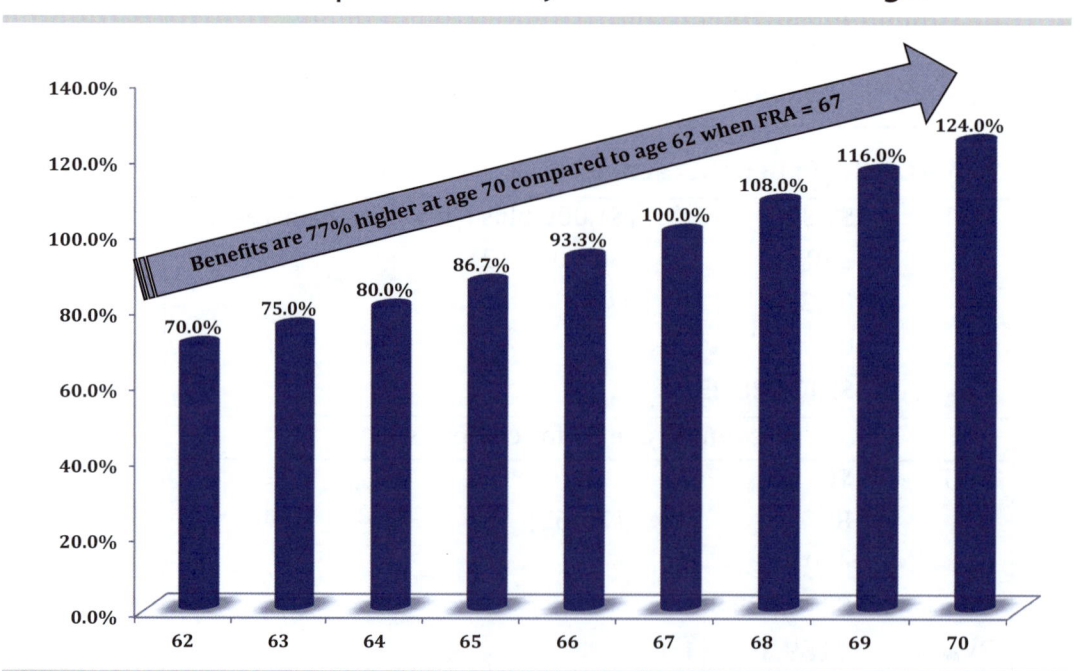

Reduction of Social Security Benefits

Besides early retirement, there are two other situations in which beneficiaries can have benefits reduced. The first instance is a reduction of benefits based on earnings, referred to as the **retirement earnings limitations test**. The other instance is through taxation of Social Security benefits. Both of these measures reduce one's net benefits.

A person may continue to work even though he is considered "retired" under Social Security. For a retiree who receives Social Security retirement benefits before normal retirement age, the earnings received by the beneficiary cannot exceed certain limitations without triggering a reduction in Social Security benefits. Beneficiaries can earn up to the limitation amount and receive all of their benefits, but if their earnings exceed the designated limit for the calendar year, then benefits will be reduced or eliminated. The law provides for earnings limitations of $18,960 for those under the full retirement age for 2021. The Social Security Administration reduces $1 in benefits for each $2 earned by those beneficiaries above $18,960. In the year that the retiree reaches full retirement age, $1 in benefits will be deducted for each $3 earned above the given year's limit but only for earnings before the month the

retiree reaches full retirement age. For 2021, the limit for earnings in the year the retiree reaches full retirement age is $50,520. The earnings limitation increases every year as median earnings nationwide increase. Once the retiree reaches normal retirement age, benefits will not be reduced regardless of the earnings limitations.

In the event that a beneficiary, who is younger than normal retirement age, has earnings that exceed the limitation, that beneficiary's benefits will be reduced depending on his or her age. The beneficiary must file an annual report of his earnings to the Social Security Administration by April 15 of the year following the year worked and must provide the exact earnings for that year and an estimate for the current year. The filing of a federal tax return with the IRS does not satisfy the filing requirement with the Social Security Administration. Also, the wages count toward the earnings limitation when they are earned, not when paid, whereas income for the self-employed normally counts when paid, not earned. If other family members receive benefits based on the beneficiary's Social Security record, then the total family benefits may be affected by the beneficiary's earnings that exceed the earnings limitation. In such a case, the Social Security Administration will withhold not only the worker's benefits but will withhold those benefits payable to family members as well. However, if a family member's benefits are reduced based on their own earnings, only that family member's benefits are reduced.

Generally, only wages and net self-employment income count towards the retirement earnings limitation, whereas income from savings, investments, and insurance does not. The following is a nonexclusive list of sources of income that DO NOT count toward the earnings limitation:

- Pension or retirement income
- 401(k) plan and IRA withdrawals
- Dividends and interest from investments
- Capital gains
- Rental income

- Workers' compensation benefits (generally not payable after a worker has retired)
- Unemployment benefits
- Court-awarded judgments, less components of award that include lost wages
- Contest winnings

Example 11.20

Rory is 64 years old and despite being retired from his occupation as an attorney, earned $21,000 in 2021 while working as a golf instructor at a local golf course. Rory's monthly retirement benefit from Social Security is normally $1,200, which totals $14,400 for the entire year. Because Rory exceeded the retirement earnings limitation, how much money will be reduced from Rory's Social Security retirement benefit for 2021?

Rory's total earnings in 2021	$21,000
Earnings limitation	($18,960)
Remainder excess	$2,040
One-half deduction	÷ 2
Benefits reduced by:	**$1,020**

The Social Security Administration will reduce Rory's benefits for the year by $1,020. Rory will receive $13,380 in retirement benefits ($14,400 annual retirement benefit less $1,020 reduction). Rory's total income for 2021 will be $34,380, instead of $35,400.

Example 11.21

Angel is 67 years old and has a full-time job working as a masseur. This year (2021) Angel anticipates earning $22,000 from her job. How much, in dollars, will Angel's Social Security benefits be reduced for the earnings test?

None, because Angel is over full retirement age.

Special Calculation of Earnings Test in the First Year of Retirement

In the first year of retirement, a special monthly earnings test can be applied so that earnings prior to the month of retirement are not counted. Beginning with the month of retirement, for any month in which earnings are below 1/12 of the annual amount ($1,580 in 2021), the Social Security benefit amount will not be reduced. This special monthly calculation only applies in the first year of retirement; after the first year, the annual test will apply.

Example 11.22

Odell will be turning age 64 on July 31, 2021. Odell's full retirement age is 66 and 6 months. If Odell retires in the month he turns age 64, his Social Security benefit will be $1,200 per month. Odell will earn $25,000 between January and July, but will reduce his hours beginning in August and earn $1,000 per month from August through December. Since Odell's monthly earnings in the months after retiring under Social Security are less than $1,580 ($18,960 ÷ 12 = $1,580), his Social Security benefits for August - December will not be reduced. For 2022, Odell will be subject to the earnings test based on his annual income.

In 2022, Odell will still be under full retirement age and he reports to Social Security that he expects to earn $23,760 in 2022. If the earnings limit remains unchanged in 2022, he will be over the $18,960 threshold by $4,800. His Social Security benefits will be reduced by $1 for every $2 that he is over the limit, or $2,400 ($4,800 ÷ 2 = $2,400). Odell will not receive a check in January or February of 2022 (those checks ($1,200 each month x 2 = $2,400) are withheld to cover the earnings test reduction in benefits), and then he will receive the full $1,200 each month from March - December. Odell's Social Security benefit will increase slightly when he reaches full retirement age to make up for the amount that was withheld due to the earnings test.

TAXATION OF SOCIAL SECURITY BENEFITS

Apart from the earnings limitation, some beneficiaries may be required to pay income tax on their Social Security benefits. For persons with substantial income in addition to Social Security benefits, up to 85 percent of their annual Social Security benefits may be subject to federal income tax. The Social Security Administration is concerned with a beneficiary's **modified adjusted gross income** (MAGI). For purposes of Social Security, MAGI is equal to the taxpayer's adjusted gross income plus tax exempt interest, including:

- interest earned on savings bonds used for higher education;
- amounts excluded from the taxpayer's income for employer-provided adoption assistance;
- amounts deducted for interest paid for educational loans;
- interest earned on tax exempt municipal bonds; and
- income earned in a foreign country, a U.S. possession, or Puerto Rico, that is excluded from income.

Key Concepts

1. How are Social Security benefits taxed?

2. What benefits are available from Social Security other than retirement benefits?

3. What is the maximum family benefit?

Example 11.23

Last year Fred and Velma had adjusted gross income of $40,000. They also had the following items:

- Velma spent three months during the year in Mexico visiting her mother. While she was there, she earned $5,000 that has been excluded from their AGI.

- While in Mexico, Velma fell in love with a little orphan girl. Luckily, Fred's company has an Adoption Assistance Program. The program paid $8,000 towards the adoption and the amount was excluded from Fred's AGI.

- Fred has been attending night school for several years and has several student loans. Last year he paid and deducted $200 in student loan interest.

- Fred and Velma had $900 in interest. $400 was from tax-exempt bonds and the remaining $500 was from corporate bonds.

Fred and Velma's MAGI for last year is:

Adjusted Gross Income (AGI)	$40,000
+ Foreign Income Excluded	$5,000
+ Adoption Assistance Excluded	$8,000
+ Student Loan Interest Deduction	$200
+ Tax-Exempt Bonds Interest	$400
= Modified Adjusted Gross Income (MAGI)	**$53,600**

Note that the $500 of corporate-bond interest has already been included in AGI for Fred and Velma.

A taxpayer's "combined" (or provisional) income is equal to: MAGI + ½ of Social Security benefits. Generally, up to 50 percent of Social Security benefits may be subject to federal income taxes for beneficiaries who file a federal tax return as an "individual" and have a combined income between $25,000 and $34,000. For those with a modified adjusted gross income plus one-half of Social Security greater than $34,000, up to 85 percent of their Social Security benefits may be subject to federal income taxation. For those beneficiaries that file a joint federal tax return and have a combined income with their spouse between $32,000 and $44,000, up to 50 percent of their Social Security benefits will be subject to federal income taxes. Finally, if beneficiaries filing a joint tax return have a modified adjusted gross income plus one-half Social Security benefits that exceeds $44,000, up to 85 percent of their Social Security benefits may be subject to federal income taxation.

In summary, for persons with substantial income in addition to their Social Security benefits, up to 85 percent of their annual benefits may be subject to federal income tax.

Exhibit 11.16 | Social Security Hurdle Amounts

	Married Filing Jointly	All Others Except MFS = 0
1st Hurdle	$32,000	$25,000
2nd Hurdle	$44,000	$34,000

If MAGI plus one half of Social Security benefits exceeds the first hurdle but not the second, the taxable amount of Social Security benefits is the lesser of:
- 50% Social Security Benefits, or
- 50% [MAGI + 0.50 (Social Security Benefits) - Hurdle 1]; which is 50% of the amount by which combined income exceeds Hurdle 1.

Example 11.24

A married couple has interest income of $18,000 and Social Security benefits of $20,000. What amount of their Social Security benefits must be included in their taxable income?

Lesser of:
- 0.50($20,000) = $10,000, or
- 0.50 [$18,000 + 0.50 (20,000) - 32,000] = Negative

They would have $0 inclusion due to a negative result.

Example 11.25

A married couple has income of $30,000 and Social Security benefits of $20,000. What amount of their Social Security benefits must be included in their taxable income?

Lesser of:
- 0.50($20,000) = $10,000, or
- 0.50 [30,000 + 0.50 (20,000) - 32,000] = $4,000

They would have $4,000 of Social Security benefits included in taxable income.

If MAGI plus one-half the Social Security benefits exceeds the second hurdle, the taxable amount of Social Security benefits is the lesser of:
- 85% Social Security Benefits, or
- 85% [MAGI + 0.50 (Social Security Benefits) - Hurdle 2], plus the lesser of:
  - $6,000 for MFJ or $4,500 for all other taxpayers, or
  - The taxable amount calculated under the 50% formula and only considering Hurdle 1.

Example 11.26

A married couple has income of $60,000 and Social Security benefits of $20,000. What amount of their Social Security benefits must be included in their taxable income?

0.85 ($20,000) = **$17,000**

0.85 [$60,000 + 0.50 ($20,000) - $44,000] = $22,100
   Plus the lesser of:
- $6,000, or
- 0.50($20,000) = $10,000, or
- 0.50[$60,000 + 0.50($20,000)-$32,000] = $19,000

$6,000
                                      $28,100

Therefore, **$17,000** must be included in their taxable income.

Example 11.27

A married couple has income of $45,000 and Social Security benefits of $20,000. What amount of their Social Security benefits must be included in their taxable income?

0.85 ($20,000) = **$17,000**

0.85 [$45,000 + 0.50 ($20,000) - $44,000] = $9,350
   Plus the lesser of:
- $6,000, or
- 0.50($20,000) = $10,000, or
- 0.50[$45,000 + 0.50($20,000)-$32,000] = $11,500

$6,000
                                        $15,350

Therefore, **$15,350** must be included in their taxable income.

Example 11.28

Last year LaWanda, a single taxpayer, received $10,400 in Social Security benefits. For the entire year, she had an adjusted gross income of $28,000. How much, if any, of her Social Security benefit is taxable?

First, determine LaWanda's modified adjusted gross income. Modified adjusted gross income is the sum of adjusted gross income, nontaxable interest, and foreign-earned income. One-half of LaWanda's Social Security benefits must then be added to her MAGI, to arrive at her combined income. For LaWanda, the equation is as follows: $28,000 + [$10,400 x 0.50] = $33,200. Since LaWanda's combined income is between the two base amounts for a single individual of $25,000 and $34,000, we can use the following formula to determine her taxable amount. The income tax base will be the lesser of 50% of her Social Security benefits _OR_ 50% of the amount by which LaWanda's combined income exceeds the base amount of $25,000. Based on this formula, LaWanda will be subject to income tax on $4,100 of her Social Security benefit.

- 0.50($10,400) = $5,200
- 0.50($33,200 - $25,000) = $4,100 (the LESSER amount)

Example 11.29

A married couple files jointly and has an adjusted gross income of $38,000, no tax-exempt interest, and $11,000 of Social Security benefits. How much, if any, of their Social Security benefits is included in gross income?

The lesser of the following:
- 0.50 ($11,000) = $5,500, or
- 0.50 [$38,000 + 0.50 ($11,000) - $32,000] = 0.50 ($11,500) = $5,750

They will include $5,500 in gross income. If the couple's adjusted gross income was $15,000 and their Social Security benefits totaled $5,000, none of the benefits would be taxable since their combined income is below the $32,000 threshold amount.

Example 11.30

Clark and Lois, married filing jointly, have tax-free municipal bond interest of $2,000. Assuming that Clark and Lois have differing AGI amounts ranging from $20,000 to $50,000, the Social Security amount includible in taxable income is shown below. Thus, if Clark and Lois have $20,000 in AGI, then only $1,000 of the Social Security benefit is included (4% of the benefit is included), but if they have AGI of $50,000 then $20,400 is includible (85% of the benefit is included). Notice that once an individual is substantially over the second hurdle they can expect to include 85% of the Social Security benefit.

Preliminary AGI	$20,000	$25,000	$30,000	$35,000	$40,000	$45,000	$50,000
Tax free bond interest	$2,000	$2,000	$2,000	$2,000	$2,000	$2,000	$2,000
MAGI	$22,000	$27,000	$32,000	$37,000	$42,000	$47,000	$52,000
50% of Social Security	$12,000	$12,000	$12,000	$12,000	$12,000	$12,000	$12,000
MAGI plus 1/2 Social Security	$34,000	$39,000	$44,000	$49,000	$54,000	$59,000	$64,000
First hurdle	$32,000	$32,000	$32,000	$32,000	$32,000	$32,000	$32,000
Second hurdle	$44,000	$44,000	$44,000	$44,000	$44,000	$44,000	$44,000
Excess of income over first hurdle	$2,000	$7,000	$12,000	$17,000	$22,000	$27,000	$32,000
Excess of income over second hurdle	$0	$0	$0	$5,000	$10,000	$15,000	$20,000
1. 50% of SSB	$12,000	$12,000	$12,000				
2. 50% [MAGI + 0.50 (SSB) - Hurdle 1)	$1,000	$3,500	$6,000				
3. 85% of SSB				$20,400	$20,400	$20,400	$20,400
4. [85% [MAGI + 0.5 (SSB)- Hurdle 2]] + 6000				$10,250	$14,500	$18,750	$23,000
5. [85% [MAGI + 0.5 (SSB)- Hurdle 2]] + 50% [MAGI + 0.50 (SSB) - Hurdle 1]				$14,450	$18,700	$22,950	$27,200
6. [85% [MAGI + 0.5 (SSB)- Hurdle 2]] + 50% of SSB				$16,250	$20,500	$24,750	$29,000
Includable portion of Social Security	$1,000	$3,500	$6,000	$10,250	$14,500	$18,750	$20,400
Percent of SS Taxed	4%	15%	25%	43%	60%	78%	85%

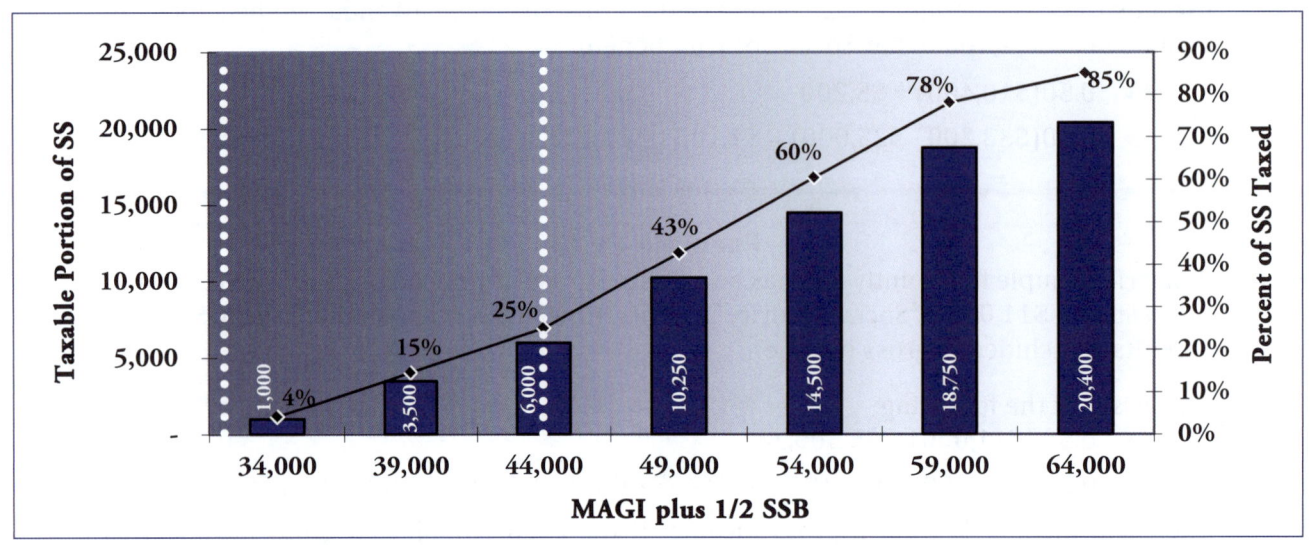

OTHER SOCIAL SECURITY BENEFITS

Disability Benefits and Disability Insured

Benefits are payable at any age to workers who have enough Social Security credits and who have a severe physical or mental impairment that is expected to prevent them from doing "substantial" work for a year or more or who have a condition that is expected to result in death. Workers are insured for disability if they are fully insured and, except for persons who are blind or disabled at age 31 or older, have a total of at least 20 quarters of coverage during the 40-quarter period ending with the quarter in which the worker became disabled. Workers who are disabled before age 31 must have total quarters of coverage equal to one-half the calendar quarters that have elapsed since the worker reached age 21 ending in the quarter in which the worker became disabled. However, a minimum of six quarters is required.

Exhibit 11.17 | Work Credits for Disability Benefits

Born After 1929, Become Disabled at Age:	Number of Credits You Need:
31 through 42	20
44	22
46	24
48	26
50	28
52	30
54	32
56	34
58	36
60	38
62 or older	40

- Before age 24 - The disabled individual may qualify if they have six credits earned in the three-year period ending when the disability starts.
- Age 24 to 31 - The disabled individual may qualify if they have credit for working half the time between age 21 and the time they become disabled. For example, if they become disabled at age 27, they would need credit for three years of work (12 credits) out of the past 6 years (between ages 21 and 27).
- Age 31 or older - In general, the disabled individual needs to have the number of work credits shown in the chart. Unless they are blind, they must have earned at least 20 of the credits in the 10 years immediately before they became disabled.

In 2021, earnings of $1,310 or more per month are considered substantial; therefore, a worker earning more than $1,310 per month would not be eligible for Social Security disability benefits. (If the individual is blind, then the amount is increased to $2,190.) The disability program includes incentives to smooth the disabled individual's transition back into the workforce, including continuation of benefits and healthcare coverage. Disability under the Social Security system is defined as an inability to engage in substantial gainful activity by reason of a physical or mental impairment expected to last at least 12 months or result in death. The impairment must be of such severity that the applicant is not only unable to do his previous work but cannot, considering age, education, and work experience, engage in any other kind of substantial gainful work that exists in the national economy.

There is a five month waiting period for Social Security disability benefits; therefore, benefits will not be paid until the sixth month after the onset of disability.

Family Benefits

If an individual is receiving retirement or disability benefits, other members of the individual's family might receive benefits as well. Family members who may receive retirement or disability benefits include the following:

- A spouse, if the spouse is 62 years old, caring for a child under age 16, or caring for a child who was disabled before age 22.
- A child, if the child is unmarried and under age 18, under age 19 but still in school, or age 18 or older but disabled before age 22.

For those workers who are entitled to retirement or disability benefits, an ex-spouse who was married to the worker for more than 10 years could also be eligible for retirement benefits based on the worker's record. For a divorced spouse to collect spousal retirement benefits, the worker must be at least age 62, but does not have to be receiving benefits him- or her- self, and the divorce must have been final for at least two years. For the current spouse, spousal benefits are available only if the worker is also receiving benefits.

A child's benefit stops the month before the child reaches 18, unless the child is unmarried and is either disabled or is a full-time elementary or secondary school student. Approximately five months before the child's 18th birthday, the person receiving the child's benefits will get a form explaining how benefits can continue. A child whose benefits stop at 18 can have them started again if the child becomes disabled before reaching 22 or becomes a full-time elementary or secondary school student before reaching 19. If the child continues to receive benefits after age 18 due to a disability, the child also may qualify for SSI disability benefits. When a student's 19th birthday occurs during a school term, benefits can be continued up to two months to allow completion of the school term.

> ### 📝 Quick Quiz 11.4
>
> 1. Up to 85% of an individual's Social Security benefits may be included in their taxable income.
>   a. True
>   b. False
>
> 2. Once divorced, non-working ex-spouses will not receive Social Security benefits.
>   a. True
>   b. False
>
> 3. The maximum family benefit establishes a limit on the benefits that can be received by one family.
>   a. True
>   b. False
>
> True, False, True.

Survivors' Benefits

If a worker earned enough Social Security credits during his lifetime, certain members of the worker's family may be eligible for benefits when the worker dies. The family members of the deceased worker who may be entitled to survivors' benefits include:

- A widow or widower age 60 (including a divorced spouse if the marriage lasted at least 10 years and the spouse has not remarried before the age of 60), age 50 if disabled, or any age if caring for a child under age 16 or a disabled child.
- A child of the deceased worker, if the child is unmarried and under age 18, under age 19 but still in school, or age 18 or older but disabled.
- Parents of the deceased worker, if the deceased worker was their primary means of support.

A surviving spouse may elect to receive the widow or widower benefit beginning at age 60, while delaying their own retirement benefit to between full retirement age and age 70, to receive delayed retirement credits. The spouse can elect to switch to their own benefit at any time between age 62 and 70.

A widow or widower who remarries after age 60 is not disqualified from obtaining benefits based on the deceased spouse's earnings. Marriage before age 60, however, will cause such disqualification while the marriage lasts.

A surviving spouse under age 60 will receive Social Security benefits until the youngest child reaches age 16. Spousal benefits will then cease until the spouse turns age 60 (50 if disabled). The years without benefits before age 60 are often referred to as the "blackout period" for the surviving spouse.

A special one-time payment of $255 may be made to a deceased worker's spouse or minor children upon death. If a spouse was living with the beneficiary at the time of death, the spouse will receive a one-time payment of $255. The payment may be made to a spouse who was not living with the beneficiary at the time of death or an ex-spouse if the spouse or ex-spouse was receiving Social Security benefits based on the deceased's earnings record. If there is no surviving spouse, a child (or children) who is eligible for benefits on the deceased's work record in the month of death may claim the payment.

THE MAXIMUM FAMILY BENEFIT

When a person dies, the deceased's survivors receive a percentage of the worker's Social Security benefits ranging from 75 percent to 100 percent each. There is a limit on the amount of monthly Social Security benefits that may be paid to a family. This limit is called the **maximum family benefit** and it is determined through a formula based on the worker's PIA. While the limit varies, it is equal to roughly 150 to 180 percent of the deceased worker's PIA. If the sum of the family members' benefits exceeds the limit, the family members' benefits are proportionately reduced. For old-age and survivor family benefits, the formula computes the sum of four separate percentages of portions of the worker's PIA. For 2021, these portions are the first $1,272 of PIA, the amount between $1,272 and $1,837, the amount between $1,837 and $2,395 and the amount over $2,395. These are the bend points for the maximum family benefit formula for the year 2021, with the following percentage calculations:

150 percent of the first $1,272 of the worker's PIA, *plus*
272 percent of the worker's PIA over $1,272 through $1,837, *plus*
134 percent of the worker's PIA over $1,837 through $2,395, *plus*
175 percent of the worker's PIA over $2,395.
This number is rounded to the next lower $0.10.

Example 11.31

If an individual has the maximum PIA for 2021, $3,148 per month, this would provide a maximum family benefit of $5,510.20 per month as shown by the calculation below:

```
            $1,272  x 1.50 =  $1,908.00
($1,837 - $1,272) x 2.72 =  $1,536.80
($2,395 - $1,837) x 1.34 =    $747.72
($3,148 - $2,395) x 1.75 =  $1,317.75
                            $5,510.27
           Rounded to $5,510.20
```

Example 11.32

Natalie and Brian, both age 50, are married and have two children, Ashley (age 15) and Kayli (age 5). Brian is disabled and has a PIA amount equal to the maximum PIA ($3,148). As calculated in **Example 11.31**, the maximum family benefit is $5,510.20 Because Brian is disabled, Natalie, Ashley, and Kayli are each entitled to receive a benefit equal to 50% of Brian's PIA, subject to the maximum family benefit limit, because the two children are under 18 and Natalie is a spouse/caretaker of a child under 16. Without regard to the maximum family benefit, they would each receive:

Brian	$3,148.00	100% of PIA
Natalie	$1,574.00	50% of Brian's PIA
Ashley	$1,574.00	50% of Brian's PIA
Kayli	$1,574.00	50% of Brian's PIA
Total	$7,870.00	

Because the benefit exceeds the maximum family benefit, the amounts for Natalie, Ashley, and Kayli must be prorated. Therefore, they will each receive $787.40 [($5,510.20 - $3,148) ÷ 3].

Brian	$3,148.00	100% of PIA
Natalie	$787.40	50% of Brian's PIA subject to maximum family benefit
Ashley	$787.40	50% of Brian's PIA subject to maximum family benefit
Kayli	$787.40	50% of Brian's PIA subject to maximum family benefit
Total	$5,510.20	

Assume instead that Ashley is 19 and no longer eligible to receive benefits under Brian. The maximum family benefit would be calculated as follows:

Brian	$3,148.00	100% of PIA
Natalie	$1,181.10	50% of Brian's PIA subject to maximum family benefit
Ashley	$0	Not eligible
Kayli	$1,181.10	50% of Brian's PIA subject to maximum family benefit
Total	$5510.20	

Now assume Ashley is 19 and Kayli is 17. In this case, Natalie is no longer eligible because she is not caring for a child under 16. The family benefit would be calculated as follows:

Brian	$3,148.00	100% of PIA
Natalie	$0	Not eligible
Ashley	$0	Not eligible
Kayli	$1,574.00	50% of Brian's PIA
Total	$4,722.00	

Notice that Kayli is limited to 50% of Brian's PIA, thus they do not reach the maximum family benefit.

CHOOSING WHEN TO BEGIN SOCIAL SECURITY RETIREMENT BENEFITS

There are many issues in deciding when to begin receiving Social Security retirement benefits. As discussed earlier in this chapter, Social Security retirement benefits may be reduced if other income is earned before full retirement age, benefits may or may not be subject to income tax, and benefits may be increased or decreased depending on the start date of benefits relative to full retirement age. In addition to these issues, there are other considerations that may impact the total benefits collected by the worker and the worker's spouse.

Ideally, the present value of the total lifetime benefits for a person with an average life expectancy would be the same whether the beneficiary takes a smaller benefit at age 62 or a larger benefit at 70, as the calculations are actuarially based. However, that is not the case. Decisions that are made by a worker can greatly impact both the present value of benefits and total lifetime benefits collected. In fact, even if a retiree's life span is cut short, delaying retirement benefits past age 62 may make sense.

As discussed earlier in the chapter, delaying retirement benefits increases the annual benefit when it is received. However, delaying commencement of receipt of retirement benefits should not be confused with a cost-of-living adjustment (COLA). Cost-of-living adjustments have averaged less than two percent over the last ten years, but once retirement benefits are being paid to a retiree, those benefits only increase based on the COLA. Nonetheless, by delaying benefits from age 62 to 63, the yet-to-be-received benefit increases approximately seven percent for that one year. Delaying benefits for anyone born in or after 1943 beyond full retirement age increases benefits by eight percent per year. That return is large for what is considered to be a very secure investment. Once the Social Security benefit is adjusted for inflation through application of the COLA, the rate is even more attractive.

Key Concepts

1. How are retirement benefits impacted by cost-of-living adjustments and by delayed credits?

2. What strategies can be used to potentially increase total lifetime benefits under Social Security?

3. How can a divorced spouse born before January 2, 1954 use "file and suspend?"

4. How does marriage or divorce affect Social Security benefits?

Is the eight percent increase worth delaying the start of benefits? That question is more complicated than it appears. Some of the important factors in this question are based on an individual's thoughts regarding wealth, cash flow needs, life expectancy, perception of the solvency of the Social Security program, as well as others.

An easy way to estimate a breakeven point for delayed benefits is to consider the benefit that is given up compared to the increase in future benefits. For example, assume a benefit of $1,000 per month or $12,000 per year at full retirement age. If the worker delayed benefits by one year, the benefits would increase by eight percent to $12,960 (without regard to a COLA). Therefore, the benefits that are received are $960 higher, but $12,000 had to be forfeited. Dividing what was given up ($12,000) by the increase ($960) results in a simple breakeven of 12.5 years. This calculation is very simplistic and does not consider the time value of money or other implications, such as taxation of benefits. However, it does provide basic guidance about how long one needs to live to justify giving up current benefits for higher future benefits.

The simplified breakeven analysis can be modified to include a COLA and a discount rate. As the spread between the COLA and the discount rate increases, so does the time it takes for the present value of the delayed benefits to exceed the present value of the benefits commencing immediately. For example, using a discount rate of four percent and a COLA of two percent (a spread of two percent) increases the breakeven point from 12.5 years to approximately 14 years. Thus, for someone to delay benefits until age 70 based solely on payback or breakeven, the person would have to live to at least age 82½, without considering the time value of money. However, there are other reasons that delaying benefits may be beneficial to the worker or their family members.

For non-married, lower wage earners who will not qualify for the maximum retirement benefit, it is important to keep in mind that the retirement benefit formula is based on the highest 35 years of work. If a non-married worker had historically lower earnings compared to earnings today, that worker might consider working longer to not only allow the automatic increase or growth of delaying the retirement benefit, but to also serve to increase the 35 year base, which is the basis for determining the retirement benefit. Delaying is especially helpful to those who do not work all 35 years, as that situation tends to have a more noticeable effect on the retirement benefit.

There has been much written on the topic of maximizing Social Security benefits over the last ten years. Strategies, such as "file-and-suspend," have been used to increase the total dollars that retirees would be receive over their lifetime. However, in 2015 Congress chose to eliminate the benefits of this strategy as they were seen by some as taking advantage of the system. In fairness, the file-and-suspend strategy did provide greater benefits to many seniors. However, the Bipartisan Budget Act (BBA) of 2015 eliminated file and suspend after April 29, 2016.

Married individuals are entitled (1) to a worker-determined retirement benefit based on their own earnings and/or (2) to a spousal benefit equal to one half of their spouse's benefit claimed at normal retirement age. The individual is entitled to receive the higher of these two amounts; however, the worker's own benefit is paid first. Therefore, if the spousal benefit is higher, the worker will receive their own benefit plus a portion of the spousal benefit, with a combined total equal to the higher spousal benefit amount. If a married individual files a claim prior to attaining normal retirement age, the laws governing Social Security deem the individual as claiming both types of benefits and the benefits will be permanently reduced.

Example 11.33

Stacy Lynn qualifies for a retirement benefit of $250 and a spouse's benefit of $400. At her full retirement age, she will receive her own $250 retirement benefit, and $150 from her spouse's benefit, for a total of $400. If she takes her retirement benefit before her full retirement age, both amounts will be reduced.

Surviving spouses are entitled to 100 percent of the deceased worker's benefit amount after the worker dies. If the spouse with the higher benefits delays benefits until age 70 and then dies, it will increase the surviving spouse's benefit. This approach was not changed by the 2015 legislation

Divorced spouses can also claim benefits based on their ex-spouse's record if they were married ten years or longer. Generally, the divorced spouse can collect based on their ex-spouse's record as long as they are unmarried, they are age 62 or older, and the ex-spouse is entitled to Social Security retirement or disability benefits. If a divorced spouse who was born before Jan. 2, 1954 has reached full retirement age and is eligible for a spouse's benefit, then he or she can choose to receive only the divorced spouse's benefits and delay receiving their own retirement benefits until a later date. If retirement benefits are delayed, a higher benefit may be received at a later date based on the effect of delayed retirement credits. Thus, in effect, the spouse is able to receive a benefit from the ex-spouse's working history and let their own benefit increase until age 70. Divorced spouses born January 2, 1954 or later no longer have the option to file for a divorced spouse's benefit and suspend their own. If these spouses file for one benefit, they are effectively filing for all of the benefits for which they are entitled.

Example 11.34

Joanie and Chachi were happily married and raised four wonderful children, who went on to become contributing members of society: a butcher, a baker, a dancer, and a home maker. However, once the children left the home, Joanie and Chachi grew apart and finally divorced after 25 years of marriage. They both were professionals early in their career and became college professors. As a result, their retirement benefits are comparable. While Chachi has remarried, Joanie remains single. If Joanie was born before January 2, 1954, at full retirement age, Joanie could claim a spouse's benefit and let her retirement benefits increase until she turns age 70.

Deciding when to begin taking Social Security benefits should be planned as it can greatly impact the total benefits received over the life of a a worker and the worker's spouse. The planning should take into consideration the health and longevity of the spouses, as well as the need for income now and into the future.

MEDICARE BENEFITS

Medicare is a federal health insurance plan for people who are 65 and older, whether retired or still working. People who are disabled or have permanent kidney failure are entitled to Medicare at any age. The Health Care Financing Administration, now known as Centers for Medicare and Medicaid Services (or CMS), part of the United States Department of Health and Human Services, administers Medicare. Medicare is the nation's largest health insurance program, covering over 59 million individuals. There are two parts to original (traditional) Medicare: Hospital Insurance (Part A) and Medical Insurance (Part B). In addition, prescription drug coverage can be added by purchasing Part D. As an alternative to traditional Medicare, an individual who is eligible for Medicare may select Medicare Advantage (Part C), with or without prescription drug coverage.

Key Concepts

1. What benefits are provided by Medicare?
2. What benefits are provided by Supplemental Security Income?
3. Explain the major decisions that must be made when an individual becomes eligible for Medicare.
4. What are the various enrollment periods for Medicare?

Exhibit 11.18 | Medicare Options

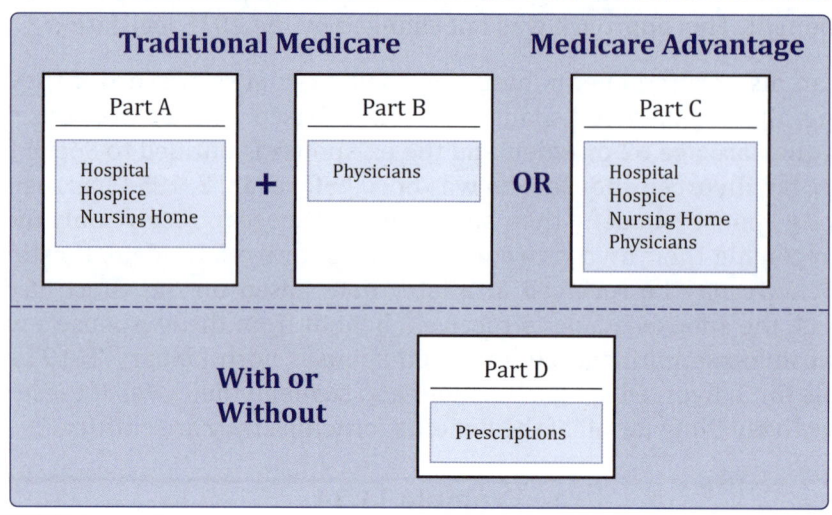

Individuals who are age 65 and over and receive Social Security benefits automatically qualify for Medicare. Also, individuals who have received Social Security disability benefits for at least two years automatically qualify for Medicare. Spouses age 65 or over who are eligible for Social Security benefits based on their spouse's earnings also qualify. All other individuals must file an application for Medicare. Those who are age 65 or over and not eligible for Social Security Benefits are permitted to enroll in Medicare by paying a fee for Part A along with the Part B premiums discussed below.[5]

Exhibit 11.19 | Medicare Parts

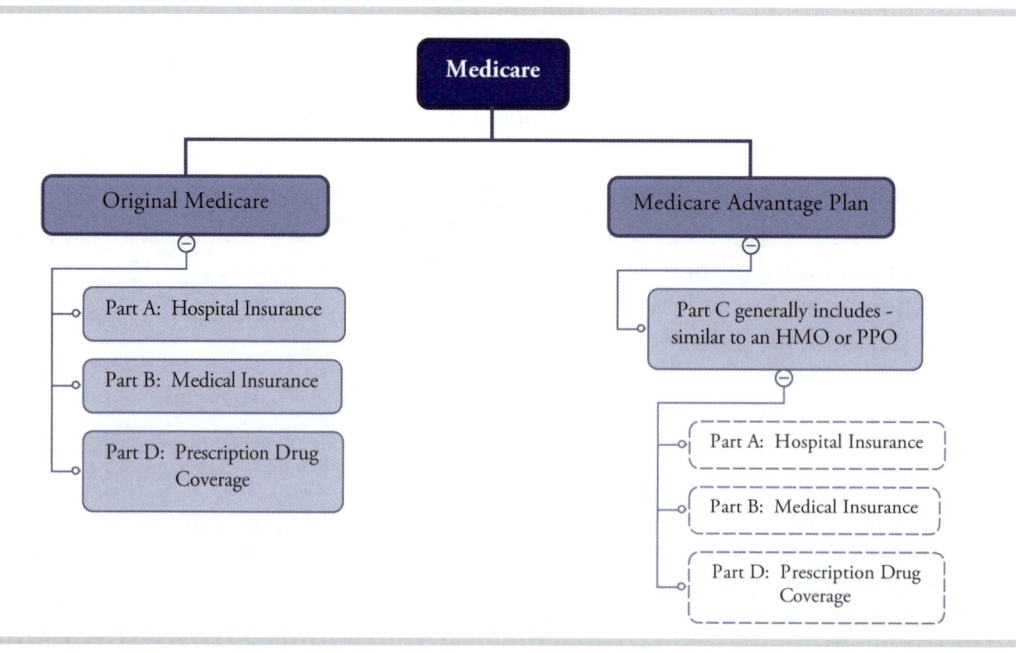

5. About 99% of Medicare beneficiaries will not pay a premium for Part A because either they or their spouse had 40 quarters of Medicare-covered employment. https://www.cms.gov/newsroom/fact-sheets/2021-medicare-parts-b-premiums-and-deductibles

TRADITIONAL MEDICARE

The original Medicare Plan (traditional Medicare, Part A and Part B) is the way most individuals obtain their Medicare benefits. This structure is the traditional payment-per-service arrangement where the individual insured may go to any doctor, specialist, or hospital that accepts Medicare, and Medicare pays its share after approved services are rendered. Medicare Administrative Contractors (MACs) are private insurance organizations that handle claims under the original Medicare Plan. The Social Security Administration does not handle claims for Medicare payments.

Medicare Part A

Part A, Hospital Insurance, is paid for by a portion of the FICA tax (as discussed previously in this chapter). Part A helps pay for necessary medical care furnished by Medicare-certified providers, including inpatient hospital care, skilled nursing care, home health care, hospice care, and other care. The number of days that Medicare covers care in hospitals and skilled nursing facilities is measured in what is termed **benefit periods.** A benefit period begins on the first day a patient receives services in a hospital or skilled nursing facility and ends after 60 consecutive days without further skilled care. There is no limit to the number of benefit periods a beneficiary may have.

Benefit periods are identified because deductibles, coinsurance, and premiums relate to a benefit period instead of a calendar year. For instance, coverage under Medicare Part A for 2021 requires a deductible of $1,484 per benefit period. For the 61st through the 90th day of each benefit period, the insured individual must pay $371 per day in the form of coinsurance. Any days over 90 in a benefit period are considered lifetime reserve days. There are 60 lifetime reserve days available with coinsurance of $742 per day. Lifetime reserve days do not renew with each benefit period. It is important, therefore, to determine the number of days used in each benefit period.

Exhibit 11.20 | Medicare Time Line

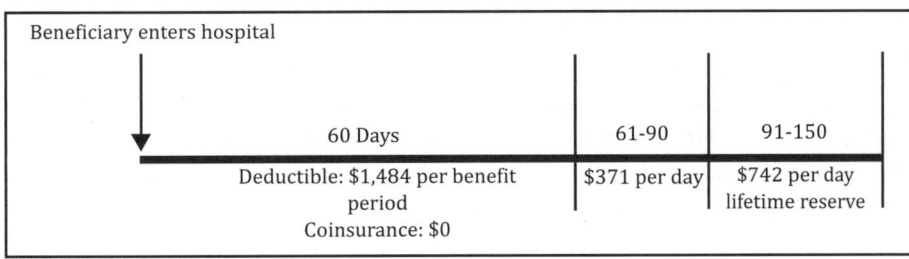

Exhibit 11.21 | Skilled Nursing Facility Time Line

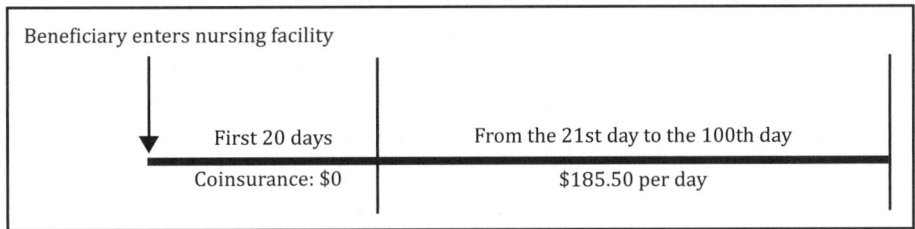

Exhibit 11.22 | Medicare Deductible, Coinsurance, and Premium Amounts (2021)

Hospital Insurance (Part A)
• **Deductible** - $1,484 per benefit period
• **Coinsurance**
• $371 a day for the 61st through the 90th day
• $742 a day for the 91st through the 150th day for each lifetime reserve day (total of 60 lifetime reserve days – nonrenewable)
• **Skilled Nursing Facility Coinsurance** - $185.50 a day for the 21st through the 100th day per Benefit Period
• **Hospital Insurance Premium** - $471 per month (Note: This premium is paid only by individuals who are not otherwise eligible for premium-free hospital insurance and have less than 30 quarters of Medicare covered employment.)

Medical Insurance (Part B)
• **Deductible** - $203 per year
• **Standard Monthly Premium** - $148.50 for new enrollees in 2021. The premium may be higher if income exceeds certain limits.

Source: medicare.gov/pubs/pdf/11579-medicare-costs.pdf

Medicare Part A helps pay for up to 90 days of inpatient hospital care during each benefit period. Covered services for inpatient hospital care include: semiprivate room and meals, operating and recovery room costs, intensive care, drugs, laboratory tests, x-rays, general nursing services, and any other necessary medical services and supplies. Convenience items such as television and telephones provided by hospitals in private rooms (unless medically necessary) are generally not covered. Medicare does not pay for custodial services for daily living activities such as eating, bathing, and getting dressed. Medicare does, however, pay for skilled nursing facility care for rehabilitation, such as recovery time after a hospital discharge. Part A may help pay for up to 100 days in a participating skilled nursing facility in each benefit period. Medicare pays all approved charges for the first 20 days relating to skilled nursing facility care, and the patient pays a coinsurance amount for days 21 through 100. Medicare may also pay the full, approved cost of covered home healthcare services, which includes part-time or intermittent skilled nursing services prescribed by a physician for treatment or rehabilitation of home-bound patients. Normally, the only cost to the insured for home health care is a 20 percent coinsurance charge for medical equipment, such as wheelchairs and walkers.

Medicare Part B

Medicare Part B, Medical Insurance, is optional and is subject to a monthly premium. Part B is financed by the monthly premiums paid by those who are enrolled and out of the general revenues from the U.S. Treasury. Medicare Part B is used to pay for doctors' services; ambulance transportation; diagnostic tests; outpatient therapy services; outpatient hospital services, including emergency room visits; X-rays and laboratory services; some preventative care; home healthcare services not covered by Part A; durable medical equipment and supplies; and a variety of other health services.

Medicare Part B pays for 80 percent of approved charges for most covered services. For those who are already receiving Social Security benefits at the time of enrollment in Medicare, the Part B premium will automatically be deducted from their Social Security benefits. Those not yet receiving Social Security benefits at the time of enrollment can choose to receive a bill from Medicare or can arrange for the premiums to be automatically deducted from a checking or savings account each month. The standard Part B premium amount is $148.50 (or higher depending on your income). The income-related monthly adjustment amount (IRMAA), as illustrated in **Exhibit 11.23**, is based on adjusted gross income from two years prior (a two-year look-back). If a Medicare enrollee's income has gone down for any of the following reasons, he or she may appeal the increase in premiums:

- marriage, divorce, or becoming widowed,
- reduction in work hours,
- loss of income-producing property due to disaster or other events beyond the insured's control,
- cessation or termination of an employer's pension plan, or
- settlement from an employer due to the employer's closure, bankruptcy, or reorganization.

The deductible for Part B is $203 per year. The insured is responsible for paying a $203 deductible per calendar year and the remaining 20 percent of the Medicare-approved charges. Medicare Part B usually does not cover charges for prescription drugs, routine physical examinations (it does cover a one-time "Welcome to Medicare" wellness visit and one yearly wellness visit), or services unrelated to treatment of injury or illness. Dental care, dentures, cosmetic surgery, hearing aids, and eye examinations are not covered by Part B.

Exhibit 11.23 | Medicare Part B Premiums 2021 (Based on 2019 Modified Adjusted Gross Income)

Premium	Filing Status: Single	Filing Status: MFJ
$148.50	$88,000 or less	$176,000 or less
$207.90	$88,001-$111,000	$176,001-$222,000
$297.00	$111,001-$138,000	$222,001-$276,000
$386.10	$138,001-$165,000	$276,001-$330,000
$475.20	$165,001-$499,999	$330,001-$749,999
$504.90	$500,000 and Above	$750,000 and Above

Medicare Exclusions

Many retirees will be more interested in what is not covered than what is covered, since they will need a plan to fill in any gaps. Part A does not cover hospital stays beyond 90 days unless lifetime reserve days remain available. Part A also excludes services provided outside the U.S., its territories, and its possessions. It also covers only up to 100 days of skilled nursing care, and only following at least three days of hospitalization. Part A does not cover custodial care.

Medicare Part B excludes prescription drugs not administered by a doctor. It does not cover services provided outside the U.S., its territories, and its possessions. Part B does not cover routine physical exams (except as required by the Affordable Care Act), routine eye exams, dental care, hearing aids, or eyeglasses. It also excludes luxury elective services, custodial care, elective cosmetic surgery, services covered by workers' compensation, and services provided free in a federal facility. Part A and Part B both exclude coverage for the first three pints of blood when a blood transfusion is needed. There is no annual maximum-out-of-pocket limit for original Medicare Parts A and B.

Many private insurance companies sell Medicare supplemental insurance policies, referred to as Medigap policies. These supplemental policies help bridge the coverage gaps in the original Medicare Plan by paying Medicare's coinsurance amounts, as well as other out-of-pocket expenses for health care.

When a worker is first enrolled in Part B at age 65, there is a six-month open enrollment period in Medigap. Enrolling during this time is highly recommended since, during the time of open enrollment, the health status of the applicant cannot be used as a reason to refuse a Medigap policy or to charge more than other open enrollment applicants. If enrollment occurs outside of the initial six-month open enrollment period, the insurer may require a six-month waiting period for coverage of pre-existing conditions and in some cases may deny coverage. The waiting period for pre-existing conditions can be reduced or eliminated if the insured had prior creditable coverage. Each month of prior coverage reduces the waiting period for coverage of preexisting conditions by one month, so if prior coverage lasted at least six months, there will be no wait. However, there cannot be a break in coverage for more than 63 days. If, however, the open enrollment period has expired, the applicant may be denied a policy based on health status or may be charged higher rates.

Medicare Part D Subsidy

Medicare prescription drug plans, known as the Medicare Part D Subsidy (Part D or Medicare Prescription Drug Plan), became available beginning January 1, 2006, to individuals with Medicare. Part D is intended to save participants money on prescription drug costs and help protect against higher drug costs in the future. Insurance companies and other private companies work with Medicare to offer these drug plans by negotiating discounts on drug prices. Both those who enroll in traditional Medicare and those who choose Medicare Advantage have the option to also enroll in Part D.

Medicare prescription drug plans provide insurance coverage for prescription drugs. Part D covers both brand-name and generic prescription drugs at certain pharmacies in a Part D participant's area. If an individual is enrolled in Medicare, then that individual is eligible under Part D regardless of income, assets, health status, or current prescription expenses. Like other insurance, if an individual joins, they pay a monthly premium and pay a share of the cost of their prescriptions. As with Part B, higher income taxpayers will pay higher premiums. In addition, the premiums increase for delayed enrollment into the program by a factor of the "national base beneficiary premium" times the number of full, uncovered months that a senior was eligible but did not join a Medicare drug plan and went without other creditable prescription drug coverage. This premium increase (penalty) will continue to apply for as long as the Medicare drug plan is maintained.

Example 11.35

Mrs. Jones did not join Part D when she was first eligible - by May 15, 2016. She joined a Medicare drug plan with an effective date of January 1, 2021. Since Mrs. Jones did not join when she was first eligible and went without other creditable drug coverage for 55 months (June 2016 to December 2020), she will be charged a monthly penalty of $19.25 in 2021 ($35 x 0.01 = $0.35 x 55 = $19.25) in addition to her plan's monthly premium.[6]

Individuals may enroll in Part D during their Initial Enrollment Period (described below) without any penalty. If Medicare was available due to a disability, the applicant can join from three months before to three months after the 25th month of cash disability payments. There are two ways to obtain Medicare prescription drug coverage. The individual can either join a Medicare prescription drug plan or join a Medicare Advantage Plan or other Medicare Health Plan that offers drug coverage. Whichever plan is chosen, Medicare drug coverage helps the participant by covering brand name and generic drugs at pharmacies.

Drug plans may vary as to what prescription drugs are covered, how much the individual must pay, and which pharmacies they can use. All drug plans will have to provide at least a standard level of coverage, which Medicare will set. The premium, deductible, co payment/co insurance, and coverage may vary from plan to plan. However, some plans might offer more coverage and additional drugs for a higher monthly premium. When an individual joins a drug plan, it is important for them to choose one that meets their prescription drug needs. A list of drugs that a Medicare drug plan covers is called a formulary, which includes generic drugs and brand name drugs. Most prescription drugs used by those with Medicare will be on the given plan formulary, whether it is in brand name or generic form. To insure coverage of an appropriate amount of drugs, a formulary must include at least two drugs in each of the categories and classes of most commonly prescribed drugs. This helps to insure that people with varying medical conditions can get the medication or treatment they need. While a specific drug may not be included, a similar drug should be available. To assist with shopping for plans under Part D, insurance plans offering Part D coverage will typically have a "Drug Calculator" available on their website on which an individual's regular prescriptions may be entered and a cost estimate will be provided. Medicare also provides assistance selecting a plan on their "Find a Medicare Plan" website.[7]

If the insured's needs change, they can change their Part D prescription drug plan each year during the open enrollment period (October 15 - December 7), with new coverage beginning January 1. Since prescription drug plans are based on service areas, a three (or four in some cases) month special enrollment period to change plans is available if the Medicare beneficiary moves.

Even individuals who do not use prescription drugs should consider joining Part D during the initial enrollment period because aging people typically need prescription drugs to stay healthy. For a relatively low premium, Medicare prescription drug coverage can protect the individual from unexpected drug expenses in the future. Enrolling during the initial enrollment period avoids the late enrollment premium penalty, saving potentially thousands of dollars through the duration of the retirement years.

---

6. The "national base beneficiary premium" of $35 is assumed for this example. The 2021 premium is actually $33.06.
7. https://www.medicare.gov/plan-compare/#/?lang=en.

Part D consists of four phases of coverage: the deductible, the copayment/coinsurance phase, the coverage gap, and the catastrophic phase:

1. **Deductible:** The deductible must be satisfied prior to any benefits being provided from the plan. Deductibles can vary between drugs plans, with some plans having no deductible, but the deductible cannot exceed $445 in 2021.
2. **Copayment/Coinsurance:** In the copayment/coinsurance phase, beneficiaries pay a portion of the expenses until the insured and the plan together have paid $4,130 in 2021.
3. **Coverage Gap:** The next phase is the paid all or most of the costs of prescription drugs. The Affordable Care Act has been gradually reducing the size of the donut hole. Within the coverage gap phase for 2021, the Medicare recipient will pay up to 25 percent of the cost of brand name prescription drugs while the manufacturer (via a discount) pays 70 percent and the plan pays five percent of the cost. This phase lasts until the total out-of-pocket costs, including the costs paid by the insured and by the manufacturer for brand name drugs, reach $6,550 in 2021 (for generic drugs, only the costs paid by the insured count as out-of-pocket expenses).
4. **Catastrophic Phase:** The catastrophic phase covers all but a small coinsurance amount for the remainder of the year.

Exhibit 11.24 | Four Phases of Coverage Under Part D

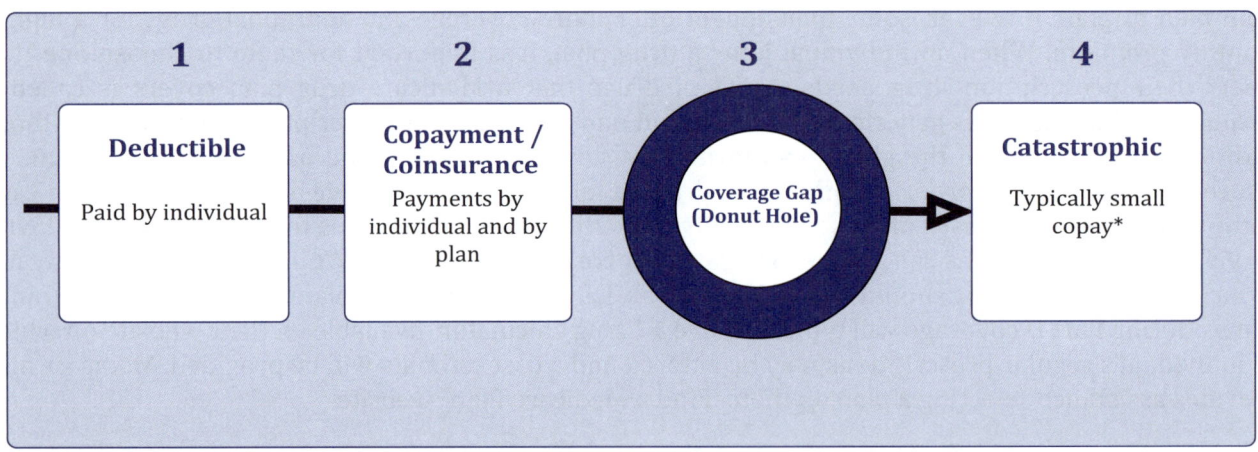

In 2017, approximately 8% of Part D enrollees reached the catastrophic phase. Those without low-income subsidies spent an average of $3,214 out-of-pocket on prescriptions. Among the top 10 conditions treated for those who reached the catastrophic phase are cancer, hepatitis, and intellectual disabilities.
https://www.kff.org/medicare/issue-brief/how-many-medicare-part-d-enrollees-had-high-out-of-pocket-drug-costs-in-2017/

MEDICARE PART C - MEDICARE ADVANTAGE

Medicare Advantage, Part C, is an option whereby those eligible for the traditional Medicare program can instead elect coverage under Medicare managed care plans such as Health Maintenance Organizations (HMOs), HMOs with a point of service option, Provider Sponsored Organizations (PSOs), and Preferred Provider Organizations (PPOs). These plans provide at least the same benefits as Medicare Parts A and B, and may also include additional benefits for an additional premium charge.

Over the past two decades, the percentage of Medicare enrollees choosing Medicare Advantage Plans has more than doubled, from 17 percent in 2000 to 39 percent in 2020.[8] One feature that makes Medicare Advantage Plans attractive for retirees who are concerned about the rising cost of health care is that they may have an annual maximum-out-of-pocket amount. Although the maximum amount may increase each year, it eliminates a large portion of the unknown potential costs of medical care for retirees. The Medicare Advantage plans tend to have lower premiums than Medigap policies, and may offer additional benefits, such as dental and vision.

A Medicare Advantage plan eliminates the need for Medigap coverage, therefore, those who enroll in Medicare Part C are not permitted to purchase a Medigap policy. Those enrolling in a Medicare Advantage Plan will still pay the Part B premium, along with a premium for the Part C coverage, which will vary based on the deductibles, coinsurance, co-pay, and maximum out-of-pocket limits of the plan chosen.[9] Medicare Advantage Plans may be limited to only doctors who are in the network, or may allow the covered individual to see doctors outside of the network as well, but with a higher out-of-pocket cost. Medicare Advantage Plans are required to offer at least the same benefits as original Medicare Parts A and B (they will never have less coverage than Parts A and B), although most plans offer greater coverage and may also include prescription drug coverage. An additional monthly premium may be charged if Part D prescription drug coverage is included.

One of the biggest decisions upon reaching Medicare eligibility age is whether to enroll in traditional Medicare with a Medigap supplement or to instead purchase a Medicare Advantage plan (Part C). One advantage to selecting traditional Medicare with a Medigap supplement is that there is little ongoing monitoring required since coverages are regulated by the government. Medicare Advantage plans often include additional services beyond what is covered under Parts A and B, but these additional services can be amended by the sponsoring insurance company each year, so an annual review will be necessary to ensure that the plan is still suitable for meeting the Medicare beneficiary's needs.

Medicare Savings Programs

For those who receive Medicare and have low income and few resources, states may pay Medicare premiums and, in some cases, other out-of-pocket Medicare expenses, such as deductibles and coinsurance. The respective state decides if individuals qualify. For more general information about Medicare, Centers for Medicare and Medicare Services' *Medicare & You* Handbook is helpful, as are the websites *www.ssa.gov* and *www.medicare.gov*.

ENROLLING IN MEDICARE

Those receiving Social Security benefits prior to age 65 are automatically enrolled in Medicare Parts A and B at age 65 and will receive a Medicare insurance card in the mail three months before turning age 65. Those not yet receiving Social Security benefits at age 65 will need to enroll for Medicare during the Initial Enrollment Period (IEP) beginning three months before the month of the 65th birthday and ending three months after the month of the 65th birthday (seven months total). Enrollment can be done at www.ssa.gov, by calling the Social Security administration, or visiting the local Social Security office.

8. https://www.kff.org/medicare/issue-brief/a-dozen-facts-about-medicare-advantage-in-2020/
9. Some Medicare Advantage plans have a $0 premium.

For individuals turning age 65 before January 1, 2023, it is usually best to enroll during the three months prior to the month of the 65th birthday so that coverage will begin on the first day of the month of the 65th birthday, unless the birthday is on the first of the month, then benefits begin the first day of the prior month. For example, if an individual's birthday is on August 15th, coverage will begin August 1st, but if the individual's birthday is August 1st, coverage will begin July 1st. If enrollment is done in the month the client turns age 65 or in the three months following, coverage will be delayed for one to three months after enrollment.

The Consolidated Appropriations Act of 2021 simplifies enrollment for individuals turning age 65 on or after January 1, 2023. For individuals who enroll during any month of their Initial Enrollment Period (IEP), coverage will begin on the first day of the month following the month during which they enroll. For individuals who do not enroll during their Initial Enrollment Period (IEP) and instead enroll during the annual General Enrollment Period (GEP), as described in **Exhibit 11.25**, coverage will begin on the first day of the month following the month during which they enroll.

When an individual applies for Part A, they are automatically enrolled in Part B as well unless they opt out of it. Anyone who does not apply for Part B when he or she is initially eligible can apply later, during general enrollment periods, which are the first three months of each year. A person who delays enrollment, however, will pay premiums, increased by 10 percent for each 12-month period that the person was eligible and did not enroll. A person who has continuous group coverage from age 65 until retirement can enroll up to eight months after termination of employment and not be subject to premium increases. The eight month Special Enrollment Period (SEP) applies from the earlier of (1) the month after the employment ends or (2) the month after group health insurance based on current employment ends, regardless of whether COBRA is elected (as discussed in Chapter 14).[10]

An individual who has group health coverage through an employer or union, may choose to wait to take the action of enrolling in Part B of Medicare and purchasing a Medigap policy. This delay makes sense when the employer plan provides similar coverage. When the employer coverage ends, the individual will have the opportunity to enroll in Part B without a late enrollment penalty during the 8-month Special Enrollment Period (SEP), and the Medigap open enrollment period will begin at that time as well.

Medicare beneficiaries can switch from original Medicare Parts A and B to Medicare Advantage, or switch from Medicare Advantage with a prescription drug plan to Medicare Advantage without a prescription drug plan (or vice versa) during Medicare open enrollment periods each year, which run from October 15th through December 7th. In addition, beneficiaries can switch between Medicare Advantage Plans, or switch from Medicare Advantage to original Medicare (but cannot switch from original Medicare to Medicare Advantage) during the Medicare Advantage Open Enrollment Period (MA OEP), which runs from January 1 - March 31 each year. It is important to note that those who originally selected Medicare Advantage and choose to change to traditional Medicare will be required to go through medical underwriting to obtain Medigap coverage as a supplement to traditional Medicare (Parts A and B).

10.Consolidated Omnibus Budget Reconciliation Act of 1985 (COBRA).

Exhibit 11.25 | Medicare Enrollment Periods

Enrollment Period	Time Frame	Noteworthy
Initial Enrollment Period (IEP)	Three months before your 65th birthday, the month of your 65th birthday, and three months after your 65th birthday (total seven months)	Two important decisions: 1. Choose between Traditional Medicare or Medicare Advantage. 2. Select your Part D Prescription Drug Plan. *Note*: If you enrolled in Medicare Advantage during your IEP, you can change to another Medicare Advantage Plan or to original Medicare in the first three months you have Medicare
Medigap Open Enrollment Period	Starts the first day of the month in which you are both age 65 or older and enrolled in Medicare Part B, and lasts for six months	No medical underwriting is required during this time, so don't delay.
Part B Special Enrollment Period (SEP)	Starts the earlier of: 1. termination of employment, or 2. termination of group coverage, and lasts for eight months	Requires continuous group coverage from age 65 to retirement or loss of group coverage. The eight months starts at termination of employment or termination of group coverage even if COBRA is elected.
Medicare Advantage and Part D Special Enrollment Period (SEP)	• If you tell the plan before you move, the SEP begins the month before the month you move and lasts for two full months after you move • If you tell the plan after you move, your SEP begins in the month you move and lasts for two full months after you move	These plans are based on service areas, so if you move you probably need to change your Medicare Advantage Plan and/or Part D prescription drug plan.
Medicare Open Enrollment Period (OEP)	October 15 - December 7 (coverage change effective January 1)	During this time you can: • enroll in or change Part D plans • change from original Medicare to Medicare Advantage • change from a Medicare Advantage plan that does not offer prescription drug coverage to one that does (or vice versa)
Medicare Advantage Open Enrollment Period (MA OEP)	January 1 - March 31	During this time, if you have a Medicare Advantage Plan, you can: • change to another Medicare Advantage plan • change from Medicare Advantage to original Medicare
Medicare General Enrollment Period (GEP)	January 1 - March 31	Allows you to enroll if you did not sign up when you were first eligible and you do not qualify for a SEP. Premiums will be higher due to late enrollment. Coverage begins July 1.

SUPPLEMENTAL SECURITY INCOME BENEFITS

Supplemental Security Income (SSI) makes monthly payments to individuals with low incomes and few assets. In order to obtain SSI benefits, an individual must be age 65 or older, disabled, or blind. The definition of disability is satisfied when the individual is unable to engage in any substantial gainful activity due to a physical or mental problem expected to last at least a year or expected to result in death. Children as well as adults qualify for SSI disability payments. As its name implies, Supplemental Security Income supplements the beneficiary's income up to various levels depending on where the beneficiary lives. If an otherwise eligible SSI applicant lives in another's household and receives support from that person, the federal SSI benefit is reduced by one-third.

The federal government pays a basic rate. The basic monthly SSI benefit for 2021 is $794 per month for one person and $1,191 per month for married couples. Some states supply additional funds to qualified individuals. To ascertain the SSI benefit rates in a certain state, the advisor or client can contact a local Social Security office in that state or visit the Social Security Administration's website. Generally, individuals who receive SSI benefits also qualify for Medicaid, food stamps, and other government assistance.

To be eligible for the monthly SSI benefit, the beneficiary must not have assets that exceed $2,000 for one person or $3,000 for married couples. This asset determination does not include the value of the home and some personal belongings, such as one car. If the potential beneficiary does not work, he may be eligible for SSI benefits if monthly income is less than $794 for one person and $1,191 for a couple. If the potential beneficiary works, more monthly income is allowed. SSI benefits are not paid from Social Security trust funds and are not based on past earnings of the beneficiary. Rather, SSI benefits are financed by general tax revenues and assure a minimum monthly income for needy elderly, disabled, or blind persons.

FILING FOR SOCIAL SECURITY CLAIMS

The Social Security Administration reports that many people fail to file claims with the Social Security Administration or fail to do so in a timely fashion. Individuals should file for Social Security or SSI disability benefits as soon they become too disabled to work or for survivors' benefits, when a family breadwinner dies. Social Security benefits do not start automatically. Social Security will not begin payment of benefits until the beneficiary files an application. When filing for benefits, applicants must submit documents that show eligibility, such as a birth certificate for each family member applying for benefits, a marriage certificate if a spouse is applying, and the most recent W-2 forms or tax returns.

To file for benefits, obtain information, or to speak to a Social Security representative, individuals must call the Social Security Administration's toll-free number, 800-772-1213, or visit the Social Security Administration's website. The toll-free number can be used to schedule an appointment at a local Social Security office. The Social Security Administration treats all calls confidentially. Periodically, a second Social Security representative will monitor incoming and outgoing telephone calls to ensure accurate and courteous service.

OTHER ISSUES - SOCIAL SECURITY

Effect of Marriage or Divorce on Benefits

Marriage or divorce may affect one's Social Security benefits, depending on the kind of benefits received. If a worker receives retirement benefits based on his own earnings record, the worker's retirement benefits will continue whether married or divorced. If an individual receives benefits based on his spouse's record, the individual's benefits will cease upon divorce unless the individual is age 62 or older and was married longer than 10 years. Widows and widowers, whether divorced or not, will continue to receive survivors' benefits upon remarriage if the widow or widower is age 60 or older. Disabled widows and widowers, whether divorced or not, will continue to receive survivors' benefits upon remarriage if the disabled widow or widower is age 50 or older.

Example 11.36

Linus was married at the following ages and to the following wives. Linus is now 62 and married to Sally.

	Wife	Current Age	Larry's Age at Marriage	Current Marital Status	Length of Marriage
1	Marcie	62	20	Single	10 years, 1 month
2	Lucy	63	31	Single	10 years, 1 month
3	Patty	64	42	Single	9 years
4	Sally	65	53	Married	9 years

Who, among the wives, may be eligible to receive Social Security retirement benefits based upon Linus's earnings if Linus is retired or not retired?

Any divorced spouse, age 62 and married to Linus for 10 years or longer is eligible to receive benefits. If Linus is retired, then his current wife is also eligible to receive benefits. However, she cannot collect benefits if he is not retired.

If Linus is retired: Marcie, Lucy, and Sally.

If Linus is not retired: Marcie and Lucy.

For all other forms of Social Security benefits, benefits will cease upon remarriage, except in special circumstances. When a person marries, it is presumed that at least one person in the marriage can provide adequate support. Likewise, Social Security benefits may recommence based on the previous spouse's benefits if the marriage ends.

Change of Name

If an individual changes their name due to marriage, divorce, or a court order, that individual must notify the Social Security Administration of the name change so the Social Security Administration will be able to show the new name in their records and properly credit that individual for earnings. This notice will ensure that the individual's work history will be accurately recorded and maintained.

Projected Benefit Statements

The Social Security Administration currently mails projected benefit statements only to those age 60 and older who are not yet receiving benefits and have not set up an online account at SSA.gov. Any individual covered under the Social Security system has the ability to establish an online account in which an individualized statement of projected benefits based on the worker's reported earnings can be viewed.[11] A detailed interactive calculator in which various parameters impacting benefits may be adjusted is also available.[12] A sample Social Security Statement is presented in **Exhibit 11.26**.

Leaving the United States[13]

Beneficiaries who are United States citizens may travel or live in most foreign countries without affecting their eligibility for Social Security benefits. However, there are a few countries where Social Security checks cannot be sent. These countries currently include:

- Cuba
- North Korea

Also, beneficiaries that go to any of the following countries can receive Social Security benefits only if they meet and agree to certain restricted conditions. These countries are:

- Azerbaijan
- Belarus
- Kazakhstan
- Kyrgyzstan
- Moldova
- Tajikistan
- Turkmenistan
- Uzbekistan

> ### 📝 *Quick Quiz 11.7*
>
> 1. In order to obtain Supplemental Social Security benefits, the individual must be 62, disabled, or blind.
>   a. True
>   b. False
>
> 2. Social Security beneficiaries who are United States citizens may live in most foreign countries without affecting their eligibility for Social Security benefits.
>   a. True
>   b. False
>
> False, True.

Beneficiaries should inform the Social Security Administration of their plans to go outside the United States for a trip that lasts 30 days or more. By providing the name of the country or countries to be visited and the expected departure and return dates, the Social Security Administration will send special reporting instructions to the beneficiaries and arrange for the delivery of their checks while they are abroad.

---

11. https://www.ssa.gov/myaccount
12. https://www.ssa.gov/oact/anypia/anypia.html
13. ssa.gov Publication No. 05-10137, June 2020.

Windfall Elimination Provision (WEP) and Government Pension Offset (GPO) Provision

The Windfall Elimination Provision (WEP) of Social Security applies to those who earned a pension in a job where no Social Security taxes were paid (such as those under the Civil Service Retirement System and some state and local government employees), but who also worked in other jobs long enough to qualify for Social Security retirement or disability benefits. Because Social Security is structured to provide a higher replacement ratio for low-income earners than it does for high-income earners, those who have low earnings from employment for which Social Security taxes are paid, but have a large pension from earnings for which no Social Security taxes are paid, would receive a "windfall" benefit from Social Security (a higher replacement ratio than they would receive if benefits were based on all earnings).

To prevent these workers from receiving a higher than usual replacement ratio from Social Security, the benefit calculation formula is altered to reduce the amount of Social Security benefits paid. The WEP calculation will result in a lower PIA for the worker; therefore, it will also reduce benefits to others who may be eligible to collect based on that worker's PIA as well. However, the reduction in Social Security benefits for the worker will not be more than ½ of the pension that is based on earnings for which no Social Security taxes were paid.

The Windfall Elimination Provision does not apply to federal workers first hired after 1983, or to those with a pension based only on railroad employment. In addition, those who paid Social Security taxes on at least 30 years of substantial earnings ($26,550 in 2021) will have no reduction.

While the Windfall Elimination Provision does not apply to survivor benefits, these benefits may be reduced under the Government Pension Offset Provision (GPO). This provision also affects spousal benefits for retirement and disability. Under the GPO provision, Social Security benefits are reduced by 2/3 of the government pension amount received by the spouse, widow, or widower who earned the government pension. This rule is to ensure that spousal benefits for those working for government employers where earnings are not subject to Social Security get treated in a similar manner to those who have earnings that are subject to Social Security. Government employees who pay Social Security taxes on their government earnings are not subject to the GPO provision.

Example 11.37

Frieda worked for the federal government and has Civil Service Retirement benefits of $800 per month. Since Frieda did not pay into the Social Security system for her earnings from the federal government, she has $0 of Social Security benefits based on her own work record. Frieda's husband, Charlie, has worked and paid into the Social Security system and Frieda is entitled to a spousal benefit of $600 based on Charlie's PIA. If there were no offset, Frieda would be entitled to both her $800 per month and the spousal benefit of $600 per month. With the GPO offset, Frieda's spousal benefit under Social Security will be reduced by 2/3 of her civil service pension (2/3 x 800 = $533), so her spousal benefit from Social Security will be $67.

Finally, **Exhibit 11.27** reflects the 2021 Social Security changes for ease of reference.[14]

---

14. ssa.gov and Social Security National Press Office press release.

Exhibit 11.26 | Sample Social Security Statement

Your payment would be about
$2,042 a month
at full retirement age

WANDA WORKER
456 ANYWHERE AVENUE
MAINTOWN, USA 11111-1111

January 2, 2021

Your Social Security Statement

This *Social Security Statement* tells you about **how much you or your family would receive** in disability, survivor, or retirement benefits. It also includes our record of your lifetime earnings. Check out your earnings history, and **let us know right away if you find an error**. This is important because we base your benefits on our record of your lifetime earnings.

Social Security benefits are not **intended to be your only source of income when you retire**. On average, Social Security will replace about 40 percent of your annual pre-retirement earnings. You will need other savings, investments, pensions, or retirement accounts to make sure you have enough money to live comfortably when you retire.

To view your *Statement* online anytime, create a **my Social Security account** at *myaccount.socialsecurity.gov*.

Social Security Administration

To view your *Social Security Statement* online anytime create a **my Social Security** account today!

my Social Security
myaccount.socialsecurity.gov

Follow the Social Security Administration at these social media sites.

Sample Social Security Statement Continued

Your Estimated Benefits

*Retirement   You have earned enough credits to qualify for benefits. At your current earnings rate, if you continue working until…

your full retirement age (67 years), your payment would be about..$ 2,042 a month

age 70, your payment would be about ....$ 2,546 a month

age 62, your payment would be about ....$ 1,406 a month

*Disability   You have earned enough credits to qualify for benefits. If you became disabled right now, your payment would be about...$ 1,841 a month

*Family   If you get retirement or disability benefits, your spouse and children also may qualify for benefits.

*Survivors   You have earned enough credits for your family to receive survivors benefits. If you die this year, certain members of your family may qualify for the following benefits:

Your child..$ 1,421 a month

Your spouse who is caring for your child..$ 1,421 a month

Your spouse, if benefits start at full retirement age...$ 1,895 a month

Total family benefits cannot be more than ....$ 3,522 a month

Your spouse or minor child may be eligible for a special one-time death benefit of $255.

Medicare   You have enough credits to qualify for Medicare at age 65. Even if you do not retire at age 65, be sure to contact Social Security three months before your 65th birthday to enroll in Medicare.

* **Your estimated benefits are based on current law. Congress has made changes to the law in the past and can do so at any time. The law governing benefit amounts may change because, by 2035, the payroll taxes collected will be enough to pay only about 80 percent of scheduled benefits.**

We based your benefit estimates on these facts:

Your date of birth (please verify your name on page 1 and this date of birth) ....   April 5, 1981

Your estimated taxable earnings per year after 2018 .... $55,492

Your Social Security number (only the last four digits are shown to help prevent identity theft)........   XXX-XX-1234

How Your Benefits Are Estimated

To qualify for benefits, you earn "credits" through your work — up to four each year. This year, for example, you earn one credit for each $1,470 of wages or self-employment income. When you've earned $5,880, you've earned your four credits for the year. Most people need 40 credits, earned over their working lifetime, to receive retirement benefits. For disability and survivors benefits, young people need fewer credits to be eligible.

We checked your records to see whether you have earned enough credits to qualify for benefits. If you haven't earned enough yet to qualify for any type of benefit, we can't give you a benefit estimate now. If you continue to work, we'll give you an estimate when you do qualify.

What we assumed — If you have enough work credits, we estimated your benefit amounts using your average earnings over your working lifetime. For 2021 and later (up to retirement age), we assumed you'll continue to work and make about the same as you did in 2019 or 2020. We also included credits we assumed you earned last year and this year.

Generally, the older you are and the closer you are to retirement, the more accurate the retirement estimates will be because they are based on a longer work history with fewer uncertainties such as earnings fluctuations and future law changes. We encourage you to use our online Retirement Estimator at *www.socialsecurity.gov/estimator* to obtain immediate and personalized benefit estimates.

We can't provide your actual benefit amount until you apply for benefits. **And that amount may differ from the estimates stated above because:**

(1) Your earnings may increase or decrease in the future.

(2) After you start receiving benefits, they will be adjusted for cost-of-living increases.

(3) Your estimated benefits are based on current law. **The law governing benefit amounts may change.**

(4) Your benefit amount may be affected by **military service, railroad employment or pensions earned through work on which you did not pay Social Security tax.** Visit *www.socialsecurity.gov* to learn more.

Windfall Elimination Provision (WEP) — In the future, if you receive a pension from employment in which you do not pay Social Security taxes, such as some federal, state or local government work, some nonprofit organizations or foreign employment, and you also qualify for your own Social Security retirement or disability benefit, your Social Security benefit may be reduced, but not eliminated, by WEP. The amount of the reduction, if any, depends on your earnings and number of years in jobs in which you paid Social Security taxes, and the year you are age 62 or become disabled. For more information, please see *Windfall Elimination Provision* (Publication No. 05-10045) at *www.socialsecurity.gov/WEP*.

Government Pension Offset (GPO) — If you receive a pension based on federal, state or local government work in which you did not pay Social Security taxes and you qualify, now or in the future, for Social Security benefits as a current or former spouse, widow or widower, you are likely to be affected by GPO. If GPO applies, your Social Security benefit will be reduced by an amount equal to two-thirds of your government pension, and could be reduced to zero. Even if your benefit is reduced to zero, you will be eligible for Medicare at age 65 on your spouse's record. To learn more, please see *Government Pension Offset* (Publication No. 05-10007) at *www.socialsecurity.gov/GPO*.

Your Earnings Record

Years You Worked	Your Taxed Social Security Earnings	Your Taxed Medicare Earnings
1997	635	635
1998	1,672	1,672
1999	3,205	3,205
2000	5,801	5,801
2001	8,033	8,033
2002	9,824	9,824
2003	12,235	12,235
2004	16,099	16,099
2005	19,810	19,810
2006	23,325	23,325
2007	26,803	26,803
2008	29,704	29,704
2009	31,275	31,275
2010	33,819	33,819
2011	36,498	36,498
2012	39,110	39,110
2013	40,897	40,897
2014	43,514	43,514
2015	46,091	46,091
2016	47,611	47,611
2017	50,129	50,129
2018	52,765	52,765
2019	55,492	55,492
2020	Not yet recorded	

You and your family may be eligible for valuable benefits:

When you die, your family may be eligible to receive survivors benefits.

Social Security may help you if you become disabled—even at a young age.

A young person who has worked and paid Social Security taxes in as few as two years can be eligible for disability benefits.

Social Security credits you earn move with you from job to job throughout your career.

Total Social Security and Medicare taxes paid over your working career through the last year reported on the chart above:

Estimated taxes paid for Social Security:
  You paid: $37,817
  Your employers paid: $39,329

Estimated taxes paid for Medicare:
  You paid: $9,198
  Your employers paid: $9,198

Note: Currently, you and your employer each pay a 6.2 percent Social Security tax on up to $142,800 of your earnings and a 1.45* percent Medicare tax on all your earnings. If you are self-employed, you pay the combined employee and employer amount, which is a 12.4 percent Social Security tax on up to $142,800 of your net earnings and a 2.9* percent Medicare tax on your entire net earnings.

*If you have earned income of more than $200,000 ($250,000 for married couples filing jointly), you must pay 0.9 percent more in Medicare taxes.

Help Us Keep Your Earnings Record Accurate

You, your employer and Social Security share responsibility for the accuracy of your earnings record. Since you began working, we recorded your reported earnings under your name and Social Security number. We have updated your record each time your employer (or you, if you're self-employed) reported your earnings.

Remember, it's your earnings, not the amount of taxes you paid or the number of credits you've earned, that determine your benefit amount. When we figure that amount, we base it on your average earnings over your lifetime. If our records are wrong, you may not receive all the benefits to which you're entitled.

Review this chart carefully using your own records to make sure our information is correct and that we've recorded each year you worked. You're the only person who can look at the earnings chart and know whether it is complete and correct.

Some or all of your earnings from **last year** may not be shown on your *Statement*. It could be that we still were processing last year's earnings reports when your *Statement* was prepared. Your complete earnings for last year will be shown on next year's *Statement*. **Note:** If you worked for more than one employer during any year, or if you had both earnings and self-employment income, we combined your earnings for the year.

There's a limit on the amount of earnings on which you pay Social Security taxes each year. The limit increases yearly. Earnings above the limit will not appear on your earnings chart as Social Security earnings. (For Medicare taxes, the maximum earnings amount began rising in 1991. Since 1994, **all** of your earnings are taxed for Medicare.)

Call us right away at **1-800-772-1213** (7 a.m.–7 p.m. your local time) if any earnings for years **before last year** are shown incorrectly. Please have your W-2 or tax return for those years available. (If you live outside the U.S., follow the directions at the bottom of page 4.)

3

Sample Social Security Statement Continued

Some Facts About Social Security

About Social Security and Medicare…

Social Security pays retirement, disability, family and survivors benefits. Medicare, a separate program run by the Centers for Medicare & Medicaid Services, helps pay for inpatient hospital care, nursing care, doctors' fees, drugs, and other medical services and supplies to people age 65 and older, as well as to people who have been receiving Social Security disability benefits for two years or more. Medicare does not pay for long-term care, so you may want to consider options for private insurance. Your Social Security covered earnings qualify you for both programs. For more information about Medicare, visit *www.medicare.gov* or call **1-800-633-4227** (TTY **1-877-486-2048** if you are deaf or hard of hearing).

Retirement — If you were born before 1938, your full retirement age is 65. Because of a 1983 change in the law, the full retirement age will increase gradually to 67 for people born in 1960 and later.

Some people retire before their full retirement age. You can retire as early as 62 and take benefits at a reduced rate. If you work after your full retirement age, you can receive higher benefits because of additional earnings and credits for delayed retirement.

Disability — If you become disabled before full retirement age, you can receive disability benefits after six months if you have:

— enough credits from earnings (depending on your age, you must have earned six to 20 of your credits in the three to 10 years before you became disabled); and

— a physical or mental impairment that's expected to prevent you from doing "substantial" work for a year or more or result in death.

If you are filing for disability benefits, please let us know if you are on active military duty or are a recently discharged veteran, so that we can handle your claim more quickly.

Family — If you're eligible for disability or retirement benefits, your current or divorced spouse, minor children or adult children disabled before age 22 also may receive benefits. Each may qualify for up to about 50 percent of your benefit amount.

Survivors — When you die, certain members of your family may be eligible for benefits:

— your spouse age 60 or older (50 or older if disabled, or any age if caring for your children younger than age 16); and

— your children if unmarried and younger than age 18, still in school and younger than 19 years old, or adult children disabled before age 22.

If you are divorced, your ex-spouse could be eligible for a widow's or widower's benefit on your record when you die.

Extra Help with Medicare — If you know someone who is on Medicare and has limited resources and income, Extra Help is available for prescription drug costs. The Extra Help can help pay the monthly premiums, annual deductibles and prescription co-payments. To learn more or to apply, visit *www.socialsecurity.gov* or call **1-800-772-1213** (TTY **1-800-325-0778**).

Receive benefits and still work…

You can work and still get retirement or survivors benefits. If you're younger than your full retirement age, there are limits on how much you can earn without affecting your benefit amount. When you apply for benefits, we'll tell you what the limits are and whether work would affect your monthly benefits. When you reach full retirement age, the earnings limits no longer apply.

Before you decide to retire…

Carefully consider the advantages and disadvantages of early retirement. If you choose to receive benefits before you reach full retirement age, your monthly benefits will be reduced.

To help you decide the best time to retire, we offer a free publication, *When To Start Receiving Retirement Benefits* (Publication No. 05-10147), that identifies the many factors you should consider before applying. Most people can receive an estimate of their benefit based on their actual Social Security earnings record by going to *www.socialsecurity.gov/estimator*. You also can calculate future retirement benefits by using the Social Security Benefit Calculators at *www.socialsecurity.gov*.

Other helpful free publications include:

— *Retirement Benefits* (No. 05-10035)

— *Understanding The Benefits* (No. 05-10024)

— *Your Retirement Benefit: How It Is Figured* (No. 05-10070)

— *Windfall Elimination Provision* (No. 05-10045)

— *Government Pension Offset* (No. 05-10007)

— *Identity Theft And Your Social Security Number* (No. 05-10064)

We also have other leaflets and fact sheets with information about specific topics such as military service, self-employment or foreign employment. You can request Social Security publications at our website, *www.socialsecurity.gov*, or by calling us at **1-800-772-1213**. Our website has a list of frequently asked questions that may answer questions you have. We have easy-to-use online applications for benefits that can save you a telephone call or a trip to a field office.

You also may qualify for government benefits outside of Social Security. For more information on these benefits, visit *www.benefits.gov*.

If you need more information — Visit *www.socialsecurity.gov* on the Internet, contact any Social Security office, call **1-800-772-1213** or write to Social Security Administration, Office of Earnings Operations, P.O. Box 33026, Baltimore, MD 21290-3026. If you're deaf or hard of hearing, call TTY **1-800-325-0778**. If you have questions about your personal information, you must provide your complete Social Security number. If your address is incorrect on this *Statement*, ask the IRS to send you a Form 8822. We don't keep your address if you're not receiving Social Security benefits.

Form SSA-7005-SM-SI (01/21)   4

Exhibit 11.27 | Social Security Fact Sheet

Fact Sheet

SOCIAL SECURITY

2021 SOCIAL SECURITY CHANGES

Cost-of-Living Adjustment (COLA):

Based on the increase in the Consumer Price Index (CPI-W) from the third quarter of 2019 through the third quarter of 2020, Social Security and Supplemental Security Income (SSI) beneficiaries will receive a 1.3 percent COLA for 2021. Other important 2021 Social Security information is as follows:

Tax Rate	2020	2021
Employee	7.65%	7.65%
Self-Employed	15.30%	15.30%

NOTE: The 7.65% tax rate is the combined rate for Social Security and Medicare. The Social Security portion (OASDI) is 6.20% on earnings up to the applicable taxable maximum amount (see below). The Medicare portion (HI) is 1.45% on all earnings. Also, as of January 2013, individuals with earned income of more than $200,000 ($250,000 for married couples filing jointly) pay an additional 0.9 percent in Medicare taxes. The tax rates shown above do not include the 0.9 percent.

	2020	2021
Maximum Taxable Earnings		
Social Security (OASDI only)	$137,700	$142,800
Medicare (HI only)	No Limit	
Quarter of Coverage		
	$1,410	$1,470
Retirement Earnings Test Exempt Amounts		
Under full retirement age	$18,240/yr. ($1,520/mo.)	$18,960/yr. ($1,580/mo.)
NOTE: One dollar in benefits will be withheld for every $2 in earnings above the limit.		

Social Security Fact Sheet Continued

The year an individual reaches full retirement age	$48,600/yr. ($4,050/mo.)	$50,520/yr. ($4,210/mo.)
NOTE: Applies only to earnings for months prior to attaining full retirement age. One dollar in benefits will be withheld for every $3 in earnings above the limit.		
Beginning the month an individual attains full retirement age	None	

	2020	2021
Social Security Disability Thresholds		
Substantial Gainful Activity (SGA)		
Non-Blind	$1,260/mo.	$1,310/mo.
Blind	$2,110/mo.	$2,190/mo.
Trial Work Period (TWP)	$ 910/mo.	$ 940/mo.
Maximum Social Security Benefit: Worker Retiring at Full Retirement Age		
	$3,011/mo.	$3,148/mo.
SSI Federal Payment Standard		
Individual	$ 783/mo.	$ 794/mo.
Couple	$1,175/mo.	$1,191/mo.
SSI Resource Limits		
Individual	$2,000	$2,000
Couple	$3,000	$3,000
SSI Student Exclusion		
Monthly limit	$1,900	$1,930
Annual limit	$7,670	$7,770
Estimated Average Monthly Social Security Benefits Payable in January 2021		
	Before 1.3% COLA	**After 1.3% COLA**
All Retired Workers	$1,523	$1,543
Aged Couple, Both Receiving Benefits	$2,563	$2,596
Widowed Mother and Two Children	$2,962	$3,001
Aged Widow(er) Alone	$1,434	$1,453
Disabled Worker, Spouse and One or More Children	$2,195	$2,224
All Disabled Workers	$1,261	$1,277

MEDICAID

Title XIX of the Social Security Act is a Federal/State entitlement program that pays for medical assistance for certain individuals and families with low incomes and resources. This program, known as **Medicaid**, became law in 1965 as a cooperative venture jointly funded by the Federal and State governments (including the District of Columbia and the Territories) to assist States in furnishing medical assistance to eligible needful persons. Medicaid is the largest source of funding for medical and health-related services for impoverished Americans. Medicaid is by far the largest source of funding for long-term care services, providing 44.1 percent of funding for long term services and support in 2018.[15]

Key Concepts

1. What is the purpose of the Medicaid program?

2. How do individuals qualify for benefits under Medicaid?

3. How long is the look-back period?

4. What is the purpose of a special needs trust?

Medicaid is the nationwide program (administered by the individual states) that provides medical assistance to those without resources to pay. The federal government oversees the Medicaid program through the Centers for Medicare and Medicaid Services (CMS). The states administer their Medicaid programs through agencies at the state and local level. The federal government establishes broad national guidelines, however, each State establishes its own eligibility standards; determines the type, amount, duration, and scope of services; sets the rate of payment for services; and administers its own program. Some states combine their Medicaid program with other programs, such as the Children's Health Insurance Program (CHIP) which provides medical insurance for children under age 19 in families whose income is too high to qualify for Medicaid.

Medicaid policies for eligibility, services, and payment are complex and vary considerably, even among states of similar size or geographic proximity. Thus, a person who is eligible for Medicaid in one state may not be eligible in another state, and the services provided by one state may differ considerably in amount, duration, or scope from services provided in a similar or neighboring state. In addition, state legislatures may change Medicaid eligibility, services, and/or reimbursement at any time.

Funding

The federal and state governments jointly fund the Medicaid program. The federal contribution to Medicaid expenditures in each state is determined by a formula that is set by federal statute. The portion that the federal government must pay is called the Federal Medical Assistance Percentage (FMAP). The formula used to calculate FMAP has resulted in the federal government paying a larger percentage to states with lower per capita income and a smaller percentage to states with higher per capita income. The minimum percentage that states can be required to pay is 50 percent of the Medicaid expenses, but states with lower per capita incomes may receive up to 75 percent of their Medicaid expenditures from the federal government. There is no limit on the amount that the federal government will pay when a state pays its share. Medicaid is a substantial part of the budget for each state and is larger than any other item in most state budgets. The state and federal payments account on average for approximately 29 percent of state budgets. Under federal law, states may obtain up to 60 percent of their share of Medicaid funding from local governments.

15.https://crsreports.congress.gov/product/pdf/IF/IF10343

Mandatory and Optional Benefits

The federal government has set broad guidelines for the benefits that states must provide under a Medicaid program. In addition to the mandatory benefits, states may provide additional optional benefits. Each state establishes and administers its own Medicaid program and can determine, within the federal guidelines, the amount and type of services it will provide.

Exhibit 11.28 | Medicaid Mandatory and Optional Benefits

Mandatory Benefits	Optional Benefits*
• Inpatient and outpatient hospital services	• Prescription drugs
• Physician services	• Dental services
• Nursing facility services	• Hospice
• Home health services	• Preventive and rehabilitative services
• Early and periodic screening, diagnostic, and treatment services	• Physical therapy
• Laboratory and x-ray services	• Chiropractic services
• Rural health clinic services	• Personal care
• Federally qualified health center services	• Clinic services
• Family planning services	• Occupational therapy
• Nurse midwife services	• Speech, hearing, and language disorder services
• Certified pediatric and family nurse practitioner services	• Respiratory care services
• Freestanding birth center services	• Podiatry services
• Transportation to medical care	• Optometry services
• Tobacco cessation counseling for pregnant women	• Dentures
	• Prosthetics
	• Eyeglasses

Other optional benefits may also be available.

It is important to distinguish home care from home health services. Home health services consist of medical care provided in the home by trained professionals such as doctors and nurses. Home care is personal care provided by family members or paid caregivers. Home health services are mandatory while home care is optional. Not all states pay for the expenses of home care, but more states are offering it due to its lower cost compared to care in nursing homes.

Nursing facility services are mandatory, and must be provided at Medicaid certified nursing homes. Medicaid will not pay for expenses at a nursing home that has not been certified. Nursing homes will often obtain certification even though most of their residents are not eligible for Medicaid. By becoming certified, these nursing homes can continue to receive payment for nursing facility services in the event their residents exhaust their resources and become Medicaid eligible.

Nursing homes, assisted living facilities, and other services are not required to accept Medicaid reimbursement, and some do not. Nursing facilities often care for individuals who are Medicaid recipients as well as those who are not. Consequently, the quality of care received may often not be much different between Medicaid recipients and others. Since some nursing homes do not accept Medicaid, however, the choices of nursing homes may be more limited for those receiving Medicaid assistance. In some states, Medicaid will not help with paying for assisted living care, so individuals may not have that option with Medicaid. A person who has his or her own resources, or who has long-term care insurance, to pay for nursing home care when first applying will have more options.

States can apply to the Centers for Medicare and Medicaid Services (CMS) for a waiver of federal law to expand health coverage beyond the mandatory eligibility groups. Many states have expanded coverage above the federal minimums, especially for children.

State and federal officials have been seeking to shift more care from nursing homes to home and community services. The cost of long-term care in nursing homes and similar institutions averaged $82,128 per person in 2016. In contrast, community-based services for long-term care beneficiaries averaged only $45,800.

Eligibility

While Medicaid will pay for most long-term care expenses for eligible low-income persons, it is often difficult to qualify for the government service. To be eligible, a person must meet both the general requirements as well as meet the financial requirements. In most cases, a person must be one of the following to meet the general requirements:

- Be age 65 or older
- Have a permanent disability as that term is defined by the Social Security Administration
- Be blind
- Be a pregnant woman
- Be a child, or the parent or caretaker of a child

A person must have limited income and limited assets to meet the financial requirements for Medicaid.

Income

The amount of income a person can have varies by state, and also varies depending on which eligibility groups each state covers. Each state's Medical Assistance Office is usually the best resource to determine the eligibility requirements within that state. In the state determination of a person's financial eligibility for Medicaid, the state will only count certain types of income. A person's income includes these sources:

- Regular benefit payments such as Social Security retirement or disability payments
- Veterans benefits
- Pensions
- Salaries
- Wages
- Interest from bank accounts and certificates of deposit
- Dividends from stocks and bonds

However, Medicaid generally does not count such things as:

- Nutritional assistance (food stamps)
- Housing assistance provided by the federal government
- Home energy assistance

The states set varying income eligibility requirements, but for applicants who live in the community (i.e., not in a nursing home, hospital, or other institution), the limit is generally a percentage of the federal poverty level. A common income standard is 133 percent of the federal poverty level. In 2021, 133 percent of the federal poverty level for an individual is $1,427.50 monthly or $17,130 annually. The amount increases for a family with two, three, four or more persons.

There is another option for those individuals whose income exceeds the state limits, called the special income level group. The special income level group is an optional group for states, meaning that states can choose to cover or not cover this group. Over 40 states have chosen to cover this group though, so it is widely available as a pathway to receiving long-term care services under Medicaid. This group is aimed specifically at people who need long-term care services. The income requirement is significantly higher for this group (typically 300 percent of the Supplemental Security Income (SSI) limit of $794 in 2021, which is $2,382 per month in 2021), but receiving benefits under this category may require the person to "share in the cost" of the service provided.[16] The group has the same general requirements and similar asset requirements. Before Medicaid will pay nursing home expenses, residents must pay all of their income toward the cost of care. Residents are permitted to retain a personal allowance of $30 to $40 per month. A married couple's income is generally counted separately, so that the income of the non-applicant spouse is not used to determine eligibility of the applicant spouse. This helps to protect the spouse of a nursing home resident from impoverishment.

Assets

In the process of a state determining a person's financial eligibility for Medicaid, certain types of assets are counted, while others are excluded. During the Medicaid application process, applicants must provide documentation of the assets they own.

The amount of countable assets a person can have and still qualify for Medicaid varies from state to state. In most states a person can retain about $2,000 in countable assets, and married couples that are still living in the same household can retain about $3,000 in countable assets. This may not sound like much, but it is important to understand that many assets are not counted at all when determining Medicaid eligibility.

Assets that are usually counted for Medicaid eligibility include:
- Checking and savings accounts
- Stocks and bonds
- Certificates of deposit
- Real property other than your primary residence
- Additional motor vehicles if you have more than one
- Retirement plan assets that can be withdrawn in a lump sum (such as IRAs and 401(k)s)

Assets that do not usually get counted for Medicaid eligibility include the following:
- Primary residence
- Personal property and household belongings
- One motor vehicle
- Life insurance with a face value under $1,500
- Up to $1,500 in funds set aside for burial
- Certain burial arrangements such as pre-need burial agreements

16.https://www.medicaidplanningassistance.org/medicaid-eligibility/

- Assets held in specific kinds of trusts
- Retirement plan assets that cannot be withdrawn in a lump sum (such as defined benefit pension plans in which a lump sum distribution is not available)

The personal residence is often a person's largest and most valuable asset and is not considered for Medicaid eligibility purposes. However, there are limits to the amount of equity that a person can maintain and still qualify for Medicaid. In 2021, the equity limit is in excess of $600,000. Medicaid must deny benefits above this limit.[17]

Community Spouse Resource Allowance

When both spouses are in a nursing home, the couple is limited to $3,000 of assets, but the law is different for married couples when only one spouse is in a nursing home. The Medicaid law provides special protection to prevent spousal impoverishment. When one spouse enters a nursing home, the law wants to make it possible for the other spouse to continue living in the community. The spouse who does not need long-term care is permitted to retain certain assets, which are called the "community spouse resource allowance." The couple's assets are counted as of the day the applicant enters the nursing home, and the community spouse is entitled to retain one-half of the couple's countable assets up to a maximum of $130,380 (2021).

Example 11.38

On the day Danny Fontaine enters a nursing home, he and his wife Sandy have a home valued at $240,000, a car worth $28,000, and a stock portfolio with a market value of $140,000. The house and car are not countable assets, so the Fontaines have countable assets of $140,000. They divide the $140,000 equally so Sandy gets $70,000 for her community spouse resource allowance. Danny can retain $2,000, so the Fontaines must spend down $68,000 before Danny will qualify for Medicaid.

When an applicant needs to spend down assets to qualify for Medicaid, the money can be spent on more than just nursing home care. The following expenditures are permitted:
- Paying off debts, including credit cards, mortgages, auto loans, taxes, and other legitimate debts
- Purchase of a new exempt asset such as a car or home
- Payments for home improvements and repairs to a home and car
- Pre-payment of funeral and burial expenses
- Payments for services under caregiver agreements, even when a child or sibling is the caregiver
- Purchase of certain annuities (Medicaid-compliant annuities are discussed below)

Partnership Programs

Middle-income individuals generally cannot qualify for Medicaid, and generally do not have enough resources to adequately self-insure. The Deficit Reduction Act of 2005 (DRA) created the Qualified State Long Term Care Partnership program to encourage more people to purchase long-term care insurance. Residents of some states may be able to find long-term care coverage through a State Partnership Program that links special Partnership-qualified (PQ) long-term care policies provided by private insurance companies with Medicaid. These Partnership-qualified policies:

---

17. CMCS Informational Bulletin for 2020: States have the option of using a higher limit, which can be as high as $893,000 in 2020. Most states have chosen to use the lower limit, but some states, especially in parts of the country where housing is expensive, use the higher amount. These limits are adjusted each year to account for inflation. (

- Help people purchase shorter term, more complete long-term care insurance
- Include inflation protection, so the dollar amount of benefits received can be higher than the amount of insurance coverage originally purchased
- Allow people to apply for Medicaid under modified eligibility rules if there is continued need for long-term care after the policy maximum is reached
- Include a special "asset disregard" feature that allows individuals to keep assets like personal savings above the usual $2,000 Medicaid limit

The following example shows how a Partnership-qualified policy works:

Example 11.39

Axel, a single man, purchases a Partnership policy with a value of $100,000. Some years later he receives benefits under that policy up to the policy's lifetime maximum coverage (adjusted for inflation) equaling $150,000.

Axel eventually requires more long-term care services, and applies for Medicaid. If Axel's policy was not a Partnership-qualified policy, in order to qualify for Medicaid, he would be entitled to keep only $2,000 in assets. He would have to spend down any assets over and above this amount.

However, because Axel bought a Partnership-qualified policy, he can keep $152,000 in assets and the state will not recover those funds after his death. Axel would only have to spend down his assets over and above the $152,000 in order to be eligible for Medicaid.

States must certify that partnership policies meet the specific requirements for their partnership program, including that those who sell partnership policies are trained and understand how these policies relate to public and private coverage options.

Only traditional long-term care insurance policies qualify; life insurance and annuity policies with LTC riders (discussed later in this chapter) do not qualify. Not all long-term care insurance (LTCI) policies are partnership-qualified, so it is important to understand the rules of the partnership program within the client's state. Partnership-qualified policies must be tax-qualified, contain certain consumer protections, and must include an inflation adjustment for applicants under age 75 in most states. Since Partnership-qualified policies must include inflation protection, the amount of the benefits received can be higher than the original amount of insurance protection purchased. The insurance company will provide notice in writing, either in a separate letter or in the policy declarations, that the policy is a partnership-qualified policy. If a separate letter is sent, it should be kept in a safe place along with the policy. The state's insurance commission websites may be consulted for state-specific requirements. Individuals who may wish to receive care in a different state, for example, to be closer to children who have moved to another area, should inquire in advance of the purchase whether the states offer reciprocity if the insured moves.

Medicaid Planning and the Look Back Period

The Medicaid program provides coverage for long-term care services for individuals who are unable to afford it. Some individuals, with assistance from financial planners and attorneys, have found ways of arranging assets so that the assets are preserved for the individual and/or family members, but are not countable when Medicaid eligibility is determined. The Deficit Reduction Act of 2005 (DRA) addresses key areas related to transfers of assets for less than fair market value and makes it more difficult for individuals with the resources to pay for their own long-term care services to inappropriately transfer assets in order to qualify for Medicaid.

When an individual applies for Medicaid coverage for long-term care, States conduct a review, or "look-back," to determine whether the individual (or his or her spouse) transferred assets (e.g., cash gifts to children, transferring home ownership) to another person or party for less than fair market value (FMV). When individuals transfer assets at less than the FMV they are subject to a penalty that delays the date they can qualify to receive Medicaid long-term care services. The DRA lengthened the "look-back period" to the 60 months (five years) prior to the date the individual applied for Medicaid.

Previously the penalty period began with the month the assets were transferred. However, under the DRA, the penalty period, for transfers made on or after February 8, 2006, begins on the later of:
1. the date of the asset transfer, or
2. the date the individual enters a nursing home and is found eligible for coverage of institutional level services that Medicaid would pay for were it not for the imposition of a transfer penalty.

The illustration below provides a time line for Medicaid eligibility. A "look-back" period applies to the 60 months prior to applying for Medicaid, while the penalty period begins after the applicant has:
1. filed for Medicaid and moved into the nursing home, and
2. spent down assets to an amount to become eligible for Medicaid.

Exhibit 11.29 | Medicaid Eligibility Timeline

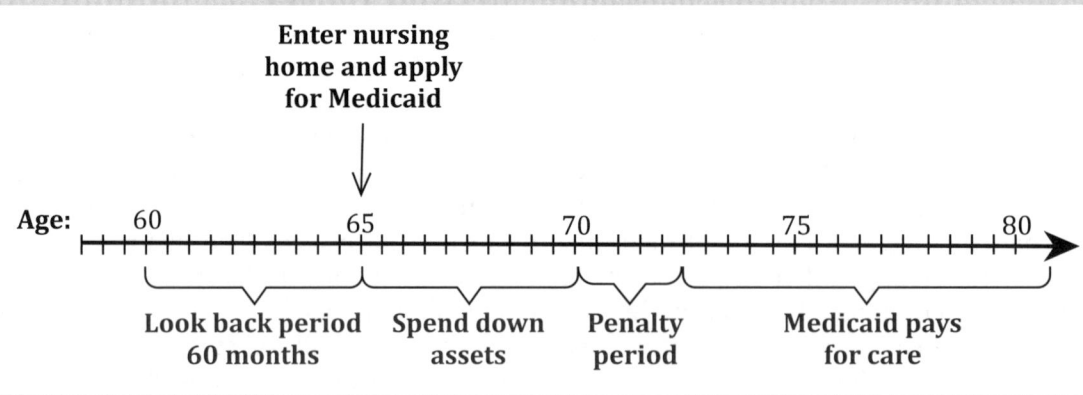

The penalty period is calculated by dividing the value of the property transferred by the average monthly cost of a nursing home in the state. If the value of the property transferred was $50,000 and the average monthly cost of nursing home care is $5,000, the penalty period is 10 months ($50,000/$5,000).

Example 11.40

Charmaine gave her two sons gifts of $15,000 each 12 months ago. This year, Charmaine will enter a nursing home that costs $6,000 per month and will apply for Medicaid benefits. She is a widow and has countable assets of $122,000. The average monthly cost of nursing home care in her state is $6,000. The look back period is 60 months, so Charmaine will have a penalty period of five months ($30,000/$6,000 = 5 months) due to the gifts to her two sons.

Medicaid eligibility will not begin until after Charmaine has spent down her countable assets to $2,000. The countable assets will be spent on the nursing home care and will be depleted down to $2,000 after 20 months. The penalty period will apply after her assets have been spent down, resulting in a total of 25 months before Medicaid will begin paying for her care.

Some transfers are permitted even after an individual enters a nursing home. The following transfers can be made without causing a period of Medicaid ineligibility:

- Transfer to a spouse
- Transfer to a child who is blind or disabled
- Transfer in trust for the benefit of a person under age 65 and disabled
- Transfer of a home to a child under the age of 21 or a child who has lived in the home for at least two years before the applicant moved to a nursing home and provided care that enabled the applicant to stay in the home during that time
- Transfer of a home to a sibling who has an equity interest in it and who lived in it at least a year before the applicant moved to a nursing home

Medicaid planning is often undertaken to preserve assets for children or relatives, or to preserve assets for a spouse. It is also done to preserve assets that could be used to enhance care above what is provided for under Medicaid. There is a valid question as to whether Medicaid planning is ethical and/or moral. There are many advisors and attorneys who assist people in transferring assets to qualify for Medicaid benefits. There are also many advisors and attorneys who believe it is unethical and will not engage in this type of planning. Consider the following two examples:

Example 11.41

Barry worked as a plumber since he was 18 years old. He worked hard his entire life and has saved a fair amount of money by not going on vacations, eating at home, and living modestly. He just turned age 65 and has been diagnosed with Alzheimer's disease. He had hoped that he would be able to leave some of his money to his daughter for his grandson's college education. However, he is concerned that he will spend his life's savings on long-term care. He is also concerned that his wife will be without the necessary funds to care for her needs.

Example 11.42

Larry worked as a plumber since he was 18 years old. He worked hard his entire life, but also enjoyed his life by buying expensive cars, vacationing every change he had, and always buying the latest in fashion trends. While he has earned a significant amount of money over his career, he has almost nothing saved and lives in an apartment. He just turned age 65 and has been diagnosed with Alzheimer's disease. He is very concerned about the progressiveness of the disease and the prospect of needing long-term care and not being able to afford it.

Despite the fact that Larry has been at least somewhat irresponsible in terms of spending, he is entitled to Medicaid. From an ethical perspective, the case can be made that Medicaid is designed for the poor and therefore Larry should receive it and Barry should not. This outcome may or may not be palatable. Barry, on the other hand, is left with the choice of spending down his assets (using them for long-term care needs) and then applying for Medicaid or engaging in Medicaid planning.

In Helvering v. Gregory, Judge Learned Hand famously wrote about tax planning: "Any one may so arrange his affairs that his taxes shall be as low as possible; he is not bound to choose that pattern which will best pay the Treasury; there is not even a patriotic duty to increase one's taxes." Considering this quote and the idea of preserving assets for a spouse, one might conclude that Medicaid planning is not unethical. Some might even conclude that Medicaid planning is not only ethical, but also prudent. However, what is certain is that there is an ethical question that must be answered before undertaking this type of planning.

Special Needs Trust

The assets of certain kinds of trusts are not considered for purposes of determining eligibility for Medicaid. These trusts are generally classified as special needs trusts. A **special needs trust** is a specific type of trust that is used to provide benefits to persons or beneficiaries with special needs. Typically, these trusts are established to ensure that benefits available from federal and state agencies are preserved and maintained. The more common special needs trusts are the Third Party Special Needs Trust, the self settled type trust that is established and exempt under 42 U.S.C. Sec. 1396p(d)(4)(A), and what is referred to as a pooled trust, which is exempt under 42 U.S.C. Sec. 1396p(d)(4)(C).

A third party special needs trust is sometimes referred to as a family trust as the trust is a receptacle for funds from a parent, guardian or other family member. The assets of these trusts, if properly structured, are not counted or considered for purposes of available federal or state benefits for the beneficiary.

> ### 📝 Quick Quiz 11.8
>
> 1. Long-term care insurance does not cover hospice care.
>   a. True
>   b. False
>
> 2. Because everyone qualifies for Medicaid, long-term care insurance is only for those who want more choices in long-term care than Medicaid offers.
>   a. True
>   b. False
>
> 3. If Tito had a home worth $300,000, it is possible he could qualify for Medicaid.
>   a. True
>   b. False
>
> 4. Paying for long-term care services out of pocket is not a wise choice for anyone.
>   a. True
>   b. False
>
> False, False, True, False.

These trusts can be funded by a parent or guardian during life or at death and are sometimes funded through the proceeds from a life insurance policy. The funds are contributed to a trust by the grantor or settlor for the benefit of the person with the special needs (beneficiary). The assets were never the property of the beneficiary and are therefore not counted as assets for purposes of federal or state benefits.

The trust must be established so as to not provide food, shelter or any asset that could be converted into food or shelter, such as cash. It may provide for other benefits, such as medical treatment, therapy, education, travel, computer equipment, or other opportunities allowing the individual with special needs to pursue new and enjoyable experiences. These types of benefits can improve the lifestyle of the beneficiary and not interfere with governmental benefits.

The assets of a pooled trust are also ignored for Medicaid purposes. However, these two trusts require that assets remaining in the trust be available for state recovery to the extent that state funds were used to care for the beneficiary.

Medicaid-Compliant Annuities

A "spend down" strategy that can be useful to the spouse of a nursing home resident is the purchase of a Medicaid-compliant (or Medicaid-qualified) annuity. An annuity is a financial product that allows a lump-sum amount to be converted to a guaranteed income stream over a set period of time or based on someone's lifetime, with no access to the principal amount once the income stream is started. The purchase of a Medicaid-compliant annuity is not available in all states and should only be undertaken with an adviser knowledgeable in the use of these annuities. It is not a very useful strategy for unmarried individuals.

In many states, the purchase of an immediate annuity that pays income to the community spouse is not a gratuitous transfer for purposes of Medicaid eligibility. The payments from the annuity must be made to the community spouse to avoid affecting the Medicaid eligibility of the nursing home resident. It is important that the annuity be immediate (with the income stream beginning immediately) because the purchase of a deferred annuity (one in which the receipt of income is delayed) is not a permitted transfer, and the deferred annuity will be a countable asset. In addition, for an annuity to avoid being treated as an impermissible transfer it must meet the following requirements:
- It must be irrevocable and non-assignable.
- It must be actuarially sound so the payments over the community spouse's life expectancy will at least equal what was paid for the annuity. If there is a term certain it must be shorter than the community spouse's life expectancy.
- Payments must be in equal amounts with no deferral or balloon payments.
- The state must be named the remainder beneficiary up to the amount of Medicaid payments made for the resident spouse.

The purchase of an immediate annuity will change a countable asset into an income stream for the community spouse. Since the spouse's income is not considered in the determination of Medicaid eligibility, the annuity will not result in any period of ineligibility.

Example 11.43

Karl and Rita Djocavich live in a state where the maximum community spouse resource allowance is $128,640 (2021). Karl is in a nursing home, and has transferred his assets to Rita so she has countable assets of $218,640. Rita can take the excess of $90,000 over her allowance and purchase an annuity. Karl will immediately be eligible for Medicaid, and Rita will receive monthly payments for life from the annuity.

The use of these annuities has been opposed by several states on the grounds that they involve impermissible transfers, but courts have recognized the annuities as part of the overall federal legislative design to assure that the healthy spouse will have sufficient income to remain in the community.

The community spouse can spend the income from the annuity as he or she wishes and can even make gifts or transfers of this income to children or relatives.

Exhibit 11.30 Strategies for Medicaid Eligibility

- Spending down of assets and income
- Transfer of assets to spouse
- Special needs trust
- Medicaid qualified annuity

Estate Recovery

The federal government requires states to try to recover Medicaid costs for long-term care. States generally pursue two approaches to cost recovery: (1) from the deceased individual's estate, and (2) from liens on the individual's property.

The extent to which a state can recover the repayment of Medicare costs from a deceased individual's estate will depend to some extent on the way state law defines an "estate." The definition will determine the type of property the state can recover, and states define the term differently. Some states will limit the property that can be recovered to the deceased person's probate estate. The probate estate includes only the property solely owned by the individual at death. Joint property, life estates, contracts with a named beneficiary, and payable on death accounts are not assets belonging to the probate estate. Other states will define the "estate" to include life insurance and assets in which the individual held an interest at death and which are not included in the probate estate, such as joint tenancy interests or life estates.

States cannot recover Medicaid costs paid for the deceased spouse while the surviving spouse is still living. Assets of surviving spouses are exempt from recovery; however, recovery may be made after the death of the surviving spouse.

Liens can be used to recover Medicaid costs by allowing the state to collect repayment when property is sold. Liens can be placed on real property during the lifetime of the individual receiving Medicaid benefits. The state collects its payment for the Medicaid costs when the property is sold. Liens may be placed on the individual's home, even though it is exempt property for purposes of eligibility. A state may waive recovery and not try to collect repayment where it would cause undue hardship to the deceased's heirs.

Estate recovery for Medicaid benefits can mean that the individual ends up paying for Medicaid expenses after death, even though the individual avoided payment during lifetime. Assets that were exempt during the individual's lifetime, such as a home or a car, are subject to the estate recovery.

DISCUSSION QUESTIONS

SOLUTIONS to the discussion questions can be found exclusively within the chapter. Once you have completed an initial reading of the chapter, go back and highlight the answers to these questions.

1. List and describe the six major categories of benefits administered by the Social Security Association.

2. How are Social Security funds collected?

3. Which individuals are covered workers under the Social Security system?

4. List the beneficiaries of Social Security benefits.

5. How is a person's Social Security retirement benefit calculated?

6. How does retiring early or retiring late affect the calculation of Social Security benefits?

7. How are Social Security benefits taxed?

8. What other benefits are available from Social Security other than retirement benefits?

9. Discuss the maximum family benefit.

10. What benefits does Medicare provide?

11. Describe the various enrollment periods for Medicare.

12. Describe Supplemental Security Income benefits and when they are available.

13. How does marriage or divorce affect Social Security benefits?

14. What are the Medicaid eligibility requirements?

15. Explain the Medicaid look back on asset transfers and the associated penalty period.

A sample of multiple choice problems is provided below. Additional multiple choice problems are available at money-education.com by accessing the Student Practice Portal.

1. Social Security is funded through all of the following except:
    a. Employee payroll tax.
    b. Employer payroll tax.
    c. Sales tax.
    d. Self-employment tax.

2. Brisco, now deceased, was married for 12 years. He had two dependent children, ages 10 and 12, who are cared for by their mother age 48. His mother, age 75, was his dependent and survived him. At the time of his death, he was currently but not fully insured under Social Security. His dependents are entitled to all of the following benefits except:
    a. A lump-sum death benefit of $255.
    b. A children's benefit equal to 75% of Brisco's PIA.
    c. A caretaker's benefit for the children's mother.
    d. A parent's benefit.

3. Medicare Part A provides hospital coverage. Which of the following persons is not covered under Part A?
    a. A person 62 or older and receiving railroad retirement.
    b. Disabled beneficiaries regardless of age that have received Social Security for two years.
    c. Chronic kidney patients who require dialysis or a renal transplant.
    d. A person 65 or older entitled to a monthly Social Security check.

4. A person receiving Social Security benefits under full retirement age can receive earned income up to a maximum threshold without reducing Social Security benefits by the earnings test. Which of the following count against the earnings threshold?
    a. Dividends from stocks.
    b. Rental income.
    c. Pensions and insurance annuities.
    d. Self-employment income.

5. All of the following statements concerning Social Security benefits are correct except:
    a. The maximum family benefit is determined through a formula based on the worker's PIA.
    b. If a worker applies for retirement or survivors' benefits before his 65th birthday, he must also file a separate application for Medicare.
    c. People who are disabled or have permanent kidney failure can get Medicare at any age.
    d. The Social Security Administration is concerned with beneficiaries' combined income, which, on the 1040 federal tax return, includes adjusted gross income and nontaxable interest income

QUICK QUIZ EXPLANATIONS

Quick Quiz 11.1
1. False. Reduced Social Security benefits can be withdrawn as early as age 62.
2. False. Social Security contributions are placed in the following trust funds: OASI, DI, and HI. The SMI Trust Fund is not funded by Social Security contributions.

Quick Quiz 11.2
1. True.
2. True.

Quick Quiz 11.3
1. False. The Social Security retirement benefit is based on the worker's PIA. A worker's PIA is based on the worker's average indexed monthly earnings during the 35 years in which the worker earned the most.
2. False. Full retirement age for Social Security is increasing because of increasing life expectancies.

Quick Quiz 11.4
1. True.
2. False. Once divorced, a non-working ex-spouse who was married to the worker for more than ten years can still receive Social Security benefits based on the worker's record.
3. True.

Quick Quiz 11.5
1. True.
2. False. The increase equals 8 percent per year times three years, which is a 24 percent increase.
3. True.

Quick Quiz 11.6
1. True.
2. False. Medicare Part C (Medicare Advantage) is an alternative to traditional Medicare (Parts A and B). Part D provides prescription drug coverage when purchased with Parts A and B.
3. False. Failure to enroll in Medicare Part B during the initial enrollment period will result in a permanent increase in premium unless the individual maintains creditable health coverage from an employer and enrolls during a special enrollment period following loss of the employer-provided coverage
4. False. Traditional Medicare does not have a maximum out-of-pocket amount, leaving the covered individual at risk for paying large out-of-pocket medical expenses. Some Medigap (Medicare Supplement) policies and some Medicare Advantage plans, however, do offer a maximum out-of-pocket provision.

QUICK QUIZ EXPLANATIONS

Quick Quiz 11.7
1. False. In order to obtain SSI benefits, an individual must be 65, disabled, or blind.
2. True.

Quick Quiz 11.8
1. False. Long-term care insurance coverage includes: nursing homes, home health, and hospice.
2. False. One must qualify financially for Medicaid.
3. True.
4. False. For those individuals with significant assets or few assets, it may make sense to pay for the services in lieu of paying for the insurance.

**Additional multiple choice problems
are available at
money-education.com
by accessing the
Student Practice Portal.
Access requires registration of the title using
the unique code at the front of the book.**

12

DEFERRED COMPENSATION AND NONQUALIFIED PLANS

LEARNING OBJECTIVES

1. Explain the general characteristics of a deferred compensation plan and when it is appropriate.*
2. Understand the significance of IRC §409A.*
3. Describe the tax benefits of a deferred compensation plan available to employees and employers.*
4. Discuss the tax issues of constructive receipt, substantial risk of forfeiture, economic benefit doctrine and income and payroll tax implications of a deferred compensation plan.*
5. Analyze the benefits and risks of filing an 83(b) election.*
6. Describe the various types of deferred compensation arrangements.*
7. Calculate the income attributable to the exercise of ISOs and NQSOs as well as the gain from the subsequent sale of the acquired stock.*
8. Explain the mechanics of restricted stock and ESPPs.*
9. Appreciate the rational for qualified equity grants and the benefits of the provision.*

Ties to CFP Certification Learning Objectives

INTRODUCTION

Employers establish **deferred compensation arrangements** to provide benefits to a select group of employees without the limitations, restrictions, and rules of a qualified plan. These types of arrangements, usually in the form of **nonqualified plans** or other executive compensation, often discriminate in favor of key employees and can exceed the dollar limits imposed on qualified plans. These arrangements may take many forms but the ultimate objective is usually to recruit and/or retain key executives. While qualified plans and the other tax-advantaged plans are effective with respect to mid and lower-paid employees, the limitations imposed by these plans, especially the dollar limits and testing requirements, do not provide sufficient retirement resources for key executives who earn in excess of $290,000, the covered compensation limit for qualified plans for 2021.

The general characteristics of the deferred compensation arrangements presented in this chapter are:
1. They do not have the tax advantages of qualified plans.
2. They usually involve some deferral of income to the executive.
3. The employer generally does not receive an income tax deduction until the key employee receives the payment and it becomes recognizable as taxable income, thus following the traditional income tax matching principle of deduction by one party only upon inclusion by another party.
4. There is generally a requirement that the employee/executive have a "substantial risk of forfeiture" or else the government will claim that the executive, while perhaps not having actual receipt of the money, has "constructive receipt" of the money and, therefore, current income subject to income tax.

Correspondingly, deferred compensation arrangements are most often used for one or all of the three following reasons:
1. to increase the executive's wage replacement ratio,
2. to defer the executive's compensation, or
3. in lieu of qualified plans.

Some different arrangements include:
1. Golden Handshakes - severance package, often designed to encourage early retirement
2. Golden Parachutes - substantial payments made to executives being terminated due to changes in corporate ownership
3. Golden Handcuffs - designed to keep the executive with the company

It is also important to understand that employers also use deferred compensation arrangements as a method of retaining key employees. This can be done either by vesting schedules or through increased benefits with additional years of service.

Wage Replacement Ratio

An individual may need approximately 70-80 percent of his pre-retirement income during his retirement years to maintain his pre-retirement lifestyle. Most low-income and middle-income employees are capable of accumulating the amounts necessary to attain their target **wage replacement ratio** utilizing qualified plans offered by their employer in conjunction with Social Security and their own savings. However, executives who earn substantially more than the qualified plan covered compensation limit, $290,000 for 2021, cannot attain a significant wage replacement ratio from qualified plans because qualified plans adhere to strict limits on either contributions (e.g., $58,000 per year in 2021 for defined contribution plans) or benefits (e.g., a defined benefit limit of $230,000 in 2021).

Key Concepts

1. What are deferred compensation arrangements?
2. What are the three common reasons employers use deferred compensation arrangements?

Example 12.1

Consider the following employer data from Meyer Group.

Person	Current Compensation	Covered Compensation	Contribution to Qualified Plan (Limit)*	Savings Rate (As a % of Gross Compensation)
Dina	$400,000	$290,000	$58,000	14.5%
Breckin	$290,000	$290,000	$58,000	20.0%
Seth	$40,000	$40,000	$20,000**	50.0%

Seth could have a larger contribution under IRC 415(c) under certain scenarios.
**Assumed*

Each employee's final compensation can be projected using a 3.5 percent assumed wage rate increase and assuming that each employee is 20 years from retirement.

Person	Current Compensation	Compensation 20 Years from Today (Assume 3.5% Raises)
Dina	$400,000	$795,916
Breckin	$290,000	$577,039
Seth	$40,000	$79,592

Assuming that each employee saves the stated contribution amount each year at year end and the funds earn eight percent per year, determine the accumulated account balance and the dollar size of a 20-year annuity paid in arrears on an annual basis.

Person	Savings from Qualified Plan Today	Future Accumulated Balance at 8% in 20 Years	Accumulation 20-Year Annuity
Dina	$58,000	$2,654,194	$270,336
Breckin	$58,000	$2,654,194	$270,336
Seth	$20,000	$915,239	$93,219

The wage replacement ratio that the annuity provides can then be calculated as a fraction of each employee's final pre retirement compensation.

Person	Wage Replacement (Annuity/Future Compensation)	
Dina	34%	($270,336 ÷ $795,916)
Breckin	47%	($270,336 ÷ $577,039)
Seth	117%	($93,219 ÷ $79,592)

As illustrated, Dina saves 14.5 percent of her gross compensation in the qualified plan, resulting in a wage replacement ratio from that qualified plan at retirement of 34 percent. This amount is substantially less than the 70-80 percent recommended wage replacement ratio that she will need.

The qualified plan restricted Dina to this wage replacement ratio of 34 percent because the maximum contribution to the plan each year was limited ($58,000 for 2021).

The establishment of a deferred compensation plan allows an employer to provide nonqualified benefits to an executive without having to provide benefits to other rank and file employees. The purpose is to increase the executive's wage replacement ratio to a level commensurate with the executive's actual compensation instead of a wage replacement ratio limited by the qualified covered compensation limit of $290,000 for 2021 and the other limits of qualified plans (defined contributions of $58,000 and defined benefits of $230,000 for 2021). A common application of deferred compensation plans is to supplement qualified retirement plans.

IRC Section 409A

The American Jobs Creation Act of 2004 was signed into law on October 22, 2004 and created IRC §409A, which deals with nonqualified deferred compensation plans. The purpose of this section is to provide clear structure and guidance for these types of plans. These rules also enact harsh penalties for those plans that do not comply with §409A. Plans failing to meet the requirements of this section are subject to acceleration of prior deferrals, interest, penalties, and a 20 percent additional tax on the amount of the deferrals. These are serious ramifications for plans that fail to comply with the new rules.

The law attempts to define nonqualified deferred compensation plans as any plan that provides for "deferral of compensation." However, it excludes most qualified plans, incentive stock option plans, nonqualified stock option plans, employee stock purchase plans, stock appreciation rights plans, and standard type bonuses that are paid within 2½ months after the close of the taxable year. Eligible plans under IRC §457(b) are also excluded. However, the new rules do apply to plans under IRC §457(f) (as discussed in Chapter 10).[1]

If deferred compensation plans meet the requirements of §409A, then IRC §409A has no effect on the employee's gross income and taxes. If the arrangement does not meet the requirements of §409A, however, §409A generally provides that all amounts deferred under a nonqualified deferred compensation plan are currently includible in gross income to the extent that the amounts are not subject to a substantial risk of forfeiture and to the extent that the amounts have not been previously includible in gross income.[2] Compensation is subject to a substantial risk of forfeiture if entitlement to the amount is conditioned on the performance of substantial future services by any person or the occurrence of an event related to a purpose of the compensation, such as the attainment of certain earnings or equity value.[3]

In order to comply with §409A, the regulations require that the plan be established and maintained in accordance with the requirements of §409A. As part of these requirements, the material terms of the plan must be set forth in writing. In addition, §409A generally provides that payments may only be made at certain times or upon certain events, including:
- separation from service
- disability
- death
- at a specified time or pursuant to a fixed schedule
- upon a change in control[4]
- upon an unforeseeable emergency

IRC §409A greatly restricts the conditions under which a plan may permit the acceleration of the time or schedule of payments under the plan. The exceptions that the law provides are minimal but include domestic relations orders, distributions for paying income tax for 457(f) plans, and the payment of employment taxes.

Deferred Executive Compensation

Deferred compensation arrangements may also be established simply to defer an executive's compensation to a future year. When an executive agrees to defer his compensation, the executive is agreeing to defer receipt of current income for a promise from the employer to pay that compensation at some later date. It is important to note that an agreement to defer compensation into the future must be made prior to the compensation being earned. Deferred compensation arrangements usually create income tax benefits for both the executive and the employer.

---

1. IRC §409A(d)(1).
2. Internal Revenue Bulletin 2006-29.
3. IRC §409A(d)(4).
4. Treas. Reg. §1.409A-3(i)(5)(vi).

Employee Tax Benefit

An executive who elects to defer compensation generally earns a significantly greater amount than the covered compensation limit, is usually in the highest marginal income tax bracket, and does not currently need the deferred income to sustain his current standard of living. If the executive chooses to defer the compensation, the executive generally defers the compensation to a time when he expects to be in a lower marginal income tax bracket and thus, at the date of receipt, expects to pay less income tax on the compensation than would have been paid currently.

Employer Tax Benefit

The IRC places a $1,000,000 limit on a public company's deduction for compensation payable to any one of the top five executives of a publicly traded company. No deduction is allowed by a public company for a covered employee's compensation to the extent it exceeds $1,000,000 for the year. A covered employee includes the following five individuals:[5]

Quick Quiz 12.1

1. Deferred compensation plans allow the employer to take a current deduction for compensation expense while the employee can defer the income tax on the compensation.
   a. True
   b. False

2. Public companies are limited to a $1,000,000 compensation deduction for some executives.
   a. True
   b. False

False, True.

- The chief executive officer (CEO) at any time during the taxable year (or was an individual acting in such a capacity),
- The chief financial officer (CFO) at any time during the taxable year (or was an individual acting in such a capacity), and
- The three highest compensated officers for the taxable year (other than the CEO and CFO).

The definition of covered employee was expanded in the TCJA 2017 to include the CFO. In addition, covered employee (and the $1 million deduction limit) applies to anyone who was a covered employee after 2016. This addition to the definition includes former CEOs, CFOs, or officers if they were a covered employee after 2016 and are receiving compensation, even if it is as a director or non-employee. Thus, a covered employee after 2016 will be a covered employee for all future years. [6]

The TCJA 2017 also modified the definition of compensation, which is referred to as remuneration in the IRC, to include cash and non-cash benefits, including commissions and performance-based compensation for tax years after 2017.[7] Previously, commissions and performance-based compensation was excluded from the definition of compensation. This exclusion allowed companies to structure remuneration for covered employees in such a way as to be able to deduct compensation above the $1 million limit, if it consisted of commissions or performance-based compensation.

The new rules provide for transitional relief if compensation is provided based on a written binding contract that was in effect as of November 2, 2017 and is not materially modified after such date.

---

5. §162(m)(3) defines covered employee and uses the term "principal executive" and "principal financial" in lieu of "chief executive" and "chief financial."
6. §162(m)(3).
7. In REG-122180-18 the IRS issued Proposed Regulations under IRC §162(m) that clarify that compensation includes an amount that is includible in the income of, or paid to, a person other than the covered employee, including after the death of the covered employee.

After 2017, public companies include all U.S. domestic publicly traded companies and all foreign public companies that are listed on exchanges or traded through ADRs (American depository receipts). The Conference Committee Report also states that the "proposed definition may include certain additional corporations that are not publicly traded, such as large private C or S corporations."[8]

These rules do not eliminate deferred compensation for the covered employees. However, they reduce the effectiveness as a covered employee retains his or her status for all future years, and any deferred income that exceeds the $1 million limit will no longer be deductible. If the deferred income is spread out over enough years to fall below the threshold amount, the payments should be fully deductible.

For example, when a CEO is paid $1,250,000 per year, the employer can only deduct $1,000,000 for income tax purposes. In this case, if the executive elects to defer any income over the $1,000,000 limit to a year in which the executive earns less than the limit, the employer would be able to deduct the total compensation over the period of deferral and subsequent payments. However, if the deferred income payments exceed the $1 million threshold, the employer would not be able to take an income tax deduction (even though the CEO picked up the payments as taxable income) for amounts over the threshold.

Example 12.2

Josephine, the CFO of Eighteen Corporation, a publicly traded company, earns $1,250,000 per year. Without an election to defer any of her compensation, Eighteen Corporation will only be able to deduct $1,000,000 in relation to Josephine's compensation.

If, however, Josephine elected to defer $250,000 of her compensation until her retirement, Eighteen Corporation would be able to deduct $1,000,000 in the current year as Josephine's compensation, and upon Josephine's retirement, would be able to deduct the additional $250,000 payment to Josephine as deferred compensation. To the extent that multiple years of deferrals results in annual payments that exceed the $1 million threshold, the employer would not be able to take an income tax deduction for the excess.

Alternative to Qualified Plans

Deferred compensation plans are also used where the employer does not have a qualified plan because the employer does not desire to cover a broad group of employees. The employer may nonetheless be compelled to provide retirement benefits to certain key executives and can accomplish this goal by utilizing a deferred compensation plan. Nonqualified plans can discriminate in favor of key employees and are not subject to the limits imposed on qualified plans.

---

8. In REG-122180-18 the IRS issued Proposed Regulations under IRC §162(m) that provide that a corporation is publicly held if, as of the last day of its taxable year, its securities are required to be registered under section 12 of the Exchange Act or it is required to file reports under section 15(d) of the Exchange Act.

INCOME TAX ISSUES

Deferred compensation arrangements are typically used to benefit the highly compensated and key executives in an organization. One of the primary benefits to these types of plans is the deferral of income taxation for the key executive. For deferral of income tax to be realized, the deferred compensation plan must comply with certain income tax provisions.

Constructive Receipt

Constructive receipt is an income tax concept that establishes the point at which income is includible by a taxpayer and therefore subject to income tax. The rules for constructive receipt are found in Treasury Regulation §1.451-2.

Income, although not actually in a taxpayer's possession, is nonetheless constructively received by the taxpayer in the taxable year during which it is credited to his account, set apart for him, or otherwise made available so that he may draw upon it at any time, or so that he could have drawn upon it during the taxable year if notice of intention to withdraw had been given. Generally, an individual will be deemed to have constructive receipt of income if he can choose to receive the income today or in the future. However, income is not constructively received if the taxpayer's control of its receipt is subject to substantial limitations or restrictions. Thus, if a corporation credits its employees with stock as a bonus but the stock is not available to the employees until some future date, the mere crediting of the stock on the books of the corporation does not constitute constructive receipt of the stock.

> ### :≡ *Key Concepts*
>
> 1. What is constructive receipt and how does it affect deferred compensation plans?
>
> 2. What is a substantial risk of forfeiture and how does it affect deferred compensation plans?
>
> 3. What is the Economic Benefit Doctrine and how does it affect deferred compensation plans?

Examples of Constructive Receipt

Amounts payable with respect to interest coupons that have matured and are payable, but which have not been cashed, are constructively received in the taxable year during which the coupons mature, unless it can be shown that there are no funds available for payment of the interest during such year. Dividends on corporate stock are constructively received when made subject to the demand of the shareholder without qualifications. However, if a dividend is declared payable on December 31 and the corporation followed its normal practice of paying the dividends by mailing checks so that the shareholders would not receive them until January of the following year, such dividends are not considered to have been constructively received in December. Generally, the amount of dividends or interest credited on savings bank deposits or to shareholders of organizations, such as building and loan associations or cooperative banks, is income to the depositors or shareholders for the taxable year when credited. However, if any portion of such dividends or interest is not subject to withdrawal at the time credited, that portion is not constructively received and does not constitute income to the depositor or shareholder until the taxable year in which the portion first may be withdrawn.

Deferred compensation plans are structured so that employees benefiting under the plan will avoid constructive receipt and will therefore be allowed the deferral of income taxation.

As mentioned, an employee who elects to defer compensation, such as a bonus, into the future under a deferred compensation arrangement must do so prior to the compensation being earned. Otherwise, the employee would effectively have the choice of receiving current income or deferring. This choice would result in the income being considered constructively received whether or not there was a subsequent substantial risk of forfeiture.

The following are some examples of what is not considered constructive receipt:

- an unsecured promise to pay
- the benefits are subject to substantial limitations or restrictions
- the triggering event is beyond the recipient's control (i.e., company is acquired)

Substantial Risk of Forfeiture

Substantial risk of forfeiture is another income tax concept that relates to when income is subject to income tax. The rules for substantial risk of forfeiture are found in Treasury Regulation §1.83-3(c).

A substantial risk of forfeiture exists when rights in property that are transferred are conditioned, directly or indirectly, upon the future performance (or refraining from performance) of substantial services by any person, or the occurrence of a condition related to a purpose of the transfer and the possibility of forfeiture is substantial if the condition is not satisfied. The issue of whether a risk of forfeiture is substantial remains a matter of facts and circumstances. When there is a substantial risk of forfeiture, the taxpayer is not required to include the income as taxable income. When there is not a substantial risk of forfeiture, the taxpayer is required to recognize the income currently as taxable income.

Often, a deferred compensation agreement is structured as a simple contractual promise from the employer to a key employee. Generally, this puts the employee at risk that the employer might default or breach the contract and not pay. The obligation of a deferred compensation agreement is reflected

> ### Quick Quiz 12.2
>
> 1. Deferred compensation plans are generally structured so that employees benefiting under the plan will avoid constructive receipt.
>   a. True
>   b. False
>
> 2. A substantial risk of forfeiture is the risk that the employee will leave the corporation prematurely and take the plan assets with them.
>   a. True
>   b. False
>
> 3. For contributions to a deferred compensation plan to be taxed because of the economic benefit doctrine, there must be no restrictions or risks that the funds would not be paid to the employee.
>   a. True
>   b. False
>
> 4. Jordan is the CEO of Colin, Inc., a publicly traded company. Jordan's salary is $2.3 million. Colin can take an income tax deduction for Jordan's entire salary.
>   a. True
>   b. False
>
> True, False, True, False.

on the balance sheet of the organization as a liability. However, in terms of the ranking of creditors in the case of liquidation, all secured and unsecured creditors would be fully paid prior to paying the deferred compensation obligation. In liquidation, a participant in a deferred compensation plan is paid before both preferred and common shareholders. Thus, it can be said that for an unfunded deferred compensation arrangement based on a simple contractual promise to pay, the employee is at a "substantial risk of forfeiture." Most deferred compensation arrangements are unfunded and, therefore, subject to the risk of nonpayment. Deferred compensation arrangements can, however, be funded.

Example 12.3

On November 25, 2021, Carb Corporation gives Edward, an employee, a bonus of 100 shares of Carb Corporation stock. The terms of the bonus arrangement obligate Edward to return the stock to Carb Corporation if he terminates his employment for any reason. However, for each year occurring after November 25, 2021, during which Edward remains employed with Carb Corporation, Edward ceases to be obligated to return 10 shares of the Carb Corporation stock. Therefore, each year occurring after November 25, 2021 that Edward remains employed, his rights in 10 shares of stock cease to be subject to a substantial risk of forfeiture. Thus, the value of 10 shares of stock will be included in Edward's income each year when the substantial risk of forfeiture expires. The value of this income is equal to the value of the stock on each November 25th, when the substantial risk of forfeiture expires.

Since one of the primary purposes of deferred compensation arrangements is to avoid current taxation for the key executive, these plans will almost always include a substantial risk of forfeiture so that the executive can defer payment of income tax. Employers may simply promise to pay the employee or may use some form of vesting schedule in an attempt to meet the substantial risk of forfeiture standard.

Economic Benefit Doctrine

The **economic benefit doctrine** provides that an employee will be taxed on funds or property set aside for the employee if the funds or property are unrestricted and nonforfeitable, even if the employee was not given a choice to receive the income currently. In other words, if an employer sets aside funds for an employee and there is no risk that the employee will not receive the funds, then the funds are taxable under this doctrine at the point in time at which there are no longer any restrictions attached to the property.

Deferred compensation plans may provide for a trust to hold the funds for the employee prior to retirement or termination. Contributions to an employee's trust made by an employer will generally be included in the gross income of the employee in accordance with IRC §83 (discussed below, except that the value of the employee's interest in the trust shall be substituted for the fair market value of the property for purposes of applying such section). This means that contributions to a trust are taxable to the employee even if there is not a distribution from the trust. To be subject to income tax, the funds simply have to be unrestricted and nonforfeitable, which could occur once the employee becomes partially or fully vested.[9] An exception to this rule can be achieved through use of a rabbi trust, discussed later in this chapter.

Under no circumstances would a simple promise to pay be subject to current income tax since there are substantial risks as to whether the payments will be made. To be taxable under the economic benefit doctrine, there must be no restrictions or risks that the funds would not be paid to the employee.

> ### ⋮≡ *Key Concepts*
>
> 1. What is the Section 83(b) election with regard to a deferred compensation plan?
>
> 2. When are payroll taxes due on compensation placed into a deferred compensation plan?
>
> 3. When does the employer receive an income tax deduction for assets contributed to a deferred compensation plan?

---

9. IRC §402(b).

IRC Section 83: Property Transferred in Connection with Performance of Service

When an employer transfers property to an employee in connection with the performance of service, the employee will be taxed on the difference between the fair market value of the property and the amount paid for that property. For example, if an employer transferred stock worth $10 to an employee and the employee paid $3 for the stock, then the employee would be taxed on the difference of $7.

The fair market value of the property is determined at the time the rights of the person having the beneficial interest in the property are transferable or are not subject to a substantial risk of forfeiture, whichever occurs earlier.

Example 12.4

Ares, Inc. grants $50,000 worth of company stock to Randi, a key executive, and provides that she can only receive it if she is employed for five additional years. There is clearly a substantial risk of forfeiture during that five year vesting period that she will not be paid. Once Randi has completed the five years, she will be taxed based on the value of the stock at that time, which may be greater or lower than $50,000.

Generally, the gain or difference between the fair market value of the property and any amounts paid by the employee is taxed as ordinary income to the employee. Usually, this amount is included in the employee's Form W-2 and is also subject to both withholding and payroll taxes. Any further appreciation from the point at which the income is included in taxable income is capital gain (assuming that the property is of a capital nature).

These rules are typically applicable to grants of stock, especially restricted stock, and employee stock options but can also be applied to other transfers of property to an employee. The Section 83(b) election allows an employee to include into income the net value of a transfer from an employer for the purpose of establishing a basis in a capital asset. This election is discussed in greater detail later in this chapter.

Payroll Tax

Deferred compensation is considered to be earned income at the time a substantial risk of forfeiture expires and, therefore, is subject to payroll taxes at that time even though the employee may not receive payment until sometime in the future. The general rule is that payroll tax will apply at the later of the time at which the deferred income is earned or the point at which the deferred income becomes nonforfeitable.[10] Restricted stock or other benefits may be subject to vesting or other restrictions that would result in an employee forfeiting benefits if employment was terminated prior to a specific point in time. Once the restrictions are lifted, the benefits are deemed nonforfeitable and payroll taxes are due. Benefits from these plans are reported on Form W-2 since it is literally deferred compensation. The taxable event occurs when there is no longer a substantial risk of forfeiture.

---

10. Treas. Reg. §31.3121(v)(2)-1(e)(1) states that except as otherwise provided in this paragraph (e), an amount deferred under a nonqualified deferred compensation plan must be taken into account as wages for FICA tax purposes as of the later of the date on which services creating the right to the amount deferred are performed or the date on which the right to the amount deferred is no longer subject to a substantial risk of forfeiture.

Example 12.5

Employer C establishes a nonqualified deferred compensation plan for Employee A on January 1, 2021. Under the plan, which is an account balance plan, Employee A obtains a legally binding right on the last day of each calendar year (if Employee A is employed on that date) to be credited with a principal amount equal to 10 percent of compensation for the year. In addition, a reasonable rate of interest is credited quarterly. Employee A's account balance is nonforfeitable and is payable upon Employee A's termination of employment. For 2021, the principal amount credited to Employee A under the plan is $25,000.

The services creating the right to the $25,000 amount deferred are considered performed as of December 31, 2021, the date on which Employee A has performed all of the services necessary to obtain a legally binding right to the amount deferred. Thus, the $25,000 amount deferred must be taken into account as of December 31, 2021, which is the later of the date on which services creating the right to the amount deferred are performed or the date on which the right to the amount deferred is no longer subject to a substantial risk of forfeiture.

Example 12.6

The facts are the same as in **Example 12.5**, except that the principal amount credited under the plan on the last day of each year (and attributable interest) is forfeited if the employee terminates employment within five years of that date.

Because Employee A's right to receive the $25,000 principal amount (and attributable interest) is conditioned on the performance of services for five years, a substantial risk of forfeiture exists with respect to that amount deferred until December 31, 2026.

Example 12.7

The facts are the same as in **Example 12.5**, except that the principal amount credited under the plan on the last day of each year (and attributable interest) becomes nonforfeitable according to a graded vesting schedule under which 20 percent is vested after one year, 40 percent after two years, 60 percent after three years, 80 percent after four years, and 100 percent after five years.

Each 20 percent (of which there are five) is treated separately and a substantial risk of forfeiture exists with respect to that amount deferred until the point at which it is fully vested. Therefore, $5,000 plus attributable interest will vest on December 31, 2022, 2023, 2024, 2025, and 2026.

CASE STUDY 12.1

James H. Dunlap and Eileen M. Dunlap v. Commissioner, U.S. Tax Court, Dkt. No. 5811-17S, Summary Opinion 2020-10 (February 18, 2020).

Over the course of several years Eileen Dunlap worked her way up from sales consultant to national sales director for Mary Kay Cosmetics, Inc. Mary Kay consultants, sales directors, and national sales directors are independent contractors and are not employees.

Once she became a national sales director, Ms. Dunlap was eligible to participate in the Family Security Program (FSP) which was designed to provide a national sales director with financial security should she retire or be unable to work. Under the FSP, at 65 years of age, Ms. Dunlap was eligible to receive FSP payments for 15 years based on her average high tiered sales activity, but her business relationship with Mary Kay would end.

A July 1, 2001 restatement of the FSP plan stated "The Plan is intended to be a non-qualified deferred compensation arrangement and is not intended to meet the requirements of Section 401(a) of the [Internal Revenue] Code. The Plan is intended to meet the requirements of Section 409A of the Code and shall be construed and interpreted in accordance with such intent." The FSP was funded from the general assets of the firm.

At age 65, Ms. Dunlap retired and began receiving payments under the FSP. Ms. Dunlap argued that the FSP payments were for the sale of a capital asset (her business or goodwill) to the firm and were, therefore, not subject to self-employment tax. The court determined that the facts of the case were unambiguous. There was no agreement between Mary Kay and Ms. Dunlap with respect to a sale of a business or goodwill. Ms. Dunlap's prior earnings were the basis for the annual FSP payments and the quantity and quality of her labor were the reason for the post retirement payments. The FSP payments were paid contemporaneously although they were earned in prior years, and were subject to self-employment tax.

Executives and key employees who participate in deferred compensation plans generally have current earnings in excess of the Social Security wage base of $142,800 for 2021 and, therefore, only pay the 1.45 percent Medicare portion on income that is deferred in the deferred compensation plan. They will also be subject to the additional Medicare taxes for deferral income above certain limits.[11] While the funds are subject to payroll tax in the year earned, the employee is better off since the OASDI portion at 6.2 percent does not have to be paid. Likewise, the employer will also avoid paying the 6.2 percent for OASDI.

11. See Chapter 11 for a complete discussion.

The Affordable care act created two additional Medicare taxes that will impact wealthier taxpayers and executives. The first is an additional Medicare tax of 0.9 percent on wages or self-employment income above specified thresholds. The second is a 3.8 percent tax on certain amounts of net investment income. Both of these are more fully discussed in Chapter 11.

The additional Medicare tax equal to 0.9 percent applies to wages or self-employment income that is above the following threshold amounts:

Married filing jointly	$250,000
Married filing separately	$125,000
Single	$200,000
Head of household	$200,000

The wages for an executive that are subject to FICA would also be subject to the additional Medicare tax of 0.9 percent, to the extent that the wages exceed the threshold amount.[12]

When the income is later paid to the executive, it will be subject to income tax. However, the payments will not constitute "earned income" in the period received and, therefore, will not be subject to payroll taxes and will not qualify for the earned income test for IRAs and other qualified plans.

Employer Income Tax Deduction

As discussed in the first chapters of the book, one of the greatest benefits of qualified plans is that the employer receives a current income tax deduction for contributions to a qualified plan and the employee is not taxed on those contributed amounts until they are received as a distribution from the plan. This tax benefit does not extend to deferred compensation arrangements. In deferred compensation plans, the employer is entitled to receive an income tax deduction for contributions to the plan only when the employee is required to include the payments as taxable income. This concept is referred to as the matching principle - the employer's deduction follows the employee's inclusion into taxable income.

12. See Treas. Reg §31.3121(v)(2)-1.

Example 12.8

On January 1, 2021, the taxpayer and corporation X executed an employment contract under which the taxpayer is to be employed by the corporation in an executive capacity for a period of five years. Under the contract, the taxpayer is entitled to a stated annual salary and to additional compensation of 10x dollars for each year. The additional compensation will be credited to a bookkeeping reserve account and will be deferred, accumulated, and paid in annual installments equal to one-fifth of the amount in the reserve as of the close of the year immediately preceding the year of first payment. The payments are to begin only upon:

- termination of the taxpayer's employment by the corporation,
- the taxpayer's becoming a part-time employee of the corporation, or
- the taxpayer's becoming partially or totally incapacitated. Under the terms of the agreement, corporation X is under a merely contractual obligation to make the payments when due, and the parties did not intend that the amounts in the reserve be held by the corporation in trust for the taxpayer.

The contract further provides that if the taxpayer should fail or refuse to perform his duties, the corporation will be relieved of any obligation to make further credit to the reserve (but not of the obligation to distribute amounts previously contributed); but, if the taxpayer should become incapacitated from performing his duties, then credits to the reserve will continue for one year from the date of the incapacity, but not beyond the expiration of the five-year term of the contract.

The additional compensation to be received by the taxpayer under the employment contract concerned will be includible in his gross income only in the taxable years in which the taxpayer actually receives installment payments in cash or other property previously credited to his account.

Example 12.9

Assume that in June 2021, Drew Brees entered into a five-year standard player's contract with the New Orleans Saints in which he agreed to play football and engage in activities related to football during the five-year term only for the Saints. In addition to a specified salary for the two-year term, it was mutually agreed that as an inducement for signing the contract the taxpayer would be paid a bonus of $10 million. He could have demanded and received payment of this bonus at the time of signing the contract, but at his suggestion there was added to the standard contract form a paragraph providing substantially as follows:

The player shall receive the sum of $10 million upon signing of this contract, contingent upon the payment of this $10 million to an escrow agent designated by him. The escrow agreement shall be subject to approval by the legal representatives of the player, the Saints, and the escrow agent.

Pursuant to this added provision, an escrow agreement was executed on June 25, 2021, in which the Saints agreed to pay $10 million on that date to the Y bank, as escrow agent;

and the escrow agent agreed to pay this amount, plus interest, to the taxpayer in installments over a period of five years, beginning at the end of this contract. The escrow agreement also provides that the account established by the escrow agent is to bear the taxpayer's name; that payments from such account may be made only in accordance with the terms of the agreement; that the agreement is binding upon the parties thereto and their successors or assigns; and that in the event of the taxpayer's death during the escrow period the balance due will become part of his estate.

Applying the principles stated in the Sproull decision to the facts here, the $10 million bonus is includible in the gross income of Drew Brees in 2021, the year in which the club unconditionally paid such amount to the escrow agent.[13] The taxpayer controlled when the funds would be received and the structure allowed for no risk of forfeiture.

CASE STUDY 12.2

Ray S. Robinson v. Commissioner, 44 T.C. 20 (1965)

This case involved the deferred payment of Sugar Ray Robinson's purse in the 15 round contest for the middleweight crown between Ray Robinson and Carmen Basilio held on September 23, 1957 at the Yankee Stadium in Bronx, New York. Robinson entered into an agreement with International Boxing Club of New York, Inc. and agreed to be paid 45 percent of the gross receipts from ticket sales. His payment was to be paid as follows: 40 percent within two weeks from the fight and 20 percent per year over a three year period, paid in quarterly installments.

The IRS argued that Sugar Ray and the Club were partners in a joint venture and that Sugar Ray should include his share of income in the year of the fight. The question before the court was when the payments should be included into income. The Tax Court found that Sugar Ray had the same rights as any unsecured creditor and that the deferred income should be included into income when received by Robinson.

13. E. T. Sproull v. Commissioner, 16 T.C. 244

Exhibit 12.1 | Summary of Deferred Compensation

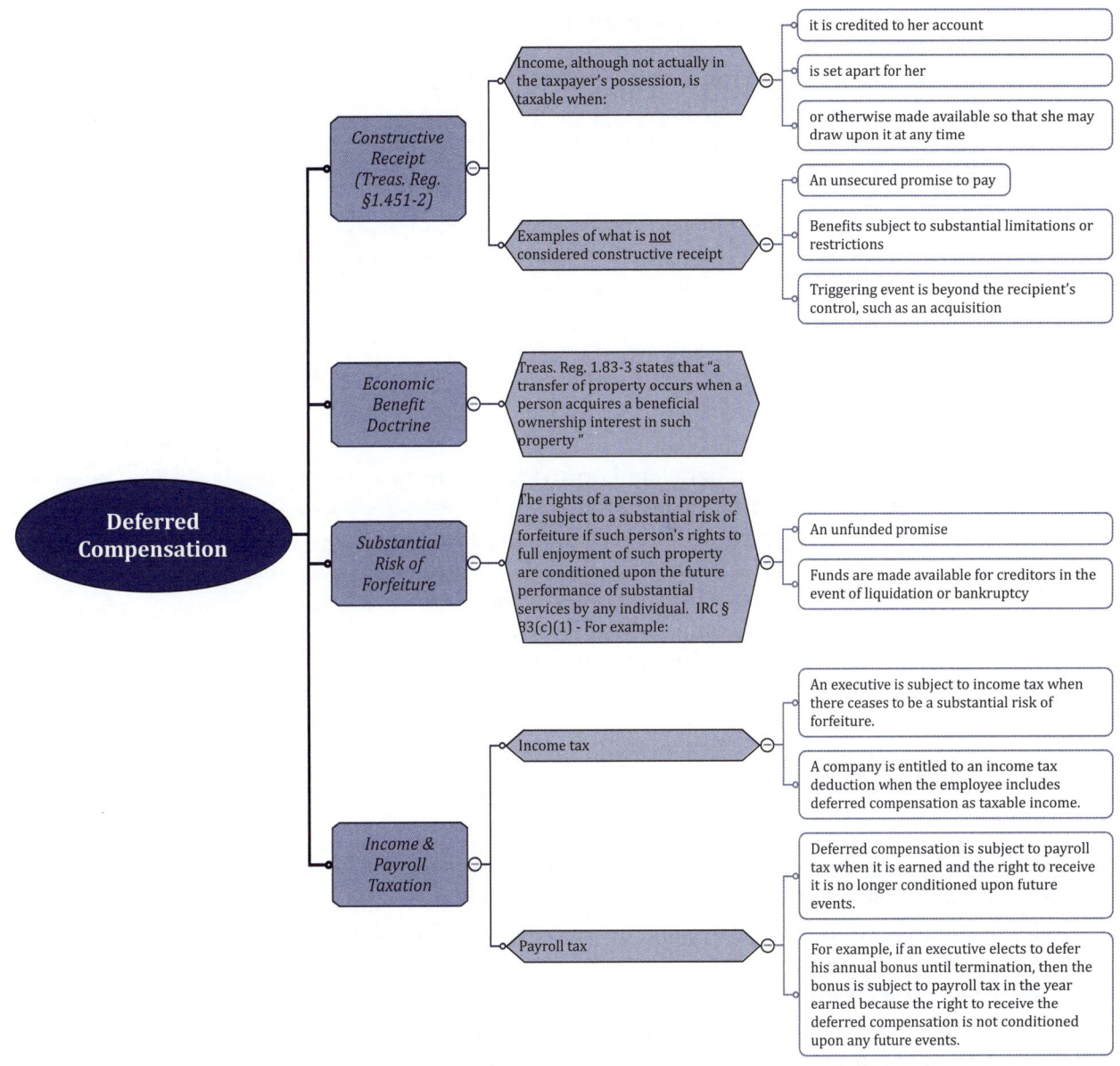

FUNDING ARRANGEMENTS AND TYPES OF NONQUALIFIED DEFERRED COMPENSATION PLANS

A **nonqualified deferred compensation plan (NQDC)** is a contractual arrangement between an employer and an executive whereby the employer promises to pay the executive a predetermined amount of money sometime in the future. The phrase "in the future" may mean at or during retirement or at or after termination of employment. These types of plans are neither required nor intended to meet the ERISA or IRC requirements to be a qualified plan. Therefore, the employer does not realize the tax advantages of a qualified plan.

There are certain benefits to employers and employees in setting up deferred compensation plans. The advantages of deferred compensation plans to the employer are:

1. cash outflows are often deferred until the future,
2. the employer will save on payroll taxes except for the 1.45 percent Medicare match (since the employee's income is probably over the Social Security wage base), and
3. the employer can discriminate and provide these benefits exclusively to a select group of key employees. The employee benefits from a deferred compensation plan by deferring the receipt of income, thus increasing the possibility of lower federal income taxes at the time of the actual payment and avoiding Social Security taxes (except the 1.45 percent for Medicare) at the time it was earned.

> ### ≔ *Key Concepts*
>
> 1. What funding arrangements are available for deferred compensation plans?
> 2. What impact does Title I of ERISA have on deferred compensation plans?
> 3. What types of deferred compensation plans are available?
> 4. What are 401(k) wraps?

In addition, both the employee and employer benefit in these types of plans because the total compensation, including deferred compensation, may exceed the $1 million annual limit on deductible compensation.

Although the characteristics discussed above apply to most NQDC plans, there are a variety of funding arrangements and types of plans to be discussed. These include unfunded promises to pay, secular trusts, rabbi trusts, phantom stock plans, and other types of deferred compensation arrangements.

Unfunded Promise to Pay

Deferred compensation may take any form due to the flexibility and lack of requirements under ERISA and the IRC. An unfunded promise to pay falls within the spectrum of deferred compensation. This type of arrangement will meet the standards of a substantial risk of forfeiture and will, therefore, meet the objective of tax deferral. However, the employee is at some risk of not being paid. The employer may choose not to pay, or claim that the employee did not meet the conditions of the contract, or the employer may not have sufficient funds to pay the obligation. Obviously, the employee has the right to claim that the employer is in violation of the agreement, which may or may not yield any tangible benefit. To mitigate against such risk, employees would prefer that the employer set funds aside for the purpose of providing for the payment of the deferred obligation. However, as discussed, if there are no restrictions on the set aside funds or there is not a risk of forfeiture, then the funds become immediately taxable, thereby defeating the tax-deferral objective.

Secular Trust

Secular trusts are irrevocable trusts designed to hold funds and assets for the purpose of paying benefits under a nonqualified deferred compensation arrangement. This type of plan provides protection for the assets in the trust. The funds are set aside for the benefit of employees and are not available to the employer or subject to the claims of the employer's creditors. Since a secular trust does not create a substantial risk of forfeiture for the employee, assets set aside in a secular trust result in immediate taxation to the employee.[14] This tax consequence is the cost of eliminating the risk that the funds will not be paid in the future.

Secular trusts are generally subject to Title I of ERISA and, therefore, have to comply with certain reporting, disclosure, vesting, and other requirements. Secular trusts may use a graduated vesting schedule, and the vesting of benefits will trigger the recognition of income for purposes of income tax. Once the funds are vested, the employee is required to include the value of the vested benefit in income and the employer will have an income tax deduction of an equal amount.

Treasury Regulation §1.402(b)-1 provides that any employer contribution made to a trust that is not exempt from taxation shall be included as compensation in the gross income of the employee for his taxable year during which the contribution is made, but only to the extent that the employee's interest in such contribution is substantially vested at the time the contribution is made.[15] Thus, the secular trust can be effectively used in combination with a vesting schedule to defer tax for the executive.

To compensate for the increased taxable income without necessarily having an increase in cash distributions, secular trusts may provide for distributions to the participants for the purpose of paying the income tax attributable to the taxability of the benefits in the trust.

The funds contributed to the trust will be invested and will generate income. The income will usually be taxable to the employee as it is earned if it is not subject to a substantial risk of forfeiture.

Example 12.10

Oxford Corporation has created a deferred compensation plan (Plan) for 50 key executives (participants), all of whom are highly compensated employees. Oxford contributes each year on behalf of each participant to a trust, T. The trust is not and never has been a qualified trust under §401(a) and is not exempt from taxation under §501(a).

T's assets are not subject to the claims of Oxford's creditors. Separate accounts that reflect the participant's share of the net trust assets and income are maintained for each participant.

A participant's entire interest in T becomes vested upon completion of three years of service with Oxford beginning on the date the individual first becomes a participant in the Plan. Participants or their beneficiaries are entitled to receive their vested interest in the net assets of T, net of applicable withholding and other taxes, on death, disability, or termination of employment. In addition, T is required to distribute to each participant each year an amount that the trustee reasonably estimates will be equal to the amount of Federal, state, and local income and employment taxes payable by the participant with

---

14. IRC §402(b) and the Economic Benefit Doctrine.
15. Such as a trust under IRC §501(a).

respect to the increase in the participant's vested accrued benefit in T during such year. T is permitted to make the distribution in part as a distribution of cash to the participant, and in part in the form of applicable employment tax withholding under Federal, state, or local law.

This arrangement is an example of a secular trust, in which assets cannot be seized by creditors, but tax is only deferred until the participant is vested.

Rabbi Trust

Rabbi trusts strike a balance between the risk of an unfunded promise to pay and the lack of substantial risk of forfeiture in a secular trust. Like a secular trust, a rabbi trust is an irrevocable trust that is designed to hold funds and assets for the purpose of paying benefits under a nonqualified deferred compensation arrangement. However, there are certain critical differences between rabbi trusts and secular trusts. Although the assets in a rabbi trust are for the sole purpose of providing benefits to employees and may not be accessed by the employer, they may be seized and used for the purpose of paying general creditors in the event of the liquidation of the company. In this regard, they do not protect the executive employee from bankruptcy of the employer. Because of this possibility, the IRS has ruled that rabbi trusts that are established and follow specific guidelines will create a substantial risk of forfeiture. When these guidelines are followed, any assets within a rabbi trust are not currently taxable to the employee yet provide significantly more protection to the employee than a simple unfunded promise to pay.

Even though assets are set aside in a trust, rabbi trusts are treated as unfunded (also can be informally funded) for purposes of Title I of ERISA due to the presence of a substantial risk of forfeiture. As a result, these plans do not have to comply with as many rules as secular trusts.

The income generated from the assets within the trust is taxed to the employer. However, the employer will receive an income tax deduction upon distribution from the trust. Many deferred compensation plans will use life insurance products to avoid taxation of income to the employer.

The American Jobs Creation Act of 2004 and the creation of IRC §409A had an impact on rabbi trusts. Section 409A(b) states that in most cases, assets set aside in a trust outside of the United States (i.e., an offshore trust account) are treated as property transferred in connection with the performance of service whether or not such assets are available to satisfy claims of general creditors. Thus, any such assets will be taxed to the executive as constructively received at the date of transfer.

The Pension Protection Act of 2006 further amended the rules regarding rabbi trusts. Under the PPA 2006, employers are prohibited from setting aside or transferring assets for the purpose of paying deferred compensation of an "applicable covered employee" under a nonqualified deferred compensation plan during a "restricted period" with respect to a qualified defined benefit plan. The term "applicable covered employee" includes certain current and past executives of the plan sponsor. The term "restricted period" means:
1. any period where the sponsor of a defined benefit plan is a debtor in a Chapter 11 proceeding;
2. the six month period prior to, and the six month period following, a qualified defined benefit plan's termination if the plan does not have sufficient assets to satisfy its liabilities upon termination; or
3. any plan year, beginning in 2008, during which a qualified defined benefit pension plan of the employer fails to meet certain minimum funding levels and is in "at-risk" status.[16]

Model Rabbi Trust

The IRS provided clear and specific rules defining a model rabbi trust in Revenue Procedure 92-64 that must be followed to make certain that the plan will result in the desired outcome. The Revenue Procedure provides for many rules, some of which are listed below:

- the model language must be adopted almost verbatim
- the trust must be valid under state law
- the trust must state that the assets are subject to the claims of creditors in the case of insolvency
- the trustee must be an independent third party, such as a bank
- the trustee must be given some level of discretion over investment of plan assets

Exhibit 12.2 | Characteristics of Alternative Deferred Compensation Arrangements

	Unfunded Promise to Pay	Rabbi Trust	Secular Trust
Funded with assets	No	Yes	Yes
Funded (for purposes of ERISA)	No	No	Yes
Risk of forfeiture without employer financial instability	Yes	No	No
Risk of forfeiture if employer is insolvent	Yes Claim is below general creditors	Yes Claim is below general creditors	No
When is there taxable income to the executive?	When actually or "constructively received"	When actually or "constructively received"	Immediately upon funding by employer or vesting
When is the payment deductible to employer?	Deferred until payment is made to executive	Deferred until payment is made to executive	When "constructively received" and taxable to executive
Accomplishes the objective of deferral	Yes	Yes	If vesting is required

---

16. Pension Protection Act of 2006.

CASE STUDY 12.3

Bank of America, N.A. v. Moglia addressed creditors' interests in a "rabbi trust" that a Chapter 7 debtor established before filing for bankruptcy to create a source of funding for its otherwise unfunded employee benefit plans.[1] The Chapter 7 debtor, Outboard Marine Corporation ("Outboard"), had approximately $14 million in assets in a "rabbi trust." Bank of America, the agent of Outboard's secured creditors, claimed rights in those assets, while the trustee in bankruptcy claimed them for the unsecured creditors. The security agreement on which Bank of America relied covers all Outboard's "general intangibles," a term of great breadth in commercial law and broadly defined in the agreement as well to include "all other intangible personal property of every kind and nature."

The Court defined a "rabbi trust" as a form of trust whose tax treatment was first addressed in an IRS letter ruling on a trust for the benefit of a rabbi.[2] Under a rabbi trust, a trust is created by a corporation or other institution for the benefit of one or more of its executives (the rabbi in the IRS's original ruling).[3]

According to the Court, the main reason for a rabbi trust is that should the control of the institution change, the trust could then be funded to cushion the fall of the old executives if the new management intends to reduce the compensation of, or even fire, the old executives. However, as the IRS explained in the letter ruling, unless an executive's right to receive money from the trust is "subject to substantial limitations or restrictions" rather than being his to draw on at any time (making it income to him in a practical sense), the executive must include any contribution to the trust and any interest or other earnings of the trust in his gross income in the year in which the contribution was made or the interest obtained.[4] Bank of America conceded that Outboard established a bona fide rabbi trust, so that its contributions to the trust and the income that those contributions generated were not includible in the executives' gross income.

The "substantial limitations or restrictions" condition was satisfied in the transaction on which the IRS ruled. The trust agreement provided that the rabbi would not receive the trust assets until he retired or otherwise ended his employment with the congregation. Until then, the corpus of the trust and any interest on it would be owned by the congregation, so the rabbi would have no right to the money.[5]

What was also key in the Moglia case, was that the trust instrument provided that "the assets of the trust estate shall be subject to the claims of [the congregation's] creditors as if the assets were the general assets of [the congregation]," thus reserving those assets for the unsecured creditors and preventing Outboard from creating a security interest in favor not only of the executives but also of any creditor.

1. *Bank of America, N.A. v. Moglia*, 330 F.3d 942 (7th Cir. 2003).
2. *See Private Letter Ruling 8113107 (Dec. 31, 1980); see also IRS General Counsel Memorandum, 39230 (Jan. 20, 1984).*
3. *See, for example, Westport Bank & Trust Co. v. Geraghty, 90 F.3d 661, 663-64 (2nd Cir. 1996).*
4. *McAllister v. Resolution Trust Corp., 201 F.3d 570, 572-73, 575 (5th Cir. 2000).*
5. Maher v. Harris Trust & Savings Bank, 75 F.3d 1182, 1185 (7th Cir.1996); Goodman v. Resolution Trust Corp., 7 F.3d 1123, 1125 (4th Cir.1993).

CASE STUDY 12.3 CONTINUED

The United States Seventh Circuit Court of Appeals concluded that the creditor's security interest in general intangibles of the debtor did not extend to the corpus of the rabbi trust and that the clause in the trust agreement creating the rabbi trust that prohibited the settlor from granting any creditor a security interest in trust corpus was enforceable. The Court explained that the creditors' security interest in general intangibles of Outboard did not extend to the corpus of "rabbi trust" because the corpus was to remain available at all times for payment of the debtor's general creditors pursuant under the terms of trust agreement and because Outboard was barred from creating any security interest in the trust corpus in favor of beneficiaries or creditors.

Funding with Insurance

For NQDC plans that have funds set aside to pay obligations under the plan, the employer will be responsible for paying income tax attributable to earnings on assets held in the plan. As assets accumulate for executives and remain "at risk," earnings will be subject to taxation by the employer. Ultimately, the employer will receive an income tax deduction when the funds are distributed to the executives. However, employers will often use insurance products because the increase in cash surrender value is not taxed if payments are not made from the policy. A permanent life insurance policy provides the cash value that can be used to fund the deferred compensation and it provides a death benefit that can be paid to the employer to offset some of the costs of the deferred compensation arrangement.

Phantom Stock Plans

A **phantom stock plan** is a nonqualified deferred compensation arrangement where the employer gives fictional shares of stock to a key employee that is initially valued at the time of the grant.[17] The stock is later valued at some terminal point (usually at termination or retirement), and the executive is then paid the differential value of the stock in cash. Phantom stock provides the same benefit as stock ownership except the final payment is made in cash. The employer has a deductible compensation expense equal to the payment made to the employee. The goal of phantom stock plans is to align the economic incentives of the executive with those of the company. Actual stock is not issued, usually because the current stockholders do not want to dilute their equity position (e.g., no non-family shareholders). This is particularly important in family and closely held business situations.

Example 12.11

Mike became the president of Tantalus, a closely held family business. At the time of Mike's employment, the value of the company is $2 million and there are 2,000,000 shares of stock outstanding. Mike is granted phantom stock at the end of the first year valued at $100,000 because the value of the company has increased to $3 million or $1.50 per share. When Mike terminates, the value of the company is $5 million and he has phantom stock representing 300,000 shares at $2.50 per share. Tantalus will pay Mike $750,000 at termination as a result of the phantom stock plan. However, at no time did Mike actually own any shares or their voting rights.

17. Phantom stock plans are sometimes referred to as shadow stock plans.

Title I of ERISA

Most NQDC plans do not have to meet the coverage, participation, funding, and discrimination requirements of ERISA imposed on qualified plans. Top-hat plans and unfunded excess benefit plans are statutorily exempted from **Title I of ERISA**. As such, these plans have minimal compliance requirements. There are, however, some reporting and disclosure requirements even for nonqualified plans (including SERP and top-hat plans). These include an initial, one-time filing of a Form 5500 disclosing that the company has such a plan. This "Alternative Reporting and Disclosure Statement" must be filed within 120 days of plan inception date. Additionally, the employer must be fair to all those in that plan and have disclosure requirements to them. Most employers establishing these types of plans will attempt to have the plan classified as a top-hat plan so that the plan is exempt from Title I.

Types and Applications of NQDC Plans

There are several types of nonqualified deferred compensation plans that can be established to benefit key executives. Salary reduction plans allow employees to elect to reduce their current salary and defer it until future years, generally until retirement or termination. Salary continuation plans typically provide benefits after retirement on an ongoing basis or for a predetermined period of time.

Supplemental executive retirement plans (generally referred to as SERPs) are nonqualified deferred compensation arrangements designed to provide additional benefits to an executive during retirement. These plans are also referred to as **top-hat plans** since they are designed to benefit a select group of top management or key employees. **Excess-benefit plans** are a type of SERP that is designed solely to provide benefits in excess of the benefits available in qualified plans based on the limits under IRC §415. As mentioned, unfunded excess benefit plans are not subject to Title I of ERISA while funded excess benefit plans are generally subject to these provisions.

Example 12.12

People's Bank and Dorothy, the vice-president and a cash-basis employee, enter into an employment agreement providing an annual total salary of $300,000 to Dorothy. People's promises to pay Dorothy $100,000 of the $300,000 in ten equal annual installments beginning at Dorothy's retirement or to her heirs beginning at her death. The agreement is a non funded, nonqualified deferred compensation agreement. The $100,000 is not constructively received by Dorothy and is not deductible to People's Bank until actually paid. The entire $300,000 is currently subject to the 1.45 percent Medicare tax. When ultimately received, the $100,000 will be subject to income tax, but not subject to Social Security taxes. Likewise, the payment will then be deductible by People's Bank as compensation. This plan could be an excess benefit plan or a SERP/top-hat plan depending on the purpose. If the only purpose is to provide excess benefits over qualified plan limits, it is an excess benefit plan. However, most plans have additional purposes and are, therefore, SERPs/top-hat plans.

Salary-reduction plans are common with professional athletes. A large signing bonus, or a part thereof, is frequently transferred to an escrow agent, subject to general creditors of team or owner, to defer the receipt of taxable income until such time as the athlete is beyond his peak earning period, thereby helping to assure the athlete's future financial security.

401(k) Wrap Plan

401(k) wrap plans are a form of salary reduction plans that enable executives who are subject to salary deferral limitations due to the nondiscrimination rules to contribute higher amounts than otherwise permitted under a 401(k) plan. From the executive's perspective, there is not a significant difference between funds being contributed in these plans and 401(k) plans. The contribution to both plans are subject to payroll tax and income tax is deferred. However, there is a risk that the funds within the wrap plan might not be paid. Otherwise, there would not be substantial risk of forfeiture and the funds would then be taxable.

The usual motivation for use of a nonqualified deferred compensation plan where a qualified plan is in existence is to increase the wage replacement ratio (WRR) for key employees. Recall that qualified plans have compensation limits ($290,000 for 2021). If a key executive makes exactly $290,000, the qualified plan may deliver a suitable wage replacement ratio at retirement. However, for a key employee whose compensation is $400,000, the qualified plan will deliver benefits as if that employee earned $290,000, not $400,000. Thus, the greater the current compensation in excess of the qualified plan limit, the smaller the wage replacement ratio delivered by the qualified plan. Nonqualified plans are used to make up for this inequity.

Example 12.13

Ren, age 50 (president), and Jen, age 50 (vice-president), are the top two executives in AFA, Inc. Jen's compensation is $290,000 and Ren's is $400,000. Jen is expected to receive $145,000 per year in retirement from AFA's qualified plan, thus achieving a wage replacement ratio of 50% ($145,000/$290,000). Unfortunately for Ren, she will also receive the same $145,000 from the qualified plan, thus producing a WRR of 36% ($145,000/$400,000). To make their retirement WRRs equal, AFA might use a NQDC arrangement to pay Ren an additional $55,000 per year in retirement [($145,000 + $55,000) ÷ 400,000 = 50%]. This type of arrangement is an example of an excess benefits plan.

NQDC plans may be established for a wide variety of key employees, shareholder employees, officers, highly compensated employees, or any particular person. Their disadvantage, when compared to qualified plans, is the lack of a current income tax deduction for the employer. Despite this fact, there is widespread use of NQDCs due to their great flexibility and the fact that they have none of the disadvantages of qualified plans.

Exhibit 12.3 | NQDC Concept Summary

Employer Viewpoint	Employee Viewpoint
• Unfunded promise to pay • Not a qualified plan • Cash outflows are deferred • Employer saves on payroll taxes • Income tax deduction deferred until paid • Sometimes used if compensation exceeds $1 million and, therefore, non-deductible • May discriminate among employees	• Employee is at risk for nonpayment • Fund by using a rabbi trust; if unfunded, best with a financially secure company • No current taxable income • Employee saves on payroll taxes • May provide future cash flow at lower income tax rate

EMPLOYER STOCK OPTIONS AND STOCK PLANS

Stock Options

An employee **stock option** gives the employee a right to buy stock at a specified price for a specified period of time. As part of an employer's overall compensation package, an employee's stock option program can be used to attract or retain talented management and to tie the financial compensation of selected key executives to the performance of the company, thus aligning the interest of management executives with outside shareholders.

Through the technology bubble and the accounting scandals of the recent past, stock options were extremely popular with publicly-traded companies and "start-ups." However, with the financial accounting requirement that options be expensed, the use of options is on a decline. Companies are choosing to reward executives in other ways that do not have the same negative impact on a firm's financial statements.

> ### ⦂≣ *Key Concepts*
>
> 1. What are stock options?
>
> 2. What are Incentive Stock Options, and what are the tax consequences associated with the grant, exercise, and sale of ISOs?
>
> 3. What are Nonqualified Stock Options and what are the tax consequences associated with the grant, exercise, and sale of NQSOs?

Stock options are usually granted to select employees for the purchase of stock of the employer or a subsidiary. The option agreement must be in writing, and the option holder has no obligation to exercise the option. The terms of the option agreement must be stated (e.g., 10 years) in the agreement.

Option Price

Generally, the **option price (exercise price)** is equal to the fair market value at the **grant date** (the date of issuance). If the option does not have a readily ascertainable fair market value at the grant date, there is no taxable income to the option holder as of the grant date. Employee stock options usually have substantial restrictions and vesting requirements such that a readily ascertainable fair market value for the options is not available. If values were available and the value was ascertainable, it would be taxable income to the recipient. An option is a form of deferred compensation if the price of the stock increases. If the stock price declines, the option holder will simply allow the option to lapse.

It is important to note that options granted at fair market value are not subject to the rules under IRC §409A. However, options issued at a discount from fair market value are subject to IRC §409A and its harsh tax results.

Vesting

Generally, stock options vest over time, thus continuing to provide an incentive to the executive who is receiving the option to remain with the employer and to be productive. As the fortunes of the company improve, it is common for more options to be granted. A common vesting schedule is 20 percent per year of service after the grant. However, the vesting schedule could take any form, even immediate 100 percent vesting, although that is uncommon.

Types of Options

There are two standard types of employer stock options: **Incentive Stock Options** (ISOs) and **Nonqualified Stock Options** (NQSOs). The goal of utilizing either type of option is to motivate employees by providing them with employer stock at a price that is expected to appreciate. From a tax perspective, however, ISOs can have more favorable tax treatment than NQSOs. The cost of this tax benefit is that ISOs have more restrictions.

Incentive Stock Options (ISOs)

An incentive stock option (ISO) is a right given to an employee to purchase an employer's common stock at a stated exercise price. If the requirements of IRC §422 are met when the incentive stock option is granted (provided the exercise price is equal to the fair market value of the stock), the employee will not recognize any taxable income at the date of grant. Further, at the date of exercise, the employee will also not be subject to ordinary income tax on the difference between the fair market value of the stock and the exercise price. However, this difference is a positive adjustment for the alternative minimum tax calculation (it increases alternative minimum taxable income). When the employee sells the stock subsequent to the exercise, the difference between the sales price of the stock and the original exercise price is considered long-term capital gain and there is a negative adjustment for the alternative minimum tax calculation (it decreases alternative minimum taxable income). For an employee in the 37 percent ordinary income tax bracket, the long-term capital gain rate of 20 percent is very attractive, but to attain this tax benefit, ISOs have strict requirements.

Exhibit 12.4 | Requirements for Incentive Stock Option

1. ISOs can only be granted to an employee of the corporation issuing the ISOs.

2. The ISO plan must be approved by the stockholders of the issuing corporation.

3. The ISOs must be granted within 10 years of the ISO plan date.

4. The exercise of the ISO is limited to a 10-year period (5 years for 10% + owners).

5. At the date of the ISO grant, the exercise price must be greater than or equal to the fair market value of the stock.

6. An ISO cannot be transferred except at death.

7. An owner of more than 10% of a corporation cannot be given ISOs unless the exercise price is 110% of the fair market value at the date of grant and the option term is less than five years.

8. To the extent that the aggregate fair market value of stock with respect to which ISOs are exercisable for the first time by any individual during any calendar year exceeds $100,000, such options shall be treated as NQSOs.

9. To qualify as an ISO, the executive must hold the stock for the greater of two years from the grant of the ISO or one year from the date of exercise of the ISO.

10. The executive must be an employee of the corporation continuously from the date of the grant until at least three months prior to the exercise.

Taxation

Grant Date

At the date of the ISO grant there is no taxable income to the employee if the exercise price is greater than or equal to the fair market value of the employer stock. If the exercise price is less than the fair market value of the employer stock, the executive will have W-2 income equal to the difference and the employer will have compensation expense for the same amount. In addition, this would cause the option to fall within IRC §409A.

Exercise of the ISO

Once the ISO is exercisable, the executive purchases the employer stock at the exercise price. At the date of exercise in a qualifying ISO transaction, the executive will purchase the stock with his own funds with an intent to hold the stock for at least the holding period requirement (as discussed below). The exercise of the ISO in a qualifying transaction will not create any regular tax impact for either the employee or the employer but will create an alternative minimum tax (AMT) adjustment for the executive equal to the difference between the exercise price and the fair market value of the stock at the exercise date.

The exercise price of the ISO creates the executive's adjusted basis in the employer stock for regular tax purposes since the executive used after-tax dollars to purchase the stock under the ISO. However, the executive's AMT adjusted basis is the fair market value at the date of exercise.

Sale of the Stock from the ISO Exercise After Holding Period Requirement

An executive will receive favorable gain treatment on the **bargain element** (defined as appreciation of employer stock above the exercise price), provided the executive does not sell the employer stock before two years from the date of grant and one year from the date of exercise, referred to as the holding period requirement. This holding period requirement is more accurately stated as a sale that occurs at least two years from the date of grant and *one year plus one day* from the date of exercise.[18] References to the required holding period in this chapter, however, will follow the common practice of stating it as two years from grant and one year from exercise. If the holding period requirement is met, the employer will never receive a tax deduction in relation to the ISO.

If the executive meets this holding period requirement and the value of the stock is greater than the exercise price of the ISO, the executive will have long-term capital gain treatment on the appreciation above the exercise price and a negative AMT adjustment equal to the AMT adjustment at the date of the exercise.

Example 12.14

On January 5, 2021, Bob, vice president of XYZ Corporation, is granted 10,000 ISOs at an exercise price of $10 (immediate vesting). On February 6, 2022, he exercises all of the options when the price of XYZ stock is $42. Bob subsequently sells the stock at $60 on February 14, 2023. What are his tax consequences?

At the date of exercise, Bob has no W-2 income, or ordinary income, but does have an AMT adjustment of $320,000 ($420,000 - $100,000) which may cause Bob to pay AMT. For regular tax, he has an adjusted basis of $100,000. When he subsequently sells the stock for $600,000, he has a long-term capital gain of $500,000 subject to a capital gains rate of 20% and a negative AMT adjustment equal to $320,000.

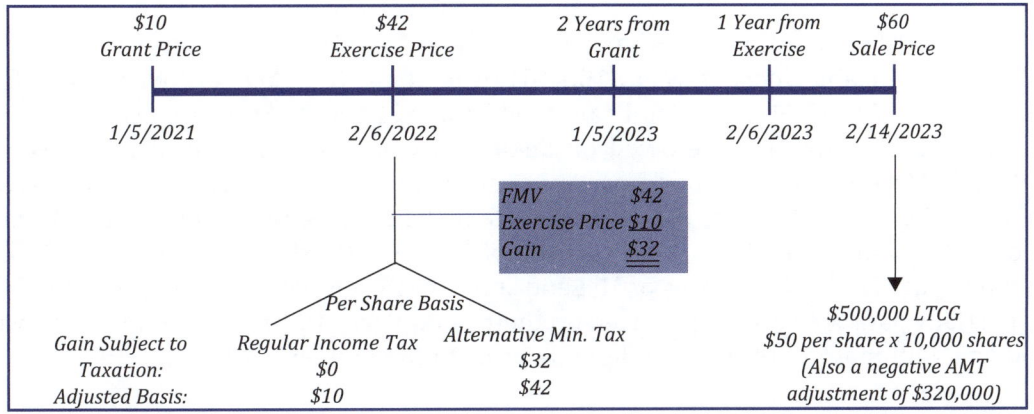

Note: This example is designed so that all the options are ISOs. If instead, the options vested when the stock price was higher, some of the options might be classified as NQSOs, due to the $100,000 limit.

---

18. Treas. Reg. §1.422-1(a) defines the required holding period as follows: "no disposition of such share before the later of the expiration of the 2-year period from the date of grant of the option pursuant to which such share was transferred, or the expiration of the 1-year period from the date *of transfer of such share to the individual* [emphasis added]." IRS Publication 525 clarifies that for ISOs and ESPPs (discussed later in this chapter) "the holding period for the property you acquire when you exercise an option begins on the day after you exercise the option."

Keep in mind that presuming the holding period rules are met, the gain at exercise is deferred and treated as capital gain upon sale of the ISO stock. However, for AMT purposes there is no deferral of gain, which results in a timing difference between regular tax and AMT.

If the executive meets the holding period requirement but the value of the stock is less than the exercise price, the executive has a long-term capital loss equal to the difference between the exercise price and the sales price. The executive also has a negative AMT adjustment equal to the AMT adjustment at the exercise date.

CASE STUDY 12.4

In *Spletz v. Commissioner of Internal Revenue,* 124 Tax Ct. No. 9 (15382-036, March 23, 2005 Ronald and June Speltz incurred AMT liability as a result of their exercise of incentive stock options in 2000. The stock declined precipitously in value after the date of exercise. Mr. and Mrs. Speltz partially paid the tax liability and submitted an offer in compromise with respect to the unpaid balance. The IRS rejected the offer in compromise and filed a lien on their property. The tax court held it was not an abuse of the IRS's discretion to reject Mr. and Mrs. Speltz's offer in compromise and to continue the lien. Mr. and Mrs. Speltz reasoned that their offer in compromise should have been accepted because of the unfair application of the alternative minimum tax (AMT).

Ronald Speltz was employed by McLeodUSA as a senior manager earning wages over $75,000 in 2000 and over $90,000 in 2004. As part of his compensation package he received ISOs for acquisition of McLeod Stock. In 2000, Mr. Speltz exercised some of the ISOs. Mr. and Mrs. Speltz filed their 1040 and the ISOs resulted in "excess of AMT income over regular tax income" of $711,118.

On their Form 1040, petitioners reported that their "regular" adjusted gross income was $142,070. Their taxable income was $105,461, and their "regular" tax was $18,678. They reported AMT of $206,191 for a total tax liability of $224,869. After application of Federal income tax withheld, the balance owed on Speltz's tax liability for 2000 was $210,065. The value of their McLeod stock dropped precipitously. On their tax return for 2000, the Speltzs reported that they sold 200 shares of McLeod stock on January 14 for a total of $14,011 and 500 shares of McLeod stock on March 10 for a total of $52,282. On their tax return for 2002, they reported that they sold 2,070 shares of McLeod stock on December 30 for a total of $1,647. The Speltzs partially paid the liability reported on their 2000 Form 1040 at the time that it was filed and paid an additional $75,000 in installments prior to November 2, 2001.

In November of 2001, they submitted to the Internal Revenue Service (IRS) a Form 656, Offer in Compromise. The Speltzs offered a cash payment of $4,457, the cash value of Mr. Speltz's life insurance policy, against the liability that then exceeded $125,000. On the Form 656, petitioners checked the box for "Doubt as to Collectibility" stating they had insufficient assets and income to pay the full amount.

Petitioners also attached to Form 656 a statement in which they explained that an offer in compromise was necessary because of the impact the AMT in 2000 had on their finances and their lifestyle.

CASE STUDY 12.4 CONTINUED

Specifically, petitioner's income in 2000 was at a comfortable level for a family of five including three young daughters; the McLeod stock they held was nearly worthless and declining and had been used to secure a $134,000 loan with a bank to pay part of the 2000 Federal and State taxes; and, in the event of a sale of the stock (forced or otherwise), petitioners would be unable to carry back the capital loss to offset their 2000 gain.

They began building a new home in 2000 and sold their prior home in 2001, using the proceeds of sale to repay the bank. Lifestyle changes were necessary, including: Petitioner June M. Speltz had to get a job instead of staying home with the children; the oldest daughter had to switch schools; petitioners were unable to contribute to their retirement and to their children's education fund; and they had to reduce their charitable donations. Finally, they could not afford to have a fourth child, which they had wanted.

In the statement, petitioners expressed their mental anguish and frustration with the unfairness of their situation. The offer was ultimately rejected because the IRS believed the Speltzs did have the ability to pay.

The Speltzs did not actually dispute the AMT, instead they claimed that the IRS abused its discretion by not allowing them to pay less because of the decline in stock. While the Tax Court was sympathetic, it found that the IRS did not abuse its discretion.

Disqualifying Disposition

If stock acquired after exercising an ISO is disposed of before either two years from the date of the grant or one year from the date of exercise, the sale is known as a **disqualifying disposition** and some of the favorable tax treatment is lost. For such a sale, any gain on the sale of the stock attributable to the difference between the exercise price and the fair market value at the date of exercise is considered ordinary income and reported on the executive's W-2, but not subject to payroll tax or federal income tax withholding.[19] Any gain in excess of the amount reported on the W-2 is short or long-term capital gain considering the executive's holding period from the time of exercise. Any AMT adjustment created at the date of exercise is reversed at the date of the disqualifying disposition. Also, at this time, the employer has a tax deductible expense equal to the amount reported on the executive's W-2.

Example 12.15

On October 12, 2021, Donald was granted 15,000 ISOs at an exercise price of $2 per share when the fair market value of the stock was also $2. On November 14, 2022, Donald exercised the stock when the fair market value was $8 per share. Subsequently, on January 1, 2023, Donald sold all the stock for $6 per share.

At the date of grant there was no taxable income because the exercise price of the stock was equal to the fair market value of the stock. At the date of exercise, there was no regular income tax but there was AMT income equal to $6 per share ($8 - $2). Because Donald did not hold the stock for at least two years from the date of the grant and one

19. See IRC Section 3121(a)(22).

year from the date of exercise, Donald has a disqualifying disposition at the date of sale. The gain on the stock of $4 per share ($6 - $2) is ordinary income, and Donald's employer will receive a tax deduction for the same amount ($60,000). Donald will also have a negative AMT adjustment equal to $6 per share at the date of sale to reverse the adjustment at the date of exercise.

Example 12.16

Assume the same facts as above, except that the stock price at the time of sale is $11 instead of $6. There is still a disqualifying disposition since the holding period was not met. However, in this case, there will be ordinary income equal to $6 ($8 - $2; the amount of the bargain element) per share and a short-term capital gain of $3 per share ($11 - $8).[20] As before, Donald has a negative AMT adjustment equal to $6 per share.

Cashless Exercise

A **cashless exercise** is an exercise of an option where the executive does not utilize any cash. Cashless exercises are quite common as many executives do not have the additional cash to exercise the option. At the time of a cashless exercise, a third-party lender lends the executive the cash needed to exercise the option and the lender is immediately repaid with the proceeds of the almost simultaneous sale of the stock. A cashless exercise of incentive stock options automatically triggers a partial disqualifying disposition since the holding period requirements will not be met.

Because the executive does not hold the stock for at least two years from grant and one year from exercise, the disposition of the stock is a disqualifying disposition and any gain recognized from the transaction will be treated as ordinary income (reportable on the W-2) not subject to payroll taxes. From the executive's perspective, the entire transaction is a form of cash bonus. Like a disqualifying disposition when the executive recognizes the ordinary income, the employer will have a tax deductible compensation expense.

Example 12.17

Annie, an executive, has 10,000 ISOs with an $8 exercise price. When the value of the stock increases to $32, the stock has a total value of $320,000. If Annie exercised today, she would need $80,000 to exercise the option (ignoring any potential AMT consequence). Like many individuals, Annie does not have the $80,000 cash available to exercise the option. Therefore, Annie makes a cashless exercise of the option and receives $240,000 (the proceeds from the sale of the stock less the exercise price of $80,000). In reality, the proceeds Annie actually receives are reduced for transaction fees.

Since the sale of the stock did not meet the holding period requirements of an ISO, $240,000 is subjected to ordinary income tax.

---

20. Short-term capital gains apply when the holding period is one year or less. Donald's holding period began the day after the exercise date of November 14, 2022. The date of sale, January 1, 2023, is one year or less from that date, resulting in a short-term capital gain.

Nonqualified Stock Options (NQSOs)

An NQSO is an option that does not meet the requirements of an incentive stock option or it is explicitly identified as nonqualified. As such, the exercise of an NQSO does not receive favorable capital gains treatment but also does not require the holding period associated with ISOs. A NQSO is designed to tie a benefit given to an executive to the stock price of the company, but unlike an ISO, it does not provide the executive or the employer with substantial tax benefits.

From a risk perspective, the executive takes no risk in an NQSO. If the stock price falls below the exercise price, the executive simply does not exercise. If the stock appreciates, the executive may choose to exercise and may immediately sell the stock or hold it (there is investment risk to holding the stock).

Taxation
Grant Date
The grant of an NQSO will not create a taxable event assuming that there is no readily ascertainable value for the NQSO. Generally an option will not have a readily ascertainable value if the exercise price of the option is greater than or equal to the fair market value of the underlying stock. If, however, the option does have a readily ascertainable value at the date of grant or at anytime after the grant, the executive will otherwise have W-2 income equal to the value and the employer will have an income tax deduction.

Exercise of the NQSO
At the exercise date of the NQSO, the executive will deliver to the employer both the option and the exercise price per share. The executive will recognize W-2 income for the appreciation of the fair market value of the stock over the exercise price (often referred to as the bargain element), income tax withholding will apply, and the employer will have an income tax deduction for the same amount.

The fair market value of the stock at the exercise date (which is equal to the sum of the exercise price plus the appreciation of the stock after the date of grant) is the executive's adjusted basis in the employer stock. The executive's holding period for calculation of subsequent gains and losses also begins on the exercise date.

Sale of the Stock from the NQSO Exercise
Stock acquired through the exercise of an NQSO does not have a specified holding period requirement. When the stock is sold, the executive's gain or loss will be considered capital gain or loss and will receive short or long-term capital gain treatment according to the elapsed time between the date of the sale and the exercise date. The employer corporation does not have a tax effect at the sale date.

Example 12.18

On January 2, 2021 (the grant date), Ned, an executive with ABC Corporation, is issued one nonqualified stock option from ABC Corporation with an exercise price of $10 (the current market price). On January 3, 2022, Ned exercises his option when the ABC stock price is $35. Ned brings the option and $10 to ABC. ABC issues the stock and Ned recognizes $25 in W-2 income from ABC. Ned's new basis in the stock is $35. He later sells the stock, on March 4, 2022 for $50, which creates a short-term capital gain of $15. If instead, Ned had sold the stock on or after January 4, 2023, the gain would be long term.

Example 12.19

On January 5, 2021, JereAnn was issued 10,000 nonqualified stock options of L&O Corporation, her employer. At the date of the grant, the fair market value of the stock was $35 and the exercise price was $35. Due to the time, vesting, and transferability provisions, there was no readily ascertainable value for the options at the time of the grant. The options vest 20% per year and are exercisable as vested. On January 5, 2022, JereAnn exercised 2,000 options when the fair market value of the stock was $48. JereAnn surrenders 2,000 options and $70,000 to L&O Corporation. She will receive 2,000 shares of L&O having a current fair market value of $96,000. She has W-2 income of $26,000 and has an adjusted basis in the stock of $96,000. If JereAnn subsequently sells the stock, she will have a capital gain or loss, depending on the sale price of the stock. L&O Corporation will deduct $26,000 as compensation expense at the time of exercise.

Cashless Exercise

As discussed above, a cashless exercise is the exercise of an option when the executive does not utilize any cash. A NQSO can be exercised with a cashless exercise just as described above with the ISO, and the executive will receive the difference between the exercise price and the fair market value of the stock at the date of the cashless exercise as W-2 income.

Gifting of ISOs and NQSOs

Lifetime transfers of unexercised ISOs by the employee are not permitted. The requirement to obtain long-term capital gain treatment for the stock received upon exercise is that the stock must be transferred only after the holding period requirement. Any transfer of ISO stock before the completion of the holding period may cause the appreciation on the stock to be taxed as ordinary income rather than capital gain.

A NQSO can be gifted provided the NQSO plan permits transfer of ownership. There are no immediate income tax consequences on the transfer. Upon exercise of the NQSO by the donee, the employee will have W-2 income for the difference between the exercise price and the fair market value on the date of exercise. The donee's basis after the exercise will be equal to the fair market value on the date of exercise (exercise price plus employee's tax recognition). If the employee also pays the exercise price, it is an additional gift to the donee. Any gift of a NQSO that is neither vested nor exercisable is an incomplete gift. Valuation of options is determined using the **Black Scholes Method**. NQSOs are not good items to transfer to charities except after the option has been exercised and the stock held for more than a year and a day, which is when the stock can qualify as long-term capital gain property and is then available for a higher charitable deduction.

> **✏ Quick Quiz 12.5**
>
> 1. A stock option agreement must be in writing and must state an option term.
>   a. True
>   b. False
>
> 2. The exercise of an ISO triggers W-2 income for the employee.
>   a. True
>   b. False
>
> 3. At the exercise date of an NQSO, the employee will recognize W-2 income for the appreciation of the fair market value of the stock over the exercise price.
>   a. True
>   b. False
>
> True, False, True.

Exhibit 12.5 | NQSO and ISO Summary

	NQSO	ISO
At Grant Date	No taxable income to holder if issued at the current or greater share price.	No taxable income to holder if issued at current or greater share price.
At Exercise	Executive gives options and exercise price to company. Company issues stock to executive to replace option.	Executive gives options and exercise price to company. Company issues stock to executive to replace option.
Employee Taxation	At exercise, executive recognizes W-2 income to extent of difference between current stock price and exercise price.	At exercise, executive does not recognize any regular taxable income but will have an AMT adjustment for the appreciation over the exercise price.
Employer Tax Deduction	Employer's income tax deduction equals the executive's taxable income at the time of exercise.	The employer will not receive a tax deduction unless the stock is disposed of in a disqualifying disposition (on the date the executive sells the stock).
Adjusted Basis	Executive's adjusted basis in stock is equal to the fair market value of stock at exercise (exercise price in cash plus the recognition of W-2 income).	Executive's adjusted basis in stock is equal to the exercise price.
When Stock is Sold	Capital gain or loss treatment.	Capital gain or loss treatment; ordinary income on bargain element if disqualifying disposition.

Stock Appreciation Rights

Stock Appreciation Rights (SARs) are rights that grant to the holder cash in an amount equal to the excess of the fair market value of the stock over the exercise price.

Example 12.20

Jamie is a key executive in NT Company. She is granted 1,000 SARs at $10, the current trading price of NT. If Jamie exercises the SARs two years from the grant when NT's stock price is $32, she will receive $22,000 as W-2 income subject to both income and payroll taxes.

The SAR is essentially a way to achieve a "cashless exercise." Notice in **Example 12.20**, Jamie did not have to come up with the exercise price of $10,000 (1,000 x $10). The rights cannot be exercised before one year, and if they are not exercised within five years, they are deemed exercised on the fifth anniversary of the grant. At that time, the employee will be paid the amount of the appreciation. Payments received for the stock appreciation rights are includible in gross income in the year the rights are exercised.

An employee who possesses stock appreciation rights is not in constructive receipt of income by virtue of the appreciation of the employer's stock. The cash payment to which the employee is entitled is includible in gross income in the year a stock appreciation right is exercised.

The grant of the SAR does not constitute constructive receipt, even if immediately exercisable, because of the future potential appreciation of the SAR. If, however, the SAR has a cap or limit, there is constructive receipt when the stock reaches that limit price, unless the SAR is issued in tandem with the option and the option is terminated if not exercised simultaneously with the SAR. In such case, there is no constructive receipt.[21]

Generally, SARs are granted with NQSOs or ISOs and may be used to provide cash to the executive, which is necessary to exercise the NQSO or ISO. Usually, the number of NQSOs or ISOs is reduced by any exercised SARs.

SARs are generally subject to the requirements of §409A. However, there are certain circumstances under which SARs are excluded from coverage under §409A because the Internal Revenue Service has determined that these circumstances do not present the potential for abuse or intentional circumvention of the purposes of 409A. Specifically, a SAR will not constitute a deferral of compensation if (1) compensation payable under the SAR is not greater than the difference between the fair market value of the stock on the date of grant and the fair market value of the stock on the exercise date, with respect to a number of shares fixed on or before the date of grant; (2) the SAR exercise price is not less than the fair market value of the underlying stock on the date of grant; and (3) the SAR does not include any feature for the deferral of compensation other than the deferral of recognition of income until the exercise of the right.[22]

Restricted Stock Plans

A **restricted stock plan** is an employer-provided plan designed to increase retention and compensate employees with a non-cash outflow. The plan pays executives with shares of the employer's stock. The executive does not pay any amount towards the allocation of the stock and is restricted by the employer from selling or transferring the stock. The restriction most often gives the employer the ability to repurchase the stock during a set period of years or prohibits the executive from selling the stock during a set number of years or until a defined occurrence or event (i.e., the executive attains 10 years of service with the company).

At receipt of the restricted stock, the executive will generally not recognize any taxable income (see §83(b) discussion below) as the restrictions generally create a substantial risk of forfeiture. In addition the employer will not have a deductible expense. However, when this substantial risk of forfeiture is eliminated the executive recognizes W-2 income equal to the value of the stock at that date and the employer will have a tax deductible expense for an equal amount. The amount recognized by the executive becomes the executive's adjusted basis in the stock for purposes of any subsequent gain or loss calculation. The executive's holding period of the stock also begins at the date the restrictions are lifted.

---

21. Revenue Ruling 82-121.
22. Treas. Reg. §1.409A-1(b)(5)(i)(B).

Example 12.21

Dana was entitled to a $100,000 incentive bonus from Significant Corp. in 2021. However, Significant was short on cash due to poor planning and instead paid Dana $25,000 and gave her $75,000 worth of restricted stock (5,000 shares at $15 per share). In 2024, after all of the restrictions were lifted, Dana's shares are worth $30 per share. In 2024, Dana has W-2 income of $150,000 and Significant has a deduction of $150,000. Dana now has an adjusted basis in the Significant stock of $150,000.

The Section 83(b) Election

If property is transferred in connection with the performance of services, the person performing such services may elect to include in gross income under **IRC Section 83(b)** the excess (if any) of the fair market value of the property at the time of transfer over the amount (if any) paid for such property as compensation for services. The fact that the transferee has paid full value for the property transferred, realizing no bargain element in the transaction, does not preclude the use of the election as provided for in this section. If this election is made, any subsequent appreciation in the value of the property is not taxable as compensation to the person who performed the services but as capital gain at the date of sale. Thus, property with respect to which this election is made shall be includible in gross income as of the time of transfer even though such property is substantially nonvested at the time of transfer and no compensation will be includible in gross income when such property becomes substantially vested.

In computing the gain or loss from the subsequent sale or exchange of such property, its basis shall be the amount paid for the property increased by the amount included in gross income under §83(b). Its holding period shall be determined based upon the date the value was included in gross income. If property for which a §83(b) election is in effect is forfeited while substantially nonvested, such forfeiture shall be treated as a sale or exchange upon which there is realized a loss equal to the excess (if any) of the amount paid (if any) for such property over the amount realized (if any) upon such forfeiture. Therefore, the taxpayer would not receive any loss for the amount included in income, only a loss for the amount paid.

The economic benefit of this election is that the appreciation from the time of the grant through the vesting period will be treated as capital gain instead of W-2 income. However, the taxpayer must consider not only the tax issues of such an election but also other issues in deciding whether or not to make the election. For example, it is important to consider the investment characteristics of the property or stock. Another important consideration is whether the restrictions will be met. If, for example, an employee is issued restricted stock that vests over five years, it would not make sense for the employee to make the 83(b) election if there is a risk he would leave his employer within five years.

Example 12.22

Assume SARs Inc. has a restricted stock plan. Stock granted to employees of SARs under this plan vest after a 5-year period. Kristi, a new executive, was granted restricted stock worth $10,000 on January 5, 2021. Kristi believes that the value of the stock will increase significantly over the next five years. Kristi can make an 83(b) election and include the $10,000 into her current income.

Assuming the stock is worth $25,000 at the end of five years, Kristi will not recognize any gain upon vesting of the stock. When the stock is sold, Kristi will have capital gain equal

---

to the difference between the sale proceeds and the value of the stock at the time of the grant. Kristi has effectively converted ordinary income into capital gain income.

If Kristi had not filed the election, then she would include the $25,000 in taxable income as ordinary income for the year in which the vesting was complete. Any future appreciation above $25,000 would be treated as a capital gain.

Example 12.23

Assume the same facts as above, including the fact that Kristi made the 83(b) election, except that Kristi quit two years after the grant. In this case, at the date of 83(b) election, Kristi would have ordinary income of $10,000 but at termination would not have a loss since she did not pay for the stock.

Making the Election

The 83(b) election must be filed no later than 30 days after the date the property is transferred and may be filed prior to the date of transfer. The election is made by filing one copy of a written statement with the internal revenue office with whom the person who performed the services files returns. Historically, one copy of such statement had to be submitted with the taxpayer's income tax return for the taxable year in which such property was transferred. However, the IRS issued proposed regulations in 2015 that eliminate the requirement that taxpayers must submit a copy of a section 83(b) election with their tax return for the year in which the property subject to the election was transferred.

The statement shall be signed by the person making the election, shall indicate that it is being made under §83(b) of the Code, and shall contain the following information:

- the name, address, and taxpayer identification number of the taxpayer,
- a description of each property with respect to which the election is being made,
- the date or dates on which the property is transferred and the taxable year (for example, "calendar year 2021" or "fiscal year ending May 31, 2022") for which such election was made,
- the nature of the restriction or restrictions to which the property is subject,
- the fair market value at the time of each property with respect to which the election is being made,
- the amount (if any) paid for such property, and
- a statement to the effect that copies have been furnished to other persons as provided in the regulations.

> ### ✒ Quick Quiz 12.6
>
> 1. SARs are generally granted with NQSOs or ISOs, and may be used to provide cash to the executive to provide that executive with the cash necessary to exercise the NQSO or ISO.
>   a. True
>   b. False
>
> 2. Employee Stock Purchase Plans allow employees to use pre-tax dollars to purchase company stock at a discount.
>   a. True
>   b. False
>
> 3. A §83(b) election allows the employer to elect to include contributions to the deferred compensation plan into the employee's income.
>   a. True
>   b. False
>
> True, False, False.

Employee Stock Purchase Plans (ESPP)

Intended to benefit all or a large portion of an employer's employees (the plan cannot be discriminatory), per IRC §423, an **employee stock purchase plan** (ESPP) gives employees an incentive to buy employer stock by allowing the employees to purchase the stock at a discounted price and receive favorable tax treatment for any gains if the stock meets certain holding period requirements. As discussed in other areas of the text, an employee who owns stock in his employer is connected to the productivity of the company and, in most cases, will work more efficiently and effectively towards the goals of the company.

Generally, an employee elects to defer after-tax compensation throughout the plan year through payroll deductions to the ESPP established by the employer. The employee is able to purchase the employer stock through the ESPP for a price equal to no less than 85 percent of a date determined stock price or an average stock price.[23] An example of a date determined price is the lesser of fair market value (1) at the beginning of the plan period, grant date, or (2) the end of the plan period, exercise date. An example of an average price is the average price for the quarter. The grant date and exercise date generally coincide with the beginning and end of the calendar year, but either could follow quarters, months, or any other time period that the employer selects.

Example 12.24

DTY Corporation's ESPP has a plan year of December 1, 2021 to November 30, 2022. DTY's employees are permitted to defer after-tax compensation into the plan from December 1, 2021 to November 30, 2022, and the ESPP will purchase the DTY stock for 85% of the lesser of the fair market value on December 1, 2021 or the fair market value on November 30, 2022. The fair market value of the stock at December 1, 2021 was $20, and the fair market value of the stock at November 30, 2022 was $28. The employee would be able to purchase the employer stock through the ESPP for $17 (85% of $20).

Example 12.25

Tribro's ESPP operates four plan periods during the year following the normal quarters of the calendar year. Employees must elect to defer their after-tax compensation prior to the beginning of each period to participate in the ESPP. After the end of each quarter, the employee purchases the employer stock for 85% of the average price during the quarter.

At the date of purchase, the employee will not have any taxable consequences but will immediately have an unrealized gain at least equal to the price discount off the fair market value of the stock. Consider an employee who was able to purchase the stock of his employer through the ESPP for $11.05, 85% of the fair market value on the date of exercise ($13.00). This employee would have $1.95 ($13.00-$11.05) or a 17.6% ($1.95÷$11.05) immediate pre-tax gain. Even with a 30% marginal tax rate, the gain would be 12.32% (17.6% x (1 - 30%)) without considering the benefits of future appreciation and lower tax rates (discussed below).

---

23. IRC §423(b)(6)(A). Most ESPPs utilize the 85% of the date determined price or average price; although, it may be any amount or percentage greater than 85%.

Employee Dollar Limit

An employee is statutorily limited to purchasing $25,000 of employer stock per year as determined based on the fair market value at the date of grant of the employer stock through the ESPP.[24] For example, if at the grant date the fair market value of the stock was $31.25 and at the exercise date the stock had a fair market value of $28.00, the employee could only purchase 800 shares ($25,000 ÷ $31.25) for $23.80 (85% of $28.00) for a total of $19,040 (800 x $23.80). If the employee deferred more to the ESPP than necessary, the difference would be returned to him. The refund would not create any taxable consequences as the funds in the ESPP are post-tax. Some employers may place additional limitations on their employees by restricting the amount of stock they may purchase (i.e., 15% of compensation or 2,500 shares) through the ESPP. Such restrictions cannot be applied on a discriminatory basis.

Qualifying Disposition

If the employee holds the stock purchased through the ESPP for two years from the date of grant and one year from the date of exercise, any subsequent sale is a qualifying disposition of the stock.[25] The employee's gain on the sale of the stock will be ordinary income to the extent the gain is attributable to the discount at the date of purchase. Any gain in excess of the ordinary income portion will be long-term capital gain. For example, if the employees were able to purchase the employer stock for $85.00 (85% of fair market value) and after meeting the required holding period requirements sold the stock for $90.00, then $5.00 ($90.00 - $85.00) would be considered as ordinary gain. This treatment occurs because the $5 represents part of the original discount. However, if after meeting the holding period requirement the employee sold the stock for $110.00, the total gain would be $25.00 ($110.00 - $85.00) and $15.00, the amount attributable to the discount, would be treated as ordinary income and the remaining $10.00 would be treated as long-term capital gain.

Example 12.26

Stanley, Inc. has an ESPP, and the stock traded on January 2, 2021 for $12.00 and on December 31, 2021 for $15.00. The plan permitted Cline, an employee, to buy at 85% of the lesser of the two prices ($12.00 x 0.85 = $10.20 per share). Cline, who contracted to purchase $25,000 worth of stock, will receive 2,083 shares of Stanley, Inc. stock ($25,000 ÷ $12.00). Note that since the stock price has risen to $15.00 per share, Cline has a portfolio worth $31,245 for which he paid $21,247. If he holds the stock two years from the date of the original purchase before selling at $20 per share, Cline will have ordinary income of $3,749 ($12.00-$10.20 x 2,083) and long-term capital gain of $16,664 ($8.00 x 2,083).

---

24. IRC §423(b)(8).

25. As discussed previously in this chapter, IRS Publication 525 clarifies that for ISOs and ESPPs the holding period for the property acquired when the employee exercises the option begins on the day after exercise. Although common practice is to state the holding period requirement as at least 2 years from grant and one year from exercise, it is more accurate to describe it as at least 2 years from grant and one year plus one day from exercise.

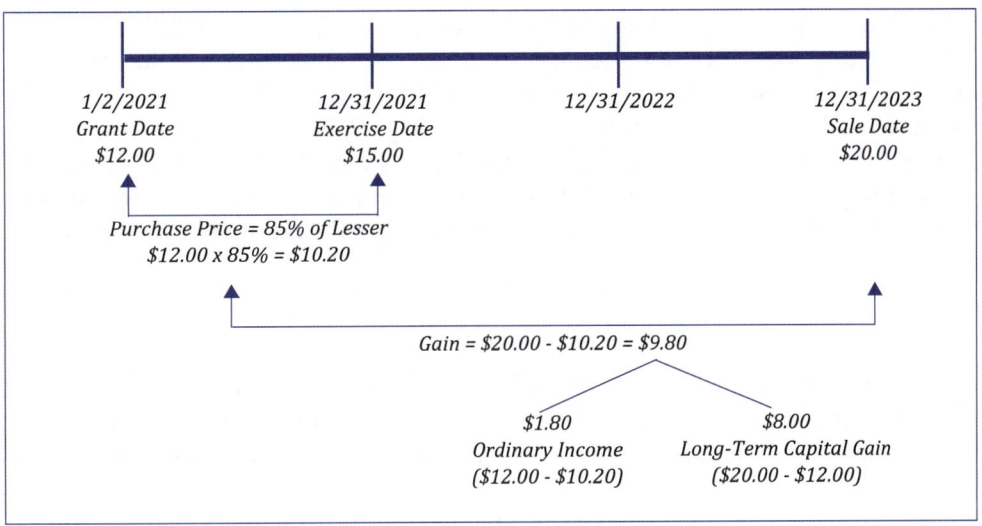

Example 12.27

Assume the same facts as above, except that Cline sells the stock for $11.00. In this case, since the entire gain, $0.80 per share ($11.00 - $10.20), is less than Cline's purchase discount, ($1.80 per share), Cline will have ordinary income equal to $1,666 ($0.80 x 2,083).

Disqualifying Disposition

If an employee does not hold the stock purchased through the ESPP for at least two years from the date of grant and one year from the exercise date, any sale is a disqualifying disposition. The primary difference as compared to a qualifying disposition is that the gain attributable to the discount will be W-2 income rather than ordinary income and therefore subject to FICA. The employee's gain on the sale will be W-2 income to the extent the gain is attributable to the purchase discount. Any gain in excess of the ordinary income portion will be long or short-term capital gain dependent upon the holding period, which begins on the day after the exercise date. For example, if an employee were able to purchase employer stock for $85.00 or 85 percent of a $100 fair market value, and before meeting the required holding period, sold the stock for $90.00, $5.00 ($90.00-$85.00) would be W-2 income. However, if the employee had sold the stock six months after the exercise date for $110.00, the total gain would be $25.00 ($110.00 - $85.00) and $15.00, the amount attributable to the discount, would be W-2 income and the remaining $10.00 would be short-term capital gain.

Example 12.28

Timer, Inc. has an ESPP and its stock traded on June 30, 2021 for $30.00 and July 31, 2021 for $25.00. Rhonda had elected to defer after-tax income to the ESPP and purchased 400 shares of the stock at 85% of the lower of the two values. Rhonda purchased 400 shares of the Timer, Inc. stock for $8,500 ($21.25 x 400 shares). Six months later, Rhonda sold the 400 shares at $27 per share. Since Rhonda did not hold the stock for the required holding period, Rhonda will have W-2 income at the date of sale of $1,500 [($25.00 - $21.25) x 400] and a short-term capital gain of $800 [($27.00 - $25.00) x 400].

Loss

If the employee sells the stock purchased through the ESPP at a price less than the exercise price, the employee will have a short or long-term capital loss as determined based upon the holding period beginning on the day following the date of exercise and the difference between the exercise price and the sales price.

Exhibit 12.6 | ESPP Summary

- Employee usually buys employer stock at 85% of fair market value.
- When the stock is sold, the price discount of 15% is ordinary income.
- The excess of the sales price over the undiscounted purchase price is long-term capital gain if a qualifying disposition.
- The stock purchase has a built-in return of 17.6% pre-tax.
- There is a $25,000 limit for purchases (based on the FMV of the stock on the date of grant).

Qualified Equity Grants

The TCJA 2017 created IRC §83(i), which provides the opportunity for employees of private companies (eligible corporations) to defer taxation on income from stock options or restricted stock units (RSUs)[26] for up to five years. This treatment to defer taxation is an election that qualified employees may elect once qualified stock vests or becomes taxable. This election is similar to the election employees can make under IRC §83(b) and must also be made within 30 days of vesting.

- **Qualified employee** - a qualified employee is an employee who is not excluded. An excluded employee is any employee:
  - who is a one-percent owner of the corporation at any time during the calendar year, or who was a one-percent owner at any time during the 10 preceding calendar years;[27]
  - who is, or has been at any prior time, the chief executive officer or chief financial officer of the corporation, or an individual acting in either capacity;
  - who is a family member of an individual described above (one-percent owner, CEO, or CFO);[28] or
  - who has been one of the four highest compensated officers of the corporation for the tax year or for any of the 10 preceding tax years.

---

26. Restricted Stock Units are similar to restricted stock, but no shares are transferred until vesting. Employees receiving RSUs are not permitted to make a §83(b) election as no tangible property is actually transferred when an RSU is granted. An employee receiving RSUs also has no voting or dividend rights until the shares are transferred at vesting.
27. A one-percent owner, as with the definition of key employee, means someone who owns more than one percent of the stock.
28. Family member is defined under IRC §318 and includes the employee's spouse, children, grandchildren, and parents.

- **Eligible corporation** - this tax deferral treatment is only available to companies that are not publicly traded and that have a written plan under which at least 80 percent of U.S. employees are granted stock options or RSUs to receive qualified stock.

- **Qualified stock** - qualified stock means stock in an eligible corporation that is received in connection with the exercise of an option or in the settlement of an RSU. However, to be qualified stock, the employee must not be able to sell the stock back to the corporation.

At the earliest time in which an amount attributable to the options or RSUs would be included in income, the employer must provide the employee with notice that the exercise of the option or settlement of the RSU is eligible for the Section §83(i) election, that the election must be made within 30 days after the first date the employee's rights in the qualified stock are transferable or aren't subject to a substantial risk of forfeiture (whichever occurs earlier), and that in the year the options or RSUs will be taxed the employer will withhold taxes based on the highest tax bracket in effect at the time (currently 37%), without regard to the employee's W-4.[29]

The election allows the employee to defer the tax until the earliest of:
1. The date the stock becomes publicly traded or becomes transferable to the corporation, or
2. The date the employee becomes ineligible (as identified above; e.g., CEO, CFO, 1% shareholder, etc.), or
3. The date the employee revokes the election, or
4. The date five years after the earlier of the date the rights of the employee in the stock are transferable or are no longer at substantial risk of forfeiture.

The election cannot be combined with the §83(b) election, and the employer's tax deduction will be delayed until the time the employee is taxed.

This provision appears to be designed to allow employees of private companies an opportunity to defer taxation on stock that has no market in which the stock could be sold. Without such a provision, these employees would have income without the ability to sell the stock to pay the tax. While this provision allows deferral for up to five years, deferral will cease if the company becomes publicly traded or the employee becomes an excluded employee. This tax treatment applies to stock received after 2017.

---

29. IRS Notice 2018-97.

SOLUTIONS to the discussion questions can be found exclusively within the chapter. Once you have completed an initial reading of the chapter, go back and highlight the answers to these questions.

1. Why are deferred compensation arrangements established?

2. List three common reasons deferred compensation arrangements are used.

3. Define "constructive receipt" and how it affects deferred compensation plans.

4. What is a substantial risk of forfeiture, and how does it affect deferred compensation plans?

5. Describe the Economic Benefit Doctrine and how it affects deferred compensation plans.

6. How is the 83(b) election used with regard to deferred compensation plans?

7. When are payroll taxes due on compensation contributed to a deferred compensation plan?

8. When will the employer receive an income tax deduction for assets contributed to a deferred compensation plan?

9. Discuss the funding arrangements available for deferred compensation plans.

10. What is the impact of Title I of ERISA on deferred compensation plans?

11. List and describe the types of deferred compensation plans available.

12. Describe 401(k) wrap plans.

13. What is an incentive stock option and what are the tax consequences associated with the grant, exercise and sale of ISOs?

14. What is a nonqualified stock option and what are the tax consequences associated with the grant, exercise, and sale of NQSOs?

15. What are stock appreciation rights?

16. What are restricted stock plans?

17. What is an employee stock purchase plan?

MULTIPLE CHOICE PROBLEMS

A sample of multiple choice problems is provided below. Additional multiple choice problems are available at money-education.com by accessing the Student Practice Portal.

1. All of the following are reasons that an employer might favor a nonqualified plan over a qualified retirement plan except:
    a. There is more design flexibility with a nonqualified plan.
    b. A nonqualified plan typically has lower administrative costs.
    c. Nonqualified plans typically allow the employer an immediate income tax deduction.
    d. Employers can generally exclude rank-and-file employees from a nonqualified plan.

2. Rick has an 18% nonqualified deferred compensation plan that is funded annually by his employer. Payments are made to a separate trustee of a secular trust who was selected by Rick and his employer. The employer contributions are discontinued at Rick's death, disability, or employment termination. When Rick retires or terminates employment, he will receive the proceeds from the trust.

    Which of the following is/are correct regarding the deferred compensation plan?
    1. The contributions are not currently taxable to Rick because they are subject to a substantial risk of forfeiture.
    2. The contributions to the plan are currently subject to payroll taxes.
    3. The employer can deduct the contributions to the plan at the time of the contribution.
    a. 3 only.
    b. 1 and 3.
    c. 2 and 3.
    d. 1, 2, and 3.

3. Courtney receives stock options for 12,000 shares of XYZ Corporation with an exercise price of $10 when the stock is trading on the national exchange for $10 per share. The XYZ company plan is an Incentive Stock Option Plan. Which of the following statements are true regarding the options?
    1. Courtney will be required to hold any ISOs for more than a year after exercise and more than two years from the grant date to have long-term capital gains.
    2. 2,000 of the options are NQSOs.
    a. 1 only.
    b. 2 only.
    c. Both 1 and 2.
    d. Neither 1 nor 2.

4. Kurt receives stock options (ISOs) with an exercise price of $18 when the stock is trading at $18. Kurt exercises these options two years after the date of the grant when the stock price is $39 per share. Which of the following statements is correct?
    a. Upon exercise Kurt will have no regular income for tax purposes.
    b. Kurt will have W-2 income of $21 per share upon exercise.
    c. Kurt will have $18 of AMT income upon exercise.
    d. Kurt's adjusted basis for regular income tax will be $39 at exercise.

5. Brynn received 1,000 NQSOs with an exercise price of $25 per share when the stock was $25 on the market. Two years from the date of grant Brynn exercises when the stock price is $102. At exercise, Brynn:
    a. Has W-2 income of $25,000.
    b. Has an AMT adjustment of $77,000.
    c. Has W-2 income of $77,000.
    d. Has an AMT adjustment of $25,000.

> **Additional multiple choice problems
> are available at
> money-education.com
> by accessing the
> Student Practice Portal.
> Access requires registration of the title using
> the unique code at the front of the book.**

QUICK QUIZ EXPLANATIONS

Quick Quiz 12.1
1. False. With a deferred compensation plan, the employer may take a compensation deduction when the deferred compensation is taxable to the employee.
2. True.

Quick Quiz 12.2
1. True.
2. False. A substantial risk of forfeiture exists when rights in property that are transferred are conditioned, directly or indirectly, upon a future performance or occurrence.
3. True.
4. False. The deduction for the salary of the CEO, CFO, and top three officers is limited to $1 million per year.

Quick Quiz 12.3
1. False. Deferred compensation is subject to payroll taxes at the time the substantial risk of forfeiture expires.
2. True.
3. True.

Quick Quiz 12.4
1. False. The use of rabbi trusts is not restricted to nonprofit organizations.
2. True.
3. False. A 401(k) wrap plan does not eliminate the substantial risk of forfeiture.

Quick Quiz 12.5
1. True.
2. False. The exercise of an ISO does not trigger W-2 income, but does create an AMT adjustment.
3. True.

Quick Quiz 12.6
1. True.
2. False. An Employee Stock Purchase Plan allows employees to use after-tax dollars to purchase company stock. An ESPP does not allow employees to use pre-tax dollars to purchase company stock.
3. False. A §83(b) election allows the employee to include in income the net value of a transfer from the employer in order to create basis in a capital asset.

13

EMPLOYEE BENEFITS: FRINGE BENEFITS

1. Understand that, unless an employer provided fringe benefit is specifically excluded by the IRC, it is taxable income.
2. Provide a general definition or description of a fringe benefit.
3. Identify the most important fringe benefits.
4. Know that, if a fringe benefit is provided by the employer to the employee, and it is not excludable, it is compensation and generally subject to both income and payroll taxes.
5. Be aware that most excludable fringe benefits have a non-discrimination requirement.
6. Be aware that employer provided fringe benefits can benefit a wide range of persons beyond the employee, including spouse, dependents, retired persons, directors, and in some cases independent contractors.
7. State the rules for exclusion of meals, lodging, athletic facilities, dependent care programs, no additional cost services, qualified employee discounts, working condition fringes, de minimus fringes, qualified moving expenses, adoption assistance, prizes and awards, and other fringe benefits when provided by employer to employee.
8. Know how fringe benefits are valued.

* Ties to CFP Certification Learning Objectives

INTRODUCTION

When an employee provides services to an employer in return for compensation, the employee will often receive certain benefits, known as fringe benefits, that otherwise would be taxable income if the Internal Revenue Code (IRC) did not statutorily exclude the value of these benefits from the employee's gross income. Many employees do not even consider using the office copier or fax machine for personal reasons as an employer-provided fringe benefit, whereas other fringe benefits are more obvious, such as employer-provided health insurance.

Generally, when a fringe benefit is provided as a requirement of employment or is for the convenience of the employer (i.e., meals, lodging), the value of the benefits will not be included in the employee's gross income. However, this general statement is not always correct as the value of some fringe benefits are excluded from an employee's gross income merely based on statutory provisions that focus on social goals, fitness, and education (i.e., health insurance, fitness center use, tuition). In order for the value of a fringe benefit to be excluded from the employee's gross income, the fringe benefit must be provided to the employees following a specific set of rules and qualifications as set forth in the IRC.

On December 22, 2017, President Trump signed the Tax Cuts and Jobs Act (TCJA 2017) into law. TCJA 2017 enacted a significant overhaul of the U.S. Income Tax System, including many changes to the deductibility of fringe benefits. Broadly, the new law reduces the deductibility by the employer of entertainment expenses and expenses related to providing meals to employees. The specific law changes that affect fringe benefits are discussed through this chapter.

Fringe Benefits Defined

A "**fringe benefit**" is a form of compensation where a benefit other than customary taxable wages is provided by the employer to the employee for the performance of services. These benefits are considered on the "fringe" because such benefits merely accompany, or are in addition to, an employee's salary, wages, or other compensation. Broadly, fringe benefits include paid vacation, sick leave, family leave, health insurance, life insurance, pension plans, profit sharing plans, the use of recreational facilities, personal use of employer's property, holidays, parking, prizes and awards, discounted products and services, and many others. When any of these fringe benefits are provided in return for the performance of services, the value of the fringe benefit is initially deemed compensation for those services. However, not all of the value of all fringe benefits will be included in the employee's current gross pay even though the employer has a current income tax deduction. The existence of an employer's income tax deduction with no current taxable income to the employee is similar to some benefits of qualified retirement plans.

KNOW THE NUMBERS

	2020	2021
Achievement Awards: Nonqualified[1]	$400	$400
Achievement Awards: Qualified[1]	$1,600	$1,600
Adoption Assistance	$14,300	$14,400
Adoption Assistance Beginning Phaseout	$214,520	$216,660
Adoption Assistance Ending Phaseout	$254,520	$256,660
Business Miles Expense	57.5 cents per mile	56 cents per mile
Dependent Care Assistance[2]	$5,000	$5,000
Educational Assistance Program[3]	$5,250	$5,250
Group Term Insurance	$50,000	$50,000
Moving Expense (Mileage)	17 cents per mile	16 cents per mile
Qualified Bicycle Commuting[4]	$0 per month	$0 per month
Qualified Parking	$270 per month	$270 per month
Transit Passes	$270 per month	$270 per month

1. IRC §274(j)(2).
2. IRC §129(9)(2).
3. IRC §127(a).
4. IRC §132(f)(5)(F). Eliminated for years after 2017 due to TCJA 2017.

Taxation of Fringe Benefits

Under IRS Treasury Regulations, all fringe benefits provided by an employer to an employee are taxable as wages unless a specific provision of the IRC excludes the benefit from taxation or unless the employee pays the fair value for the fringe benefit. Although a fringe benefit may not be specifically excluded by the regulations, the value of the fringe benefit is not taxable if it is fully paid for by the employee. The IRC and regulations, while providing no definition for the phrase "fringe benefit," list various examples of fringe benefits. Of paramount importance with fringe benefits is the issue of whether the fringe benefit is subject to income taxation and withholding requirements by the employer and employee.

> ### ⋮☰ *Key Concepts*
>
> 1. Define "fringe benefit."
> 2. In general, what are the tax consequences with regard to employee fringe benefits?
> 3. What are the nondiscrimination rules that apply to employee fringe benefits?

The value of a fringe benefit provided to an employee is deductible as compensation expense by the employer unless the fringe benefit is excludable from the employee's taxable income. Even if the expenditure by the employer is not deductible as compensation expense, it may very well be deductible under ordinary and necessary business expense. Employers should be aware that providing certain fringe benefits may trigger reporting requirements on W-2s for employees, K-1s for partners, or 1099s for independent contractors. The employer may also be required to withhold monies as a result of any taxable amount for FICA, FUTA, SUTA, or federal and state income taxes. Other issues that arise with fringe benefits are whether any exclusion has a limit, the amount of any such limit, who is eligible for the fringe benefit, and whether nondiscrimination requirements apply to the provision of the fringe benefit.

TCJA 2017 generally provides no deduction for:
- Activity broadly deemed to be entertainment, amusement, or recreation;
- Membership dues for any clubs;
- A facility (or portion of a facility) used in conjunction with any of the above; and
- Expenses for qualified transportation fringes (except those related to the safety of employees).

Meanwhile, beginning on January 1, 2018, the TCJA generally limits to 50 percent deductions for expenses of the employer for providing food for employees through an eating facility (de minimis fringes and those for the convenience of the employer).[1] After December 31, 2025, these amounts will no longer be deductible at all. Finally, TCJA 2017 limits the exclusion for awards to those meeting the new definition of tangible personal property.

---

1. Under the Taxpayer Certainty and Disaster Tax Relief Act (TCDTRA) of 2020, an exception to the 50% deduction limit applies to food and beverages provided by a restaurant, allowing such meals to be fully deductible by the employer when paid or incurred after December 31, 2020 and before January 1, 2023.

Exhibit 13.1 | TCJA 2017 Changes to Fringe Benefits

Expense Category	Before TCJA 2017	After TCJA 2017
Entertainment, amusement, or recreation.	50% deductible if ordinary and necessary to taxpayer's trade or business	Not deductible
Qualified transportation fringe.	Deductible	Not deductible
Costs for providing meals through an eating facility.	100% deductible	50% deductible from 2018 – 2025, and not deductible after 2025
De minimus food or beverages	100% deductible	50% deductible
Taking a client or customer to lunch or dinner (cannot be entertainment)	50% deductible	50% deductible*
Moving expenses	Fully excludable by employee if rules were met	Exclusion suspended from 2018 – 2025, except for members of the Armed Forces (or their spouse or dependents) on active duty that move pursuant to a military order and incident to a permanent change of station

Under the Taxpayer Certainty and Disaster Tax Relief Act (TCDTRA) of 2020, an exception to the 50% deduction limit applies to food and beverages provided by a restaurant, allowing such meals to be fully deductible by the employer when paid or incurred after December 31, 2020 and before January 1, 2023.

Nondiscrimination of Fringe Benefits

A vital area of concern with some fringe benefits is the requirement that the employer not discriminate against different classes of employees. When these "nondiscrimination requirements" apply, and the fringe benefit is provided only to a "highly compensated employee," and is not available on substantially the same terms to all employees, then the fringe benefit is deemed discriminatory. If the provision of a fringe benefit is discriminatory, then the exclusion may be lost, resulting in the value of the fringe benefit being included or added to an employee's income. As discussed below, some fringe benefits have nondiscrimination requirements while others do not.

Benefiting Individuals

An employee performing services in return for a fringe benefit need not be the person who actually uses or enjoys the fringe benefit. For instance, a spouse or child of an employee may receive or use the fringe benefit of an employer-provided athletic facility. Other individuals beyond current employees who may be taxed on the value of the fringe benefit or who may be eligible to receive the fringe benefit without taxable income include retired employees, spouses of employees, dependent children, spouses of deceased employees, partners who perform services for a partnership, directors, and independent contractors. The description of each fringe benefit includes a detail of those individuals who may receive or benefit from the fringe benefit.

Summary of Available Fringe Benefits

The fringe benefits that will be addressed in this chapter are those that are normally addressed in the regulations and are as follows:

1. Meals and lodging furnished for the convenience of the employer[2]
2. Athletic facilities furnished by the employer[3]
3. Educational assistance programs[4]
4. Dependent care programs[5]
5. No additional cost services (airlines/hotels/line of business)[6]
6. Qualified employee discounts (products versus services)[7]
7. Working condition fringe benefits[8]
8. *de minimis* fringe benefits[9]
9. Qualified moving expense reimbursement (W-2) for AGI[10]
10. Qualified transportation and parking[11]
11. Adoption assistance programs[12]
12. Prizes and awards[13]
13. Qualified tuition reduction plans[14]

SPECIFIC FRINGE BENEFITS

Meals and Lodging Provided by the Employer to the Employee

Meals

In general, an employee may exclude from gross income the value of all meals provided in-kind (not as cash reimbursement) to the employee, the employee's spouse, or any dependents. Meals are provided in-kind when the meal is actually served or supplied to the employee, as opposed to providing a cash reimbursement for food. In addition, the in-kind meals must meet the following two conditions:

- the meals are furnished for the convenience of the employer, and
- the meals are furnished on the employer's business premises.

---

2. IRC §119.
3. IRC §132(j)(4).
4. IRC §127.
5. IRC §129.
6. IRC §132(b).
7. IRC §132(c).
8. IRC §132(d).
9. IRC §132(e).
10. IRC §132(g).
11. IRC §132(f).
12. IRC §137.
13. IRC §274.
14. IRC §117.

The Convenience of the Employer

Meals furnished by an employer without charge to the employee will be regarded as furnished for the convenience of the employer if the meals are furnished for a substantial business reason of the employer, not just as a means of providing additional compensation to the employee. The determination of "for the convenience of the employer" is made based on all of the surrounding facts and circumstances. The IRS provides some of the following examples as guidance when determining which meals provided by an employer would qualify, or be deemed, as furnished for the convenience of the employer.

≔ *Key Concepts*

1. What requirements are necessary for meals to be excluded from income?

2. What requirements are necessary for lodging to be excluded from income?

Exhibit 13.2 | Meals Deemed for the Convenience of the Employer

- Meals furnished to the employee during working hours so that the employee will be available for emergency calls. It must be shown that emergencies have actually occurred or can reasonably be expected to occur in the employer's business during mealtime. For example, when a hospital provides a meal to an on-call doctor.

- Meals furnished to the employee during working hours because the employer's business requires restricted short meal periods, 30 or 45 minutes, and the employee could not be expected to eat elsewhere in such a short meal period.

- Meals furnished to the employee during working hours because the employee could not otherwise secure proper meals within a reasonable meal period and when there may be insufficient eating facilities in the vicinity of the employer's premises.

- Meals furnished to restaurant employees for each meal period in which the employee works, despite whether the meal is furnished during, immediately before, or immediately after the employee's working hours.

- If the employer furnishes a meal to all employees, and the reason for furnishing the meal for more than 50% of the employees is deemed for the convenience of the employer, 100% of the meals are deemed to be for the convenience of the employer.

- If the employer would have furnished a meal to an employee for any reason deemed to be for the convenience of the employer during the employee's working hours, but the employee's duties prevented him from obtaining a meal during those working hours, a meal provided by the employer immediately after the employee's working hours is deemed for the convenience of the employer.

- If an employer charges the employee a fixed amount for the meal, the meal will be regarded as furnished for the convenience of the employer if the employee pays the fixed charge regardless of whether he accepts the meal or provides his own meal.

The IRS also provides specific examples as to what is not considered "for the convenience of the employer."

Exhibit 13.3 | Meals Deemed Not for the Convenience of the Employer

- Any meal provided to promote the morale or goodwill of the employee or to attract prospective employees does not qualify for the exclusion.

- If the employer charges the employee for the meal, the meal will not be regarded as furnished for the convenience of the employer if the employee has a choice of accepting the meal and paying for it or of not paying for it and providing his own meals.

The Employer's Business Premises

The term "**business premises of the employer**" is defined as the place of employment of the employee. For example, meals provided in the employer's home to a domestic servant would constitute meals furnished on the business premises of the employer. Similarly, meals furnished to cowhands while herding their employer's cattle on leased land would be regarded as furnished on the business premises of the employer.[15]

Example 13.1

Flo, a waitress at Circle Bar and Grill, works from 7 a.m. to 4 p.m. five days a week. Each workday she is furnished, without charge, two meals. The manager of Circle Bar and Grill encourages her to eat breakfast in the employee break room each day before 7 a.m. but does not expressly require her to do this. The manager does, however, require her to eat her lunch in the employee break room. Since Flo is a food service employee and works during the normal breakfast and lunch periods, she can exclude the value of the breakfast and lunch from her gross income.

CASE STUDY 13.1

Dr. Walter Jacob was the executive director of the Training School Unit of the American Institute for Mental Studies. He was required, as a condition of his employment, to reside on the premises of Institute and be available 24 hours a day. Because of this requirement, the Institute provided his family housing and free groceries from the Institute's commissary. The provision of groceries to Mr. Jacob's family is excluded from his gross income as in-kind because the groceries were prepared into meals and consumed by Mr. Jacobs and his family on the Institute's premises.[1] In addition, the court held that the value of non-food items such as napkins, toilet tissue, and soap was an integral part of either lodging or meals and was excluded from gross income.

1. 74-1 USTC 9316.

---

15. Treas. Reg. §1.119-1(c)(1).

Example 13.2

Mobile Processing and Manufacturing (MPM) built a cafeteria in its main building. Mark, a foreman at MPM, can purchase his lunch in the cafeteria or bring his lunch from home, but there are no other dining facilities nearby. Mark cannot exclude the value of any meals purchased in the cafeteria from his gross income because Mark has the choice to pay for and eat the cafeteria meal or to not pay for the cafeteria meal and bring his lunch from home.

Example 13.3

In **Example 13.2**, had MPM required Mark to pay $40 each month for food from the cafeteria whether he ate the food or not, the $40 would be excludable from Mark's gross income. This exclusion only applies because Mark is required to pay for the meal whether he eats it or not. The payment of $40 for the meal can be through payroll withholding or can be a cash payment by Mark. In either case, the payment will be excluded from Mark's gross income.

Lodging

The IRC also provides an exclusion from an employee's gross income for the value of lodging furnished by an employer to an employee if all three of the following qualifications are met:

1. The lodging is furnished on the employer's business premises,
2. The lodging is furnished for the convenience of the employer, and
3. The employee is required to accept the lodging as a condition of employment.

If all three elements of this test are satisfied, the exclusion applies regardless of whether the employee is charged a fee for the lodging.

The Employer's Business Premises

The requirement that lodging be provided on the employer's premises is similar to the requirement that meals be provided on the employer's business premises. Generally, the business premises of the employer means the place of employment of the employee. Lodging furnished in the home of an employer to a domestic servant constitutes lodging furnished on the business premises of the employer.[16] Likewise, lodging for cowhands while herding their employer's cattle on leased land is deemed lodging furnished on the business premises of the employer.

The Convenience of the Employer

Similar to the rules concerning meals above, lodging furnished by an employer without charge to the employee will be regarded as furnished for the convenience of the employer if the lodging is furnished for a substantial business reason of the employer, not just as a means of providing additional compensation to the employee. The determination of "for the convenience of the employer" is made based on all of the surrounding facts and circumstances of each employer.

---

16. IRC §119(c).

Condition of Employment

The value of lodging is not includible in an employee's gross income if the employee is required to accept the lodging as a condition of employment. Requiring the employee to accept the lodging as a condition of employment is defined as the employee being required to accept the lodging to "enable him to perform the duties of his employment." In other words, the lodging is furnished because the employee is required to be available for duty at all times or because the employee could not perform the services required unless the employee is furnished such lodging.[17] If the employer provides lodging to the employee and the employee is charged a fixed amount whether or not the employee actually accepts the lodging, then the amount of the charge by the employer is not included in the employee's gross income.

Includible Lodging

If the lodging is not furnished on the business premises of the employer, or the lodging is not furnished for the convenience of the employer, or the employee is not required to accept the lodging as a condition of the employment, then the employee must include the value of the lodging in gross income irrespective of whether the value exceeds or is less than the amount charged. Unless evidence is shown to the contrary, the value of the lodging is considered to be equal to the amount charged.[18]

CASE STUDY 13.2

Even if an employee is convenienced by the lodging, this has no effect on the exclusion. This was one of the issues raised in *Wilhelm v. United States*.[1] In *Wilhelm*, supervisory employees of a cattle ranch, who were required to be available for duty at all times, were allowed to exclude from gross income the lodging furnished by their employer. Although there was alternative housing available within a short distance, the *Wilhelm* court stated at the outset of its discussion that "there is no requirement... that the employee be deprived of his free choice in lodging and boarding or that he be inconvenienced. There is no statutory provision that the employee may not exclude from his gross income the value of the food and lodging furnished by his employer because the employee, too, is convenienced."

1. *Wilhelm v. United States*, 257 F.Supp. 16, 20-21 (D.Wyo.1966).

Example 13.4

An employee of an institution is given the choice of residing at the institution free of charge or of residing elsewhere and receiving a cash allowance in addition to her regular salary. If she elects to reside at the institution, the value to the employee of the lodging furnished by the employer will be includible in the employee's gross income because her residence at the institution is not required in order for her to perform properly the duties of her employment.

17. IRC §119(b).
18. IRC §119(b).

Example 13.5

A construction worker is employed at a construction project at a remote job site in Alaska. Due to the inaccessibility of facilities for the employees who are working at the job site to obtain food and lodging in the prevailing weather conditions, the employer is required to furnish meals and lodging to the employee at the camp site in order to carry on the construction project. The employee is required to pay $40 a week for the meals and lodging. The weekly charge of $40 is not part of the compensation includible in the gross income of the employee, and the value of the meals and lodging is excludable from his gross income.

There has been significant litigation concerning what constitutes the business premises of the employer. The courts have been somewhat flexible on this issue and consider all facts and circumstances.[19]

TCJA 2017 and TCDTRA 2020 Modifications

As noted earlier, TCJA 2017 modified the rules regarding the employer's deduction for meals furnished for the convenience of the employer after 2017, whereby such expenses are subject to a 50 percent limitation through 2025, and not deductible by the employer after 2025. Under the Taxpayer Certainty and Disaster Tax Relief Act (TCDTRA) of 2020, an exception to the 50 percent deduction limit applies to food and beverages provided by a restaurant, allowing such meals to be fully deductible by the employer when paid or incurred after December 31, 2020 and before January 1, 2023.

CASE STUDY 13.3

In the case of ***Erdelt v. United States***, 715 F.Supp. 278 (D.N.D. 1989), the school district purchased a house that was occupied by the district's superintendent. The house was located one block from the school facility. The fact that the house was not on the same contiguous piece of real estate as the school facility did not prevent the house from being considered on the district's business premises. The house was a "residence required as a condition of employment." The nature of the superintendent's position and uniqueness of the school district itself, the court reasoned, required that the superintendent be available to the community at all times through his presence and availability near the school. As such, the reasonable rental value of the house was not includible in his gross income for income tax purposes.

Nonetheless, some exclusions have been found to not apply under somewhat similar circumstances, like in ***Wilson v. United States***, 412 F.2d 694 (1st Cir. 1969). There, a state trooper was reimbursed for "mid-shift" meals or lunches if he was more than 10 miles from his home. The court considered this to be includible in gross income of the state trooper.

---

19. This flexible position was seen in the case of Saunders v. Commissioner, 215 F.2d 768, 771 (3rd Cir. 1954), where the court articulated: "... (T)he rationale of the rule should make it applicable to determine the extent of gross income either when quarters and meals are furnished in kind or cash is paid in lieu thereof ... Admittedly, the payment of cash to an employee is normally compensatory and probably more obviously so than payment in kind. Nevertheless, just as an employee is often furnished tangible property which cannot be regarded as compensation, an employee may be furnished cash which is not compensation ..."

CASE STUDY 13.4

In *Coyner v. Bingler*, 344 F.2d 736, 738 (3rd Cir. 1965), a park foreman for the City of Pittsburgh volunteered to become a resident caretaker at a community cultural center while still working and receiving his salary as a park foreman. Mr. Coyner lived free of charge at the cultural center where he acted as caretaker. The Tax Court ruled that the value of the lodging should have been included in gross income, but the United States Third Circuit Court of Appeals disagreed, overturning the Tax Court and finding that the value of the lodging was excludable from gross income because Mr. Coyner had to live there in proper performance of his duties as caretaker. Mr. Coyner's occupancy of the apartment was not simply for his convenience and benefit, but was of distinct benefit to the City and, therefore, "for the convenience of the employer" within the terms of the statute.

The Court recognized the facts that his presence was required to prevent vandalism, to perform certain janitorial services, to be present to admit persons entitled to use the facilities and to secure and lock the building at night. Because the cultural center was almost constantly in use, Mr. Coyner could exclude the lodging from his gross income because it related to the practical working necessity of performing his duties with any sort of efficiency.[1] The Court did acknowledge that, had the commissioner introduced any evidence that Mr. Coyner was not required to be available for duty at all times, a different result may have been in order.

---

1. Excluding the value of lodging for officers and employees of a family owned funeral business was allowed where the lodging was furnished as a matter of company policy and the nature of the business required that close personal contact be made available on a 24-hour per day basis. *In the Matter of Harry Schwartz*, 22 T.C.M. 835 (1963).

Athletic Facilities Furnished by the Employer

Under the regulations, the value of any "on premises athletic facility" provided by an employer to an employee is not included in the employee's gross income.[20] An "**on premises athletic facility**" is defined as a gym or other athletic facility such as a tennis court, pool, or golf course that meets all of the following requirements:

1. Operated by the employer,
2. Located on the employer's premises, and
3. "Substantially all" of the use of the facility is by employees of the employer, their spouses or their dependent children.[21]

Key Concepts

1. What requirements are necessary for athletic facilities provided to an employee as a fringe benefit to be excluded from income?

2. What requirements are necessary for education assistance programs provided to an employee as a fringe benefit to be excluded from income?

---

20. Treas. Reg. §1.132-1(e)(1).
21. Treas. Reg. §1.132-1(e). See also Treas. Reg. §1.132-1(b)(5) for the definition of dependent children. A dependent child or children of an employee under this § is a child or step-child who is a dependent of the employee or who is twenty-four years of age or younger whose parents are both deceased.

Operated by the Employer

The employer is deemed to operate an athletic facility when the employer operates the facility by hiring its own employees or hires an independent contractor to operate the athletic facility. If the athletic facility is operated by an unpaid separate unrelated entity, then the exclusion does not apply and the value of the athletic facility will be included in an employee's taxable income. Also, the facility may be operated by more than one employer, and as long as an employer pays rent either directly to the owner of the premises or to a sub-lessor of the premises, that employer is eligible for the exclusion.[22]

Located on the Employer's Premises

The requirement that the athletic facility be located on the employer's "premises" does not necessarily mean that the employer must own the facility or that the facility be located on the employer's *business* premises.[23] In other words, the premises could be leased or rented by the employer. As long as the employer pays reasonable rent for the premises, the facility may be considered the employer's premises. If the athletic facility is for "residential use" (like a tennis court, pool, or gym that are part of a resort), then this exclusion is lost (unless, of course, if the resort is owned by the employer).[24]

Use by Employees

General Public

The exclusion for on-premises athletic facilities is inapplicable to any athletic facilities made available to the general public through the sale or rental of memberships or similar arrangements.[25, 26] For example, if the on-premises facility is a health club where others from the general public pay monthly membership dues, then the value of the use of the facility is included in an employee's gross income.

Discriminatory

Nondiscrimination requirements do not apply to on-premises athletic facilities.[27, 28] Thus, the employer has discretion to determine who may or may not have access to on-premises athletic facilities without jeopardizing the eligibility for the exclusion from the employee's gross income.

Covered Employees

The following individuals are treated as employees for the purposes of the athletic facility exclusion:

- current employees;
- former retired or disabled employees;
- widow(er)s of those who died while employed;
- widow(er)s of former retired or disabled employees;
- partners who perform services for a partnership; or
- leased employees providing services to an employer on a substantially full-time basis for at least a year where the services are performed under the employer's primary control.

---

22. Treas. Reg. §1-132.1(e)(4).
23. Treas. Reg. §1.132-1(e)(2).
24. Treas. Reg. §1.132-1(e)(2).
25. Treas. Reg. §1.132-1(e).
26. Treas. Reg. §1.132-1(e)(1).
27. The nondiscrimination requirements of §132 and §1.132-A do not apply to the on-site athletic facility.
28. Treas. Reg. §1.132-1(e)(5).

Example 13.6

Thomas works at ABC Insurance Company in a high rise building in downtown Austin, Texas. Adjacent to the main office, ABC rents out a gym from the building management. Under these circumstances, as long as the general public does not use the gym, the ABC employees may exclude the value of the use of the on-premises gym from their gross income. However, if the high rise building was a resort for residential use, then the value of the use of the athletic facility would need to be included in each employee's gross income.

Educational Assistance Programs

The value of an educational assistance program provided by an employer for the benefit of an employee is excluded from the employee's gross income subject to certain limitations and requirements.[29] Under the regulations, a **qualified educational assistance program** is a plan established and maintained by an employer that provides employees with educational assistance.[30] The program need not be funded, nor must the employer apply to the IRS for a determination of whether the plan is qualified.[31] The program must be a separate written plan of the employer set forth in a separate document and must only provide educational assistance.[32]

The gross income exclusion for educational assistance is limited to the value of $5,250.[33] Nonetheless, as discussed below, an employer may exclude part or all of the excess of educational assistance over $5,250 from an employee's taxable income as a working condition benefit, assuming that the working condition benefit tests apply. Amounts above $5,250 that do not qualify as a working condition fringe benefit are treated as W-2 income.

Note that any educational expense reimbursed by an employer or paid for by an employer cannot be used as the basis for the American opportunity credit or lifetime learning credit.

Educational Assistance

"Educational assistance" is defined as either:

1. the employer's payment of expenses incurred on behalf of an employee for education, or
2. the employer's provision of education to an employee.[34]

Qualifying educational assistance can be provided for tuition, fees, books, supplies, and equipment related to either undergraduate or graduate education. The CARES Act of 2020 and the Taxpayer Certainty and Disaster Tax Relief Act (TCDRA) of 2020 expanded the definition of qualifying educational assistance to include eligible student loan repayments made to either the employee or directly to the lender after March 27, 2020 and before January 1, 2026, subject to the overall $5,250 per year limitation. Eligible student loans are qualified higher education loans of the employee only; loans of spouses or dependents do not qualify.

---

29. IRC §127.
30. Treas. Reg. §1.127-2.
31. Nonetheless, an employer may request that the IRS determine whether a plan is a qualified program.
32. Treas. Reg. §1.127-2(b).
33. IRC §127(a).
34. Treas. Reg. §1.127-2(c)(1).

If the program provides the employee with a choice between the employer providing educational assistance or the employer providing other remuneration to the employee that is includible in the employee's gross income, the value of any benefit received from the plan is taxable to the employee.[35] More particularly, educational assistance does not include:

- the employer's payment for tools or supplies other than textbooks that the employee may retain after completion of the course,
- the employer's payment for meals, lodging, or transportation, or
- the employer's payment for education involving sports, games, or hobbies, *unless* the education involves the employer's business or is a required part of a degree program.

The value of any of the above are included in the employee's gross income if provided by the employer.

Eligible Individuals

An educational assistance program must be an exclusive benefit for employees (defined below) of the employer. An educational assistance program must also be nondiscriminatory. Any educational assistance program for an employee's spouses or dependents does not apply to this exclusion.

Nondiscrimination

The IRC prohibits discrimination in the provision of the educational assistance program. If the program discriminates in favor of officers, shareholders, self-employed, or highly compensated employees, then the exclusion from gross income is lost. In other words, if the program is discriminatory, then the value of any benefit paid from the plan on behalf of an employee will be taxable to the employee. Specifically, the program meets the nondiscrimination requirements if the following conditions are met:

- the program benefits employees and does not favor highly compensated employees (as defined in Chapter 3);
- the program does not provide more than five percent of its benefits during the year to shareholders or owners (or their spouses or dependents) who own more than five percent of the stock, of the capital, or of the profit interest in the employer;
- the employees are not allowed to choose cash that must be included in gross income in lieu of educational assistance; and
- reasonable notice is given to the employees that the program is provided to eligible employees.

Covered Employees

The following individuals are considered employees under this exclusion:

- current employees
- former employees who are retired, disabled, or laid off
- leased employees who provide services on a substantially full-time basis for at least a year and the services are performed under the employer's primary control
- sole proprietors
- partners performing services for the partnership

35. Treas. Reg. §1.127-2(c)(2).

Example 13.7

Barbie is a covered employee of Toys, Toys & More Toys. The company implemented a qualified educational assistance program and offered educational assistance to Barbie and all other employees. Barbie incurred $5,000 of educational expenses that were paid for by the company. Barbie and other employees had a choice between the company providing educational assistance or the company providing other remuneration that would be includible in employees' gross income. In this case, any benefit paid from the plan is taxable to Barbie because the plan offered a choice between the company providing educational assistance or the company providing other remuneration that would be includible in the employees' gross income. If Barbie's only choice was to either receive educational assistance or nothing at all, then the full $5,000 would be excluded from her gross income.

Qualified Tuition Reduction Plans

An employee may exclude from gross income any amount representing a qualified tuition reduction.[36] **Qualified tuition reduction** is defined in the IRC as the amount of any reduction in tuition provided to an employee of an educational organization for education below the graduate level of:[37]

- current employees,
- former employees who retired or left on disability,
- widow(er)s of a person who died while employed,
- widow(er)s of former employees who retired or left on disability, or
- dependent children or spouses of any of the above.

Qualified Educational Organizations

Although this exclusion normally does not apply to the graduate level, if the individual is a graduate student teaching or performing research activities for an educational organization, then that individual may be eligible if he or she meets all other requirements of this exclusion.[38] To be qualified, an educational organization must normally maintain a regular faculty and curriculum and have a regularly enrolled body of students in attendance at the place where its educational activities are carried out in the normal course of business. This educational organization can be elementary, secondary, a college, or university.

Nondiscriminatory

For the exclusion to apply, the tuition reduction must not discriminate in favor of highly compensated employees, or stated differently, the reduction must be made available on substantially the same terms to each member of a group of employees defined under a reasonable classification set up by the employer that does not discriminate in favor of highly compensated employees.[39]

> ### ✒ Quick Quiz 13.3
>
> 1. Athletic facility dues provided to employees for an off-site gym are excludable from income.
>   - a. True
>   - b. False
>
> 2. Educational assistance programs lose their tax benefits if the plan is discriminatory.
>   - a. True
>   - b. False
>
> 3. A qualified tuition reduction plan may never apply to graduate level work.
>   - a. True
>   - b. False
>
> False, True, False.

---

36. IRC §117(d)(1).
37. IRC §117(d)(2).
38. IRC §117(d)(5).
39. IRC §117(d)(3).

Example 13.8

Dr. Bob is a professor of Ancient Roman History at Cool University. His daughter, Ainsley, decided she would pursue her undergraduate degree in journalism at CU. The waiver of her tuition by the university can be excluded from income. However, if Ainsley were pursuing a graduate degree, then the tuition waiver would be included in income.

Dependent Care Assistance

The IRC allows an employee to exclude the value of dependent care assistance (as defined below) provided by an employer from the employee's gross income.[40] This exclusion for **dependent care assistance** applies to household and dependent care services paid for or provided by the employer to an employee under a dependent care assistance program. The services must be provided under the following conditions:

1. The services must be provided for one of the following qualifying persons:[41]
   - dependent children under 13 years of age,
   - dependent children who are physically or mentally incapable of caring for themselves, or
   - an employee's spouse if the spouse is physically or mentally incapable of caring for himself.
2. The services must also allow an employee to work.
3. An employee may exclude up to the lesser of:
   - $5,000 annually ($2,500 for married couples filing separate returns) in benefits received through a dependent care assistance program from his gross income,[42] or
   - the earned income of the employee or his spouse.
4. The plan must provide beneficiaries with advance notice of the program to permit them to make informed decisions about dependent care.[43]

Dependent care benefits include:
1. Amounts an employer paid directly to either the employee or the care provider for the care of a qualifying person while the employee works,
2. The fair market value of care in a daycare facility provided or sponsored by the employer, and
3. Pre-tax contributions the employee made under a dependent care flexible spending arrangement (FSA). FSAs are discussed in more detail in Chapter 14.

Nondiscrimination

Nondiscrimination requirements apply to the dependent care assistance exclusion. Highly compensated employees may not exclude any benefits paid as dependent care assistance from their taxable wages unless the benefits provided under the program do not favor highly compensated employees and are not discriminatory as to the other employees. In addition, not more than 25 percent of the amounts paid or incurred by the employer for dependent care assistance during the year may be provided for the class of individuals who are shareholders or owners. In the event that the plan fails to meet certain requirements, it may be treated as a valid dependent care assistance program for employees who are not highly compensated.

---

40. These are programs under IRC §129.
41. IRC §21(b).
42. IRC §129(a)(2). Increased by ARPA of 2021 to $10,500 ($5,250 for married filing separately) for 2021 only.
43. This was the precise situation in *American Family Mut. Ins. Co. v. United States,* 815 F.Supp. 1206 (W.D.Wis.1992), where the Court found that the exclusion was unavailable because the plan did not provide the beneficiaries with advance notice.

Excluded Employees

The plan must define eligible employees. Similar to a qualified plan, a company does not have to include employees who have not attained age 21 and completed 1 year of service. In addition, employees who are covered by a collective bargaining agreement may be excluded if there is evidence that dependent care was part of the bargaining between the employer and the employee representatives.[44]

"No-Additional-Cost Services"

The exclusion for **no-additional-cost services** applies to any service provided by an employer to an employee that does not cause the employer to incur any substantial additional cost or lose revenue. The service provided as a fringe benefit must be offered to customers in the ordinary course of the line of business in which the employee performs substantial services. Examples of no-additional-cost services include providing free airline, bus, or train tickets, and hotel accommodations or telephone services either free or at reduced prices to employees working in those lines of business.[45] Also, an employee working as a parking lot attendant would have parking provided as a no-additional-cost service if the parking lot is not at capacity on a given day.[46]

Lost or Forgone Revenue

One of the most important distinctions in determining whether a no-additional-cost service is excludable from an employee's gross income involves whether the employer loses revenue or incurs an opportunity cost by providing the fringe benefit to the employee. Stated differently, any lost or **forgone revenue** is deemed to be a cost when determining whether the employer has incurred substantial additional costs when providing a service to an employee. The employer is considered to incur substantial additional cost if the employer or the employee spends a substantial amount of time providing the service even if the time spent would otherwise be inactive or idle or if the services are provided outside normal business hours.

Covered Employees

The following individuals are considered employees under the no-additional-cost service exclusion:

- current employees,
- former employees retired or on disability,
- widow(er)s of an individual who died while employed,
- widow(er)s of a former employee who retired or left on disability,
- leased employees providing services to the employer on a substantially full-time basis for at least a year if the services were performed under the primary control of the employer, or
- a partner who performs services for a partnership.

Providing this service to an employee's spouse or dependent child is viewed as being provided to the employee individually. Use of air transportation by an employee's parents is also considered use by the employee.

---

44. IRC §129(d)(9).
45. Treas. Reg. §1.132-2(a)(2).
46. Note that other exclusions could apply to this as well, such as a working condition fringe or de minimis fringe benefit if applicable.

Exception - Special Flight Rule

Airlines frequently provide personal flights at no charge, or at reduced costs, for employees or family members of employees. Whether the no-additional-cost exclusion is available depends upon seat availability to other customers and if reserved seating is provided to the employee. The key distinction is that the airline must not forego revenue in order to provide the excludable fringe benefit.

Example 13.9

Commercial Airline permits its employees to take personal flights on the airline at no charge and receive reserved seating. Because Commercial Airline foregoes potential revenue by permitting the employees to reserve seats, employees receiving such free flights are not eligible for the no-additional-cost exclusion and must include the value of the flight in their gross income.[47] However, if the employees are not allowed to reserve seats and only board the flight if there is available capacity, then employees receiving those flights are eligible for the no-additional-costs exclusion and may exclude the value of the flight from their gross income.

Unrelated Employers - Reciprocal Agreements

There is an exception for reciprocal agreements that meet certain requirements between unrelated employers. These written agreements are between unrelated entities in the same type of business or industry and there is no substantial cost in providing these services to employees of the other business. These agreements are common in the airline industry.

A no-additional-cost service provided to an employee by an unrelated employer may qualify as an excludable benefit if the following requirements are met:

1. the service is the same type of service provided generally to customers in both the line of business of the employee and of the service provided;
2. the employer of the employee and the employer providing the service have a written reciprocal agreement whereby a group of employees of each employer in the same line of business receive no additional cost services from the other employer; and
3. the employer of the employee and the unrelated employer do not incur any substantial additional cost in providing this service or because of the written agreement.[48]

Example 13.10

Assume that commercial airline A and B have a reciprocal agreement that permits employees of A to fly on B's airlines subject to space available and allows B's employees to fly on A's airlines subject to space available. Because neither employer forgoes revenue or incurs substantial cost in offering this benefit, employees receiving these free flights are eligible for the no-additional-cost exclusion.

---

47. Treas. Reg. §1.132-2(c).
48. Treas. Reg. §1.132-2(b). If one employer receives a substantial payment from the other employer with respect to the reciprocal agreement, the paying employer will be considered to have incurred a substantial additional cost pursuant to the agreement, and consequently services performed under the reciprocal agreement will not qualify for exclusion as no-additional-cost services.

Nondiscrimination

Employers may not exclude the value of the services to highly compensated employees if the value of the no-additional-cost service is not available on the same terms to all employees or at least to a group of employees defined under a reasonable classification that does not favor highly compensated employees. If the provision of the no-additional-cost service is discriminatory, then no aspect or portion of the exclusion applies to highly compensated employees. Therefore, the entire value of the exclusion is disallowed with the amount of the benefit included in the highly compensated employees' gross income.[49]

CASE STUDY 13.5

In ***Charley v. Commissioner of Internal Revenue Service***, Dr. Philip Charley, in his capacity as an employee of Truesdail Laboratories, traveled to various accident sites to inspect machinery.[1] Truesdail had an "unwritten policy" that frequent flyer miles earned during employee travel became the sole property of the employee. If Dr. Charley chose to travel to an inspection by air, Truesdail would bill the client for round-trip, first class air travel. However, Dr. Charley would instruct the travel agent to arrange for coach service to and from the site but to charge Truesdail for first class travel. Dr. Charley would then use his frequent flyer miles (largely earned in connection with his business travel for Truesdail) to upgrade the coach ticket to first class and would instruct the travel agent to transfer funds equal to the difference in price between the first class ticket for which Truesdail was charged and the coach ticket to his personal travel account. Over the course of the taxable year, the travel agent maintained separate travel accounts for Dr. Charley and Truesdail. Dr. Charley took four business trips that year and using the procedures outlined above, received $3,149.93 in his personal travel account from his "sale" of the frequent flyer miles.

The IRS argued that Dr. Charley was wealthier after the transaction than before, showing that he received income. While the travel credits converted to cash can be characterized as additional compensation, Dr. Charley received property from his employer in the account upon which he could draw up to $3,149.93. Truesdail paid for first class airfare and allowed the travel agent to credit Philip's account with the difference between the first class price and the coach price. The funds constituting the difference therefore came from Truesdail, and the fact that travel credits were exchanged for frequent flyer miles was, according to the Court, irrelevant to their analysis. Dr. Charley asserted that the credits were "no-additional-cost services" that should be excluded under the IRC. However, the service in question must, among other things, be "offered for sale to customers in the ordinary course of the line of business of the employer in which the employee is performing services."[2] Truesdail did not offer frequent flyer miles to customers in the ordinary course of its business; thus, the travel credits at issue could not be deemed an excludable no-additional-cost service.

1. *Charley v. Commissioner of Internal Revenue Service*, 91 F.3d 72 (9th Cir. 1996).
2. IRC §132(b).

---

49. Treas. Reg. §1.132-8(a)(2).

Qualified Employee Discounts

Under the regulations, the value of "**qualified employee discounts**" on property or services offered to an employer's customers in the ordinary course of the employer's business may be excluded from an employee's income (subject to certain limits).[50] However, this exclusion does not apply to discounts on real property or on personal property commonly held for investment purposes.[51]

Limits

The exclusion for an employee discount is limited based on whether the discount is for a service or merchandise:

- twenty percent (20%) of the price at which the service is offered to nonemployee customers, or
- for merchandise or other property, the employer's gross profit percentage multiplied by the price the employer charges nonemployee customers for the property.[52]

Covered Employees

The following individuals are treated as employees for the purposes of the qualified employee discount exclusion:

- current employees,
- former retired or disabled employees,
- widow(er)s of those who died while employed,
- widow(er)s of former retired or disabled employees,
- partners performing services for the partnership, or
- leased employees providing services to an employer on a substantially full-time basis for at least a year where the services are performed under the employer's primary control.

> ### ✎ Quick Quiz 13.4
>
> 1. Dependent care assistance can be excluded up to $2,500 for single individuals and $5,000 for married individuals filing jointly.
>   a. True
>   b. False
>
> 2. No-additional-cost services provided to employees may be discriminatory and be excluded from the employee's gross income.
>   a. True
>   b. False
>
> 3. Qualified employee discounts are discounts given to the employees on property or services offered to an employer's customer in the ordinary course of business.
>   a. True
>   b. False
>
> False, False, True.

Nondiscrimination

Nondiscrimination rules apply to the exclusion for qualified employee discounts. The discount must be made available to all employees or to a group of employees defined under a reasonable classification designated by the employer that does not favor highly compensated employees.

Example 13.11

Randy's Parts Depot sells radiators for $100 to its customers. The radiator cost Randy's $80. If Randy's allows its employees to purchase the radiator for $90, the employees can exclude the $10 discount from gross income. If, however, Randy's sold the radiator to the employees at $75, then they would be required to include $5 in their gross income. The maximum excludable discount in this situation is $20 (20% x $100).

---

50. Treas. Reg. §1.132-3.
51. For instance, stocks and bonds are personal property commonly held for investment purposes.
52. An employer's gross profit percentage is determined based on all property offered to customers during the year preceding the year the discount is available, by subtracting the total cost of the property from the total sales price, and dividing the result by the total sales price of the property.

Working Condition Fringe Benefits

The value of "**working condition fringe benefits**" provided by an employer are excluded from an employee's gross income.[53] Working condition fringes are defined as any property or service provided to an employee that enables the employee to perform his work and, if paid for by the employee, would be deductible as a trade or business expense.[54]

Covered Employees

Under the regulations, the following individuals are considered to be employees under the working conditions fringe exclusion:

- a current employee,
- a partner who performs services for a partnership,
- a director of the company, and
- an independent contractor performing services for the employer.[55]

Discriminatory

Working condition fringes are not subject to nondiscrimination requirements; therefore, the exclusion applies even if they favor highly compensated employees.

Eligible Benefits

The working condition fringe exclusion applies to cash payments provided for an employee's expenses for a business activity as long as the employee may deduct the expenses had the employee paid for the expenses without reimbursement. It is imperative that the employee keep sufficient documentation to verify the payment is actually used for those expenses and any unused portion of the payment is returned to the employer.

The exclusion will not apply to:

- a service or property provided under a flexible spending account that provides the employee a certain level of unspecified non-cash benefits with a pre-determined cash value,
- a physical examination program provided by the employer, and
- any employee expense the employee may deduct as an expense for a trade or business other than the employer's trade or business.[56]

The property or service must be received by the employee, and there must be a legitimate business expense that relates to the employee's work. Business-related security devices, job-related education, parking, and use of company cars are some examples of working condition fringes.[57]

> ### ☰ *Key Concepts*
>
> 1. What are working condition employee fringe benefits, and when are they excluded from income?
>
> 2. What are "de minimis" employee fringe benefits, and when are they excluded from income?

---

53. IRC §132.
54. IRC §162 or §167.
55. Treas. Reg. §1.132-1(b)(2).
56. Treas. Reg. §1.132-5(a)(1).
57. Treas. Reg. §1.132-5.

Company Car as a Working Condition Fringe Benefit

As listed above, a common working condition fringe benefit is the provision of a company car. If the employee utilizes the car for both personal and business purposes, the portion used for business is considered the value of the working condition fringe benefit, whereas the personal use value of the car will be included in the employee's gross income. Also, use of a demonstration car by full-time automobile salespersons qualifies as a working condition fringe benefit if the demonstration car is predominately used to facilitate the services the sales person provided to the employer and there are restrictions on personal use of the automobile.[58]

Example 13.12

Assume that an employer makes available to an employee an automobile and a chauffeur. Assume further that the value of the chauffeur services is $30,000 and that the chauffeur spends 30 percent of each workday driving the employee for personal purposes. There may be excluded from the employee's income 70 percent of $30,000, or $21,000, leaving an income inclusion with respect to the chauffeur services of $9,000.

Qualified Vehicles for "Non-Personal Use"

A **qualified non-personal use vehicle** is a vehicle that the employee does not use more than a minimal amount for personal reasons due to the design of the vehicle. If an employee is provided a vehicle that is deemed to be a qualified non-personal use vehicle, the value of the provision will be excluded from his gross income.

Qualified non-personal use vehicles may include:
- clearly marked police and fire vehicles
- unmarked vehicles utilized by law enforcement individuals if the use is officially authorized
- an ambulance or hearse
- any vehicle designed to carry cargo with a loaded gross weight over 14,000 pounds
- delivery trucks with seating for the driver only or the driver with a folding jump seat
- a passenger bus with the capacity of at least 20 passengers
- school buses
- tractors or other farm-type vehicles

Pickup truck: A pickup truck with a loaded gross vehicle weight of 14,000 pounds or less may be a qualified non-personal use vehicle if it has been modified so that it will unlikely be used more than for minimal personal use. Such pickup trucks that are clearly marked with decals, special painting, or other advertising associated with the function of the business may qualify if the pickup truck is equipped with a hydraulic lift tank, permanent tank or drum, permanent side boards that materially raise the level of the sides of the truck or the bed, or other heavy equipment are part of the vehicle. Also, if the pickup truck is primarily used to transport a particular type of load in construction, manufacturing, farming, drilling, timbering, or other similar operation for which it was specially designed, it will be considered a qualified non-personal use vehicle.

Vans: A van with a loaded gross vehicle weight of 14,000 pounds or less is a qualified nonpersonal-use vehicle if it has been specially modified so it is not likely to be used more than minimally for personal purposes. For example, a van qualifies if it is clearly marked with permanently affixed decals, special

---

58. Treas. Reg. §1.132-5(o).

painting, or other advertising associated with the business and has a seat for the driver only (or the driver and one other person) and either of the following items: (1) permanent shelving that fills most of the cargo area, or (2) an open cargo area and the van always carries merchandise, material, or equipment used in the trade or business.

Education: Certain job-related education provided to an employee may qualify for exclusion as a working condition benefit. To qualify, the education must meet the same requirements that would apply for determining whether the employee could deduct the expenses had the employee paid the expenses. The education must meet at least one of the following tests:
1. The education is required by the employer or by law for the employee to keep his present salary, status, or job. The required education must serve a bona fide business purpose of the employer, or
2. The education maintains or improves skills needed in the job.

However, even if the education meets one or both of the above tests, it is not qualifying education if it is needed to meet the minimum educational requirements of the employee's present trade or business, or is part of a program of study that will qualify the employee for a new trade or business.

Employer provided transportation for security reasons:[59] The employee may not generally exclude the value of employer-provided transportation as a working condition fringe if such transportation is primarily personal. If, however, for bona fide business-oriented security concerns, the employee purchases transportation that provides him with additional security, the employee may generally deduct the excess of the amount actually paid for the transportation over the amount the employee would have paid for the same mode of transportation absent the bona fide business-oriented security concerns.

A bona fide business-oriented security concern exists only if the facts and circumstances establish a specific basis for concern regarding the safety of the employee. A generalized concern for an employee's safety is not a bona fide business-oriented security concern. Once a bona fide business-oriented security concern is determined to exist with respect to a particular employee, the employer must periodically evaluate the situation for purposes of determining whether the bona fide business-oriented security concern still exists. Example(s) of factors indicating a specific basis for concern regarding the safety of an employee are:
1. A threat of death or kidnapping of, or serious bodily harm to, the employee or a similarly situated employee because of either employee's status as an employee of the employer, or
2. A recent history of violent terrorist activity (such as bombings) in the geographic area in which the transportation is provided, unless that activity is focused on a group of individuals which does not include the employee (or a similarly situated employee of an employer), or occurs to a significant degree only in a location within the geographic area where the employee does not travel.

In addition, the employer must establish an overall security program with respect to the employee involved. This program must include 24-hour protection and must be provided at the employee's residence and work place. However, an employer may make use of an independent security study and follow such recommendations, even if the security is not provided on a 24-hour basis. For example, the security concerns may simply involve travel to a specific geographic area.

59.Treas. Reg. §1.32-5(m).

Example 13.13

Assume that in response to several death threats on the life of A, the president of X a multinational company, X establishes an overall security program for A, including an alarm system at A's home and guards at A's workplace, the use of a vehicle that is specially equipped with alarms, bulletproof glass, and armor plating, and a bodyguard/chauffeur. Assume further that A is driven for both personal and business reasons in the vehicle. Also, assume that but for the bona fide business-oriented security concerns, no part of the overall security program would have been provided to A. With respect to the transportation provided for security reasons, A may exclude as a working condition fringe the value of the special security features of the vehicle and the value attributable to the bodyguard/chauffeur. Thus, if the value of the specially equipped vehicle is $40,000, and the value of the vehicle without the security features is $25,000, A may determine A's inclusion in income attributable to the vehicle as if the vehicle were worth $25,000. A must include in income the value of the availability of the vehicle for personal use.

Example 13.14

Assume that company Z retains an independent security consultant to perform a security study with respect to its chief executive officer. Assume further that, based on an objective assessment of the facts and circumstances, the security consultant reasonably recommends that 24-hour protection is not necessary but that the employee be provided security at his workplace and for ground transportation, but not for air transportation. If company Z follows the recommendations on a consistent basis, an overall security program will be deemed to exist with respect to the workplace and ground transportation security only.

"De Minimis" Fringe Benefits

The term **"de minimis" fringe benefit** is defined in IRC §132(e) as any property or service provided by an employer to an employee that is so small in value that it makes accounting for it unreasonable or administratively impracticable when taking into account the frequency that similar fringes are provided by the employer to employees. "De minimis" is a term that means minimal, very trifling, or small.

Examples of De Minimis Fringe Benefits

The following is an illustrative, but not exclusive, list of de minimis fringe benefits as discussed in the regulations:[60]

- occasional typing of personal letters by a secretary hired by an employer
- occasional personal use of an employer's copying machine, providing that the employer exercises sufficient control and imposes significant restrictions on the personal use of the machine so that at least 85 percent of the use of the machine is for business purposes
- occasional cocktail parties, group meals, or picnics for the employees and their guests
- traditional birthday or holiday gifts or property (not cash) with a low fair market value
- occasional theater or sporting event tickets
- coffee, donuts, or soft drinks
- local telephone calls
- flowers, fruit, or books, or similar property provided to employees under special circumstances (i.e., on account of illness, outstanding performance or family crisis)[61]

---

60. Treas. Reg. §1.132-6.

Examples of Fringe Benefits that are not De Minimis

The regulations also discuss examples of benefits that are not excludable as de minimis benefits:

- season tickets for sporting or theatrical events
- the commuting use of an employer-provided automobile or other vehicle more than one day a month
- membership in a private country club or athletic facility, regardless of the frequency with which the employee uses the facility
- employer-provided group term life insurance on the life of the spouse or child of an employee
- use of employer-owned or leased facilities (such as an apartment, hunting lodge, boat, etc.) for a weekend, unless required for work[62]

The Exclusion

The value of some or all of de minimis fringe benefits may be excluded from an employee's gross income under other statutory provisions or regulations such as the exclusion for meals furnished for the convenience of the employer discussed later in this section.[63]

The frequency of which similar fringes are furnished by the employer to the employee is generally calculated by reference to the frequency of which the employer furnishes the fringes to each individual employee.[64] An example of this employee-measured frequency is where an employer provides a free meal to one employee on a daily basis but not to any other employee, and the value of such meals is not de minimis concerning that one employee even though the meals are infrequently furnished to the employer's entire work force.[65]

Example 13.15

Make You Well Hospital provides meals in the hospital cafeteria free of charge to nurses that work shifts greater than 24 hours. On average, each nurse receives one free meal every two weeks. The hospital also provides the director of the hospital a free meal in the hospital cafeteria every day. While the free meals to the nurses may be de minimis because they are infrequent, the meals to the director are not because they are provided everyday.

Irrespective of the "employee-measured frequency" rule above, the frequency with which the benefits are furnished in the aggregate to the entire work force is used where it would be administratively difficult to determine frequency considering individual employees. [66]

A cash fringe benefit is never excludable unless the cash is for reasonable, occasional meal money or local transportation fare.[67,68] The "occasional" requirement depends on the frequency, availability, and regularity of the benefit. The furnishing of meals, money, or local transportation fare on a regular or routine basis is not considered to be "occasional."[69] Further, the meals, meal money, or local

---

61. Treas. Reg. §1.132-6(e)(1).
62. Treas. Reg. §1.132-6(e)(2).
63. Treas. Reg. §1.132-6(e)(2).
64. Treas. Reg. §1.132-6(b)(1).
65. Treas. Reg. §1.132-6(b)(1).
66. Treas. Reg. §1.132-6(b)(2).
67. IRC §132(a).
68. Treas. Reg. §1.132-6(d)(2).
69. Treas. Reg. §1.132-6(d)(2)(i)(A).

transportation fare must be provided due to overtime work necessitating an extension of the employee's normal work schedule.[70] The meals or meal money are excludable if they are provided to allow the employee to work overtime. For instance, meal money given to the employee for meals consumed during overtime work satisfies this test.[71]

Example 13.16

MAD Dog LLC is a well respected publisher of financial planning materials. MAD Dog requires its employees to work overtime when projects have to be completed by certain deadlines. When employees work overtime, MAD Dog often brings in food for the staff. As long as the overtime is deemed occasional and the meals are provided to allow employees to work longer hours, it will not be included in the income of the employees.

De Minimis Meals

When meals or meal money furnished is so small in value that accounting for it is unreasonable or administratively impractical, the de minimis fringe benefits exclusion will apply. There is some overlap between de minimis meals and meals furnished for the "convenience of the employer" under IRC §119. In numerous lawsuits, employers attempt to argue that meals furnished satisfy both de minimis fringe benefit requirements and meals for the convenience of the employer.[72] Aside from coffee, donuts, soft drinks, occasional meals or meal money to enable the employee to work overtime, and occasional picnics and parties, this exclusion deals largely with employer-operated eating facilities.[73] Employer-operated eating facilities for employees qualify for this exclusion if:

- the facility is located on or near the business premises of the employer, and
- the annual revenue of the facility is equal to or greater than the direct operating costs of the facility.[74]

Quick Quiz 13.5

1. Working condition fringe benefits may be discriminatory and still maintain the favored tax treatment.
   a. True
   b. False

2. A de minimis employee fringe benefit is property or service provided to an employee that is so small in value that accounting for it is unreasonable.
   a. True
   b. False

True, True.

If access to the facility is available on substantially the same terms to all members of a group of employees defined under a reasonable classification set up by the employer that does not discriminate in favor of highly compensated employees, then this de minimis fringe benefit is excludable from the gross income of all employees including highly compensated employees.[75] The revenue from furnishing a meal is presumed to be equal to the facility's direct operating costs if its value can be excluded from an employee's gross income.[76] It is here where the de minimis meal rule overlaps with meals furnished for the convenience of the employer rule.[77] Under §119, an employee may exclude meals furnished on the business premises of the employer for the convenience of the employer.[78]

---

70. Treas. Reg. §1.132-6(d)(2)(i)(B).
71. Treas. Reg. §1.132-6(d)(2)(i)(C).
72. See *Boyd Gaming Corp. v. Commissioner of Internal Revenue Service,* 17 F. 3d. 1096 (9th Cir. 1999), discussed later in this Chapter. See also IRC §119.
73. The facility may be operated "directly or through a hired third party" by the employer and owned or leased by the employer as well.
74. IRC §132(e).
75. IRC §132(e)(2).
76. *Id.*
77. See also *Boyd Gaming Corporation, supra,* at page 1099.

TCJA 2017 Modification

One attractive feature of de minimis meals prior to 2018 was that they were fully deductible for income tax purposes by the employer without the 50 percent statutory limit on deductions for cost of meals yet excludable from the employee's gross income. However, for tax years 2018 through 2025, TCJA 2017 expanded the 50 percent limitation to employer expenses for food for employees to include de minimus meals, and completely removed deductibility after 2025. However, under the Taxpayer Certainty and Disaster Tax Relief Act (TCDTRA) of 2020, an exception to the 50 percent deduction limit applies to food and beverages provided by a restaurant, allowing such meals to be fully deductible by the employer when paid or incurred after December 31, 2020 and before January 1, 2023.

De Minimis Transportation

Transportation provided with minimal value may also qualify as a de minimis" fringe benefit. If an employer furnishes an employee with taxi fare based on unusual circumstances and due to unsafe conditions, the excess of the value of each one way trip over $1.50 is excluded from the employee's gross income.[79] Unusual circumstances are determined by consideration of all facts and circumstances relating to the situation, like a temporary change in employee's work schedule or being called to the work place at 1:00 a.m. when an employee usually works from 8:00 a.m. to 4:00 p.m.[80] Factors indicating whether it is unsafe for an employee to use other available means of transportation are the history of crime in the geographic area surrounding the employee's workplace or residence and the time of day during which the employee must commute.

Prior to 2018, a public transit pass, tokens, or fare cards provided to the employee at a discount to defray commuting costs could be excluded from the employee's gross income as a de minimis fringe benefit if the discount or net value of the employee's costs did not exceed $21.00 per month.[81] However, TCJA 2017 created IRC §274(l), which provides that no deduction is permitted for any expense incurred for providing any transportation, or any payment or reimbursement, to an employee in connection with travel between the employee's residence and place of employment, except as necessary for ensuring the safety of the employee for years after 2017.

Benefits Exceeding Value and Frequency Limits - All or Nothing

If a benefit is provided to an employee that is not deemed de minimis due to excess value or excess frequency, then no amount is considered a de minimis fringe.[82] If, for example, an employer reimburses an employee $40.00 per month for taxi fare, then the entire $40.00 per month will be included in the employee's gross income, not merely the $19.00 ($40 minus the $21 total cost threshold) per month excess value.

Example 13.17

Jane works for ABC Company. ABC reimburses Jane $15 per month for a ferry pass. The ferry pass costs Jane $40 per month. In this situation, $15 is excluded from Jane's gross income. If in the same example, ABC reimburses Jane $21 per month for the ferry pass, $21 is excluded from Jane's income. If in the same example, ABC reimburses Jane $25 per month, then none of the $25 could be excluded from Jane's income.

---

78. IRC §119(a).
79. Treas. Reg. §1.132-6(d)(2)(iii).
80. Treas. Reg. §1.132-6(d)(2)(iii)(B).
81. Treas. Reg. §1.132-6(d)(1).
82. Treas. Reg. §1.132-6(d)(4).

Nondiscrimination Rules

The nondiscrimination rules do not apply in determining the amount of a de minimis fringe benefit or working condition fringe benefit.[83] However, the nondiscrimination rules do apply to most other types of fringe benefits. Thus, the ability to classify a benefit that would ordinarily not allow discrimination as a de minimis fringe benefit may allow the employer to in effect discriminate.

CASE STUDY 13.6

The issues of de minimis meals for the convenience of the employer were presented to the United States 9th Circuit Court of Appeals in **Boyd Gaming Corp. v. Commissioner of Internal Revenue Service.**[1]

Although decided in 1999, the Boyd Gaming case dealt with facts occurring in the 1987 - 1988 taxable years when 26 U.S.C. §274(n) provided for an 80% cap on meal and entertainment expenses. Concerned with tax laws that purportedly "unfairly allowed high income taxpayers to structure their business affairs in a manner that generated deductions for personal living expenses," Congress imposed a cap on the amount of deductions for business meals and entertainment.[2] Boyd Gaming Corporation and California Hotel and Casino and their subsidiaries were hotel and casino operators that required their employees to stay on the business premises throughout their work shift, resulting in the employees receiving free meals at onsite cafeterias. Boyd asserted that it was exempt from the then 80% cap on deductions because the meals provided were "de minimis fringe benefits."[3]

The Tax Court rejected Boyd's argument and ruled that Boyd's deductions were limited to 80% under §274(n). The United States Ninth Circuit disagreed and reversed the Tax Court, finding that Boyd's stay-on-the-premises policy rendered the employee's meals furnished for the convenience of the employer and the meals constituted de minimis fringe benefits under 26 U.S.C. §132(e)(2).[4]

More specifically, Boyd offered reasons for its stay-on-the-premises policy, including security and efficiency concerns,[5] maintaining work force control,[6] handling business emergencies and continuous customer demands, and the impracticability of obtaining meals within a reasonable proximity.

1. *Boyd Gaming Corp. v. Commissioner of Internal of Revenue,* 177 F. 3d 1096 (9th Cir. 1999).
2. 177 F. 3d at 1097.
3. Id. (citing 26 U.S.C. §274(n)(2)); 26 U.S.C. §132 (e)).
4. *Boyd Gaming,* 177 F. 3d at 1097.
5. The Court described the facts behind Boyd's stay on the premises policy. The casino environment is one in which vast amounts of cash flow in fast-moving transactions and special security precautions are imposed by state regulations, and many of Boyd's employees handle or have easy access to cash and gambling chips. Consequently, each property performs special check-out procedures for certain employees before they are permitted to leave the premises. The "stay-on-premises" policy minimizes the number of entries and departures during each work shift, thereby reducing security risks and the costs of security measures.
6. Boyd contends that the "stay-on-premises" requirement allows it to maintain tight control over its workforce, thereby reducing the chances of employees succumbing to the distractions and temptations of the "festive" Las Vegas atmosphere.

83. Treas. Reg. §1-132-5(q).

CASE STUDY 13.6 CONTINUED

The Court analyzed the statutes that dealt with the test of deductibility and indicated that §132(e)(2) defined de minimis fringe benefits as an employer's operation of an eating facility for employees if the facility was located on or near the business premises of the employer and the revenue derived from the facility met or exceeded the direct operating costs of the facility.

Because there was no evidence as to the revenue derived, Boyd had to rely on the statutory presumption in §132(e)(2) that treats revenue as equal to operating costs if employees are entitled to exclude the value of the meals under IRC §119. Thus, in order to determine the applicability of the 80% cap on deductions, the Court resorted to §132(e)(2), which in turn required an analysis of §119's "convenience of the employer" test.[1] Boyd asserted that the stay-on-the-premises requirement constituted a "substantial non-compensatory business reason" for furnishing meals. The Court reasoned that Boyd furnished meals as a consequence of its stay-on-the-premises policy, as employees could not leave the premises during their shifts. The Court articulated that common sense dictated that, once the policy was embraced, the employees had no choice but to eat on the premises and were "indispensable to the proper discharge of the employee's duties."[2] Because Boyd supported its "closed campus policy" with adequate evidence of legitimate business reasons, the Court found that non-compensatory business reasons existed, and thus the employees could exclude the meals under §119, which consequently meant that the presumption in §132(e)(2) applied. Once the presumption of §132(e)(2) applied, the cap on deductions was inapplicable and Boyd was allowed to deduct all meal expenses from its income.

1. IRC §119 (B) (4) considers meals to be furnished for the convenience of the employer if they are provided to more than half of the employees for a "substantial non-compensatory business reason." *Boyd Gaming,* 177 F.3d at 1099-1100.
2. *Boyd Gaming,* 177 F.3d at 1100.

Exhibit 13.4 | Rules for Selected Fringe Benefits (2021 IRS Pub. 15b)

	Treatment Under Employment Taxes		
Type of Fringe Benefit	Income Tax Withholding	Social Security and Medicare (including Additional Medicare Tax when wages are paid in excess of $200,000)[1]	Federal Unemployment (FUTA)
Accident and health benefits	Exempt,[2] except for long-term care benefits provided through a flexible spending or similar arrangement.	Exempt, except for certain payments to S corporation employees who are 2% shareholders.	Exempt
Achievement awards	Exempt[2] up to $1,600 for qualified plan awards ($400 for nonqualified awards).		
Adoption assistance	Exempt[2,3]	Taxable	Taxable
Athletic facilities	Exempt if substantially all use during the calendar year is by employees, their spouses, and their dependent children, and the facility is operated by the employer on premises owned or leased by the employer.		
De minimis (minimal) benefits	Exempt	Exempt	Exempt
Dependent care assistance	Exempt[3] up to certain limits, $5,000 ($2,500 for married employee filing separate return).		
Educational assistance	Exempt up to $5,250 of benefits each year.		
Employee discounts	Exempt[3] up to certain limits.		
Employee stock options	Discussed in Chapter 12.		
Employer-provided cell phones	Exempt if provided primarily for noncompensatory business purposes.		
Group-term life insurance coverage	Exempt	Exempt[2,4,6] up to cost of $50,000 of coverage. (Special rules apply to former employees.)	Exempt
Health savings accounts (HSAs)	Exempt for qualified individuals up to the HSA contribution limits.		
Lodging on your business premises	Exempt[2] if furnished on your business premises, for your convenience, and as a condition of employment.		
Meals	Exempt[2] if furnished on your business premises for your convenience.		
	Exempt if de minimis.		
No-additional-cost services	Exempt[3]	Exempt[3]	Exempt[3]
Retirement planning services	Exempt[5]	Exempt[5]	Exempt[5]
Transportation (commuting) benefits	Exempt[2] up to certain limits if for rides in a commuter highway vehicle and/or transit passes ($270) or qualified parking ($270).		
	Exempt if de minimis.		
Tuition reduction	Exempt[3] if for undergraduate education (or graduate education if the employee performs teaching or research activities).		
Working condition benefits	Exempt	Exempt	Exempt

[1] Or other railroad retirement taxes, if applicable.

[2] Exemption doesn't apply to S corporation employees who are 2% shareholders.

[3] Exemption doesn't apply to certain highly compensated employees under a program that favors those employees.

[4] Exemption doesn't apply to certain key employees under a plan that favors those employees.

[5] Exemption doesn't apply to services for tax preparation, accounting, legal, or brokerage services.

[6] You must include in your employee's wages the cost of group-term life insurance beyond $50,000 worth of coverage, reduced by the amount the employee paid toward the insurance. Report it as wages in boxes 1, 3, and 5 of the employee's Form W-2. Also, show it in box 12 with code "C." The amount is subject to social security and Medicare taxes, and you may, at your option, withhold federal income tax.

Qualified Moving Expense Reimbursements

Before 2018, and for tax years beginning after December 31, 2025, qualified moving expense reimbursements from an employer are excluded from gross income by employees. TCJA 2017 eliminated both the deduction for qualified moving expenses and the exclusion from income of qualified moving expense reimbursements. TCJA 2017 provided only one exception to this rule - Members of the Armed Forces (or their spouse or dependents) on active duty who move pursuant to a military order and incident to a permanent change of station may deduct amounts attributable to in-kind moving and storage expenses, and may exclude from income any reimbursements or allowances received for these expenses.

For tax years before 2018 and after 2025, a **qualified moving expense reimbursement** includes direct or indirect payment by the employer to pay for the cost of moving an employee's family and belongings. In order to qualify for exclusion by the employee, the reimbursement must be for expenses that would be deductible (for AGI) by the employee as moving expenses under IRC Section 217 if paid by the employee. Expenses such as house hunting expenses and meals are not eligible to be deducted as moving expenses.

Example 13.18

Monica paid $3,800 to move her family and belongings to her new work location with the same employer. All $3,800 would be deductible under IRC Section 217. If her employer paid her $3,800 as reimbursement for her moving expenses, she can exclude the $3,800 from gross income (but she could not also deduct the $3,800). If Monica had deducted the moving expenses in one year and received the reimbursement in the next year, the tax benefit rule would prevent her from excluding the reimbursement from gross income. If the employer had reimbursed Monica for nondeductible expenses, the reimbursement would have to be included in Monica's gross income as well. After 2017, aforementioned tax treatment for Monica would only be correct if she were an active member of the armed forces and moved pursuant to a military order.

Before 2018 and after 2025, both employees and leased employees qualify for the exclusion of qualified moving expense reimbursements. Moving expense reimbursements can discriminate in favor of highly compensated employees.

Qualified Transportation and Parking

The regulations provide for an exclusion of the value of qualified transportation benefits from an employee's gross income.[84] This exclusion for transportation benefits is subject to the following limitations:
- $270 per month (2021) for commuter highway transportation and transit passes combined.
- $270 per month (2021) for qualified parking.

For any given month, if the value of a benefit is more than the limit, then any excess amount above the limit, less any amount the employee paid, is included in the employee's income. The excess may not qualify as a de minimis benefit.

---

84. Treas. Reg. §1.132-9.

After 2008 and before 2018, an employee who does not receive any of the transportation fringe benefits explained above, may exclude up to $20 per month of qualified bicycle commuting reimbursements from an employer. Qualified bicycle commuting reimbursements are employer reimbursements for the purchase, improvement, repair, or storage of a bicycle that is regularly used for travel between the employee's residence and place of employment. TCJA 2017 suspends the exclusion for qualified bicycle commuting reimbursement from 2018 through 2025.

Covered Employees

The provision of the benefit may be discriminatory. Current employees and leased employees providing services substantially full time for at least a year under the employer's control are considered employees under this exclusion. Nonetheless, those who own two percent or more of the stock of an S corporation are not considered employees.

Excludable Transportation and Parking Benefits

The following examples are excludable transportation and parking benefits:
- a transit pass
- a ride in a commuter highway vehicle between the home of the employee and the workplace
- qualified parking[85]

The value of each one of these benefits are excludable from an employee's gross income without regard to whether one or all are provided by the employer to the employee. **Qualified parking** is parking provided by the employer on or near the employer's business premises. It also includes parking on or near the location where employees commute to work using mass transit, carpools, or commuter highway vehicles but not at the employee's home.

Qualified transportation benefits may be given by the employer directly or through a bona fide reimbursement arrangement. However, cash reimbursements for transit passes may qualify only when a voucher is not readily available for direct distribution by the employer.

TCJA 2017 Modification

TCJA 2017 disallows a deduction by the employer for expenses associated with providing any qualified transportation fringe to employees of a taxpayer after 2017. In addition, the new law disallows deductions for any expense incurred for providing transportation (or any payment or reimbursement) for commuting between the employee's residence and place of employment, except as necessary for ensuring the safety of an employee. Thus, while the fringe is excludable from employee's taxable income, it is not deductible by the employer after 2017.

85. Treas. Reg. §1.132-9.

Adoption Assistance Programs

Ordinarily, an employee may exclude from an employee's gross income amounts paid for, or expenses incurred, by the employer for qualified adoption expenses concerning the adoption of a child by an employee if these amounts are furnished according to a written adoption assistance program.[86, 87] An employer may establish a written **adoption assistance program** intended to promote adoption and that will pay expenses related to an adoption not exceeding $14,400 for 2021 to an employee. The limitation of $14,400 for 2021 applies to an adoption for each child. The amount paid is excluded from the employee's income, but there is a phaseout of this exclusion starting at $216,660 of adjusted gross income (AGI) for 2021 through $256,660. If the employee's AGI is greater than or equal to $256,660 for 2021, then the exclusion is eliminated.

The plan must comply with nondiscrimination requirements. The plan may pay for qualified adoption expenses consisting of adoption fees and related charges, court costs, attorney's fees, and other expenses directly tied to the adoption of a child under age 18 or who is physically or mentally incapable of caring for themselves.[88] While the payments or reimbursements made under the program are excluded from an employee's gross income, such payments continue to be subject to Social Security, Medicare, and federal unemployment taxes.

Taxpayers are also able to claim a credit for expenses incurred that are associated with adopting an eligible child. The credit, which is no longer refundable for years after December 31, 2011, has the same limits and income phase out ranges as discussed above with adoption assistance programs. Taxpayers may be able to make use of both the exclusion and the credit in certain circumstances.

Example 13.19

Madelyn paid $10,000 in qualified adoption expenses for the adoption of an eligible child. Under a qualified adoption assistance program, Madelyn's employer reimbursed her for $4,000 of those expenses. Madelyn may exclude the $4,000 reimbursement from her income. However, because of the employer reimbursement, $4,000 of her expenses no longer meets the definition of qualified adoption expenses. As a result, Madelyn's maximum adoption credit is limited to $6,000 ($10,000 - $4,000).

Example 13.20

Haylee paid $10,000 in qualified adoption expenses for the adoption of an eligible child. Under a qualified adoption assistance program, Haylee's employer paid an additional $6,000 of qualified adoption expenses on her behalf. Her total qualified adoption expenses are $16,000 ($10,000 + $6,000). Because the expenses paid by Haylee were different from the expenses paid by her employer, Haylee may exclude the $6,000 that her employer paid from her income and may claim a credit for the $10,000 of qualified adoption expenses she paid.

86.IRC §137.
87.IRC §137(a).
88.IRC §23(d)(2).

Example 13.21

Mitchell paid $30,000 in qualified adoption expenses to adopt an eligible foreign child, and the adoption became final in 2021. Under a qualified adoption assistance program, Mitchell's employer reimbursed him for $14,400 of those expenses. Mitchell may exclude the $14,400 reimbursement from his income. The remaining $15,600 of expenses ($30,000 - $14,400) continue to be qualified adoption expenses that are eligible for the credit. However, Mitchell's credit is dollar-limited to $14,400. The remaining amount of expenses may never be claimed as a credit or excluded from gross income.

Awards and Prizes

Certain prizes and awards (as defined below) given to employees by their employer may be excluded from the employees' gross income.[89] An employee achievement award is defined in the IRC as an item of tangible personal property that is:

- transferred by an employer to an employee for length of service achievement or safety achievement,
- awarded as part of a meaningful presentation, and
- awarded under conditions and circumstances that do not create a significant likelihood of the payment of disguised compensation.[90]

> **Key Concepts**
>
> 1. What requirements are necessary for awards and prizes to be excluded from income?
>
> 2. What requirements are necessary for qualified tuition reduction plans to be excluded from income?

For purposes of this section, the term "tangible personal property" does not include cash. Other items that will not be considered tangible personal property include vacations, meals, lodging, tickets to theater and sporting events, and stocks, bonds, and other securities.

Limits on Value of Awards

An employee is allowed to exclude from gross income the value of any employee achievement awards insofar as the cost of the award does not exceed the following limitations:[91]

- $400 for all nonqualified plan awards when added to the employer's cost for all other employee achievement awards made to such employee during the taxable year that are not qualified plan awards, and
- $1,600 for all qualified plan awards when added to the employer's cost for all other employee achievement awards made to such employee during the taxable year (including employee achievement awards that are not qualified plan awards).[92]

Only the excess amount over the $400 and $1,600 limitations is included in the employees income (but not deductible by the employer); the initial $400 or $1,600 limitations are not included in the employees' income (and deductible by the employer). In other words, if an employee achievement award exceeds the $1,600 limit and constitutes a qualified plan award, then only the excess amount above $1,600 is included in the employee's gross income and no penalty occurs that would render the entire amount taxable.

---

89. IRC §274.
90. IRC §§274(j)(3)(A) and 74(c).
91. IRC §§274(j)(1) and (2).
92. IRC §274(j)(2).

If the cost of the award provided to an employee is more than the employer's allowable deduction, then the larger of the following amounts must be included in the employee's wages: (a) the portion of the cost that is more than the employer's allowable deduction (up to the value of the award), (b) the amount of the value of the award that exceeds the employer's allowable deduction.

Qualified Plan Award

A "**qualified plan award**" is defined as an employee achievement award bestowed as part of an established written plan of the taxpayer that does not discriminate in favor of highly compensated employees (within the meaning of §414(q)) for eligibility or benefits.[93] However, there are limitations on this exclusion. If the "average cost" of all employee achievement awards provided by the employer during the year exceeds $400, then such employee achievement award shall not be treated as a qualified plan award for any taxable year.[94]

Example 13.22

In 2021, J Company presents employee length of service awards to seven employees for a total cost to the employer of $2,100. The average cost of all awards is $300 ($2,100÷7). Since the average cost of all awards does not exceed $400, the awards are considered qualified plan awards provided there is a written plan that does not discriminate in favor of highly paid employees.

Special Rules

In the event that an employee achievement award is granted by a partnership, the deduction limitations apply to the partnership as well as to each member.[95] For length of service awards, an award is not deemed as being provided for length of service achievement if it is accepted during the recipient's first five years of employment, or within any other five year period.[96] Meanwhile, an item is not considered a safety achievement award if:

- such safety achievement awards have been granted to more than 10 percent of the employees of the employer during the taxable year, or
- such item is awarded to a manager, administrator, clerical employee, or other professional employee.[97]

Covered Employees

Under this exclusion, employees are considered (1) current employees, or (2) leased employees providing services to an employer on a substantially full-time basis for at least a year if the services performed are under the

Quick Quiz 13.7

1. A cash award of $300 given to an employee as part of a written plan is excludable from the employee's income.
   a. True
   b. False

2. Adoption assistance benefits may be excluded from the employee's gross income and are not subject to Social Security and Medicare taxes.
   a. True
   b. False

False, False.

---

93. IRC §274(j)(3)(B)(i).
94. IRC §274(J)(3)(ii). For purposes of this provision, average cost shall be determined by including the entire cost of all qualified plan awards given by the employer without taking into account employee achievement awards of nominal value (less than $50).
95. IRC §274(j)(4)(A).
96. IRC §274(j)(4)(B).
97. IRC §274(j)(4)(C).

greater shareholders of S corporation are not considered employees of the corporation for this exclusion.

Example 13.23

Kathleen is a professor at the University of Georgia. She receives an employee achievement award for her work during the year. She is given a crystal trophy and matching serving dishes for a total value of $1,500. The award is a qualified plan award. Is this amount excluded from her income for that taxable year?

Answer: Yes. In this scenario, Kathleen can exclude from her income $1,500 because it is a qualified plan award. If the plan was not qualified, then Kathleen could only exclude up to $400.

TCJA 2017 Modification

TCJA 2017 did not include a repeal for awards and prizes but did clarify that tangible personal property awards for employee achievement are still deductible by an employer and may be excluded from employee's taxable gross income. TCJA 2017 provides a definition for tangible personal property, which shall not include cash, cash equivalents, gift cards, vacations, meals, lodging, tickets to theatre or sporting events, stocks, bonds, or other similar non-tangible personal items.

Example 13.24

Fiona has been an awesome employee of DE for the last ten years. As part of the recognition of her ten years of service as of June 2021, she is presented with a plaque recognizing her ten years of service and a gift card worth $300 to a local restaurant. The definition of tangible personal property requires that the $300 for the gift card be included into income for Fiona.

Example 13.25

Robin has been an awesome employee of ME for the last ten years. As part of the recognition of her ten years of service as of June 2021, she is presented with a $395 watch with an inscription recognizing her ten years of service. Robin does not have to recognize any income as a result of the award because the watch qualifies as tangible personal property.

VALUATION RULES APPLYING TO FRINGE BENEFITS

In determining whether a fringe benefit is excludable from taxation, a common problem is the valuation of the fringe benefit in the event that the entire fringe benefit is taxable or a portion of the fringe benefit is taxable. Various taxation rules apply in determining the value of a fringe benefit. Ordinarily, the general valuation rule applies to the value of a fringe benefit. However, there are special valuation rules for certain benefits, which are discussed in this section. Aside from the general valuation rule, there are special valuation rules for employee transportation benefits, which include the cents per mile rule, the commuting rule, the lease value rule, and the unsafe conditions commuting rule.

The General Valuation Rule

Most fringe benefits are valued under the general valuation rule. Basically, the fair market value should be the value assigned to a fringe benefit. Under the regulations, the amount that an employee would be required to pay a third party in an arm's-length transaction to purchase or lease the benefit, or what one would pay in the market place, is considered the fair market value of a fringe benefit. This figure is different than the cost an employer may incur in providing the benefit to an employee. Likewise, this figure is not what an employee considers to be the value or the amount the employer would be willing to pay for the fringe benefit. Instead, the amount that is determined to be fair market value depends on the facts and circumstances of the particular situation.

For instance, with employer-provided vacations, the fair market value of an employer-provided vacation is the amount the employer would have to pay a third party, travel agent, or directly to the service provider for the same or similar vacation on the same or comparable terms in the geographic area where the vacation is taking place. Additionally, when ascertaining the value of an employer-provided vehicle, the fair market value is the amount the employee would need to pay a third party or dealership to lease the same or similar vehicle in the same or similar terms in the geographic area where the employer uses the vehicle. The duration of the lease is also relevant in this determination, so the comparable lease term should be a similar period as the period provided by the employer-provided vehicle. In other words, if the employer is providing the vehicle to the employee for a two year period, then comparable lease terms of two years should be used in determining the fair market value.

> **⠿ Key Concepts**
>
> 1. How are employee fringe benefits valued under the general rule?
> 2. What is the cents per mile rule?
> 3. What is the commuting rule?
> 4. What is the lease value rule?
> 5. What is the unsafe conditions commuting rule?

The Cents Per Mile Rule

Valuation under the **cents per mile rule** requires multiplying the standard mileage rate by the total miles the employee drives the vehicle for personal purposes. Personal use is any use of the vehicle other than use in the employer's trade or business. The standard business mileage rate is 56 cents per mile (2021). Of course, the vehicle must be provided by an employer to the employee for both business use and personal use. Under the regulations, a vehicle is considered to be any motorized wheeled vehicle, which would include those manufactured primarily for use on public roads, streets, and highways.[98] One important issue in using this valuation is whether the vehicle is used regularly in the employee's business.[99]

---

98. Treas. Reg. §1.61-21(f)(4).
99. Treas. Reg. §1.61-21(f).

The test for determining whether the vehicle is used regularly in the employee's business requires that any of the following conditions are satisfied:

- 50 percent or more of the total annual mileage of the vehicle is for the employer's trade or business,
- the employer sponsors a commuting pool that uses the vehicle each work day to transport no less than three employees to and from work, or
- the vehicle is "regularly used," and not subject to infrequent business use such as occasional trips between multiple business premises, and this regular use is in the employer's business based on all the facts and circumstances.[100]

The employer cannot use the cents per mile rule for an automobile if its value when first made available to any employee for personal use is more than an amount determined by the IRS as the "maximum automobile value" for the year. The cents per mile rule can be utilized, however, if the employer reasonably expects the vehicle to be regularly used in its business during the calender year or if the vehicle meets the mileage test.

The "mileage test" is satisfied if: (1) the vehicle is driven at least an annual rate of 10,000 miles per year, and (2) where the vehicle is used "primarily" during the year by employees.[101] However, use of the vehicle by another individual who is not an employee should not be treated as use by an employee.

Notably, the value of maintenance and insurance for the vehicle are "built in" the cents per mile rate. The rate of any other service provided by the employer to the employee for a vehicle is not included in the cents per mile, and therefore use of the general valuation rule should be utilized to value those services.

The Commuting Rule

The value of this fringe benefit is determined by multiplying each one way commute from home to work or from work to home by $1.50. This value applies to more than one employee irrespective of whether one or more employees ride in the vehicle during the commute. The **commuting rule** is allowed if all of the following requirements are satisfied:

- the employer provides the employee the vehicle for use in the employer's business and the employer requires the employee to commute in the vehicle for bona fide non-compensatory business reasons,[102]
- a written policy is established and implemented whereby the employer does not permit the employee to use a vehicle for personal use other than for commuting or minimal personal use,[103]
- other than de minimis personal use and commuting, the employee does not use the vehicle for personal use, and[104]
- if the vehicle used is an automobile, the employee who uses the automobile for commuting must not be a control employee.[105] Rather than using the definition of a control employee, an employer may choose to define a control employee as a highly compensated employee.[106]

---

100. Treas. Reg. §1.61-21(e)(1)(iv).

101. For instance, if the vehicle was owned or leased only during a portion of the year, the 10,000 mile requirement is reduced proportionately.

102. As a general rule this requirement is satisfied if the vehicle is used each work day to carry no less than three employees to and from work in a commuting pool sponsored by the employer.

103. Minimal, or de minimis, personal use is considered use of the vehicle for a personal errand either going to and from work or between employee's home and a business delivery.

104. This is the essential difference between commuting rule and the cents per mile rule. Under the cents per mile rule, valuation is determined by taking a snap shot of the miles used for personal miles v. the miles used for work-related business. However, the commuting rule zeroes in simply on the commuting and de minimis personal use, and therefore prohibits significant or more than minimal personal use of the vehicle.

The Lease Value Rule

According to the **lease value rule**, the value of an employer-provided automobile is determined by using the automobile's annual lease value. According to the general rule, the lease value of the automobile used by the employee in the employer's business is reduced by the amount excluded from the employee's wages as a working condition fringe benefit. Notably, the employer may choose to include the entire lease value in the employee's wages. The annual lease value of an automobile is determined by first ascertaining the automobile's fair market value on the first day it is available to any employee for personal use. Next, through reference to the Annual Lease Value Table (**Exhibit 13.5**), the annual lease value is provided by the applicable fair market value of the automobile. Automobiles with a fair market value exceeding $59,999 will have an annual lease value that is equal to 25 percent of the automobile's fair market value plus $500.

Example 13.26

$60,000 automobile (25% x $60,000) = $15,000, plus $500 = $15,500. Under this example, the annual lease value of a $60,000 vehicle would be $15,500.

As discussed earlier in this section, the fair market value of an automobile is the amount an individual would pay to purchase the automobile in an arm's-length transaction from a third party in the geographic area that the same automobile is bought or leased. The fair market value would therefore include an amount for all expenses related to the sale including tax, title and license, sales tax, and applicable fees. Only under these circumstances would a true fair market value be provided.

Importantly, safe harbor provisions apply to the determination of fair market value of an automobile. The safe harbor value may be used for an automobile purchased at arm's-length by utilizing the employer's costs (including tax, title, license, and other purchase expenses) as long as the employer is not the manufacturer of the automobile.

If the automobile is leased, safe harbor value for the lease can be any of the following:
- Invoice price including options and additions of the manufacturer, plus four percent,
- The suggested retail price of the manufacturer, minus eight percent, or
- The nationally recognized retail value of the automobile if that retail value is reasonable for the automobile.

Similar to the commuting rule, the annual lease value in the table provided includes, and has built in, the value of maintenance and insurance on the automobile. The annual lease value should not be reduced by the value of any services that were not provided by the employer. For instance, annual lease value should not be reduced by the value of a maintenance service contract or insurance if the employer did not provide the maintenance or insurance. Conversely, the annual lease value does not include the value of

---

105. A control employee is defined by the Treasury Regulations for the year 2021, as (1) an officer whose pay is $115,000 or more, (2) a director, (3) an employee who makes $235,000 or more, (4) an employee owning 1% interest or more in the employer's business, or (5) an elected official. See IRS Publication 15-b.

106. Under the Treasury Regulations, a highly compensated employee for 2021 is an employee who (1) was a 5% owner at any time during the year or preceding year, or (2) the employee was paid more than $130,000 for the preceding year unless the employee was not also in the top 20% for employee compensation the preceding year.

fuel provided to an employee for personal use. The value of the fuel must be included separately in the employee's wages. If any other service other than maintenance and insurance is provided by the employer to the employee for an automobile, the fair market value of that service must be determined based on the fair market value of that service.

The annual lease values that are determined on an automobile may be prorated if an employee was provided an automobile for a period of 30 or more days but less than the entire calender year. The annual lease value is prorated by multiplying the annual lease value by a percentage derived by dividing the number of days of availability by 365 days. Treasury Regulations prohibit use of a prorated annual lease value if the reduction of federal taxes is the main reason the automobile is unavailable during the remainder of the calender year. Nonetheless, if the employer provides an automobile to an employee for a period continuously that is less than 30 days, a daily lease value is assigned. The daily lease value is determined by multiplying the annual lease value by the percentage derived by dividing four times the number of days of availability by 365.[107] The equation is as follows:

$$\text{Daily Lease Value} = \text{Annual Lease Value} \times \frac{(4 \times \text{Number of Days of Availability})}{365}$$

For instance, if the employee used the automobile continuously for 25 days and the annual lease value was $5,100, the daily lease value is calculated as follows.

$$\$5,100 \times \frac{(4 \times 25)}{365} = \$1,397 \text{ Daily Lease Value}$$

107. Treas. Reg. §1.61-21(d)(4)(ii).

Exhibit 13.5 | Annual Lease Value Table

(1) Automobile FMV	(2) Annual Lease
$ 0 to 999	$ 600
1,000 to 1,999	850
2,000 to 2,999	1,100
3,000 to 3,999	1,350
4,000 to 4,999	1,600
5,000 to 5,999	1,850
6,000 to 6,999	2,100
7,000 to 7,999	2,350
8,000 to 8,999	2,600
9,000 to 9,999	2,850
10,000 to 10,999	3,100
11,000 to 11,999	3,350
12,000 to 12,999	3,600
13,000 to 13,999	3,850
14,000 to 14,999	4,100
15,000 to 15,999	4,350
16,000 to 16,999	4,600
17,000 to 17,999	4,850
18,000 to 18,999	5,100
19,000 to 19,999	5,350
20,000 to 20,999	5,600
21,000 to 21,999	5,850
22,000 to 22,999	6,100
23,000 to 23,999	6,350
24,000 to 24,999	6,600
25,000 to 25,999	6,850
26,000 to 27,999	7,250
28,000 to 29,999	7,750
30,000 to 31,999	8,250
32,000 to 33,999	8,750
34,000 to 35,999	9,250
36,000 to 37,999	9,750
38,000 to 39,999	10,250
40,000 to 41,999	10,750
42,000 to 43,999	11,250
44,000 to 45,999	11,750
46,000 to 47,999	12,250
48,000 to 49,999	12,750
50,000 to 51,999	13,250
52,000 to 53,999	13,750
54,000 to 55,999	14,250
56,000 to 57,999	14,750
58,000 to 59,999	15,250

For automobiles with an FMV of more than $59,999, the annual lease value equals (0.25 × the FMV of the automobile) + $500.

Publication 15b (2020), Table 3-1

The Unsafe Conditions Commuting Rule

The **unsafe conditions commuting rule** determines the value of commuting transportation provided by an employer to a qualified employee solely because of unsafe conditions as $1.50 for a one-way commute.[108] The excess of the value of each one-way trip over $1.50 per one-way commute is excluded from gross income. The unsafe conditions commuting rule requires that a "qualified employee" be provided with the subject commuting transportation. If, however, the employer does not comply with record keeping requirements concerning the wages of the employee, as well as the employee's hours and other conditions and practices, then the employee may not be deemed a qualified employee. For the unsafe conditions commuting rule to apply, the employee must ordinarily walk or use public transportation; the employer must have a written policy against transportation for personal purposes other than commuting because of unsafe conditions; and the employee does not use the transportation for personal reasons beyond commuting due to unsafe conditions.

Finally, whether other "unsafe conditions" exist is determined based on the facts and circumstances of each individual situation. Unsafe conditions exist if a reasonable person would consider it unsafe for the employee to walk or use public transportation at the time of day that the employee is required to commute. Another factor used in determining whether conditions are unsafe is the history of criminal activity in the area surrounding the workplace or home of the employee at the time of day that the employee commutes.

108. Treas. Reg. §1.132-6(d)(2)(iii)(C).

Exhibit 13.6 | Summary Chart

Fringe Benefits	Key Aspects
Meals for the Convenience of the Employer	• The meals are for the convenience of the employer, and • The meals are furnished on the employer's business premises. • 50% deductible from 2018-2025 and not deductible after 2025 (100% deductible in 2021-2022 if provided by a restaurant).
Lodging for the Convenience of the Employer	• The lodging is furnished on the employer's business premises, • The lodging is furnished for the convenience of the employer, and • The employee is required to accept the lodging as a condition of employment.

Athletic Facilities Furnished by the Employer*	• The facility must be:
	  • Operated by the employer,
	  • Located on the employer's premises, and
	  • Substantially all of the use of the facility is by employees or spouses or dependents.
	• Could be gym, pool, tennis court or golf course.
	• Cannot be operated by unrelated entity.

Educational Assistance	• Must be a separate written plan. • Must not be discriminatory. • Not more than 5% of the benefits can go to owners. • Employees cannot have a choice of cash or the education. • Limit: $5,250. • Amounts above the limit are generally W-2 income.
Qualified Tuition Reduction Plan	• Tuition reduction for education below the graduate level. • For an employee, spouse or dependent of the employee. • Must be an eligible educational institution - regular faculty with a regular student body.
Dependant Care Assistance	• Qualifying persons - include children under 13, children who are unable to care for themselves or a spouse who is unable to care for himself. • Services must allow employee to work. • Limit of $5,000 ($10,500 in 2021, ARPA 2021).
No Additional Cost Services	• The service is offered to customers in the ordinary course of business, and • The employer incurs no additional cost (including foregone revenue).
Qualified Employee Discount	• Value of discounts on services or property offered to customers may be excluded. • Limit is 20% for services or the gross profit percentage for merchandise or other property. • Does not apply to real property or investment property.

Summary Chart Continued

Fringe Benefits	Key Aspects
Working Condition Fringe*	• Property or service provided to an employee that enables the employee to perform his work and if paid for by the employee would be deductible as a trade or business expense. • Examples: company car or chauffeur, security.
De Minimis Fringe*	• Any property or service provided to an employee that is so small in value that it makes accounting for it impracticable. • Examples of de minimis: occasional typing of personal letters by a secretary, occasional use of a copy machine, overtime meals, etc. • Examples of what is not de minimis: season tickets to sporting events, membership to a country club, group term life insurance on life of a non employee spouse or child.
Qualified Moving Expense Reimbursement	• TCJA 2017 generally suspends the deduction for moving expenses for taxable years 2018 through 2025. However, during that period, the IRC retains the deduction for moving expenses and the rules providing for exclusions of amounts attributable to in-kind moving and storage expenses (and reimbursements or allowances for these expenses) for members of the Armed Forces (or their spouse or dependents) on active duty that move pursuant to a military order and incident to a permanent change of station.
Qualified Transportation and Parking*	• Includes transportation in a commuter highway vehicle, transit passes and qualified parking. • No longer deductible by the employer after 2017. • 2021 limit of $270 for commuter highway transportation and transit passes combined. • 2021 limit of $270 for qualified parking. • $0 monthly limit for qualified bicycle commuting after 2017.
Adoption Assistance Programs	• Must be a written plan. • Expenses of up to $14,400 for 2021 can be paid by the employer. • Applies to the adoption of a child under the age of 18 or who is physically or mentally unable to care for themselves.
Awards and Prizes	• An employee can exclude the value of an award as long as it does not exceed $400 for nonqualified awards and $1,600 for qualified plan awards. • A qualified plan award requires that the average cost of all employee achievement awards does not exceed $400. • Must meet new definition of tangible personal property.

The fringe benefit can be discriminatory.

DISCUSSION QUESTIONS

SOLUTIONS to the discussion questions can be found exclusively within the chapter. Once you have completed an initial reading of the chapter, go back and highlight the answers to these questions.

1. Define the term "employee fringe benefits" and identify common types of fringe benefits.

2. What are the normal tax consequences to the employer and to the employee of employee fringe benefits?

3. Describe the nondiscrimination rules that apply to employee fringe benefit plans.

4. List the requirements necessary for the value of meals provided by an employer to be excluded from the employee's gross income.

5. List the requirements necessary for the value of lodging provided by an employer to an employee to be excluded from the employee's gross income.

6. List the requirements necessary for the value of athletic facilities provided by an employer to an employee to be excluded from the employee's income.

7. List the requirements necessary for the value of an educational assistance program provided by an employer to an employee to be excluded from the employee's gross income.

8. Describe the requirements necessary for the value of a dependent care assistance program provided by an employer to an employee to be excluded from the employee's gross income.

9. What are employer-provided no-additional-cost services and identify when the value of this fringe benefit may be excluded from an employee's gross income?

10. What are employer-provided qualified employee discounts and identify the requirements for excluding the value of this fringe benefit from an employee's gross income?

11. List the requirements necessary for the value of working condition fringe benefits to be excluded from an employee's gross income.

12. List the requirements necessary for the value of employer provided "de minimis" fringe benefits to be excluded from an employee's gross income.

13. What is an employer provided qualified moving expense reimbursement and what are the requirements for the value of this fringe benefit to be excluded from an employee's gross income?

14. Describe employer provided qualified transportation and parking and identify the requirements for the value of the fringe benefit to be excluded from an employee's gross income.

15. Explain the limitations of excluding the value of employer-provided adoption assistance programs to an employee's gross income.

16. Describe the requirements necessary for the value of employer-provided awards and prizes to be excluded from an employee's gross income.

17. Describe the requirements necessary for employer-provided qualified tuition reduction plans to be excluded from an employee's income.

18. How are employee fringe benefits generally valued?

19. Describe the cents per mile rule.

20. Describe the lease value rule.

21. Describe the unsafe conditions commuting rule.

MULTIPLE CHOICE PROBLEMS

A sample of multiple choice problems is provided below. Additional multiple choice problems are available at money-education.com by accessing the Student Practice Portal.

1. Which of the following benefits provided by an employer to its employees is currently taxable to the employee?
   a. Employees of the DEF Department Store are allowed a 15% discount on store merchandise. DEF's normal gross profit percentage is 20%.
   b. On a space-available basis, undergraduate tuition is waived by Private University for the dependent children of employees (value of $15,000 per semester).
   c. Fly Airline allows its employees to fly free when there are open seats available on a flight (average value of $200).
   d. Incidental personal use of a company car.

2. Norman the manager of Airline Highway Motel. He lives in Unit 12. Norman was given the option to live at the motel if he would also look after the night auditing (the value of his reviews is $400 per month) responsibilities. The value of the motel unit on a monthly basis is $800, but Unit 12 rents on a daily basis for $100 per day. How much, if any, does Norman have to include in his gross income for living on the premises of his employer?
   a. $0 lodging for the convenience of the employer.
   b. $400 per month.
   c. $800 per month.
   d. $3,000 per month.

3. Meredith is an employee of a large company. They are very interested in the betterment of the health of all employees. The company has a health facility on its premises for the exclusive use of its employees and their dependents. A comparable private health club membership at a public facility would cost $2,400 per year. How much, if any, must Meredith include in her gross income if her 10-year old daughter uses the facilities for one-half of the year?
   a. $0.
   b. $600.
   c. $1,200.
   d. $2,400.

4. Which of the employee fringe benefits listed below, if provided by the employer, are both deductible by the employer and not included in an employee's gross income after 2017?
   1. Business periodical subscriptions.
   2. Season tickets to professional football games.
   3. Parking provided near its business (employer pays $90 per month).
   4. The use of an on-premises athletic facility (value of $180 per employee per month).
   a. 2 only.
   b. 1 and 4.
   c. 1, 3, and 4.
   d. 1, 2, 3, and 4.

5. Oscar holds two jobs - a full-time job with R Corporation and a part-time job with Z Corporation. He uses his car to drive to work. The mileage is as follows: from Oscar's home to R is 70 miles; from R to Z is 10 miles; and from Z to Oscar's home is 70 miles. Oscar's deductible mileage for each work day is:

    a. 10 miles.
    b. 70 miles.
    c. 80 miles.
    d. 150 miles.

> **Additional multiple choice problems**
> **are available at**
> **money-education.com**
> **by accessing the**
> **Student Practice Portal.**
> **Access requires registration of the title using**
> **the unique code at the front of the book.**

QUICK QUIZ EXPLANATIONS

Quick Quiz 13.1
1. False. An employee fringe benefit is a form of compensation, and as a result, it is taxable as compensation unless specifically exempted from taxation under the Internal Revenue Code.
2. True.
3. False. Not all employee fringe benefits are subject to nondiscrimination requirements.

Quick Quiz 13.2
1. True.
2. True.

Quick Quiz 13.3
1. False. Only the value of an on-premises athletic facility furnished by the employer may be excluded from the employee's gross income.
2. True.
3. False. If a student is a graduate student and is teaching or performing research activities for an educational organization, then the student may be eligible for a qualified tuition reduction plan.

Quick Quiz 13.4
1. False. Dependent care assistance can be excluded up to the lesser of (1) $2,500 ($5,250 in 2021 only, ARPA 2021) for married filing separately individuals and $5,000 ($10,500 in 2021 only, ARPA 2021) for married individuals filing jointly and single individuals, or (2) the earned income of the employee or the employee's spouse.
2. False. No-additional-cost services must be provided to all employees in a nondiscriminatory manner in order to avoid inclusion in the employee's gross income.
3. True.

Quick Quiz 13.5
1. True.
2. True.

Quick Quiz 13.6
1. False. Meals during the move are not a deductible moving expense.
2. True.

Quick Quiz 13.7
1. False. Cash awards may not be excluded from gross income.
2. False. Adoption assistance benefits may be excluded from the employee's gross income, but are subject to Social Security, Medicare, and federal unemployment taxes.

Quick Quiz 13.8
1. True.

14

EMPLOYEE BENEFITS: GROUP BENEFITS

LEARNING OBJECTIVES

1. Understand that group insurance plans, if paid for by the employer, are generally considered by that employer as part of an overall compensation plan.*
2. Explain the rules regarding the various insurance and other group benefit plans.*
3. Describe the rules related to COBRA.*
4. Explain the income tax treatment of group life insurance provided to an employee in excess of $50,000.*
5. Describe a cafeteria plan and articulate its benefits.*
6. Describe a flexible spending account (FSA) and articulate its benefits and rules.*
7. Compare and contrast medical savings accounts (MSAs) and health savings accounts (HSAs).*
8. Explain the major benefits that a Voluntary Employees' Beneficiary Association (VEBA) can and cannot provide. *
9. Describe the importance of business succession planning and why it is complex and challenging.*
10. Identify factors a business owner should consider when creating a succession plan, including the ability and motivation of a successor and the degree of idiosyncrasy in the business.*
11. Describe other employer / employee insurance arrangements such as buy-sell agreements, business disability, split dollar, and key person life and disability insurance.*
12. Describe the purpose of a buy-sell agreement as a business succession planning tool.*
13. Illustrate how a buy-sell agreement can be designed and implemented.*

Ties to CFP Certification Learning Objectives

INTRODUCTION

Most employees value fringe benefits, especially insurance benefits such as medical, life, and disability, as a core element of their compensation package. With a large number of employees, employers can often provide lower group insurance premiums and better coverage than an individual employee is able to acquire in the open market. Thus, where insurance coverage is desired by a large number of employees, the employer may adopt an insurance plan as part of an overall compensation package. This may also enable the employer to be more competitive in the labor market. The federal government, in the case of some fringe benefits and insurance plans, also promotes employer insurance arrangements by allowing the employer to pay the premiums for employees and immediately deduct the cost for income tax purposes without requiring the participant employee to include such premium cost in their taxable income.

Most employer-provided health and other insurance is provided under group insurance coverage that is paid in part by the employer. Any premiums paid by the employer are generally deductible by the employer or included in the employee's gross income. Although the employee is usually required to pay a portion of the premiums, the employee may still benefit through a pre-tax payment of the insurance premium or through better rates. To receive the potential tax benefits for the employer or the employee, each type of group benefit has specific requirements.

This chapter addresses the following group benefits and details the benefits, requirements, and exemptions of each:

- Group medical plans
- Group term life insurance
- Group disability insurance
- Cafeteria plans used to provide diverse employee groups with a greater selection of employee benefits
- Flexible spending accounts
- Medical savings accounts
- Health savings accounts
- Voluntary Employee's Beneficiary Association
- Salary continuation plans
- Group long-term care insurance
- Group retirement planning services
- Business continuation plans
- Business overhead disability plans
- Split-dollar life insurance
- Key person life insurance

KNOW THE NUMBERS

	MSA		HSA	
Established	Before 2006		2004 and Later	
	Single	**Family**	**Single**	**Family**
Health Insurance Deductible	$2,400 - $3,600	$4,800 - $7,150	At least $1,400	At least $2,800
Maximum Out-of-Pocket	$4,800	$8,750	$7,000	$14,000
Maximum Contribution	65% of deductible	75% of deductible	100% of deductible limited to $3,600	100% of deductible limited to $7,200
Catch-Up Contribution Available	No		Yes $1,000 for 2021	

MEDICAL PLANS

There are several ways that employers can provide employees with benefits for medical expenses that result from personal injury or sickness. Many employers use these types of group health insurance plans as a part of the overall compensation package provided to their employees. Included in these health insurance plans are both private insurance plans and self-insurance plans. Any premium payments or costs made to or for these plans are deductible for federal income taxes by the employer and excluded from the employee's gross income.

Group Medical Insurance

A group accident or health plan is an arrangement that provides benefits for employees, their spouses, and their dependents in the event of personal injury or sickness. The plan may be insured or noninsured and plans must provide certain disclosures and plan information in writing to eligible employees or participants. The premiums paid by the employer for health insurance are not includible in the employee's taxable income but are a deductible business expense for the employer under IRC §162. Group medical insurance includes hospitalization coverage, major medical, indemnity coverage, health maintenance organization, exclusive provider organizations, preferred provider organizations, point of service plans, and dental and vision plans.

Income Tax Implications

When the employer pays all or a portion of the premium for health insurance on the employee (including premiums for the employee's spouse and dependents), the employer is permitted a tax deduction for the premiums paid.

When insurance benefits are paid, they are includible in the employee's income with the exception of payments received for medical care of the employee, spouse, and dependents, and payments for permanent loss or the loss of the use of a member or function of the body or permanent disfigurement of the employee, spouse, or dependent. Therefore, the employer can generally exclude the value of accident or health benefits provided to an employee from the employee's gross income.

Self-Employed Individuals

Self-employed individuals (sole proprietors, partners in a partnership, LLC members, and greater-than-2% S corporation owners) cannot be treated as employees for purposes of the exclusion from income of employer-paid health insurance premiums, causing the premiums to be included in the owner's taxable income, subject to income tax withholding but not subject to Social Security, Medicare, and FUTA taxes. However, self-employed individuals who do not have an employer-provided health plan available through another employer or spouse's employer may deduct the premiums as an above-the-line tax deduction on the owner's federal income tax return (Form 1040). The deduction for health insurance premiums cannot exceed the earnings from the business; therefore, if the business produced a loss for the year, no premium deduction will be permitted. For greater-than-2% S corporation owner-employees, the premiums will be included as taxable income on the owner-employee's W-2, and are then deducted above-the-line on the Form 1040. Benefits paid from the insurance policy are generally excluded from the self-employed individual's income when the payments are for medical care of the self-employed individual, spouse, or dependents.

Self-Insured Plans

A **self-insured plan** is a plan that reimburses employees for medical expenses not covered by an accident or health insurance policy.

If the employer's plan is a self-insured medical reimbursement plan that favors highly compensated employees, the employer must include all or part of the amounts the employer pays to these employees as benefits in the employee's wages subject to federal income tax withholding. However, the employer can exclude these amounts (other than payments for specific injuries or illnesses) from the employee's wages subject to Social Security, Medicare, and FUTA taxes.

For self-insured plans, a highly compensated employee is any individual who is one of the five highest paid officers of the company or an employee who owns (directly or indirectly) more than 10 percent in value of the employer's stock. In addition, an employee who is among the highest paid 25 percent of all employees (other than those who can be excluded from the plan) is also considered a highly compensated employee.

Eligibility

To be eligible to purchase group health insurance, an individual has to be affiliated with a group that is covered by a group health insurance policy. Typically, all individuals who are employed on a full-time basis (or are a member of a qualifying group) at a company that provides group health coverage are eligible to participate in the group plan. Sometimes non-employer groups provide coverage for their members as well. Common examples are local Chambers of Commerce (which may offer a group plan that can cover the employees of all member companies), labor unions, and professional associations (such as The American Bar Association or the American Institute of Certified Public Accountants). However, the Patient Protection and Affordable Care Act (ACA) has changed the way heath care is purchased and made available to individuals. As a result, some groups have ceased offering health insurance.

Features of Group Health Insurance

Group policies are underwritten based on the characteristics of the group to be covered as a whole and include factors such as the average age of the group, the geographical location, and tobacco use. Most group contracts require that either all full-time employees or all members of a qualifying group be automatically covered (enrolled) under the plan. This requirement helps to prevent adverse selection risk for the insurer, which is the risk that healthy members of the group will opt out of coverage, leaving only those with greater expected health care needs covered in the plan.

The employer typically enrolls all eligible employees in the plan, and pays some or all of the premiums for coverage. If the employee pays part of the health insurance costs, those costs are typically paid through payroll deduction. Since the employer shoulders a large part of the administrative burden by enrolling employees and paying premiums, part of the administrative cost savings realized by the insurer is passed on to the employer in the form of lower group-health insurance premiums.

The ACA requires large employers (an employer that, at any time during the year, employs at least 50 people) to provide a minimum level of health insurance coverage to employees or face significant tax penalties. Small employers (those employing fewer than 50 workers at all times during the year) are encouraged by means of tax credits to provide health insurance to their employees.

Most large employers will allow the employee to choose from multiple types of policies with various choices of deductibles and coinsurance amounts. Employees may also be permitted to choose coverage for self-only, self plus spouse, or family (covering the employee, spouse, and all dependents). These selections typically must be made during the group's open enrollment period; for example, employees may have to choose their benefits for the upcoming year during October of the current year. When new dependents are added during the year (for example a child is born), there will be a limited time period, usually 30 days, following the event to add that dependent, and coverage will commence as of the date the dependent becomes eligible.

Types of Group Health Insurance

There are two primary types of group health insurance:
- group basic medical insurance
- group major medical insurance

When the features of these plans are combined into one policy, the policy is referred to as a Group Comprehensive Major Medical Insurance plan.

Group Basic Medical Insurance

Historically, group basic medical insurance covered hospital, physician, and surgical bills, but typically had low policy limits. Due to the low policy limits, group basic medical coverage was often used in conjunction with group major medical insurance. However, today, the Affordable Care Act prohibits health plans from putting annual or lifetime dollar limits on most benefits so group basic medical insurance on a stand alone basis will not meet the requirements of minimum essential coverage under The Affordable Care Act.

Group Major Medical Insurance

Group major medical insurance coverage supplemented basic medical coverage by permitting a wider array of services and increasing policy maximums. As as result of the Affordable Care Act, lifetime maximums are no longer permitted. Sometimes these policies are referred to as group supplemental insurance plans.

Group Comprehensive Major Medical Insurance

The vast majority of group plans are comprehensive major medical insurance plans which combine the benefits of basic medical coverage and major medical coverage and are simply referred to as health insurance plans. Typically, plan deductibles are relatively low, and the employee may be required to make a copayment when receiving services. After the plan deductible has been met for the year, the insurance company usually pays 80 percent of the cost of health care and the participant pays the remaining 20 percent until a maximum annual out-of-pocket limit is reached. Once the annual out-of-pocket maximum is reached, the insurance company pays 100 percent of the costs of care for the remainder of that year. There are various ranges of coinsurance between the insurer and the insured, including 60/40, 70/30, 80/20 and 90/10.

Example 14.1

Dylan is a participant in his employer's Group Comprehensive Major Medical Insurance Plan. The plan has a $200 deductible, an 80/20 coinsurance after the deductible has been met, and a $1,500 out-of-pocket maximum. If Dylan is injured in an accident and his medical costs total $2,000, Dylan will have to pay the first $200 to cover the deductible, and will pay $360 (20% of the remaining $1,800 in medical costs), for a total of $560. The plan will pay the remaining portion of the cost, or a total of $1,440. The next time that Dylan needs medical attention within the same year, he will pay 20% of those costs (but he would not have to pay another deductible, since the deductible has to be satisfied only once per year) until his total out-of-pocket costs for the year (including the deductible) is $1,500. In other words, Dylan will have to pay a maximum of $940 more for the year before the insurer pays 100% of future costs for the year.

To meet the definition of a Qualified Health Plan (QHP) under the ACA, health insurance plans must meet ACA guidelines for cost sharing (deductibles, coinsurances, and maximum out-of-pocket limits) and must cover 10 specified essential health benefits, including hospital, emergency, outpatient, and rehabilitative services, lab tests, mental health services, pregnancy and baby care, preventive and wellness services, prescription drugs, and, for children only, dental and vision services.[1]

Traditionally, comprehensive major medical plans were not favored by employees, since they resulted in the employee paying up to the out-of-pocket maximum each year. Many employees and unions favored first-dollar pay type plans, where the employee would make a small co-payment (of, perhaps $5 or $10) each time they visited a physician, and the insurance company would pay for the balance of the bill. First-dollar-pay type plans have higher premiums than comprehensive plans due to the increase in benefit payments made by the insurance company, and the increased administrative costs incurred. More recently, however, with the creation of Health Savings Accounts (HSAs) and the new federal requirements concerning health insurance coverage for employees, high deductible plans have enjoyed a renaissance as a means to provide adequate healthcare coverage while lowering premium costs for employers.

Indemnity Health Insurance

Indemnity health insurance is also referred to as a traditional health insurance plan or fee-for-service plan. Indemnity health insurance plans allow participants the benefit of having a whole range of health care practitioners at their disposal. Indemnity plan participants are not limited to a service network system for medical care. Indemnity health insurance is the most flexible type of insurance policy, but participants also pay some of the highest premiums in order to have the flexibility of choosing their own health care providers. Typically, indemnity plans have deductibles and coinsurance for medical expenses.

Managed Care Insurance

Managed care insurance emerged from a desire to reduce the costs of health care while increasing competition among service providers. When compared to major medical plans, managed care approaches to health care restrict participant choice of health care providers, and often require participants to obtain pre-approval from insurance company representatives as a condition of obtaining covered treatment that is not considered emergency care. Companies offering managed care have also been criticized for prohibiting physicians from discussing alternative options to care with the patients, creating an ethical

> ### Key Concepts
>
> 1. Describe the similarities and differences between an HMO and a PPO.
>
> 2. Explain the reasoning behind the criticism of managed care insurance plans.

dilemma for the health care provider who is determined to act in the best interest of the patient. Despite their shortcomings, managed care approaches to health insurance have assisted in somewhat containing the cost of medical services over time.

There are four main types of managed care approaches to health insurance coverage:
- Health Maintenance Organization (HMO)
- Preferred Provider Organization (PPO)
- Point-of-Service Plans (POS)
- Exclusive Provider Organization (EPO)

Health Maintenance Organizations (HMOs)

Health Maintenance Organizations (HMOs) were authorized by the HMO Act of 1973. HMOs consist of a group of physicians who provide comprehensive care for their patients, and are organized in an effort to control the rising cost of healthcare. Physicians may be employed by the HMO directly or may be

---

1. Some health plans were grandfathered when the ACA rules came into effect and may not cover the 10 essential health benefits, so each policy should be examined carefully.

physicians in private practice who have chosen to participate in the HMO network. The independent physicians are paid a flat annual fee, called a capitation fee, for agreeing to provide medical service for each HMO member, whether or not the member uses them as a **primary care physician** or receives services from them. The flat capitation fee is paid, regardless of the extent or complexity of the service provided to a patient, thus serving to discourage physicians from providing unnecessary medical treatment.

One of the most important disadvantages of an HMO is the limited range of choices that the plan participant has as to where he or she may receive medical care. In most circumstances, the hospital or the physician must be a member of the HMO in order for the plan participant to be eligible for medical care from that provider (except for cases of true emergencies). Those insured under an HMO will typically have a primary care physician (PCP) who serves as gatekeeper, making referrals for specialist care when the PCP deems it necessary. The advantage of having a primary care physician, however, is coordination of care. The PCP serves as the quarterback calling the plays on the field and all of the team members (physicians and specialists) work as one unit to provide efficient care and share information about care needs.

Some HMOs permit their members to obtain service outside of the insurance company's provider network, but payments for services performed by an out-of-network provider will typically be smaller than claims allowed for similar services provided within the network, which effectively increases the cost to the participant. Typically, the HMO does not cover care received out-of-network as a result of patient choice. However, the HMO is responsible for providing medically necessary services as needed, so if the network lacks a specific type of provider, the insured can petition, with the support of the PCP, to have the HMO cover an out-of-network provider.

Exhibit 14.1 | Advantages and Disadvantages of HMOs

Advantages
• Coordination of care
• Pre-set fees for health care/no unexpected bills (surprise bills)
• Low co-payments; little use of deductibles and coinsurance
• Total health care costs is generally lower and more predictable than with PPO or POS
Disadvantages
• Gatekeeper for specialists services so it is often difficult and complicated to get specialized care
• Potentially longer waits for non-emergency doctor appointments
• Any health care costs from out-of-network providers, except in emergencies, are generally not covered

Preferred Provider Organizations (PPOs)

A **Preferred Provider Organization** is an arrangement between insurance companies and health care providers that permits members of the PPO to obtain discounted health care services from the preferred providers within the network. Unlike an HMO, which limits choice of physicians and other health care providers, a PPO typically has a larger provider pool from which participants may choose. Participants are not required to receive services from preferred providers, but higher deductibles and coinsurance payments may apply when services are obtained from providers outside of the network.

Exhibit 14.2 | Advantages and Disadvantages of PPOs

Advantages
• Health care costs are low when using in-network providers
• No gatekeeper required for specialist consultations, including out-of-network providers
• Primary care physician is not required
• Yearly out-of-pocket costs are limited

Disadvantages
• Out-of-network treatment is more expensive
• Copayments are generally larger than with HMOs
• May need to satisfy a deductible, especially with out-of-network providers
• Coinsurance may apply, and be higher when out of network

Point of Service Plans (POS)

A **point of service plan (POS)** is considered a managed care/indemnity plan hybrid, as it mixes aspects of in-network and fee-for-service, for greater patient choice. Members choose which option that they will use each time they seek health care.

Like an HMO and a PPO, a POS plan has a contracted provider network. POS plans encourage members to choose a primary care physician from within the health care network. This physician becomes the patient's "point of service." If the patient prefers an out-of-network provider, the in-network primary care physician may make referrals, but higher deductibles and coinsurance payments may apply if the insured is receiving services on the indemnity side.

POS plans are becoming more popular because they offer more flexibility, lower costs, and freedom of choice than standard HMOs, PPOs, or indemnity plans.

Exhibit 14.3 | Advantages and Disadvantages of POS Plans

Advantages
• Freedom of choice for managed care
• Not limited to only HMO network providers
• Costs are lower for in-network care
• Annual out-of-pocket costs are limited
• No referral is needed for choosing an out of network doctor

Disadvantages
• Copays for out-of-network providers are high
• There are deductibles for out-of-network providers
• It is sometimes difficult and complicated to get specialized care with in-network providers

Exclusive Provider Organizations (EPOs)

An **Exclusive Provider Organization** is a managed care plan under which services are covered only when received from in-network doctors, specialists, or hospitals. No coverage is provided outside the network unless due to an emergency. An EPO is similar to an HMO but typically does not require a primary care physician to serve as the gatekeeper to specialist care (no referrals are needed to see a specialist), although a PCP may be selected if coordination of care is desirable. With an EPO, hospital stays often must be approved in advance (unless an emergency). Premiums tend to be higher than an HMO due to the flexibility of seeing a specialist without a referral, but tend to be lower than a PPO since only in-network care is covered.

Exhibit 14.4 | Advantages and Disadvantages of EPO Plans

Advantages
• Ability to select a PCP for coordination of care if desired • Typically have a low copay for in-network care • Premiums are typically lower than PPO or POS (but higher than HMO) • No referral is needed to see a specialist
Disadvantages
• No out-of-network coverage (unless an emergency) • Limited to in-network providers

Upcoming Changes: Advance Cost Estimates and Restrictions On Surprise Medical Billing

The No Surprises Act (which was part of the Consolidated Appropriations Act of 2021) requires that, for plan years beginning on or after January 1, 2022, group health plans must provide the participant with a notification (Advanced Explanation of Benefits) based on billing and diagnostic codes provided by the service provider. The notice must include information regarding whether the provider is an in-network provider along with a good faith estimate of the amount the plan will pay and the cost-sharing amount to be paid by the participant.

For plan years beginning on or after January 1, 2022, group health plans must cover emergency services in a hospital emergency department or independent freestanding emergency department without the need for prior authorization and regardless of whether or not the provider is an in-network provider. In addition, the participant's cost sharing for these services can be no greater than would apply for services at an in-network provider. While limited to emergency services, these requirements will eliminate many unexpected (surprise) medical bills for participants.

Health Reimbursement Arrangement (HRA)

Health reimbursement arrangements, also known as "health reimbursement accounts" or "personal care accounts," are a type of health insurance plan that reimburses employees for qualified medical expenses. An HRA is an arrangement that: (1) is paid for solely by the employer and not provided pursuant to salary reduction election or otherwise under a §125 cafeteria plan, (2) reimburses the employee for medical care expenses incurred by the employee and the employee's spouse and dependents, and (3) provides reimbursements up to a maximum dollar amount for a coverage period. Any unused portion of the maximum dollar amount at the end of a coverage period is carried forward to increase the maximum reimbursement amount in subsequent coverage periods. To the extent that an HRA is an employer-provided accident or health plan, coverage and reimbursements of medical care expenses of an employee and the employee's spouse and dependents are generally excludable from the employee's gross income under IRC §106 and IRC §105.

Medical care expenses submitted for reimbursement must be substantiated under the HRA and the HRA may not reimburse a medical care expense that is attributable to a deduction allowed for medical expenses for any prior taxable year. Additionally, an HRA may neither reimburse a medical care expense that is incurred before the date the HRA is in existence nor reimburse a medical care expense that is incurred before the date an employee first becomes enrolled under the HRA.

The objective of these plans, like many other fringe and group benefits, is to provide benefits to employees that are excludable from the employee's taxable income. As long as the plan is not discriminatory and as long as the expenses are valid under IRC §213 (medical expenses), then the expense will be deductible and the benefit received will not be subject to taxation.

> **Quick Quiz 14.1**
>
> 1. PPOs typically have a wider network of health care providers, from which to choose, than HMOs.
>   a. True
>   b. False
>
> 2. The emergence of managed care plans was born from a desire to decrease competition amongst health care providers.
>   a. True
>   b. False
>
> True, False.

HRAs may be implemented by small or large companies and as stand-alone plans or in conjunction with other health plans of the employer.

Individual Coverage HRAs

Historically, HRAs received the tax benefits discussed previously because they were considered a group health plan offered in conjunction with an Affordable Care Act-compliant group health policy (ACA requirements are discussed below). This precluded the use of HRA funds from being used in conjunction with individual health insurance policies. In an effort to expand opportunities for workers to access affordable quality health care coverage, the Departments of Health and Human Services, Labor (Employee Benefits Security Administration), and Treasury (IRS) in June 2019 issued final rules[2] allowing integration of HRAs and other account-based group health plans[3] with individual health insurance coverage, provided that the individual health insurance policy does not impose annual dollar limits on health care coverage and covers preventive services without cost sharing.[4] A qualifying Individual Coverage HRA will have the same tax treatment as a traditional HRA. The expectation is that Individual Coverage HRAs will be an attractive way for small employers to offer health coverage to employees without the higher level of administration required for a group health plan.

The Individual Coverage HRA must require participants to verify enrollment in an individual health insurance plan (a plan sold in the individual market, on the Health Care Exchange, or Medicare).[5] An Individual Coverage HRA cannot be offered to any employee to whom a group health plan is offered, but

2. "Health Reimbursement Arrangements and Other Account-Based Group Health Plans." Federal Register Vol. 84, No. 119, page 2888; applicable to plan years beginning on or after January 1, 2020.
3. Eligible account-based group health plans include health care FSAs, but not MSAs or HSAs (FSAs, MSAs, and HSAs are discussed later in this chapter).
4. PHSA §2711 and PHSA §2713.
5. All of the plans listed are assumed to be compliant with PHSA §2711 and §2713 without further substantiation by the employee or employer. Short-term, limited duration coverage and policies that cover only dental or vision are not included in the definition of individual health insurance plan.

employers are permitted to offer a group health plan to certain classes of employees while offering the Individual Coverage HRA to other classes of employees.[6] As with the traditional HRAs described above, each sponsoring employer has discretion to determine which expenses are eligible for reimbursement under the Individual Coverage HRA. For example, an employer may choose to offer reimbursement only for the premiums for the individual market policy, or only for out-of-pocket costs and not premiums. If an employee receives an "affordable" Individual Coverage HRA, he will be prohibited from receiving premium tax credits under IRC §36B.[7] However, employees offered an Individual Coverage HRA may elect to opt out, enabling them to qualify for the tax credit if otherwise eligible.

Excepted Benefit HRAs

The new rule also created another new form of HRA called an "Excepted Benefit HRA." Excepted benefit policies are exempt from many federal health care requirements, which allows these HRAs to be made available to employees who decline the group coverage (although they must still be offered group coverage). An Excepted Benefit HRA can be funded by the employer with contributions up to $1,800 (in 2021) per year and unused funds can roll over from year-to-year. The funds can be used to reimburse out-of-pocket expenses such as deductibles and copays, and they can be used for premiums for dental or vision coverage; however they cannot be used to reimburse individual health insurance premiums, group health plan premiums (other than COBRA, covered later in this chapter) or Medicare premiums.[8]

The Health Insurance Portability and Accountability Act of 1996 (HIPAA)

President Clinton signed HIPAA into law in 1996. The law offers protections for millions of American workers that improve portability and continuity of health insurance coverage in addition to insuring that the privacy of individual's health information is maintained.

HIPAA includes protections for coverage under group health plans that:
- Limit exclusions for preexisting conditions
- Prohibit discrimination against employees and dependents based on their health status
- Allow a special opportunity to enroll in a new plan to individuals in certain circumstances
- Provide privacy of medical information

One of the most important protections under HIPAA is that it assists those with preexisting conditions in obtaining health coverage. Prior to HIPAA, some employers' group health plans limited, or even denied coverage if a new employee had such a condition prior to enrolling in the plan. Under HIPAA, that is not permitted. If the plan generally provides coverage but denies benefits to an employee because that employee had a condition before the coverage began, then HIPAA applies.

Under HIPAA, a plan is allowed to look back only six months for a condition that was present prior to the start of coverage in a group health plan. Specifically, the law says that a preexisting condition exclusion may be imposed on a condition only if medical advice, diagnosis, care, or treatment was recommended or received during the six months occurring just prior to the enrollment date in the plan. If an employee had prior creditable coverage for at least twelve months without a break of more than 63 days, no waiting period can be imposed before coverage begins for the preexisting condition. Since the enactment of the ACA, under which qualified health plans cannot deny coverage for any preexisting condition, HIPAA is somewhat less prevalent in protecting insureds with preexisting conditions. However, for

---

6. The rule provides a list of 11 classes of employees.
7. See Treas. Reg. §1.36B-2(c)(5).
8. https://www.irs.gov/pub/irs-utl/health_reimbursement_arrangements_faqs.pdf; Q11.

insureds covered by grandfathered health plans that existed prior to ACA which are exempt from the preexisting conditions rules of the ACA, HIPAA still provides at least some level of protection against denial of coverage due to preexisting conditions.

A major goal of the Privacy Rule is to assure that individuals' health information is properly protected while allowing the flow of health information needed to provide and promote high quality health care and to protect the public's health and well being. The Rule strikes a balance that permits important uses of information, while protecting the privacy of people who seek care and healing. Given that the health care marketplace is diverse, the Rule is designed to be flexible and comprehensive to cover the variety of uses and disclosures that need to be addressed.

The Patient Protection and Affordable Care Act (ACA) of 2010

The ACA was enacted in 2010 and survived a Supreme Court challenge. The act sets out to:
- End pre-existing conditions.
- End lifetime limits on coverage.
- Increase the age that children can remain on their parent's heath insurance policy to age 26.
- Require that insurance providers offer a Summary of Benefits and Coverage (SBC) document that provides individuals with easy-to-understand information about their policy and make it easier to compare to other policies.
- Set a maximum waiting period before which employee group health plan coverage becomes effective.
- Create federal and state exchanges that permit individuals to purchase insurance without the need to prove insurability. The exchanges may be referred to as the Health Insurance Marketplace or Health Care Exchange.

Children under age 26 can remain on their parent's plan even if the child is married, does not live with the parents, is not financially dependent on the parents, or is eligible to enroll in his or her own employer's plan.

For group health plan years beginning on or after January 1, 2015, the maximum time an otherwise eligible employee can be required to wait before coverage becomes effective is 90 calendar days, following a maximum 30-day orientation period. For example, if the employee begins work on September 15th, the 30-day orientation period ends on October 14th (as measured by adding one month and subtracting one day) and group health insurance coverage must begin no later than January 13th (the 91st day from the end of the orientation period).[9]

COBRA Provisions

Under the **Consolidated Omnibus Budget Reconciliation Act of 1985 (COBRA)**,[10] an employer that maintains a group health plan and employs 20 or more people on more than 50 percent of the calendar days in a year is required to continue to offer coverage under the plan to covered employees and qualified beneficiaries following the occurrence of a statutorily defined qualifying event as depicted in **Exhibit 14.5**.[11]

9. Reg § 54.9815-2708.
10. Public Law 99-272 (April 7, 1986).
11. 29 USCA §1161.

Exhibit 14.5 | Summary of COBRA Provisions

Event	Beneficiary (Qualifying)			Period of Coverage
	Worker	**Spouse**	**Dependant**	
Normal termination (resigned, laid off, or fired; except gross misconduct) *(29 USCA 1163(2))*	✓	✓	✓	18 months
Full time to part time *(29 USCA 1163(2))*	✓	✓	✓	18 months
Disabled employee or dependent (must meet Social Security definition of disabled) *(29 USCA 1162(2)(A))*	✓	✓	✓	29 months
Qualified dependent (child reaches age no longer eligible for plan) *(29 USCA 1163(5))*			✓	36 months
Death of employee *(29 USCA 1163(1))*		✓	✓	36 months
Employee reached Medicare age *(29 USCA 1163(4))*		✓	✓	36 months
Divorce *(29 USCA 1163(3))*		✓	✓	36 months
Plan terminates* *(29 USCA 1163(6))*	✓	✓	✓	36 months

Applies to retirees who retired on or before the date of elimination of coverage when a plan terminates as a result of the employer filing Chapter 11 bankruptcy. 29 USCA 1163(6) and Treas. Reg. §54.4980B-4.

COBRA Premiums

While the employer may pay for the COBRA coverage, generally the employer shifts the burden of paying the premium to the beneficiaries. If the employer pays for the medical coverage, then the exclusion from the employee's income for accident and health benefits applies to amounts the employer pays to maintain medical coverage under COBRA. The exclusion applies regardless of the length of employment, whether the employer pays the premiums directly or reimburses the former employee for premiums paid, and whether the employee's separation is permanent or temporary.

During the statutory COBRA period, the premium charged to the employee cannot exceed 102 percent of the cost to the plan for similarly situated individuals who have not incurred a qualifying event.[12] The 102 percent includes both the portion paid by beneficiary employees and any portion paid by the employer before the qualifying event plus two percent for administrative costs. If a qualified beneficiary receives the 11 month disability extension of coverage, the premium for the additional 11 months may be increased to 150 percent of the plan's total cost of coverage. COBRA premiums may be increased if the costs to the plan increase, but generally must be fixed in advance of each 12-month premium cycle.[13]

> ### ✏ Quick Quiz 14.2
>
> 1. The value of health benefits provided to all employees or owners can be excluded from the employee or owner's income.
>   a. True
>   b. False
>
> 2. COBRA premiums paid by the employer on behalf of a former employee can be excluded from the employee's taxable income.
>   a. True
>   b. False
>
> False, True.

---

12. 29 USCA 1162(3).

13. The American Rescue Plan Act of 2021 created a short-term COBRA premium subsidy, available between April 1, 2021 and September 30, 2021, for Assistance-Eligible Individuals (AEIs; beneficiaries eligible for COBRA due to a qualifying event of involuntary termination of employment or reduction of hours).

The election period for COBRA begins on the date of the qualifying event and must last at least 60 days from the time the beneficiary receives notification from the administrator.[14] Each of the qualified beneficiaries can choose COBRA continuation independently. When the election for coverage is made, coverage is retroactive to the date of the qualifying event. If no action is taken and medical expenses are incurred during the 60-day election period, the election can still be made and coverage will begin retroactively to the day of the qualifying event, so that those recently incurred medical expenses will be paid by the plan. Of course, this also means premiums must be paid retroactively, but if the medical expenses are significantly higher than the total premiums, it can be a large savings to the insured. If coverage is initially waived, the waiver can be revoked during the 60-day election period, however coverage need not be retroactive to the date of the qualifying event and instead may begin on the date the revocation is sent to the employer or plan administrator.[15]

Individuals whose coverage terminates due to a job change will often have a probationary period before becoming eligible for coverage under the health plan of the new employer. If the employee and family members are healthy and will be eligible for the new coverage before the 60-day COBRA election period ends, a strategy some employees take is to wait and see if any medical expenses are incurred before electing COBRA. If no or low costs are incurred before the new coverage begins, the family will have saved the cost of the premiums. If the family incurs significant medical costs during that 60-day time-frame, the election for COBRA can be made retroactively. Care must be used when employing this strategy, however, because if the family has any pre-existing conditions and there is a period of more than 63 days between the old health plan coverage and the new health plan coverage, the new plan may be permitted to exclude coverage for preexisting conditions for up to six months.

When the maximum period for continuation coverage under COBRA terminates, an employee must be able to exercise the conversion rights that are otherwise available under the plan, or, as an alternative, will be eligible for the special 60-day enrollment period in the Healthcare Marketplace (policies purchased though the Marketplace have no exclusions for pre-existing conditions).

Example 14.2

Brandy recently terminated her employment. Her major medical insurance ended on her last day of employment. Brandy started a new job one week after leaving her previous job. Coverage under her new employer's plan will begin after 30 days of employment. Since Brandy has 60 days to elect COBRA coverage, which will then be retroactive to the date she terminated employment, if she is healthy, she can wait to see if she has any significant medical expenses during the 37 days until her new group coverage begins. If she incurs costs higher than the COBRA premiums, she can elect COBRA, pay the premiums retroactive to the date her group coverage terminated, and receive benefit payments for the retroactive coverage period. If her medical costs during that time are lower than the COBRA premiums, she will not need to elect COBRA and will save the cost of the premiums.

---

14. 29 USC §1165 and 1166.
15. Treas. Reg. §54.4980B-6, Q.4.

Example 14.3

Assume the same facts as above except Brandy is going to take 18 months off to find herself. Now is COBRA an appropriate election? In this instance, the answer is maybe. She needs medical insurance coverage of some type, but COBRA may or may not be the best option. Brandy should compare the coverage and costs of the group policy under COBRA with the cost of purchasing an individual policy, either through the marketplace or outside the marketplace, where she can purchase an individual policy without evidence of insurability during the 60-day election period for COBRA (which is also the time-frame for the special enrollment period for purchase of an individual policy). She may find that an individual policy is less costly than COBRA while still providing adequate coverage. Purchases of insurance on the Health Care Exchange are generally only permitted during the open enrollment period (November 1 - December 15 of the prior year, for coverage to begin January 1st); however, loss of group coverage due to termination of employment creates a 60-day special enrollment period.

Employees age 65 and older who have chosen not to enroll in Medicare Part B due to the employer-provided coverage should generally not elect COBRA coverage at termination of employment and should instead enroll in Medicare Part B. This enrollment is recommended because failure to enroll in Medicare Part B within eight months of termination of employment will cause the Part B premium to be permanently increased, and because COBRA premiums are typically more expensive than Medicare Part B premiums. The 8-month period is always measured from the earlier of:

1. the month after termination of employment, or
2. the month after termination of group health insurance based on the current employment, regardless of whether COBRA is elected.

GROUP TERM LIFE INSURANCE

Amounts paid by the employer for group term life insurance also receive favorable tax treatment. The employer can deduct the amounts paid for the insurance, and the employee can exclude a portion, if not all, of the value from the employee's income (discussed below). To receive such favorable treatment, the life insurance must provide a general death benefit to a group of employees, and the coverage must provide an amount of insurance to each employee based on a formula that prevents individual selection. This formula must use factors such as the employee's age, years of service, pay, or position.

Key Concepts

1. What is required for a life insurance policy to be considered group term life insurance?

2. What are the tax implications of employer-provided group term life insurance?

Group term life insurance is pure insurance protection that pays a predetermined sum if the insured dies during a specified period of time (i.e., the term, which may be 1, 5, 10, 20 years or longer). Term insurance generally has no cash value savings or investment component and essentially states, "If you pay x, we will pay y if you die during the term." The protection ceases at the end of the term unless renewed. Term insurance is very inexpensive at young ages (substantially less than whole life). The premium pattern may be level or increasing on an annual or set period basis (i.e., five-year renewable term). The face amount may be level, decreasing, or increasing (i.e., there may be a cost of living provision that increases the face).

Group term life insurance is usually renewable on an annual term, and does not include the following types of insurance:

- Insurance without general death benefits, such as travel insurance or a policy providing only accidental death benefits;
- Life insurance on the life of the employee's spouse or dependent. However, the employer may be able to exclude the cost of this type of insurance from the employee's wages as a de minimis fringe benefit (as discussed in Chapter 13);
- Permanent life insurance; or
- Life insurance where the employer is the beneficiary of the policy.

Definition of Employee and Requirements

Generally, life insurance provided by the employer is not considered group term life insurance unless the employer provides it to at least 10 full-time employees at some time during the year. For this purpose, employees are typically defined as current common-law employees, full-time life insurance agents who are current statutory employees, and leased employees who have provided services to the employer on a substantially full-time basis for at least a year (if the services are performed under the employer's primary direction and control).

The employer should count employees who choose not to receive the life insurance unless, to receive the coverage, the employee must pay for benefits other than group term life insurance. For example, the employer should count an employee who is eligible to benefit from the group term life insurance by paying part of the premium, even if that employee chooses not to receive the life insurance coverage. However, the employer does not count an employee who must pay part or all of the cost of permanent benefits to benefit from the group life insurance unless that employee chooses to pay the costs and benefit from the life insurance coverage.

If the employer does not meet the general 10-employee-rule, the employer may still be eligible to receive the benefits of the group term life insurance coverage if the employer's provision of the coverage meets the following three requirements:

1. The employer provides coverage under the plan to all of its full-time employees who provide evidence of insurability.
2. The coverage provided under the plan must be based on either a uniform percentage of pay or a set amount of coverage depending upon age, years of service, compensation, or position.
3. The required evidence of insurability must be limited to a medical questionnaire (completed by the employee) that does not require a physician.

When applying this exception, employers should not consider employees who were denied insurance for any of the following reasons:

1. The employees were 65 or older;
2. The employees customarily work 20 hours or less a week or five months or less in a calendar year; or
3. The employees have not been employed for a waiting period stated in the policy (which cannot exceed six months).

S Corporation Shareholders

When an employer provides group term life insurance coverage for a more than two percent shareholder of an S Corporation, the cost of the coverage is included in the shareholder's gross income and is subject to Social Security and Medicare taxes. However, the employer does not pay federal unemployment tax (FUTA) on the cost of any group term life insurance coverage provided to a more than two percent shareholder.

Income Tax Treatment

Group term life insurance premiums paid by the employer on the first $50,000 of death benefits are deductible by the employer and are excludable from an employee's gross income. The cost, as determined under the Uniform Premium Table provided by the IRS, of any death benefit coverage in excess of $50,000 is taxable to the employee. The monthly cost of the insurance to include in the employee's gross income is determined by multiplying the number of thousands of dollars of insurance coverage over $50,000 (rounded to the nearest $1,000) by the cost shown in the following table. The table corresponds with the employee's age as of the last day of the tax year and the includible amount is reduced by any contribution payments made by the employee.

Exhibit 14.6 | Uniform Premium Table: Cost Per $1,000 of Protection For One Month[16]

Age	Cost
Under 25	$0.05
25 through 29	$0.06
30 through 34	$0.08
35 through 39	$0.09
40 through 44	$0.10
45 through 49	$0.15
50 through 54	$0.23
55 through 59	$0.43
60 through 64	$0.66
65 through 69	$1.27
70 and older	$2.06

The employee can always receive the first $50,000 of death benefit coverage tax-free. Thus, if an employee's death benefit under the employer-provided term life insurance is $90,000, the employee will be taxed (as determined above) on $40,000 ($90,000 - $50,000) of the coverage. Also, if an employee pays an amount towards the cost of the taxable death benefit coverage, the taxable amount is decreased by the employee's payment.

---

16. Treas. Reg. 1.79-3(d).

Example 14.4

BigBully Corp provides all of its employees with group term life insurance coverage equal to their salary. Steve earns $40,000 per year and is 40 years old. Steve is not considered a key employee. In this instance, Steve's term policy will provide a death benefit of $40,000. Since the benefit is below the taxable limit, Steve's benefit will be excluded from his income.

Example 14.5

BigBully Corp provides all of its employees with group term life insurance coverage equal to their salary. Fred earns $100,000 per year and is 40 years old. Fred is not considered a key employee. The cost of the insurance that must be included in Fred's compensation is calculated as follows:

Salary	$100,000
Less exclusion	- $50,000
	$50,000
Divided by 1,000	÷ 1,000
	50
Times cost (as provided in table)	x 0.10
	$5.00
Times 12 months	x 12
Yearly inclusion in employee's income (W-2)	$60.00

BigBully Corp provides all of its employees with group term life insurance coverage equal to their salary. Ralph earns $100,000 per year and is 40 years old. Ralph is not considered a key employee and pays $50 per year toward the cost of the insurance. The cost of the insurance that must be included in Ralph's compensation is calculated as follows:

Salary	$100,000
Less exclusion	- $50,000
	$50,000
Divided by 1,000	÷ 1,000
	50
Times Cost (as provided in table)	x 0.10
	$5.00
Times 12 months	x 12
Yearly premium cost	$60.00
Premium paid by employee	- $50.00
Yearly inclusion in employee's income (W-2)	$10.00

Key Employees

To qualify for favorable tax treatment, a group term life insurance plan must be nondiscriminatory. To be nondiscriminatory, the plan must cover either:[17]

- 70% or more of all eligible employees, or
- 85% of the non-key employees.

If the plan does not meet either of the two tests, the plan is considered discriminatory and the key employee must include the greater of either the cost as determined in the Uniform Premium Table or the actual cost of the life insurance coverage to the employer in the employee's gross income. In addition, if the plan is discriminatory, there is no exclusion for the key employee for the first $50,000 of coverage.

Coverage for Dependents

The cost of group term life insurance coverage paid by the employer for the spouse or dependents of an employee may be excludable from an employee's gross income as a de minimis fringe benefit. The cost of the coverage is determined by the Uniform Premium Table.

GROUP DISABILITY INSURANCE

Disability insurance provides benefits in the form of periodic payments to a person who is unable to work due to sickness or accidental injury. The cost of disability insurance varies depending on occupation, age, and sex of the insured, as well as the benefit term, coverage, and the length of the waiting period (elimination period) provided under the policy.

Disability insurance can be provided under a group or individual plan. Group disability policies are often cheaper than individual polices but may actually have additional restrictions as compared to individual policies.

> **Key Concepts**
>
> 1. What are the tax implications of employer-provided group disability insurance?
>
> 2. What are cafeteria plans and how are they used?
>
> 3. What are the tax implications of employer-provided cafeteria plans?

In addition, there is a clear difference between **group short-term disability policies** and **group long-term disability policies**. Short-term disability will generally begin after a very brief period of time (1-14 days), often corresponding to the employer's sick leave. Long-term disability benefits typically begin after short-term and will often continue for a fixed period of time, until retirement or in some cases for life. Many of the differences between short and long-term group disability plans, including coverage period, elimination periods, eligible employees, and definition of disability, are identified in **Exhibit 14.7**.

---

17. IRC §79(d)(3).

Exhibit 14.7 | Group Short-Term Disability vs. Group Long-Term Disability

	Short-Term Disability	Long-Term Disability
Definition of Disability	Generally more liberal than long-term disability	May be any occupation, own occupation, or split-definition
Begins	After sick-leave - usually a short period of time (may be 0-14 days)	After elimination period - often 6 months (but may be from 90 - 180 days)
Benefit Period	• Generally 3-6 months for group policies • Will often tie to the elimination period for the long-term policy • Range: 3, 6, 12, 24 months	• May be a term of years (5, 10), or: • To an age 65, 67, 70 (or other) • For life (benefits may be shorter for blue collar workers and longer for white collar workers)
Benefit	Up to 100% of income but usually 40-65% of salary and usually with a dollar cap and a time cap	Generally up to 60% - 70% of income

Exhibit 14.8 | Disability Coverage Phases

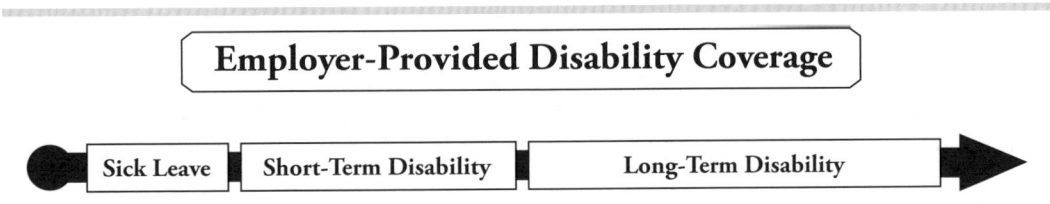

Taxation of Disability Benefits

Premiums paid by the employer are deductible by the employer and are not included in the employee's gross income. However, when the employer pays the premium and the value is excluded from the employee's gross income, any disability income benefit received by the employee is taxable to the employee. If the employee pays the entire premium with after-tax income or the employer pays the premium and the employee includes the premium payment in income, any benefits received will be considered tax-exempt. As such, many employees choose to include the cost of the premiums in their taxable income even when paid by the employer because any disability benefits paid from such a plan would then be received tax-free. If the employer and employee each pay part of the premium, the prorated part of the benefits associated with the employer's contribution is taxable to the employee.

Types of Disability Insurance Policies

Disability insurance policies typically cover periods when the insured is unable to work due to suffering an accident or sickness. There are three primary types of disability policies, as determined by the definition of disability:
- own occupation policies,
- any occupation policies, and
- split definition policies.

Exhibit 14.9 | Types of Disability Policies

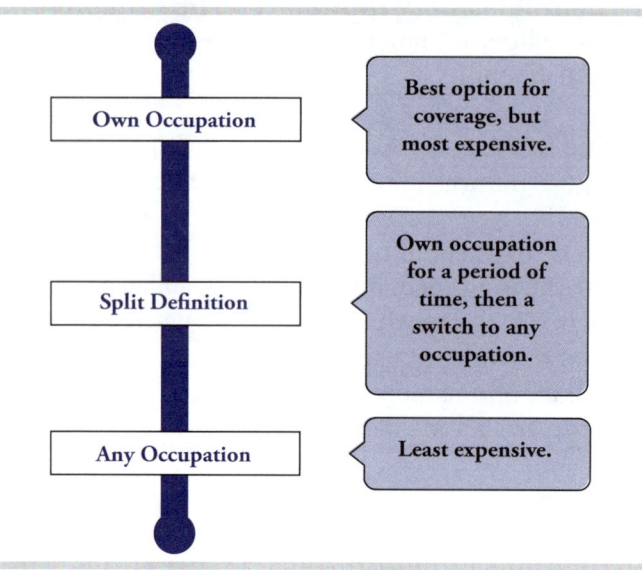

An **own occupation** policy states that if the insured is unable to perform each and every duty associated with his own occupation (specified e.g., orthopedic surgeon) the insured is deemed to be disabled and the policy will provide benefits.

Example 14.6

Rosemary is a concert pianist and has spent her lifetime practicing and performing piano concertos around the world. She recently contracted a disease which affected the dexterity of her hands and prevented her from being able to perform at concerts. She purchased an own occupation disability insurance policy 25 years ago so the insurance policy will pay disability benefits to Rosemary since she can no longer perform the duties of her own occupation as a pianist.

Own occupation policies were popular disability tools in the late 1980s and early 1990s, particularly with physicians, musicians, and other professionals whose income was dependent on their ability to perform specific tasks. Over time insurance companies recognized that there was a large adverse selection risk associated with these policies, which are now less available. When an own-occupation policy (as they are referred to) is issued, the premium is high due to the risks undertaken by the insurance company.

An **any occupation** disability insurance policy provides benefits to a policy owner if the policy owner is unable to perform the duties of any occupation. This type of policy is not attractive to individuals in high-skill professions. The surgeon, for example, would probably not want a policy that will not pay benefits unless the surgeon could not perform telemarketing services. The courts have limited the interpretation of this definition of disability to mean that the insured can collect benefits if the insured is unable to perform any occupation for which he is suited based on training, experience, and educational degrees. Continuing our example, if the surgeon is unable to perform surgery due to an injury to his hands, but could teach medical school to new physicians, he would be expected to earn income in that fashion, and would not receive benefits under the policy. The surgeon would not, however, be required to perform telemarketing services as a means of minimizing benefits received under the policy.

Many disability insurance policies today use a **split definition** of disability in their disability insurance policies. Under a split definition policy, an insured is covered against the risk of not performing his own occupation for a period of time and, after that period expires, an any-occupation definition of disability is used. This gives the insured a period to adjust to his new reality and perhaps get the training necessary to perform other occupations that will allow him to replace the lost income from the old occupation.

CAFETERIA PLANS

A **cafeteria plan** is a written plan, under which the employee may choose to receive cash as compensation or tax-free fringe benefits. Provided the cafeteria plan meets the requirements defined below, the value of the fringe benefit, if chosen by the employee, will be a deductible expense for the employer and will not be included in the employee's gross income. These plans are referred to as §125 plans because they are permitted by IRC §125, which requires a cafeteria plan to offer at least one taxable benefit, usually cash, and one qualified nontaxable benefit. The usual nontaxable benefits include group term life insurance in any amount, medical reimbursements or insurance plans, accident and disability benefits, dependent care assistance, and paid vacation.

Uses and Applications

A cafeteria plan is appropriate when employee benefit needs vary within the employee group; the employee mix includes young, unmarried people with minimal life insurance and medical benefits needs, as well as older employees with families who need maximum medical and life insurance benefits. A cafeteria plan is also appropriate when employees want to choose the benefit package most suited to their individual needs, and when an employer seeks to maximize employee satisfaction with the benefit package, thereby maximizing the employer's benefit from its compensation expenditures. A cafeteria plan is also appropriate when the employer is large enough to afford the expense of such a plan. A cafeteria plan is a way of managing fringe benefit costs to the employer by individually pricing each benefit, and providing a total dollar equivalency to each employee to effectively shop for the best mix of benefits for that employee.

Cafeteria plans help give employees an appreciation of the value of their benefit package by allowing them to choose the cash or purchase the benefit. Cafeteria plans can also help control employer costs of providing benefit packages because the employer does not pay for benefits that are not used by the employees. Cafeteria plans are more complex and expensive to design and administer and usually include some insured benefits such as medical and life insurance.

Exhibit 14.10 | Cafeteria Plans

Qualified Benefits	Benefits Not Allowed
• Accident and health benefits (but not medical savings accounts or long-term care insurance) • Adoption assistance • Dependent care assistance • Group term life insurance up to $50,000 • Group term life insurance above $50,000 can be provided, but is includible in an employee's gross income • Long-term or short-term disability coverage • A qualified cash or deferred arrangement (401(k) plan) • Contributions to Health Savings Accounts (HSAs)	• Archer Medical Savings Accounts (see accident and health benefits) • Athletic facilities • De minimis (minimal) benefits • Deferred compensation arrangements • Educational assistance • Employee discounts • Lodging on employer's business premises • Meals • Moving expense reimbursements • No-additional-cost services • Transportation benefits • Tuition reduction • Working condition benefits

Benefits Provided

Qualified benefits include benefits that the employer could provide tax-free to the employee (except for the items listed above). More specifically, qualified benefits include accident and health insurance benefits (but not medical savings accounts or long-term care insurance), adoption assistance, dependent care assistance, and group term life insurance coverage (including costs that cannot be excluded from wages). A cafeteria plan cannot include an Archer medical savings account, the payment of athletic facilities dues, de minimis (minimal) benefits, educational assistance, employee discounts, lodging on the employer's business premises, meals, moving expense reimbursements, no-additional-cost services, transportation (commuting) benefits, tuition reduction, working condition benefits, and scholarships or fellowships.

Generally, a cafeteria plan can not include any plan that offers a benefit that defers an employee's compensation, like a contribution to a retirement plan. However, a cafeteria plan can include a qualified 401(k) plan as an available nontaxable benefit.

The flexible spending account (FSA) is a cafeteria plan funded through employee salary reductions. FSAs are discussed in detail in the next section.

Example 14.7

Employer NR provides group-term life insurance coverage to its employees only through its cafeteria plan. Employer NR's cafeteria plan allows employees to elect salary reduction for group-term life insurance. Bambi, age 42, elected salary reduction of $200 for $150,000 of group-term life insurance. None of the group-term life insurance is paid through after-tax employee contributions. Implications:

- Bambi's $200 of salary reduction for group-term life insurance is excludable from her gross income.
- Bambi has a total of $150,000 of group-term life insurance. The group-term life insurance in excess of the dollar limitation of section 79 is $100,000 (150,000 - 50,000).
- The Table I cost is $120 (100 x $0.10 x 12 months) for $100,000 of group-term life insurance for an individual between ages 40 to 44. The Table I cost of $120 is reduced by zero (because Bambi paid no portion of the group-term life insurance with after-tax employee contributions).
- The amount includible in Bambi's gross income for the $100,000 of excess group-term life insurance is $120 for the year.

Income Tax Implications

Because the employee who benefits from a cafeteria plan has the choice to either receive cash as compensation or use the value to "purchase" fringe benefits tax-free within the cafeteria plan, the cafeteria plan must meet the rules of IRC §125. Under this section, the IRC provides the benefits payable from a fringe benefit plan with an exclusion from the constructive receipt rule, which would otherwise require the employee to include the value of the benefits purchased in his taxable income.

A cafeteria plan meets the qualifications of the IRC if the benefits provided under the plan are qualified (as discussed above), the plan does not favor the highly compensated employees, and the nontaxable benefits provided to key employees is less than 25 percent of the total nontaxable benefits provided under the plan to all employees.

Benefits under the plan cannot discriminate in favor of highly compensated employees or key employees. Cafeteria plans cannot discriminate in favor of highly compensated individuals as to eligibility to participate, or highly compensated participants as to contributions and benefits. If benefits provided to key employees exceed 25 percent of the aggregate of nontaxable benefits provided for all employees through the cafeteria plan, each key employee must include in gross income an amount equal to the maximum taxable benefits that he could have elected for the plan year.

Highly compensated employees for purposes of cafeteria plans are defined as an officer, a greater than five percent owner, or an employee with income in excess the annual limit ($130,000 for 2021).

Key employees are defined in the same manner as for qualified plans. A **key employee** is any employee who is any one or more of the following:

- A greater than five percent owner,[18] or
- A greater than one percent owner with compensation in excess of $150,000 (not indexed), or
- An officer (defined below) with compensation in excess of $185,000 for 2021 as determined last year.[19]

---

18. The definition of a five-percent owner under top-heavy rules is the same as it is for determining whether an employee is highly compensated and includes family attributions.

When a cafeteria plan meets the requirements of the IRC, the employee will not be taxed on the value of the nontaxable fringe benefits chosen, and the employer can deduct the value of the nontaxable fringe benefits chosen by the employee. In the case where the plan provides a benefit that is not qualified, the value of the benefit will be included in the employee's gross income. Also, in the case where the plan is deemed discriminatory by favoring the highly compensated or providing more than 25 percent of the benefit to key employees, the value of the nontaxable benefits chosen by the key employees or highly compensated will be included in their gross income.

Simple Cafeteria Plans for Small Businesses

After December 31, 2010, small employers meeting contribution requirements and eligibility and participation requirements can establish a simple cafeteria plan. Simple cafeteria plans do not have to meet the same nondiscrimination rules that a regular cafeteria plan generally must meet. Simple cafeteria plans are treated as meeting the nondiscrimination requirements of a cafeteria plan and certain benefits under a cafeteria plan.

Eligible employers will generally have 100 or fewer employees. The test for this rule is that the employer had an average of 100 or fewer employees on business days during either of the two preceding years. In addition, small companies that increase in size retain small employer status until such time as the average number of employees equals or exceeds 200.

Employers must make a contribution to provide qualified benefits on behalf of each qualified employee in an amount equal to:

1. A uniform percentage (not less than 2%) of the employee's compensation for the plan year, or
2. An amount which is at least six percent of the employee's compensation for the plan year or twice the amount of the salary reduction contributions of each qualified employee, whichever is less.

> ### ☑ Quick Quiz 14.4
>
> 1. If an employer pays for and provides disability insurance to an employee, the benefits received from such a policy will be tax-free.
>   a. True
>   b. False
>
> 2. Cafeteria plans allow an employee to exclude from income the value of the nontaxable fringe benefits selected.
>   a. True
>   b. False
>
> False, True.

If the contribution requirements are met using option (2) above, the rate of contribution to any salary reduction contribution of a highly compensated or key employee can not be greater than the rate of contribution to any other employee.

Employers must generally cover any employee who has attained the age of 21, has one year of service and works at least 1,000 hours during the year.

19.IRC §416(i)(1).

FLEXIBLE SPENDING ACCOUNTS

A **flexible spending account (FSA)** is a cafeteria plan under which employees can choose between receiving cash or deferring income tax-free to fund the cost of certain employee selected benefits. Because of the consequences of forfeiture of unused benefits, these are often referred to as "Use It or Lose It" accounts.

A flexible spending account is appropriate in any of the following situations:

1. An employer wants to expand employee benefit choices without significant employer out-of-pocket costs (or possibly realize some actual dollar savings).
2. Many employees have employed spouses with duplicate medical coverage.
3. Employees contribute to health insurance costs.
4. The employer's medical plans have large deductibles or coinsurance (co-pay) provisions.
5. There is a need for benefits that are difficult to provide on a group basis, such as dependent care.
6. The costs of employee benefit plans, such as health insurance, have increased, and the employer must impose additional employee cost sharing in the form of increased employee contributions and deductibles.

The FSA approach minimizes employee outlay since the FSA converts what would have been after-tax employee expenditures for the benefits selected to pre-tax expenditures. The plan provides employees a degree of choice to receive either cash as compensation or the cash to pay for the costs of certain benefits. The FSA is funded entirely through employee salary reductions, only requiring the employer to bear the administrative costs. Salary reductions elected by employees to fund the nontaxable benefits available under the plan are not subject to income taxes or payroll taxes. There are many nontaxable benefits available from a FSA, which include many benefits that employers might not otherwise provide to their employees such as dependent care, dental, etc.

Flexible Spending Account Limit

Flexible spending accounts have an annual limit on the amount that employees can contribute from salary and spend tax-free on health care. The dollar limit is indexed for inflation annually, and is $2,750 for 2021.[20]

Use it or Lose it Rule

FSAs must comply with the use-or-lose rule since they are not permitted to defer compensation. However, a "run-out period" allows extra time during the following year for submission of invoices for reimbursement of expenses incurred during the plan year (a plan year is not always a calendar year). During this time, the employee can still be reimbursed from the FSA for expenses incurred during the prior year (the year for which funds were contributed). The period of time permitted for these claims (the run-out period) will vary from employer-to-employer and can be found in the Summary Plan Description provided by the employer.

In 2005, the IRS modified the "use it or lose it" rules to extend the time period through which employees can use FSA funds.[21] This extension of time, referred to as a grace period, must apply to all participants in the FSA cafeteria plan. Expenses for qualified benefits incurred during the grace period may be paid or reimbursed from benefits or contributions remaining unused at the end of the immediately preceding plan year. The grace period must not extend beyond the fifteenth day of the third calendar month after

---

20. IRC Section 125(i).
21. IRS Notice 2005-42.

the end of the immediately preceding plan year to which it relates (i.e., "the 2½ month rule"). The effect of the grace period is that the participant may have as long as 14 months and 15 days (the 12 months in the current cafeteria plan year plus the grace period) to use the benefits or contributions for a plan year before those amounts are "forfeited" under the "use-it-or-lose-it" rule.

Exhibit 14.11 | Run-Out Period vs. Grace Period

Run-Out Period	Allows extra time to be reimbursed for expenses incurred in the prior year.
Grace Period	Allows funds from the prior year to be used for expenses incurred during the first 2½ months of the current year.

Example 14.8

Employee A plans to have eye surgery in 2021. For the 2021 plan year, Employee A timely elects salary reduction of $2,750 for a health FSA. During the 2021 plan year, Employee A learns that she cannot have the eye surgery performed, but incurs other medical expenses totaling $1,400. As of December 31, 2021, she has $1,350 of unused benefits and contributions in the health FSA. Consistent with the use-it-or-lose-it rules she would forfeit the $1,350 if it is not used by March 15, 2022.

The Affordable Care Act, enacted in March 2010, established a uniform standard that, effective January 1, 2011, applied to FSAs. Under the standard, the cost of an over-the-counter medicine or drug could not be reimbursed from the FSA account unless a prescription was obtained. The change did not affect insulin, even if purchased without a prescription, or other health care expenses such as medical devices, eye glasses, contact lenses, co-pays and deductibles. As a result of the COVID-19 pandemic in 2020, the CARES Act (Coronavirus Aid, Relief, and Economic Security Act of 2020) repealed this rule, once again allowing over-the-counter drugs to be purchased from an HSA or FSA without the need for a prescription after December 31, 2019.

Over the last decade, the IRS has considered various methods of relief for taxpayers using FSAs. In October 2013, the IRS made modifications to the "use-or-lose" rule for FSAs, and made further modifications to the same rule in 2020.[22] These modifications allow §125 cafeteria plans to be amended to allow up to $550 (in 2021) of unused amounts remaining at the end of a plan year in a health FSA to be paid or reimbursed to plan participants for qualified medical expenses incurred during the following plan year, provided that the plan does not also incorporate the grace period rule discussed above. This carryover of up to $550 does not affect the maximum amount of salary reduction contributions that the participant is permitted to make to the FSA for the year. This carryover option provides an alternative to the grace period rule. As a result of the COVID-19 pandemic in 2020, temporary special rules were implemented regarding the carryover of unused amounts in health care FSAs, as discussed below.

☰ Key Concepts

1. What are flexible spending accounts, and when are they appropriate?

2. What are the tax implications of employer-provided flexible spending accounts?

---

22. IRS Notice 2013-71 and IRS Notice 2020-33.

Example 14.9

Employer sponsors a §125 cafeteria plan and health FSA with a calendar plan year, an annual run-out period from January 1 through March 31 in which participants can submit claims for expenses incurred during the preceding plan year, and an annual open enrollment season in November in which participants elect a salary reduction amount (not to exceed $2,750) for the following plan year. The plan is timely amended to provide for a carryover that allows all participants to apply up to $550 of unused health FSA amounts remaining at the end of the run-out period to the health FSA for expenses incurred at any time during that plan year. The plan does not provide for a grace period with respect to the health FSA.

In November 2021, Participant A elects a salary reduction amount of $2,750 for 2022. By December 31, 2021, A's unused amount from the 2021 plan year is $800. On February 1, 2022, A submits claims and is reimbursed with respect to $350 of expenses incurred during the 2021 plan year, leaving a carryover on March 31, 2022 (the end of the run-out period) of $450 of unused health FSA amounts from 2021. The $450 amount is not forfeited; instead, it is carried over to 2022 and available to pay claims incurred in that year so that $3,200 (that is, $2,750 + $450) is available to pay claims incurred in 2022. A incurs and submits claims for expenses of $2,700 during the month of July 2022, and does not submit any other claims during 2022. A is reimbursed with respect to the $2,700 claim, leaving $500 as a potential unused amount from 2022 (depending upon whether A submits claims during the 2022 run-out period in early 2023).

Uniform Coverage Rules Applicable to Health FSAs

The maximum amount of reimbursement from a health FSA must be available at all times during the year (properly reduced as of any particular time for prior reimbursements for the same period of coverage). Thus, the maximum amount of reimbursement at any particular time during the year cannot relate to the amount that has been contributed to the FSA at any particular time prior to the end of the plan year. Similarly, the payment schedule for the required amount for coverage under a health FSA may not be based on the rate or amount of covered claims incurred during the coverage period. Employees' salary reduction payments must not be accelerated based on employees' incurred claims and reimbursements. The uniform coverage rule applies only to health FSAs and does not apply to FSAs for dependent care assistance or adoption assistance.

✏️ Quick Quiz 14.5

1. An employee should consider carefully whether to use a flexible spending account for child care expenses as the FSA is usually more beneficial than the child and dependent care credit.
   a. True
   b. False

2. An employee who contributes to an FSA reduces his taxable income but must still pay payroll taxes on the contributed amount.
   a. True
   b. False

True, False.

Example 14.10

Employer C maintains a calendar year cafeteria plan, offering an election between cash and a health FSA. The cafeteria plan prohibits accelerating employees' salary reduction payments based on employees' incurred claims and reimbursements.

For 2021, Employee N timely elects salary reduction of $2,750 for a health FSA. N pays the $2,750 salary reduction amount through salary reduction of $229 per month throughout the year. Employee N is eligible to receive the maximum amount of reimbursement of $2,750 at all times throughout the year (reduced by prior reimbursements).

N incurs $2,750 of medical expenses in January of the current year. The full $2,750 is reimbursed although N has made only one salary reduction payment of $229. After N submits a claim for reimbursement and substantiates the medical expenses, the cafeteria plan reimburses N for the $2,750 of medical expenses. Employer C's cafeteria plan satisfies the uniform coverage rule.

The employer is at risk for the total annual amount an employee elects to allocate to health benefits under his FSA even if the employee terminates employment before funding the amount used from the plan. In addition, if the employee fails to use all contributed amounts within a certain time period, contributions are forfeited back to the employer (use-it-or-lose-it).

Dependent Care Expenses: FSA vs Child and Dependent Care Credit

As described in the Dependent Care Assistance section in Chapter 13, a dependent care FSA allows the employee to contribute up to $5,000 ($2,500 if married filing separately) on a pre-tax basis similar to the health care FSA. Using a flexible spending account to pay for dependent care expenses (if provided) may provide more tax savings than utilization of the Child and Dependent Care Credit. In general, an employee is better off using an FSA unless the employee's income (AGI) is less than $43,000.[23]

The $5,000 limit on contributions to a dependent care FSA is not indexed for inflation; however, the dollar limit was temporarily increased by the American Rescue Plan Act (ARPA) of 2021. In 2021 only, plans are permitted to adopt an amendment increasing the limit to $10,500 ($5,250 for married taxpayers filing separately). ARPA also temporarily increased, for 2021 only, the amount of qualified expenses under the Child and Dependent Care Credit and made the credit refundable. The examples below are based on the permanent limits applicable in all years except 2021.

---

23. Form 2441.

Example 14.11

Ruth is a single parent with three children. Ruth's income is $25,000 per year. She has $4,000 in child care expenses. In this instance using the dependent care credit will provide a greater tax savings than a dependent care flexible spending account. The calculation is as follows:

Dependent Child Care Credit		Flexible Spending Account	
$4,000	Expenses (limit is $6,000)*	$4,000	Expense
x 0.30	Rate for $25,000 of income	x 0.12	Tax bracket
$1,200	Tax savings (Credit)	$480	Tax savings
		+ 306	7.65 Payroll tax saved by Ruth
		$786	Total taxes saved

Limit is $3,000 for one qualifying dependent or $6,000 for two or more (in all years except 2021).

Example 14.12

Assume Ruth marries Marty, whose income is $150,000. Ruth's income is $25,000 per year and she has $4,000 in expenses for their three children. In this instance using the dependent care flexible spending account would be more beneficial because of the income tax rate differential on the dependent care credit. The calculation is as follows:

Dependent Child Care Credit		Flexible Spending Account	
$4,000	Expenses*	$4,000	Expense
x 0.20	Rate for income above $43,000	x 0.22	Tax bracket
$800	Tax savings (Credit)	$880	Tax savings
		+ 306	7.65 Social Security saved by Ruth
		$1,186	Total taxes saved

Limit is $3,000 for one qualifying dependent or $6,000 for two or more (in all years except 2021).

It should be noted that any dependent care expenses that are excluded or deducted from taxable income will reduce the availability of the dependent care credit. This offset is illustrated in the next two examples.

Example 14.13

Javier is a widower with one child and earns $24,000 a year. He pays work-related expenses of $2,900 for the care of his 4-year-old child and qualifies to claim the credit for child and dependent care expenses. His employer pays an additional $1,000 under a qualified dependent care benefit plan. This $1,000 is excluded from Javier's income.

Although the dollar limit for his work-related expenses is $3,000 (one qualifying person), Javier figures his credit on only $2,000 of the $2,900 work-related expenses he paid. This is because his dollar limit is reduced as shown next.

Maximum allowable expenses for one qualifying person	$3,000
Minus: Dependent care benefits Javier excludes from income	-$1,000
Equals: Reduced dollar limit on expenses Javier can use for the credit	**$2,000**

In summary, Javier had $1,000 excluded from his income and can take a credit on $2,000 of expenses.

Example 14.14

Maya is married and both she and her husband are employed. Each has earned income in excess of $6,000. They have two children, Jonah and Charlotte, ages 2 and 4, who attend a daycare facility licensed and regulated by the state. Maya's work-related expenses are $6,000 for the year.

Maya's employer has a dependent care assistance program as part of its cafeteria plan, which allows employees to make pre-tax contributions to a dependent care flexible spending arrangement. Maya has elected to take the maximum $5,000 exclusion from her salary to cover dependent care expenses through this program.

Although the dollar limit for her work-related expenses is $6,000 (two or more qualifying persons), Maya figures her credit on only $1,000 of the $6,000 work-related expense paid. This lower credit amount of $1,000 is because her dollar limit is reduced by the $5,000.

An FSA must meet the nondiscrimination requirements as previously discussed for cafeteria plans. FSAs also require that employees evaluate their personal and family benefit situations, and file a timely election form each year indicating their deferral choice. The plan could result in adverse selection that would ultimately raise benefit costs.

Income Tax Implications

Employee salary reductions applied to nontaxable benefits are not subject to income taxes or payroll taxes. The employer gets a tax deduction for any amounts it pays under the plan coverage.

Temporary Special Rules Regarding Health and Dependent Care FSAs[24]

The Taxpayer Certainty and Disaster Tax Relief Act (TCDTRA) of 2020 provided special rules for health and dependent care FSAs in 2020 and 2021, including:

1. For plan years ending in 2020, a plan may allow unused amounts in a health or dependent care FSA to carry over to 2021 without limit (carryovers are normally limited to $550).
2. For plan years ending in 2021, a plan may allow unused amounts in a health or dependent care FSA to carry over to 2022 without limit.
3. Health or dependent care FSA grace periods for plan years ending in 2020 or 2021 may be extended to 12 months from the end of the plan year (grace periods are normally limited to 2.5 months).
4. Plans may allow an employee who ceased participation during 2020 or 2021 (calendar year) to receive reimbursements from unused benefits through the end of the year in which the employee ceased participation (including grace periods).
5. Dependent care FSAs are permitted to extend the maximum age from 12 to 13 for eligible dependents.
   - Eligible dependents are those who aged out during a plan year with an enrollment period ending on or before January 31, 2020.
   - Unused balances for the plan year (as described in part a) may be permitted to pay claims for reimbursement in the following year.
6. Employees may be permitted to modify FSA contributions prospectively, for plan years ending in 2021, without a change in status.

The above changes require timely plan amendments.

24. Additional details regarding these special rules can be found in IRS Notice 2021-15.

FSA contributions not only affect taxes, but may affect disability benefit calculations. In ***Brosted v. Unum Life Ins. Co. of America***,[1] Mr. Daniel Brosted was employed by Dreisilker Electric Motors, Inc., which was also the plan administrator for Dreisilker Electric Motors, Inc. Group Long Term Disability Income Plan, a single-employer employee benefit plan. Mr. Brosted was employed by Dreisilker as a purchasing manager from 1974 until January 3, 2000, and was a member of the Plan from its inception. Another defendant, Unum Life Insurance Company of America, provided the insurance coverage for the Plan. Mr. Brosted sought to recover $22,086.09 for past benefits he felt were wrongfully not paid, as well as an increase of his current benefits by $513.63 per month.

Mr. Brosted was diagnosed with multiple sclerosis at age thirty-two. In 2000, Mr. Brosted was hospitalized for his illness and subsequently was prevented from returning to work by Dreisilker. In June 2000, Mr. Brosted applied for long-term disability benefits under the Plan, and by August 1st, Mr. Brosted reached an agreement with Dreisilker concerning his severance from the company. Shortly thereafter, an Unum accountant reviewed Mr. Brosted's file and discovered that his disability benefits had been improperly calculated. According to the policy, benefits were to be either sixty percent of the claimant's monthly earnings prior to disability or $6,000, whichever was less. The monthly earnings used to calculate the benefit were not to include "pre-tax contributions to a qualified deferred compensation plan, §125 plan, or other flexible spending account." Unum's original calculations neglected to take into account Mr. Brosted's pre-tax contributions to his §125 flexible spending account and to his deferred compensation plan. As a result, his monthly benefits were reduced by $513.

Mr. Brosted argued that the Plan and Unum were legally prevented from changing his benefit amount and that Unum breached its fiduciary duty to him under ERISA. The Court disagreed, and granted the defendants' pretrial motion to dismiss because the pre-tax contributions to his §125 flexible spending account and to his deferred compensation plan should not have been included in calculating his disability benefits.

1. ***Brosted v. Unum Life Ins. Co. of America,*** 349 F.Supp.2d 1088, 34 Employee Benefits Cas. 1523 (N.D.Ill. 2004).

OTHER EMPLOYEE BENEFITS

Medical Savings Accounts

The Health Insurance Portability and Accountability Act (HIPAA) established a tax-favored savings account for medical expenses called an **Archer Medical Savings Account (MSA).**[25] The MSAs could be established after 1996 and before 2006 for employers with 50 or less employees and self-employed individuals. Employees could not establish the MSA but could contribute (subject to the limitations discussed below) to the account if their employer established an MSA on their behalf. After 2005, an MSA cannot be established and has been replaced by the Health Savings Account (HSA), which is discussed later. However, the MSAs that were established prior to 2006 are still in existence, may still be maintained, and retain their tax-favored status.

25. Public Law 104-191 (August 21, 1996); IRC §220.

For MSAs to be established, the employer must have provided its employees with a high-deductible health plan with a maximum out-of-pocket cost.[26] A high deductible plan for purposes of meeting the requirements of the MSA is a major medical health insurance plan with a deductible between $2,400 and $3,600 (2021) for individual coverage and between $4,800 and $7,150 for 2021 for family coverage. The maximum out-of-pocket costs for the plan is $4,800 for individual coverage and $8,750 for family coverage. These same limitations apply for self-employed individuals.

Contributions can be made to the MSA by the employee or the employer. Employee contributions are deductible from the employee's gross income. In addition, employer contributions are tax deductible by the employer, not subject to payroll taxes, and not taxable income to the employee. The aggregate contributions to the plan by the employee and the employer cannot exceed 65 percent of the deductible for individual coverage and 75 percent of the deductible for family coverage.

The earnings on the assets within an MSA are tax deferred until a distribution is taken from the account. If a distribution is for qualified medical expenses, the distribution, including any earnings, is not taxable. If the distribution is not for qualified medical expenses, the entire distribution is taxable as ordinary income. In addition, if the distribution is taken before the owner of the account is age 65, the distribution is subject to an additional 20 percent excise penalty tax.

Health Savings Accounts

The Medicare Act of 2003 created **Health Savings Accounts (HSAs)**, which are very similar to MSAs but less restrictive. Specifically, HSAs can be established by anyone with a high deductible health insurance plan (see below), and allow a higher contribution amount.

To be eligible to make HSA contributions, the individual's health insurance plan's deductible must be at least $1,400 for single coverage and the annual out-of-pocket costs cannot exceed $7,000 for 2021.[27] For family coverage under an HSA, the health insurance plan deductible must be at least $2,800, and the annual out-of-pocket costs cannot exceed $14,000 for 2021. Individuals who are covered by Medicare, another health insurance policy, or individuals who are dependents of another person for income tax purposes are not eligible to make contributions to HSAs.

Individuals who are married should also be aware that they will be ineligible for an HSA if they are covered under any other health plan which is not a high deductible plan (HDHP). Ineligibility applies even to a spouse's non-HDHP or a spouse's FSA if it is permitted to be used for the individual's medical expenses. However, if the FSA is limited to paying only the individual's dental and vision expenses and the individual is not covered under the spouse's health insurance policy, then the individual may still be eligible for an HSA as long as the other HSA rules are met.

> **⋮☰ *Key Concepts***
>
> 1. What are the tax implications of employer-provided Archer MSAs, and when can they be established?
>
> 2. What are the tax implications of employer-provided HSAs, and when can they be established?
>
> 3. What are VEBAs, and what are the tax implications of payments made by the employer to the VEBA?

---

26. IRC §220(c)(2)(A); Rev. Proc. 2004-71.
27. IRC §§223(b) and (c); Rev. Proc. 2019-25.

Contributions to the HSA can be made by the individual or by the individual's employer on a pre-tax basis. In either case, the aggregate contributions cannot exceed the maximum contribution of $3,600 for individuals and $7,200 for families for 2021. However, individuals between 55 years old and 64 years old can make additional catch-up contributions of $1,000 over these limits for 2021.[28] The full amount of the contributions may be deducted regardless of the actual amount of the deductible or maximum out-of-pocket expenses.

Those who enroll in a HDHP and become eligible to make HSA contributions part way through the year are permitted to make the full annual contribution so long as they were eligible for an HSA as of the first day of the last month of the tax year (December 1 for most taxpayers); however, the insured must continue to be covered under a HDHP for a full year afterward (the "testing period," through December 31 of the following year for most taxpayers) or taxes and a 10 percent penalty will apply to contributions allocated to months prior to becoming HSA-eligible. Alternatively, the annual maximum contribution can be prorated to a monthly amount and only the amount allowable for the number of months the insured is actually covered by the HDHP contributed. The insured must be covered by the HDHP on the first day of each month to be eligible for that month.

Example 14.15

Bellamy and Charlie, who are both under the age of 55, have three children, named Denver, Emerson, and Finley. Bellamy works for Acme and has an HSA as a health care option. Bellamy signs up for the HSA family option and includes the three kids. Charlie works for Pinnacle and also has access to an HSA. Bellamy and Charlie thought that they could defer $7,200 for the family and $3,600 for Charlie. However, they cannot exceed a total deferral of $7,200 for the entire family. Charlie could certainly choose the HSA coverage for family as well, but, since they cannot contribute any additional funds to the HSA as a result of this election, it might be better for Charlie to select a different option with a lower deductible or to opt out of insurance from Pinnacle because he is included under Bellamy's family plan.[29]

Example 14.16

Shae, who earns $60,000 from Onyx Inc., signed up for the HSA health care option for her family. She pays a $500 premium on a monthly basis and has elected to contribute $7,200 to the HSA for 2021. Shae's monthly compensation of $5,000 is reduced by the premium and one-twelfth of the HSA contribution. Shae's monthly income subject to federal income tax equals $3,900 ($5,000 - $500 - $600).

Shae will be able to pay qualified medical expenses from her HSA. The funds in the account are hers and are portable in the event she changes employers or leaves the workforce. She is also able to invest the funds, which may generate interest, dividends, and/or capital gains. These investment earnings are not subject to income tax unless distributions are used for purposes other than qualified medical expenses.

---

28. IRC §223(b)(3)(B).
29. See IRS Notice 2008-59.

Earnings within the HSA are not taxable, and amounts distributed from an HSA are also not taxable provided the distributions are used to pay for qualified medical expenses. If a distribution is not for qualified medical expenses, the entire distribution is taxable as ordinary income. If the distribution is taken before the owner of the account is 65, the distribution is subject to an additional 20 percent excise penalty tax.[30]

Qualified medical expenses include:
- Medical expenses for the taxpayer, spouse, or dependents that are not reimbursed by a health insurance policy,
- COBRA health insurance premiums,
- Long-term care insurance premiums,
- Health insurance premiums if the taxpayer is receiving unemployment compensation, and
- Personal Protective Equipment (PPE), such as masks, hand sanitizer, and sanitizing wipes for the primary purpose of preventing the spread of COVID-19 (COVID-19 PPE).[31]

Death of an HSA Owner

Owners of HSAs should establish beneficiaries for their accounts when they are set up. When the owner of an HSA dies prior to distributing all of the assets in the account, the remaining balance can be transferred to the named beneficiary. If the beneficiary is the spouse, the spouse is treated as the owner of the HSA and the normal HSA distribution rules apply. If the account is left to anyone other than the spouse, the death of the participant terminates the HSA, and the remaining balance will be subject to income tax (but not penalty) in the hands of the beneficiary. In the event there is no beneficiary named, the account will be distributed and taxed to the account owner's estate.

Exhibit 14.12 | Comparison of MSA (Archer) and HSA for 2021

	MSA (Archer)		HSA	
Established	Before 2006		2004 and Later	
Creators	• Employers with less than 50 employees • Self-employed individuals		Any individual	
	Single	**Family**	**Single**	**Family**
Health Insurance Deductible	$2,400- $3,600	$4,800 - $7,150	At least $1,400	At least $2,800
Maximum Out-of-Pocket	$4,800	$8,750	$7,000	$14,000
Maximum Contribution	65% of deductible	75% of deductible	Limited to $3,600	Limited to $7,200
Catch-Up Contribution Available	No		Yes $1,000 for 2021	
Penalty for Nonqualified Expenditures	Ordinary income tax on earnings and 20% penalty if owner is < 65		Ordinary income tax on earnings and 20% penalty if owner is < 65	

---

30. IRC §223(f)(4).

31. COVID-19 PPE added by IRS Announcement 2021-7. COVID-19 PPE expenses are also eligible expenses for FSAs and HRAs.

Voluntary Employees' Beneficiary Association (VEBA)

A **Voluntary Employees' Beneficiary Association (VEBA)** is a welfare benefit plan, into which an employer deposits funds that will be used to provide specified employee benefits in the future. Technically, the VEBA is either a trust or a corporation set up by an employer to hold funds used to pay benefits under an employer benefit plan. However, generally they are trusts that are exempt from tax under the provisions of IRC §501(c)(9) and subject to the "welfare benefit fund" rules under §419 and §419A. While welfare benefit funds can also be taxable trusts, most welfare benefit funds apply for exempt status as VEBAs in order to reduce or eliminate income taxes at the trust level. VEBA's file Form 990, whereas taxable trusts file Form 1041.

VEBAs must meet all of the following requirements:
1. The organization is an employees' association,
2. Membership in the association is voluntary,
3. The organization provides for the payment of life, sick, accident, or other benefits to its members or their dependents or designated beneficiaries, and substantially all of its operations are in furtherance of providing such benefits, and
4. No part of the net earnings of the organization inures, other than by payment of the benefits referred to above, to the benefit of any private shareholder or individual.

Generally, all ordinary and necessary expenses are deductible under IRC §162. However, expenses for deferred compensation are not deductible until included into income by the employee as discussed in Chapter 12.

Welfare benefit plans provide for deferral of funds used for the purpose of providing future benefits to employees and are not subject to the same taxation rules as deferred compensation plans. This exception is largely because it is society's interest to provide these type of benefits to employees. IRC §404(a), which governs the taxation of qualified plans and deferred compensation, does not apply to a plan that does not defer the receipt of compensation. Furthermore, §404(a) does not apply to deductions for contributions under a plan which is solely a dismissal wage or unemployment benefit plan, or a sickness, accident, hospitalization, medical expense, recreation, welfare, or similar benefit plan, or a combination thereof. For example, if under a plan an employer contributes five percent of each employee's compensation per month to a fund out of which employees who are laid off will be paid benefits for temporary periods, but employees who are not laid off have no rights to the funds, such a plan is an unemployment benefit plan, and the deductibility of the contributions to it is determined under section 162.

Under IRC §419 and §419A, employers can make contributions to welfare benefit plans without the benefits being currently distributed and avoiding current taxation. These sections limit the amount of deductions for contributions to these type of plans. However, there is an exception to these limits for plans with ten or more employers contributing to the plan.

> ### ☑ Quick Quiz 14.6
>
> 1. Archer MSAs cannot be established after April 15, 2004.
>   a. True
>   b. False
>
> 2. Distributions from an HSA that are not used for medical expenses are taxed as ordinary income and subject to a 10% penalty if the owner of the HSA has not reached age 59½.
>   a. True
>   b. False
>
> 3. A VEBA allows an employer to take a current deduction for future benefits that will be provided to employees.
>   a. True
>   b. False
>
> False, False, True.

As with other areas of the Code that allow for current deductions and no corresponding current income, the exception for these plans has been subject to abuse and the current rules are much less favorable then in the past. The IRS Notice 95-34 discusses tax problems raised by certain trust arrangements seeking to qualify for exemption from IRC §419. Additionally, it puts taxpayers on notice that deductions for contributions to some of these arrangements are disallowable for any one of several reasons (e.g., the arrangements may provide deferred compensation, the arrangements may be separate plans for each employer, the arrangements may be experience rated in form or operation, or the contributions may be nondeductible prepaid expenses).

Despite the abuses with these types of plans, VEBAs and other welfare benefit plans continue to be beneficial to some companies and employees.

Application and Benefits

By creating and funding a VEBA, an employer can reduce the employer's income tax burden by accelerating an income tax deduction for the payment of welfare type benefits that would have been funded by the employer in the future. An employer can also potentially reduce future cash flow and the total cost of the benefits as the earnings within the VEBA are not taxed, which will provide the employer with additional funds to provide the benefits.

VEBAs also provide employees with benefit security, because after the funds are deposited into the VEBA, the funds can only be used for the exclusive benefit of the employees, are beyond the reach of the employer's creditors, and generally cannot revert to the employer.

Life insurance benefits provided by a VEBA will generally be subject to current taxation, similar to the tax treatment for life insurance. However, the proceeds are generally tax-free and are not included in the gross estate of the decedent since the decedent had no incidents of ownership.

Contributions

The level of annual contributions to the VEBA in order to fund benefits is determined actuarially. This amount is paid annually or in more frequent installments if the employer desires and, provided the plan meets the qualification requirements, is fully deductible by the employer in the year of the contribution.

Exhibit 14.13 | VEBA Benefits that Can and Cannot be Provided

VEBAs Can Provide	VEBAs Cannot Provide
• Life insurance before and after retirement • Other survivor benefits • Sickness and accident benefits • Other benefits including vacation and recreation benefits • Severance benefits paid through a severance pay plan • Unemployment and job training benefits • Disaster benefits • Legal service payment for credits	• Savings • Retirement • Deferred compensation • Coverage of expenses such as commuting expenses • Accident or homeowners insurance covering damage to property • Other items unrelated to the maintenance of the employee's earning power

Salary Continuation Plans

A **salary continuation plan** is an arrangement between an employer and an employee where the employer agrees to continue to pay an employee after retirement or to pay the employee's spouse if the employee dies prior to retiring. A salary continuation plan can be provided on a discriminatory basis and provides the benefit of shifting the income to the employee to a period when the tax burden is not as heavy (i.e., retirement).

When the payments are made from the salary continuation plan, the value is included in an employee's gross income, is subjected to payroll tax, and is deductible by the employer. Some employers fund the salary continuation plan through the use of a permanent life insurance policy on the employee. Premiums for this type of insurance are not deductible by the employer, but amounts paid to the employee or to the employee's dependents are deductible by the employer at the time of payment.

Group Long-Term Care Insurance

The premium payments for qualified group long-term care insurance are tax deductible if paid by the employer and tax-free to the employee (see below for a discussion of self-employed individuals). In addition to the tax advantages, group long-term care insurance generally also provides the following advantages:

> ### ⋮≡ *Key Concepts*
>
> 1. What are the tax implications of employer-provided salary continuation plans?
>
> 2. What are the tax implications of employer-provided group long-term care insurance?
>
> 3. What are the tax implications of employer-provided group retirement planning services?

- lower rates than individual policies (generally 30% - 60% less)
- guaranteed coverage for all employees, even those who might not be insurable under an individual policy
- increase eligibility for extended family members including parents, grandparents, and in-laws
- the policy must be guaranteed renewable
- the coverage can be provided in a discriminatory manner
- "qualified" benefits are non-taxable to the recipient of the care

To be a qualified long-term care insurance plan, the plan must meet the provisions of the IRC, specifically the plan must:
- only provide long-term care insurance coverage
- not duplicate benefits paid by Medicare
- be guaranteed renewable
- only pay benefits when the employee or beneficiary of the plan is certified by a licensed health care practitioner as chronically ill

Long-term care premiums cannot be paid for within a cafeteria plan or flexible spending account nor can the premium payment be made with pre-tax employee salary deferrals. If, however, the employee pays the premiums with after-tax dollars, the employee may deduct, as an itemized medical expense deduction (subject to the 7.5% hurdle), the costs on the employee's income tax return for the year. The deduction limit is the lesser of the premium paid or the amount corresponding to the employee's age in the table below.[32]

---

32. IRC §213(d)(10) adjusted for inflation. See Rev. Proc. 2020-45.

Exhibit 14.14 | Eligible Long-Term Care Premiums for 2021

Age	Maximum Deductible Amount for 2021
≤ 40	$450
41 - 50	$850
51 - 60	$1,690
61 - 70	$4,520
≥ 71	$5,640

Self-Employed Individuals

Self-employed individuals as well as individuals that are considered self employed, including partners of partnerships, greater-than-2% S corporation owners, and members of limited liability companies that are taxed as partnerships, must include the cost of long-term care insurance paid by the employer in their gross income. The self-employed individual can deduct the premiums as an above-the-line deduction (not subject to the 7.5% floor hurdle), but the deduction is limited by the dollar amounts discussed above. The premiums paid for by the employer for any other employees who are not considered self-employed will continue to be a deductible business expense for the employer that is not included in the employee's income.

Group Retirement Planning Services

An employer may exclude from an employee's gross income the value of any retirement planning advice or information the employer provides to the employee or his spouse if the employer maintains a qualified retirement plan.[33] In addition to employer plan advice and information, the services provided may include general advice and information on retirement. However, the exclusion does not apply to the value of services for tax preparation, accounting, legal, or brokerage services.

> ### ✒ Quick Quiz 14.7
>
> 1. A salary continuation plan allows employees to shift income to future years.
>   a. True
>   b. False
>
> 2. Long-term care plans are frequently a benefit option of a cafeteria or FSA plan.
>   a. True
>   b. False
>
> 3. An employer can exclude from an employee's gross income the value of any retirement planning advice provided to an employee whether or not the employer has a retirement plan.
>   a. True
>   b. False
>
> True, False, False.

The employer may not discriminate in favor of highly compensated executives. The nondiscrimination rule states that the exclusion is allowable for highly compensated employees only if the retirement planning services are available on substantially the same terms to each member of the group of employees normally provided education and information regarding the employer's qualified employer plan.

---

33. IRC §132(m).

Prepaid Legal Services

A prepaid legal services plan provides broader access to legal services for an employee base at a discounted rate.These plans can be funded by employees, employers or partially paid by both the employee and employer. These plans work in a similar fashion to group life, health, or disability insurance. The risk of needing a lawyer is pooled together and costs are reduced. However, these plans no longer receive favorable tax treatment.

Under IRC §120, qualified group legal services plans received special tax treatment prior to July 1992. Employer contributions to the plan were deductible by the employer if the plan provided personal legal services for its employees, their spouses, and their dependents and the plan met the requirements of IRC §120. In addition, the value of the legal services provided under the plan was not subject to taxation for the employee receiving the benefits. However, this tax benefit is no longer available.

SUCCESSION PLANNING AND INSURANCE ARRANGEMENTS

Succession Planning Overview

Companies use business succession planning to ensure leadership continuity, which helps to ensure effective future operations. Through this process, current leaders identify and develop employees who have the potential to be trained to take on additional leadership roles in the future. While succession planning is routinely conducted in the corporate world, it is also conducted in the small business setting, and there are clear differences.

For large private and publicly-traded companies, succession planning is often an ongoing process that happens at many levels of the organization. It is often a part of the annual review process, in which a manager seeks out individuals who have the requisite skills, desire, work ethic, and experience to take over the manager's own role. Employees who have been identified to advance in the organization are often selected for continued development, which may involve internal or external leadership training. In addition, these individuals may often change leadership roles within the organization periodically to increase exposure to other functions within the company.

Key Concepts

1. Explain the purpose of succession planning.

2. Describe various long-term objectives available to a small business owner.

3. Identify factors and issues that a business owner should consider when creating a succession plan.

4. Consider the complications of transferring a small business to children or other family members.

Example 14.17

Andrea has worked for N-ergy for the last 25 years in various roles. She was moved to a management role in the IT department five years ago and has continued to be one of the top performers in the organization. She has been reporting to the Chief Information Officer (CIO) for the past two years. The CIO has moved Andrea several times to run different departments within the IT organization. Andrea is being groomed to take over the CIO position in the future.

In large organizations, leadership positions are often vacated when leaders advance within the organization or leave the organization entirely. For example, talented managers may be enticed to go to work for competitors with higher compensation packages. To avoid the leadership gaps this practice can cause, successful companies have formalized programs to identify and develop leadership so that there is continuity of management. These programs also help mitigate the risk of losing talented employees.

In the small business setting, especially ones in which the original entrepreneur(s) function as senior leadership, the major business functions tend to reside with a small group of people. These companies may have less risk of an owner leaving to work for a competitor, as they are vested in the business; however, these organizations often have significant challenges filling leadership roles.

Owners of small businesses should consider their long-term objectives for the business. These options are usually:
- Close the business and walk away
- Sell the business to a third-party buyer (or go public)
- Sell the business to employees
- Transfer the business to family members
- Continue to own the business but transition out of management
- Transfer the business to the other owners in the event of an untimely death

Closing the Business
Closing the business is not a commonly considered choice, as most entrepreneurs believe there is a significant amount of value in their businesses. The owners have often worked for years in their businesses and have a vested interest in them. However, for some owners, simply closing the business is the best option regardless of value.

It often takes decades for a small business to become successful. During this time, entrepreneurs often sacrifice many aspects of their lives. Once successful, many entrepreneurs, who have worked in their businesses for much of their lives, look to their businesses as sources of funding for retirement. This funding could be from the sale of the businesses or from distributions from the businesses as they continues to operate.

Owners who want to sell their businesses have a few choices in terms of potential buyers. However, selling a business is not always easy or guaranteed. Owners can sell to a third party, employees, current owners, or to family members.

Selling to a Third Party
Selling to a third party is not always an option but may be quite lucrative. Third-party buyers include strategic buyers and private equity firms. Strategic buyers make acquisitions for a variety of purposes, including:
- Acquiring a new, innovative process or product
- Expanding its product offering through the acquisition
- Eliminating a competitor, which may result in a better product offering and costs savings
- Other reasons, such as gaining competent management or research and development

Private equity (PE) firms generally make acquisitions to earn a return on invested capital. PEs attempt to purchase companies at a relatively low multiple (price to EBITA or net income), grow net income, and sell at a higher multiple.

Example 14.18

Hyper Growth Horizons Firm (HGH) is a private equity firm. They just purchased Muscle Chem, Inc., which is a nutritional supplements company, for $7 million. Muscle Chem's net income is $1 million, so HGH paid seven times net income for the company. HGH believes that they can help management double the net income over the next three-to-five years and can sell to a larger nutritional supplements company for 14 times net income. Based on those assumptions, HGH expects to quadruple its money - $2 million times 14 equals $28 million.

Typically, an acquiring company wants key employees to remain with the company for a minimum period of time. This aspect of an acquisition agreement normally applies to the owners, also, which means that the owners should be open to staying employed after the purchase for a period of time. However, in some acquisitions, the acquiring company has less interest in personnel and more interest in a company's products, services, or cash flows.

Another option is to take the company public and hold an initial public offering. This choice is more appropriate and realistic for larger companies and requires significant cost and, usually, the assistance of an investment banker.

Example 14.19

Both Dropbox and Spotify went public in 2018. Prior to going public, Dropbox, a cloud-based storage provider, had over $1 billion in revenue, while Spotify, the world's largest music streaming business had nearly $5 billion in revenue. Dropbox used traditional investment bankers, while Spotify went public in a more unique fashion. Unlike traditional IPOs, Spotify did not raise new capital but simply listed existing shares directly on the NYSE.

In some cases, finding a company to purchase a business is difficult or even impossible. In these cases, an owner may attempt to sell the business to an individual or an employee. The challenge with this approach is often that the buyer does not have the funds to purchase the company and wants to finance the purchase with the internally-generated future cash flows of the business. This approach is usually a bad idea for the owner, as the owner effectively continues to retain the risk of operating the business after the sale with little or no upside potential. If the business declines, the owner may not be repaid. However, if the business succeeds, he is repaid but does not participate in the growth. It's not advisable to retain the risk side of a transaction without the return side.

Selling to Employees

The final selling option is to sell it to the employees. As discussed above, the employees do not always have enough funds to acquire the company. In this situation, the owner can use a leveraged ESOP, which was discussed earlier in the text and involves using borrowed funds to finance the purchase.

In many cases, owners are concerned about ensuring the continuing operation of the business in the event of an untimely death of one of the owners. This risk can often be managed with buy-sell agreements, discussed below.

Transferring to Family Members

Small businesses are often family businesses, meaning that various family members work in the business. In these situations, as an owner gets older, it is common to want to transfer the business to a child or to children. This process of transferring the business, if done correctly, requires a great deal of planning. This type of planning attempts to ensure that the business continues to operate effectively and that the transferee (often a child) has the requisite skills and experience to effectively manage the business. One of the biggest problems occurs when parents put their adult children in roles for which they are inexperienced and ill-equipped to successfully manage.

To successfully run a small business, a successor must have an understanding of:
- Basic aspects of accounting and finance (including some tax law)
- The company's product offerings, industry and competitors
- The company's operations, including supply chain management and distribution
- Basic human resources, including hiring, managing, inspiring, and firing
- Basic strategic planning

Because running a small business requires an enormous number of skills, many small businesses fail in the first or second generation. Large businesses have the resources to hire personnel who can specialize in one or a few of these areas, while a small business owner must have a basic understanding of most of these skills.

Once the decision to transfer the business has been made, the method must be chosen. The owner has the option to either sell or donate the business to a child immediately or over time. This choice and its implications are discussed in more detail in the Money Education *Estate Planning* textbook.

In the event that the owner/transferor of a small business is dependent on the future cash flows from the business, there will have to be simultaneous financial planning for the transferor and strategic planning for the transferee. This requirement is one of the reasons that succession planning in a small business can take a significant number of years to complete.

Transition Out

In some cases, owners may want to continue to own the business but transition out of management. The objective of this approach is to continue to benefit from the fruits of prior labor. The owner has worked for years building a company and often has an emotional attachment to the business. Often the idea of selling the business is somewhat frightening, as it signifies an abrupt change in the owner's life, as opposed to a more gradual change by "transitioning out". The transitioning out option allows the owner to maintain ownership and control while continuing to receive income from the business.

Transitioning is a nice compromise between continuing to run the business and selling. However, it has potential issues for the owner that range from working too much to not paying enough attention to what is going on in the business. In some cases, owners may have a hard time not going into the office and may end up working more than they had imagined. In other cases, they are so far removed from the business that they miss potential issues that could be devastating to the business. It often takes a lifetime to build a great reputation and only a short time to tarnish it. This option of transitioning out absolutely does not work unless a succession plan is successfully executed, resulting in a competent leadership team that can run the business with little or no input from the owner. Without a reliable leadership team, it is only a matter of time before the company goes out of business.

Untimely Death of a Business Owner

The untimely death of a business owner can be devastating to the business, the remaining owners, as well as the family of the deceased owner. The section below discusses how buy-sell agreements can provide needed liquidity for the business as well as for the deceased owner's family.

Succession Planning Issues

While some financial professionals and business owners equate a buy-sell agreement with succession planning, true succession planning is more broad-based. The goal of business succession planning should be twofold: (1) to ensure a graceful, fulfilling, and lucrative exit for the owner; and (2) to position the business to grow and prosper well into the future.

An exit strategy is important to business owners for a number of reasons, including:
- Achieving business and personal goals
- Facilitating retirement of the owner
- Controlling how and when the owner exits the business
- Ensuring the survival and growth of the business
- Preserving family harmony
- Reducing family and employee uncertainty
- Maximizing company value
- Minimizing, deferring, or eliminating income and estate taxes

Failure to have a succession plan in place often results in undervaluation of the company, payment of more taxes than necessary, loss of control over the exit process, and failure to realize personal, financial, or business goals during the exit process. When family ownership is involved, it is common for emotional factors and family dynamics to outweigh rational decision-making unless a carefully thought-out plan has been established.

Underestimating the Amount of Time Needed to Put a Plan in Place

One of the biggest mistakes business owners make is waiting too long to establish an exit strategy. **Succession planning is a process, not an event.** It should be proactive, not reactive.

The best time to start planning for succession of the business is the day the business is opened, the day an existing business is purchased, the day the business is inherited, or the day a partner is brought into the business. The second best time is today.

The sooner the succession planning process is started, the more likely it is that a plan can be established that will meet the goals of the owners and of the business. Implementation can take many years. For example, if the reputation and knowledge of the owner is a key factor in driving revenue, it may take a number of years to locate, hire, and train a successor. In some cases, it may even be necessary to hire and train multiple people to handle the many facets of the business that the current owner handles. Another example of a succession plan requiring significant time for implementation is a gradual transfer of ownership to a junior generation by annual exclusion gifts (up to $15,000 can be given to each donee each year without payment of gift taxes). A third example is planning for the owner who would like to retire and sell the business for a lump sum payment or for a combination of a large lump sum and installment payments. Negotiating the terms of sale in advance can ensure a fair sale price, and can also enable the buyer to establish a sinking fund to provide the cash for the purchase when the owner reaches retirement age.

Strain on the Business due to Death, Disability, or Retirement of an Owner and Lack of a Ready Market to Sell the Business

In the absence of a prearranged plan for transfer of the business interest, a great amount of strain can be placed on the business, the employees, the remaining owners, and the family members of a deceased, disabled, or retired owner.

Family members who may not be qualified to run the business or who may be incompatible with the remaining owners could end up owning a substantial portion of the business. Creditors and suppliers may become uneasy when the future of the business is unstable. Employees may leave due to the uncertainty of the future of the business. Having a succession plan in place can provide assurance that the business will continue to operate smoothly throughout the transition.

Failure to Plan for Retirement Outside the Business

When the establishing owner of a small business does not plan for retirement by accumulating funds outside the business and must continue to draw an income from the business in retirement years, it often creates cash flow and/or liquidity problems for the business. Advance planning can help to mitigate the strain on the business by ensuring that the retiring owner has retirement funds available in a separate fund, as well as preparing the business for cash outflows to the retired owner.

Management/Personnel Issues

With a family-owned business, the owner often desires that the business stay in the hands of family members after the establishing owner is no longer active in the day-to-day operations of the business. Ownership of the business may be transferred by making gifts or by selling ownership interests to family members. Unfortunately, family members often do not have the same skills and management ability that the departing owner had. In these situations, it will be imperative for the ongoing success of the business that key non-family personnel remain. The succession plan will address who the key employees are, and it will define a process to ensure that these key employees are rewarded for staying with the business throughout the transition and beyond.

Family Issues

Another common problem is that the senior family member who built the business may feel the need to treat all children "equally" in providing an inheritance. This attitude may arise even though not all children are involved in the business. A senior family member who leaves equal ownership interests to all children almost always causes discord. Those who work in the business will want profits retained in the business to facilitate growth, and those not involved in the business will want profits to be distributed. A good succession plan will overcome these issues before they become a problem.

Example 14.20

Matrix Software is a software engineering company owned and operated by the founders, Dakota and Denver, who are married and have three children. Their children, Emerson, Justice, and Skyler, are 26, 23, and 17 years old, respectively. Emerson graduated from Georgia Tech in computer science and is working at Matrix and loves it. Justice just graduated from Colorado College and is working for REI guiding expeditions in and around Colorado. Justice has embraced the outdoor life and is uninterested in coding software in a closed in office. Skyler is in a high school for gifted music students and wants to go to Belmont University in Nashville and focus on music. Matrix has grown substantially over the last decade and represents 85% of Dakota and Denver's net worth.

They would like to think about developing a succession plan and an estate plan. It appears that one of their children will work in the business and the other two will not. Dakota and Denver will have to consider how to benefit their children appropriately (as they see fit), while developing a succession plan for Matrix.

In many cases, the success of a family-owned business is hampered by successor family members who insist on running the business even if they are not qualified. In other cases, because the number of family shareholders often increases exponentially from generation to generation, infighting over control may occur.

The selection of a successor (or multiple successors) should not be taken lightly. An open and honest discussion among family members (or owners of a non-family-owned closely held business) is imperative. Everyone involved, including the departing owner, successor owner(s), key employees, and other family members will need to agree with the plan. All family members must share the desire to ensure a successful transition, and they should have an interest in doing their part (even if their part does not include being directly involved with the day-to-day operations of the business). Everyone needs the motivation and commitment to follow through with their part in the plan.

Management versus Ownership

In some cases, two succession plans that work together may be necessary. Ownership and management are not one and the same. The new owner of the business may not have the skills required or the desire to manage the day-to-day operations, and may instead hire someone else to manage the business.

Part of the planning process will be an assessment of the current managers in the business to identify their strengths and to determine who the best replacement may be.

- What are the strengths of the retiring owner?
- What are the strengths of the other owners?
- What role does the retiring owner play in the business?
- What roles do other owners play in the business?
- Who will replace the retiring owner (or who will replace an owner who dies, become disabled, or leaves)?
- Who does the owner call on (if anyone) in the business when he or she is on vacation? Why that person? What skills does the person possess that are necessary to the success of the business when the owner is absent?

Family Successor Issues

In some cases with a family business, the senior family member will simply assume that the children will be the successor owners. Again, an open and honest conversation is required. Is a career in the family business what the child really wants, or is the decision to take over the business influenced by a feeling of obligation? What does the child expect from his career and can he reasonably expect to achieve it in the family business?

If it is decided that the child has a sincere desire to own and work in the family business, a skill evaluation will be necessary. For non-family successor-owners, a skill evaluation will also be necessary to determine whether the successor's skills are a "match" for those of the retiring owner. If not, further training and experience will be required to get the successor prepared. Alternatively, the business may decide to hire a manager who already possesses the necessary skills, and the successor owner can contribute to the business in a different way that utilizes his own skills to the advantage of the business.

Skill Evaluations
Financial management skills
Project management skills
Planning skills
Interpersonal skills
Analytical skills
Technical/trade skills
Personal presentation skills
Industry knowledge

Skill Diversification

In family businesses, the life cycle of the business is often tied to the work life cycle of the founder (25 – 40 years). At the time of transfer, the business may be in its maturity or declining phase and may need to be regenerated by updating product and technology, developing new markets, addressing new competitive pressures, or implementing long-range strategies and goals. In other words, a successor with skills different from those of the original owner may be exactly what the business needs to survive and grow. Thus, skill assessments should not be focused solely on replacing those of the current owner, but should also consider the skills needed going forward.

Establishing Guidelines for Family Members to Work in the Business

Family businesses may want, or need, to establish clear guidelines for how family members prepare for work in the family business.

It may be desirable to require family members to work outside the family business for a period of time to allow them to gain knowledge and perspective. This experience in non-family businesses will provide family members with an opportunity to show employees and managers that they are competent and have made a contribution to another business (rather than having "inherited" a leadership position). It will also give a family member the confidence that he can make it elsewhere on his own merit.

Other guidelines might include requiring family members to go through the interview and hiring process as if they were not related to the owner, and holding family members accountable to follow the same rules as other employees, with formalized job descriptions, regular performance reviews, and promotions based on merit.

Note that some of these guidelines for the next generation may require development of a more formalized business structure than the first generation has ever used, but these guidelines will go a long way to minimize conflict among family members.

Documenting the guidelines for family participation in the business should include (but need not be limited to):

1. Education and experience requirements for employment in the business.
2. Supervision of family member performance: Parents will most often have a conflict in providing an unbiased and objective evaluation of the job performance of a child; it may be best to have an unrelated manager responsible for these performance evaluations.
3. Family compensation practices: It is in the best interest of the business to pay salaries based on market value, which is the amount the job duties would earn the family member if working for a competitor. Without clearly defined guidelines, there may be an expectation of being paid based on desired lifestyle rather than on value to the business.
4. Procedures for hiring and termination decisions.
5. The extent to which the business will or will not provide special opportunities and consideration to family members.

Facilitating Retirement of the Owner

Holistic succession planning will focus not only on the technical and tax aspects of business succession, but also on ensuring that the retiring owner and spouse are emotionally prepared to begin a new phase of their lives. The owner and spouse must determine how to use their time, talents, and interests in a fulfilling manner when they are less involved with the business. Some will volunteer time with various charities that they support, some may start charitable foundations, some may move on to other business interests, and some may pursue various types of recreation. Some owners will provide consulting services, or they may serve on the board of directors of various businesses.

This is a period of great change – clear expectations will maintain healthy relationships and facilitate a successful transition.

Ensuring Financial Needs Are Met

In many family and closely held business situations, the owners will reinvest substantial amounts of their profits in their business throughout most of their lives. Owners may assume that they will either sell the business or draw an income from the business upon retirement. Business owners should be encouraged to diversify their retirement portfolio by contributing to qualified plans and IRAs, but the fact remains that many do not do so. If an owner does not save enough to fully fund retirement, part of the succession plan will revolve around how to ensure that the retiring owner can continue to receive income from the business or from the sale of the business.

Consulting Services

A retiring owner may continue to work in the business with reduced hours or as a consultant, helping both to ease the transition of ownership and to provide some ongoing income for the retiring owner. Remaining an employee of the business may also be desirable in order to maintain health insurance or other employee benefits.

Corporate Recapitalization

Another way to provide ongoing income to the owner of a C-corporation is to restructure the business to include both preferred and common stock. The common stock with voting rights can then be transferred to the successor owner, and the retiring owner can retain preferred shares that will pay a regular dividend, providing a source of retirement income.

Note that a similar strategy cannot be used with an S-corporation because of the limitation to only one class of stock.

Lease Income from Real Estate or Other Assets

Many businesses will operate under multiple, separate entities. One common division is to separate the ownership of the real estate from the operating business, and the business pays rent to use the real estate. A simple plan to provide income to the retiring owner is for the owner to retain ownership of the real estate. The owner might also include in the terms of sale of the operating business an agreement to lease the building at the current rate (or other agreed upon amount) for a certain number of years.

Selling the Business

The sale of the business will also provide funds to be invested that can produce income for retirement. A buy-sell agreement (discussed below) can be used to ensure that there will be a buyer who will pay a fair price under acceptable terms of sale (e.g., a lump sum plus installment payments, with the selling owner retaining a collateral interest in business assets until the note is fully paid).

Preserving Family Harmony

Communication between parents and children is key to any strategy used for succession of the family-owned business.

Equal and Fair Are Not the Same Thing

A common issue for family businesses is how to handle transfer of ownership from one generation to the next when one child is involved in the family business and others are not. Parents will often feel that they need to treat their children equally in terms of gifts and inheritances, but if the business makes up a large portion of wealth, transferring equal ownership interests can cause discord among the children. The child working in the business is likely to desire that earnings be retained to grow the business, while children not involved in the business are likely to desire distributions of earnings.

Example 14.21

Assume the same facts as **Example 14.15**, but that ten years later (when Emerson is 36, Justice is 33, and Skyler is 27) Dakota and Denver are simultaneously killed in a car accident. Their wills left Matrix to all three children equally. Emerson is running the business and it remains quite profitable. He has plans to reinvest the profits in another business line that will diversify Matrix's portfolio of products. However, Justice has fallen in love with a drifter who likes to spend her money on lavish vacations, causing Justice to pressure Emerson to distribute profits. Justice recruits Skyler to vote with her in favor of the distribution, forcing Emerson to forego the growth and diversification of the business and distribute profits instead. Emerson becomes resentful of his siblings for teaming up against him when he is the only sibling working overtime to ensure the success of the business. Justice and Skyler believe that he is overreacting because their parents clearly wanted them all to share equally in the future success of the business. The relationship between the siblings is shattered, perhaps irreparably.

One way to resolve this issue is to leave the full ownership in the hands of those children who actually work at the business, and the parents use life insurance to provide an equivalent value for children who do not work in the business. It is recommended, however, that a family meeting be held to discuss this strategy before it is implemented, since a child who runs the business may feel cheated – his inheritance requires work and everyone else is getting cash.

Another way to deal with the issue is to restructure the business. If the business is a C-corporation or S-corporation, ownership interests can be changed to voting and nonvoting stock. If the business is a family limited partnership, it can be changed to general partnership interests (which control business decisions) and limited partnership interests (with no management control). If the family owns an LLC, it can be restructured with managing and non-managing membership interests. The children who are involved in the business can then be given the voting shares, general partnership interests, or managing membership interests, while children not involved in the business are given nonvoting shares, limited partnership interests, or non-managing interests.

If the business has been structured under several entities (for example, the operating entity might be set up as a C-corporation and the real estate owned by an S-corporation), it may seem like a good idea to transfer ownership of the operating entity to the child involved in the business and transfer the entity owning the real estate to the children not involved in the business. Again, caution is needed. Tenants and landlords often do not agree on numerous issues, and family harmony can be destroyed along with the ongoing viability of the business.

Of course, there is no reason that children have to be "given" anything. A better solution may be to sell the business at fair market value to those who desire to be owners. Buy-sell agreements are appropriate when the business is to be sold to anyone, whether it is a family member, a key employee, another unrelated owner, or a competitor.

> ## Quick Quiz 14.8
>
> 1. Generally, selling a small business to a third party is fairly easy and straight forward.
>   a. True
>   b. False
>
> 2. It is often extremely helpful for children who will run a small business in the future to have spent time working outside the family business.
>   a. True
>   b. False
>
> 3. Life insurance or voting and non-voting classes of stock can be used effectively to mitigate potential problems when leaving a small business to children, some of whom are working in the business and some of whom are not working in the business.
>   a. True
>   b. False
>
> False, True, True.

Business Continuation (Buy/Sell) Agreements

Closely-held business interests often represent a considerable portion of business owner's net worth and gross estate at the death of the owner. These business interests are generally illiquid, which creates a need for liquidity within the estate and often for a surviving spouse. Life insurance can be used to fund buy-sell agreements for closely held and family-owned business owners.

In the absence of a pre-arranged plan for transfer of the business interest, a great amount of strain can be placed on the business, the remaining owners, and the family members of a deceased, disabled, or retired owner. A buy-sell agreement funded with life insurance and disability income insurance guarantees a buyer for a retiring, disabled, or deceased owner's interest and assures a fair sale price.

The agreement also fosters the continuation of the business by not allowing the departing owner's interest to fall into the hands of outsiders, persons who may not be qualified to run the business, or persons who may be incompatible with the remaining owners. While a complete discussion of buy-sell agreements and their tax consequences is beyond the scope of this chapter, an overview of this common planning technique is warranted.

Buy-sell agreements are legal arrangements that require the sale of a business interest owned by one individual to another individual or entity upon a specified triggering event. Buy-sell agreements are commonly used by business owners to plan for the orderly transfer and control of a business interest, to create a market for stock that is not traded on securities exchanges, and to plan for liquidity in the estate of a deceased business owner.

Additional benefits of having a properly funded buy-sell agreement in place include:
- The agreement defines the events that will trigger a sale of the business.
- The sale of the business provides liquidity for the estate of a deceased owner.
- The agreement avoids conflicts between heirs and surviving owners (e.g., the remaining owners do not become unwilling partners with the surviving spouse of a deceased owner).
- The orderly transfer of the business helps to maintain stability of business operations.
- Having an agreement in place assures suppliers that the business will continue to operate smoothly when an owner leaves the business.
- Having an agreement can improve the creditworthiness of the business.
- The agreement ensures a fair price, and proper funding ensures that resources will be available to pay the agreed-upon price.
- The agreement can ensure that existing owners maintain control and prevent outsiders from becoming owners.
- Having a succession plan and funded buy-sell agreement in place gives employees peace of mind regarding the stability of the company and their jobs. Without such a plan, employees may "jump ship," for example, when an owner dies, because of the fear that the business will not survive.

The most common triggering event that invokes obligations under a buy-sell agreement is the death of the business owner. A properly structured buy-sell agreement requires the estate of the business owner to sell the decedent's business interest to another entity or person, who is often a family member or close business associate of the decedent. Since an obligation to purchase a business interest is triggered at the death of the owner, life insurance is an ideal funding vehicle for buy-sell agreements triggered at death. Typically, either the business itself, or the individual or entity who is obligated to purchase the decedent's business interest will hold a life insurance policy on the decedent's life that has a death benefit sufficient to cover the purchase price of the decedent's business interest.

Other triggering events for buy-sell agreements include disability, divorce, retirement, and withdrawal from the business, but a full discussion of these is beyond the scope of this chapter.

When working with business owners to establish the buy-sell agreement, the financial planner will need to assemble a team of professionals to ensure that all of the important elements are addressed. An attorney will be needed to draft the document to ensure that the agreement will be enforceable. In addition, in some cases the corporate bylaws, partnership agreement, or LLC operating agreement may contain some form of buy-sell agreement within them. When that is the case, either a new agreement will need to be drafted in such a way as to avoid violating any terms of that existing agreement, or the consent of everyone affected may be required to change the agreement. The attorney will be able to provide guidance on these issues. In addition, a CPA or other tax advisor will likely be needed to advise regarding the income and estate tax implications of transfers under the agreement. Also, an insurance professional will be necessary to provide guidance on the best types of life and disability policies to be used for funding the agreement.

Buy-sell agreements generally are of one of three types:
- entity purchase (sometimes referred to as redemption agreements)
- cross-purchase agreements
- wait-and-see agreements

Entity (Redemption) Agreements

The simplest form of buy-sell agreement is the **entity purchase**, or redemption, agreement. This type of buy-sell agreement obligates the business entity to purchase an owner's interest in the entity upon that owner's death. This type of buy-sell agreement works well for organizations that have a separate legal existence from their owners but would not be appropriate for a sole proprietorship. Sole proprietorships are wholly owned by one person, and when that person dies, so does the proprietorship. The business of a sole proprietor may be transferred to another person or entity at the death of the sole proprietorship through a one-way agreement (discussed below), but the proprietorship cannot purchase itself.

Example 14.22

Cecil is part owner of a luxury resort hotel, Fawlty Towers. Fawlty Towers is organized as a C corporation, and the corporation is wholly owned by members of Cecil's family. To ensure that the ownership of the hotel stays within the family and to make sure that Cecil's estate has sufficient liquidity to cover its expenses at his death, Cecil enters into a buy-sell agreement with Fawlty Towers, Inc. whereby Cecil (through his estate) agrees to sell, and Fawlty Towers agrees to purchase his stock when he dies. The agreement between Cecil and Fawlty Towers is an entity purchase buy-sell agreement.

To fund the purchase obligation under an entity-purchase buy-sell agreement, the business can acquire a life insurance policy on the owner's life with a death benefit sufficient to cover the purchase amount. Life insurance is an ideal vehicle to use for this purpose, since it provides funds at the exact time they are needed (the death of the insured). Furthermore, using the death benefit to meet the purchase obligation under the buy-sell agreement does not affect cash holdings or other assets that the company may need for continued business operations.

Disadvantages

While entity buy-sell agreements have the advantage of simplicity, there is at least one disadvantage to using this structure.

Key Concepts

1. Highlight the parties to an entity agreement versus a cross-purchase agreement.

2. Distinguish between an entity agreement, a cross-purchase agreement, and wait-and-see buy-sell agreement.

3. Explain why life insurance is a perfect hedge for buy-sell agreements that are triggered on the death of the owner.

If an entity buy-sell agreement is used, and the surviving owners plan to sell their business interests after the death of the first owner but prior to their own deaths, the entity buy-sell agreement will increase their taxable gain upon sale of their interests. Of course, this would not be an issue for family businesses that are not sold during the lifetimes of the family members. This disadvantage of entity buy-sell agreements is easily remedied by using a cross-purchase buy-sell agreement.

Cross-Purchase Agreements

A **cross-purchase buy-sell agreement** is an arrangement between individuals who agree to purchase the business interest of a deceased owner. Unlike an entity-type agreement, which involves the business itself, a cross-purchase agreement only involves the owners of the business.

Example 14.23

Cecil and his sister, Sybil, are equal owners of a luxury resort hotel, Fawlty Towers. Fawlty Towers is organized as a C corporation, and the corporation has been wholly owned by members of Cecil & Sybil's family since it began. Neither Cecil nor Sybil are married, and neither has any children. To ensure that the ownership of the hotel stays within the family, and to make sure that their estates have sufficient liquidity to cover expenses at death, Cecil and Sybil enter into a buy-sell agreement whereby the first sibling to die agrees to sell (through her estate), and the surviving sibling agrees to purchase the decedent's interest when she dies. The agreement between Cecil and Sybil is a cross-purchase buy-sell agreement.

To fund a cross-purchase buy-sell agreement with life insurance, each party to the agreement purchases a life insurance policy on the life of all of the other parties to the agreement so that the death benefit is sufficient to purchase the interest of any deceased owner. If there are only two parties, this approach is relatively straightforward – each party purchases one policy on the life of the other. When more than two owners are involved, however, things can get complicated, and as the number of owners grows, so does the complexity of the arrangement and the number of life insurance policies that must be purchased.

Example 14.24

Bertie, Claude, and Eustice are equal owners of Wooster Enterprises, Ltd. They have entered into a cross-purchase buy-sell agreement triggered upon death. If Bertie dies first, his 1/3 interest would have to be purchased by Claude and Eustice in equal shares. To fund the agreement, both Claude and Eustice should purchase a life insurance policy on Bertie's life that will pay a death benefit equal to 1/6 (1/3 x 1/2) of the value of the company. Bertie and Claude should each purchase a life insurance policy on Eustice's life for the same amount (in case Eustice dies first), and Eustice and Bertie should purchase a life insurance policy on Claude's life in case Claude dies first. As this example illustrates, for a three-owner agreement, six life insurance policies would have to be purchased to fund this buy-sell agreement.

The number of cross purchase policies needed to fully fund the buy-sell agreement can be calculated by using the formula:

$$\text{Number of policies} = N(N-1)$$

Where N = the number of owners subject to the agreement. The greater the number of owners, the greater the number of life insurance policies that should be purchased. For example, four owners would require twelve policies or 4(4-1).

While applying for a large number of life insurance policies does somewhat complicate the administration of a cross-purchase agreement, the real issues emerge in the annual maintenance of the agreement. Each year, each of the owners will pay the premiums on policies they own covering the lives of other owners in order to keep those policies in force. If just one owner fails to pay the premium and another owner dies, the benefits of entering into the buy-sell agreement may be in jeopardy. For this reason, the agreement may contain a clause creating a legal obligation for each owner to keep the policies in force by paying the premiums as required by the policy.

An entity agreement is a simple arrangement in which only one policy is purchased on the life of each owner and the premiums are paid by the entity. A cross-purchase agreement is much more complex than an entity agreement.

One of the advantages to a cross-purchase agreement is the ability to increase the surviving owner's basis in his or her shares of the business entity. When life insurance death benefits are received (on a tax-free basis), and are used to purchase the business interest of a deceased owner, each surviving owner's share of the business increases, but so does his or her basis in the business entity. Basis is that portion of the sale proceeds not subject to income tax, so a higher basis results in a higher after-tax benefit to the taxpayer. This benefit is unavailable with entity buy-sell agreements and is often the reason that financial advisors prefer cross-purchase arrangements.

Example 14.25

Bertie, Claude, and Eustice are equal owners of Wooster Enterprises, Ltd. The adjusted basis for each 1/3 interest is $100,000. They have entered into a cross-purchase buy-sell agreement triggered upon death. Bertie passed away, and his 1/3 interest in Wooster enterprises was valued at $334,000. The entire business was worth $1 million, leaving $333,000 each for Claude and Eustice. As specified in the buy-sell agreement, Claude and Eustice each purchase half of Bertie's 1/3 interest in Wooster Enterprise, Ltd. for $167,000. After the purchase, Claude's and Eustice's ownership percentages increased from 33% to 50%. Their basis in the ownership interests increased from $100,000 to $267,000 each ($100,000 original adjusted basis + $167,000 paid for acquisition of the interest from Bertie's estate). If Claude and Eustice immediately sold Wooster Enterprises, Ltd. for $1 million, each of them would receive $500,000 (1/2 the proceeds) and would have to pay income tax on a capital gain of $233,000 ($500,000 amount realized - $267,000 adjusted basis).

How would this result differ if the buy-sell agreement was structured as an entity buy-sell, and Claude and Eustice sold the business after Bertie died? As described above, Claude and Eustice would each receive $500,000 (1/2 the proceeds) but would have to pay income tax on a capital gain of $400,000 ($500,000 amount realized - $100,000 adjusted basis). In this instance, the basis of the surviving shareholders is not affected because the corporation, not the individual shareholders, purchased the shares from Bertie's estate.

Cross-purchase agreements are typically preferred from a tax planning standpoint because:

1. they permit the surviving shareholders to increase their basis in the business interest;
2. life insurance owned by business owners outside of a corporation does not trigger any potential accumulated earnings tax.

One-Way Buy-Sell Agreements

When the business is a sole proprietorship (one owner), an LLC with only one member, or a corporation with one shareholder, it is possible to have a one-way buy-sell agreement. A one-way agreement is similar to a cross-purchase agreement, but with only one buyer and one seller and no reciprocity because the buyer does not expect to sell a business interest to the sole owner. The owner will agree only to sell, and the buyer will agree only to buy. Often either a family member or a key employee will have a desire to purchase the business when the owner dies. If that is the case, the buyer will purchase a life insurance policy on the current owner.

Wait-and-See Buy-Sell Agreements

Wait-and-see buy-sell agreements are a cross between entity and cross purchase buy-sell agreements. Using this approach, the business has the first option to purchase the interest of a deceased owner. If the business entity chooses not to purchase the interest, the surviving owners of the company are given the opportunity to purchase the deceased owner's interest in proportion to his or her ownership interest. If the surviving owners do not exercise their right to purchase the interest, any interest remaining is purchased by the business.

By giving both the company and the owners the right to purchase an interest, the wait-and-see buy-sell maintains flexibility between the simplicity of the entity agreement and the tax advantages of the cross-purchase agreement. Both the company and the surviving owners can assess their respective situations when the death of an owner occurs and act in a way that maximizes their combined benefits.

Wait-and-see buy-sell agreements are very useful for C corporations with large amounts of retained earnings. When retained earnings are distributed to shareholders, they are usually treated as dividend distributions and are subject to income tax. If a corporation redeems shares from the estate of a deceased owner, and the redemption does not exceed the estate and inheritance taxes plus funeral expenses incurred by the deceased owner's estate, the redemption is typically exempt from income tax. This approach results in a reduction in retained earnings at the corporate level (IRC Sec. 303). The reduction in retained earnings reduces the amount of future corporate distributions that are subject to taxes as dividends, which is a significant benefit for C corporations and their surviving shareholders. Under a wait-and-see buy-sell agreement, the corporation will typically exercise its first option to purchase the number of shares necessary to effectuate a Sec. 303 redemption (thereby reducing its retained earnings) and give the surviving shareholders the option to purchase the remaining interest. If the surviving shareholders exercise this option, they will receive an increase in their basis in the business interest, which will reduce their taxable gain in the business entity should they decide to sell their interests before their deaths.

While wait-and-see buy-sell agreements are often used for C corporations, they are not frequently used for S corporations, partnerships, limited liability companies, or limited liability partnerships. Only C corporations issue taxable dividends, so the tax features of the wait-and-see buy-sell agreements are applicable only to C corporations. Wait-and-see buy-sell agreements could still be used with other types of business entities if the primary objective is to maintain flexibility in the repurchase of interests.

Life Insurance is the Perfect Hedge for a Buy-Sell Agreement Triggered at Death

As illustrated in the discussion above, life insurance is a perfect hedge for buy-sell agreements that are triggered on the death of the owner. If life insurance is purchased on the owner's life, the proceeds can be used to purchase the business interest from the decedent owner's estate. This facilitates effective transfer of ownership and control of the business entity and provides liquidity for the deceased owner's estate so that estate and inheritance taxes, funeral expenses, and end-of-life medical care costs can be paid.

What type of life insurance policy should be purchased to fund the buy-sell agreement? The answer, of course, depends on the facts. If the business is family owned, and the owner of the interest is a family member, or if there has been a long-term relationship between the owner and the business with no definitive date when that relationship will end (such as a retirement date), a permanent life insurance policy should be considered. Whole life insurance costs more up front but provides protection for longer periods of time with guarantees from the insurance company. Using term life, universal life, or variable universal life may be risky, since those policies will only remain in force as long as there is money to pay premiums or in the policy cash value to pay the annual mortality and expense charges. Whole life insurance guarantees that the money needed to buy the business interest will be there no matter how long the owner lives or continues to be involved in the operation of the business activity.

Tax-Related Issues for Buy-Sell Agreements

With an entity purchase agreement, the business entity will be the owner and beneficiary of a life insurance policy on each owner. The business entity will pay the premiums for this life insurance and the payments are not deductible by the entity. The life insurance death benefit proceeds are received income tax-free so long as the rules under IRC §101(j) are met.[34] Section 101(j) of the tax code sets forth rules regarding employee notice and consent when a business entity wishes to purchase a life insurance policy in which the employee will be the insured and the business will be the owner and beneficiary. In order to retain the income tax-free nature of the death benefit, the business is required, before the contract is issued, to:

1. Notify the employee in writing that the business (policyholder) intends to insure the employee's life, and the notice should include the maximum face amount for which the employee could be insured at the time the contract is issued, and
2. Obtain from the employee written consent to be insured under the contract and to allow continued coverage after the insured terminates employment, and
3. Inform the employee, in writing, that the business (policyholder) will be a beneficiary of any proceeds payable upon the death of the employee.

---

34. Public Law 109-280 (August 17, 2006), The Pension Protection Act of 2006.

In addition to the notice and consent requirements, one of the following must also apply:

1. At the time the policy is issued, the employee is a highly compensated employee (defined under the law as: a director, a five percent or greater owner, one of the five highest paid officers, among the 35% highest paid employees under Section 105(h)(5), or an employee with compensation of at least $130,000 per year as indexed for inflation under Section 414(q) in 2021), or

2. At the time of death, the employee was still employed with the business at any time during the 12 months prior to death, or

3. The death benefit is paid to the insured's heirs, or

4. The death benefit is used to purchase the insured's ownership interest in the business from the insured's heirs or estate (e.g., under a buy-sell agreement).

Failure to comply with these requirements will result in the death benefit being taxed as ordinary income, to the extent that it exceeds the employer's cost basis in the policy. Each year that the business continues to own the policy, it will be required to file Form 8925 with its income tax return to report information regarding the policy.

With a cross-purchase agreement, the premiums paid by each owner to purchase insurance on the lives of the other owners are not tax deductible, but the death benefits received will be income tax-free, provided a transfer for value problem does not exist. IRC Sec. 101(a) provides that the death benefit of life insurance is income-tax-free. The major exception to this provision is the transfer-for-value rule. If a policy is transferred to a party that is not one of the statutorily defined exceptions (see below), then the death benefit in excess of the total amount paid for the transfer and any subsequent premiums, is received as ordinary income.

Example 14.26

Thelma sells her $100,000 life insurance policy to her sister, Louise, for $60,000. Louise pays the $1,000 annual premium for four years before Thelma dies. The profit to Louise is calculated as follows:

$100,000 - $60,000 - $4,00 0 = $36,000

This profit is received as ordinary income and is, therefore, fully taxable.

The transfer of an insurance policy is exempt from the transfer for value rules and will not cause the loss of the death proceeds' tax-free nature if the transfer is one of the statutorily defined exceptions. Examples of exceptions to the transfer-for-value rule are:

- A transfer of the policy to the insured.
- A transfer to a partner of the insured or to a partnership of which the insured is a partner.
- A transfer to a corporation of which the insured is a shareholder or officer.
- A transfer in which the transferee's basis is determined, in whole or in part, by reference to the transferor's basis (e.g., a substituted or carryover basis).

Several of these exceptions to the transfer-for-value rule are useful in planning for buy-sell agreements for business owners, particularly if an owner is currently uninsurable but owns a policy that is no longer necessary in fulfilling his personal financial plan. For example, the ability of business partners to transfer existing policies either to each other or to the partnership is a valuable exception that allows the buy-sell agreement to be funded with an existing policy without adverse tax consequences. It should be noted, however, that the same flexibility is not available when the business is a corporation. There is no exception to the transfer-for-value rule when shareholders transfer policies to each other. The only exception for a corporation is for the insured (who is an officer or shareholder) to transfer an existing policy to the corporate entity.

A transfer-for-value situation can be reversed by a later transfer that falls under one of the exceptions listed above. For example, if the policy were later transferred back to the insured, it would no longer be considered a transfer-for-value.

When an existing policy is transferred from the employee to the employer, the transfer itself is sufficient to meet the Notice and Consent requirement of §101(j) regarding written consent, maximum face amount, and notice that the employer will be the beneficiary of the policy.[35]

Trusteed Agreements

To avoid the transfer-for-value problem with a corporate cross-purchase agreement funded with existing policies, or if the owners simply want to avoid purchasing separate life insurance policies on one another due to the large number of policies required for multi-owner cross-purchase agreements, they can use a trusteed cross-purchase agreement. Under such an agreement, a trustee owns the life insurance policy on each owner, and the owners contribute their individual share of the insurance premiums.

Trusteed agreements are a way to avoid a large number of policies while still achieving the increase in basis associated with a cross-purchase agreement. For tax purposes, the trustee is treated as a straw man (one with no substance) and the surviving owners are treated as having received the death benefit and purchased the shares of the deceased owner upon death, thus providing them with an increased cost basis.

Business Disability Plans

Disability overhead insurance is designed to cover the expenses that are usual and necessary expenses in the operation of a business should the owner become disabled. Premiums are deductible as a business expense, and benefits payable from the plan are taxable income to the entity. Disability buyout policies are policies to cover the value of an individual's interest in the business should they become disabled.

Split-Dollar Life Insurance Arrangement

A split-dollar arrangement is a discriminatory benefit plan using life insurance. The employer and employee share the cost of a life insurance policy on the employee (usually permanent insurance such as whole life insurance or variable universal life insurance). Such arrangements are typically used by businesses to provide low cost insurance to key employees. A **split-dollar life insurance arrangement** is generally structured in one of either of the two following ways:
1. The endorsement method, or
2. The collateral assignment method.

> ### ≔ *Key Concepts*
>
> 1. What are the tax implications of business overhead disability plans?
>
> 2. What is split-dollar life insurance, and what are the income tax consequences associated with such plans?
>
> 3. What is key person insurance, and what are the income tax consequences associated with such plans?

35.Notice 2009-48.

The Endorsement Method

Under a split-dollar life insurance plan using the endorsement method, the employer owns the life insurance policy on the employee and the employer pays the policy premium. The employer withholds the right in the plan to be repaid for all of its premium either at the employee's death or the surrender of the life insurance policy. Usually any death benefit or cash surrender value in excess of the employer's refund is paid to the policy beneficiaries.

The Collateral Assignment Method

Under a split-dollar life insurance plan using the collateral assignment method, the employee owns the life insurance policy and the employer makes a loan to the employee to pay the policy premiums. In this case, at the employee's death or at the surrender of the policy, the employer loan will be repaid and any excess will be paid to the policy beneficiaries.

Uses of Split-Dollar Life Insurance

A split-dollar life insurance policy is appropriate when an employer wishes to provide an executive with life insurance benefits at a low cost and low cash outlay to the executive (the premiums are essentially paid for by the employer). Split-dollar life insurance plans are best suited for executives in their 30s, 40s, and early 50s since the plan requires a reasonable duration to build adequate policy cash value and the cost to the executive at later ages is usually prohibitive. Split-dollar life insurance can be used as an alternative to an insurance-financed nonqualified deferred compensation plan or in conjunction with a nonqualified, unfunded, deferred compensation plan. A split-dollar policy is also effective when an employer is seeking a totally selective executive fringe benefit as the nondiscrimination rules do not apply.

A split-dollar plan allows an executive to receive the benefit of current value using employer funds with minimal or no tax cost to the executive. In most types of split-dollar plans, the employer's outlay is at all times fully secured. Upon the employee's death or termination of employment, the employer is reimbursed from policy proceeds for its premium outlays. The net cost to the employer for the plan is merely the loss of the net after-tax income the funds could have earned while the plan was in effect.

Income Taxation Issues

The income tax treatment of split-dollar life insurance arrangements will be determined under one of two sets of rules depending on who owns the policy. If the executive, or someone designated by the executive, owns the life insurance policy, then the loan taxation rules apply. If the employer owns the policy, the economic benefit rules apply.

If the executive owns the policy, the employer's premium payments are treated as below-market loans from the employer to the executive. Consequently, unless the executive is required to pay the employer market-rate interest on the loan, the executive will be taxed on the difference between market-rate interest and the actual interest charged.

If the employer is the owner of the policy, the employer's premium payments are treated as providing taxable economic benefits to the executive. The executive recognizes as taxable income the value of life insurance coverage, as well as any increase in equity currently accessible to the executive. By taxing the executive on the increase in equity each year, this arrangement is discouraged.

Death Benefit - Transfer for Value

Death benefits payable from a split-dollar life insurance plan including both the employer's share and the employee/beneficiary's share are generally received income tax-free. However, the tax-free nature of the death proceeds is lost if the policy has been transferred for value (as discussed previously in this chapter).

Estate Consequences of Split-Dollar Life Insurance

Incidents of ownership will cause inclusion in the gross estate if the decedent retained the ownership or had the right to name or change the beneficiary. Inclusion in the gross estate could result from a policy transferred or assigned with the three year period prior to the insured/owner's death.

Key Person Life and Disability Insurance

Key person life and disability insurance covers employees who are considered critical to the success of a business; and whose death or disability might cause financial loss to the company. The company has an insurable interest in the person. Therefore, the company pays the premiums and is the beneficiary of the insurance policy. The premiums are not deductible, and the benefits are not taxable, so long as the previously discussed Notice and Consent requirements of § 101(j) are followed.

1. The premiums paid for a cross purchase life insurance policy are deductible by the payor.
   a. True
   b. False

2. An entity must include in income any benefits received from a business overhead disability plan.
   a. True
   b. False

3. Key person insurance premiums are not deductible by the employer until the death benefit is paid.
   a. True
   b. False

False, True, False.

DISCUSSION QUESTIONS

SOLUTIONS to the discussion questions can be found exclusively within the chapter. Once you have completed an initial reading of the chapter, go back and highlight the answers to these questions.

1. Discuss the tax implications of employer-provided group medical plans.

2. Describe COBRA and discuss the tax implications of employer-paid premiums.

3. Describe the requirements for a life insurance policy to be considered group term life insurance.

4. Discuss the tax implications of employer-provided group term life insurance.

5. Discuss the tax implications of employer-provided group disability insurance.

6. Describe cafeteria plans and discuss how they are used to provide employee benefits.

7. Discuss the tax implications of employer-provided cafeteria plans.

8. Describe flexible spending accounts (FSAs).

9. Discuss the tax implications of employer-provided Flexible Spending Accounts.

10. Discuss the tax implications of employer-provided Archer MSAs, and when they can be established.

11. Describe VEBA's and discuss the tax implications of payments made by the employer.

12. Discuss the tax implications of employer-provided salary continuation plans.

13. Discuss the tax implications of employer-provided group long-term care insurance.

14. Discuss the tax implications of employer-provided group retirement planning services.

15. Describe buy-sell agreements and describe the income tax consequences associated with such plans.

16. Discuss the tax implications of business overhead disability plans.

17. Describe split-dollar life insurance and discuss the income tax consequences associated with such plans.

18. Describe key person insurance and discuss the income tax consequences associated with such plans.

MULTIPLE CHOICE PROBLEMS

A sample of multiple choice problems is provided below. Additional multiple choice problems are available at money-education.com by accessing the Student Practice Portal.

1. Medical Trials Inc. has a cafeteria plan. Full-time employees are permitted to select any combination of the benefits listed below, but the total value received by each employee must be $6,500 a year or less.
    1. Group medical and hospitalization insurance for employee only, $3,600 a year.
    2. Group medical and hospitalization insurance for employee's spouse and dependents, $1,200 additional a year.
    3. Child-care payments, actual cost not to exceed $5,000.
    4. Cash required to bring the total of benefits and cash to $6,500.
    5. Universal variable life insurance $1,000.

    Which of the following statements is true? (All employees are full time.)
    a. Chadwick chooses to receive $6,500 cash because his wife's employer provides medical benefits for him. Chadwick has $2,900 of taxable income ($6,500 - $3,600).
    b. Erik chooses 1, 2, 5, and $700 cash. He must include $700 in taxable income.
    c. River chooses 1 and 2 and $1,700 in child care. He must include the $1,700 in gross income.
    d. Suri chooses 1 and 2 and $1,700 cash. Suri must include $1,700 in taxable income.

2. Which of the following circumstances suggest the use of a cafeteria plan?
    1. A cafeteria plan is appropriate when the employee mix is comprised only of older employees with families who need maximum medical and life insurance benefits.
    2. A cafeteria plan is appropriate when employers want to choose the benefit package most suited to their employee's individual needs.
    3. A cafeteria plan is appropriate when an employer seeks to maximize employee satisfaction with the benefit package, thereby maximizing the employer's benefit from its compensation expenditures.
    4. A cafeteria plan is appropriate for a small employer who does not have much money to spend on benefits.
    a. 3 only.
    b. 4 only.
    c. 1, 2, and 4.
    d. 1, 2, 3, and 4.

3. Which of the following is/are advantages of cafeteria plans?
    1. Cafeteria plans help to give employees an appreciation of the value of their benefit package.
    2. The flexibility of a cafeteria benefit package helps to meet varied employee needs.
    3. Cafeteria plans can help control employer costs for the benefit package because the cost of benefits that employees do not need is minimized.
    4. Cafeteria plans are less complex and less expensive to design and administer than general group benefit plans.
        a. 2 only.
        b. 1 and 2.
        c. 1, 2, and 3.
        d. 1, 2, 3, and 4.

4. Dani is covered by a $90,000 group-term life insurance policy, her daughter is the sole beneficiary. Dani's employer pays the entire premium for the policy; the uniform annual premium is $0.60 per $1,000 per month of coverage. How much, if any, is W-2 taxable income to Dani resulting from the insurance?
        a. $0.
        b. $24.
        c. $288.
        d. $648.

5. The beneficiary of key person life insurance is usually:
        a. The spouse of the employee.
        b. The employee's spouse and dependents.
        c. The company.
        d. The estate of the employee.

> **Additional multiple choice problems
> are available at
> money-education.com
> by accessing the
> Student Practice Portal.
> Access requires registration of the title using
> the unique code at the front of the book.**

QUICK QUIZ EXPLANATIONS

Quick Quiz 14.1
1. True.
2. False. Managed care plans emerged from a desire to decrease health care costs and increase competition amongst health care providers.

Quick Quiz 14.2
1. False. Health benefits provided to employees can be excluded from income. Employees who are also greater than two percent owners of S corporations must include the benefit into their income. However, they may be entitled to an above-the-line deduction for the amount of premiums paid and included in income.
2. True.

Quick Quiz 14.3
1. False. To be considered a group term life insurance policy, the employer must provide life insurance benefits to at least 10 employees.
2. False. If an employer provides a group term policy with a benefit over $50,000, then the employee must include in income an amount determined by multiplying the number of thousands of dollars of insurance coverage over $50,000 (rounded to the nearest $1,000) by the cost shown in the Uniform Premium Table provided by the IRS.

Quick Quiz 14.4
1. False. When the employer pays the premium and the premium value is excluded from the employee's gross income, any disability income benefit received by the employee is taxable to the employee.
2. True.

Quick Quiz 14.5
1. True.
2. False. Salary reductions elected by employees to fund nontaxable benefits available under the plan are not subject to income taxes or payroll taxes.

Quick Quiz 14.6
1. False. An MSA cannot be established after 2005.
2. False. Distributions from an HSA that are not used for medical expenses are taxed as ordinary income and subject to a 20 percent penalty if the owner of the HSA has not reached age 65.
3. True.

QUICK QUIZ EXPLANATIONS

Quick Quiz 14.7

1. True.
2. False. Long-term care premiums cannot be paid for within a cafeteria plan or flexible spending account nor can the premium payment be made with pre-tax employee salary deferral.
3. False. An employer may exclude from an employee's gross income the value of any retirement planning advice or information the employer provides to the employee or his spouse if the employer maintains a qualified retirement plan.

Quick Quiz 14.8

1. False. It is often very difficult to sell a small business to a third party. However, private equity firms and potential strategic buyers should be considered.
2. True.
3. True.

Quick Quiz 14.9

1. True.
2. False. An entity approach buys one policy per owner, therefore five policies not 20.
3. True.

Quick Quiz 14.10

1. False. The premiums for a cross-purchase life insurance policy are not deductible.
2. True.
3. False. Key person insurance premiums are not deductible, and the benefits of such a policy are not taxable.

15

ITEM SETS AND THE MIKE & MARIA ROMAN CASE

ITEM SET 1: CAPITAL NEEDS ANALYSIS

Troy and Kristy Reynolds (both currently age 56) have determined that they will require retirement income equal to $93,000 in today's dollars, based on their current income. They plan to retire in eight years and wish to assume an after-tax return on their investments, prior to retirement, of eight percent. They plan to readjust their assets after retirement and believe that their net return will drop to six percent. Troy's parents are both in their late eighties, and Kristy's parents are in their seventies. Troy and Kristy assume that retirement will last for 30 years, and that inflation will average two percent.

1. How much income will Troy and Kristy need in their first year of retirement?

Answer:

_____

_____

_____

_____

_____

_____

_____

_____

2. What is the amount of capital necessary at the start of retirement to support their income needs throughout retirement?

Answer:

_____

_____

_____

_____

_____

_____

_____

_____

3. For purposes of Social Security retirement benefits, the Reynolds reach full-retirement age at age 67. Their full benefit is expected to be $30,000 in today's dollars. If the Reynolds decided to factor in Social Security and begin taking Social Security benefits when they retire at age 64, how much personal capital would they need to accumulate at retirement?

Answer:

_____

_____

_____

_____

_____

_____

_____

_____

_____

4. If the Reynolds wanted to leave a specific bequest to their favorite charity (Wounded Warrior Project) in the amount of $2 million (actual amount of donation at death), how much additional capital would they need to have accumulated at the time they retire at age 64?

Answer:

_____

_____

_____

_____

_____

_____

_____

_____

_____

5. The Reynolds would like to know how much they need to save each year to fund retirement. For purposes of this calculation, assume they have accumulated retirement savings of $162,491, they want to retire at age 64, they will live until age 95, and they expect to inherit $1,000,000 at age 64 (just when they are retiring). Social Security benefits are the same as described above.

Answer:

_____

_____

_____

_____

_____

_____

_____

_____

6. The Reynolds modified their thinking and would like to know how much they need to save each year to fund retirement including a few changes. For purposes of this calculation, assume they have retirement savings of $900,000 (from the sale of a few assets), they want to retire at age 62, they will live until age 95, and they will plan on not receiving an inheritance. They also believe that they can live off of $86,000 instead of $93,000, annually in today's dollars. Social Security benefits are the same as described above.

Answer:

_____

_____

_____

_____

_____

_____

_____

_____

_____

ITEM SET 2: RETIREMENT PLAN DISTRIBUTIONS

Chad Boudreaux is a 58-year-old riverboat captain. He grew up in New Orleans and has worked on the Mississippi River his entire life. He works for a private company in New Orleans called Crescent River Pilots Inc. (CRP) and is married to Patricia, who is 35 years old. They have a seven-year-old son, named River. CRP sponsors a 401(k) plan that offers a Roth account and a separate ESOP. Chad has the following retirement plan accounts:

Account Description	Current FMV	Beneficiary
ESOP account from CRP - consists of CRP shares. The cost basis for the shares is $75,000.	$400,000	Patricia
401(k) Plan From CRP Inc.	$800,000	Patricia
401(k) Plan from Schlumberger, where he worked in his thirties	$90,000	Patricia
Roth IRA (established in 2000 with a $2,000 initial contribution; three years ago he rolled over a traditional IRA with a balance of $10,000)	$45,000	Patricia
Traditional IRA (established twenty years ago with $15,000 of after-tax contributions)	$90,000	River
Inherited IRA from the death of his mom. She died in the same year Chad turned 50 years old.	$120,000	River

1. Chad plans on retiring in March of this year, and he and his wife would like to go to Rome for an extended vacation. He wants to take a distribution of $20,000 from one of his retirement accounts to pay for the vacation. Which of his retirement plans would allow him to take a penalty-free withdrawal to fund his vacation?

Answer:

_____

_____

_____

_____

_____

_____

_____

_____

_____

2. Can Chad change the beneficiary designations on his IRAs without spousal consent?

Answer:

_____

_____

_____

_____

_____

_____

_____

_____

3. Can Chad change the beneficiary designations on his non-IRA retirement plans without spousal consent?

Answer:

_____

_____

_____

_____

_____

_____

_____

_____

_____

4. If the balance in Chad's mom's IRA was $120,000 at the end of 2020 when Chad was age 58 and $140,000 at the end of 2021 when Chad is age 59, how much, if any, must he take out from this account in 2021 and 2022 to satisfy the minimum distribution rules?

Answer:

_____

_____

_____

_____

_____

_____

_____

_____

5. If Chad were to die in 2021, and River was to inherit the inherited IRA, how would he comply with the minimum distribution rules?

Answer:

_____

_____

_____

_____

_____

_____

_____

_____

_____

6. Assuming Chad decided to take out the entire balance in the Roth IRA to purchase a new fishing boat, how would the distribution be taxed?

Answer:

_____

_____

_____

_____

_____

_____

_____

_____

7. If Chad took a $20,000 distribution from his traditional IRA to pay for the vacation, what are the tax implications?

Answer:

_____

_____

_____

_____

_____

_____

_____

_____

_____

8. If Chad retires, what should he do with the CRP shares and why?

Answer:

_____

_____

_____

_____

_____

_____

_____

_____

9. If Chad were to die in 2021, what options would Patricia have for satisfying the minimum distribution rules on the Roth IRA account?

Answer:

_____

_____

_____

_____

_____

_____

_____

_____

_____

10. Assume Chad takes a distribution of the CRP stock several years from now when the stock is valued at $500,000. A few years later, Chad has a terrible accident and dies. The value of the CRP stock at the time of his death is $700,000. Patricia inherits the stock and sells it six months after Chad dies for $800,000. What are the tax implications of the sale?

Answer:

_____

_____

_____

_____

_____

_____

_____

_____

_____

ITEM SET 3: REQUIRED MINIMUM DISTRIBUTIONS (RMDs)

Carley, who turned age 72 on September 10th of 2021, owns 32 percent of Big Company, and is its current CEO. She has amassed $15 million in her qualified plan account as of December 31st of 2020 and $17 million as of December 31st of 2021. She has named her son, Simon (age 9 at the end of 2021), as her beneficiary.

1. What is the minimum distribution that Carley must receive for 2021?

Answer:

_____

_____

_____

_____

_____

_____

_____

_____

_____

2. If she only receives a distribution of $200,000 during 2021, then how much in penalties will she be required to pay for 2021?

Answer:

_____

_____

_____

_____

_____

_____

_____

_____

_____

3. Assume that the market crashes in 2021 and the value of the qualified plan drops to $1 million. As a result of the market drop, Carley dies in September of 2021 (after having taken her required distribution for 2021) and Simon inherits the IRA. If the value of the IRA is $1 million at the end of 2021, $1.2 million at the end of 2022, and $1.5 million at the end of 2023, how much, if any, must Simon take out to satisfy the minimum distributions in Years 2021, 2022, and 2023 if his goal to stretch distributions over the longest period possible?

Answer:

_____

_____

_____

_____

_____

_____

_____

_____

_____

4. Can Carley delay taking minimum distributions from her Big Company Plan since she is still employed? Explain why or why not.

Answer:

_____

_____

_____

_____

_____

_____

_____

_____

_____

ITEM SET 4: ISOS AND NQSOS

David Goggins' employer, Run Hard, Inc., granted him 1,000 ISOs and 1,000 NSOs on January 1st last year. The exercise price was $5 per share for both sets of options. David exercised both sets of options on July 1st last year, when the stock was worth $8 per share. David sold 400 shares acquired from the ISO grant and another 400 shares acquired from the NSO grant on April 1st this year for $14 per share. David sold the remaining shares from both the ISO and NSO grants on December 31st of this year for $20 per share.

1. How much ordinary income did David recognize when his employer granted him the ISOs?

Answer:

_____

_____

_____

_____

_____

_____

_____

_____

_____

2. How much ordinary income did David recognize when his employer granted him the NSOs?

Answer:

_____

_____

_____

_____

_____

_____

_____

_____

_____

3. How much ordinary income did David recognize when he exercised the ISOs?

Answer:

_____

_____

_____

_____

_____

_____

_____

_____

4. How much ordinary income did David recognize when he exercised the NSOs?

Answer:

_____

_____

_____

_____

_____

_____

_____

_____

_____

5. How much ordinary income did David recognize when he sold the shares acquired from the ISO grant on April 1st of this year?

Answer:

_____

_____

_____

_____

_____

_____

_____

_____

_____

6. How much ordinary income did David recognize when he sold the shares acquired from the NSO grant on April 1st of this year?

Answer:

_____

_____

_____

_____

_____

_____

_____

_____

_____

7. How much ordinary income did David recognize when he sold the shares acquired from the ISO grant on December 31st of this year?

Answer:

_____

_____

_____

_____

_____

_____

_____

_____

8. How much ordinary income did David recognize when he sold the shares acquired from the NSO grant on December 31st of this year?

Answer:

_____

_____

_____

_____

_____

_____

_____

_____

ITEM SET 5: ISOs AND NQSOs

Dottie is the CEO of Chaos Baseball Equipment, Inc. (Chaos). It is a rapidly growing publicly traded company. She was awarded the following stock options from her company:

Option Grant	Grant Date	Type	Exercise Price	# Shares
A	February 1, Year 1	ISO	$20	100
B	July 1, Year 2	NQSO	$25	100
C	August 1, Year 3	ISO	$30	100
D	May 1, Year 4	NQSO	$30	100

During Year 5, Dottie had the following transactions regarding the above stock options:

Option Grant	Date	Action	# Shares	Market Price on Action Date
A	February 1	Exercised	100	$42
A	February 1	Sold	100	$42
B	February 14	Exercised	100	$45
C	February 14	Exercised	100	$45
D	May 1	Exercised	100	$50
D	June 1	Sold	100	$60

1. How much income would Dottie have when her ISOs are granted?

Answer:

_____

_____

_____

_____

_____

_____

_____

_____

_____

2. What are the tax implications for the A options during Year 5?

Answer:

_____

_____

_____

_____

_____

_____

_____

_____

3. What are the tax implications for the B options during Year 5?

Answer:

_____

_____

_____

_____

_____

_____

_____

_____

_____

4. What are the tax implications for the C options during Year 5?

Answer:

_____

_____

_____

_____

_____

_____

_____

_____

_____

5. What are the tax implications for the D options during Year 5?

Answer:

_____

_____

_____

_____

_____

_____

_____

_____

_____

_____

6. Over the last five years, Dottie's salary has increased from $450,000 to $900,000 and her annual bonus has increased to $400,000 as the market value of the company has increased. What are some of the tax implications?

Answer:

_____

_____

_____

_____

_____

_____

_____

_____

ITEM SET 6: QUALIFIED PLAN RULES

Bubbles LLC is a web design company that operates out of Boulder, Colorado. Jesse and Skyler started Bubbles twenty years ago and it has grown to be one of the more sizable web development firms in Colorado. Bubbles offers a 401(k) /profit sharing plan with a Roth account option. The plan has the following characteristics:

- Eligibility: age 21 and one-year of service
- Match: dollar for dollar match
- Vesting: 20% per year (years 1 through 5)
- Highly compensated definition: uses top 20% election
- Profit-sharing contribution: Bubbles generally makes a sizeable contribution, but the percentage varies.
- The plan has been amended to permit in-plan Roth rollovers.
- The plan permits rollovers from other qualified plans and IRAs.

EE#	Employee	Ownership	Age	Tenure	Salary	Deferral
1	Jesse	60%	48	20 Years	$200,000	$10,000
2	Skyler	30%	49	20 Years	$150,000	$15,000
3	Walter	6%	33	15 Years	$75,000	$5,250
4	Marie	4%	42	10 Years	$85,000	$5,100
5	Hank	0%	58	8 Years	$60,000	$0
6	Lydia	0%	29	6 Years	$75,000	$4,500
7	Jane	0%	53	4 Years	$50,000	$0
8	Hector	0%	19	2 Years	$60,000	$0
9	Gale	0%	25	8 Months	$24,000	$0
10	Gus	0%	19	6 Months	$18,000	$0

Note: Lydia is Skyler's daughter. She graduated from the art institute five years ago.

1. Who is not eligible for the 401(k) plan?

Answer:

2. Who is highly compensated?

Answer:

_____

_____

_____

_____

_____

_____

_____

_____

3. What is the most that Bubbles could contribute to the profit-sharing plan for the current year assuming the salary deferrals stay constant?

Answer:

_____

_____

_____

_____

_____

_____

_____

_____

_____

4. What is the actual deferral percentage for the highly compensated employees?

Answer:

_____

_____

_____

_____

_____

_____

_____

_____

5. What is the actual deferral percentage for the non-highly compensated employees?

Answer:

_____

_____

_____

_____

_____

_____

_____

_____

6. Does the plan pass the ADP test? Why or why not and what can the company do if the plan does not pass the test?

Answer:

_____

_____

_____

_____

_____

_____

_____

_____

7. Assume the company decided to make a profit-sharing contribution that was integrated with Social Security, with an integration level equal to the Social Security wage base. If the base percentage was 10 percent with a maximum excess percentage, how much would be contributed to the plan on behalf of Jesse (disregard the salary deferral)?

Answer:

_____

_____

_____

_____

_____

_____

_____

_____

_____

8.   How many years of service does Hector currently have for purposes of vesting?

Answer:

_____

_____

_____

_____

_____

_____

_____

_____

_____

9.   Jesse has $702,000 accumulated in the 401(k) plan. The balance consists of deferrals, employer matching contributions, earnings, and profit-sharing contributions. Jesse also has an NOL carryover on his personal return from another business investment. Discuss whether Jesse can execute an in-plan Roth rollover and the tax implications.

Answer:

_____

_____

_____

_____

_____

_____

_____

_____

_____

_____

ITEM SET 7: 403(b) PLANS

Roger, age 46, works for the local public school teaching Physics to advanced science high school students. Roger has been with the school for 21 years, earns $65,000 per year, and has never contributed to the 403(b) retirement plan that is offered. The 403(b) plan offers dollar for dollar matching on all contributions. The school district is considering adopting a 457 plan.

1.   Which plan will offer Roger the highest tax deferral in 2021?

Answer:

_____

_____

_____

_____

_____

_____

_____

_____

_____

_____

2.   If Roger's wife makes enough money for them to live on and they decide to save as much of his income as possible, how much is the maximum that he can defer in tax-deferred retirement savings vehicles assuming the school adopts the 457 plan?

Answer:

_____

_____

_____

_____

_____

_____

_____

_____

_____

3. What type of investments is Roger permitted to make in the 403(b) plan?

Answer:

_____

_____

_____

_____

_____

_____

_____

_____

4. What type of employers may adopt a 403(b) plan?

Answer:

_____

_____

_____

_____

_____

_____

_____

_____

_____

5.   What types of employees benefit the most from the implementation of a 403(b) plan?

Answer:

_____

_____

_____

_____

_____

_____

_____

_____

ITEM SET 8: SIMPLE IRAs

Penelope's Paint -N- Plumbing, Inc. (3P) has been in business for 33 years. Penelope is retiring and passing the business on to her two children in equal shares to manage and operate according to their skills and experience. The children, Derek and Morgan, decide to adopt a retirement plan for both current and future employees in an attempt to attract and retain talent. They have decided to adopt a SIMPLE IRA, funded by both employee and employer contributions.

1. What are the advantages and disadvantages of offering a SIMPLE IRA over a qualified plan, such as a 401(k) plan?

Answer:

_____

_____

_____

_____

_____

_____

_____

_____

_____

2. If Reid (age 55), a long-time employee of 3P, wants to contribute both to the SIMPLE IRA at work and to a traditional IRA, what are the limits on his contributions and deductibility regarding the traditional IRA?

Answer:

_____

_____

_____

_____

_____

_____

_____

_____

_____

3. What are the annual dollar limits for contributing to a SIMPLE IRA and Traditional IRA? Also what are the phase-out levels for making these contributions, including spousal IRA contributions?

Answer:

_____

_____

_____

_____

_____

_____

_____

4. Gideon has been with 3P for a year and a half. He has deferred some of his compensation and has received a company match in the SIMPLE. Gideon's daughter is about to attend college, however, he has not saved any money for her education. What are the tax implications if Gideon takes a distribution from his SIMPLE IRA with 3P to pay for her college education expenses?

Answer:

_____

_____

_____

_____

_____

_____

_____

_____

_____

ITEM SET 9: SEPs

Robert "Bubba" Breaux, 32, owns and operates a po'boy shop in New Orleans, called Ya Mama's Po Boys. It is a family business that sells authentic New Orleans fare, just like "ya mama would serve," assuming she was from New Orleans. Bubba wants to establish a retirement plan so he can save for his retirement and the retirement of his employees on a tax-deferred basis. He has recruited you to assist in making a plan selection.

Bubba only wants to contribute in years that he makes a profit and does not want to incur much if anything on administrative expenses. Since the employees of Ya Mama's are all family members, Bubba is happy to contribute on behalf of the employees when the restaurant is doing well.

1. Based on Bubba's objectives, what type of retirement plan is most suited for his needs?

Answer:

_____
_____
_____
_____
_____
_____
_____
_____

2. Why might you recommend that Bubba utilize a qualified profit sharing plan with a CODA in lieu of the suggestion in question 1? (If you suggested a profit sharing plan with a CODA for question 1, reconsider.)

Answer:

_____
_____
_____
_____
_____
_____
_____
_____

3. Bubba employs the following individuals. Which employees may he exclude if the plan was a SIMPLE, SEP, or 401(k) profit-sharing plan?

Name	Age	Years of Service	Full-Time / Part-Time (< 1,000 hours)	Annual Income
Bubba	32	13	Full-Time	$160,000
Mama	49	4	Full-Time	$35,000
Trey	22	2	Full-Time	$32,000
Aaron	28	4	Part-Time (650 hours)	$26,000
Dixie	18	1	Part-Time (400 hours)	$12,000

Answer:

_____

_____

_____

_____

_____

_____

_____

_____

_____

ITEM SET 10: REQUIRED MINIMUM DISTRIBUTIONS (RMDs)

Charlie and Rose have been married for 40 years and have three children together. They are currently semi-retired and enjoying life at the beach in Florida. Rose turned 70 on February 14th 2019 and Charlie turned 70 on October 15th 2019. Rose is fully retired as a fashion model from Burl's Boutique, which marketed to older customers. Charlie still works part-time for a company that rents sailboats and provides sailing guides for customers renting boats. The company, called Set Sail, sponsors a 401(k) plan, in which Charlie continues to make contributions. Charlie gave up his corporate job at IBM several years ago and plans to continue working at Set Sail because he loves it.

Charlie's rich uncle, Alan, died earlier during 2019 and left his Roth IRA to Charlie. Charlie is sad about Alan, but happy about the IRA and even happier that it is a Roth IRA. Alan started the Roth IRA over ten years ago.

They need to know whether they need to take minimum distributions and if so, how much and from what accounts. The balances in the accounts are shown below.

Plan Owner	Plan #	Account /Plan Type	December 31, 2018 Balance	December 31, 2019 Balance	December 31, 2020 Balance	December 31, 2021 Balance
Rose	1	Self Directed IRA	$22,000	$23,500	$20,500	$19,800
Rose	2	Self Directed Roth IRA	$58,000	$67,000	$68,000	$70,000
Rose	3	Self Directed IRA	$45,000	$51,300	$50,300	$49,100
Rose	4	Burl's MPPP	$270,000	$267,000	$260,000	$252,000
Charlie	5	Inherited Roth IRA	$180,000	$200,000	$220,000	$218,500
Charlie	6	Self Directed IRA	$17,000	$18,000	$20,000	$20,500
Charlie	7	IBM 401(k) Roth Account	$40,000	$41,500	$49,000	$51,000
Charlie	8	IBM MPPP	$600,000	$650,000	$700,000	$723,000
Charlie	9	Set Sail 401(k) Roth Account	$80,000	$89,000	$92,000	$99,000

1. What is the required beginning date (RBD) for Rose and Charlie (without regard to the CARES Act waiver of RMDs for calendar year 2020)?

Answer:

2. What is the factor for Rose and for Charlie's first required minimum distribution (RMD)?

Answer:

_____

_____

_____

_____

_____

_____

_____

3. Which plans must they take a distribution from during 2020 (without regard to the ability to delay a distribution and without regard to the CARES Act waiver of RMDs for 2020)?

Answer:

_____

_____

_____

_____

_____

_____

_____

_____

4. What is the total amount of Charlie's RMD for 2021 (the year he turns age 72)?

Answer:

_____

_____

_____

_____

_____

_____

_____

_____

5. What is the minimum number of RMDs Rose has to take each year?

Answer:

_____

_____

_____

_____

_____

_____

_____

_____

_____

6. If Rose delays her first RMD to April 1st of 2020, how much is the total amount of her RMDs for 2020 (without regard to the CARES Act waiver of RMDs for calendar year 2020)?

Answer:

_____

_____

_____

_____

_____

_____

_____

_____

7. How is the life expectancy factor for the inherited Roth IRA determined for 2021 compared to the life expectancy factor for Charlie's other accounts?

Answer:

_____

_____

_____

_____

_____

_____

_____

_____

_____

8. Assume that Rose falls off the sailboat in 2020 and is eaten by a great white shark. Also assume that she named her three children, ages 50, 48, and 45, as equal beneficiaries on her self-directed Roth IRA. What are the implications for the beneficiaries regarding minimum distributions?

Answer:

_____

_____

_____

_____

_____

_____

_____

_____

ITEM SET 11: 401(k) PLANS

Kryptonite is a telecommunications provider located in Iowa with hundreds of thousands of employees. Their CEO, Clark Kline, is considering the replacement of their expensive defined benefit (DB) pension plan which requires large contributions every year with a 401(k) where the employees will bear the investment risk. The majority of the workforce is young and the top executives are all in their 50's and 60's.

1. As Clark's top financial advisor, what type of qualified retirement plan would you recommend instead of the 401(k) if he wants the majority of the benefits to accrue to the top executives?

Answer:

_____

_____

_____

_____

_____

_____

_____

_____

2. An intern who works for you recommends utilizing a DB/K plan. What is your opinion of using such a plan in this case?

Answer:

_____

_____

_____

_____

_____

_____

_____

_____

_____

3. Who would benefit the most from the change away from the DB plan to a 401(k)?

Answer:

_____

_____

_____

_____

_____

_____

_____

_____

4. What is the maximum contribution to a 401(k) of a worker age 56, who earns $20,000 per year as a factory worker with Kryptonite?

Answer:

_____

_____

_____

_____

_____

_____

_____

_____

5. Lois has been with Kryptonite for 10 years but is nervous now that Clark has taken over operations. She wants to know her options regarding taking money out of the 401(k) at a later date. You correctly tell her that she can access her 401(k) funds without penalty under what eight circumstances?

Answer:

_____

_____

_____

_____

_____

_____

_____

_____

6. Clark has heard that the ADP testing is an issue for 401(k) plans. What are three ways to minimize this issue?

Answer:

_____

_____

_____

_____

_____

_____

_____

_____

_____

ITEM SET 12: MEDICARE

Gaye is a 68-year old individual who retired from Yosimiti Corporation last year. Yosimiti is a multi-national corporation employing over 10,000 employees. She worked for the company for over 20 years, and was fully insured for purposes of Social Security retirement benefits, which she began receiving at age 63. At age 65, her Medicare Part A coverage began, and she opted to receive Medicare Part B coverage. Gaye has come to you with the following questions regarding her Medicare coverage.

1. What types of costs are covered under Medicare Part A?

Answer:

_____

_____

_____

_____

_____

_____

_____

_____

2. What types of costs are covered under Medicare Part B?

Answer:

_____

_____

_____

_____

_____

_____

_____

_____

3. Assume that Gaye suffered a severe fall and spent 100 days in the hospital. How much would she have to pay under Medicare for 2021?

Answer:

_____

_____

_____

_____

_____

_____

_____

_____

4. Unfortunately, while traveling in a foreign country, Gaye broke her ankle and had to go to the hospital emergency room. Which part of Medicare will cover the emergency room fees?

Answer:

_____

_____

_____

_____

_____

_____

_____

_____

ITEM SET 13: CAPITAL NEEDS ANALYSIS

Callie and Trinity Jackson are married and interested in planning for their retirement. Callie is 47 years old, while Trinity is three years younger. They would like to plan on retiring when Callie is age 65, which is when their mortgage on their home will be paid off. Their mortgage payment is $2,000 per month. Callie earns $75,000 and Trinity earns $105,000. They have current savings of $250,000 and would like to plan on a wage replacement ratio (WRR) of 80 percent, including Social Security. They currently save $15,000 each in their respective 401(k) plans. Neither of their plans offer an employer match.

They have been reading that 70 percent to 80 percent for wage replacement is optimal. They both reach full retirement age under Social Security at age 67. Callie and Trinity's Social Security retirement benefit at full retirement age is projected to be $2,500 and $3,000 per month, respectively. They want to plan on living until Trinity is age 95.

Assume that inflation is two percent and they can earn seven percent on their investments.

1. Calculate their needs at age 65 and their annual savings requirement.

Answer:

_____

_____

_____

_____

_____

_____

_____

_____

_____

2. Comment on the wage replacement ratio assumption.

Answer:

_____

_____

_____

_____

_____

_____

_____

_____

3. Recalculate their needs at age 65 based on adjusting the WRR (include assumptions for the new WRR).

Answer:

_____

_____

_____

_____

_____

_____

_____

_____

4. After spending time discussing retirement scenarios and what they want in their future, the Jacksons ask if they could afford to buy a beach house if they worked until age 70. Assume that the beach house they really want is expected to cost $1.5 million when they retire.

Answer:

_____
_____
_____
_____
_____
_____
_____
_____

5. The Jacksons like the idea of a $1.5 million beach house, however, they do not like the idea of working until Callie is 70 years old. You suggest that they consider retiring at age 65 with a 65 percent WRR and sell their current house at retirement and buy a beach house they can live in full time. They like the idea and ask how much they could afford for a beach house. Assume that their current house is worth $570,000 and is expected to increase at four percent per year. Ignore real estate closing costs for the calculation.

Answer:

_____
_____
_____
_____
_____
_____
_____
_____
_____

ITEM SET 14: QUALIFIED PLANS, INHERITED IRAS, & OTHER

Conor turned 48 years old in July this year and owns Kelly's Bar & Grill (known as "Kelly's"). Conor is in fairly good health, despite drinking too much alcohol. He enjoys running Kelly's, which produces a healthy profit. Cara is 47 years old, as of January, and is a speech therapist at a Catholic elementary school making $75,000 per year. She has worked there for the last 20 years. Cara has diabetes but is otherwise in reasonably good health.

Conor and Cara have been married for 22 years. Although Conor never went to college, Cara graduated from the Ohio State University. They have two children, Sean age 24, and Aoife, age 23. Sean is working at Kelly's and recently got married to Sam. Aoife is studying nursing in graduate school. Sam is 26 and working as a chemical engineer at Shell, after graduating with from USC. Sean and Sam met while at Mardi Gras in New Orleans a few years ago.

Conor's parents died in a small airplane crash while vacationing in Ireland. Conor's dad was a pilot in the U.S. Air Force and flew as a hobby. It was a tragic death. Cara's parents, on the other hand, are healthy and are expected to live to be 100 years old. They decided to move in across the street from Conor and Cara.

Being in the "bar" business much of his life, Conor has developed a love for music and has amassed quiet a collection of music and guitars.

Kelly's Bar & Grill (Kelly's)
Conor bought Kelly's 24 years ago when Sean was born. He realized he needed a steadier source of income and has worked to improve it over the years. Conor never incorporated the business but does have a separate checking account that he manages for the business.

Sean started working as a bus boy at Kelly's when he was 15 years old. He started full time at Kelly's after dropping out of his first year of college. Sean has made dramatic improvements to the bar over the last two years. He has upgraded the inside and outside of the building and, most importantly, brought in a young, energetic chef who has drastically improved the food menu. Kelly's was more of a bar for locals but is now more of a "grill" with great drinks and great food. Sean even helped Kelly's get the attention of several TV food shows. The expanded building now includes a snooker room and an area for darts. The new snooker league and a dart league helps increase nighttime customers.

Retirement Planning
Conor inherited a Roth IRA from his mom when she died in 2019. At the end of last year, the IRA had a balance of $255,000. Conor also started contributing to his first Roth IRA three years ago. That account has a balance of $20,000.

Cara has a 403(b) plan at school. The balance in the account is $350,000. She has not contributed the maximum every year but is now contributing $15,000.

Kelly's Employee Census

Employee	Age	Years of Service	Compensation	Role
Conor	48	24	$240,000	Owner
Sean	24	9	$150,000	General Manager
Aoife	23	7	$15,000	Part-Time Server
Daniel	32	2	$80,000	Executive Chef
Emily	38	4	$65,000	Office Manager
Finley	55	30	$30,000	Prep Cook
Gracie	31	8	$30,000	Bartender
Hogan	50	32	$30,000	Server
Irean	26	1	$20,000	Server
Jasmine	27	1	$18,000	Server
Total			**$678,000**	

Kelly's Profit & Loss Statement

Statement of Income and Expenses Kelly's Bar and Grill		
CASH INFLOWS		Totals
Revenue	$1,400,000	
Total Cash Inflows		$1,400,000
CASH OUTFLOWS		
Food Cost	$420,000	
Labor	$438,000	
Rent	$75,000	
Utilities	$100,000	
Marketing / Web	$65,000	
Other	$62,000	
Total Cash Outflows		$1,160,000
NET INCOME		**$240,000**

1. Sean implemented an HSA for Kelly's a couple of years ago. If Sean had $15,000 in the HSA, could he use it as part of a down payment on a house?

Answer:

_____

_____

_____

_____

_____

_____

_____

_____

_____

2. If Kelly's set up a profit-sharing plan and contributed 25 percent for the employees, how much would Sean and Conor receive?

Answer:

_____

_____

_____

_____

_____

_____

_____

_____

3. If Kelly's set up a profit-sharing plan, could they exclude the servers from the plan?

Answer:

_____

_____

_____

_____

_____

_____

_____

_____

4. If Kelly's adopted a qualified plan, would vesting begin as of the adoption date?

Answer:

_____

_____

_____

_____

_____

_____

_____

_____

_____

5. Describe the minimum distribution requirements for Conor for the inherited Roth IRA. How are distributions from the Roth IRA taxed?

Answer:

_____

_____

_____

_____

_____

_____

_____

6. Could Conor take a distribution from his Roth IRA? How much could he take and how would it be taxed?

Answer:

_____

_____

_____

_____

_____

_____

_____

_____

7. There was a fight in the bar about a year ago and one of the two people involved was severely injured. Sean called the police as soon as the altercation started and there did not appear to be any fault on the bar. As is common, Kelly's was also named in the lawsuit as a defendant. Discuss the credit risks Conor faces, including his IRAs and Cara's retirement plan.

Answer:

_____

_____

_____

_____

_____

_____

_____

_____

8. One of Conor's neighbors asks him if he set up Roth IRAs for his kids when they started working at Kelly's when they were around 16 years old. What would you tell Conor about whether that is possible or not?

Answer:

_____

_____

_____

_____

_____

_____

_____

_____

ITEM SET 15: TAXATION OF SOCIAL SECURITY BENEFITS

Tim and Tammy are the same age and have greatly enjoyed their life. They began taking Social Security benefits in 2016 at age 67 and are living off their benefits and a small amount ($1,050) of municipal bond interest. They have been able to save money in an IRA which they have contributed to over the years. The balance at the end of 2020 was $640,000.

1. Assuming their combined Social Security benefits are $36,500 in 2021, how much of their Social Security benefit is taxable? How much federal income tax do they have for 2021? Only consider their municipal bond income and their Social Security.

Answer:

_____

_____

_____

_____

_____

_____

_____

_____

_____

_____

2. Assume the same facts as in question 1, but also assume that Tammy took a job making $21,000 for 2021. They do not need the money, but Tammy wanted to help out and get out of the house. How much of their Social Security benefit is taxable? How much federal income tax do they have for 2021?

Answer:

_____

_____

_____

_____

_____

_____

_____

_____

_____

3. Assume the same facts as in questions 1 and 2. However, near the end of the year, Tammy receives a call from their broker who reminds them that they have a minimum distribution for 2021. How much of their Social Security benefit is taxable? How much federal income tax do they have for 2021?

Answer:

_____

_____

_____

_____

_____

_____

_____

_____

_____

4. Assume the same facts as in questions 1, 2, and 3. However, when Tammy took the job, she decided to defer $19,000 into her employer's 401(k) plan. How much of their Social Security benefit is taxable? How much federal income tax do they have for 2021?

Answer:

_____

_____

_____

_____

_____

_____

_____

_____

_____

5. Would deferral of most of Tammy's income into the 401(k) plan be a reasonable strategy for reducing the taxation of Social Security benefits?

Answer:

_____

_____

_____

_____

_____

_____

_____

_____

6. How would converting the traditional IRA to a Roth IRA before minimum distributions began or before Social Security benefits started impact the current taxation of their Social Security benefits?

Answer:

_____

_____

_____

_____

_____

_____

_____

_____

_____

MIKE AND MARIA ROMAN CASE

MIKE AND MARIA ROMAN

Mike and Maria have come to you, a financial planner, for help in developing a plan to accomplish their financial goals. From your initial meeting together, you have gathered the following information.

PERSONAL BACKGROUND AND INFORMATION COLLECTED

The Family

Mike and Maria Roman live in the country and operate a baseball academy on their property. They have a quaint home with a baseball field to the left of their house and two covered baseball batting and pitching cages. Mike played professional baseball for 15 years and now provides baseball instruction through RBI to children ages six to the early twenties. Mike currently coaches several college baseball players and is one of the most respected hitting and pitching coaches in the area. He also coaches a 9-year-old team and a 14-year-old team, both competing at the major division level. Maria has the tireless job of scheduling all of the lessons.

Mike and Maria Roman

Mike is 44 years old and loves his job. He is also an avid hunter and fisherman. Maria is also 44 years old and has done a wonderful job of raising their two kids, while helping with the family business.

The Children

Emily is 20 years old and is a Junior at Florida State University where she is double majoring in anthropology and communications. She has always been an excellent student and has a full academic scholarship. She also works part time to earn additional spending money. Her brother, Michael, is 17 years old and is a junior at Mission High School, where he plays shortstop on the baseball team and is hitting over 300 for the year.

Roman's Baseball Institute (RBI)

Mike started RBI seven years ago after he left professional baseball. He has built his reputation, as well as that of RBI over that time period. RBI is one of the premier baseball academies in the area.

The primary source of income for RBI is fees from baseball lessons. Lessons are priced at $70 per hour. Mike has three other coaches who help him provide lessons (Mickey, Mr. Joe, and Joey). His dad, Mickey, who is now retired from the Post Office, taught him how to play baseball, coached him growing up, and works with him now that he is retired. Mr. Joe also coached Mike as a child and now coaches for Mike. Joey is 20 years old, played baseball for Mike growing up and played in college during his freshman year before getting injured.

RBI generates $245,000 in gross annual revenue and has the following expenses:

Coaching fees to his coaches	$60,000
Utilities	$2,500
Field Maintenance	$7,000
Equipment (balls, etc.)	$1,000
Other Expenses	$3,000

Mike works 1,500 hours and the other coaches total 2,000 hours. His three coaches work the following number of hours and are paid $30 per hour:

Mickey	1,100
Joey	500
Mr. Joe	400

Mike's coaches have worked with him for at least five years. Mike's net income equals the fees less the expenses listed above. He reports his revenue and expenses on Schedule C of his personal income tax return.

Personal and Financial Objectives for Mike and Maria Roman

1. Provide for retirement. They would like to retire when Mike is age 60. They want to plan on $100,000 of retirement income in today's dollars. They expect to receive Social Security and Mike has a pension with Major League Baseball (MLB). They would like to plan on funding potential retirement expenditures until they turn age 95 and would like to maintain the same level of spending, even if Mike or Maria died early.
2. Provide for the cost of Michael's college education. They expect Michael to receive a partial baseball scholarship, but they plan on paying $15,000 per year for each of his five years for college.
3. Establish a retirement plan for the income he earns at RBI.

EXTERNAL INFORMATION

Economic Information

- Inflation is expected to be 3.0% annually.
- There is no state income tax.
- The yield curve is slightly upward sloping, but relatively flat.
- The historic and expected correlation between the equity markets in the modernized countries is relatively high. The correlation between these markets increase especially during economic crisis.
- They have a required rate of return of 9 percent.
- The economy is in a steady slow growth expansion phase with moderate unemployment.

Bank Lending Rates
- 15-year mortgage rate is 5.0%.
- 30-year mortgage rate is 6.0%.
- Secured personal loan rate is 10.0%.

Education Information
- Mike and Maria believe strongly in education. They want Michael to attend a college for learning, as well as baseball. As mentioned, they expect to fund $15,000 per year for five years in today's dollars for Michael's education. Tuition has been increasing at a 7 percent rate, which is expected to continue indefinitely.

INTERNAL INFORMATION
Insurance Information

Life Insurance

	Policy A	Policy B
Insured	Mike	Maria
Face Amount	$150,000	$40,000
Type	Term	Term
Cash Value	$0	$0
Monthly Premium	$156	$50
Who pays premium	Mike	Mike
Beneficiary	Maria	Mike
Policy Owner	Mike	Maria
Settlement options clause selected	None	None

Health Insurance
Mike and Maria are covered under the Major League Baseball policy. The plan includes a family deductible of $12,600 at a cost of $500 per month.

Long-Term Disability Insurance
- Neither Mike nor Maria are covered by any disability insurance.

Homeowners Insurance
- The Romans have a HO3 policy with endorsements for replacement value and open perils for personal property. The current dwelling coverage is 100% replacement value with an inflation rider.

Automobile Insurance
- Both of their cars are covered.

Type	PAP
Bodily Injury	$100,000/$300,000
Property Damage	$50,000
Medical Payments	$5,000 per person
Physical Damage	Actual Cash Value
Uninsured Motorist Bodily Injury	$100,000/$300,000
Uninsured Motorist Property Damage	$50,000
Comprehensive Deductible	$1,000
Collision Deductible	$1,000
Premium (annual)	$3,300

Personal Liability Insurance
- Neither Mike nor Maria have PLUP coverage.

Income Tax Information

The Romans filing status for their federal income tax return is married filing jointly.

Retirement Information

Mike would like to retire at age 60 and quit working. Mike met the requirements for the MLB minimum pension of $34,000 per year, which is what he expects to receive. This pension begins at age 62 and the amount is fixed for life (both his and his spouse's life). It is not inflation adjusted from today or during retirement. Mike expects his Social Security benefits will equal $30,000 in today's dollars at full retirement age, which is age 67. Maria does not have 40 quarters of Social Security coverage.

Gifts, Estates, Trusts, and Will Information

Neither Mike nor Maria have prepared a will or any other estate planning documents.

Mickey Roman

Mickey is Mike's dad and is an "old school" baseball coach. He turned 70 on December 22, 2019. He has a pension payment from the USPS of $2,000 per month and he and his wife receive a monthly payment from Social Security of $2,200. He also has an IRA with the following balances:
- $80,000 as of December 31, 2019
- $85,000 as of December 31, 2020
- $90,000 as of December 31, 2021
- $99,000 as of December 31, 2022

Since his wife will continue to receive Social Security and his pension in the event he dies, he has named his grandson Michael as the beneficiary of his IRA.

Mickey also has Exxon stock that was distributed from a qualified plan 30 years ago. The distribution was a lump-sum distribution in which the FMV of the stock from the plan was $100,000. Mickey deposited the stock in his brokerage account and included $20,000 in his taxable income in the year of the distribution, based on the Form 1099-R. Mickey still owns the stock, which is now worth $324,340 and is held in the same brokerage account. He is hoping to leave it to Mike when he dies.

Financial Statements

Statement of Income and Expenses

Statement of Income and Expenses Mike and Maria Roman Statement of Income and Expenses for 2020 and Expected (Approximate) For 2021		
CASH INFLOWS		Totals
Salaries		
RBI Gross Revenue	$245,000	
Total Cash Inflows		$245,000
CASH OUTFLOWS		
Taxes		
Federal Estimated Tax Payments	$40,000	
Property Tax Principal Residence & Land	$10,000	
		$50,000
Debt Payments		
Principal Residence	$22,547	
Auto Loan - Jeep	$3,488	
Auto Loan - Ram	$7,968	
Credit Card Payments	$13,000	
Total Debt Payments		$47,002
Living Expenses		
Utilities Principal Residence	$3,900	
Gasoline for Autos	$3,500	
Gifts	$1,000	
Entertainment	$1,750	
Vacations	$2,000	
Church Donations	$500	
Clothing	$2,000	
Auto Maintenance	$2,000	
Satellite TV	$2,000	
Food	$4,650	
Total Living Expenses		$23,300
RBI Expenses		
Fees Paid to the Three RBI Coaches	$60,000	
Utilities for Batting Cages	$2,500	
Baseball Field Maintenance	$7,000	
Baseball Equipment	$1,000	
Other Baseball Business Expenses	$3,000	
Total RBI Expenses		$73,500
Insurance Payments		
MLB Health Insurance Premium	$6,000	
HO Insurance Principal Residence	$3,000	
Auto Insurance Premiums	$3,300	
Life Insurance Premiums (Policy A &B)	$2,472	
Total Insurance Payments		$14,772
Total Cash Outflows		$208,574
NET DISCRETIONARY CASH FLOWS		$36,426

Statement of Financial Position 1/1/2021

Statement of Financial Position Mike and Maria Roman Balance Sheet as of 1/1/2021					
Assets[1]			**Liabilities and Net Worth**		
Cash and Cash Equivalents			**Liabilities[2]**		
Cash	$5,000		Home Mortgage[3]	$307,808	
Savings Account	$25,000		Credit Card Balance Visa[4]	$2,000	
Total Cash and Cash Equivalents		$30,000		$1,200	
Investment Assets			Auto Loan - Mike[5]	$26,444	
Brokerage Account[6]	$70,000		Auto Loan - Maria[7]	$9,918	
Municipal Bond Portfolio[8]	$20,000		**Total Liabilities**		$347,370
Education Portfolio	$10,000				
IRA	$20,000				
Total Investment Assets		$120,000	**Total Net Worth**		$335,630
Personal Use Assets					
Personal Residence	$200,000				
Land for Home & Baseball Field	$200,000				
Jeep - Maria	$18,000				
Ram Truck - Mike	$35,000				
Furniture & Personal Property	$80,000				
Total Personal Use Assets		$533,000			
Total Assets		$683,000	**Total Liabilities & Net Worth**		$683,000

1. Assets are stated at fair market value.
2. Liabilities are stated at principal only as of January 1, 2021 (prior to January payments).
3. The home and land were financed with a $350,000 loan, seven years ago at 5 percent over 360 months.
4. They typically spend about $1,000 per month on each credit card, but the balances are higher after the holidays. They do not maintain these balances.
5. The Ram truck was financed with a loan of $30,000, six months ago at 3 percent over 48 months.
6. Mike's brokerage account is highly correlated to the market. In fact the account has a correlation with the market of about 99 percent. However, because Mike has some leveraged mutual funds in the account, the beta of the portfolio is approximately 20 percent greater than the market. Mike's brokerage account is a margin account, which has an initial margin of 50 percent and a maintenance margin of 35 percent.
7. The Jeep was financed with a loan of $13,000, 12 months ago at 3.5 percent over 48 months.
8. The municipal bond portfolio has a modified duration of 5 and a current YTM of 7 percent.

CASE ASSUMPTIONS

- Required return - use the required return as stated in the case.
- For retirement and other long-term goals, assume cash and cash equivalents are added to investment accounts for purposes of projections and asset allocation decisions.
- Assume the education portfolio is not available to fund retirement.
- Assume Social Security benefits begin at age 67.

APPENDIX

A

GLOSSARY

A

ABLE ACCOUNT - ABLE accounts are designed to help people with disabilities and their families save and pay for disability-related expenses. Though contributions are not deductible, distributions, including earnings, are tax-free to the designated beneficiary if used to pay qualified disability expenses.

ACTIVE PARTICIPANT - Individuals who participate in a qualified plan under IRC 401(a), a 403(b) plan, a government retirement plan, a SEP, or a SIMPLE. Participating means receiving a benefit under the plan.

ACTUAL CONTRIBUTION PERCENTAGE TEST (ACP) - A nondiscrimination test that limits the sum of employee after-tax contributions and employer matching contributions for the HC based on the sum of employee after-tax contributions and employer matching contributions for the NHC.

ACTUAL DEFERRAL PERCENTAGE TEST (ADP) - A nondiscrimination test that limits employee elective deferrals for the highly compensated employees (HC) based on the elective deferrals of non- highly compensated employees (NHC).

ACTUARY - An expert professional who makes quantitative calculations and assumptions about inflation, wage increases, life expectancy of the assumed retirees, investment returns on plan assets, mortality rates for retirees, and forfeitures resulting from termination in order to determine funding for a retirement plan.

ADEQUATE CONSIDERATION STANDARD - Fair market value determined in good faith.

ADJUSTED BASIS (AB) - The portion of a distribution that is not subject to income tax. Usually, the return of after-tax contributions or nondeductible contributions.

ADJUSTED GROSS INCOME (AGI) - A tax return amount that includes an individual's income less certain deductions, known as "above-the-line" deductions. AGI is calculated before subtracting the standard or itemized deductions and the personal and dependency exemptions. The calculated AGI affects the deductibility of traditional IRA contributions and the ability to make Roth IRA contributions.

ADOPTION ASSISTANCE PROGRAM - An employee-provided program that pays adoption expenses up to $14,400 in 2021. The employee is not taxed on the payments or reimbursements made on his behalf.

AGE-BASED PROFIT SHARING PLAN - A qualified profit sharing plan that uses a combination of age and compensation as the basis for allocating the contribution to a participant's account.

AIME (AVERAGE INDEXED MONTHLY EARNINGS) - A worker's highest 35 years of earnings adjusted for inflation and averaged on a monthly basis. AIME is used as the basis for the PIA calculation.

ALIMONY - Support payments from one ex-spouse to the other. Alimony received is considered earned income for purposes of making IRA contributions if the divorce agreement was signed prior to 2019.

ANNUITY CONTRACTS - While the contracts are not specifically defined in the Internal Revenue Code, an annuity contract must be purchased for the employee from an insurance company and may give a fixed benefit or a variable benefit depending on the performance of the investment. Any contract or certificate that is transferable to a person other than a trustee is not an annuity contract.

ANNUITY METHOD - Determines how much a client needs to fund their retirement based on the assumption that the person will die exactly at the assumed life expectancy with a retirement account balance of zero.

ANTI-ALIENATION PROTECTION - An ERISA-afforded protection for qualified plans that prohibits any action that may cause a qualified plan's assets to be assigned, garnished, levied, or subjected to bankruptcy proceedings. Exceptions to the anti-alienation rule apply for tax levies and QDROs.

ANY OCCUPATION - Type of disability insurance policy that provides benefits to a policy owner if he is unable to perform the duties of any occupation.

ARCHER MEDICAL SAVINGS ACCOUNT (MSA) - A medical savings account available for employers with 50 or less employees and self-employed individuals (must have been established by 12/31/05). The account allows participants to make pretax contributions (subject to limitations) to the account and benefit from tax-free earnings provided they are covered under a high deductible health insurance policy. Further, if the funds are utilized for qualified medical expenses, the distributions from the plan will not be taxable.

Average Benefits Percentage Test - One part of the average benefits coverage test that requires the average benefit percent of the nonhighly compensated employees to be at least 70 percent of the average benefit percentage of the highly compensated employees.

Average Benefits Test - A qualified plan coverage test that determines whether the plan adequately benefits the nonhighly compensated employees by comparing the benefits received by the nonhighly compensated to the benefits of the highly compensated employees and also determines whether the employee classification is nondiscriminatory. The test consists of the Average Benefits Percentage Test and the Nondiscriminatory Classification Test.

B

Back Loading - A practice of delaying the accrual of benefits until late in someone's career so that if they were to leave the company they would forfeit all or a large portion of their benefits.

Backdoor Roth - A technique whereby a high-income taxpayer contributes to a traditional IRA with the intent of converting those funds to a Roth IRA.

Bargain Element - Appreciation of employer stock above the exercise price.

Benefit Periods - Begins on the first day an individual receives services as a patient in a hospital or skilled nursing facility and ends after 60 consecutive days without further skilled care.

Black Scholes Method - An option valuation model.

Business Premises of the Employer - The employee's place of employment.

Buy-Sell Agreements - Legal arrangements that require the sale of securities owned by one individual to another individual or entity upon a specified triggering event.

C

Cafeteria Plan - A written plan where the employee may choose to receive cash as compensation or, alternatively, the employee may choose from among a range of tax-free fringe benefits.

Capital Needs Analysis - The process of calculating the amount of investment capital needed at retirement to maintain the pre-retirement lifestyle and mitigate the impact of inflation during the retirement years.

Capital Preservation Model (CP) - A capital needs analysis method that assumes that at the client's life expectancy, the client has exactly the same account balance as he did at the beginning of retirement.

Capitalization of Earnings Model (CP) - A capital needs analysis method based on producing a perpetual stream of income.

Cash Balance Pension Plan - A defined benefit pension plan that shares many of the characteristics of defined contribution plans but provides specific defined benefits based on a mandatory contribution and earnings rate.

Cash or Deferred Arrangement (CODA) - Permits an employee to defer a portion of his salary on a pretax or Roth basis to a qualified plan or receive the salary as current taxable income. Generally, these are referred to as 401(k) plans.

Cashless Exercise - An exercise of an employer stock option where the option holder does not utilize any cash. The option is exercised and the stock is sold simultaneously.

Catch-Up Contribution - A contribution that allows those nearing retirement to increase their deferral contributions to improve their financial situation for retirement. An elective contribution for employees 50 and over that allows the employee to increase their elective deferral limit by up to $6,500 for 2021. The catch-up contribution is $1,000 for IRAs and $3,000 for SIMPLEs in 2021.

Cents per Mile Rule - To determine the value of the personal use of an employer-provided automobile, multiply the standard mileage rate (55 cents for 2021) by the total miles the employee drives the vehicle for personal purposes.

Cliff Vesting Schedule - A vesting schedule that provides the participant's full rights to the plan's assets immediately upon the passage of a certain number of years.

Commuting Rule - To determine the value of the personal use of an employer-provided vehicle, multiply each one-way commute from the employee's home to work or from work to home by $1.50.

CONDUIT IRAS - Accounts that hold rollover funds are often referred to as IRA rollover accounts or conduit IRAs.

CONSOLIDATED OMNIBUS BUDGET RECONCILIATION ACT OF 1985 (COBRA) - Requires an employer that employs 20 or more people in a typical business day and has a health insurance plan to continue to offer health insurance coverage under that health insurance plan to covered employees and qualified dependents following the occurrence of a statutorily defined qualifying event.

CONSTRUCTIVE RECEIPT - An income tax concept that establishes when income is includible by a taxpayer and therefore subject to income tax. Income is constructively received in the taxable year during which it is credited to the employee's account, set apart for him, or otherwise made available so that he may draw upon it at any time or so that he could have drawn upon it during the taxable year if notice of intention to withdraw had been given.

CORRECTIVE DISTRIBUTION - A distribution to satisfy the ADP or ACP test that reduces the elective deferrals or contributions of the HC employees by distributing or returning the funds to the HC employees.

COST OF LIVING ADJUSTMENT (COLA) - The cost-of-living adjustments applied to Social Security benefits.

COVERED COMPENSATION LIMIT - The maximum employee compensation that may be considered for contributions to qualified plans or the accrual of benefits to a qualified plan. For 2021, the covered compensation limit is $290,000.

COVERED EMPLOYEE - An employee who benefits from a qualified plan during the year.

CREDIT FOR PRIOR SERVICE - To give employees credit for years of service (with the plan sponsor) prior to the establishment of the qualified plan.

CROSS PURCHASE LIFE INSURANCE - A partner or shareholder purchases a sufficient amount of life insurance on the lives of each other partner or shareholder to assure sufficient liquidity to buyout a deceased partner or shareholder's interest.

CURRENTLY INSURED WORKERS - A worker who has earned at least six quarters of coverage out of the previous 13 quarters for Social Security.

CUSTODIAL ACCOUNTS - Accounts generally maintained by a bank or other financial institution for the benefit of participants.

CUSTODIANS - Brokerage company, bank, or mutual fund company that holds an individual's IRA.

D

DB(k) RETIREMENT PLAN - For plan years beginning in 2010 and later, a DB(k) retirement plan incorporates, under one single plan with a single trust, a defined benefit plan combined with a 401(k) arrangement.

DEFERRED COMPENSATION ARRANGEMENTS - An arrangement to pay an executive compensation in a future year.

DEFINED BENEFIT PLAN - A qualified retirement plan that provides its participants with pre-determined formula-based benefits at retirement.

DEFINED CONTRIBUTION PLAN - A qualified retirement plan that provides its participants with either a contributory or noncontributory retirement account which benefits from tax-deferred growth for contributions and earnings in the plan.

"DE MINIMIS" FRINGE BENEFIT - A benefit of any property or service provided by an employer to an employee that is so small in value that it makes accounting for it unreasonable or administratively impracticable when taking into account the frequency with which similar fringes are provided by the employer to all employees.

DEPARTMENT OF LABOR - Governmental department charged with enforcing the rules governing the conduct of plan managers, investment of plan assets, reporting and disclosure of plan information, enforcement of the fiduciary provisions of the law, and workers' benefit rights as regulated by ERISA.

DEPENDENT CARE ASSISTANCE - Assistance that applies to household and dependent care services paid for or provided by the employer to an employee under a dependent care assistance program covering employees. The employee is not taxed on the value of the program or service paid on his behalf under the program (up to $5,000 per year; $10,500 in 2021 (ARPA 2021)).

DETERMINATION LETTER - A request filed with the IRS requesting a determination on a particular topic. In the case of a retirement plan, they are used when a plan is adopted, amended, or terminated to assure the plan sponsor that the qualified plan complies with applicable provisions.

DILUTION - The reduction in the monetary value or voting power of an owner's stock as a result of contributions to stock bonus plans and ESOPs.

DIRECT ROLLOVER - Occurs when the plan trustee distributes the account balance directly to the trustee of the recipient account.

DISABILITY BENEFIT - A Social Security benefit available to recipients who have a severe physical or mental impairment that is expected to prevent them from performing "substantial" work for at least a year or result in death. To qualify for these benefits, the recipient must have the sufficient amount of Social Security credits.

DISABILITY INSURANCE - Insurance that provides benefits in the form of periodic payments for a person who is unable to work due to sickness or accidental injury.

DISABILITY INSURANCE (DI) TRUST FUND - The trust fund that pays benefits to workers with disabilities and their families. It is funded by 0.90 percent of an individual's taxable earnings up to $142,800 (2021).

DISABILITY OVERHEAD INSURANCE - Insurance that is designed to cover the expenses that are usual and necessary expenses in the operation of a business should the insured owner or key employee become disabled.

DISCRETIONARY - The choice for a plan sponsor of a profit sharing plan as to the amount and frequency of a contribution.

DISCRETIONARY CONTRIBUTIONS - Allows an employer to decide each year whether to make a matching contribution and then inform the plan participants.

DISQUALIFIED PERSONS - Any person who owns with other family members 20 percent or more of the stock of the company, or in the case of someone without other family ownership, owns 10 percent or more of the stock of the company.

DISQUALIFYING DISPOSITION - If stock acquired after exercising an ISO is disposed before either two years from the date of the grant or one year from the date of exercise.

DISTRESS TERMINATION - Termination that occurs when the employer is in financial difficulty and is unable to continue with a defined benefit plan.

DIVERSIFIED INVESTMENT PORTFOLIOS - An investment portfolio invested in a broad range of investment classes to reduce investment risk.

E

EARLY WITHDRAWAL PENALTY - A 10 percent penalty on distributions made before the participant attains the age of 59½ (exceptions apply).

EARNED INCOME - Any type of compensation where the individual has performed some level of service for an employer or is considered self-employed, plus alimony received (for divorce decrees in effect before 2019) and taxable fellowship or stipends for graduate or postdoctoral study (for tax years after 2019).

ECONOMIC BENEFIT DOCTRINE - An employee will be taxed on funds or property set aside for the employee if the funds or property are unrestricted and nonforfeitable even if the employee was not given a choice to receive the income currently.

ELIGIBLE CORPORATIONS - Under §83(i), companies that are not publicly traded and that have a written plan under which at least 80 percent of employees are granted stock options or RSUs to receive qualified stock.

EMPLOYEE CENSUS - A matrix of information that is used in plan selection and identifies each employee, their age, compensation, number of years of employment, and any ownership interest in the plan sponsor.

EMPLOYEE ELECTIVE DEFERRAL CONTRIBUTIONS - Pretax employee contributions to a qualified retirement plan with a CODA. The employee must choose to defer the compensation before earning the compensation.

EMPLOYEE PLANS COMPLIANCE RESOLUTION SYSTEM (EPCRS) - The system provided by the IRS that allows plan sponsors to voluntarily correct any disqualifying actions within two years of the plan year end in which the problem occurred.

EMPLOYEE RETIREMENT INCOME AND SECURITY ACT (ERISA) - Legislation enacted by Congress in 1974 as a result of various abuses by plan sponsors to provide protection for an employee's retirement assets, both from creditors and from plan sponsors.

EMPLOYEE STOCK OWNERSHIP PLAN (ESOP) - A qualified profit sharing plan that utilizes employer contributions to the plan to purchase the stock of the employer's company and allocates the ownership to the plan participants.

EMPLOYEE STOCK PURCHASE PLAN - A plan designed to benefit all or a large portion of an employer's employees that gives employees an incentive to buy employer stock by allowing the employees to purchase the stock at a discounted price (up to a 15% discount) and receive favorable tax treatment for any gains if the stock meets certain holding period requirements.

EMPLOYER MATCHING CONTRIBUTIONS - Employer-provided contributions to a qualified retirement plan, usually a 401(k) plan, that are based on the employee contributions.

ENTITY INSURANCE - Insurance in which the entity purchases a life insurance policy on the life of each partner or shareholder that is used for buyouts triggered by death of a shareholder or partner.

ERISA ATTORNEY - An attorney who specializes in ERISA law.

EXCESS BENEFIT PLANS - A type of SERP that is designed solely to provide benefits in excess of the benefits available in qualified plans based on the limits under IRC §415.

EXCLUSIVE PROVIDER ORGANIZATION (EPO) - A form of managed care in which participants receive all of their care from in-network providers. Unlike an HMO, a referral is not necessary to see a specialist.

F

FAIR MARKET VALUE - The price that a willing buyer would pay a willing seller, both having reasonable knowledge of the pertinent facts and neither under duress.

FAMILY BENEFIT - A Social Security benefit available to certain family members of workers eligible for retirement or disability benefits.

FICA (FEDERAL INSURANCE CONTRIBUTIONS ACT) - A law allowing Social Security taxes, including Medicare taxes, to be deducted from employee's paychecks.

FIDUCIARY - An individual that has a special relationship of trust, confidence, and responsibility in certain financial obligations.

15-YEAR RULE - A special catch-up provision for 403(b) plan participants that have worked for the plan sponsor for 15 years. The catch-up allows them to defer up to an additional $15,000 during the plan year, however, no more than $3,000 per year.

50/40 COVERAGE TEST - A coverage test applicable only to a defined benefit pension plans that requires the plan to cover for every day during the plan year the lesser of 50 employees or 40% of all eligible employees.

FINAL 3-YEAR CATCH-UP PROVISION - A special catch-up provision for public and private 457(b) plans that allows an individual to defer an additional $19,500 for 2021 to the plan in their final three years before the plan's normal retirement age.

501(c)(3) ORGANIZATIONS - Nonprofit tax-exempt organizations that are established under IRC §501(c)(3) of the Internal Revenue Code.

FINANCIAL INDEPENDENCE - The ability to live comfortably without having to work for an income.

FIXED AMORTIZATION METHOD - The substantially equal periodic payment is calculated over the participant's life expectancy if single, or the joint life expectancy if married, and the interest rate is reasonable.

FIXED ANNUITIZATION METHOD - The participant takes substantially equal periodic distributions of the account over a number of years determined by dividing the account balance by an annuity factor using a reasonable interest rate and mortality table.

FLAT AMOUNT FORMULA - A benefit formula of a defined benefit pension plan that provides each of its participants with an equal dollar benefit at retirement.

FLAT PERCENTAGE FORMULA - A benefit formula of a defined benefit pension plan that provides all plan participants with a benefit equal to a fixed percentage of the participant's salary, usually the final salary or an average of the participant's highest salaries.

FLEXIBLE SPENDING ACCOUNT (FSA) - A cafeteria plan under which employees can choose between receiving cash or deferring income tax-free to fund the cost of certain employee selected benefits. If the participant does not utilize the money in the account by the end of the year, the participant forfeits the deferred funds. The 2021 limit for a health care FSA is $2,750, and for a dependent care FSA is $5,000 (not indexed).

FORFEITURES - The percentage or amount of a participant's accrued benefit that was not vested to the employee at the employee's termination from the plan sponsor. The forfeited amount stays in the plan and may be allocated to the other plan participants (defined contribution plan) or reduce future plan costs (defined contribution plan or defined benefit plan).

FORGONE REVENUE - The lost revenue or opportunity cost incurred by an employer for providing the fringe benefit to the employee.

FORM 5304-SIMPLE - The IRS form used to establish a SIMPLE IRA plan when the employees choose the financial institution.

FORM 5305-SIMPLE - The IRS form used to establish a SIMPLE IRA plan when the employer chooses the financial institution.

401(k) WRAP PLANS - A form of salary reduction plan that enable executives who are subject to salary deferral limitations due to the nondiscrimination rules to contribute higher amounts than otherwise permitted under a 401(k) plan.

457 PLAN - A nonqualified deferred compensation plan for employees of state and local government and tax-exempt entities.

457(b) PLANS - 457(b) plans for governmental and tax- exempt organizations under 501(c) that allow employees to defer income taxation on savings for retirement into future years. Eligible plans are available to most of an employer's employees.

457(f) PLANS - 457(f) plans for employees of governmental entities and tax-exempt entities under 501(c)(3). Ineligible plans are only available to highly compensated and management employees.

FRINGE BENEFIT - A benefit, other than customary taxable wages, provided by an employer to an employee for the employee's performance (in most instances) of services for the employer.

FULLY INSURED - A worker who has earned 40 quarters of coverage under the Social Security system.

FUTA (FEDERAL UNEMPLOYMENT TAX ACT) - A tax on an employee's wages.

G

GRACE PERIOD - If an employer meets the 100-employee limitation in a given year, then the employer will have a two-year "grace period" when the employer can exceed the limitation without losing eligibility to maintain the SIMPLE.

GRADUATED VESTING SCHEDULES - A vesting schedule that provides an employee with full rights to a certain percentage (less than 100%) of benefits after completing a number of years of service and provides the employees with an additional percentage for each additional years of service.

GRANT DATE - The date of issuance of a stock or option.

GROUP LONG-TERM DISABILITY POLICIES - Benefits typically begin after short-term disability and will often continue for a fixed period of time, until retirement or for life.

GROUP SHORT-TERM DISABILITY POLICIES - Benefits generally begin after a short period of time, often corresponding to the employer's sick leave.

GROUP TERM LIFE INSURANCE - Pure insurance protection purchased as a group that pays a predetermined sum if the insured dies during a specified period of time (i.e., the term, which may be 1, 5, 10, 20 years or longer). The value of the premiums, up to $50,000 of death benefit coverage, provided by an employer may be excluded from an employee's gross income.

H

HARDSHIP DISTRIBUTIONS - A distribution from a 401(k) plan because the employee has an immediate and heavy financial need and the withdrawal is necessary to satisfy the need. The distribution is taxable and subject to penalties to the extent the participant has other resources to have satisfied the financial need.

HEALTH SAVINGS ACCOUNTS (HSAs) - A medical savings account, similar to an MSA but less restrictive, that allows anyone with a high deductible health insurance plan to make pretax contributions (subject to limitations). The earnings within the account and the value of the contributions will not be taxed to the extent they are used to pay for qualifying medical expenses.

HEALTH MAINTENANCE ORGANIZATIONS (HMOS) - A form of managed care in which participants receive all of their care from participating providers. Physicians may be employed by the HMO directly, or may be physicians in private practice who have chosen to participate in the HMO network. The independent physicians contract with the HMO to serve HMO participants, receiving a flat annual fee (capitation fee) for each HMO member, whether the member receives medical services from the provider or not.

HEALTH REIMBURSEMENT ARRANGEMENT (HRA) - A type of health insurance plan that reimburses employees for qualified medical expenses.

HIGHLY COMPENSATED EMPLOYEE - An employee who is either a more than five percent owner at any time during the plan year or preceding plan year, or had compensation in excess of $130,000 for the prior plan year (2021). A special election can be made to count only those employees whose compensation is in excess of $130,000 and are in the top 20% of employees as ranked by compensation.

HOSPITAL INSURANCE (HI) TRUST FUND - The trust fund that pays for services covered under the hospital insurance provisions of Medicare (Part A). It is funded by 1.45 percent of an individual's taxable earnings (no limitation).

HYPOTHETICAL ACCOUNT - The account statement that displays hypothetical allocations and hypothetical earnings. The accounts are hypothetical because the cash balance pension plan assets are managed by the plan sponsor in the same manner as a defined benefit pension plan.

I

INCENTIVE STOCK OPTIONS (ISOS) - A right given to an employee to purchase an employer's common stock at a stated exercise price. If the requirements of IRC §422 are met, the employee will not recognize any taxable income at the date of grant. Further, at the date of exercise, the employee will also not be subject to ordinary income tax on the difference between the fair market value of the stock and the exercise price. This

difference is a positive adjustment for the alternative minimum tax calculation. When the employee sells the stock subsequent to the exercise, the difference between the sales price of the stock and the original exercise price is considered long-term capital gain and there is a negative adjustment for the alternative minimum tax calculation.

INCLUDIBLE COMPENSATION - An employee's taxable wages and benefits for the most recent year of service.

INDEMNITY HEALTH INSURANCE - Traditional, fee-for-service health insurance that does not limit where a covered individual can get care.

INDIRECT ROLLOVER - A distribution to the participant with a subsequent transfer to another qualified account (or IRA).

INDIVIDUAL 401(k) PLAN - An easy-to-administer, low-cost retirement plan designed for self-employed individuals and owner-only businesses.

INDIVIDUAL RETIREMENT ACCOUNT (IRA) - Two general types under present law: traditional IRAs, to which both deductible and nondeductible contributions may be made, and Roth IRAs, to which only nondeductible contributions may be made.

INDIVIDUAL RETIREMENT ANNUITY - An annuity contract or endowment contract issued by an insurance company that follows many of the same rules for deductibility of premium payments and the limits for premium payments as a traditional IRA.

IN-SERVICE WITHDRAWAL - Any withdrawal from a qualified retirement plan other than a loan while the employee is a participant in the plan.

INTERESTED PARTIES - Present employees who are eligible to participate in the plan and present employees who are not eligible for the plan but whose principal place of employment is the same as the principal place of employment of any employee who is eligible to participate.

INVOLUNTARY TERMINATION - Termination initiated by the PBGC for a defined benefit plan that is unable to pay benefits from the plan.

IRA ANNUITY - An annuity contract or endowment contract issued by an insurance company that follows many of the same rules for deductibility of premium payments and the limits for premium payments as a traditional IRA.

IRC SECTION 83(b) ELECTION - Election to include in gross income the difference between the fair market value of restricted stock and its purchase price.

J

JOINT LIFE EXPECTANCY TABLE - The life expectancy table used to determine a participant's RMD when the participant's sole designated beneficiary is the participant's spouse and that spouse is more than 10 years younger than the participant.

K

KEOGH PLAN - A qualified plan for a self-employed individual.

KEY EMPLOYEE - Any employee who is a greater than five percent owner, a greater than one percent owner with compensation in excess of $150,000 (not indexed), or an officer with compensation in excess of $185,000 (2021).

KEY PERSON LIFE AND DISABILITY INSURANCE - Life insurance coverage for employees who are considered critical to the success of a business and whose death might cause financial loss to the company.

L

LEASE VALUE RULE - To determine the value of an employer-provided automobile, use the automobile's annual lease value.

LEPTO-KURTIC - A distribution that appears to be normal but has more area under the two tails than a normal distribution (i.e., fat tails).

LEVERAGED ESOP - An ESOP that borrows the funds necessary to purchase the employer's stock. The interest and principal repayments on the loan are tax deductible for the employer.

LOAN OFFSET - A reduction in the amount of a direct rollover distribution's outstanding loan balance. The loan offset is treated as an actual distribution from the plan equal to the unpaid loan balance (rather than a deemed distribution), and (unlike a deemed distribution) the amount of the distribution is eligible for tax-free rollover to another eligible retirement plan.

LUMP-SUM DISTRIBUTION - A complete distribution of a participant's account balance within one taxable year on account of death, disability, attainment of age 59½, or separation from service. Some lump- sum distributions from qualified plans are eligible for special taxation options.

M

MANAGED CARE INSURANCE - Health-care delivery systems that integrate the financing and delivery of health care. Managed care plans feature a network of physicians, hospitals, and other providers who participate in the plan. Managed care includes HMOs, PPOs, POS, and EPO plans.

MANDATORY FUNDING REQUIREMENT - An amount or percentage that must be contributed to a qualified pension plan by the employer each plan year.

MASTER PLAN - Provides a single trust or custodial account that is jointly used by all adopting employers.

MAXIMUM FAMILY BENEFIT - The limit on the amount of monthly Social Security benefits that may be paid to a family.

MEDICAID - Provides medical assistance for persons with low incomes and resources.

MEDICARE - A federal health insurance plan for those who have attained age 65 or have been disabled whether retired or still working.

MODIFIED ADJUSTED GROSS INCOME - When calculating taxable Social Security, it is the sum of an individual's adjusted gross income plus tax exempt interest, including interest earned on savings bonds used for higher education; amounts excluded from the taxpayer's income for employer provided adoption assistance; amounts deducted for interest paid for educational loans; amounts deducted as qualified tuition expense; and income earned in a foreign country, a U.S. possession, or Puerto Rico that is excluded from income.

MONEY PURCHASE PENSION PLAN - A defined contribution pension plan that provides for mandatory employer contributions to the plan each year of a fixed percentage of the employees' compensation. The employer does not guarantee a specific retirement benefit.

Monte Carlo Analysis - A mathematical tool used to calculate the success of an individual's retirement portfolio using changing variables.

N

Net Unrealized Appreciation (NUA) - A special taxation treatment for a lump-sum distribution from a qualified plan that treats the appreciation in the value of employer stock after the date of contribution to the plan until the date of distribution as capital gain.

New Comparability Plan - A qualified profit sharing plan in which contributions are made to employees' accounts based on their respective classification in the company as defined by the plan sponsor.

No-Additional-Cost Services - Services provided by an employer to an employee that do not cause the employer to incur any substantial additional cost or lost revenue.

Nonallocation Year - Any plan year of an employee stock ownership plan that holds employer securities consisting of stock in an S corporation, and disqualified persons own at least 50 percent of the number of shares of stock in the S corporation.

Noncontributory Plans - Qualified retirement plans that do not include employee contributions.

Nondiscriminatory - A requirement of all qualified plans. The eligibility rules, coverage requirements, and contributions allocations of a qualified plan cannot discriminate against the rank-and-file employees for the benefit of shareholder, officers, and highly compensated employees.

Nondiscriminatory Classification Test - As the second requirement of the average benefits test, it helps to determine whether a plan adequately benefits nonhighly compensated employees.

Nonelective Contributions - Contributions to a qualified plan on behalf of all eligible employees.

Nonexcludable - An employee who must be considered as eligible to participate in a qualified plan.

Nonqualified Deferred Compensation Plan (NQDC) - A contractual arrangement between the employer and an executive whereby the employer promises to pay the executive a predetermined amount of money sometime in the future.

Nonqualified Plans - Plans that do not meet the requirements of the IRC §401(a) and therefore do not have the benefits of qualified plans.

Nonqualified Stock Options (NQSOs) - An option that does not meet the requirements of an incentive stock option. The exercise of an NQSO does not receive favorable long- term capital gains treatment but also does not require the holding period associated with ISOs.

Nonrecognition of Gain Treatment - A delay in the recognition of gain available to owners of a company that sell company stock to an ESOP. The transaction must meet the stated requirements of the IRC and the owner must reinvest the proceeds from the sale within 12 months of the sale into qualified domestic replacement securities.

O

Officer - An administrative executive who is in regular and continued service and has the executive authority normally associated with an officer.

Old Age, Survivor, and Disability Insurance (OASDI) - An inclusive title given to the Social Security benefit system.

Old Age and Survivors Insurance (OASI) - The trust fund that pays retirement and survivors' benefits funded by 5.30 percent of an individual's taxable earnings up to $142,800 (2021).

On-Premises Athletic Facility - A gym or other athletic facility such as a tennis court, pool, or golf course that is operated by the employer, located on the employer's business premises, and "substantially all" of the use of the facility is by employees of the employer, their spouses, or their dependent children. The value of the use of on premises athletic facilities is not taxable to the employee as long as its availability is nondiscriminatory.

One Year of Service - 1,000 hours of service with an employer within a 12-month period.

Option Price (Exercise Price) - Usually the fair market value at the grant date.

Own Occupation - Type of disability policy which states that if the insured is unable to perform the duties associated with his own occupation, the insured is deemed to be disabled and the policy will provide benefits.

P

PASS THROUGH VOTING RIGHTS - The voting rights of the stock pass through from the ESOP or the stock bonus plan to the participant.

PAYROLL TAXES - The combination of OASDI and Medicare tax paid by an employee and employer on an employee's compensation.

PENSION BENEFIT GUARANTY CORPORATION (PBGC) - Established in 1974 when President Gerald R. Ford signed the Employee Retirement Income Security Act (ERISA) into law. The PBGC guarantees qualified pension benefits. It is a federal corporation that acts as an insurance provider to maintain the benefits promised to employees by their defined benefit pension plans.

PENSION PLAN - A qualified retirement plan that pays a benefit, usually determined by a formula, to a plan participant for the participant's entire life during retirement.

PERMITTED DISPARITY (SOCIAL SECURITY INTEGRATION) - A technique or method of allocating qualified plan contributions to an employee account that provides a higher contribution to those employees whose compensation is in excess of the Social Security wage base ($142,800 for 2021) or selected integration level for the plan year.

PHANTOM STOCK PLAN - A nonqualified deferred compensation arrangement where the employer gives fictional shares of stock to a key employee that are initially valued at the time of the grant. The stock is later valued at some terminal point and the executive is then paid in cash the differential value of the stock as compensation.

PHASEOUT - The AGI range that will affect the deductibility of IRA contributions and an individual's ability to make contributions to a Roth IRA.

PIA (PRIMARY INSURANCE AMOUNT) - The amount on which a worker's retirement benefit is based; the PIA determines the amount the applicant will receive at full retirement age based on the year in which the retiree turns 62. The PIA is indexed to the Consumer Price Index (CPI) annually.

PLAN ENTRANCE DATE - The date an eligible employee becomes a participant in a qualified plan.

PLAN FREEZE - Employer will no longer make any contributions to the plan, but does not want to fully terminate the plan.

PLAN LOANS - Loans from a qualified plan made available to all participants on an effectively equal basis that are limited in amount (no greater than $50,000 or half of the vested account balance), are repaid within a certain time period (usually five years), bear a reasonable rate of interest, are adequately secured, and require the administrator to maintain a proper accounting.

POINT OF SERVICE PLAN (POS) - A form of managed care that is considered a managed care/indemnity plan hybrid, as it mixes aspects of HMOs, PPOs, and indemnity plans for greater patient choice. A primary care physician coordinates patient care, but there is more flexibility in choosing doctors and hospitals than in an HMO.

PRE-1974 CAPITAL GAIN TREATMENT - A special taxation treatment for lump-sum distributions from qualified plans that treat the distribution attributable to pre-1974 participation in the plan as long-term capital gain.

PREFERRED PROVIDER ORGANIZATION - A form of managed care in which participants have more flexibility in choosing physicians and other providers than in an HMO. The arrangement between insurance companies and health care providers permits participants to obtain discounted health care services from the preferred providers within the network.

PRIMARY CARE PHYSICIAN - A physician that is designated as a participant's first point of contact with the health care system, particularly in managed care plans.

PROFIT SHARING PLAN - A qualified retirement plan established and maintained by an employer where the employer makes deductible contributions on behalf of the employees, the assets grow tax-deferred, and if there is a CODA feature, the employee also makes pretax contributions.

PROHIBITED TRANSACTIONS - Transactions between the plan and a disqualified person that are prohibited by law.

PROTOTYPE PLAN - A prepackaged plan that allows the sponsor to use a check the box approach to plan choices.

PURCHASING POWER PRESERVATION MODEL (PPP) - A capital needs analysis method that assumes that at a client's life expectancy, the client will have a capital balance with purchasing power equal to the purchasing power at the beginning of retirement.

PURE ANNUITY CONCEPT - The basic capital needs analysis approach, which is generally prepared on a pretax basis.

Q

QUALIFIED AUTOMATIC CONTRIBUTION ARRANGEMENT (QACA) - A plan that contains a "qualified automatic enrollment feature" and is eligible for a new nondiscrimination safe harbor under PPA 2006.

QUALIFIED DISTRIBUTION - A distribution from a Roth IRA that is made after a five-taxable-year period and on account of the account owner's death, disability, attainment of age 59½, or first time home purchase. This definition also applies to qualified distributions from a Roth account, except first time home purchase does not apply.

QUALIFIED DOMESTIC RELATIONS ORDER (QDRO) - A court order related to divorce, property settlement, or child support that can divide a participant's interest in a qualified plan.

QUALIFIED EDUCATIONAL ASSISTANCE PROGRAM - A plan established and maintained by an employer that provides employees with educational assistance. The employer may exclude $5,250 of benefits from an employee's taxable income.

QUALIFIED ELECTION PERIOD - The term "qualified election period" means the 6-plan-year period beginning with the first plan year in which the individual first became a qualified participant.

QUALIFIED EMPLOYEE - Under §83(i), an employee who is not excluded. An excluded employee is any employee (1) who is a one-percent owner of the corporation at any time during the calendar year, or who was a one-percent owner at any time during the 10 preceding calendar years; (2) who is, or has been at any prior time, the chief executive officer or chief financial officer of the corporation, or an individual acting in either capacity; (3) who is a family member of an individual described above (one-percent owner, CEO, or CFO); or (4) who has been one of the four highest compensated officers of the corporation for the tax year or for any of the 10 preceding tax years.

QUALIFIED EMPLOYEE DISCOUNTS - A discount on the value of property or services offered to an employer's customers in the ordinary course of the employer's business may be excluded from an employee's income (subject to certain limitations).

QUALIFIED JOINT AND SURVIVOR ANNUITY (QJSA) - The QJSA pays a benefit to the participant and spouse as long as either lives; although, at the death of the first spouse, the annuity may be reduced.

QUALIFIED MATCHING CONTRIBUTION (QMC) - Additional matching contributions made by the employer to satisfy the ADP or ACP test that increases the ACP or ADP of the NHC employees by who had deferred compensation during the plan year.

QUALIFIED MOVING EXPENSES REIMBURSEMENT - Members of the Armed Forces (or their spouse or dependents) on active duty who move pursuant to a military order and incident to a permanent change of station may deduct amounts attributable to in-kind moving and storage expenses, and may exclude from income any reimbursements or allowances received for these expenses. For tax years before 2018 and after 2025, qualified moving expense reimbursements from an employer are excluded from gross income by employees.

QUALIFIED NONELECTIVE CONTRIBUTION (QNEC) - A contribution made by the employer to satisfy the ADP or ACP test that increases the ADP or ACP of the NHC employees by making additional contributions to all NHC eligible employees without regard to any elective deferral election made by the employees.

QUALIFIED NON-PERSONAL USE VEHICLE - A vehicle that the employee does not use more than a minimal amount for personal reasons due to the design of the vehicle. The value of a qualified non- personal use vehicle is excluded from an employee's gross income.

QUALIFIED OPTIONAL SURVIVOR ANNUITY (QOSA) - An annuity for the life of a participant with a survivor annuity for the life of the participant's spouse that is equal to a specified applicable percentage of the amount of the annuity that is payable during the joint lives of the participant and the spouse (and that is actuarially equivalent to a single life annuity for the life of the participant).

QUALIFIED PARKING - Parking provided by the employer on or near the employer's business premises. An employee may exclude up to $270 per month (for 2021) from his gross income for employer provided parking. This expense is not deductible after 2017 (TCJA 2017).

QUALIFIED PARTICIPANT - The term "qualified participant" means any employee who has completed at least 10 years of participation under the plan and has attained age 55.

QUALIFIED PLAN - A retirement plan that meets the qualifications of IRC §401(a).

QUALIFIED PLAN AWARD - An employee achievement award bestowed as part of an established written plan of an employer that does not discriminate in favor of highly compensated employees (within the meaning of §414(q)) for eligibility or benefits. The value of an award provided under the plan, up to $400 for a nonqualified award and $1,600 for a qualified award, is excluded from the employee's gross income. TCJA 2017 adds a definition for tangible personal property, which shall not include cash, cash equivalents, gift cards, vacations, meals lodging, tickets to sporting events, stocks, bonds or other similar items.

QUALIFIED PLAN LOAN OFFSET AMOUNT - A plan loan offset amount that is treated as distributed from a qualified retirement plan, a section 403(b) plan or a governmental section 457(b) plan solely by reason of the termination of the plan or the failure to meet the repayment terms of the loan because of the employee's severance from employment.

QUALIFIED PRE-RETIREMENT SURVIVOR ANNUITY (QPSA) - Provides a benefit to the surviving spouse if the participant dies before attaining normal retirement age.

QUALIFIED REPLACEMENT SECURITIES - Securities in a domestic corporation, including stocks, bonds, debentures, or warrants, which receive no more than 25% of their income from passive investments.

QUALIFIED STOCK - Under §83(i), stock in an eligible corporation that is received in connection with the exercise of an option or in the settlement of an RSU.

QUALIFIED TRUST - A trust established or organized in the U.S. that is maintained by the employer for the exclusive benefit of employees.

QUALIFIED TUITION REDUCTION - The amount of any reduction in tuition provided to an employee of an educational organization for education below the graduate level is excluded from the employee's gross income.

R

RABBI TRUST - An irrevocable trust that is designed to hold funds and assets for the purpose of paying benefits under a nonqualified deferred compensation arrangement. The assets in a rabbi trust are for the sole purpose of providing benefits to employees and may not be accessed by the employer, but they may be seized and used for the purpose of paying general creditors in the event of a liquidation of the company. Assets within a rabbi trust are not currently taxable to the employee.

RANK-AND-FILE EMPLOYEES - The non-key, non-highly compensated employees.

RATIO PERCENTAGE TEST - A coverage test that compares the ratio of nonhighly compensated covered by a retirement plan to the ratio of highly compensated covered by the plan. The comparative ratio must be at least 70%.

RECHARACTERIZATION OF DEFERRALS - To change the nature of any excess employee deferrals from pretax employee contributions to after-tax employee contributions.

RECHARACTERIZE - Transferring a contribution and its attributable earnings from a traditional IRA to a Roth IRA or vice versa. The recharacterization must occur by the tax return filing date including extensions for the year of the recharacterization. TCJA 2017 prohibits recharacterization of Roth conversions after 2017.

REMAINING WORK LIFE EXPECTANCY (RWLE) - The work period that remains at a given point in time before retirement.

REPURCHASE OPTION (PUT OPTION) - An option that allows a terminating employee to receive in cash the fair market value of the employer's stock within a stock bonus plan or ESOP if the employer stock is not readily tradeable on an established market. An option to sell to the employer.

REQUIRED BEGINNING DATE (RBD) - The date on which lifetime minimum distributions must begin. Generally April 1st of the year following the year the participant attains age 72.

REQUIRED MINIMUM DISTRIBUTION - A minimum amount that must be withdrawn from a qualified plan each year after the participant attains the age of 70½ (age 72 if age 70½ is attained after December 31, 2019). The amount is calculated using the uniform distribution table, the single life expectancy table, or the joint life expectancy tables.

REQUIRED MINIMUM DISTRIBUTION METHOD - The substantially equal periodic payment is calculated in the same manner as required under minimum distribution rules. Note that payments are recalculated annually.

RESTRICTED STOCK PLAN - An employer provided plan designed to increase retention and compensate employees with a non-cash outflow. The plan pays executives with shares of the employer's stock. The executive does not pay any amount towards the allocation of the stock and, in fact, is restricted by the employer from selling or transferring the stock.

RETIREMENT BENEFIT - The most familiar Social Security benefit, full retirement benefits are payable at normal retirement age and reduced benefits as early as age 62 to anyone who has obtained at least a minimum (40 quarters) amount of Social Security credits.

RETIREMENT EARNINGS LIMITATIONS TEST - A test that may reduce the Social Security benefit paid to an individual based on their other income.

RETIREMENT FUNDING (CAPITAL NEEDS ANALYSIS) - The process of calculating the amount of investment capital needed at retirement to maintain the pre-retirement lifestyle and mitigate the impact of inflation during the retirement years.

RETIREMENT LIFE EXPECTANCY (RLE) - The time period beginning at retirement and extending until death; the RLE is the period of retirement that must be funded.

RETIREMENT NEEDS ANALYSIS - The process of determining how much money a person needs to accumulate to be financially independent during retirement.

ROLLOVER - To elect to transfer funds from one tax-advantaged account to another tax-advantaged account to continue to defer the recognition of income taxes until the ultimate distribution of the assets.

ROTH CONVERSION - When a traditional IRA is converted to a Roth IRA. At the date of conversion, an individual includes the fair market value of the traditional IRA into his adjusted gross income.

ROTH IRA - An IRA created by the Taxpayer Relief Act of 1997. Contributions to a Roth IRA are nondeductible and qualified distributions are excluded from an individual's taxable income.

S

S CORPORATIONS - Small corporations taxed as pass-through entities that cannot have more than 100 individual shareholders and have only one class of stock.

SAFE HARBOR COVERAGE TEST - A coverage test that requires the employer to cover at least 70% of the nonhighly compensated employees.

SAFE HARBOR 401(k) PLANS - A 401(k) plan that satisfies a minimum contribution or matching test and allows the plan sponsor to bypass the ADP test, the ACP test, and the top-heavy tests.

SALARY CONTINUATION PLAN - An arrangement between an employer and an employee where the employer agrees to continue to pay an employee after his retirement or to the employee's spouse if the employee dies prior to retirement.

SALARY REDUCTION PLANS - A nonqualified plan designed to receive deferral contributions from executives to reduce their current taxable income.

SALARY REDUCTION SIMPLIFIED EMPLOYEE PENSION (SARSEP) - A plan that can no longer be established but allowed employees to elect to defer a portion of their current salary into a SEP-IRA in a similar fashion to a 401(k) plan.

SAVERS CREDIT (RETIREMENT SAVINGS CONTRIBUTIONS CREDIT) - A tax credit for making eligible contributions to an IRA or employer-sponsored retirement plan.

SAVINGS INCENTIVE MATCH PLANS FOR EMPLOYEES (SIMPLEs) - Retirement plans for small employers with 100 or fewer employees who earn more than $5,000 in a year. SIMPLEs may be established as SIMPLE 401(k)s or SIMPLE IRAs.

SAVINGS RATE - The average savings amount in the U.S. based on consumption.

SECTION 83(b) ELECTION - Election to include in gross income the difference between the fair market value of restricted stock and its purchase price.

SECULAR TRUSTS - Irrevocable trusts designed to hold funds and assets for the purpose of paying benefits under a nonqualified deferred compensation arrangement. A secular trust does not create a substantial risk of forfeiture for the employee. Assets set aside in a secular trust results in immediate inclusion of income to the employee.

SEE-THROUGH TRUST – A trust that is the beneficiary of a custodial IRA. For participant deaths before January 1, 2020, it provides for more control over distribution of IRA assets after the owner's death, as well as providing increased creditor protection for the beneficiaries of the trust. For participant deaths after December 31, 2019, it is more advantageous for eligible designated beneficiaries for whom required minimum distributions may be spread over the beneficiary's lifetime.

SELF-INSURED PLAN - A plan that reimburses employees for medical expenses not covered by an accident or health insurance policy.

SENSITIVITY ANALYSIS - A tool used to understand the range of outcomes for each variable in a retirement plan. It rotates each variable toward the undesirable side of the risk to determine the impact of a small change in that variable on an overall plan.

SEPARATE INTEREST APPROACH - Divides the participant's retirement benefit into two separate portions: one for the alternate payee and one for the participant.

SHARED PAYMENT APPROACH - Splits the actual benefit payments made between the participant and the alternate payee.

SIMPLE 401(k) - A SIMPLE plan that utilizes a 401(k) plan as the funding vehicle of the plan.

SIMPLE IRA - A SIMPLE plan that utilizes an IRA account as the funding vehicle of the plan.

SIMPLIFIED EMPLOYEE PENSION (SEP) - A practical retirement plan alternative to a qualified plan that can be used by small businesses and sole proprietors. It follows many of the same limits as qualified plans but may require the employer to cover more employees.

SINGLE LIFE EXPECTANCY TABLE - Tables used to calculate the required minimum distribution for beneficiaries.

SOCIAL SECURITY INTEGRATION (PERMITTED DISPARITY) - A technique or method of allocating qualified plan contributions to an employee account that provides a higher contribution to those employees whose compensation is in excess of the Social Security wage base ($142,800 for 2021) or selected integration level for the plan year.

SPLIT DEFINITION - Type of disability policy where an insured is covered against the risk of not performing his own occupation for a period of time, and after that period expires, an any-occupation definition of disability is used.

SPLIT-DOLLAR LIFE INSURANCE ARRANGEMENT - A single life insurance policy in which two parties, employer and employee, have an ownership interest. The two parties generally split ownership, premiums, and beneficiaries any way they wish.

SPOUSAL IRA - An IRA created on behalf of a spouse who does not have the necessary earned income to make a contribution to an IRA of their own but can borrow earned income from their spouse.

SSI (SUPPLEMENTAL SECURITY INCOME) - A program administered by the Social Security Administration and funded by the general Treasury that is available to those age 65 or the disabled who have a low income and few assets.

STANDARD ELIGIBILITY - The general eligibility requirement that requires an employer to consider an employee eligible when he attains 21 years of age and has completed one-year of service (defined as 1,000 hours of service with an employer within a 12-month period).

STANDARD ELIGIBILITY REQUIREMENTS - IRC eligibility rules for participation in a qualified plan. Provides that an employee must be considered eligible to participate in the plan after completing a period of service with the employer extending beyond the later of the date on which the employee attains the age of 21 or the date on which the employee completes one year of service (1,000 hours of service within 12 months).

STANDARD TERMINATION - Termination in which the employer has sufficient assets to pay all benefits (liabilities) at the time of final distribution.

STOCK APPRECIATION RIGHTS (SARs) - Rights that grant to the holder cash in an amount equal to the excess of the fair market value of the stock over the exercise price.

STOCK BONUS PLAN - A qualified profit sharing plan funded solely with employer stock.

STOCK OPTION - A right to buy stock at a specified price for a specified period of time.

SUBSTANTIAL AND RECURRING - IRC standard defining the frequency requirement of contributions by employers to profit sharing plans.

SUBSTANTIAL RISK OF FORFEITURE - An income tax concept that relates to when income is subject to income tax. A substantial risk of forfeiture exists when rights in property that are transferred are conditioned, directly or indirectly, upon the future performance (or refraining from performance) of substantial services by any person, or the occurrence of a condition related to a purpose of the transfer and the possibility of forfeiture is substantial if the condition is not satisfied.

SUITABILITY - Having a reasonable basis to believe that a recommended transaction or investment strategy is appropriate for a client, after considering the client's age, other investments, financial situation and needs, tax status, investment objectives, investment experience, investment time horizon, liquidity needs, risk tolerance and other relevant issues. See FINRA Rule 2111.

SUMMARY ANNUAL REPORT - A summary of the annual financial report that the plan files with the Department of Labor each year.

SUMMARY OF MATERIAL MODIFICATIONS - Document that provides in plain language the modifications made to a qualified plan.

SUMMARY PLAN DESCRIPTION - Document that explains in plain language the details of a retirement plan and how it operates. It provides information on when an employee can begin to participate in the plan, how service and benefits are calculated, when benefits become vested, when and in what form benefits are paid, and how to file a claim for benefits.

SUPERANNUATION - The risk of outliving available savings.

SUPPLEMENTAL EXECUTIVE RETIREMENT PLANS (SERP) - Nonqualified deferred compensation arrangements designed to provide additional benefits to an executive during retirement.

SUPPLEMENTARY MEDICAL INSURANCE (SMI) TRUST FUND - The trust fund that pays for services covered under the medical insurance provisions of Medicare, known as Part B. The coverage is funded by general federal tax revenues and monthly Medicare premiums paid by enrollees.

SURVIVORS' BENEFIT - Social Security benefit available to surviving family members of a deceased, eligible worker.

T

TANDEM PLAN - A 10% money purchase pension plan combined with a 15% profit sharing plan. These were popular prior to TRA 2001.

TARGET BENEFIT PENSION PLAN - A special type of money purchase pension plan that determines the contribution to the participant's account based on the targeted benefit that will be paid from the plan at the participant's retirement rather than on the value of the contribution to the account. Requires an actuary at inception.

TAX SHELTERED OR DEFERRED ANNUITIES (403(b) PLANS) - Retirement plans for certain qualified non-profit organizations or employees of public educational systems – often called 401(k)s for nonprofit organizations.

10-YEAR FORWARD AVERAGING - A method of income tax calculation for certain lump-sum distribution from qualified plans that divides the taxable portion of the lump-sum distribution by 10 and applies the result to the 1986 individual income tax rates. The resulting calculation is then multiplied by 10 to determine the total income tax due on the distribution.

TERM INSURANCE POLICY - A life insurance contract which states if the insured dies within the term of the contract, the insurance company will pay a stated death benefit.

THIRD PARTY ADMINISTRATOR - An organization unrelated to the plan sponsor who is paid to administer the plan sponsor's qualified or other retirement plan.

THRIFT PLAN - A qualified retirement plan that permits employees to make after-tax contributions to the plan. Although the contributions are taxable before being contributed to the plan, the account still benefits from tax-deferred growth on earnings.

THRIFT SAVINGS PLAN (TSP) - A retirement savings and investment plan for Federal employees and members of the uniformed services, including the Ready Reserve.

TITLE I OF ERISA - Coverage, participation, funding, and discrimination requirements of ERISA imposed on qualified plans.

TOP HAT PLANS - Plans designed to benefit a select group of top management or key employees. A plan is top heavy if more than 60 percent of either the account balance or accrued benefits are for the benefit of key employees.

TOP-HEAVY - Rules that were designed to ensure that plans established primarily to benefit the owners and executives of the company also provided some minimum level of benefits for the rank-and-file employees.

TRADITIONAL IRA - An IRA that may accept deductible and nondeductible contributions and whose assets grow tax-deferred until distribution.

TRUSTEED IRA – A trust established within the United States that holds IRA assets, which is an alternative to a custodial IRA. It allows for ultimate control over the distribution of the IRA assets by the owner after his or her death and provides creditor protection for the beneficiaries. Post-SECURE Act, a trusteed IRA is not as advantageous, but may remain useful when the IRA beneficiaries are eligible designated beneficiaries for whom required minimum distributions may be spread over the beneficiary's lifetime.

TWO-YEAR ELIGIBILITY ELECTION - A special election that overrides the standard eligibility requirements and permits the employer to only consider those employees who have two years of service as eligible to participate in a plan. If the employer elects the two-year requirement, than the employer must also provide 100% vesting at the completion of two years of service. This exception is not available for 401(k) plans

U

UNIFORM LIFETIME TABLE - A table used to calculate the RMD for the plan participant unless the participant's sole designated beneficiary is the participant's spouse and that spouse is more than 10 years younger than the participant.

UNIT CREDIT FORMULA - A benefit formula of a defined benefit pension plan that utilizes a combination of the participant's years of service and salary to determine the participant's accrued benefit.

UNIVERSAL LIFE INSURANCE - A term insurance policy with a cash accumulation account attached to it.

UNSAFE CONDITIONS COMMUTING RULE - The value of commuting transportation provided by an employer to a qualified employee solely because of unsafe conditions is $1.50 for each one way commute.

V

VEST - To give an employee rights to employer contributions and earnings in their retirement plan benefits.

VOLUME SUBMITTER PLAN - A plan that is designed by a professional, such as an attorney, CPA or third party administrator, which contains language that has been pre-approved by the IRS. This type of plan allows for more customization than a standard prototype plan, but is generally much less costly than an individualized plan.

VOLUNTARY EMPLOYEES' BENEFICIARY ASSOCIATION (VEBA) - A welfare benefit plan into which employers deposit funds that will be used to provide specified employee benefits in the future. The deposits are deductible for the employer at the date of the contribution rather than at the date when the employee benefits are provided.

W

WAGE REPLACEMENT RATIO (WRR) - An estimate of the percent of income needed at retirement compared to earnings prior to retirement.

WHOLE LIFE INSURANCE POLICY - A permanent life insurance policy that guarantees that the policy will remain in force as long as the premium is paid. The life insurance policy has a cash account that grows tax deferred.

WORK LIFE EXPECTANCY (WLE) - The period of time a person is expected to be in the work force, generally 30-40 years.

WORKING CONDITION FRINGE BENEFITS - Any property or service provided to an employee that enables the employee to perform his work and, if paid for by the employee, is deductible as a trade or business expense (i.e., parking).

Y

YEAR OF SERVICE - At least 1,000 hours of service for an employer and 12 months of continuous employment.

APPENDIX

B

INDEX

Numerics

A

R